Photoshop® CS5 All-in-One For Dummies®

Published by
Wiley Publishing, Inc.
111 River Street
Hoboken, NJ 07030-5774

www.wiley.com

Copyright © 2010 by Wiley Publishing, Inc., Indianapolis, Indiana

Published by Wiley Publishing, Inc., Indianapolis, Indiana

Published simultaneously in Canada

For general information on our other products and services, please contact our Customer Care Department within the U.S. at 877-762-2974, outside the U.S. at 317-572-3993, or fax 317-572-4002.

For technical support, please visit www.wiley.com/techsupport.

Wiley also publishes its books in a variety of electronic formats. Some content that appears in print may not be available in electronic books.

Library of Congress Control Number: 2010925703

ISBN: 973-0-470-60821-0

Manufactured in the United States of America

10 9 8 7 6 5 4 3 2

WILEY

About the Author

Barbara Obermeier is principal of Obermeier Design, a graphic design studio in Ventura, California. She's the author or co-author of over 19 publications, including *Photoshop Elements 8 For Dummies, How-to-Wow with Illustrator,* and *Digital Photography Just the Steps For Dummies,* 2nd Edition. Barb also teaches graphic design at Brooks Institute.

Dedication

I would like to dedicate this book to Gary, Kylie, and Lucky, who constantly remind me of what's really important in life.

Author's Acknowledgments

I would like to thank my excellent project editor, Nicole Sholly, who kept me and this book on track; Bob Woerner, the world's best Executive Editor; Andy Cummings, who gives Dummies a good name; David Busch, for his great contribution to the first edition; Dennis Cohen, for his technical editing; and all the hard-working, dedicated production folks at Wiley. A special thanks to Ted Padova, colleague, fellow author, and friend, who always reminds me there is eventually an end to all those chapters.

Publisher's Acknowledgments

We're proud of this book; please send us your comments at http://dummies.custhelp.com. For other comments, please contact our Customer Care Department within the U.S. at 877-762-2974, outside the U.S. at 317-572-3993, or fax 317-572-4002.

Some of the people who helped bring this book to market include the following:

Acquisitions, Editorial, and Media Development

Project Editor: Nicole Sholly

Executive Editor: Bob Woerner

Copy Editors: Heidi Unger, Brian Walls

Technical Editor: Dennis R. Cohen

Editorial Manager: Kevin Kirschner

Media Development Project Manager: Laura Moss-Hollister

Media Development Assistant Project Manager: Jenny Swisher

Media Development Associate Producers: Josh Frank, Marilyn Hummel, Douglas Kuhn, Shawn Patrick

Editorial Assistant: Amanda Graham

Sr. Editorial Assistant: Cherie Case

Cartoons: Rich Tennant (www.the5thwave.com)

Composition Services

Project Coordinator: Katherine Crocker

Layout and Graphics: Claudia Bell, Samantha Cherolis, Joyce Haughey, Erin Zeltner

Proofreader: Melissa D. Buddendeck

Indexer: Sherry Massey

Publishing and Editorial for Technology Dummies

Richard Swadley, Vice President and Executive Group Publisher

Andy Cummings, Vice President and Publisher

Mary Bednarek, Executive Acquisitions Director

Mary C. Corder, Editorial Director

Publishing for Consumer Dummies

Diane Graves Steele, Vice President and Publisher

Composition Services

Debbie Stailey, Director of Composition Services

Contents at a Glance

Table of Contents

Book IV: Painting, Drawing, and Typing..................... 285

Chapter 1: Painting and Drawing with Photoshop..............287

Chapter 2: Filling and Stroking 311

Chapter 3: Creating and Editing Type 329

Introduction

There's a reason why Photoshop is the world's industry standard in image-editing software. The depth and breadth of the program is unparalleled. Photoshop immediately sucks you in with its easy-to-use interface and powerful tools and commands. It's so feature rich that you soon begin to lose track of time and start blowing off your commitments just to try one more thing. And just when you think you've finally explored every nook and cranny and mastered the program, you suddenly read a tip in a book or magazine that enlightens you about something you didn't know. Or even more likely, you stumble upon some great effect while working on a late-night project. That's the beauty of Photoshop. It's the program that just keeps giving.

The depth and breadth of Photoshop has downsides too, of course. You must make a major time commitment and invest much effort to master it — hence the large number of books written on the program. Walk into your neighborhood bookstore or type Photoshop in the Search field at any online bookseller's site, and you see a barrage of choices. Some books are general reference books, some are targeted toward the novice user, and others focus on a specific mission, such as color management or restoration and retouching.

About This Book

This book is written for the person who has a good grasp of using a computer and navigating the operating system and at least a cursory knowledge of Photoshop. It is intended to be a comprehensive reference book that you can read cover to cover or reach for when you're looking for specific information about a particular task.

Wherever I can, I sneak in a useful tip or an interesting technique to help you put Photoshop to work for your project needs.

Sometimes, knowing *how* to use a tool doesn't necessarily mean that you know *what* to do with it. That's why this book contains several Putting It Together exercises that help you make a connection between the multiple Photoshop tools at your disposal and the very specific task you need to accomplish. Want to get the red out of a subject's eyes or create a collage?

Just check out the Putting It Together sections in Books III through IX. These sections present info in easy-to-follow numbered steps, in a hands-on style, building on what's presented in the chapter so that you can go to the next level, put concepts to work, and move on to the next task.

You can find images that appear within the Putting It Together sections on this book's companion Web site (www.dummies.com/go/photoshopcs5 aiofd), so you can follow along precisely with the steps.

What's in This Book

This book is broken into minibooks, each covering a general topic. Each minibook contains several chapters, each covering a more specific topic under the general one. Each chapter is then divided into sections, and some of those sections have subsections. I'm sure you get the picture.

You can read the book from front to back, or you can dive right into the minibook or chapter of your choice. Either way works just fine. Anytime a concept is mentioned that isn't covered in depth in that chapter, you find a cross-reference to another book and chapter where you find all the details. If you're looking for something specific, check out either the Table of Contents or the Index.

The Cheat Sheet at Dummies.com (find more information inside the front cover) helps you remember all the shortcuts you'll use most often. Print it, tape it to your monitor, and glance over it when you need to.

And finally, I have pictures. Lots of them. In full, living color. Many of these pictures have callouts that point to specific steps or identify important concepts, buttons, tools, or options. With a program like Photoshop, an image often speaks louder than words.

This book contains nine minibooks. The following sections offer a quick synopsis of what each book contains.

Book 1: Photoshop Fundamentals

Ready to get your feet wet with the basics of Photoshop? Head to Book I. Here's where you get familiar with the Photoshop environment — the desktop, menus, and panels. I also briefly introduce the key tools and explain what each one does.

Photoshop has such an abundance of tools — and so many ways to use those tools — I can't possibly cover them all in this book. But if you're looking for details on the less commonly used features or perhaps more information about using tools you're already familiar with, you'll find them on this book's companion Web site (www.dummies.com/go/photoshopcs5aiofd).

In this book, I cover how to get started on Photoshop and how to view and navigate your image window. Here's also where I give you all the important details about the o'mighty Adobe Bridge, and the new Mini Bridge, and how to customize your workspace and preference settings.

Finally, I go into the bare basics of printing, and then how to save files and close Photoshop.

Book II: Image Essentials

This book covers all those nitpicky — but critical — details about images, such as size, resolution, pixel dimension, image mode, and file format. Turn to this book to find out how to safely resize your image without causing undue damage.

You can also find out how to crop images and increase their canvas size. In addition, I breeze through basic color theory and get you started using and managing color.

But wait — there's more. I give you the lowdown on the History panel and brushing and erasing to history. And, if that's not enough, I throw in a chapter on using and creating actions for enhanced productivity.

Book III: Selections

This important book gives you all the juicy details and techniques on creating and modifying selections and paths. You find out about each of the selection tools and also the powerful — albeit sometimes unruly — Pen tool and its accompanying Paths panel.

Book IV: Painting, Drawing, and Typing

If you want to know about the drawing and painting tools, this book is for you. Here I cover the Brush and Pencil tools, including the new Mixer Brush tool, along with the multifaceted Brush panel and new Brush Preset Picker panel. I also show you how to create vector shapes by using the shape tools, and how to fill and stroke selections.

Head to this book to find out how to create both gradients and patterns and, last but not least, become familiar with the type tools and how to use them to create and edit standard type, type on and in a path, and type with special effects.

Book V: Working with Layers

Layers are an integral component in a Photoshop image, and Book V is where I explain them. In this book, you discover how to create and edit layers and how to use multiple images to create a multilayered composite image. You find out various ways to manage layers for maximum efficiency, including using the Layer Comps panel. I also show you how to enhance layers by applying different blend modes, opacity settings, layer styles, and styles. I round out the minibook by covering Smart Objects. And finally, I introduce you to working with the Auto Align and Auto Blend features.

Book VI: Channels and Masks

This book gives you all the how-tos you need to work with channels and masks. I show you how to save and edit selections as alpha channels so that you can reload them later. And I show you how to work with the various kinds of masks — quick masks, clipping masks, layer masks, and channel masks — and how you can use each to select difficult elements. I also cover other masking techniques, such as erasing and using the Color Range command. Finally, I introduce you to the Masks panel, a powerful ally to the masking arsenal.

Book VII: Filters and Distortions

I filled this book with tons of handy tips and techniques on using filters to correct your images to make them sharper, blurrier, cleaner, and smoother — whatever fits your fancy. I give you the scoop on the Smart Filters feature, which enables you to apply filters nondestructively. You also find out how to use filters to give your image a certain special effect, such as a deckled edge or water droplets. Finally, I introduce the Liquify command so that you can see the wonder of its distortion tools — and how they can turn your image into digital taffy.

Book VIII: Retouching and Restoration

You find everything you need to know about color correction or color enhancement in Book VIII — getting rid of colorcasts, improving contrast and saturation, remapping, and replacing colors.

In addition, I include a chapter on using the focus and toning tools to manually lighten, darken, smooth, soften, and sharpen areas of your image. You get to see how you can use the Clone Stamp tool, the Healing tools, and the Red Eye tool to fix flaws and imperfections in your images, making them good as new. I also show you the Color Replacement tool and how to replace your image's original color with the foreground color. Finally, you get some tidbits on how to work with the fascinating Vanishing Point feature, which can make editing and compositing images a whole lot easier.

Book IX: Photoshop and Print

This book gives you the lowdown on preparing your images for print. You find details on how to get the right resolution, image mode, and file format. You also discover how to set up both process and spot color separations for those offset print jobs.

About the Web Site

For those Web graphics enthusiasts, you find lots of great bonus chapter material on this book's companion Web site (www.dummies.com/go/ photoshopcs5aiofd). Find out how to optimize your images for maximum quality and quick download times. You also find information on slicing and animating your images and creating a photo gallery that you can easily post on the Web.

Conventions Used in This Book

You'll find that this book is cross-platform. Windows commands are given first, followed by Mac commands in parentheses, like this:

Press Enter (or Return on the Mac) to begin a new line.

And occasionally, text is specific to one platform or another. You'll find that figures are divided into both platforms as well.

Often, the commands given involve using the keyboard along with the mouse. For example, "Press Shift while dragging with the Rectangular Marquee tool to create a square," or "Alt-click (Option-click) on the eyeball to redisplay all layers."

When you see a command arrow (⇨) in the text, it indicates that you should select a command from the menu bar. For example, "choose Edit⇨Define Custom Shape" means to click the Edit menu and then choose the Define Custom Shape command.

This book has been written using Photoshop CS5 and, more specifically, the Standard version. Despite that fact, you can still glean valuable info if you're using version CS4 or CS3. It may take a little more time to understand how a panel or options have changed, and of course, the topics covering new features won't be applicable.

Speaking of new features, when writing this book, it wasn't exactly crystal clear what new CS5 features Adobe would be including in the Standard versus Extended versions of Photoshop. So if I've included (or not) a particular tool or command that you don't have, my apologies in advance.

Icons Used in This Book

While perusing this book, you'll notice some icons beckoning you for your attention. Don't ignore them; embrace them! These icons point out fun, useful, and memorable tidbits about Photoshop, plus facts you'd be unwise to ignore.

Seasoned users will appreciate this icon, which kindly points out new features introduced in Photoshop CS5.

This icon indicates information that makes your Photoshop experience easier. It also gives you an icebreaker at your next cocktail party. Whipping out, "Did you know that pressing the bracket keys enlarges or shrinks your brush tip?" is bound to make you the center of conversation.

This icon is a reminder of things that I already mentioned and want to gently re-emphasize. Or I might be pointing out things that I want you to take note of in your future Photoshop excursions.

The little bomb icon is a red flag. Heed these warnings, or else Photoshop may show its ugly side.

This icon marks eggheady graphics or Photoshop info that goes beyond the basics.

This icon points to related content you'll find on this book's companion Web site, which you can find at www.dummies.com/go/photoshopcs5aiofd.

Book I
Photoshop
Fundamentals

The 5th Wave   By Rich Tennant

"I've got the red—eye reduction, I'm just seeing if there's a button that'll fix your hair."

Don't know where to start? Well, unless you have a burning question on something very specific, this is a great place to dive in. And I promise you won't flounder. There's nothing like a general overview to get you feeling confident enough to tackle more sophisticated features.

In this book, I introduce you to the Photoshop environment with all its components, from the desktop to the many panels. I show you each of the 71 tools and briefly explain what each tool does. From there, I show you how to open existing files or create new ones and then how to save and print those files, as well as how to view and navigate around your image window. In that same chapter, I give you details on using Adobe Bridge, a powerful browser and file-management tool, as well as the new mini Bridge. Finally, I explain how to customize your workspace and preferences so you can tailor Photoshop to better suit your personal image-editing needs and interests. I guarantee you won't find a more accommodating image editor around.

Wright Beach, Ca

Chapter 1: Examining the Photoshop Environment

In This Chapter

✓ **Starting Photoshop**

✓ **Examining the Photoshop desktop**

✓ **Working with panels**

✓ **Discovering the Application bar**

✓ **Investigating the Menu bar and the Options bar**

*A*s environments go, the Photoshop working environment is pretty cool: as inviting as a landscaped backyard and not nearly as likely to work you into a sweat. Each of Photoshop's many tools — with more options than a Swiss Army knife — is custom-designed for a specific chore. When you're familiar with your surroundings, you'll be eager to make like Monet in his garden, surrounded by panels, brushes, buckets of paint, and swatches of color, ready to tackle the canvas in front of you.

Launching Photoshop and Customizing the Desktop

You start Photoshop the same way you launch any other program with Windows or the Mac OS. As with other programs, you can choose the method you find the easiest and most convenient. In Windows, you can launch programs from the Start menu or an icon on the taskbar. In Mac OS X, you may have a Photoshop icon on the Dock. In either Windows or Mac OS X, you can double-click a Photoshop shortcut or alias icon if you have one on your desktop. Finally, you can double-click an image associated with Photoshop, which then launches Photoshop along with the file.

When you launch Photoshop, the workspace, shown in Figure 1-1, appears. Like the real-world desktop where your keyboard and monitor reside, the Photoshop desktop is a place for you to put all the images you're working with.

Within the Photoshop application window, you see a variety of other windows and boxes, such as the image window that enables you to view and edit images. The application window contains the stuff you're probably used to seeing in other programs — a title bar at the top of the window, a status bar at the bottom (unless you have it turned off) if you're a Windows user, and menus to help you execute commands and get important information about your image files. However, the arrangement of controls may be a little unfamiliar to you. Photoshop arranges controls into groups, or *panels*.

Your virtual desktop can become as cluttered as the real thing, but Adobe has built in some special features (located on the Options bar, which I discuss later in this chapter) that let you keep stuff close at hand but tuck things away so they're not constantly underfoot (or under-mouse, so to speak).

Options bar   Document window   Dock

Tools panel   Panels

Status bar

Digital Vision

Figure 1-1: The Photoshop desktop consists of many components, including an image window, panels, and bars.

After you arrange your Photoshop desktop the way you like it for a specific project, you can even save the desktop and reuse it whenever you work on that project (see Book I, Chapter 5 for details).

Every image you work on appears within the confines of the image window. However, you can move some components, such as the various panels and the Options bar, both inside and outside the Photoshop application window.

The following sections show you how to customize the workspace so you can get to work.

Setting display settings with the Window menu

The Window menu, shown in Figure 1-2, controls the display of panels and some other elements of the Photoshop workspace. (Find out more about maneuvering panels in the section "Playing with Panels," later in this chapter.)

The top two entries on the Window menu enable you to control the display arrangement of your open documents and manage your workspaces.

On the Window➪Arrange submenu, you can tell Photoshop to *cascade* (stack) or *tile* (butt edge to edge) all open documents. Your images must be floating in their windows to enable this option (Window➪Arrange➪Float All in Windows).

Photoshop also sports what's referred to as an application frame. Open documents are tabbed together neatly, one stacked behind the other. If you yearn for the old days and want your images to float within the application, choose Float in Window (for the currently selected image only) and Float All in Windows (for all your images) commands in the Arrange submenu.

Table 1-1 gives you the lowdown about the other options on the Window➪Arrange submenu.

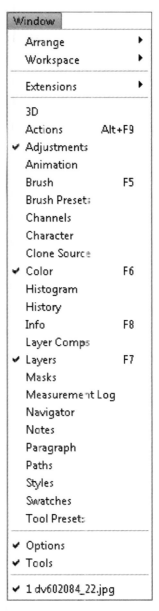

Figure 1-2: Access all panels via the Window menu.

The remaining bulk of the Window menu contains a list of panels (in alphabetical order) and currently open documents.

Table 1-1	The Window⇨Arrange Submenu
Menu Command	*What It Does*
Consolidate All to Tabs	Takes your open floating documents and tabs them together under the Options bar.
Match Zoom	Takes your open documents and matches the magnification percentage of your active document.
Match Location	Takes your open documents and matches the location of your active document. For example, if you're viewing the lower-left corner of your active document and choose Match Location, all your open documents display from the lower-left corner.
Match Rotation	Takes your open documents and matches the canvas rotation of your active document.
Match All	Employs all Match commands simultaneously.
New Window	Opens another view of the same image, allowing you to work on a close-up part of the image while viewing results on the entire image.
Minimize (Mac only)	Hides the image while placing the image's thumbnail on the Dock. Click the thumbnail to restore the image in Photoshop.
Bring All to Front (Mac only)	If you have multiple applications launched, thus multiple document windows open, this command brings all Photoshop documents to the front, ahead of any document windows from other open applications.

Setting up the status bar

Each Photoshop image window comes equipped with a status bar. Many people tend to associate status with wealth, so I think there's a good reason to accept the free wealth of information that the status bar offers:

✔ On the far left of the bar is a box that displays an active image's current zoom level (such as 33.33%). Incidentally, the title bar of the document itself also shows the zoom level.

If you installed Photoshop to a networked computer and you activate the workgroup features, which enable file sharing and other perks, you see the icon for the Workgroup Services pop-up menu just to the right of the zoom-info box.

✔ To the right of the zoom level is the display area for file and image information — which, by default, shows the document profile.

To display other types of information, click the right arrow in the status bar, choose Show, and select one of the following options from the menu that appears (as shown in Figure 1-3):

✔ **Adobe Drive:** If you're a Version Cue user, you can select this option, which enables you to connect to Version Cue servers. When you connect via Adobe Drive, you can open and save Version Cue files. Adobe has decided to discontinue Version Cue, so the future of the Adobe Drive feature is unknown.

PhotoDisc

Figure 1-3: The status bar provides a wealth of vital information about your image.

✔ **Document Sizes:** When you select this option, Photoshop displays two numbers to approximate the size of the image. The first number shows you the size of the file if you were to flatten (combine) all the layers into one and save it to your hard drive in the native Photoshop file format. The number on the right shows the size of the file, including layers, channels, and other components, and how much data Photoshop has to juggle while you're working on the file. You want this option active when you need to keep track of how large your image is.

✔ **Document Profile:** When you select this option, the status bar displays the name of the color profile that the image uses, as well as the number of bits per channel. You probably won't use this option unless you need to know the profiles of all the open documents while making complex color corrections. (You can find more information about profiles in Book II, Chapter 3.)

✔ **Document Dimensions:** When you select this option, the status bar shows you the size of the image by using the default measurement increment you've set in Photoshop's Preferences (pixels, inches, picas, and so on). You might need this information to reference the physical dimensions of your open files. For information on setting preferences in Photoshop, see Book I, Chapter 5.

✔ **Measurement Scale:** Displays the scale of the document. For example, 1 pixel=1.0000 pixels.

✔ **Scratch Sizes:** Scratch space is the virtual memory set aside on your hard drive to simulate RAM and make editing large files easier. Enabling this option shows two measurements for an active image. On the left, you see the amount of real memory and virtual memory that all open images are using. On the right, you see the total amount of RAM available for working with images. Photoshop needs a lot more memory and disk space to work on an image while that image is open, shown by the Scratch Sizes display, as opposed to the Document Size display that shows only the file size of the document.

✔ **Efficiency:** This indicator helps you gauge whether you really have enough RAM to perform a task. It shows the percentage of time Photoshop spends actually working on an operation, compared to the time it must spend reading or writing image information to or from your hard disk. If the value dips below 100 percent most of the time, you need to allocate more memory to Photoshop (if you're using a Windows PC). For more information on parceling out RAM, see Book I, Chapter 5.

✔ **Timing:** This number shows you how long it took you to complete your most recent incredible feat.

✔ **Current Tool:** This option shows you the name of the tool currently in use.

✔ **32-Bit Exposure:** This option is for adjusting the preview image for viewing 32-bit High Dynamic Range (HDR) images. The slider control is available only if you have an HDR image open. Book IX, Chapter 2 covers HDR.

Playing with Panels

Many image-oriented programs use panels of a sort, and Photoshop has had panels (formerly called palettes) since version 1.0 (released in January 1990). However, since Photoshop 3.0, the program has used a novel way of working with panels. Rather than standalone windows, Photoshop uses grouped, tabbed panels, which overlap each other in groups of two or three (or more, if you rearrange them yourself). To access a panel that falls behind the one displayed on top, click the panel's tab. By default, some panels, such as Tool Presets, appear alone.

Panels may contain sliders, buttons, drop-down lists, pop-up menus (as shown in Figure 1-4), and other controls. You also find icons at the bottom of many panels. For example, at the base of the Layers panel are command icons that let you create a new layer, add a layer style, or trash a layer that you no longer want. Many panels — such as the Brush, Styles, Actions, and Color panels — include options for defining sets of parameters (called *presets*) that you can store for reuse at any time.

Whatever name you call them, palettes or panels, they still hold the same information. They're streamlined and easily tucked away and expanded, as needed. By default, the panels are anchored in the top-right by a multitiered dock.

Here's how to open, close, and otherwise manipulate a panel group, which can be accessed easily from the Window menu:

Dock Panel group bar

Panel tab Collapse to icons

Panel pop-up menu

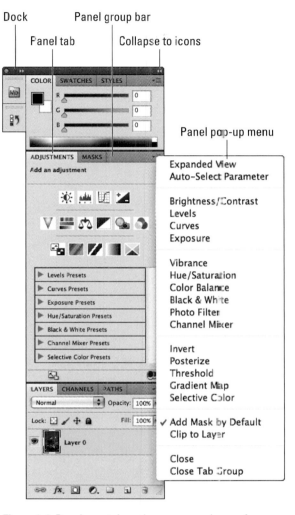

Figure 1-4: Panels contain various command icons for editing and managing your image.

✔ **To expand a panel:** Panels are represented by icons when collapsed. To expand a panel, simply click its icon. You can also select a panel by choosing it in the Window menu.

✔ **To bring a panel to the front of its group:** When the panel group is expanded, the visible panel is the panel that has a check mark next to it on the Window menu. In this mode, you can select only one panel in any group because only one tab in a group can be on top at one time. When you select a panel from the Window menu, you have no way of knowing which panels are grouped together because Adobe lists panels alphabetically, rather than by groups. To bring a specific panel to the front, click its tab (when expanded) or icon (when collapsed).

✏ **To move a panel out of its group:** Grab the panel's tab with your mouse and drag it to its new location, such as another group, the panel dock, or the Photoshop desktop. If you move the panels out of their groups or drag them onto the desktop so they stand alone, any of them can be selected in the Window menu.

✏ **To collapse a panel:** Click the gray area next to the tab.

✏ **To close a panel:** Select a check-marked panel in the Window menu. The whole panel group closes. You can also select Close or Close Tab Group from the panel's pop-up menu.

Here are some more panel-manipulation tips:

✏ **Expand or collapse the dock.** To do so, click on the double triangles at the top of the dock.

✏ **Reduce a panel to its icon.** Drag the panel by its tab and position it below the existing column of icons. Release your mouse button to make the panel collapse to its corresponding icon.

✏ **Save space by keeping panels in groups.** You can move all the panels in a group by dragging the gray area to the right of the group's tab. Access an individual panel by clicking its tab to bring it to the front. As a result, several panels occupy the screen space required by only one.

✏ **Use the Window menu if you can't find a panel.** On the Window menu, select the panel's name to make it visible or to bring it to the top of its group.

✏ **Customize, customize, customize.** After you use Photoshop for a while, creating your own custom panel groups based on the panels you most often use can be a real timesaver. For example, if you don't use the Paths panel very often but can't live without the Actions panel, you can drag the Paths panel to another group or to the panel dock area, and put the Actions panel in the same group as the mission-critical Layers and Channels panels.

✏ **Restore default panel locations, when desired.** If you decide you don't like the way you've arranged your panels, you can choose Window⇨Workspace⇨Essentials (Default) to return them to the default configuration (the way they were when Photoshop was installed).

Many panels (for example, the Swatches and Character panels) allow you to reset the settings back to their defaults. To do so, select Reset from the panel's pop-up menu located in the top-right corner.

Working with Your First Photoshop File

So many menus, so little time! The second you begin working with Photoshop, you may be convinced that Adobe's flagship image editor has approximately 8,192 different menu selections for you to choose from. In truth, Photoshop has only about 500-plus separate menu items, including some duplicates. That figure doesn't count the 100 or so entries for filter plug-ins (which can expand alarmingly when you add third-party goodies). However, even 500-plus menu items are considerably more than you find in the most ambitious restaurants. Basically, if you want to do something in Photoshop, you need to use the Menu bar (or its equivalent command snuggled within a panel menu). If you're using the Mac OS, the Photoshop Menu bar may share space with Finder components (such as the Apple menu).

The following sections offer a summary of what you can find and where you can find it.

Photoshop also helps you by providing efficient context menus, which change their listings depending on what you're doing. You don't see options you don't need; you see options appropriate to what you're working on. Right-click (Right-click or Control-click on the Mac) to bring up the menu.

Opening, printing, and saving files

The File menu offers a cornucopia of file options, from opening new images and opening saved files to browsing existing files, closing files, and saving files. You'll find automate, scripts, and print commands, too. To open a file, choose File➪Open and navigate to the folder containing the file you want to open. Select the file and click Open. For detailed instructions on the many ways you can open files, see Book I, Chapter 3.

Making selections

Selections let you work with only part of an image. You can select an entire layer or only portions of a layer with one of the selection tools, such as the Marquee or Magic Wand tool. The Select menu offers several commands to modify your selection — from capturing more pixels to softening the edges of the selection. The Select menu (shown in Figure 1-5) is short and sweet, but the capability and control that the menu unleashes is nothing short of an image-editing miracle.

Understanding selections is such an important cornerstone to your Photoshop knowledge that I devote an entire minibook (Book III) to showing you how to use them.

Making simple image edits

The Edit menu contains tools that enable you to cut, copy, or paste image selections in several ways. You can fill selections or *stroke* their outlines (create a line along their edges), which I explain in more detail in Book IV, Chapter 2. You can use the Edit menu to rotate, resize, distort, or perform other transformations (changes in size or shape) on your selections (see Book III, Chapter 3). Additionally, you can undo the last change you made in Photoshop, fade a filter, check your spelling. or find and replace text.

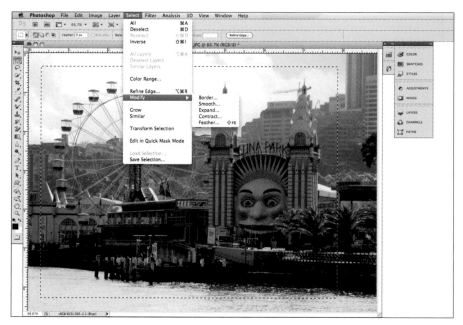

Purestock

Figure 1-5: The Select menu offers commands for making, modifying, saving, and loading your selections.

Adjusting size, color, and contrast

You'd think the Image menu (shown in Figure 1-6) might have something to do with making changes to an entire image document, wouldn't you? In practice, some of the entries you find here do apply to the whole document, but others can apply to only particular layers or selections.

For example, the Mode menu item allows you to change an entire image from color to grayscale. The Image Size, Canvas Size, Image Rotation, Crop, and Trim selections all change the whole document in some way. On the other hand, you can only apply the changes wrought from the Adjustments submenu to an entire image if the document consists of only a background and has no layers. If the document has more than one layer, then adjustments such as Color Balance, Hue/Saturation, or Levels work only with a single layer or a selection on that layer.

The Variables and Apply Data Set commands work with data-driven graphics. Briefly, data-driven graphics make it possible to quickly produce multiple versions of an image for print and Web projects. Multiple versions allow for target audience customization for projects such as direct mail pieces. For example, you can base hundreds of versions of a brochure or Web banner on a single template. The Variables define which elements change within a template. A Data Set is a collection of variables and associated data.

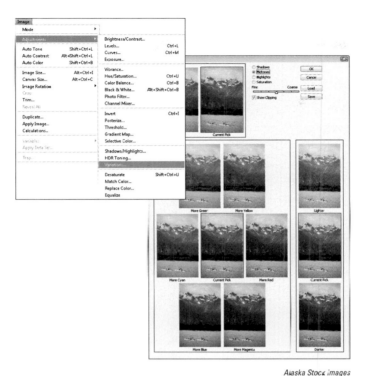

Alaska Stock Images

Figure 1-6: The Image menu is where you find commands for adjusting the size, color, and contrast of your image.

You'll find yourself turning to the Image menu more often than many of the other menus, partially because it's so useful and partially because, for some reason many of the options don't have keyboard shortcuts that let you bypass the menu.

Creating layers

Layers give you a way of stacking portions of an image — like sheets of acetate — on top of one another so that you can work on individual pieces separately. Then, when you're satisfied with your changes, you can either combine the changes into a final image or leave them in layers for maximum editing flexibility.

The Layers feature, which gets an entire book of its own (Book V), lets you create new and duplicate layers, delete one or several layers, change layer properties (such as a layer's name), or add special features, such as drop shadows or beveled edges, to objects in a layer. You can also create special kinds of layers to make adjustments or mask portions of an image. The menu has selections for changing the order of the layers (moving a specific layer to the front or top of the stack, and so on) and grouping layers. Figure 1-7 shows an image that has three layers: The first layer is the symphony image, the second layer is the instrument, and the third layer contains the type.

You also can merge layers down, combine them with all other visible layers, or flatten them into one single-layer image (or background). Although consolidating your layers makes the file smaller, flattening is irreversible after you close the file. Storing an unflattened version of a file is always a good idea in case you want to make more changes later on.

Applying filters

A filter is an effect that changes an entire layer, channel, or selection. Some common filters include the Blur and Sharpen filters, as well as the Distort filters, such as Spherize. The Filter menu, shown in Figure 1-8, consists almost entirely of cascading categories of image-transmogrifying plug-ins. You can wade through this menu to find the perfect effect to apply to an image or selection. Book VII has everything you need to know about filters.

PhotoSpin

Figure 1-7: Layers enable you to edit elements individually in your document.

After you apply a filter, Photoshop copies the filter command to the top of the Filter menu for easy accessibility, in case you want to reapply the filter with the exact same settings.

The Filter Gallery command allows you to apply several filters simultaneously in one neat editing window.

Liquify and Vanishing Point are more like mini-programs than filters. The rest of the Filter menu consists of 14 filter categories, each containing from two to more than a dozen options:

Figure 1-8: The Filter menu is bursting at the seams with plug-ins to improve, enhance, or completely transform your image.

- ✔ Single-step filters, such as Blur, Facet, and Clouds, are simple to use but make a huge impact on an image. Just select each filter to apply it; it has no options to specify.

- ✔ Dialog box-based filters let you select options galore. These filters utilize preview windows, buttons, slider controls, and menus to distort, pixelate, sharpen, stylize, apply textures, and perform other functions.

- ✔ The Filter menu also provides an opportunity to convert for Smart Filters. If you convert your layer to a Smart Object, you can then apply a Smart Filter. A Smart Filter is smart because it doesn't alter your image pixels, but merely hovers above them, thereby allowing you to re-edit, or even remove, the filter if necessary. For the scoop on this cool (and very useful) feature, see Book VII, Chapter 1.

If you install additional filters from third parties, Photoshop lists them at the very bottom of the Filter menu. You can find third-party filters at such Web sites as www.alienskin.com, www.andromeda.com, and www.autofx.com.

Unifying with the Application bar

The Application bar, shown in Figure 1-9, located at the far end of the main menu in Windows and directly below the main menu on the Mac, consolidates commands and features previously found, or also found, elsewhere in the application. For more details on most of these commands, check out Book I, Chapter 4. Here's what you can find on this bar:

- ✔ **Application icon:** The Photoshop icon is displayed to simply identify the application. In Windows, clicking the icon displays the standard system menu.

✔ **Launch Bridge:** This button allows you to access the image-management application, Bridge, with a mere click.

✔ **View Extras:** Click this icon to select whether to show guides, the grid, or rulers from the drop-down list. For more on these items, see Book I, Chapter 4.

✔ **Magnification Percentage:** Displays the current magnification percentage. Click the down arrow to select from preset percentages of 25%, 50%, 100%, and 200%. Or enter your desired magnification percentage in the text field.

✔ **Hand and Zoom tools:** Select these tools from the Application bar or Tools panel — your choice. Use the Hand tool to move around your image window and the Zoom tool to zoom in and out. For more on these two tools, see Book I, Chapter 4.

✔ **Rotate View tool:** Select this tool from either the Application bar or Tools panel. This tool actually rotates your entire image window, not just the image within the boundaries of the window.

✔ **Arrange Documents tool:** Click the down arrow to select various viewing configurations. Depending on the number of open images you have, various configurations will be available. You can also choose to float, rather than tab, your open images; create a new window; and display actual pixels or fit your entire image onscreen. See explanations of the Match commands in the earlier "Setting display settings with the Window menu" section in this chapter.

✔ **Screen Mode Switcher:** Click the down arrow to select from standard, full screen with Menu bar, and full screen modes.

✔ **Workspace Switcher:** Click the down arrow to select a different workspace. Selecting the Essentials workspace resets all your panels and menus to the default settings.

If you're a Mac user and don't care for this bar, hide it by choosing Window➪Application Bar to deselect it. Also, if you use other CS5 applications, you may find a similar Application bar.

Simplifying your edits with the Options bar

The Options bar, shown in Figure 1-10, is a great feature because it eliminates the need to access a separate options panel for each tool. The bar remains available at all times, docked below the Menu and Application bars (unless you decide to hide it for some bizarre reason), and the options change when you switch tools. If the default location doesn't work for you, feel free to move it anywhere you please.

Application bar

Figure 1-9: The Application bar unifies commonly used features in one centralized location.

Options bar

Alaska Stock Images

Figure 1-10: The ubiquitous Options bar is dynamic and reflects various options
for the tool in use and operation being performed.

Because the Options bar changes its appearance with each active tool, I can't explain all the components you might find there, but all Options bars do have some common characteristics:

- **Gripper bar:** Grab this little bar, on the far left, with the mouse and drag to undock or dock the Options bar. You can let the Options bar float anywhere in the workspace.

- **Tool Presets/Options pop-up menu:** This box displays the icon of the currently active tool. Click the down arrow to access a drop-down list that includes a selection of brush tips (for painting and erasing tools); a flyout menu that lets you select presets (saved settings) for various tools; and additional options to set, such as the size of the icons used to represent brush tips. You may also reset a particular tool — or all tools — to the Photoshop default values.

- **Bar options:** Additional options, such as mode, opacity, feather, type styles, and fonts are arrayed on the rest of the Options bar.

Viewing and navigating the image

A hodgepodge of functions is sprinkled throughout the View menu. Some of them, such as Proof Setup, Proof Colors, and Gamut Warning, won't trouble you until you've become a fairly advanced Photoshop user. For new Photoshop users, the commands to zoom into and out of the image are likely the most familiar. You can also choose your screen mode, which lets you view your image full-screen with the Menu bar and panels, or full-screen with just panels.

You're better off accessing some functions, especially the zoom features, through keyboard shortcuts. See Book I, Chapter 5 for details.

From the View menu, you can select which extras Photoshop displays. You can choose to show (or hide) the following, as shown in Figure 1-11:

- **Layer Edges:** Displays a blue-stroked box that surrounds the boundaries of the content of the selected layer.

- **Selection Edges:** Moving lines that define the boundary of a selection, which are very useful for obvious reasons.

Figure 1-11: Viewing and navigating your image are the main tasks on the View menu.

- **Target Path:** Lines and curves that define a shape or select part of an image. You definitely want to see them if the paths need editing.

- **Grid and Guides:** Lines that display onscreen, which are great when you're aligning selections, objects, or other components, and potentially distracting when you're not.

- **Count:** Bulleted numbers indicating your counted elements will appear. The Count feature is only in the Extended version of Photoshop.

- **Smart Guides:** Smart Guides enable you to precisely position and align layer content, and only appear when needed.

- **Slices:** Rectangular pieces of an image to which you can optimize or apply Web features. If you slice the image, you probably want to view the results.

- **Notes:** Onscreen notes that you can create and view. Notes can sometimes be confusing, unless you're already confused; then notes can help you sort out what's what.

- **Pixel Grid:** Displays a pixel grid when you are zoomed into your image at a magnification greater than 500%.

- **3D Axis:** Show the X, Y, and Z Axis orientation of a 3-D object. This option is only in the Extended version of Photoshop.

The View menu holds the controls for turning on and off the snap feature in Photoshop. (The *snap feature* makes objects magnetically attracted to grids, guides, or other objects.) You can also create new guides, lock and clear slices (see Bonus Chapter 2 for slice-and-dice information), and turn rulers on or off. (The Introduction has details about finding bonus chapters on this book's companion Web site.)

Introducing Adobe ConnectNow

Adobe provides a useful and, more importantly, free Web conferencing application that enables users to share ideas and collaborate on projects online. Using any computer platform and any browser, users can participate in online meetings and work sessions. ConnectNow enables users to share their files, audio, and video. You can participate via chats, whiteboard, Webcam, and notes.

With CS5, Adobe moved the ConnectNow feature to Acrobat.com (https://acrobat.com) and added even more functionality. The only requirements are

- **An Adobe.com user ID:** Get one at www.adobe.com.

- **An Adobe ConnectNow account:** Sign up at www.adobe.com/accm/connectnow.

- **Adobe Flash Player:** Download it at www.adobe.com/shockwave/download/download.cgi?P1_Prod_Version=ShockwaveFlash.

Follow these steps to access Adobe ConnectNow (shown in Figure 1-12) from within Photoshop:

1. **Choose File⇨Share My Screen to launch Adobe ConnectNow.**

   You can also access Adobe ConnectNow from this Web address: `www.adobe.com/acom/connectnow`.

   You can go directly to `https://acrobat.com`.

2. **From the Menu bar, choose Files to create a new document, presentation, table, or PDF. Choose Meetings to start a meeting, invite participants, or share your screen or Webcam.**

This great application deserves far more space than I can cram into this section. In fact, it probably deserves its own mini user manual. Be sure to visit `www.adobe.com/acom/connectnow` if you're interested in trying Adobe ConnectNow. You can find a ton of detailed information on using this great tool.

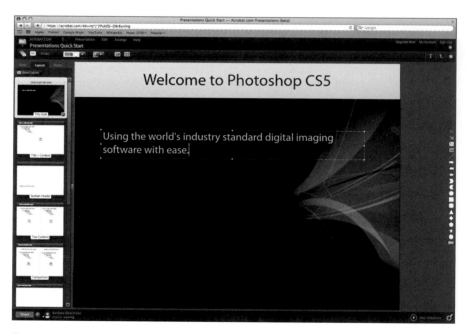

Figure 1-12: Use Adobe ConnectNow to participate in an online Web conference.

Chapter 2: Getting to Know the Tools Panel

In This Chapter

✓ Using the Tools panel

✓ Looking at what each tool does

✓ Creating tool presets

*A*fter you have a good grasp of the overall Photoshop environment (described in Book I, Chapter 1), you're ready to dive into the cache of gadgets that — along with the menus, panels, and dialog boxes — make it all happen. Just like you can use a saw, hammer, and nails to transform a pile of 2x4s into a garden gazebo, you can use the Lasso, Healing Brush, and Smudge tools to convert a mediocre photo into a masterpiece that's fit for framing. But remember, behind every garden gazebo is a carpenter who knew how to use the tools required to build it.

Turning On the Tools Panel

You can access the Tools panel by choosing Window➪ Tools. Here are a few tips for using the Tools panel:

✓ To quickly hide and show the Tools panel (along with the other panels), press Tab.

✓ To move the Tools panel anywhere within the Photoshop window, drag the title bar. Re-dock the Tools panel by dragging it back to its original location.

By default, the Tools panel is a single column. Click the double triangle at the top of the panel to display a two-column configuration.

Selecting tools

To select a tool, simply click it in the Tools panel. A small black triangle in the bottom-right corner of a tool slot indicates that more tools are hidden behind that tool on a *flyout menu,* shown in Figure 2-1 (note that the Tools panel in Figure 2-1 is from the Extended Version of Photoshop). Click and hold down your desired tool to access the flyout menu. You can also access tools by using keyboard shortcuts (which are listed in the Cheat Sheet at Dummies.com; find more information inside the front cover).

Note: 3D tools are in the Photoshop CS5 Extended version only.

Figure 2-1: The Photoshop Tools panel offers a multitude of tools for your editing pleasure.

For the most part, you can access a hidden tool by pressing the Shift key along with the keyboard letter of the visible tool. For example, to select the Pencil tool, which shares the flyout menu with the Brush tool, press Shift+B.

If you don't like having to press the Shift key to access a hidden tool, choose Edit⇨Preferences⇨General (Photoshop⇨Preferences⇨General on the Mac) and deselect the Use Shift Key for Tool Switch option. You can then rotate through the tools by pressing the same letter repeatedly.

When you hover your mouse pointer over a tool, color control, or icon, you see a tooltip. The *tooltip* tells you the name of the tool or icon and its keyboard shortcut, if any. Although helpful at first, it can get annoying after a while. Turn it off by deselecting the Show Tool Tips option in the Interface section of the Preferences dialog box.

Getting to know your tools

The Tools panel is divided into three sections: tools, color swatches, and icons for Quick Mask or Standard mode. The following sections introduce you to the tools. The following list details the other residents of the Tools panel shown in Figure 2-2:

✓ **Foreground Color and Background Color:** *Color swatches* represent the current foreground and background colors. When using some of the tools and applying some commands, you may apply one of these colors. The small black-and-white swatches represent the default colors.

  • Click the Default Colors icon to reset the colors to the default.

  • Click the curved arrow icon to switch the foreground and background colors.

  For everything you need to know about color, see Book II, Chapter 3.

✓ **Edit in Quick Mask Mode:** The default editing mode is Standard mode. To edit in Quick Mask mode, click the icon. I cover Quick Masks, which offer a way to view, make, and edit a selection, in Book VI, Chapter 2.

Color swatches

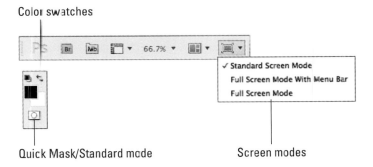

Quick Mask/Standard mode   Screen modes

Figure 2-2: The Tools panel's color, masking, and viewing options.

The Screen modes can be found in the Application bar (Window↔Application Bar on the Mac only). This bar is located at the top of the application window, to the right of the Menu bar on the PC and directly below the Menu bar on the Mac. Click the icon located on the far right of the Application bar to access various view modes. The default Standard Screen Mode enables you to see your entire Photoshop desktop. You can also select Full Screen Mode with Menu Bar, which hides your desktop background and other open images. Or click Full Screen Mode, which hides everything but your current image. When you select Full Screen Mode, a warning tells you that you must press F to return to Standard Screen mode. In addition to viewing modes, you can also find other handy items in the Application bar; see Book I, Chapter 1 for details.

Introducing the Photoshop Tools

I'm giving you just a very brief description of what each tool does. You're thoroughly initiated on each of the tools while you go through the book. Don't want to go page by page through the book? Okay, you're in luck; I also give you the exact spot where you can find more on each of the tools. For what it's worth, I've organized the tools into logical groupings — although some can cross over into other groups, and some are so unique that they don't fit well in any group.

Using selection tools

The selection tools are the workhorses of Photoshop. They allow you to capture and isolate pixels so that you can edit or manipulate just a portion of an image. Marquee tools capture rectangular or elliptical selections, or single rows or columns of pixels. Figure 2-3 shows an example of an elliptical selection. Whereas the lasso tools make freeform selections, the Magic Wand tool creates selections by picking up pixels of similar colors. The Quick Selection tool enables you to "paint" your desired selection. And the Move and Crop tools do just what their names describe — move and crop images. See Book III, Chapter 1 for details on all the selection tools except the Move and Crop tools. You can find Move-tool details in Book III, Chapter 3, and Book V, Chapters 1 and 5. Crop-tool details reside in Book II, Chapter 1.

Creating and modifying paths

The path tools create and modify *paths,* which are elements comprised of straight and curved segments and anchor points. You can then use these paths as a basis for a selection or to define a shape.

Because of their precision, you may find that using path tools to create a difficult selection usually yields better results than you can achieve with the selection tools.

Figure 2-3: The Elliptical Marquee tool (left) lets you make an elliptical selection; the Move tool (right) enables you to move a selection within your image.

The Path Selection and Direct Selection tools select your paths and path components after you draw the path. Figure 2-4 shows examples of using the Pen tool and Direct Selection tool, respectively. (For more on the Pen tools, see Book III, Chapter 2.)

Corbis Digital Stock

Figure 2-4: The Pen tool creates a path of anchor points and segments; use the Direct Selection tool to select and manipulate those points and segments.

Using painting tools

Generally, the painting tools allow you to apply color or erase pixels. In the case of the Gradient tool, you can apply multiple colors simultaneously. And with the Art History Brush tool, you paint on a stylized effect rather than color. The Color Replacement tool lets you replace the color within your image with the foreground color. Figure 2-5 shows an example of a heart drawn with the Custom Shape tool, painted with the Brush tool (using the Scattered Rose brush tip), Special

Figure 2-5: The painting tools can add texture and color to a basic shape; the Eraser tool erases pixels to reveal your background color.

Effects brush (left), and later (right) partially erased with the Eraser tool.

 The new Mixer Brush tool simulates traditional, natural media painting methods, such as blending and mixing color together and varying the wetness within a brushstroke. See Book IV, Chapter 1 for more on the Mixer Brush tool.

 All the painting tools rely on the Brushes panel for the size, shape, texture, and angle for the tip of the tool. See Book IV, Chapters 1 and 2, for details on most of the painting tools. You can find an explanation of the Eraser's Erase to History option in Book II, Chapter 4.

Using tools for cloning and healing

The cloning and retouching tools are the powerhouse tools to break out when you need to do some image repairs. These tools allow you to duplicate portions of your image, paint with a pattern, or seamlessly fix scratches, wrinkles, and other blemishes. The unique History Brush tool lets you actually paint a previous version of your image back into your current image — perfect for undoing mistakes.

The Spot Healing Brush quickly removes small blemishes and hickeys of all kinds. The Red Eye tool removes the nasty red reflections in the eyes of your loved ones, as shown in Figure 2-6. Be sure to check out Book VIII, Chapter 3 for info on cloning, pattern stamping, and healing. You can find History Brush details in Book II, Chapter 4.

Figure 2-6: The Red Eye tool is a quick and easy way to correct demon eyes.

Creating effects with typographical tools

Type tools pretty much do what their moniker suggests — create type of varying sorts. The Horizontal Type tool and Vertical Type tool create regular old type, and type on a path; the Mask Type tools create selections in the shape of letters — which you can then fill with images, patterns, colors, and so on. Figure 2-7 shows text created using both the Horizontal Type and Horizontal Type Mask tools. (For type tool details, see Book IV, Chapter 3.)

life's a beach

Corbis Digital Stock

Figure 2-7: You can easily create vector type (left) or a type mask (right) in Photoshop.

Using focus and toning tools

The focus and toning tools allow you to enhance your image by altering the pixels in various ways. You can lighten, darken, blur, smudge, sharpen, saturate, or desaturate color in selected portions of your image.

These tools work best for touching up smaller areas, rather than the entire image. For example, in Figure 2-8, I used the Smudge tool to spike the groom's hair. (I hope he doesn't take it personally.) To saturate the orange on the right, I used the Sponge tool. See Book VIII, Chapter 2 for all you want to know about focus and toning tools.

Creating shapes

The shape tools allow you to create vector-based elements in your image. You can fill these elements with the foreground color or leave them as an empty path.

Although vector-based elements are the heart and soul of the shape tools, you can also create shapes filled with pixels of the foreground color. For shape details, see Book IV, Chapter 1. For more on resolution, see Book II, Chapter 1. Figure 2-9 shows the Custom Shape (left) and Rectangle and Ellipse tools (right) in action.

Corbis Digital Stock

Figure 2-8: You can make your images stand out from the crowd with the Smudge (left) or Sponge (right) tool.

Figure 2-9: Create shapes from large preset libraries (or from your own imagination) with the shape tools.

Viewing, navigating, sampling, and annotating tools

Photoshop has an abundance of tools to help you view and navigate your image window. These tools allow you to zoom in (as shown in Figure 2-10) and out, move your image within the window, and measure distances and angles. The Eyedropper and Color Sampler tools let you pick up and sample color respectively — handy for grabbing or evaluating color in an image. The Notes tool creates written notes that you can leave within an image window — useful for collaboration purposes or simply for reminders to yourself. (See Book II, Chapter 3 for more on the Eyedropper and Color Sampler tools. For the lowdown on the Measure, Zoom, and Hand tools, see Book I, Chapter 4.)

Figure 2-10: The Zoom tool enables you to zoom in and out of your image.

ON THE WEB

Bonus Chapter 3 covers the Notes tool. See the Introduction for details about this book's companion Web site.

Using tools for the Web

Photoshop doesn't have a whole lot of tools dedicated to the preparation of Web images. That's mainly because Adobe's other programs (Fireworks, Dreamweaver, and Flash) take up the slack in that department. In the Tools panel, you find the Slice tool and Slice Select tool, which allow you to create and select slices. *Slices* are rectangular sections from an image that you can optimize and turn into Web features. For example, you might slice an image and, in Dreamweaver, apply rollovers and image maps to those slices separately for the best viewing experience on your Web page.

See Bonus Chapter 2 for all you need to know about slicing. The Introduction has all the details about this book's Web site.

Photoshop also provides a whole array of 3-D tools, which you can use to create graphics for Web animation, but only in the Extended version.

Saving Time with Tool Presets

Tool presets enable you to create tool settings that you can save and use again. Creating tool presets is a real timesaver if you use specific tool settings on a frequent basis. For example, I make numerous 2-x-2-inch and 2-x-3-inch rectangular selections on images I use in a newsletter. Because I saved the settings as presets, I don't have to redefine them each time I want to select an image for my project.

Creating custom tool presets

Follow these short and simple steps to create your own custom tool preset:

1. **Select the tool you want to create a preset for.**

2. **Select the option you want for the tool on the Options bar.**

   For example, if you selected the Rectangular Marquee tool in Step 1, you may want to select Fixed Size from the Style pop-up menu and then enter your desired Width and Height values.

3. **Click the Tool Preset Picker button on the Options bar, as shown in Figure 2-11 (it's on the far-left side of the Options bar).**

   Or you can choose Window⇨Tool Presets to work through the Tool Presets panel.

Tool Preset Picker button   Create a new tool preset

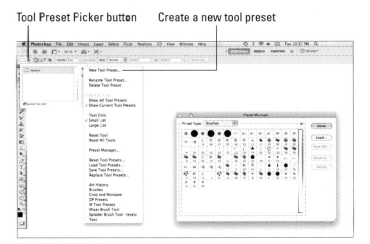

Figure 2-11: Create a custom tool preset for tool settings that you use often.

4. Click the Create New Tool Preset button (the dog-eared-page icon).

Or, if you're using the Tool Presets panel, choose New Tool Preset from the panel menu. If the tool doesn't allow for presets, such as the Measure tool, for example, the Create New Tool Preset button is gray.

5. Name the preset and click OK.

Your new preset is saved and ready for reuse.

6. To select the tool preset, you can do one of three things:

- Click the Tool Preset Picker button and select a preset from the picker's pop-up menu.

- Select a preset in the Tool Presets panel.

- Select a preset in the Preset Manager (Edit⇨Preset Manager). Then, choose Tools from the pop-up menu and select your preset.

The Tool Presets panel contains a trash can icon that enables you to delete a preset quickly. Select the preset and drag it to the trash.

Managing your presets

You can manage your presets by selecting options from the Tool Preset Picker pop-up menu. Table 2-1 describes these options.

Table 2-1	The Tool Preset Picker Pop-Up Menu
Option	*What It Does*
New Tool Preset	Creates a new preset.
Rename Tool Preset	Renames the preset. (Select the preset in the list and then select this option.)
Delete Tool Preset	Deletes a preset. (Select the preset in the list and then select this option.)
Sort by Tool	Groups your presets by tool.
Show All Tool Presets	Shows the presets for all your tools.
Show Current Tool Presets	Shows the presets for the active tool only.
Text Only	Gives you the name of the preset without the icon.
Small List	Shows a small icon, along with the preset name.
Large List	Shows a larger icon with the preset name.
Reset Tool	Closes the active preset and returns to the default tool setting.
Reset All Tools	Returns all tools to their defaults.
Preset Manager	Opens the Preset Manager, which manages all the various libraries of preset brushes, swatches, gradients, styles, patterns, contours, custom shapes, and tools. You can also load other libraries and the custom preset libraries you've created. Additionally, you can rename or delete a preset.
Reset Tool Presets	Replaces your current tool presets with the default presets. If you want to restore the defaults but keep your custom tool presets, select Append.
Load Tool Presets	Loads tool presets that you've previously saved or acquired elsewhere.
Save Tool Presets	Saves a custom set of tool presets for later retrieval. The saved file has a `.tpl` extension.
Replace Tool Presets	Replaces your current tool presets. Allows you to load a `.tpl` file that replaces your current tool presets.
Art History, Brushes, Crop and Marquee, DP Presets, M Tool Presets, Mixer Brush Tool, Splatter Brush Tool Presets and Text options	Allows you to either append or replace your current tool presets with the tool presets from each of those individual libraries.

Chapter 3: Starting, Finishing, and Getting It on Paper

In This Chapter

✔ Opening images

✔ Saving images

✔ Closing down Photoshop

✔ Printing from Windows and the Mac

*A*lthough you can create some interesting images from scratch in Photoshop, most of the time you work with digital pictures that already exist. These pictures may be images captured by your scanner or photos you've snapped with your digital camera.

Photoshop offers you a lot of different options for opening existing images, creating new images, and saving original files or copies to your hard drive. After you open, edit, and save your files, you may want to transfer those images from screen to paper. This chapter takes you through the steps you need to know to get your photos in and out of Photoshop.

Browsing for Files

If you don't know the exact filename or location of an image, you can use Adobe Bridge to search for and open files. (Check out Book I, Chapter 4 for a complete description of Bridge.) Finding a file is about as easy as you might expect: Choose File➪Browse in Bridge or press Alt+Ctrl+O (Option+⌘+O on the Mac). The Bridge window opens, as shown in Figure 3-1.

You can also just click the Launch Bridge button, which is a Br icon on the Application bar.

You can also now browse in the new Mini Bridge, which can even remain within your application window as a panel. For more on this handy new addition, see Book I, Chapter 4.

iStockphoto

Figure 3-1: Adobe Bridge allows you to efficiently search for your images.

In the default workspace, to navigate to a folder you want to search, click the Folders tab and locate your desired folder from the list. Click an image in the lightbox area to see it in the Preview window (which shows up on the right side of the Bridge). Bridge graciously provides information about the file in the Metadata panel located below the Preview.

When you find a file you're sure you want to open, either double-click it, choose File⇨Open, or choose File⇨Open With (and then choose your desired application) on the Bridge menu.

Opening an Image

If you know where an image file is stored, you can open the file in a similar way to opening a word-processing, spreadsheet, or other file. Follow these steps to open a file:

1. **In Photoshop, choose File⇨Open.**

    Or press Ctrl+O (⌘+O on the Mac).

    The standard Open dialog box for Windows or the Mac OS (operating system) appears. The layout of the dialog box differs slightly between the two. Figure 3-2 shows the Windows version and Figure 3-3 the Mac version.

Figure 3-2: Opening a file in Photoshop on a PC in Windows.

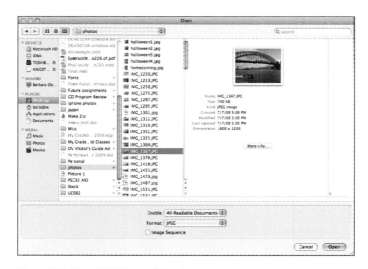

Figure 3-3: Mac OS X Open dialog box.

2. **Navigate to the folder that contains your file.**

   From the Files of type list (Windows) or Enable list (Mac OS), you can select which types of files you want to display.

   To view all files, select All Formats (Windows) or All Readable Documents (Mac OS).

3. **Click the name of the image file you want to open.**

   To select multiple files, click the first file and then Ctrl-click (⌘-click on the Mac) each additional file.

   You may see a preview of the image in the Open dialog box's Preview window.

4. **After you select the file you want, click the Open button.**

   The file opens in Photoshop.

   If you choose File⇨Open Recent, a submenu lists the last files you worked on. Click a filename to open it or simply type the number next to the filename. You can specify the number of files that appear on this menu in the File Handling section of the Preferences dialog box. (For the lowdown on how to specify this value, jump ahead to Book I, Chapter 5.)

Opening special files

Photoshop needs to know the image format of a file (whether it's a TIFF, PCX, PSD, or JPEG file, for example) before it can open the file. Photoshop uses different methods in Windows and Mac OS to determine the format of an image file:

- ✔ In Windows, Photoshop looks at the file extension (.tif, .pcx, .psd, and so forth), and if it finds a standard image format extension, it assumes that the file was saved using that format.

  File extensions are hidden by default in Windows. You, like many other users, may have changed the default to display file extensions.

- ✔ Mac OS X uses a similar system based on filename extensions. File extensions may or may not be hidden in the Mac OS. Showing or hiding file extensions can be accomplished via any file's Info dialog box. Select the file in the Mac OS X Finder and press ⌘+I to make the Info dialog box pop up. In this dialog box, you can show or hide the extension for that file and change what application is associated with that file (or all files with the same extension).

For compatibility reasons, Macintosh applications such as Photoshop usually use the Windows file extension. However, when you move files from one platform to the other, they can easily be misidentified. With Photoshop's

Open As feature, you can specify the format that you think (or know) a given file uses. This facility works slightly differently in Windows than in the Mac OS.

Opening specific files using the Windows OS

In Windows, follow these steps to open a specific file:

1. **Choose File⇨Open As and navigate to the file you want to open.**

2. **From the Open As drop-down list, select the file format you want to use.**

3. **Double-click the file's icon.**

   If you selected the right format in Step 2, the file opens in Photoshop. If the file doesn't open, you may have selected the wrong format. Select another and try again.

Opening specific files using the Mac OS

The standard Open dialog box includes an Enable option at the bottom. Select All Documents from the Enable pop-up menu. Then, you can select the file format you want to try directly from the Format list.

Opening as a Smart Object

Photoshop enables you to open a file as a Smart Object. Choose File⇨Open as Smart Object to create a special layer that can contain both raster and vector data. Smart Objects are beneficial because they allow you to transform and manipulate your image data non-destructively. (For details on Smart Objects, see Book V, Chapter 5.)

Placing Files

In Photoshop, use File⇨Place to put PDF (Portable Document Format), Adobe Illustrator (AI), EPS (Encapsulated PostScript), PSD, JPEG, TIFF, BMP, GIF, PNG, and several other lesser-used file formats into separate layers of their own. These files are often created by programs other than Photoshop (such as Adobe Acrobat or Adobe Illustrator) or acquired from your digital camera. Although Photoshop can open these files independently, you can use the Place feature if you want to combine them with an existing image.

Follow these steps to place a PDF, Adobe Illustrator, or EPS file:

1. **Open an existing document into which you want to place a file.**

2. **Choose File⇨Place.**

   The Place dialog box opens.

3. **Navigate to the file you want to insert and then double-click the file.**

   If you're placing an Illustrator file, make sure it was saved with PDF Compatibility selected in the Illustrator Options dialog box. Otherwise, it may not be placed.

   For some types of files, such as multipage PDF files, you may see a dialog box like the one shown in Figure 3-4, which lets you specify which page you want to place. You can also select either the entire Page or just a particular Image on the page. Finally, select how much of your image you want to place from the Crop To pop-up menu. The default bounding box crops to the smallest area that includes text and graphics.

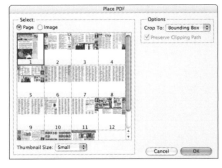

Figure 3-4: Use the Place command when importing a page from a multipage PDF into an existing file.

   Photoshop automatically places PDFs, JPEGs, TIFFs, or PNGs (among other image types) as Smart Objects. For more on Smart Objects, see Book V, Chapter 5.

   Your image appears in a bounding box in the center of your Photoshop image.

4. **If you want, reposition the artwork by positioning your cursor inside the bounding box and dragging.**

   You can also transform (scale, rotate, and so on) your placed artwork, if you want — by dragging or rotating the handles on the bounding box or by entering values on the Options bar. Hold down the Shift key to constrain the proportions when scaling.

   You don't have to be concerned if your placed image is a Smart Object, but be careful about sizing non–Smart Object images. If you enlarge them too much, you may degrade the quality of your image. For more information on transforming images, see Book III, Chapter 3. Avoid degradation of quality by creating a Smart Object, which I explain in Book V, Chapter 5.

   Note that when you place a file, you can't edit the text or vector artwork in it within Photoshop. Why? Because Photoshop rasterizes the file, using the resolution of the file into which you placed it. You can, however, edit a Smart Object in the program it was created in, such as Illustrator. See Book V, Chapter 5 for details. Note that when art is larger than the Photoshop image, Photoshop downsizes the art so that it fits the image. See Book II, Chapter 1 for more on rasterizing and resolution.

5. **If you're placing vector artwork, select Anti-Alias on the Options bar if you want to soften the edges of the artwork during the transformation.**

   Not selecting the option produces a hard edge.

6. **Double-click inside the bounding box to commit the placed image to a new layer.**

   You can also press Enter (Return on the Mac) or click the Commit button (the check icon) on the Options bar.

Creating a New Image

At some point, you'll want to create a new image from scratch. You may want an empty canvas to paint on or need a blank image as scratch space. Or you may want to paste a copied selection into a new document.

Follow these steps to use the New feature to create a new image:

1. **Choose File⇨New.**

   Or press Ctrl+N (⌘+N on the Mac).

   The New dialog box appears, as shown in Figure 3-5.

2. **Type a name for the new file.**

   If you don't specify a name, Photoshop creates one for you, such as Untitled-1, Untitled-2, and so forth.

3. **If you want to create content for mobile devices (such a cellphone, PDA, or mini portable PC), click the Device Central button.**

Figure 3-5: Specify all your desired options in the New dialog box.

   What follows is a fairly quick, easy process:

   a. *Specify your desired preferences by choosing Edit⇨Preferences (Device Central⇨Preferences on the Mac) and selecting your default Phone ID, language, and fonts in the Preferences dialog box. Click OK.*

      You may also specify your levels of Undo.

   b. *In the dialog box's main window, click the Browse tab to select a category from the Library Filter in the bottom left and then choose one or more devices from the list in the Device Library, as shown in Figure 3-6.*

c. *Click the Create tab and then under the New Document tab, select the type of content you want to create, such as a full-screen graphic or wallpaper, from the Content Type drop-down menu.*

To create a custom size, check the Custom Size option at the bottom and enter your desired dimensions.

d. *Click Create.*

Your new, blank document, sized and ready for art, opens in Photoshop. Note that the default is 72 ppi, RGB color mode, using an sRGB color profile. For more on resolution and modes, see Book II, Chapter 2.

If you want to preview how your content will look, choose File⇨Save for Web & Devices. See Bonus Chapter 1 on this book's Web site for details.

Note that you can also access the Device Library dialog box by choosing File⇨Device Central. And you find the same command in both Adobe Illustrator and Flash.

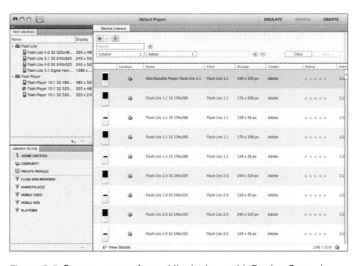

Figure 3-6: Create content for mobile devices with Device Central.

4. **In the New dialog box, select a preset image category from the Preset pop-up menu.**

Choose from common categories such as U.S. Paper, Photo, Web, Mobile and Devices, and Film and Video.

The Clipboard provides the size that corresponds with an image that you copied. Here are a couple of other preset tips:

- You can also choose to match the size of any open file. Open files are listed at the bottom of the Preset list.

- If you select Custom, Photoshop also allows you to create a user-defined custom preset based on your defined settings: After you define your values, click the Save Preset button in the New Document Preset dialog box. Name your preset. Choose any or all the options you want to include in your preset. When you choose not to include an option, Photoshop displays the last used value for that option. Click OK. Your custom preset row appears near the top of the Preset list.

5. **If you selected an image category from the Preset menu in Step 4, select your desired preset Size for that category.**

6. **Or, if you chose Custom in Step 4, enter the width and height of your image manually by typing the width and height of your choice in the text boxes.**

   Note that any Preset sizes automatically revert to Custom when any of the preset's values are changed, and that when you change the units for either the width or height, the other dimension also changes. You can hold down the Shift key to change both width and height independently.

   Like with other Photoshop dialog boxes, you may change from the default unit of measurement of pixels to another, such as inches.

7. **Enter the resolution for the new document.**

   When you select a Preset image category and size, the recommended resolution is entered for you. You can change this resolution if desired, but remember that selecting the right resolution at this point in the creation process is important because if you need to change the resolution later, you degrade image quality. (For more information on selecting an appropriate resolution, see Book II, Chapter 1.)

   Note that Photoshop gives you the size of your image file, based on your settings, in the lower-right portion of the dialog box. This information is good to know if you're targeting a specific file size for your image.

8. **From the Color Mode drop-down list, select a color mode.**

   Your choices include Bitmap, Grayscale, RGB Color, CMYK Color, and Lab Color.

9. **Select your desired color depth for your document.**

   Only 1-bit color depth is available for bitmap images. (Each pixel is either black or white.) The 8-bit and 16-bit color depths are available for the other color modes. And you may also create a new 32-bit image in RGB or Grayscale modes. For details on modes and color depths, see Book II, Chapter 2

10. **In the Background Contents drop-down list, select an option for how you want the background layer to be filled.**

    Your choices are white, the current background color, or transparent.

11. **Click the Advanced button to display a couple of additional options:**

    • *Color Profile:* Assigns a *color profile* (a definition of the way color looks in a document) to your new document. The default, Adobe RGB (1998), is fine when creating a new document unless you have good reason not to. This setting provides a nice, large *gamut* (range) of RGB colors.

    • *Pixel Aspect Ratio:* Selects an *aspect ratio* (the relationship of width to height of a pixel). The default setting of Square Pixels is fine for print or Web images. Images for digital video content may require a non-square aspect ratio, such as D1/DV NTSC.

12. **Click OK when you finish entering your options.**

    Photoshop creates the new image.

Saving a File

Before you exit Photoshop, you want to save your file on your hard drive or other media. Don't worry if you forget to do this; Photoshop won't let you exit without first asking you if you want to save any files that you've changed or newly created.

Saving files from time to time while you work on them is a good idea so that you always have a recent copy safely stored on your drive.

Follow these steps to save a file:

1. **Choose File⇨Save to store the current file with its present name.**

   Choose File⇨Save As to store a file already saved with a different name, or even a file with the same name but in a different location.

   The dialog box appears, as shown in Figure 3-7.

2. **Navigate to the folder where you want to store the file.**

3. **Type a name in the File Name (Save As on the Mac) text box.**

4. **Select a format from the Format drop-down list.**

   Some file formats have special capabilities and requirements. For details on file formats, see Book II, Chapter 2.

Figure 3-7: Saving a file frequently is one of the smartest things you can do in Photoshop.

5. **In the Save and Color options areas, select or deselect (if available) the following check boxes, as desired:**

   - *As a Copy:* Save the file as a copy.

   - *Notes:* Include or delete notes you have created with the Note tool in the saved copy. (See Bonus Chapter 3 for more on notes. The Introduction has details about this book's bonus material on the Web.)

   - *Alpha Channels:* Include or ignore *alpha channels* (stored selections). (See Book VI, Chapter 1 for a discussion of channels.)

   - *Spot Colors:* Enable spot colors in the saved file. (For more information on spot colors, see Book IX, Chapter 1.)

   - *Layers:* Include layers or simply flatten the image to one layer. (See Book V, Chapter 1 for the lowdown on layers.)

   - *Use Proof Setup:* Enable proof setup, which includes an onscreen preview of how the image will look when printed or viewed on a specific device. (See Book II, Chapter 3 for more information.)

- *ICC Profile (Windows)/Embed Color Profile (Mac):* Embed a color profile in the file based on the settings established in your Color Settings dialog box. Leave this value at the default setting, but check out Book II, Chapter 3 for information on the specialized situations when you might want to change it.

- *Thumbnail (Windows only):* Embed a thumbnail image in the file if you've defined thumbnails as optional in Photoshop's Preferences. (You can find more on preferences in Book I, Chapter 5.)

- *Use Lower Case Extension (Windows only):* Use lowercase extensions (that is, .tif rather than .TIF), regardless of how you type the filename.

6. **Depending on which file format you select, you may get an additional dialog box of options.**

   For specifics on these file format options, see Book II, Chapter 2.

7. **Click Save to store the image.**

Closing and Quitting

When your session is finished, you want to close up shop and quit Photoshop. PC users, in addition to using the traditional File⇨Exit option, can close Photoshop in any of the following ways:

- Choose Close from the Windows Control menu in the upper-left corner of the Photoshop title bar.

- Click the Close (X) button in the upper-right corner of the Photoshop title bar below Windows.

- Press Ctrl+Q.

Mac users can choose Photoshop⇨Quit Photoshop or press ⌘+Q.

When you use any of these methods, Photoshop asks you whether you want to save any open file that hasn't been saved (or hasn't been saved since it was modified in this session). Click the Yes button to save and close the files.

You can also close any open files without exiting Photoshop by pressing Ctrl+Alt+W (⌘+Option+W on the Mac).

You want to have a backup copy of an image safe on your hard drive prior to an editing session. If you change your mind about the modifications you make to an image, you can always return to the backup copy. Choose File⇨ Save As and enter a new name for the file. You can also select the As a Copy check box and append the word "copy" to the current filename.

Getting It on Paper

Hard-copy prints have become a hugely popular output option, thanks largely to the swarm of inexpensive photo-quality inkjet printers that are vying for your discretionary dollars. Today, anyone can afford a printer capable of producing sparkling prints from digital images. The chief problem is restraining the urge to print everything in sight before your ink tank (and wallet) runs dry.

Actually, making the prints is only a minor puzzle, and one addressed in the following sections. You can print most images with just a few clicks. Most of the advanced options I discuss in this chapter are needed only for special situations or specialized applications, and they're not discussed in detail; the following sections cover only the basics. If you need more detailed information on printing, see Book IX, Chapter 1.

Many photofinishers, service bureaus, or even retail outlets can make prints from your Photoshop-edited images if you burn them to a CD, save them to a USB flash drive, or upload them to an FTP site over the Internet. Vendors such as Shutterfly (`www.shutterfly.com`), Kodak Gallery (`www.kodakgallery.com`), and Snapfish (`www.snapfish.com`) offer prints of all sizes, calendars, and professionally printed and bound photo books. One of my favorite places to get great quality photos, photo books, and even photos printed on canvas is Costco.

Taking a look at printers

You can print Photoshop images on any kind of printer — but aside from the occasional 200-copy print run of black-and-white "Have You Seen This Kitty?" posters, monochrome laser printers are not high on the list of favored Photoshop output hardware.

More often, you're choosing a full-color printer — probably an inkjet model, but possibly other models (such as dye-sublimation, thermal-wax, solid-ink, or even color laser) — as your printer. Although all these printers produce roughly similar results, they do have some differences, as detailed in the following list:

- **Inkjet printers:** These printers paint the page by spraying a jet of ink one dot at a time, under precision computer control. They produce better results when used with photo paper designed especially for inkjets. Inkjet printers generally provide excellent full-color output, but the cost of consumables (ink and paper) can add up fast.

- **Dye-sublimation printers:** These printers potentially offer better-looking prints, but the printers and materials are more expensive than inkjet printers. They use a continuous ribbon of color panels in a roll that's the same width as the print, with each panel used only once. The print head's tiny heating elements can melt dots of dye over a range of 256 values to generate up to 16.8 million colors.

✔ **Thermal-wax printers and solid-ink printers:** These printers use blocks of wax or resin that are melted and sprayed directly onto a page. These devices are commonly used in printing barcodes and labels for clothing, autos, and aircraft.

✔ **Color Laser:** Color laser printers use colored toner and apply ink in four passes. They tend to be a little more expensive, and the quality isn't as good as a nice inkjet print. They do usually print much faster than inkjet printers.

Printing an image

The process of printing an image in Photoshop is slightly different in the Windows and Mac operating systems. The chief differences are in the Print Settings (previously the Page Setup) dialog box, in which you can select a printer and specify orientation, paper size, and other parameters. The following sections take a closer look at the Print Settings dialog box in the two operating systems. Note that unlike the old Page Setup command, the Print Settings command cannot be accessed via the File menu, but instead it's tucked away as a button in the Print dialog box.

Print settings in Microsoft Windows

With Windows applications such as Photoshop, you open the Print Settings dialog box by choosing File➪Print and clicking the Print Settings button. The Properties dialog box then appears. On the Main and Page Setup tabs, you can select the paper size, orientation (portrait or landscape), and other things — such as which paper tray to use, as shown in Figure 3-8. Click Save, or Preview, to return to the main Print dialog box.

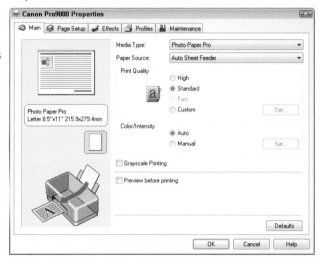

Figure 3-8: Set your desired paper size in the Windows Properties dialog box.

Print settings in the Mac OS

Choose File➪Print and click the Print Settings button. You can set the desired printer, page size, and additional parameters, depending on your printer, as shown in Figure 3-9. Click Save, or Preview, to return to the main Print dialog box.

 In Mac OS X, you can also select a printer directly from the Print dialog box, just like you can in Windows. Also in Mac OS X, if you're connected directly to a printer via the USB port, the system automatically detects the printer. If you're on a network, select a printer from the Printer pop-up menu in the Print dialog box.

Figure 3-9: The Mac Print dialog box offers options for a printer and paper size.

Setting printing options

Photoshop has a couple printing modes to choose from, depending on how much control you need and how much of a hurry you're in. Here are your options:

- ✏ **Print One Copy:** A quick way to print a hard copy using the default settings.

- ✏ **Print (Ctrl+P on a PC, ⌘+P on the Mac):** Opens a generous Print dialog box that includes a Preview pane and many options. This dialog box is almost identical in Windows and Mac operating systems. Figure 3-10 shows the Windows version.

Digital Vision

Figure 3-10: The Print dialog box gives you a multitude of options.

To set your print options, follow these steps:

1. **Choose File➪Print.**

   The Print dialog box opens.

2. **Select your desired printer from the Printer drop-down list.**

3. **Specify the number of copies you want.**

4. **(Mac only) Select Send 16-Bit Data if your image is 16-bit.**

5. **Click the Print Settings button if you need to revisit that dialog box.**

   In Windows, this dialog box may look different than the one you see when choosing File➪Page Setup, depending on which printer you selected in the Print dialog box. You may see specific settings customized for your printer, such as print quality, special effects, and so on. These settings vary from printer to printer, so be sure to consult your printer's instruction manual.

6. **Change your page orientation in the Print dialog box by clicking the Portrait or Landscape button next to the Print Settings button.**

7. **Use the Top and Left boxes in the Position area to indicate where you want the image to appear on the page.**

   To center the image, select the Center Image check box. You can also click and drag the image in the preview window to position it if the Bounding Box option is selected.

8. **If you aren't centering your image, select your desired unit of measurement from the Units drop-down list at the bottom of the dialog box.**

9. **If you want to scale the image up or down, select the scale percentage and/or enter height and width values in the Scaled Print Size area.**

   You can also scale the image by clicking and dragging the corner handles of the image in the preview window. However, make sure the Bounding Box option is selected. Scaling in the Print dialog box doesn't change the physical dimensions of the image, just the print size. But keep in mind that scaling up may give you a less-than-optimum printout. Additional options include

   • *Scale to Fit Media:* Sizes your image to fit on a particular paper size.

   • *Match Print Colors:* Gives you a soft proof in your preview. For more on soft proofs, see Book II, Chapter 3.

   • *Gamut Warning:* This option displays colors that will be *out of gamut,* or out of the range of printable colors. These colors appear as gray pixels by default.

   • *Show Paper White:* This option simulates the white point of the paper you choose in the Printer Profile submenu. (Choose Color Management from the menu at the top-right to access the Printer Profile submenu.)

TIP

The Match Print Colors, Gamut Warning, and Show Paper White options are available only when your Color Handling is set to Photoshop Manages Colors. For details on color management when printing, see Book IX, Chapter 1.

- *Bounding Box:* Places the handles around the image area and allows for visual sizing.

- *Print Selected Area:* Allows you to print only part of a large image. You need to make the selection before choosing the Print command.

- *Units:* Select your desired unit of measurement.

Your document's resolution is now displayed, as well.

10. Choose Output from the drop-down list located in the top-right.

The other option on the drop-down list, Color Management, controls advanced proofing and color-profile tasks. (Check out Book IX, Chapter 1 for information on printing using color management and Book II, Chapter 3 for more detail on general color-management topics.)

11. Select the Output printing options you want to apply:

- *Background:* The area surrounding the printed image is called the *background,* not to be confused with the *background color* on the Colors panel or the *background layer* of an image. You can change this color from the default (white) to any other color.

- *Border:* The dialog box that pops up lets you add a black border around an image in any width from 0 to 10 points, 0 to 3.5 millimeters, or 0 to 0.15 inches.

- *Bleed:* A *bleed* is an image that extends right up to the edge of the paper size on one or more edges. In effect, you're cropping inside the image area. In practice, most printers don't actually print right to the edge, so to bleed, say, a 5-x-7-inch image, you need to print it on a larger sheet of paper, such as 6 x 8 inches. Clicking the Bleed button opens a dialog box in which you enter a width in inches, millimeters, or points inside the edge of the image.

- *Interpolation:* This option is available with only some printers, particularly PostScript Level 2 (or higher models), to even out the jagged appearance of diagonal lines. Just be aware that interpolation can help only so much, and in some cases, it can be damaging. For more on interpolation, see Book II, Chapter 1.

- *Include Vector Data:* If you have vector artwork in your image, be sure to include this option. For more info on printing vector data, see Book IX, Chapter 1.

12. Select options for marking the area outside the print area.

These options include several items that appear only when the print area is smaller than the paper size:

- *Calibration Bars:* This option adds an 11-step grayscale bar outside the image area when printing to a paper size that's larger than the image area. You can use calibration bars to gauge how accurately the gray tones of an image are being reproduced.

- *Registration Marks:* Registration marks are handy when you're printing with multiple plates for color separations, such as those used in four-color or duotone processes. These marks help keep the plates aligned so the image is printed properly.

- *Corner Crop Marks:* Selecting this box prints crop marks at the corners of the image, which indicate where trimming should take place. You can see these and other marks in Figure 3-11.

- *Center Crop Marks:* These crop marks show where the page will be trimmed at the top, bottom, and each side.

- *Description:* To include a description on a printout, choose File⇨File Info and enter the text you want to appear. Then, select the Description box in the Print dialog box.

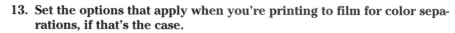

Corner crop marks   Center crop mark

Registration mark   Label

Corbis Digital Stock

- *Labels:* Selecting this check box prints the document name and

Figure 3-11: Crop marks are handy to print.

channel name on the image. (See Book VI, Chapter 1 for more on channels.)

13. **Set the options that apply when you're printing to film for color separations, if that's the case.**

Be sure to talk to your service bureau or offset printer representative for their recommendations. (For more tips, see Book IX, Chapter 1.)

Here are your choices:

- *Emulsion Down:* The side of a film or photographic print paper that's light-sensitive is called the emulsion side. You must specify whether you want the emulsion side up or side down for film output. Emulsion Down is the most common film output choice, although some publications may request Emulsion Up. The default is Emulsion Up. (The check box isn't selected.) This option isn't available with all printers.

- *Negative:* When you print an image on paper, you usually want a positive image; in which case, you shouldn't select the Negative check box. If you're printing the image on film (as is the case if you're printing color separations), your printer will probably request a negative.

14. **Click Print.**

Chapter 4: Viewing and Navigating Images

In This Chapter

- ✐ Exploring the image window
- ✐ Zooming within an image
- ✐ Moving with the Hand tool
- ✐ Traveling around with the Navigator
- ✐ Selecting screen modes
- ✐ Positioning and measuring precisely
- ✐ Finding images with Adobe Bridge
- ✐ Sharing images in a PDF or Web gallery
- ✐ Introducing Mini Bridge

*P*hotoshop offers a variety of ways to view your image documents while you work with them. You can pull back to look at the big picture or zoom in to work on a tiny portion of the image in minute detail. A useful Navigator panel is also at hand to show you exactly where you are in an image and help you move to a specific spot with a click of the mouse button. Should you want to align objects precisely on the screen, Photoshop offers grids and guides with some "magnetic" properties. If you're having trouble finding the image you want, using an uber-browser, called Adobe Bridge, helps you search visually. And the new Mini Bridge is a compact browsing tool that docks itself as a panel in your Photoshop window.

This chapter introduces you to all these viewing and navigating aids, each designed to help you spend less time cruising around the images and more time working with them.

Looking at the Image Window

Each Photoshop image document resides in its own window. A great feature of this window is that you can open multiple image windows for the same image. This feature comes in handy because sometimes you want to look at an image from two perspectives. For example, you may want to get up close and personal with an image to edit pixels, but you still want to view the full image in a fairly large size, as shown in Figure 4-1. In either case, all you need to do is create a new image window for the same image. You can size each window separately, and you can center the window on any portion of the image you want.

Corbis Digital Stock

Figure 4-1: Creating a new image window enables you to view the overall image while editing an area in close-up view.

Here's a quick list of what you can do with multiple windows:

- ✓ **Keep different parts of an image straight by creating multiple windows.** Select the document window you want and then choose Window⇨ Arrange⇨New Window for (*filename*) from the Menu bar. You can size and position the new window, and zoom in or out, without affecting the view of the original window.

- ✓ **Keep windows organized by cascading them.** If you find that you've created so many windows that you can't view them all easily, Photoshop can automatically arrange them for you in its working space. Choose Window⇨Arrange⇨Cascade to create an overlapping stack of windows arranged from the upper-left to the lower-right side of your display. Be sure, however, that your images are all floating in windows. (Choose Window➪Arrange➪Float All in Windows.)

✔ **Keep from losing important windows by tiling them.** Choose Window➪Arrange➪Tile to arrange the windows side by side without overlapping. Photoshop shrinks the document windows so they all fit onscreen, but it doesn't change the zoom amount.

You can also click the Arrange Documents icon (next to the last icon) in the Application bar. Select from among a variety of layouts for your image windows. For example, you can choose to Tile All Vertically.

✔ **Tidy up by closing windows you don't need anymore.** To close a specific window when your images are tabbed, click its Close button in the upper-right (upper-left on the Mac) corner of its title bar. If your images are in floating windows, click in the top-right (top-left on the Mac) corner.

✔ **Close all windows in one fell swoop.** To close all windows, choose File➪ Close All. You can also press Alt+Ctrl+W (Option+⌘+W on the Mac).

✔ **Minimize/maximize a document.** Note that your images must be in floating windows to view the Minimize and Maximize icons.

✔ **Bring all Photoshop documents to the front (in Mac OS).** The Mac OS allows you to work in multiple applications and multiple files simultaneously. Choose Window➪Arrange➪Bring All to Front to bring all your Photoshop documents to the forefront.

One image, two monitors

For many image-editing enthusiasts and professionals, one monitor simply isn't enough. If you have Windows Vista or 7 installed, or any recent Mac OS, you can set up your computer so that you can use two monitors to edit an image. The extra space offers advantages for viewing and navigating your images.

In Windows, you can drag the image window anywhere in the Photoshop working space. If you want to drag it to a second display screen (and your video card supports spanning two displays), you have to stretch the Photoshop working space (or application window) across both displays. This works great if both monitors are the same size. But if the monitors are significantly different sizes, it doesn't work so well. Either way, make sure your monitors are set to the same resolution. Remember that you can also move panels and dialog boxes onto a second monitor.

Although explaining how to set up multiple monitors on various operating systems is beyond the scope of this book, you can likely find details on how to set up an additional monitor in your operating system's Help feature.

Zooming In and Out of Image Windows

Photoshop offers several ways to zoom in or out of an image, but you'll probably find yourself using one method, such as the keyboard shortcuts, almost instinctively. Each method has advantages of its own. The following sections offer a quick discussion of the main zoom features, as well as some of the lesser-known zooming tricks.

Zooming with keyboard shortcuts

The keyboard shortcuts are the quickest and easiest way to zoom, after you use them enough to remember what they are. Table 4-1 offers a rundown of the handiest zoom keyboard shortcuts, which work no matter what tool you're using. When you press a keyboard shortcut, Photoshop zooms in or out by one of its preset increments (such as 200%, 100%, 50%, 33%, 25%, and so forth). The maximum magnification Photoshop now allows is 3,200%; the minimum magnification is less than 1%, way more than you'd ever need.

Table 4-1	Zooming with Keyboard Shortcuts	
To Do This	*Windows Shortcut*	*Mac Shortcut*
Zoom in.	Ctrl+the plus key (Press Ctrl and the + key.)	⌘+the plus key
Zoom out.	Ctrl+the minus key (Press Ctrl and then the − key.)	⌘+the minus key
Zoom in to a point centered on where you click the mouse button.	Spacebar+Ctrl-click	Spacebar+⌘-click
Zoom out from a point centered on where you click.	Spacebar+Alt-click	Spacebar+Option-click

Using the Zoom tool

Click the Zoom tool in the Tools panel or press Z to activate it. Click anywhere in the image to magnify it by one of the preset magnifications mentioned in the preceding section. Hold down the Alt key (or the Option key on the Mac) and click with the Zoom tool to zoom out. In either case, the zoom centers on the point you click.

Double-click the Zoom tool in the Tools panel to display your image at 100% magnification.

The Zoom tool's big advantage is its zoom selection facility. With the Zoom tool, drag in your image to create a temporary selection. When you release the button, Photoshop zooms in to fill the image window at the highest magnification that includes the selected area.

When the Zoom tool is active, you also have additional zoom tools on the Options bar, as shown in Figure 4-2. Selecting plus (+) or minus (−) sets the default magnification of the Zoom tool to either enlarge or reduce the image.

When you zoom in and out, Photoshop doesn't alter the size of the document window, so your image may become too large for its window (in which case, scroll bars appear so you can view the rest of the image) or too small (in which case, a gray border appears around the image).

Figure 4-2: Zoom options include handy buttons for fitting your image onscreen and displaying the image's print size.

Select the Resize Windows to Fit option on the Options bar to make Photoshop automatically change the size of the document window to show the full document in view, up to the size of the Photoshop working area.

within your screen; make the image fill your application working space; or make the document appear in the size it'll be when printed.

✔ **Use the Hand tool while zooming.** When the Hand tool is active, you can hold down the Alt key (Option key on the Mac) and click the image to zoom out, or hold down the Ctrl key (⌘ key on the Mac) and click to zoom in — without needing to press the spacebar like you would with the normal keyboard shortcut.

✔ **Scroll All Windows.** When the Hand tool is active, this option, in the Options bar, enables you to move around all open documents simultaneously.

✔ **Double-click the Hand tool.** Resizes the document image to a Fit on Screen magnification.

✔ **Press the Page Up or Page Down buttons to change the view.** These buttons move the view up or down by a window.

Now that you've become friendly with the Zoom and Hand tools, here's one last tip. If you hold down the Shift key while scrolling with the Hand tool or zooming with the Zoom tool, all open image windows scroll or zoom together. This trick can come in especially handy, for example, when you create another view of the same document. (Choose Window⇨ Arrange⇨New Window.)

Rotating with the Rotate View tool

Sharing the flyout menu with the Hand tool is the Rotate View tool. This tool actually rotates your entire image window, as shown in Figure 4-3.

Follow these steps to use the Rotate View Tool:

1. **Select the Rotate View tool from the Tools panel or Application bar.**

2. **Place your tool cursor in the image window and hold down the mouse button.**

   A compass rose appears.

Figure 4-3: Rotate your entire image window.

3. **Drag the cursor clockwise (or counterclockwise) to rotate the image window.**

   Note that you can see the numeric rotation angle in the Options bar. Check the Rotate All Windows option to simultaneously rotate all open documents.

4. **When you reach your desired rotation angle, release the mouse button.**

5. **If you want to undo your rotation, click the Reset View button in the Options bar.**

   Choosing Edit⇨Undo or using the History panel to undo doesn't revert your image to the original 0-degree rotation.

If you're a MacBook user, or if you are using a Windows 7 computer with a multi-touch trackpad, you may be aware that you can use your trackpad to flick, rotate, or zoom. You may also have been annoyed when you did these things inadvertently, in which case you can disable Gestures in your General Preferences settings.

Cruising with the Navigator Panel

Some Photoshop users don't use the *Navigator panel* (which is a roadmap to your image document) nearly as often as they could, and there's a simple reason for that: In its default size, the Navigator panel is just too darned small to be of use.

Most new Photoshop users see the tiny Navigator window and decide that working with such a small thumbnail image isn't worth the bother. There's a quick fix, and after you've seen exactly what the Navigator panel can do for you, it may become one of your favorite tools. Here are the keys to using the Navigator panel, which you open by choosing Window⇨Navigator:

✐ **Resize the Navigator panel.** Before you begin working with the Navigator panel, shown in Figure 4-4, grab the size box at the lower-right corner of the Navigator panel and drag it down and to the right to create a jumbo version with a much larger, more viewable thumbnail. It's easiest to resize when you pull the panel out of the dock and let it float.

Resizing works really well if you're using a second monitor. Placing the jumbo-sized Navigator panel on the second monitor works great. For more on working with two monitors, see the sidebar "One image, two monitors," in this chapter.

The Navigator panel is one panel that you probably want readily accessible. It's most useful when it's visible at all times. Undock the Navigator panel by pulling the tab of the panel to the left. Position the Navigator panel to one side of your image so it's ready for instant use.

✔ **View the thumbnail.** The entire Navigator window shows the full document image, with an outline called a *View box* showing the amount of image visible in the document window at the current zoom level.

✔ **Change the view.** Click anywhere in the thumbnail *outside* the View box to center the box at that position. The comparable view in your main document window changes to match.

✔ **Move the view.** Click anywhere in the thumbnail inside the View box and then drag to move the box to a new position. The main document window changes to match the new view.

Corbis Digital Stock

Figure 4-4: The Navigator panel is more productive and user-friendly when enlarged.

✔ **Zoom in or out.** Click the Zoom In button (which has an icon of two large pyramids) or Zoom Out button (which has an icon of two smaller pyramids) to zoom in or out. Or drag the Zoom slider that resides between the two icons. The View box changes size when you zoom in or out, and Photoshop magnifies or reduces the view in the original document window to match, as well.

✔ **Specify an exact magnification.** The lower-left corner of the Navigator panel has a Magnification box. It shows the current magnification, and you can type a new value to zoom to the exact magnification level you need.

If the View box color is too similar to a dominant color in your image, you can select a new color for its outline by selecting Panel Options from the Navigator panel pop-up menu.

Choosing a Screen Mode

Photoshop's working area can become horribly cluttered. And here's a secret: The more adept you become, the more cluttered the desktop becomes. Just when you begin to appreciate a neatly docked Options bar and the convenience of displaying panels, you realize that you've gobbled up all your free working space.

Photoshop now has three different screen modes (or maybe five, depending on what you consider to be a screen mode). Each mode shows or hides some of the elements on the screen at the press of a key or click of the mouse button. Select a mode by clicking the Screen Mode icon at the right end of the Application bar, or by choosing View➪Screen Mode. The final two modes are accessible via keyboard commands. Table 4-2 shows you how to unclutter your screen quickly.

Table 4-2	Cleaning Up Working Space Clutter	
Do This . . .	*. . . To Change to This Screen Mode*	*What's Happening*
Press Shift+Tab.	Hide all panels.	All the panels in your working space — except for the Tools panel — vanish. When you need to access them again, press Shift+Tab again.
Press the Tab key.	Hide all panels and the Options bar.	All the panels (including the Tools panel) and the Options bar vanish, leaving you with a clean workspace showing only the Menu bar, Application bar, and any open documents (on the Mac, the Application bar may not display).
Click the Screen Mode button in the Application bar.	Full Screen mode with Menu bar.	Only the active document window is visible, along with the panels, Menu bar, Application bar, and Options bar. The document window is maximized, and the other documents are hidden.
Click the Screen Mode button in the Application bar.	Full Screen mode.	View the image alone with all other components hidden, as shown in Figure 4-5.
Click the Screen Mode button in the Application bar.	Standard Screen mode.	The default Photoshop screen appears, displaying all menus and panels.

Press the F key to cycle between the last three screen modes in Table 4-2.

If you hide the Tools panel in any Screen Mode, simply hover your mouse over the left side of the screen to make your Tools panel reappear.

Getting Precise Layout Results

Photoshop includes numerous useful features that help you lay out your images precisely. There are dozens of reasons to make a selection in a particular place, position an object at an exact location, or align several objects along the same imaginary line. Here are a few examples:

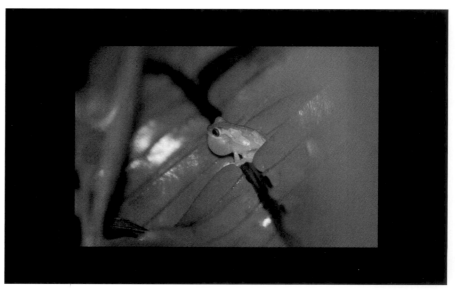

Dynamic Graphics, Inc.

Figure 4-5: View your image in Full Screen mode.

- You want to draw parallel lines exactly 50 pixels apart to create a "window blind" effect.
- You're creating a set of thumbnails that need to be aligned in neat rows and columns.
- You want to create an object that's the exact same size (in one or more dimensions) as another object already in your image.

You have several tools to help you do this and more.

Creating guides

Guides are nonprintable horizontal and vertical lines that you can position anywhere you like within a document window. Normally, they're displayed as solid blue lines, but you can change guides to another color and/or to dashed lines.

To use guides, choose Edit⇨Preferences⇨Guides, Grid & Slices (or Photoshop⇨Preferences⇨Guides, Grid & Slices on the Mac), as I discuss in Book I, Chapter 5. Guides would be useful even if they were only, well, guides. However, they have another cool feature: Objects and tools dragged to within 8 screen pixels of a guide are magnetically attracted to the guide and snap to it. That makes it ridiculously easy to align objects precisely. Because the objects snap to the guides, you can be confident that you've placed the objects exactly on the guide and not just near it. You can turn off the Snap to Guides feature if you want a little more control in your arrangements.

To place guides, follow these steps:

1. **Make sure that rulers are visible in your image.**

   Choose View➪Rulers to display them, if necessary.

2. **Click in the horizontal ruler and drag down to create a new horizontal guide. Release the mouse button when the guide is in the location you want.**

   Anytime you create a guide by dragging from the ruler, the Show Guides option automatically switches on. At other times, you can show or hide guides by choosing View➪Show➪Guides or by pressing Ctrl+semicolon (⌘-semicolon on the Mac).

3. **Click in the vertical ruler and drag to the right to create a new vertical guide.**

   When you release the mouse button, your new guide stops.

   You can also create a horizontal guide by Alt-clicking in the vertical ruler (Option-clicking on the Mac), or create a vertical guide by Alt-clicking in the horizontal ruler (Option-clicking on the Mac). Use whichever method is faster for you.

   Finally, you can choose View➪ New Guide and enter your desired orientation and position.

4. **Use the Move tool (press V to activate it) to reposition your guides.**

   Look for the guides in Figure 4-6.

Corbis Digital Stock

Figure 4-6: Nonprinting guides allow you to precisely position your elements.

Using guides

After the guides are in place, here are a few of the things you can do with them:

- ✔ **Turn the Snap to Guides feature on or off.** Choose View➪Snap To➪Guides.

- ✔ **Lock all guides so you don't accidentally move them.** Choose View➪Lock Guides. You can also press Alt+Ctrl+semicolon (Option+⌘+semicolon on the Mac).

- ✔ **Remove all guides and start from scratch.** Choose View➪Clear Guides.

✔ **Change a horizontal guide to a vertical guide (or vice versa).** Hold down the Alt key (Option key on the Mac) while you drag the guide with the Move tool.

✔ **Align a guide at a precise location on the ruler.** Hold down the Shift key while you drag a guide to force it to snap to the ruler ticks.

✔ **Create a new guide in a precise location.** Choose View➪New Guide, click the Horizontal or Vertical option, and type a distance from the ruler where you want the new guide to reside.

✔ **Hide and show guides.** Click the View Extras icon in the Application bar and select Show Guides from the drop-down list to toggle the view off and on.

Using grids

The Photoshop grid feature offers a convenient canned set of guidelines already nicely arranged for you at preset intervals. You can use a grid for any application where you want to align objects in a pleasing, geometrically precise arrangement.

Grids share some features in common with guides but boast a few differences, too:

✔ Like guides, grids don't print with your image. They're used only as reference lines in your onscreen image, as shown in Figure 4-7.

✔ Objects and tools can optionally snap to the lines on a grid, depending on whether you have View➪Snap To➪Grid turned on or off.

✔ You can show or hide grids by choosing View➪Show➪Grid. Or click the View Extras icon in the Application bar and select Show Grids from the drop-down list to toggle the view off and on.

Corbis Digital Stock

Figure 4-7: Grids enable you to arrange elements along evenly spaced lines.

✔ You can change the color of the grid and select solid lines, dashed lines, or dots for the grid by choosing Edit➪Preferences➪Guides, Grid, Slices (Photoshop➪Preferences on the Mac).

✔ You can specify the distance between grid lines and the number of sub-divisions between grid lines in the Preferences dialog box. For more information on setting grid and guide preferences, see Book I, Chapter 5.

Measuring Onscreen

You can measure distances and objects within Photoshop many different ways. The rulers, used in combination with guides, are a good way to mark distances precisely so that you can create objects of a particular size. You can change the increments used for these measurements in Photoshop's Preferences, as I detail in Book I, Chapter 5.

However, Photoshop also has a handy Ruler tool that you can use to lay measurement outlines in any direction. These lines tell you a great deal more than just the size of the object you're measuring. You can also measure angles and determine the exact coordinates of an object.

When you use the Ruler tool, the Options bar offers a readout of information that includes the following values:

- ✓ **X, Y — the X and Y coordinates of the start of the line:** For example, if you start at the 1-inch position on the horizontal ruler and the 3-inch position on the vertical ruler, the X and Y values on the Options bar are 1.0 and 3.0, respectively. (You select the increments for the X and Y values on the ruler in Photoshop's Preferences.)

- ✓ **W, H — the horizontal (W) and vertical (H) distances traveled from the X and Y points:** A 1-inch long, perfectly horizontal line drawn from the X,1 and Y,3 positions shows a W value of 1.0 and an H value of 0.0.

- ✓ **A:** The angle of the first line or the angle between two lines.

- ✓ **L1:** The total length of the line.

- ✓ **L2:** The total length of the second line.

- ✓ **Clear:** Press the Clear button to delete your current measurement.

You can now straighten your image using the Ruler tool. Simply drag along the horizontal axis you wish to align to with the Ruler. Then click the Straighten button in the Options bar.

Measuring an object

To measure an object, follow these steps:

1. **Select the Ruler tool.**

   It's tucked away in the Tools panel with the Eyedropper. Press I, or Shift+I, to cycle between the Eyedropper, Color Sampler, Note, and Ruler tools until the Ruler tool appears.

2. **Click at a starting location for the measuring line and then drag to the end location.**

Hold down the Shift key while dragging to constrain the line to multiples of 45 degrees.

3. **Release the mouse button to create the measurement line, as shown in Figure 4-8.**

Measuring an angle

You can measure an angle by drawing two lines and reading the angle between them from the Options bar. Just follow these steps:

1. **Select the Ruler tool in the Tools panel.**

   It's tucked away with the Eyedropper. Press I, or Shift+I, to cycle through the tools until the Ruler tool appears.

Figure 4-8: The Ruler tool is your onscreen measuring device.

2. **Click at a starting location for the first line and drag to the end location.**

   You can hold down the Shift key while you drag to constrain the line to multiples of 45 degrees.

3. **Release the mouse button to create the first line.**

4. **Hold down the Alt key (the Option key on the Mac) and click the endpoint of the first line that you want to use to measure the angle.**

5. **Drag the second line and release the mouse button when you reach your desired length.**

6. **On the Options bar, read the angle between the two lines (labeled A).**

   You can also see the length of each line, as shown in Figure 4-9.

Using the Info Panel

The Info panel, accessible under the Window menu, shown in Figure 4-10, displays a variety of information, depending on what tool you're using. To specify which status info options you want displayed, or whether you want Tool Hints shown, select Panel Options from the Info panel pop-up menu. For example, if you're using the Ruler tool, the information in the Info panel duplicates the measurements shown on the Options bar. Selecting other tools modifies the Info panel's appearance to reflect the functions of that tool. Here's some of the information you can find out by keeping the Info panel visible on your desktop:

✔ When using most tools, the Info panel displays the X and Y coordinates of the cursor, as well as the color values of the pixel directly beneath the cursor.

Peter Adams/Digital Vision

Figure 4-9: The Ruler tool also serves as a digital protractor.

✔ When making a selection with the marquee tools, the Info panel shows both the X and Y coordinates of the cursor, as well as the width (W) and height (H) of the selection.

✔ When dragging with the Crop or Zoom tools, the Info panel shows the width and height of the marquee used to define the cropping or zoom borders. The Crop tool's current angle of rotation (A) is also displayed.

✔ With the Line, Pen and Gradient tools, the Info panel shows the X and Y coordinates of the starting position for the line, path, or gradient you're defining, as well as the distance (L) of the line you've dragged, the change in X and Y directions (Delta X and Delta Y), and the angle (A).

 ✔ When you use a transformation command, the Info panel displays the percentage change in the Width, Height, Angle, Angle of Horizontal Skew (H), and Angle of Vertical Skew (V). For more on transformations, see Book III, Chapter 3.

 ✔ When you use a color adjustment, such as Levels, and that adjustment dialog box or adjustment layer is active, the Info panel displays before-and-after color values beneath the mouse cursor. See Book VIII, Chapter 1 for more on color adjustments.

 ✔ After you make a selection with the Lasso or Magic Wand tools, the Info panel shows the Width and Height of the selection's bounding rectangle.

 ✔ Select Panel Options from the Info panel's pop-up menu. In the Info Panel Options dialog box that appears, you can define a second color readout, in addition to the default readout, using a different color model if you want, as shown in Figure 4-11. In addition to the regular color modes, the default Actual Color option displays values in the current mode of the document. Proof Color displays values based on the setting chosen in View➪Proof Setup. The Total Ink option displays the percentage CMYK ink under the cursor based on the settings in the CMYK Setup dialog box in the Color Settings (Advanced). You can also define a measurement increment for the mouse cursor (in inches, pixels, millimeters, and so forth)

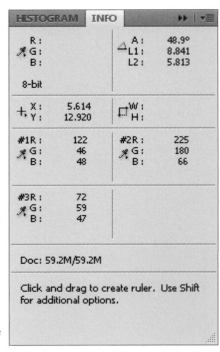

Figure 4-10: The Info panel displays useful file information, such as measurements and color readouts.

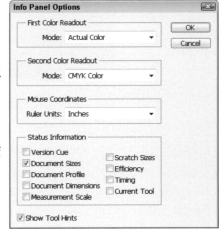

Figure 4-11: Set a different color mode in the Info Panel Options dialog box.

independently of the increment you've selected in Preferences. You can also choose to display other types of information about your file. For more info on these options, see Book I, Chapter 1.

Working with Extras

Extras are the optional items displayed on your screen, such as grids, pixel grids, guides and Smart Guides, selection and layer edges, notes, slices, and the *target path* (a line drawn with the Pen tool). Although you can turn on and off the display of each option independently, the Extras function helps you to create a set of extras that you want to see or hide. You can then turn them all on or off at the same time.

The following list explains how to show or hide these extras:

- To turn one extra on or off, choose View➪Show and then select the extra you want to show.

- You can also hide and show your guides, grid, and ruler by clicking the View Extras icon in the Application bar.

- To show or hide extras in a group, choose View➪Show➪Show Extras Options. Select each extra that you want to show in the dialog box that appears, as shown in Figure 4-12.

Figure 4-12: Pick and choose the extras you want to show in your image window.

- To show or hide all the extras you've selected in the Extras Options dialog box, choose View➪Extras or press Ctrl+H (⌘+H on the Mac).

Managing Images with Adobe Bridge

Adobe Bridge, shown in Figure 4-13, is command and control central for not just Photoshop, but the entire Adobe Creative Suite. So, if you haven't embraced Bridge yet, it won't be long before you appreciate the omnipresent power of this application.

Adobe Bridge enables you to visually browse your network, hard drives, and external media to find the exact image you need, and it has a multitude of viewing, sorting, cataloging, and organizing features to manage all your assets — photographic, illustrative, video, written, and so on. Bridge is so multifaceted that, although you can access it from any Adobe application, it's also a standalone program.

Favorites panel

Menu bar

Folders panel

Application bar

Metadata panel

Preview panel

Keywords panel

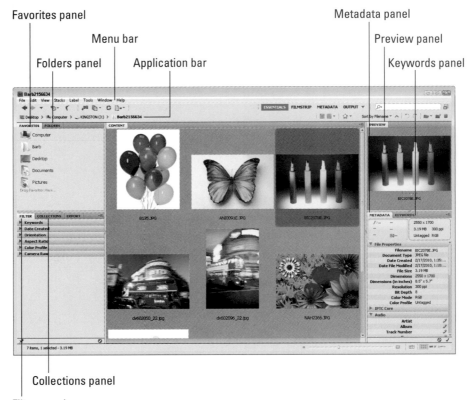

Collections panel

Filter panel

Figure 4-13: Adobe Bridge enables you to visually explore and locate your digital media assets.

Here's a brief description of what Bridge offers:

- **File browsing and asset management:** View, search, organize, and process your files. You can open, move, delete, rotate, label, and rate your images. You can also import and edit your photos from your digital camera.

- **Camera Raw:** You can open and edit Camera Raw files directly from Bridge and save them in a format that's compatible with Photoshop. You can edit JPEG and TIFF files, as well.

- **Color management:** You can use Bridge to synchronize the color settings across all your Creative Suite applications to ensure color accuracy and consistency. This capability requires you have the applications installed on your computer.

✔ **Perform automated tasks:** You can perform automatic tasks like batch processing directly from Bridge.

✔ **Create projects:** Finally, you can create projects, such as slide shows, PDF presentations, and Web galleries.

You can access Bridge in several ways:

✔ In Photoshop, choose File➪Browse in Bridge.

✔ Click the Bridge icon in the Application bar.

✔ To launch Bridge directly, choose Start➪Adobe Bridge in Windows. (Click the Bridge icon in the Dock or double-click the Bridge icon in the `Applications/Adobe Bridge CS5` folder on the Mac.)

Brief anatomy of Bridge

Before I dive headlong into the applicable operations of Bridge, let me give you a brief anatomical breakdown of each of its main components. (Refer to Figure 4-13.)

✔ **Menu bar:** Commands found on the Menu bar allow you to open or delete images, get photos from your camera, create stacks, add file info, and search for images. You can also label files and append their *metadata* (information about your file). The Menu bar also offers options for sorting and viewing files. Finally, on the Tools➪Photoshop menu, you have access to basically the same Automate menu that you find in Photoshop itself, plus a couple unique commands, which I cover in the section "Using the Menu bar and buttons," later in this chapter.

✔ **Application bar:** You find some often-used commands on the Application bar at the top of the application window. Click the right- and left-arrow buttons to go forward and back among your files and folders. Click the down-pointing arrow button to go to a parent or favorites location. Click the Boomerang icon to go back to Photoshop. Click the arrow-and-clock icon to access a recent file or folder. Click the camera icon to get photos from a camera. The Refine icon offers several options:

  • *Review Mode:* This mode leaves the Bridge interface and displays your images full screen. You can find more details about this mode in the section "View menu," later in this chapter.

  • *Batch Rename:* In this dialog box, you can rename, move, or copy a folder of images in one fell swoop. Bridge runs a script and processes the images simultaneously.

  • *File Info:* This command brings up a comprehensive metadata panel in which you can edit info about your file. For more details, see Bonus Chapter 3 on the Web.

Click the shutter icon to open an image in Camera Raw. Click the page icon to Output to the Web or PDF (more on this feature coming up in this chapter).

✏ **Folder hierarchy:** A bar that appears below the Menu and Application bars lists the current location (such as a folder on your hard drive) on display. Click the right-pointing arrow to view the particular folder's hierarchy, as well as Favorites and Recent Folders.

✏ **Shortcut buttons:** Open a recent file, create a new folder, and rotate or delete files with a click of the button. You can also switch to Compact mode (which I explain how to do in the following section). Enter a description of what you're looking for in the Search field and choose where you search via the drop-down menu.

✏ **Favorites panel:** Located in the upper-left of the Bridge window, this panel provides easy access to folders, files, and, if you're a Creative Suite user, the Bridge Home. Drag whatever hard drives, folders, or files you want to include in your Favorites panel.

✏ **Folders panel:** Also located in the upper-left portion of the Bridge window, this panel shows the folder hierarchy on your computer. If an image file is available to your computer, Bridge lets you use this panel to find it.

✏ **Filter panel:** Enables you to see your assets sorted by various criteria. For example, you can view your images by date created, keywords, file type, and even the ISO setting of your camera. Select your criteria in the Filter panel, as shown in Figure 4-14, and view the results in the Content window. Click the No icon (a circle with a diagonal line) at the bottom of the Filter panel to clear all filters. Click the pushpin icon to keep the filter intact when browsing for files in Bridge.

✏ **Collections panel:** If you've already gone through the trouble of meticulously naming your files, or you're like me and are too darned lazy to do so, then the Collections panel is for you. It's a lot less time-consuming than using keywords — simply select, or find, your desired images

Figure 4-14: The Filter panel sorts and displays your assets.

in the Content area (technically referred to as the *light table*) and click the New Collection icon at the bottom of the panel. If you want to include selected files into a new collection, click Yes when prompted. Name your collection. To add a file to an existing collection, simply select the image(s) and drag it (or them) into the folder icon in the Collections panel. To delete a collection, select the collection and click the trash icon. Click the time-saving New Smart Collection icon to have Bridge go out and collect your files based on established criteria. Choose where to look and by what criteria. To add another criterion, click the plus sign. Specify match settings — any or all — and specify whether you want to include subfolders and non-indexed files. Click Save. If all goes well, you have a collection, or digital photo album, in short order.

✔ **Export panel:** Drag files from your light table area onto the Export panel. Click the up-pointing arrow to export the files to your hard drive. In the Export dialog box, under the Destination tab, choose what folder you would like to export your files to. Choose your image specifications under the Image Options tab. Click Export. This is a quick and easy way to copy files you need for a project onto your desktop.

✔ **Workspace controls:** Select from a variety of presets — Essentials (the default workspace), Filmstrip, or Metadata located at the top of the Bridge window. You can find additional workspaces in the pop-up menu to the right of the Metadata button. You can also find commands to create a new workspace, and delete and reset workspaces. Find details on creating a new workspace in the following section.

✔ **Preview panel:** In the top-right portion of the Bridge window is a preview of the currently selected file. You can reduce or enlarge the preview by dragging the separator bars on the left and bottom of the Preview panel. To more closely examine a portion of your image in the Preview panel, simply click the image. That portion then appears in a loupe window over your image. Hold down and drag the loupe to view other portions of the image. To close the loupe, simply click in the loupe window.

✔ **Content light table:** The largest area of the Bridge window is reserved for displaying the content. This window shows thumbnail images of all the files in the currently selected folder, along with information about each file. In addition, any subfolders are shown with a folder icon.

✔ **Keywords panel:** This feature lets you tag your images with keywords, such as the names of people or places, to enable easier locating and sorting of images.

✔ **Metadata panel:** The Metadata panel shows information about your images. The File Properties section shows items such as filename, date of creation, date last modified, image format, size, and so on. Any file information for images added via File⇨File Info appears in the IPTC section of the Metadata panel. Likewise, you can also enter or edit file information directly in the IPTC section in Bridge. Finally, the Camera Data section displays information associated with your digital photos, such as the make and model of your camera, exposure, and ISO speed. You can also display other types of metadata, such as Camera Raw information, by selecting them in the Preferences dialog box, accessed via the Metadata panel pop-up menu.

In Bonus Chapter 3 on this book's companion Web site, you can find out about the Notes feature and advanced features of the Metadata panel. See the Introduction for details about this book's Web site.

✔ **Viewing controls:** At the bottom of the Bridge window is a slider that reduces or enlarges the content thumbnails. Note that you can enlarge thumbnails up to 640 pixels. There are also icons to view your content as thumbnails, details, or a list.

Configuring the Bridge window

Bridge, being as enormous and full-featured as it is, is surprisingly flexible when it comes to how you configure its various panels. Here's a rundown of how to customize your Bridge window:

✔ To size the entire Bridge window, diagonally drag any corner or edge of the window. (On the Mac, drag the lower-right corner.)

✔ To resize panels, drag the bar that divides them. Position your cursor over the bar (the cursor changes to a double-headed arrow), and then click and drag the bar to size the panel.

✔ Switch to Compact mode by clicking the icon in the upper far-right corner of the Application window. This command condenses your Bridge window to just a portion of your light table and the Application bar. Click the Ultra Compact Mode icon to reduce the window to just the Application bar. Click the Switch to Full Mode icon to revert. Other viewing options are available in the drop-down menu in the top-right corner when you're in one of the compact modes.

✔ You can drag and regroup the tabbed panels in Bridge, just like you can with Photoshop panels. To collapse a panel, double-click its tab.

✔ After you configure your Bridge, you can save it as a workspace preset that you can then call up at anytime. For example, you may want one workspace for working with photos and yet another when working with layout or word-processing files. Simply choose Window⇨Workspace⇨ New Workspace. Provide a name, choose to save your window location and sort order of images as part of the workspace, and click Save. Note that you can also select New Workspace from the Workspace drop-down menu in the Application bar. To access the workspace, choose Window⇨ Workspace and then select the name of your saved preset. It also appears as its own icon in the Workspace area at the top of the Bridge window. You may also select from several preset workspaces designed for specific tasks. For example, if viewing files is your most important task, then select the Light Table preset, shown in Figure 4-15. Not happy with a workspace?

Choose Window➪Workspace➪Delete Workspace and select your workspace from the Workspace drop-down list in the Delete Workspace dialog box. Or simply reset your workspace back to the Essentials workspace, the default.

Figure 4-15: The Light Table workspace focuses on the best viewing configuration in the Bridge.

Using the Menu bar and buttons

The Menu bar is a visual testimony to the numerous capabilities of Bridge. The following sections provide a brief rundown of what you find on each menu.

File menu

Here's what you find on the Bridge's File menu:

- ✓ **New Window:** If you want one window to remain displayed as is, choose this command to create another Bridge window.

- ✓ **New Folder:** This command creates a new folder in the location listed in the folder hierarchy. You can also click the Create a New Folder button in the row of shortcut buttons.

- ✓ **Open:** After you select a thumbnail in the Content window, you can choose the Open command to open the image in Photoshop or another CS5 application. Of course, you can also simply double-click the selected file(s). To open multiple files, just hold down Ctrl (⌘ on the Mac) while selecting.

- ✓ **Open With:** Select a file and choose the Open With command. Select your program of choice from the submenu that appears.

✔ **Open Recent:** Choose from your most recent ten files.

✔ **Open in Camera Raw:** Select a Camera Raw file and choose this command to edit the Raw settings. You can also open JPEG or TIFF files.

✔ **Test in Device Central:** Select a file and then this command, which launches the Adobe Device Central mini-application. In this mini-application, you can see how your image will look on a variety of mobile devices. See Book I, Chapter 3 for details on Device Central.

✔ **Close Window:** When you have enough of Bridge, choose this command.

✔ **Delete (Move to Trash on the Mac):** If you want to eliminate a file, select it and choose this command. Kiss that file goodbye by emptying the trash. You can also click the trash can icon in the top-right portion of the Bridge window. Remember that when you trash things via the Bridge, you're actually deleting them from the desktop, as well.

✔ **Eject (Mac only):** Select your media and then this command to eject that media from your computer.

✔ **Return to (*program*):** Choose this command to leave the Bridge and return to your program of choice.

✔ **Reveal in Explorer (Finder on the Mac):** This command brings up your operating system's window and reveals the location of the selected file.

✔ **Reveal in Bridge:** This command visually escorts you to where your selected file resides.

✔ **Get Photos from Camera:** Select your desired device (camera or card reader) and import your images into your chosen folder and subfolder. Click Get Photos to start the download. Click Advanced Dialog if you want to apply metadata to the imported images.

✔ **Move to:** Select a file and move it to another location on your computer or network.

✔ **Copy to:** Select a file and copy it to another location on your computer or network.

✔ **Export to Hard Drive:** This command can be used in lieu of the Export panel, which is described earlier in this chapter.

✔ **Place:** Select a file, choose Place, and then choose one of the CS5 applications, such as InDesign, from the submenu. That program then imports your selected file.

✔ **Add to Favorites:** You can choose to add or remove a folder from your Favorites. If you're not familiar with Favorites, it's a special folder that lists your favorite files, folders, programs, and drives for quick and handy access. You can easily find the Favorites panel and the Folders panel in the top-left portion of the Bridge window. And, depending on your operating system, you'll come across numerous ways to access your Favorites.

✔ **File Info:** This feature lets you add some of your own metadata, such as title, author, copyrights, dates, credits, and so on. This information can come in handy for photographers and reporters. You can also edit (replace, append, save, and delete) some other data, such as IPTC data. But feel free to leave this data as it is.

Many commands, such as Open, Copy, Delete, and Label, are available via a context menu. Simply select an image or folder and right-click (Control-click on the Mac) to access the menu.

Edit menu

On the Bridge's Edit menu, here are your options:

✔ **Preferences:** Mac users can access the Preferences window from the Adobe Bridge CS5 menu, rather than Edit. Briefly, **General** preferences control the way the Bridge looks and feels. For example, you can control how light or dark to make the Content window for your files. **Metadata** preferences control which type of data is displayed in the Metadata panel. Check out Bonus Chapter 3 to find out more about metadata. You can assign names and keyboard shortcuts to your colored **Labels.** Specify which application to use to open files of certain types. The **File Type Associations** are specific to the Bridge only. **Thumbnails** settings have to do with items such as showing additional lines of data along with the thumbnail image. I suggest leaving those settings at their default unless you're certain you want to change them.

✔ **Undo/Cut/Copy/Paste/Duplicate:** I lumped these commands together because they're all self-explanatory. Undo undoes your last executed command. Select a file(s) and cut, copy, duplicate, or paste it from or into your folder.

✔ **Select All/Deselect All:** These two commands quickly select or deselect all the files in your selected folder.

✔ **Invert Selection:** Selects everything that's currently not selected and deselects everything that is.

✔ **Find:** This command enables you to find files in selected folders, including subfolders, based on a variety of criteria such as filename, dates, labels, or keywords. Click Find, and the files matching your criteria appear in the Bridge Content window.

✔ **Develop Settings:** If you have Camera Raw images, you can open them directly in the Bridge and apply the default Camera Raw settings or settings from a previous conversion. You can also copy, paste, and clear settings via this submenu.

✔ **Rotate:** The rotate commands rotate your images in varying degrees and directions. When you open the image, Photoshop applies the rotation. You can also click the rotate buttons.

✓ **Creative Suite Color Settings:** See whether the color settings of all your Creative Suite applications are synchronized. (The Creative Suite applications must be installed on your computer.) If they aren't, and you want them to be, select your desired setting from the list and click Apply.

✓ **Camera Raw Preferences:** Choose this command to establish your Camera Raw image, cache, and DNG (Digital Negative) File Handling settings. Mac users can find the Camera Raw Preferences window on the Adobe Bridge CS5 menu, rather than Edit. For more on Camera Raw, see Book II, Chapter 2. For more on Camera Raw Preferences, see Book I, Chapter 5.

View menu

Here's what the View menu has to offer:

✓ **Full Screen Preview:** Select this option to fill your screen with your selected image only. Press Esc to return to the Bridge application window.

✓ **Slideshow:** This neat option leaves the Bridge interface and displays just the images, full screen, from your selected folder.

✓ **Slideshow Options:** Choose settings for your slide show, including the duration of your slide display, type and duration of your transitions, and whether to display a caption, among others.

✓ **Review Mode:** This mode leaves the Bridge interface and displays your image(s) full screen. Click the forward- and back-arrow buttons to cycle through the images. Click the down-pointing arrow button to eliminate an image from the Review mode display. Click the magnifying glass icon to open a window in which you can enlarge portions of your image for a more detailed view. Click the Next icon to create a new collection from the images displayed in Review mode and then return to the Bridge interface. Click the X icon to just return to the Bridge interface.

✓ **Compact Mode:** Select this option to get a pared-down Bridge with just a Content window and Application bar — no panels.

✓ **As Thumbnails/Details/List:** Display your content in the default view of thumbnails. View it with Details, where you get a large thumbnail along with metadata, ratings, and labels, as shown in Figure 4-16. Or view it as a list, with smaller thumbnails, filenames, and some metadata.

✓ **Show Thumbnail Only:** This option shows just the thumbnail of the image without the accompanying data, such as filename, date, and so on.

✓ **Grid Lock:** This option provides a grid of horizontal and vertical lines around your thumbnails in the Content light table.

✓ **Show Reject Files:** Display files that you've labeled with the harsh moniker of Reject.

✔ **Show Hidden Files:** Select this option to see files that Photoshop doesn't recognize.

✔ **Show Folders:** This option enables you to view folder icon thumbnails, in addition to image thumbnails.

✔ **Show Items from Subfolders:** Select this option to have all the files within your subfolders displayed.

✔ **Show Linked Files:** Select this option to display content files linked to a specific file that uses links, or reference files, or OLE (Object Linking and Embedding).

✔ **Sort:** From this menu, select the criteria by which you want to sort your files. The default is by the name of your file, but a ton of other options, such as label, rating,

Figure 4-16: View your content as Details.

or date, are up for grabs. After you select the criteria, Bridge displays your files accordingly.

✔ **Refresh:** If you've renamed a file, the order of your files isn't updated in the Bridge's window. Choose Refresh to get your files in order.

Stacks menu

You can select a group of images and create a stack, which makes the images easier to manage and cuts down on clutter in your Content window. The top image thumbnail in the stack is visible in the Content window, and the number of images in the stack is visible on the top-left corner of that thumbnail, as shown in Figure 4-17. It's not mandatory, but normally, you want to create stacks from similar images, such as multiple exposures of the same subject, multiple poses of a portrait, and so on. Here are the options found in the Stacks menu:

✔ **Group as Stack:** Select your desired photos and choose this command to create a stack.

✔ **Ungroup from Stack:** Select a photo and choose this command to remove it from the stack.

✔ **Open/Close Stack:** Select Open to display each image in the stack (surrounded by an outline). Choose Close to collapse the stack.

Closed stack   Open stack

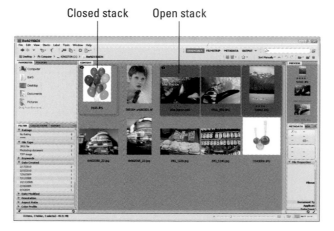

Figure 4-17: Create stacks from groups of images.

✔ **Promote to Top of Stack:** First, open the stack and select your desired image. Choose this command to have that image appear on top of the stack.

✔ **Expand/Collapse All Stacks:** Opens and displays, or closes, all images in all stacks.

✔ **Auto Stack Panorama/HDR:** This script looks at the metadata (EXIF) of your images, and if it finds two or more files that have a timestamp within 18 seconds of each other, it first inspects the images by using the Auto Align algorithm. If everything is good to go, it creates a group, or stack, of panorama shots. It also creates a stack for HDR (High Dynamic Range) shots if it also finds different exposure value (EV) settings in the metadata. You can then process these stacks in Photoshop by choosing Tools⇨Process Collections in Photoshop.

Label menu

The Label menu offers commands for rating and labeling your files:

✔ **Rating:** Rank your files using the one- to five-star system. You can now also apply a Reject rating, for those images that aren't up to par. Use the View⇨Sort menu or the Rating shortcut button to choose your desired ranking. Files with that ranking then appear in the Content window.

✔ **Labels:** Label your files for quick identification and organization. Again, use the View⇨Sort menu, or the Sort shortcut or Rating shortcut buttons to choose and view the labeled files.

Note that you can also assign labels and ratings to folders.

Tools menu

Here are the offerings on the Tools menu:

- ✔ **Batch Rename:** Choose this command to rename multiple image files within a folder in one execution. You can rename the files and keep them in the same folder or move them to a new folder. Click the Browse button to select that folder. Then, designate how your files are named by selecting an option from the pop-up menu or typing your own name. Choose the starting number for renamed images and specify whether you want to enable the naming convention to be compatible with another platform.

- ✔ **Device Central:** This command launches Adobe's Device Central, a mini-application that lets you create graphics for mobile devices, such as cell phones. See Book I, Chapter 3 for more details.

- ✔ **Create Metadata Template and Edit Metadata Template:** Choose which metadata you want to include in the template. Name the template and save it. Choose Edit Metadata Template if you need to later modify the template.

- ✔ **Append Metadata and Replace Metadata:** Allow you to add or substitute existing metadata based on a template. To create a template, choose Tools⇨Create Metadata Template.

- ✔ **Cache:** *Cache* is memory that stores frequently used data, such as thumbnails and file info, to allow for quicker loading when you display a previously viewed image or folder. Building a cache for a subfolder enables you to store the information for a selected folder. If you purge the cache, you delete ranking and thumbnail information, thereby creating more disk space. Exporting a cache lets you export to the folder selected in the Folders panel. Cache allows you to burn a CD without generating thumbnails. Purging the cache can also fix problems with thumbnails and previews that aren't displaying properly.

- ✔ **Photoshop:** Some of the features are the same as those on the Photoshop File⇨Automate submenu. See Book IX, Chapter 2 for more on Photomerge and Merge to HDR Pro. For more info on batch processing, see Book II, Chapter 5. For details on the Lens Correction feature, see Book VII, Chapter 2. The Load Files into Photoshop Layers command takes your selected images in Bridge and creates a new layered file in Photoshop, using those selected images. The Process Collections in Photoshop command searches for stacked Panorama and HDR images (see the "Stacks menu" section, earlier in this chapter), and imports them into Photoshop for processing into composite images.

Window menu

If you've configured the Bridge just to your liking and want to save it as a workspace for future retrieval, choose Workspace⇨New Workspace. You can also select from preset workspaces that are configured for specific tasks, such as optimum viewing of thumbnails or pinpointing metadata. Finally, under the Workspace submenu, you find commands to reset and delete your various Bridge workspaces. See details on workspaces in the section "Managing Images with Adobe Bridge," earlier in this chapter.

You can also choose to display or hide your various panels in the Window menu. Finally, you can open a new synchronized Bridge window, enabling you to perform your Bridge activities within two windows.

You should be aware that Photoshop has bestowed the Content window with light table powers. You can drag images around to reorder, group, or rank them. What the heck? You can just drag them around to give them a little exercise, if you want. Sitting in the Bridge window all day can make a file a little stiff.

Using keywords

Keywords are descriptive labels that you attach to files. They help to categorize your images, enabling you to more efficiently and quickly locate your desired files. Here's the lowdown on creating and using keywords:

- ✔ **To create a new keyword (a categorical folder which contains keywords):** Click the plus sign (+) icon at the bottom of the Keywords panel, as shown in Figure 4-18, or select New Keyword from the Keywords panel pop-up menu. Specify your keyword and press Enter (Return on the Mac).

- ✔ **To create a new sub keyword:** Select your desired keyword, click the arrow-and-plus-sign (+) icon at the bottom of the Keywords panel, or select New Sub Keyword from the Keywords panel pop-up menu. Type the keyword you want to add and press Enter (Return on the Mac).

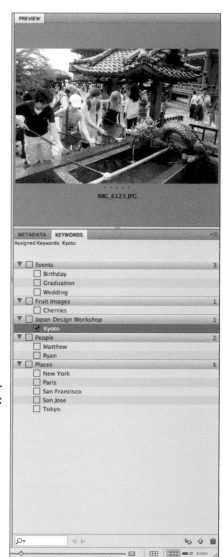

Figure 4-18: Create keywords to organize, and later sort, your images.

✔ **To rename an existing keyword or sub keyword:** Select the keyword and then select Rename from the Keywords panel pop-up menu. Provide a new name and press Enter (Return on the Mac).

Renaming a keyword in the panel doesn't also rename it if you've applied it to a file.

✔ **To delete a keyword or sub keyword from the panel:** Select the keyword; then click the Trash icon or select Delete from the Keywords panel pop-up menu. Again, deleting the keyword doesn't delete it from any files that you've previously applied it to.

✔ **To apply a keyword or sub keyword:** Select the file or files, and then check the box to the left of the keyword in the panel.

✔ **To remove a keyword or sub keyword from a file:** Select the file(s) and deselect the check box to the left of the keyword in the panel

✔ **To search for images labeled with certain keywords:** Select Find from the Keywords panel pop-up menu. Choose your desired folder or disk from the Look In menu or choose Browse to navigate to your desired location. Select your criteria from the pop-up menus and select your matching specifications — any or all. To add additional criteria fields, click the plus sign (+). Specify whether to include all subfolders and non-indexed files. When you finish, click the Find button. All images containing your entered keyword appear in the Content window of the Bridge. Select your desired images and then click the New Collection button in the Collections panel to store and arrange your images in a digital photo album, referred to as a *collection.*

✔ **To search for keywords:** Use the Quick Find field (the magnifying glass icon) by entering a keyword and selecting Contains, Equals, or Starts With from the pop-up menu.

Creating PDF Presentations

In Bridge, you can use the ultra-efficient PDF generation feature to create a single, multipage document from multiple images. This feature is great for several reasons. First, your recipient doesn't need to have any specific hardware, software, utilities, or fonts to open and view the presentation. Your recipient needs only the Acrobat Reader program, a free download from www.adobe.com. In addition, sending a single file that contains multiple images is a great way to share your photos with family and friends. You avoid the hassle of having to e-mail your images as separate attachments. Finally, the PDF format offers excellent compression, thereby squeezing your file size down significantly without sacrificing image quality. Just be sure to check your final file size so that you don't choke your recipients' e-mail inboxes!

Follow these steps to create a PDF presentation:

1. **Select your desired images and choose Window⇨Workspace⇨Output.**

   You can also select Output from the Workspace shortcut menu in the top-right portion of the Application window. Finally, you can also click the Output to Web or PDF button in the Application bar.

   The Output panel appears, as shown in Figure 4-19.

   Click PDF

   Figure 4-19: Create a PDF presentation by using Bridge's Output panel.

2. **Click the PDF icon, as shown in Figure 4-19.**

3. **Select a Template from the pop-up menu.**

   Presets, such as 2-UP Greeting Card and 4*5 Contact Sheet, are available. The Maximize Size preset places one image per page at the maximum size. I chose the Fine Art Mat template, which surrounds each image with significant white space, similar to a framing mat.

4. **In the Document area, select a page preset and size.**

   Note that you can enter a custom size in the Width and Height fields. Select either Portrait or Landscape orientation. Select your desired background color. Specify whether you want High or Low Quality. Select High if you want to be able to print the PDF with optimum results. Select Low if your PDF is meant to be viewed only onscreen. Finally, if you want to secure your PDF via a password or disable printing, select those options. Both options can be good when sending a PDF for approval purposes only.

5. **In the Layout section, specify how you want your images to be arranged on the page.**

   Because I want one image per page, I'm leaving it as 1 Column and 1 Row. Specify your margin measurements and other options for spacing and rotation.

6. **In the Overlays section, if you want the filename and/or file extension below each image, select your desired font size and color.**

   In addition, you have the option of adding a header or footer to each of the pages in your PDF.

7. **If you want your file to be viewed as a slide show, specify your viewing options in the Playback area:**

   - *Open in Full Screen Mode:* Opens the PDF in Full Screen mode, where the page fills the screen.

   - *Automatic advance to the next page:* Specify how long each image appears onscreen in the Duration field.

   - *Loop After Last Page:* Enables the presentation to continually run. If not selected, the presentation stops after the last image.

   - *Transition:* From the pop-up menu, select how you want one image to transition to the next. For certain transitions, you can also specify the Direction and Speed of the transition.

8. **Finally, if you want watermarked text (which will be overlaid on the images), such as a copyright notice, enter the text and specify the font attributes and colors.**

   You can also specify the Opacity (transparency) percentage.

9. **Select View PDF After Save to have your PDF file open in Acrobat or Acrobat Reader.**

   Preview may open for Mac users, depending on your settings.

10. **Click Save. Name your file and click Save again.**

    Bridge then creates your PDF, as shown in Figure 4-20.

Figure 4-20: A PDF created by Bridge.

Creating a Web Gallery

If you're proud of your Photoshop artistry and you want to show it off to the world on a Web page, doing it in Bridge is the way to go. It's a breeze to use, so even if you don't know anything about HTML — except that it's an acronym you hear a lot — you can create a Web-based display page for your images with very little trouble.

All you need to do is select the images you want to include on your Web page, select a style, enter a little information, and sit back and watch while Bridge does the rest. Of course, tell all your friends and colleagues where to find it.

If you want to know more about creating Web pages and posting them for anyone and everyone who has Internet access to see, check out *Web Sites Do-It-Yourself For Dummies,* by Janine Warner (Wiley).

A Web gallery is a Web page that includes small thumbnails and links that enable visitors to view those images in a larger size. But using thumbnails isn't your only option. The gallery can also showcase one image at a time in large form and change the view at intervals, just like a slide show.

The advantage of displaying your images in a Web gallery (compared to simply constructing one humongous page that shows all the images at their full file sizes) is that viewers who have slow Internet connections don't have to wait for all the images to download. Even visitors who have fast Internet connections will appreciate not being inundated with a flood of images.

To create your Web gallery, follow these steps:

1. **Select your desired images and choose Window⇨Workspace⇨ Output.**

   You can also select Output from the Workspace shortcut menu in the top-right portion of the Application window. Finally, you can also click the Output to Web or PDF in the Application bar. The Output panel appears.

2. **Click the Web Gallery icon.**

3. **Select a template from the pop-up menu.**

   Presets, such as Filmstrip and Slideshow, are available. I chose the Lightroom Flash Gallery template, as shown in Figure 4-21. Photoshop will automatically select the Style, based on your chosen template.

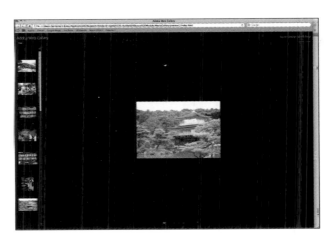

Figure 4-21: A finished Web Gallery in Adobe Bridge.

4. **(Optional) To get an idea of what the template will look like, click the Refresh Preview button.**

   You can also click Preview in Browser to see how your Web gallery looks in your default Web browser.

5. **In the Site Info area, specify your desired site, gallery titles, and description. Also, enter your contact info and e-mail or Web address, if desired. If you want everyone to know that your Web gallery is copyrighted, tell them so.**

   Be aware that putting an e-mail link on a Web page invites spam. So, be sure to have your e-mail client's spam filter on full bore if you plan to include your e-mail address.

6. **Specify the colors you want for your text, headers, menu, background, border, and controls in the Color Palette section.**

   I left mine at the default colors.

7. **In the Appearance area, specify whether you want your Web page to be laid out as scrolling, left-aligned, paginated, or a slide show.**

   I chose paginated so that visitors can navigate through the site by page.

8. **Select the size of your preview and thumbnails.**

9. **In the Create Gallery section, click either Save to Disk or Upload.**

   If you select Save to Disk, click Browse to navigate to the location where you want to save your Web gallery files. Then, click Save.

If you select Upload, enter the FTP server address, your username, your password, and the folder name. Then, click a second Upload button. If you're unsure about this information, check with your ISP (Internet service provider).

Introducing Mini Bridge

Mini Bridge is a new extension in Photoshop CS5 that enables you to easily and quickly browse for files without leaving the application, like you must with full-blown Bridge. Once you open Mini Bridge, it remains on your screen as a panel until you choose to close it. The Mini Bridge panel is divided into what is referred to as *pods,* or mini panels.

To open Mini Bridge, do one of the following:

- ✔ Choose File⇨Browse in Mini Bridge.
- ✔ Click the Mini Button icon in the Application bar.
- ✔ Choose Window⇨Extensions⇨Mini Bridge.

Click the Settings button to specify these Mini Bridge preferences:

- ✔ **Bridge Launching:** Choose how Mini Bridge launches and how it communicates with the big cheese Bridge.

- ✔ **Appearance:** Adjust the brightness of the user interface (UI) by lightening the panel background. You can also adjust the lightness of the Content and Preview pod backgrounds. Select Color Manage Panel to apply your monitor's ICC profile to thumbnails and image previews. See Book II, Chapter 3 for more on ICC profiles.

- ✔ **Manage Modules:** Select which applications you want enabled when you launch Mini Bridge. You can check for updates by clicking the gear icon.

Here are few things you can do with Mini Bridge, shown in Figure 4-22:

- ✔ Browse for files by clicking the Browse Files button on the Home page.

- ✔ Open or place a file using Mini Bridge by selecting it in the Content pod and dragging it into Photoshop. You can also double-click to open it in its associated application.

- ✔ Click the Tools button above the Content pod to access Photoshop-automated commands such as Batch processing and Photomerge.

✔ Click the Panel view button to bring up the various pods such as Navigation, Preview, and Path.

✔ Search for files using the Search button (magnifying glass icon).

✔ Adjust the view of your panel and how it displays thumbnails and content using the controls at the bottom.

✔ Sort your files in the Content pod by using the Sort, Filter, and Select buttons above the pod.

✔ Click the Preview button in the bottom-right corner and preview files by opening a panel-sized preview, full-screen preview, or slide show preview, or you can compare images in Review mode.

✔ Add an item to Favorites or a Collection by dragging it from the Content pod to the list in the Navigation pod.

✔ Go to Bridge by clicking the Br icon in the top-right corner.

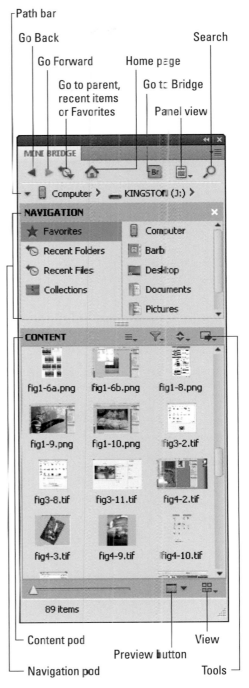

Path bar
Go Back
Go Forward
Go to parent, recent items or Favorites
Home page
Search
Go to Bridge
Panel view

Content pod
Navigation pod
Preview button
View
Tools

Figure 4-22: Browse the Mini Bridge and keep it docked as a panel.

Chapter 5: Customizing Your Workspace and Preferences

In This Chapter

✓ Saving your workspace as a preset

✓ Customizing keyboard shortcuts and menus

✓ Defining preferences in Photoshop

✓ Managing settings with the Preset Manager

*N*ow, more than ever, Photoshop lets you have it your way without having to make a trip down to the local burger shack. You can easily customize the look of your workspace, specifying everything from the location of panels to the arrangement of dialog boxes when you begin a session. You can even store these physical layouts and recall them anytime you like. And, in addition to customizing your keyboard shortcuts, you can also customize your menus to highlight certain workflow commands.

Photoshop also makes it easy to choose how certain tools and features operate. You can choose how the cursors for tools such as brushes look, tell Photoshop your preferred way of storing files, and specify just how much memory you want to set aside for image editing. You can set all these preferences once and then forget them, or you can change them from time to time when your needs change. This chapter shows you how to customize your workspace and preferences so that Photoshop works your way.

Creating Workspace Presets

Photoshop is a complicated program; the more you learn, the more complicated (and routine) your activities become. For one project, you may find yourself using the Styles panel repeatedly to add special effects to layers. For your next project, you may never use the Styles panel but require frequent access to the Paths panel to create curves that you use to make selections. And so it goes.

Use custom workspaces to save time and effort, or to instantly clean up a messy desktop.

Custom workspaces come in handy if you share a computer with students, family members, or coworkers. Those who prepare images for various mediums and purposes have different needs that may call for special workspaces, too.

You can start with one of the many preset workspaces. Select a workspace from the Workspace Switcher in the Application bar, or by choosing Window➪Workspace. Photoshop CS5 offers preset workspaces for various workflows, such as design, motion, and photography. These presets can modify menu and/or keyboard shortcuts. They can also modify which panels are visible. You can select a preset, then establish your panel preferences, and save the modified workspace as your own custom workspace. Read on to find out how.

You can tailor your workspace in these ways:

✔ **Combine panels to group together the ones you use most often.** Drag a panel's tab into another panel group to add it to that group. If the Layers, Channels, and History panels are the ones you use most often, you might want to group them together. You can collapse panels that you rarely use down to space-saving icons, minimize them to just their title bars, or close them altogether.

Before saving your workspace preset, show or minimize, collapse, or close the panels (however you prefer them) and move them to the locations you want on your screen.

✔ **Position dialog boxes.** Although they don't save with the workspace, per se, Photoshop's Menu bar dialog boxes pop up in the same location they appeared the last time you used them. You may want to drag them to a specific place on your screen so that they appear there every time. When I'm working with a large image, I sometimes position dialog boxes on the screen of my second monitor to maximize the area for the image on my main display.

✔ **Customize the Options bar.** You can grab the gripper bar at the left edge of the Options bar and drag it to another location. For example, you can dock the bar on the right, along with your other panels, or have it float in a specific place on your Photoshop desktop. Photoshop stores these settings with your workspace preset.

✔ **Set Photoshop's font size.** You can change the size of the font for text that's displayed on the Options bar and panels. Choose Edit➪ Preferences➪Interface (Photoshop➪Preferences➪Interface on the Mac). Select Small, Medium, or Large from the UI Font Size pop-up menu in the Interface dialog box. The change takes place the next time you start Photoshop.

Other settings concerning the appearance of screen modes, menu colors, and the actions of panels are located in the Preferences settings, described in the section "Setting Your Preferences," later in this chapter.

Creating and Deleting Workspace Presets

After you set up your custom workspace, you can save it by choosing Window⇨Workspace⇨New Workspace. In the New Workspace dialog box that appears, type a name for your saved workspace.

Panel locations are saved by default. You have the additional options of selecting which components — keyboard shortcuts and menus — you want to capture in your custom workspace, as shown in Figure 5-1. After you adjust your desired settings, click the Save button.

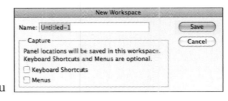

Figure 5-1: Select which components to save in your custom workspace.

Your saved workspace now appears as an item on the Workspace submenu.

Want to return to the way Adobe sees the world of Photoshop? Choose Window⇨Workspace⇨Essentials (Default).

To delete a saved workspace, choose Window⇨Workspace⇨Delete Workspace. In the Delete Workspace dialog box that appears, select the name of the workspace you want to remove from the drop-down list. Click the Delete button, and your preset is gone, gone, gone.

You can create a workspace, as well as delete it or select a preset, by using the handy Workspace Switcher on the right side of the Application bar. The Workspace Switcher highlights the name of the current workspace. Simply click the other workspaces displayed in the bar or click the down-pointing arrow and make your selection from the submenu.

Customizing Keyboard Shortcuts

For those of you who are like me — I avoid using a mouse, and prefer the ease and speed of keyboard shortcuts — Photoshop offers customizable keyboard shortcuts. You can assign shortcuts to menu commands, panel commands, and tools. You can edit, delete, or add to the Photoshop default set or create your own custom set. Follow these steps to customize keyboard shortcuts:

1. **Choose Edit⇨Keyboard Shortcuts. In the Keyboard Shortcuts and Menus dialog box that appears (see Figure 5-2), make sure the Keyboard Shortcuts tab is selected.**

   You can also choose Window⇨Workspace⇨Keyboard Shortcuts & Menus.

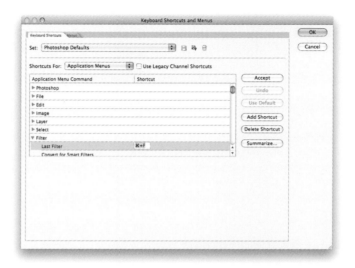

Figure 5-2: Customize keyboard shortcuts for enhanced productivity.

2. **Select your desired set of keyboard shortcuts from the pop-up menu.**

   You can also create a new set by clicking the New Set button (the disk with a down-pointing arrow icon).

   Clicking New Set makes a copy of the selected set for you to then edit and customize. If you create a new set, name the set (leaving it with a .kys extension) and keep it stored in the Keyboard Shortcuts folder.

3. **Select Application Menus, Panel Menus, or Tools from the Shortcuts For drop-down list.**

   Click the triangle next to the menu heading to expand the particular menu headings.

4. **Select your desired command from the list. Type the shortcut keys you want to assign to that command in the shortcut field.**

   If a shortcut has already been assigned to that command, you can simply type over it.

   If the keyboard shortcut you type is already being used, Photoshop warns you that if you accept the shortcut, it'll be removed from the original command.

5. **Click Accept to assign the shortcut to the command or tool.**

   If you later change your mind and want to use the original keyboard shortcut (if there was one), click Use Default. If you decide you don't want the shortcut at all, click Delete Shortcut. And if you make a mistake, just click Undo.

Application and Panel menu commands must include a Ctrl (⌘ on the Mac) and/or a Function (F) key in the keyboard shortcut.

6. **When you finish, click the Save Set button (the disk icon).**

   If you want to delete the set, click the Delete Set button (the trash icon).

7. **Click the Summarize button to save the keyboard shortcut set as an .htm file, which loads in your Internet browser.**

   You can then print the file and keep it as a handy reference of your shortcuts.

8. **Click OK to exit the dialog box.**

Customizing Menus

Adobe takes the customization club to yet another level by adding the ability to customize menus, as shown in Figure 5-3. You have the choice of colorizing chosen menu items or hiding the menu items altogether.

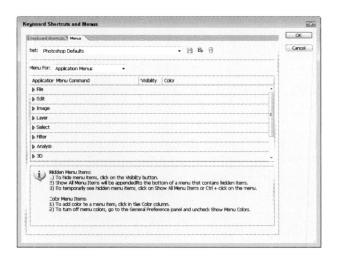

Figure 5-3: Customize menu items to show only those you use.

Follow these steps to make the Photoshop menus your own:

1. **Choose Edit➪Menus.**

   You can also choose Window➪Workspace➪Keyboard Shortcuts & Menus.

   The Keyboard Shortcuts and Menus dialog box appears. (Refer to Figure 5-3.)

2. **Click the Menus tab, and in the Set drop-down list at the top, select the Photoshop Defaults set or another preset.**

   Or to create a new menu, click the New Set button (the disk with a down-pointing arrow icon).

   Clicking New Set makes a copy of the selected set for you to then edit and customize. If you select a new set, name the set (leaving it with a .mnu extension), and keep it stored in the Menu Customization folder.

3. **Select Application Menus or Panel Menus from the Menu For drop-down list. Click the triangle to expand the individual menu headings.**

4. **Select one of the following options for your desired command:**

   - *Visibility:* To hide or show a menu item, click the Visibility button.

     Be careful not to hide the really critical commands, such as Open or Save.

   - *Color:* To add color to a menu item, click the Color swatch (or the word None) and select a color from the drop-down list.

5. **When you finish making changes, click the Save All Changes to the Current Set of Menus button (the disk icon).**

   To delete a menu set, click the Delete Set button (trash can icon).

   Or, to create a new set based on the current menu, click the Create a New Set Based on the Current Set of Menus button.

6. **In the Save dialog box, enter a name for the set and click Save.**

7. **Click OK to exit the dialog box.**

If you've hidden some menu items and decide you want to temporarily show them while working in Photoshop, choose Show All Menu Items from the menu that has the hidden items.

To turn off menu colors (they're on by default), choose Edit⇨Preferences⇨ Interface (Photoshop⇨Preferences⇨Interface on the Mac) and deselect Show Menu Colors.

Setting Your Preferences

Photoshop stores settings for many different options in various Preferences files on your hard drive. The first time you run Photoshop after a new installation, you probably want to customize preferences to suit your own needs.

You can access the Preferences dialog box by choosing Edit⇨Preferences (Photoshop⇨Preferences on the Mac). The first category of settings that appears in the submenu are the General Preferences (shown in Figure 5-4). You can choose any of the other Preferences categories from the submenu.

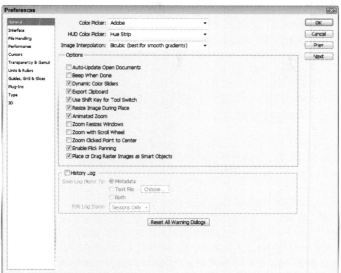

Figure 5-4: The General Preferences pane specifies a lot of the "look and feel" of your Photoshop interface.

After you're in any Preferences dialog box, you can move between the pane by clicking the Prev or Next buttons that appear in each of the Preferences panes. If you like keyboard shortcuts, you can switch to the other Preferences pane by pressing Ctrl+1, Ctrl+2 (⌘+1, ⌘+2 on the Mac), and so forth. The following sections give you a rundown of what you can do with the settings in the different Preferences panes.

Setting general preferences

The General Preferences pane is where you select some options that are, well, general in nature. You can select some choices from drop-down lists, and others are check boxes you can select or deselect to activate or disable that option. Here's a rundown of options in the upper part of the pane:

- ✔ **Color Picker:** Use the familiar Adobe Color Picker to select precise colors or work with the Windows or Macintosh system color pickers, as desired. You might want to use the Windows or Apple color picker, for example, if you've previously defined some custom colors outside Photoshop and now want to make them available for a Photoshop project.

- ✔ **HUD Color Picker:** The HUD (heads-up display) Color Picker lets you quickly select colors within the image window without having to access the Color Picker. Choose whether you want a strip or wheel of color. For more on using the HUD Color Picker, see Book II, Chapter 3.

✔ **Image Interpolation:** When Photoshop resizes an image, it must either create new pixels (when making the image larger) or combine existing pixels (to make the image smaller). To do this, the program examines neighboring pixels and uses the information to derive the new or replacement pixels. You can select the type of mathematical algorithm Photoshop uses to do this, though you likely want to stick with the default option, Bicubic (Best for Smooth Gradients). You can find out more about interpolation and the other algorithms in Book II, Chapter 1.

In the Options section of the General Preferences dialog box, you find nearly a dozen check boxes that you can select or deselect, as described in the following list:

✔ **Auto-Update Open Documents:** When you're working on an image and move to another application to work on the same image, you'll probably want the changes made in the other application to reflect in the document still open in Photoshop. Select this check box so that Photoshop monitors the document and updates its version whenever the document is changed in the other application.

✔ **Beep When Done:** I remember the bad old days when computers were slow and Photoshop would take a minute or two to apply the Gaussian Blur filter or perform calculations when merging even moderate-sized image layers. The Beep When Done signal was my cue to stop watching television and resume working with Photoshop. Although most operations are a lot faster today, if you're working with very large images or simply like to be notified when a step is finished, the beep option can be useful (or incredibly annoying to your coworkers).

✔ **Dynamic Color Sliders:** The sliders in the Color panel change colors to match the settings you make. If your computer is on the slow side, you can turn off this feature to improve performance.

✔ **Export Clipboard:** When this feature is active, Photoshop transfers its private clipboard (used only within Photoshop) to the general Windows or Macintosh Clipboard so that you can paste information into other applications. If you activate this option, switching from Photoshop to other applications takes a little longer, and Photoshop's clipboard contents replace whatever was in your system Clipboard when you switched.

The clipboard is generally a poor vehicle for moving image data between applications because the transferred information may not be of the best quality. Instead, save your file and open it in the other application. If you do this, you can turn off the Export Clipboard option, saving you some time when switching between applications. Additionally, many applications support the dragging and dropping of files between programs.

✔ **Use Shift Key for Tool Switch:** When this feature is active, you can change from one tool in the Tools panel to another in the same flyout menu (say, to change from the Gradient tool to the Paint Bucket tool) by pressing the Shift key and the keyboard shortcut for that tool.

✔ **Resize Image During Paste/Place:** By default, when you place or paste files that are larger than the document they're being pasted or placed into, the files are resized to fit. Deselect this option to have the file import with its exact dimensions, as shown in Figure 5-5.

✔ **Animated Zoom:** This option enables you to zoom in smoothly, rather than in increments, when holding down the mouse button or pressing Ctrl+plus/equal sign (+/=) (⌘+plus/equal sign [+/=] on the Mac).

✔ **Zoom Resizes Windows:** Select this check box if you want your document windows to grow and shrink to fit your document while you zoom in and out. Deselect this check box if you want the document's window to always remain the same size; you might want to deselect the check box if you frequently work with several documents side by side and don't want them to change relative size while you zoom in and out.

Not resized

Resized

Photo Disc

Figure 5-5: Select the Resize Image During Paste/Place check box to have your image automatically resized upon import.

- ✔ **Zoom with Scroll Wheel:** This handy option enables your mouse scroll wheel to become a zooming tool, regardless of which tool you're using.

- ✔ **Zoom Clicked Point to Center:** If selected, when you click the Zoom tool at a specific location, that location then becomes the center of your image window.

- ✔ **Enable Flick Panning:** If selected, when you quickly drag and release with the Hand tool, the image continues to move, slowly decelerating to a stop.

- ✔ **Place or Drag Raster Images as Smart Objects:** Select this option to create Smart Object layers when using the File➪Place command or when dragging and dropping raster images from other applications from the browser or from your desktop.

In the History Log section, you can have Photoshop record all your editing commands. The History Log feature is handy if you want to present a finished, fully edited image to a client or manager, but need to be able to show the steps of how you got there. Or maybe you want a record of the steps so that you can repeat them on other images and don't want to rely on your memory.

You have a few formats in which you can save your history log:

- ✔ **Metadata:** Saving the log to *metadata* (information embedded in your image file) allows you to view the log in the Bridge window and in the History tab of the File➪File Info dialog box. For more on Bridge, see Book I, Chapter 4.

- ✔ **Text File:** You can save the log to a text file. Click the Choose button to provide a name and location for the file.

- ✔ **Both:** This option saves the log as both metadata and a text file.

- ✔ **Edit Log Items:** You select Sessions Only, Concise, or Detailed. The Sessions Only option records your editing until you close the file or quit Photoshop. The Concise option keeps a comprehensive log (multiple sessions), but in short and sweet steps. The Detailed option provides a comprehensive, detailed log. For example, a concise log entry may be just Crop, whereas a detailed log entry may be Crop to rectangle, also providing the original and cropped dimensions, the angle, and the resolution values.

The last option in the General Preferences dialog box is the Reset All Warning Dialogs button. If you've turned off the display of certain warnings by selecting the Don't Show Me This Dialog Box Again check box, you can reactivate all the warnings by clicking this button.

Customizing the interface

The Interface preferences, shown in Figure 5-6, deal with the "look" of Photoshop. Here's the scoop:

✓ **Screen Modes:** When using the Application Frame, you can select the color of the background around your image. You can also select whether your image edge is surrounded by a line, drop shadow, or nothing at all.

✓ **Show Channels in Color:** When selected, this option tells Photoshop to show each of the color channels (for example, Red, Green, and Blue; or Cyan, Magenta, Yellow, and Black) in their respective colors in the Channels panel. In most cases, you don't want to use this feature. You need to be able to see the channels in their grayscale form to perform image-editing tasks such as converting from color to grayscale or channel masking, or for selective sharpening on certain channels. Book VI, Chapter 1 introduces channels.

✓ **Show Menu Colors:** Check this option to have the ability to view customized menus in color.

✓ **Show Tool Tips:** Photoshop can display little pop-up reminders about tools and other objects on your screen. If you find these reminders distracting, deselect this check box to turn off tool tips.

✓ **Enable Gestures (Mac only):** Enables you to use your Macintosh trackpad for controls such as rotation of the document canvas. If you are annoyed by the inadvertent rotation of your canvas, deselect this option.

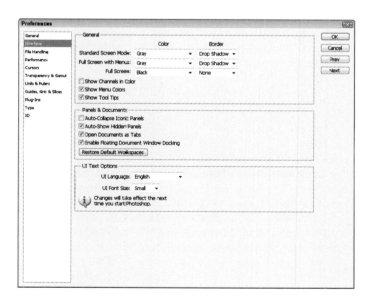

Figure 5-6: The Interface Preferences category specifies the "look" of Photoshop.

✔ **Auto-Collapse Iconic Panels:** If selected, panels automatically collapse down to just their icons when you click somewhere else within the Photoshop application.

✔ **Auto-Show Hidden Panels:** If selected, this option automatically shows any hidden panels.

✔ **Open Documents as Tabs:** Selecting this new option opens documents tabbed to the Application Frame. If you deselect this option, images "float," like in previous versions of Photoshop.

✔ **Enable Floating Document Window Docking:** Lets you dock floating document windows as tabs when dragging one document window to another document window. Holding down Ctrl (Control on the Mac) while dragging a floating window also temporarily turns on the preference while you're working in Photoshop.

✔ **Restore Default Workspaces:** Click this button to reset all of your workspaces back to their default settings.

✔ **UI Text Options:** Specify the size of the text displayed in dialog boxes, panels, and so on. Select from Small, Medium, or Large.

Deciding how you want files handled

The options in the File Handling Preferences pane, shown in Figure 5-7, control how Photoshop handles files when they're opened and closed. Here's the lowdown on these options:

✔ **Image Previews:** Storing a preview thumbnail with an image can speed up browsing for the image you want. You can tell Photoshop to save a preview by default or to ask you first (in case you want to create images that are a little smaller in size, especially for the Web). Or you can also choose not to ever save a preview. Mac users need to select the kinds of image previews they need. Select the Icon option to enable an image icon to appear on the desktop. Select the Macintosh Thumbnail option to see a preview in the Open dialog box. Select the Windows Thumbnail option to see a preview in a Windows OS dialog box. Finally, select the Full Size option to save a low-resolution version of the file to use in applications that can open only low-resolution (72 ppi) Photoshop images.

✔ **File Extension (Append File Extension on the Mac):** You can select whether the file extensions appended to filenames (such as .psd, .tif, and so forth) are consistently uppercase or lowercase, as you prefer. On the Mac, you can choose whether to add extensions by selecting from the Always, Never, or Ask When Saving options. If you want cross-platform compatibility with PCs or you're creating Web graphics, select the Always option. Mac users, select the Use Lower Case option to save extensions as lowercase characters.

Figure 5-7: The File Handling Preferences dialog box offers settings for opening and saving files.

✔ **Save As to Original Folder:** When you choose File⇨Save As, your file will save to the folder you last saved that image.

✔ **Camera Raw Preferences:** Here are the details on these preferences, as shown in Figure 5-8:

- When a Camera Raw (CR) file is processed, the image settings can be saved in two different places — a sidecar .xmp file or a Camera Raw database file. Create a separate sidecar .xmp file if you want to archive your images or exchange them with other people because it's a collaborative workflow. If you archive the files to a CD or DVD, copy them to a hard drive before opening them because CR can't write an XMP file to read-only media. If you store your setting to a CR database file, the settings are saved in the folder Document and Settings/[*username*]/Application Data/Adobe/CameraRaw (Users/[*user name*]/Library/Preferences on the Mac).

- When you reopen a CR image, the image settings you used when the file was last opened are reapplied. Select which Default Image Settings you want applied. The only settings that aren't stored are color profile, bit depth, pixel dimensions, and resolution.

- The cache in Camera Raw stores data for file thumbnails, metadata, and file info. You can choose to increase the cache, if desired. Note that 1GB holds data for around 200 images. If your cache gets bloated or corrupted, clicking the Purge Cache button deletes the data.

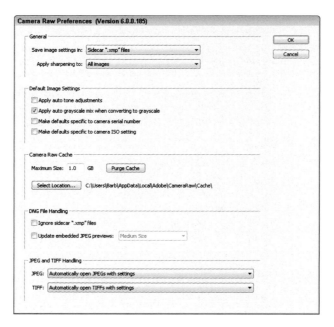

Figure 5-8: Establish preferences for Camera Raw images.

- DNG stands for Digital Negative, a popular format for storing CR images. DNG image settings are usually embedded in the file itself. If you want to stick with the norm, select the Ignore Sidecar ".xmp" Files option. If you want a JPEG preview of your image, select the option and choose from a Medium or Full Size preview.

- Another important setting is the JPEG and TIFF Handling option. Camera Raw (CR) enables you to open and edit both JPEGs and TIFFs. If you select Automatically Open All Supported JPEGs (or TIFFs), any JPEG or TIFF automatically opens in CR, rather than Photoshop. If you select Automatically Open JPEGs (or TIFFs) with Settings, CR opens any JPEG or TIFF with Camera Raw (crs) tags. So, any files that you have previously opened and edited, and then closed by clicking Done in CR, will open in CR. Because working with Camera Raw images can be a little complex, Adobe offers a lot of documentation and videos on working with these types of images. Check out www.adobe.com.

✔ **Prefer Adobe Camera Raw for Supported Raw Files:** Select this setting to have ACR open any and all Raw file formats supported by Photoshop.

✔ **Ignore EXIF Profile Tag:** When this option is selected, Photoshop ignores the sRGB tag that many digital cameras add to their EXIF (camera) data. The sRGB tag is widely used by digital cameras, but it's not well respected among many high-end digital photography professionals.

✓ **Ask Before Saving Layered TIFF Files:** Photoshop can save an advanced type of TIFF file that includes layers, exactly like with its own native PSD files. However, many applications can't read these files. If you always open TIFF files in Photoshop, or you're using recent versions of other Creative Suite applications that can accept layered TIFFs and you don't mind creating larger TIFF files in the process, you can disable this option. Otherwise, Photoshop asks you for confirmation each time you want to save a TIFF file that contains layers.

✓ **Maximize PSD File and PSB File Compatibility:** Photoshop lets you choose an option for file compatibility.

Not all applications can handle the more sophisticated features that may be stored in a PSD file (such as fancy layer effects). If you frequently open PSD files in applications other than later versions of Photoshop, you may want to set this option to Always. Keep in mind that you may lose some features when you choose this option. Select Ask to have Photoshop prompt you when you save a file about whether you want to apply the option. Or select Never to ignore the option completely.

When you maximize compatibility, Photoshop saves a *composite* (flattened) version along with the layered file to ensure that older applications (such as Photoshop version 2) can read the files. However, this option can make your file size balloon significantly.

The PSB (large file) format is like the PSD format in that it supports most Photoshop features. Currently, only Photoshop CS (along with Photoshop Elements 7 and 8) and higher can open PSB files. Again, keeping this option selected ensures maximum compatibility with any future programs that may accept this format.

If you plan to use your PSD files in InDesign or Illustrator, you should have the Maximize Compatibility feature selected because the performance of these programs is faster when you have a composite along with the layers, especially with large files that have a lot of layers.

✓ **Adobe Drive:** Select this option if your computer is located on a network and you need to share your files with others in your collaborative workgroup by using a server.

✓ **Recent File List Contains:** Type a value from 0 to 30 to specify the number of recently used files you want displayed in the Open Recent list on the File menu.

Handling performance options

Everything you need to specify Photoshop's performance can be found in the Preferences pane. Here are the options, as shown in Figure 5-9:

✔ **Memory Usage:** The perennial question: How much memory does Photoshop require? The perennial answer: As much as you can cram into your computer! Memory is so inexpensive right now that you have no excuse for not having at least a gigabyte of RAM, and more is even better if you're using an operating system that can handle extra memory efficiently, such as Windows Vista or 7, or Mac OS X. Version CS5 runs at its best with at least 2 gigabytes of RAM, even better with 4 gigabytes.

When you cram your RAM, you want to make sure Photoshop can use as much as you can spare. You can use the Memory Usage slider, shown in Figure 5-9, to allocate your memory. Use a value of 50 to 80 percent, depending on how much memory you have to spare. Allocating more to Photoshop reduces the RAM for other applications, so if you have other programs that need a lot of memory, select a prudent value.

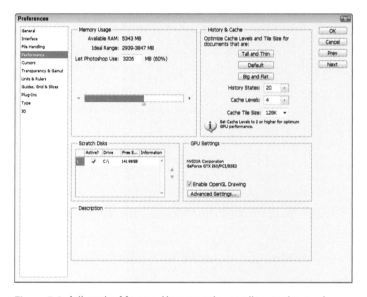

Figure 5-9: Adjust the Memory Usage setting to allocate the maximum amount of RAM Photoshop gobbles up.

✔ **History States:** Photoshop remembers how your document looks at various stages of editing, storing all the image information on your hard drive and listing the individual states in the History panel. (For more information on using the History panel, see Book II, Chapter 4.) Keeping track of every change you make requires a lot of memory and hard drive space, so you can specify how many resources to use by typing a value into this box. The default is 20. (The max is 1000.) If you have resources to burn and frequently find yourself stepping way back in time to modify or delete a step, you can type a larger number. If your resources are skimpy and you don't anticipate making many changes to earlier steps (or are willing to take frequent snapshots or save interim images), you can enter a smaller number.

✔ **Cache Levels:** You can set aside the amount of memory for storing screen images in the Cache Levels setting, to speed up redraws of a reduced-view image on your screen while you make changes. You can specify the number of copies of your image stored in memory, from the default value of 4 up to 8 levels. CS5 has added Cache Optimize buttons to make it easier to decide the number of cache levels. You can use Tall and Thin (2 cache levels) if you have a smaller file with lots of layers. You can choose Big and Flat (5 cache levels) if your file is bigger with fewer layers. The Default setting gives a cache level of 4. In addition, you are able to specify the Cache Tile Size, which determines the amount of data Photoshop processes at one time. Bigger tiles can result in faster processing of larger files. Smaller tiles may be better for smaller files with more layers.

✔ **Scratch Disks:** Scratch disks are areas on your hard drive that Photoshop uses to substitute for physical RAM when you don't have enough RAM to work with the images you open. Scratch disks are no replacement for physical memory, but Photoshop needs scratch disks many times, even if you have huge amounts of memory.

Photoshop uses your startup drive (the drive used to boot your operating system) as its first scratch disk by default. That may not be the best choice because your startup drive is usually pretty busy handling requests of your operating system. Ideally, your scratch disk(s) should be a different hard drive and, preferably, the fastest one you have available.

If you have more than one hard drive, select one other than your startup drive as your first scratch disk.

If you don't have a second hard drive, you can improve scratch disk performance by creating a *partition* on an existing drive for use as a scratch disk. Remember to keep the scratch disk *defragmented* (that is, with the files all organized together on your hard drive) by using your favorite defragmentation utility.

✔ **GPU Settings:** Photoshop attempts to auto-detect your video card and lists the make and model. Select Enable OpenGL Drawing to enhance the performance of your graphics display and speed up your screen redraw. If some of your tool cursors don't appear while you edit an image, try deselecting this option to see whether it fixes the problem. You must select this option to enable viewing options such as flick panning, animated zooms, and the Rotate View tool.

Adjusting your cursors

The Cursors Preferences pane, shown in Figure 5-10, enables you to set several options that control how cursors display onscreen.

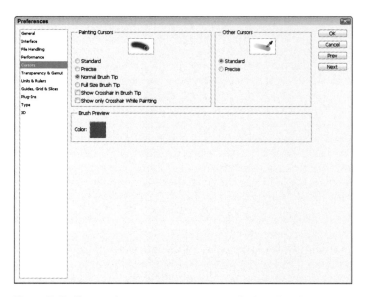

Figure 5-10: Choose the way your cursors are displayed — from crosshairs to brush tips.

The following list describes the Cursor options:

✔ **Painting and Other Cursors (shown in Figure 5-11):** Select the Standard option to show a tool's cursor as an icon representing the tool itself (although I don't know why you'd want to do this). Here's the lowdown on the other settings:

- *Precise:* Switches to a cursor that has crosshairs, which is useful for positioning the center of a tool's operational area in a particular place.

- *Normal Brush Tip:* Displays a 50% point for the brush tip, which means that the diameter of the brush tip reflects feathering of 50% or more. The wispier feathered areas of 50% or less are outside the diameter area shown.

- *Full Size Brush Tip:* Displays the full size of the diameter of the brush tip.

- *Show Crosshair in Brush Tip:* A great hybrid. It shows a crosshair in the center of either of the brush tips — great for precision retouching.

- *Show Only Crosshair While Painting:* Cursor switches to just a crosshair when painting. This can be helpful when using large brushes. Showing the diameters of very large brushes can be cumbersome and slow.

Most users prefer to set the painting cursors to Normal or Full Size Brush Tip and the other cursors to Precise. Some folks complain that precise cursors are hard to see against some backgrounds, but you can always press the Caps Lock key to toggle precise cursors on or off.

- **Brush Preview:** To change the color of your brush editing preview, click the color swatch, which takes you to the Color Picker, where you can select your desired color.

Adjusting transparency and gamut

Photoshop uses colors and patterns to represent information about an image that's normally invisible, such as areas that are transparent or parts of an image that contain colors that can't be represented by your current display or printing system. The Transparency & Gamut Preferences pane, shown in Figure 5-12, enables you to tailor these displays to your own preferences.

For example, transparency is typically shown onscreen by using a gray-and-white checkerboard pattern. You can change the pattern and colors if you prefer another type of display.

Here's a rundown of the options you find in this pane:

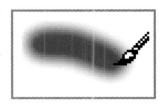

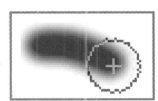

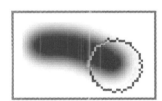

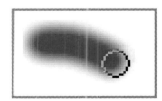

Figure 5-11: Photoshop offers six brush tips.

✒ **Grid Size:** You can choose small, medium, large, or no grid at all. You may want to switch from the default medium-sized grid to a large grid if you're using a very high-resolution setting (such as the 1920 x 1200 pixel setting I use on my monitor) so that the grid is a little easier to see. (I don't bother with this, myself.) Or you can switch to a smaller grid if you're working at a lower resolution.

✒ **Grid Colors:** The default light grid is the least obtrusive, but you can switch to a medium or dark grid, if you want. Also, you're not limited to gray-and-white checkerboard squares. To select custom colors, click the white and gray squares below the Grid Colors list.

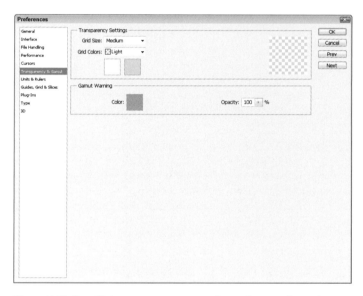

Figure 5-12: Specify how transparency and out-of-gamut (meaning out-of-range) colors are displayed in the Transparency & Gamut Preferences pane.

✒ **Gamut Warning:** You can adjust the color used to represent out-of-gamut colors and to specify the transparency for the warning color. Double-click the Color box to set the hue and select the transparency with the Opacity slider. The gamut warning is generally used before converting RGB images to CMYK to see which colors will be lost. For more information on color gamuts, see Book II, Chapter 2.

A *gamut* is the range of colors that can be displayed or printed. In Photoshop talk, out-of-gamut colors generally are those that can't be represented by cyan, magenta, yellow, and black and, therefore, can't be printed. To turn gamut warnings on or off, choose View➪Gamut Warning. I recommend leaving the gamut warning on. That way, you know what's happening with your image's colors.

Setting measurement preferences

In the Units & Rulers Preferences pane, shown in Figure 5-13, you can set the
units used to measure things onscreen (inches, pixels, millimeters, and so
forth) and to define a default column size when typing text in multiple columns. In addition, you can define the resolution of the image when you
choose File⇨New and select a preset from the Preset Sizes list. (See Book I,
Chapter 3 for more on preset sizes.)

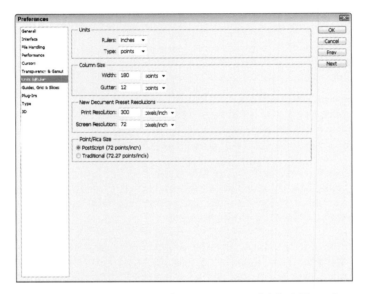

Figure 5-13: Specify your units of measurement and default Photoshop
resolution settings in the Units & Rulers Preferences dialog box.

In the Units area of the pane, you find these options:

- **Rulers:** Select the measurement units that Photoshop uses for rulers.
  Your choices are pixels, inches, centimeters, millimeters, points, picas,
  or percent. The most popular units are inches and millimeters, but if
  you're working with publications and specifying in picas, you might prefer that increment instead. If you're prepping Web graphics, you may
  prefer to have your rulers incremented in pixels.

- **Type:** Select the measurement used to represent the dimensions of type.
  Point size is almost universally used, but pixels and millimeters are also
  available. You may want to use pixels if you're trying to fit type into a
  specific-sized area of an image.

In the Column Size area, you can specify the following:

- ✓ **Width:** The width of the column in inches, centimeters, millimeters, points, or picas.

- ✓ **Gutter:** The width of the area separating columns, also in inches, centimeters, millimeters, points, or picas.

In the New Document Preset Resolutions area, you can set the following:

- ✓ **Print Resolution:** The default is 300 pixels per inch, a good overall print setting to keep. You can change to another value and use pixels per centimeter as a measurement, if you want. This resolution setting affects the Photo, International Paper, and U.S. Paper presets found in the New dialog box.

- ✓ **Screen Resolution:** Generally, 72 pixels per inch works with most images that are prepped for screen viewing. You can select another resolution and use pixels per centimeter, if you like. This resolution setting affects the Web and Film and Video presets found in the New dialog box.

Changing the resolution of an image after you created it can impact the sharpness of your image and degrade quality. Choosing the final resolution you want when you create a document is best, whether you specify the resolution manually or use these presets.

In the Point/Pica Size area, you can select whether you want to use a measurement of 72 points per inch (which first became relevant in the Macintosh realm and spread as desktop publishing became widespread) or the traditional 72.27 points per inch definition used in the precomputer era. Unless you have a special reason to choose otherwise, use the PostScript (72 points per inch) option.

Setting up guides, grids, and slices

Guides are nonprinting lines you can create on your screen to make it easier to align objects. *Grids* are vertical and horizontal lines in the background that make lining up objects even easier. *Slices* are sections of an image you can create for Web page graphics so that each slice can be loaded and treated separately (usually in a table or similar arrangement). For more information on using grids and guides, see Book I, Chapter 4. Figure 5-14 shows the Guides, Grid & Slices Preferences pane.

In the Guides and Smart Guides areas, you can set these options:

- ✓ **Color:** Either select a color from the drop-down list or click the color sample swatch to select your own color. You may want to change the default color if that color is too similar to a dominant color in your image.

- ✓ **Style (for guides only):** Select from lines or dashed lines. If you work with images that contain many horizontal and vertical lines that extend across most of an image, dashed lines may be more visible.

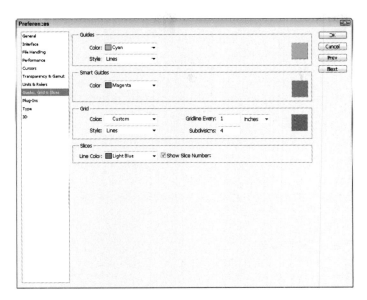

Figure 5-14: Change the colors and styles of your guides and grids for maximum contrast against your image in the Guides, Grid & Slices Preferences pane.

In the Grid area, these are your options:

- **Color:** Select a color from the drop-down list or click the color sample patch to define a specific hue.

- **Style:** You can select lines, dashed lines, or dots.

- **Gridline Every:** Select the distance between gridlines.

- **Subdivisions:** Select the number of subdivisions for each gridline.

In the Slices area, these are your choices:

- **Line Color:** From the drop-down list, select a color for the lines that surround each slice.

- **Show Slice Numbers:** If you select this check box, Photoshop adds a slice number to the display of slices, which makes it easier to keep track of individual slices.

For a full explanation of slices, check out Bonus Chapter 2. See the Introduction for details about this book's companion Web site.

Adding plug-ins

Plug-ins are mini software programs that add features to Photoshop. The Plug-Ins folder is where Photoshop stores all your filters and other plug-in add-ons. A default folder is created when you install Photoshop.

Photoshop allows you to specify an additional folder to search other than its own Plug-Ins folder. This additional folder may come in handy if you want to keep your third-party add-ons separate from Photoshop's native plug-ins. An auxiliary plug-ins directory (not nested within Photoshop's own Plug-Ins folder) can simplify managing those extra filters, and you can turn off their use (potentially speeding up Photoshop's load time) by deselecting the Additional Plug-Ins Folder check box in this dialog box, as shown in Figure 5-15. You can also use this option when you have some plug-ins installed for another application and want to share them with Photoshop without having to make extra copies in your Photoshop Plug-Ins directory.

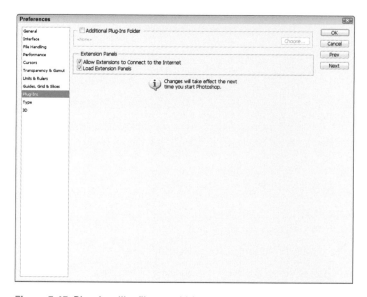

Figure 5-15: Plug-ins, like filters, add features to Photoshop.

Here are a couple tips on using plug-ins:

✐ **To activate a new plug-ins folder:** Select the Additional Plug-Ins Folder check box. In the dialog box that appears, navigate to the folder you want to use and select it. Click Choose. You then need to exit Photoshop and restart the program to activate the new directory.

✐ **If you have a plug-in or folder you want to deactivate:** Use a tilde (~) as the first character of the plug-in or folder name. Photoshop ignores the plug-in(s) or folder(s) specified. Just remove the tilde from the name to activate the plug-in or folder. This can come in handy if you're having a program glitch and want to deactivate your plug-ins to troubleshoot whether they're causing the problem.

✔ **Extension Panels:** Choose whether to allow Extension panels like Kuler and CS Live to connect to the Internet for updates and new goodies. Also choose whether to have your Extension panels load when you start Photoshop.

Specifying type options

The Type Preferences enable you to establish your font options, shown in Figure 5-16, as follows:

✔ **Use Smart Quotes:** Smart quotes are the curly quotes that typographers use for quotation marks and apostrophes. Straight quotes should be used for abbreviations for feet and inches. I recommend leaving this option selected by default.

✔ **Show Asian Text Options:** If deselected (the default), Photoshop hides Asian text options in the Character and Paragraph panels.

✔ **Enable Missing Glyph Protection:** If certain *glyphs* (characters) are missing, Photoshop makes a substitution if this option is selected.

✔ **Show Font Names in English:** Photoshop displays Asian font names in English if this option is selected (and you select the Show Asian Text Option).

✔ **Font Preview Size:** Specify whether you want a small, medium, or large font for the font menu display of your Type tool.

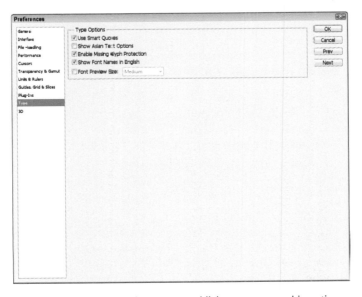

Figure 5-16: The Type preferences establish your typographic options.

Using the Preset Manager

Many of the panels and tools Photoshop works with can use settings that you store on your hard drive as presets. For example, you can create custom colors and brush tips, build your own gradients, create a library of shapes, or compile a set of styles to apply to layers.

You want to become familiar with the Preset Manager, which provides a central management tool for all the options that are individually available from the panels and tools themselves. Just like with the tools, you can select, edit, and delete presets. The only thing you can't do with the Preset Manager is actually create a preset. You must do this with the Tool Preset Picker, Tool Presets panel, Gradient Editor, Brushes panel, and other locations. For more details, see Book I, Chapter 2. Here are some tips on using the Preset Manager, shown in Figure 5-17:

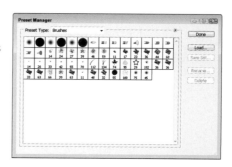

Figure 5-17: The Preset Manager is the central management tool for all Photoshop presets for all panels.

✔ To show the Preset Manager, choose Edit➪Preset Manager. To hide it, click Done.

✔ To select a specific type of preset to work with, select it from the Preset Type drop-down list.

✔ To load an existing set of presets from your hard drive, click the Load button and navigate to the presets you want to access. You can also select a preset library listed on the pop-up menu of each preset type.

✔ To store a new or modified group of settings, click the Save Set button and type a name.

✔ To give a particular preset a new name, select the preset in the dialog box, click the Rename button, type the new name, and click OK.

You can rename multiple presets consecutively by clicking and Ctrl-clicking (⌘-clicking) the items that you want to rename, and then clicking the Rename button. Photoshop asks you to supply a new name for each, in turn.

✔ To quickly load the default preset library for any tool or panel, select Reset *[Preset]* from the Preset Manager pop-up menu. You can also replace your current preset library with another.

✔ Different preset display options are available on the Preset Manager pop-up menu.

Book II
Image Essentials

*T*o me, when people say that a bit of information is *essential,* they mean, "Hey, you really gotta know this stuff or else!" Well, technically, you could skip this book, and Photoshop wouldn't be any wiser — but I don't recommend it. In this book, I cover the nitty-gritty of topics like resolution, image modes, and file formats. Fun? Nope. Dry? Most likely, unless you're the type who gets excited about pixel dimensions. But having a good handle on the information in this book is critical to ensuring good-looking images.

I show you how to safely size your images without causing them to turn to mush. You can also find information on cropping images and increasing canvas sizes, as well as an important chapter on both applying color and color managing your files. If you want to know more about how to undo your mistakes, you'll want to check out the chapter on the History panel. And finally, if all this information makes your head spin and you need a breather, look at the chapter on Actions. Actions can automate a lot of your frequently executed Photoshop techniques, giving you more time to stop and smell those roses you just photographed.

Chapter 1: Specifying Size and Resolution

In This Chapter

✓ Comparing raster (pixel) and vector images

✓ Understanding how pixels appear on different monitors

✓ Working with the Image Size command

✓ Resampling images (if you must)

✓ Adjusting the canvas size

✓ Cropping an image

Size and resolution are slippery subjects. A digital image's size may refer to its file size, how big you want it to be on a printed page (such as 3 x 5 or 8 x 10 inches), the size you want it be onscreen (full screen or just part of the screen), or how densely packed the pixels are (its resolution). To use Photoshop's tools so that an image looks good in print *or* onscreen, you need to know not only what type of size you're working with, but also what the image's resolution is — and how both of these factors might affect the image's appearance.

Given all the factors in size and resolution, it's not surprising that Photoshop has evolved into a Swiss Army knife. It offers multiple tools for specifying, viewing, or changing an image's size. In this chapter, I give you a bit of background in both size and resolution so that you know what tools to use and how to use them. In Book IX, you can find out how to use the basics I cover here in order to tailor size and resolution specifically for print.

I also explain how to change image size without harming your image. Yes, you can harm your image. Not intentionally, of course. But it can happen quicker than you can close a dialog box. However, with a firm understanding of how pixels live and breathe, you can ensure that your images are safe from damage.

Putting Images under the Microscope

Digital images fall into two camps — *vector* images, which are created by mathematical formulas, and *raster* images, which are made up of pixels arranged in a grid. Photoshop allows you to produce both types of images and even to combine both types within a single file. Table 1-1 gives you the skinny on vector and raster images.

Table 1-1	Characteristics of Vector and Raster Graphics			
Graphic Type	*How It Works*	*File Size*	*Image Degradation Possible?*	*Resolution-Dependent?*
Vector	Mathematical formulas precisely locate and connect geometric objects and segments.	Usually small	No	No
Raster	Breaks pieces of an image into a grid made up of pixels.	Usually large	Yes	Yes

Even though Photoshop can produce vector graphics, its primary mission is to create awe-inspiring raster images. And because the issue of resolution is so critical to raster images, this chapter primarily discusses methods for sizing and resizing raster images. I cover producing vector art in more detail in Book IV, Chapter 1.

Vector images

One cool thing about vector images — also called *object-oriented images* — is that when you zoom in on them, they don't look blocky. That's because vector images are made of *segments* (whether curved or straight) and *anchor points,* which are elements that indicate the endpoints of the segments. Both segments and anchors are defined by mathematical objects called *vectors*. Vectors use a unique mathematical formula to define the specific location of an object, as well as its geometric shape. Vector images, one of which is shown in Figure 1-1, are usually the product of drawing programs, such as Adobe Illustrator, but Photoshop is also capable of producing a vector or two.

Figure 1-1: Graphics that need clean lines work great in vector format.

Here are a few more handy things to know about vector graphics:

- **A curve is still a curve, even at 20,000 feet.** Because they're mathematically defined, vector graphics can be sized and otherwise transformed without an inkling of quality loss. Take that little 2-inch spot illustration and size it up to mural size, and it appears identical.

- **You can get pretty pictures in small packages.** Vector-image files can be small because file size depends on the complexity of the vector objects, not on the size of the illustration.

- **Vector images are independent — resolution-independent, that is.** Not only can they be transformed and printed without degrading their quality, but they also have no built-in resolution — they take on the resolution of the output device. For example, if you print my logo in Figure 1-1 to an *imagesetter* (a high-end printing device used for color separations) at 3600 dots per inch (dpi), the image comes out at 3600 dpi. Print it to a 300-dpi laser printer, and what do you get? A 300-dpi image.

Because your monitor can display images only on a grid, vector images display onscreen as pixels. This accounts for the jagged appearance you sometimes see when you zoom into a curved vector object. But don't worry; it prints just fine.

Raster images

Raster images are usually the result of the digitizing of *continuous-tone* images, such as photographs or original painted or drawn artwork. Raster images are made up of a grid of squares called pixels. (*Pixel* is short for picture element; it's the smallest component of a digital image.) If you've ever looked at a bathroom wall made up of those small square tiles reminiscent of the '40s, you're familiar with what a grid of pixels looks like up close: Each pixel lives in a specific location on that grid, and each contains a single color. When you edit a raster image, you're editing one or more pixels, rather than an object-oriented shape.

But how do you fit a round peg into a square hole? By faking it. Unlike the true mathematical curve that's possible when you're drawing vector shapes, raster images must try to approximate a curve by mimicking the overall shape with square pixels. So, the elliptical shapes of my beanie (shown in Figure 1-2) have to fit within this system of squares. Fortunately, the pixels'

Figure 1-2: Raster images are composed of a grid of square pixels.

mimicry is unnoticeable in high-resolution images viewed at a reasonable distance. But when you zoom in, you can see that a curve in an image (such as the curve of my beanie) is indeed made up of square pixels.

Raster graphics work great for photorealistic or painterly images in which subtle gradations of color are necessary. On the downside, because they contain a fixed number of pixels, raster graphics can suffer a degradation of quality when they're enlarged or otherwise transformed. They're also large in file size.

Bitmap (another name for raster) images are resolution-dependent. Because they contain a fixed number of pixels, the resolution of the device they're being printed to is only one of two factors that influence the quality of the image. The quality of the output also depends heavily on the resolution of the image. For example, an image with 72 dots per inch (dpi) doesn't look any better printed on a 600-dpi printer than it does on a 1200-dpi printer. Likewise, a 300-dpi image doesn't look as good printed on an old 72-dpi dot-matrix printer as it does on a 1200-dpi printer.

Viewing Raster Images Onscreen

When you view images onscreen, pixel dimensions come into play — especially if you're putting images on the Web — because the display of images is based on 1 image pixel per 1 screen pixel. The most important issue, then, is making sure that your image fits inside your (or your audience's) monitor when viewed at 100 percent.

When you view an image onscreen, the display size is determined by the pixel dimension, plus the size and setting of the monitor. You therefore need to determine what monitor resolution your audience is likely using and size your graphics accordingly. Table 1-2 illustrates how an 800-x-600-pixel image might display differently, depending on monitor resolution.

Table 1-2	Displaying an Image on Different Monitors	
Size of Monitor	*Resolution (in Pixels)*	*How Does an 800-x-600-Pixel Image Display?*
24-inch monitor	1920 x 1080	The image fills a small portion of the screen.
22-inch monitor	1680 x 1050	The image fills a small portion of the screen.
17-inch monitor	1024 x 768	The image fills part of the screen.
	800 x 600	The image fills the screen, with each pixel appearing larger.
15-inch monitor	800 x 600	The image fills the screen.
		Larger images can't be viewed in their entirety.

You may also hear people referring to monitor resolution in graphic display standards, such as XGA (1024 x 768 pixels), UXGA (1600 x 1200 pixels), WQXGA (2560 x 1600 pixels), and so on.

Resolution is measured in pixels per inch, or *ppi*. You may also run across the term *samples per inch (spi)*, often used when talking about scanners. Another term you see often is *dots per inch (dpi)*, always used in reference to printers, imagesetters, and other paper-outputting devices. You may hear people refer to dpi as *printer resolution*.

When displaying images onscreen, the recommended resolution setting is somewhere between 72 ppi and 96 ppi, even though resolution isn't really a factor in preparing screen images. That's just because monitors display somewhere in the 72- to 96-ppi range.

So, if you change the physical dimensions of an image, it's always at a one-to-one ratio with the monitor. If you view an image whose resolution is higher than that of the monitor, the image appears larger onscreen than in print. For example, try opening (or dragging and dropping) a 300-ppi JPEG file into a browser window. It explodes on your screen. Because the monitor can display only 72 to 96 ppi, it needs a ton of space to show all the pixels.

Using the Image Size Command

A time will come when you need to mess with the resolution or dimensions of an image. You may want to

- Change the file size.
- Make sure the resolution is appropriate for print.
- Adjust the dimensions so that they're just right for viewing onscreen.
- Change the width, height, and/or resolution of your image for printing or some other kind of output.

Photoshop — powerhouse that it is — allows you to size an image in all these ways with the Image Size command on the Image menu. Follow these steps to resize your image:

1. **Open the image and then choose Image⇨Image Size.**

   The Image Size dialog box opens, as shown in Figure 1-3. This is where the magic happens.

2. **Note the current state of your image and decide whether any of the following values need to change in order to get a nice-looking image for the desired output (print or the Web):**

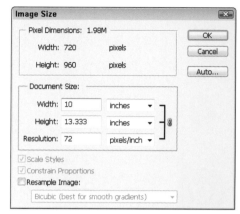

Figure 1-3: The Image Size dialog box is one of the most important in Photoshop.

- *The current pixel dimensions and the resulting file size:* My example shows 720 pixels in width and 960 pixels in height for a file size of 1.98MB (megabytes).

- *The current document size:* The size of your image when it prints on media, such as paper.

- *The resolution:* My example is 72 ppi, which is good for displaying onscreen or on the Web, but inadequate for printing. I'll see some *pixelation* (visible little squares) on my printout. Therefore, to print, I need to reduce the size of the image so that my total pixels are packed into a smaller area, to give the image cleaner lines.

3. **Make sure the Constrain Proportions check box is selected.**

The chain-and-bracket icon in the Document Size area indicates that the Constrain Proportions check box is selected. Nine times out of ten, you want your image to stay proportional. With the option selected, changing one value in the Document Size area makes the other values change automatically so that the proportions stay intact.

You can also select the Scale Styles check box, which allows you to scale or not scale any effects or styles that you've applied to your layer(s). This option is available only if you select Constrain Proportions. (For more on styles, see Book V, Chapter 4.)

4. **Make sure that the Resample Image check box is deselected.**

When you *resample,* you add or delete pixels in the image. Although you sometimes need to resample, doing so isn't good for your image. (I explain why in the following section.)

5. **Enter any new values in the dialog box.**

For example, because I want to print my image, I enter a new value of 300 pixels per inch for my resolution in the Document Size area. The other values automatically change.

6. Click OK.

You won't notice any difference in the way your image appears onscreen because you haven t added or deleted any pixels; you've merely compacted them into a smaller space.

Congratulations! You've just safely resized your image. You can proudly say, "No pixels were harmed in the making of this image."

Resampling Images

Resampling means you're changing the pixel dimensions of an image. When you *downsample* (or resample down), you're eliminating pixels and therefore deleting information and detail from your image. When you *upsample* (or resample up), you're adding pixels. Photoshop adds these pixels by using interpolation. *Interpolation* means Photoshop analyzes the colors of the original pixels and "manufactures" new ones, which are then added to the existing ones.

You can specify the interpolation method in the Image Size dialog box. The default that appears in the dialog box is based on the interpolation method you specified in your General Preferences dialog box. Here are your five choices:

- ✔ **Nearest Neighbor:** This method is fast and provides for the smallest file size, but it's less precise than the other options and therefore the lowest quality.

- ✔ **Bilinear:** Considered a medium-quality method, it works by averaging the color of the pixel above, below, and to the right and left of each pixel.

- ✔ **Bicubic:** This method is the slowest but most precise.

- ✔ **Bicubic Smoother:** A good method to use when you must upsample images, but it can slightly affect the sharpness of the image.

- ✔ **Bicubic Sharper:** This is a good method when downsampling an image.

If you really must resample, especially when upsampling, I recommend leaving the method set to Bicubic Smoother. Notice I said *if you really must.* Here are some reasons why you might choose to add or delete pixels

- ✔ You no longer have access to the original artwork, which you could otherwise rescan at the proper resolution and size.

- ✔ You no longer have access to the original high-resolution version of the file.

- ✔ You want to print a photo at a specific dimension, but the image's current resolution won't allow for decent-quality output.

- ✔ You absolutely can't replace the low-resolution image with another of higher resolution

Resampling isn't a recommended activity, especially when it pertains to upsampling. As smart as Photoshop is, having to manufacture pixels isn't an exact science. Your image tends to lose detail and sharpness and get blurry and mushy. Overall blurriness and goopy edges tend to be an unfortunate side effect of interpolation, as shown in Figure 1-4. The bottom line is that your resampled image never looks as good as the original. Downsampling isn't as scary. You're deleting pixels, and therefore detail, but the degradation is virtually undetectable to the eye.

Original   Resampled

Figure 1-4: Fuzzy, blurry images are a result of resampling.

Adding pixels to an image

To add pixels to an image, follow these steps:

1. **With your desired image open, first choose Image⇨Duplicate to make a copy of your original. With the duplicate active, choose Image⇨Image Size.**

   The Image Size dialog box appears.

   This is where the havoc happens. Be careful!

2. **Make sure that the Resample Image option is selected.**

   The Width and Height in the Pixel Dimensions area are now text boxes into which you can enter values. They're no longer fixed values as they are when Resample Image is deselected.

3. **Enter a higher value for the resolution and, if desired, enter a higher value for the width or height.**

In my example, I entered a resolution of 300 ppi.

The pixel dimensions increased dramatically, and so did the file size (from a mere 299.5K to 5.08MB), as shown in Figure 1-5.

If you get all discombobulated when working in the dialog box, press Alt (Option on the Mac). The Cancel button changes to a Reset button. Click it, and you're back to where you started. This is a good shortcut to remember because it holds true for many of Photoshop's dialog boxes.

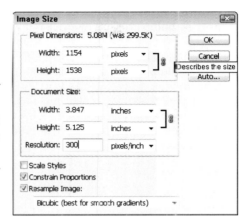

Figure 1-5: Increasing the pixel dimensions in an image causes your image to degrade in quality.

4. **Leave your Interpolation method set to Bicubic (Best for Smooth Gradients), which is a good option when upsampling.**

5. **Click OK.**

Photoshop now goes through its interpolation ritual and churns out a newly resampled image. Do a side-by-side comparison to the original, looking at both at 100% view. Your original should look a whole lot better than the resampled image. And, for a real shocker, try printing out the two images and seeing what kind of degradation takes place.

Taking pixels out of an image

When you *downsample,* you eliminate pixels and therefore delete information and detail from your image. Although I've emphasized the pitfalls of resampling up, you can sometimes damage your image by downsampling, as well.

Granted, downsampling is sometimes necessary when you're converting high-resolution print graphics into Web graphics. For example, you may be forced to take images used for a corporate brochure and repurpose them into content for the company's Web site. You probably won't notice much degradation in image quality because the images are just being viewed onscreen. In addition, downsampling can occasionally camouflage the moiré patterns caused by scanning halftones. (For more on halftones, check out Book VII, Chapter 1.) Keep in mind, however, that 72 ppi isn't sufficient for printing an image, as shown in Figure 1-6.

You should never need to make an image smaller than 72 ppi.

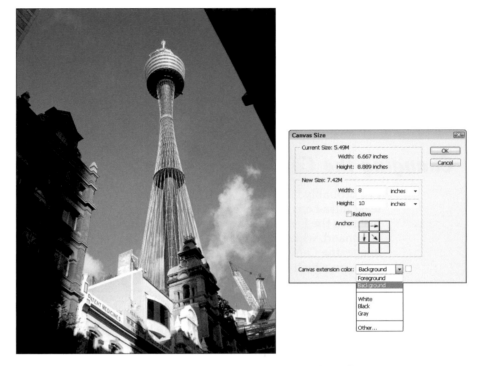

Figure 1-7: Increasing your canvas size adds to the area around your image.

4. **Select your canvas color from the Canvas Extension Color pop-up menu and click OK.**

   Choose from Foreground, Background, White, Black, Gray, or Other. If you select Other, Photoshop transports you to the Color Picker, where you can select any color you desire. The small swatch to the right of the pop-up menu displays the current background color. You can also click this swatch to access the Color Picker (which I explain how to use in Book II, Chapter 3).

Cropping an Image

Even a novice photographer knows that cropping an image can make a composition stronger. *Cropping* entails cutting away background clutter or endless expanses of empty space in order to focus in on your desired subject.

This simple process can transform a ho-hum photograph into a visually exciting one. Take a look at my example in Figure 1-8. I mean, it doesn't take Ansel Adams to figure out which image is stronger. (It would be even better if the fence weren't in the background, but hey, that's nothing that a little Photoshop retouching can't take care of. Check out Book VIII; it's all about retouching and restoration techniques.)

Figure 1-8: Cropping is one of the easiest ways to improve the composition of your image.

Sure-fire cropping tips

Even though cropping is about as simple an image-editing maneuver as you can get, you need to know about a few other options:

✔ **Perspective:** If you need a nonrectangular cropping marquee, select this check box on the Options bar. (Your crop marquee must be active.) This feature allows the corner handles to move independently. Note that when you apply the actual crop, the photo is transformed into a rectangular shape, thereby distorting the image based on your applied perspective.

✔ **Front Image:** Also in the Options bar, this setting enables you to crop one image so that it's the exact same size as another image. Open two images and crop the first one. Click Front Image. Photoshop enters the width, height, and resolution values from the first image on the Options bar. Drag the Crop tool on your second image and adjust the marquee, as desired. Double-click inside the marquee. Photoshop automatically crops your second image to match your first.

✔ **Delete and Hide:** If your image doesn't contain any layers — that is, it consists only of a background — any cropped areas are permanently deleted from your file. However, if your image consists of one or more layers (see Book V for the lowdown on layers), you have the choice of deleting or hiding your cropped area. Delete eliminates the cropped area, whereas Hide just hides the cropped area. You can see the hidden areas if you move the layer by using the Move tool. Another way to see the hidden area is to choose Image⇨Reveal All. Photoshop expands the canvas to show all areas in all layers, except for the Background layer.

✔ **Width, Height, and Resolution:** If you want to crop an image to an exact measurement, enter a value in these text boxes on the Options bar. These options are available only when the Crop tool is active and you haven't yet dragged a cropping marquee. But be careful about the value you use for the Resolution setting. Remember, resampling isn't a good thing. To remove the entered settings, click the Clear button on the Options bar.

Using the Crop tool

The most popular way to crop an image is by using the Crop tool. This simple tool is as easy and effective to use as a T-square and an X-ACTO knife, just without the possibility of bodily injury. Select the Crop tool in the Tools panel or press C on the keyboard. Then, follow these steps:

1. **With the Crop tool, drag around the part of the image you want to keep and then release your mouse button.**

   While you drag, a *marquee* (a dotted outline) appears and displays the cropping boundaries. Don't worry if your cropping marquee isn't exactly correct. You can adjust it in Step 2.

   The area outside the cropping marquee appears darker than the area inside in order to better frame your image. Adobe calls this a *shield.* You control the color and *opacity* (the amount of transparency) of the shield by adjusting the settings on the Options bar. If, for some strange reason, you don't want the shield, deselect the Shield check box.

Version CS5 gives you an added aid in framing your image. Choose None, Grid, or Rule of Thirds from the new Crop Guide Overlay setting in the Options bar. The Rule of Thirds is a photographic principle that advocates placing elements most appealing to the eye at one of the four intersecting points of the rule of thirds grid.

Figure 1-9 shows a great example of way too much useless background. I dragged around the only thing I want to retain — the pirate girl.

2. **Adjust the cropping marquee by dragging the handles.**

   The small squares on the sides and corners of the cropping marquee are called *handles.* When you hover your mouse over any handle or the marquee itself, your cursor changes to a double-headed arrow, indicating that you can drag.

Handle Cropping marquee Shield

Rule of Thirds grid

Figure 1-9: The area around your cropping marquee appears darker so that you can better frame your image.

To move the entire marquee, position your mouse inside the marquee until you see a black arrowhead cursor and then drag. Adjust the marquee until you're satisfied.

You can also drag the *origin point* (the circle icon in the center) to change the axis of rotation.

If you move your mouse outside the marquee, the cursor changes to a curved, double-headed arrow. Dragging with this cursor rotates the marquee. This feature can be extremely useful when you need to rotate and crop a crooked image. By using the Crop tool, you can perform both commands in one step and often more quickly and accurately. Just be aware that rotation, unless it's in 90-degree increments, resamples your image — which, if done repeatedly, can damage your image. (See the earlier section, "Resampling Images," for more on resampling.) Getting the rotation right the first time around is for the best.

3. **Double-click inside the cropping marquee.**

    You can also just press Enter (Return on the Mac) or click the Commit (check mark icon) button on the Options bar. Photoshop discards the area outside the marquee, as shown in Figure 1-10. If you want to cancel the crop, just press Esc or click Cancel (the slashed circle icon) on the Options bar.

Figure 1-10: Eliminating background clutter allows you to hone in on your subject.

Cropping with the Marquee tool

If you get bored with using the Crop tool, you can also crop a selected area by choosing Image➪Crop. Simply make a selection with any of the tools and then choose this command. Although using the Rectangular Marquee tool for your selection makes the most sense, you don't have to.

You can use Image➪Crop with any selection — circular, polygonal, kidney bean, even feathered. Photoshop can't crop to those odd shapes, but it gets as close to the outline as it can. (For all you need to know on selections, see Book III Chapter 1.)

Using the Trim command

The fabulous Trim command trims away transparent or solid-colored areas around your image. Choose Image➪Trim, and a dialog box appears. Select Transparent Pixels (for layered images), Top Left Pixel Color, or Bottom Right Pixel Color as a basis for the trim. Then, choose to trim away the Top, Bottom, Left, or Right side(s) from the image, and click OK.

This command works great for quickly eliminating black-and-white borders around images.

Using the Crop and Straighten Photo command

Choose File➪Automate➪Crop and Straighten Photos. Photoshop then looks for rectangular areas in your document, extracts each one into its own document, and straightens those individual images, as shown in Figure 1-11.

The Crop and Straighten Photos command is fabulous if you want to save time by scanning multiple images initially into one document. (And the command works on single images, as well.) This command is a real manual-labor timesaver, and I wholeheartedly endorse it.

You can now also straighten images using the Ruler tool. Here's how:

1. **Select the Ruler tool from the Tools panel.**

   It shares a flyout menu with the Eyedropper tool. You can also press I or Shift I to cycle through the tools.

2. **Click at the starting point of the axis you wish to straighten. Drag the tool at the ending point of that axis. Release the mouse.**

3. **Click the Straighten button in the Options bar.**

Figure 1-11: The Crop and Straighten command extracts and straightens your images into separate files.

Chapter 2: Choosing Color Modes and File Formats

In This Chapter

✓ **Choosing the right color mode**

✓ **Switching a file's color mode**

✓ **Focusing on file formats**

In addition to choosing a size and resolution (discussed in Book II, Chapter 1), you need to decide on a color mode and file format for your image. Usually, you base this decision on the final use for the image. Are you importing it into a page-layout program for offset printing? Posting it on a Web page? Using it for a newspaper article?

When you know an image's final destination, you can make intelligent choices about which color mode and file format are best. This chapter gives you some background information to help you make those choices so that you don't end up having to do extra work, spend extra time, or waste extra money.

Selecting a Color Mode

Every file has a *color mode*, also called an *image mode* or just plain *mode*. To determine the color mode of an image, look in the title bar of the image window or choose Image⇨Mode. Color modes define the color values used to display the image. Photoshop offers eight modes and enables you to convert images from one mode to another. The color mode you choose for a particular image depends on a couple of factors:

✓ **The file format you plan to save it in:** Some modes call for specific file formats. You may find that a certain format is unavailable because your file isn't in the appropriate color mode.

✓ **The end use for the image:** Do you plan to post the image on the Web? Or are you putting it in a brochure that will be offset printed? For more on prepping images for print, see Book IX, Chapter 1. For details on getting images ready for the Web, see Bonus Chapter 1.

Basic RGB and CMYK color theory

When you view an RGB image, you're looking at an image made of three colors — red, green, and blue. These colors are

⤙ The primary colors of light (additive color)

⤙ The colors that correspond to the three types of cones inside your eyes

⤙ The colors that comprise white light from the sun

⤙ The colors your monitor uses when displaying images

The CMYK color scheme (subtractive color) is based on the light-absorbing quality of ink on paper. In theory, a white light hits these inks. Some visible wavelengths are absorbed, or subtracted, and others are reflected back to your eyes. CMYK images comprise various percentages of only four colors of ink — cyan, magenta, yellow, and black. These colors correspond to the inks used in the offset printing process.

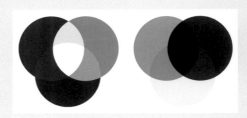

The following sections provide a brief description and example of each mode and any file-format or usage connections.

Color modes affect the number of colors that display, as well as the size of the file and the number of channels. One or more channels — in which the color data is stored — represents each mode. Grayscale images have one color channel — Black. CMYK images have four color channels — Cyan, Magenta, Yellow, and Black. (For the lowdown on channels, see Book VI, Chapter 1.)

RGB Color

Uses: RGB is the gold standard for most scanners, all monitors, all digital cameras, and some desktop inkjet printers. And it's the primary color mode (with Indexed Color being secondary) to use with any images to be viewed onscreen (whether on the Web or in any kind of multimedia presentation).

File formats: Just about every file format, except GIF, can handle an image in RGB mode.

RGB is a very good overall work mode. Images in RGB mode have full access to all Photoshop commands, including filters and image adjustments. RGB images contain values of 0 to 255 for each of three colors — red, green, and blue. With

8 bits of color information for each of the three colors, these 24-bit images can reproduce up to 16.7 million colors onscreen. 48-bit images (16 bits per color) can display even more. Most scanners also scan images in RGB, all monitors display in RGB, and most desktop inkjet printers prefer to print RGB (rather than CMYK) images. But always do a test print with both modes to be sure.

The RGB mode in Photoshop varies according to the RGB Working Space setting you select in the Color Settings dialog box. For details on color settings, see Book II, Chapter 3.

RGB also supports High Dynamic Range, or HDR, (32-bit per color) images.

CMYK Color

Uses: CMYK is the standard for images that are color-separated for offset printing. Some other composite printing devices also require images to be in CMYK mode.

File formats: CMYK can handle just about every major format except GIF.

CMYK images, such as the one shown in Figure 2-1, contain a percentage of one or more four-process color inks — cyan, magenta, yellow, and black. Darker colors have higher percentages, whereas lighter colors have lower percentages. Pure white is created when all four colors have a value of 0 percent. Like RGB mode, the CMYK mode in Photoshop can vary according to the CMYK Working Space setting you select in the Color Settings dialog box.

Corbis Digital Stock

Figure 2-1: CMYK is the mode needed for offset-printed images.

Make sure that you do your image editing in RGB mode, where you have access to the full range of filters and adjustments. When you complete your editing, convert the image from RGB to CMYK. (For details see the section "Converting from RGB to CMYK," later in this chapter.)

Grayscale

Uses: Grayscale mode, shown in Figure 2-2, is for black-and-white (and all shades of gray in between) images.

File formats: All the most commonly used file formats accept Grayscale mode.

Corbis Digital Stock

Figure 2-2: Images in grayscale mode contain 256 levels of gray.

Grayscale images contain up to 256 levels of gray. Each pixel has a brightness value ranging from 0 (black) to 255 (white). You can scan an image in Grayscale mode, or you can convert color images to grayscale. If you convert a color image to grayscale, Photoshop discards all the color information, and the remaining gray levels represent the luminosity of the pixels. (Check out the "Converting to grayscale" section, later in this chapter.) You can also convert a grayscale image to a color image; although this process doesn't actually convert your grayscale image to color, it enables you to apply color on top of the grayscale image.

High Dynamic Range (HDR) images can also support Grayscale mode. For more on HDR images, see Book IX, Chapter 2.

Monotone, Duotone, Tritone, and Quadtone

Uses: Because printing presses can print only about 50 gray levels per ink color, duotones and multitones — which use two to four inks — are used to increase the range of tones of grayscale images. Duotones and multitones are often created by using black and spot colors (premixed inks), although you can also use process colors. (For more on spot colors, see Book IX, Chapter 1.)

File formats: The only file formats that can save duotones, tritones, and quadtones are native Photoshop, Photoshop 2.0, EPS, PDF, Large Document Format, or Photoshop Raw.

These modes create one-color, (monotone), two-color (duotone), three-color (tritone; shown in Figure 2-3), and four-color (quadtone) images. Photoshop lumps all the various tone modes under duotone. You can find a pop-up menu in the Duotone options dialog box, from which you can select the various options. Unlike RGB and CMYK images, in which the components of the image display with different colors, the monotones, duotones, tritones, and quadtones have the colors mixed throughout the image. The colored inks are often used to reproduce tinted grays, not the different colors you find in RGB and CMYK images.

To access the Duotone mode, you must first convert the color image to grayscale (see how later in this chapter). Then, choose Image➪ Mode➪Duotone. In the dialog box that appears, select Monotone, Duotone, Tritone, or Quadtone from the pop-up menu. Then, select ink colors — either spot or process — by clicking the appropriate swatches. Finally, you can adjust the

Corbis Digital Stock

Figure 2-3: Tritone images mix three inks throughout the image.

Curves settings by dragging the graph line. This tells Photoshop how to distribute the ink(s) among the various tones. You don't have access to the individual color channels in Duotone mode. The only manipulation you can do in that mode is to specify the Curves settings.

If you're new to these modes, you need to know that Photoshop offers numerous preset duotones, tritones, and quadtones. To access these presets, select one from the Preset pop-up menu. Sometimes, printing these types of images can be challenging, so starting with these presets is a good idea if you're inexperienced.

Indexed Color

Uses: Indexed Color mode is primarily for Web graphics and multimedia displays.

File formats: Indexed Color mode supports a variety of formats, with GIF being the most popular. Other formats supported include Photoshop, Photoshop 2.0, Photoshop Raw, BMP, EPS, IFF Format, ElectricImage, Large Document Format, PCX, PDF, PICT, PICT Resource, PNG, Targa, and TIFF.

Indexed Color mode, shown in Figure 2-4, uses 256 colors or less; what graphics aficionados call 8-bit color. When you convert an image to indexed color, Photoshop builds a Color Lookup Table (CLUT), which stores and indexes the color. (The Color Table option appears in the Mode menu.) If a color in the original image isn't in the table, Photoshop chooses the closest match or makes a new one from the available colors. Using fewer colors reduces the file size, which is why the GIF file format — a very popular Web-graphics format — uses this mode. (See the "GIF" section, later in this chapter.)

Corbis Digital Stock

Figure 2-4: Indexed Color mode uses 256 colors or less.

The Indexed Color mode doesn't support layers, and editing capabilities are limited. For more on indexed color, see Bonus Chapter 1 on this book's Web site. (The Introduction has details about the companion Web site.)

Lab Color

Uses: Lab Color mode provides a consistent color display, which is ideal for high-end image retouching.

File formats: You can save an image in Lab Color mode in native Photoshop, Photoshop Raw, EPS, TIFF, PDF, JPEG 2000, Large Document Format, or Photoshop DCS 1.0 and 2.0 formats. You can save images containing 48 bits (16 bits per channel) in Photoshop, Photoshop Raw, PDF, Large Document Format, and TIFF formats.

Lab Color mode is usually thought of as the internal color mode that Photoshop uses when converting from one color mode to another — for example, when going from RGB to CMYK. It's also the mode preferred by color-retouching experts because it's considered to be *device-independent* (it appears consistent on various devices).

Lab Color mode consists of a lightness channel and two additional channels (*a* and *b*), shown in Figure 2-5, which contain the range of colors from green to red *(a)* and blue to yellow *(b)*.

HDR images containing 32 bits per color can be saved in Photoshop, FXG, Large Document Format, OpenEXR, Radiance, Portable Bit Map, and TIFF file formats. OpenEXR and Radiance are two types of HDR file formats. OpenEXR images are used in film visual effects. Radiance images are often used in 3-D modeling programs. See more on HDR images in Book IX, Chapter 2.

Bitmap

Uses: This mode is best for scanned *line art* (that is, art composed entirely of lines, such as a line drawing of a camera you might see in a manual) and signatures (your John Hancock).

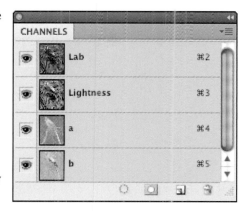

Figure 2-5: Lab Color mode is the preferred editing mode for color experts because it's device-independent.

When scanning line art, be sure to crank up your scanning resolution to 1200 ppi or so to ensure a good-quality bitmap image.

File formats: Photoshop, Photoshop 2.0, EPS, TIFF, PDF, BMP, PNG, GIF, Large Document Format, PCX, PICT, PICT Resource, Portable Bit Map, and Wireless Bitmap.

Bitmap images contain pixels that are either black or white, exclusively. You must convert color images to grayscale before you can access Bitmap mode. When you choose Image➪Mode➪Bitmap, a dialog box appears, offering options for resolution and method. The various methods give several appearances, one of which is shown in Figure 2-6, so try each one to see which you prefer. When you select Custom Pattern, you can then select a pattern from the drop-down menu.

If you save a file in Bitmap mode as an EPS (see the section "EPS," later in this chapter), you can convert the white areas in the image to transparent areas. Transparency enables you to overlay the file on a background containing color or an image, and only the dark pixels show.

Corbis Digital Stock

Figure 2-6: Bitmap mode enables you to choose a method, such as Pattern Dither.

Multichannel

Uses: Multichannel mode is for special printing needs or as an intermediate mode when converting between color modes.

File formats: The only file formats available for multichannel images are native Photoshop, Photoshop 2.0, Photoshop DCS 2.0, Large Document Format, or Photoshop Raw formats.

The Multichannel mode, shown in Figure 2-7, comprises multiple grayscale channels, each containing 256 levels of gray. Whenever you delete or mix channels, you end up with a multichannel image. You can also convert any image with more than one channel to this mode. In a multichannel image, each channel becomes a spot channel, with 256 levels of gray.

Corbis Digital Stock

Figure 2-7: Deleting or mixing channels creates a multichannel image.

For more on channels, see Book VI, Chapter 1.

You'll also find various bit depths under the Mode menu. For info on bit depth, see the Book VI, Chapter 1 sidebar, "A little bit about bit depth."

Converting to a Different Color Mode

Sometimes, your image starts out in one color mode and then you find you need to convert the image to another mode. Maybe you have to strip the color out of an image you're submitting to the local newspaper. Or maybe you have to convert your RGB image to CMYK to get it ready for an offset print job.

When you convert modes, you're permanently changing the color values in your image, so save a backup image, just in case.

The following sections offer pointers for the most common conversions you'll make. If you want to convert an image into an indexed color for the Web, your best bet is to use the Save for Web option, which I cover in Bonus Chapter 1 on this book's companion Web site (you can find out about the Web site in the Introduction).

Converting from RGB to CMYK

As I mention several times in this book, CMYK is the image mode necessary for high-end composite printing and offset printing. You first want to perform all your necessary image-editing tasks in RGB mode for the following reasons:

- ✔ The image size is smaller because RGB mode has only three channels.
- ✔ The RGB color space provides more device independence because it isn't reliant on inks.
- ✔ You have full accessibility to filters and image adjustments.
- ✔ RGB mode provides a large color gamut, so Photoshop preserves more colors after it makes image adjustments.

When you finish editing the image in RGB mode, you can convert the image from RGB to CMYK (you can perform any fine-tuning in CMYK mode, if necessary). If you're new to this procedure, you may be surprised at what can result. You may see a *color shift* (from slight to major) because the *color gamut* (range of colors) of the RGB model (16.7 million) is much larger than that of CMYK (approximately 55,000).

The extent of the shift depends on the colors in the RGB image and how many of them are out of gamut. Photoshop replaces RGB colors that are out of gamut with the closest match available within the CMYK gamut, often replacing the electric blues, fiery reds, and sunny yellows with duller, muddier CMYK equivalents. Unfortunately, you can't do anything to prevent this replacement. It's just the way of the world of color. However, if you can select colors (instead of acquiring them from a scan), be sure that you don't select any colors that are out of gamut to begin with. You can also *soft proof* colors (preview the effects of your CMYK conversion without actually converting) by choosing View➪Proof Setup➪Working CMYK. Check out Book II, Chapter 3 for details about selecting colors and soft proofing.

Converting to grayscale

You can convert a color image to grayscale in a multitude of ways, as shown in Figure 2-8. The following sections cover a few that you may want to try.

Quick-and-dirty method

Choose Image➪Mode➪Grayscale. Photoshop then asks you whether you want to discard color information. Click Discard. If your image contains multiple layers, Photoshop first asks whether you want to merge your layers. If you want to keep your layers, click the Don't Merge button.

Although this method does the job in stripping color from your image, you may be left with an image that's flat and lacking contrast. You can apply a Levels adjustment (choose Image➪Adjustments➪Levels) to boost the contrast, or you can try one of the other conversion methods.

3. **Delete the Alpha 2 channel.**

   That leaves you with the lightness channel, which is now named Alpha 1.

4. **Choose Image➪Mode➪Grayscale.**

   Your color image is now a grayscale one.

Best channel method

If you look at the individual channels in the image, one often stands out as being a very good grayscale image by itself. (If channels are a mystery to you, check out Book VI, Chapter 1 for details.) You may find that the Red channel provides a good grayscale image when the subject is people because humans have a lot of red in their skin. Or you may find that the Green channel looks good in a scenic shot. The Blue channel rarely yields a nice image, though. Most of the crud picked up in a digital image finds its way into the Blue channel.

In the Channels panel, select each channel and view its contents. Find the channel that looks the best, select it, and then choose Image➪Mode➪Grayscale. If you have layers, Photoshop asks whether you want to flatten your layers. Click OK. Photoshop then asks whether you want to discard all the other channels. Click OK.

You can also use the Channel Mixer to create custom grayscale images. For more on the Channel Mixer, see Book VI, Chapter 1.

Finally, you have yet one more way to convert to grayscale, via the Black & White feature in the Image➪Adjustments submenu. For details, see Book VIII, Chapter 1.

Using the Conditional Mode Change command

Photoshop enables you to specify instances in which one mode changes into another so that you can utilize the conversion command in an action. Briefly, an *action* is a collection of recorded and saved commands that you can replay repeatedly. (For details on actions, see Book II, Chapter 5.) Sometimes, when you incorporate a mode conversion as part of an action, you get an error message because the file you're opening may not have the same mode you specified as the source mode in the action. For example, you may have specified CMYK as your source mode in the action, but the action opens a file in Grayscale mode. You get an error message because the Grayscale mode of the file doesn't match the CMYK source mode. The Conditional Mode Change command takes care of this problem. Follow these steps to add this command to your action:

1. **Start creating and recording your action.**

2. **Choose File➪Automate➪Conditional Mode Change.**

   The Conditional Mode Change dialog box, shown in Figure 2-9, appears.

**Book II
Chapter 2**

**Choosing Color
Modes and File
Formats**

Image⇨Mode⇨Grayscale   Lab mode   Best channel

Corbis Digital Stock

Figure 2-8: Photoshop gives you many ways to convert a color image to grayscale.

Be aware that you can no longer apply color to your image after you convert it. If you choose a color in the Color panel, the color appears gray in the foreground and background color icons. If you *want* to apply color to your grayscale image, convert it back to RGB or CMYK mode.

Lab Color mode method

This method most likely provides a better grayscale image than the quick-and-dirty method I describe in the preceding section. Make sure that you finish all your edits that require layers before you follow these steps:

1. **Choose Image⇨Mode⇨Lab Color.**

   As I mention in the earlier "Lab Color" section, converting to Lab Color mode converts the channels into a lightness channel and *a* and *b* channels containing ranges of color. If you have layers, you're prompted for whether you want to merge your layers. You can choose either option because, in Step 2, you have to flatten the image if you want to proceed with the operation. For details on working with layers, see Book V.

2. **Choose Window⇨Channels. Delete the *a* channel by dragging it to the trash can icon at the bottom of the panel.**

   Again, if you have layers, click OK to flatten your layers. If you select Cancel, you abort the operation.

   If you delete the *a* channel, the *b* channel then changes its name to Alpha 2.

Although praising the qualities of JPEG 2000 is fine, be warned that you currently need a plug-in to view these files on the Web, and support is still spotty. In the future, this format may become a standard for the Web and for digital cameras.

GIF

GIF is another file format used for Web graphics. GIFs support transparency — but on the down side, you must save GIFs in the Indexed Color mode, which offers only 256 colors (or even fewer). Although this format is great for making tiny files, it's not so great for continuous-tone images in which the number of colors displayed is critical. Therefore, the GIF format is usually reserved for illustrations (spot illustrations, buttons, logos, and so on) and type with large areas of flat colors and sharp details. For the whole story on GIFs, head to this book's companion Web site (discussed in the Introduction) and check out Bonus Chapter 1.

PNG is the last major file format used for Web images. PNGs support transparency and 24-bit color. For more info, see Bonus Chapter 1 (located at this book's companion Web site).

EPS

EPS is short for *Encapsulated PostScript.* PostScript is a page-description language developed by Adobe and used by many printers. The EPS format can contain both vector and raster graphics. (For details on vector and raster graphics, see Book II, Chapter 1.) The EPS format tends to create larger file sizes and doesn't have a built-in compression scheme as do JPEGs or TIFFs. EPS is a recommended file format for creating color separations for high-end, four-color print jobs. This is also the file format to use for images with clipping paths (explained in Book III) and one of the few formats that supports Duotone mode. In addition to duotones, EPS supports Lab Color, CMYK, RGB, Indexed Color, Grayscale, and Bitmap modes. Additionally, you use this format when creating a DCS (Desktop Color Separations) file. It doesn't support alpha channels. Finally, EPS is the format of choice for importing to and from drawing programs, such as Illustrator and CorelDRAW.

Here are the options when saving in the EPS format, as shown in Figure 2-12:

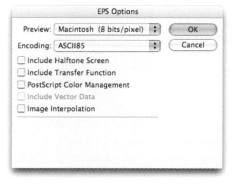

Figure 2-12: When saving an EPS, specify your options.

✓ **Preview:** If you import your EPS into another application, this option provides a low-resolution image for you to view. I recommend choosing 8-bit TIFF, which works on both PC and Mac.

✓ **Encoding:** This option specifies the way an image is sent to the PostScript printer. Choose Binary if you can; it produces smaller files and keeps all original data. If you're having printing problems, choose ASCII. JPEG compresses the file, but discards data and may cause color-separation problems. Avoid it, if possible.

✓ **Include Halftone Screen** and **Include Transfer Function:** Use these options for offset print jobs. Let your friendly service bureau or commercial printing expert specify these options.

✓ **Transparent Whites:** If your image is in Bitmap color mode, this option enables white areas to appear transparent.

✓ **PostScript Color Management:** This option converts the file's color data to the printer's color space. I don't recommend selecting this option if you're importing your image into a document that's color managed. (For more on color management, see Book II, Chapter 3.)

✓ **Include Vector Data:** When selected, this option preserves any vector graphics, such as type and shapes. However, that data is preserved only when you import the file into another program. If you reopen the EPS in Photoshop, your vector data is rasterized.

✓ **Image Interpolation:** This option *anti-aliases* low-resolution images — softens their edges when they're printed.

PDF: The universal donor

PDF is the acronym for *Portable Document Format,* which is the native format of Adobe Acrobat. This format, developed by Adobe, can contain editable text, vector, and raster data. PDF files are often used for electronic documentation that will be downloaded from the Web.

PDFs are extremely useful in the imaging world. Anyone with a computer running Windows, Mac OS, or Unix can read a PDF. All you need to view a PDF file is Adobe Acrobat Reader, which is available as a free download from the Adobe Web site. If you save your image as a PDF and e-mail it to (or post it on the Web as a downloadable file for) a colleague, manager, client, or friend, that person can see your image — colors, fonts, and all — exactly the way you see it. The other nice thing about PDFs is that they have an automatic compression process that makes the files small and manageable for mail transfer or loading on the Web.

When you save a file as a Photoshop PDF, you have all the same save options of the native Photoshop format. PDF supports layers, alpha channels, spot colors, and annotations, so select these options if you have any. It also supports the same image modes as the native Photoshop format. Additionally, you can also save 16-bit images as PDFs. After choosing your initial options, you get an alert dialog box that informs you that the settings you just chose may be overridden by the settings you choose next.

The Save Adobe PDF dialog box offers a multitude of options. At the top of the dialog box are settings for presets, standards, and compatibility, as shown in Figure 2-13:

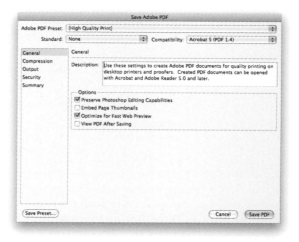

Figure 2-13: The Save Adobe PDF dialog box offers a smorgasbord of options.

> ✔ **Adobe PDF Preset:** Select a preset setting from the pop-up menu. Photoshop then kindly gives you a description of that setting, including what versions of Acrobat can open that PDF. The default setting of High Quality Print creates PDF files suitable for good-quality printing on desktop printers. Stick with the default as an overall setting — unless you want to create a PDF specifically to view onscreen or e-mail for approval purposes, in which case, select Smallest File Size.

PDF/X is an ISO (International Organization for Standardization) standard for graphic content exchange designed for the prepress purpose workflow. Ask your service provider or offset print house if it prefers one of the PDF/X formats, rather than the generic PDF, for final file output. For specifics on the criteria of each PDF/X format, check the Acrobat Help file.

> ✔ **Standard:** Accept the default associated with your chosen preset or choose a flavor of PDF/X from the pop-up menu.

> ✔ **Compatibility:** Specify the version of Acrobat you want your file to be compatible with. Note, however, that Acrobat 4 and 5 don't support layers. When you change either the Standard or Compatibility options, (Modified) is added to your preset name.

In addition to the options along the top, described in the preceding list, this massive, multi-tiered dialog box offers the following categories in which you can refine your choices, if you want:

✔ **General:** The General category of settings contains the PDF presets, editing options, Acrobat version compatibility choices, and viewing options.

✔ **Compression:** The PDF format, by nature, includes excellent compression, but you can compress and downsample your image even further to reduce (or maybe to simply adjust) the size of the PDF file. You can find details about downsampling in Book II, Chapter 1.

If optimum print quality is a concern, you're better off not downsampling your image at all.

✔ **Output:** The Output area covers how to handle the color data in your file when you export to PDF. I recommend keeping the default settings of your presets, unless you're sure of what you're doing. An understanding of color management, explained in Book II, Chapter 3, helps you interpret the options in this area.

✔ **Security:** If you want to apply some restrictions on who can open your PDF, including what they can then do with it, you've come to the right spot. You can assign a password for opening the file in either Acrobat or Photoshop (or Preview on a Mac), but if you forget the password, there's no way to extract it from your file. Make sure you write it down somewhere! You can also choose whether you want your user to be able to print or change the document.

✔ **Summary:** This option gives you a rundown of all your specified options and alerts you to anything it finds not so kosher.

Acrobat 4 users can't open PDFs that have 128-bit RC4 encryption.

You can also combine multiple images into a single, multi-paged PDF document or slide show. This is a great way to e-mail images to coworkers, family, and friends. The best way to accomplish this is to do it within Adobe Bridge, where you have a multitude of options to customize your PDF. Click the PDF button on the Output tab in the top-right corner in Bridge and specify your options.

Photoshop

Of course, I can't forget the native Photoshop format (.psd). This format offers several benefits. First, along with TIFF and PDF, Photoshop enables you to save layers in your image. The other formats flatten the layers into a single background. This format works well if you're going to spend a considerable length of time working on your image. The Photoshop format also supports all image modes, is the fastest format for opening and saving, and offers all the various save options.

Like TIFF, the Photoshop format uses a lossless compression process, although it's invisible to you. If you need to open a file in an older version of Photoshop, be sure to save it as a native Photoshop file. Finally, almost all drawing and layout programs now support the importing of Photoshop files.

QuickTime users should be aware that it provides a PSD translator that allows you to open PSD files in any application, such as Microsoft Word, that has the QuickTime translators enabled.

Photoshop Raw

This format is designed to transfer images among applications and platforms. The Photoshop Raw format can be useful if you want to transfer an image to or from a mainframe computer or other device that doesn't support the standard graphic formats. Don't confuse it with the Camera Raw format I describe in the following section. The Photoshop Raw format supports CMYK, RGB, Lab Color, Grayscale, and Multichannel images. The format allows for any pixel or file size, but it doesn't support layers.

You may never have to save a file in the Photoshop Raw format. If you do, you can likely accept the defaults for File Type, Creator, and Header. Save Channels In and Byte Order are similar to Pixel Order and Byte Order, discussed earlier in this chapter.

Camera Raw

The Camera Raw file format is the format used by many digital cameras to capture and save image data and the image's metadata, as shown in Figure 2-14. This format captures everything about an image and is the closest possible thing to a digital negative. Each camera has its own proprietary raw image format. Fortunately, Photoshop can support most camera models, especially higher-end cameras. If, by chance, your new camera isn't supported, check www.adobe.com periodically for updates.

Camera Raw files utilize a lossless scheme to capture and save image data, similar to TIFFs (explained in the "TIFF" section, earlier in this chapter). This approach is advantageous because no data is lost through compression as it is with the JPEG format. Camera Raw files also have the advantage of being smaller than uncompressed TIFFs. Of all the digital camera file formats, only Camera Raw images contain the actual, unadulterated data captured by the digital camera's sensor without any camera adjustments, filters, and other processing. Many die-hard photographers consider this file format to be the pure digital "negative," so to speak. They prefer to analyze, manipulate, and adjust the image data themselves, instead of leaving those decisions to the mercy of the camera. This file format also prevents the loss of any image data that can sometimes occur when a file is converted from its native format to a more commonly used format, such as TIFF or PSD. But Camera Raw can save your files as DNG (Digital Negative), TIFF, PSD, or JPEG formats, if you desire.

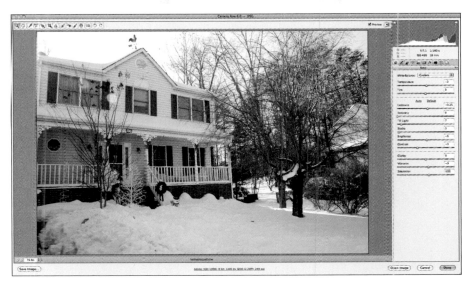

Figure 2-14: The Camera Raw format is as close to a digital negative as you can get.

Version CS5 introduces Camera Raw 6.0 and incorporates newer processing (version 2.0) that employs better sharpening and noise reduction. Here's just a brief sampling of some of the capabilities of Camera Raw:

✔ Select multiple Camera Raw files, as well as JPEGs and TIFFs, in Adobe Bridge and then edit the settings in one fell swoop.

✔ Make adjustments in white balance, exposure, shadows, contrast, saturation, sharpness, and so on. Your settings are applied to all selected files.

✔ Save your files in Adobe Bridge or import them into Photoshop for further enhancements.

✔ Rate your files inside Camera Raw.

✔ Crop, rotate, straighten, and sharpen your images.

✔ Correct lens distortion, reduce noise, color fringe, spots, red-eye, and other flaws.

✔ The Fill Light feature is similar to the Shadow function in Photoshop's Shadow/Highlight feature. Move the slider (0 to 100) to lighten dark areas while leaving light areas undisturbed.

✔ Camera Raw files are processed in their own thread, which means you can do double duty — editing some files while saving others simultaneously.

✔ Camera Raw also offers what's referred to as *localized corrections* — using an Adjustment Brush, you can "paint" areas by using varying brush sizes to correct very specific portions of your image. Similarly, you can use the Graduated Filter to apply more or less adjustment to your image in a gradual, gradient-like manner. This is Camera Raw's digital answer to using a Neutral Density analog filter when capturing a shot. The Graduated Filter can come in handy, especially when adjusting landscape shots.

Adobe has added additional camera support in version CS5 — but if, by chance, the Camera Raw feature still doesn't support your particular camera model, contact Adobe to see whether it will be supporting your model in the near future. If your camera doesn't capture images in the Camera Raw format at all, don't worry. You're fine with TIFF or JPEG, especially because you can edit these two formats in the Camera Raw dialog box. However, if your camera is capable of saving images in Camera Raw format, check out its capabilities. Visit www.adobe.com/products/photoshop/cameraraw.html for detailed information showing all you need to know about working with Camera Raw.

BMP

BMP (Bitmap) is a standard Windows file format commonly used for saving images that you want to make part of your computer's resources, such as the wallpaper that you see on your Windows desktop. BMP is also a format used by computer programmers. BMP supports RGB, Indexed Color, Grayscale, and Bitmap image modes.

Here are your options when saving a BMP file:

✔ **File Format:** Choose between Windows and OS/2.

✔ **Depth:** Although you can select a bit depth, I recommend leaving the default setting Photoshop selects for you.

✔ **Compress (RLE):** The compression scheme used is lossless, which is great, but don't select this option if you're creating wallpaper. Windows won't recognize it.

✔ **Flip Row Order:** This option enables Windows to recognize the file by reading the first row of pixels first and the last row last. It's for programmers who are coding for Windows applications. Leave it deselected unless you're one of them.

Don't worry about the Advanced Modes option. It's even more eggheady than the other options and strictly programming territory.

Large Document Format (PSB)

Work with humongous files? Then you'll be pleased to know that the Large Document Format supports files of any size. Besides the Photoshop Raw and TIFF file formats, the Large Document Format is the only other format that can save files larger than 2GB. Even better, the coveted features, such as layers, layer effects, and filters, are all supported by this format. If you want to work with large files, just make sure you have the Maximize PSD and PSB File Compatibility option set to Always in the File Handling pane of your Preferences.

Large Document Format files can be opened in Photoshop CS or later, *only* (and Photoshop Elements 7 and 8 if you happen to also own those programs). So, make sure any recipients of your files have the latest and greatest version of Photoshop. This limitation isn't confined to older versions of Photoshop, either. Be forewarned that many other applications, and even some operating systems, fall to their knees when presented with a file size larger than 2GB.

Other file formats

Although you may never need to use any of these formats, just to satisfy any curiosities, here's a quick description of each.

- ✔ **Cineon:** A Kodak film format containing 10-bits per channel.
- ✔ **Dicom (Digital Imaging and Communications in Medicine):** Used for transfer and storage of medical images (PS Extended only)
- ✔ **Digital Negative (DNG):** Archival format for Camera Raw images containing raw image data as well as metadata.
- ✔ **FXG:** A vector graphics XML file format used to describe graphic files and intended for new Flash-authoring applications.
- ✔ **IFF:** Includes Maya IFF and Amiga IFF, supporting image, sound and video files.
- ✔ **PCX:** An old PC vector drawing format.
- ✔ **PICT:** Stands for Macintosh Picture and is Apple's original format for Mac graphics. Not used much since 2001, except for occasional old slides and screen presentations.
- ✔ **Photoshop DCS 1.0 and 2.0:** Version of the EPS format that enables you to save desktop color separations (DCS).
- ✔ **Pixar:** High-end format used for 3-D images and animation.

✔ **Portable Bit Map:** Supports monochrome (1-bit) images used for exchanging files between various platforms.

✔ **Scitex:** Used for high-end imaging on a Scitex system.

✔ **Targa:** An old PC video format.

✔ **WBMP:** Supports 1-bit images used for mobile devices.

Chapter 3: Using and Managing Color

In This Chapter

✓ Choosing foreground and background colors

✓ Defining color

✓ Establishing color management settings

✓ Getting consistent color among multiple applications

✓ Soft proofing colors

Color in Photoshop takes on two personalities. On one hand choosing colors and applying them is easy, fun, and stress-free. On the other hand, managing color — that is, making what you see onscreen match what comes out on paper (or in your browser) — can be difficult and frustrating.

Unfortunately, you have to be well-versed in both picking great colors and managing colors for print. What's the use of creating the next *Mona Lisa* in Photoshop only to find that it looks like a fifth-generation color Xerox copy? In this chapter, I start by showing you how to define and apply color; then, I ease you into the world of color management.

If you haven't already read the section on color theory in Book II. Chapter 2, you might want to give it a gander before you dive into this chapter. Knowing a little color theory may make this chapter a little more understandable.

Dealing with Foreground and Background Colors

Photoshop has two categories of color — a foreground color and a background color. You apply the *foreground color* when you use the type tools, the painting tools, or the shape tools. The foreground color is also the beginning color of a default gradient applied by the Gradient tool. The *background color* is the color you apply with the Eraser tool (assuming you don't have layers) and is the ending color of the default gradient. When you increase the size of your canvas, you fill the additional canvas with the background color (also assuming you don't have layers). You can find the swatches that represent the two color categories in the lower part of the Tools panel, as shown in Figure 3-1.

The default color for the foreground is black; the background is white. Click the small icon labeled in Figure 3-1 or simply press the D key to return the colors to the defaults. To switch the foreground and background colors, click the curved arrow in the Tools panel or press the X key.

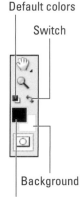

Default colors

Switch

Background

Foreground

Figure 3-1:
Photoshop
color swatches
are at the
bottom of the
Tools panel.

Here are a few tips to help you get a handle on using tools with foreground and background colors:

- **Blend the foreground and background by using the Gradient tool.** When you drag with the Gradient tool across the canvas and the gradient is set to the default, you get a blending of the foreground and background colors.

- **Fill selected areas with the foreground color.** Just click your canvas with the Paint Bucket tool to select areas based on a Tolerance setting and fill those areas with the foreground color.

- **Apply the background color by erasing.** If you're working on a background, rather than a layer, you can use the Eraser tool to apply the background color. Some people prefer to say you're erasing to the background or canvas color.

    If you use the Eraser tool on a layer, you erase to transparency. See Book V for the scoop on layers.

- **Add more background to your canvas and fill it with the background color.** When you enlarge your canvas size, Photoshop, by default, automatically fills the added canvas with the background color.

    If you enlarge a layer, the extra canvas is transparent. See Book II, Chapter 1 if the word *canvas* seems foreign to you.

Defining Color

Like with nearly everything else in Photoshop, you can select color in several ways. In the following sections, I explain each of these color-definition options:

- Click a color in the Color Picker.

- Move the sliders in the Color panel.

- Sample color from your image (or elsewhere) with the Eyedropper tool.

- Grab a color from the Swatches panel.

Poking around Color Picker

When you click either the Foreground or Background color swatch in the Tools panel, you're transported magically to the Color Picker. This huge dialog box, shown in Figure 3-2, allows you to select a color from the color spectrum (called a *color slider*) or define your color numerically.

Color field   Color slider Color values

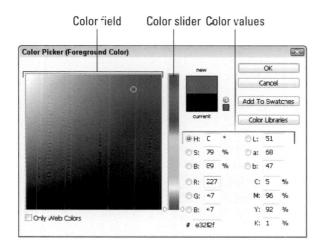

Figure 3-2: Using the Color Picker is one of the many ways to specify color in Photoshop.

Choosing a color visually is fine for Web or multimedia work, but not recommended for print work. Among other reasons, your monitor uses an RGB (red, green, and blue) color model, whereas printers use a CMYK (cyan, magenta, yellow, and black) model. For more on this and other color-management issues, see "Color Management Essentials," later in this chapter. For the basics of color theory, see Book II, Chapter 2.

To select a color visually, follow these steps:

1. **Click either the Foreground or Background color swatch in the Tools panel.**

   The Color Picker dialog box appears. (Refer to Figure 3-2.)

2. **Drag the color slider to get in the ballpark of the color you want.**

3. **To fine-tune your choice, click in the large square on the left.**

   This square area is called a *color field.* The circular icon targets your selected shade. The dialog box displays your new chosen color as well as the current, or original, foreground or background color.

   The numeric values also change accordingly to represent the exact shade you've chosen.

Alternatively, if you know the numeric values of the color you want to use, you can plug in the values in the text boxes on the right side of the Color Picker. For example, RGB values are based on brightness levels, from 0 to 255, with 0 being black and 255 being the pure color or white. CMYK values are based on percentages (0 to 100) of the four process colors — cyan, magenta, yellow, and black. You can enter the hexadecimal formula (six digit alpha numeric color code) for Web colors.

4. **When you're satisfied with the color, click OK. Note that you can add your new color to your Swatches panel, if desired. Click the Add to Swatches button. Name your new swatch and click OK.**

5. **Click OK to exit the Color Picker.**

The new HUD (Heads Up Display) Color Picker is a nifty onscreen tool that lets you quickly select colors. This can come in handy when you want to choose colors based on your image and want to have your Color Picker adjacent to those colors. To choose a color from the HUD Color Picker, select any painting tool. Then press Shift+Alt+right-click (Control+Option+⌘ on the Mac) and click in your image window to display the HUD Color Picker. Drag to select your desired hue and shade (you can release the keys while you drag). You'll see the appearance of a circle target to help pinpoint your desired color, as shown in Figure 3-3.

Figure 3-3: Using the new HUD Color Picker enables you to quickly choose colors in your image window.

You can do pretty much the same thing in the Color panel that you can do with the Color Picker. I prefer the Color panel, so I go into more detail about that approach in the following section.

Mixing with the Color panel

To open the Color panel shown in Figure 3-4, choose Window➪Color. A couple of swatches in this panel may look vaguely familiar. That's because they represent the foreground and background colors — just like the swatches in the Tools panel. And (also like the Tools panel swatches) the infamous Color Picker appears if you click the swatches in the Color panel. But forget the Color Picker; you don't need to go there. Everything you need is right here in this tiny panel.

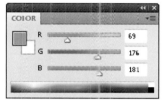

Figure 3-4: The Color panel is a compact but efficient way to select colors.

Before you use the Color panel to define your colors, you should know which color model you want to use. Here's a short description of each:

- **Grayscale:** For working strictly in black, white, and shades of gray. You get one slider, K, which represents black. Move the slider to get shades of gray, including complete white and complete black.

- **RGB (Red-Green-Blue):** For anything that's viewed onscreen — from multimedia and slide presentations to content for the Web. You can use it for printing on most desktop inkjet printers.

- **CMYK (Cyan-Magenta-Yellow-Black):** Used in printing.

- **Web Color:** Used strictly for the Web. If you select this model, make sure that you also select Make Ramp Web Safe from the Color panel options menu. The Ramp is the color spectrum bar at the bottom of the Color panel.

- **HSB (Hue-Saturation-Brightness):** Based on percentages of saturation and brightness, and an angle (0 to 360 degrees), which corresponds to a location on the color wheel. (I don't cover this model in Book II, Chapter 2.)

- **Lab (Lightness, a, b):** Contains three channels: one for lightness, one (a) that contains colors from green to red, and one (b) that contains colors from blue to yellow. Lab is more complex to understand and work with than the other models — and it's the color model of choice for high-end color experts. (By the way, Lab is also Photoshop's native color mode.)

When you want to define a color according to a color model, I think the Color panel is the way to go. Follow these quick-and-easy steps to define a color by using the Color panel:

1. **Open the Color panel by choosing Window⇨Color.**

2. **Make sure the color swatch you want to define, Foreground or Background, is selected on the left side of the Color panel.**

   An outline appears around the selected swatch.

3. **Select your desired color model from the Color panel pop-up menu by clicking the down-pointing arrow in the upper-right corner.**

   You'll probably be using RGB, CMYK, or Web Color the majority of the time.

    If you want to use the RGB color model but also want to ensure that any color you choose is printable, select CMYK Spectrum from the Color panel options menu. By default, all the colors in the ramp are printable. Just be sure to choose your colors by clicking in the ramp.

4. **In the Color panel, move the sliders for each component of the color model or enter numeric values.**

   You can also select a color by clicking inside the color ramp at the bottom of the Color panel. Click the small swatches at the far-right end of the color ramp to change your color to black or white.

5. **To make sure your desired color works with the color mode you've selected, keep an eye open for an alert icon.**

   Here are a few more tips to keep in mind when working with the Color panel:

   - If you're working in RGB or CMYK, this alert icon is known as the *gamut alarm* and looks like the triangular warning. Its appearance is Photoshop's way of saying, "Hey, you! That color you mixed won't print the way you think it will because it's out of gamut." Remember, *gamut* is the range of colors a device can either display or print.

   - Because the RGB color model has a much wider gamut than the CMYK color model, some of the colors can be viewed only onscreen and not reproduced on paper.

   - If a color is out of gamut, Photoshop offers you a substitution. Inside a little square to the right of the gamut alarm icon, the closest printable color to the one you chose appears.

   - If you're working in Web Colors, be on the lookout for a small cube icon. Click either the icon or the square to use the closest Web-safe color. The cube indicates that the color you mixed isn't a Web-safe color. Clicking the cube tells Photoshop that you want to use its Web-safe alternative, instead. A Web-safe color ensures that the color won't *dither* (mix available colors to simulate a missing color) when displayed in the browser.

6. **Click either the icon or the square if you want to use the closest printable color, rather than your original choice.**

Grabbing color from the Swatches panel

Another way to define a foreground or background color is by clicking a color in the Swatches panel, shown in Figure 3-5. Choose Window⊅Swatches to bring up the panel.

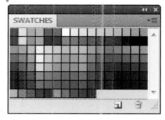

You can have any tool active when you use the Swatches panel to define a color because as soon as you move the tool over the Swatches panel, it temporarily changes to an Eyedropper icon that samples the color.

Figure 3-5: The Swatches panel allows you to grab and store colors.

TIP

Besides being a way to select your foreground and background colors, the Swatches panel acts like a traditional artist's paint palette in digital form by letting you store as many colors as you want in the panel for later use.

To change the background color, either select the background swatch icon in the Color panel or simply Ctrl-click (⌘-click on the Mac) a swatch in the Swatches panel.

Here are some of the things you can do with the Swatches panel:

- ✓ **Customize the Swatches panel's display.** You can choose how to display the Swatches panel by selecting Small or Large Thumbnail (swatch thumbnails) or Small or Large List (swatch thumbnails along with a name) from the Swatches panel pop-up menu. (Click the down-pointing triangle in the upper-right portion of the panel to open the menu.)

- ✓ **Use preset colors.** To load a particular preset swatch library, select it from the list on the Swatches panel pop-up menu. Click Append to add the library to the existing swatches or OK to replace the existing swatches. You can find libraries specific for Web graphics and for implementing spot colors, such as those created by Pantone, Toyo, and Focoltone.

  You can also select Load Swatches from the Swatches panel pop-up menu. In the Load dialog box, navigate to the Color Swatches folder by following this path: `Adobe\Adobe Photoshop CS5\Presets\Color Swatches`; then, select your desired library.

  You can also work with swatches by using the Preset Manager. (For more on the Preset Manager, see Book I, Chapter 5.)

- ✓ **Customize your own Swatches panel.** To add a color to the Swatches panel, do one of the following:

  - • Click the New Swatch icon at the bottom of the Swatches panel.

  - • Select New Swatch from the Swatches panel pop-up menu. Name your swatch and click OK.

- Click an empty spot in the Swatches panel. (Your cursor changes to a paint bucket icon.) Name your swatch and click OK. Or Alt-click (Option-click on the Mac) on an empty spot to add the color and bypass the Name dialog box. Note that the color that's added depends on whether your foreground or background swatch is selected.

✔ **Delete swatches that you don't want anymore.** To delete a swatch, drag it to the trash can icon at the bottom of the Swatches panel.

✔ **Create your own library of swatches.** To save a set of swatches as a library, select Save Swatches from the Swatches panel pop-up menu. Name your swatch library (leave the file extension as .aco) in the Save dialog box. Click Save.

✔ **Save swatches to share with other Adobe Creative Suite applications.** Select Save Swatches for Exchange from the Swatches panel pop-up menu, and your color panel is saved in a format (with an .ase extension) that you can then load into sister applications, such as Illustrator and InDesign.

I recommend saving libraries in a subfolder of the Presets folder. Follow this path: Adobe\Adobe Photoshop\Presets\Color Swatches; then, create your own folder, name the file, and click Save.

✔ **Restore your default swatch libraries.** To return to the default library of swatches, select Reset Swatches from the Swatches panel pop-up menu. You can choose to either replace or append to the current library.

Lifting and sampling color

Photoshop lets you change foreground or background colors by lifting them from the image with the Eyedropper tool. Using the Eyedropper tool comes in handy when you want to sample an existing color in an image for use in another element. For example, if I want my text to be the same color as the flower in my image, I click a petal with my Eyedropper tool, which then lifts (samples) the color and makes it my new foreground color. I then create my type, which uses that foreground color. *Voilà* — color coordination at its finest.

Here are some handy tips for using the Eyedropper tool to suck up color from one place and use it elsewhere in your image:

✔ **Select any color you want from any image that's open.** If you have multiple images open, you can click inside an image that you're not working on. In fact, if that doesn't knock your socks off, you can lift any color you see onscreen, even from a file in another application, such as Illustrator, or from your desktop. Just click and drag your Eyedropper from the image window onto the color you want to sample. Be sure that you can see both application windows simultaneously.

✔ **Select your sampling area.** You have only two options (found on the Options bar) to worry about when using the Eyedropper tool. You can select the color of just the single pixel you click (Point Sample). Or Photoshop averages the colors of the pixels in a 3-x-3-, 5-x-5-, 11-x-11-,

31-x-31-, 51-x-51-, or 101-x-101-pixel radius. You can also choose to sample from just your currently active layer or all your layers.

✓ **Make colors Web ready with a right-click of your mouse button.** For you Webbies out there, if you right-click (Control-click on the Mac) your image to bring up the context menu, you have one more option — Copy Color as HTML. This option converts the sampled color to a hexadecimal color code and copies the code to the Clipboard so that you can paste the code into an HTML file.

✓ **Toggle between the Eyedropper and other tools.** For your productive painting pleasure, when you're using the Brush, Pencil, Color Replacement, Gradient, Paint Bucket, or Shape tool, holding down Alt (Option on the Mac) allows you to temporarily access the Eyedropper tool. Release the key to return to your original tool.

✓ **Toggle between the background and the foreground.** If the foreground color swatch is active, Alt-click (Option-click on the Mac) with the Eyedropper tool to lift a new background color. If the background color swatch is active, Alt-clicking (Option-clicking on the Mac) lifts a new foreground color

To use the Eyedropper tool, you first need to decide whether you want to change the foreground or background color. Then, follow these steps:

1. **Select the foreground (or the background) in the Tools panel or the Color panel.**

2. **Select the Eyedropper tool in the Tools panel (or press the I key).**

   Fortunately, the Eyedropper looks exactly like a real eyedropper.

3. **Click the color in your image that you want to use.**

   That color becomes your new foreground (or background) color.

Using the Color Sampler tool to measure color

The Eyedropper's cousin, the Color Sampler tool, looks like an eyedropper with a small target next to the icon. It also shares the Eyedropper's flyout menu.

The "Sampler" moniker is kind of misleading because this tool only *measures* the colors you click. In addition to merely obtaining the numeric value of a color, the Color Sampler tool can monitor changes to your image after you apply color-correction techniques and filters.

Follow these steps to use the Color Sampler tool:

1. **Select the Color Sampler tool in the Tools panel and then click the color you want to measure.**

   A target icon, labeled #1, appears on your image.

**Book II
Chapter 3**

**Using and
Managing Color**

Photoshop opens the Info panel automatically and shows you the numeric values for that color (as shown in Figure 3-6).

2. **Repeat Step 1 up to three more times for a total of four targeted colors.**

   Target icons appear for your second, third, and fourth samples.

3. **With the Color Sampler tool, drag the targets to sample new areas of your image, if you want. Delete a target by Alt-clicking (Option-clicking on the Mac) it.**

   You can actually measure a fifth color by just moving the Color Sampler cursor around the image. The numeric value appears in the upper portion of the Info panel.

Color target icons

Corbis Digital Stock

Figure 3-6: The Color Sampler tool measures up to five colors in your image.

Finding and Sharing Color Themes with Kuler

Kuler is an online community that provides color themes for you to browse, download, create, edit, and upload for sharing with others. Use these themes when creating graphic print projects or Web sites. All you need to participate is an Internet connection and an Adobe ID. (See www.adobe.com to sign up if you don't have one already.)

Here are basics of how to use Kuler:

1. **Choose Window➪Extensions➪Kuler.**

2. **Click the Browse button. In the Browse panel, enter your desired tag word in the Search field (magnifying glass icon) and press Enter (Return on the Mac).**

   For example, I entered the word *organic,* as shown in Figure 3-7. All the themes tagged with the word *organic* then appear in the list of themes. You can also search by criteria such as Highest Rated or Most Popular from the Search Results drop-down list. Click the up- and down-pointing arrow buttons at the bottom of the panel to view previous and next sets of themes. Click the double curved arrow to refresh the themes from the Kuler community.

3. **Choose a theme from the list, click the right-pointing arrow, and choose one of the following submenu items:**

   • *Edit the Theme:* Choosing this option takes you to the Create panel, as shown in Figure 3-8. In the color wheel, select your desired color by clicking on the color's associated circle icon. To edit the color, move the circle icon within the wheel or drag your color sliders (or enter a hexadecimal formula) at the bottom of the panel. You also have icons above the color sliders to add your foreground or background color as the base color (the color around which your theme is based) and to add and delete colors from the theme. Finally, to change your base color, select a color in your theme and click the button labeled Affect the Other Colors in the Theme Based on a Harmony. Hover your mouse over the buttons, and a tooltip indicates which button is which.

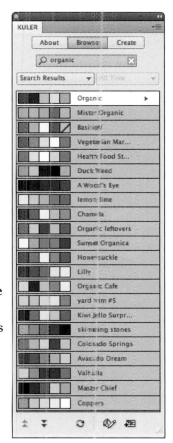

Figure 3-7: Search for color themes in Kuler.

You can also click the Color Wheel/Pencil icon at the bottom of the panel to edit the theme.

- *Add to Swatches Panel:* This option adds the colors in the theme to your Swatches panel. (Choose Window⇨Swatches.)

  You can also click the Swatches icon at the bottom of the panel to add to the Swatches panel.

- *View Online in Kuler:* Selecting this option launches your browser and opens your theme in the Kuler community Web site.

4. **Click the Save Theme button at the bottom of the panel.**

   You can also click the Swatches icon at the bottom of the panel to add the theme to your Swatches panel. Finally, click the up arrow icon in the bottom right of the Create panel to upload the theme to the Kuler community Web site.

To create a new theme, click the Create panel and basically follow the same steps as editing the theme, described in Step 3.

Figure 3-8: Edit your color theme using the color wheel.

Color Management Essentials

Grab some Tylenol. You're about to delve into the rather confusing and sometimes cantankerous world (or as some users would call it — underworld) of color management. It's by far the biggest headache of every graphics professional's day-to-day experience. And I'm sure quite a few home users also scratch their heads wondering why their digital photos looked so great onscreen and turned into a muddy mess on paper.

Reproducing color isn't an exact science. In fact, sometimes you'd think it takes an act of voodoo magic to get the output you want. Don't throw up your hands and live with whatever output comes out the other end; if you can't change the color, you can at least change your attitude toward color. Getting a handle on color management requires four things — some knowledge, some patience, a significant amount of time to experiment and test, and (most importantly) acceptance. Acceptance of the unfortunate fact that you don't live in a WYSIWYG world: What you get in one medium is sometimes merely an approximation of what you see in another.

Why? Well, I start with the basic gripe of many users while they look disapprovingly at their printout — "But it didn't look like that on the screen!" As detailed in Book II, Chapter 2, you can work with two major color models — RGB (Red-Green-Blue) and CMYK (Cyan-Magenta-Yellow-Black). The RGB color model (16.7 million colors), which all monitors use, has a significantly wider range of color (called a *gamut* in computer lingo) than the CMYK color model (approximately 55,000 colors) that printers use. So, many of the colors you see onscreen fall outside the CMYK gamut — and therefore can't be reproduced on paper. And, in some cases, some CMYK colors fall outside the RGB gamut. Programs such as Photoshop do their best by providing colors that are the closest match. But those out-of-gamut bright and vibrant colors are matched with duller, darker versions, at best.

And, if that difference alone isn't enough to complicate matters, hardware devices that share the same color model can possess different gamuts within that color model. For example, the RGB color space of a monitor can differ from the RGB color space of a scanner. Not only that, but you can also have different color spaces within the same type of device. A 15-inch generic monitor doesn't display color equal to a 24-inch Samsung or Apple monitor. Likewise, an Epson printer may not share the same color space as a Hewlett-Packard or Canon printer. So, when you take into account the differences that can occur among platforms, monitors, printers, browsers, scanners, applications, paper and other substrates, or any of the almost infinite number of possible permutations, it makes you want to return to the days of quill and parchment. Techies often call this mind-numbingly large number of possible inconsistencies *device-dependent color*. In other words, the color is dependent upon the hardware device. And device-dependent color varies. That's just the cold, harsh reality, and nothing's changing that.

But Adobe, being the kind and benevolent software mega-giant that it is, has developed a color-management system designed to be *device-independent*. The 5-cent explanation of this system is that you first identify your working color spaces. Photoshop then *tags* your files with that color space by embedding a color profile (also known as an ICC profile) with your files. The program analyzes any color space in which you either view or output a file and makes adjustments on the fly so that the color is viewed and printed reasonably accurately and consistently, in theory, independent of the device. Photoshop also reads the embedded color profile (or lack thereof) of any file you open and addresses how you want to deal with that profile if it doesn't match your working color space.

In the following sections, I give you the 25-cent explanation — which I hope is enough to get you started in managing color. If color management is an extremely critical workflow issue for you, I recommend buying a book or two strictly devoted to nothing but managing color. It's well worth the money. One of my personal favorites is *Color Management for Digital Photographers For Dummies,* by Ted Padova and Don Mason (Wiley).

**Book II
Chapter 3**

**Using and
Managing Color**

Setting up your work environment

One aspect of color management that people often overlook is setting up a good working environment for digital image editing. You may wave your hand impatiently and say, "Yeah, yeah, I just want to get to the important stuff." This *is* the important stuff. Don't worry. Setting up a good work environment won't cost you much. Just do these things:

- **Keep your computer desktop a neutral gray.** Colors and patterns behind your images influence the way that you perceive those images. Creating a neutral, gray desktop is the closest you can get to mounting your work on gray, black, or white matte board (and not neon green or paisley), the way professional graphic designers and photographers do.

- **Keep your lighting as consistent as possible.** For example, avoid working on images in full, bright afternoon sun and then again under a single desk lamp late at night. Likewise, view onscreen images and your printed output under the same lighting.

- **Keep the walls of your work environment as neutral as your monitor desktop.** You don't have to paint your office gray, but try to avoid a lot of colorful posters and artwork around and behind your monitor.

- **Speaking of monitors, if you're using an LCD (flat screen) monitor, be sure you're sitting directly in front of it.** Color shifts quite a bit on LCDs if you're viewing it at even a slight angle. So, no slumping in your chair!

- **Keep a swatch book (or two) handy, such as those from Pantone or Trumatch, to select your colors.** Don't make a decision based on what you see onscreen. These books give you a true representation of how onscreen color looks when printed on paper. Just be sure to keep them out of the light and update them periodically when the colors start to fade.

Be prepared for a healthy monetary investment when you buy a swatch book. These little buggers can cost anywhere from $75 to $200. You can purchase swatch books from some larger art supply stores or order them online. You can purchase Pantone books from www.pantone.com. Do a Web search for others, such as Trumatch, Focoltone, and Toyo.

- **Take some time to test your *workflow* (production methods) and your computer system.** Scan images using multiple settings, print images using multiple settings, and view your images using different browsers on different monitors and different platforms.

Get to know the strengths, limitations, and quirks of every piece of your equipment. Experiment with Photoshop. I know; I know. You have a life. But trust me — it's an investment with great returns.

Calibrating your monitor

Calibrating your monitor and creating an ICC profile of your monitor ensures that your monitor doesn't display any red, green, or blue *colorcasts* (traces of color) and that it provides as neutral a gray screen as possible. Calibration is incredibly important if you want to standardize your image display — knowing that how you view your image today will be how you view your image tomorrow or next week.

If you really want to do a good calibration job, consider investing in a combination hardware/software calibration package. These products used to be really pricey, but you can get a starter package for as little as $79. You can choose from several manufacturers, including Datacolor (http://spyder.datacolor.com) and X-Rite (www.xrite.com).

If you're a Windows 7 user, you can check out Display Color Calibration. Choose Start➪Control Panel and type calibrate display in the Search field. Click Calibrate Display Color. Click Next and follow the instructions. If you're a Mac OS X user and on a super-tight budget, you can use the Display Calibrator Assistant. Choose Apple➪System Preferences and click Displays in the System Preferences dialog box. Then click the Color tab and click the Calibrate button. Answer the questions in the Display Calibrator Assistant. (See Figure 3-9.)

Figure 3-9: Mac users can use the Display Calibrator Assistant to calibrate their monitors.

The Display Calibrator Assistant attempts to remove any colorcasts and get as neutral a gray background as it can. It also creates a profile of your monitor for Photoshop, Illustrator, and other programs so that those applications know how your monitor displays color.

TIP

When you calibrate your monitor, display an image for which you already know the color values. For example, use an image that you've worked with and for which you have a good print, and then use that image each and every time you calibrate. Your goal is to match the digital image on your screen to the printed image. You should calibrate every so often because monitors can drift and degrade. Some experts say weekly is best; others are more liberal and say monthly is fine.

Not only is letting your monitor warm up a prerequisite before you calibrate, it's also a good idea before you sit down to tackle any image-adjustment work.

Establishing Your Settings

After you calibrate your monitor (see the preceding section) and adequately arrange your work environment (described earlier in this chapter), you need to nail down the color settings and make sure they're the right match for your intended output.

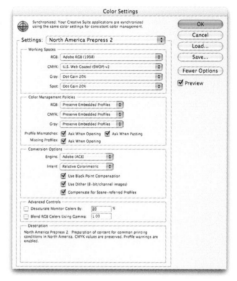

Figure 3-10: The Color Settings dialog box is command central for establishing your color-management system.

You establish these settings in the Color Settings dialog box, the rather intimidating dialog box shown in Figure 3-10. To open it, choose Edit⇨Color Settings. In the Color Settings dialog box, you can choose from predefined settings established for specific types of output, or you can customize your own settings to fit your individual needs. The following sections offer more details about the settings you can choose in the Color Settings dialog box.

While you're perusing the dialog box, hover your cursor over any item to make a great description of that item appear at the bottom of the dialog box.

Handling Photoshop's predefined settings

In the Color Settings dialog box, Photoshop allows you to take the easy route and select from a long list of predefined color settings based on your desired output. After you set up the predefined settings, Photoshop provides all the appropriate working color spaces and color-management policies you need to get good color results.

Being the smart program that it is, Photoshop won't steer you down the wrong path with its predefined settings. The only way you can mess up the predefined settings is if your output doesn't match the setting. For example, the Web Graphics Defaults setting isn't appropriate for your high-end, four-color print job because these two mediums use color in completely different ways. (See Book II, Chapter 2 for details if you're curious why this is so.)

Be sure to click the More Options button in the Color Settings dialog box to access the full set of predefined color settings. Here's a brief description of the main settings in the Settings drop-down list at the top:

- **Custom:** Allows you to manually assign your own settings. When you define a custom configuration, save your settings so that you can reload them later, if necessary.

- **Monitor Color:** Emulates the color of most video applications. Reserve it for screen images only. Avoid it for producing print images.

- **North America General Purpose 2:** Provides all-purpose general color settings for screen and print images in North America. It uses the same CMYK, Grayscale, and Spot working spaces as North America Prepress 2, but uses the Web standard of sRGB for the RGB working space.

- **North America Newspaper:** For prepping content for North American newspaper presses. CMYK values are preserved, and all profile warnings are enabled.

- **North America Prepress 2:** Provides color settings for print images in North America. Preserves the CMYK working space and brings any profile warnings to your attention.

- **North America Web/Internet:** Gives color settings for Web images in North America. Uses sRGB for the RGB working space.

- **ColorSync Workflow (Mac only):** Uses ColorSync 3.0 Color Management System and ColorSync profiles. It's not recognized by the Windows platform.

- **Europe General Purpose 2:** Provides general color settings for screen and print images in Europe. Profile warnings are disabled.

- **Europe General Purpose 3:** Same as 2, but it offers updated CMYK ICC profiles for offset printing on coated paper.

- **Europe Prepress 2:** Provides color settings for print images in Europe. Preserves the CMYK working space and brings any profile warnings to your attention.

- **Europe Prepress 3:** Same as 2, but it offers updated CMYK ICC profiles for offset printing on coated paper.

- **Europe Web/Internet:** Gives color settings for Web images in Europe. Uses sRGB for the RGB working space.

- **Europe Web/Internet 2:** Same as Web/Internet, but it offers updated CMYK ICC profiles for offset printing on coated paper.

- **Japan Color for Newspaper:** Provides settings to be used for newspaper presses in Japan. Preserves the CMYK working space and alerts you to any profile warnings.

- **Japan General Purpose 2:** Provides general color settings for screen and print images in Japan.

✔ **Japan Magazine Advertisement Color:** Gives color settings for preparing images by using the color standards of the Japanese Magazine Publisher Association.

✔ **Japan Prepress 2:** Provides color settings for print images in Japan. Preserves the CMYK working space and brings any profile warnings to your attention.

✔ **Japan Web/Internet:** Gives color settings for Web images in Japan. Uses sRGB for the RGB working space.

✔ **Photoshop 5 Default Spaces:** Uses the default color settings found in Photoshop 5, the first version to use color management.

You can always use a predefined setting as a starting point and adjust whatever individual settings you need to. If you do, your predefined setting name automatically changes to Custom.

Indicating your working spaces

If you select one of the predefined color settings from the Settings drop-down list, Photoshop plugs in all the necessary remaining options in the dialog box. (If you select the Custom option, Photoshop leaves whatever settings were there previously because it knows you're going to choose your own settings, anyway.)

When you select one of the predefined color settings, the first group of settings that Photoshop plugs in contains your working spaces. *Working spaces* are the color profiles associated with the RGB, CMYK, Grayscale, and Spot color modes. If you select the Custom color setting, you need to choose your own working spaces.

Each of the four working spaces is equally important, so I advise you to read all the following sections — and read them in order — if you're serious about color management.

RGB working spaces

Table 3-1 gives you a quick view of your RGB working space options.

Table 3-1	RGB Working Space Options	
Working Space	*What It Does*	*Recommendation*
Monitor RGB	Sets the working space to your current monitor space (which it gets from the monitor profile you established during calibration). Forces Photoshop to turn off color management.	I don't recommend this setting unless you have a specific need to use it.

Working Space	What It Does	Recommendation
ColorSync RGB	Sets the working space to the profile specified in the Apple ColorSync control panel. This is the default setting for the ColorSync Workflow pre-defined setting.	For Macintosh only.
Adobe RGB (1998)	The default setting for all the Prepress predefined settings. It's the best color profile to use for viewing 24-bit (8-bit mode) images and converting RGB files to CMYK. Provides a large gamut of RGB colors.	I recommend this option as a general setting for all print work and as an overall setting if you're unsure what to choose.
Apple RGB	Can be used for older Mac OS scanners and monitors.	Unless you're the proud owner of a 13-inch Apple monitor, I'd avoid it.
ColorMatch RGB	Use this working space only with Radius PressView monitors.	I don't think I need to give you a recommendation on this one! You Radius PressView users know who you are.
ProPhoto RGB (also called ROMM RGB)	Provides a large color gamut. Good for viewing 48-bit (16-bit mode) images. You may see banding in 24-bit (8-bit mode) images.	Good for output to dye sublimation and inkjet photo printers.
sRGB	The default setting for Web Graphics Defaults. This color profile represents a standard, Trinitron PC monitor — the monitor of choice for many of the world's Web surfers. This option can also be used with Windows scanners. Avoid it for print work because of its limited RGB color gamut.	If your goal is to ensure your Web graphics look relatively the same in Los Angeles as they do in Bangladesh, sRGB is a good profile to use.

If you click the More Options button in the Color Settings dialog box, you get even more RGB, as well as CMYK, Grayscale, and Spot settings. These settings include profiles for monitors, printers, and various video formats. For the most part, you can stick with the main working spaces and be covered.

You can save and load any custom settings, including the individual RGB, CMYK, Grayscale, and Spot working spaces, as well as your entire group of color settings.

After you set RGB working spaces, don't forget that you also have to configure the other three working spaces, as described in the following sections.

CMYK working spaces

CMYK working spaces are a little more involved than RGB options (listed in the preceding section). CMYK working spaces serve a threefold purpose:

- ✔ Photoshop converts your RGB file to the CMYK color space when you choose Image⇨Mode⇨CMYK.

- ✔ You view your RGB image in the CMYK color space when you choose View⇨Proof Setup⇨Working CMYK. See the section "Proofing Colors in the Final Output (Soft Proofing)," later in this chapter, for more on soft proofing colors.

- ✔ The CMYK color space determines how a CMYK file is displayed on an RGB monitor.

Europe (FOGRA), Japan, and the United States have specific color profiles for printing. Those CMYK options are divided between those for coated and uncoated paper, and sheet-fed or Web printing presses. The latter two have different percentages of ink coverage and paper stock. Macs also have a ColorSync Generic CMYK profile. I'd leave the setting at U.S. Web Coated (SWOP) v2 unless your commercial printer tells you otherwise.

Grayscale working spaces

Grayscale working spaces have to do with two parameters — viewing and dot gain of grayscale images (Image⇨Mode⇨Grayscale). You can select Gray Gamma 1.8 for a Macintosh monitor or Gray Gamma 2.2 for a PC monitor. You can also view an image according to how it will print, based on typical dot gain.

For those Mac users using Mac OS 10.6, Snow Leopard, you can set your Gray Gamma to 2.2.

Dot gain is how much ink the paper absorbs, thereby increasing the size of every halftone dot. When continuous-tone images are digitized, they're converted into a series of dots known as a *halftone*.

If you're preparing graphics for the Web, you may want to set your working space to Gray Gamma 2.2 — whether or not you're using a Mac — because most of the Web surfers worldwide are PC users.

For print work, leave the setting at Dot Gain 20% unless your commercial printer tells you otherwise. You can enter any desired percentage in the Custom Dot Gain option.

Don't forget — you still have to adjust another working space, which I cover in the following section.

Spot working spaces

Spot working spaces have to do with spot colors. *Spot colors* are premixed inks that are printed in addition to, or in lieu of, the four process colors — cyan, magenta, yellow, and black. Unless your commercial printer tells you otherwise, stick with a setting of Dot Gain 20%.

Working with your newly defined settings

After you define your color profiles in the Color Settings dialog box, you may want to get a handle on how these newly established settings affect how Photoshop works. Although the settings typically affect only how Photoshop works in the background, you nevertheless might want to be aware of the following key changes:

- **By default, any new images you create use the color profile you selected in the Color Settings dialog box.** Every file you create on your computer now uses the colors within the gamut of your color profiles (either RGB or CMYK, depending on your document color mode). Overall, this default setting should make managing color in Photoshop easier. For example, if you mostly work with multimedia or Web images and have specified your color settings accordingly, you don't need to worry about whether each color will display accurately because you've set the defaults to reflect that color mode. But, if you want to prep an image for print, those defaults won't work, and you need to change your individual working spaces to those that are print oriented or to a preset, such as North American Prepress.

- **The color settings you select are used to display any *untagged images* (images that don't have an embedded color).** An example of an untagged image is a Photoshop file created before version 5 — that is, before Photoshop supported embedded color profiles.

- **Your settings define how Photoshop converts your images from one working space to another.** For example, say you choose North America Prepress 2 from the Settings drop-down list in the Color Settings dialog box. In this case, the default for CMYK is U.S. Web Coated (SWOP) v2, which is a specific CMYK setting for a Web printing press and coated paper, among other things. (This setting appears in the Working Spaces area of the Color Settings dialog box.) When you convert an RGB image to CMYK (Image➪Mode➪CMYK) prior to sending it off to the printer, Photoshop automatically tags the image with the U.S. Web Coated (SWOP) v2 color profile.

✔ **When you save a file, make sure that you select the ICC Profile (Embed Color Profile on the Mac) option in the Save or Save As dialog box, if it's available.** See Figure 3-11. (Some file formats don't support color profiles.) This selection ensures that Photoshop tags the file with the specified color profile and that its origins are always known.

Figure 3-11: Select the ICC (or Color) Profile check box when you save an image.

Setting color-management policies

After you establish working color spaces, the next step is to establish the default color-management policy for each color mode. In other words, you need to tell Photoshop how to interpret and manage the color profiles of files it opens.

Photoshop looks at the color profile of a file, compares it to your working spaces, and then employs the default policies you've established. If the file has the same color profile as yours, there isn't an issue. You're good to go.

But sometimes, this isn't the case — like in these situations:

✔ **The file you open has no profile.** These can be older files, files that were created with color management turned off, or files created in other applications that don't employ color management.

✔ **The file you open has a color profile that doesn't match your working space.** Say that you have a Web designer friend, and his settings are based on the North America Web/Internet option. He gives you a file, and you open it in Photoshop on your computer. You do mostly print work, so your settings are based on the North America Prepress 2 option. Photoshop then displays an alert that says the file has an embedded color profile that doesn't match your current RGB working space — his working space is sRGB and yours is Adobe RGB (1998). The alert then goes on to describe the default policy that's invoked on the file, as shown in Figure 3-12.

If you've selected a predefined setting, the policies have already been established for you, and those should work fine. I do recommend, however, that if you change the policies of any of the predefined settings, don't choose Off as your option, unless you have a good reason. (***Remember:*** Color management is a *good* thing.)

To set your color-management policies, follow these steps:

1. **Open the Color Settings dialog box by choosing Edit⇨Color Settings.**

2. **In the Color Management Policies area, select from the following three options for each color mode:**

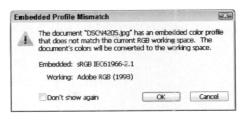

Book II
Chapter 3

Figure 3-12: Photoshop alerts you when you open a file whose color profile doesn't match yours.

   - *Off:* This option turns color management off for any new files you create, import, or open. However, if the opened or imported file's color profile matches your current working space, the profile is preserved.

   - *Preserve Embedded Profiles:* This option displays the files in their original embedded color space. No color conversion occurs. Untagged files remain untagged but use the current working space for display.

   - *Convert to Working RGB (or CMYK or Grayscale, depending on your image mode):* This option converts any files with missing or mismatched embedded profiles to your working RGB space. Untagged files remain untagged but use the current working space for display.

3. **Decide whether you want to select the Ask When Opening check box for Profile Mismatches.**

   If you don't select the Ask When Opening option for Profile Mismatches, Photoshop displays the Embedded Profile Mismatch alert message (see Figure 3-12), describing which default policy will occur. You can then select the Don't Show Again check box, and from that point forward, Photoshop executes the policy without displaying an alert. For files with missing profiles, Photoshop simply invokes the default policy without an alert.

   If you select the Ask When Opening check box for Profile Mismatches, Photoshop not only displays an Embedded Profile Mismatch alert, but also provides you with options for handling the color of that file, thereby overriding the default policy, as shown in Figure 3-13.

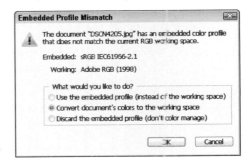

Figure 3-13: Selecting the Ask When Opening option allows you to override your default color-management policy setting.

The options in the alert are similar to the default policies of the Color Settings dialog box. Here's a brief explanation of each option in the alert:

- *Use the Embedded Profile (Instead of the Working Space):* Photoshop displays the file in its original embedded color space and doesn't perform any color conversions.

- *Convert Document's Colors to the Working Space:* Photoshop converts the file from its embedded color space to your working color space.

- *Discard the Embedded Profile (Don't Color Manage):* Photoshop doesn't utilize any color management when opening files but displays the file in your working space.

Be cautious about making any CMYK conversions. If you encounter a Profile Mismatch with a CMYK image, you probably want to preserve the image's embedded profile unless you're absolutely sure it should be converted to another CMYK working space. But, if the image doesn't have a profile, then, by all means, convert it to your CMYK working space.

4. **Decide whether you want to select the Ask When Pasting check box for Profile Mismatches.**

   If you select the Ask When Pasting option for Profile Mismatches, Photoshop prompts you when you drag and drop layers or selections that have the same color mode (see Book II, Chapter 2 for more on modes) but different color profiles. In the Paste Profile Mismatch alert dialog box, you have two options:

   - *Convert (Preserve Color Appearance):* Photoshop converts and matches the appearance of the color, rather than the RGB numerical values. For example, the RGB color of R 152, G 122, B 250 may be a different shade of purple in one RGB working space versus another. If you preserve the numerical values, the shades won't match. If you preserve the appearance, Photoshop attempts to maintain the two shades.

   - *Don't Convert (Preserve Color Number):* Photoshop doesn't convert the appearance of the color, but instead matches the RGB numerical values.

   If you don't select the Ask When Pasting check box, Photoshop pastes the color appearance between RGB images and pastes the numerical values between CMYK images.

5. **Decide whether you want to select the Ask When Opening check box for Missing Profiles.**

   If you do select the check box, Photoshop displays a Missing Profile alert and also provides you with the following options, as shown in Figure 3-14:

Figure 3-14: Photoshop alerts you when opening an image without a color profile and asks you how you want to proceed.

- *Leave As Is (Don't Color Manage):* This option leaves the image untagged and without a color profile, but displays the image in your working space.

- *Assign Working RGB (or CMYK or Grayscale, depending on your image mode):* your working space. Photoshop tags the image with your working space and displays it in that working space. If you change your working space, the image retains the old working space.

- *Assign Profile:* This option allows you to assign any color profile contained within the pop-up menu. You can use this option if you know where the untagged image originated. For example, if you scanned your image and your scanner doesn't embed profiles, you can assign the scanner profile.

Unless you have a specific reason not to, I recommend that you assign your working RGB space to those orphan files.

6. If you're done working in the Color Settings dialog box, click OK to exit.

I recommend selecting the Ask When Opening and Ask When Pasting check boxes. With these boxes selected, you know when a profile mismatch occurs — and you have the choice of picking your course of action, which includes overriding the defaults you set in the policy settings. So, you can evaluate whether you want to preserve or convert on a file-by-file basis. For example, if you're a print designer and a Web designer gives you a file, you get a profile mismatch alerting you that the file has the sRGB color space and that it doesn't match your working space of Adobe RGB (1998). If you're going to use the image as-is for Web content, you tell Photoshop to preserve the embedded profile and not to make any conversion. But if you want to repurpose the image (for, say, a logo), you have to instruct Photoshop to convert the file to your working RGB space. (Of course, ultimately, you have to also convert the image mode to CMYK for printing purposes.)

To find out the color profile of an image, select Document Profile from the pop-up menu at the bottom of the image window (which I describe in detail in Book I, Chapter 1). Also, if an image has a color profile that differs from your working space, an asterisk appears outside the parentheses in the title bar. An untagged image displays a pound sign. By the way, when you select More Options in the Color Settings dialog box, you have a few additional options regarding color conversion engines and rendering intents, which are methods of color translation. I recommend putting your trust in Photoshop and leaving these options at their defaults unless you're a bona fide color expert.

Getting Consistent Color among Adobe Applications

If you have a complete Adobe workflow (like I do), you may want to use the same color settings for all your Adobe applications. Illustrator, InDesign, and

**Book II
Chapter 3**

**Using and
Managing Color**

Acrobat share a similar Color Settings dialog box. They have a few minor differences, but nothing major. If an element doesn't exist in one application's Color Settings dialog box, Adobe merely plugs in the default setting. You can choose the same predefined color setting from the Settings pop-up menu in each application, or you can use a shortcut.

With the advent of Adobe Bridge (explained in Book I, Chapter 4), getting consistent color across all your Creative Suite applications is merely a button click away. Just follow these steps:

1. **Simply launch Bridge and choose Edit⇨Creative Suite Color Settings.**

   In the Suite Color Settings dialog box, shown in Figure 3-15, you can immediately tell whether the color settings across all your Creative Suite applications are synchronized. (*Synchronized* is Adobe's cool name for *the same.*)

2. **If they're not and you want the settings to be the same, first click the Show Expanded List of Color Settings Files to ensure you have the full list of possibilities.**

3. **Then, just select your desired predefined color setting from the list and click the Apply button.**

Figure 3-15: Get consistent color among your Adobe Creative Suite apps.

   Bridge then ensures that each Creative Suite application uses that color setting. You can also select a previously saved custom setting. If you want to see where your saved color settings files reside, just click the Show Saved Color Settings Files button.

You don't have to synchronize your color settings. You may want to have different settings in InDesign, a page-layout program, than you have in Dreamweaver, a Web-page-creation application. In the Color Settings dialog box in each Creative Suite application, a message appears at the top to let you know whether your suite color settings are synchronized.

You can save your custom Color Settings in Photoshop by clicking the Save button in the Color Settings dialog box. To ensure that all your Adobe applications can access the settings file, save it to a default location:

  ✔ For Microsoft Windows, the default location is the `AppData/Roaming/Adobe/Color/Settings` folder.

  ✔ For Mac OS X users, the default folder is `Users/CurrentUser/Library/ApplicationSupport/Adobe/Color/Settings`.

You can also place saved custom color settings files that you've received from other people (for example, reps from your offset print house) in this location.

Proofing Colors in the Final Output (Soft Proofing)

Photoshop allows you to preview onscreen how your image will look on a variety of output devices. First, choose View➪Proof Setup and select your desired setup. The Working options are based on the working spaces you specified in the Color Settings dialog box (described earlier in this chapter):

  ✔ **Legacy Macintosh RGB:** Display your image as it'll appear on a standard Macintosh monitor running Mac OS 10.5 or earlier.

  ✔ **Internet Standard RGB (sRGB):** Display your image as it'll appear on a standard Windows monitor or a Macintosh monitor running Mac OS 10.6 or earlier.

  ✔ **Monitor RGB:** Allows you to view the image by using your current monitor's color space. This setting essentially turns off your RGB working space and lets you see the image without any color management.

  ✔ **Custom:** Allows you to choose a specific device. For example, choosing U.S. Web Coated (SWOP) v2, from the Device to Simulate drop-down menu, lets you to see how your RGB images will look when they're converted to CMYK for printing. Or you can choose your desktop inkjet printer profile from the Device to Simulate drop-down menu to see how your images will look when printed to that device.

After you select your setup, choose View➪Proof Colors to view the image in your chosen working space. For the most reliable results, use a good-quality monitor and set up a good viewing environment (described earlier in this chapter). Also, keep in mind that although soft proofing is a good thing, it's no substitute for a good-quality hard-copy proof. Some things — such as the type and quality of paper, certain inks, and so on — can't be accurately simulated onscreen.

Photoshop also offers two proof setup settings to view how images will appear to those who are colorblind. Color Blindness Protanopia mimics red-green colorblindness with less sensitivity to red light. Color Blindness Deuteranopia mimics red-green color blindness with less sensitivity to green light.

Chapter 4: Time Travel — Undoing in Photoshop

In This Chapter

✔ Undoing and redoing

✔ Reverting to the state you last saved

✔ Exploring the History panel

✔ Viewing an image's states

✔ Looking at the History options

✔ Taking snapshots

✔ Erasing with the Erase to History option

✔ Brushing back in time with the History Brush tool

*W*hen Thomas Wolfe said, "You can't go home again," he wasn't talking about Photoshop. If you change your mind about something you do and want to return to your starting place (or any point in between), Photoshop is very forgiving. My favorite image editor offers many different ways to reverse actions, undo what you did, reapply effects you've cancelled, and change your mind as often as a new apartment owner deciding where to put the couch.

This chapter helps you master Photoshop's powerful time-traveling features, including the Undo command, the History panel, and such tools as the Art History Brush and the Eraser.

Undoing What's Done with the Undo Command

Your first stop in your journey through time is the Undo/Redo command. This command simply reverses the last action you took or reapplies that action if you just undid it. For example, if you apply a brush stroke that you don't like, use Undo to remove that stroke. Then, if you immediately change your mind, you can redo it by using the command again.

To undo your last action, choose Edit⊃Undo or simply press Ctrl+Z (⌘+Z on the Mac).

Press the Undo/Redo shortcut keys rapidly to toggle an effect on and off if you want to compare the before and after effects quickly. When you decide which way to go, stop toggling. This procedure works best if you press Ctrl+Z (⌘+Z on the Mac) to apply both Undo and Redo.

The Undo/Redo command works for only a single command. If you do anything else after you apply a command and then change your mind about that command, you have to resort to one of the other time-travel techniques described later in this chapter.

If you can't undo or redo an action, Undo/Redo is gray in the menu, showing that it's unavailable. However, you can often use the History panel to remove the action. See the section "Working with the Almighty History Panel," later in this chapter, for details on how to use the History panel.

If you want to free the memory that the Undo command uses, choose Edit⊃Purge⊃Undo. If the item is gray, the buffer is already empty. You can't undo this action, so do it only if Photoshop is acting sluggish.

Reverting to What's Saved

Revert replaces your current file with the last saved file, effectively wiping out everything you've done since you last saved the file. You can revert to the last version of the file by choosing File⊃Revert. Although you lose all the changes in your current file when the last saved version replaces it onscreen, the Revert command is stored on the History panel. You can find out how to remove a command from the History panel in the section "Introducing History panel options and tools," later in this chapter.

Working with the Almighty History Panel

Undoing and redoing commands, explained in the preceding sections, are kid's stuff compared to the power of the almighty History panel. (Choose Window⊃History.) Think of this tool as a recipe that lists the steps (how many appear depends on what you specify in your preferences, which I talk about in the following section) that you took to cook up your image in its present state. By using the History panel, you can browse through the recipe and return to any step in the list to begin work anew from that point.

Understanding states and snapshots

You can't go too far in your use of the History panel without understanding two important concepts, as well as how the concepts are different

✔ **States:** *States* is just another way of saying steps. At any given point in your image-editing activities, Photoshop saves your edits into states.

By default, Photoshop remembers 20 states for an image. You can increase the number to as many as 1,000 in the Performance Preferences dialog box. Choose Edit➪Preferences➪Performance (or Photoshop➪ Preferences➪Performance in Mac OS X) and enter a new value (or move the slider) in the History States box.

Boosting this number can eat up your available memory quite quickly. You may want to leave the states set to 20 and save snapshots of your image, as I describe in the section "Taking Snapshots," later in this chapter. When you reach the limit of 20 steps, the oldest step (at the top of the list) is deleted to make room for the latest one at the bottom.

✔ **Snapshots:** You can save temporary copies of an image at any state. This enables you to revert to a previous state any time during your work session by selecting a particular snapshot to work from. See "Taking Snapshots," later in this chapter, to find out how to use snapshots.

When you have these concepts down, you can get to the business of understanding how the tools in the History panel use states and snapshots to help you go back in time (and back to the future again) to undo, redo, and modify each miniscule edit you make to your images.

Introducing History panel options and tools

The History panel has several useful components you should know about, as shown in Figure 4-1:

✔ **Snapshot thumbnail:** This miniature image of the saved snapshot image gives you a copy of your document that has all the current states included. (For more on snapshots, see the section "Taking Snapshots," later in this chapter.)

✔ **Source state column:** Click in this column to the left of a particular snapshot or state, and when you begin painting with the History Brush tool or erasing with the Erase to History option, Photoshop uses the snapshot or state that you select in this column as the source.

✔ **History state:** A particular step or edit in your document's list of steps. An icon appears in this column showing what kind of action occurred in that state.

Source state column

Source state

Snapshot thumbnail

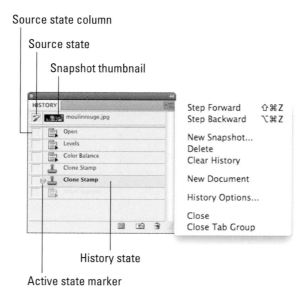

History state

Active state marker

Figure 4-1: The indispensable History panel lets you undo up to 1,000 steps.

✔ **Active state marker:** This slider points to the currently active state. You can drag it up or down to change the current state.

✔ **Create new document from current state:** Click this icon to create a duplicate copy of your image at the currently selected state. Your new document starts out with a nearly empty history list. The only state that's present is Duplicate State.

✔ **Create new snapshot:** Click this icon to store an image of your document, preserving all the states listed.

✔ **Delete current state:** Click this icon to remove a selected state.

✔ **Undone states:** These gray states are undone when you select an earlier state in the list.

✔ **Open state:** The original document that you first opened.

✔ **Current history state:** The active state that you've selected in the history list.

Viewing an Image's Various States

You can move back to any state listed in the History panel, remove a state to cancel a step, or perform other time-travel stunts by using the History panel. The following sections outline some basic time-shifting techniques that you can use.

Going back to a particular state

To go back in time and resume editing at a particular point, just click the state to which you want to return. All subsequent states appear gray, or *undone*. Then, begin editing your image as usual. As soon as you perform a new step, all the states that follow your reentry point vanish. It's like applying the Undo command (Ctrl+Z on a PC, ⌘+Z on the Mac) to a group of steps with one click.

If you intentionally (or accidentally) begin editing while a previous state is highlighted, and then you change your mind, immediately undo your action — press Ctrl+Z (⌘+Z on the Mac). The subsequent steps that were removed reappear.

Reviewing your image at different states

To review how your image looked at previous states, just click the state that you want to see. (You can also drag the active state marker up and down the list.) The document image immediately changes to reflect that earlier state. You can move back and forth between any two points in the history list, if you like. As long as you don't make any editing changes during your time-traveling jaunt, your current history list is preserved.

Purging and clearing all states

To remove a state and all the steps that follow it, select the state and then press the Delete key or click the trash can icon.

You can clear all the states except the most recent one from the panel by selecting Clear History from the panel pop-up menu. (Click the down arrow in the upper-right corner of the panel to make this menu appear.) All your snapshots will be preserved. You can undo your clearing only if you choose Edit⇨Undo immediately after you execute the command. You can also delete all the states except the last one in the history list and keep the snapshots you've saved by choosing Edit⇨Purge⇨Histories. You can clear or purge your history list when you no longer need the states it includes — if you either want to save memory or return to the original state of your document. When purging, just be sure that you really, seriously are not interested in going back later to make changes because you can't undo this command.

Navigating the history list

You can move up and down the history list, even if the list isn't visible on your screen. Choose Edit⇨Step Forward to move forward in the history list and Edit⇨Step Backward to move back. The best way to access these commands is to use the keyboard shortcuts:

- Press Alt+Ctrl+Z (Option+⌘+Z on the Mac) to move backward (up the history list).

- Press Shift+Ctrl+Z (Shift+⌘+Z on the Mac) to move forward (down the history list).

Looking at the History Options Dialog Box

The History panel has five options that change its behavior. To access these options, select History Options from the History panel pop-up menu, which opens the History Options dialog box, shown in Figure 4-2. For a rundown of the various settings, see Table 4-1.

Figure 4-2: Change the History panel's behavior in this dialog box.

Table 4-1	Setting History Panel Options	
Option	*What It Does*	*Recommended Setting*
Automatically Create First Snapshot	This option, selected by default, tells Photoshop to create a snapshot of the image when you first open it, before you make any changes. You can return to this snapshot at any time by clicking its name in the History panel.	Checked. Consider it free insurance — you can always return to your original image, if necessary.
Automatically Create New Snapshot When Saving	This option tells Photoshop to create a new snapshot each time you save the image.	Depends. If you're like me and save every couple of minutes, you probably don't want to select this option; otherwise, you end up with a panel filled with unwanted snapshots.
Allow Non-Linear History	Selecting this option lets you edit or delete a state without removing all the states that follow it. When the Non-Linear History capability is active, you can edit an intermediate state in the history list, leaving the other steps below it unchanged.	Unchecked. Use this option with caution because steps are interdependent. A change that you remove may form the basis for another edit later on, so deleting it can cause weird results.

Option	What It Does	Recommended Setting
Show New Snapshot Dialog by Default	This option ensures that Photoshop asks you to name any new snapshot that you create.	Checked. Applying names to snapshots makes remembering the state of the image when you saved the snapshot easy. Even if this option is unchecked, however, you can still access the dialog box by pressing the Alt (Option on the Mac) key when you click the camera icon.
Make Layer Visibility Changes Undoable	This option records the toggling on and off of the visibility of your layers.	Unchecked. Showing and hiding layers doesn't affect image pixels.

Taking Snapshots

Snapshots are duplicates of your image at a particular point in time, similar to saving a document with an alternate name to create a copy of that document. (Photoshop automatically names the snapshots Snapshot 1, Snapshot 2, and so on.) However, snapshots are temporary copies, available only during your current work session.

You can use snapshots to alternate between versions of an image when you're making major changes. For example, if you plan to apply several filters and adjustments that will drastically modify your image, you may want to save a snapshot before you apply the filters and adjustments and then save another snapshot after you apply them. You can then click either snapshot to switch from one version to the other quickly, as shown in Figure 4-3.

The second you close a file, the snapshots you've taken disappear forever. If you want a more permanent way to save versions of your file, see the Layer Comps panel discussion in Book V, Chapter 2.

Digital Vision

Figure 4-3: Use snapshots to compare before and after images when you apply a filter or adjustment.

To take a snapshot, follow these steps:

1. **Select the state at which you want to take a snapshot.**

   You can select the most recent state that has all your latest editing changes, or you can select an earlier state. Just make sure that you take the snapshot before your desired state is eliminated.

2. **Select New Snapshot from the panel pop-up menu.**

   You can also click the New Snapshot icon at the bottom of the History panel. Either way, the New Snapshot dialog box opens. Photoshop names your first snapshot Snapshot 1.

3. **In the Name box, enter a name for the snapshot.**

   Use a name that helps you remember the contents of that particular snapshot.

You can add or change the name of the snapshot later by double-clicking the snapshot name in the history list and typing the new name.

4. If you like, select a snapshot subtype in the From menu.

Full Document, which is the default, creates a snapshot of all the layers in the image at the currently selected state. This keeps all of your separate layers. You can also take a snapshot of merged layers. This merges all of your layers into a single layer. Finally, you can just snap the Current Layer. Book V explains working with layers.

5. Click OK to create the snapshot.

If you no longer need a snapshot, you can select the snapshot and click the trash can icon, drag the snapshot to the trash can icon, or select Delete from the History panel's options menu.

Restoring Part of an Image

Although the concept may seem like quantum physics, you can erase and brush on an image by using previously saved states or snapshots.

What? Okay, let me try this again. You can erase portions of an image to a history state, as well as paint on an image from a history state. So, traveling through time doesn't have to be an all-or-nothing experience; you can erase or paint portions of a different state onto your currently active state.

For example, suppose you apply a blur filter to a face and decide later that you want to make the eyes sharp again. You can use the Eraser tool with the Erase to History option selected, or use the History Brush tool, to paint over the eyes with information from an earlier state before you blurred them, as shown in Figure 4-4.

Using the Eraser with the Erase to History option

Use the Eraser with the Erase to History option when a portion of an earlier state or snapshot contains information that you want to include in an image that you've extensively edited. To erase and restore to a portion of an earlier state or snapshot, just follow these steps:

1. In the History panel, click in the far-left column of the state or snapshot that you want to use as the source for the Eraser tool with the Erase to History option.

A brush icon appears to the left of the state's listing in the History panel, indicating that Photoshop will use this state as the source for the Eraser tool with the Erase to History option.

Purestock

Figure 4-4: You can easily restore portions of your edited image to an earlier state.

2. Select the Eraser tool.

You can also press the E key to access the tool.

3. Select the Erase to History option on the Options bar.

4. Select any other Eraser tool options that you want to use, such as Brush size and type, Mode, Opacity and Flow percentages, or Airbrush.

The Mode options include a Brush, Pencil, or Block tip for your brush. For details on the other options, see "Selective Erasing with the Eraser Tools" in Book VI, Chapter 2.

5. Select your desired layer in the Layers panel and, in the History panel, select the state that you want to erase to.

6. Drag your eraser on the portion of the image you want to erase.

Photoshop removes the image in the layer and replaces it with the image in the state that you specified as the source in Step 1.

You can convert the Eraser tool so that it temporarily uses the Erase to History option by holding down the Alt key (Option key on the Mac) while you erase or paint.

Using the History Brush tool

You can use the History Brush tool to apply an image area from a different state or snapshot to your current state. Use this tool to restore a portion of an image to an earlier state, while leaving the rest of the heavily modified image alone. The History Brush has an advantage over the Eraser tool because the History Brush gives you access to many blend modes. Just follow these steps to use the History Brush:

1. **In the History panel, click in the far-left column of the state or snapshot that you want to use as the source for the History Brush tool. (Refer to Figure 4-1.)**

   A brush icon appears in the column, indicating that Photoshop will use this state as the source for the History Brush tool.

   In my example, I chose my original image just after I cropped it.

2. **Select the History Brush tool in the Tools panel.**

   You can also press Y to select the tool.

3. **On the Options bar, select any other brush options that you want to use — such as Brush size and type, Mode, Opacity and Flow percentages, and Airbrush.**

   For details on the brush options, see Book IV, Chapter 1.

4. **Select your desired layer in the Layers panel and, in the History panel, select the state that you want to paint back to.**

5. **Drag with the History Brush tool to paint over the portion of the image you want to restore.**

   Photoshop paints over the image in the layer with the image from the state you specified as the source in Step 1.

   In Figure 4-5, I painted my original faces by using a 10–15% Opacity setting over my Water Paper-filtered image.

Figure 4-5: Painting with the History Brush tool

Using the Fill with History feature

If you can easily select the area that you want to replace with a specific state, you can use the Fill with History feature. Suppose you don't like the sky in a particular image. You select the sky area and then add clouds by using the Clouds filter. After you make those changes, you want to put the original sky back, but you don't want to reverse any of the other edits you performed. Just follow these steps to replace an area by using the Fill with History feature:

1. **Click in the far-left column of the state you want to use as the source for the Fill with History function in the History panel.**

   For example, select the state that has the original sky.

2. **With your current state active, use your favorite selection tools to select the area that you want to replace.**

   For example, if you remembered to save your original sky selection before you added clouds, you can choose Select⇨Load Selection and retrieve that selection. Book III covers selection tools in detail.

3. **Choose Edit⇨Fill and then select History from the Use pop-up menu.**

4. **Click OK to fill the selection with the image area from the selected state.**

Using the Art History Brush tool

The Art History Brush tool is an interesting variation on the plain old History Brush tool. Both tools paint over an image by using information from a previous state. The Art History Brush tool, however, includes several choices on the Options bar that let you apply brush-stroke effects to your image when you paint:

- ✔ **Style:** The Style menu contains various-shaped brush stroke styles, such as Tight Short, Loose Medium, Dab, or Loose Curl.

- ✔ **Area:** This option controls the area that the paint stroke covers, independent of the brush size you select. The larger the brush size, the more area it covers.

- ✔ **Tolerance:** This option adjusts the amount of the change applied to your image. A low tolerance value lets you apply strokes anywhere in the image, regardless of color values. A high tolerance value limits Art History strokes to areas that are very different from the source state or snapshot, making your image less dramatically different from the original.

You can use these options to create an interesting hand-painted effect, which you can control quite easily after you have some practice.

When Photoshop won't let you go back

Sometimes, you may see a No symbol (a slashed circle) when you try to use the Eraser with the Erase to History option, the History Brush tool, or the Fill with History command. Your current image must be the same file size (have the same number of pixels) as the state you're trying to go back to. Such actions as cropping, trimming, using the Image Size or Canvas Size commands, or rotating any amount other than 180 degrees can prevent you from going back to a previous state. However, if you happen to have a square image, you can still use the Eraser with the Erase to History option if you rotate that image in 90-degree increments.

The Art History Brush tool often works best when you use a state that's quite different from the state you're painting over. For example, you can apply a heavy filter that makes the image almost unrecognizable and then use that filtered image to paint with the Art History Brush tool. You can even completely fill an image with color or texture and then work with that.

To paint with the Art History Brush tool, follow these steps:

1. **Apply any effects and filters that you want to use to a chosen state.**

   See Book V, Chapter 4 for the details on effects. See Book VII, Chapters 1 and 2 for filter info.

   I started by applying a Rough Pastels filter to my beach scene.

2. **Click in the far-left column in the History panel to select the state that you want to use as the source for the Art History Brush tool.**

3. **Select the Art History Brush tool from the Tools panel.**

   You can also press Y to select it.

4. **Select from the choices on the Options bar.**

   Several of the options, such as Brush, Mode, and Opacity, are similar to the options available with the ordinary Brush tool. The new options are Style, Area, and Tolerance, explained earlier.

5. **Paint with the brush to get the effect you want, as shown in Figure 4-6.**

Don't forget that you can use the History panel to reverse Art History strokes if you change your mind about them!

Purestock

Figure 4-6: The Art History Brush tool lets you paint back to history with artistic flair.

Chapter 5: Creating Actions for Productivity and Fun

In This Chapter

✐ Working with actions in the Actions panel

✐ Playing preset actions

✐ Recording a new action

✐ Editing and organizing actions

✐ Using actions sets

✐ Processing batches of files

✐ Creating droplet applets

*P*ractice makes perfect — but when repeating the same steps in Photoshop over and over, the result is often tedium and impatience. You don't want to have to reinvent the wheel each time you go for a spin around the block, so why repeat the actions that carry out specific tasks in Photoshop if you don't have to? Photoshop lets you record steps by using a fast and fun feature called Actions. Photoshop also has presets for popular actions, such as creating a wood frame, simulating water reflections, or providing a molten-lead look. This chapter shows you how to take advantage of Photoshop's presets, as well as its macro recording and editing capabilities.

Using the Actions Panel

Not surprisingly, Photoshop has a panel dedicated to the automation of various chores. To view the Actions panel, choose Window⇨Actions (or press F9 on a PC, Opt+F9 on the Mac) or click the Actions icon in the panel dock. You can view the Actions panel in two modes, Button and List. Each mode is useful in its own way. You can access the mode you're not currently using via the Actions panel pop-up menu:

✐ **Button mode:** A convenient, compact mode that hides all the inner workings of the actions, presenting only a list of buttons that you can click to trigger a particular macro. Button mode is fast and easy; just click and go.

✔ **List mode:** Shown in Figure 5-1 is the default display in which each action appears as a folder-like heading. You can open a heading to reveal all the steps within that action or collapse the heading to hide those steps. You need to be in List mode when you record an action and when you edit individual steps. List mode also lets you perform only a select number of the steps in an action.

When you're working in List mode, the Actions panel has these three columns:

✔ **The left column:** Contains check boxes that you can select or deselect to include or exclude actions (or steps within an action).

Figure 5-1: The Actions panel lets you create and store actions — a set of recorded steps that automate repetitive tasks.

✔ **The middle column:** Toggles on or off whether actions display dialog boxes. Some actions include options that you can select while running the macro. For example, the Vignette (Selection) action, which creates a faded frame around a selection, includes a dialog box that lets you specify the width of the fading. This dialog box appears only after you select this middle column; if you deselect the column, the action uses a default value. Adobe refers to this setting as Modal control.

✔ **The right column:** This widest column shows the name of the set of actions (folder icon) or the individual action. Click the right-pointing arrow to the left of the action's name to reveal the individual steps of the action. If you've assigned any keyboard shortcuts to your action, they also appear in this column.

Introducing Preset Actions

Preset actions are the actions created by the kind folks at Adobe that come with Photoshop. You can also get other preset actions from Adobe's Web site, as well as from third-party vendors. You may need to load an action into the panel so that it's ready to use. After an action is loaded, you can apply all the steps in that action in one fell swoop by playing the action. The following sections explain how to work with preset actions in more detail.

Loading preset actions

Photoshop's preset actions are located in a series of files in the Actions folder. The default actions load by, um, default when you first open Photoshop. However, you can open and use other preset actions. They include Frames (for putting frames around your images), Text Effects (for enhancing your text), and Image Effects (which let you give your image the appearance of being aged or neon, for example), among others.

Photoshop CS5 adds a couple new preset actions. Using LAB-Black and White Technique is a nice way to convert a color image into gray-scale. Star Trails Rotation creates circular, glowing motion trails, as shown in Figure 5-2.

Follow these steps to load preset actions:

1. **In the Actions panel, click the panel pop-up menu arrow and select Load Actions.**

   In the Load dialog box, Photoshop opens the Actions folder in the Presets folder. This folder contains several sets of actions presets. If the folder is empty,

Book II
Chapter 5

Creating Actions for Productivity and Fun

Original

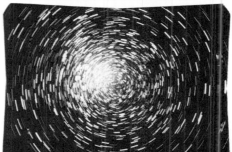

Star Trails Rotation applied

NASA

Figure 5-2: Photoshop comes with a wide array of interesting preset actions that can quickly transform your image.

navigate to `C:\Program Files\Adobe\Adobe Photoshop CS5\Presets\Actions`. (On the Mac, go to `Macintosh HD\Applications\Adobe Photoshop CS5\Presets\Actions`.)

2. **Select one of the actions sets.**

3. **Click the Load button.**

Easier, Photoshop's additional actions presets also appear at the bottom of the Actions panel pop-up menu. You can add any of them to your current list of actions by selecting the set's name.

The new actions presets appear in the Actions panel below the default actions. You can show or hide the actions in Default Actions or any of the other sets by clicking the expand/collapse arrow in the third column.

You can also make actions available — or unavailable — for an entire set by clicking the first column in the Actions panel to the left of the actions set's folder icon.

Here are some other tidbits about loading and working with preset actions:

- ✔ Any actions sets that you create (as I describe in the section "Creating and Saving Actions Sets," later in this chapter) appear in the pop-up menu if you save them in the Photoshop Actions folder. If you save them somewhere other than the Actions folder, you can navigate to that folder by using the usual file navigation commands.

- ✔ To remove the existing actions and replace them with the set you're loading, select Replace Actions from the panel pop-up menu.

- ✔ To reset the Actions panel to the Default Actions set (removing all other sets that you may have loaded), select Reset Actions from the panel pop-up menu.

- ✔ To clear all actions from the Actions panel, select Clear All Actions from the panel pop-up menu. (You might want to do this if you're creating your own set of actions from scratch.)

- ✔ To rename an actions set, select it and then select Set Options from the panel pop-up menu.

If you do a Google search for *Photoshop Actions*, you get a barrage of user-created actions, ranging from functional to funky. You can save these actions to your computer so that you can then load them into Photoshop. **Remember:** Check any file that you download from the Internet for viruses and other malware, using an antivirus program or a similar utility.

Playing a preset action

You perform an action on an image by playing that action. To play a preset action, just open the file that you want to apply the action to, and then do one of the following:

- ✔ In Button mode, click the action that you want to play. You don't have any other options.

✔ In List mode, select the action that you want to play, and then click the Play Selection button at the bottom of the Actions panel or select Play from the panel pop-up menu.

If you want to play back just one step of an action (say, for testing purposes), select the step that you want to play in List mode, and then Ctrl-click (⌘-click on the Mac) the Play button in the Actions panel. You can also simply double-click the step in the list while holding down the Ctrl key (the ⌘ key on the Mac).

Creating a New Action

When you create an action, you automate a series of steps. The hardest part about creating a new action is figuring out what functions you want to automate. Think about steps that you carry out over and over, and whether you could be more productive if you had an action that could do them for you. For example, you might want to create your own action to reduce images to a constant width of 500 pixels for display in an eBay auction. However, performing color-correction tasks for your eBay images is more difficult to automate because your images may vary in their original color and contrast.

Note that you can now even record your custom print settings as part of your action. This can save loads of time, if you have taken a bit of time to set up custom print settings that you want to use time and time again.

After you decide what you want to automate, examine the actual steps so that you can record them. After you record the steps, creating a new action involves little more than starting Photoshop's macro recorder and carrying out the steps that you want to include in the action.

While you're working out the kinks in your action, I highly recommend that you do so on a *copy* of your original file. That way, if things go awry, your original file is safe from harm.

Here are the steps to follow to create a new action:

1. **Open an image.**

2. **Display the Actions panel in List mode by unchecking Button Mode in the panel pop-up menu.**

3. **Click the Create New Action button at the bottom of the Actions panel.**

   You can also select New Action from the panel pop-up menu.

   The New Action dialog box opens, as shown in Figure 5-3.

Figure 5-3: Name your new action and specify your other options.

4. **In the Name text box, enter a name for the action.**

5. **In the Set pop-up menu, select the actions set in which you want to save the new action.**

   An *actions set* is merely a folder that contains individual actions for organizational purposes. Feel free to use an existing set or create your own.

6. **(Optional) To associate the action with a function-key shortcut, select the name of the function key from the Function Key drop-down list.**

   This step associates the action with a button on the keyboard. Associating an action with a function key, such as F2, F3, and so on, can cut down the time it takes you to perform common actions. Try to use keyboard shortcuts that aren't already associated with other Photoshop tasks.

   Select the Shift or Ctrl (Shift or ⌘ on the Mac) check box to use either one of these keys with the function key.

   Any keyboard shortcut that you assign to an action overrides the default function already assigned to the keyboard shortcut. A few exceptions exist in which the operating system wins in the case of a conflict. You can revert to the original shortcut by choosing Edit⇨Keyboard Shortcuts. See Book I, Chapter 5 for details.

   To avoid conflicts, Mac users can check for system keyboard shortcuts. To do so, look under the Keyboard Shortcuts tab in the Keyboard & Mouse section of the Systems Preferences under the Apple menu.

7. **In the Color drop-down list, select a color to mark your action in Button mode.**

   This option enables you to group related actions by color.

8. **Click the Record button in the New Action dialog box to begin recording.**

9. **Carry out all the steps that you want to record.**

10. **Click the Stop Playing/Recording button at the bottom of the Actions panel to finish the action.**

    Your new action appears in the Actions panel, in both List and Button modes.

Editing and Managing Actions

After you create a new action, you can try it out by opening an image and clicking the Play button in the Actions panel. If the action doesn't perform the way you expect, you may need to edit your action to fine-tune it. You also may need to edit an action to add features or change the action's behavior in some way. (For example, you might decide that you want your resizing action to change the size to 45 percent, rather than 50 percent.) Photoshop enables you to edit your actions fairly easily. However, certain actions won't run on certain files. For example, if your action involves adjusting the opacity of a layer and you run it on an image without layers, it won't work. You have to include a step that creates a layer first.

You have a lot of editing options; you can change the action's name, keyboard shortcut, or color coding. Just double-click the action name in the Actions panel and then enter a new name; or select the action, select Action Options from the panel pop-up menu, and change the information in the dialog box, as desired. You can also hold down the Alt key (Option key on the Mac) and double-click the action's name in the Actions panel to open the Actions Options dialog box.

Rerecording an action

As easy as editing an action is, your best option is often to simply rerecord the action from scratch. If the action isn't long or complex, you can often rerecord it in less time than editing the existing action. You can rerecord an action two ways:

✔ **Create a new action from scratch.** Perform all the steps again to replace the old action with a new one, saving the action with the same (or a different) filename.

✔ **Use the clever Record Again feature.** Photoshop runs through the steps that you already recorded, opening the dialog boxes that you used the first time so that you can enter new values.

This Record Again method is very handy if you want to change only some of the parameters, keeping the steps the same and in the same order. You don't even have to remember what steps you used. Photoshop runs through them for you while you record the steps, or macro, again.

To rerecord a macro with the Record Again option, select the name of the macro that you want to rerecord and select Record Again from the panel pop-up menu. When the different dialog boxes appear, enter the new values that you want and click OK until the macro is finished.

Editing an action

You can edit individual steps of an action. Here are some of the editing changes that you can make:

✔ **Move a step.** To move a step from one place in the action to another, click the step that you want to relocate and drag it to its new place in the action list.

✔ **Add a step in the middle.** To add a new step in the middle of an existing action, select the step that you want to precede the new step. Click the Record button and perform the steps that you want to add. Click the Stop Recording button when you finish.

✔ **Add a step to the end.** To add a new step at the end of an existing action, select the name of the action, click the Record button, and perform the steps that you want to add. Click the Stop Recording button when you finish.

✔ **Remove a step.** Click the step that you want to delete and then drag the step to the trash icon, or click the trash icon and then click OK in the dialog box that appears. (Alt-click the trash icon [Option-click on the Mac] to bypass the dialog box and delete the step without confirmation.) You can also select a step and select Delete from the panel pop-up menu.

✔ **Duplicate a step.** Hold down the Alt key (Option key on the Mac) and drag the step that you want to duplicate to another location in the Actions panel. Photoshop then creates a copy of the step, leaving the original step where it was, as shown in Figure 5-4.

Figure 5-4: Duplicate a step in an action.

Slowing down action playback

When you play back an action to test it, the action may run too quickly for you to see exactly what's going on. To slow things down, select Playback Options from the panel pop-up menu and select a playback speed in the Playback Options dialog box.

Select Accelerated to zip through an action at normal speed, Step by Step to command Photoshop to briefly stop between actions so that you can examine what's happened, or Pause For to create a short pause before moving on. (Make sure that you specify for how many seconds you want to pause.) If you want to get really fancy, you can select the Pause for Audio Annotation check box and use your microphone to describe what each step does.

You can remove or duplicate an entire action by using the procedures described in the preceding list for removing a step or duplicating a step.

Creating and Saving Actions Sets

If you create your own sets of actions, you may want to include them in custom sets that you can load or remove, as needed. Just follow these steps:

1. **Display the Actions panel in List mode.**

2. **Click the Create New Set button in the Actions panel or select New Set from the panel pop-up menu.**

   The New Set dialog box appears.

3. **Enter a name for your actions set in the New Set dialog box and click OK.**

4. **Drag any existing actions that you want to include from their locations in the Actions panel to a new location within your new set folder.**

5. **Create any new actions that you want to include within the new set.**

   See the section "Creating a New Action," earlier in this chapter.

6. **Select the name of the set and choose Save Actions from the panel pop-up menu.**

7. **Save the set in the Actions folder (which you can find in the Presets folder within the Adobe Photoshop CS5 folder).**

**Book II
Chapter 5**

**Creating Actions for
Productivity and Fun**

Batch Processing Actions

Photoshop's Batch feature lets you apply an action to a group of files. Suppose you want to make changes to a series of files. You can open each file in Photoshop, play the desired macro, and then save the file. However, that might take a few minutes (or much longer if you have several files to process). If you want to keep your original file, too, you have to remember to save each file in a new folder. Batch processing can automate tedious chores for you.

To try this useful tool, copy some files (at least five or six) to a new folder and follow these steps:

1. **Make sure that all the files are in a single folder of their own.**

   Any subfolders will be included in that folder.

   Photoshop, by default, works on all the files in a folder. You have to use Adobe Bridge if you want to choose only some of those files by using the Batch feature. You can find out more about Adobe Bridge in Book I, Chapter 4.

2. **Choose File➪Automate➪Batch.**

   The Batch dialog box opens, as shown in Figure 5-5.

3. **In the Set pop-up menu, select the set that contains the action you want to apply.**

   If you have only one set of actions loaded, that set appears by default.

4. **In the Action pop-up menu, select the action that you want to apply.**

5. **In the Source pop-up menu, select Folder.**

Figure 5-5: By batch-processing an action on a group of files, you can take a coffee break and still get work done.

You can also select Opened Files to process files that you already opened in Photoshop, Import to process a series of files captured with your scanner or transferred from your digital camera, or Bridge to process files that you selected in Adobe Bridge.

6. **Click the Choose button, navigate to the folder that you want to use, and click OK (in Windows) or Choose (in Mac OS).**

7. **Select other options in the Source area, as desired.**

   Here's a description of your choices:

   • *Override Action "Open" Commands:* Normally, Photoshop opens each of the files in the selected folder automatically and processes them — so your action doesn't have to contain an Open command. However, if the macro *does* contain an Open command, select this option. With this option active, Photoshop overrides Open commands in the actions that use specific files (rather than batched files).

   • *Include All Subfolders:* Select this option to process files in subfolders within the folder that you specify.

   • *Suppress File Open Options Dialogs:* Select this option to have Photoshop disregard any options that possibly could be selected upon opening a file.

   • *Suppress Color Profile Warnings:* When Photoshop opens a file that contains its own color profile, it asks whether you want to use that profile or Photoshop's default profile. Selecting this check box suppresses that choice; Photoshop always uses its own default color profile. I explain color profiles in Book II, Chapter 2.

8. **In the Destination area, tell Photoshop what to do with each file after the action has been applied to it.**

   Choose one of the following options from the drop-down list:

   - *None:* Leaves the file open on your Photoshop desktop without saving it (unless the action itself contains a Save command).

   - *Save and Close:* Closes the files in the same folder in which Photoshop found them. Your original file is overwritten, so use this option only when you don't want to save the original or you have another copy.

   - *Folder:* Saves the document in a folder.

9. **If you chose Folder in Step 8, click the Choose button and navigate to a destination folder for your files.**

10. **Select the Override Action "Save As" Commands check box to ignore any Save As parameters in the action and use the filenames of the files (as specified in the File Naming section described in Step 11).**

11. **In the File Naming section, specify how you want Photoshop to create the filenames for the new, processed files by selecting options from the drop-down lists.**

    You can select options from six pop-up menus, depending on how long and complicated you want the filenames to be.

    When you process large numbers of files, these naming tools can help you keep track of when and how the files were created.

12. **Select the Windows, Mac OS, or Unix check box to specify what operating system you want the saved filenames to be most compatible with.**

13. **In the Errors pop-up menu, select whether you want Photoshop to stop processing a batch when it encounters an error or whether you want it to simply continue and list the errors in a file. If you select the latter option, click the Save As button and, in the Save dialog box, specify a name and location for the log.**

    If you want to apply several different actions to a set of files or apply the same action to multiple folders of files, just create an action that includes multiple batch-processing directives. To process multiple folders, you can also deposit shortcuts (in Windows) or aliases (in Mac OS) to each of the additional folders in the main source folder, and then select the Include All Subfolders check box in the Source area.

14. **When you finish selecting options in the Batch dialog box, click OK to start the batch processing.**

Creating Droplets

Droplets are drag-and-drop mini-applications — essentially applets — in macro form that can exist outside Photoshop on your desktop, on your taskbar, or within a folder. They're always available, so you can apply them to any image files you want. Think of them as batches waiting to happen.

You just need to drag the file or files that you want to process onto the droplet. Photoshop doesn't even have to be open at the time. When you drop the file or files, the droplet opens Photoshop and carries out the steps in the action embedded in the droplet's instructions. You must use an existing action as the core of the droplet.

To create a droplet, follow these steps:

1. **Choose File⇨Automate⇨Create Droplet.**

   The Create Droplet dialog box opens, as shown in Figure 5-6.

2. **In the Save Droplet In area, click the Choose button and enter a name and location on your hard drive for the droplet application.**

   The location isn't of overriding importance because after you create the droplet, you can drag it to your desktop, a toolbar, or wherever you like.

Figure 5-6: Create and manage your droplets in this dialog box.

   The rest of the Create Droplet dialog box is the same as the Batch dialog box (described in the preceding section), except that you don't have to specify a source. Droplets use the files dropped on them as their source files.

3. **In the Play area, select the actions set, action, and options.**

4. **Select a destination from the Destination pop-up menu.**

5. **Specify any file-naming options you want.**

6. **Specify how Photoshop should process errors.**

7. **When you finish, click OK to create the droplet.**

   To use the droplet, just select the file, files, or folders that you want to process and drag them to the droplet applet.

Book III
Selections

The 5th Wave   By Rich Tennant

"How's it going? You get a handle on that Lasso function yet?"

1 f there's one technique that separates the really good Photoshop users from the wannabes, it's the ability to make a top-notch selection. Pick up any tabloid and you'll agree with me that a lot of those wannabes seem to be gainfully employed! This book, along with Book VI, gives you a complete arsenal of selection commands, methods, and techniques. In this book, I give you information on how to create and modify selections and paths by using various Photoshop tools, such as the Marquee, Lasso, Magic Wand, Quick Selection, and Pen tools. After you go through this book, you can put those wannabes to shame.

Chapter 1: Making Selections

*N*o matter how much you know about Photoshop, if you can't make a good selection, your work will look like it belongs with the creatively (but poorly) composed images in those weekly tabloid rags. You know what I'm talking about — those pictures that go alongside headlines like "Bat Boy Wins Bake-Off" and "Woman with 16 Fingers Wins Typing Contest."

Making accurate selections is the key to creating and editing images effectively so that the result looks flawless. Fortunately, Photoshop offers a bevy of tools and techniques for creating selections, from the simple to the complex. Photoshop offers three basic methods of creating a selection: using a selection tool or method, using the Pen tool, or creating a mask.

In this chapter, I give you the foundation you need to use the selection and Pen tools. In fact, the rest of Book III covers these tools in detail. I cover the more complex method of masking in Book VI.

Defining Selections

The tools I discuss in this chapter require you to take a little piece of a larger image so that you can dig in and make some serious edits. Defining a selection means that you specify which part of the image you want to work with. Everything within a selection is fair game for manipulation and is considered *selected*. Everything outside the selection is protected, or *unselected*. Simple enough, right? Well, you can also have partially selected pixels. Confused yet? A *partially selected* pixel has usually been anti-aliased, feathered, or masked. (I cover anti-aliasing and feathering in the section "Using the Marquee options," later in this chapter. You can find out about masking in Book VI.)

When you use a selection tool to define a selection, a moving dotted outline called a *selection marquee* appears.

Marqueeing When You Can

Photoshop geeks call the selection marquee by a variety of names. Sometimes it's referred to as a marquee, other times as a selection, and you might even hear people call it a selection outline, an outline, selection edges, or just plain old edges. A favorite name for these dotted lines is marching ants. Throughout the book, I usually call them *selection marquees.* Boring? Maybe. Accurate? Yup. Whatever you want to call the selection marquee, how you create one depends on the particular Marquee tool or command you use.

The Marquee tools are the easiest selection tools to use — so I suggest that you use them when you can.

In the Photoshop repertoire of tools, you find four types of Marquee tools: Rectangular Marquee, Elliptical Marquee, Single Row Marquee, and Single Column Marquee.

Using the Rectangular Marquee tool

The Rectangular Marquee tool creates rectangular, including square, selections. Use this tool when you want to zero in on an image, plucking it out of a larger background to provide a better focal point.

Follow these steps to make a selection with the Rectangular Marquee tool:

1. **Select the Rectangular Marquee tool from the Tools panel.**

   You can also use the keyboard shortcut — press the M key.

2. **Click and drag from one corner of the area that you want to select to the opposite corner.**

   While you drag, the selection marquee appears. The marquee follows the movement of your mouse cursor (a crosshair or plus sign icon). For example, in Figure 1-1, I dragged from the lower-left corner to the upper-right corner.

Selection marquee

Purestock

Figure 1-1: The Rectangular Marquee selects part of your image.

3. **Release your mouse button.**

   You now have a full-fledged rectangular selection.

If you want to create a perfect square, hold down the Shift key after you begin dragging. When you have your desired selection, release the mouse button and then the Shift key.

If you want to drag your selection from the center outward, rather than from corner to corner, hold down the Alt (Option on the Mac) key after you begin dragging. When you have your desired selection, release your mouse button and then release the Alt (Option on the Mac) key.

Using the Elliptical Marquee tool

The Elliptical Marquee tool is designed for elliptical, including circular, selections. You can easily select objects such as clocks, balls, and full moons by using this tool.

When you select with the Elliptical Marquee tool, you don't drag from corner to corner per se; you drag from one corner of the ellipsis's bounding box to the other, which makes the process a little tougher. Here are the steps:

1. **Select the Elliptical Marquee tool from the Marquee flyout menu in the Tools panel.**

   You can also use the keyboard shortcut. If the Elliptical Marquee tool is visible, press the M key. If the Rectangular Marquee is visible, you must press Shift+M.

2. **Position the crosshair near the area that you want to select and then drag around your desired element.**

   While you drag, the selection marquee appears.

   You may find it easier to create an elliptical selection by holding down the Alt (Option on the Mac) key and dragging from the center outward. First, click the mouse button, and then before you move the mouse, hold down Alt (Option on the Mac) and drag. Release your mouse and then the key when you have your desired selection. If you want to draw from the center out and want a perfect circle, hold down the Shift key, as well. When you have your desired selection, release your mouse button and then the Shift+Alt (Shift+Option on the Mac) keys. This technique works for creating squares, also.

3. **When you're satisfied with your selection, release your mouse button.**

   Your elliptical selection is alive and well, as shown in Figure 1-2.

   • If you need to move the selection marquee to better center your selection, click and drag inside the marquee.

- You can move a selection with any of the Marquee tools by pressing the spacebar while you're drawing.

- If the selection isn't quite the right shape and size, jump to Book III, Chapter 2 to find out how to make perfect selections.

Using the Single Column and Single Row Marquee tools

The Single Row and Single Column Marquee tools select a single row or single column of pixels. If you don't go blind using them, these tools can occasionally come in handy for selecting and repairing a thin scratch or fold line on an image, or for getting rid of an artifact, such as a colored line, that has somehow appeared on a scanned image. (You can find out more about making repairs in Book VIII.)

Photodisc

Figure 1-2: The Elliptical Marquee is the tool of choice for selecting round objects.

To use either of these tools, click either the row or column of pixels that you want to work on. You don't have to do any dragging, but it does help to zoom into your image so that you can better position the tool on the offending row or column.

For more on zooming, see Book I, Chapter 4. Check out Figure 1-3 to get familiar with a single-row selection.

The Single Row and Single Column Marquee tools don't have keyboard shortcuts, so you're stuck with having to click the tools to select them.

Using the Marquee options

If drawing from the center outward or creating a perfect circle or square doesn't give you enough control, you may want to look at the marquee settings provided by the Options bar. These options allow you to make selections that are even more precise by specifying exact measurements.

You must select the options on the Options bar *before* you make your selection with the Marquee tools.

Figure 1-3: The Single Row Marquee tool selects just one row of pixels.

For now, you can ignore the first five icons on the left side of the Options bar, as shown in Figure 1-4. The first icon has to do with tool presets, which I cover in Book I, Chapter 2. The next four icons are the selection-option icons (which I discuss in Book III, Chapter 3).

Figure 1-4: Specify all your marquee settings on the Options bar.

Here's the lowdown on each of the remaining options:

✐ **Feather:** *Feathering* softens, or feathers, the edges of a selection. The amount of softening depends on the radius — the higher the radius, the softer the edge, as shown in Figure 1-5. The radius measures how far in all directions the feather effect extends.

You can use feathering to create a subtle and natural transition between selections or to create a special effect in which an image slowly fades out to the background or to transparency. To feather while you're selecting, select the Feather option on the Options bar before you use the Marquee tools. You can feather a selection after the fact by using the Select➪Modify sub-menu. Check out Book III, Chapter 2 for more feathering details.

Feather radius 4 pixels

Feather radius 20 pixels

Corbis Digital Stock

Figure 1-5: Applying a feather to your selection blurs the edges.

✔ **Anti-Alias:** Whereas feathering completely blurs edges, anti-aliasing just slightly softens the edge of an elliptical selection so that very hard, jagged edges aren't quite so prominent, as shown in Figure 1-6. You don't have an option in which you can enter a pixel value for anti-aliasing. An anti-aliased edge is always 1 pixel wide.

For the most part, I recommend keeping the Anti-Alias option selected, especially if you plan to create composite images. Anti-aliasing helps create natural-looking blends between multiple selections. However, if want a crisp, linear edge, deselect this option.

✔ **Style:** The Style drop-down list contains these three settings:

• *Normal:* This setting enables you to freely drag a selection to any desired dimension.

- *Fixed Aspect Ratio:* This option allows you to specify a ratio of width to height in a selection. For example, if you enter 2 for width and 1 for height, you *always* get a marquee selection that's twice as wide as it is high, no matter what the size. If you enter 1 for both dimensions, you get perfect circles or squares.

- *Fixed Size:* Select this option to specify exact values for the Width and Height. This option comes in handy when several images need to be the same exact size, such as in a row of headshots in a corporate brochure.

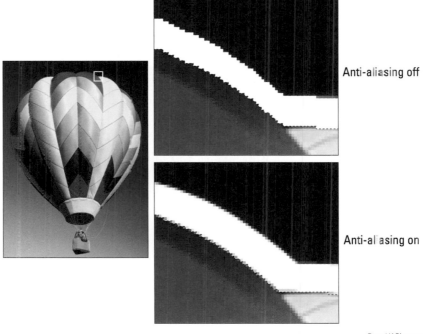

Anti-aliasing off

Anti-aliasing on

Figure 1-6: Anti-aliasing slightly softens your selection edges.

✔ **Width and Height:** When you select a Fixed Size from the Style drop-down list, you can enter values in the Width and Height text boxes. To swap the Width and Height values, click the double-headed arrow button.

Even though the default unit of measurement in the Width and Height text boxes is pixels (px for short), you can enter any unit of measurement that Photoshop recognizes — pixels, inches, centimeters, millimeters, points, picas, or percents. After the number, simply type the word or abbreviation of your desired unit of measurement. Photoshop even lets you enter mixed units of measurements, so if you want a selection 100 pixels by 1.25 inches, you can specify that.

✔ **Refine Edge:** Although you probably won't need to fine-tune a simple marquee selection, that's what this option does. You can apply Refine Edges to any selection, and it appears on the Options bar of the Marquee, Lasso, Magic Wand, and Quick Selection (where it'll come in handy) tools. You can even use it to refine a layer mask. (See Book V, Chapter 3 for more on layer masks.) You can also apply this command to any existing selection by choosing Select⇨Refine Edge.

Here's the lowdown on this option's settings (shown in Figure 1-7), which are greatly improved in CS5:

- *View Mode:* Choose a mode from the pop-up menu to preview your selection. For example, Marching Ants shows the moving marquee, Overlay displays the red overlay you get when working in Quick Mask mode, and On Black and On White show the selection against a black or white background. Hover your cursor over each mode to get a tooltip. Press F to cycle through the various modes. Show Original shows the image without a selection preview. Show Radius displays the image with the selection border.

- *Smart Radius:* Select this option to have Photoshop automatically adjust the radius for hard and soft edges near your selection border.

- *Radius:* Specify the size of the selection border you will refine. Increase the radius to improve the edge of areas with soft transitions or a lot of detail. Move the slider while looking at your selection to find a good setting.

- *Smooth:* Smoothes out jigs and jags along the selection edge.

- *Feather:* Move the slider to create an increasingly softer, more blurred edge.

- *Contrast:* Removes artifacts while tightening soft edges by increasing the contrast. Try using the Smart Radius option first before playing with Contrast.

- *Shift Edge:* Decreases or increases your selection border. Slightly decreasing your selection border can help to *defringe* (eliminate undesirable background pixels) your selection edges.

- *Decontaminate Colors:* Replaces background fringe with the colors of your selected element. Note that because decontamination changes the colors of some of the pixels, you will have to output to, or create, another layer or document to preserve your current layer. To see the decontamination in action, choose Reveal Layer for your View mode.

- *Amount:* Changes the level of decontamination.

- *Output To:* Choose whether you want to output your refined, decontaminated selection to a selection on your current layer, layer mask, layer, layer with layer mask, new document, or new document with layer mask.

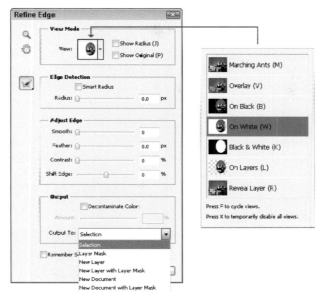

Figure 1-7: Fine-tune your selections with Refine Edges.

- *Refine Radius tool:* Brush around your border to adjust the area you are refining. To understand exactly what area is being included or excluded, change your View mode to Marching Ants. Use the right and left brackets to decrease and increase the brush size.

- *Zoom tool:* Enables you to zoom into your image to see the effects of your settings.

- *Hand tool:* Lets you pan around your document window to see the effects of your settings in various portions of your image.

**Book III
Chapter 1**

Making Selections

Lassoing (When You Can't Marquee)

Unfortunately, not much in life is perfectly rectangular or elliptical. Most of the time, you have to deal with irregular shapes that have *extrusions* and *protrusions* (otherwise known as bumps or bulges) of some sort. That's where the Lasso tools come in handy. This group of tools allows you to make freeform selections.

Photoshop offers three Lasso tools: the Lasso tool itself (which I call the regular Lasso to distinguish it from the others), the Polygonal Lasso tool, and the Magnetic Lasso tool. Each of the Lasso tools has its own special purpose in the realm of freeform selections. But, in the category of simplicity, the Lasso tools are almost as easy to use as the Marquee tools. You just have to drag around the part of the image that you want to select. Just don t indulge in too much caffeine. A steady lasso hand is a good lasso hand.

The selection you make is only as good as how accurately you can trace around your desired element. If you don't make an exact selection the first time around, you can always go back and make corrections (which I cover in Book III, Chapter 3).

If, when making a selection, you find yourself fighting with your mouse (and losing), you may want to invest in a digital drawing tablet, such as a Wacom tablet. Using the stylus and the tablet can make mastering tools such as the Lasso a whole lot easier.

The Lasso and Polygonal Lasso tools both have only three choices on the Options bar to worry about — Feather, Anti-Aliased, and Refine Edges. These options work exactly the way they do with the Marquee tools. To find out more, check out the earlier section "Using the Marquee options."

To make a selection by using the Lasso tool, follow these steps:

1. **Select the Lasso tool from the Tools panel.**

   The tool looks like (well, yeah) a rope. You can also use the keyboard shortcut; press the L key.

2. **Position the cursor somewhere on the edge of the element that you want to select.**

   The *hot spot* (the lead point) of the Lasso cursor is the end of the rope. If you need a little visual assistance, press your Caps Lock key, which switches your cursor to a crosshair.

   Zoom in on the image if the element and the background don't have a lot of contrast.

   In my example, I started at the top of the butte, as shown in Figure 1-8.

3. **Trace around the element and try to capture only what you want to retain in your selection.**

   While you trace, a line forms that follows the movement of your mouse.

   Don't release your mouse button until you complete the selection by returning to the starting point to close the loop. When you release your mouse button, Photoshop thinks you're done and closes the selection, as shown in Figure 1-9.

4. **Continue tracing until you return to your starting point; release the mouse button.**

   Recognizing that you're now done, Photoshop presents you with a selection marquee that matches your Lasso line. (See Figure 1-10.)

Lasso cursor

Corbis Digital Stock

Figure 1-8: The Lasso tool is for freeform selections.

Closed selection marquee

Corbis Digital Stock

Figure 1-9: Don't release your mouse button too soon.

Selected area

Corbis Digital Stock

Figure 1-10: After tracing around your object, release your mouse, and Photoshop presents you with an accurate selection marquee.

Selecting straight sides with the Polygonal Lasso tool

Whereas the regular Lasso tool is great for selecting undulating, curvy elements, the Polygonal Lasso tool shines when it comes to the more regimented, straight-sided subjects, such as city skylines, buildings, and stairways.

Unlike the regular Lasso tool, the Polygonal Lasso tool has rubber band-like qualities, and instead of dragging, you click and release the mouse button at the corners of the object that you're selecting. It's like digital connect-the-dots. (Bonus: Less manual dexterity required.)

The following steps show you how to select with the Polygonal Lasso tool:

1. **Select the Polygonal Lasso tool in the Tools panel.**

   You can also use the keyboard shortcut. Press the L key and then press Shift+L until you get the Polygonal Lasso tool. It looks like the regular Lasso tool, but it has straight sides.

2. **With the Polygonal Lasso tool selected, click to establish the beginning of the first line of your selection.**

   A corner is always a good place to start.

3. **Move the mouse and click at the next corner of the object. Then, continue clicking at the various corners of your object.**

   The line stretches out from each corner that you click, like a rubber band.

4. **To close your selection, return to the first point that you clicked and click one last time.**

When you place your cursor over the starting point, a small circle appears next to your cursor, a sure sign that you're at the right place for closing the selection. A selection marquee that matches your Polygonal Lasso line appears, as shown in Figure 1-11.

Figure 1-11: The Polygonal Lasso tool is perfect for selecting straight-sided objects.

Which tool do you use if you have an object with both curves and straight sides? You can have two, two, *two* tools in one! Hold down the Alt (Option on the Mac) key to have the Polygonal Lasso tool temporarily transform into the regular Lasso tool. Then, click and drag to select the curves. Release the Alt (Option) key to return to the Polygonal Lasso tool. This trick works with the other Lasso tools, as well.

**Book III
Chapter 1**

Making Selections

Attracting with the Magnetic Lasso tool

The last member of the lasso tool trio is the Magnetic Lasso, which I admit can be somewhat tricky to use and sometimes even downright obstinate. The Magnetic Lasso tool works by analyzing the colors of the pixels between the elements in the foreground and the elements in the background. Then, it snaps to the edge between the elements, as if the edge had a magnetic pull.

The Magnetic Lasso tool performs best when your image has a lot of contrast between the foreground and background elements — for example, a dark mountain range against a light sky or a shadow against a stucco wall.

The Magnetic Lasso tool also has some unique settings — which you can adjust on the Options bar — to tame its behavior. I cover those settings in the following section. For now, follow these steps to use the tool:

1. Select the Magnetic Lasso tool in the Tools panel.

You can also use the keyboard shortcut: Press the L key and then press Shift+L until you get the Magnetic Lasso tool. The tool looks like a straight-sided lasso with a little magnet on it.

2. Click the edge of the object you want to select.

You can start anywhere; just be sure to click the edge between the element you want and the background you don't want.

3. Move your cursor around the object without clicking.

The Magnetic Lasso tool creates a selection line similar to the other lasso tools. It also adds little squares, called *points,* along that selection line, as shown in Figure 1-12. These points pin down the selection line the way you might section off an area of your yard with ropes and stakes.

Magnetic Lasso point

iStockphoto

Figure 1-12: The Magnetic Lasso tool detects the edge of your object.

Here are a couple more tips to keep in mind when working with the Magnetic Lasso tool:

- If the Magnetic Lasso tool starts veering off the edge of your object, back up your mouse and click to force a point down on the line.

- If the Magnetic Lasso tool adds a point where you don't want one, simply press your Backspace (Delete on a Mac) key to delete it.

4. **Continue moving your mouse around the object; return to your starting point and click the mouse button to close the selection.**

Like with the Polygonal Lasso tool, a small circle appears next to your cursor, indicating that you're at the correct place to close the selection. The selection marquee appears when the selection is closed.

Adjusting the Magnetic Lasso options

The Magnetic Lasso tool comes equipped with a few settings on the Options bar that control the sensitivity of the tool.

I recommend starting out by messing around with the Magnetic Lasso tool using its default settings. If the tool isn't cooperating, then play with the options.

The first icon, on the far left, has to do with tool presets, and the next four icons are the selection option icons. (Check out Book III, Chapter 3.) The Feather, Anti-Alias, and Refine Edge options work the way they do with the Marquee tools. (See the earlier section "Using the Marquee options.") The following list explains the remaining options:

- **Width:** This option, measured in pixels from 1 to 256, determines how close to the edge you have to move your mouse before the Magnetic Lasso tool recognizes the object you're selecting. Decrease the value if the object's edge has a lot of indentations and protrusions or if the image has low contrast. Increase the value if the image has high contrast or smooth edges.

    When using the Magnetic Lasso tool, you can change the Width value from the keyboard by pressing the left bracket ([ ) key to lower the value and the right bracket ( ]) key to increase the value.

- **Edge Contrast:** Measured in percentages from 1 to 100, this option specifies the required contrast between the object you're selecting and its background before the Magnetic Lasso tool hugs the edge between them. If your image has good contrast between the foreground and background, use a high percentage.

- ✔ **Frequency:** This setting, measured in percentages from 0 to 100, specifies how many points to place on the selection line. The higher the percentage, the greater number of points. If the object you want to select has a fairly smooth edge, keep the percentage low. If the edge is jagged or has a lot of detail, a high percentage may be more effective in getting an accurate selection line.

- ✔ **Tablet Pressure (Pen icon):** If you own a pressure-sensitive drawing tablet, select this option to make an increase in stylus pressure causing the edge width to decrease.

Performing Wand Wizardry

The Magic Wand. The name is intriguing, isn't it? Any tool that has the audacity to call itself the Magic Wand must be so powerful that it can grant your every selection wish with a mere swoosh. Unfortunately, it's not quite so awe-inspiring. A better name for this tool would be the Click-'n-Select tool. You click your image, and the Magic Wand tool makes a selection that contains areas of similar color based on the color of the pixel you clicked.

Simple enough. What's not quite so simple is how to determine *how* similar the color has to be to get the Magic Wand tool to select it. That's where the important Tolerance setting comes in. Before you tackle tolerance (and find out how it affects the Magic Wand tool's performance), you first need to get the hang of using the Magic Wand tool. In case you haven't used the Magic Wand before, I ordered the following sections with this in mind, so read them in order.

Selecting with the Magic Wand tool

Like with the Magnetic Lasso tool (covered in the section "Attracting with the Magnetic Lasso tool," earlier in this chapter), the Magic Wand tool works best when you have high-contrast images or images that have a limited number of colors. As shown in Figure 1-13, a black-and-white checkered flag is a perfect example of something that the Magic Wand tool effectively selects. I click the top of a black square, and the Magic Wand tool picks up all the other surrounding black pixels. I can now easily change the color of my black squares to red or yellow in one fell swoop.

Figure 1-13: The Magic Wand tool works best on images with limited colors.

As you can see, Figure 1-14 is a poor candidate for the Magic Wand tool. This image contains a ton of colors — and no definitive contrast between the glass, the wine, and the background. Although it takes only one click to select the black squares on the flag, other high-contrast candidates may take a few clicks. And some images may need you to make a tweak or two to the Tolerance setting, described in the following section.

Setting your tolerance

Sometimes, an image may contain a few shades of a similar color. Consider a cloudless sky, for example. A few shades of blue make up the bright blue yonder. By using the Magic Wand tool, if you click a darker shade of blue in the sky, Photoshop selects all similar shades of blue, but the lighter shades remain unselected. This is usually a sure sign that you need to increase your Tolerance level. The *Tolerance* setting determines the range of color that the Magic Wand tool selects. Tolerance is based on brightness levels that range from 0 to 255:

Corbis Digital Stock

Figure 1-14: Trying to select an image with a lot of color variation can be an exercise in futility.

  ✓ Setting the Tolerance to 0 selects one color only.

  ✓ Setting the Tolerance to 255 selects all colors — the entire image.

To use the Magic Wand tool and adjust Tolerance settings, follow these steps:

1. **Select the Magic Wand tool in the Tools panel.**

   Press the W key and then press Shift-W until you get a tool that looks like the weapon of choice for many Disney characters.

2. **Click the portion of the image that you want to select; use the default Tolerance setting of 32.**

   The pixel that you click determines the base color. The default value of 32 means that the Magic Wand tool selects all colors that are 16 levels lighter and 16 levels darker than the base color.

   If you selected everything you wanted the first time you used the Magic Wand tool, stretch your arm and give yourself a pat on the back. If you didn't (which is probably the case), go to Step 3.

3. **Enter a new Tolerance setting on the Options bar.**

   If the Magic Wand tool selected more than you wanted it to, lower the Tolerance setting. If it didn't select enough, raise the setting.

4. Click the portion of the image that you want to select.

Changing the Tolerance level doesn't adjust your current selection.

The Magic Wand tool deselects the current selection and makes a new selection — based on your new Tolerance setting, as shown in Figure 1-15. If it still isn't right, you can adjust the Tolerance setting again. I regret that I can't give you a magic formula that you can use to determine the right value. It's all about trial and error.

Tolerance of 16   Tolerance of 64

iStockphoto

Figure 1-15: Finding the right Tolerance is the key to selecting with the Magic Wand.

Using the Magic Wand Options bar

If you get a selection close to what you want, stop there and then use the selection-refining techniques I discuss in Book III, Chapter 2. But before you do that, you need to know about the other Magic Wand settings on the Options bar. Besides Anti-Alias and Refine Edge, which I discuss in the earlier section "Using the Marquee options," the three remaining options are as follows:

- **Contiguous:** When you turn on this option, the Magic Wand tool selects *only* pixels that are adjacent to each other. If you turn off the option, the Magic Wand tool selects all pixels within the range of tolerance, whether or not they're adjacent to each other.

- **Sample All Layers:** This option is valid only when you have multiple layers in your image. (For more on layers, see Book V.) If you have multiple layers and this option is on, the Magic Wand tool selects color from all visible layers. If you turn off this option, the Magic Wand selects colors from the active layer only.

✓ **Sample Size:** Although this option affects the Magic Wand tool, it appears on the Options bar *only* when you select the Eyedropper tool. (For more on the Eyedropper, see Book II, Chapter 3.) Select the Eyedropper tool and, in the Sample Size pop-up menu that appears, select from the following options:

- *Point Sample:* Samples just the color of the pixel you clicked.

- *3 by 3 Average:* Averages the color of the pixel you clicked and the surrounding eight pixels.

- *5 by 5 Average:* Averages the color of the pixel you clicked and the surrounding 24 pixels.

- *11 by 11 Average:* Averages the color of the pixel you clicked and the surrounding 120 pixels.

- *31 by 31 Average:* Averages the color of the pixel you clicked and the surrounding 960 pixels.

- *51 by 51 Average:* Averages the color of the pixel you clicked and the surrounding 2,600 pixels.

- *101 by 101 Average:* Averages the color of the pixel you clicked and the surrounding 10,200 pixels.

Saving Time with the Quick Selection Tool

We all never have enough time. Luckily, Adobe heard our cries and gave us a great tool. Think of it as a combo Brush, Magic Wand, Lasso tool. Easy to use — with surprisingly good results — it's sure to become part of your selection arsenal. To make short work of selecting by using this tool, follow these steps:

1. **Select the Quick Selection tool from the Tools panel.**

   The tool looks like a wand with a marquee around the end. It shares the Magic Wand tool's flyout menu. You can also press the W key and then press Shift+W until you get the tool.

2. **If you're making a new selection, be sure that the selection option is set to New Selection or Add to Selection on the Options bar.**

3. **Select your desired brush settings from the Brush picker on the Options bar.**

4. **If your image has layers and you want to make a selection from all the layers, select the Sample All Layers option.**

   If you leave this option unselected, you select only from the current layer.

Book III
Chapter 1

Making Selections

5. **Select the Auto-Enhance option to have Photoshop assist you by automatically refining your selection by implementing an algorithm.**

6. **Click and drag over the desired areas of your image.**

   Your selection grows while you drag, as shown in Figure 1-16.

   If you stop dragging and click in another portion of your image, your selection includes that clicked area.

7. **Change your selection as needed.**

   You have three options to change your selection:

   • To add to your selection, hold down the Shift key while dragging across your desired image areas. (If the Add to Selection option is selected on the Options bar, you don't have to hold down the Shift key.)

   • To delete from your selection, press the Alt (Option on the Mac) key while dragging across your unwanted image areas.

   • You can also select the Add to Selection and Subtract from Selection options on the Options bar.

Purestock

Figure 1-16: Paint a selection with the Quick Selection tool.

8. **If you need to further fine-tune your selection, click the Refine Edges option on the Options bar.**

   I explain settings in detail in the "Using the Marquee options" section, earlier in this chapter.

Chapter 2: Creating and Working with Paths

In This Chapter

✓ Working with the Pen tools

✓ Using the Paths panel

✓ Loading paths as selections (and vice versa)

✓ Editing, saving, and selecting paths

Although the Marquee, Lasso, and Magic Wand tools are fun, friendly, and easy to wield (see Book III, Chapter 1), sometimes they don't quite have the horsepower to make a precise selection. Therefore, either you spend a lot of time cleaning up what you've selected (see Book III Chapter 3 for more on that topic), or you live with a ho-hum selection. That's where the Pen tool and its related cronies come to the rescue. The Pen tool creates paths that you can then convert into selections.

Because the Pen tool (along with the related path-editing tools) offers control and precision, it can nail that accurate selection. The only problem is that the Pen tool is far from fun, friendly, and easy. Many new users try the Pen a few times but end up muttering in disgust and returning gratefully to the Lasso tool. However, I guarantee that if you dedicate a good chunk of time to mastering the Pen tool, you can turn up your elite little nose at the simple Lasso tool.

Introducing Paths

Unlike the other selection tools, the Pen tool doesn't initially produce a selection marquee. When you select the Pen tool and start clicking and dragging around your image, you create a path. Paths have three types of components — anchor points, straight segments, and curved segments.

Curved paths are *Bézier paths* (after Pierre Bézier — who, in the 1970s, invented the equation used for CAD CAM programs). They're based on a mathematical cubic equation in which the path is controlled by direction lines that end in direction points (often referred to as *handles*), as shown in Figure 2-1. The length and angle of direction lines control the pitch and angle of the Bézier curve.

The following list introduces the different kinds of anchor points (refer to Figure 2-1) that Photoshop puts at your disposal. You can use some or all of these anchor points in a single path:

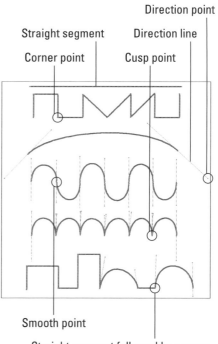

- ✔ **A true corner point:** Has no direction lines. Use corner points when you're selecting objects that have straight sides, such as stairs or barns.

- ✔ **A smooth point:** Has two direction lines pointing in opposite directions that are dependent on one another. Use smooth points when selecting objects that have alternating curves, such as a sea of rolling waves.

Figure 2-1: The Pen tool creates Bézier curves, which are comprised of many different components.

- ✔ **A cusp point:** Has two direction lines that are independent of one another. Use cusp points when you're selecting an object that has curves going the same direction, such as the petals on a daisy.

- ✔ **A point between a straight segment and a curve:** A corner point that has only one direction line.

After you create a Bézier path, you can then edit the path by moving, adding, deleting, or converting anchor points and by manipulating the direction lines. You can also transform paths by choosing Edit⇨Transform Paths. When you transform a path, you can scale, rotate, skew, distort, change the perspective of, or warp the path. (See Book III, Chapter 3 for details.)

The path hovers over the image in its own space. You control the path via the Paths panel, where you can save it, duplicate it, stroke it with color (apply color to the edge only), fill it with color or a pattern, and (most importantly) load it as a selection. I say "most importantly" because nine times out of ten, you painstakingly create a path as a means to an accurate selection marquee. You may use the path as a clipping path one other time: to hide a part of a layer or part of an image.

Creating a Path with the Pen Tool

The best way to get the hang of the Pen tool is to dive right in and work with it. Start with straight lines, which are very easy, and then move on to the more difficult curves. The more you practice with the Pen, the more comfortable and proficient you can become. It definitely is an example of the old adage, "You get out what you put into it."

Knowing your Pen tool options

Although every path consists of three basic components — segments, points, and direction lines — the Pen tool enables you to use these components to create a few different types of paths. See Book IV, Chapter 1 for more information on the following options, accessible from the Pen tool's Options bar. You must choose one of the following:

- **Shape Layers:** This option creates a shape on a new layer that's called, not surprisingly, a shape layer. After you create the path that defines the shape, Photoshop fills the shape with the foreground color and stores the path as a vector mask (see Book VI, Chapter 3) in the Paths panel. A shape layer is a unique entity.

- **Paths:** This option enables you to create a traditional path that hovers over the image. The path you create is a *work path* — which is temporary, appears in the Paths panel, and is unsaved. If you're creating a path that you eventually want to load as a selection, this is your option.

- **Fill Pixels:** This option is available only when you're using the shape tools. It allows you to create a shape and fill it with the foreground color, but it doesn't create a shape layer, nor does it retain the path.

For a detailed explanation of vector images (shape layers and paths) and raster images (such as those created with fill pixels), see Book II, Chapter 1.

Creating your first work path

Making a work path is the easiest of the three options, and you'll use it frequently after you get the hang of using the Pen tool. The following steps show you how to create a simple, straight path:

1. **Open an image you want to practice on.**

    I suggest choosing an image that has an element with straight edges and curves, if you also want to practice creating curved paths in the next few sections.

2. **Select the Pen tool from the Tools panel.**

    You can just press the P key, too.

3. **On the Options bar, click the Paths button.**

   You can see this button in Figure 2-2.

4. **To create a straight line, click and release your mouse button at the points where you want the line to begin and to end, leaving anchor points at those positions.**

   You don't need to do any dragging to create straight segments. When you click and add your anchor points, Photoshop creates straight segments that connect the anchor points, as shown in Figure 2-3.

5. **To draw a constrained line — horizontal, vertical, or 45-degree angle — hold down the Shift key while you click.**

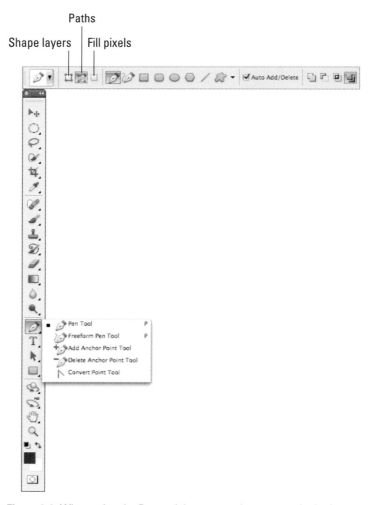

Figure 2-2: When using the Pen tool, be sure to choose your desired path type from the Options bar.

Straight segment Anchor points

Corbis Digital Stock

Figure 2-3: Drawing straight lines with the Pen tool requires nothing more than clicks.

6. **To end the path, click the Pen tool in the Tools panel to deselect it.**

   Or use this very handy shortcut:

   a. *Hold down the Ctrl key (⌘ on the Mac).*

      The Direct Selection tool (the white arrow) appears.

   b. *Click away from the line and release the Ctrl key (⌘ on the Mac).*

      The Pen tool reappears.

      With your path now deselected, you're free to start another, unconnected path, if you need to.

Check out the following sections if you want to add other kinds of segments to the path. Otherwise, skip to the section "Closing a path," later in this chapter.

Drawing curves

You're probably never going to create a simple work path that doesn't have curves as well as straight lines. I mean, not much in life is perfectly linear. Most things have undulations here and there. Picking up from the preceding section, follow these steps to create curved paths:

1. **If you're adding on to a previously created open path, be sure to position your cursor on the last anchor point you created on that open path before you continue.**

   A slash mark or a small square appears next to your cursor. If you're starting a new path, position the cursor where the curve begins.

2. **Whichever appears — the slash mark or the square — click and drag toward the direction you want the bump of the curve to go. Release the mouse button when you're done.**

   Here are some quick pointers for this stage of the procedure:

   - If you're creating a new path, an anchor point and two direction lines (which have direction points at their ends) appear. If you're adding a curve to your straight segment, an anchor point and one direction line with one direction point appear. The direction lines and direction points control the angle and pitch of the curve.

   - How do you know how far you should drag? Use the Rule of Thirds. Imagine that your curve is a piece of string that you've laid out in a straight line. Divide that line into thirds. Generally, the distance you drag your mouse cursor is approximately one-third the length of that line.

   - How do you establish the angle? Drag straight from the anchor point for a steeper curve and at an angle from the anchor point for a flatter curve. The element in my example is a flatter curve; therefore, I dragged up and to the right at an angle of just a few degrees, as shown in Figure 2-4.

Anchor point   Direction line

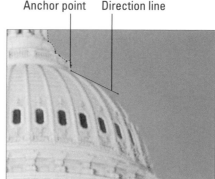

Corbis Digital Stock

Figure 2-4: Dragging at an angle of about 45 degrees or less begins the path of the flat curve.

3. Move the cursor to the end of the curve and click and drag in the opposite direction, away from the bump.

Another anchor point and a set of two direction lines and points appear. Photoshop creates the curve segment between the anchor points, as shown in Figure 2-5. Here are a couple other handy pointers:

- If you drag both direction lines in the same direction, you create a curve shaped like an *S*.

- On the Options bar, click the down arrow at the end of the row of tools and choose the Rubber Band option. With this option selected, Photoshop draws a segment between the last anchor point you created and wherever your cursor is located, which gives you a kind of animated preview of how the path will appear. I find the option distracting, but some users love it.

Second anchor point

Curve segment   Direction line

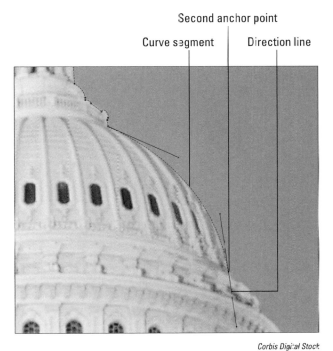

Figure 2-5: Finish the curve by dragging in the opposite direction.

4. To draw more alternating curves, repeat these steps, dragging in an opposite direction each time.

Book III
Chapter 2

Creating and Working with Paths

Connecting a straight segment to a curve segment

If you need to create a straight segment after creating a curve (or vice versa), you need to convert the point where the path changes from curved to straight. To convert a point, follow these steps:

1. **Position your cursor over the second anchor point in the existing curve and hold down the Alt key (Option on the Mac).**

   A caret (which looks like an upside down V) appears next to the Pen cursor.

2. **Click and release your mouse button over the anchor point. Also release the Alt key (Option on the Mac).**

   The bottom direction line disappears. You've converted a smooth point into a corner point with one direction line. This action now allows you to create a straight segment.

   It's no coincidence that the icon for the Convert Point tool is also a caret. Whenever you see a caret symbol in Photoshop, it's an indication that you're converting an anchor point, from smooth to corner or vice versa.

3. **Move your mouse to the end of the straight edge that you want to select, and then click and release your mouse button.**

   You can press the Shift key while you click if you want the line to be constrained horizontally, vertically, or at an angle that's a multiple of 45 degrees.

   Photoshop connects the two anchor points with a straight segment, as shown in Figure 2-6.

Corner point with one direction line   Straight segment

Corbis Digital Stock

Figure 2-6: To connect a straight segment to a curve segment, you must first convert the point.

Connecting curve segments with cusp points

If you want to create a curve that goes in the same direction as a curve that's adjacent to it, you have to take a couple additional steps, in addition to following the steps in the earlier "Drawing curves" section:

1. **Convert the point — this time from smooth to cusp — by positioning your cursor over the second anchor point in the existing curve and holding down the Alt (Option on the Mac) key.**

2. **Click and drag toward the bump of the curve. Release the mouse button and then release the Alt (Option on the Mac) key.**

   Essentially, your actions are pulling the direction line out from the anchor point. Both direction lines move to the same side of the anchor point, yet they're independent of each other, creating the cusp point, as shown in Figure 2-7.

3. **Move your cursor to where you want the curve to end and drag away from the bump to create your second curve.**

Cusp point

Corbis Digital Stock

Figure 2-7: You can connect two curves that go in the same direction with a cusp point.

Try to keep anchor points on either side of the curve, not along the top. Also, try to use the fewest number of anchor points possible to create your path. That way, the path results in a much smoother curve. It also can reduce the possibility of printing problems.

Book III Chapter 2

Creating and Working with Paths

Closing a path

To close the path, return to your first anchor point and click. A small circle appears next to your Pen cursor, indicating that you're closing the path.

Congratulations! You're now the proud owner of a work path. (See Figure 2-8.) Don't worry if the path isn't perfect; you can find out how to edit paths in the section "Editing Paths," later in this chapter. If your path is perfect and you want to save it, skip ahead to the section "Working with the Paths Panel," later in this chapter.

If your path is incomplete and you want to continue drawing it, either click or click and drag the endpoint with the Pen tool. A slash mark or small square appears next to the Pen cursor.

Creating subpaths

You can create a series of lines or curves. For example, you may want to create a border consisting of some decorative curve shapes, which you could later stroke with color. (See Book IV, Chapter 2.) You can then save these *subpaths* under a single path name. To create a series of subpaths, simply end one path before starting another. Make sure that the paths aren't hidden when you do so; otherwise, Photoshop eliminates the previous path when you start another.

3. **In the dialog box that appears, enter a Tolerance value.**

   The Tolerance value controls how sensitive Photoshop is to the nooks and crannies in the selection when it creates the path:

   - The lower the value, the more sensitive it is, and the more closely the selection follows your path.

   - Too low a value, such as 0.5, may create too many anchor points.

   - Too high a value, such as 10 (the max), rounds out your path too much. Start with the default setting of 2.0.

   You can always tweak the path later (check out the section "Editing Paths," later in this chapter).

4. **If the path is still showing, simply click in the gray area below the path names in the Paths panel.**

   This action deselects the path.

5. **Select the work path in the Paths panel and select Save Path from the Paths panel pop-up menu. Name the path and click OK.**

Using the Kinder Freeform Pen

Confession: There's a more amicable incarnation of the Pen tool — the Freeform Pen tool. This tool is kind of a hybrid Lasso/Pen tool. Just click and drag around the element you want to select, and the tool creates an outline that follows your cursor, exactly like the Lasso.

After you release your mouse button, Photoshop provides the anchor points, lines, and curves for that path. In this way, the Freeform Pen works exactly like the Pen.

In my humble opinion, the Freeform Pen rates just an okay. The downside is that you're back to needing a steady hand in order to get an accurate selection. The Freeform Pen tool's probably one notch better than the Lasso tool because you get a path that you can refine before you load it as a selection. I'd rather pay my dues and get skilled with the regular Pen.

Here are some Freeform Pen tips:

- To create straight segments by using the Freeform Pen, hold down Alt (Option on the Mac) while pressing the mouse button and then click to create the anchor point.

✔ Holding down Alt (Option on the Mac) temporarily turns the Freeform Pen into the regular Pen. When you want to return to using the Freeform Pen, release Alt (Option on the Mac), keeping the mouse button clicked.

If you release Alt (Option on the Mac) after releasing the mouse button, Photoshop ends your path, and you can do nothing about it.

The following sections give you the scoop on the options (which you can find by clicking the down arrow on the Options bar) that go hand in hand with the Freeform Pen tool. (See Figure 2-13.)

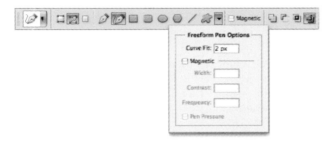

Figure 2-13: The Freeform Pen is a cross between the Lasso and the Pen tools, and it requires a steady hand to create paths.

Curve Fit

The Curve Fit option lets you adjust the amount of error Photoshop allows when trying to fit your cursor movement to a path. You can enter a value from 0.5 to 10 pixels; the default setting is 2 pixels.

At the default setting Photoshop doesn't register any movement of your cursor that's 2 pixels or less. Setting the value to 0.5 pixels makes the Freeform Pen very sensitive to your movement and forces the tool to follow the edge closely.

The disadvantage of this option is that using it also causes unnecessary anchor points. Although a value of 10 pixels corrects this problem by making the option less sensitive, your path may not be as accurate if you back off on the sensitivity.

I recommend trying the Freeform Pen at each of these settings and then getting a feel for the kind of path it makes.

Magnetic

When selected, the Magnetic option makes the Freeform Pen act much like the Magnetic Lasso tool. (See Book III, Chapter 1.) Click anywhere on the edge of the element you want to select. Release your mouse button and then move the cursor around the edge. The tool snaps to the edge of your element, creating anchor points and segments. You can

- ✔ **Manually control the magnetism.** If the Freeform Pen tool starts to veer off course, you can force an anchor point down manually by clicking. To delete the most recent anchor point, press Backspace (delete on the Mac).

- ✔ **Create straight segments.** To create straight segments, Alt-click (Option-click on the Mac) to temporarily get the regular Pen. Alt-drag (Option-drag on the Mac) to temporarily access the regular Freeform Pen. To return to the Magnetic Freeform Pen tool, release Alt (Option on the Mac), click again, and continue moving the cursor.

To close a path by using the magnetic Freeform Pen, double-click or return to your starting anchor point.

Width, Contrast, Frequency, and Pen Pressure

The Width, Contrast, and Frequency settings are specifically for the Magnetic option and work just like the Magnetic Lasso options. Width specifies how close to the edge (1–256) the tool must be before it detects an edge. Contrast (1–100) specifies how much contrast must be between pixels for the tool to see the edge. Frequency (0–100) specifies the rate at which the tool lays down anchor points. For more details, see Book III, Chapter 1.

The Pen Pressure option is available only if you're using a pressure-sensitive drawing tablet. It allows you to adjust how sensitive the tool is based on how hard you press down with the stylus.

Creating Paths without the Pen

I want to let you in on a fun way to create paths. Yes, I said fun. (You have to assume that by *fun,* I mean no Pen tool is involved in the method.)

You can grab any of the shape tools and create a work path. However, before you do, be sure to click the Paths icon on the Options bar. The icon looks like a Pen cursor with a square path around it. Click and drag the shape tool of choice or to your canvas and presto, an instant path These shapes can come in handy for creating small spot illustrations, logos, and Web buttons.

Follow these steps:

1. **Open an existing image and select a shape tool.**

   In the example shown in Figure 2-14, I used the Custom Shape tool. For details on the shape tools and their options, see Book IV, Chapter 1.

2. **Choose a shape from the Custom Shape Picker drop-down panel on the Options bar.**

   I chose a fish shape for my example.

3. **Choose the Paths option on the Options bar. Using the Shape tool, click and drag a path in your image window. Press the Shift key while dragging to constrain the shape's proportions.**

   You can then use the Paths panel to load the path as a selection. (See the section "Loading Paths as Selections," earlier in this chapter.)

Photodisc

Figure 2-14: Using the Custom Shape tool is a fun and painless way to create paths.

4. **Choose Layer⇨New⇨Layer via Copy.**

   You just put the selection on its own layer. You can hide your original background image by clicking the eyeball icon in the Layers panel. For more on layers, see Book V.

5. **If you want, add some type with the Type tool.**

   Then, you can jazz it up — like this, for example:

   - If you want to give your type some motion, click the Create Warped Text button on the Options bar. You can also apply drop shadows, bevels, and other effects by choosing Layer⇨Layer Style.

   - For my example, I chose the Arc style warp in the Warp Text dialog box.

   - I also applied a Bevel and Emboss and Drop Shadow Layer Style to both the selection and the type. (For more on type, see Book IV, Chapter 3.)

6. **Delete the original image layer.**

   Figure 2-15 shows the image I ended up with — fun and very easy.

Photodisc

Figure 2-15: After adding some type and a few effects, you have a fun composite image.

Editing Paths

Often, using the Pen tool to get a reasonably decent, but not perfect, path is easier and less time consuming. After you have that path, go back and edit it for more accuracy. Although following the Eyeball-It-Then-Fix-It strategy is valuable at any time in your Photoshop career, it's especially true when you're figuring out how to use the Pen tool.

Photoshop offers you a bevy of editing tools that can make your path repair a snap. These tools even share the Pen tool's flyout menu. Additionally, the arrow tools, which Adobe calls the Path Selection and Direct Selection tools, are extremely helpful when it comes to fine-tuning your path. You may find (as I do) that the Direct Selection tool is one of your favorite tools — so simple to use, yet so functional. Figure 2-16 shows both sets of tools.

To edit a path, follow these steps:

1. **If you can't see the path you want to edit, select the path in the Paths panel.**

   This selection activates the path.

2. **To see the individual anchor points so that you can edit them, select the Direct Selection tool (the white arrow) and then click anywhere along the path.**

   You now see the individual anchor points and segments that comprise the path. Most of the anchor points, if not all, are hollow because they're unselected, as shown in Figure 2-17.

3. **If you need to move an anchor point, click it with the Direct Selection tool.**

   When selected, the point becomes solid, also shown in Figure 2-17.

4. **Drag to move the anchor point.**

   If you need to, you can move a curved or straight segment in the same fashion.

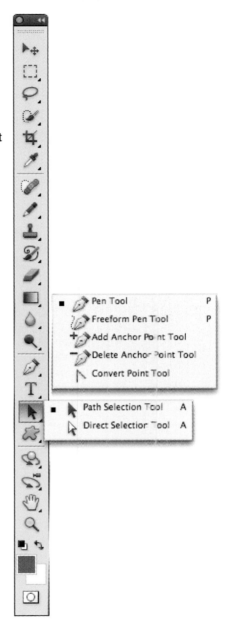

Figure 2-16: The compadres of the Pen tool help to refine your paths to perfection.

Book III
Chapter 2

Creating
and Working
with Paths

5. If you need to move an entire path, use the Path Selection tool (the black arrow).

You can also select multiple paths by holding down the Shift key while clicking the paths.

REMEMBER

If you move any part of the path beyond the boundary of the image canvas, it's still available — just not visible. Use the Zoom tool to zoom out until you see the hidden portion of the path.

6. Using the Direct Selection tool, manipulate the direction lines to change the shape of the curve. First, click the anchor point of the curve to select it. Then, click and drag the direction point going the same direction as the bump.

By lengthening or shortening the direction line, you can control how steep or flat the curve is. By rotat-ing the direction line, you change the slope of the curve, as shown in Figure 2-18. Here are a few more editing pointers:

Selected anchor point

Unselected anchor point

Corbis Digital Stock

Figure 2-17: Hollow anchor points are unselected; solid points are selected.

Corbis Digital Stock

Figure 2-18: By manipulating the direction lines, you can change the shape of a curve.

- **To add an anchor point in your path:** Use the Add Anchor Point tool. Click in the path where you need an anchor point. This tool always adds a smooth point, no matter where you click.

- **To delete an anchor point:** Select the Delete Anchor Point tool, position the cursor over the anchor point, and click it. The anchor point disappears while you keep your path intact.

- **To convert an anchor point from smooth to corner or vice versa:** Select the Convert Point tool. Position your cursor over your desired anchor point. If the anchor point is a corner point, drag away from the anchor point to create the direction lines that create a smooth point. If the point is a smooth point, simply click and release the anchor point to convert it into a corner point.

  To convert a smooth point to a cusp point, make sure the direction lines are showing and then drag a direction line to break it into independent direction lines. Finally, to convert a cusp point back to a smooth point, just drag out from the anchor point.

- **To copy a path:** Select the path by using the Path Selection tool. Then, hold down Alt (Option on the Mac) and drag away from the path. While you drag, you carry a copied path with you.

- **To delete a path:** Select the path by using the Path Selection tool and press the Backspace key (Delete key on the Mac). You can also select a point on the path by using the Direct Selection tool and pressing Backspace (Delete on the Mac) twice.

Using the Options Bar

Quite a few options appear on the Options bar when the Pen tool or Path Selection/Direct Selection tools are active. Here's the scoop on those options:

- ✔ **Auto Add/Delete:** Enables you to add or delete an anchor point by using the regular Pen tool.

- ✔ **Show Bounding Box:** Places a box around the path, allowing you to transform the path. The bounding box isn't a path or part of your image. It's merely a visual guide to assist you in transformations. For more on transformations, see Book II, Chapter 3.

- ✔ **Path state buttons (Add, Subtract, Intersect, and Exclude):** Combine all visible paths by adding, subtracting, intersecting, or excluding paths. Click your desired button to direct Photoshop on how to control the overlapping portions of the path(s) when you convert it to a selection. For example, clicking the Add button selects all areas, whether or not they overlap. Clicking Intersect selects only the overlapping areas.

**Book III
Chapter 2**

**Creating
and Working
with Paths**

✔ **Combine button:** Allows you to group paths as a single unit. Select your desired paths and click the Combine button. When you select any one of the paths, all the paths within the group are selected.

✔ **Align and Distribute buttons:** Align two or more paths, and distribute three or more paths. The icons give you a good visual clue as to how the alignment or distribution will appear.

Chapter 3: Modifying and Transforming Selections and Paths

In This Chapter

✔ **Adding and subtracting from a selection**

✔ **Using the Select commands**

✔ **Feathering selections**

✔ **Moving and cloning a selection**

✔ **Transforming pixels, selections, and paths**

f you're like me, you may find it tough to get the perfect selection the first time around. I mean, all you need is one too many cups of coffee, and that Lasso tool seems to take on a mind of its own. That's okay. Photoshop is too benevolent to leave you hanging with a mediocre selection. Multitudes of techniques are available to modify and transform your selections. You can add or remove pixels from your selection, scale your selection outline, smooth jagged edges, or switch what's selected for what isn't. Knowing how to clean up and modify your selections helps you to nail your desired element with precision.

If you haven't already thumbed through the first two chapters of Book III and gotten a good grasp of how to create selections by using the mighty Photoshop Tools panel, go ahead and browse those chapters now.

Achieving Selection Perfection

Although the selection tools, such as the Lasso, Quick Selection, and Magic Wand tools, usually do a decent job of capturing the bulk of your selection, making an accurate selection often requires another sort of tool — concentration. Give your selections a little extra attention, and you'll be amazed by the results. By adding and subtracting from the outline here and there, you can refine a selection and ensure that you capture only what you really want — and nothing that you don't.

The following sections show you how to use keyboard shortcuts, along with your mouse, to make perfect selections. If you're not one for keyboard shortcuts, you can use the selection option buttons on the Options bar to create a new selection, add to a selection, subtract from a selection, or intersect one selection with another. You just need to grab the selection tool of your choice, click the selection option button you want, and drag (or click if you're using the Magic Wand or the Polygonal Lasso tool).

When adding to a selection, a small plus sign (+) appears next to your cursor. When subtracting from a selection, a small minus sign (–) appears. When intersecting two selections, a small multiplication sign (×) appears.

Adding to a selection

If your selection doesn't quite contain all the elements you want to capture, you need to add those portions to your current selection.

For you keyboarders, to add to a current selection, simply hold down the Shift key and drag around the pixels you want to include when using the regular Lasso tool or the Rectangular or Elliptical Marquee tools. You can also hold down the Shift key and click the area you want when using the Magic Wand tool, or drag the area you want when using the Quick Selection tool.

To include an area that has straight sides in your selection, you can hold down the Shift key and click around the area when using the Polygonal Lasso tool. And although you may not have much need to do it, you can hold down the Shift key and click when using the Single Column or the Single Row Marquee tool. I wouldn't use the Magnetic Lasso tool to add to a selection; it's excessively cumbersome.

To add to your selection, you don't have to use the same tool that you used to create the original selection. Feel free to use whatever selection tool you think can get the job done. (See Book III, Chapters 1 and 2 for details on selection tools and methods.)

Follow these steps to add to the circular selection, such as the one shown in Figure 3-1:

1. **Make your first elliptical selection by selecting the larger circle with the Elliptical Marquee tool.**

   Be sure you hold down the Alt key (Option on the Mac) to draw from the center out. See the left image in Figure 3-1.

2. **To add the smaller circular area you will need to hold down two keys. Hold down the Shift key to add to the selection and then hold down the Alt key (Option on the Mac) to draw from the center out. You must press and hold down the keys in this order.**

3. **Drag around the smaller selection by using the Elliptical Marquee tool.**

   The resulting selection is shown in the example on the right in Figure 3-1.

 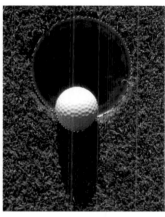

Figure 3-1: The original selection appears on the left; the selection after adding is on the right.

Subtracting from a selection

Just like you can add to a selection marquee, you can also subtract from, or take a chunk out of, a selection. Here's how to subtract from a current selection using the following tools:

- ✔ **The regular Lasso tool or the Rectangular and Elliptical Marquee tools:** Hold down the Alt (Option on the Mac) key and drag around the pixels you want to subtract.

- ✔ **The Magic Wand and the Quick Selection tools:** Hold down the Alt (Option on the Mac) key and click the area you want to remove.

- ✔ **The Polygonal Lasso tool:** To subtract a straight-sided area, hold down the Alt (Option on the Mac) key and click around the area.

- ✔ **The Single Column and the Single Row Marquee tools:** You can hold down the Alt (Option on the Mac) key and click. The Single Column and the Single Row Marquee tools come in handy when you want to get rid of just the edge of a selection.

In Figure 3-2, I selected the outside of the frame by using the Polygonal Lasso tool. I didn't use the obvious tool of choice — the Rectangular Marquee tool — because the frame wasn't completely straight. To deselect the inside of the frame from the selection, I held down the Alt (Option on the Mac) key and clicked each corner of the inside of the frame when using the Polygonal Lasso tool, resulting in the selection shown in Figure 3-2.

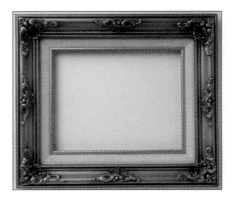

Figure 3-2: Press Alt (Option on the Mac) to delete from your existing selection.

Intersecting two selections

What happens when you hold down the Shift and Alt (Option on the Mac) keys together? Not a collision, but an intersection. Holding down both keys while dragging with the Lasso or the Marquee tool, or clicking with the Magic Wand tool, creates the intersection of the original selection with the second selection.

To retain only the part of an image where two selections overlap, hold down Shift+Alt (Shift+Option on the Mac) and then drag.

You can select a portion of an image by using the Polygonal Lasso tool. Then, hold down Shift+Alt (Shift+Option on the Mac) and drag with the Rectangular Marquee tool. The resulting intersection of the two selections appears.

Getting the Keys to Behave

Photoshop has a little glitch in its way of doing things. Well, not so much a glitch as a conflict. With so many ways of doing things, somewhere along the line you may have to jigger with Photoshop to get it to do what you want. For example, how does Photoshop know whether you want to create a perfect square or add to a selection when you press the Shift key?

Let me lay this out for you:

- ✔ When you make an initial selection with the Rectangular or the Elliptical Marquee tool, holding down the Shift key constrains the proportions of the selection, thereby allowing you to create a perfect square or a perfect circle.

- ✔ If you hold down Alt (Option on the Mac) when using either of these tools, you can draw from the center out.

- ✔ If you hold down Alt (Option on the Mac) when using the Lasso tool, the Lasso tool temporarily becomes the Polygonal Lasso tool.

Unfortunately, despite numerous requests, the capability to read users' minds wasn't a Photoshop CS5 upgrade feature. The following steps show you what you have to do to get Photoshop to recognize your wishes.

To add a perfectly square or round selection to an existing selection, follow these steps:

1. **Hold down Shift and drag when using the Rectangular or the Elliptical Marquee tool.**

   Your selection is unconstrained.

2. **While you drag, keeping your mouse button pressed, release the Shift key for just a moment and then press and hold it again.**

   Your unconstrained selection suddenly snaps into a constrained square or circle.

3. **Release the mouse button before you release the Shift key.**

   If you don't release the mouse button before you release the Shift key, the selection shape reverts to its unconstrained form.

To delete part of a selection while drawing from the center out, follow these steps:

1. **Hold down Alt (Option on the Mac) and drag when using the Rectangular or the Elliptical Marquee tool.**

2. **While you drag, keeping your mouse button pressed, release the Alt (Option on the Mac) key for just a moment and then press and hold it again.**

   You're now drawing from the center outward.

3. **Release the mouse button before you release the Alt (Option on the Mac) key.**

   See Figure 3-3.

Digital Vision

Figure 3-3: You can delete from an existing selection and draw from the center out simultaneously.

Use the preceding steps when you're selecting a doughnut, tire, inflatable swim ring, and other circular items that have holes in the middle.

Using the Select Menu

Although you can add, subtract, and intersect selections by using the Shift and Alt (Option on the Mac) keys and the selection option buttons on the Options bar, you can do much more with the commands on the Select menu. In this menu, you can find ways to expand, contract, smooth, and fuzz your selection, and even turn your selection inside out. You can also use this

Book III
Chapter 3

Modifying and
Transforming
Selections and Paths

menu to automatically select similar colors and create selection borders. I show you how to do all this in the following sections. With this kind of knowledge, imperfect selections will soon be a thing of the past.

Selecting all or nothing

The All and the Deselect commands are pretty self-explanatory. To select everything in your image, choose Select➪All. To deselect everything, choose Select➪Deselect. The key commands Ctrl+A (⌘+A on the Mac) and Ctrl+D (⌘+D on the Mac), respectively, come in very handy and are easy to remember.

In most cases, you don't have to select everything in your image. If you don't have an active selection marquee, Photoshop naturally assumes that you want to apply whatever command you execute to the entire image.

Reselecting a selection

If you've taken 20 minutes to carefully lasso a spiny sea anemone from its ocean home, the last thing you want is to lose your coveted selection marquee. But that's exactly what happens if you accidentally click the canvas when you have an active selection tool in hand. The selection marquee disappears.

Sure, you can choose Edit➪Undo if you catch your mistake right away. Technically, you can also access the History panel to recover your selection. (See Book II, Chapter 4 for more on history.) However, a much easier solution is to choose Select➪Reselect. This command retrieves your last selection.

Besides immediately bringing back a selection you accidentally deselected, the Reselect command can come in handy if you decide to select an element for a second time. For example, if you do such a great job retouching your spiny anemone that you decide to add, by copying, another anemone to your image, go ahead; it's all up to you. By using the Reselect command, you can easily load the selection again, rather than start the selection from scratch.

The Reselect command works for only the last selection you made, so don't plan to reselect a selection you made last week — or even ten minutes ago — if you've selected something else in the meantime.

Swapping a selection

Sometimes, selecting what you don't want is easier than selecting what you do want. For example, if you're trying to select your pet dog, photographed against a neutral background, why spend valuable time meticulously selecting him with the Pen or the Lasso tool, when you can just click the background with the Magic Wand tool? (Don't forget to use the Shift key to select bits of background you might have missed the first time.)

After you select the background, just choose Select➪Inverse. Presto, you now have Fido the Retriever selected and obediently awaiting your next command, as shown in Figure 3-4.

Feathering a selection

In Book III, Chapter 1, I describe how to *feather* (blur the edges of) a selection when using the Lasso and the Marquee tools by entering a value in the Feather box on the Options bar. This method of feathering requires that you set your feather radius *before* you create your selection.

Unfortunately, using this method, a problem arises if you want to modify the initial selection. When you select with a feather, the marquee outline of the selection adjusts to take into account the amount of the feather. Therefore, the resulting marquee outline doesn't resemble your precise mouse movement. As a result, modifying, adding, or subtracting from your original selection is pretty tough.

A much better way to feather a selection is to make your initial selection without a feather, as shown in the top image of Figure 3-5. Clean up your selection as you need to, and then apply your feather by choosing Select➪Modify➪Feather. In the dialog box, enter a Feather Radius value and click OK. The resulting selection appears in the bottom image of Figure 3-5.

The *radius* is how far out in all directions the feather extends. A radius of 8 means the feather extends 8 pixels from the selection outline. A large feather radius makes the image appear to fade out.

Figure 3-4: Sometimes, you want to select what you don't want and then invert your selection.

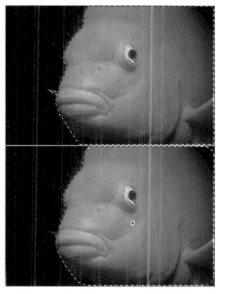

Corbis Digital Stock

Figure 3-5: You can more easily clean up your selection prior to applying a feather.

Deleting a straight-sided selection

If you have an existing selection, holding down Alt (Option on the Mac) when using the Lasso tool subtracts from the selection. If you want to subtract a straight-sided selection from an existing selection, you can hold down Alt (Option on the Mac) and begin to drag. Then, release Alt (Option on the Mac) and select the Polygonal Lasso tool. But this process can be tricky and is really unnecessary. I recommend just grabbing the Polygonal Lasso tool itself to delete your straight-sided selection. Ditto for adding and getting intersections with straight-sided selections.

Using the other Modify commands

In addition to the Feather command, the Select⇨Modify menu contains a group of other modification commands that are lumped categorically. With the exception of the Contract command, you probably won't use these options every day. When you do use them, however, you'll find they prove pretty handy. Here's the lowdown on each command:

- **Border:** This command selects the area around the edge of the selection marquee. You specify the width of the area, from 1 to 200 pixels, and you get a border marquee. Select a foreground color, choose Edit⇨Fill, pick Foreground Color from the Use drop-down list, and then click OK to fill your border with color. (By the way, you can also achieve a similar look by choosing Edit⇨Stroke. See Book IV, Chapter 2 for details.)

- **Smooth:** If your selection marquee seems a bit ragged around the edges, try selecting the Smooth command to round the nooks and crannies. Enter a sample radius value from 1 to 100 pixels. Photoshop examines each selected pixel and then includes or deselects pixels in your selection based on the range specified by the radius amount. If most of the pixels are selected, Photoshop includes the strays; if most of the pixels are unselected, Photoshop removes the pixels. Start with 2 pixels — and if that doesn't seem like enough, increase it by a few more pixels or so.

  Use this command with great caution. It's just too easy to get mushy, ill-defined selections.

- **Expand:** This command allows you to increase the size of your selection by a specified number of pixels, from 1 to 100. This command can come in handy if you just missed the edge of a circular selection and want to enlarge it, as shown in Figure 3-6.

- **Contract:** To shrink your selection by 1 to 100 pixels, choose Contract. I use this command a lot, in conjunction with the Feather command, when compositing multiple images.

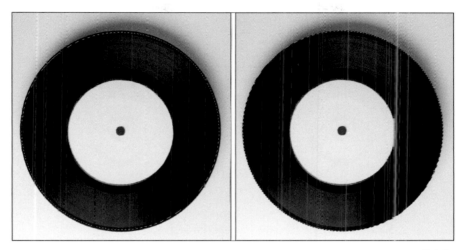

Figure 3-6: The Expand command increases your selection, enabling you to pick up missed pixels around the edges.

Applying the Grow and Similar commands

The Grow and the Similar commands are close cousins to the Magic Wand tool, and to a lesser extent, the Quick Selection tool. (For more on the Magic Wand tool and the Tolerance setting, check out Book III, Chapter 1.) If you're familiar with the modus operandi of the Magic Wand tool, you know that you rarely get the perfect selection on the first click. That's because you're making an intelligent guess about what Tolerance setting can pick up the pixels you want.

The Grow command compensates a little for the Magic Wand tool's inaccuracy. For example, if you need to include more in your selection, you can increase the Tolerance setting and try again — hold down Shift and click the area you need to include. Or you can choose Select⇒Grow. The Grow command increases the size of the selection by including adjacent pixels that fall within the range of Tolerance.

The Similar command is like Grow, only the pixels don't have to be adjacent to be selected. The command searches throughout the image and picks up pixels within the Tolerance range, wherever they may fall.

Both commands use the Tolerance value that's displayed on the Options bar when you have the Magic Wand tool selected. Adjust the Tolerance setting to include more or fewer colors by increasing or decreasing the setting, respectively.

The Refine Edge command, which has been upgraded in version CS5, helps to fine tune your selection. Find out the details in Book III, Chapter 1.

Moving and Cloning Selections

When you have your selection refined to ultimate perfection, you may then want to move it or clone it. To move a selection, simply grab the Move tool (the four-headed arrow) at the top right of the Tools panel, and then drag the selection.

Sounds easy enough, right? When you move the selection, however, be warned that the area where the selection used to reside fills with the background color, as shown in Figure 3-7. The background appears, of course, only if you're moving both the selection outline and the image pixels. You can move just the selection outline (without the pixels), as I explain in the section "Moving the selection outline, but not the pixels," later in this chapter. Additionally, if you're moving a selection on a layer, you're left with transparent pixels. When you use the Move tool, your cursor icon changes to a pair of scissors, letting you know that you're cutting out the selection.

Photodisc

Figure 3-7: When you move a selection by using the Move tool, you leave a hole that reveals the background color.

The Move tool has some notable options on the Options bar:

- **Auto-Select Layer:** Select the topmost layer directly under the Move tool cursor, not necessarily the selected area.

- **Auto-Select Group:** Select the entire layer group that the selected layer belongs to.

- **Show Transform Controls:** Show handles on the bounding box of your selected area.

Cloning

If the idea of leaving a big hole in your image doesn't appeal to you, you can copy and move the selection, leaving the original image intact, as shown in

Figure 3-8. Just hold down Alt (Option on the Mac) and drag when using the Move tool. This action is often referred to as *cloning* because you're essentially making a duplicate of a selected area and then moving that duplicate elsewhere.

When cloning, your cursor icon changes to a double-headed arrow, notifying you that you're duplicating the selection.

Figure 3-8: Hold down Alt (Option on the Mac) while dragging to clone your selection and not leave a nasty hole.

Moving the selection outline, but not the pixels

If all you want to do is move the selection marquee without moving the pixels underneath, avoid using the Move tool. Instead, grab any selection tool — a Marquee tool, a Lasso tool, or the Magic Wand tool — and then click inside the marquee and just drag. That way, you move only the outline of the element, not the element itself. You can also use the arrow keys to nudge a selection marquee.

Transforming Pixels

After you perfectly select your element, you may find you need to resize or reorient that element. *Transforming* involves scaling, rotating, skewing, distorting, warping, flipping, or adjusting the perspective of your pixels.

Follow these steps to transform a selection:

1. Create your selection.

I'll leave this task up to you; just use your well-honed selection expertise (or refer to earlier sections in this chapter for help).

You can also apply transformations to a layer or to multiple layers. (For more on this topic, see Book V.)

2. Choose Edit⇨Transform.

If all you want is a single transformation, this command is adequate. However, if you want multiple transformations, you're wise to stick with the Free Transform command.

3. Choose a transformation type from the submenu:

- *Scale.* Increases or decreases the size of your selection.

- *Rotate:* Freely rotates your selection in either direction.

- *Skew:* Distorts your selection on a given axis.

- *Distort:* Distorts your selection with no restrictions on an axis.

- *Perspective:* Applies a one-point perspective to your selection.

- *Warp:* This option is like a mini-Liquify command, which you can use to distort your selection by manipulating a mesh grid that overlays your image. (Book VII, Chapter 3 covers Liquify.)

- *Rotate 180°, 90° CW (Clockwise), or 90° CCW (Counterclockwise):* Rotates the selection by specified amounts.

- *Flip Horizontal or Vertical:* Flips your selection along the vertical and horizontal axes, respectively.

As soon as you select your desired distortion and release the mouse button, the *bounding box* or *transform box* surrounds your selection, complete with handles on the sides and corners. You don't get a bounding box when you select the Flip or Rotate (by degrees) transformations (which just get applied to your image).

4. **Depending on which transformation type you choose in Step 3, drag the appropriate handle:**

   - *Scale:* Corner handles work best for this transformation. Hold down Shift to scale proportionately. You can also click the Maintain Aspect Ratio (lock icon) on the Options bar to do the same. Hold down Alt (Option on the Mac) to scale from the center.

   - *Rotate:* Move your cursor outside the bounding box. When the cursor becomes a curved arrow, drag clockwise or counterclockwise. Hold down Shift to rotate in 15-degree increments.

   - *Skew:* Drag a side handle.

   - *Distort:* Drag a corner handle.

   - *Perspective:* Drag a corner handle.

   - *Warp:* Drag any control point or line on the default custom mesh grid to distort your selection. You can pretty much drag anywhere on the image, even in between mesh lines, to apply the warp. You can't, however, add or delete control points.

With the Warp transformation, you have some additional options. The Options bar has a drop-down list with various warping styles, such as arch, wave, and twist. In fact, these styles are the same ones you find on the Warp Text menu. (See Book IV, Chapter 3.) When you choose one of the styles, Photoshop then applies the mesh grid for that style. Here's the lowdown on the remaining options:

- *Change the warp orientation:* Change the direction of some styles, such as wave, flag, and fish.

- *Bend:* Increase or decrease the value, or drag the handle on the warp style, to increase the distortion.

- *H% and V%:* Increase the percentages to increase the horizontal (H) and vertical (V) distortions.

- *Switch between Free Transform and Warp mode:* Switch between the Free Transform box and the Warp mesh grid.

To warp an image in an even more flexible way, check out the new Puppet Warp feature in Book VII, Chapter 3.

Choosing Rotate 180°, 90° CW, or 90° CCW, or Flip Horizontal or Vertical executes the command. Handle-dragging isn't necessary.

Photoshop executes all the transformations, except Warp, around a point called the *reference point* (dotted square icon). The reference point appears in the center of the transform box by default.

You can move the center point anywhere you want, even outside the bounding box. Additionally, you can set your own reference point for the transformation by clicking a square on the reference point locator on the Options bar. Each square corresponds with a point on the bounding box.

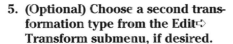

Alaska Stock Images

Figure 3-9: Apply all transformations at the same time to minimize interpolation.

5. **(Optional) Choose a second transformation type from the Edit⇨ Transform submenu, if desired.**

If you're an ultra-precise type of person, you can also numerically transform the selection by entering values on the Options bar.

In Figure 3-9, I executed all the transformations at the same time.

Execute all your transformations in one fell swoop, if possible. In other words, don't scale a selection and five minutes later rotate it and five minutes after that distort it. Every time you apply a transformation to an image, you're putting it through an interpolation process. You want to limit how many times you interpolate an image because it has a degrading effect — your image starts to appear soft and mushy. Only flipping or rotating in 90-degree increments is interpolation-free. For more on interpolation, see Book II, Chapter 1.

For best results when transforming, make sure to set your interpolation method to Bicubic. This setting can be found in your Preferences settings under General.

**Book III
Chapter 3**

**Modifying and
Transforming
Selections and Paths**

If you want to be able to transform your image nondestructively, and indefinitely, use Smart Objects. See Book V, Chapter 5 for details.

6. **After you transform your selection to your liking, click the Commit button on the Options bar, or press Enter (Return on the Mac).**

   To cancel the transformation, press Esc or click the Cancel button on the Options bar.

Your image is now magically transformed. If your image isn't on a layer, you can leave a hole filled with the background color after your image is transformed. Check out Book V to avoid this calamity.

To repeat a transformation, choose Edit⇨Transform⇨Again.

To duplicate an item while transforming, hold down the Alt (Option on the Mac) key when selecting the Transform command.

Transforming Selection Marquees

To transform just the selection marquee — without affecting the underlying pixels — make your desired selection and then choose Select⇨Transform Selection. Photoshop doesn't have a submenu with individual transformations to choose from. Instead, you must apply the transformations as you do with the Free Transform command: by using the keyboard shortcuts. You can also enter values on the Options bar to transform numerically, or you can access the context menu. To move the selection marquee and the bounding box, simply drag inside the marquee or nudge it by pressing the keyboard arrow keys. Transforming selections is particularly handy when you're trying to select elliptical objects. Getting a precise selection the first time around is often hard, so you may need to apply a transformation. For example, in Figure 3-10, I scaled, rotated, and distorted the marquee around my clockface to get a more accurate selection.

Corbis Digital Stock

Figure 3-10: Transform a selection marquee without affecting underlying pixels.

Using Content-Aware Scaling

Content-aware scaling is a cool image-sizing feature also known as *seam carving*. This method of scaling enables you to resize and reshape your images without overdistorting the content and composition of those images. It also preserves image quality much better than traditional transformations. Although the exact way the algorithm works is technically complex, don't worry. It's pretty darn simple to use. Here's how to apply content-aware scaling:

1. **Choose your desired layer in the Layers panel. If you want to isolate the scaling to a selection on the layer, make that selection now.**

   Content-aware scaling doesn't work on adjustment layers, layer masks, individual channels or Smart Objects. For more on layers and Smart Objects, see Book V. For more on channels, see Book VI. If you're scaling a Background layer, choose Select⇨All.

2. **Choose Edit⇨Content-Aware Scale.**

3. **Specify your options on the Options bar as follows:**

   - *Reference Point:* Click a square in the reference point box to specify the axis point. The default location is the center.

   - *Use Relative Positioning for Reference Point (triangle icon):* Select this option to specify the new axis point in relation to its current position.

   - *Amount:* This option specifies the ratio of content-aware scaling to normal scaling. To minimize distortion, specify your Threshold amount. Start with a higher percentage and then adjust accordingly, if necessary.

   - *Protect:* You can designate areas that you want to protect from scaling by selecting them and saving them as alpha channels. (See Book VI, Chapter 1.) If you have an alpha channel, choose it from this submenu.

   - *Protect Skin Tone (man icon):* Select this option to preserve skin tones from distorting when scaling.

4. **Click and drag one of the handles of the scale box that surrounds your layer or selection to resize your image.**

   You can upscale (make your image bigger) or downscale (make your image smaller). You can also use the Horizontal and Vertical Scale numerical fields on the Options bar. Select Maintain Aspect Ratio to keep the scaling proportional (chain icon).

5. **When you have completed your scale, double-click inside the scale box, or press Enter (Return on the Mac) on your keyboard.**

   Check out Figure 3-11 to see the difference between a layer resized with Content-Aware Scale and a layer resized with Free Transform. Note how there is less distortion with the first method.

**Book III
Chapter 3**

**Modifying and
Transforming
Selections and Paths**

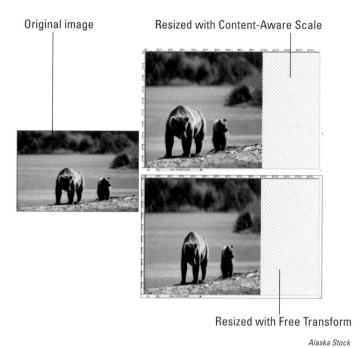

Original image

Resized with Content-Aware Scale

Resized with Free Transform

Alaska Stock

Figure 3-11: Resize your image using content-aware scaling.

Transforming Paths

After you create a bounding box around the path (see Book III, Chapter 2 for more on paths), the transformation technique for paths is the same as it is for selections and selection marquees, except that you can apply the Distort, Perspective, and Warp commands only to whole paths. The major difference between transforming paths and transforming selections is in how you select the path.

To select all paths, follow these steps:

1. **Choose Window⇨Paths.**

2. **Click the pathname in the Paths panel.**

3. **Choose Edit⇨Transform Path and choose your desired transformation from the submenu.**

   You can also choose Edit⇨Free Transform Path.

To select a single path, follow these steps:

1. **Choose Window⇨Paths.**

2. **Click the pathname in the Paths panel.**

3. **Select the Path Selection tool.**

4. **Click the path with the Path Selection tool.**

5. **Choose Edit⇨Transform Path and choose your desired transformation from the submenu.**

   You can also choose Edit⇨Free Transform Path. In Figure 3-12, I transformed the path by rotating it.

To select part of a path, follow these steps:

1. **Choose Window⇨Paths.**

2. **Click the pathname in the Paths panel.**

3. **Select the Direct Selection tool.**

4. **Select the points you want with the Direct Selection tool.**

5. **Choose Edit⇨Transform Points and choose your desired transformation from the submenu.**

You can also choose Edit⇨Free Transform Points.

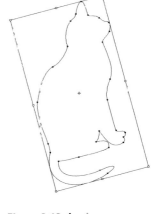

Figure 3-12: Apply transformations to paths.

Putting It Together

Removing a Person (Without Getting in Trouble with the Law)

Follow these steps to seamlessly remove an unwanted element (in this case, a person) from an image:

TIP

When you first attempt this technique, start with an image that has an element that isn't attached to something you want to keep in the image.

1. **Open an image that contains something you want to remove.**

2. **Use the selection tool of your choice to select the element that you want to remove.**

   You don't have to be super-precise, so feel free to grab the Lasso tool. If you need a Lasso refresher, see Book III, Chapter 1. When you make your selection, be careful not to cut off any portion of your element. Otherwise, you leave some stray pixels — a dead giveaway that something was once there. Using the Lasso tool, I made a rough outline around the woman on the right, as shown in the figure.

Selection marquee

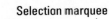

Purestock

continued

Book IV
Painting, Drawing, and Typing

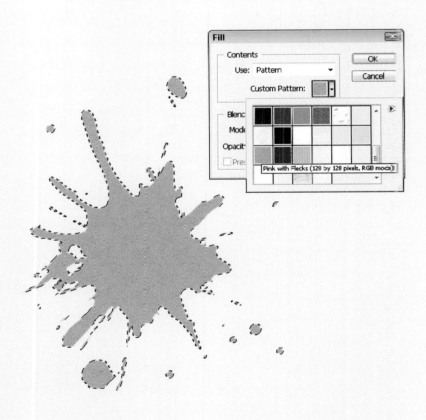

Like a Swiss Army knife, Photoshop does it all. This book describes all you need to know about Photoshop's drawing and painting tools. I first give you the lowdown on the ubiquitous brush. The brush — which is found not only in the Brush tool itself but within several other painting and editing tools — has more variations than you can shake a stick at. I also cover how to create vector shapes with the Shape tools and how to fill and stroke your selections with color. If one color is not enough, keep reading until you get to the section on gradients and patterns. I give you the steps for using the many Photoshop presets and also for creating your own gradients and patterns. Rounding out this section will be an introduction to the 3-D tools. And finally, because man doesn't communicate by images alone, you can find lots of useful information about creating type. Not just regular old run-of-the-mill type, mind you (which is covered, of course), but type on a path, type with shadows and bevels, type filled with images, type warped into shapes — you get the . . . um . . . picture.

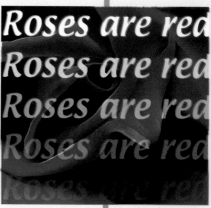

Chapter 1: Painting and Drawing with Photoshop

In This Chapter

✔ **Making pencil sketches and brush strokes**

✔ **Managing brushes with the Brush panel**

✔ **Using Brush presets**

✔ **Understanding vectors**

✔ **Creating basic and custom shapes**

✔ **Setting Geometry options**

You're definitely going to want to brush up on your painting and drawing techniques now that you don't have to worry about messing up your clothes. Painting is one of the basic skills you need to work in Photoshop. After you master the art of painting strokes and working with brushes, you're well on your way to mastering more-advanced techniques, such as masking and retouching, which benefit from strong painting skills. (I introduce the full range of Brush tools in Book I, Chapter 2.)

Hand in hand with painting, of course, is drawing. Photoshop's shape tools add an important dimension to your drawing capabilities. This chapter introduces you to a plethora of tools and techniques. I start with painting and then move on to drawing. Embrace both, and they can serve you well.

Introducing the Pencil and Brush Tools

The Pencil and Brush tools are like peanut butter and chocolate. Not only do they work well together, but they also share many important traits. Just as important, however, are their differences. You can access these tools in the Tools panel. Press B to make the Brush tool appear by default. To access the Pencil, press Shift+B. You can toggle between these tools, along with the Color Replacement tool and Mixer Brush tool, by pressing Shift-B again. Find out more about using these tools in the following sections.

Finding out what the Pencil tool does

The Pencil and Brush tools are very much alike, except that the Pencil tool has hard edges by default (as shown in Figure 1-1) and the Brush tool can have soft, feathered edges. The Pencil tool can also erase what it creates!

Figure 1-1: The Pencil tool draws hard-edged strokes and is perfect for digital sketches.

You can do all the following with the Pencil tool:

- Drag the mouse to draw freehand lines.
- Click at one point, release the mouse button, and then Shift-click at a second point to draw a straight line between the points. As long as you hold down the Shift key, you can keep clicking to draw straight lines between each of the points.
- Press the Alt key (the Option key on the Mac) and click any area of your drawing to switch the foreground color to that hue.
- When using the Pencil, as well as the Brush, Color Replacement, and Mixer Brush tools, press and hold down the V key to access the Move tool temporarily. Release the V key to return to the original tool. This handy shortcut enables you while drawing or painting to move a layer or selection without having to go back and forth to the Tools panel.

The Pencil tool also offers the Auto Erase option, which you activate from the Options bar at the top. Auto Erase is a handy feature that lets you remove portions of your pencil strokes without switching to the Eraser tool. When you have Auto Erase turned on, the operation of the Pencil tool is slightly different from the default. The effect of either of the following actions is that Photoshop erases lines you've drawn:

- When you click an area of the drawing other than an area that's foreground colored (for example, the pencil lines you've already drawn), the Pencil tool begins drawing a line in the foreground color (this is the default mode).

- When you click an area of the drawing that's foreground colored (such as the pencil lines you've drawn), the Pencil tool draws by using the background color

Because the Pencil tool doesn't use soft-edged lines to draw, anything other than straight vertical or horizontal lines has rough, jagged edges (often called *jaggies*), as shown in the close-up image in Figure 1-2. Jaggies aren't objectionable in some cases, especially in higher-resolution images, but if you zoom in on an area containing pencil lines, the jaggies are readily apparent. I show you how to modify the characteristics of the lines drawn with the Pencil tool in the section "Working with the Brush panel," later in this chapter.

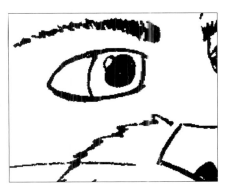

Figure 1-2: Zooming in on hard-edged strokes displays jagged edges.

Using the Pencil tool

If you're ready to start using the Pencil tool, keep in mind that lines that aren't vertical or horizontal look jagged up close. However, this doesn't necessarily pose a problem in all cases, especially when working with Web graphics. Those same hard edges can lend themselves to producing crisp-edged images for display in a browser window. To try out the Pencil tool, follow these steps:

1. **Activate the Pencil tool by selecting it from the Tools panel.**

   The Pencil tool shares a flyout menu with the various Brush tools. You can press Shift+B to make it appear if it's hidden underneath the Brush tool.

   The Pencil tool's current brush tip (usually the 1-pixel brush, unless you select something else) appears in the Brush Preset Picker on the Options bar.

   Click the thumbnail or arrow in the Brush box to summon the Brush Preset Picker panel if you want to select a different-size pencil tip.

2. **If you want to draw using anything other than Normal mode, select a mode from the Mode options menu.**

   Blend modes other than Normal cause colors to interact and blend in different ways. (You can find more about modes in Book V, Chapter 3.)

3. **Select opacity for your pencil strokes.**

   If you want whatever is in the background to show partially through your strokes, select opacity of less than 100 percent by using the slider or by typing an opacity percentage directly into the text box.

4. **Click and drag with the mouse to create your pencil lines.**

Painting with the Brush tool

The Brush tool is a basic tool used throughout Photoshop in various incarnations, so master its use as quickly as possible.

The most important difference between the Brush and the Pencil tools is that, by default, the Brush tool produces soft-edged lines that Photoshop renders smoother by a process known as *anti-aliasing*. This technique substitutes partially filled pixels along the edges of lines to produce the illusion of gradual fading. Our eyes merge the transparent pixels together, so the line looks smooth rather than hard-edged.

Although jagged edges are most apparent in diagonal lines, Photoshop applies anti-aliasing to brush stroke edges, even in horizontal and vertical lines. The fuzzier the brush, the more semi-filled pixels used to produce the effect, as shown in Figure 1-3.

Pencil line   Hard-edge brush line

Soft-edge brush line

Figure 1-3: Strokes from the Pencil and Brush tools vary in the softness of their edges.

The Brush tool shares most of the basic features found in the Pencil tool, except the Auto Erase feature isn't available:

- Select the Brush tool from the Tools panel or press B or Shift+B until you get the Brush.

- Select a brush tip from the Brush Preset Picker on the Options bar.

- Select a mode and opacity from the options on the Options bar.

✔ Drag to paint, click and Shift-click to paint straight lines, and hold down the Shift key while dragging to constrain the Brush tool to horizontal or vertical lines.

✔ Press the Alt key (the Option key on the Mac) and click an area of color to switch the foreground color to that color.

The Brush tool has several other options to select from:

✔ **Flow:** *Flow* determines how quickly the Brush tool applies the paint. You can set a flow rate from 1 to 100 percent by using the Flow slider or by typing a percentage directly into the text box. You might think of it as controlling how liquid the paint is. At low flow rates, Photoshop applies the paint slowly so the color is less intense; at higher flow rates, the paint quickly reaches its full strength while you drag.

✔ **Airbrush:** Click the Airbrush button on the Options bar to switch the Brush tool (as well as many of the other tools that use brush tips) to Airbrush mode. This mode produces the spray effect you get with a traditional airbrush. The longer you hold down the mouse button, the more paint pumps out of the tool, and the wider the airbrush effect spreads, as shown in Figure 1-4.

Figure 1-4: Using the Airbrush option with the Brush tool enables you to create smoky strokes.

✔ **Toggle the Brush Panel:** On the left side of the Options bar is a button (a panel icon) that shows or hides the Brush panel. This button is a quick way to access this valuable panel, and it's available with the Pencil tool and other tools that use brush tips, too. I show you how to use the Brush panel in the upcoming "Working with the Brush panel" section.

Blending with the Mixer Brush tool

The new Mixer Brush tool takes painting one notch higher toward achieving a more realistic, natural media look to the brush strokes. This tool allows you to blend colors (see Figure 1-5) and vary your wetness within a single brush stroke. The Mixer Brush tool uses two paint wells — a "reservoir" that deposits color (Adobe calls it paint) on the canvas and a "pickup" that receives, or picks up, color from the canvas (which can be an image or color you've applied). This is a great tool to try if you want to paint over a photo to make it look more painterly but don't want to apply a filter.

Here's how to use the Mixer Brush tool:

1. **Select the Mixer Brush tool from the Tools panel.**

   This tool shares the same flyout menu as the Brush, Pencil, and Color Replacement tools.

2. **To load color into your reservoir, Alt+click (Option+click) where you wish to sample that color. You can also choose your desired Foreground color from the Tools panel.**

   When you load color from your canvas, your brush tip reflects any color variation in the sampled area. If you want the brush tip to use a single color based on your sampled area, select the Load Solid Colors Only from the Current Brush Load (swatch icon) drop-down menu on the Options bar.

3. **Choose a brush from the Brush Presets panel.**

4. **Set your desired options in the Options bar.** For a description on the various options, see "Painting with the Brush tool" earlier in this chapter and "Choosing a brush-tip shape" later in this chapter.

   Here is a brief rundown on options specific to the Mixer Brush tool:

   - *Current Brush Load Swatch:* Load Brush fills your brush with reservoir color. Clean Brush removes color from your brush. Load Solid Colors Only, as mentioned above, enables you to pick up a uniform versus varied color from your sampled area.

   - *Load Brush after Each Stroke/Clean Brush after Each Stroke:* Automatically loads your brush with reservoir color and then cleans your brush after each stroke. These two options are good options if you want to paint over a photo, for example, to make it look like a painting.

   - *Blending Brush Combinations:* Choose presets, from Dry, Moist, Wet, Very Wet, with variations of mixing levels. Experiment with these combos to see the look they provide.

   - *Specify percentages of Wet, Load, Mix, and Flow:* Wet percentages specify how much color the brush picks up from the canvas. Higher numbers give more paint. Load specifies how much color is loaded in the reservoir. Lower percentages enable the stroke to "dry" out more quickly. Mix controls the ratio of canvas color to reservoir color. A mix percentage of 100% grabs all color from the canvas, whereas 0% gets all color from the reservoir. Flow specifies how much color is pumped out when the Airbrush option is enabled.

   - *Sample All Layers:* Enables you to pick up or blend color from all layers, not just your active layer.

5. **Drag on your image to paint. If you have selected the Airbrush option, you can also hold down your mouse to "build" your color.**

Mixer Brush applied

Original

Figure 1-5: The Mixer Brush tool enables you to blend two colors or more.

Working with the Brush panel

You'll find the Brush panel extremely useful for changing the characteristics of preset brush tips and for creating your own. You can also access and select brush presets, as I discuss in the section "Using the preset brushes," later in this chapter.

You can view the Brush panel in several ways:

- Choose Window⇨Brush from the menu bar.
- Click the Brush panel's icon in the Photoshop panel dock.
- Toggle the Brush panel's button on the left side of the Options bar.
- Press F5 to toggle the Brush panel open or closed.
- Grab the Brush panel's icon and drag it out of the dock and onto your Photoshop desktop. This mode keeps the Brush panel easily accessible until you put it away by dragging it to the dock, clicking its Close box, or rendering it hidden by choosing Window⇨Brush.

The Brush panel displays a list of brush properties on the left and includes a brush-stroke preview at the bottom of the panel.

The largest pane in the panel, on the right, shows various types of information, such as the size and type of brush tip, or the different controls offered for any of the 11 properties you can set.

Book IV Chapter 1

Painting and Drawing with Photoshop

No longer does the Brush panel have to share a space with the Brush presets. Click the new Brush Presets button located in the upper-left of the Brush panel; a separate Brush Presets panel appears. Additionally, preset previews appear on the right side of the Brush panel, as well as a Size (diameter) slider.

Choosing a brush-tip shape

When you select Brush Tip Shape on the left side of the Brush panel, a scrolling box shows the available brush tips, as shown in Figure 1-6.

The 11 brush parameters you can choose to apply and edit display in the left column. You can select any of these options to apply them to the currently selected brush. Click the option name to edit its characteristics. You must select the parameter name to access the options. Toggling the parameter on by checking the check box doesn't work. Here are the Brush Tip Shape characteristics:

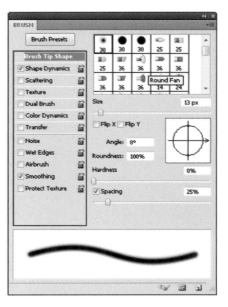

Figure 1-6: The Brush panel offers a multitude of different brush tips.

- ✔ **Shape Dynamics:** Controls the amount of jitter (randomness or variation) produced when you draw a stroke, the minimum diameter, tilt, angle and roundness jitter, minimum roundness, and other options. The higher the value, the greater the variance for each option.

Some of these options apply only when you're using a pressure-sensitive digital tablet. Check your digital tablet's instruction manual for more information on how to customize brushes for your tablet.

The Flip X and Flip Y jitter option flips the brush shape across the horizontal axis (X) or the vertical axis (Y). For example, if your brush is an L shape and you select Flip X, your brush shape becomes a backward L. Check Flip Y to make your brush shape an upside-down L shape. Check both to make your brush shape an upside-down, backward L shape.

- ✔ **Scattering:** Controls the number and position of brush marks in a stroke. The higher the value, the higher the number of brush marks and the farther apart they are. When you select Both Axes, Photoshop distributes the brush marks radially, as if on a curve. Count controls the number of brush marks at each spacing point. The higher the value, the greater the number of marks.

✔ **Texture:** Allows you to impart a texture pattern (using the foreground color) to a brush stroke; a Photoshop preset texture or one of your designs. Select Invert to reverse the light and dark pixels in the pattern. Scale sizes the pattern in each stroke. Texture Each Tip renders each tip when it's stroked, giving a more saturated effect. Depth controls how prominent the pattern appears against the brush stroke. Minimum Depth specifies the minimum depth that the paint of each stroke shows through the pattern. Mode lets you choose one of Photoshop's blending modes, as I describe in Book V, Chapter 3. You can find more about creating and working with patterns in Book IV, Chapter 3.

✔ **Dual Brush:** You can use two tips to draw with a single brush. This option lets you select the characteristics of the second tip by using the same type of attributes — such as diameter, spacing, and scatter — that you applied to the first tip. You can also specify a blending mode between the two tips.

✔ **Color Dynamics:** Uses your foreground and background colors to adjust how the color varies during a stroke, allowing you to create a multicolored brush. Slight variations give the stroke a more natural, organic look. You can introduce slight (or major) jitter to the hue, saturation, brightness, and purity of the colors, as well as some randomness between the foreground and background colors when you draw a stroke. Without color dynamics, the stroke color remains constant.

✔ **Transfer:** Controls the buildup of color; that is, how much color transfers onto the brush tip. Options include introducing randomness into the opacity and flow factors of a brush, again making the brush stroke look more natural and less machine-generated. The new Wet and Mix options are available when you select the Mixer Brush tool. Experiment with all the dynamics to see exactly how they can affect your image. The Flow and Opacity settings in the Brush panel don't override those settings on the Options bar.

Here's a list of brush-tip characteristics, which you can find on the left side of the Brush panel:

✔ **Noise:** Adds random pixels to brush tips, giving them texture and an organic quality. This option is more apparent in feathered brushes.

✔ **Wet Edges:** The brush tip leaves a stroke that looks more like watercolor, with paint building up along the edges.

✔ **Airbrush:** Gives the brush tip a soft, airbrushed look.

✔ **Smoothing:** Smoothes curves when you draw arcs with the brush. This option is more noticeable when you use a pressure-sensitive drawing tablet.

✔ **Protect Texture:** Ensures that all brush tips that use a texture use the same texture. Therefore, you can switch back and forth between brush tips while painting and still achieve a consistent texture.

Figure 1-7 shows the range of possibilities these options offer.

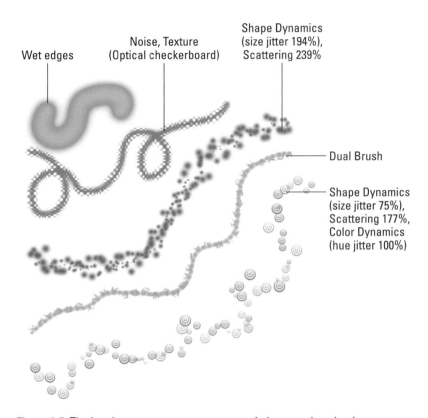

Shape Dynamics
(size jitter 194%),
Scattering 239%

Wet edges

Noise, Texture
(Optical checkerboard)

Dual Brush

Shape Dynamics
(size jitter 75%),
Scattering 177%,
Color Dynamics
(hue jitter 100%)

Figure 1-7: The brushes you can create are as varied as your imagination.

You can lock any of the brush characteristics by clicking the small lock icon to the right of the characteristic. Locking a characteristic ensures that the settings don't change after you have your brush just so. This works especially well if you want the size of your brush to correlate with the amount of pressure you apply to a stylus when using a drawing tablet. By locking settings, you override any specifications set by preset brushes. You can select the Reset All Locked Settings option from the Brush panel pop-up menu to bring back the default settings of the brush. To clear all brush options, select Clear Brush Controls from the Brush panel pop-up menu.

If you really like a brush you've created, feel free to save it as a preset that you can access again and again. Simply select New Brush Preset from the pop-up menu on the Brush panel or from the Brush drop-down panel on the Options bar.

Using the preset brushes

Photoshop has two brush panels, in a sense. In addition to the Brush panel, the Brush Preset Picker (shown in Figure 1-7) on the Options bar appears when you click the down arrow next to the box displaying the active brush tip.

With CS5, Photoshop offers a separate, dedicated Brush Presets panel, as shown in Figure 1-8.

Photoshop has a large number of pre-designed brush presets that you can use. The default set includes round, hard-edged brushes (which still have softer edges than the Pencil tool) and round soft-edged brushes. There are also airbrush, spatter, and natural media brush-tip presets, as well as a group of brush-tip shapes, such as stars, leaves, and other shapes. In CS5, you also get a set of new "bristle" tip brushes. You can also download brushes galore from the Web, so go crazy. Just Google "photoshop brushes" and watch in amazement as you get page after page of available downloads.

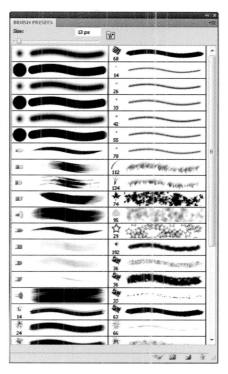

Figure 1-8: The Brush Presets panel offers a deluge of premade brushes.

A preset brush's pixel diameters appear as text next to a thumbnail image of the brush shape when the panel's display is in default mode. To use one of these brushes, just click the Brush Preset Picker arrow or thumbnail on the Options bar, or click the brush in the Brush Presets panel and then select the brush you want from the scrolling preset list. You can augment your choices with any of the following options:

✔ **Move the Size slider to change the diameter of the selected brush.** This is a quick way of getting a slightly larger or smaller brush when none of the presets meets your needs exactly. For example, the hard-round brush preset is 13 pixels in diameter. You can click this brush tip and move the slider to the right to get a hard-edged brush in any size up to 2,500 pixels.

To change the brush size by using the keyboard when a tool is active, press the] key (the right bracket) to increase the size and the [key (the left bracket) to decrease the size. The amount of change varies according to the initial size of the brush. To adjust the size more dramatically, continue to press the bracket key.

✔ **Click the curved arrow icon to restore the brush to its original size.**

✔ **Select any of the libraries of additional brush-tip presets provided with Photoshop.** Click the Brush Preset Picker or the Brush Presets panel's pop-up menu and select one of the brush libraries shown at the bottom. They have names like Special Effect Brushes and Faux Finish Brushes. Select whether to append the brushes to your current set or to replace the current set with the library you select from the dialog box that appears.

✔ **CS5 has provided a new set of preset brush tips referred to as "bristle" brushes.** These brushes create realistic brush stokes that appear to have been made using natural, not digital, media. You can specify options for the brush tips to change the shape, bristles (density), length, thickness, stiffness (flexibility), angle, and spacing.

You can also manage brush-tip libraries by using the Preset Manager. (See Book I, Chapter 5 for information on using the Preset Manager.) Click the Preset Manager icon at the bottom of the Brush Presets panel to access it directly.

✔ **Select a custom library of brush tips that you've created.** Click Load Brushes to append new brushes to your current collection or to replace them with the new library.

✔ **In the Brush Preset Picker, if the Hardness option is available, adjust the slider to make the brush more (higher) or less (lower) fuzzy.**

In addition to the presets Photoshop offers, you can create your own presets to use when you need them. Book I, Chapter 2 explains how to create your own presets.

Viewing preset brushes

You can change the way brushes are shown in the Brush Preset Picker, the Brush panel, and the Brush Presets panel by selecting a viewing mode from the Picker's or panels' pop-up menus:

✔ **Text Only:** Displays the names of the brush tips in several columns (depending on how wide you've made the panel).

✔ **Small Thumbnail:** The default view, with a thumbnail image of the brush tip and its diameter in pixels.

✔ **Large Thumbnail:** Provides a closer look at the brush tip.

✔ **Small List:** Shows a column list of the brush tips with their text names and small thumbnails.

✔ **Large List:** Shows a column list of the brush tips with their text names and larger thumbnails.

✔ **Stroke Thumbnail:** Shows a typical stroke from the selected brush so you can see how it looks when applied.

✔ **Bristle Brush Preview** (in the Brush Preset panel): Click the first icon on the bottom left to toggle a preview window of the Bristle Brush tip, which appears on the image window. Click the preview window to view the brush from different angles.

Putting It Together

Colorizing Black-and-White Images

Just as there are valid artistic reasons for shooting a photo in black and white, there are equally reasonable rationales for changing a grayscale image into a color one. Perhaps the picture is an old one, taken before color film was widely used, and you want to colorize it. Or you may come across a monochrome image that would look even better in color. Photoshop lets you restore black-and-white pictures to their original colors or create entirely new color schemes. If you can imagine an image in color, use Photoshop to add the hues you want to see.

IT Stock Free

In my example, which you can find on this book's Web site (see the Introduction for details), I chose a black-and-white photo of an adorable boy. Rather than a full-color treatment that attempts to duplicate a color photograph, I want to apply a technique that mimics the hand-colored look of the venerable Marshall's Photo Coloring System of

continued

continued

pigments, photo oils, spot colors, retouch pencils, and other products so popular in the '50s and '60s (and enjoying a rebirth today). Although I've worked with a Marshall's kit myself, Photoshop is a lot faster and easier, and less messy.

1. **Open a grayscale image in Photoshop.**

2. **Choose Image⇨Mode⇨RGB Color to convert the grayscale image to a full-color image (even though it presently still lacks any color).**

3. **Choose Layer⇨New⇨Layer.**

   This creates a new transparent layer to paint on, as shown in the figure. Although you can paint directly on an image layer (or a copy of an image layer), using an empty layer is safer and gives you more flexibility in backtracking when you make a mistake. (For more information on working with layers, consult Book V.)

4. **In the New Layer dialog box that appears, name the layer and then click OK.**

   You can paint all your colors on a single layer, but you may find that using a separate layer for each part of the face lets you fade that color in and out as required to blend smoothly with your other hues.

5. **Select the Color mode from the Blend Mode drop-down list in the Layers panel.**

   Photoshop uses this mode to combine the painting layer with the image layer, enabling you to apply color while retaining the details of the underlying image.

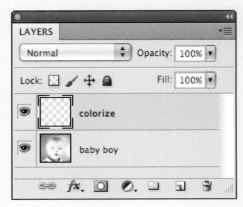

6. **Select a color you want to apply from the Swatches panel or use the Color panel to mix your own.**

   You can find information on color in Book II, Chapter 3.

7. **Select the Brush tool in the Tools panel.**

8. **Click the down arrow next to the Brush Preset Picker on the Options bar and select a brush from the list.**

   Hard-edged brushes appear first, and the soft-edged brushes follow. I would start with a soft-edged brush.

   The Airbrush option on the Options bar creates a very subtle and soft effect. Just be sure you pick the kind of brush that works best for the area of the picture you're colorizing. (Use a small, fuzzy brush for smaller areas, and use a bigger, sharper brush for more defined lines and wider areas.)

9. **Paint all the parts of the image where you want to apply color.**

If you make a mistake, you can erase the bad strokes without affecting the underlying grayscale image because you're painting on a separate layer.

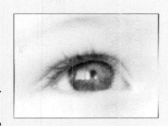

In my example, I chose a nice, light blue color to change the color of the boy's eyes, as shown in the figure. A small fuzzy brush is perfect for a small area such as the eyes.

Change brushes as necessary by clicking the Brush Preset Picker on the Options bar and selecting a larger or smaller brush.

10. **When you finish with that area of the image, create a new layer for each of the main components of the photograph and repeat Steps 4 through 9 with an additional color.**

I painted the eyes, lips, cheeks, hair, and hair highlights separately because creating natural, subtle effects with people's skin, hair, and eyes takes a special touch:

- ✔ *Eyes:* When painting the eyes, paint only the irises and leave the pupils their original black color. Don't paint over the catchlights in the eyes, either. (*Catchlights* are reflections of light sources, such as windows or the flash.

- ✔ *Lips:* Color the inner surface of the lips a darker, rosier pink than the outer surface. Lips look best when portrayed in at least two shades. Don't forget to color the gums with an even lighter pink.

- ✔ *Hair:* Hair looks best when the highlights and darker portions are slightly different colors.

- ✔ *Cheeks:* To put a little blush in the cheeks, choose the Airbrush option on the Options bar and work with a relatively large brush size. Apply a good dash of color to each cheek and a lighter bit of color to the forehead and chin. (I used a 300-pixel brush for this high-resolution image.)

  I left the clothes and background uncolored to emphasize that the focal point is the boy's face.

11. **For the overall skin tone, I chose a different technique, using the Hue/Saturation command. This technique works especially well with those who have naturally dark complexions. You can choose to paint the skin with a brush or use this technique:**

- ✔ Duplicate the grayscale image layer and then choose Image➪Adjustments➪Hue/Saturation.

- ✔ Choose the Colorize option and move the Hue slider to the left to produce a sepia tone. I set my Hue to 36. Set Saturation to 25 percent and click OK to colorize this layer.

continued

continued

TIP

✔ Use the Eraser tool to remove everything in the colorized layer that isn't skin. In my example, I removed the hair, background, eyes, lips, teeth, and clothing. The result is a nice sepia tone to the face.

Be sure to pick a color that's as close to real life as possible. If the subject has darker skin, you may need to move away from rosier blush tones.

12. **When you finish coloring your layers, you can experiment with different opacity levels for each colorized layer to see whether more-transparent hues might look better.**

Drawing with Vector Shapes

Although I'm a big fan of photos and all the pixels that make up those photos, sometimes you have to call on a vector or two. Maybe you need to create a simple line art graphic for a Web page. Or perhaps you want to add a logo to a poster. In these instances, drawing a vector shape with the Pen or Shape tool is the way to go.

Before you begin creating vector shapes in Photoshop, having a firm grasp on the basics of pixels versus vectors is a big help. Vectors describe a shape mathematically; pixel images, on the other hand, describe the same shape in terms of a map of pixels. The key difference is that, while you increase the size of a pixel-based image, it begins to look blocky. Because vector images are based on mathematical formulas, they look good at any size. Figure 1-9 shows both types of image. I explain the difference between vector and pixel-based images in more detail in Book II, Chapter 1.

When you create vector objects in a program like Photoshop, they're comprised of paths, which are made of anchor points, and straight and curved segments, or *lines*. You can create these points and lines by working with the preset shapes or by creating your own shape. The presets are easier to work with, but the custom shapes enable you to be more creative. In the following sections, I walk you through the steps for creating vector shapes, as well as the various options.

Vector image   Pixel image

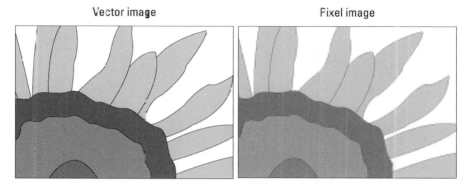

Figure 1-9: Photoshop images fall into one of two camps — vector or pixel.

Drawing a preset shape

Follow these steps to draw a preset shape in your document:

1. **Select a Shape tool from the Tools panel.**

   You can also press U and select the shape tool from the Options bar. You can select from the following shape tools (shown in Figure 1-10):

   - *Rectangle/Ellipse:* The rectangle and ellipse have no special parameters on the Options bar; however, they both behave much like their counterparts among the selection tools. For example, you can hold down the Shift key while dragging a shape to produce a perfect square or circle; hold down Shift+Alt (Shift+Option on the Mac) to draw the shape outward from the center. You have other Geometry options that let you determine how you draw the shapes (unconstrained, fixed size, from center, and so forth).

   - *Rounded Rectangle:* This shape has the same options as the rectangle shape, with the addition of a box in which you can type the radius of the circle used to round the corners of the rectangle.

   - *Polygon:* This shape includes a box in which you can enter the number of sides (from 3 to 100) you want for the polygon, as well as Geometry options.

Shape mode   Shape tools   Custom shape panel

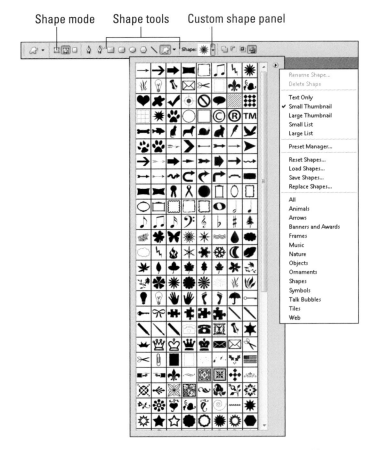

Figure 1-10: The shape tools and Options bar give you everything you need to make shapes, from simple squares to ornate *fleur-de-lys*.

- *Line:* You can give the line shape a width from 1 to 1,000 pixels and assign a layer style and/or fill color. You can also enter parameters for an arrowhead at either or both ends.

- *Custom:* You can find numerous preset custom shapes to choose from. As with any shape, you hold down Shift to constrain proportions or Alt (Option on the Mac) to draw from the center out.

2. **Select the mode for the shape you want to draw from the three icons on the Options bar.**

   Here's a list of ways in which you can create a shape (all options are on the Options bar):

   - *Shape Layers:* Click this icon to create the shape in a new layer of its own. When you select this mode, icons appear on the Options bar that let you select a layer style and/or fill color.

Shape Layers is a good choice if you want to keep your shapes in separate layers so you can manipulate them further. (Some options include making the shapes appear to have been added together, subtracted from each other, and so on.) Photoshop links shapes in a shape layer to a vector mask, which can show or hide portions of an image. You can find out more about shape layers and vector masks in the sections "Creating your own custom shape" and "Using vector masks," later in this chapter. The shapes remain scalable until you change them into pixels by choosing Layer➪Rasterize➪Shape.

- *Paths:* Click this icon to create the shape with a path, which "hovers" over your image. The shape appears as a path that you can edit by using the Pen tools and the Paths panel. (For everything you need to know about paths, check out Book III, Chapter 2.)

- *Fill Pixels:* Click this icon to create a shaped area filled with the foreground color. This option doesn't produce a vector shape, but instead fills the shape with pixels. The process is similar to filling a selection created with the Rectangular or Elliptical Marquee tools or painting on your canvas with a painting tool. When you select this mode, the Options bar includes choices that let you specify a blending mode, the transparency of the filled area, and whether you want the area anti-aliased. You can't edit a shape created with this option, except to modify the pixels.

3. **Select your options — on the Options bar (if any) and in the Geometry options drop-down panel, which also resides on the Options bar.**

   The Options bar changes to reflect each type of shape; each type has its own options, which are listed in Step 1. For detailed explanations on the various Geometry options, see the section "Setting Geometry options," later in this chapter.

   If you chose the Custom Shape tool in Step 1, click the drop-down arrow to access the Shapes panel. Select the shape that works for you. You can access more preset shape libraries via the pop-up menu at the top of the panel (refer to Figure 1-10).

4. **Drag in the document to draw the shape you've defined.**

   The shape appears in the image window. If you chose the Shape Layer mode in Step 2, the shape also appears in the Layers panel in its own layer. A rectangle filled with the foreground color appears in the image column, and the shape itself is shown in the mask column as a vector mask, as you can see in Figure 1-11. The black layer peeks through my vector mask, which is in the shape of pinwheels.

Drawing multiple shapes in a shape layer

After you create a shape layer, you can draw additional shapes in the layer, adding to the vector mask associated with that layer. You can add, subtract, overlap, and intersect shapes in exactly the same way you do with selections, as described in Book III, Chapter 3. Follow these steps:

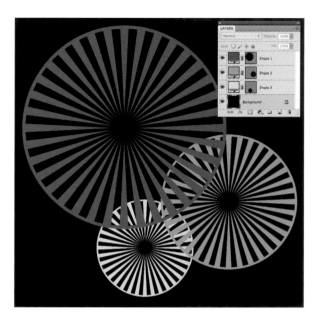

Figure 1-11: When you create a shape layer, you're creating a layer of color that shows through a vector mask (path) in the form of your shape.

1. **After you create the first shape, as I explain in the preceding section, select your desired state button on the Options bar:**

   - *Add to Shape Area:* Combines and joins two or more shapes

   - *Subtract from Shape Area:* Subtracts one shape from another shape

   - *Intersect Shape Areas:* Creates a shape only from the areas that overlap

   - *Exclude Overlapping Shape Areas:* Creates a shape only from the areas that don't overlap

2. **Grab your desired shape tool and draw the next shape.**

Hold down the Shift key to temporarily switch to Add to Shape Area while drawing a new shape. Hold down the Alt (Option on the Mac) key to temporarily switch to Subtract from Shape Area. This works just like adding or subtracting selections.

Setting Geometry options

Geometry options for your shapes (rectangle/rounded rectangle, ellipse, polygon, line, and custom) help define how the shapes look. Click the down arrow on the Options bar to access the Geometry options. The following sections show you what you can do with these options.

Rectangular-shape Geometry options

Here are the Geometry options for the rectangle and rounded rectangle shapes, as shown in Figure 1-12:

- **Unconstrained:** When you select this option (the default), Photoshop defines the size and proportions of the rectangle while you drag.

- **Square:** Select this button to constrain the shape to a perfect square. (You can also hold down the Shift key to do the same thing on the fly.)

- **Fixed Size:** This option lets you draw rectangles only in fixed sizes. Specify the exact size by entering a width and height.

Figure 1-12: Geometry options define how your particular shape appears.

- **Proportional:** This option lets you define an aspect ratio, or proportion, for the rectangle. Type 3 into the W box and 4 into the H box to constrain yourself to drawing any size rectangle with fixed proportions in a 3:4 ratio.

- **From Center:** Select this option to expand the shape from the center point you click.

- **Snap to Pixels:** This option snaps the edges of a rectangle or rounded rectangle to the pixels on your screen.

Elliptical-shape Geometry options

The ellipse shape has the same options that are available for rectangles (also shown in Figure 1-11). Of course, instead of being able to create a perfect square, you can restrain the shape to be a perfect circle. Also, the Snap to Pixels option (available for rectangles) doesn't exist for ellipses.

Polygonal-shape Geometry options

The Geometry options for the polygon shape, as shown in Figure 1-13, include:

- **Radius:** Controls the distance from the center of a polygon to its outer points.

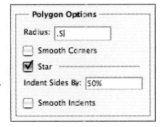

Figure 1-13: Choose between a polygon and a star.

✓ **Smooth Corners:** Select this option to round off the corners.

✓ **Star:** Select this option to create a star shape — that is, a polygon in which the sides indent inward, rather than extend outward from the corner points.

✓ **Indent Sides By:** The value entered here determines the amount the sides indent inward.

✓ **Smooth Indents:** Rounds off the inner corners created by indenting the sides.

✓ **Sides:** Directly in the Options bar, indicate the number of sides for your polygon or the number of points for your star.

Line Geometry options

The line's Geometry settings include whether to put arrowheads at the start or end of the line, as shown in Figure 1-14, or both. Figure 1-14 also shows how changing the width, length, and concavity settings affect the arrowhead shapes.

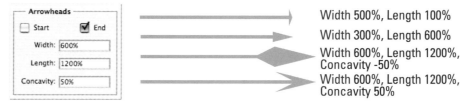

Width 500%, Length 100%

Width 300%, Length 600%

Width 600%, Length 1200%, Concavity -50%

Width 600%, Length 1200%, Concavity 50%

Figure 1-14: By specifying the width, length, and concavity, you can change the appearance of your arrowheads.

Custom-shape Geometry options

The custom shape options are similar to those you find for the other Geometry shapes — with a couple additions, shown in Figure 1-15:

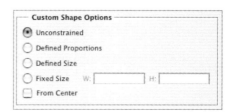

Figure 1-15: You can size your shape without losing its original proportions by checking the Defined Proportions option.

✓ **Defined Proportions:** When you use this option, Photoshop limits any shapes created by using this new custom shape to the *proportions* you use when you create it now. That is, you can change the size of a new shape, but only in proportion with the original custom shape that you created.

✓ **Defined Size:** When you use this option, Photoshop limits any shapes generated based on this new custom shape to the size you set now.

Creating your own custom shape

You can create your own custom shape by defining the shape with a vector mask. work path, or saved path. You can find out more about creating work paths and saved paths in Book III, Chapter 2. To create a shape and add it to your shape library, follow these steps:

1. **Select the Pen tool from the Tools panel or press Shift+P until the Pen tool is selected.**

2. **Select the Shape Layers icon on the Options bar and use the pen to draw the shape you want to create.**

   Book III, Chapter 2 describes the techniques for adding, removing, and adjusting the shapes of curves with the Pen tool.

   Photoshop automatically places the shape you create in its own shape layer as a vector mask. Find out more about what you can do with a vector mask in the following section.

3. **In the Paths panel, select the path or vector mask you want to convert into a custom shape.**

4. **Choose Edit⇨Define Custom Shape from the menu bar.**

   The Shape Name dialog box appears, as shown in Figure 1-16.

   Figure 1-16: Create your own shapes when you tire of the presets.

5. **Enter a descriptive name for your new shape in the dialog box and then click OK.**

   The new shape appears in the custom shapes pop-up panel on the Options bar.

6. **Select Save Shapes from the Shapes panel's pop-up menu to store your new library on your hard drive.**

Although you can't create a shape with the Preset Manager, you can use the Preset Manager to manage the shapes in your shape library.

Using vector masks

When you create a shape in Shape Layer mode, Photoshop automatically saves the shape as a vector mask. Essentially, a shape layer has two components. First, Photoshop entirely fills the layer with color. Then, Photoshop places the shape, which (again) is comprised of a path, on top. The thumbnails in the Layers panel visually display this concept. The color peeks through the outline of the shape, and Photoshop hides (or masks) the rest of the layer. In other words, vector masks clip away the color of a shape layer. If you delete a vector mask, you're left with just a layer of solid color.

Like all vector objects, vector paths print at the full resolution of the printer and are resolution-independent.

You can edit a shape that Photoshop has saved as a vector mask at any time. Simply click the vector mask thumbnail to select it. Then, use the Shape and Pen tools to edit the shape.

Here are some additional things you can do with a vector mask:

- ✓ To remove a vector mask, drag its thumbnail in the Layers panel to the Trash icon at the bottom of the panel. You can also select the layer and choose Layer➪Vector Mask➪Delete.

- ✓ To enable or disable a vector mask, Shift-click its thumbnail in the Layers panel, or select the layer and choose Layer➪Vector Mask➪Disable (or Enable). Photoshop marks the thumbnails of disabled vector masks with an X.

- ✓ You can convert a vector mask to a layer mask by selecting the layer and choosing Layer➪Rasterize➪Vector Mask.

There is an additional tool to refine masks — both vector and pixel. Choose Window➪Masks to bring up this useful panel. Move the Feather slider to soften the edges of your hard-edged vector mask. Drag the Density slider to control the opacity of the areas outside the vector mask. For more details on this great panel, see Book VI, Chapter 3.

Manipulating shapes

You can manipulate shapes you create by using a variety of tools. Here's a quick list of the things you can do:

- ✓ **Move:** Select the Move tool (press V) to move shapes in their layer.

- ✓ **Delete:** Select a shape and press Delete to remove it.

- ✓ **Adjust anchor points:** Use the Direct Selection tool to manipulate anchor points, direction handles, lines, and curves.

- ✓ **Transform shapes:** Choose Edit➪Transform Path or with the Move tool selected, select the Show Transform Controls option on the Options bar to transform shapes. For more information, see Book III, Chapter 3.

- ✓ **Align and distribute shapes:** Use active buttons on the Options bar when you have the Move tool selected to change alignment and distribution along an imaginary line (shown on the button).

- ✓ **Clone a shape:** Hold down Alt (Option on the Mac) and move the shape with the Path Selection tool.

You can find more information on manipulating shapes in Book III, Chapter 2.

Remember that if you select the Fill Pixels option on the Options bar, you're stuck with limited editing capabilities.

Chapter 2: Filling and Stroking

In This Chapter

✓ **Filling and stroking selections or paths**

✓ **Building and applying gradients**

✓ **Creating and applying patterns**

*P*hotoshop offers several ways to create elements, such as geometric shapes, out of pixels. Filling and stroking these elements are two of the most venerable commands at your disposal. You can also paint geometric elements on your canvas by hand or convert vector shapes to pixels (see Book IV, Chapter 1 for more on that topic). Therefore, if you need pixels arranged into regular circles, ellipses, and polygons, the Fill and Stroke facilities of Photoshop are worthy of your consideration.

Here's how they work:

✓ The Fill command adds color, a pattern, or content to a selection of any shape (or form) you've created.

✓ The Stroke command applies color around the selection outline only.

This chapter shows you how to create these objects by filling and stroking selections and paths, how to add smooth gradient blends, and the best ways to apply patterns. After reading this chapter, you'll have your fill of different strokes.

Another way of filling is by using a fill layer, which you can use to fill a shape. Because fill layers work a little differently from the types of fills discussed in this chapter, I cover them in Book V, Chapter 1.

Filling a Selection with a Solid Color

When you just want to add a solid color, you use either the foreground or the background color. (These colors appear at the bottom of the Tools panel, as I explain in Book I, Chapter 2.) The following steps show you the basics of filling a selection with either the foreground or the background color (you have plenty of other Fill options, which I discuss in the following sections):

1. **Create your selection on a layer.**

   See Book III for all you need to know about selections and Book V for the scoop on layers.

2. **Select a fill color as the foreground or background color.**

   Choose Window➪Color. In the Color panel, use the color sliders to mix your desired color. For more on choosing color, see Book II, Chapter 3.

3. **Choose Edit➪Fill.**

   The Fill dialog box, shown in Figure 2-1, appears. In this dialog box, under Contents, you can select whether to fill with the foreground or the background color. You also can select Color (which launches the Color Picker), Black, 50% Gray, White, History, Pattern, or the new Content-Aware option.

4. **Click OK.**

   The color that you choose fills the selection.

Figure 2-1: You can fill your selection with color, history, a pattern, or content.

You can select a blending mode, the fill opacity, and choose whether to fill the entire selection or only the portions of the selection that contain pixels (the nontransparent areas). I recommend not adjusting your Blending Mode or Opacity settings in the Fill dialog box; instead create a new layer for your fill and adjust those settings in the Layers panel, where you have more flexibility. For all you need to know about layers, check out Book V.

Fill Options and Tips

After you make a selection, you're ready to use one of the Fill options. You can use the Fill dialog box (as described in the preceding section) to fill the selection with the foreground or the background color; you can also choose to fill the selection with color, black, white, gray, a pattern, history, or content. Photoshop is full of shortcuts and options. Here are just a few:

> ✔ With the selection active, press Alt+Backspace (Option+Delete on the Mac) to fill the selection with the foreground color. All areas within the selection, including transparent areas, fill with the color.

> ✔ Fill only the pixels in a selection with the foreground color, leaving any transparent pixels transparent, by pressing Alt+Shift+Backspace (or Option+Shift+Delete on the Mac). For more on transparency, see Book V, Chapter 1.

> Lock the transparent pixels in a layer (and its selections) by clicking the Transparency icon in the Lock area of the Layers panel.

✔ If you're working on the Background layer, you can also fill the selection with the background color by pressing the Backspace (Delete on the Mac) key. This opens the Fill dialog box. Choose your desired Fill option from the Use drop-down menu. (Pressing Backspace/Delete on other layers creates a transparent area that shows the image in the layer underneath the selection.)

✔ By selecting the Color option in the Fill dialog box, you access the Color Picker where you can select any color of the rainbow to fill your selection. For more on using the Color Picker, see Book II, Chapter 3.

✔ Select the Content-Aware option in the Fill dialog box to fill the selection with similar content that's close to your selection, as shown in Figure 2-2. If you are trying to create a realistic composite, be sure to look at the results closely. Sometimes this option can create soft or choppy edges.

Selection marquee

Selection filled with content

Figure 2-2: Fill your selection with content from your image.

✔ Select the Pattern option in the Fill dialog box to fill the selection with a pattern. Click the arrow next to the pattern swatch and select a pattern from the pop-up panel. Click the Pattern panel pop-up menu to select more pattern libraries.

✔ Select the History option in the Fill dialog box to restore the selection to a state or snapshot of the image. For more on working with the History panel, see Book II, Chapter 4.

✔ Paint part or all the interior of the selection by using any of the Brush tools, as shown in Figure 2-3. This option lets you partially fill a selection by using a bit of flexibility and creativity. When you paint a selection by using Brush tools, Photoshop confines the paint inside the boundaries of your selection. For more on painting, see Book IV, Chapter 1.

✔ Pour color from the Paint Bucket tool into the selection.

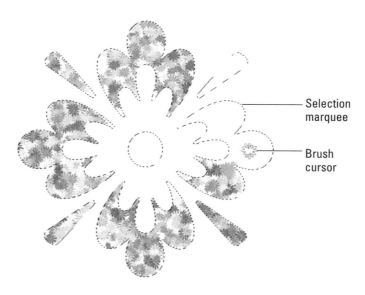

Selection marquee

Brush cursor

Figure 2-3: The marquee confines your brushstrokes to your selected area.

Pouring with the Paint Bucket Tool

The Paint Bucket tool, available in the Tools panel (where it shares a flyout menu with the Gradient tool), operates much like a combination of the Brush tool and the Magic Wand tool, as you can see by looking over its options.

To use it, select the tool (press Shift+G until it's active) and click inside the selection you want to fill. Here are your options, all of which are on the Options bar:

- ✔ **Fill:** You can select whether to fill with the foreground color or a pattern.

- ✔ **Pattern:** When you select Pattern on the Options bar, you can select a preset pattern, load patterns from your pattern libraries, or create a pattern of your own. You can find more information on patterns in the section "Working with Patterns," later in this chapter.

- ✔ **Mode:** You can select a fill blend mode, too, although you'll be better served to set your blend mode via your Layers panel due to better editing flexibility. You can find more information on these modes in Book V, Chapter 3.

- ✔ **Opacity:** Adjust this value to make your fill semitransparent.

- ✔ **Tolerance:** Like the Magic Wand tool, you can choose a Tolerance level (0 to 255) that specifies how similar in color a pixel must be before it's selected for painting. You can find more information on Tolerance levels in Book III, Chapter 1.

- ✔ **Anti-Alias:** Choose this option to blend in the paint smoothly with the areas not filled.

- ✔ **Contiguous:** When selected, the paint fills only pixels that are touching within your selection. When deselected, paint fills all pixels within the Tolerance level that you specify within your selection.

- ✔ **All Layers:** This option applies paint based on the colors in all layers that are within the selection and Tolerance level you specify.

 As with other tools that fill, you can prevent the Paint Bucket tool from filling the transparent pixels. Just select the Transparency icon in the Lock area of the Layers panel.

Stroking a Selection

Stroking enables you to create outlines of selections, layers, or paths. Stroking a selection creates a border around the selection. It's up to you to decide whether to put the border inside, outside, or centered on the selection. (Photoshop doesn't care.)

To stroke a selection, follow these steps:

1. **In the Tools or Colors panel, choose a foreground color and make a selection of your choice.**

2. **Choose Edit⇨Stroke.**

3. **In the Stroke dialog box, adjust the settings and the options, as shown in Figure 2-4:**

- *Width:* You can select 1 to 250 pixels. You can also type a value by using another measurement, such as inches, but Photoshop converts it to pixel values before applying.

- *Color:* Click in the Color box to select the hue you want from the Color Picker.

- *Location:* Select where Photoshop should apply the stroke in relation to your selection border. The Inside option always gives you sharp corners on a rectangle. The Center and Outside options can result in blunt, mitered corners.

- *Mode:* This determines how the stroke color merges with other colors on the same layer.

Figure 2-4: Apply strokes to your selection up to 250 pixels wide.

- *Opacity:* The default value is 100%. If you want the stroke to be semi-transparent, type another value.

- *Preserve Transparency:* Select this option to apply the stroke only to nontransparent pixels.

4. Click OK to apply the stroke.

I recommend leaving the Blending Mode and Opacity setting options in the Stroke dialog box alone. Instead of adjusting these settings, create a new layer for your stroke and then choose different Blending Mode and Opacity settings in the Layers panel. This approach maximizes your ability to make edits.

Working with Gradients

A *gradient* is a wonderful blend of colors that you can apply to a layer or selection, gradually fading from one hue to another. Gradients can involve more than two colors, producing a veritable rainbow of variations. You can apply gradients by using preset selections of colors, or you can create your own gradient.

You can create the following gradient effects:

- **Foreground to background:** A transition from the current foreground color to the background color.

- **Foreground to transparent:** A transition from the current foreground color to transparent, allowing whatever's under the transparent portion to show.

- **Black to white:** A transition from black to white.

- **An array of colorful selections:** Including rainbows, coppery sheens, and other effects.

You can load other libraries of gradients from the Gradient panel menu's libraries. They have names such as Color Harmonies, Metals, and Special Effects. For more information on managing preset libraries, see Book I, Chapter 5.

In addition to being able to control the appearance and application of a gradient, you also have the opportunity to adjust the Gradient tool's options, all of which are on the Options bar:

- **Mode:** Select any of Photoshop's blending modes.

- **Opacity:** Select how transparent the gradient is.

- **Reverse:** Reverse the order in which the colors are applied

✔ **Dither:** Add *noise,* or random information, to produce a smoother gradient that prints with less *banding* (color stripes caused by the limitations of the printing process to reproduce a full range of colors).

✔ **Transparency:** This option determines whether Photoshop ignores the gradient's transparency settings when you apply a gradient. If you deselect this option, all portions of the gradient are fully opaque. I show you how to work with a gradient's transparency in the section "Adding transparency to a gradient," later in this chapter.

Applying a preset gradient to a selection

Here's how to apply a preset gradient:

1. **Select the layer from the Layers panel and/or make the selection that you want to apply the gradient to.**

2. **Select the Gradient tool from the Tools panel (or press G or Shift+G) until the Gradient tool becomes active.**

3. **Select one of the preset gradients from the Gradient Picker drop-down menu on the Options bar.**

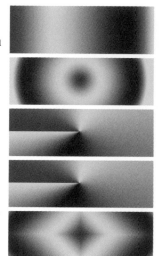

NEW FEATURE CS5

CS5 now provides a new preset called Neutral Density. Based on an analog-graduated, neutral-density lens filter, this preset is great when you want to correct an image that may have an overly bright (or overexposed) sky in comparison to the rest of the image. Create a new layer over your image layer and drag the Gradient tool (set to Linear) from the top to the bottom, using this preset. Then play with various blend modes for that layer. Overlay and Soft Light usually work well. You can also try using this new preset when layer masking. (See Book VI, Chapter 3.)

4. **Select the gradient type by clicking one of the icons on the Options bar.**

Figure 2-5 illustrates each gradient type:

Figure 2-5: You can choose from five gradients.

• *Linear:* Blends the colors of the gradient from start color to end color in a straight line

• *Radial:* Blends the colors outward in a circular pattern

• *Angle:* Creates a counterclockwise sweep around the starting point, resembling a radar screen

- *Reflected:* Blends the colors by using symmetrical linear gradients on either side of the starting point

- *Diamond:* Blends the colors outward in a diamond pattern

5. **Choose any other options you want from the Options bar.**

   I explain these options in the section "Working with Gradients," earlier in this chapter.

6. **Place the cursor at the position in the layer or selection where you want to place the starting color of the gradient.**

7. **Drag in any direction to the point you want to place the end color.**

   Longer drags result in a subtle transition between colors, whereas shorter drags result in a more abrupt transition. Press the Shift key while dragging to restrain the direction of the gradient to an even 45-degree angle, as well as perfectly horizontal or vertical.

8. **Release the mouse button to apply the gradient.**

   The gradient I created is shown in Figure 2-6.

Figure 2-6: Indulge your love of color with Photoshop gradients.

Customizing and editing gradients

Although Photoshop includes dozens of gradient presets, you may want to create your own. Perhaps you want to create a gradient with your company colors or build one to match the predominant colors in an image. Or, you might want to create a gradient that includes more than two colors. The Gradient Editor lets you create your own gradient preset, using as many colors as you want, which you can save and reuse at any time.

The Gradient Editor has many options, but it's easy to use when you know what all the controls and options do. Follow these steps to create a simple smooth gradient:

1. **Select the Gradient tool from the Tools panel.**

2. **Click in the gradient sample window (not the arrow) on the Options bar.**

   The Gradient Editor dialog box opens, as shown in Figure 2-7.

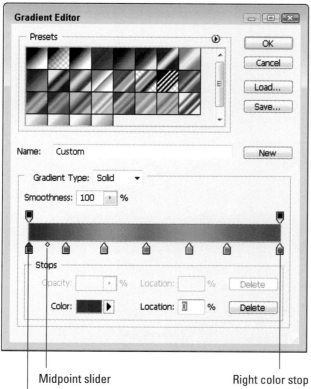

Midpoint slider   Right color stop

Left color stop

Figure 2-7: The Gradient Editor enables you to create custom gradients.

3. **Pick an existing gradient preset from the Presets area to use as the basis for your new gradient.**

4. **Select Solid or Noise from the Gradient Type pop-up menu.**

   As soon as you start to edit the existing gradient, the name of the gradient changes to Custom. A Noise gradient is one containing random colors. Because the colors are random, each time you create a noise gradient, the result is different. If you choose Noise, you can select which color mode to use and the roughness of the gradient, and then select a range of acceptable colors.

5. **Adjust the Smoothness slider.**

   Click and drag the slider (click the right arrow) or enter a value to determine how smoothly to blend your colors into one another.

   If you choose Noise in Step 4, the slider changes to Roughness. This option affects how smoothly or abruptly a color transitions into another.

6. **You can set the following options only if you choose Noise in Step 4:**

   - *Color Model:* Select your desired color model or limit the range of colors by adjusting the sliders. See Book II, Chapter 2 for more on color models.

   - *Restrict Colors:* Limits the colors to printable CMYK colors only. See Book II, Chapter 2 for details.

   - *Add Transparency:* Lets you include transparency in your gradient, if desired.

   - *Randomize:* Changes the colors in your gradient. Each time you click Randomize, you get a new set of colors.

7. **To define the color of the starting point for your gradient, click the left color stop button under the gradient bar.**

   The triangle above the stop turns black to indicate you're working with the starting point of the gradient. Because Noise gradients are random, you can't define the colors.

8. **Select the starting color by using one of these methods:**

   - Double-click the left color stop and select a color from the Color dialog box that appears.

   - Click the Color box in the Stops area of the dialog box and choose a color from the Select Stop Color dialog box that opens.

   - Select Foreground, Background, or User Color from the Color pop-up menu in the Stops area of the Gradient Editor dialog box.

If you select color with the Foreground or Background option, the color in the gradient changes automatically when you change the foreground or the background color. The change doesn't affect any gradients you've already created, but it does affect any future gradients. However, when you open the Gradient Editor again, you can revert to the original foreground or background color you used when you created the gradient by selecting the User Color option from the Color pop-up menu in the Stops area.

- Position the cursor (it appears as an Eyedropper icon) anywhere in the gradient bar to select a start color from the bar, or position the cursor anywhere within an image on your screen and then click to select the color under the cursor.

9. **Click the end point color stop at the right side of the gradient bar and use any of the methods described in Step 8 to choose the end color of the gradient.**

10. **Change the location of the start and end points of the colors by moving the color stops to the left or right. Click and drag the midpoint slider (a diamond icon that appears when you click an adjacent color stop) to adjust where the color mixes equally, 50-50.**

   You can also change the position of the midpoint by typing a value into the Location box. The position of the color stops can also be changed this way.

   Because the center point of the gradient is halfway between the start and end points, the gradient proceeds smoothly from one color to the other, meeting to blend evenly in the middle. Moving the color stops and the midpoint changes the proportions.

11. **(Optional) Want to add another color? Just click below the gradient bar at the position you want to add the next color, and then define a color for the new color stop.**

12. **(Optional) Repeat Step 11 for additional colors.**

   Heck, you can keep going like this for hours.

13. **For the additional color stops, move the stops to the left or right to adjust the location of the start and end points for each color. Then, adjust the midpoint sliders between the colors.**

14. **If you change your mind, you can redefine the color or click the Delete button.**

   You can also remove a color stop by dragging it down or up from its position on the gradient bar.

15. **After your edits are complete, give your gradient a name, if you want, and click the New button.**

Your gradient is added to the Presets menu. Figure 2-8 shows an example of a unique gradient that I created in the Gradient Editor.

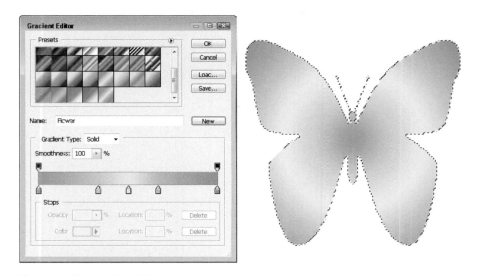

Figure 2-8: The Gradient Editor gives you more creative license than the presets.

Adding transparency to a gradient

By default, a gradient has 100-percent opacity in the start color and progresses to 100-percent opacity in the end color. If you like, you can have the gradient fade out to transparency so that the portion of the image under the gradient shows through. To add transparency to a gradient, follow these steps:

1. **Create a gradient, as described in the preceding sections.**

2. **Select the left opacity stop.**

This stop is located just above the gradient bar, as shown in Figure 2-9.

3. **Use the Opacity slider to specify the amount of transparency for the gradient at its start point.**

You can also type a value into the Opacity box.

4. **Select the right opacity stop, and then slide the Opacity slider or enter a percentage in the text box to specify transparency for the gradient at its end point.**

The lower the percentage, the less opaque the color.

Opacity stop   Opacity slider

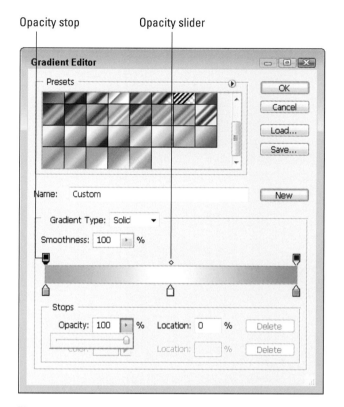

Figure 2-9: Lighten your gradients by adjusting the opacity of your colors.

5. **Move the opacity stops to the right or left to adjust the location where Photoshop applies each stop's opacity setting.**

6. **Move the midpoint slider (a diamond icon) to adjust how the color and the transparency mix.**

7. **Click above the gradient bar to add more opacity stops if you want to vary the transparency of the gradient at different points.**

   For example, you could fade transparency from 100 percent to 50 percent and back to 100 percent to produce a particular effect. Figure 2-10 shows a gradient with varying levels of transparency.

Gradients ordinarily proceed smoothly from one color to another. If you want a less homogeneous appearance, adjust the Smoothness slider to a value of less than 100 percent (click the right arrow to access the slider).

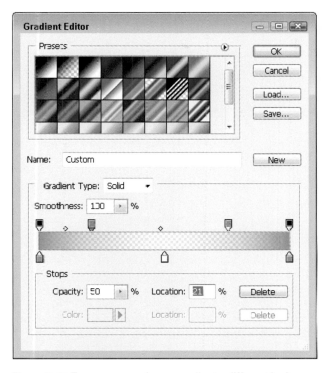

Figure 2-10: Transparency gives a gradient a different look.

Managing and Saving Gradients

If you're smart, you'll store the gradients you create so that you can use or edit them again later. Before you can save them, however, be sure to add them to the gradient Presets (see "Customizing and editing gradients" earlier in this chapter). Here are some tips for managing your gradients:

- ✔ To save a gradient, click the Save button in the Gradient Editor dialog box. You save the current presets, including your new gradient, under the current library's name or another name that you choose.

- ✔ To load gradient presets into the Gradient Editor, click the Load button and select the name of the gradient library that you want to add to the Presets list.

- ✔ To add an additional set of presets to the current presets, select the name of the presets from the Gradient Editor's pop-up menu

For more information about managing gradient presets with the Preset Manager, see Book I, Chapter 5.

Working with Patterns

Patterns are textures or repeating configurations of pixels that you use to fill selections or layers. You can apply patterns with painting tools, smear them around your image with the Pattern Stamp tool, or use them as a basis for the Healing Brush and Patch tools. Photoshop offers a large selection of patterns; you can download an even larger selection, and you can even create your own.

You select patterns from panels that appear on the Options bar for many of the tools just mentioned, much like brush tips and gradients, and you manage them in much the same way, using the Preset Manager (see Book I, Chapter 5). The following sections show you how to apply a preset pattern and create your own pattern.

Applying a preset pattern

Although you can apply patterns with many tools, this chapter sticks with applying patterns as fills. To fill a layer or selection with a preset pattern, follow these steps:

1. **Choose the layer from the Layers panel and/or make the selection you want to fill with a pattern.**

2. **Choose Edit⇨Fill and then select Pattern from the Use pop-up menu.**

3. **In the Custom Pattern panel, select the pattern you want to fill with.**

   Here are some tips in choosing a pattern:

   • Choose a pattern from the drop-down panel, as shown in Figure 2-11.

   • Replace the current patterns with new patterns by selecting Replace Patterns from the panel pop-up menu (click the arrow on the right side of the dialog box). Then, select the new pattern library from the dialog box that appears.

   • Append new patterns to the current set by selecting Load Patterns from the panel pop-up menu.

   • Append one of the preset libraries that come with Photoshop by selecting the pattern from the list at the bottom of the panel pop-up menu.

4. **Choose any other Fill options you want to apply, such as Mode, Opacity, or Preserve Transparency.**

   The Preserve Transparency option prevents Photoshop from filling the transparent areas on your layer with a pattern.

   I recommend adjusting the Mode and Opacity settings in the Layers panel rather than the Fill dialog box. This approach allows you maximum flexibility if you want to make edits later.

5. **Click OK to fill the layer or selection with the chosen pattern.**

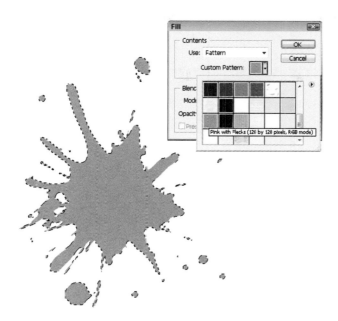

Figure 2-11: Fill your selection with pink flecks or one of the many other Photoshop preset patterns.

Creating a new pattern

You can create your own pattern, basing it on an existing image or one you create yourself. Select a small portion of an image to build an abstract pattern or use a recognizable object to define that object as a pattern stamp. You can use anything from a logo to your signature, as a pattern.

To create your own pattern, follow these steps:

1. **Open the image that contains the area you want to use as a pattern or create an image from scratch.**

2. **Make any modifications to the image to produce the exact pattern that you want.**

3. **Use the Rectangular Marquee tool to select the area you want to convert into a pattern.**

   If you don't make a selection, Photoshop uses your entire image as a basis for the pattern.

   If you're using a selection to define your pattern, you must use a rectangular selection. You can't use a feathered selection of any kind.

4. **Choose Edit⇨Define Pattern.**

5. **Enter a name for your pattern in the Define Pattern dialog box.**

    Your new pattern appears in the Pattern panel for use.

Chapter 3: Creating and Editing Type

In This Chapter

✔ Discovering different kinds of type

✔ Getting to know the type tools

✔ Entering text

✔ Making type follow a path

✔ Using the Character and Paragraph panels

✔ Editing text

✔ Creating character and paragraph styles

✔ Exploring masking, shaping, and warping effects

*F*or an image-editing program, Photoshop has surprisingly good tools for creating type. Over time, features have been added that let you create paragraphs of text or simple lines of text used as headlines or labels. You can change the spacing between characters, warp your type, check your spelling, or create selections in the shape of text. Drop shadows, beveled type, and other special effects are yours quickly and easily. And you can even place text on or inside a path.

You may still want to use Adobe Illustrator or InDesign to create professional layouts in which you can keep text and image files separate, or where you have to place buckets full of text at small point sizes. But if what you're looking for is a great-looking image that includes great-looking snippets of text, Photoshop can do the job. This chapter introduces you to Photoshop's basic type tools, as well as its more advanced type capabilities.

Selecting a Type Mode

The text you create in Photoshop can be categorized in several different ways, but ultimately, you're either adding just a little text (such as a word or single line of text) or a lot (maybe a paragraph or so). Accordingly, Photoshop separates type into two modes:

✔ **Point type:** Use this mode to create a headline or label. You can create point type by clicking in your image and typing; the line appears while you type and grows to whatever length you need (even if that length is wider or taller than your image). Point type never wraps around to a new line. To wrap to the next line, you must insert a hard return by pressing Enter (Return on the Mac).

✔ **Paragraph type:** Use this mode to enter longer blocks of text on an image. It's (unsurprisingly) similar to the kind of type you're accustomed to working with in word processing programs. In Paragraph mode, all the text goes into a resizable bounding box, and if a line is too long, Photoshop automatically wraps it around to the next line.

There is a third way to enter type — on a path. This unique way to create type is described in the later section, "Creating Type on or in a Path."

The Point type and Paragraph type modes each operate a bit differently, although they share many features and options. I explain each of them separately in the sections "Entering Text in Point Type Mode" and "Entering Text in Paragraph Type Mode," later in this chapter.

Understanding Different Kinds of Type

Whether you're using Point type mode or Paragraph type mode, you can select several type options, each designed to help you work with, display, print, and edit text. These options determine how Photoshop enables you to work with text in a file:

✔ **Vector type:** All text in Photoshop is initially created as vector-based type. Vector type provides scalable outlines that you can resize without producing jaggy edges in the diagonal strokes. You can also edit type in this mode, adding or subtracting characters or adjusting attributes, such as kerning and tracking. Vector type is always of optimum quality and appears crisp and clean. (See Book II, Chapter 1 for more details on vector and rasterized images.)

✔ **Rasterized type:** When Photoshop converts vector type into pixels, that text is *rasterized.* When text is rasterized, it's no longer editable; instead, it's a frozen graphic of what the text looks like. When you finish editing vector type and want to merge the text with the other pixels in an image (or to perform some manipulations that can be done only with rasterized text, such as applying filters), you can transform the vector type into pixels by rasterizing it. You can't resize rasterized type without losing some quality or risking a bad case of the jaggies.

✔ **Pixel fonts:** *Pixel fonts* are tiny fonts designed for display at small sizes on computer screens, especially Web sites. Pixel fonts are designed so that every pixel corresponds to a pixel on your screen. These fonts, with names such as MINI 7, MiniSerif, and Tenacity, are created in fixed sizes (say, 7 pixels high for MINI 7 or 10 pixels high for Tenacity and PixelDust). Diagonal lines are avoided as much as possible, with the font designs favoring horizontal and vertical strokes. As a result, pixel fonts look crisp and clear at small sizes without anti-aliasing (smoothing around the edges). Indeed, you shouldn't use anti-aliasing with pixel fonts, nor should you attempt to resize or rescale them. You can buy or download pixel fonts, install them on your computer, and use them just like you use other fonts. You can see some examples of pixel fonts in Figure 3-1.

FFF NADADOR BOLD

FFF MANAGER BOLD

FFF HARMONY

FFF FORWARD

Figure 3-1: Unlike traditional fonts, pixel fonts are designed to fit into the pixel grid of your screen.

Exploring the Type Tools

Strictly speaking, Photoshop has four type tools (found in the Tools panel), but two of them are simply vertically oriented versions of the main two text implements. You can use either Paragraph or Point type mode with any of the type tools:

- ✔ **Horizontal Type:** Use this tool to enter point or paragraph type oriented horizontally on your screen. If you want text that's oriented at an angle other than vertical, you can rotate it by choosing Edit⇨Transform⇨ Rotate after you enter the text. This tool creates the type on its own type layer, except when used in Bitmap, Multichannel, or Indexed Color modes, which don't support layers. (Book II, Chapter 2 covers these modes.)

- ✔ **Vertical Type:** The Vertical Type and Vertical Type Mask tools (described in the following bullet) are handy for entering Asian characters. However, you can also use this tool to enter Roman character point type oriented in a vertical column. You can also use the Vertical Type tool to create columns of paragraph text, but the results look a little strange. Note that the columns also go from right to left. After you enter your text columns, you can rotate the text to an orientation other than vertical by choosing Edit⇨ Transform⇨Rotate. Like the Horizontal Type tool, this tool creates type in its own type layer, except with file formats that don't support layers.

- ✔ **Horizontal Type Mask/Vertical Type Mask:** These tools operate identically to their siblings described in the two preceding bullets, with two exceptions. Instead of adding filled type, both the Horizontal and Vertical Type Mask tools create a selection border in the shape of the type you enter. Both tools add a selection marquee to the current active layer. You can do anything with a type selection that you can do with any other selection, including saving it (Select⇨Save Selection) for reuse later. You can find a longer discussion of the type mask tools in the section "Creating type outlines," later in this chapter.

**Book IV
Chapter 3**

**Creating and
Editing Type**

The Horizontal and Vertical Type tools have some interesting options, which I explain in the following section. You can also set controls in the Paragraph and Character panels, which I discuss in the sections "Working with the Character Panel" and "Working with the Paragraph Panel," later in this chapter.

Entering Text in Point Type Mode

If you're image oriented (and why wouldn't you be if you're using Photoshop?), you're probably not planning to include a novella with your graphics.

Point type is great for headlines, labels, and similar small amounts of text. You can also use it to create logos and headings for Web pages. The Web is one place where text that isn't tack-sharp can still do the job.

Although a Photoshop image is generally not the place you want to insert a whole lot of text, you can add larger blocks of text that are professional and effective — read the section "Entering Text in Paragraph Type Mode," later in this chapter. You can modify how point type and paragraph type are displayed by using the Paragraph and Character panels.

To enter point type, just follow these steps:

1. **Open a saved image or create a new Photoshop document.**

2. **Select either the Horizontal or Vertical Type tool from the Tools panel, or press T to select the type tool if the one you want is visible.**

   Press Shift+T to cycle through the four available type tools until the one that you want is active.

   Your cursor looks like an I-beam, similar to the one you see in a word processing program.

3. **Click the area of the image where you want to insert the text.**

   Where you click is called the *insertion point.*

   A small horizontal line about one-third of the way up the I-beam shows where the baseline (on which the line of text rests) is for horizontal type. If you select the Vertical Type tool, the cursor is rotated 90 degrees. The baseline is centered in the I-beam and represents the center axis of the vertical column of text you type.

4. **Select any of the type options from the Options bar, Character panel, or Paragraph panel.**

   To access the panels, click the Character and Paragraph toggle button on the Options bar or select either panel on the Window menu.

   I describe these options in the sections, "Working with the Character Panel" and "Working with the Paragraph Panel," later in this chapter.

5. **Type your text. Press Enter (or Return on the Mac) to begin a new line.**

   Lines of point type don't wrap around. When you press Enter or Return, you're inserting a hard carriage return that doesn't move. You have to remove hard returns if you want to change the length of the lines you type.

6. **When you finish entering the text, click the Commit (the check mark icon) button on the Options bar. You can also press Ctrl+Enter (⌘+return on the Mac).**

   A new type layer with your text is created. The layer appears in your Layers panel, as indicated by the T icon.

Entering Text in Paragraph Type Mode

Paragraphs are best allocated to captions, text descriptions, or slightly longer chunks of text that accompany an image.

Paragraph type is similar to the text you enter in a word processing program, except that it's contained inside a border, called a text box or a *bounding box*. While you type into a text box, the lines of text wrap around to fit the dimensions of the box. If you resize the box, Photoshop adjusts the wrapped ends to account for the new size.

You can type multiple paragraphs, use typographical controls, and rotate or scale the type. You can easily resize paragraph type (and point type, too) by entering a new point size value in the Character dialog box without having to reselect all the text. Just make sure the text layer is selected in the Layers panel and the Text tool is active. This approach works for all the other text characteristics, as well.

To enter paragraph type, follow these steps:

1. **Open a saved image or create a new Photoshop document.**

2. **Select either the Horizontal or Vertical Type tool from the Tools panel, or press T to select the type tool if the one you want is active.**

   Press Shift-T to cycle through the four available type tools until the one you want is active.

   Your cursor looks like an I-beam, similar to the one you see in a word processing program.

3. **Insert and size the text box by using one of the following methods:**

   • Drag to create a text box of an arbitrary size. After you release the mouse button, you can drag any of the handles at the corners and sides of the box to customize the size.

**Book IV
Chapter 3**

**Creating and
Editing Type**

✐ **Change Text Orientation:** Use this handy button to toggle between vertical and horizontal text orientations. Just select the type layer you want to transform and with the type tool selected, click the Text Orientation button on the Options bar. This option works with point type and paragraph type, although the results you get from switching the paragraph type to vertical orientation may look odd.

✐ **Font Family:** Select the font/typeface you want from the drop-down list.

You will find one of these abbreviations before the font name: a (Adobe Type 1 [PostScript]) fonts; TT (TrueType); O (OpenType). Those fonts with no abbreviations are bitmapped fonts.

✐ **Font Style:** Some fonts can have additional styles, such as light or demibold, and other styles are assigned as separate typefaces. Only the styles available for a particular font appear in the list.

If a font you want to use doesn't offer bold or italic style, you can simulate either or both by selecting a faux style in the Character panel.

✐ **Font Size:** Select the size of the text from this list or type a size in the text box. Generally, text sizes are shown in points, with 72 points equaling approximately 1 inch. (A 36-point font is ½ inch in size at 72 pixels per inch [ppi].)

If you don't like points, you can switch to millimeters or pixels in the Units & Rulers Preferences dialog box. (You can find instructions for doing this in Book I, Chapter 5.)

✐ **Anti-Aliasing:** This list includes four different types of smoothing to use on your text, plus *none* (which leaves your text unsmoothed). For small type, try Sharp to avoid your type from being too fuzzy around the edges. But the exact results depend on the typeface, so be sure to take a gander at your type. Bonus Chapter 1 (on this book's Web site) explains anti-aliasing in detail. See the Introduction for details about the Web site.

✐ **Text Alignment:** Three buttons specify whether Photoshop aligns your Horizontal Type tool text left, center, or right. When you use the Vertical Type tool, the buttons transform into Top, Center (vertically), and Bottom choices.

✐ **Text Color:** Click in this box to select a color from the Color Picker.

✐ **Create Warped Text:** This option lets you warp and bend text by using 15 different types of distortion.

✐ **Toggle Character and Paragraph Panels:** Click this button anytime a type tool is active to show or hide the Character and Paragraph panels.

✐ **Cancel:** Click this button (or press the Esc key) to cancel the text entry you're making.

✐ **Commit:** Click this button to apply the text to a type layer.

Working with the Character Panel

The Character panel (shown in Figure 3-5), which is usually paired with the Paragraph panel, lets you format the appearance of individual type characters. Choose Window➪ Character or click the Character panel icon (capital letter A) in the dock. Five of the options in the Character panel are exactly the same as those on the Options bar. The duplicated features include Font Family, Font Style, Font Size, Anti-Aliasing, and Text Color. The other menus, buttons, and text boxes provide additional functions. I discuss these options in the following sections.

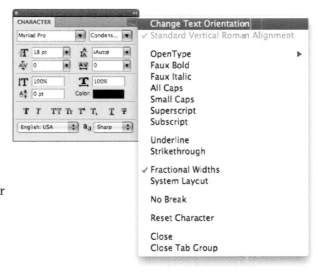

Figure 3-5: The Character panel offers type specification options galore.

Leading

Leading is the amount of space between the baselines of consecutive lines of type, usually measured in points. (The *baseline* is the imaginary line on which a line of type rests.) You can select a specific amount of leading or allow Photoshop to determine the amount automatically by choosing Auto from the Leading menu.

Wider line spacing can make text easier to read (as long as you don't go overboard!) or can be used for artistic effect. Tighter line spacing makes for more compact text but can decrease readability if your tightening goes too far.

When you select Auto Leading, Photoshop multiplies the type size by a value of 120 percent to calculate the leading size. So, Photoshop spaces the baselines of 10-point type 12 points apart. You can change this automatic value by clicking the Paragraph panel and selecting Justification from the panel's menu. A dialog box appears, containing several values. Type the amount you want in the Auto Leading box. If all this seems confusing, I recommend experimenting with leading to get a true idea of how various values affect the space between lines of text.

Tracking

Tracking is the amount of space between letters in a word, line, or paragraph. You can specify negative tracking to squeeze all the letters together more closely or positive tracking to let them spread out a bit.

Don't confuse tracking with *kerning,* which deals with the space between two individual letters. Tracking sets a value to evenly space all the letters you select, and kerning helps you close or widen the gap between two individual letters, officially called a *letter pair.*

One use for tracking is to help lines of text fit a specified horizontal space, and you can make this technique work if you use it judiciously. Beginners typically overdo tracking, squeezing letters together so tightly they touch, or spreading them apart so that wide gaps appear. You can see examples of tracking in Figure 3-6.

This is normal tracking.
This is loose tracking.
This is tight tracking.

Figure 3-6: Tracking adjusts the spaces between your selected letters.

To track a set of characters or a line, select the text you want to squeeze or expand, and select a value either from 0 to –100 or 0 to 200 from the Tracking menu, or type a specific value (from –1000 to 10000) in the Tracking text box. Each unit is equal to $\frac{1}{1,000}$ of an *em* (the width of an em dash in a particular typeface), so a setting of –100 reduces the space between characters by $\frac{1}{10}$ the width of an em dash (quite a lot!).

Kerning

Kerning is a technique for adding or removing space between pairs of letters to make them fit together more closely and aesthetically. For example, the letters A and V are a natural fit and often look better when kerned slightly closer. If you select Metrics in your Kerning option, Photoshop automatically tries to kern the characters to provide an attractive look, like that shown in the kerned pair in Figure 3-7. The Optical option kerns a pair of letters based on their particular shape. The kerning tables are built into the individual font. Be warned that cheap fonts sometimes have poorly created kerning tables or no tables at all — another good reason to stick with quality fonts.

To manually kern letters, click the point between the two characters and select a percentage either from 0 to –100 or 0 to 200 from the Kerning menu or type a specific value (from –1000 to 10000) in the Kerning text box. Like with the Tracking menu, the values represent $\frac{1}{1,000}$ of an em.

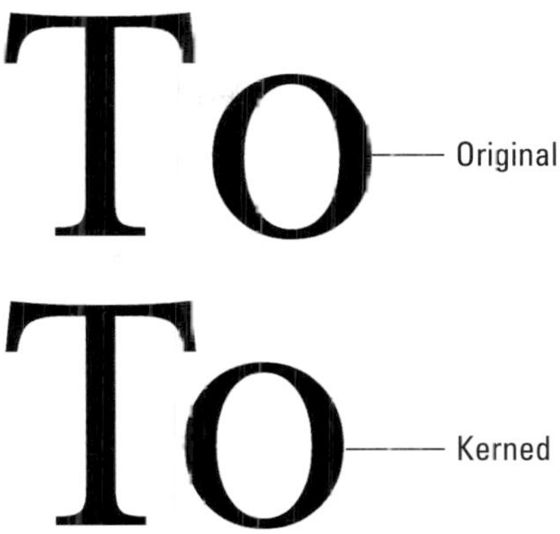

Figure 3-7: Kerning a pair of letters can enhance their appearance.

Vertical and Horizontal Scale

The Vertical and Horizontal Scale options represent the relationship between the height and width of the text. By default, this relationship is 100%. To make the width of the type proportionately 50% more than the height, enter 150% into the Horizontal Scale box. You can see examples of scaling in Figure 3-8.

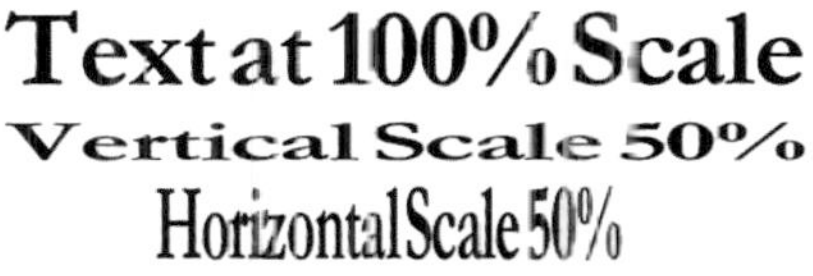

Figure 3-8: Be wary of using Vertical or Horizontal Scale.

Be careful about using the Scale options. Type designers create fonts with very specific proportions. When you deviate from those proportions, you can destroy what was once a beautifully designed typeface.

Baseline shift and text attributes

The Baseline option adjusts the height above or below a typeface's normal baseline. You can employ this option to adjust the height of bullets and symbols, such as trademark and registration marks. A bar with several buttons in the Character panel lets you turn on or off several type attributes with a single click. Table 3-1 covers the many text attributes.

**Book IV
Chapter 3**

**Creating and
Editing Type**

Table 3-1		Character Panel Text Attributes
Icon	*Name*	*What It Does*
T	Faux Bold	Creates a fake bold. ***Warning:*** Applying faux styles can distort the proportions of a font. It's really best to use fonts as they were originally designed — and if there's no bold font style, *c'est la vie.*
T	Faux Italic	Creates a fake italic. Like with faux bold, take caution when using this attribute to prevent distortion.

continued

Table 3-1 *(continued)*

Icon	Name	What It Does
TT	All Caps	Changes the case of the characters in selected text to all capitals or back to their original case when you turn it off.
Tᴛ	Small Caps	Creates uppercase letters about the size of lower-case letters in a font. Less obtrusive than full-size caps in text passages. Photoshop either uses the small caps characters built into many fonts or creates faux small caps for you.
T^1	Superscript	Raises and reduces a character automatically to create a superscript, as in $E=MC^2$.
T_1	Subscript	Lowers and reduces the character below the baseline, creating a subscript.
T	Underline	Underlines the selected characters.
₸	Strikethrough	Provides a ~~strikethrough~~ effect to the selected characters. In legal applications, strikethrough is widely used to show sections that have been removed, but in their original context.
English: USA	Character Set	Selects the language you want to use for Photoshop's spell checker and for hyphenation. The option includes variations, such as English: USA or English: UK, and French or Canadian French.

You can also find the attributes in Table 3-1 on the Character panel pop-up menu. And the menu lists a few other attributes that aren't displayed directly in the panel:

- ✔ **Change Text Orientation:** Rotates your text horizontally or vertically.

- ✔ **Standard Vertical Roman Alignment:** Displays the text in the standard alignment you're used to seeing — across the page.

- ✔ **OpenType:** When you work with OpenType fonts, you may find that they include tables of various font attributes. These tables allow you to apply various styles, such as true diagonal fractions; alternate Old Style numerals; fancy cursive type uppercase letters (Swash and Titling); ligatures (designed to fix the kerning of certain awkward letter combinations, such as fi and tt); and ornamental fonts (think dingbats or wingdings), such as leaves and flowers.

- ✔ **Fractional Widths:** This setting is the default display. When type gets small, the spacing between characters may vary by fractions of a pixel.

Photoshop has to favor one pixel or the other, and sometimes the appearance is strange. Overall, however, it provides the best spacing for the legibility and appearance of the type. But, for small type to be displayed on the Web, the readability may be impaired due to some characters running together and words having gaps.

✔ **System Layout:** Displays the text by using the operating system's default text handling, similar to what you see in WordPad or TextEdit. This option doesn't allow fractions of pixels and removes any anti-aliasing. This is a good option for text to be displayed on the Web.

✔ **No Break:** Prevents words from breaking at the end of lines. You may want to select this option to prevent words such as proper names, dates, initials, and so forth from breaking. Select your text and then select the option.

✔ **Reset Character:** Select this option to reset your character attributes (font family, size, style, and so on) back to Photoshop's default.

Working with the Paragraph Panel

You can use the Paragraph panel, shown in Figure 3-9, to format any or all paragraphs in a type layer. Choose Window⇨Paragraph or click the Paragraph panel icon (backward P icon called a pilcrow) in the dock. Simply select the paragraph or paragraphs that you want to format by clicking an individual paragraph with the Type tool. You can drag a selection to select multiple paragraphs, or in the Layers panel, click a type layer that contains the paragraphs to format all of them at the same time.

The Paragraph panel's pop-up menu gives you access to Justification and Hyphenation dialog boxes. You can use these to customize the default settings that Photoshop uses for these functions. As a side note, if you're not familiar with the word *glyph* used in the Justification dialog box, it's another word for a font character.

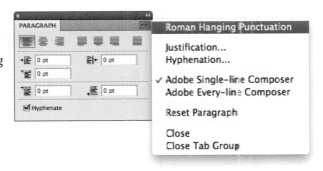

Figure 3-9: Use the Paragraph panel to align and indent your text.

Book IV
Chapter 3

Creating and
Editing Type

Changing paragraph alignment

At the top of the Paragraph panel, you see a set of seven alignment buttons. Three of these buttons align nonjustified text. They include the following:

✔ **Left Align Text:** All text is even with the left margin and allowed to be ragged on the right side of the column.

✔ **Center Text:** Text is evenly centered in its column and ragged on both right and left edges.

✔ **Right Align Text:** All text is even with the right margin and allowed to be ragged on the left side.

With vertical type, these choices align the text to the top, a center axis, and the bottom of a column.

Changing paragraph justification

Four options in the Paragraph panel produce justified text, in which Photoshop inserts spaces between characters as necessary so that each line is flush on both left and right sides. In addition, you choose to make the last line flush left, flush right, centered, or force justified on both sides with spaces inserted by Photoshop. This last option sometimes calls for some manual tweaking to avoid a final line that's squeezed or expanded too much. You can apply justification options to paragraph type only, not point type.

The "rules," or criteria, that Photoshop uses for creating justified text can be found in the Justification dialog box, accessible via the Paragraph panel pop-up menu.

For vertical type, the justification choices are Top align, Center, Bottom align, or Justify (four options).

Changing paragraph indentation

Three options in the Paragraph panel let you enter an amount of indentation between the sides of the text bounding box and the actual text. You can specify the amount of indentation from the left or right, and for the first line of the paragraph (creating a first line that's indented more than the others in the paragraph). For vertical type, the indentations are rotated 90 degrees.

Changing spacing between paragraphs

Two options in the Paragraph panel let you specify the amount of space between paragraphs. You can specify the amount of space before every paragraph, the amount after every paragraph, or both.

Breaking long words across two lines

The final option in the Paragraph panel is the Hyphenate check box, which specifies whether Photoshop hyphenates words that are too long to fit on a line or leaves them intact. Turning on hyphenation can prevent awkward spacing, particularly with justified text that would otherwise contain a lot more spaces between characters to make a line fit.

The criteria that Photoshop uses for creating hyphenated text can be found in the Hyphenation dialog box, accessible via the Paragraph panel pop-up menu.

The Paragraph panel's pop-up menu has a few additional options:

- **Roman Hanging Punctuation:** Controls whether punctuation marks (quotations, dashes, colons, and so on) appear inside or outside the margins. Select this option to have the punctuation marks appear outside.

- **Adobe Single-Line Composer:** Composition includes using a host of parameters (such as word and letter spacing, and hyphenation) to determine where a line should break. This option composes type one line at a time and offers more manual control over where lines break. The option favors compressing or expanding word spacing over hyphenation, but prefers hyphenation over compressing or expanding letter spacing. This option is selected by default.

- **Adobe Every-Line Composer:** Looks at multiple, possible breaking points for a range of lines. The option can optimize earlier lines in the paragraph to avoid weird breaks later on in the paragraph. Emphasis is given to even spacing of letters and words over hyphenation. This option can provide more even spacing and fewer hyphens.

- **Reset Paragraph:** Resets all the paragraph attributes back to the Photoshop defaults.

Editing Text

You can apply all the options described in this chapter while you enter text, or later, when you're rearranging words or fixing typos and other errors. To make changes to the text itself, just follow these steps:

1. **Open a saved image or create a new Photoshop document.**

2. **Select the appropriate Type tool.**

3. **In the Layers panel, select the existing type layer you want to modify or, for a new type layer, click the Type tool in the document.**

4. **To modify existing text, drag the mouse from the insertion point to select characters to copy, delete, or format. For new type, begin typing at the place you clicked. Press the Backspace or Delete key as you type to eliminate characters.**

5. **When you're done entering your changes, click the Commit button.**

Finding and replacing text

You can make global changes in a text layer, switching all occurrences of a set of characters to another string. For example, you might have typed

Book IV
Chapter 3

Creating and
Editing Type

Ghandi a few dozen times before remembering that Mahatma's name is spelled *Gandhi*. To replace text, follow these steps:

1. **Open a saved image or create a new Photoshop document.**

2. **In the Layers panel, select the type layer you want to modify.**

3. **Choose Edit⇨Find and Replace Text.**

   The Find and Replace Text dialog box appears, as shown in Figure 3-10.

Figure 3-10: Make global changes to your text with the Find and Replace command.

4. **Type or paste the text you want to replace in the Find What box.**

5. **Enter the replacement text in the Change To box.**

6. **(Optional) If you want the search to locate only text that exactly matches the case of the Find string (for example, *FREEdom* but not *Freedom*), select the Case Sensitive option.**

7. **(Optional) To ignore the search word embedded in another word (say, to find *the* but not *there* or *they*), select Whole Word Only.**

8. **Click Find Next.**

9. **When each string is found, select whether you want to**

   - *Change:* This option changes only the string of text just located. Click this button if you're looking for one particular occurrence.

   - *Change All:* This option changes all occurrences of the search text with the replacement string in your text.

   - *Change/Find:* This option changes the found text and then looks for the next occurrence.

Checking your spelling

Photoshop can check your spelling by using an internal dictionary that you can update with words of your own. Even though you're not likely to enter huge amounts of text in Photoshop, that's no excuse for misspelling the words that you do include. Indeed, because it's so difficult to change text after you've rasterized a text layer, the spell checker can save you a great deal of work. Follow these steps to use it:

1. **Open a saved image containing type layers.**

2. **Make sure that you've specified the correct language in the Character panel's Character Set menu.**

3. **Select the text that you want to check or select a type layer, in the Layers panel, to check all the text on that layer.**

4. **Choose Edit⇨Check Spelling.**

5. **When Photoshop identifies a possible error in the Not in Dictionary box, click Change to substitute the recommended correction for the word that's spelled incorrectly.**

   Or you can choose from one of these options:

   - *Ignore:* Leaves the word alone and continues to check the rest of the text.
   - *Ignore All:* Ignores all instances of the word for the rest of the spell-check session.
   - *Suggestions:* Select a different word from the Suggestions text box or type in the correct spelling yourself.
   - *Change All:* Corrects all occurrences of the misspelled word.
   - *Add:* Adds the unfamiliar word to Photoshop's dictionary.

   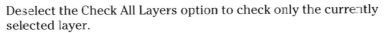

   Deselect the Check All Layers option to check only the currently selected layer.

6. **Click Done when you finish.**

   The Check Spelling dialog box closes.

Masking, Shaping, and Warping Type

You can do a lot more with type than create labels, captions, or paragraphs of text. Type can become an integral part of your decorative design, especially when you stylize, warp, or otherwise transform it in interesting ways.

Your Photoshop text can have character, too, communicating messages with more than just words. The text of a beach scene can appear to be wavy, or watery and translucent. Halloween type can take on a ghostly or spooky appearance. Type can be romantic, otherworldly, cheerful, or comical. It all depends on how you create and apply it.

The following sections show you some of the tricks you can perform by masking, warping, and shaping your type so that your words come to life and add something special to your images.

Playing with type layer opacity

Layers are like stacks of digital overlays on which each of the elements of your image reside. (Check out Book V, Chapter 1 for the lowdown on layers.) You can change the transparency of a type layer, like you can with any other layer in Photoshop, reducing the *opacity* (transparency) of the type so that it allows the underlying layer to show through. Take a look at Figure 3-11, which shows type at varying levels of opacity over an image.

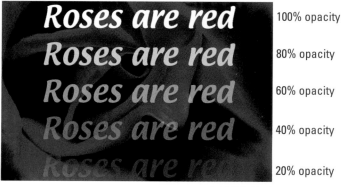

Corbis Digital Stock

Figure 3-11: Varying the opacity of your type is as easy as dragging a slider.

Changing the opacity of a type layer can convey an idea of gradual visibility of words onto an image. When working with opacity in multiple layers of type, you can create a sort of nonanimated fade-in, each with a greater opacity. Figure 3-12 shows an example of this effect.

Another way to alter the transparency of type is to use a layer mask. (Check out Book VI, Chapter 3 for more information on layer masks.) By using a layer mask, you can customize your transparency with maximum flexibility and still edit the text to change the wording, font size, font, or anything else. Simply apply a gradient, or grab a brush and paint on the layer mask. I used the fun Drippy Water Color Brush and painted on my layer mask, as shown in Figure 3-13.

The first Putting It Together project in this chapter, "Ghosting Your Type," shows you another way to use type opacity to create a ghostly effect.

Figure 3-12: Gradually fade your type to get the message across.

PhotoSpin

Figure 3-13: Creating a layer mask on your type layer gives you more flexibility with your transparency effects.

Creating fade effects

To create text that appears to fade out, just follow these steps:

1. **Enter the words** `fading out slowly` **(or other text of your choice) into a new type layer.**

   You can find out how to enter text in the section "Entering Text in Point Type Mode," earlier in this chapter.

2. **Choose Layer⇨Layer Mask⇨Reveal All.**

   This step creates a mask that can show or hide some of the layer. With Reveal All selected, the layer defaults to showing everything on the layer without hiding any of it. For details on layer masks, see Book VI, Chapter 3.

3. **Press D to make sure that Photoshop's colors are the default black and white.**

4. **Select the Gradient tool from the Tools panel.**

   Or press Shift+G until the Gradient tool is active. For more on working with gradients, see Book IV, Chapter 2.

5. **Select the Linear Gradient fill from the Options bar.**

6. **In the Options bar, click the Gradient picker (down-pointing arrow) and select the Foreground to Background gradient.**

   This is, by default, the first one in the panel, unless you've changed the defaults.

7. **Click the layer mask's icon in the Layers panel to make sure it's active. You will see brackets around the layer mask thumbnail icon.**

8. **Click on the left side of the type layer and drag to the right side.**

   Photoshop creates a gradient in the layer mask that's black on the right and fades to white on the left, as shown in Figure 3-14. So, the mask is most transparent on the left side (where the mask is white) and least transparent on the right side (where the mask is black). It reveals more of the original type on the left and fades it out on the right, as you can see in the figure.

FADING OUT SLOW

Figure 3-14: Fade your text gradually by applying a gradient on a layer mask.

Putting It Together

Ghosting Your Type

Need some ghostly, semitransparent type? You can twist, transmogrify, and transform your text by using Photoshop's arsenal of features. Create your type from scratch in an empty document or add the type to an existing picture or background. (You can find my example image on this book's Web site.) For the heck of it, these steps show you how to add ghostly writing to an existing image. Just follow these steps:

1. **Open the background image you want to overlay with the ghost type.**

   Any image, ectoplasmic or not, will do.

2. **Select the color you want to use for your text from the Swatches panel.**

   Black and orange are good Halloween colors, but you can use any contrasting color.

   You can also sample a color from your image by using the Eyedropper tool. Simply click your desired color, and it then becomes your new foreground color.

3. **Select the Horizontal Type tool from the Tools panel and then click the area where you want to add the text.**

   The vertical cursor that appears is the size that the text will be.

4. **Select a font, style, and size from the drop-down lists on the Options bar.**

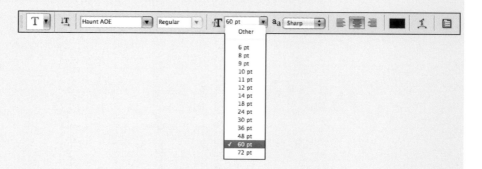

5. **Select an anti-aliasing method to help smooth the edges of your type.**

   Anti-aliasing, which I cover in the section "Using the Options Bar," in this chapter, softens a hard edge by adding partially transparent pixels.

6. **Type your text.**

   The text appears on top of the background.

7. **Click the Commit button (the check mark icon) on the Options bar to insert the text you've typed into a layer of its own. You can also press Ctrl+Enter (⌘+return on the Mac).**

8. **To change the opacity of the type, adjust the Opacity setting in the Layers panel.**

   To make additional changes to the text, use a filter. For example, if you want to make the text wavy, select the Wave filter from the Filter⇨Distort menu. Or you can use other filters from the array discussed in Book VII. Just remember, when you use a filter, a warning pops up, informing you that the type layer must be *rasterized* (converted from editable text to pixels) first. Click OK, and you're on your way.

9. **When you're satisfied with the look, save your image for additional editing later or choose Layer⇨Flatten Image to combine the text and background.**

Creating type outlines

In addition to its Vertical and Horizontal Type tools (discussed in the section "Exploring the Type Tools," earlier in this chapter), Photoshop includes Vertical and Horizontal Type Mask tools. These tools function almost identically to their conventional counterparts, with one important exception: Type mask tools don't create a new layer. Instead, they create a selection that hovers over the currently active layer, like the one shown in Figure 3-15.

TYPE SELECTION

Figure 3-15: Type mask tools create selection marquees from your letter shapes.

You can treat the selections created with the type mask tools just as you can any other selection. Try the following:

Here are the chief things to know about type converted into a shape or path:

✔ Like a type layer, you can resize it without producing jagged diagonal lines.

✔ You can edit the shape of the characters, but you can't edit the text itself, as shown in Figure 3-17.

✔ You must rasterize the converted type before you can merge it with pixel-based layers or apply special effects with filters. You can apply layer styles to any kind of type, however. Be sure to check out Book V, Chapter 4 for all you need to know about layer styles.

✔ If you've converted your type into a shape, it becomes a vector mask exactly like other vector masks in Photoshop, and you can edit the shape of the characters by using the Pen tools. You can find detailed information on editing vector masks in Book VI, Chapter 3.

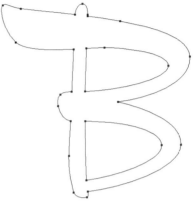

Figure 3-17: Converting your type to a path allows you to alter the shape of the letters.

Wreaking havoc on your type

Photoshop's great automated Warp feature can twist your type in predictable ways that are not only repeatable but, thanks to the controls in their dialog boxes, also customizable. The cool part is that even though type has been warped, it remains fully editable until you rasterize it. All you need to do to warp your text is click the Warp icon on the Options bar, which opens the multifaceted Warp Text dialog box (shown in Figure 3-18), and then choose your warp style and distortion options in that dialog box.

Web designers take note: You can't warp text that has a faux bold style applied (found in the Character panel).

You can find a whole list of special effects in the Warp Text dialog box, such as Arc, Arch, Bulge, Flag, Wave, Fish, Fisheye, and Twist. Each of these effects provides a special look to your type, as shown in Figure 3-19.

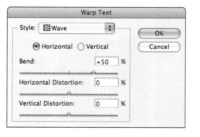

Figure 3-18: Choose from a number of warp styles.

Each effect has a dialog box of its own that allows you to set the parameters for the amount, direction, degree of distortion, amount of bend, and so forth. You can watch your type warp right onscreen and tailor the distortion however you like. You can apply most asymmetrical warp effects to type in either horizontal or vertical directions. Fisheye, Inflate, and Twist are among those effects that can't be rotated because they're already oriented in horizontal and vertical directions that you can control with sliders.

Figure 3-19: Even after you warp your text, it remains fully editable.

Putting It Together

Carving Your Type in Stone

You can use a type tool to create selections shaped like text and then use images themselves as textures for the type. A type selection can cut out any part of a picture for use any way you want.

Follow these steps to carve letters into a stone texture image:

1. **Open the stone texture image you want to use.**

I'm using a sandstone wall, but you can use other kinds of stone, wood, or any texture that interests you. Best of all, the embossed look that results is only one of many different looks you can achieve simply by making small changes in the layer style that you apply to the text.

2. **Select the Horizontal Type Mask tool from the Tools panel and then click the area where you want to enter your text.**

3. **Select the font, font style, font size, and other text parameters from the drop-down lists on the Options bar.**

4. **Enter the text you want to use onto the texture you've chosen. Then, click the Commit button (the check mark icon), or press Ctrl+Enter (⌘+return on the Mac) on the Options bar to set your text.**

The selection in the shape of the text appears where you typed the text.

Corbis Digital Stock

Book IV
Chapter 3

Creating and
Editing Type

continued

continued

5. **Press Ctrl+C (⌘+C on the Mac) to copy the selected area of your chosen texture (the brick in the shape of the text, in my example), and then press Ctrl+V (⌘+V on the Mac) to paste a text-shaped section of that texture in a layer of its own.**

The text blends in with what's in the background layer (in my example, the sandstone) and is invisible (for now).

6. **Choose Layer⇨Layer Style⇨Bevel and Emboss to open the Layer Style dialog box.**

In the Layer Style dialog box, you can find dozens of different effects that you can create.

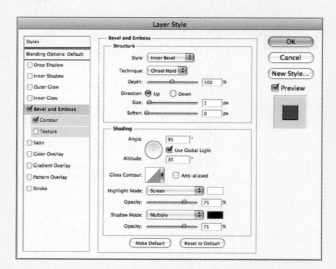

7. **Experiment with the settings in the Layer Style dialog box to try out different looks and achieve various effects:**

↙ Select the kind of beveling or embossing you want from the Style and Technique drop-down lists in the Structure area.

I selected Inner Bevel and Chisel Hard to produce a dramatic, hard-edged embossing effect.

↙ Move the Depth slider to the right to increase the depth of the bevel.

I set the value at 500% for a raised effect. A lower value produces a less 3-D effect, and a higher value produces a more drastic 3-D effect.

↙ Select the Contour check box in the layer styles column on the left side of the dialog box for an even more pronounced 3-D look.

↙ In the Shading area, you can adjust controls that allow you to change the apparent angle of the illumination that produces the bevel's shadow.

I moved the angle to 95 degrees (roughly straight overhead), but I left the other controls alone.

You can find details about how to use the other options in the Layer Style dialog box in Book V, Chapter 4.

8. **Click OK to apply the effects that you've chosen.**

9. **(Optional) As a last touch, choose Image➪Adjustments➪Levels to darken the text layer so that it stands out even more distinctly from the background. Drag the midtones (gray triangle) and shadows (black triangle) adjustments to the right, while keeping an eye on your image.**

For more info on how to use the Levels adjustment, see Book VIII, Chapter 1.

Book V
Working with Layers

*L*ayers are like modern appliances. Sure, you could live without a microwave, a dishwasher, and a vacuum cleaner, but cooking and cleaning would take a lot longer — and it wouldn't be nearly as convenient. Layers give Photoshop users the ultimate in editing flexibility. This in turn saves production time, giving you more time to let your creative juices flow.

In this book, I give you information about how to create and edit layers. You see how to take multiple images and create single composite images. I also cover how to manage your layers by using layer sets and layer comps. And you find out how to enhance your layers by using adjustment layers, layer styles, blend modes, and various opacity settings. Finally, you'll want to check out the chapter on Smart Objects. These intelligent objects allow you to transform elements indefinitely without loss of quality.

Chapter 1: Creating Layers

In This Chapter

✔ Backgrounds versus layers

✔ Taking a look at the types of layers

✔ Working with the Layers panel

✔ Creating layers

✔ Compositing with multiple layers

✔ Transforming layers

✔ Automatically aligning and blending layers

*P*eople are often surprised and even downright shocked when I tell them that pretty much everything they can do with layers they can also do without them. Not using layers would be more technically challenging and a heck of a lot more tedious, but you could still get the job done. The benefit to using layers is that you have tremendous flexibility. The changes you make to the pixels on the individual layers are permanent, but the interaction between the pixels on different layers is dynamic. You can make endless edits as long as those layers exist. Layers make working in Photoshop a lot more forgiving, allowing you to make changes quickly and productively.

But hey, it's not just the technical and practical aspects that make layers so wonderful. Layers also allow you to express your creative side, compositing several images into one with just a drag of the mouse. The only downside to layers is that each one makes your file size grow and, therefore, can slow your system performance. Additionally, you can save layers in only a few file formats. Nevertheless, the downsides are a small price to pay for something that makes your image-editing life so much easier.

Getting to Know the Layers Panel

In terms of a real-world analogy, think of layers as sheets of acetate similar to those clear plastic sheets used with overhead projectors. You draw different elements on the various sheets. What you draw on one sheet doesn't affect the other sheets. You can show just one sheet, or you can stack several on top of one another to create a combination image. You can reshuffle the order of the sheets, add new sheets, or delete old sheets. Any space on the sheet that doesn't have a mark on it is clear, or transparent.

That's how layers work in Photoshop. You can place elements on separate layers, yet show them together to create a combination image, or *composite*. You can also add, delete, or rearrange layers. Unlike sheets of acetate, however, you can adjust how opaque or transparent the element on the layer is, as well as change the way the colors between layers interact (blending modes).

As with every other important aspect of Photoshop, the program houses layers in a single location, called a panel. It's time to formally meet the powerful panel that controls the operations of layers. To display the Layers panel, shown in Figure 1-1, choose Window⇨Layers or, easier yet, press F7.

Active layer

Type layer

Figure 1-1: Layers give you tremendous editing flexibility.

The order of the layers in the Layers panel represents the order in the image. The top layer in the panel is the top layer in your image, and so on.

For some tasks, you can work on only one layer at a time. For other tasks, you can work on multiple layers simultaneously.

Here's the lowdown on how to work with the Layers panel:

- **Select a layer.** Simply click its name or thumbnail. Photoshop then highlights the *active layer*.
- **Select multiple contiguous layers.** Click your first layer and then Shift-click your last layer.
- **Select multiple noncontiguous layers.** Ctrl-click (⌘-click on the Mac) your desired layers.

✓ **Select all layers except the background.** Choose Select➪All Layers.

✓ **Select layers of similar type.** If you want to select all the type layers, for example, select a layer and then choose Select➪Similar Layers.

✓ **Deselect all layers.** Choose Select➪Deselect Layers or click in the area below the bottom layer or background.

✓ **Select the actual element (the nontransparent pixels) on the layer.** Ctrl-click (⌘-click on the Mac) the layer's thumbnail in the panel. If you forget this handy shortcut, you can also select your layer in the Layers panel and then choose Select➪Load Selection. Make sure that the layer name that appears in the Channel pop-up menu is *[layer name]* Transparency and click OK.

 ✓ **Create an adjustment or fill layer.** Click the Create a New Fill or Adjustment Layer icon at the bottom of the panel. You can also click an adjustment icon in the new Adjustments panel. See "Introducing Different Types of Layers," later in this chapter, for more on these layers.

 ✓ **Duplicate an existing layer.** Drag the layer to the Create a New Layer icon at the bottom of the panel. See the following section for more on creating layers.

✓ **Rename a layer.** When you create a new layer, Photoshop provides default layer names (Layer 1, Layer 2, and so on). If you want to rename a layer, simply double-click the layer name (the name, not the thumbnail) in the Layers panel, enter the name directly in the Layers panel, and press Enter (Return on the Mac).

Although it may seem tedious to give your layers meaningful names, it can help your productivity, especially when the number of layers in your file starts to increase.

This renaming shortcut works throughout Photoshop (the Channels panel, the Paths panel, and so on). You can also select the layer and select Layer Properties from the Layers panel options menu or choose Layer➪Layer Properties.

✓ **Determine what layer holds the element you want to edit.** Select the Move tool and Ctrl-click (⌘-click on the Mac) the element. Photoshop automatically activates the appropriate layer. Or you can right-click (Control-click on the Mac) the element. A context menu appears, telling you what layer the element resides on and enabling you to select that layer.

You can use the keyboard shortcut Alt+] (right bracket) (Option+] on the Mac) to move up one layer; Alt+[(left bracket) (Option+[on the Mac) to activate the next layer down.

✓ **Adjust the interaction between colors on layers and adjust the transparency of layers.** You can use the blending modes and the Opacity and Fill options at the top of the panel to mix the colors between layers and adjust the transparency of the layers. For details, see Book V, Chapter 3.

> ✔ **Delete a layer.** Drag it to the trash icon at the bottom of the Layers panel. You can also choose Layer➪Delete➪Layer or choose Delete Layer from the panel options menu.
>
> If you've gone a little layer crazy and created a bunch of empty layers, you can get rid of them quickly. Just choose File➪Scripts➪Delete All Empty Layers to delete layers that don't contain any content.
>
> ✔ **Change the size of the layer thumbnails.** Choose Panel Options from the panel menu and select a thumbnail size. You can also choose whether to display just the boundary of the layer contents or the whole document in the thumbnail. Finally, you can choose to have a layer mask on your fill layer by default and have your layer effects appear in expanded view. Fill layers are described in the section "Taking advantage of fill layers," later in this chapter, and layer effects are covered in Book V, Chapter 3.

The remaining icons at the bottom of the Layers panel allow you to link layers, and create layer styles, layer masks, and layers groups, all of which warrant sections of their own. See Book V, Chapter 4 for more on layer styles and Book V, Chapter 2 for more on layer groups. Check out Book VI, Chapter 3 for more on layer masks.

The preceding list represents just the tip of the iceberg. You can also view and hide layers, and link, lock, color-code, rearrange, merge, flatten, and animate layers. Book V, Chapter 2 covers most topics in detail.

Looking at the Background and Layers

When you create a new image with white or background colored contents, scan an image into Photoshop, or open a file from a stock photography CD or your own digital camera, basically, you have a file with just a *background.*

An image contains at most only one background, and you can't do much to it besides paint on it and make basic adjustments. You can't rearrange the background in the stack of layers — it's always on the very bottom of the Layers panel. You also can't change the opacity or blend mode of a background. What you can do is convert a background to a layer, and then the world's at your feet.

To convert a background into a layer, follow these steps:

1. **Double-click Background in the Layers panel.**

   Alternatively, you can choose Layer➪New➪Layer from Background. Note that Background is italic in the Layers panel, as shown in Figure 1-2.

2. **Name the layer or leave it at the default name of Layer 0.**

PhotoSpin

Figure 1-2: A newly opened image in Photoshop contains only a background.

You can also color-code your layer in this dialog box or by selecting Layer Properties from the panel pop-up menu. Color-coding your layer just makes it stand out more noticeably in the Layers panel.

3. **Click OK.**

Photoshop converts your background into a layer, as indicated in the Layers panel. Note that the layer name is no longer italic, as shown in Figure 1-3.

When you create a new image with transparent contents, the image doesn't contain a background; instead, the image is created with a single layer. You can also convert a layer into a background by selecting it and then choosing Layer⇨New⇨Background from Layer. However, this option is available only when no background exists.

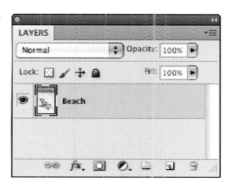

Figure 1-3: Double-click the background to convert it into a layer.

Introducing Different Types of Layers

Although turning the background into a layer (discussed in the preceding section) is a popular activity, Photoshop refers to *layers* in the plural for a reason. Image editing would be no fun if you didn't have a variety of different layers to mess around with.

Photoshop Standard offers five types of layers (Extended gives you two more — Video and 3D). Four of the five have very specific purposes in the life of your image. Some you may never use, and some you'll use only occasionally. But the vanilla-flavored type, which you'll use the most, is simply called a layer.

Using plain vanilla layers

The regular layer is the one that most closely matches the acetate analogy (discussed in the section "Getting to Know the Layers Panel," earlier in this chapter). You put various elements on separate layers to create a composite image. You can create blank layers and add images to them, or you can create layers from images themselves. You can create as many layers as your computer's RAM lets you. Sometimes, layers are created automatically by a specific action.

Because each layer in an image is a separate entity, you can edit, paint, transform, mask, or apply a filter on a layer without affecting the other layers. After an element is on a layer, you no longer have to make a selection (get the selection outline) to select it — you simply drag the element with the Move tool. The element freely floats in a sea of transparency. Because showing "clear" areas or transparency is impossible on a computer monitor, Photoshop uses a gray-and-white checkerboard, by default, to represent the transparent areas of a layer.

Because you'll work with regular layers on a daily basis, I spend the majority of Book V discussing them.

Playing around with layer masks

A *layer mask* is like a second sheet of acetate that hovers over a layer. You can use layer masks with regular layers, adjustment layers, fill layers, and Smart Filters. For example, you may paint on a layer mask (typically with black, white, and various shades of gray) to selectively hide or display an adjustment (or an image on a regular layer). Any black areas on the mask hide the adjustment, any white areas show the adjustment, and anything in between (gray) partially shows the adjustment. The Masks panel gives you even more flexibility because it includes options for controlling the density and feather of the mask. I cover layer masks in detail in Book VI, Chapter 3.

Using adjustment layers

An *adjustment layer* is a special kind of layer used mostly for color correction. What's great about adjustment layers is that you can apply that color correction without permanently affecting any of your layers. Adjustment layers apply the correction to all the layers below them, without affecting any of the layers above them.

Because the color correction actually resides on a layer, you can edit, delete, duplicate, merge, or rearrange the adjustment layer at any time. You have more flexibility in your image-editing chores and more freedom for experimentation. Additionally, none of this experimentation harms your image because it takes place above the image on an adjustment layer.

Photoshop has 15 kinds of adjustment layers, and you can use as many as your heart desires. The adjustments offered are the same adjustments you find on the Image➪Adjustments menu. For specifics on each adjustment, including what it corrects, see Book VIII, Chapter 1. Here's how to create an adjustment layer:

1. **Open an image of your choice.**

   Because you're applying an adjustment layer, you may want to use an image that's in need of some color correction. In the case of adjustment layers, you don't need to convert your background into a layer. I chose an image that was oversaturated.

2. **Choose Layer➪New Adjustment Layer. From the submenu, choose your desired adjustment. In the New Layer dialog box, name the layer (if you want), leave the other options at their defaults, and click OK.**

   For my example, I chose Hue/Saturation.

   You can also just click the Create a New Fill or Adjustment Layer icon (the black and white circle icon) at the bottom of the Layers panel and choose an adjustment from the pop-up menu that appears.

   The dialog box pertaining to your adjustment appears in the Adjustments panel The adjustment layer also appears in the Layers panel, shown in Figure 1-4. The adjustment layer icon and a thumbnail appear on the adjustment layer. The thumbnail represents a layer mask. For more on layer masks, check out the "Playing around with layer masks" sidebar, in this chapter.

3. **Make the necessary corrections and then click OK.**

The adjustment layers have their own panel. Choose Window➪Adjustments to bring up the panel, shown in Figure 1-4. Click an icon to apply one of the 15 adjustments. The dialog box pertaining to your adjustment appears within the panel. You can also select a preset for an adjustment. Presets appear in the list window of the Adjustments panel (click the right-pointing arrow next to the adjustment name) or, after you select the adjustment, in the pop-up menu directly to the right of the adjustment name in that particular adjustment's dialog box. Here are a few tips to keep in mind when working with this panel:

 ✔ Click the arrow at the bottom of the panel to switch between the adjustment list and adjustment controls windows.

 ✔ Click the manila envelope icon to switch between compact and expanded views of the panel.

 ✔ Click the triple circle icon to have the new adjustment affect all the underlying layers. Click again (to return to the default setting) to have the new adjustment clip to, or just affect, only the layer directly under the adjustment layer.

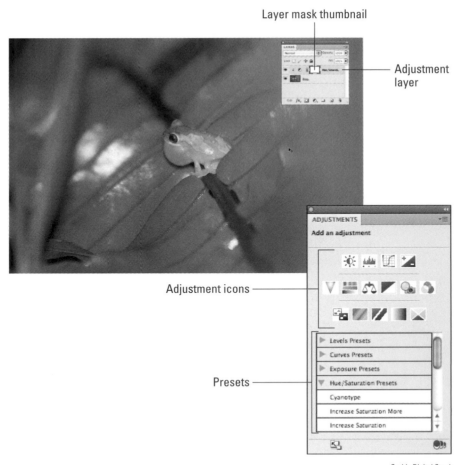

Corbis Digital Stock

Figure 1-4: Applying your corrections with an adjustment layer, rather than directly on the image, allows for more editing flexibility.

In the adjustment controls window, you can

✔ Click the double circle to toggle between having the adjustment layer affect all layers or just the layer directly below the adjustment.

✔ Click the eye icon to toggle visibility of the adjustment layer.

✔ Click the eye and curved arrow icon to view a previous state

✔ Click the curved arrow to reset the default settings for the adjustment layer.

✔ Click the Trash icon to delete the adjustment layer.

✔ Access the panel pop-up menu to make adjustments, reset an adjustment, change the view of the panel, save and load presets, or close the panel.

In my example, the layer mask is white, so my adjustment shows up full strength over my image. You can also apply an adjustment layer to a selected portion of your image by painting on your layer mask. Like with regular layers, you can also adjust the opacity, fill, and blending modes of an adjustment layer. For more on these options, see Book V, Chapter 3.

If you want to view your image without the adjustment, click the eye icon in the left column of the Layers panel to hide the adjustment layer. You can find more about viewing layers in Book V, Chapter 2. If you want to delete the adjustment layer, simply drag it to the trash icon in the Layers panel, or choose Delete➪Layer from the Layer menu or the Layers panel options menu. You can also perform these commands via the new Adjustments panel.

Editing adjustment layers

After you create an adjustment layer, you can easily edit it. Simply click the adjustment layer icon in the Layers panel. In the adjustment's dialog box, make any edits and then click OK. The only adjustment layer that you can't edit is the Invert adjustment. It's either on or off.

Isolating your adjustments

If you don't use an adjustment layer when you make color corrections, the correction you apply affects only the *active layer* (the layer highlighted in the Layers panel). However, you can also isolate your adjustment layer to a single layer or a portion of a single layer.

Here are some tips for using and isolating adjustment layers:

✔ **Correct part (but not all) of a layer.** To enable the adjustment layer to correct only a portion of a layer, make a selection before you create the adjustment layer. The adjustment affects only the pixels within the selection outline.

The adjustment affects the pixels within the selection outline *on each layer that resides below the adjustment layer.* In addition to selecting a part of a layer, you can also create and select a closed path (see Book III, Chapter 2 for more on paths).

Another way to correct part of a layer is to paint on the adjustment layer mask. Painting with black hides the adjustment, painting with various levels of gray partially hides the adjustment. For more on layer masks, see Book VI, Chapter 3.

✔ **Clip to the layer.** By default, when you apply a new adjustment layer, that adjustment clips to the layer directly below the adjustment layer. This means that the adjustment layer will affect only that underlying layer. However, you can click the circles icon at the bottom of the Adjustment Layers panel to have the adjustment affect all underlying layers.

✔ **Create a layer group.** You can create a *layer group* (described in Book V, Chapter 2) and place the layers you want adjusted in that group. Then, make sure that the blending mode is set to any mode except Pass Through. For more on modes, see Book V, Chapter 3.

Taking advantage of fill layers

A *fill layer* lets you add a layer of solid color, a gradient, or a pattern. Like adjustment layers, fill layers also have layer masks, as indicated by the mask icon thumbnail in the Layers panel.

You can create as many fill layers as you want, just as you can with regular layers and adjustment layers. You can also edit, rearrange, duplicate, delete, and merge fill layers. Additionally, you can blend fill layers with other layers by using the opacity, fill, and blending mode options in the Layers panel.

Like with an adjustment layer, to confine the effects of a fill layer to a portion of the image, make a selection, or create and select a closed path, before you create the fill layer (see Book III, Chapter 2 for more on paths). Editing or changing the contents of a fill layer is similar to editing or changing the contents of an adjustment layer (see the preceding section for details), except that fill layers don't have their own panel. To edit a fill layer, double-click the fill layer thumbnail in the Layers panel.

Here's how to create a fill layer:

1. **Open an image of your choice.**

   In this case, open an image that would look good with a border or text. For my example, I created the word *fujiyama* by using the Horizontal Type Mask tool (for details, see Book IV, Chapter 3). If you don't have an active selection, the fill layer encompasses your entire canvas.

2. **Choose Layer➪New Fill Layer. From the submenu, choose your desired adjustment. Name the layer, leave the other options at their defaults, and click OK.**

    For my example, I chose Pattern from the submenu.

     You can also just click the Create a New Fill or Adjustment Layer icon at the bottom of the Layers panel and select a fill from the pop-up menu.

3. **Follow the steps that correspond with the option you chose in Step 2:**

    -   *Solid Color:* Select your desired color from the Photoshop Color Picker. (For more on color, see Book II, Chapter 3.)

    -   *Gradient:* Select a preset gradient from the pop-up panel or click the gradient preview to display the Gradient Editor, where you can create your own gradient. Set additional gradient options, as desired. (For gradient details, see Book IV, Chapter 2.)

    -   *Pattern:* Select a pattern from the pop-up panel. Drag the scale slider to adjust the size of the pattern. I scaled my Crayon on Vellum pattern 120%, as shown in Figure 1-5. Click Snap to Origin to position the origin of the pattern with the document window. Finally, select the Link with Layer option to specify that the pattern moves with the fill layer if you move it.

Figure 1-5: Choose from a variety of preset patterns for your fill layer.

4. **Click OK.**

    After you close the dialog box, the fill layer appears in the Layers panel. Similar to adjustment layers, a layer mask is created on the fill layer. In my example, shown in Figure 1-6, *fujiyama* appears white on the layer mask, thereby allowing my pattern to show through. The remaining areas are black, hiding my pattern. I added a couple layer styles (Drop Shadow and Inner Bevel) to my type to jazz it up a bit. If you want to do the same, jump ahead to Book V, Chapter 4.

    If you want to delete the fill layer, do one of four things: Drag it to the trash icon in the Layers panel; choose Delete➪Layer from the Layer menu; choose Delete Layer from the Layers panel options menu; or the easiest, press the Backspace key (Delete on the Mac) on your keyboard.

You can rasterize a fill layer to convert it to a regular raster image. Choose Layer➪Rasterize➪Fill Content. A raster image enables you to use painting tools or filters on the layer. I introduce raster images in Book II, Chapter 1.

Figure 1-6: Your chosen fill shows through your selected areas.

Making use of shape layers

Believe it or not, Photoshop isn't just about photos and painting. Photoshop also has a whole slew of shape drawing tools — six, to be exact. You can fill those shapes with solid color, gradients, or patterns. When you create a shape, it resides on its own unique shape layer. A shape layer contains a *vector mask,* similar in concept to the adjustment layer mask described in the section "Using adjustment layers," earlier in this chapter.

If you look at the Layers panel, you can see that the Shape layer has two thumbnails: One is filled with color, and the other contains the path of the shape, as shown in Figure 1-7. To state it simply, the color is peeking through the path of the shape, and the rest of the layer is hidden or masked. The paths that constitute a shape are *vector paths;* when printed, they retain their smooth curves without the jagged edges you often see from bitmap editing programs. Although you can edit, move, and transform shapes, your ability to edit shape layers is limited. To apply filters and most other special effects, you must first *rasterize* the shape layers — that is, convert the vector paths to pixels. For more details on shapes, see Book IV, Chapter 2.

Using type layers

To create type, such as the type shown in Figure 1-8, click your canvas with the Type tool (horizontal or vertical) and type your desired text. After you commit your text by pressing Enter on the numeric keypad or clicking the Commit button on the Options bar (it looks like a check mark), you've created a type layer. In the Layers panel, you see a layer with a T icon, indicating that it's a type layer. Initially, the name of the type layer corresponds to the text you typed (you can change the layer name, if you want). Like shapes the text in Photoshop is true vector type and, if left in that format, always prints smooth and without jaggies.

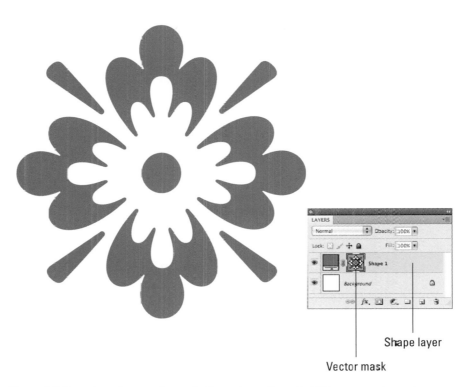

Shape layer

Vector mask

Figure 1-7: On a shape layer, color peeks through a path and is hidden everywhere else.

Another great thing about type in Photoshop is that it's live; you can edit the text at any time. You can also change the orientation, apply anti-aliasing (softening of the edges), create paths from the type, and even warp it into various distortions. You can also convert the type to a shape. Like with regular layers, you can move, re-arrange, copy, and change the layer options (opacity, fill, and mode) of a type layer. If, however, you want to apply certain special effects, such as filters, you must first *rasterize* (convert into pixels) the text. For everything you need to know about type, see Book IV, Chapter 3.

Figure 1-8: Type layers automatically appear when you create and commit type.

Making Layers

As I mention in the section "Using plain vanilla layers," earlier in the chapter, good, old-fashioned, regular layers are the backbone of the layers world. The following sections look at the various ways to create these layers.

Creating a new layer

You can create a new layer in a couple ways:

- **To create a new blank layer in an image that's open:** Click the Create a New Layer icon at the bottom of the Layers panel. You can also create a new layer by selecting New Layer from the panel pop-up menu or by choosing Layer⇨New⇨Layer. Both methods open a dialog box in which you name your layer and specify other options for grouping, color-coding, blending, and opacity (all of which I explain in other chapters in Book V). Provide a name for your layer and click OK. If you chose the first method, a layer with the default name of Layer 1 appears in the Layers panel.

    When you click the Create a New Layer icon, the layer is added above your active layer. By holding down the Ctrl key (⌘ on the Mac) when you click, Photoshop adds the new layer below the active layer.

- **To create an entirely new document with a layer:** Choose File⇨New. In the New dialog box that appears, select the Transparent for the Background Contents option. Your new file then appears with Layer 1, rather than a background.

When your new transparent layer is ready and waiting, you can put content on the new layer in several ways:

- Use one of the painting tools and paint directly on the layer.

- Make a selection on another layer or the background (for the difference between the two, see the preceding sections in this chapter) within the same document or from another image entirely. Then, choose Edit⇨Copy. Select your new blank layer in the Layers panel and choose Edit⇨Paste.

- Make a selection on another layer (or the background) within the same document or from another image and then choose Edit⇨Cut. Select your new blank layer and choose Edit⇨Paste. Remember that Photoshop deletes the selection from the source and adds it to your new layer, as shown in Figure 1-9.

- Transfer an entire image to your new layer by choosing Select⇨All and then either Edit⇨Copy or Edit⇨Cut. Select your new blank layer and choose Edit⇨Paste.

Figure 1-9: Cutting and pasting a selection from one layer to another leaves a transparent hole on the original layer.

Using Layer via Copy and Layer via Cut

Another way to create a layer is to use the Layer via Copy command on the Layer menu. Make a selection on a layer or background and choose Layer⇨ New⇨Layer via Copy. The copied selection is placed on a new layer with the default name of Layer 1. You can do the same with the Layer via Cut command, but in this case, Photoshop deletes the selected area from the source layer or background, and places it on the new layer. The source layer is left with a gaping transparent hole (refer to Figure 1-9). If you used the background for the source, your background color fills the space. Remember that you can use these two commands only within the same image. You can't use them between multiple images.

Duplicating layers

If you want to duplicate an existing layer, select it in the Layers panel. Then, drag the layer to the Create a New Layer icon at the bottom of the panel. You can also duplicate a layer by selecting Duplicate Layer from the panel pop-up menu or by choosing Layer⇨Duplicate Layer. As with creating a new layer, both methods prompt you with a dialog box to name your layer and include other options. Provide a name for your layer and click OK. If you chose the first method, Photoshop provides the default name of the original layer with the word *Copy* appended to the name.

Duplicating layers can be especially handy when you want to experiment with a special effect but don't want to harm your original image.

Compositing with Multiple Images

Often, when working with layers, you're not confined to using a single image. I mean, you can do only so much to that family portrait taken at the local photo studio. But take your family and put them in front of the ruins at Machu Picchu or the summit at Mount Everest (you can even add faux snow with a technique I show you in Book VII), and you have endless hours of fun. When you get the hang of working with several images, you'll find myriad new creative possibilities. And you're not limited to just plain old snapshots. You can incorporate type, vector illustrations, and scans of just about anything you can place on a scanning bed. Apply some layer styles, maybe a filter or two (see Book VII), and you have an image worthy of some major wall space.

Copying and pasting images

In the "Creating a new layer" section, earlier in this chapter, I explain how to use the Copy, Cut, and Paste commands within the same image or between two images when you want to fill a new blank layer with content. You can also use the Copy and Paste commands without having a blank layer ready. When you copy and paste a selection without a blank layer, Photoshop automatically creates a new layer from the pasted selection. You can go about your merry way and perform all your layer creations by using only those commands. However, I rarely use them when working with multiple images. I prefer the drag-and-drop method, which I describe in the following section.

The Copy Merged command on the Edit menu creates a merged copy of *all* the visible layers within the selection.

Dragging and dropping layers

To copy an entire layer from one document to another, simply select your desired layer in the Layers panel, grab the Move tool, and in your image window, drag and drop that layer onto your destination document. Or simply drag the thumbnail of your layer in the Layers panel onto your destination document. Photoshop automatically introduces the dropped layer as a *new* layer above the active layer in the image. You don't need to have a selection outline to copy the entire layer. However, if you want to copy just a portion of the layer, make your desired selection, as shown in Figure 1-10, before you drag and drop with the Move tool. If you want the selected element centered on the destination image, hold down the Shift key while you drag and drop. See the "Bypassing the clipboard" sidebar for more on dragging and dropping.

In CS5, you can also drag and drop a file, not just within Photoshop, but from most anywhere — your desktop, your Web browser, and other applications. Simply open a Photoshop document and drag and drop from your source onto that document. By doing so, you create a new layer in that document.

To drag and drop your images, be sure to specify that your images float rather than specifying they're tabbed. To do so, choose Window➪Arrange➪Float All in Windows.

Bypassing the clipboard

Yes, you can always cut and paste, or copy and paste, a layer from one image to another, but I prefer to drag and drop, rather than copy and paste, between two images. By dragging and dropping, you bypass the temporary storage area for copied and stored data, the *clipboard*. (Whenever you copy or cut a selection, Photoshop stores the selection on the clipboard until you're ready to paste it to its new home.) So, what's wrong with that? Well, nothing, unless you're working with high-resolution images. Storing images on the clipboard, even on a temporary basis, can slow down your system.

Keeping your clipboard clear of data ensures that Photoshop is running lean and mean so that you can drag and drop more images, selections, and layers more quickly and more efficiently. If you want to perform a little spring cleaning on your clipboard, you can always choose Edit➪Purge➪Clipboard, which empties your clipboard of any stored data. Take my advice and try the drag-and-drop method. I guarantee that, like me, you'll be flexing your trigger finger — all the better to drag and drop even faster.

Figure 1-10: Dragging and dropping a selection keeps your clipboard lean and mean.

What if you have multiple elements on one layer and want to select only one of the elements to drag and drop? Simply grab the Lasso tool and draw around the object. You don't have to be super-precise, but don't include any portion of the other elements on the layer. Then, hold down the Ctrl key (⌘ key on the Mac) and press the up-arrow key once. The element then is neatly selected. Not only can you drag and drop the element, but you can also move or edit it without affecting the other pixels on the layer. Flip to Book III, Chapter 1 for help with making selections.

Using the Paste Special commands

Photoshop has added a couple new paste commands. In addition to Paste Into, you will find Paste in Place and Paste Outside. All three commands are lumped under the new Edit➪Paste Special submenu.

Paste Into

Let's start with my favorite — Paste Into. You may occasionally want to place an image on a separate layer, yet have it fill a selection. That's where this command comes into play. Paste Into enables you to insert a copied or cut selected image into a selection outline.

For example, if you want to make it appear as if a snake is poking its head out of the opening of a cave, or a bottle is poking out of a can, as shown in Figure 1-11, Paste Into is your command. Be sure to check out the Putting It Together project, in this chapter, to get more practice at this practical technique.

Layer mask

PhotoSpin

Figure 1-11: Use the Paste Into command to make one layer appear as though it is emerging from another.

Follow these steps to insert a copied or cut selected image into a selection outline:

1. **Make the selection on the layer that you want the image to fill.**

   I call this the destination layer.

2. **Select the image that will fill that selection.**

   I call this the source image.

3. **Choose Edit⇨Copy.**

4. **Return to the destination layer and choose Edit⇨Paste Special⇨ Paste Into.**

   Photoshop converts the selection outline on the destination layer into a layer mask. The pasted selection is visible only inside the selection outline. In my example, my bottle is showing only inside my selection. The bottom of the bottle is hidden, making it look like my bottle is sitting inside the can.

Paste Outside and Paste in Place

The opposite of Paste Into is Paste Outside. The Paste Outside command pastes a copied selection outside another selection, rather than inside. If you are copying between two images and you want to paste the selection of your source image into the same relative location in your target image, choose the Paste in Place command.

Transforming Layers

When compositing multiple images, you'll no doubt have to scale some of your image to fit it into your layout. Fortunately, Photoshop makes scaling an easy chore by providing you with the Transform and Free Transform commands on the Edit menu. Transforming layers is almost identical to transforming selections, except that you don't need to make a selection first. After an element is on a layer, you can just choose the appropriate transformation command and off you go. Additionally, you can apply a transformation to multiple layers simultaneously if you select the multiple layers first. I explain each transformation in detail in Book III, Chapter 3.

Try to perform all your transformations in one execution. Don't go back numerous times and apply various transformations. Each time you transform pixels, you're putting your image through the *interpolation* process (increasing, decreasing, or remapping pixels). Done repeatedly, your image may start to turn into mush. If not mush, it won't be as pristine and crisp as it was before.

If your image looks jagged after you transform it, you may have your preferences set incorrectly for your interpolation method. Choose Edit⇨ Preferences⇨General (Photoshop⇨Preferences⇨General on the Mac) and select the Bicubic option from the Image Interpolation pop-up menu. Bicubic enables a smoother appearance to your interpolated pixels. You can also try Bicubic Smoother when resampling up (upsampling) and Bicubic Sharper when resampling down (downsampling). For more on resolution and resampling, see Book II, Chapter 1.

When the Move tool is active, you can transform a layer without choosing a command. Simply select the Show Transform Controls option on the Options bar. This option surrounds the contents (or an active selection) of the layer with a bounding box with handles. Drag these handles to transform the contents.

Using Puppet Warp

Being a puppet master is an easy task with CS5's new transform command — Puppet Warp. Think of Puppet Warp as a lighter-weight Liquify filter (see Book VII, Chapter 3). This command enables you to distort specific areas of an image via a mesh overlay and the placement of pins.

You can apply a Puppet Warp on regular layers, shape layers, type layers, Smart Objects, and even vector masks. Here's how:

1. **Select your desired layer in the Layers panel.**

2. **Choose Edit⇨Puppet Warp.**

3. **On the Options bar, shown in Figure 1-12, specify your desired settings:**

Figure 1-12: Specify your Puppet Warp distort settings.

- *Mode:* Determines the elasticity of the mesh. Distort will give you an ultra-stretchy mesh, while Rigid will do the opposite.

- *Density:* Specifies the spacing of the mesh, where small changes in moving the pins result in larger warps. Also a good mode for larger images. Rigid is the opposite and recommended when your object is more stiff, as with human appendages.

- *Expansion:* Expand or contract the outer edges of the mesh.

- *Show Mesh:* Deselect to display only the pins, and not the mesh.

4. **On your image, click to add a pin to an area you want to distort or anchor.**

5. **Drag a selected pin to warp the mesh, as shown in Figure 1-13.**

6. **To rotate around a pin automatically, select Auto on the Options bar, and drag. To rotate a fixed number of degrees, select Fixed on the Options bar, press the Alt (Option on the Mac) key and position your cursor near, but not over, the pin. Drag to rotate.**

Your degree of rotation appears on the Options bar.

Original

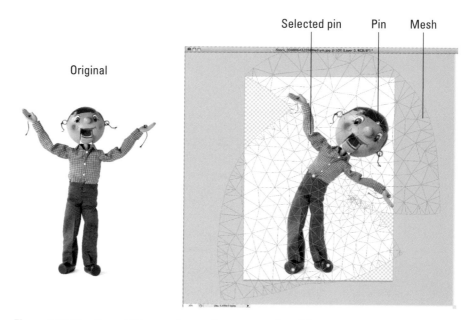

Selected pin   Pin   Mesh

Figure 1-13: Use Puppet Warp to give marionettes newfound flexibility.

7. **You can also do the following:**

   - To show a mesh area that you've overlapped over another, click the Pin Depth buttons on the Options bar.

   - To select multiple pins, Shift+click on your desired pins. Release the Shift key to drag all pins simultaneously.

   - To delete a pin, select it and press Backspace (Delete on the Mac). Or Alt (Option on the Mac) and click over a pin.

   - Click Remove All Pins (the curved arrow icon) on the Options bar to do just that.

   - To select all pins, press Ctrl (⌘ on the Mac). To deselect all pins, press Ctrl+D (⌘+D on the Mac). To hide the mesh, press Ctrl+H (⌘+H on the Mac).

   - To exit Puppet Warp, click the slashed circle icon, or press Esc.

8. **After you warp to your desired result, press Enter (Return on the Mac) or click the check icon on the Options bar.**

Auto-Align Layers

One of the coolest features in Photoshop is the Auto-Align Layers command. How many times have you taken photos at a reunion, wedding, or other family event where not one of the shots is perfect? In one shot, Aunt Marlene has her eyes closed. In another, Momma Sue is looking to the side for Junior who should be in the photo. The Auto-Align Layers feature enables you to take these multiple images and composite them into that perfect shot by aligning your image and then letting you mask out the parts of the image that you don't want.

You can also use the Auto-Align Layers feature to stitch together images, such as panoramic shots or scans of oversized images — that is, any series of images that have even a slight overlap.

Follow these steps to Auto-Align your layers:

1. **Create a new document with the same dimensions as your source images.**

2. **Open all your source images. With the Move tool, drag and drop each image into the new document.**

   Each image should be on a separate layer.

3. **If you desire, you can choose a layer to use as a reference. Lock the reference layer.**

   If you don't set a reference layer, Photoshop analyzes the layers and then selects the layer in the center of the final composite as the reference.

4. **In the Layers panel, select all the layers you want to align and choose Edit⇨Auto-Align Layers.**

5. **Choose one of the projection methods:**

   - *Auto:* Photoshop analyzes the layers, decides which method would create the best composite, and then applies the alignment.

   - *Perspective:* Photoshop designates one of the layers as the reference layer. The remaining layers are transformed so that content is aligned.

   - *Collage:* This option enables you to move, rotate, and scale your layers to get your desired layout.

   - *Cylindrical:* This is a good option for panoramic shots. It places the reference layer in the center and then places remaining layers on an unfolded cylinder to minimize distortion.

   - *Spherical:* This option also places the reference layer in the center and places the remaining layers on a sphere to correct distortion. This option comes in handy when you want to align shots taken with a wide-angle lens.

   - *Reposition:* A good option when you need to stitch together oversized scanned images. And the option to select if you're trying to create the perfect shot I describe in the introduction of this section.

6. **Check options to correct for lens problems, such as Vignette Removal and Geometric Distortion.**

Vignetting is an exposure problem caused when light at the edges of the images is reduced and the edges become darkened. *Geometric Distortion* refers to such problems as barrel (bulging out) and pincushion (pinching in) distortions.

7. **Click OK.**

Photoshop finds and aligns the common areas of the layers, as shown in Figure 1-14. If you're stitching together images, you're done. If the composite has visible seams or inconsistencies, you can apply the Auto-Blend Layers command described in the following section.

Figure 1-14: Use Auto-Align Layers to stitch or composite multiple images.

If you're creating the perfect shot, add a layer mask to your top layer, set your foreground color to black, and use the Brush tool (with the appropriate tip size) to paint over the portions you want to hide or delete. In a mask, black hides pixels, so the layer underneath shows through. Repeat this process of layer masking your content until you have the shot you want. For more on layer masks, see Book VI.

Auto-Blend Layers

You may have images that need to be stitched together. For example, you may need to stitch together a series of panoramic shots you took or an oversize image you had to scan in several sections because it couldn't fit on your scanner. As you can see in Figure 1-15, the Auto-Blend command helps to smooth out the telltale seams or weird color inconsistencies that occur when stitching together shots with different exposures or contrast settings. You can also use the File⇨Automate⇨Photomerge command to stitch together images. For more on Photomerge, see Book IX, Chapter 2.

Figure 1-15: Seamlessly blend your images with the Auto-Blend command.

You can also use this command to blend a stack of several images together. For example, say you took several shots, at varying depths of field, of a group of flowers, which caused some flowers to be in focus and others to be blurry. You can blend them together to get a composite shot with all the flowers in focus.

Follow these steps to blend layers:

1. **Create a new document and then open all your source images. With the Move tool, drag and drop each image into the new document.**

   Each image should be on a separate layer.

2. **Select all the layers and choose Edit⇨Auto-Align Layers.**

   Note that you can try to align the layers yourself manually.

3. **Choose a projection method (see details in the preceding section), then click OK.**

4. **Select all the layers (avoiding the Background layer, if you have one) and choose Edit⇨Auto-Blend Layers.**

5. **Select your Blend Method — either Panorama or Stack Images.**

   Select Panorama for, well, panoramic shots. Select Stack Images for non-panoramic images, such as shots of flowers with varying depths of field. Select the Seamless Tones and Colors option to optimize the blending of the multiple images.

6. **Click OK.**

   This command automatically applies layer masks to each layer, as necessary. These layer masks attempt to hide under- and overexposed areas.

You can apply this command only on RGB or Grayscale images. You can't apply it to background layers and Smart Objects (and video or 3-D layers in the Extended version of Photoshop).

Putting It Together

Creating Layers and Using the Paste Into Command to Make a Collage

If you remember your elementary-school days, you probably remember cutting out a bunch of pictures from magazines and pasting them on a piece of construction paper. Well, with Photoshop, the idea of a collage isn't much different, but the activity is a little more refined. Maybe you want to let loose your artistic side. Or maybe you need to combine several images as part of a job. Whatever your reason, you can use the steps here to get started on your first collage. And, if *collage* is too froufrou a word for you, you can substitute it with *composite* — which has the definition "derived from many components." I usually do.

REMEMBER

Creating a collage takes many steps. Throughout Book V, you can find several ongoing Putting It Together projects, all of which lead you to a finished collage. Be sure to save your collage file so that you can work on it while you make your way through this minibook.

If you're short on photos, you can go to www.gettyimages.com. Be sure to register so that you can have access to a huge gallery of free comping images. *Comping images* are small, low-resolution images used for internal corporate or personal non-commercial use only. You can also purchase high-resolution images for a song ($1 to $5) at www.istockphoto.com or www.stockxpert.com.

To create the first layer of your collage, follow these steps:

1. **Decide on two images you want to use in your collage and open them by choosing File⇨Open.**

   I recommend picking an image to use as your main canvas and then opening up a supporting image that you can select and then drag onto that main image. However, if you want, you can also start with just a blank document. For my example, I chose a travel theme and opened an image of the Grand Canyon and another image of a passport, as shown in the figure.

2. **Choose Window⇨Layers to open the Layers panel.**

   Always be sure that the Layers panel is visible whenever you're creating a composite from multiple images. You need to see what's happening while you drag and drop, and be aware of what layer you're working on at all times.

continued

continued

3. **Select the desired element in the supporting image.**

   Feel free to use whatever selection method suits your fancy, but remember, the finished collage will look only as good as its individual selections. For more on making selections, see Book III.

   Because the contrast between my passport and the background behind it was very good, I grabbed the Magic Wand tool, set the Tolerance to 50, and clicked the passport. I then held down the Shift key and, with the Lasso tool, circled the remaining pixels in the gold type that the Magic Wand tool didn't pick up.

4. **Choose Select⇨Modify⇨Contract and, in the Contract Selection dialog box, enter a value. Then, choose Select⇨Modify⇨Feather and enter a value in the Feather Selection dialog box.**

   Contract the selections lightly (I chose a value of 1 pixel) before you apply a feather (I chose a 0.5 pixel value) to avoid picking up some of the background during the feathering process. Note that the values you choose depend on the resolution of your images — the lower the resolution, the smaller the value needed.

   Using a small feather helps to avoid the harsh, I-cut-it-out-with-a-pair-of-pinking-shears look.

5. **With the Move tool, drag and drop the selection onto the background image.**

   The Layers panel shows that you've produced a layer. You'll notice that your main image remains as the background below the layer, as shown in the figure.

   Don't worry if your element isn't the right size. You can find a Putting It Together project in Book V, Chapter 2 that shows you how to scale the layer.

6. **Choose File⇨Save As. In the Save As dialog box, name the file *collage* and make sure the format is Photoshop.**

   Keep the file in a handy spot on your hard drive so that you can find it when you're ready to do more with your collage.

In the preceding steps, I showed you how to create a layer by dragging and dropping a passport onto a background image of the Grand Canyon. The process I demonstrate in the following steps is a little different. It entails pasting one selection into another.

Sticking with my travel theme, I opted to take the image of a compass and paste it into the background so that the compass looks like it's peeking out from the side of the canyon. To paste one selection into another on your collage, follow these steps:

1. **Choose File⇨Open. Select the file you saved from the preceding exercise. Also, open a new supporting image.**

2. **Choose Window⇨Layers to open the Layers panel.**

   Always keep the Layers panel visible whenever you're creating a composite from multiple images.

3. **Select the part of the supporting image that you want to use.**

   Feel free to use whatever selection method you desire, but try to get as accurate a selection as you can.

   For my compass image, I used the Elliptical Marquee tool, while holding down the Alt key (Option on the Mac), to draw from the center out to select the bottom portion of the compass. With the same tool, I held down the Shift key, then the mouse button, and then the Alt key (Option) to add the top portion of the compass, as shown in the figure.

4. **Contract and feather the selection (as described in Step 4 in the preceding set of steps).**

   Unless you're going for some special effect, be consistent with the treatment of the edges of each of your elements in your composite.

5. **Choose Edit⇨Copy.**

6. **In your saved collage file, move the first supporting image (the image you added in the preceding set of steps) to the side with the Move tool. Then, use the Lasso tool (or any other selection tool) to create a selection in which to paste your new supporting image.**

   I want the compass image to look like it's peeking up from behind the side of the canyon, so I made a selection in the cliffs of the Grand Canyon.

continued

continued

7. **Choose Edit⇨Paste Special⇨Paste Into.**

If you use the Move tool to move the pasted image around the canvas, you see that the pasted image is invisible outside the boundaries of the selection outline, as shown in my collage.

Don't be concerned if your element isn't the right size. I show you how to scale your layer in Book V, Chapter 2.

The Layers panel shows a second thumbnail next to the compass thumbnail. This thumbnail represents the layer mask created automatically when you pasted into a selection. A layer mask allows portions of the layer to show and be hidden. In my example, the white areas on the layer mask are where my compass shows through. Those white areas correspond to the selection I made in Step 6. The black areas represent where my compass would be hidden if I were to move it into those areas. For more on layer masks, see Book VI, Chapter 3.

8. **Choose File⇨Save.**

Chapter 2: Managing Layers

In This Chapter

✔ **Viewing, shuffling, and moving layers**

✔ **Aligning and distributing layers**

✔ **Linking and locking layers**

✔ **Creating layer sets**

✔ **Flattening and merging layers**

✔ **Using the Layer Comps panel**

*H*opefully, you had the time and inclination to check out the first chapter of Book V. That's where you get all the basic information on creating layers. In this chapter, you get the scoop on how to manage the layers you've created. And unlike some coworkers, clients, or family members, layers are downright agreeable to being managed — even micromanaged, for that matter. The beauty of layers is that they're so darn easy to get along with. You can hide them, shuffle them, link and lock them, herd them into groups, and even smush them together into one loving, collective layer. Yes, Photoshop has a whole slew of ways to get your layers in the orderly and organized fashion you deserve.

Often, hiding all the layers in your image except for the one you want to edit is useful. You can focus on the element at hand without the distraction of all the other components of the image. You can hide a layer with a single quick click of the mouse button, as I describe in the following list:

✔ **Hide all the layers but one.** Select the layer you want to display. Alt-click (Option-click on the Mac) the eye icon for that layer in the left column of the Layers panel. To redisplay all the layers, Alt-click (Option-click on the Mac) the eye icon again.

✔ **Hide an individual layer.** Click the eye icon for that layer, as shown in Figure 2-1. To redisplay the layer, click the blank space in the eye column.

You can also hide layer styles or entire layer groups by using the same method as with layers. You can find out more about layer groups in the section "Creating Layer Groups," later in this chapter. For the lowdown on layer styles, see Book V, Chapter 4.

Figure 2-1: You can hide and show individual layers to better focus your tasks.

 Only layers that are visible will print. Hiding layers for printing can be useful if you want to have several versions (each on a separate layer) of an image for a project within the same document. You can view selective layers, print them, get approval from the powers-that-be, and then delete the layers with the scrapped versions. Only one file to manage — even I can handle that.

 If clicking is just too strenuous for you, try this neat trick: Drag through the eye column to hide or display multiple layers in one fell swoop. Now that's technology.

Rearranging Layers

You can shuffle the order of layers like clear sheets of acetate used with overhead projectors. The *stacking order* of the layers in the Layers panel corresponds to the order of the layers in the document. If you want to move a layer to another position in the stacking order, drag the layer (or layer group) up or down in the Layers panel. While you drag, you see a fist icon. Release your mouse button when a highlighted line appears where you want to insert the layer.

Alternatively, you can change the order by selecting the layer (or layer group) and then choosing Layer➪Arrange. Then, select one of the following commands from the submenu:

- ✔ **Bring to Front and Send to Back:** Send the layer to the very top or very bottom of the stacking order.

- ✔ **Bring Forward and Send Backward:** Move the layer one level up or down.

- ✔ **Reverse:** Switches the order of your layer stack if you have two or more layers selected.

If your image has a background, it always remains the bottommost layer. If you need to move the background, first convert it to a layer by double-clicking the name in the Layers panel. Enter a name for the layer and click OK.

Moving Layer Elements

Rearranging layers is different from moving the content on the layer. Because the elements on a layer are free floating on a bed of transparency, it's a piece of cake to move the element whenever necessary. Moving the element has no effect on any of the other layers, and it doesn't harm the image one iota.

To move an image on a layer, first select that layer in the Layers panel and then just drag it with the Move tool (the arrow pointer with a tiny four-headed arrow), located in the Tools panel; it doesn't get any simpler than that. Here are a few more handy tips when moving an image and using the Move tool:

- ✔ **Move the layer in 1-pixel increments.** Press an arrow key (located between the keyboard and keypad) when you have the Move tool selected. To move the layer in 10-pixel increments, press Shift when you press the arrow key.

- ✔ **Find out what layer holds the element you want to move (or edit in some other way).** If you have the Auto-Select and Layer options selected in the Options bar, select the Move tool and click the element. Photoshop automatically activates the layer that the element resides on. If you don't have this option selected, then Ctrl-click (⌘-click on the Mac) the element. Or you can right-click (Control-click on the Mac) the element. A context menu appears, telling you what layer the element resides on, and then enables you to select that layer from the context menu. It also lists the background layer.

- ✔ **Switch to a layer when you click with the Move tool on any part of a layer.** Select the Auto-Select and Layer options on the Options bar. But be careful if you use this option, especially if you have a lot of overlapping elements; you may inadvertently select a layer when you don't want to.

- ✔ **Select the Auto-Select and Group options on the Options bar to select the layer group that the selected layer is in.** For more on groups, see the section "Creating Layer Groups," later in this chapter.

✔ **Display a bounding box that has handles around the elements on your layer.** Select the Show Transform Controls check box on the Options bar. This box can be useful if all your elements are melting into one another in an indistinguishable conglomeration.

I recommend keeping this option selected so that you essentially have the same controls (scale, rotate, and so on) you have if you chose Edit⇨ Free Transform. For more on transformations, see Book III, Chapter 3.

Putting It Together

Transforming and Moving Layers in a Collage

When you have a couple images in your collage (see the Putting It Together project in Book V, Chapter 1), you can start transforming them to your liking. Moving and scaling are the manipulations you'll probably do the most. Photoshop enables you to transform layers without affecting any other layer within the image. (For more on transformations, see Book V, Chapter 1 and Book III, Chapter 3.) To transform and move images in a collage, follow these steps:

1. **Choose File⇨Open. Select your saved collage file in the dialog box that opens.**

2. **Choose Window⇨Layers to open the Layers panel.**

3. **In the Layers panel, select the layer you want to transform.**

In my example, I chose the layer that has the passport on it.

4. **Choose Edit⇨Free Transform.**

By choosing Free Transform rather than Transform, you interpolate the image only once, rather than twice. For more on interpolation, see Book II, Chapter 1.

5. **Shift-drag a corner transformation handle to scale the image down to the desired size but maintain the proportions, which reduces the amount of distortion.**

I reduced the passport in my example to about half its original size.

6. **Position the cursor just outside the handle until a curved arrow appears. Rotate the image the desired amount.**

The figure shows my example; I rotated the passport about 35 degrees.

7. **When you transform the selection to your liking, double-click inside the transform box or press Enter (Return on the Mac).**

8. **Transform the element that has a layer mask. In the Layers panel, choose the layer and follow Steps 4 through 7.**

In my example, that's the compass layer.

Be sure to click the layer's thumbnail and not the layer mask thumbnail. Otherwise, you transform the layer mask thumbnail, rather than the element.

9. **When you transform the selection to your liking, double-click in the transform box.**

   I scaled the compass slightly so that the top of the compass became visible. Then, I rotated the compass to show more of the compass face, rather than the cover.

10. **Choose File⇨Save.**

You probably already have a pretty good sense of the possibilities (which are infinite) available to you when you create and change collages. Of course, you can always add more stuff to a collage and rearrange the layers, as needed. Just follow these steps:

1. **Choose File⇨Open and select your collage file. Also open another image.**

   I chose a boarding pass image.

2. **Choose Window⇨Layers to open the Layers panel if it isn't already visible.**

3. **Select the desired element in the supporting image.**

   It goes without saying that making the selection accurate can only enhance your composite. I selected the boarding pass with the Polygonal Lasso tool.

4. **Contract and feather the image's edges and use the Move tool to drag the selection into the collage file.**

   For the most professional appearance possible, use consistent values for modifying and feathering all the selections in this composite.

5. **Position and transform the selection, as needed.**

   Follow the directions provided in the preceding steps list. In my example, I scaled the boarding pass to the same size as the passport, rotated it clockwise, and positioned it a little lower than the passport.

continued

continued

6. **In the Layers panel, rearrange your layers, if needed, by selecting a layer and dragging it above another layer.**

   In my image, I dragged my passport layer above my boarding pass layer, as shown in the figure.

   Because the layers are independent entities, you can shuffle them indefinitely like a deck of cards.

7. **Choose File⇨Save.**

Aligning and Distributing Layers

If you're a precision junkie like me, you'll appreciate Photoshop's capability to align and distribute your layers. These commands can be especially useful when you need to align items such as navigation buttons on a Web page mock-up or a row of headshots for a corporate publication. Follow these steps to align and distribute your layers:

1. **In the Layers panel, select the layers you want to align, as shown in Figure 2-2.**

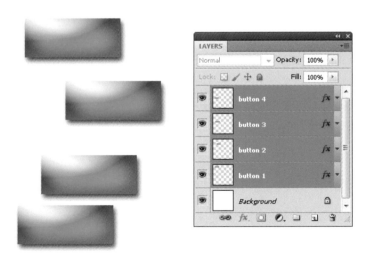

Figure 2-2: Select the layers you want to align in the Layers panel.

2. **Choose Layer⇨Align and select one of the alignment commands.**

Photoshop provides you with handy little icons that illustrate the various alignment types. You also find these icons as buttons on the Options bar when you have the Move tool selected, as shown in Figure 2-3. Feel free to use either method.

Figure 2-3: The Options bar offers different alignment buttons.

Depending on which alignment type you choose, Photoshop aligns to the layer element that's the farthest to the top, bottom, left, or right. If you align to the center, Photoshop splits the difference among the various layer elements.

3. **In the Layers panel, select three or more layers that you want to distribute evenly.**

4. **Choose Layer⇨Distribute and select one of the distribute commands.**

The distribute commands evenly space the layers between the first and last elements in either the row or column.

For the word-challenged, you can find an icon illustrating the distribution types. And like alignment, the distribute icons appear as buttons on the Options bar when you have the Move tool selected. You can see the buttons from Figure 2-2 precisely aligned and evenly distributed in Figure 2-4.

You can also align a layer to a selection outline by following these steps:

1. **Make your desired selection in the image.**

2. **Select a layer or layers in the Layers panel.**

3. **Choose Layer⇨Align Layers to Selection and choose an alignment type from the submenu.**

Note that the Align Layers to Selection command doesn't appear in the Layer menu until you have both layers and an active selection outline.

Figure 2-4: The aligned and evenly distributed buttons.

For the Auto-Align Layers option, the last icon on the Options bar, check out Book V, Chapter 1.

Linking Layers

You'll probably find that you don't need to link layers in most cases. Simply select multiple layers and apply your command — moving, scaling, rotating, and so on. Occasionally, however, you may want to link layers so that they stay grouped as a unit until you decide otherwise. To link layers, follow these short steps:

1. **Select the layers or layer groups in the Layers panel.**

2. **Click the Link Layers icon at the bottom of the Layers panel, as shown in Figure 2-5.**

   A link icon appears to the right of the layer name in the Layers panel.

   To remove a link, click the Link Layers icon again.

Link layers

Figure 2-5: Use the Link command if you need a longer-term grouping of your layers.

If you find the need to quickly select all the linked layers in your Layers panel, select just one of the layers and then choose Select Linked Layers from either the Layer menu or the Layers panel pop-up menu. This technique can come in handy, for example, when working on Web pages with a lot of linked layers containing buttons or labels in a navigation bar.

Putting It Together

Selecting Layers in a Collage and Adjusting Their Size

When you're working on composites, you may find the need to adjust the size or angle of more than one layer. You can select the layers you want to scale or rotate and transform all the layers at the same time. This strategy enables you to adjust all the layers the same amount at the same time — thus ensuring that they stay proportional in size. If you want to be certain that all the layers stay selected during the transformation process, you can link them for extra insurance. Follow these steps:

1. **Open your saved collage file.**

   Make sure that the Layers panel is visible.

2. **Select the layers you want to transform. If you want to link them, simply click the Link Layers icon at the bottom of the Layers panel.**

   In my example, I selected Layers 1 and 3 — my passport and boarding pass.

3. **Choose Edit⇨Free Transform and Shift-drag the corner transformation handle to scale the layers. When you're satisfied, double-click inside the transform box or press Enter (Return on the Mac).**

   Because both layers are selected, any transformation you apply, including moving and scaling, affects both layers, as shown in the figure.

4. **Save the file when you're done.**

Locking Layers

After you get your layers the way you want them, you may want to lock them to prevent them from being changed, as shown in Figure 2-6. To lock a layer, select it in the Layers panel and select one or more of the lock options at the top of the Layers panel. See Table 2-1 for details about each option.

TIP

You can also choose Layer⇨Lock Layers or select Lock Layers from the Layers panel pop-up menu.

When you select the Lock All option, a solid, dark gray lock icon appears on the layer, indicating the layer is fully locked. When you select any of the other lock options, the lock appears light gray and hollow, indicating the layer is partially locked.

Lock options   Fully locked

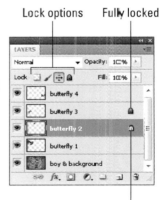

Partially locked

Figure 2-6: Locking prevents unwanted edits.

✓ Like with regular layers, you can select, duplicate, show, hide, lock, and rearrange layer groups. See other sections in this chapter for more on these commands.

✓ You can nest layer groups. Create (or drag) one layer group into another layer group. In CS4, you were limited to five or fewer levels of nested groups. Now, however, in CS5, you can nest more than five.

✓ You can create a layer group from selected layers. Select the layers that you want to be in a group, and then select New Group from Layers from the Layers panel pop-up menu or choose Layer⊏>New⊏>Group from Layers. Name the group in the dialog box that appears and click OK.

✓ If you select a layer within a group and then choose Layer⊏>Arrange, the command applies to the stacking order only within the layer group.

✓ You can merge layer groups. Select the group and select Merge Group from the Layers panel pop-up menu or choose Layer⊏>Merge Group. For more on merging, see the following section.

✓ You can rename your group by double-clicking the group name in the Layers panel. You can also choose Layer⊏>Group Properties or select Group Properties from the Layers panel pop-up menu.

✓ In addition, you can lock layers within a group. Select Lock All Layers in Group from the Layers panel pop-up menu or choose Layer⊏>Lock All Layers in Group.

Flattening and Merging Layers

Being the true layers evangelist that I am, I tout the glories of layers in the first two chapters of this minibook. And layers are wonderful. But they do have a dark side. They can make your file go from slim and trim to bulky and bloated. You not only get a larger file size that slows your computer system performance, but you're also limited to the file formats that allow you to save layers: Photoshop's native format (.psd), TIFF (.tif), Large Document Format (.psb), and PDF (.pdf). If you save your file in any other format, Photoshop smashes your layers down into a background. This file limitation often forces users to save two versions of every layered file — one as a native Photoshop file and one as something else, such as EPS or JPEG, to import into another program. For more on file formats, see Book II, Chapter 2. To curb large file sizes or use layered images in a wider range of formats, you have a couple options:

✓ **Merging layers:** Combines visible, linked, or adjacent layers into a single layer (not a background). The intersection of all transparent areas is retained. You can merge layers or layer groups. You can also merge adjustment or fill layers (see Book V, Chapter 1 for details), but they can't act as the target layer for the merge. Merging layers can help decrease your file size and make your document more manageable. You're still restricted to the layer-friendly file formats, however.

✔ **Flattening an image:** Combines all visible layers into a background. Photoshop deletes hidden layers and fills any transparent areas with white. Flattening is usually reserved for when you're completely finished editing your image.

When you convert an image from one color mode to another, that conversion may cause the file to flatten. Look out for the warning dialog box that prompts you of this result, and go back and save a copy of your file as a native Photoshop file, thereby preserving your layers. See Book II, Chapter 2 for details about color modes.

Merging layers

You can merge your layers several ways. To use the first option, follow these steps:

1. **Ensure that all the layers (and layer sets) that you want to merge are visible, as shown in Figure 2-9.**

Figure 2-9: Merging layers can make your file size a lot smaller.

2. **Choose Merge Visible from the Layers panel pop-up menu or the Layer menu.**

   All visible layers are smushed into a single layer, as shown in Figure 2-9.

Hold down Alt (Option on the Mac) when choosing Layer⇨Merge Visible. Photoshop merges those layers onto a new layer.

You can also merge layers by following these steps:

1. **Position the layer or layer groups that you want to merge adjacent to each other in the Layers panel.**

2. **Select the top layer of those you want merged.**

3. **Choose Merge Down from the Layers panel pop-up menu or the Layer menu.**

   If the top layer is a layer group, the command is called Merge Group.

   Merge Down merges your selected layer with the layer directly below it.

Flattening layers

To flatten an image, follow these steps:

1. **Ensure that all the layers you want to retain are visible.**

   Photoshop discards all hidden layers.

2. **Choose Layer➪Flatten Image or select Flatten Image from the Layers panel pop-up menu.**

   The transparent areas of your flattened image are filled with the background color and appear as a background layer in the Layers panel, as shown in Figure 2-10.

   Figure 2-10: Flatten your layers only if you're reasonably sure you won't need individual layers any longer.

   Photoshop doesn't prompt you with a warning like, "Are you sure you really want to do this?" But if you mistakenly flatten your image, you can undo the command immediately by choosing Edit➪Undo. If you go ahead and perform another action, then undo your mistake by using the History panel. However, if the flattening step is no longer in the History panel, there's no way to undo the flattening. See Book II, Chapter 4 for the scoop on the History panel.

 Putting It Together

Checking Your Collage for Flaws and Consolidating Layers

When you begin a project, you may think you know what you want the final result to look like. But when your creative juices start flowing, you may decide that something doesn't look right. For example, while I was working on my collage, I discovered that the sky behind and above the canyon was a little on the ordinary side.

1. **Open the saved collage file and open a new image that you want to incorporate into the collage.**

   In my example, I thought the sky needed some kick, so I opened an image that contained a sky I liked.

2. **Select the part of the image that you want to add to your collage, as shown in the figure.**

   Most of the time, consistency is key. In my example, however, I didn't need to feather the image. Because I'm going to paste it into the old sky, the edges of the element won't be seen.

Photodisc

3. **Choose Edit⇨Copy.**

4. **In the collage image, select the portion of the image into which you want to paste your copied element.**

   Because I'm pasting the image into the background image, I first needed to make the selection I wanted to paste into. I used the Magic Wand tool. After a couple of additional Shift-clicks, I selected the entire sky behind the canyon.

5. **Choose Edit⇨Paste Into.**

   The element you copied (in my case, the new sky) appears inside the selected area of your collage, as shown in the figure.

When you're close to finalizing your collage, you might want to consolidate layers. Minimizing the number of layers makes projects easier to manage and your file size smaller, which is great when you get ready to add the finishing touches to your collage.

Be sure that before you merge your layers, you'll never have to manipulate them separately, especially if the elements on the layer overlap each other, as mine do.

To consolidate two layers, follow these steps:

1. **Select the layers in the Layers panel.**

continued

continued

2. **Select Merge Layers from the Layers panel pop-up menu.**

   The two layers merge and become one.

3. **Choose File⇨Save.**

Working with the Layer Comps Panel

The Layer Comps feature doesn't really add more layer functionality, but because it shares a similar moniker, I explain it in this minibook.

What Layer Comps does is enable you to create and save multiple versions of your project within a single master file. Through the Layer Comps panel, Photoshop records all the vital statistics of your layers, including their visibility, position, and blending options. These statistics come in handy when you want to show a client or art director various design versions within a single document. That's right: No longer do you have to save the various renditions of a design or project in multiple files. Just be aware that layer comps do add to your file size.

The following steps walk you through the day-to-day operation of the Layer Comps panel:

1. **Choose Window⇨Layer Comps to display the panel, shown in Figure 2-11.**

Corbis Digital Stock

Figure 2-11: The Layer Comps panel enables you to create and save multiple versions of a project within a single document.

2. **Create all your desired layer content.**

   If you perform all your editing on just a background layer, you can't save the document as a layer comp.

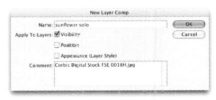 3. **When you have a version of the document that you want to save as a comp, click the New Layer Comp button at the bottom of the panel or select New Layer Comp from the panel pop-up menu.**

   The New Layer Comp dialog box appears.

   To create a comp and bypass the options dialog box, hold down the Alt (Option on the Mac) key when you click the New Layer Comp button.

4. **Name your layer comp and select the attributes you want recorded — Visibility, Position, and Appearance (Layer Style) of the layers. Click OK.**

   You can also add an optional comment about the configuration you're capturing, as shown in Figure 2-12.

   Figure 2-12: Add project details in the Comment field.

   If you add a comment, you see a triangle just to the left of the layer comp name. (Refer to the sunflower solo comp shown in Figure 2-11.) Click the triangle to see your comment in the panel.

5. **Continue creating your various configurations of the document, capturing a layer comp after each.**

6. **To display a particular layer comp, click in the left column in the Layer Comps panel.**

   A document icon appears, which indicates that particular layer comp is selected.

7. **To efficiently cycle through all your layer comps, click the Apply Next Selected Layer Comp or Apply Previous Selected Layer Comp icon (the arrows) at the bottom of the Layer Comps panel.**

   You can also, less efficiently, apply layer comps by selecting the particular layer comp and selecting Apply Layer Comp from the panel pop-up menu. The document icon moves to that layer, and Photoshop displays that layer comp.

Here are a few more Layer Comp tidbits:

✔ **To rename a layer comp:** Simply double-click its name in the panel.

 ✔ **To delete a layer comp:** Select it and click the trash can icon in the Layer Comps panel. You can also drag the layer comp to the trash can icon or select Delete Layer Comp from the panel pop-up menu

✔ **To duplicate a layer comp:** Select it and drag it onto the New Layer Comp icon in the panel or select Duplicate Layer Comp from the panel pop-up menu.

✔ **To update a particular layer comp with the currently active configuration of the document:** Select the layer comp, and then select Update Layer Comp from the panel pop-up menu or click the Update Layer Comp button at the bottom of the panel.

✔ **To display your document at its latest configuration (but not necessarily the latest saved layer comp):** Select Restore Last Document State from the panel pop-up or simply click in the column to the left of the Last Document State item in the Layer Comps panel.

✔ **To rearrange the order of the layer comps:** Simply drag it to a new location in the panel.

To output your layer comps, choose File➪Scripts➪Layer Comps to Files. Select this command to make Photoshop export your layer comps to individual files. In the dialog box that appears, shown in Figure 2-13, provide a destination and prefix name for your file. Indicate whether you want to include Selected Layer Comps Only. (You must select them before you choose the command.) Leave that option deselected to have Photoshop export all layer comps. Then, choose your desired file type and specify whether you want to Include ICC Profile (see Book II, Chapter 2) and Maximize Compatibility. (See Book I, Chapter 5.) Click Run and then sit back and watch the magic happen.

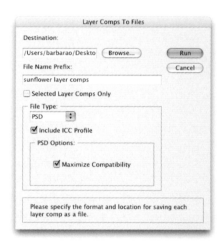

Figure 2-13: Have Photoshop automatically export your layer comps into individual files.

The Layer Comps to WPG (Web Photo Gallery) command is an optional plug-in that you'll find on your installation disc in the Goodies folder. And you won't find the Layer Comps to PDF command in the Scripts submenu at all. You can find it in the Adobe Output Module in Adobe Bridge. For more on creating PDFs and Web galleries, see Book I, Chapter 4.

Chapter 3: Playing with Opacity and Blend Modes

In This Chapter

✓ Adjusting opacity and fills

✓ Applying blend modes for effects

✓ Setting the blend options

In this chapter, I show you how to let down your hair and get those creative juices flowing. Yes, I'm about to say the "F" word: Fun.

This chapter, along with Book V, Chapter 4, focuses on how to tweak the layers you've made. Maybe you want to make one of your layers semitransparent so that you can see the layer beneath it; or say you want to try blending the colors between a couple layers in a way that's slightly offbeat. Look no further.

Although some techniques in this chapter may reek of complexity, keep in mind that you don't need to totally understand them. Take these techniques as far as you want. And remember, there's no substitute for good, old experimentation. Before you jump into these techniques, it helps to have a handle on the methods of layer creation and management that I explain in Book V, Chapters 1 and 2.

Adjusting Layer Opacity

By far one of the easiest ways to make your image look oh-so-sophisticated is to have one image ghosted over another, as shown in Figure 3-1. Creating this effect is a snap with the Opacity option in the Layers panel. You adjust the opacity in two ways:

✓ Select your desired layer in the Layers panel. Then, either access the slider by clicking the right-pointing arrow, entering a percentage value in the Opacity text box, or simply scrubbing over the word Opacity (it converts to a two-way arrow).

You can now select more than one layer at a time and change the Opacity (or Fill Opacity) values in one fell swoop.

NEW FEATURE CS5

Figure 3-1: Adjusting the opacity enables one image to ghost over another.

🖛 You can also double-click a layer thumbnail, choose Layer⇨Layer Style⇨ Blending Options, or select Blending Options from the Layers panel pop-up menu. (Click the triangle in the upper-right corner to open the menu.)

Any of these methods brings up the Layer Style dialog box, where you can enter a value or drag the slider for opacity.

The Opacity setting allows you to mix the active layer with the layers below it in varying percentages from 100% (completely opaque) to 0% (completely transparent). Remember that you can adjust the opacity only on a layer, not a background.

You can also change the Opacity percentage by using keyboard shortcuts. With any tool active, except a painting or editing tool, press a number key. Press 5 for 50 percent, 25 for 25 percent. If you're entering a two-digit value, just be sure you type the numbers quickly, or else Photoshop interprets the numbers as two different values. You get the picture. Note that for the default of 100 percent, you must press 0.

Adjusting the Fill Opacity

In addition to adjusting the regular opacity for a layer, you can also adjust the fill opacity. Fill opacity works a little differently from regular opacity. The regular Opacity setting affects layer styles (see Book V, Chapter 4) and blend modes (see the following section) that have been applied to the layer. Fill opacity, however, affects only the pixels or shapes that reside on the layer. It doesn't affect the styles or blends. As you can see in Figure 3-2, the drop shadow and emboss styles in the bottom example show through full strength.

Figure 3-2: Fill opacity (bottom) affects only layer pixels, not styles or blend modes that have been applied to the layer.

To adjust the Fill Opacity setting, select your desired layer, or layers, in the Layers panel, and then enter a value in the Fill Opacity text box or drag the pop-up slider. The other methods for adjusting fill opacity are similar to the regular opacity option.

Creating Effects with Blend Modes

Photoshop's 25 blend modes (27 when you work with the painting and editing tools) determine how the colors in different layers interact with each other. Blend modes can produce a multitude of interesting, sometimes even bizarre, effects. And what's more, you can easily apply, change, or discard blend modes with no permanent damage to your layers.

Most options in the Blend Mode pop-up menu (located under the Layers tab) in the Layers panel are the same as those on the Mode pop-up menu on the Options bar. The exceptions are the Behind and Clear modes, which you can find only on the Options bar because they're available for use only with painting and editing tools.

I urge you to pick an image with a few layers and apply each blend mode to get a good handle on what the various blend modes do. In fact, try a few different images because the effects may be subtle or intense, depending on the colors in the image. Throw in some different opacity percentages, and you're on your way to endless hours of creative fun.

You'll find these modes called *blend modes, painting modes, brush modes, layer modes, calculations,* or just plain *modes.* They're usually referred to as *blend modes* or *layer modes* when used with layers and painting modes, and *brush modes* when used in conjunction with a painting or editing tool.

General blend modes

In the General category, you find the following modes, which are shown in Figure 3-3 and explained in Table 3-1.

Table 3-1	General Blend Modes
Blend Mode	*Description*
Normal	You're probably very familiar with the Normal blend mode by now. It's the default that lets each pixel appear in its very own unadulterated state. The other three modes are used only in certain circumstances.
Dissolve	The effects of Dissolve can be seen only with a layer that has an opacity setting of less than 100% — the lower the opacity, the more intense the effect. The effect is created by allowing some pixels from lower layers, which are randomized, to show through the target layer.
Behind	Available only when you have a painting or editing tool active. Type must be rasterized, and Lock Transparency must be deselected. It allows you to edit or paint only on the transparent areas of the layer, giving the illusion that the strokes are behind the layer.
Clear	Available only when you have a painting or editing tool active. Type must be rasterized, and Lock Transparency must be deselected. It allows you to edit or paint with transparency, giving the appearance that holes are being punched into your image.

Blend modes that darken

Overall, the blend modes in this category all produce effects that darken your image, as shown in Figure 3-4. However, one of my favorite uses for the Darken blend mode is a little different. Scan a handwritten letter or sheet of music and layer it over an image. Apply the Darken blend mode to the letter or sheet-music layer. The white areas of the paper become transparent, and only the letters or musical notes display, creating a nice composite image. Table 3-2 describes these modes.

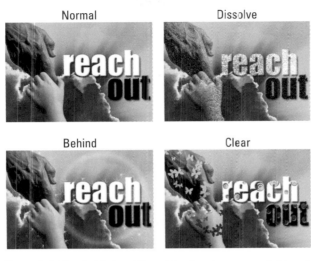

Figure 3-3: The Behind and Clear blend modes are available only with a painting or editing tool.

Figure 3-4: These blend modes darken, or burn, your layers.

Table 3-2	Blend Modes That Darken
Blend Mode	*Description*
Darken	If the pixels on the layer are lighter than those below, the lighter pixels turn transparent. If the pixels on the layer are darker, they appear unchanged. It's a great mode, as is Darker Color, for superimposing scanned text or line art because it allows the white color of the paper to essentially drop out, leaving only the dark letters or lines.
Multiply	Burns the layer into the layers underneath. The Multiply mode darkens all colors where they mix. With layers, it's comparable to sticking two slides in the same slot in a slide projector. If you're painting, each successive stroke creates a darker color, as if drawing with markers.
Color Burn	Darkens the layers underneath and burns them with color. Increases contrast. Blending with white pixels has no effect. It's like applying a dark dye to your image.
Linear Burn	Darkens the layers underneath by decreasing the brightness. This is similar to Multiply but tends to make portions of your image pure black. Blending with white pixels has no effect.
Darker Color	When blending two layers, the darker of the two colors will be visible.

Blend modes that lighten

If you have blend modes that darken, having modes that lighten just makes good sense. So, if you have the need to throw some digital bleach on your brightly colored pixels, try a couple of these blend modes, which I describe in Table 3-3. Figure 3-5 shows examples of these effects.

Table 3-3	Blend Modes That Lighten
Blend Mode	*Description*
Lighten	If the pixels on the layer are darker than those below, the darker pixels turn transparent. If the pixels on the layer are lighter, they appear unchanged. This is the opposite of Darken.
Screen	Lightens the layer where it mixes with the layer underneath. Blending with black pixels has no effect. It's like putting two slides in two different projectors and pointing them at the same screen. Screen is the opposite of Multiply.

Blend Mode	Description
Color Dodge	Lightens the pixels in the layers underneath and infuses them with colors from the top layer. This is like bleaching your layer. Blending with black pixels has no effect.
Linear Dodge (Add)	Lightens the layers underneath by increasing the brightness. It's similar to Screen but tends to make parts of your image pure white. Blending with black pixels has no effect.
Lighter Color	When blending two layers, the lighter of the two colors will be visible.

Figure 3-5: These blend modes lighten, or dodge, your layers.

Lighting blend modes

This group of blend modes plays with the lighting in your layers. Some of these blend modes, such as Pin Light, are reserved for the occasional wacky special effect. The following list and images explain and show each mode:

✔ **Overlay:** Multiplies the dark pixels in the top layer and screens the light pixels in the underlying layers. Enhances the contrast and saturation of colors.

Overlay

✔ **Soft Light:** Darkens the dark pixels and lightens the light pixels. If the pixels on the top layer are lighter than 50% gray, the lighter pixels are lightened further. If the pixels on the top layer are darker than 50% gray, the mode darkens pixels. Blending with black or white results in darker or lighter pixels, but it doesn't make parts of your image pure black or pure white. It's similar to Overlay, but softer and subtler, like shining a soft spotlight on the image.

Soft Light

✔ **Hard Light:** Multiplies the dark pixels and screens the light pixels. It's like shining a bright, hard spotlight on the image. If the pixels on the top layer are lighter than 50% gray, they're screened. If the pixels on the top layer are darker than 50% gray, the mode multiplies the pixels. You can use this mode to add highlights and shadows to an image. Blending with black or white gives you black and white.

Hard Light

✔ **Vivid Light:** If the pixels on the top layer are darker than 50% gray, this mode burns (or darkens) the colors by increasing the contrast. If the pixels on the top layer are lighter than 50% gray, the mode dodges (or lightens) the colors by decreasing the contrast. Vivid Light is a combination of Color Burn and Color Dodge.

Vivid Light

✔ **Linear Light:** If the pixels on the top layer are darker than 50% gray, the mode burns (or darkens) the colors by decreasing the brightness. If the pixels on the top layer are lighter than 50% gray, the mode dodges (or lightens) the colors by increasing the brightness. It's a combination of Linear Burn and Linear Dodge.

Linear Light

✔ **Pin Light:** Replaces the colors of pixels, depending on the colors in the top layer. If the pixels on the top layer are darker than 50% gray, the mode replaces pixels darker than those on the top layer and doesn't change lighter pixels. If the pixels on the top layer are

Pin Light

lighter than 50% gray, the mode replaces the pixels that are lighter than those pixels on the top layer and doesn't change pixels that are darker. Pin Light is a combination of Darken and Lighten and it's useful for special effects.

Hard Mix

✔ **Hard Mix:** Similar to Vivid Light, but it reduces the colors to a total of eight — cyan, magenta, yellow, black, red, green, blue, and white. Although the results depend on the mix of existing colors on the top and bottom layers, this mode usually creates a highly posterized effect.

Blend modes that invert

If the blend modes discussed in the preceding sections are a tad too tame for you, you may want to check out the inverters — Difference and Exclusion (described in Table 3-4). These blend modes invert your colors and can produce some interesting special effects, as shown in Figure 3-6.

Difference

Exclusion

Figure 3-6: The Difference and Exclusion blend modes invert colors.

Table 3-4	Blend Modes That Invert
Blend Mode	*Description*
Difference	Produces a negative, or inverted, effect according to the brightness values on the top layers. If the pixels on the top layer are black, the mode doesn't change the colors of the underlying layers. If the pixels on the top layer are white, the mode inverts the colors of the underlying layers. This can produce bizarre results.
Exclusion	Similar to Difference, but with less contrast and saturation. If the pixels on the top layer are black, the mode doesn't change the colors of the underlying layers. If the pixels on the top layer are white, the mode inverts the colors of the underlying layers. Medium colors blend to create gray.

HSL color model blend modes

These blend modes use the HSL (Hue, Saturation, and Lightness) color model to mix colors. My favorite blend mode in this group is Color, which allows you to apply color to images without obscuring the tonality. The Color mode is great for "hand painting" grayscale images. See details on this technique in Book IV, Chapter 1. Table 3-5 lists these modes, and Figure 3-7 shows their effects.

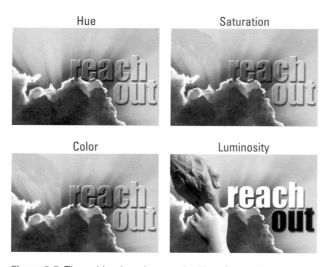

Figure 3-7: These blend modes use the Hue, Saturation, and Lightness color model to mix colors.

Table 3-5	HSL Color Model Blend Modes
Blend Mode	**Description**
Hue	Blends the luminance (brightness) and saturation (intensity of the color) of the underlying layers with the hue (color) of the top layer.
Saturation	Blends the luminance and hue of the underlying layers with the saturation of the top layer.
Color	Blends the luminance of the underlying layers with the saturation and hue of the top layer. This mode is great for colorizing gray-scale (with a color mode set to RGB) images because it preserves the shadows, highlights, and details of the underlying layers.
Luminosity	Blends the hue and saturation of the underlying layers with the luminance of the top layer. Preserves the shadows, highlights, and details from the top layer and mixes them with the colors of the underlying layers. Luminosity is the opposite of Color.

The following blend modes work with 8-, 16-, and 32-bit images: Normal, Dissolve, Darken, Multiply, Lighten, Linear Dodge, Difference. Hue, Saturation, Color, Luminosity, Lighter Color, and Darker Color.

Working with the Advanced Blending Options

If you want to get serious about layers, then you need to know about the Advanced Blending Options, which you can find in the Layer Style dialog box. These options allow you to tailor the way your layer styles and blend modes interact with your layers. Getting to the advanced options is just like accessing opacity and blend modes: You can double-click a layer thumbnail, choose Layer➪Layer Style➪Blending Options, or select Blending Options from the Layers panel pop-up menu. The massive Layer Style dialog box rears its multi-paneled head, as shown in Figure 3-8.

(By the way, if you're ready to know more about these blending features, skip to Book V, Chapter 4, where I cover layer styles.)

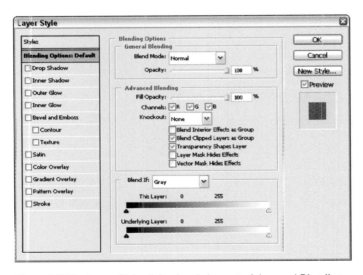

Figure 3-8: The Layer Style dialog box is home to Advanced Blending Options.

Advanced options to blend with

The advanced options aren't for the faint of heart. To be frank, the options are, well, advanced, so you might find them a tad too eggheady for your taste. But if not, here you go:

✔ **Fill Opacity:** I cover this in the section "Adjusting the Fill Opacity," earlier in this chapter.

✔ **Channels:** This option allows you to restrict your blending options to specific channels only. For all you need to know about working with channels, check out Book VI.

✔ **Knockout:** This option allows you to specify which layers have holes in them so that you can view the layers underneath. You first have to use the Fill Opacity option to set the opacity of the knockout. The lower the opacity, the more the hole shows; therefore, set it to 0% (like in my example in Figure 3-9) to see all the way through. Set the Knockout to Shallow to create a hole through one layer group (see Book V, Chapter 2) or a clipping group. (See Book V, Chapter 4.) Set the Knockout to Deep to create a hole all the way through to the background. If you're working with just layers, and not layer groups or clipping groups, the knockout cuts through to the background. If there's no background, it cuts through to transparency.

Figure 3-9: A knockout cuts holes in your layers to enable you to view the layers underneath.

✔ **Blend Interior Effects as Group:** This option applies the blend mode of the layer to interior layer effects, such as inner glows, satin and color overlay, and so on. Deselect this option to prevent the blend mode from affecting the layer effects. You can see the difference in Figure 3-10.

✔ **Blend Clipped Layers as Group:** The blend mode of the bottom layer in the clipping group affects all the other layers in the group. Deselect this option to make each layer retain its own blend mode and appearance.

✔ **Transparency Shapes Layer:** Confines layer effects and knockouts to opaque areas of a layer. Deselect this option to apply the mode's layer effects and knockouts to the entire layer. (See Figure 3-11.)

Blend Interior Effects as Group selected

Deselected

Figure 3-10: The Blend Interior Effects as Group option applies
the blend mode of the type layers to the layer's inner glow, bevel
and emboss, and color overlay.

- ✓ **Layer Mask Hides Effects:** Confines layer effects to the area designated by the layer mask. (For more on layer masks, see Book VI, Chapter 3.)
- ✓ **Vector Mask Hides Effects:** Confines layer effects to the visible area designated by a vector mask, as shown in Figure 3-12. (For more on vector masks, see Book VI, Chapter 3.)

Transparency Shape Layer selected   Deselected

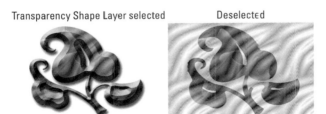

Figure 3-11: The Transparency Shapes Layer restricts layer styles
to the opaque areas of a layer.

Figure 3-12: Choose to confine your effects to the vector mask, or not.

Blend If options

By using the slider bars, you can specify which colors are visible in the active layer and which colors show through from the underlying layers. You can select a specific channel from the Blend If pop-up menu to apply the option to a single channel. The default channel, Gray, affects all channels in the image. The two sliders at the bottom of the Layer Style dialog box do the following:

- ✓ **This Layer:** Allows you to set a blending range. In other words, you can hide certain colors according to the brightness values in the active layer. By dragging the black triangle to the right, you exclude darker colors. By dragging the white triangle to the left, you exclude lighter colors.

- ✓ **Underlying Layer:** Forces the colors from the underlying layers to show through the active layer. Again, dragging the black and white triangles excludes ranges of colors.

Excluding and forcing colors can result in some harsh color transitions. You can provide for a smoother transition between blended and unblended areas by splitting the slider into two parts, allowing the pixels to gradually fade to transparency. Alt-drag (Option-drag on the Mac) on either the black or white triangle in either slider bar to split the triangle into two halves. The left and right triangles mark the beginning and end of the blending range, where pixels fade into or out of view.

Putting It Together

Fine-Tuning and Adjusting Opacity Settings in Your Collage

If you've followed along with the Putting It Together projects I discuss in Book V, Chapters 1 and 2, you may have a collage that you're pretty satisfied with. You just need to make the final tweaks and then go to sleep (or go home to your spouse and children).

One of the most important tweaks you can make is to opacity. Follow these steps to adjust the opacity settings on some of the layers:

1. **Open your saved collage file.**

   If the Layers panel isn't already visible, open it.

2. **Select a layer in your collage and move the opacity slider to the left or right.**

   If you want the layer to be more opaque, move the slider to the right. If you're interested in making the layer more transparent, move the slider to the left.

   I chose Layer 4 and adjusted the opacity to 75%. I like the blue sky in my collage, but it's a tad too vibrant in comparison to the rest of the image. Adjusting the opacity tones it down and allows the blue to blend in more naturally.

3. **Save the file and move on to the next layer you want to adjust.**

   If you have more complicated opacity settings to adjust, keep reading.

4. **Select the background layer and then select Duplicate Layer from the Layers panel pop-up menu. Click OK to close the Duplicate Layer dialog box.**

continued

groups. For more on backgrounds, see Book V, Chapter 1. For details on locking layers and creating layer groups, see Book V, Chapter 2.

✔ Layer effects are *dynamically linked* to the contents of a layer. If you move or edit the contents of the layers, the effects are updated.

✔ When you apply effects, they become part of the layer's style. A styled layer has an fx symbol next to the layer's name in the Layers panel. You can expand (to view the individual effects) or collapse the layer style by clicking the triangle icon next to the florin.

✔ Drag the fx symbol from one layer to another to move it. Or Alt+drag (Option+drag on the Mac) the fx symbol from one layer to another to copy the style easily.

✔ If you create a style so fantastic that you want to save it for later use, you can save a custom style as a preset and store it in the Styles panel. (See the section "Saving your own style," later in this chapter.)

✔ Feel free to cut loose and have some fun. Layer styles are completely nondestructive. They don't muck around with your actual pixel data. If you don't like them, edit them. If you really don't like them, delete them to go back to your original unstylized image.

Introducing the Many Layer Styles

Layer effects fall into a few categories. You can add shadows, glow effects, beveled and embossed edges, and overlay colors and patterns, and you can, of course, tweak to your heart's content. This list introduces the various effects that you can apply. (In the following sections, I explain how you apply each layer style and tweak its settings.)

✔ **Shadows:** Add a soft drop or inner shadow to the contents of a layer. You can adjust the blend mode, color, opacity, angle, size, and contour to suit your needs. Figure 4-1 shows examples of both types of shadows.

Drop Shadow   Inner Shadow

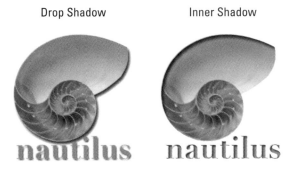

Figure 4-1: Add dimension by applying an inner or drop shadow to your object or type.

✔ **Glows:** Add a soft highlight that appears on the outside or inside edges of the contents of a layer, as shown in Figure 4-2. Like shadows, you can fine-tune the appearance by adjusting numerous options.

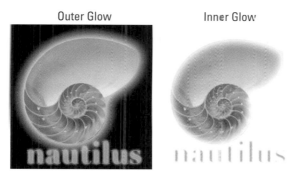

Outer Glow   Inner Glow

Figure 4-2: Inner and outer glows add a soft highlight to edges.

✔ **Bevels:** Create a 3-D edge on either the outside or inside edges of the contents of a layer, giving the element some dimension. Similarly, emboss effects make elements appear raised off of or punched into the page. Satin creates a satiny or draped fabric effect over your element. All these effects (shown in Figure 4-3) offer numerous options to adjust their appearances.

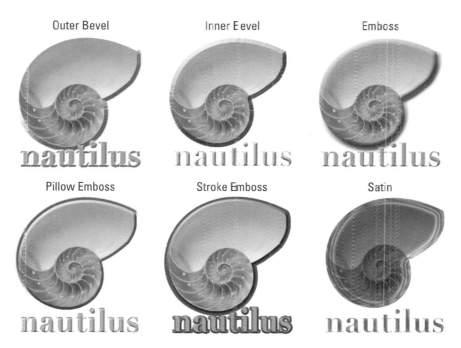

Outer Bevel   Inner Bevel   Emboss

Pillow Emboss   Stroke Emboss   Satin

Figure 4-3: Bevel and Emboss make your element look raised or punched.

✔ **Overlays:** Apply a fill of color, a gradient, or a pattern over the contents of your layer, as shown in Figure 4-4. You can adjust the opacity of the overlay, among other options, so that your original element shows through more clearly. You can also surround your layer with a stroke consisting of a color, gradient, or pattern.

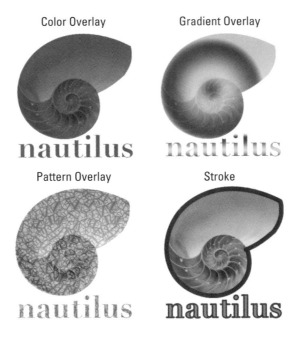

Figure 4-4: Overlays cover your object or type.

Applying a Layer Effect

Follow these steps to apply a layer effect:

1. **Select your desired layer in the Layers panel.**

2. **Choose Layer➪Layer Style and choose an effect from the submenu.**

   You can also click the Add a Layer Style icon in the Layers panel and select an effect from the pop-up menu.

   An intimidating Layer Style dialog box with a ton of options rears its head, as shown in Figure 4-5.

3. **Select the Preview check box in the top-right portion of the dialog box so you can see your effects while you apply them.**

4. **To accept the default settings, just click OK.**

    Or you can experiment with the settings.

    You can use sliders or check boxes, enter values in the text boxes, and so on. The following sections in this chapter describe the options and settings in detail.

5. **If you refine your effect settings, click OK when you finish.**

    Photoshop applies your effect to your layer, as indicated by the fx icon.

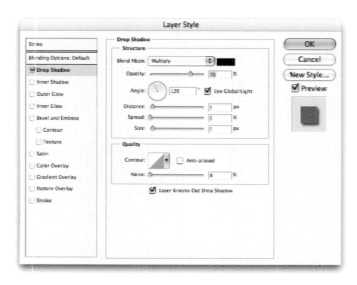

Figure 4-5: The Layer Style dialog box allows you to easily turn effects off and on with a mere check of a box.

Managing and Editing Layer Styles

You can always just apply the layer effect with Photoshop's default settings, but what fun is that? To edit a style, double-click the Effect name or the Effects label, double-click the layer thumbnail or double-click the Layer Style icon in the Layers panel, and make your desired adjustments in the Layer Style dialog box. If you double-clicked the layer thumbnail or the icon, be sure to select your desired effect from the left side of the dialog box to get access to your effect's settings.

The following sections give you the details on each of the options. But a picture is worth a thousand words. Experiment to see these effects come alive.

Managing layer styles

Here are a few pointers to keep in mind when working with and editing layer styles:

- ✔ **Choose several effects at one time.** Simply select the check box for the effect on the left side of the Layer Style dialog box. To access the options for each effect, you must click the effect name so that it's highlighted.

- ✔ **Remove an effect.** Deselect the check box associated with it.

- ✔ **Move a style onto a separate layer.** By default, layer styles are attached to a layer. To put a style on a separate layer, select the styled layer and choose Layer⇨Layer Style⇨Create Layer. You see a new layer in the Layers panel with a name, such as `Layer 0's Drop Shadow`.

Although separating a style onto its own layer may give you more manual editing capability and allow you to apply filters, you lose all editing ability with the Layer Style dialog box. Also, the style won't dynamically update when you change the layer itself. Your style basically becomes just a generic mass of colored pixels.

- ✔ **Copy and paste effects onto other layers.** Select the layer containing the effect and choose Layer⇨Layer Style⇨Copy Layer Style. Select the layer or layers on which you want to apply the effect and choose Layer⇨Layer Style⇨Paste Layer Style. Even easier, you can also just hold down the Alt (Option on the Mac) key and then drag and drop an effect from one layer to another.

- ✔ **Hide effects.** Choose Layer⇨Layer Style⇨Hide All Effects to hide all effects on the image, not just the selected layer.

- ✔ **Display hidden effects.** Choose Layer⇨Layer Style⇨Show All Effects.

- ✔ **Remove all the effects on a layer.** Choose Layer⇨Layer Style⇨Clear Layer Style. You can also drag the *Effects bar* (what Adobe calls the name Effects) or fx icon to the trash can icon in the Layers panel.

- ✔ **Remove a single effect.** Simply drag and drop the single effect to the trash can icon in the Layers panel.

- ✔ **Resize a layer effect.** Select your desired layer in the Layers panel. Choose Layer⇨Layer Style⇨Scale Effects. Select Preview and enter a value between 1 and 1,000 percent. This command allows you to scale the effect without scaling the element.

Editing drop shadow or inner shadow effects

If you used the default settings to apply your drop shadow or inner shadow and want to do some tweaking, edit by following these steps:

1. **In the Layers panel, double-click the Effect name.**

   Or you can double-click the layer thumbnail or the Layer Style icon (fx icon).

   The Layer Style dialog box opens. If you double-clicked the layer thumbnail or the Layer Style icon, you need to click the Drop Shadow or Inner Shadow name on the left side of the dialog box.

2. **Change the Blend Mode setting to adjust how the colors of the shadow mix with the colors of your elements.**

   Usually, the default mode, Multiply, works best.

3. **Adjust the Opacity setting to change how transparent the shadow appears.**

4. **To select a shadow color, open the Color Picker by clicking the swatch to the right of the Blend Mode setting.**

5. **Establish the angle of your light source.**

6. **Select the Use Global Light option to ensure that all the shadows and highlights of all your elements are consistent.**

   You don't want one layer to look like it's 6 a.m. and another to look like it's 2 p.m. The neat thing is that if you change the angle on one layer style, all the styles (with the Use Global Light option selected) you've applied to your layers adjust to that new angle dynamically.

7. **Specify how far the shadow is offset from your element with the Distance setting.**

8. **Adjust the Spread, Choke, and Size settings to specify the boundary, intensity, and size of the shadow.**

9. **Select the Layer Knocks Out Drop Shadow option if you have a transparent object on top of the shadow.**

   This option prevents the shadow from showing through the object.

10. **After you refine your effect settings, click OK.**

    Your effect is edited and ready to go, as shown in Figure 4-6.

    You can also choose to apply various contours and noise to your shadow. See the section "Playing with Contours," later in this chapter, for details.

Figure 4-13: A Ring-Triple contour on the drop shadow of
my beveled text and oval adds a metallic touch.

Adjusting contour settings

You're using Photoshop, the Swiss Army Knife of the graphics-editing world,
so you can do a whole lot more than select a preset contour and apply it to a
layer. Depending on the effect you're working with, you can change the
appearance of the contour in a variety of ways:

- **Noise:** Randomizes the colors of selected pixels in the drop or inner
  shadows to give a gritty effect.

- **Anti-Aliasing:** Slightly softens the edge pixels of a contour.

- **Range:** Controls how much of the glow is targeted for the contour.
  Reduce the Range setting to get a less feathered, tighter, and larger
  glow.

- **Jitter:** Doesn't affect the appearance of the default glow, but with other
  gradients, the Jitter setting varies the color and opacity of selected pixels to give a roughened effect.

- **Invert:** Turns the colors of the satin effect inside out.

- **Gloss Contour:** Changes the distribution of color in the effect over the
  layer. It creates a metallic effect when used with the Bevel and Emboss
  styles. The Contour option that appears indented below the Bevel and
  Emboss style in the Styles list does the same for the edges of the layer. It
  creates shaded and highlighted nooks and crannies when used with the
  Bevel and Emboss styles.

Modifying contours with the Contour Editor

If the preset contours just don't do it for you, feel free to create your own by
following these steps:

1. **Open the Contour Editor dialog box, shown in Figure 4-14, by clicking the Contour thumbnail in the Layer Style dialog box.**

2. **Click the line on the Mapping grid to add points and drag the line to adjust the slope.**

   You can also select a point on the Mapping line and enter values in the Input and Output boxes.

3. **To create a sharp corner, rather than a curve, select a point and click the Corner option.**

4. **When you have the contour to your liking, click the New button, give it a name in the Contour Name dialog box that appears, as shown in Figure 4-15, and click OK.**

   Photoshop saves your custom contour as a preset and makes it available in the Contour panel.

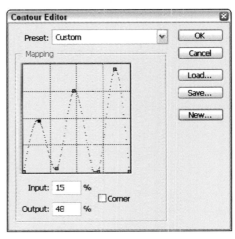

Figure 4-14: Create a custom contour if the presets don't meet your needs.

Figure 4-15: Name your custom contour.

 You can save custom contours for reloading later or for trading with friends and neighbors. (Try giving them away on Halloween.) Photoshop saves a contour as a .shc file in the Contours folder in the Presets folder in the Photoshop application folder.

Applying and Modifying Preset Styles

In addition to layer effects, Photoshop also offers you a multitude of preset layer styles that you can access via the Styles panel, in the Window menu, shown in Figure 4-16.

You can also access these styles by using the Style picker drop-down panel on the Options bar, when the Pen or shape tools are active and you have the Shape Layer option selected. And you can find the Styles panel nestled at the top of the Layer Style dialog box, as well.

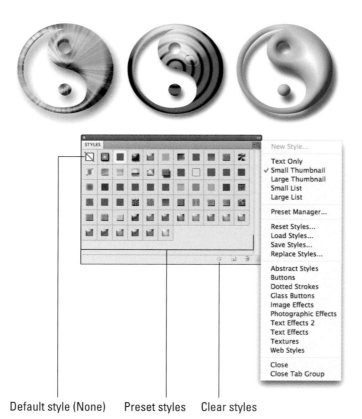

Default style (None)   Preset styles   Clear styles

Figure 4-16: Use the Styles panel to apply effects such as Angled Spectrum (left), Striped Cone (center), and Star Glow (right).

Here are the many splendid ways to apply a preset style:

- Select the layer and click a style in the Styles panel.

- Drag and drop a style from the Styles panel onto a layer in the Layers panel.

- Drag and drop a style directly onto the image window. When your cursor is over the element to which you want to apply the style, release your mouse button.

- Double-click the layer thumbnail in the Layers panel. Select Styles in the upper-left side of the Layer Style dialog box. Choose a style from the panel. Click OK to close the Layer Style dialog box.

✔ If you're using a Pen or shape tool, select the Shape Layer option. Then, select a style from the Style picker drop-down panel on the Options bar before drawing the shape.

By default, applying a style over another style replaces it. To add a style along with another, hold down the Shift key while clicking or dragging the style.

Managing preset styles

Here are some additional points to remember when using the Styles panel. You can do any of the following:

✔ **Load another Style preset library.** In the Styles panel, the Style picker drop-down panel in the Options bar, or the Styles panel in the Layer Style dialog box, you can select Load Styles from the panel pop-up menu to add a library to your current preset list. (Refer to Figure 4-16.) Select the library and click Load. You can also select Replace Styles. Even easier, just select a preset library from the bottom of the menu and click OK to replace or append your current list.

✔ **Use the Preset Manager to load Style preset libraries.** You can also rename, delete, and save whole libraries of presets. See Book I, Chapter 5.

✔ **Return to the default library of presets.** Select Reset Styles from the Styles panel pop-up menu.

✔ **From the Styles panel pop-up menu, select a viewing option for your panel.** You can select Small or Large Thumbnail or Small or Large List. And, of course, there's also Text Only, but what fun is it if you can't see the presets?

✔ **Rename a preset style.** Although there are a lot of ways to rename a preset style, it's easiest to double-click the style in the Styles panel. If you're in Thumbnail view, type a new name in the dialog box and click OK. If the view is set to Small List or Large List, simply type a new name directly in the Styles panel and press Enter (Return on the Mac).

✔ **Save a set of preset styles as a library.** Select Save Styles from the Styles panel pop-up menu, from the Styles panel of the Layer Style dialog box pop-up menu, or from the Style picker drop-down panel pop-up menu on the Options bar. Name the library, navigate to the Styles folder in the Presets folder in the Photoshop folder, and click Save.

✔ **Delete a preset style.** Drag the style to the trash can icon in the Styles panel or Alt-click (Option-click on the Mac) the style. You can also select Delete Style from the Styles panel of the Layer Style dialog box or the Style picker drop-down panel on the Options bar.

✔ **Clear a style (that is, remove it from the layer).** Select your desired layer in the Layers panel and click the Clear Style button in the Styles panel. You can also click the Default Style (None) swatch in the stand-alone Styles panel or the ones located in the Layer Style dialog box or on the Options bar.

✔ **Change the style or color of the currently active shape layer.** Click the link icon on the Options bar and select a different style or color. This option allows you to experiment with different styles for that shape.

Conversely, if you deselect the link icon, Photoshop doesn't change the style of the active shape layer when you select a different style. This option allows you to select a different style or color for a new shape layer without affecting the previous shape layer.

Saving your own style

If you get bored using the preset style libraries, or if you really went to town and created a custom style that you think is so fabulous that you'll want to use it again and again, you can easily save it to the Styles panel. Just follow these steps to save a custom style:

1. **Create your own custom style by applying layer effects and/or styles to your layer.**

   Starting with an existing preset style and modifying the settings to suit your needs is also easy.

2. **After you complete your style, click the Create New Style button in the Styles panel or select New Style from the Styles panel pop-up menu.**

   You can also simply click in an empty space in the Styles panel. Or you can double-click the fx icon or effect name to open the Layer Style dialog box, in which you can click the New Style button.

3. **In the New Style dialog box, shown in Figure 4-17, name your style and select your desired options.**

   The Include Layer Effects check box includes any effects you applied via the Effects section of the Layer Style dialog box — drop shadows, bevels, and so on.

   The Include Layer Blending Options check box includes any blending you did by using the Blending Options section of the Layer Styles panel. Photoshop adds your new style to the end of the Styles panel. If you want to edit your custom style, you must select each individual effect in the Layers panel and adjust the settings in the Layer Styles dialog box.

In the Styles panel, Alt-click (Option-click on the Mac) to create a new style and bypass the dialog box. Your style gets the default name of Style 1.

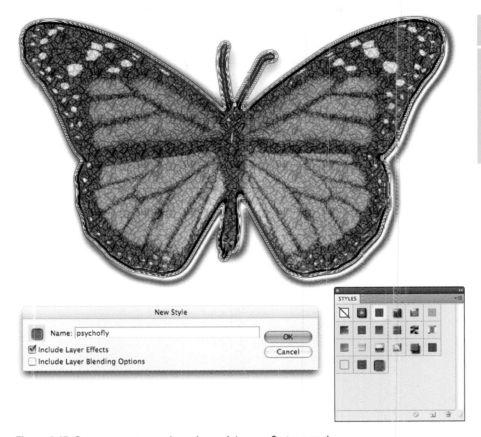

Figure 4-17: Create a custom style and save it in your Styles panel.

Clipping Layers into Masks

In a *clipping mask,* the bottommost layer (also known as the *base layer*) acts as a mask for the layers above it. The layers in the group clip to the opaque areas of the base layer and don't show over the transparent areas of the base layer.

At this point, you might be saying, "Huh?" Instead of trying to decipher the definition, a better way to understand a clipping mask is to just create one. Follow the steps in this section, and I know that rather than "Huh," you'll be saying "Yeah, baby," just like Austin Powers.

Creating a clipping mask works well if you want to fill type with different images on multiple layers.

Managing clipping masks

Here's some clipping mask trivia:

- To remove a single layer from the clipping mask, you can simply Alt-click (Option-click on the Mac) the line between the two layers in the Layers panel. Or you can select the layer and choose Layer➪Release Clipping Mask. Both commands remove the selected layer and any layers above it from the clipping mask.

- To ungroup all the layers in the clipping mask, select the clipped layer and choose Layer➪Release Clipping Mask.

- You can also apply clipping masks to adjustment and fill layers. If you clip between a regular layer and an adjustment layer, or a regular layer and a fill layer, the adjustment or fill layer affects only the pixels of the adjacent underlying layer, rather than all the underlying layers. For more on adjustment and fill layers, see Book V, Chapter 1.

Using the steps that follow, I created a new document with a white background. I took the Custom Shape tool, selected the Fill Region option (see Book IV, Chapter 1 for more on shapes), and drew a heart on my second layer. I added a drop shadow and inner bevel to my heart for added dimension, but this step isn't mandatory.

I then opened an image of an island and dragged and dropped that image onto my composite. I opened an image of some dolphins, selected a couple dolphins, and dragged and dropped them onto my composite.

And, finally, I created some type and applied a drop shadow and inner bevel to the type, as shown in Figure 4-18.

Follow these steps to create your own clipping mask:

1. **Open or create an image that has several layers.**

2. **Hold down Alt (Option on the Mac) and position your mouse cursor over the line dividing two layers in the Layers panel.**

   Your cursor changes to two overlapping circles with a small arrow icon. You can also choose Layer➪Create Clipping Mask.

Figure 4-18: In a clipping mask, layers clip to the opaque areas of a base layer

3. Click your mouse button.

I did this three times: in between my type and the dolphin layer, in between the dolphin and the island layer, and in between the island layer and my heart shape. Notice how all my images and my type clip to the base layer (the heart shape) in the Layers panel. (Refer to Figure 4-18.)

Nothing outside the boundaries of the heart shape is visible on any of the layers in the clipping mask, as shown in Figure 4-18. The down-pointing arrow icons beside each layer on the Layers panel indicate that the layers are clipped. The clipping mask takes on the opacity and blend mode of the base layer.

Putting It Together

Adding Text and Layer Styles to a Collage

If you've been reading Book V from the beginning, then you may have a nearly complete collage on your hands. If you're at all interested in using words with your images, then now (at the end of the project, not the beginning) is the time to add them. Adding type can turn a good composite into a dynamite and cohesive image that conveys exactly what you want. I'm no Shakespeare and can't help you create the perfect tag line, but I can show you how to add text to your collage. Adding layer styles gives you versatility in the kinds of effects you can apply to layers, so I show you how to apply those to a collage. To add and adjust type, follow these steps:

1. **Open the saved collage file.**

Make sure that the Layers panel is open.

2. **Select the Eyedropper tool from the Tools panel. Click a color in the collage that you like.**

The color you sampled is now the foreground color.

3. **Select the Type tool. On the Options bar, select a font, style, point size, and other formatting options.**

I recommend choosing an easy-to-read serif font and applying a bold style to it. I'm using Times Bold, and I set the point size to 100.

I set the Anti-Aliasing option to Crisp and the Alignment option to Left, but you can explore your options until you're dizzy (or your deadline passes).

4. **Click inside your image and type some text.**

I typed Go outside for my travel collage.

5. **Select the Move tool from the Tools panel and position the type in the collage.**

I put my text in the upper-left corner.

6. **Adjust your settings as you desire.**

If you want to add a second, smaller line of text, grab the Type tool again, click the image, and reduce the point size from the Options bar. You can change other settings, as well.

7. **When you're satisfied with your changes, click under the first line of text and type your next line.**

Under Go outside, I typed and play, as shown in the figure.

With the Move tool, fine-tune the position of the type.

When you're satisfied with the size, style, color, and appearance of the type in your collage, you can make some more large-scale changes by creating layer styles. Follow these steps:

1. **Add a drop shadow.**

Make sure that you select Use Global Light so that all the layers use the same angle.

In the Layers panel, select the layer that includes the first line of text. Then, choose Layer⇨Layer Style⇨Drop Shadow. Make sure the Drop Shadow box is selected in the left column.

You can change the angle so that the light source is coming from one direction or another. (Mine's set at 120% so that the light's coming from the upper-left.)

2. **Add bevels and embossing.**

Click the Bevel and Emboss style in the left column.

Make sure that you actually select the style and not just the box; otherwise, the right panel with all the options doesn't appear.

In my example, I selected Inner Bevel from the Style pop-up menu in the right panel. Then, I selected Chisel Soft from the Technique pop-up menu. My idea was to give the type a carved-in-stone look.

3. **Click OK when you're satisfied with the styles you've created in the layer so far.**

continued

continued

4. **Apply the same styles to the layer that includes the second line of text, as shown in the figure.**

To get the exact same settings without having to make every adjustment again, right-click (Control-click on the Mac) the fx icon on the first layer you worked on and select Copy Layer Style from the context menu that appears. Select the second type layer and right-click (Control-click on the Mac) on the layer name, and then select Paste Layer Style from the context menu that appears.

5. **Make any last adjustments and choose File⇨Save.**

You're all done. If you feel like it, keep adding to or refining the collage when you figure out new tricks.

Chapter 5: Working with Smart Objects

In This Chapter

✔ Creating Smart Objects

✔ Converting Smart Objects

✔ Editing Smart Objects

*W*ith the advent of Smart Objects Photoshop has significantly cut your editing time while letting you transform your objects indefinitely without fear of quality loss. That's right. Vector files, raster files — it doesn't matter to these intelligent fellows. And with Smart Objects, you create the art once, and then if you want to show the art again, you use what are called *instances*. These instances can be linked to your original art, which makes editing a breeze. This chapter tells you all about this feature — the ultimate in digital recycling.

Introducing Smart Objects

A Smart Object is actually what Adobe refers to as a *container,* in which a bitmap (raster) or vector image's source data is embedded. So, in essence, a Smart Object is composed of two files, one inside the other. Adobe uses the analogy of a new file, the *child,* which is embedded into the original file, the *parent.* This source data of the child is contained in the Smart Object parent but keeps all its native characteristics and is fully editable.

Here are a few advantages of Smart Objects:

✔ **Transform with minimum degradation.** In Book III, Chapter 3, I warn you about the negative side of transformations. When transforming traditional layers, your image goes through the process of resampling, which then causes degradation of quality. With Smart Objects, you can perform multiple transformations on your artwork without losing any additional image quality. Photoshop does this by actually using your *original* source data to render the additional transformations.

✔ **Preserve nonnative file data.** Photoshop transforms any nonnative image information, such as Illustrator vector artwork, into a format it can recognize without altering the native data.

✔ **Edit the Smart Object, and all instances are dynamically updated.** If you make changes to the original Smart Object, all instances (duplicates of the original) are automatically changed, as well. No need to change them individually. This can be a real timesaver, especially if you've gone crazy with the number of instances you've used, such as on a map or Web home page.

✔ **Apply a Smart Filter.** Layers must first be converted to Smart Objects before you can apply a Smart Filter. Smart Filters are a totally non-destructive way to apply filters that can then be edited indefinitely. For details on this great feature, see Book VII, Chapter 1.

Creating Smart Objects

You can create a Smart Object in a few ways. You can import the artwork via the Place command. You can also copy and paste the artwork from Illustrator into Photoshop. Or you can convert a Photoshop layer into a Smart Object. Finally, you can create one Smart Object from another. I discuss the specific steps for each way in the following sections.

Placing artwork

You may not have much experience in using the Place command in Photoshop because most activities involve opening images and creating new ones. But with the advent of Smart Objects, you may call on this command more frequently. Follow these steps to place artwork:

1. **Choose File⇨New and create a new blank Photoshop document, using your desired size and settings.**

   If you're unsure about creating a new file, see Book I, Chapter 3. You can also use an existing Photoshop file.

2. **Choose File⇨Place. In the Place dialog box, locate and select your desired artwork. Click the Place button.**

   If your file is in any format besides Illustrator or PDF, it pops right onto your canvas, as shown in Figure 5-1. Note the bounding box and X around and across the image, which is an indication that the image has been placed.

Figure 5-1: Create a Smart Object by placing your artwork into a Photoshop file.

If your file is a native Illustrator or PDF file, the Open as Smart Object dialog box appears, asking you for additional information, as shown in Figure 5-2. If it's a multipaged PDF, you can select the page or image you want placed. Select your cropping options. Not sure what they mean? Just select one and view the thumbnail to see how the image appears in relationship to the page. By the way, you can also select between a Small, Large, and Fit Page thumbnail view.

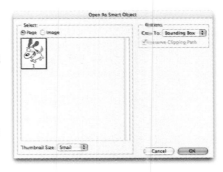

Figure 5-2: When placing an Illustrator or PDF file, specify your options in the Open as Smart Object dialog box.

If you happen to deselect the Create PDF Compatible File option when saving your native Illustrator file, you see a nasty warning in the Place PDF dialog box telling you to go back and resave your file with the option checked and then place the file again. Don't take it personally. Illustrator was programmed based on PDF core code and sometimes doesn't like it when you strip it of the connection.

You can also select the image in Adobe Bridge and choose File➪Place➪ In Photoshop. See Book I, Chapter 4 for details on working with Bridge.

3. **Using the bounding box, transform (scale, rotate, and so on) your image to your desired dimensions and then position it on your canvas, as shown in Figure 5-3.**

   Remember, you can rest assured that your transformations are applied without degrading the quality of your image.

   If your image is larger than the Photoshop canvas, it's automatically sized to fit within the canvas dimensions. If you need a refresher on transforming and moving, see Book III, Chapter 3.

Figure 5-3: Transform and position your image before committing it into your file.

   If you're placing a PDF, EPS (most of them), or native Illustrator file, specify the Anti-Alias option on the Options bar. Select it to create a softer, blended edge. Deselect it to produce a hard edge.

4. **After you have your image the way you want it, you can double-click inside the bounding box, press Enter (Return on the Mac), or click the Commit (check mark icon) button on the Options bar.**

   When the artwork is committed, the native file data is embedded into the Photoshop file, and the artwork is rasterized on its own layer. The Smart Object icon appears on those layers, as shown in Figure 5-4.

   If you change your mind and don't want to commit the image, press Esc or click the Cancel button on the Options bar.

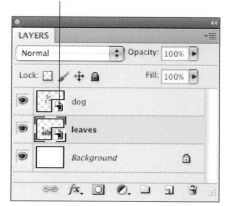

Figure 5-4: The Smart Object icon.

Copying and pasting

Before you copy and paste artwork from Illustrator into Photoshop as a Smart Object, be sure to check the PDF and AICB (no transparency support) options in the File Handling and Clipboard preferences in Illustrator.

Leave the default of Preserve Appearances and Overprints selected. By doing so, you can control how your artwork is rasterized in Photoshop. If left deselected, Photoshop rasterizes the art without your vital input. Follow these steps to copy and paste artwork as a Smart Object from Illustrator into Photoshop:

1. **Open your desired Adobe Illustrator file in Illustrator.**

2. **Select your artwork and choose Edit⇨Copy.**

3. **Switch to Photoshop. Open your desired Photoshop document or create a new document.**

4. **Choose Edit⇨Paste.**

5. **In the Paste dialog box, shown in Figure 5-5, select the Smart Object option and click OK.**

   Your image is imported and appears in a bounding box, and the Layers panel shows that you pasted the image as a Smart Object, as shown in Figure 5-5.

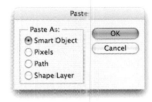

6. **Using the bounding box, transform (scale, rotate, and so on) your image to your desired dimensions and position it on your canvas.**

   Perspective, Distort, and Warp transformations are unavailable to Smart Objects.

Figure 5-5: Specify how you want the artwork pasted.

   Because you chose Smart Object in the Paste dialog box in Step 4, remember that you can transform your artwork without degrading it before you place it into Photoshop Like with the Place command, the native file data is embedded into the Photoshop file, and the art is rasterized on its own layer after the artwork is committed.

7. **Commit the artwork by double-clicking inside the bounding box, pressing Enter (Return on the Mac), or clicking the Commit (check mark icon) button on the Options bar.**

Converting a layer into a Smart Object and vice versa

If you want to convert a layer into a Smart Object, follow these steps:

1. **Select your desired layer in the Layers panel.**

2. **Choose Layer⊅Smart Objects⊅Convert to Smart Object.**

   You can also select the command from the Layers panel pop-up menu. After you convert a layer into a Smart Object, you see the Smart Object icon in the lower-right corner of the layer thumbnail.

You can also convert a Smart Object into a layer. You may want to do this if you need to paint on your artwork.

Follow these steps to make the conversion:

1. **Select your desired layer in the Layers panel.**

2. **Choose Layer⊅Rasterize⊅Smart Object.**

   Your Smart Object is rasterized at its current size, so be sure it's the size you want before you execute the command. Your Smart Object icon disappears, and you're left with a normal, run-of-the mill layer.

Creating one Smart Object from another

Sometimes, you may want to use one Smart Object as the basis for another. Depending on your needs, you can keep the new Smart Object linked to or unlinked from the original. If it remains linked, modifying the original automatically modifies the duplicate. If unlinked, you can modify the original without changing the duplicate. In addition, you're free to change the duplicate without worrying about affecting the original.

Follow these steps to create a Smart Object from another:

1. **Select the Smart Object layer in the Layers panel.**

2. **Create a duplicate Smart Object that's linked to or unlinked from the original:**

   - *An unlinked object:* Choose Layer⊅Smart Objects⊅New Smart Object via Copy.

   - *A linked object:* Choose Layer⊅New⊅Layer via Copy.

   A new Smart Object layer appears in the Layers panel, as shown in Figure 5-6.

You can also drag and release the Smart Object layer over the Create a New Layer icon at the bottom of the Layers panel. This action creates a duplicate Smart Object that's linked.

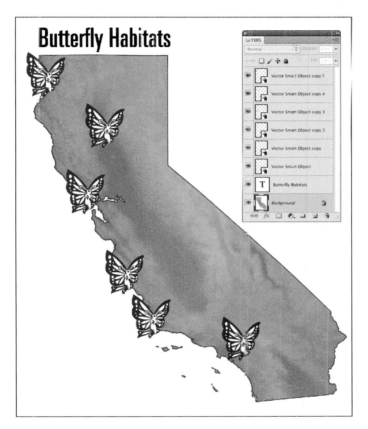

Figure 5-6: You can duplicate a Smart Object and either have it linked to or unlinked from its original.

Editing Smart Objects

One of the great things about Smart Objects is that you can edit the contents, or source data. If the source content is a vector-based PDF, AI, or EPS file and was prepared in Illustrator, it opens in that program. If the source content is raster-based, a Camera Raw file or a vector file (like a shape layer) and created in Photoshop, the file opens in Photoshop. (For details on vector versus raster images, see Book II, Chapter 1.)

Follow these steps to edit the contents of a Smart Object:

1. In your document, select the Smart Object layer in the Layers panel.

2. **Choose Layer⇨Smart Objects⇨Edit Contents.**

Or you can simply double-click the Smart Objects layer thumbnail in the Layers panel.

A dialog box appears, telling you to save your changes and save the file in the same location.

3. **Click OK to close the dialog box.**

The Smart Object opens in the program in which it was created, either Illustrator or Photoshop.

4. **Edit your file *ad nauseam*.**

5. **Choose File⇨Save to incorporate the edits.**

6. **Close your source file.**

7. **Return to your Photoshop document, which contains your Smart Object.**

If all goes as expected, all instances of the Smart Object are updated. For example, my butterflies went from purple in Figure 5-6 to blue in Figure 5-7.

Replacing contents

When replacing the contents of a Smart Object with new contents, you automatically update all instances of that Smart Object in your document, which can be a real productivity enhancer. Just follow these short steps:

1. **Select the Smart Object layer in the Layers panel.**

2. **Choose Layer⇨Smart Objects⇨Replace Contents.**

3. **In the Place dialog box, locate your new file and click the Place button.**

Butterfly Habitats

Figure 5-7: The Photoshop document automatically reflects any editing you do to your Smart Object.

4. **Click OK if you're presented with a dialog box, and the new contents pop into place, replacing the old contents, as shown in Figure 5-8.**

All instances of that Smart Object are also updated in your document.

To replace the contents of a single instance of a Smart Object, you have to make sure that the Smart Object isn't linked to other Smart Objects. To create an unlinked Smart Object, select the Smart Object instance you want to change, choose Layer➪Smart Objects➪New Smart Object via Copy. Make your desired replacement and then delete the original Smart Object.

Exporting contents

You can export your Smart Object and save it to a hard drive or external media. Photoshop exports the contents of your Smart Object in its original placed format, such as JPEG, native Illustrator (.ai), TIFF, PDF, and so on. Follow these steps:

Butterfly Habitats

Figure 5-8: I replaced the contents of my blue butterflies with that of a rarer species.

1. **Select the Smart Object in the Layers panel.**

2. **Choose Layer➪Smart Objects➪Export Contents.**

3. **In the Save dialog box, navigate to your destination and click Save.**

   If your Smart Object was created from layers, it exports in the PSB format. Remember, you can open the .psb file only in Photoshop. It won't open in another program.

The last command in the Layer➪Smart Objects submenu is Stack Mode. Unfortunately, this command is available only in the Extended version. People in the science, forensics, medical, and pro video fields are probably thrilled over its capabilities. How about the rest of us? Well, using image stacks can help to decrease the noise in your images across multiple exposures. In this case, *noise* can be defined not just as the grainy or wavy little artifacts throughout your image, but also anything that you don't want in the picture — cars, birds, annoying people walking in front of your scenic shot. If this sounds like something worthwhile for your workflow, it may be worth checking out an upgrade.

Book VI

Channels and Masks

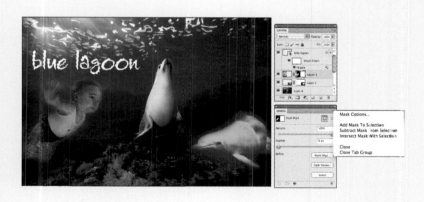

*1*f you have the basics down and are ready for something a little more challenging, this is your book. Here, I help you start working with channels and creating masks. Creating masks is one of the most accurate ways to make a selection and is especially useful in tackling more difficult selections.

In this book, I show you different ways of creating a mask, from quick masks to layer masks to channel masks. If you've ever flung your mouse or stylus pen in frustration because you couldn't select the hair on your loved one's photo, you'll be well-served by reading this book and getting up to speed on masking techniques.

Chapter 1: Using Channels

In This Chapter

- ✔ Understanding what a channel is
- ✔ Working with the Channels panel
- ✔ Editing channels
- ✔ Creating alpha channels
- ✔ Using the Channel Mixer

*I*f you're reading this, it probably means that you didn't quickly thumb through this chapter, say "Yuck, bocrrrrringgg!" and move on to sexier topics such as blending, filtering, and retouching. You knew that would be a huge mistake.

The wonderful thing about channels is that they offer you greater control and selectivity when doing those very things — blending, filtering, and retouching. Channels give you one more level of control when editing your images. You can use individual channels for layer-blending options and filters, as well as starting points for masks.

Channels also come into play when saving selections for later use or for adding spot (custom) colors to your image. You can also use channels to turn color images into nicely contrasted grayscale images. And finally, you can play around with the colors in an image by mixing up the channels. So bear with me. The topic of channels may be a bit dry and technical, but in the end, channels enable you to hold the envious title of Master Editor.

To understand how channels work, you ll find it helpful to know a few things about colors — specifically, the various color modes, which I cover in Book II, Chapter 2.

Understanding Channels

When you look at a color image, you see one big, 24-bit, composite collection of colored pixels. Technically speaking, however, Photoshop doesn't see that at all. Photoshop perceives a color image as individual bands of 8-bit, grayscale images. RGB images have three bands; CMYK images have four bands.

I know it's strange to think of a color image as being composed of several grayscale images, but it's true. Each one of these bands, or grayscale images, is a *channel*. Specifically, they're color channels. If you just can't get past the fact that a color image is the sum of several grayscale channels, as shown in Figure 1-1, then just think of channels as holding tanks for color data.

Purestock

Figure 1-1: A color image is composed of 8-bit grayscale images referred to as channels.

Another way of relating channels to the real world is in terms of hardware. Here's how the most common hardware handles color:

- When you offset-print a CMYK image, the process separates the colors (see Book IX, Chapter 1) into four colors — cyan, magenta, yellow, and black. Paper passes through four individual rollers on the printing press, and each roller contains one of those four colored inks.

- Scanners scan in RGB via a pass of red, green, and blue sensors over your image.

- Digital cameras capture images in RGB.

- CRT screens display images via red, green, and blue tubes.

In addition to color channels, there are channels called *alpha channels* (covered in the section "Introducing Alpha Channels," later in this chapter) and others called *spot channels* (discussed in Book IX, Chapter 1). Photoshop now supports up to 56 channels per file. So knock yourself out! Just remember that each channel you add increases your file size.

TIP

A little bit about bit depth

When you're standing around the water cooler or the color printer and hear people talking about a 1-bit or an 8-bit image, they're referring to something called bit depth. *Bit depth* measures how much color information is available to display and print each pixel. A higher bit depth means the image can display more information — specifically, more colors. For example, a 1-bit image can display two color values — black and white. That's why a purely black-and-white image is called a bitmap image. Likewise

✔ An 8-bit image can contain up to 256 grayscale levels (2^8). Grayscale images are 8 bit (1 channel, 8 bits).

✔ A 24-bit image can contain about 16 million colors (2^{24}). RGB images are 24 bit (3 channels $\times$ 8 bits).

✔ CMYK images are 32 bit (4 channels $\times$ 8 bits). CMYK images, however, are limited to the number of colors that are physically reproducible on paper, which is around 55,000.

✔ High Dynamic Range (HDR) images are 96 bit (3 channels [RGB] $\times$ 32 bits). Theoretically, they're capable of having about 65 million colors, but in reality, the maximum range is determined by what colors were captured by the camera.

Bit depths typically range from 1 to 64 bits.

Book VI
Chapter 1

Using Channels

Briefly, you can use alpha channels to create, store, and edit selections, defining them not by a selection outline but by black, white, and varying shades of gray pixels — in other words, a grayscale image. Black pixels represent unselected areas of the image, white pixels represent selected areas, and gray pixels represent partially selected pixels.

You can create spot channels when you want to add a spot (or custom) color to your image. Spot colors are premixed inks often used in addition to or in lieu of CMYK colors.

All images, no matter what their color mode, have at least one channel. Grayscale, Bitmap, Duotone, and Indexed Color (for GIF Web images) modes have only one channel. RGB and CMYK images have three and four channels, respectively. They also contain a composite channel, which reflects the combination of the individual color channels and gives you the full color display.

Working with Channels

Like with layers (which I discuss in Book V), channels have their own panel that acts as command central for viewing, creating, and managing tasks. The first step is accessing channels by choosing Window⇨Channels. The Channels panel appears, as shown in Figure 1-2.

Viewing channels without a remote

Selecting a channel in the Channels panel automatically makes it appear in the image window. To select a channel, click the channel thumbnail or name in the panel. To select more than one channel, Shift-click. To show or hide a channel, click in the eye column in the far left of the panel. You can also drag through the column to hide or show the channels quickly.

CMYK, RGB, and Lab images have a *composite* channel, in addition to their individual channels. This composite channel is the combination of all the channels in the image and is named after the color mode. For example, the composite channel in Figure 1-2 is the first one, called CMYK.

Corbis Digital Stock

Figure 1-2: The Channels panel stores all the image's channels, from spot to alpha channels.

Changing the default channel view

The default setting is to view your channels in grayscale. You can, however, view them in color. To do so, choose Edit⇨Preferences⇨Interface (Photoshop⇨ Preferences⇨Interface on the Mac) and select Show Channels in Color.

Although this option *graphically* exemplifies the way an image comprises separate color channels, it really does you no good if you want to work with your channels for editing. That's because the color view obscures details and makes measuring the impact of adjustments and filters more difficult. You need to see the channels in their true grayscale form for that.

If you select or show more than one channel, even in the default grayscale view, the channels always appear in color.

To change the size of the thumbnail that appears, select Panel Options from the Channels panel pop-up menu. Select your desired thumbnail size. If you're working with several channels and you have a dinosaur of a computer, you can also choose None to turn off the thumbnails — which improves performance.

Duplicating and deleting channels

Duplicating channels is something you may do quite often. I know I do. And deleting channels isn't just for neat freaks: Channels take up a lot of memory, so getting rid of the ones you no longer need is always good.

Here are some instances when duplicating channels is a good idea

- **When you want to create a channel mask:** First, you find a suitable channel and then make a duplicate. (For more on this technique, see Book VI, Chapter 3.) You can use channel masks to select difficult elements involving fine details, such as hair, fur, smoke, and so on.

- **When you want to make a backup copy of the channel before doing some editing:** Having a backup, just to be on the safe side, is always a good idea. For example, you may want to apply an Unsharp Mask filter to one or two channels to improve the focus of the image. For more on the Unsharp Mask filter, see Book VII, Chapter 1.

- **To insert a copy of an alpha channel into another image:** For example, maybe you spent an hour creating elaborate alpha channels for shadows and highlights on a product photographed in flat lighting.

  You may have 12 products, all the same shape but different colors, that you need to apply those highlights and shadows to. Instead of re-creating the wheel each time, you could simply duplicate the alpha channels into each file.

Duplicating channels

To duplicate a channel, follow these short steps:

1. **Select your desired channel in the Channels panel.**

2. **Select Duplicate Channel from the panel pop-up menu.**

   The Duplicate Channel dialog box appears, as shown in Figure 1-3.

3. **In the Duplicate section, in the As field, name the channel.**

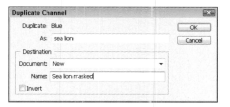

Figure 1-3: Name and provide a destination for your duplicate channel.

You can also drag the channel to the New Channel icon at the bottom of the panel. If you do this, Photoshop provides a default name and bypasses Steps 3 through 6.

You can also duplicate a channel to another image by dragging the channel. Open your destination image and drag the desired channel from your current image into the destination image window. The duplicated channel appears in the Channels panel.

4. **In the Destination section, select a file from the Document drop-down list.**

   Or choose New to create a new image.

   You can choose your current image or any open image with the same pixel dimensions as your current image. (For more on pixel dimensions, see Book II, Chapter 1.)

   If you choose New, Photoshop creates a new image that has a single channel. Provide a name for the file.

5. **Select Invert if you want to reverse the selected and unselected areas of the duplicate channel.**

   You use the Invert option primarily when you duplicate an existing alpha channel. For more on alpha channels, see the section "Introducing Alpha Channels," later in this chapter.

6. **Click OK.**

   The dialog box closes. Your duplicate channel appears in the Channels panel, as shown in Figure 1-4.

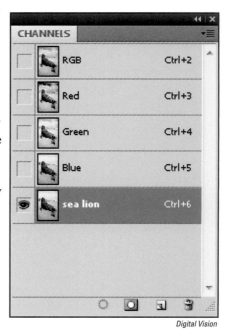

Digital Vision

Figure 1-4: You can duplicate channels for masking, as well as for backup purposes.

Replacing one channel over another

To replace the contents of one channel with another, you can use the copy-and-paste method. In your current image, select your desired channel in the Channels panel. Choose Select⇨All and then Edit⇨Copy. Select the channel in the destination image that you want to replace and choose Edit⇨Paste. The pasted content of the channel replaces the original content.

Deleting unwanted channels

To delete an unwanted channel — something you definitely want to do because channels can eat up a lot of space — select the channel in the Channels panel and do one of the following:

   ✔ Drag the channel to the trash at the bottom of the panel.

   ✔ Select Delete Channel from the panel pop-up menu.

   ✔ Click the trash and then click Yes in the dialog box.

   ✔ Alt-click (Option-click on the Mac) the trash.

Rearranging and renaming channels

Although you can't shuffle or rename color channels, you can do so with spot and alpha channels. To move a spot or alpha channel, simply drag it up or down in the Channels panel. When you see a dark line appear where you want the channel to go, release your mouse button. You can move a spot or alpha channel above a color channel only in a multichannel image. In short, in a multichannel image, each channel becomes an independent spot channel, and the channels no longer have a relationship with each other. Multichannel images don't support layers. For more details, see Book II, Chapter 2.

To rename a spot or alpha channel, double-click the name in the Channel panel and type a new name. You can also select Channel Options from the panel pop-up menu.

Splitting channels

You can split the channels of your image into separate images in separate files. For example, in Figure 1-5, you see the Red, Green, Blue, Alpha, and Spot channels split into individual channels. Choose Split Channels from the panel pop-up menu. When you do so, your original image closes. The channel files have the name of your original image plus the channel name. You can split channels only on a flattened image — in other words, an image that has no individual layers.

Corbis Digital Stock

Figure 1-5: Be sure to save all changes in your original image before you split it because Photoshop closes your file.

You might want to split channels if you need to save your original file in a format that doesn't preserve channels — such as EPS, which doesn't support alpha channels. Or you may want to split channels to merge them later on.

Merging channels

You can merge channels into a single image. The channels must be opened as separate images, in grayscale mode, and have the same pixel dimensions. You can merge channels only when they're flattened images and have no layers.

Merging color channels can create some unique special effects. For example, by mismatching your channels when you merge them, you can create bizarre, and sometimes beautiful, color shifts.

To merge channels, follow these steps:

1. **Open your split channel files and activate any one of them.**

2. **Choose Merge Channels from the Channels panel pop-up menu.**

3. **In the Merge Channels dialog box, choose your desired color mode, as shown in Figure 1-6.**

   Any modes that are unavailable are grayed out. You may not have enough channels for the grayed-out modes.

   Figure 1-6: Choose the color mode and number of channels in this dialog box.

4. **Enter the number of channels you want.**

   When you choose your mode in Step 3, Photoshop automatically fills in the number of channels for the mode. If you deviate and enter something different, the file becomes a multichannel file.

5. **Click OK.**

6. **Select your channels in the dialog box that appears.**

   In my example, the Merge CMYK Channels dialog box appears. If you want to merge the channels normally, make sure that each channel matches (Red for Red, and so on). If you want to rearrange the channels, you can mix them, as I did in Figure 1-7, so that the Cyan channel is mixed with the Magenta channel, and so on.

7. **If you're merging into a multi-channel image, click Next.**

   Repeat this step for each channel.

8. **Click OK.**

   You've now merged your files into a single image, which appears in your Photoshop window.

   Figure 1-7: You can mismatch your channels when merging them to create a unique effect.

Photoshop closes individual channel files and merges any spot channels as alpha channels.

Check out Figure 1-8 to see how my sunflower went from yellow to magenta just by merging the layers a little differently.

Original

 TIP

If you have an image that includes alpha or spot channels, select Multichannel from the Mode drop-down list in Step 3; otherwise, Photoshop doesn't include those channels in the merged image. After you merge the image, Photoshop gives all the channels the names Alpha 1, Alpha 2, Alpha 3, and so on. To get back to a color composite, choose Image⇨Mode⇨RGB Color or CMYK Color.

Split and merged

Using Painting and Editing Tools with Channels

Sometimes, it's better to edit individual channels rather than the composite image. Mediocre flat-bed scanners often reproduce, and digital cameras sometimes capture, an image that's slightly soft or out of focus. You may want to counteract that effect by applying an Unsharp Mask or Smart Sharpen filter. Before you do, you should examine each channel separately. You may find that the Blue channel contains a lot of garbage — artifacts, dithering, and other nasty crud.

Photodisc/Getty Images

Figure 1-8: When you split and merge channels, you can create botanical specimens from another world.

 REMEMBER

Blue channels are notorious for acquiring this junk, so try to avoid sharpening this channel unless you *really* want to accentuate what's already ugly.

Instead of applying the Unsharp Mask or Smart Sharpen filter on Blue channels, select the Red and Green channels in the Channels panel and then choose Filter⇨Sharpen⇨Unsharp Mask or Smart Sharpen. Similarly, you can apply a Gaussian Blur filter to a channel to soften the unsightly pattern (called a *moiré* pattern) caused by scanning a halftone. (See Book VII, Chapter 1 for more on moiré patterns, and filters are covered throughout Book VII.)

Although Unsharp Mask, Smart Sharpen, and Gaussian Blur are a few corrective filters that you'll use frequently, I also find it useful to apply a special-effect filter to individual channels. Sometimes, applying a filter to the composite image produces an effect that's, well, overdone. Applying the filter to one or two channels can produce an effect that's subtler and less in-your-face. For example, in Figure 1-9, I applied a filter to just the Blue channel for the flower on the top. Using individual channels can also be useful for applying filters that produce monochromatic images, such as the Graphic Pen or Photocopy filters. (Be sure your foreground and background colors are black and white.) If you apply the filter to the entire image, you get a black-and-white image. If you apply it to an individual channel, you retain some color.

You can select a color channel and then edit that channel by using a painting or editing tool in the image. Keep these facts in mind:

Photodisc/Getty Images

Figure 1-9: By editing individual color channels, you can selectively and subtly apply filters (top) or adjust color (bottom).

- ✒ Painting with white adds the color channel's color at full intensity in the composite image.

- ✒ Painting with black removes the color in the composite image.

- ✒ Painting with a value of gray adds color at varying levels of intensity in the composite image.

For example, if you paint with white on the Blue channel in an existing image, Photoshop adds more blue to the color composite image. But if you paint with black, Photoshop adds yellow to the image because when you remove blue, you're left with the opposite (or complementary) color — yellow. To perform this channel magic, select the Brush tool and then select your desired brush size from the Options bar. Select your desired color in the Color panel. Select the channel you want to edit in the Channels panel and paint on the image. You can see the results by selecting the composite channel in the Channels panel. Refer to Figure 1-9 to see how I gave a flower a channel-color makeover.

The results are a little different if you try this technique on a blank CMYK canvas. For example, when you paint with black on the Cyan channel, your composite color image displays cyan. When you paint with white, you get no change.

Introducing Alpha Channels

You use alpha channels for selections that are incredibly detailed or that you want to save and reuse. To make that selection, an alpha channel uses black, white, and shades of gray to create a mask. The selected pixels are white, and unselected pixels are black. For example, in the alpha channel of the image shown in Figure 1-10, the selection includes the lanterns and trees;

they appear white in the alpha channel. If an alpha channel includes gray areas, those areas are partially selected (or partially unselected, depending on whether you think the glass is half full or half empty).

Original image

Alpha channel mask

Corbis Digital Stock

Figure 1-10: The alpha channel makes selecting this shape much easier than using the Lasso or Magic Wand tool.

Book VI
Chapter 1

Using Channels

You can create a mask by first duplicating a color channel and then editing that channel with painting and editing tools and filters. (See Book VI, Chapter 3 for the details.) You can also create an alpha channel by saving a selection you've created. After you create a channel mask or save a selection as an alpha channel, you can load that channel to use it as a selection in any image. The following sections explain how to save a selection as an alpha channel and load a selection.

Saving a selection as an alpha channel

One of the great things about alpha channels is that you can save them and then retrieve them time and time again, which can be especially handy if you've taken a lot of time and effort to create the selection. Why reinvent the wheel if you want to select the element again in the future? Sure, you can create a mask by using Quick Mask mode and Color Range (see Book VI, Chapter 2), but those masks are only temporary.

After you make the initial selection, saving it is a piece of cake. Follow these steps:

1. **Make a selection in your image. (See Book III for help.)**

2. **Choose Select⇨Save Selection.**

   You can also click the Save Selection as Channel button (a circle on a square icon) at the bottom of the Channels panel. A new channel appears with the default name of Alpha 1, bypassing Steps 3 and 4.

3. **Select a destination image in the Document pop-up menu.**

   You can select your current image, any other open image that has the same pixel dimensions, or a new image.

4. **Select a destination channel from the Channel pop-up menu.**

   You can select a new channel, an existing alpha channel, or a layer mask. (See Book VI, Chapter 3 for more on layer masks.)

   • If you select New, name the channel.

   • If you select an existing alpha channel or layer mask, select your desired operation: Replace, Add To, Subtract From, or Intersect. These commands add to, subtract from, or intersect your current selection with the existing alpha channel.

5. **Click OK.**

   Your alpha channel is complete and appears in the Channels panel, as shown in Figure 1-11.

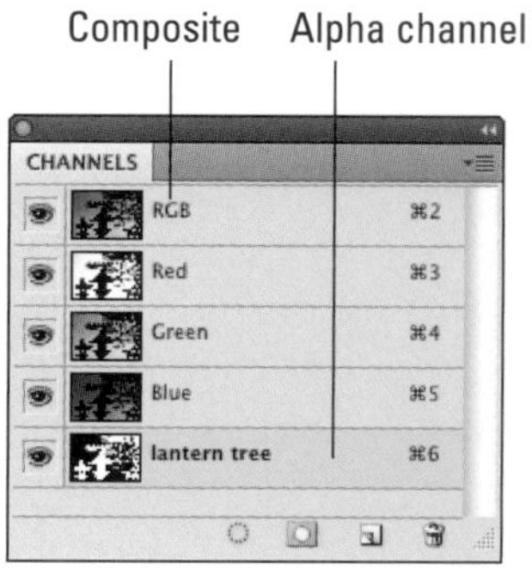

Composite   Alpha channel

Figure 1-11: Saving your selection as an alpha channel allows you to efficiently reuse the selection.

Loading an alpha channel

If you've gone through the trouble of creating an alpha channel, it's no doubt because you want to easily load (or access) the selection again and again. To load an alpha channel, use any one of these many methods:

✔ Choose Select⇨Load Selection. In the Load Selection dialog box, select your document and channel. Click Invert to swap selected and unselected areas. If your image has an active selection, choose how you want to combine the selections.

✔ Select the alpha channel in the Channels panel, click the Load Channel as Selection icon at the bottom of the panel, and then click the composite channel.

✔ Drag the channel to the Load Channel as Selection icon.

✔ Ctrl-click (⌘-click on the Mac) the alpha channel in the Channels panel.

✔ Ctrl+Shift-click (⌘+Shift-click on the Mac) to add the alpha channel to an active selection.

✔ Ctrl+Alt-click (⌘+Option-click on the Mac) to subtract the alpha channel from an active selection.

✔ Ctrl+Alt+Shift-click (⌘+Option+Shift-click on the Mac) to intersect the alpha channel with an active selection.

Adding channels can start to bloat your file size, so use them judiciously. The Photoshop native format and TIFF format compress channel information and therefore are good file formats to use when working with a lot of channels. The only formats that preserve alpha channels are Photoshop, TIFF, PDF, PICT, Pixar, Photoshop Raw. BMP, TGA (Targa), and PSB (Photoshop large format).

Using the Channel Mixer

The Channel Mixer actually does what its name implies — it mixes color channels. This feature lets you repair bad channels and produce grayscale images from color images. It also allows you to create tinted images and more intense special effects. Finally, it allows you to do the more mundane tasks of swapping or duplicating channels.

Although some Photoshop elitists worldwide tout the Channel Mixer as an advanced feature not to be mucked with by amateurs, I say, "Give it a whirl." Intimidation is a nasty roadblock to creative fun. Just make a backup copy of an image before diving into the mix by following these steps:

1. **Select the composite channel in the Channels panel.**

   If you have an RGB image, the composite channel is the RGB channel; for CMYK images, it's the CMYK channel.

2. **Choose Image⇨Adjustments⇨ Channel Mixer.**

   The Channel Mixer dialog box appears, as shown in Figure 1-12.

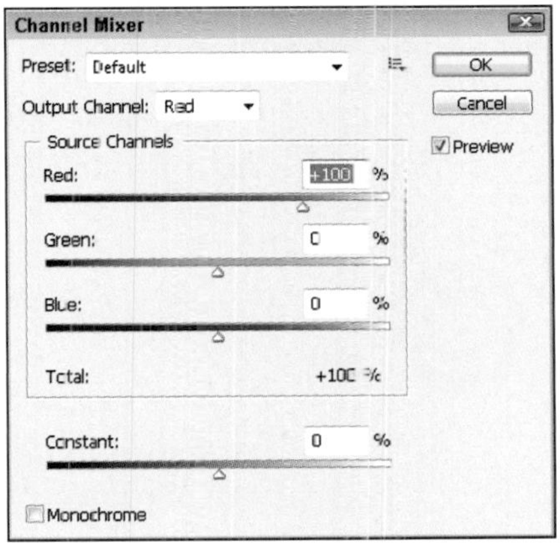

3. **If desired, select a Preset from the pop-up menu.**

   CS5 provides an assortment of Black and White presets you can use to convert your color images to grayscale. This is a great conversion method because it preserves detail and provides very good contrast control.

Figure 1-12: Among its many capabilities, the Channel Mixer enables you to repair bad channels.

4. **For Output Channel, select the channel in which to blend one or more source (existing) channels.**

For example, if your Blue channel is lousy, select it from the Output Channel drop-down list. Note that if you're using one of the black and white presets, you have only the Gray channel available.

5. **Drag any source channel's slider to the left to decrease the channel's effect on the Output channel or drag to the right to increase the effect.**

Because my Blue channel contains artifacts and dithering picked up by the scanner, I'm raising the Red and Green values from 0% to 25% and lowering the Blue value from 100% to 50%. To retain good contrast, try to use a combo of Red, Green, and Blue values that add up to close to 100%.

You can also enter a value from –200% to +200%. Using a negative value inverts the color data of the source channel.

6. **Tinker with the Constant option to add a Black or White channel of varying opacity.**

This option adjusts the grayscale value of the selected Output channel. Drag the slider to a negative value to get a Black channel. Positive values give a White channel.

This option brightens or darkens the overall image, but it may cause strange color shifts if adjusted to the extreme. I recommend leaving it at 0 most of the time. But try it. It may help.

7. **Select Monochrome to apply the same settings to all output channels, producing a color image that has only values of gray.**

This is another great way to produce a grayscale image from a color image. Adjust the individual sliders to mix the values until you're satisfied with the contrast.

You can save (and load) any of your custom settings by clicking the Preset Option button just to the left of the OK button.

8. **Click OK to exit the Channel Mixer.**

After you exit the Channel Mixer, choose Image➪Mode➪Grayscale to complete the conversion.

If you select and then deselect the Monochrome option, you can modify the blend of each channel separately. By doing so, you can create color images that appear to be hand-tinted with color inks. Go for the subtle treatment or a more intensely colored look.

Swapping color channels can produce some bizarre color effects. For example, try selecting the Red channel from the Output Channel drop-down list. Set the Red source channel to 0 and then set the Green source channel to 100. Try other combinations, Green for Blue, Blue for Red, and so on. Sometimes, they can be downright freakish, but occasionally you may stumble on one that's worthy.

Putting It Together

Book VI
Chapter 1

Using Channels

Giving Flat Art Highlights and Shadows

Sometimes, you need to give your art — whether it's a photo or another type of image — a little shine and shadow to bring it to life. You can do this by creating and saving your selections as alpha channels and filling them with translucent color. The great thing about alpha channels is that because you save them with your document, you can use them time and time again. Just follow these steps:

1. **Create a simple piece of artwork to use as a basis for your shadows and highlights.**

I created a pool ball by creating two layers. On each layer, I used the Elliptical Marquee tool to create different-sized circles. I filled each circle with a separate color, as shown in the figure. To follow along with these steps, you can download this image from this book's Web site. (See the Introduction for details.)

2. **Choose Window⇨Channels.**

The Channels panel appears.

Be sure to keep this panel visible because you'll be creating new channels for the highlights.

3. **Select the Pen tool from the Tools panel and create a path for the highlight.**

I created a path for the highlight on the top-left portion of the ball in my example, assuming that the light source is coming from the upper-left corner. If the Pen tool seems like a foreign object to you, check out Book III, Chapter 2.

4. **Choose Window⇨Paths.**

The Paths panel appears.

5. **Click the Load Path as Selection icon (a dotted circle) at the bottom of the Paths panel.**

Your work path disappears and a selection marquee appears.

6. **Choose Select⇨Save Selection.**

The Save Selection dialog box appears.

continued

continued

7. **Name the channel. Make sure to select New Channel under Operation and click OK.**

An additional channel appears in the Channels panel, as shown in the preceding figure. This new channel is the alpha channel — your saved selection.

8. **Click the Create a New Layer icon (the dog-eared page) in the Layers panel. Double-click the layer name and rename it.**

I named mine *large highlight.*

Putting your highlights and shadows on separate layers is important so that you can apply different opacity settings and also retain the ability to tweak them later, if needed.

9. **Choose Edit⇨Fill, select the White option for Contents, and leave all the other options at their default settings. Click OK to close the Fill dialog box.**

Your highlight is now filled with white. Don't worry; it won't stay this opaque.

10. **In the Layers panel, adjust the Opacity setting to 50%.**

The highlight now appears translucent. (Refer to the preceding figure.)

11. **Select the Pen tool and create a path for the highlight on the bottom of the object, as shown in the figure.**

Make sure the path matches up to the edge of the object. Use the Direct Selection tool if you need to adjust the anchor points or curve segments of the path.

12. **In the Paths panel, click the third icon from the left at the bottom of the panel.**

The work path disappears, and a selection marquee appears.

13. Choose Select⇨Save Selection. In the Save Selection dialog box that appears, name the channel. Make sure to select New Channel under Operation and click OK.

   Mine is called *bottom highlight.* Another alpha channel appears in the Channels panel.

14. Repeat Steps 8 through 10, but adjust the opacity to only 30% as shown in the figure.

15. Use the Pen tool to create a path for the smaller shadow.

   For example, I created a path on the bottom-right portion of the ball.

16. Load the path as a selection in the Paths panel and choose Select⇨Modify⇨Feather. In the Feather Selection dialog box, enter 3 pixels and click OK.

   The idea is to give the shadow a softer edge.

17. Repeat Steps 6 through 10, but fill the selection with black, rather than white, and adjust the opacity to 20%.

   The shadow is shown in the figure.

18. Use a selection tool to add a cast shadow.

   In my example, I used the Elliptical Marquee tool to create an ellipse at the base of the ball by holding down Alt (Option on the Mac) and dragging the mouse. The resulting selection is shown in the figure.

   Then, I feathered the selection 25 pixels before I saved the selection.

   The cast shadow needs to have really fuzzy edges, thus the large number of pixels for the feather.

19. Repeat Steps 8 and 9, filling the selection with black.

   My highlighted and shadowed pool ball is ready to roll, shown in the figure.

   If your cast shadow layer is above your object, you have to change the stacking order and move your shadow layer so that it's below your object.

   Now that you've spent all this time on the front end creating your alpha channels, you can save time on the back end by using those alpha channels to apply highlights and shadows to similar artwork.

continued

continued

20. **To load alpha channels, choose Select⇨Load Selection and select an alpha channel from the Channel pop-up menu. Then, repeat the applicable steps for creating new layers, filling them with color, and adjusting their opacity.**

In my example, I took the highlights and shadows I created with lucky pool ball number 7 and loaded them as alpha channels in pool ball number 5.

Chapter 2: Quick-and-Dirty Masking

In This Chapter

✓ **Using Quick Masks**

✓ **Working with Color Range**

✓ **Selecting by erasing**

Masking is essentially just another way of making a selection. Instead of defining your selection with a selection outline, masks define your selection with up to 256 levels of gray, which allows you to have varying levels of selection. Photoshop *masks* (or protects) unselected pixels from any commands you execute. Photoshop doesn't mask selected pixels, making them fair game to any executed commands.

Different types of masks have different purposes — channel masks, layer masks, and vector masks. You can use them to temporarily make a selection, save and load selections, define vector shapes, selectively apply an adjustment layer or filter, blend one layer into another, and so on. Although selecting with the Marquee, Lasso, Magic Wand, and Pen tools can be fine, you'll soon find that these tools have a limited repertoire: You can't use them with much accuracy on more complex images. That's when you turn to masking.

Most things that pack a powerful punch are either expensive or hard to master, or both. Well, you already forked out a pretty penny for Photoshop. And yes, masking isn't for those who get their selections via a drive-thru window. To help you with the learning curve, in this chapter I ease you into masking by using Photoshop's automated masking tools. Although they aren't quite as accurate as the hardcore masking I cover in Book VI, Chapter 3, they're easier on you, and with certain images (or a serious time crunch), the quick-and-dirty masking tools get the job done.

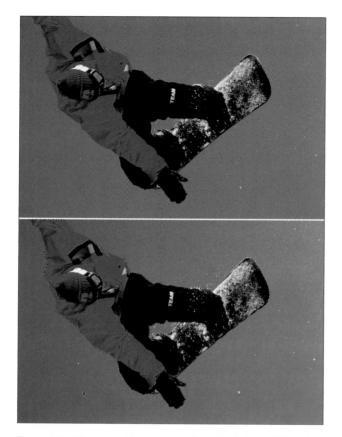

Figure 2-3: After you refine your mask (top), click the Edit in Standard Mode button (Q) to convert your mask into a selection outline (bottom).

Using the Color Range Command

The Color Range command allows you to select similarly colored pixels in a selection or within an entire image. You can think of it as a smarter Magic Wand tool (which I talk about in Book III, Chapter 1). Unlike the Magic Wand tool, however, Color Range lets you adjust your selection before you ultimately get the selection outline. It does this by using Fuzziness (a cousin of Tolerance, also discussed in Book III, Chapter 1), which allows you to select colors relative to how closely they resemble the sampled colors. Photoshop selects all the identical colors, partially selects similar colors, and doesn't select dissimilar colors. You adjust the fuzziness, and Photoshop adjusts the selection.

Starting with Color Range basics

Here are some Color Range command tips before you get started:

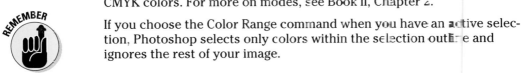

 ✔ You can save and load Color Range settings by clicking the appropriate buttons in the dialog box. But heck, after you have a selection you can also choose Select➪Save Selection to save it as an alpha channel.

 ✔ You can select a color range based on preset colors or tones that you choose from the Select drop-down list. For example, choosing red automatically selects all the red in the image. Choosing midtones selects all the medium-range tones in the image. And Out-of-Gamut (only available for RGB and Lab modes) selects all colors that can't be printed by using CMYK colors. For more on modes, see Book II, Chapter 2.

If you choose the Color Range command when you have an active selection, Photoshop selects only colors within the selection outline and ignores the rest of your image.

Executing the Color Range command

Follow these steps to work with the Color Range command:

1. **Choose Select➪Color Range.**

   The Color Range dialog box appears in full glory.

2. **Choose Sampled Colors from the Select drop-down list and then select the Eyedropper tool in the dialog box.**

3. **Select a display option — Selection or Image.**

   I recommend leaving the setting at the default of Selection so that you can see the mask while you build it. You can toggle between the two views by pressing Ctrl (⌘ on the Mac).

4. **Either in the image itself or in the image preview in the Color Range dialog box, click to sample your desired colors.**

   The image preview changes to a mask. Black areas show unselected pixels, white areas show selected pixels, and gray areas show partially selected pixels.

   Your goal is to try to make what you want to select all white and what you don't want to select all black, as shown in Figure 2-4. And if you want some things partially selected, they can remain gray.

Figure 2-4: When using the Color Range command, your desired selection area appears white in the preview box.

5. **Adjust the selection by adding or deleting colors.**

   You can select or delete as many colors in your image as you want.

   Use the Add to Sample tool (the plus eyedropper icon) to add, and use the Subtract from Sample tool (the minus eyedropper icon) to delete.

   You can be lazy like me and just stick with the regular eyedropper icon. Simply hold down Shift+Alt (Shift+Option on the Mac) to add and delete.

6. **Fine-tune the range of colors by dragging the Fuzziness slider.**

   The Fuzziness ranges extend from 0 to 200. A higher value selects more colors, and a lower value selects fewer colors. While you adjust the fuzziness, the mask dynamically updates.

   If you can't quite get the control you want with the Fuzziness slider, try selecting the Localized Color Clusters option. Instead of just maintaining a single color cluster from the colors you select, this option enables you to select multiple color clusters. This option can help with obtaining cleaner, more precise selections, especially when you're trying to select more than just one color. Adjust the Range slider to fine-tune the range, or area, of your selection.

   The Invert option selects what's currently unselected and deselects what's currently selected. And if you totally muck things up, you can reset the dialog box by holding down Alt (Option on the Mac) and clicking Reset.

7. **Select a Selection Preview from the drop-down list to preview the selection in the image window.**

   - *None:* Displays the image normally.
   - *Grayscale:* Displays just the grayscale mask.
   - *Black Matte and White Matte:* Displays the selection against a black or white background.
   - *Quick Mask:* Shows the mask over your image, using your Quick Mask settings.

8. **Click OK.**

   Your image appears with a selection outline based on the Color Range mask.

   Now, do what you will with your nice, clean selection.

   I decided my Thai dancer needed to be in a more exotic locale, so I transported her (by dragging and dropping with the Move tool onto another image) to a mystical Shangri-La, shown in Figure 2-5.

Corbis Digital Stock, Digital Vision

Figure 2-5: With a clean selection made with the Color Range command, you can send people to locales never before visited.

Selective Erasing with the Eraser Tools

The eraser tools let you erase portions of an image to the background color, to transparency, or even to the way your image looked earlier in your editing session. There are three eraser tools — the regular Eraser, the Magic Eraser, and the Background Eraser. All three share a tool flyout menu.

The eraser tools look like real erasers, so you can't miss them. But just in case you do, press E and then Shift+E to toggle through the three tools.

When you erase pixels, those pixels are gone. Gone. For good. Before using the eraser tools, it might be wise to make a backup of your image. You can save the image either as a separate file or as another layer. That way, if things run amok, you have some insurance.

Erasing to the background or transparency

The Eraser tool allows you to erase areas on your image to either the background color or to transparency. Select the Eraser tool, drag through the desired area on your image, and you're done.

If the image contains just a background, you erase to the background color, as shown in Figure 2-6. If the image is on a layer, you erase to transparency.

Corbis Digital Stock

Figure 2-6: The Eraser tool erases either to the background color (left) or, if on a layer, to transparency (right).

I rate this tool in the same category as the Lasso tool. It's quick; it's easy, but it has limited applications. Use it only for minor touchups. The Eraser tool definitely isn't a tool to use on its own for making accurate selections.

The most useful function I find for the Eraser tool is to clean up my channel masks. Set the mode to Block, zoom into your mask, and clean up those black and white pixels. See Book VI, Chapter 3 for more on channel masks.

These options on the Options bar control the Eraser tool:

- ✔ **Mode:** Select from Brush, Pencil, and Block. When you select Brush or Pencil, you have access to the Brush Preset picker panel on the far left of the Options bar.

  Use the Brush Preset drop-down picker panel to select from a variety of brush sizes and styles. Block has only one size, a square of 16 x 16 pixels. But because the block size remains constant, if you zoom way in, you can perform some detailed erasing.

- ✔ **Opacity:** Specify a percentage of transparency for the erasure. Opacity settings less than 100 percent only partially erase the pixels. The lower the Opacity setting, the less it erases. This option isn't available for the Block mode.

- ✔ **Flow:** Set a flow rate percentage when using Brush mode. Flow specifies how fast Photoshop applies the erasure and is especially handy when using the Airbrush option.

- ✓ **Airbrush:** Click the button when using Brush mode to turn your brush into an airbrush. With this option, the longer you hold your mouse button down, the more it erases.

- ✓ **Erase to History:** This option allows you to erase back to a selected source state or snapshot in the History panel. You can also hold down Alt (Option on the Mac) to temporarily access the Erase to History option. See Book II, Chapter 4 for more information.

- ✓ **Brush Panel:** Click the toggle button to bring up the full Brushes panel.

Selecting and erasing by color

The Magic Eraser tool works like a combination Eraser and Magic Wand tool. It both selects and erases similarly colored pixels:

- ✓ **When you click a layer:** The Magic Eraser tool erases pixels of a similar color based on a specified range and leaves the area transparent, as shown in Figure 2-7.

- ✓ **When you click the background:** The Magic Eraser tool automatically converts the background to a layer and then does the same thing.

- ✓ **When you click a layer with locked transparency:** The Magic Eraser tool erases the pixels and replaces the area with the background color.

The Tolerance value defines the range of colors that Photoshop erases, just like it does with the Magic Wand tool. The value determines how similar a neighboring color has to be to the color that you click. A higher value picks up more colors, whereas a lower value picks up fewer colors. In my example in Figure 2-7, I set my Tolerance value to 8 and clicked in the upper-left of my image. Photoshop selected and erased only a limited shade of black due to my lower Tolerance setting.

Here are the other options:

- ✓ **Anti-Alias:** Creates a slightly soft edge around the transparent area.

- ✓ **Contiguous:** Selects only similar colors that are adjacent to each other. Deselect this option to delete similar-colored pixels wherever they appear in your image.

Corbis Digital Stock

Figure 2-7: Clicking with the Magic Eraser simultaneously selects and erases similarly colored pixels.

✔ **Sample All Layers:** Samples colors using data from all visible layers, but erases pixels on the *active* layer only.

✔ **Opacity:** Works like it does for the regular Eraser tool.

Removing an image's background

The Background Eraser tool is probably the most sophisticated of the eraser-tool lot. It erases away the background (in the composition of the image, not the Layers panel) from an image and leaves the foreground untouched — in theory, anyway.

Like the Magic Eraser tool, the Background Eraser tool erases to transparency on a layer. If you drag on the background, Photoshop converts the background into a layer.

To use the Background Eraser tool, you need to carefully keep the crosshair that appears in the center of the cursor, also known as the *hot spot,* on the background pixels while you drag. Then Photoshop deletes all background pixels under the brush circumference. But, if you get close to a foreground pixel with the hot spot, that pixel is gobbled up, as well. As you can see from my example in Figure 2-8, I got a little too close to the man's face in some spots, and it left him a little chewed up.

Here's the rundown on the options, found on the Options bar, for the Background Eraser:

✔ **Brush Preset picker:** Provides various settings to customize the size and appearance of your eraser tip. The size and tolerance settings at the bottom are for if you use a pressure-sensitive drawing tablet. You can base the size and toler-ance on the pen pressure or position of the thumbwheel.

Background Eraser chews up man's face.

Corbis Digital Stock

Figure 2-8: Be careful when using the Background Eraser, or else you can inadvertently eat up pixels.

✔ **Sampling:** The three settings (represented by icons) determine what areas should and shouldn't be erased. The default Continuous setting allows you to sample colors continuously while you drag through the image. The Once setting erases only areas that contain the color you first clicked. If the background is pretty much one color, you can try this option. The Background Swatch setting erases only the areas containing the background color.

✔ **Limits:** The Contiguous setting erases similar colors that are adjacent to one another. The Discontiguous setting erases similar colors to whatever's under the brush tip, regardless of whether they're adjacent. The Find Edges setting erases contiguous pixels while retaining the sharpness of the edges.

✔ **Tolerance:** Works just like the Magic Eraser Tolerance setting.

✔ **Protect Foreground Color:** Prevents you from erasing areas that match the foreground color.

Putting It Together

Framing a Photo with Quick Mask

Sometimes, you may want to add a decorative border or edge to your image. Maybe you're creating a postcard or greeting card, and the standard rectangular shape image just doesn't provide enough pizzazz. Although adding a border or edge might look difficult, it is a snap with the Quick Mask command. Just follow these steps:

1. **Using any selection tool, create a selection on your image.**

   I started with a rectangle in my image and then chose Select⇨Inverse to turn the selection inside out.

2. **Click the Edit in Quick Mask Mode button in the Tools panel.**

   A color overlay covers and protects the area outside the selection, as shown in the figure.

   Your selected area is open for you to edit as you so desire.

3. **Grab the Brush tool, choose the Heavy Stipple brush, and set the brush diameter to 168 pixels.**

   You can find the Heavy Stipple brush in the Wet Media Brushes library of the Brushes panel. See Book IV, Chapter 1 for more on the Brushes panel.

4. **Paint around the edges of the mask with black to add to the masked area.**

5. **Adjust the Flow setting to 35% to get a semitransparent area and then click a few more times.**

   You can also paint with gray to get the same effect.

continued

continued

6. **Again, adjust your brush diameter (this time to 80 pixels) and add a few random clicks here and there.**

7. **Switch your color to white and repeat the steps, clicking around the image and also in the interior of the mask.**

   Because white adds to the selected area, your image starts to show through.

   I ended up with a mottled mess, shown in the figure.

   You can also apply a filter or adjustment (Image⇨Adjustment) to the Quick Mask. See this technique in action in Book VII, Chapter 2.

8. **Click the Edit in Standard Mode button to exit the Quick Mask mode.**

   The overlay disappears, leaving you with a selection outline, shown in the figure.

   The selection outline correlates with the unmasked or selected areas of the Quick Mask. If you had a feathered mask, such as mine, the selection outline runs halfway between the selected and unselected areas of the mask, creating a soft transition.

9. **Your selection is ready and waiting for your next command.**

   In my example, I deleted my selection, thereby filling the hole with my background color of white and leaving me with a stippled image. Note that because my brush was feathered and also varied in the Flow settings, some of my image is also feathered and semitransparent.

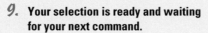

Chapter 3: Getting Exact with Advanced Masking Techniques

In This Chapter

✔ Creating and editing layer masks

✔ Using vector masks

✔ Working with channel masks

If you haven't already checked out Book VI, Chapter 2, which covers Photoshop's quick-and-easy masking tools, you might want to breeze through that chapter first, especially if the word *mask* brings to mind an image from Halloween rather than a selection technique. In this chapter, I dive into some manual masking techniques.

Layer masks are tremendously useful, and if you're like me, you'll find yourself addicted to them. They can be fantastic for blending layers and making multiple images dissolve into one another. Vector masks create shapes defined by vector paths and produce clean, smooth-edged graphic elements.

Channel masks are probably the most time-consuming of the masking lot, but they're powerful and accurate. Like anything in life, the more you practice using them, the faster and better you get.

But Photoshop CS5 includes a feature to help in your masking tasks — the Masks panel. This handy panel enables users to add, control, and refine masks of all sorts.

After you get through this final chapter of Book VI, you'll be familiar with every masking technique Photoshop has to offer. By then, you'll be prepared to use masks to select a very hairy orangutan, dyed green, perched in a tree in a lush rainforest. And how many people can say that?

Working with the Masks Panel

The Masks panel, shown in Figure 3-1, enables you to add, control, and refine your layer, vector, and filter masks. I explain layer and vector masks in the sections "Working with Layer Masks" and "Creating and Editing

Vector Masks," later in this chapter. Details on filter masks can be found in Book VII, Chapter 1. For now, I cover just the features in this panel because they may assist you in getting your mask exactly the way you want it:

- ✔ **Thumbnail:** Shows what layer or mask is currently selected in your file.

- ✔ **Add Pixel Mask/Select Pixel Mask:** Click this icon to add a layer mask. If you added a layer mask by another means, such as via the Layers panel or Layer menu, the icon is automatically selected. Remember that when working with masks, black hides areas of your image, white shows areas of your image, and any gray areas are partially hidden at varying percentages, depending how dark or light the gray is.

- ✔ **Add Vector Mask/Select Vector Mask:** Click this icon to add a vector mask. If you added a vector mask by another means, the icon is automatically selected.

- ✔ **Select Filter Mask:** This icon appears only when a Smart Filter has been applied. For more on Smart Filters, see Book VII, Chapter 1.

- ✔ **Density:** Think of this option as a kind of opacity control for your mask. To lessen the transparency of the masked (or hidden) area, select the mask and drag the slider to the left.

- ✔ **Feather:** The Feather option softens the edges of the mask, creating more of a dissolve between your layers when creating a composited image. To see the effect on the actual mask itself, hold down Alt (Option on the Mac) and click the mask thumbnail in the Layers panel, which temporarily hides the layer and shows only the mask. Hold down Alt (Option on the Mac) and click to display the layer again.

- ✔ **Mask Edge:** Click this button to bring up the Refine dialog box. In this dialog box, you can fine-tune the edges of your masks to your liking. For an explanation of the Refine Edge dialog box, see Book III, Chapter 1.

- ✔ **Color Range:** Click this button to open the Color Range dialog box. Color range is yet another way to create a selection or mask. For details on this feature, see Book VI, Chapter 2.

- ✔ **Invert:** This option reverses the colors of the mask. Therefore, black areas become white, white becomes black, dark gray converts to light gray, and so on.

- ✔ **Load Selection from Mask:** Click this option to load your mask as a selection. Note that the black areas of your mask are unselected, the white areas are selected, and the gray areas are partially selected. For more on selections, see Book III.

- ✔ **Apply Mask:** Click this icon to have your mask permanently applied to the layer. The mask is then deleted. Be careful when applying this option because you can no longer edit the mask and refine your visible areas.

- ✔ **Disable/Enable Mask:** Click this icon to show or hide your mask.

- ✔ **Delete Mask:** Click the trash can icon to delete the mask.

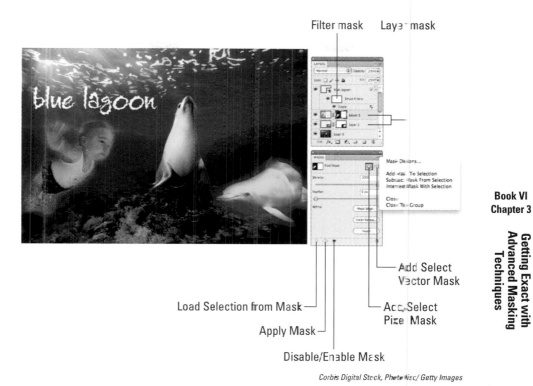

Filter mask   Layer mask

Add Select
Vector Mask

Add Select
Pixel Mask

Load Selection from Mask

Apply Mask

Disable/Enable Mask

Figure 3-1: The Masks panel aids in adding and refining various types of masks.

- ✏ **Mask Options:** This first command in the panel pop-up menu enables you to change the color and opacity of your mask overlay.

- ✏ **Add Mask to Selection, Subtract Mask from Selection, Intersect Mask with Selection:** These commands, also in the panel pop-up menu, allow you to add to, delete from, or intersect with existing selections made from your masks.

- ✏ **Close/Close Tab Group:** The final commands in the panel pop-up menu close the Masks panel and the group that the Mask panel belongs to, respectively.

Working with Layer Masks

Like any other mask, a *layer mask* is a grayscale image that you can edit to your heart's content. Layer masks are excellent for blending layers of images together and creating soft transitions between elements.

For versatility, layer masks are unparalleled. They allow you to gradually brush in transparency and opacity on a selective pixel basis. Paint with black to hide portions of the layer; paint with white to display portions; and paint in varying shades of gray to partially show elements. You can even apply gradients, image adjustments, and filters to your layer masks to create interesting special effects.

After you get the concept of layer masks, you'll never use the eraser tools (covered in Book VI, Chapter 2) again. You won't have to because one of the great things about layer masks is that you can forever edit, or even delete them, with no permanent harm whatsoever to the image.

Creating layer masks

To create a layer mask, select your desired layer and choose Layer⇨Layer Mask⇨Reveal All or Hide All.

- **Reveal All:** Creates a mask filled with white, which shows the layer.

- **Hide All:** Creates a mask filled with black, which hides, or *masks,* the layer and shows nothing but transparency.

You can also click the Add Layer Mask icon at the bottom of the Layers panel (which, by default, selects Reveal All). Or you can click the Add a Pixel Mask icon in the Masks panel.

You can't add a layer mask to a background layer. You must convert the background layer to a regular layer if you want to use a layer mask on the background of an image.

You can also use an existing selection to create a layer mask. Select your desired layer and make a selection by using one of the selection tools. Choose Layer⇨Layer Mask⇨Reveal Selection or Hide Selection. You can also click the Add Layer Mask button in the Layers panel to create a mask that reveals the selection.

After you create the layer mask, you can grab the painting tool of your choice and apply your grayscale color. ***Remember:*** Add white to the mask to display the image. Add black to hide the image. Add gray to make the layer semitransparent.

Using the Gradient and Brush tools on a layer mask

I must confess: I use two of the layer masking tools more than the others:

- **The Gradient tool:** Setting this tool to a linear gradient of black to white or white to black is truly awesome. Select the layer mask in the Layers panel and drag with the Gradient tool on the layer mask to create the gradient. The darker areas of the gradient gradually hide the image, whereas the lighter areas gradually show the image.

✏ **The Brush tool:** With a large, feathered tip, using the Airbrush option and the Flow set to around 10%, this tool is amazing. With these settings in place, you can create feathered edges that blend one layer into another without any harsh lines. Again, select the layer mask in the Layers panel and drag with Brush tool on the layer mask.

In Figure 3-2, which is an image with two layers (the flag on the bottom and the girl on top), I used a combination of both these tools. I started with the black-to-white linear gradient, which I dragged from the left edge of my image through to the right edge. I then took the Brush tool with a large feathered tip (265 pixels), selected the Airbrush option, set the Flow to 10%, set my foreground color to black, and worked my way around the profile of the girl's face to get rid of some more of the background behind her.

 To edit a layer mask, click the Layer Mask thumbnail in the Layers panel. Select your desired painting or editing tool, and paint or edit the mask to perfection. Just be sure that you're working on the layer mask, rather than editing the image itself. Otherwise, you apply paint directly to your image. You can tell because you see brackets around the layer mask thumbnail in the Layers panel. You also see the Pixel Mask icon highlighted and the mask thumbnail displayed in the Masks panel.

No layer mask

With layer mask

Figure 3-2: Layer masks enable you to seamlessly blend two layers.

continued

5. **Choose Image⇨Mode⇨Grayscale and click OK in the Discard Other Channels alert box.**

Photoshop has now stripped the color from the image, shown in the figure.

This is only one way to convert a color image to grayscale. There are a lot of others. Check them out in Book II, Chapter 2.

6. **Choose Window⇨Layers.**

The Layers panel appears.

7. **Holding down the Shift key with the Move tool selected, drag and drop your grayscale image onto your color image.**

This action automatically creates a new layer from the grayscale image. (See Book V for more information about layers.)

By holding down the Shift key, you keep the grayscale image centered over the color image.

8. **Close your duplicate image.**

9. **Press D to access the default colors.**

This step gives you a black foreground swatch and a white background swatch in your Tools panel.

Now, I show you how to use one of my favorite techniques, a black-to-white gradient, on the layer mask.

10. **Make sure that the grayscale layer is the active layer in the Layers panel and click the Add Layer Mask icon at the bottom of the panel.**

It's the icon that looks like a dark square with a white circle on top. Photoshop adds a second thumbnail on your layer, indicating that a layer mask has been applied.

A layer mask acts like a piece of clear acetate over your layer.

11. **Select the Gradient tool and then select the default gradient of Foreground to Background.**

To get the default gradient, click the Gradient Picker on the Options bar and select the first gradient.

It should be a gradient of white to black because it's based on the current foreground and background colors, which reverse when you select the Layer Mask thumbnail. For a gradient refresher, see Book IV, Chapter 2.

12. **Drag the gradient from the top of your image to the bottom.**

Or from left to right. Or at a diagonal. It's your call.

13. **Experiment with long drags and short drags. The angle and length of your mouse movement determine how the layer mask reveals the underlying image.**

In my example, I dragged from the bottom of the image to the top and stopped about two-thirds of the way up.

Where black appears on the layer mask, the grayscale image is hidden. Where white appears on the mask, the grayscale image shows through and everything in between allows the grayscale image to partially show.

Although I used a linear gradient in my example, you can experiment with the other types, as well. Radial gradients can provide some interesting effects.

14. **When you complete your mask, save and close the file.**

Creating and Editing Vector Masks

Whereas layer masks let you create soft-edged masks, vector masks create hard-edged masks defined by shapes created by a vector path on a layer. Vector-based shapes produce clean, smooth, and well-defined edges that are never jagged. And you can size and transform vector shapes without ever degrading the appearance of the element. (For an introduction to vector images, see Book IV, Chapter 1.)

You create a vector mask when you create a shape with any one of the shape tools. You can also create a vector mask when you convert type to a shape. (Choose Layer➪Type➪Convert to Shape.) See Book IV, Chapter 3.

Adding a vector mask to a layer

To add a vector mask to layer, follow these steps:

1. **Select the layer in the Layers panel and choose Layer➪Vector Mask➪Reveal All or Hide All.**

   I describe Reveal All and Hide All in the "Creating layer masks" section, earlier in this chapter. Remember that you can't add a vector mask to a background layer. You can also click the Add a Vector Mask icon in the Masks panel.

2. **Select the Paths icon in the Options bar. On the vector mask, create a path with the Pen tool or grab any shape tool and create a shape.**

   See Book III, Chapter 2 for more on paths and Book IV, Chapter 1 for more on shapes.

   I selected the Custom Shape tool and dragged a sunburst shape on my vector mask. Notice how everything inside the path (represented by the white area on the vector mask thumbnail) is visible and everything outside the path (represented by the gray areas on the vector mask thumbnail) is hidden, or masked, as shown in Figure 3-4.

   Like layer masks, you can add vector masks only to layers, not backgrounds. If necessary, simply convert your background to a layer by double-clicking the background in the Layers panel.

3. **If your vector mask is satisfactory, save your file and then close it.**

Figure 3-4: Everything outside of a vector mask is hidden, or masked, from display.

Another way to add a vector mask is to select your desired layer, draw a work path with the Pen tool or one of the shape tools, and then select Layer➪ Vector Mask➪Current Path.

Managing vector masks

Here are a few vector mask tips. You can perform the following tasks:

- ✔ **Edit a vector mask path.** Use the pen tools and the Direct Selection tool, as described in Book III, Chapter 2.

- ✔ **Add multiple shapes or paths to the existing vector mask.** All you need to do is drag another shape with any of the shape tools. Or add another path with the Pen tool. You can also add, delete, and intersect shapes and paths using the Add, Subtract, Intersect, and Exclude icons in the Options bar.

- ✔ **Remove a vector mask from a layer.** Drag the thumbnail to the trash can icon in the Layers panel or choose Layer➪Vector Mask➪Delete. You can also click the Delete (trash can) icon in the Masks panel.

- ✔ **Disable (temporarily hide) or enable a vector mask.** Shift-click the vector mask thumbnail or choose Layer➪Vector Mask➪Disable (or Enable). You can also click the Disable/Enable Mask icon in the Masks panel.

- ✔ **Rasterize a vector mask.** *Rasterizing* (or turning the mask into a pixel-based image) converts the vector mask into a layer mask. Choose Layer➪Rasterize➪Vector Mask.

- ✔ **Apply layer styles to vector shapes.** This is a quick-and-easy way to create buttons for a Web page or a custom logo, as shown in Figure 3-5. Just select the layer, not the vector mask, and choose Layer➪Layer Style. Select your style of choice. For details on layer styles, see Book V, Chapter 4.

Book VI
Chapter 3

Getting Exact with
Advanced Masking
Techniques

Figure 3-5: Adding layer styles to your shapes can make them really shine.

Creating Channel Masks

Photoshop's channel masks are probably the most time-consuming masks to use because they require a lot of manual labor. Not heavy lifting, mind you, but work with the tools and commands in Photoshop.

But, don't get me wrong; it's time well spent. Channel masks can usually accurately select what the other Photoshop tools can only dream about — wisps of hair, tufts of fur, a ficus benjamina tree with 9,574 leaves.

You can create a channel mask in a lot of ways, but I'm here to offer you one that works most of the time. To create a channel mask, follow these steps:

1. **Analyze your existing channels to find a suitable candidate to use to create a duplicate channel.**

   This is usually the channel with the most contrast between what you want and don't want. For instance, in my example, the Blue channel provided the most contrast between the windmills and the sky, which I wanted to mask, and the background, which I didn't.

   To duplicate the channel, drag your desired channel thumbnail to the New Channel icon at the bottom of the Channels panel. After you duplicate the channel, it then becomes an alpha channel and is named (channel) copy.

2. **Make sure the alpha channel is selected in the Channels panel and choose Image⇨Adjustments⇨Levels.**

   Using the histogram and the sliders in the Levels dialog box, increase the contrast between the element(s) you want and don't want selected. Click OK when you're done to close the dialog box.

3. **Select a tool, such as the Brush or Eraser tool, and paint and edit the alpha channel to refine the mask.**

   See Figure 3-6. I used the combo of the Brush and Eraser set to Block mode to clean up my mask.

4. **When you complete the mask, click the Load Channel as Selection icon (the dotted circle icon on the far left) at the bottom of the Channels panel. Then, click your composite channel at the top of the list of channels.**

   This step loads your mask as a selection, giving you that familiar selection outline. You can also use one of my favorite keyboard shortcuts: Ctrl-click (⌘-click on the Mac) directly on the alpha channel to load the mask as a selection.

   Your selection is now ready to go.

5. **You can leave it within the original image, or drag and drop it onto another image with the Move tool, as I did in Figure 3-7.**

   Because my new sky was darker than my original, I also darkened my windmills so the lighting would be more consistent. If you've done a good job, nobody will be the wiser that the two images never met in real life.

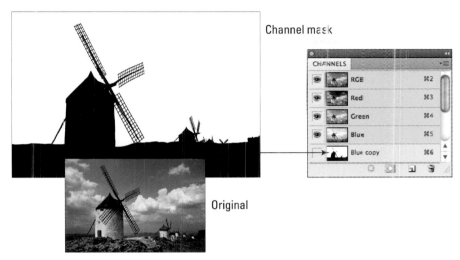

Channel mask

Original

Corbis Digital Stock

Figure 3-6: Use the Levels and Photoshop painting and editing tools to refine your channel mask.

Corbis Digital Stock

Figure 3-7: When combining multiple images, masking is usually the most accurate method.

Putting It Together

Masking Hair, Fur, and Other Wispy Things

Hair, fur, fuzz, and other objects with complex or loosely defined edges can prove difficult to select with the run-of-the-mill selection techniques. But that's where masking can save the day. Because a mask allows for a 256-level selection, it does a great job of picking up those elusive strands of hair and such that would otherwise probably be cut off in the selecting process.

Perhaps you've seen those photos where everyone in a composite image appears to have helmet hair? Here are the steps to avoid the Aqua Net look and select even the smallest wisp of hair:

1. **Choose File⇨Open.**

Select an image that contains something hairy, furry, or fuzzy. A portrait is an ideal choice (unless the subject is hair challenged).

For your first attempt at this technique, starting with an image that has a pretty simple and uncluttered background is best.

In my example, I used an image of a pensive, young urban professional shown in the figure.

2. **Choose Window⇨Channels.**

View each channel by clicking the channel name in the Channels panel.

Each channel is an independent grayscale image and a potential starting point for a mask.

It's best to start with the channel that contains the most contrast between what you want to select and what you don't. If it's a toss-up, go with the channel that makes selecting the difficult part of the image easiest. (In my example, that's the hair, so I chose the Blue channel.)

3. **Choose Duplicate Channel from the Channels panel pop-up menu. In the Duplicate Channel dialog box, name the channel *mask* and click OK.**

You've created an alpha channel for the mask, shown in the figure. Now, you can edit the mask without harming the original channel.

4. **Make sure the alpha channel is selected in the Channels panel and choose Image⇨Adjustments⇨Levels. Boost the contrast in the image by dragging the Input sliders for shadows, midtones, and highlights.**

Make the element(s) you want to select to be all white or all black with a little gray in the wispy areas. In other words, you want to change most of the pixels in the image to either black or white.

If you need help using the Levels adjustment, see Book VIII, Chapter 1.

Remember, the goal is to select the person and his or her hair. You can do that in one of two ways:

- ✔ By selecting the person
- ✔ By selecting the background first and then inverting the selection

In a mask, traditionally, white represents a selected area, black represents an unselected area, and gray represents a partially selected area.

In my example, because my guy is darker than the background, I adjusted the contrast to make the subject as black as I could while making the background lighter. You can see the result in the figure.

5. **When you're done, click OK to close the Levels dialog box.**

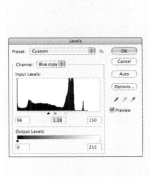

6. **Refine the mask by selecting the Eraser tool and selecting Block Mode from the Options bar.**

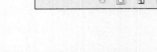

The Block Eraser is a great tool for cleaning up masks. It allows you to paint inside the mask without creating any feathered edges.

7. **Press D to access the default colors.**

Remember, the Eraser tool paints with the background color, so be sure you have the color you want before you drag. Press X to switch the foreground and background colors.

continued

continued

8. **Clean up your mask by painting with black and white, as shown in the figure.**

Make sure to use short strokes so you can undo any mistakes you make.

9. **Use the Zoom tool if you need to touch up the details.**

The Block Eraser tool has only one size, so you have to zoom in to paint thinner strokes and zoom out to erase a larger area.

Remember to leave some gray around the wispy areas, as seen in the figure; otherwise they may look chopped off.

Take your time and be as accurate as you can. Patience makes a big difference.

If you're not sure what you need to paint on the mask and you want to refer to the color image, simply click the composite channel (either RGB or CMYK, depending on your image) at the top of the Channels panel. Then click the mask channel again to return to your mask. Or you can view both the mask and the composite simultaneously. Your mask appears as a red overlay.

Your mask is refined and ready to go.

10. **Click the first icon on the left at the bottom of the Channels panel to load the mask as a selection.**

Or Ctrl-click (⌘-click on the Mac) the channel mask.

A selection marquee appears around your mask.

If you want to soften the edge a little, you can choose Select⇨Modify⇨Feather and enter a value somewhere between 0.5 pixel (for a low-resolution image) to 2 pixels (for a high-resolution image). Feathering allows for a soft, natural-looking transition between your masked element and the background. I used a 1-pixel feather for my image.

11. **Return to the composite image by clicking the RGB channel (or CMYK, if warranted).**

The selection outline appears in your composite image, shown in the figure.

12. **If you need to invert your selection, choose Select⇨Inverse.**

In my example, I just filled my background with a solid color, so I left the background selected.

13. **Choose Window⇨Color and mix a color of your choice. Choose Edit⇨ Fill, and in the Fill dialog box, choose Foreground Color for your Contents. Click OK.**

Photoshop now replaces the background with a solid color. Check the edges to see how clean your mask is.

14. **Make any final edits you need to make.**

My guy looked like he spent too much time at the local tanning booth, so I toned down the redness in his skin by using the Variation commands (see Book VIII, Chapter 1), as shown in the figure.

15. **When you're happy with your channel mask, save and close the file.**

It takes practice to get masking down to a science, but, believe me, it's worth your time. Nine times out of ten, a channel mask lends a much better selection than any of the easier, quicker selection tools and techniques.

TIP

Instead of filling the background with a color, you can also open a second image and, with the Move tool, drag and drop your masked element into the second image. A couple of things to keep in mind when compositing with two images: First, try to use two images whose lighting isn't so dissimilar that it looks artificial. Take into account the time of day, the angle of the light, and so on. Second, try to select two images whose levels of focus make sense. If you need to soften one of the images, apply the Gaussian Blur filter. If your mask is good, your person should look right at home in his or her new digs.

Book VII
Filters and Distortions

The 5th Wave   By Rich Tennant

"Hey — let's put scanned photos of ourselves through a ripple filter and see if we can make ourselves look weird."

*G*ot an image that needs to be sharper or maybe less dusty? How about an image that needs to look like it was wrapped in plastic and then Xeroxed on a circa-1970 photocopier? Either way, this is the book that describes the fine-tuning and the folly of filters.

Filters can do wonders in correcting your images, making them look better than the original. And if it's special effects you're interested in, look no further. Filters can make your image look ripped, sprayed, wet, hot — and just about any other adjective you're interested in. The best news is that Photoshop offers Smart Filters: filters that work their magic without damaging your pixels. If distortions are more your thing, you won't be disappointed with the Liquify command, for which image warping, pushing, bloating, and puckering are daily activities.

Chapter 1: Making Corrections with Daily Filters

In This Chapter

↳ **Understanding how filters work**

↳ **Introducing Smart Filters**

↳ **Sharpening soft areas**

↳ **Improving an image with blurring**

↳ **Smoothing defects with Median and Facet filters**

↳ **Fading a filter's effects**

↳ **Applying filters repeatedly or selectively**

Filters have a long and glorious history, ranging from performing essential tasks (such as removing abrasive particles from the oil in your car's crankcase) to even more important chores involving the pixels in your Photoshop images. In both cases, filters (also called *plug-ins* because they can be installed or removed from Photoshop independently) seize tiny, almost invisible bits of stuff and rearrange them in useful ways. The results are something you'd never want to do without.

This chapter introduces you to the basics of Photoshop's filter facilities and starts you on the road to plug-in proficiency.

You Say You Want a Convolution?

All filters do one simple thing in a seemingly complicated way: They make Photoshop do your bidding. Deep within a filter's innards is a set of instructions that tells Photoshop what to do with a particular pixel in an image or selection. Photoshop applies these instructions to each pixel in the relevant area by using a process the techies call *convolution* (creating a form or shape that's folded or curved in tortuous windings), but which we normal folk simply refer to as *applying a filter*.

Here are the steps to apply a Smart Filter:

1. **Create a Smart Object by doing one of the following:**

   - Choose File⇨Open as Smart Object. Select your file and click Open.

   - In an existing file, choose File⇨Place. Select your file size and position the image to your liking, and press the Commit button in the Options bar in Photoshop.

   - Select a layer in the Layers panel and choose Layer⇨Smart Objects⇨ Convert to Smart Object.

   - Select a layer in the Layers panel and choose Filter⇨Convert for Smart Filters.

   - Copy and paste Illustrator content as a Smart Object into Photoshop.

2. **Select your desired filter from the Filter menu.**

   Any filter applied to a Smart Object becomes a Smart Filter.

   Your Smart Filter is appended beneath your Smart Object layer, as shown in Figure 1-3.

Corbis Digital Stock

Figure 1-3: Apply Smart Filters for nondestructive effects.

You can also apply the Shadows/ Highlights and Variations adjustments as Smart Filters. These are found under the Image⇨ Adjustments submenu.

When you add a Smart Filter to a layer, Photoshop automatically adds a layer mask. Technically, when a layer mask is applied to a Smart Filter, it's called a *filter mask*. Correspondingly, an alpha channel appears in the Channels panel, as shown in Figure 1-4.

By default, the entire filter is displayed, as evidenced by an all-white filter mask. But the application of a filter mask enables you to selectively hide and show the effects of the filter, shown in Figure 1-4, where I applied the filter to the background (as indicated by the white in the filter mask) but not to the sea lion (as indicated by the black in the filter mask). If you made a selection on the layer before applying a Smart Filter, the mask will reflect that selection. For more Smart Filter masking details, see the following bulleted list. For information on masking in general, check out Book VI.

Note that the Masks panel enables you to control and fine-tune masks of all types, including layer masks, vector masks, and filter masks. Check out Book VI, Chapter 3 to find out details on using this great panel.

3. **Edit the filter as often as you like by simply double-clicking the filter name in the Layers panel.**

You can also right-click (Control-click on the Mac) the filter name to access a context menu from which you can select Edit Smart Filter. (Refer to Figure 1-3.)

Filter Mask

Alpha channel

Figure 1-4: Smart Filters come equipped with their own mask.

Book VII Chapter 1

Making Corrections with Daily Filters

Your filter's dialog box appears, enabling you to adjust the parameters, as desired. You can't edit *single-step filters* (those that don't display a dialog box but are automatically applied). You can, however, double-click to reapply certain filters, such as Clouds and Difference Clouds, that reside in the Render filter submenu.

4. **(Optional) If desired, adjust the blend modes and opacity settings of the Smart Filter by right-clicking (Control-clicking on the Mac) on the filter line in the Layers panel to access a context menu. From that menu, select Edit Smart Filter Blending Options.**

   In the dialog box that appears, select your desired blend mode from the Mode pop-up menu. Adjust your opacity by entering a percentage or moving the slider. This is a great way to tone down the effect of the filter and achieve a more subtle appearance. Doing so is similar to fading a filter (described in the section "Fading a Filter," later in this chapter), only better because you can infinitely edit the settings.

5. **Add as many filters as you need to the Smart Object.**

   Filters reside in a grouped stack.

6. **(Optional) If you no longer want the filter, delete it by selecting it in the Layers panel and dragging it into the trash at the bottom of the panel.**

   To delete an entire Smart Filter group (multiple filters), grab the Smart Filters line in the Layers panel and drag it into the trash. You can also delete the filters by right-clicking (Control-clicking on the Mac) the filter name and selecting Delete Smart Filter from the context menu that appears. You can also delete all filters by right-clicking (Control-clicking on the Mac) the Smart Filters line in the Layers panel and choosing Clear Smart Filters from the context menu.

Here's everything else you need to know about the ins and outs of working with Smart Filters:

- Any file format that supports layers, such as PSD, TIFF, and PDF, supports Smart Filters.

- You can't apply Liquify or Vanishing Point as Smart Filters.

- Click the eye icon next to the filter name in the Layers panel to display or hide the individual Smart Filter. Click the eye of the Smart Filters group to toggle on or off all the filters.

- When executing commands, such as a transformation (scale, rotate, and so on), on a layer that has a Smart Filter, Photoshop alerts you that it'll turn off the Smart Filter in the preview during the transformation and reapply it after the transformation is complete. You may select the Do Not Show Again option to bypass the alert box from then on.

✔ You can rearrange the order of multiple filters by dragging them up or down the list in the Layers panel.

✔ To move a smart filter, drag the filter from one Smart Object layer to another. To copy Smart Filters, hold down Alt (Option on the Mac) while dragging.

✔ In the cases of multiple filters, only a single filter mask is applied to all filters within the group.

✔ You can use most of the same tools used to edit regular layer masks, such as the Brush and Gradient tools, to edit filter masks.

✔ You can adjust the Density and Feather options of the filter mask by using the Masks panel. See Book VI, Chapter 3 for details.

✔ Filter masks aren't linked to the Smart Objects, so if you move either one with the Move tool, the other doesn't move along with it.

✔ To hide the filter mask, hold down Shift and click the filter mask thumbnail in the Layers panel. You can right-click (Control-click on the Mac) the filter mask thumbnail and select Disable Filter mask from the context menu that appears.

✔ To delete the filter mask, drag the thumbnail to the trash at the bottom of the Layers panel. You can also right-click (Control-click on the Mac) on the filter mask thumbnail and select Delete Filter Mask from the context menu that appears. In addition, you can also add, subtract, or intersect the mask as a selection in this same context menu.

✔ To display just the filter mask, hold down Alt (Option on the Mac) and click the filter mask thumbnail in the Layers panel.

✔ To add a filter mask, right-click (Control-click on the Mac) the Smart Filter line in the Layers panel and select Add Filter Mask from the context menu that appears.

Book VII Chapter 1

Making Corrections with Daily Filters

Sometimes, when converting from one color mode to another, such as when going from RGB to CMYK, certain filters can't be supported. Photoshop prompts you with an alert box saying so and asks you whether you want to rasterize the layer. Rasterizing essentially converts your Smart Object into a regular layer and fuses your Smart Filters onto that layer. Bye-bye, Smart Filter. If you choose not to rasterize, any Smart Filters that can't be displayed are annotated with an alert icon (a triangle with an exclamation mark) in the Layers panel.

Sharpening What's Soft

Sometimes, your images aren't as sharp as you want. Sometimes, your images have a tiny bit of softening caused by scanning an image or perhaps by capturing a photo on your digital camera. Or perhaps you want only a particular part to be sharper so that it stands out from its surroundings.

All sharpening tools operate by increasing the contrast between adjacent pixels. If you look at a sharpened image side by side with the original version (as shown in Figure 1-5), you see that no new information has been provided. Instead, the contrast is boosted so edges are more distinct. The dark parts of the edges are darker; the light parts at their boundaries are lighter.

Photoshop has six main sharpening features, only five of which are actually filters, on the Filter⇨Sharpen menu. The sixth (the Sharpen tool) isn't a filter, strictly speaking. It is a tool in the Tools panel and is more like a paintbrush that lets you sharpen areas selectively by using strokes.

Figure 1-5: Sharpening an image boosts the contrast of neighboring pixels and gives the illusion of improved focus.

Sharpen

The Sharpen filter is best used for minimal touchups in small areas. This single-step filter increases the contrast between all the pixels in the image or selection. Although this filter makes the image look sharper, it can add a grainy look to solid areas that aren't part of the edges.

Sharpen More

The Sharpen More filter, a single-step filter, increases the contrast between pixels even more than the regular Sharpen filter. Like the Sharpen filter, Sharpen More is best relegated to noncritical sharpening because it doesn't do a very good job of sharpening large areas. Also, it doesn't provide the control you need for more intense projects.

Sharpen Edges

The Sharpen Edges filter is a single-step filter that's superior to the Sharpen and Sharpen More filters because it concentrates its efforts on the edges of images, adding sharpness without making the image grainy or noisy. It's best used for quickie fixes.

Smart Sharpen

The newest member of the Sharpen team is definitely a keeper: Smart Sharpen does a great job of detecting edges and sharpening them less destructively. Like the veteran Unsharp Mask filter, discussed in the next section, this filter gives you a lot of control over the sharpening settings, as shown in Figure 1-6. Here's the scoop on those settings:

Corbis Digital Stock

Figure 1-6: The Smart Sharpen filter gives the most control over your sharpening specifications.

- ✔ **Preview:** Obviously, keep this option selected so that you can take a gander at what's happening as you sharpen. You'll appreciate the large preview.

- ✔ **Basic and Advanced:** The only difference between the two views is that with the Advanced view, you can control the amount of sharpening in the Shadow and Highlight areas of your image. Use the following controls to fine-tune the amount of sharpening in your light and dark areas:

  - *Fade Amount:* Determine the amount of sharpening.

  - *Tonal Width:* Specify the range of tones you want to sharpen. Move your slider to the right to sharpen only the darker of the shadow areas and the lighter of the highlight areas.

- *Radius:* Specify the amount of space around a pixel that's used to determine whether a pixel is in the shadow or the highlight area. Move your slider to the right to specify a greater area.

✔ **Settings:** You can save your sharpening settings so that you can load them for later use without having to re-create them. Click the disk/down-pointing arrow icon to do so.

✔ **Amount:** Use this control to vary the amount of edge sharpening. A higher value increases the contrast between pixels around the edges. Your choices range from 1 percent to 500 percent. For subtle amounts of sharpening, anything around 100 percent or less provides the effect you're looking for without making the image appear overly contrasty (yes, that's a technical term) or unrealistic.

✔ **Radius:** This slider controls the width (in pixels) of the edges that the filter will modify. The higher the value, the wider the edge that's affected. Your range varies from 0.1 pixel (for fine control) to 64 pixels (for broader sharpening effects). How you use this control varies chiefly on the resolution of your original image. Low-resolution images (100 pixels per inch and lower) look best when you use only a small radius value, from a fraction of a pixel up to 3 or 4 pixels.

TIP

A good rule to consider when you select a radius is to divide your image's ppi resolution by 150 and then adjust from there. For example, if you have a 150 ppi image, set the radius at 1 and then tweak from there.

✔ **Remove:** Specify the algorithm to be used to remove the blurriness in the image. Gaussian Blur is the method used by Unsharp Mask and is good for removing that hazy type of blurriness. Lens Blur detects and sharpens the edges and detail in the image, and it does a good job of reducing those nasty halos that can occur from sharpening. Motion Blur reduces the blurriness that can occur when you move your camera (or your subject moves).

✔ **Angle:** Specify the direction of motion if you choose Motion Blur as your algorithm.

✔ **More Accurate:** Check this option to make Photoshop provide a more accurate removal of blurriness. It takes longer, but it's worth the wait, as shown in Figure 1-7.

Corbis Digital Stock

Figure 1-7: Smart Sharpen can take your soft, mushy photo and make it come to life.

Unsharp Mask

Don't feel bad: Everyone is confused by the name *Unsharp Mask* the first time they encounter it. This filter provides a sophisticated attempt to duplicate a sophisticated photographic effect called (you guessed it) *unsharp masking,* in which two sheets of film are sandwiched together to create a final image. One sheet is the original film negative (or a duplicate), and the second is a positive image (the "normal" photograph) that's blurred slightly. When the two are put together, the light and dark areas cancel each other out, except at the edges — because of the blurring of the positive mask, which causes the edges to spread at those points.

Unsharp masking is a tricky procedure in the darkroom. It's much more precise in the digital realm because Photoshop can easily control the width of the areas to be masked, as well as a relative brightness level to use before beginning to apply the masking effect.

In the Unsharp Mask dialog box, you can find two of the same controls that you have with Smart Sharpen (see the preceding section) — Amount and Radius. You also have another option, called Threshold. Threshold controls the difference in brightness that must be present between adjacent pixels before the edge is sharpened. That is, you need to have a distinct contrast between adjacent pixels along an edge in order to sharpen the edge. Your choices range from brightness values of 0 to 255. Selecting a low value emphasizes edges with very little contrast difference (which is usually what you want). You're generally better off leaving this control at 0 unless your image has a lot of noise. Higher values force Photoshop to provide edge sharpening only when adjacent pixels are dramatically different in brightness. Increasing the threshold too much can cause some harsh transitions between sharpened and unsharpened pixels.

In most cases, the Amount and Radius sliders are the only controls you need to use. Threshold is most useful when the first two controls create excessive noise in the image. You can sometimes reduce this noise by increasing the Threshold level a little.

Sharpening always increases contrast, so keep this in mind if you plan on adjusting the contrast of your image with other commands and tools. Sharpening is usually one of the last commands you apply when correcting and enhancing your images.

Blurring What's Sharp

What, me blurry? The answer is yes, if you have an image that contains unwanted *grain* (the roughness or noise added by the photographic film) or perhaps an ugly pattern of halftone dots used in a printed image.

Applying the Lens Blur filter

If you've ever played with the aperture settings on a camera, you're probably well aware that you can determine how shallow or deep your depth of field is. Depth of field relates to the *plane of focus* (the areas in a photo that are in front of or behind the focal point, and that remain in focus) or how in-focus the foreground elements are when you compare them to the background elements. If you use a Lens Blur filter on an alpha channel (see Book VI, Chapter 1 for more on alpha channels), the alpha channel acts as a depth map. This approach is great for taking a fully focused image and creating a shallow depth of field in which the foremost object is in focus and the background elements get blurrier the farther they are from the focal point. You can achieve this effect by creating an alpha channel filled with a white-to-black gradient — black where you want the most focus, white where you want the least focus or most blur.

Here's a brief description of setting the Lens Blur filter options:

- ✔ **Source:** If you have an alpha channel, select it from this pop-up menu. The Lens Blur option interprets the various grayscale values of the alpha channel and applies the blur according to the value set in the Blur Focal Distance option. Choose Transparency to make an image get blurrier while it gets more transparent. Choose Layer Mask to apply the blur according to the grayscale values on the layer mask. (See Book VI, Chapter 3 for more on layer masks.) If your image contains none of these options, choose None. Photoshop applies the blur on the image.

- ✔ **Blur Focal Distance:** Specifies how blurry or in focus an area of the image is. Drag the slider to specify the value or click the crosshair cursor on the part of the image that you want to be in full focus.

- ✔ **Iris:** The Iris settings are meant to simulate a camera lens. Specify the shape of the lens, as well as the radius (size of the iris), curvature, and rotation of that shape.

- ✔ **Specular Highlights:** The Lens Blur filter averages the highlights of an image, which, if left uncorrected, cause some highlights to appear grayish. These controls help to retain *specular highlights,* or those highlights that should appear very white. Set the Threshold value to specify which highlights should be *specular* (remain white). Set a Brightness value to specify how much to relighten any blurred areas.

- ✔ **Noise:** Blurring, of course, obliterates any noise (or *film grain*) that an image may have. This absence of noise can cause the image to appear inconsistent or unrealistic, in many cases. Drag the slider to add noise back into your image.

You might need to blur a background to make the foreground seem sharper or blur a portion of an image to create an angelic glow. Here are your blurring options (all in the Filter⇨Blur menu):

- ✔ **Average:** This single-step filter calculates the average value (or color) of the image or selection and fills the area with that average value. This option can help you smooth the values of areas that contain a lot of noise.

✓ **Blur:** Also a single-step filter, Blur provides overall blurring of an image.

✓ **Blur More:** This filter provides a significantly increased amount of blurring compared to the regular, old-fashioned Blur filter.

✓ **Box Blur:** The Box Blur filter blurs your image in the shape of, well, a box or square.

✓ **Gaussian Blur:** This filter offers a radius control to let you adjust the amount of blurring more precisely. It also has a really cool name.

The Gaussian Blur filter is an excellent tool because it gives you a great deal of control over the amount and type of blurring you get, especially when compared to the single-step Blur and Blur More filters, which apply a fixed amount of blur. Use these latter two filters when you simply want to desharpen an image a tad, and turn to Gaussian Blur when you're looking for a specific effect.

✓ **Lens Blur:** This filter simulates the blurring that can occur when you capture an image with a camera. For details, see the sidebar "Applying the Lens Blur filter" in this chapter.

✓ **Motion Blur:** This filter simulates the blur you see in objects that are moving.

✓ **Radial Blur:** This filter produces the kind of blur you might get when photographing a revolving automobile tire. You can also get a zoom effect with this filter.

✓ **Shape Blur:** The Shape blur basically blurs your image according to the shape you choose from the panel. The shape choices you have are the same as those with the Custom Shape tool. Move the Radius slider to the right for a larger blur. You can see an example of different shape blurs in Figure 1-8.

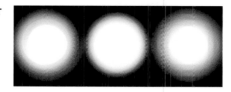

Figure 1-8: The Shape Blur blurs your image in a variety of shapes.

✓ **Smart Blur:** This filter lets you control how Photoshop applies the blur to edges and other details of the image.

✓ **Surface Blur:** This filter blurs the surface or interior of the image, rather than the edges. If you want to preserve your edge details but blur everything else, this is your filter.

**Book VII
Chapter 1**

Making Corrections with Daily Filters

Smoothing with the Facet and Median Filters

One reason you might want to blur an image is to reduce dust and scratches, or to smooth away sharp edges. In the following sections, I show you how to use the versatile Facet and Median filters to soften an image.

Although the Facet and Median filters smooth images by eliminating some detail, you can compensate for the blurring effect by applying the Smart Sharpen filter or Unsharp Mask (covered earlier in this chapter) with a low radius setting to sharpen things up a little.

The Facet filter

The Facet filter breaks up an image by using a posterizing effect. It gathers blocks of pixels that are similar in brightness and converts them to a single value, using geometric shapes. (When you posterize an image, you reduce it to a very small number of tones.)

The geometric shapes make the image look more randomly produced, while eliminating much of the banding effect you get with conventional posterizing filters.

The effects of the Facet filter are subtle and best viewed at close range. The original image in Figure 1-9 contains some dust, scratches, and a few other defects. Instead of retouching them one by one, I used Facet.

Facet is a single-step filter, so you don't need to adjust any controls. Just choose Filter⇨Pixelate⇨Facet and evaluate your results. You can apply the filter multiple times. However, even one application smoothes out the picture and eliminates the worst of the artifacts.

Original	Single Facet filter	Multiple Facet filter

iStockphoto

Figure 1-9: The Facet filter can simply eliminate annoying artifacts or convert your image into a "painted" piece.

If you apply the Facet filter multiple times, your image takes on a kind of pointillist, stroked look that becomes obvious. Using the filter over and over on the same image can yield quite interesting special effects.

The Median filter

The Median filter (look for it on the Filter⇨Noise menu) operates similarly to the Facet filter in that it reduces the difference between adjacent pixels by changing the values of some of them. In this case, it assigns the median values of a group of pixels to the center pixel in the group. Unlike the Facet filter, the Median filter gives you a bit of control. You can choose the radius of the group that Photoshop uses to calculate the median value. Median tends to make an image look a bit blurrier because it reduces the contrast of adjacent pixels. However, it does a good job of smoothing the image and removing artifacts.

Putting It Together

Creating an Angelic Glow

Sometimes, a little blur can add a soft, romantic mood or angelic glow that can improve glamour photos, pictures of kids, or even something as mundane as a flower. The secret is to apply only enough blurring to provide the soft effect you want without completely obliterating your original subject. Assuming, of course, that your subject doesn't *deserve* obliteration; that the kids are your own (or those of a close friend or relative); and that they are, in fact, of that rare angelic variety.

You don't want to use this effect on other subjects, such as men, who generally like a rugged, masculine appearance. Many senior citizens regard the age lines on their faces as badges of distinction earned over a long, rewarding life. Don't try softening them up with glowing effects, either.

To add an angelic glow to your little angel, just follow these steps:

1. **Open the image in Photoshop.**

   I used one of a cute little girl.

2. **Choose Layer⇨Duplicate Layer to create a copy of the image layer.**

3. **Select Filter⇨Blur⇨Gaussian Blur.**

   Gaussian Blur softens the upper layer, producing an airy glow.

continued

continued

4. **Move the Radius slider to the right to produce a moderate amount of blur and then click OK to apply the blurring effect, as shown in the figure.**

   I used a value of 7.

5. **In the Layers panel, select Lighten from the Blending Modes pop-up menu.**

6. **Use the Opacity slider (click the right-pointing arrow to access the slider) to reduce the amount of glow (if it's too much for your tastes).**

   I reduced my Opacity to 65 percent.

7. **Choose Layer⇨Flatten Image to combine all the layers.**

   Experiment with different amounts of Gaussian Blur until you find the perfect glowing effect, as I did in my figure.

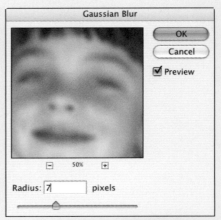

Applying a Filter Again

You can reapply the last filter you worked with — using the same settings — by pressing Ctrl+F (⌘+F on the Mac). (It's also the first command on the Filter menu.) You might want to do this to strengthen the effect of a filter on a particular image, layer, or selection. Or you simply may want to apply the same filter to a succession of images or selections.

To bring up the dialog box for the last filter you applied, press Ctrl+Alt+F (Windows) or ⌘+Option+F (Mac). This shortcut can be very useful when you apply a filter and then decide you want to go back and use different settings. After applying the filter, press Ctrl+Z (⌘+Z on the Mac) to undo, and then press Ctrl+Alt+F (⌘+Option+F on the Mac) to bring up the filter's dialog box. The dialog box opens with the settings you used last time, allowing you to make adjustments and then reapply the filter.

Fading a Filter

Sometimes, you may not want the full effects of a filter applied to your image or selection. Often, applying a filter full strength tends to give it that artificial "Photoshopped" look. Photoshop has a handy Fade Filter facility that lets you control the intensity of the filter's effects. You can access this feature by choosing Edit⇨Fade or by pressing Shift+Ctrl+F (Shift+⌘+F on the Mac). The Fade Filter facility also has a Preview option, so you can preview the changes you're making to the original image.

You must fade your filter *immediately after* you use the filter. If you use a painting or editing tool after applying the filter, for example, Fade Filter doesn't appear on the Edit menu anymore. Photoshop replaces it with Fade Brush Tool or whatever your last execution was.

You can fade the effect in the Fade dialog box in the following ways:

- **Adjust opacity settings.** Just about every filter allows you to adjust opacity, so most of the time, the Opacity slider is all you need to adjust the strength of the filter applied to your image.

- **Use a blending mode.** Use one of the blend modes in Photoshop to merge the filter effect with the original image. For more on blend modes, see Book V, Chapter 3.

  You can also fade a filter's effect by applying a filter to a duplicate layer or to a selection on that layer. Then adjust the opacity or blend mode of the filtered layer so that it merges with the unfiltered layer underneath it.

You can also apply a Smart Filter to your layer or selection. By doing so, you get the utmost flexibility in editing the filter's opacity and blend modes — not just once, but infinitely. For more about Smart Filters, see the section "Introducing Smart Filters," earlier in this chapter.

Selectively Applying a Filter

You don't need to apply filters to an entire image or an entire layer. You can achieve some of the best effects when you apply a filter to only a portion of an image — say, to an object in the foreground but not on the background. Your choices include the following:

- **Selections:** Make a selection and apply the filter only to that selection. You can use Quick Mask mode (see Book VI, Chapter 2) to paint a selection. This technique can give you a high degree of control; it even lets you feather the edges of the selection so the filter effect fades out.

✔ **Channels:** You can store selections as alpha channels (visible in the Channels panel, of course). But you can also choose to apply a filter to only one of the other channels, such as the Red, Green, or Blue channels in an RGB image. By using this technique, you can create a filter effect that's applied to only one color in an image. (Check out Book VI, Chapter 1 for information about channels.)

✔ **Layer Masks:** You can use a layer mask to create a selection where you apply the filter to that selection only. Or you can actually apply the filter to the layer mask itself for a special effect, as shown in Figure 1-10.

✔ **History Brush:** Use the History Brush tool to paint a filter onto a portion of the image. Apply the filter to the entire image. Then in the History panel, select the state just before you applied your filter. Set your source state to the filter state and then paint the part of your image you want filtered. For details on working with the History panel, see Book II, Chapter 4.

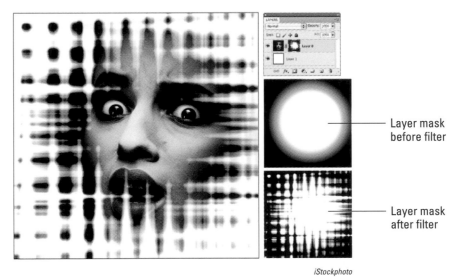

Layer mask
before filter

Layer mask
after filter

iStockphoto

Figure 1-10: Apply a filter to your layer mask to create a special effect.

Because a Smart Filter comes equipped with its own layer mask, you can selectively apply the filter to your layer in varying percentages. For details, see the section "Introducing Smart Filters," earlier in this chapter.

Putting It Together

Sprucing Up a Scanned Halftone

Publications use only a limited number of ink colors to reproduce a photograph. Every tone you see in a black-and-white image must be reproduced by using pure black ink and the white (okay, dirty beige) of the paper. Full-color images are represented by combining CMYK (cyan, magenta, yellow, and black). Printers can't use various shades of grey ink to create grayscale photos. They also can't use different strengths of color inks to generate the rainbow of hues you see in an image onscreen. To get at least some of that subtlety, photographs have to be converted to a pattern of dots before they can be printed.

Our eyes blend the dots together to produce the illusion of a grayscale or color image with smooth gradations of tone. However, a problem arises if you want to reuse a photograph and don't have access to the original. Scanners can capture the halftone dots, but the resulting image usually has an unpleasant pattern called *moiré*.

You have several ways of reducing the moiré effect, usually by blurring the image so that the dots merge and the underlying pattern vanishes. Many scanners have a *descreen* setting that partially eliminates the effect, but that setting sometimes actually blurs your image more than you want. Fortunately, you can usually do a pretty good job in Photoshop. But remember that, if there's any way possible, scanning from continuous-tone images always yields the best quality.

In the following steps, I demonstrate an easier way to eliminate a moiré pattern. (Over the years, I managed to lose the original negative and print.) You can see the dreadful moiré pattern that resulted when I scanned the clip.

To rid your scanned halftone print of bothersome moiré, follow these steps:

1. **Open the image in Photoshop.**

2. **Zoom in so that you can see the halftone pattern clearly while you work, as shown in the figure.**

3. **Choose Filter➪Blur➪Gaussian Blur.**

   The Gaussian Blur dialog box appears.

   You can also first convert your image to a Smart Object and then apply your Gaussian Blur and Smart Sharpen filters as Smart Filters. See the section "Introducing Smart Filters," in this chapter.

**Book VII
Chapter 1**

**Making Corrections
with Daily Filters**

continued

continued

4. **Move the Radius slider to the right until the halftone pattern is blurred, and then click OK to apply the blur.**

   I used a value of 1.7 pixels in my figure.

5. **Choose Filter⇨Sharpen⇨Smart Sharpen to restore some of the image's sharpness now that you've eliminated the pattern. Choose Gaussian Blur for the Remove algorithm.**

   As long as the Radius value for the Smart Sharpen filter doesn't exceed the radius of the Gaussian Blur that

you first applied, the two filters won't cancel each other out. You want the sharpening to make the details of the image crisper without bringing back those blurred halftone dots.

6. **Move the Amount slider to the right to sharpen the image.**

   Try to find a setting that does the job without making the image appear unnaturally sharp or show too much contrast. I used 150 percent in my figure.

   Calculate a starting Radius value by dividing the ppi (pixels per inch) of the scanned image by 150. If a moiré pattern reappears, reduce the Radius value.

7. **Click OK to apply the sharpness.**

   The result of my blur-and-sharpen exercise is shown in the final figure.

Chapter 2: Applying Filters for Special Occasions

In This Chapter

✓ Using the Filter Gallery

✓ Applying artsy effects and brush strokes

✓ Adding distortion and noise — on purpose

✓ Breaking up an image

✓ Rendering different effects

✓ Sketching and texturizing images the easy way

✓ Putting other filters to work

*P*hotoshop has dozens of filters that let you enhance your image in unusual ways. You can create Old Masters portraits from common snapshots, shatter your image into a thousand sparkling pieces, create clouds in a cloudless sky, create stained glass, or perform hundreds of other tricks.

The big challenge in using these filters is figuring out what each filter can do and how to apply it to the best effect. This chapter builds on Book VII, Chapter 1 by introducing you to more of those fabulous Photoshop plug-ins — and shows you some typical applications for them. Several Putting It Together projects have step-by-step instructions. For the first few examples, I provide you with the settings I used to achieve particular looks. However, filter effects vary greatly when applied to different images, so you have to play with the filter controls yourself when you use these techniques with your own images.

You can apply a filter to a layer, selection, or channel. And you can also fade a filter, change opacity settings, and use layer masks to soften the effects of filters. In fact, in some cases, you may *have* to decrease the effect of a filter because full strength can look overdone. On the other hand, when applied selectively, the same filter may look subtle and sophisticated. Although filters can be a blast to play with, you want to exercise some restraint when applying them for a real project. Getting carried away with the effects is easy, but the simplest effect is often the most beautiful.

Working in the Filter Gallery

The Filter Gallery (a dialog box-like gizmo that Adobe refers to as an *editing window*) gives you an alternative route to access and apply filters. To put it onscreen, choose Filter➪Filter Gallery. In this window, you can apply multiple filters, as well as edit or delete them later. This feature has made filters more flexible, more user-friendly, and easier to apply.

Follow these steps to get up and running in the Filter Gallery:

1. **Choose Filter➪Filter Gallery.**

   The Filter Gallery dialog box appears, as shown in Figure 2-1.

2. **Click your desired filter category folder.**

   The folder expands and displays the filters in that category. A thumbnail illustrating the filter's effect accompanies each filter. To collapse the filter category folder, simply click it again.

3. **Select the filter you want to apply.**

4. **Specify any settings associated with the filter.**

   You get a large preview of your image in the left side of the dialog box. Use the magnification controls to zoom in and out of the preview. When you change your settings, the preview dynamically updates itself. To preview a different filter, simply select that filter.

   If you want your custom settings to be the new default for the filter, simply hold down the Ctrl key (⌘ key on the Mac) while you are specifying your settings. The Cancel button changes to Default. After you have established your settings, release the Ctrl (or ⌘) key. Your new settings then become the new default.

5. **When you're happy with the filter, click OK to apply the filter and exit the dialog box. But if you want to apply another filter, leave the dialog box open and proceed to Steps 6, 7, and 8.**

6. **If you want to apply another filter, click the New Effect Layer button at the bottom of the dialog box.**

   Clicking this button duplicates the existing filter.

7. **Select your new filter, which then replaces the duplicate.**

   Photoshop lists each of the filters you apply to the image in the bottom-right of the dialog box.

8. **When you're done, click OK to apply the second filter and exit the dialog box.**

   You can apply as many filters as you want to your image. But, often, less is more.

Show/Hide

Preview   Filter category folders   Filter menu

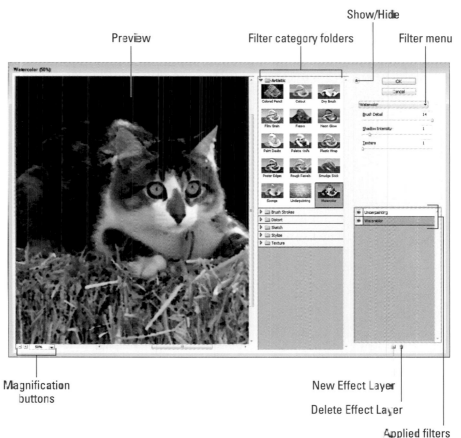

Magnification
buttons

New Effect Layer

Delete Effect Layer

Applied filters

Figure 2-1: The Filter Gallery enables you to apply and edit multiple filters within a single dialog box.

Here are some other helpful tips to keep in mind when you're using the Filter Gallery:

- ✓ To delete an applied filter, select it in the list in the lower-right portion of the dialog box and click the Delete Effect Layer button (the trash can icon) at the bottom of the dialog box.

- ✓ To edit an applied filter's settings, select it in the list and make any necessary changes. Click OK to reapply. Although you can edit a particular filter's settings, that edit affects any subsequent filters you've made after applying that particular filter.

✔ You can rearrange the order of the applied filters. Simply select and drag the filter up or down within the list.

Rearranging the order of the applied filters changes the resulting effect of the filters.

✔ To resize the Filter Gallery dialog box, drag the lower-right corner.

✔ To hide the Filter menu and provide the maximum real estate for the preview box, click the arrow to the left of the OK button.

✔ You can choose any of the filters found in the Filter Gallery from the Filter menu itself. Choosing a Filter menu filter launches the Filter Gallery automatically — but not all filters are available in the Filter Gallery. You have to access some of them individually from the Filter menu.

Don't be misled into thinking that the Filter Gallery is like layer styles, where the styles can be removed and the underlying pixel data is returned to its pristine, original state. Regular filters change the pixels of an image permanently, and after you apply one, you can't remove it. So, be sure that you really like what you've done and that you have a backup copy of that precious family photo or critical project image.

That being said, if you do want your filters to act like layer styles, they can. You can apply a Smart Filter to any layer that you first convert into a Smart Object. Smart Filters enable you to apply a filter nondestructively, without altering any underlying pixels. For more on Smart Filters, see Book VII, Chapter 1.

Getting Artsy

Quite a few Photoshop filters produce artistic effects. You can find a large collection of them in the Sketch and Stylize submenus. However, the Artistic menu contains 15 versatile filters that you can use to add brush strokes to your images, wrap them in plastic, create posterlike effects, and manufacture other interesting looks.

Many Photoshop users employ these filters to create images that look as if they were painted. What those users might not tell you, unless pressed, is that artsy filters can make terrible photos look better — or, in some cases, pretty darn good. These filters can disguise a multitude of photographic sins, turning shoebox rejects into pretty decent digital transformations. The photo of a clock in Figure 2-2 is, arguably, not very interesting — and (worse) it's blurry. I moved the camera while I was taking the photo.

Figure 2-2: This photo isn't that interesting and is slightly out of focus.

To improve this image, I employed filters on the Filter➪Artistic menu. Try one of the following filters:

- ✔ **Poster Edges:** A quick application of this filter improves the photo 100 percent. (See the left photo in Figure 2-3.) The filter not only gives the picture an artsy, posterlike look, but it also enhances the edges to make the clock's outline appear sharper.

  I set the Poster Edges filter's Edge Thickness to 4, bumped the Edge Intensity up to a value of 6 to create dramatic-looking edges, and set the Posterization level to 6 to allow more tones for a bit more realism.

- ✔ **Rough Pastels:** This filter, shown in the right photo in Figure 2-3, gives the look of a fine art piece created with oil pastels. I used the settings of 8 for the Stroke Length and Stroke Detail, 100% Scale, and 20 for Relief. I left my light source at Bottom.

- ✔ **The Dry Brush:** This filter can add an even more stylistic effect, reducing details to a series of broad strokes.

- ✔ **Colored Pencil:** This filter crosshatches the edges of your image to create a pencil-like effect.

- ✔ **Cutout:** This effect assembles an image from what looks like cut-out paper shapes, which resemble a kid's art project.

- ✔ **Film Grain:** This photographic effect diffuses an image with thousands of tiny dots that simulate clumps of film grain. (Think of old home movies.)

- ✔ **Fresco:** This effect looks (supposedly) like pigments applied to fresh, wet plaster. Okay, I guess . . . if you squint.

- ✔ **Paint Daubs:** This effect uses smears of color from your choice of a half-dozen different brush types. Very Jackson Pollock.

Figure 2-3: The Poster Edges filter (left) and the Rough Pastels filter (right) help.

- ✓ **Plastic Wrap:** This filter can produce a wet look, particularly when you apply it to a selection and then fade the filter so it doesn't overpower the detail in your image.

- ✓ **Watercolor:** This nice pastel effect diffuses an image while adding an interesting, watery texture.

Stroking Your Image with Filters

You can find more stroking filters on the Brush Strokes submenu, along with some interesting texturizing filters that can spruce up less-than-perfect photos and add a new look to even your best shots.

Choose Filter➪Brush Strokes to find the stroking filters that can provide hours of fun, including

- ✓ **Ink Outlines:** Adobe describes this filter as producing the look of a corroded ink drawing.

- ✓ **Spatter:** This filter generates the look you might get from a sputtering airbrush, as shown in Figure 2-4. I set my Spray Radius to 25 and my Smoothness to 10.

- ✓ **Accented Edges:** Use this filter to make a subject jump out from its background by emphasizing the edges of all the objects in the picture.

Corbis Digital Stock

Figure 2-4: The Spatter filter gives this portrait a nice painted texture.

Putting It Together

Creating Exotic Edges for Your Images

An attractive border can give your image an edge. If you want an edgy look or want to take your work right to the edge, you can apply this technique faster than you can say, "Over-worked metaphor!" Photoshop lets you apply deckled looks and other effects to the borders of your image by using any of several plug-ins built right into your trusty Filters menu.

Follow these easy steps to the edge of image immortality:

1. **Choose a photo that you think could use a decorative border and open it in Photoshop.**

2. **With the Rectangular Marquee tool, select the portion of the image you're framing, as shown in the figure.**

3. **Double-click the Quick Mask Mode icon in the Tools panel. In the Quick Mask dialog box that appears, choose Selected Areas in the Color Indicates area.**

4. **Click OK to enter Quick Mask mode.**

   Photoshop highlights the rectangle you selected in color, as shown in the figure.

Imagestate

5. **Choose Filter⇨Blur⇨Gaussian Blur, set the Radius, and click OK.**

   To give the image a softer edge when the selection is deckled, I've set the Radius to 30.

6. **Choose Filter⇨Brush Strokes⇨ Sprayed Strokes.**

7. **Adjust the Stroke Length and Spray Radius sliders to acquire the desired effect.**

   The higher the resolution, the higher the value you may need. In this case, I moved the Stroke Length and Spray Radius sliders to the max of 20 and 25 (respectively).

continued

**Book VII
Chapter 2**

**Applying Filters for
Special Occasions**

continued

8. **Select your desired Stroke Direction from the drop-down list.**

   I selected Right Diagonal for my image.

9. **Click OK to apply the effect to the Quick Mask selection.**

   After application, the edges of the quick mask overlay (highlighted area) appear frayed, as shown in the figure.

10. **Press Q to exit Quick Mask mode.**

    A selection border with ragged edges appears around the selection.

11. **Press Ctrl+C (⌘+C on the Mac) to copy the selected area, and then press Ctrl+V (⌘+V on the Mac) to paste it into a new layer.**

12. **Create a new layer and fill it with the color you want for the background.**

    I filled my background with white.

13. **In the Layers panel, move the colored background layer underneath your deckled image.**

14. **Choose Layer➪Flatten Image. When prompted, if you want to discard hidden layers, click OK.**

    The finished image appears, as shown in the final figure.

Distorting for Fun

With a couple exceptions, Photoshop's Distortion filters twist, turn, and bend your images in surprising ways, turning ordinary objects into wavy images, pinched shapes, and bloated spheres.

The first exception? The Diffuse Glow filter distorts images only to the extent that it imbues them with a soft, romantic, fuzzy look that can make the sharpest image look positively ethereal.

I've never figured out why Adobe dumped this useful filter into the Distort submenu, but there it is. (And here it is applied to a girl in Figure 2-5.)

Corbis Digital Stock

Figure 2-5: Give your photo a heavenly aura with the Diffuse Glow filter (left).

The second exception was the Lens Correction filter when it resided under the Distort submenu. It got moved out and supersized in CS5. This awesome filter fixes distortions caused by the camera lens. Choose Filter⇨Lens Correction. In the dialog box, you will find Auto Correction and Custom tabs. Make it easy and try the Auto Corrections or move right to the Custom settings and manually make corrective adjustments.

Here's the lowdown on the new Automatic Correction settings:

- ✔ **Correction:** Select the problem you want to correct. Find explanations of each in the Custom tab information. Note that if the corrections extend or contract your image beyond its original dimensions, choose Auto Scale Image. Choose how you want your edges filled from the Edge pop-up menu — with black, white, transparency, or extended with pixels from the image.

- ✔ **Search Criteria:** Choose your camera make and model, as well as your lens model. Choosing the correct equipment will assist Photoshop in making more accurate corrections.

✔ **Lens Profiles:** Select a matching profile. For zoom lenses, right-click (Control-click on the Mac) and choose the most similar focal length. If you don't find your lens profile, click the Search Online button to find profiles uploaded by other photographers. If you want to save a profile for later use, click the Lens Profiles pop-up menu and choose Save Online Profile Locally.

Here are the settings under the Custom tab:

✔ **Geometric Distortion:** Correct abnormalities such as *barrel* and *pincushion* distortions, in which straight lines appear (respectively) bowed out or in. Select the Remove Distortion tool and drag on the image — or you can also drag the Remove Distortion slider.

✔ **Chromatic Aberration:** Got colored fringe around your subjects? Photographers call this nastiness *chromatic aberration.* Fringe, aberration, whatever it's called — get rid of it by using the Red/Cyan or Blue/ Yellow Fringe sliders. The Move Grid, Hand, and Zoom tools can help make your adjustments more user-friendly.

✔ **Vignette:** If your images suffer from vignetting, in which the edges are darker than the center, slide the Amount slider to specify the amount of lightening or darkening. Slide the Midpoint slider to specify the width affected by the Amount.

✔ **Transform:** Correct perspective issues, often caused by tilting your camera when shooting, by using the Transform sliders of Vertical and Horizontal Perspective. Adjust the Angle to rotate the image to compensate for camera tilt or tweak your perspective adjustments. You may also use the Straighten tool to rotate a tilted image, as shown in Figure 2-6. Drag along the line in your image that you wish to straighten. Finally, to eliminate blank areas in your image created by correcting geometric distortions, use the Scale setting, which will crop off those areas.

✔ **Preview/Show Grid:** Choose whether to see your image with or without a grid overlay (of which you can specify the size). Many problems, such as perspective issues, are easier to fix using a grid as a guide.

✔ **The Move grid, Hand, and Zoom tools:** Can help make your adjustments more user friendly. You can also control your magnification using the zoom controls in the lower-left corner of the dialog box.

The Lens Correction filter works with 8-bit and 16-bit images only.

You can fix several photos simultaneously by batch-processing them with the Lens Correction automated command. Choose File⇨Automate⇨Lens Correction.

Other filters of this ilk can produce wavy images, add pond ripples, pinch images, or transform them into spheres. Check out Figure 2-7 to see distortions of a wall clock.

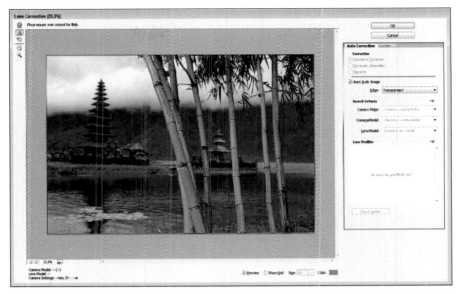

Figure 2-6: Use the Straighten tool to fix the horizon line in the Lens Correction dialog box.

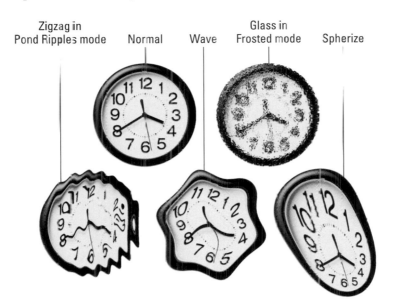

Figure 2-7: A normal clock takes on Dali-esque qualities with various Distort filters.

The Glass filter can do the following to your images:

- Add a glass-block texture
- Add a canvas texture
- Create frosted-glass fuzziness
- Break up your image with tiny lenses

Don't like any of Photoshop's textures? No biggie; you can also load your own texture. Click the Texture pop-up menu (the right-pointing arrow) and select Load Texture.

Pumping Up the Noise

Noise in images consists of any graininess or texture that occurs, either because of the inherent quality of the image or through the editing process. Noise filters, such as the Photoshop Add Noise plug-in, produce random texture and grain in an image. If you're new to image editing, you might wonder why you'd want to add noise to an image in the first place. Wouldn't it be smarter to remove it? Well, sometimes. In practice, you can find a lot of applications, including the following, that call for a little noise here and there:

- **Adding texture:** Objects that become too smooth, either because of blurring or other image editing you may have done, often look better when you add some noise to give them a texture. This technique is particularly useful if one object in an image has been edited, smoothed, or blurred more than the other objects in the image.

- **Blending foreign objects into a scene:** When you drop a new object into the middle of an existing scene, the amount of grain or noise in the new object is often quite different from the objects it's joining.

  For example, say you've decided to take a photo of your house and want to insert a certain luxury car in your driveway. Unfortunately, your digital photo of your brother-in-law's luxo-mobile is a lot sharper than the picture of your house. Adding a little noise can help the two objects blend more realistically. You may even forget that the car isn't yours.

- **Improving image quality:** Images that contain smooth gradients often don't print well because some printers can't reproduce the subtle blend of colors from one hue to another. The result is *objectionable banding* in your printed image: You can see distinct stripes where the colors progress from one to another. Adding a little noise can break up the gradient enough that your printer can reproduce the blend of colors, and the noise/grain itself is virtually invisible on the printed sheet.

Pumping Down the Noise

Although the Add Noise filter adds grain, the other filters in the Noise sub-menu don't add noise at all; instead, they make noise and *artifacts* (flaws, such as the dust and scratches on old film) less noticeable. Choose Filter⇨ Noise to find your tools, which include

✔ **Despeckle:** This filter makes dust spots in your image less noticeable by decreasing the contrast of your entire image — except at the edges. That translates into a slightly blurry image (which masks the spots) that still retains sharpness along the edges of image components. You end up with a little blur to soften the image but enough detail in the edges that the picture still looks good.

✔ **Dust & Scratches:** This filter concentrates its blurring effect on only those areas of your image that contain scratches and other artifacts. Photoshop performs this magic by looking at each pixel in an image and moving out in a radial direction until it encounters an abrupt transition in tone. (That's a signal that a spot or scratch has been found.) You can specify the radius in which Photoshop searches for the little culprits, from 1 to 100 pixels. Be careful not to overdo it. Too much of this filter can obliterate the detail in the image. Leave the Threshold at 0. If you journey into the world of mush, try using Edit⇨Fade right after you apply the filter.

When working with any of the Noise filters, be very conservative at first. All the Noise filters involve destruction of image data. Remember, that's just the nature of filters, in general — changing pixel data. A little bit can help — and be just the effect you're looking for. Just a little bit more, however, may completely wreck things.

✔ **Median:** This filter reduces contrast around dust motes, thus hiding them, in a slightly different way. This filter looks at the pixels surrounding each pixel in the image and replaces the center one with a new pixel that has the median brightness level of that group. The process is a little hard to describe succinctly, but basically, the bright spots darken while the rest of the image isn't affected. For more on the Median filter, see Book VII, Chapter 1.

✔ **Reduce Noise:** This filter, shown in Figure 2-8, is designed to remove luminance noise and JPEG artifacts that can appear on digital photos. *Luminance noise* is grayscale noise that makes images look overly grainy. Here's some info on the options:

• *Strength:* Specify the amount of noise reduction. You can reduce noise in the overall image or (if you click the Advanced button) channel by channel.

Be sure to check out the Blue channel, in particular. It's often the channel that captures all the crud.

• *Preserve Details:* A higher number preserves edges and details but reduces the amount of noise removal. Find a happy medium.

- *Reduce Color Noise:* Removes random colored pixel artifacts.

- *Sharpen Details:* Counteracts the fact that removing noise reduces sharpness, as well.

- *Remove JPEG Artifact:* Check this option to remove the annoying blocks and halos that can occur because of low-quality JPEG compression.

You can also save and reload your settings. Click the disk/arrow icon. In the New Filter Settings dialog box, enter a name for your settings and click OK. To load your settings, choose your desired settings from the Settings drop-down list.

Figure 2-8: The Reduce Noise filter attempts to remove noise while retaining some sharpness in edges and details.

Breaking Your Image into Pieces

The Pixelate filters in Photoshop break your images into bits and pieces, providing more of those painterly effects you can get with brush strokes and artistic filters.

The Pixelate submenu includes the Crystallize filter (applied to the little girl shown in Figure 2-9), as well as plug-ins that produce color halftone effects, fragmented images, and the pointillize effect (used in the "Creating Snow and Rain" Putting It Together project, in this chapter).

Corbis Digital Stock

Figure 2-9: The Crystallize filter breaks your image into polygonal shapes.

Rendering

In computerese, *rendering* means creating something from nothing, in a way. That's why all rendering filters in Photoshop produce special effects by creating a look, object, or lighting effect that's melded with your original image.

Using the Clouds filter

The Clouds filter can muster a sky full of clouds from scratch with a few clicks of the mouse, as in the now-cloudy picture shown in Figure 2-10. This filter creates clouds using random values from the foreground and background colors. Indeed, most Photoshop veterans use this filter so much that they have a surprising number of clouds in their images. Find it at Filter⇔Render⇔Clouds. To create a more contrasty cloud effect, hold down Alt (Option on the Mac) quickly when choosing the command. If you don't like the first set of clouds you get, apply the filter again and again until you do. If you want a more "realistic" sky, try using a dark sky blue for your foreground color and a very light blue, or white, color for your background color. Be sure to apply the filter on its own layer, if you don't want to obliterate the original contents of your image.

Brand X Pictures

Figure 2-10: Got clouds? Make your own with the Clouds filter.

Need a quick Web background image? Create a 128-x-128-pixel (or some multiple of that size) image and apply the Clouds filter. It tiles seamlessly on your Web page.

Creating fibers

This filter can create a textilelike effect out of thin air. Choose Filter⇨Render⇨Fibers. In the dialog box that appears, move the Variance slider to increase the contrast between light and dark areas. Move the Strength slider to increase the tightness of the weave of the fibers. Click the Randomize button to get another variation of the effect of the filter.

Using other rendering filters

Other useful filters on the Render submenu (at Filter⇨Render) include

✔ **Difference Clouds:** Use this filter to create puffy objects in the sky (or foggy clouds at lower levels). Instead of performing this magical feat the way the Clouds filter does, the Difference Clouds filter uses image information to figure the difference in pixel values between the new clouds and the image they're joining. The result is a unique cloud effect. Try applying the filter repeatedly to create a marbleized effect.

✔ **Lens Flare:** This filter creates the reflection effect that plagues photographers when they point their cameras toward a strong light source, such as the sun. Photoshop mimics several different kinds of photographic lenses, giving you useful flares that can spice up concert photos, add a sunset where none existed, and create other kinds of lighting bursts. In the Lens Flare dialog box, specify a location for the center of the flare by clicking the image thumbnail or dragging the crosshair.

✔ **Lighting Effects:** As a sort of photo-studio lighting setup, this filter uses pixels to do its work. You can set up 16 different lights and manipulate how they illuminate your photo.

Putting It Together

Creating Snow and Rain

Sometimes, you may come across a photo that needs a little bit of atmosphere thrown in to give it extra punch. And I mean *atmosphere* literally. By using a couple of filters and a blend mode, you can add some rain or snow to any image. Just follow these steps to create either rain or snow:

1. **Open a color image. If it isn't currently in RGB mode, choose Image➪Mode➪ RGB Color.**

Make sure you're in RGB mode; the blend mode used in these steps doesn't work correctly with CMYK images.

2. **Drag the background layer to the Create a new layer icon at the bottom of the Layers panel.**

You now see a layer named Background Copy in the Layers panel.

3. **Double-click the name Background Copy and type** Snow.

This isn't a mandatory step. I'm just being ultra-organized.

continued

continued

4. **First, set your background color to white. With the Snow layer active, choose Filter⇨Pixelate⇨Pointillize. In the dialog box, set your cell size to whatever value you prefer. Click OK.**

The bigger the cell size, the bigger the snowflakes or raindrops.

For rain, you might try a cell size of 3 (which is the minimum) or 4. For snow, try a larger cell size, between 6 and 9. I used a value of 7 in my image.

5. **On the Snow layer, choose Image⇨Adjustments⇨Threshold. Move the slider all the way to the right, to a max value of 255.**

This adjustment takes the colored cells and turns them to either black or white.

By using a value of 255, all brightness values less than 255 turn black, and the remaining value turns white.

6. **On the Snow layer, select Screen from the Mode pop-up menu in the Layers panel.**

The Screen blend mode lightens the Snow layer, where it mixes with the background. Blending with black pixels has no effect; therefore, they drop out, as shown in the figure.

7. **Choose Filter⇨Blur⇨Motion Blur. In the dialog box that opens, specify the Angle and Distance values.**

If you want the wind to appear to be blowing hard, set the angle more diagonally, around 45 degrees. If you want the precipitation to appear to be coming straight down, set the angle to 90 degrees. Setting the distance elongates the pointillized cells that you created in Step 4, making them look a little more realistic. For snow, start with a range of about 8 to 12 pixels. For rain, start a little higher, around 15 to 25 pixels. I used a value of 12 pixels in my figure.

If you're creating rain, proceed to Step 8. If you're a snow person, you're done, as shown in the figure.

8. **Choose Filter➪Sharpen➪Unsharp Mask.**

   The Unsharp Mask dialog box appears.

9. **Specify the Amount, Radius, and Threshold values and click OK.**

   The Unsharp Mask filter gives the illusion of sharpening the focus of the image by increasing the contrast between the pixels.

   I used an amount of 500%, a Radius of 1, and kept the Threshold at 0. This gives the raindrops a little more definition.

10. **Choose Filter➪Blur➪Motion Blur. In the dialog box that appears, specify the Angle and Distance values.**

    Again, the angle is up to you, but make it consistent with the value that you used in Step 7. Set the distance according to how you want your rain to appear — a moderate spring rain or a torrential, close-to-hurricane type of downpour. In the image shown here, I used 45 degrees and 25 pixels.

**Book VII
Chapter 2**

**Applying Filters for
Special Occasions**

Getting Organic with the Sketch Filters

The Sketch filter submenu contains a few filters that don't really belong there. That's because many current Photoshop filters were acquired from Aldus Corporation (now defunct), and Adobe had to shoehorn them into the organizational structure of Photoshop. But no matter — they work nonetheless.

If you were to encounter a picture of Michelangelo's *David,* shown in Figure 2-11, you might be tempted to sketch the famous sculpture by using one of the filters you can find when you choose Filter➪Sketch.

Perhaps a Conté Crayon effect or a Graphic Pen and Ink look would be nice. But the Sketch submenu also includes other artistic effects, such as the Note Paper look, a halftone screen, chalk and charcoal, and even a bas-relief effect that turns flat images into a Michelangelo-esque sculpture.

Normal

Conté Crayon

Graphic pen

Note Paper

Corbis Digital Stock

Figure 2-11: Give your digital photos a more organic feel with the Sketch filters.

You can also experiment with these other Sketch filters:

- **Chrome:** Creates a polished chrome effect. Use the Levels adjustment to add more contrast, if necessary.

- **Photocopy:** Gives that infamous, anachronistic look (dating back to the days when photocopiers didn't do a very good job of reproducing half-tone images). Creates areas of black and white with little gray value when the default foreground and background colors of black and white are selected.

✔ **Plaster:** Creates a look that resembles molten plastic more than it looks like plaster. The filter uses the foreground and background values to color the image.

✔ **Stamp:** Mimics a rubber or wooden-block stamp (not very sketchlike, indeed!).

✔ **Reticulation:** Adds texture by reproducing a veritable photographic disaster — the wrinkling of film emulsion that occurs when you move film from one developing chemical to another that has an extremely different temperature. (Think hot developer followed by a bath in cold water.) The highlights look grainy; the shadow areas look thick and goopy.

✔ **Torn Edges:** Creates the look of ragged paper and colorizes the image, using the foreground and background colors.

✔ **Water Paper:** Creates the look of paintlike daubs on fibrous wet paper.

Even if the Sketch filters don't all produce sketchy effects, they do have one thing in common: They give your images an organic look that's decidedly uncomputerlike.

Putting It Together

Adding Water Droplets and Other Wet Effects

**Book VII
Chapter 2**

You can find a lot of techniques for creating nice, neat, round crops of water by using Photoshop. Unless you've just waxed your car and expect a rain shower within moments, however, perfectly beaded water droplets can be fairly rare. In real life, you're likely to encounter some sloppy drops and driblets. This technique simulates that look. You could use it to add sparkling water drops to a flower, create a wet-look texture for artistic effect, or add a three-dimensional *trompe l'oeil* ("fools the eye") optical illusion. Find the flower image I use on this book's companion Web site if you want to follow along. Follow these steps to add wet effects:

Applying Filters for Special Occasions

1. **Open a plain old bone-dry photograph in Photoshop.**

I'm using a flower photograph, which will look great wet.

2. **Press D to make sure you have the foreground and background colors in Photoshop set to the default values of black and white.**

3. **Choose Window➪Channels to bring up the Channels panel. From the Channels panel menu, choose New Channel.**

This choice creates a new alpha channel for the water droplets. (For more on channels, see Book VI.)

continued

continued

4. In the Color Indicates area of the New Channel dialog box, select the Selected Areas radio button and set Opacity to 100%. Click OK.

5. Select Filter⇨Render⇨Clouds to create a motley cloud effect to use as the basis for your random water droplets.

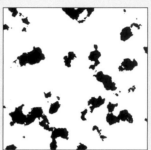

To view your alpha channel, select it in the Channels panel.

6. Choose Image⇨Adjustments⇨Threshold, and then move the slider to create black blotches that will become water droplets, as shown in the figure. Click OK.

I used a value of 83, but because the Clouds filter produces random results, you may find that a different value works better for you.

7. Choose Filter⇨Blur⇨Gaussian Blur and move the Radius slider enough to blur the jagged edges of the droplets. Click OK.

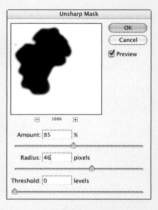

I used a value of 3.8 pixels.

8. Choose Filter⇨Sharpen⇨Unsharp Mask and adjust the Amount and Radius sliders to firm up the edges of the droplets. Click OK.

I found that an Amount of 85% and a Radius of about 46 creates soft-edged-but-distinct water droplets, as shown in the figure.

9. Ctrl-click (⌘-click on the Mac) the new channel in the Channels panel to load the selection you've created, as shown in the figure.

10. Click the RGB Channel in the Channels panel to return to your full-color picture.

The droplets appear as selections.

11. Choose Layer⇨New⇨Layer via Copy to create a new layer for the droplets to reside in.

12. Choose Layer⇨Layer Style and select Bevel and Emboss. Specify your options and click OK.

The bevel/embossing effect adds a third dimension to the crops. You can experiment with the depth and size controls to get the exact effect you want. I used the Inner Bevel style, set to the Smooth Technique in the Structure area of the dialog box. I used the sliders to increase the Size of the bevel to 27 pixels and Softened the edges by 11 pixels.

13. **If you like, you can choose Image⇒Adjustments⇒Levels to darken the droplets against their background. Click OK.**

The final image looks like a print that has been drenched with liquid.

Adding Texture

Photoshop lets you add a lot of interesting textures (which are in the Filter⇒ Texture menu) to your image, such as the cracked canvas effect generated by the Craquelure filter (see Figure 2-12) or the pixel effect produced by the Patchwork filter.

**Book VII
Chapter 2**

**Applying Filters for
Special Occasions**

Corbis Digital Stock

Figure 2-12: The Craquelure filter gives an Old-World painting feel to your image.

You can find other filters on this menu to help you create mosaic effects, add yet another kind of film grain, and create stained-glass effects in your images. But the most versatile filter in this set is the Texturizer, shown in Figure 2-13. The Texturizer filter enables you to apply various kinds of textures to your images or selections, including Canvas, Sandstone, Burlap, or Brick.

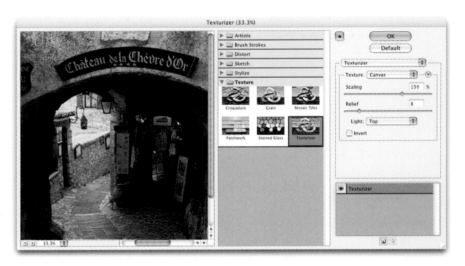

Corbis Digital Stock

Figure 2-13: You can apply either preset or custom-made textures to your images with the Texturizer filter.

You can select the relative size of the texture compared to the rest of your image by using the Scaling slider and adjust the amount of 3-D relief effect. You can even select the direction of the light source that produces the 3-D look, selecting from top, bottom, either side, or any of the four corners of the image. If those variations aren't enough for you, then create your own texture, save it as a Photoshop PSD file, and use that file to texturize your image.

You can find a handful of other filters that allow you to load your own textures, including Rough Pastels, Underpainting, and Conté Crayon.

Looking at the Other Filters

The Video and Other categories are the homes of the oddest of the odd. For example, the Other submenu is home to the Custom filter, which is no filter at all — it's a dialog box that has a matrix in which you can type numbers that Photoshop uses to process the pixels in your image in unexpected ways. The center box in the matrix represents a pixel in your image; the surrounding boxes represent the pixels that surround that pixel. The numbers you type tell Photoshop whether to darken or lighten pixels. You can experiment to see what will happen, and, if you like the effect, tell all your friends that you *meant* to do that.

The High Pass filter, also in the Other category, applies an effect opposite to the Gaussian Blur filter. It finds and keeps the details in the edges where it finds distinct color or tonal differences and turns the rest of the image gray. When converting a continuous-tone image into a bitmap (black and white only) image, applying this filter is useful before applying the Threshold adjustment. See Book VIII, Chapter 1 for more on the Threshold command. The High Pass filter is also handy for creating a channel mask. (See Book VI, Chapter 3 for details about working with channel masks.)

Two other filters that help with masking are the Minimum and Maximum filters. The Minimum filter expands the black areas while decreasing white areas (a process known as *choking* in traditional photography). The Maximum filter expands the white portions while decreasing black areas (known as *spreading*). The radius value you enter tells the filter how many pixels to expand or decrease from the edges of your selection.

The Video menu contains its own share of strange filters, including the NTSC Colors filter, which performs the rather obscure function of converting all the colors in your image to match the colors used for television reproduction. (NTSC stands for *National Television Systems Committee*.) You can use this filter to process digital presentations or slides that you want to show on television, if you're really, really particular about how the colors are portrayed.

Chapter 3: Distorting with the Liquify Command

In This Chapter

✔ **Checking out the Liquify window**

✔ **Liquifying an image**

✔ **Protecting/unprotecting with freezing and thawing**

✔ **Canceling your transformations with Reconstruction**

✔ **Extending transformations to other areas**

L iquify is the only Photoshop filter that gets a chapter of its own. But, then again, Liquify is no ordinary filter; it's the ultimate in image distortion tools and is therefore a good deal more complex than most of its kin on the Filter menu. What other filter has its own hefty tools panel, loads of buttons, several different modes, and more than a dozen option categories that amount to dozens more variations?

The Liquify command lets you push and pull on parts of your image; twist, turn, and pinch other parts; bloat sections; freeze portions in place so that they remain immune to the transformations going on around them; and perform selective reconstructions if you don't like everything you've done. You can perform this magic with a remarkable degree of control, too. You can almost be assured that every celebrity photo that appears on a magazine cover has been run through the Liquify gauntlet a time or two.

This chapter explores all the features of the Liquify command and shows you how to use these features to create sensational images.

Exploring the Liquify Window

At first glance, the Liquify window is a little daunting. It's a little daunting on second, third, and fourth glances, too. But when you quit glancing and dive into this versatile filter, you'll find that the tools and options make a lot of sense.

You open the Liquify window by choosing Filter⇨Liquify, and there, the Liquify Tools panel appears on the left, as shown in Figure 3-1. The other options available with Liquify (which I describe in the section appropriately named "The Options Areas," later in this chapter) appear on the right side of the window. The Tools panel includes a dozen tools that you can use to paint and distort your image.

Like with Photoshop's main Tools panel, you can activate each tool by pressing a letter associated with its name.

Purestock

Figure 3-1: The intimidating Liquify window is really quite user-friendly after you get familiar with its tools and settings.

The painting tools

The first group of tools is used to paint distortions on your image. Shown in this list with their keyboard shortcuts in parentheses, the painting tools (refer to Figure 3-1) are the following:

✓ **Forward Warp (W):** This tool is faintly reminiscent of the Smudge tool, but it doesn't blur the pixels quite as much as it pushes them forward while you drag, creating a stretched effect. Use the Warp tool to push pixels where you want them to go, using short strokes or long pushes.

When compared to a tool like the Smudge tool, which tends to destroy detail, the Warp tool can preserve detail within distortions.

Imagestate

✓ **Twirl Clockwise (C):** Place the cursor in one spot, press the mouse button, and watch the pixels under your brush rotate like a satellite photo of a tropical storm. Or drag the cursor to create a moving twirl effect. Pixels move faster in the center than along the edges of the brush. To twirl the other way, hold down the Alt (Option on the Mac) key while you drag or hold down the mouse button.

Try this technique with the other tools I describe in this list. (With some tools, the effect is more obvious than with others.) Simply hold down the mouse button. The longer you hold down the mouse button the more prominent the effect becomes.

✓ **Pucker (S):** This tool is the equivalent of the Pinch filter, squishing pixels toward the center of the area covered by the brush while you hold down the mouse button or drag. To reverse the pucker direction, which essentially applies a bloat, hold down the Alt (Option on the Mac) key while you hold down the mouse button or drag.

**Book VII
Chapter 3**

**Distorting with the
Liquify Command**

✓ **Bloat (B):** Here is an analog to the Spherize filter, pushing pixels toward the edge of the brush area while you hold down the mouse button or drag the mouse. To reverse the bloat direction — doing so applies a pucker — hold down the Alt (Option on the Mac) key while you hold down the mouse button or drag.

✓ **Push Left (O):** Formerly known as the Shift Pixels tool, this odd tool moves pixels to the left when you drag the tool straight up. Drag down to move pixels to the right. Drag clockwise to increase the size of the object being distorted. Drag counterclockwise to decrease the size. To reverse any of the directions, hold down the Alt (Option on the Mac) key while you hold down the mouse button or drag.

✔ **Mirror (M):** Formerly known as the Reflect tool, the Mirror tool drags a reversed image of your pixels at a 90-degree angle to the motion of the brush. Hold down the Alt key (Option key on the Mac) to force the reflection in the direction opposite the motion of the brush (for example, to the left of a brush moving right, or above a brush moving down). This tool is a good choice for producing shimmery reflections.

 ✔ **Turbulence (T):** This tool adds a random jumbling effect to your pixels when you click and hold down your mouse. It acts similarly to the Forward Warp tool when you click and drag. You can use the Turbulence tool to re-create maelstroms of air, fire, and water with (well, yeah) clouds, flames, and waves.

The other tools

The remaining tools in the Liquify Tools panel (refer to Figure 3-1) are

 ✔ **Reconstruct (R):** This tool lets you reverse or alter — completely or partially — the distortions you've made. You can retrace your steps if you went overboard in your warping activities.

 ✔ **Freeze Mask (F):** Use this tool to protect areas from changes. It paints the frozen area with a red overlay, just like Quick Mask mode.

 ✔ **Thaw Mask (D):** This tool unprotects areas by erasing the red protective "freeze" tone. This is a lot like erasing areas you've painted in Quick Mask mode.

 ✔ **Hand (H):** The Hand tool works exactly like the standard Photoshop Hand tool. Click and drag the image to move it around within the Preview window. You can find more about the Hand tool in Book I, Chapter 4.

 ✔ **Zoom (Z):** The Zoom tool works exactly like the standard Photoshop Zoom tool. Indeed, you can also zoom in and out by using Ctrl and the plus sign (⌘ and the plus sign on the Mac) and Ctrl and the minus sign (⌘ and the minus sign on the Mac) shortcuts. See Book I, Chapter 4, for more on using the regulation Zoom tool.

Separate from the Liquify Tools panel and in the lower-left corner of the Liquify window is a magnification box with a pop-up menu that you can use to select magnifications from 6 percent to 1600 percent. Or, if you like buttons, click your way to magnification by using the +/– zoom control buttons.

The Options Areas

On the right side of the Liquify window (refer to Figure 3-1), you can find some menus and buttons that let you specify options for the tools, for reconstructing and freezing, and for viewing. I point them all out to you here and cover exactly how to use them in the rest of this chapter:

- **Load Mesh and Save Mesh:** Liquify lets you show or hide a crisscross area called a *mesh,* shown in Figure 3-2. The mesh provides a visual map of the distortions you've applied. The mesh starts out as a square grid and changes while you apply distortions. The mesh lets you clearly see exactly what you've done to the image and, even better, provides a way to save those distortions on your hard drive so that you can load and reapply them to the same (or a different) image later.

- **Tool Options:** You can use the Tool Options area to apply parameters to the painting tools. You can specify the following options:

  - *Brush Size:* Specifies the width of the brush from 1 to 1500 pixels.

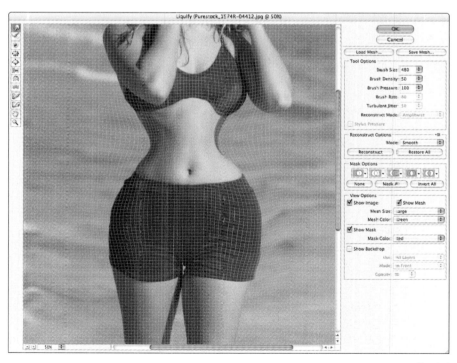

Purestock

Figure 3-2: The mesh provides a visual map of your applied distortions.

- *Brush Density:* Specifies how fast the brush effect levels off at its edges. For example, with a feathered brush, the effect is stronger in the center and lighter at the edges.

- *Brush Pressure:* Specifies the speed at which you distort while you drag. Lower is slower.

- *Brush Rate:* Specifies the speed at which you distort while you keep a tool, such as the Twirl tool, stationary. Again, lower is slower.

- *Turbulent Jitter:* Determines how tightly the brush jumbles pixels. When using the Turbulence tool, this option gives the stroke a more natural, organic look.

When you select the Reconstruct tool, you can also select a Reconstruct mode from the pop-up menu. (I explain each of these modes in the section "Extending and Cloning Distortions," later in this chapter.)

If you have a pressure-sensitive stylus tablet, you can also choose to use the amount of pressure you apply to control the width of your brush stroke.

✔ **Reconstruct Options:** Here, you can select one of several Reconstruct modes. Reconstruct and Restore All buttons let you reverse all changes made on unfrozen areas (a little at a time) or revert to your last set of distortions. I show you how to use these options in the section "Reconstructing an Image," later in this chapter.

✔ **Mask Options:** Consider freezing and masking one and the same when you're immersed in the Liquify dialog box. The mask options let you freeze areas from existing selections, layer masks, transparent areas, or alpha channels in your image. You can also invert the frozen area (thawing frozen portions of the image and freezing the previously thawed areas), and thaw all the areas that were frozen with one click. Here's the lowdown on the options, each of which is indicated by a double-circle icon:

- *Replace Selection:* Allows you to freeze or mask areas of your image based on an existing selection, transparent area, alpha channel, or layer mask. (For more on alpha channels and layer masks, see Book VI, Chapters 1 and 3, respectively.)

- *Add to Selection:* Displays the mask in the image and then enables you to add to the frozen areas by using the Freeze tool. Adds pixels to the currently frozen areas.

- *Subtract from Selection:* Subtracts pixels from the currently frozen areas.

- *Intersect with Selection:* Masks only those pixels that are selected and currently frozen.

- *Invert Selection:* Inverts selected pixels and currently frozen areas.

  Click None to remove frozen areas. Click Mask All to freeze the entire image. Click Invert All to exchange frozen and thawed areas.

✓ **View Options:** You can show or hide frozen (masked) areas, the mesh, or the image. Also, if you select the Show Mesh option, you can select the mesh size and color. If you select the Show Mask option, you can select the color that indicates frozen areas. For example, if your image contains a lot of red, you may want to change the freeze color to blue to create more contrast.

Finally, you can also apply a backdrop that shows how the image being liquified will appear when merged with other layers. To view your distorted image along with other layers, select the Show Backdrop option and then select the particular layer you want to view, or select All Layers from the Use pop-up menu. You can now choose whether you want the backdrop in front, behind, or blended with the distorted image. Specify an opacity percentage for the displayed layers so they won't obliterate the image being distorted. The default (50%) allows you to see both your image and layers well so that you can keep track of your distortions.

Transforming an Image

Liquify seems impossibly complex on the surface, but it's as easy to apply as finger paint after you play with it a little. Here's a step-by-step scenario of the things you might do to apply some distortion to your own image:

1. **Select and open an image you want to transmogrify with Liquify; select a layer.**

2. **If you don't want to distort the whole layer, you can make your desired selection.**

   You can also use a layer mask, alpha channel, selection, or transparent area to define what portions you want to distort.

3. **Choose Filter➪Liquify.**

   The Liquify dialog box appears.

4. **If applicable, load your selection, layer mask, transparent area, or alpha channel into the Mask Options area.**

   Make sure you select the Show Mask option in the View Options area. If you have a saved selection (also known as an alpha channel), you have an alpha channel option to choose from. Otherwise, you don't see that option.

5. **You can also select the Freeze Mask tool and paint over the areas that you want to mask or protect.**

   After you freeze an area, you may want to get rid of the freeze highlighting for a while. Deselect the Show Mask option in View Options to turn off the display.

6. **In the View Options area, make sure that the Show Mesh and Show Image options are both selected.**

You can hide any or all of these at any time to get a different view of your image. For example, you might want to hide the frozen areas and mesh to view only your image with the distortions you've applied so far. Or you might want to look only at the mesh, as shown in Figure 3-3, to get a look at the distortions by themselves. Being able to examine the liquification process in several different ways is one reason that Liquify is so controllable.

7. **If you're having trouble seeing the mesh (or think the mask color will blend in with a dominant color in your image), use the View options to change the size and color of the mesh and the hue of the mask.**

If you want to see your image distortions against a backdrop, you can select that option, as well.

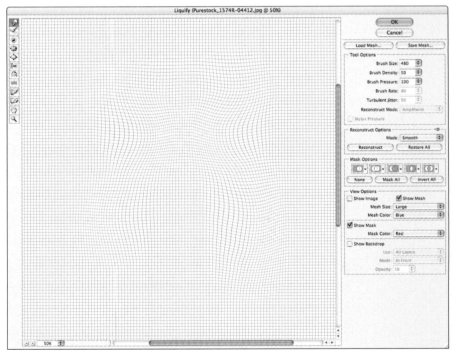

Purestock

Figure 3-3: You can choose to view just the mesh if you want a good look at how the actual distortions are mapped.

8. **Use the painting tools to apply various effects to your image, as shown in Figure 3-4.**

   Remember to adjust the brush size and pressure to get the exact coverage you want.

   At various points while you work, you may decide you want to freeze parts of the image from further changes (either temporarily or permanently).

9. **If you decide you want to work on an area again, select the Show Mask option to display the frozen areas (if necessary). Then select the Thaw Mask tool and erase all or part of the freeze.**

10. **Use the Reconstruct tool or options to partially or fully reverse or modify your distortions.**

    If you want to start over, click Restore All to get back to your original image All option settings stay as is. Hold down the Alt (Option on the Mac) key and click Reset to revert back to your original image and reset all options to their default settings.

**Book VII
Chapter 3**

Distorting with the
Liquify Command

Purestock

Figure 3-4: Use the various Painting tools to apply your desired distortions.

11. **When you finish, save the mesh you created by clicking Save Mesh. Give the mesh a name and store it on your hard drive.**

    This step is totally optional, but saving your work is a good idea if you really like what you've done.

12. **Apply the distortion to your image by clicking OK and exiting the Liquify dialog box.**

Mastering Freezing and Thawing

Liquify's capability to protect areas by freezing, and unprotect areas by thawing, deserves a closer look. Consider freezing the equivalent to masking. Here's a summary of the things you need to know:

Purestock

Figure 3-5: Protect areas from distortion by freezing them.

✔ **The easiest way to freeze/ unfreeze is to use the Freeze Mask and Thaw Mask tools to paint the areas you want to protect or unprotect, as shown in Figure 3-5.** Use the brush controls to modify how either tool paints or erases. When you set brush pressure to less than 100 percent, the opacity of the mask you're painting determines how frozen that area is. For example, if an area is only 25-percent frozen, using a distortion tool on that area produces only three-quarters the distortion you get in an area that's completely thawed.

✔ **You can use active or saved selections to define a frozen or masked area.** This is a great capability; you can use all the selection tools in Photoshop to define frozen/unfrozen areas before you invoke Liquify. You can, for example, select a portion of your image by using the Magic Wand or Quick Selection tool, another portion by using Quick Mask mode, and then save them all (choose Selection⇨Save Selection) as alpha channels. Then, when you use Liquify, choose any of those saved selections, or alpha channels, to freeze an area.

✔ **Select the basis that you want to use for your mask from the pop-up menu of the Replace Selection command (the far-left icon under Mask Options).**

You can also select a layer mask to define your mask. This is a great way to apply your distortions at varying degrees of intensity. Where the mask reveals more, the distortion is more prominent. Where the mask hides more, the distortion is subtler. For details on layer masks, see Book VI, Chapter 3.

✔ **To thaw all frozen areas, click the None button in the Mask Options area.**

✔ **To freeze all thawed areas, click the Mask All button in the Mask Options area.**

✔ **To reverse your frozen/unfrozen areas, click the Invert All button.** That which was frozen is thawed, and that which was unfrozen is frozen. Amen!

Reconstructing an Image

One of the most powerful capabilities of Liquify is that it can reconstruct your image fully or partially — restoring some or all of the image to its pre-Liquify state. This capability gives you a great deal of control over exactly how Photoshop transforms your image; you can backtrack any part of the transformation exactly the way you want. Here are some of your options:

**Book VII
Chapter 3**

Distorting with the
Liquify Command

✔ **To cancel all the changes made on your image (say, you really, really messed up), click the Restore All button in the Reconstruct Options area.** The image returns to its original state (as it was when you first opened the Liquify window) and removes distortions in both frozen and unfrozen areas.

✔ **To change only unfrozen areas of your image to their original states, select the Revert mode in the Reconstruct Options area of the dialog box, and then click the Reconstruct button multiple times until you get to your desired image.** The frozen areas remain distorted, but everything else returns to normal.

Use this option when you're displeased with some sections but like the distortions in others. Freeze the stuff you like and let Liquify cancel the changes elsewhere.

✔ **To paint portions of your image back to normalcy, select Revert mode in the Tool Options area, and then select the Reconstruct tool from the Liquify Tools panel.** You can use the Reconstruct tool to restore the areas that you paint. The image reverts more quickly at the center of the brush, so you have an extremely fine degree of control in how you revert your image. The mesh may help you see exactly what portions are being restored, too.

✔ **You can also click the Reconstruct button to have Photoshop apply an overall reconstruction.** Click the button to make Photoshop reconstruct once. Click it again to remove even more distortion.

If you don't necessarily want to reconstruct your image back to its original condition, but rather want to alter, extend, or clone your distortions, you can select Reconstruct modes other than Revert. See the following section, which talks about the other Reconstruct modes.

Extending and Cloning Distortions

Liquify allows you to extend distortions you've made in frozen areas into parts of the image that are unfrozen. If you have an image that has the requisite frozen and unfrozen portions, first select a mode — which determines specific ways in which Photoshop extends the image from the frozen areas into the unfrozen area.

Reconstruct modes

The Reconstruct modes include the following four:

✔ **Rigid:** This mode keeps rigid right angles in the mesh's grid, which can generate some mismatches (Adobe calls these *discontinuities*) at the edges where the frozen and unfrozen portions meet. This mode restores unfrozen areas to close approximations of their original states.

✔ **Stiff:** Adobe describes this as a *weak magnetic field,* attracting the edges between the frozen and unfrozen areas strongly where they meet and producing less distortion in unfrozen areas farther away from the edges.

✔ **Smooth:** This mode smoothly spreads the frozen areas' distortions through the unfrozen areas. It produces a smooth blending effect, as shown in Figure 3-6.

✔ **Loose:** This mode generates an even smoother blending effect between frozen and unfrozen areas than the Smooth mode.

Corbis Digital Stock

Figure 3-6: The Smooth mode smoothly blends frozen distortions into unfrozen areas.

Use the Reconstruct tool to expand the frozen-area distortions into the unfrozen area, using the mode you've selected to blend the pixels while you paint. You can drag to paint, or click and Shift-click to paint in straight lines (much like you do with Photoshop's regular Brush tools).

More Reconstruct modes

There are three Reconstruct modes that work slightly differently than the four discussed in the preceding section. These modes more or less clone particular distortions you've already applied elsewhere in the image. Like the Clone Stamp tool, these modes allow you to select part of the distortion and apply (or clone) copies of the selection to other parts of your image:

- ✓ **Displace:** Displace copies the amount of displacement at the starting point of the distortion to unfrozen parts of your image. You can use this mode to displace parts of your image to a different position in the image.

- ✓ **Amplitwist:** Amplitwist displaces, scales, and rotates unfrozen areas to match the distortion that exists at the starting point.

- ✓ **Affine:** Affine does much the same thing as Amplitwist, using displacement, scaling, rotation, and skew in the distortion to modify unfrozen areas to match those distortions that exist at the starting point.

Each time you click the mouse button, you create a new starting point, so if you're trying to extend a distortion effect from a single starting point, don't release your mouse button until you're done using the Reconstruct tool.

Using Displace, Amplitwist, and Affine

The Displace, Amplitwist, and Affine Reconstruct modes use different combinations of distortion factors — such as displacement, scaling, rotation, or skew. Unlike the other modes, the Reconstruct button isn't available for these three. You can use these modes only with the Reconstruct tool. To use Displace, Amplitwist, or Affine, follow these steps:

1. **Open an image to work on and choose Filter⇨Liquify.**

2. **Select the Reconstruct tool.**

3. **Select one of the three modes — Displace, Amplitwist, or Affine — from the Reconstruct Mode pop-up menu in the Tool Options area.**

4. **Click a place in the image where you want to clone the applied distortion.**

5. **Drag with the mouse in the unfrozen areas to apply that distortion.**

6. **To change the origin of the distortions being copied, click again anywhere in a distorted area to select a new sampling point. Then resume dragging in unfrozen areas.**

   Your image takes on a distorted appearance, like the one shown in Figure 3-7.

7. **When you finish, click OK to apply the distortion.**

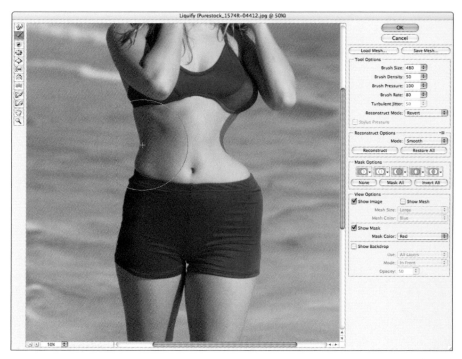

Purestock

Figure 3-7: Undo your distortions by using one of the various flavors of the Reconstruct tool.

Book VIII

Retouching and Restoration

Although taking the perfect photo is a great goal, it's one that is often just beyond our reach. Not to worry though, if you're a Photoshop owner. In this book, you find out what you need to know about correcting color in all its permutations — contrast, saturation, replacing, remapping, and so on. You find details on using the focus and toning tools to manually adjust the tones, textures, and colors in your images. I also give you details on how you can give your images a digital spa day with the two Healing Brushes and the Patch and Red Eye tools. You learn how to remove blemishes, wrinkles, and every other one of nature's imperfections. After you master these techniques, you'll be on your way to doing your own digital extreme makeovers. But whatever you do, don't leave this book without checking out the Vanishing Point feature. This single command alone may be well worth the money you plunked down for Photoshop.

Chapter 1: Enhancing Images with Adjustments

*P*hotoshop can provide magical transformations to images, making them unrecognizable from the original. But sometimes what you really want is simply to make an image look the same as the original — only better. Perhaps the colors are a little too warm, or the shadows a bit inky, but you don't want an image that looks more processed than a freeze-dried floral arrangement. You'd be happy to have everyone admire your image without a clue that you've made major corrections in Photoshop.

Welcome to the world of image enhancements. This chapter concentrates on the things you can do to correct color, contrast, hue, and color saturation. After you master the basic tools, you can explore some even more sophisticated things that you can do by using features such as Photoshop's Adjustment Layers (in Book V, Chapter 1), which let you dynamically apply your changes in remarkably flexible ways. But before you dive into image adjustments, make sure you remove any flaws, such as dust, scratches, blemishes, and other nasty items, from your image. Check out Book VIII, Chapter 3 to find out about fixing imperfections.

Introducing the Histogram Panel

One of the first things you want to do before you make any color or tonal adjustments to your image is to take a good look at the quality and distribution of the tones throughout your image. I don't mean just eyeballing the composite image on your screen. I'm talking about getting inside your image and looking at its guts with the Histogram panel — and keeping it onscreen so you can see its constant feedback on your image adjustments.

A histogram displays the *tonal range* (also referred to as the *key type*) of an image, as shown in Figure 1-1. It shows how the pixels are distributed by graphing the number of pixels at each of the 256 brightness levels in an image. On this graph, pixels with the same brightness level are stacked in bars along a vertical axis. The higher the line from this axis, the greater the number of pixels at that brightness level. You can view the distribution for each color channel separately or for the composite image as a whole.

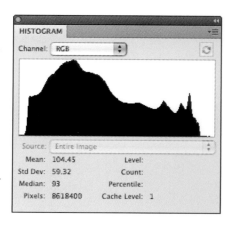

Figure 1-1: The Histogram panel displays how pixels are distributed at each of the 256 brightness levels.

From this graph, you can then determine whether the image contains enough detail in the shadow, midtone, and highlight areas. This information helps you determine what image adjustments you may need to make. The following steps walk you through the basics of using the panel and interpreting the information you find there:

1. **Choose Window⇨Histogram to bring up this graphical wonder.**

   By default, the histogram displays the tonal range of the whole image, in the composite image's color mode, such as RGB, CMYK, Grayscale, and so on. For details on color modes, see Book II, Chapter 2.

2. **Select Compact View, Expanded View, or All Channels View from the Histogram panel pop-up menu:**

   • *Compact View:* The default. Displays only a histogram of the whole image (or your chosen selection or channel) with no controls or statistics.

   • *Expanded View:* Shows a histogram with statistics and controls for selecting and viewing the histogram of individual channels. This view also has controls for refreshing the histogram to show uncached data and choosing a selected layer (on the Source pop-up menu). Refer to Figure 1-1 to see this view.

   • *All Channels View:* Shown in Figure 1-2, this view displays all the options of the Expanded View, plus the individual histograms for each color channel. You may also choose to view your channels in color.

3. **Choose a different source in the Channel and/or Source pop-up menu, if needed.**

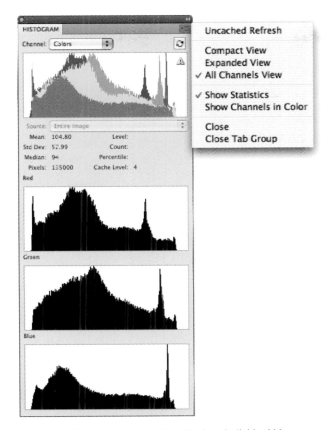

Figure 1-2: The All Channels View displays individual histograms for each color channel, as well as the composite channel.

For example, instead of seeing a histogram for an entire image, you can display the histogram of an individual channel, alpha channel, or spot channel from the Channel pop-up menu. You can also focus on the selected layer or an adjustment layer. Just select the layer in the Layers panel and choose Selected Layer or Adjustment Composite from the Source pop-up menu.

For more on adjustment layers, see Book V, Chapter 1.

4. **If the Cached Data Warning icon (a triangle with an exclamation mark) appears in the upper-right corner of the histogram, click the Uncached Refresh button just above the icon to see a histogram that reflects the image's current state.**

The warning lets you know that Photoshop is reading the histogram from cache rather than showing your image's current state. *Cache* is a reserved, high-speed section of your computer's memory. The image cache allows the histogram to display faster because it's calculating the histogram based on a representative sampling of the pixels in your image.

Unless it's really bogging down your workflow, I recommend viewing your image's histograms by using uncached data.

5. **With the Histogram panel displaying the controls and data you want to check, examine the tonal range in the histogram.**

   An image with good tonal range displays pixels in all areas. An image with poor tonal range has gaps in the histogram, as shown in Figure 1-3.

   The rest of this chapter explains ways you can correct color problems that you find.

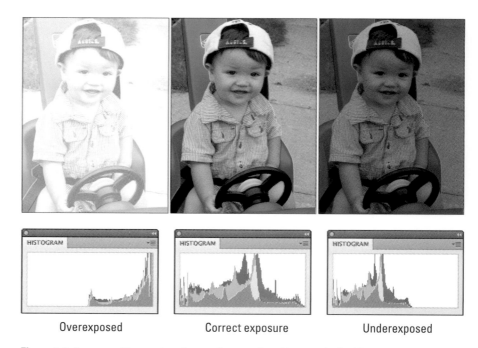

Overexposed Correct exposure Underexposed

Figure 1-3: Images with poor tonal range have noticeable gaps in the histogram.

6. **If you're into numbers, check the statistics to evaluate your image, as well.**

   See the sidebar "Understanding the histogram statistics," in this chapter, for how to interpret these details.

   Position your cursor within the histogram to see statistics about a specific value. Drag your cursor within the histogram to see statistics about a range of values. (Photoshop highlights the range.)

Understanding the histogram statistics

The Histogram panel gives you all kinds of statistics about the pixels in your image. Some of these statistics, such as Standard Deviation, may be for those who live in the land of Probability and Statistics. But you may be able to glean some useful information from the other statistics that can help you in your image-adjusting tasks. Here's a brief explanation of each statistic:

✓ **Mean:** Average intensity value

✓ **Standard Deviation:** How much the intensity values vary

✓ **Median:** Middle value of the intensity values.

✓ **Pixels:** Total number of pixels used to represent the histogram

✓ **Cache Level:** The current level of image cache used to calculate the histogram

These statistics display a value only when you position or drag your cursor in the histogram. (Each value corresponds only to the portion of the histogram under your cursor.)

✓ **Level:** Intensity level

✓ **Count:** The total number of pixels corresponding to that intensity level

✓ **Percentile:** The number of cumulative pixels (in percentages) at or below that level, from 0% (left) to 100% (right)

When you make adjustments based on problems you see in the histogram, be sure to select any Preview options in the dialog boxes of your image adjustments, such as Levels. That way, the Histogram panel displays both the original and adjusted histograms, as shown in Figure 1-4.

Choosing Automatic Color Correctors

Photoshop has three automatic correction tools that can, in many cases, improve appearance with a simple click of a menu command: Auto Tone, Auto Color, and Auto Contrast. Before you use them, first note their pros and cons:

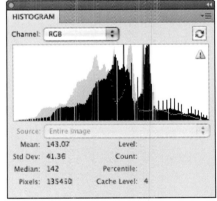

Figure 1-4: View both the original and adjusted histograms.

✓ **The upside:** These controls are easy to use. You don't need to know much about toning, color balance, or contrast to use the automatic correctors. (That's why they're automatic.) But you can find out more about correcting tone, color balance, and contrast in sections later in this chapter, when I explain how to make adjustments manually.

> ✔ **The downside:** An automatic control's ease of use almost always comes with a downside. In the case of the color correctors, none likely can do as good a job as you can do manually, and sometimes automatic controls even do more harm than good.

If you have an average image (one that doesn't require a great deal of correction), you can try the automatic color correctors to see whether they help. I explain how in the following sections. If you don't want to try the automatic controls, apply the manual tools explained in sections later in this chapter to produce the exact look you want.

You have the choice of applying the automatic color correctors, as well as any of the other image adjustments, to all or just a portion of your image. To isolate any adjustment to just a portion of your image, either make a selection (see Book III) or apply the adjustment to a layer. (See Book V.)

Auto Tone

The Auto Tone command, formerly known as Auto Levels, uses a bit of built-in Photoshop intelligence to automatically apply the Levels command (discussed in the section "Leveling for better contrast," later in the chapter) to your image.

Auto Tone works best with average images that could use a bit of tweaking but have a lot of detail in the *highlights* (the brightest portions of an image that contain detail), *shadows* (the darkest portions of an image that contain detail), and midtones.

Auto Tone defines the very lightest and darkest pixels of each of the three colors as white and black, respectively, and then arranges the midtone pixels in between. While it balances the tones in your image, the command may reduce colorcasts or even introduce some. You can fine-tune the color manually after Auto Tone has done its work.

To try out the Auto Tone command, just choose Image➪Auto Tone or press Shift+Ctrl+L (Shift+⌘+L on the Mac).

Although Auto Tone can improve your contrast, it may also produce an unwanted *colorcast* (a slight trace of color). If this happens, cancel the command and try the Auto Contrast command. If that still doesn't improve the contrast, try the Levels command instead. Even better, try your Levels adjustment on an adjustment layer. If it doesn't work, you can always delete it. No harm, no muss. For more on adjustment layers, see Book V, Chapter 1.

Auto Color

The Auto Color command adjusts both the color and contrast of an image, based on the shadows, midtones, and highlights that it finds in the image. You usually use this command to remove a colorcast (or bias) or balance the color in your image. Sometimes, using Auto Color can be helpful in correcting oversaturated or undersaturated colors, as well. You can access the command by choosing Image⇨Auto Color or by pressing Shift+Ctrl+B (Shift+⌘+B on the Mac).

Although Auto Color can do a good job on its own, you can customize the parameters it uses to make its color corrections in the Auto Color Correction Options dialog box, which I discuss in the section "Setting Auto Color Correction Options," later in this chapter. Figure 1-5 shows an image corrected by using Auto Tone and Auto Color.

Figure 1-5: Using Auto Tone and Auto Color quickly improved the contrast and colors of this snapshot.

Auto Contrast

Like its manually operated cousin, the Brightness/Contrast command, the Auto Contrast command fiddles with the overall contrast and colors (if you're working with a color image) in an image, instead of making adjustments to each color individually. Auto Contrast converts the lightest and darkest pixels to white and black, respectively, making all highlights in the image lighter and all shadows darker without changing the color values. This command may not do as good a job at improving contrast as Auto Tone does, but it retains the color balance of an image and doesn't cause any nasty colorcasts.

Book VIII
Chapter 1

Enhancing Images with Adjustments

Try using this command on hazy images. If you find it overdoes the adjustment, try choosing Edit➪Fade and bringing down the Opacity level to blend the adjusted image with your original image. For more on using the Fade command, see Book VII, Chapter 1.

To use Auto Contrast, choose Image➪Auto Contrast or press Alt+Shift+Ctrl+L (Option+Shift+⌘+L on the Mac).

Setting Auto Color Correction Options

You can use the Auto Color Correction Options dialog box to tweak exactly how Photoshop applies its Auto Tone, Auto Color, and Auto Contrast controls, as well as for the manually operated Levels and Curves commands. You can apply the settings only to a particular image-editing session or save the settings as defaults for all your Photoshop work.

Setting color correction options is a more advanced task, and you can make best use of the tools if you already understand manual color and contrast corrections. You can brush up on your color theory, too, in Book II, Chapter 3.

To customize the automatic options, follow these steps:

1. **Open an image and choose Image➪Adjustments➪Levels or press Ctrl+L (⌘+L on the Mac).**

   You can also use the Curves command by pressing Ctrl+M (⌘+M on the Mac).

2. **Click the Options button in the dialog box to access the Auto Color Correction Options dialog box, shown in Figure 1-6.**

3. **In the Algorithms area, click the method you want Photoshop to use to adjust the tones.**

   Your choices include

   Figure 1-6: After you know the basics, customize the auto correction options.

   • *Enhance Monochromatic Contrast:* This option applies the same changes to the Red, Green, and Blue channels, making brighter areas appear lighter and shadow areas appear darker, with no changes made to the colors. (This is the method used by the Auto Contrast command.)

   • *Enhance Per Channel Contrast:* This option individually adjusts the red, green, and blue colors so that each has its own best balance of light and dark tones, even if the color balance changes a bit. (This is the algorithm used by the Auto Tone command.)

- *Find Dark & Light Colors:* This option locates the average lightest and darkest pixels, and uses their values to maximize the contrast of the image. (This is the algorithm used by the Auto Color command.)

4. **Select the Snap Neutral Midtones check box if you want Photoshop to base its gamma, or midtone, correction values around a neutral color located in the image.**

The Auto Color command uses this option.

5. **In the Target Colors & Clipping area, enter a value in each of the Clip text boxes.**

Setting clipping values between 0.5% and 1% eliminates the too-dark and too-light pixels.

These values adjust the percentage of black and white pixels that Photoshop removes from the darkest and lightest areas of the image. This option is useful because every image includes some very dark pixels that contain no real image information, as well as some very light pixels that are completely washed out. Factoring in these two kinds of pixels when you adjust tonal values is a waste. By setting the clipping values between 0.5% and 1%, you leave these no-good pixels out of the picture, so to speak.

6. **Click the Shadows, Midtones, or Highlights swatch.**

The Color Picker appears, allowing you to set a preferred value for the darkest, medium, and lightest areas.

7. **Select the Eyedropper tool from the Tools panel.**

8. **Move your mouse over the image and locate the dark, middle, or light tone you want to use. Click it when you find it.**

9. **Click OK to exit the Color Picker. Repeat Steps 6 through 8 for each of the three colors you want to change.**

When you move the mouse over the image, the values in the Info panel change, helping you pick the shadow, midtone, or highlight area you want.

10. **Back in the Auto Color Corrections Options dialog box, select the Save as Defaults check box to store the settings you just made for subsequent use in any Photoshop session.**

If you don't select the check box, Photoshop applies the changes you made to only the current session.

11. **Click OK to exit the Auto Color Correction Options dialog box.**

Your options are now customized. Note that these changes also affect the Auto buttons in the Levels and Curve dialog boxes.

Using Simple Color Correctors

Photoshop has several simple manual tools you can use to fix color in ways that are different from the Auto Tone, Auto Contrast, and Auto Color commands. They're the Brightness/Contrast control, Color Balance, Shadows/Highlights, Exposure, HDR Toning, the ever-popular Variations tool, and the Desaturate command (all found in the Image⇨Adjustments menu). In the following sections, you can find out when to use (and when not to use) each of them.

Applying Brightness/Contrast

Beginners gravitate to the Brightness/Contrast control because it seems so intuitive to use. If your image is too dark, move a slider to make it lighter; if it's too light, move the same slider to make it darker. Right? You can fix an image that's overly contrasty or overly flat-looking the same way. Right?

Maybe.

I say *Maybe* and not flat out *No* because, in recent versions, Adobe has improved the command, as demonstrated in Figure 1-7. Instead of applying all its adjustments equally to all areas of your image (whether they need it or not), it now applies adjustments proportionately to your image, like the Levels and Curves adjustments do. Just avoid the Use Legacy option, which reverts the Brightness/Contrast command back to its pre-CS3 algorithm, thereby turning your image into a mess.

Even though Adobe has improved the Brightness/Contrast command, you're better off using Levels and Curves, which can tailor your image enhancements to the exact portions of the image you want to work with.

Figure 1-7: The Brightness/Contrast command attempts to improve tonal values in your image.

Tweaking with the Color Balance controls

With an understanding of color theory (which I explain in Book II, Chapter 3), you can probably use the Color Balance controls to make some simple changes to the color in your image. The difficult part is recognizing exactly which color you need to add or subtract from your image in the first place.

Resisting the urge to go nuts with sliders

If you're like me, you like clicking options, adjusting values, and sliding sliders back and forth. Thankfully, Photoshop is happy to oblige you with options to make you feel so powerful that you can take on any project.

Was that a sinister laugh I heard? Easy there, partner. I'm about to tell you something that will break your heart at first — but you'll thank me later: Always pick a single slider and stick with it when you're trying to compensate for any colorcast. Moving two sliders is a waste because you can accomplish anything you want with just one.

For example, if you move both the Cyan/Red and Magenta/Green sliders an equal amount to the left (adding cyan and magenta), you're actually just adding blue. Moving three sliders is even worse because, depending on the amount and direction of movement, the three sliders are likely to at least partially cancel each other out or multiply the effects. However, if a cast is in just one area, such as the shadows, and a different colorcast is in another area, it may be useful to do more than one adjustment.

Colors are subtler than you might think. For example, a slight colorcast toward cyan can look a lot like a slightly green or blue colorcast. Is your image too red, or does it have too much magenta?

Use the Variations command that I describe in the section "Correcting colorcast with Variations," later in this chapter, to figure out how to tell the various colorcasts apart. The Variations command displays each of the different types of colorcasts in an array so you can compare them.

To use the Color Balance controls, follow these steps:

1. **Choose Image⇨Adjustments⇨Color Balance or press Ctrl+B (⌘+B on the Mac) to access the Color Balance dialog box.**

2. **Choose the Shadows, Midtones, or Highlights option to select the tones of an image you want to work on.**

   Usually, Midtones is the best choice, unless your image has a colorcast in the shadows or highlights that doesn't affect the overall image. That can sometimes happen when a subject is close to a colored wall or other object that reflects light onto, say, the shadowed side of a subject.

3. **Select the Preserve Luminosity option.**

   When this option is selected, Photoshop modifies the colors of the image, but the brightness and contrast of the tones stay the same. If you're not happy with the results, deselect the option.

4. **Move the Cyan/Red, Magenta/Green, or Yellow/Blue slider to add or subtract color, watching the effects of your adjustments on the original image.**

The Color Levels boxes show the amount of each color that Photoshop adds and subtracts while you move the sliders. Figure 1-8 shows an example of subtracting green to improve the color in an image.

Purestock

Figure 1-8: Use the Color Balance adjustment to remove colorcasts from an image.

The colors are arranged by their opposites on the color wheel. Dragging the slider toward Cyan adds cyan to the image and subtracts its complement, red. Dragging toward Green adds green to the image and subtracts magenta.

Fixing lighting with Shadows/Highlights

The Shadows/Highlights adjustment is a great feature that offers a quick and easy method for correcting over- and underexposed areas in your image. This command works well on a subject photographed with the light source coming from behind (backlit), giving that subject a dark foreground. The adjustment can also bring out the detail in harsh shadow areas in subjects shot in bright, overhead light, as shown in Figure 1-9.

Original   Adjusted with Shadows/Highlights

Figure 1-9: The Shadows/Highlights adjustment is a quick way to correct the lighting in your images.

To familiarize yourself with this tool, follow these steps:

1. **Open an image in dire need of repair and choose Image⇨Adjustments⇨ Shadows/Highlights.**

   Note that you can also adjust CMYK images, as well as RGB.

   When the dialog box appears, the correction is automatically applied in your preview. If you don't see any change, make sure you've selected the Preview check box. The default settings in the dialog box are meant to correct backlit images, so they may or may not do the right correction job for you with the default settings.

2. **Move the Amount slider to adjust the amount of correction for your Shadows and/or your Highlights.**

   The higher the percentage, the lighter the shadows and the darker the highlights. You can also enter a value in the percentage text box.

3. **If you're happy with the results, you can click OK and be done with the adjustment. However, if you crave more control, click the Show More Options check box at the bottom of the dialog box.**

   A whole array of sliders magically appears, as shown in Figure 1-10.

4. **Drag the Tonal Width slider to increase or decrease the range of tones adjusted in the shadows or highlights.**

The lower the percentage, the narrower the range of tones that are affected. For example, by using a very low percentage, only the darkest parts of the shadow or the lightest parts of the highlight are corrected. A higher percentage includes a wide range of tones, including midtone areas. The appropriate percentage to use varies among images, so start with the default setting of 50% and work in small increments from there.

If, when lightening the shadow areas, you find the midtones and highlights getting too light, reduce the Tonal Width percentage of the Shadows. But, if you start seeing artifacts, you've set the percentage too high.

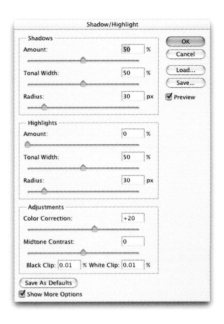

Figure 1-10: The Shadows/Highlights dialog box offers controls for adjusting the amount of correction in your shadow, midtone, and highlight areas.

5. **Drag the Radius slider to increase or decrease the number of pixels used in the local neighborhood.**

   To fix lighting, this command lightens or darkens pixels according to the luminance (brightness) of the surrounding pixels, technically called a *local neighborhood.* The best local neighborhood size depends on the particular image, so play with this slider and view the results. If the Radius is too small, your main subject may lack contrast. Conversely, if it's too large, your background may be overly bright or dark. Adobe recommends setting the radius to approximately half the size of the main subject in your image. So, if your subject takes up roughly 600 pixels, then set your radius to 300 pixels.

6. **Make additional changes in the Adjustments area, as needed:**

   - *Color Correction:* Available for color images only, this control enables you to correct the colors in *only* the adjusted portions of your image. Often, when you increase or decrease the Amount of Shadows or Highlights, you bring out the "hidden" colors. Generally, higher Color Correction values make colors more saturated, whereas lower values make colors more desaturated.

   - *Brightness:* Available for grayscale images only. Move the slider left to darken and right to lighten.

- *Midtone Contrast.* Move the slider left to reduce contrast and right to increase contrast. Just be aware that when you increase the Midtone Contrast, you may also undesirably darken shadow areas and lighten highlight areas.

- *Black Clip/White Clip:* As I explain in the section "Setting Auto Color Correction Options," earlier in this chapter, setting clipping values between 0.5% and 1% eliminates the too-dark and too-light pixels.

7. **Click the Save as Defaults button to save and make your settings the defaults.**

   If you want to reset the settings back to the original defaults, hold down Shift and click the Save as Defaults button. You can save as many settings as you want. Click the Load button to reload a particular setting. To save the settings as new settings, but not as the defaults, click the Save button.

8. **Click OK to apply the adjustment and exit the dialog box.**

Adjusting exposure

This Exposure adjustment is primarily meant to correct tonal values of High Dynamic Range (HDR) images, which are 32 bits. (In layman's terms, the bits indicate how much information is stored about the color. The more bits, the better the color.) But you can apply Exposure adjustments to 16-bit or even 8-bit images, as well. This command works by using a linear color space, also known as gamma 1.0, rather than your image's color space, to make tonal adjustments. Figure 1-11 shows an example of an image helped by this adjustment.

If you use the Exposure adjustment with 16-bit or 8-bit images, the slider's adjustments may be too drastic. Hold down the Ctrl (⌘ on the Mac) key when your mouse is over the number field and drag to access the scrubby sliders, which offer a less-dramatic adjustment when you slide the control. Also, keep an eye on your image. The Exposure adjustment sometimes *clips,* or loses, data on lower-bit images.

1. **Choose Image↷Adjustments↷Exposure.**

2. **Adjust any of the following:**

   - *Exposure:* This option adjusts mainly the highlights and pretty much ignores the darkest shadows.

   - *Offset:* This option darkens the shadow and midtone values, and leaves the highlights alone.

   - *Gamma Correction:* This option adjusts the image's gamma, or *midtone,* values.

Figure 1-11: Fix tonal values with the Exposure adjustment.

To apply the Exposure adjustment, follow these steps:

3. **Use the Eyedroppers to adjust the luminance, or *brightness*, values in the image.**

   Note that this is different from Levels, where the eyedroppers adjust all the color channels:

   - *Set Black Point Eyedropper:* Sets the Offset. The pixel you click becomes the black point.

   - *Set White Point Eyedropper:* Sets the Exposure. The pixel you click becomes the white point.

   - *Midtone Eyedropper:* Sets the Exposure. The pixel you click becomes the middle gray value.

4. **Click OK to apply the adjustment.**

   To save the settings, click the Save Preset button (to the right of OK). Name the preset and click Save in the Save dialog box. Apply the preset later by clicking the Load button.

Using HDR Toning

This new adjustment enables you to apply HDR contrast and exposure settings to your images. While mostly aimed toward 32-bit images, it can also be applied to 16-bit and 8-bit images.

To apply the HDR Toning adjustment, follow these steps:

1. **Open a 32-, 16-, or 8-bit image.**

   Make sure the image is in RGB or Grayscale mode. Also, your image cannot contain any layers and must consist of a Background only

2. **Choose Image⇨Adjustments⇨HDR Toning.**

3. **Choose your desired method from the pop-up menu and any subsequent settings.**

   For an explanation of these settings, see Book IX, Chapter 2.

You can use HDR Toning to create a stylized appearance — oversaturated, overly sharp, and illustrative, as shown in Figure 1-12. Play with the Glow and Detail sliders under the Local Adaptation method and experiment.

Original   Adjusted with HDR Toning

Figure 1-12: Create a stylized look with HDR Toning.

Correcting colorcast with Variations

Photoshop's Variations feature is a variation (so to speak) on the professional photographer's *ring around* (a set of color prints, each made with slightly different color balance) or *test strip* (a single print of an image made so that each section is shown using a different color balance). Both tools let you view several renditions of an image and choose the best one visually by comparing them. You might want to use Variations when you're unsure exactly how the color is biased and you want to compare several versions of an image to see exactly what the colorcast is.

Although not as sophisticated as some color correction techniques, the Variations feature has the advantage of being quick and simple, and it doesn't require a lot of training to use.

The Putting It Together project "Correcting Tinted, Faded Photos," in this chapter, walks you through the steps for using the Variations dialog box.

Washing out color with Desaturate

Sometimes, you don't want any color at all. Photoshop's Desaturate command can wash all the color out of a layer or selection.

Just because you can do something doesn't mean you should. Use this command with caution because neither the Desaturate command nor Photoshop's Image⇨Mode⇨Grayscale command is the best technique for converting a color image to monochrome. Simply removing the color can produce an image that appears to be too low in contrast, which is another kettle of fish altogether. See Book II, Chapter 2, along with the section "Converting to Black & White," later in this chapter, for a better way to create grayscale images.

However, if you simply want to eliminate the color from a layer or image selection quickly, the Desaturate command does the job. To apply it, select your desired layer in the Layers panel, select the area you want to operate on, and then choose Image⇨Adjustments⇨Desaturate or press Shift+Ctrl+U (Shift+⌘+U on the Mac).

Using the Saturation control in the Hue/Saturation command gives you better control over the degree of desaturation you desire, while leaving the image looking richer. I show you how to play with saturation by using the Hue/Saturation controls in the section "Getting colorful with Hue/Saturation," later in this chapter.

Putting It Together

Correcting Tinted, Faded Photos

In this Putting It Together project, I employ the Variations feature to restore the color in a scan of a color print originally made in 1965. Unfortunately, the years have not been kind to this photo; it has a slight, but annoying, greenish tinge because the magenta dye layer of the print has faded. As a result, the other two color layers, cyan and yellow, appear proportionately stronger when compared to the magenta that remains, and cyan and yellow make a shade of green.

I plan to use the Variations feature of Photoshop to restore the magenta layer in this photo that's green with age.

To correct colorcast in an old photograph by using the Photoshop Variations feature, follow these steps:

1. In Photoshop, open an old, fading photo that needs color correction.

In this case, I'm using an old, faded, greenish-looking picture, shown in the figure, but any colorcast works.

continued

continued

2. **Choose Image⇨Adjustments⇨Variations from the menu bar.**

The Variations dialog box appears.

3. **Select the Show Clipping option to tell Photoshop to show any areas of the image that will be "overwhelmed" by the correction you're contemplating.**

That is, no new information is added.

4. **If you want to use corrections you saved, load those settings by clicking the Load button. Otherwise, skip to Step 5.**

5. **Make adjustments with the Fine/Coarse slider.**

In my example, the greenish picture needs some magenta, so I dragged the Fine/Coarse slider to the left. I wanted to have a smaller increment of change when I adjusted the color.

You can also click one of the tick marks to move the slider to that position. Photoshop doesn't allow setting the control to any of the intermediate positions between the marks.

6. **Make sure that you've selected the Midtones radio button, and then click the Preview window containing the amount of color you want to add.**

Watch the Current Pick thumbnail, which reflects the correction.

In my case, I need to click the More Magenta image.

Click several times if your initial application isn't enough or click other Preview windows to add additional colors.

Photoshop applies your corrections only to the middle tones of the image. In many cases, that's sufficient. However, sometimes shadows take on a particular hue, or the highlights may gain colorcasts of their own.

7. **Click the Highlights and/or Shadows radio buttons to add colors only to those parts of the photo.**

Variations isn't the best tool to make complex color corrections, so be careful.

You might be able to see a highlight color in the shadows under the pillow, most noticeable in the More Magenta preview. The highlight is the Clipping indicator showing that the change made by that Preview window is too much for that particular area of the picture. That is, Photoshop can't add any more magenta to the highlighted area without losing detail in the image.

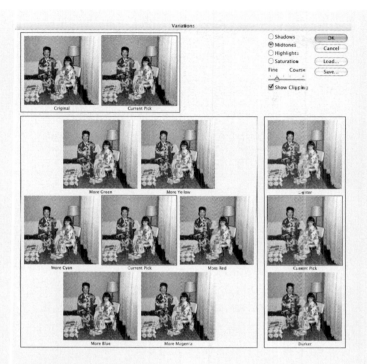

8. **Click the Darker preview (in the lower-right corner of the dialog box) to make the photo a little darker.**

   Adjust the Fine/Coarse slider to adjust the amount of change, or gradually darken and lighten the image by clicking multiple times.

   In my case, only one click is necessary.

9. **Click the Saturation radio button to brighten the colors and use the Fine/Coarse slider to control how much saturation you add or remove.**

   The Variations feature also lets you adjust the purity of color, or *saturation,* of the colors in an image. Now, only three previews appear: a less-saturated version, the current choice, and a more-saturated version. My photo was washed out, or under-saturated, so I clicked the More Saturation button.

10. **To save your settings, click the Save button, apply a name to the settings, and store them in the folder of your choice.**

continued

**Book VIII
Chapter 1**

**Enhancing Images
with Adjustments**

continued

I recommend saving your settings, especially if you're working on a copy of the original image and want to apply the same corrections later, or if you plan to correct several photos that have the same color defects.

Working with Professional Color Correctors

The simple color correctors I discuss in the section "Using Simple Color Correctors," earlier in this chapter, usually aren't enough to provide thorough color correction if you have a really problematic image on your hands. Fortunately, Photoshop has the kind of professional tools needed to make sophisticated color corrections for higher-end color printing. You don't have to be a pro to use the Levels or Curves commands, nor to work with the Hue/Saturation controls. But you'll feel like one after you master these powerful tools.

Leveling for better contrast

If you want to adjust tonal values of images (the brightness or darkness of tones) or correct colors (the relationship between the colors), the Levels command is the tool for you. It offers more control than the Auto Tone command, which I discuss in the section "Auto Tone," earlier in this chapter. The

Levels command is also a much more sophisticated tool than the Brightness/Contrast control because you can work with individual tones, brightening or darkening individual tones as you want, and you have a great deal more information to help you make your choices.

Open the Levels dialog box, shown in Figure 1-13, by pressing Ctrl+L (⌘+L on the Mac) or choosing Image➪Adjustments➪Levels. The graph shown in the center of the dialog box is a histogram, which I describe in detail in the section "Introducing the Histogram Panel," earlier in this chapter. You can use this dialog box, histogram and all, for evaluating and adjusting levels in the following ways:

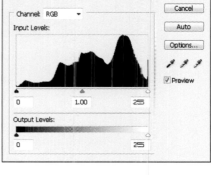

Figure 1-13: The Levels dialog box offers controls for adjusting the contrast in your image.

✔ **Visually check the distribution of dark, midtone, and light values.**

✔ **View separate histograms for each channel.** The default histogram displays information for the entire image. To see the histogram of an individual channel, select it from the Channel pop-up menu. For an RGB image, you can view the Red, Green, and Blue channels. For a CMYK image, you can view the Cyan, Magenta, Yellow, and Black channels. You can view the histograms of each channel simultaneously by using the Histogram panel.

✔ **Adjust the black and white points based on the histogram.** The three triangles at the bottom of the histogram, in black, gray, and white, represent the shadow on the left, midtone in the middle, and highlight on the right. Even though they're located where they are, many images have no black tones at the far-left side of the scale nor white tones at the far-right side.

One of the simplest corrections you can do is to move the black and white sliders so that they actually correspond to the pixels containing dark and light tones. Simply slide the black triangle so that it corresponds to the first true black pixels in the image (the beginning of the histogram), and then move the white triangle to align it with the lightest pixels (the end of the histogram). That ensures that Photoshop doesn't waste tones by allocating them to areas of the image that actually have no image detail. Figure 1-14 shows an example of an image that was rescued by the use of the Levels adjustment.

Book VIII
Chapter 1

Enhancing Images
with Adjustments

Figure 1-14: Applying the Levels command to a dark photo dramatically improves the contrast.

✔ **See exactly what happens when you use the Auto Tone command.**
When you click the Auto button, which applies the same adjustments as the Auto Tone command, Photoshop applies its own suggested changes, resetting the white point and the black point, and redistributing the gray values of the pixels in between. Afterward, the histogram shows that the pixels fill the complete range from white to black.

Setting black and white points manually

For more control, you can use the Eyedropper tools in the Levels dialog box to set the black and white points. Just follow these steps:

1. **Open an image and choose Image⇨Adjustments⇨Levels.**

   Make sure you have the Info panel open (Window⇨Info), and display the HSB and RGB color modes. (To do this, select Panel Options from the Info panel pop-up menu and select HSB and RGB from the Color Readout pop-up menus.) See Book II, Chapters 2 and 3 for more on color modes.

   Remember that you can also apply certain adjustments, such as Levels, via an adjustment layer rather than directly to the image itself. Adjustment layers provide more editing flexibility if you later decide you need to tweak the adjustment. For more on adjustment layers, see Book V, Chapter 1.

2. **Select the White Eyedropper tool and move it around the image while watching the Info panel.**

3. **Look for the lightest white in the image, which may be anywhere from 90% to 100% in brightness (the B under HSB). Select that point by clicking.**

4. **Using the Black Eyedropper tool, repeat the process outlined in Steps 2 and 3 to select the darkest black in the image, which may be anywhere from 0% to 10% in brightness (B).**

   The combination of these two choices redistributes the pixels from pure white to pure black.

You can also set the white and black points by moving the position of the white and black triangles on the input sliders (just under the histogram). Or you can enter numbers in the Input Levels boxes. The three boxes represent the black, gray, and white triangles, respectively. Use the numbers 0 to 255 in the white and black boxes.

5. **Use the Gray Eyedropper tool to remove any colorcasts. Select an area of your image that should be neutral gray, one in which the Info panel shows equal values of red, green, and blue.**

   Note that the Gray Eyedropper tool isn't available when you're working on grayscale images.

   Although you generally make changes to the entire document by using the RGB channel, you can apply changes to any one of an image's component color channels by selecting the specific channel in the Channel pop-up menu at the top of the Levels dialog box. (Refer to Figure 1-13.) You can also make adjustments to selected areas only. This can be helpful when one area of your image needs adjusting but others don't. See Book III, Chapter 1 for details on making selections.

6. **Adjust the output sliders at the very bottom of the Levels dialog box.**

   Moving the black triangle to the right reduces the contrast in the shadows and lightens the image. Moving the white triangle to the left reduces the contrast in the highlights and darkens the image.

7. **Adjust the midtones with the gray triangle slider. (It appears between the black and white input sliders, just under the histogram.)**

   The values you're adjusting are called the *gamma values*.

   Dragging this triangle to the left lightens the midtones. Dragging it to the right darkens the midtones while leaving the highlights and shadows alone. You can also move the gray triangle by entering numbers from 9.99 to 0.1 in the center option box. The default value (1.0) lies exactly in the middle of the range.

   If you're working with a series of similar images (such as a bunch of video captures), you can save the settings to reuse them later.

   You can also select a preset Levels setting, such as Increase Contrast or Lighten Shadows, from the Preset pop-up menu in the Levels dialog box. Use a preset as your starting point and then fine-tune the adjustment manually by adjusting the input sliders, as described in the preceding steps.

8. **Click the Save button to store your settings.**

   This step saves the settings, but it doesn't apply them. Just click the Load button to retrieve them.

9. **Click OK to apply your settings and exit the dialog box.**

Adjusting curves for hard-to-correct photos

The Curves command is one of the most advanced Photoshop correction tools available, offering sophisticated control over the brightness, contrast, and midtone *(gamma)* levels in an image; I'm talking about control that's far beyond what the Levels and Brightness/Contrast dialog boxes offer. This section introduces you to the functions of the Curves command, but you'll want to practice using it a great deal to gain the kind of experience you need to work with it effectively.

Whereas the Brightness/Contrast dialog box lets you change an image globally, and the Levels command allows you to change the shadows, highlights, and midtones separately, Curves goes far beyond either of those settings. It lets you change pixel values at 16 different points (which include start and end points) along an image's tonal range. You can work with the combined Red, Green, and Blue color channels (or CMYK channels) or apply your changes to the individual colors. Often, images that just can't be fixed to your satisfaction with Levels can be helped with the Curves adjustment, as shown in Figure 1-15.

PhotoDisc/Getty Images

Figure 1-15: The Curves adjustment offers more control and sophistication than many other color correction tools.

Working with the Curves dialog box

You access the Curves dialog box, shown in Figure 1-16, by choosing Image⇔Adjustments⇔Curves or by pressing Ctrl+M (⌘+M on the Mac).

The following tips help you to begin understanding how to interpret the information and use the tools in this dialog box:

✔ **The horizontal axis maps the brightness values as they are before image correction (input).**

✔ **The vertical axis maps the brightness values after correction (output).** Each axis represents a continuum of 256 levels, divided into four parts by finely dotted lines. In the default mode, the lower-left corner represents 0,0 (pure black) and the upper-right corner is 255,255 (pure white). By default, the dialog box shows a 4-x-4 (quarter tone) grid; Alt-click (Option-click on the Mac) inside the grid to toggle it to a 10-x-10 (10% increment) grid. If you have the Curve Display Options visible, you can use the Quarter Tone or 10% Increment display buttons.

✔ **Whenever you open the Curves dialog box, the graph begins as a straight line.** Unless you make changes, the input is exactly the same as the output, a direct 1-to-1 correlation.

✔ **You can expand the Curve Display Options and specify the following:**

  • *Show Amount Of:* Choose between Light and Pigment to display the brightness levels or percentages. To keep things simple, I'd leave them at the default of Light (levels), where darker values are at the bottom-left and lighter values are at the top-right. Choose between a simple or detailed grid (icons).

  • *Show:* If you're adjusting curves for individual channels, choose Channel Overlays to superimpose those individual curves.

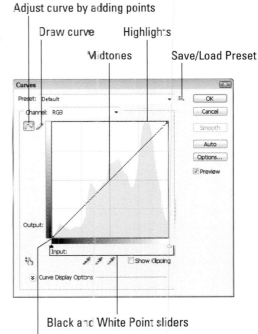

Adjust curve by adding points

Draw curve   Highlights

Midtones   Save/Load Preset

Black and White Point sliders

Shadows

Figure 1-16: The Curves dialog box offers maximum control for adjustment of your image's color and tones.

Select Baseline to show your original straight line curve. Choose to display a histogram overlay. For more on histograms, see the section "Introducing the Histogram Panel," earlier in this chapter. Select Intersection Line to display horizontal and vertical lines to help you align your points while you drag them on the curve.

- ✔ **The Eyedropper can show you pixel values.** When you use the Eyedropper tool to click in the image, a circle appears on the graph to show you the value of the pixel being sampled. At the bottom of the Curves grid box, you can read the pixel's input and output values.

- ✔ **Auto sets black and white values.** When you click the Auto button, the darkest pixels in the image (the deep shadows) are reset to black, and the lightest areas are set to white. Like with the Levels dialog box, this option is the easiest way to make a correction but may not be the best.

- ✔ **Eyedropper tools can also set black, white, and gray values.** The Curves dialog box has black, white, and gray Eyedropper tools you can use to set the black, white, and midtone points, just like you can with Levels.

- ✔ **Select the Show Clipping options to have Photoshop display where clipping occurs in the image during your corrections.** Remember, clipping occurs when a pixel's values are lighter or darker than the highest or lowest value that can be displayed in the image, resulting in loss of detail in those areas.

Adjusting curves

If you click at any point on the curve other than the end points, Photoshop adds a control point that shows your position. You can remove a control point by dragging it downward until it's completely off the graph or by dragging it on top of the next point up or down from it on the graph. You can add up to 14 points to the curve.

Curve presets are located at the very top of the Curves dialog box. If you're a Curves novice, trying one of these presets is a good way to get your feet wet in how curves work. Note that when you select a preset, a curve is loaded into your dialog box. You can also use a preset as a starting point and then tweak it further with your own adjustments. Experiment with the curves to see how they affect the image. For example:

- ✔ Click the Auto button to have Photoshop analyze your image's color and tonal values and make an automatic adjustment. Again, you can use this preset as a starting point and tweak from there.

- ✔ Flattening a curve lowers contrast.

- ✔ Making a curve steeper heightens contrast.

- ✔ Moving a curve downward (if the display is set to Light) darkens the image. Moving it upward lightens.

 ✔ If your display is set to Light, adjust your highlights by moving points in the top-right of the curve, shadows by adjusting points in the bottom-left of the curve, and midtones by moving points in the center of the curve.

 ✔ A gently sloped S-shaped curve increases contrast, especially in the highlight and shadow areas. Using a curve like this also helps to define the midtones.

 ✔ For ultimate control, Photoshop lets you draw a curve with the precise shape you want, creating an arbitrary curve or map. Click the Pencil tool and then draw peaks and valleys in the Curves dialog box. Watch the changes in your original image.

 ✔ You can also add points to the curve by holding down Ctrl (⌘ on the Mac) and clicking your image. Adding points is beneficial if you want to preserve an area in your image.

 ✔ If you want to adjust the color in your image, select your desired channel from the Channel pop-up menu and then adjust the curve. For more on channels, see Book VI.

Arbitrary maps, such as the one shown in Figure 1-17, create distinctive solarization color effects when Photoshop warps the colors of your image. They're fun to play with, maybe useful now and then, but not nearly as practical as S curves.

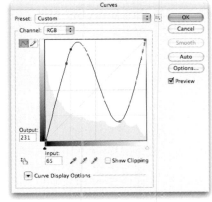

**Book VIII
Chapter 1**

**Enhancing Images
with Adjustments**

Corbis Digital Stock

Figure 1-17: Going crazy with the Curves maps can result in a solarization-like effect.

After you create a custom curve, you may want to save it (a good idea) to load and apply it to other photos with similar contrast issues. Click the Preset Options button (just to the left of the OK button) and select Save Preset from the pop-up menu that appears.

Converting to Black & White

Photoshop provides a great way to convert a color image to grayscale with the Black & White feature. For other ways to make your image grayscale, see Book II, Chapter 2 and the section "Washing Out Color with Desaturate," earlier in this chapter.

The great thing about the Black & White feature is that, like the Channel Mixer (which you can read about in Book VI, Chapter 1), you have a lot of control over how your colors are converted.

Here's how to go to grayscale by using Black & White:

1. **Choose Image⇨Adjustments⇨Black & White.**

    Your Black and White dialog box appears, as shown in Figure 1-18. In addition, Photoshop automatically applies a default conversion to your image.

Dreamstime

Figure 1-18: Convert color images to grayscale with the Black & White adjustment.

2. **Adjust the conversion to your liking by doing one of the following:**

    *   *Choose a Preset:* Select a preset conversion (or a custom one you saved previously) from the pop-up menu. Note that you can also use one of the presets as a starting point and then adjust from there.

    *   *Click Auto:* This option analyzes your image's color values and then converts to grayscale, while trying to maximize your gray tonal values. Again, this conversion can be used as a starting point.

- *Adjust the sliders:* Do your own thing. Drag the sliders left to darken and right to lighten the tones. That's what I did in my example in Figure 1-18. Note that your mouse turns into an eyedropper when you move or click over your image. Click areas of your image to highlight that dominant color in your dialog box. Click and drag on the image itself with the eyedropper to move the color slider for that color, making it darker or lighter.

3. If desired, select the Tint button to apply a tone of color to the black-and-white image.

Adjust the Hue and Saturation sliders to choose a tint color and intensity of that color. Click the color swatch to access the Color Picker, where you can select another color.

If you totally goof up your image, hold down Alt (Option on the Mac) and click the color chip to reset that adjustment. To reset all adjustments, hold down Alt (Option on the Mac) to convert the Cancel button into Reset, and then click that button.

After you establish a custom conversion setting, save it to apply to other similar images by selecting Save Preset from the Preset Options pop-up menu, just to the left of the OK button.

Getting colorful with Hue/Saturation

Photoshop's Hue/Saturation controls let you adjust colors based on their hue, saturation, and lightness. The Hue/Saturation dialog box doesn't work with the Red, Green, and Blue (or Cyan, Magenta, Yellow, and Black) channels of an image. Instead, it operates on the different colors, or hues. You can select all the colors (Master) or one color to modify from the Edit pop-up menu.

Three sliders are in the Hue/Saturation dialog box. (See Figure 1-19.)

- **Hue:** Shifts all the colors clockwise or counterclockwise around the color wheel, depending on the direction you move the slider. I moved my Hue slider to the left to turn the image green and purple.

- **Saturation:** Increases or decreases the richness of the colors in an image. I moved my Saturation slider to the right to increase the saturation and make the image almost glow.

- **Lightness:** Modifies the brightness values.

You can adjust any of these values by moving the sliders and watching the results in the image window. The top color bar at the bottom of the dialog box represents the colors in their order on the color wheel before you made any adjustment. The lower color bar shows how the modifications you make affect the colors.

ImageState

Figure 1-19: The Hue/Saturation command enables you to adjust colors based on their hue (color), saturation (intensity), or lightness (brightness).

Select the slider (the pointing finger icon) to adjust your Hue and Saturation values. With the icon selected, drag directly on your image to adjust the Saturation. Hold down the Ctrl (⌘ on the Mac) key and drag on your image to adjust the Hue.

When you select an individual color to adjust, sliders appear between the color bars so that you can define the range of color to be adjusted. You can select, add, or subtract colors from the range by selecting one of the Eyedropper tools and clicking in the image.

You can also select a Hue/Saturation preset, such as Old Style or Sepia, from the Preset pop-up menu in the Hue/Saturation dialog box.

The Hue/Saturation dialog box also lets you colorize images, a useful option for creating sepia-colored images, like in the Putting It Together project "Making a New Photo Look Old," in this chapter.

Using the Colorize option

Use the Colorize option in the Hue/Saturation dialog box to change the color of any selected area to a new, solid color. This option is unlike the Hue slider, which changes only individual pixels based on their present color values. Just follow these steps:

1. **Open an image and access the Hue/Saturation dialog box by choosing Image⇨Adjustments⇨Hue/Saturation or pressing Ctrl+U (⌘+U on the Mac).**

2. **Select the Colorize option.**

3. **Drag the Hue slider in either direction to change a color.**

   Photoshop doesn't colorize pure white pixels and pure black pixels because colorization affects only gray pixels (from a brightness value of 1 to 254).

   You can also adjust the Saturation and Lightness, if desired.

Pumping up the Vibrance

Think of the Vibrance adjustment as a souped-up, more intelligent Hue/Saturation command. This adjustment increases the saturation in an image but does it in a nonlinear fashion. Therefore, pixels with a lower saturation get more adjustment, and pixels with a higher saturation get less. As a bonus, the adjustment includes a built-in skin-tone protector to prevent faces from becoming overly red. Choose Image⇨Adjustments⇨Vibrance. In the Vibrance dialog box, move the Vibrance and Saturation sliders to the right to increase each. But use a light touch with this adjustment. A little goes a long way, as shown in Figure 1-20.

Figure 1-20: The Vibrance command increases saturation in a nonlinear way.

Making a New Photo Look Old

Black-and-white photography is a newer phenomenon than you might think. Daguerreo-types and other early photographs frequently had a brownish or bluish tone to them. You can create sepia-toned masterpieces of your own. (Or, if you want, you can create a tint in green, blue, or another shade.) Toned pictures can create a mood or otherwise transform a mundane photo into something interesting.

In this Putting It Together project, I chose a recent photo of a boy and his donkey in Java, Indonesia. Without any nasty anachronisms, such as automobiles or satellite dishes, aging this image is easy.

The Photoshop Hue/Saturation feature is all you need to perform this time-traveling magic. Just follow these easy steps:

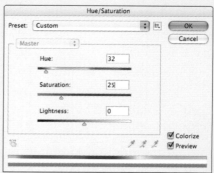

Corbis Digital Stock

1. **Open the image in Photoshop and convert it to black and white by choosing Image⇨Adjustments⇨ Black & White. Click OK.**

   You choose this command rather than the Image⇨Mode⇨Grayscale command to convert the photo to black and white because you're going to continue to work with it as a color image — the image just won't have colors until you add them. For more info on the Black & White adjustment, see the earlier section, "Converting to Black & White."

2. **Choose Image⇨Adjustments⇨ Hue/Saturation.**

   The Hue/Saturation dialog box appears.

3. **Select the Colorize check box so that you can add color to the image.**

4. **Adjust the Hue slider to produce the tone you're looking for.**

Corbis Digital Stock

   To produce a rich sepia tone, move the Hue slider to the far left. If you prefer green, blue, or some other shade, you can experiment with this slider to get the exact color you want.

5. **Adjust the Saturation slider to modify the richness of the color.**

   I used a setting of 25, as shown in the figure. When you move the slider to the right, the color becomes more pure. You end up with a striking red at the far-right position.

6. **Adjust the Lightness slider to lighten or darken the photo, depending on your mood.**

   Generally, you want to leave the Lightness slider at the default middle position. To create a darker, moodier picture, move it to the left; to produce a more faded look, move it to the right.

7. **When you're satisfied with your changes, click OK.**

   Now, my photo looks like a vintage postcard.

   You can create similar effects by using the Photoshop Duotones, Tritones, and Quadtones features. See Book II, Chapter 2 for more information on these tools. You can also try the Tint options in the Black & White adjustment. (See the section "Converting to Black & White," in this chapter.)

Corbis Digital Stock

Matching Color between Documents

The Match Color command enables you to match colors in a single image or between images — a source image and a target image. But it doesn't stop there. You can also match colors between layers or even selections. You can further refine your correction by adjusting the luminance and color intensity (saturation).

This command is great for getting rid of colorcasts in a single image. It also works wonders for matching the color of the lighting between two images or layers — for example, use it if you want to realistically composite an image shot under fluorescent lighting and one shot in natural light.

The Match Color command works only with RGB images, but be sure to apply this command before you perform any color conversions.

Follow these steps to use the Match Color command to match one image with another:

1. **Open the two images you want to match.**

   If you want, you can make selections in one or both of those images — for example, if you're creating a composite image from two separate images and want to match the lighting color or skin tones. Without selections, the overall target image is matched to the source image. In my example in Figure 1-21, I selected an image taken outdoors in natural

**Book VIII
Chapter 1**

**Enhancing Images
with Adjustments**

light and one taken inside under fluorescent lights (which give that image a nasty green colorcast). I want to use the girl in each image in a composite and therefore want to try to match the skin tones.

Figure 1-21: The Match Color command lets you match colors within a single image or between two images.

2. **Make sure your target image (the one that needs to be corrected) is the active file, and choose Image⇨Adjustments⇨Match Color.**

   If you're using a specific layer in your target image, select that layer prior to choosing the command. Make sure you select the Preview option so that you can view your adjustments on the fly.

3. **In the Match Color dialog box, shown in Figure 1-22, select your source image from the Source pop-up menu in the Image Statistics area.**

   Select None if you're working with only one image (if the source image and target image are the same).

   Remember, the source image contains the colors you want to match in the target image.

4. **If you're using a particular layer in your source image, select it from the Layer pop-up menu.**

   Or choose the Merged option to match the colors from all the layers.

Figure 1-22: Match color between two images with different lighting.

5. **If you have selections in your images, you can select one of the following options:**

   - If you have a selection in your target image but want to match the colors from the whole image, select the Ignore Selection when Applying Adjustment option.

   - Select the Use Selection in Source to Calculate Colors option if you want to use the colors in the selection in the source image to calculate the adjustment. Deselect this option to ignore the selection in the source image and match the colors from the entire source image.

   - Select the Use Selection in Target to Calculate Adjustment option if you have a selection in the target image and want to use the colors in the selection to calculate the adjustment. If it's deselected, the adjustment is calculated using the colors of the whole image.

6. **Select the Neutralize option to remove any colorcasts in the target image.**

   When using the Match Color command, your cursor becomes the Eyedropper tool. This allows you to sample colors on your images and look at the color values in the Info panel while making your adjustments.

7. **Adjust the luminance by moving the slider or entering a value.**

   A higher value increases the brightness in the target image. A lower value decreases brightness.

8. **Adjust the color intensity of your target image.**

   A higher value increases the color saturation, and a lower value decreases the saturation. Moving the slider to 1 desaturates the image to grayscale.

9. **Use the Fade option to control the amount of adjustment that is applied to the target image, moving the slider to the right to reduce the amount.**

   If you move the slider all the way to the right, the image returns to its original colors.

10. **If you want to save your settings to use on other images, click the Save Statistics button. Then, in the Save dialog box that appears, name the file, specify the location, and click Save.**

    To reload the settings later, click the Load Statistics button and navigate to the file.

11. **Click OK to apply the adjustment and exit the dialog box.**

Figure 1-23: These tones are a better match with the target image.

My image, shown in Figure 1-23, has less of that nasty green cast from the fluorescent lighting.

Switching Colors with Replace Color

The Replace Color command creates interesting creative effects by allowing you to substitute one set of colors for another. It builds a mask, using colors you select, and then replaces the selected colors with others that you specify. You can adjust hue, saturation, and lightness of the masked colors.

Just follow these steps:

1. **Choose Image⇨Adjustments⇨Replace Color.**

   The Replace Color dialog box appears, as shown in Figure 1-24.

2. **Choose either Selection or Image:**

   • *Selection:* Shows the mask in the Preview window. The masked area is black, semitransparent areas are shades of gray, and unmasked areas are white.

For details on masks, see Book VI, Chapter 2.

* *Image:* Shows the full image itself in the Preview window. Use this option if you zoomed in on the original image to select colors more easily, but you still want to be able to see the full image in the preview.

3. **Click the colors you want to select.**

   You can click the colors in either the image itself or the Preview window.

4. **Shift-click or use the plus (+) Eyedropper tool to add more colors.**

5. **Press the Alt key (Option key on the Mac) and click, or use the minus (–) Eyedropper tool and click, to remove colors.**

6. **To add colors similar to the ones you select, use the Fuzziness slider to refine your selection, adding or subtracting from the selection based on the tolerance value.**

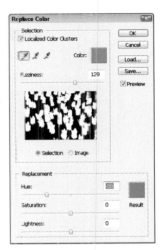

Corbis Digital Stock

Figure 1-24: The Replace Color adjustment enables you to substitute one color for another.

If your selection isn't quite cooperating, try selecting the Localized Color Clusters option to assist you in obtaining a cleaner, more precise selection. The Localized Color Clusters option is especially handy if the color you're trying to select is somewhat varied.

7. **Move the Hue, Saturation, and Lightness sliders to change them to new values.**

8. **When you like the result, click OK to apply the settings.**

Figure 1-25 shows my images before and after replacing color.

Corbis Digital Stock

Figure 1-25: Don't like the color of your flowers? Use the Replace Color command to change it.

Increasing and Decreasing Color

Increasing and decreasing color is a popular Photoshop activity, so the fact that Photoshop offers more than one way to do so is no surprise. In addition to the Selective Color command, which I describe in the following section, several other commands are a lot easier to understand — and a lot easier to use.

This is the place to start reading if you want to know all about the Gradient Maps command and the various color mapper tools, all of which are designed to change the arrangement of the colors in your photos in ways that *don't* produce realistic-looking images. Images that have been color-mapped are certainly interesting to look at.

Using the Selective Color command

You use the Selective Color command (in the Image⇨Adjustments menu) chiefly to manipulate the amount of process colors (that is, cyan, magenta, yellow, and black) used in printing an image. In the Selective Color dialog box, select the color you want to edit from the Colors pop-up menu. Adjust the CMYK sliders to modify the selected color.

With the Relative method selected, you can add or subtract color. For example, if a pixel is 30 percent cyan and you add 20 percent cyan, Photoshop adds 6 percent cyan to the pixel (20 percent of 30 percent is 6 percent).

With the Absolute method selected, Photoshop bases the amount of change on the exact value you enter. For example, if a pixel is 30 percent cyan and you add 20 percent cyan, the pixel changes to a total of 50 percent cyan.

Using gradient maps

Gradient maps convert your image to grayscale and then replace the range of black, gray, and white tones with a gradient of your choice, in effect colorizing your image — often, in startling ways.

Photoshop maps the lightest tones of your image to one color in the gradient and changes the darkest tones to the other color of the gradient (assuming you're using just two colors for the gradient). Photoshop changes all the formerly gray tones to an intermediate color between the two. When you use multiple colors or fancy gradients, the image really gets interesting. Just follow these steps to try out this feature:

1. **Open an image and access the gradient map, shown in Figure 1-26, by choosing Image⇨Adjustments⇨Gradient Map.**

2. **Choose the gradient you want from the gradient list.**

    This list is exactly like the one offered with the Gradient tool. You can edit the gradient used for your map exactly like you do for the

Gradient tool. For more information on choosing gradients, see Book IV, Chapter 2.

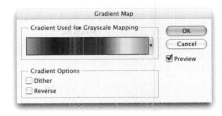

Figure 1-26: A gradient map replaces the tones in your images with a gradient.

3. **Choose either or both of these options:**

   - *Dither:* Adds random noise to smooth out the gradient and reduces banding.

   - *Reverse:* Changes the direction of the gradient. Use the Reverse option to create a negative quickly.

4. **Click OK to apply the gradient map.**

   If the effect is a little too intense for your taste, try fading the gradient map (Edit➪Fade Gradient Mask) and then adjusting the opacity percentage and/or applying a different blend mode.

Adding color with photo filters

Photographers will appreciate the Photo Filter command, which is reminiscent of the analog method of placing a colored filter in front of a camera lens to tweak the color balance and color temperature of the light coming through the lens. This is a great way to make an image appear cooler or warmer. Have a portrait where your subject appears a little too bluish? Apply a Warming filter and bring some rosiness back into his or her cheeks. You can also apply a colored filter to add a tint of color to your image. Figure 1-27 shows how I warmed up an overly cool image.

To apply the Photo Filter adjustment, follow these steps:

1. **Open your image and choose Image➪Adjustments➪Photo Filter to apply the filter to the entire image.**

   If you want to apply the filter to one or more layers, choose Layer➪New Adjustment Layer➪ Photo Filter.

Corbis Digital Stock

Figure 1-27: Photo Filters adjust the color balance and color temperature of an image.

2. **Make sure you have the Preview option selected so you can view the results.**

3. **In the Photo Filter dialog box, select the Filter radio button to choose a preset filter from the Filter pop-up menu or select the Color radio button to select a custom color for your filter.**

   See Table 1-1 for a brief description of the filters in the Filter pop-up menu.

   If you opt for the custom color, click the swatch to select a color from the Color Picker.

4. **Select the Preserve Luminosity check box if you don't want the filter to darken your image.**

   Note that some photo pros advocate not selecting this option, but it's up to you.

5. **Adjust the Density slider to control the amount of color applied to your image.**

   A higher value provides a stronger adjustment. Use the Density control with restraint. Anything above 50 percent produces a severe effect.

6. **Click OK to apply the adjustment and exit the dialog box.**

Table 1-1	Photo Filters
Name	*Effect of Filters*
Warming Filter (85, LBA) and Cooling Filter (80, LBB)	Adjusts the white balance in an image. A photo shot in a high color temperature of light makes an image blue. Warming Filter (85, LBA) makes the colors warmer, more yellow. Similarly, an image shot in light of a low color temperature benefits from the Cooling Filter (80, LBB), which makes the colors more blue.
Warming Filter (81) and Cooling Filter (82)	Similar to the preceding filters but for minor adjustments.
Colors	These filters adjust the hue of an image. You can select a color to get rid of a colorcast. For example, if your image is too green, select magenta. If it's too blue, select yellow. You can also select a color to apply a special effect.

Playing with the color mappers

Photoshop also includes some fun-filled color mapping commands (in the Image⇨Adjustments menu), so-called because they change the colors of your image in specific ways. Two of them, Invert and Equalize, don't even have any options. They're akin to single-step filters that you apply and forget. (I cover filters in Book VII.) I show all the color mappers in Figure 1-28.

Invert	Equalize	Threshold	Posterize

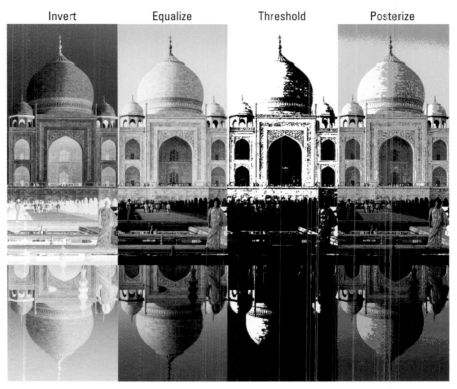

Corbis Digital Stock

Figure 1-28: The Color Mappers change the colors in your image in specific ways, such as reversing colors or converting your image to black and white.

Invert

Invert simply reverses all the colors and tones in your image, creating a negative image. Photoshop changes black tones to white, white tones to black, dark grays to light grays, and colors to their complements. For example, a light yellow color becomes a dark blue, and so forth.

Some folks mistakenly think they can use this command to create a positive (or color-correct) version of a scanned color negative. It isn't so simple because color negatives have an orange mask overlaying the color information. Converting a color negative correctly requires a lot of color correcting and tweaking. If you have sophisticated scanning software, you may have a command that does the conversion. A couple third-party Photoshop filters also do the duty. But to do it manually requires a lot of color correcting and tweaking. Something you may not want to try at home!

Equalize

This command locates the lightest and darkest pixels in an image, defines them as white and black, respectively, and then changes all the other pixels in between to divide the grayscale values evenly. Depending on your image, this process may increase contrast or otherwise alter the color and tones when the values are evenly distributed.

Threshold

Threshold converts your image to black and white, with all pixels that are brighter than a value you specify represented as white, and all pixels that are darker than that value as black. You can change the threshold level to achieve different high-contrast effects.

Posterize

This color mapper creates an interesting graphic effect by reducing the number of colors in your image to a value you specify, from 2 to 255. Low values provide distinct posterlike effects. While you increase the number of color levels, the image begins to look either more normal or a bit like a bad conversion to Indexed Color.

 Putting It Together

Cleaning Up a Line Art Scan

Line art consists of (you guessed it!) lines, rather than the continuous tones of a photograph or painting. Line art can consist of outlines, shapes (like you find in a bar chart), patterns (like the fills in the bar chart), or freehand drawings (like those produced in pen or pencil).

What you don't want to see when you scan line art is an extra color: the background color of the paper. Often, the paper appears as a dull gray, and you may see other artifacts you don't want, such as wrinkles or spots in the paper.

Luckily, Photoshop has a handy Threshold command that you can use to determine which tones appear as black and which are dropped altogether. You end up with a nice black-and-white line art image with all the intermediate tones removed.

 Follow these instructions to clean up a piece of line art (to test-drive these steps, download my example image from this book's Web site, which I talk about in the Introduction):

1. **Open a line drawing in Photoshop, as shown in the figure.**

2. **Choose Image⇨Adjustments⇨ Threshold from the menu bar.**

   The Threshold dialog box includes a chart called a *histogram*. The histogram includes a series of vertical lines showing how many of an image's tones are represented by a certain brightness level. You can see that a relatively small number of tones are represented by a brightness value of 93, marked by the gray triangle at the bottom of the histogram. Many more tones are used at the other levels, forming a sloping mountain in the chart.

Chris Blair

3. **Move the slider to the right until the tones you want to appear in the image are shown.**

   The more you move the slider to the right, the darker the image gets. A threshold of about 170 seems about right for this image.

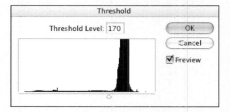

4. **Click OK to apply the modification.**

   Some small artifacts may remain in your image, as shown in the figure. These are spots and parts of wrinkles that are darker than the page background, approaching the darkness of the line art itself.

5. **To clean up these slight defects, use the Eraser tool.**

Chapter 2: Repairing with Focus and Toning Tools

In This Chapter

- ✔ **Dodging and burning**
- ✔ **Manipulating color with the Sponge tool**
- ✔ **Smudging rough spots smooth**
- ✔ **Blurring for effect**
- ✔ **Focusing on sharpness**

*O*ne of the coolest things about Photoshop is the way it offers several tools to accomplish similar results, but with distinctly individualized looks. The focus and toning tools in Photoshop are examples of this. The focus tools blur, sharpen, and smudge your image in much the same way as the Blur, Sharpen, and Liquify filters (which I cover in Book VII). The toning tools lighten, darken, and change the richness of color in your image a bit like commands, such as Levels, Curves, and Hue/Saturation (covered in Book VIII, Chapter 1).

But where their counterparts operate only on layers or selections, the focus and toning tools let you *paint* the effects you want directly onto your image. Using these tools, you can often create subtler, natural looks tailored to meet your exact needs, as I explain in this chapter.

While you work through this chapter, keep in mind all the tips I give you in Book IV, Chapter 1 about using brushes. Most of that information applies to the brushlike focus and toning tools, as well.

Lightening and Darkening with Dodge and Burn Tools

Dodging and burning originated in the darkroom, where photographers salvage negatives containing areas that are too dark or too light by adding or subtracting a bit of exposure when an enlarger makes prints.

An enlarger makes a print by projecting an image of a negative onto a piece of photosensitive paper. During the exposure, the darkroom technician can reduce the amount of light falling onto the paper by placing some object (often a disc-shaped piece of cardboard or metal impaled on a piece of wire) in the light path to *dodge* part of the image. The worker can *burn* other parts of an image by exposing only a small portion through an opening, such as the fingers in a cupped pair of hands. The Dodge and Burn tools in Photoshop adopt their icons from those popular real-world tools used to achieve these darkroom effects.

However, the Photoshop counterparts are a great deal more flexible. For example, the worker in a darkroom varies the size of the dodging or burning tool by moving it up or down in the light path. Unfortunately, the closer the real-world tool gets to the paper, the sharper it appears, forcing the darkroom worker to move the tool more rapidly and frequently to blur the edges of the effects. With the Photoshop Dodge and Burn tools, you can set the size of the tool and its softness independently by selecting a brush of the size and the hardness or softness you require.

You can also set the Photoshop tools to operate primarily on shadows, midtones, and highlights. You can adjust the degree of lightening and darkening applied by specifying an exposure, too.

The Dodge (used to lighten) and Burn (used to darken) tools can be very effective, but you can't add detail that isn't there. Keep the following in mind:

- When you lighten very dark shadows that contain little detail, you end up with grayish shadows.

- Darkening very light areas that are completely washed out doesn't look very good, either.

In either case, you want to use the Dodge and Burn tools in moderation and work only with small areas. To dodge or burn a portion of an image, just follow these steps:

1. **Open an image with under- or overexposed areas and select the Dodge or Burn tool from the Tools panel.**

   Press the O key to choose the active toning tool or press Shift+O to cycle through the available toning tools until the one you want is active.

2. **In the Options bar, make these adjustments:**

   a. *Select a brush from the Brush Preset Picker or toggle open the larger Brush panel.*

   Larger, softer brushes spread the dodging and burning effect over a larger area, making blending with the surrounding area easier.

   You can choose the same brushes available with any of the painting tools, including preset brushes from your library.

   b. *Under the Range options, select Shadows, Midtones, or Highlights.*

Use Shadows to lighten or darken detail in the darker areas of your image, Midtones to adjust the tones of average darkness, and Highlights to make the brightest areas even lighter or (more frequently) darker.

In Figure 2-1, the original image (top) had mostly dark areas, so I dodged the shadows. Note the increased detail in the eyes, teeth, and hair. I also gave a couple swipes to the highlight areas with the Burn tool.

c. *Select the amount of the effect to apply with each stroke by using the Exposure slider or text box.*

d. *Enable the airbrush option for a softer, more gradual effect.*

e. *Check the Protect Tones option.*

This setting provides more natural and subtle dodging and burning results by preserving the hues and tones of the image pixels.

f. *If you are using a pressure-sensitive tablet, click the last icon. Doing so overrides any settings you made in the Brush panel.*

Figure 2-1: The Dodge and Burn tools are effective when touching up smaller dark and light areas.

3. **Paint over the areas you want to lighten or darken with the toning brush, gradually building up the desired effect.**

Using a soft-edged brush is often best when dodging and burning. You want to create a realistic, not retouched, appearance.

The Exposure control is similar to the Opacity control offered by other painting tools, but it's especially important with dodging and burning.

Using a low value is best (I often work with 10-percent exposure or less) so that you can carefully paint in the lightening or darkening you want.

High exposure values work too quickly and produce unnatural-looking, obviously dodged or burned areas in your images.

4. **If you go too far, press Ctrl+Z (⌘+Z on the Mac) to reverse your most recent stroke.**

5. **When you finish, choose File⇨Save to store the image.**

Turning Down the Color with the Sponge Tool

The Sponge tool, which soaks up color like, well, a sponge, reduces the richness or intensity (or saturation) of a color in the areas you paint. It can also perform the reverse, imbuing a specific area with richer, more vibrant colors.

Surprisingly, the Sponge tool also works in grayscale mode, pushing light and dark pixels toward a middle gray, providing a darkening or lightening effect to those pixels. Unlike the Hue/Saturation or Desaturate commands (Image➪Adjustments), which work only on layers or selections, you can use the Sponge tool on any area that you can paint with a brush.

You can use the Sponge tool on an image in subtle ways to reduce the saturation in selected areas for an interesting effect. For example, you may have an object that's the center of attention in your picture simply because the colors are so bright (or even garish). The Sponge tool lets you reduce the color saturation of that area (and only that area) to allow the other sections of your image to come to the forefront. You can also use the Sponge tool to make an artistic statement: You could reduce or increase the saturation of a single person in a group shot to make that person stand out (perhaps as being more colorful than the rest). To use the Sponge tool, just follow these steps:

1. **Open an image and select the Sponge tool from the Tools panel.**

    Press the O key to choose the Sponge if it's the active toning tool or press Shift+O to cycle through the Sponge, Dodge, and Burn tools until the Sponge tool is active.

2. **In the Options bar, make the following changes:**

    a. *Select a brush from the Brush Preset Picker or the larger Brush panel.*

        Use large, soft brushes to saturate/desaturate a larger area.

        Smaller brushes are useful mostly when you need to change the saturation of a specific small object in an image.

    b. *Select either Desaturate (reduce color richness) or Saturate (increase color richness) from the Mode pop-up menu.*

    c. *Select a flow rate (the speed with which the saturation/desaturation effect builds up while you apply the brush) with the Flow slider or text box.*

    d. *If you want an even softer effect, select the Airbrush icon.*

    e. *Select the Vibrance option.*

        This setting allows saturation for each color to reach its fullest level, but the setting stops saturation after that point to avoid *clipping* (when colors fall outside the printable range). At the same time, it allows saturation to continue for any colors that haven't reached the clipping point.

    f. *If you are using a pressure-sensitive tablet, click the last icon. Doing so overrides any settings you made in the Brush panel.*

3. **Paint carefully over the areas you want to saturate or desaturate with color.**

   In Figure 2-2, I saturated the little girl to make her a focal point and desaturated the parents and surroundings.

Purestock

Figure 2-2: The Sponge tool saturates (increases richness) and desaturates (decreases richness) color.

Smoothing with the Smudge Tool

Although grouped among the focus tools, the Smudge tool performs more of a warping effect, something like the Warp tool in the Liquify dialog box (see Book VII, Chapter 3 for information on this command).

Smudge pushes your pixels around on the screen as if they consisted of wet paint, using the color that's under the cursor when you start to stroke. However, don't view the Smudge tool as a simple distortion tool that produces only comical effects. I use it on tiny areas of an image to soften the edges of objects in a way that often looks more natural than blurring tools. The Smudge tool can come in handy when retouching images to create a soft, almost painted look, as shown in Figure 2-3. Just don't go gung-ho, or you may obliterate detail that you want to preserve.

> **TIP**
>
> Smudged areas may be obvious because of their smooth appearance. Adding a little texture by using the Noise filter after you smudge is often a good idea if you want to blend in a smudged section with its surroundings. You can find tips on applying the Noise filter in Book VII, Chapter 2.

Book VIII
Chapter 2

Repairing
with Focus and
Toning Tools

To apply the Smudge tool, just follow these steps:

1. **Open the image and select the Smudge tool from the Tools panel.**

2. **Select the settings you want from the Options bar:**

   a. *Select a brush from the Brushes panel.*

   Use a small brush for smudging tiny areas, such as edges. Larger brushes produce drastic effects, so use them with care.

   b. *Select a blending mode from the Mode pop-up menu.*

   c. *Select the strength of the smudging effect with the Strength slider or text box.*

   Low values produce a lighter smudging effect; high values really push your pixels around.

   d. *If your image has multiple layers and you want Photoshop to use the color information from all the visible layers to produce the smudge effect, select the Sample All Layers option.*

   The smudge still appears only on the active layer, but the look is a bit different, depending on the contents of the underlying layers.

Photodisc

Figure 2-3: The Smudge tool can give your fruit, or other elements, a soft, painted look.

3. **Use the Finger Painting option to begin the smudge by using the foreground color.**

You can get some interesting effects with this option. You can switch the Smudge tool into Finger Painting mode temporarily by holding down the Alt key (the Option key on the Mac) while you drag. If you are using a pressure-sensitive tablet, click the last icon. Doing so overrides any settings you made in the Brush panel.

4. **Paint over the areas you want to smudge.**

5. **Watch the screen carefully while you smudge so that you can redirect your daubs to achieve the look you want.**

This tool can be a little on the destructive side. If you're looking to preserve reality, use it with restraint. If you want to get wild, go crazy.

6. **When you finish, choose File⊅Save to store your image.**

Softening with the Blur Tool

Adding a little blur here and there can save an image with a few defects. Blurring can also be used for artistic effect — say, to add a little motion to a soccer ball frozen in time by a too-fast shutter speed. You can also blur portions of your image to emphasize and focus on a particular element, as shown in Figure 2-4, where I blurred the empty slide cases a bit to draw attention to the image. The Photoshop Blur tool makes painting your blur effects exactly where you want them easy.

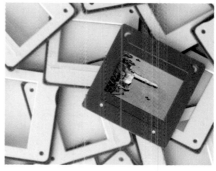

iStockphoto

Figure 2-4: Use the Blur tool to soften a rough edge or make your element a focal point by blurring its surroundings.

The Blur tool doesn't push pixels around the way the Smudge tool does. Instead, the Blur tool decreases the contrast among adjacent pixels in the area painted.

The mechanics of using the Blur tool and several of its options are similar to those of the Smudge tool (which I talk about in the preceding section). Just follow these steps:

1. **Open an image and select the Blur tool from the Tools panel.**

2. **In the Options bar, specify these settings:**

   a. *Select a brush from the Brush Preset Picker or the larger Brush panel.*

      Use a small brush for applying small areas of blur. Use larger brushes with caution to, for example, blur the entire background to make a foreground object appear sharper in comparison.

   b. *Select a blending mode from the Mode pop-up menu.*

   c. *Select the strength of the blurring effect with the Strength slider or text box.*

   d. *If your image has multiple layers and you want to blur based on the pixel information in all the visible layers in your image, select the Use All Layers option.*

      Selecting this option can produce a smoother blur when you merge the layers later.

   e. *If you are using a pressure-sensitive tablet, click the last icon. Doing so overrides any settings you made in the Brush panel.*

3. **Paint over the areas you want to blur.**

4. **When you finish, choose File➪Save to store your image.**

Cranking Up the Focus with the Sharpen Tool

In theory, the Sharpen tool is nothing more than the Blur tool (discussed in the preceding section) in reverse — instead of decreasing contrast among pixels, the Sharpen tool increases the contrast. In practice, however, you need to use this tool with a bit more care than the Blur tool. Where blurred areas tend to fade from a viewer's notice (at least, in terms of how his or her eyes perceive them), sharpened areas of an image jump out at people.

If you blur an area a little too much, you may not even notice. But even a small area that has been oversharpened can change the entire appearance of an image — and not flatteringly.

You can often successfully sharpen small areas with the Sharpen tool. Sometimes, the eyes in a portrait can benefit from a little sharpening, as shown in Figure 2-5. Or you might want to sharpen an area to make it stand out more distinctly against a slightly blurred background.

Stockphoto

Figure 2-5: Use the Sharpen tool sparingly and in small areas, such as in the eyes of this portrait.

Follow these simple steps to use the Sharpen tool:

1. **Select the Sharpen tool from the Tools panel.**

2. **Make the following changes in the Options bar:**

   a. *Select the brush of your choice from the Brushes panel.*

   b. *Select a blending mode from the Mode pop-up menu.*

   c. *Select the strength of the sharpening effect with the Strength slider or text box.*

   Using a fairly low value (say, 25 percent or less) is a good idea because you can build up sharpness slowly, being careful not to overdo it. You know you've gone too far with the sharpness when the pixels start to look noisy and grainy.

   d. *Use the information on all your layers for Photoshop's contrast-increasing algorithms by selecting the Use All Layers option.*

   e. *Choose Protect Detail to enhance the details in the image and minimize artifacts. If you leave this option unselected, your sharpening is more pronounced.*

   f. *If you are using a pressure-sensitive tablet, click the last icon. This overrides any settings you made in the Brush panel.*

3. **Paint over the areas you want to sharpen.**

4. **When you finish, choose File⇨Save to store your image.**

Sharpening increases contrast so be careful when using the Sharpen tool if you plan to adjust the Levels or Curves controls, too. Any change that increases contrast in the whole image also boosts the contrast of an area you've sharpened.

The Unsharp Mask and Smart Sharpen filters offer more options and better overall control, so unless you really need to paint the sharpening effect, you're usually better off using a filter. If you really want to apply the effect with brushstrokes, you can always apply the Unsharp Mask filter to a whole layer, take a snapshot, undo the filter operation, and then use the snapshot as a source to paint from, using the History panel. See Book II, Chapter 4 for information on how to paint from the History panel. Finally, for maximum flexibility, try using Smart Filters, which enable you to endlessly edit your filter. For more on Smart Filters, see Book VII, Chapter 1.

Putting It Together

Fixing an Underexposed Foreground

Sometimes, editing tools just don't cut the mustard when it comes to fixing large areas of an underexposed image. Instead, you have to use three tools together to repair the damage: a filter, a fill, and a blend mode.

If you're like me, you've taken at least a couple photos where your subject was lit from behind, thereby underexposing the foreground and burying the subject in the shadows. You can try the Shadows/Highlights adjustment, on the Image⇨Adjustments menu, which usually does a good job of fixing the problem. But if you're not satisfied with that adjustment, you can follow this old-school method. Or you can even go for a combo plate and use them both. Follow these steps to bring your subject back into the light:

1. **Open the image in need of repair.**

2. **Choose Image⇨Duplicate.**

3. **In the dialog box that appears, name the duplicate file (I named mine Nick after my friend) and click OK.**

4. **On the duplicate image, choose Image⇨Mode⇨Grayscale. Click Discard in the dialog box that appears to discard the color information.**

Photoshop has now stripped the color from the image. Don't worry; this is just an intermediary step.

continued

Book VIII
Chapter 2

Repairing
with Focus and
Toning Tools

continued

5. On the duplicate image, choose Filter⇨Blur⇨Gaussian Blur. In the Gaussian Blur dialog box, enter a radius value and click OK.

For a low-resolution image (72 ppi), a value of 5 pixels is enough. For higher-resolution images (300 ppi), use 20 pixels. Your goal is to get rid of the detail in the image.

6. Return to the original image and choose Select⇨Load Selection.

In the Load Selection dialog box, make sure the Document drop-down list shows your file from Step 2.

7. Select Gray for the Channel. Select the Invert box. In the Operation area, leave the setting as New Selection, as shown in the figure. Click OK to load the selection.

You're loading the only available channel in the duplicate grayscale image as a selection. A selection outline appears, which corresponds to the blurry gray areas in your duplicate image.

8. Choose Edit⇨Fill.

9. In the Fill dialog box that appears, shown in the figure, select 50% Gray from the Use pop-up menu. Select Color Dodge from the Mode pop-up menu. Leave the Opacity at 100%. Click OK.

Although Photoshop fills the selection with 50-percent gray, the Color Dodge mode *lightens* the pixels in the image, creating a kind of bleaching effect.

10. You can now see the subject of your image in a better light, like in my image.

Chapter 3: Fixing Flaws and Removing What's Not Wanted

In This Chapter

⌐ **Making copies with the Clone Stamp tool**

⌐ **Healing digitally with the Healing Brush tool**

⌐ **Applying patches with the Patch tool**

⌐ **Zapping with the Spot Healing Brush tool**

⌐ **Applying color with the Color Replacement tool**

⌐ **Eliminating red-eye**

⌐ **Using Vanishing Point**

Say that you want to duplicate an element in your image. That's easy enough, right? Make a selection and copy and paste it into the new location. Presto. That works fine most of the time. But what if the element has a shadow behind it, next to it, above it, or below it? What a pain. The better method is to clone the element by using the Clone Stamp tool. It's quick, easy, and no one will know that only one element was there originally.

Here's another hypothetical situation: What if some unsightly flaw mars your otherwise perfect image? Or maybe the corporate executive, whose head shot you took last week, has requested a little digital Botox around the eyes and mouth.

In this chapter, I reveal secrets of cloning that won't make medical ethicists scream. I show you how to heal scars, scratches, and other imperfections without calling a plastic surgeon. And you can use Vanishing Point to add or remove windows or doors without forking out a dime to a contractor.

Cloning with the Clone Stamp Tool

The Clone Stamp tool, one of Photoshop's more popular tools, always arouses a "Wow," "Cool," or similar remark of approval when demonstrated.

Believe it or not, you can also reach for this tool when retouching imperfections, such as scratches, scars, bruises, and other minor flaws. In fact, that used to be one of its major functions. In some retouching instances, it does a great job, although the advent of the Healing Brush and Patch tools has relegated the Clone Stamp tool more to the pure cloning functions and less to the hard-core retouching jobs.

Using the Clone Stamp tool

The Clone Stamp tool works its magic by taking sampled pixels from one area and *cloning* (or copying) them onto another area. Cloning often works better than making a selection and then copying and pasting it because cloning allows you to retain soft edges on details such as shadows, giving you a more realistic duplicate image. To assist you with your cloning tasks, the Clone Source panel enables you to see a preview (in an overlay style) of the source pixels you're cloning.

Follow these steps to clone an element without any genetic engineering:

1. **Open an image and select the Clone Stamp tool from the Tools panel.**

   Press the S key (or Shift+S if the Pattern Stamp is currently active) on the keyboard.

   You have several options to choose from on the Options bar.

2. **Select a brush and change its size or hardness in the Brush Preset Picker to better control the area that you're cloning.**

   For more information on brushes, see Book IV, Chapter 1.

   I recommend having your Clone Stamp tool cursor display your Full Size Brush Tip so you can judge the amount of the area you're cloning. To do so, choose Edit➪Preferences➪Cursors (Photoshop➪Preferences➪ Cursors on the Mac). Select the Full Size Brush Tip radio button in the Painting Cursors area of the dialog box.

   I used a 65-pixel, feathered brush.

   Click the Tablet icon (at the end of the Options bar) to control the size of the brush. The pressure you apply will then override any settings in the Brush panel.

3. **Select the blend mode of your choice on the Options bar.**

   Selecting a mode such as Difference, Multiply, or Color can produce some interesting special effects. For more on modes, see Book V, Chapter 3. I left my setting at Normal.

4. **To make the clone more or less opaque, use the Opacity slider or text box on the Options bar.**

   I left the opacity at 100%. If you are using a pressure-sensitive tablet, and you want the pressure you apply to set the opacity, click the Tablet Opacity icon.

5. **Specify how fast the Clone Stamp tool applies the clone by adjusting the Flow Rate percentage.**

   Again, I left my option at 100%.

6. **Select the Airbrush option for airbrushing capabilities, if desired.**

7. **Select or deselect the Aligned option, depending on your preference.**

   With Aligned selected, the clone source moves when you move your cursor to a different location. If you want to clone multiple times from the same location, deselect the Aligned option. I left mine selected.

8. **Select the All Layers option from the Sample drop-down list to clone part of an image with multiple layers.**

   Selecting this option enables you to sample pixels in all the visible layers for the clone. If you select the Current Layer option, the Clone Stamp tool clones only from the active layer. If you select the Current and Below option, you sample pixels from the current layer and all layers below it.

9. **If you select All Layers in Step 8, you can choose whether to ignore any adjustment layers when cloning. To do so, click the Adjustment Layer icon on the Options bar.**

   By ignoring adjustment layers, you may prevent the bizarre results that can sometimes occur by double-applying your adjustment layers during the cloning process.

10. **Choose Window➪Clone Source to open the Clone Source panel, as shown in Figure 3-1. Specify the following options:**

    • *Sampling Sources:* In Step 11, you define a sampling source by Alt-clicking (Option-clicking on the Mac) the area of the image that you want to clone. However, if you want to create multiple sampling sources, you can do so in the Clone Source panel by selecting a different Clone Source button and repeating this Alt-clicking (Option-clicking on the Mac) process on other areas of your image. You probably don't need to use more than one source. Multiple sampling sources are useful for video editors who have to work with tight registration between frames that need cloning.

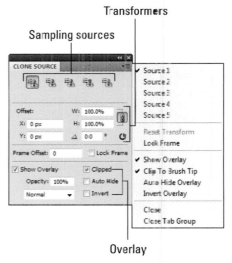

Figure 3-1: The Clone Source panel assists in the cloning process.

- *Transformations:* Adjust the rotation, position, or scale of your clone. Select the link icon to maintain your Width (W) and Height (H) aspect ratio. Click the small curved arrow below the link icon to reset your transformation settings (W, H, and Rotation). I wanted my cloned tiger to be a twin of the one that's already in the image, so I left the settings at their default.

You can use scrubby sliders by hovering over the transformation label (H, W, and so on) of a field and dragging left or right. Hold down Alt (Option on the Mac) while dragging to make your changes slower. Hold down Shift while dragging to make your changes faster.

- *Overlay:* If desired, select the Show Overlay option. Applying an overlay is especially useful when cloning subjects that need to be in alignment with the underlying image. Adjust the Opacity to your desired percentage. I used 30% in my example. If you want, select the Auto-Hide option. If you select this option, when you release your mouse, you see a ghosted preview of how your cloned pixels will appear on the image. While you're painting, however, the overlay is hidden. Select a blending mode for your overlay from the Blending Mode drop-down list. Depending on your source pixels, a blend mode other than Normal may work better in aligning your cloned image with the underlying image. Check Invert to reverse the colors and tones in your overlay. This setting may also assist you in aligning areas.

To display the overlay temporarily, hold down Alt+Shift-click (Option+Shift-click on the Mac) after setting your source. You can drag your overlay around and then, after you have your desired location, release the mouse to set it down.

You can find most of the same options in the Clone Source panel pop-up menu.

If you select the Clipped option, the overlay is clipped, or contained, only within the boundaries of your brush. In my opinion, this makes it a lot easier to clone exactly what you want.

11. **Alt-click (Option-click on the Mac) the area of your image that you want to clone.**

By clicking the area you want to clone, you're defining the *source.*

12. **Click or drag along the area where you want the clone to appear, as shown in Figure 3-2.**

While you drag, Photoshop displays a crosshair icon along with your Clone Stamp cursor. The crosshair represents the source you're cloning from, and the Clone Stamp cursor shows where the clone is being painted. While you move the mouse, the crosshair moves, as well. This provides a continuous reference to the area of your image that you're cloning. Keep an eye on the crosshair, or you may clone something you don't want. Try to clone your entire object in one fell swoop so it doesn't get fragmented.

Photo Disc/Getty Images

Figure 3-2: When using the Clone Stamp tool, drag along the area where you want your clone to appear.

When you successfully complete the cloning process, you have two identical objects. Figure 3-3 shows my identical twin Siberian tigers.

Figure 3-3: My twin Siberian tigers are the products of cloning.

13. Save the image and close it.

Tips for excellent cloning results

Here are a few useful tidbits regarding the Clone Stamp tool:

- ✔ **Use the Clone Stamp tool to fix simple flaws.** To clean up a flaw that's pretty straight, such as a stray hair or scratch, Alt-click (Option-click on the Mac) with the tool to define the source. Then, click at one end of the straight flaw and Shift-click at the other end. The cloned source pixels then cover up the flaw.

- ✔ **Pay attention to the origin point for sampling.** Depending on what you're cloning (for example, when covering up a flaw), if you keep sampling from the same point without ever varying it, the area you're cloning starts to look like ugly shag carpeting. Or, at best, starts to appear blotchy and overretouched.

- ✔ **Zoom out occasionally to check how your image looks overall.** Doing so helps you avoid those funky telltale clone stamp repetitive patterns and blotches.

 ✔ **When cloning patterns, use the Pattern Stamp tool,** which shares the flyout menu with the Clone Stamp tool. Select a custom pattern from the Pattern Picker on the Options bar. Drag with the Pattern Stamp tool, and you see the pattern appear.

Digital Bandaging with the Healing Brush Tool

The Healing Brush and Patch tools are similar to the Clone Stamp tool. They let you clone pixels from one area and apply them to another area. But that's where the similarities end; the healing tools leave the Clone Stamp tool eating their dust.

The problem with the Clone Stamp tool is that it doesn't take the tonality of the flawed area — the shadows, midtones, and highlights — into consideration. Therefore, if the pixels you're sampling from aren't shaded and lit exactly like the ones you're covering, you have a mismatch in color, which makes seamless and indecipherable repairs hard to achieve.

That's where the Healing Brush tool comes in. This very intelligent tool clones by using the *texture* from the sampled area (the source) and then the *colors* around the brush stroke when you paint over the flawed area (the destination). The highlights, midtones, and shadows remain intact, and the result of the repair is more realistic and natural — not retouched and phony. Follow these steps to heal your favorite, but imperfect, photo:

 1. **Open your image and select the Healing Brush tool.**

   My guy, shown in Figure 3-4, looks like he could stand to get some "work done," as they say in Hollywood. You can also heal between two images. Just make sure that they have the same color mode.

2. **On the Options bar, click the Brush Preset Picker.**

   In the drop-down panel, select your desired diameter and hardness, as well as spacing, angle, and roundness if you want, for your brush tip. You will most likely specify your brush settings several times while retouching your image. Using the appropriate brush size for the flaw you're repairing is important.

   Click the Tablet icon (at the end of the Options bar) to control the size of the brush. The pressure you apply will then override any settings in the Brush panel.

Figure 3-4: The Healing Brush can make these wrinkles practically disappear.

3. **On the Options bar, leave the blending mode set to Normal.**

   You can change your blending mode, if necessary. The Replace mode preserves textures, such as Noise or Film Grain, around the edges of your strokes when using a soft brush. For most simple retouching jobs, such as this one, you can leave it at Normal.

4. **Select a Source option.**

   You have a choice between Sampled and Pattern:

   - *Sampled:* You'll probably use this option, which uses the pixels from the image, 99 percent of the time.

   - *Pattern:* You can probably infer that it uses pixels from a pattern you select from the Pattern Picker.

   For my example, I'm sticking with Sampled because I don't think my guy would look that good with a Tie-Dye or Nebula pattern across his face. He's just way too corporate for that.

5. **Select how you want to align the sampled pixels.**

   When you click or drag with the Healing Brush tool, Photoshop displays a crosshair along with the Healing Brush cursor. The crosshair represents the sampling point, also known as the *source*. While you move the Healing Brush tool, the crosshair also moves, providing a constant reference to the area that you're sampling. However, if you deselect the Aligned option on the Options bar, Photoshop applies the source pixels

Book VIII Chapter 3

Fixing Flaws and Removing What's Not Wanted

from your original sampling point, despite how many times you stop and start dragging. I left the Aligned option selected in my example.

6. **Select the All Layers option from the Sample drop-down panel to heal an image by using all visible layers. Select Current Layer if you want to heal only from the active layer. Choose Current Layer and Below to heal from your active layer and all layers beneath it.**

You can use the Clone Source panel with the Healing Brush tool and the Clone Stamp tool. For details, see the section "Cloning with the Clone Stamp Tool," earlier in this chapter.

For maximum flexibility, select the Sample All Layers option and, in the Layers panel, add a new, blank layer above the image you want to heal. Select this blank layer and when you heal the image, the pixels appear on the new layer and not on the image itself. You can then adjust opacity and blending modes, and make other tweaks to the "healed" pixels.

7. **If you selected All Layers in Step 6, you can choose whether to ignore any adjustment layers when healing.**

By ignoring adjustment layers, you may prevent the bizarre results that can sometimes occur when your adjustment layers get double-applied during the healing process. To do so, click the Adjustment Layer icon on the Options bar.

8. **Establish the sampling point by Alt-clicking (Option-clicking on the Mac).**

Make sure to click the area of your image you want to clone *from*.

In my example, I clicked the smooth area on the chin and portions of the forehead.

9. **Release the Alt (Option on the Mac) key and click or drag over the area of your image that contains the flaw.**

Pay attention to where the crosshair is located because that's the area you're sampling from.

In my example, I brushed over the wrinkles under and around the eyes and on the forehead, as shown in Figure 3-5. I also zapped some dark spots here and there.

10. **Save the file, close it, and send in your invoice for your digital dermabrasion.**

Figure 3-5: In just 5 or 10 minutes, this gentleman lost about 10 years.

Patching without Seams

Although the Patch tool is similar to the Healing Brush tool in theory, its application method is slightly different. Instead of painting over the flaws with a brush, you select your flawed area and apply a patch to that selection.

The Patch tool does a good job in fixing larger flawed areas or isolated imperfections, rather than a few wrinkles or scars here and there. What's more, it's a breeze to use.

Follow these steps to patch an area in need of repair:

Figure 3-6: The Patch tool can fix the flaws on the wall.

 1. **Open your image and select the Patch tool.**

   It looks like a patch of material. The girl in my image, shown in Figure 3-6, is virtually flawless, although I can't say the same for the wall she's leaning against.

2. **Select Source or Destination on the Options bar.**

   Select Source if you want to select the flawed area. Select Destination if you want to select the good area you want to clone from.

   Select the Transparent option to patch from your source pixels with less opaqueness.

   You can use the Clone Source panel with the Patch tool. For details, see the section "Cloning with the Clone Stamp Tool," earlier in this chapter.

3. **Drag around the flawed area of your image, as shown in Figure 3-7.**

   Think of the Patch tool as a kind of super-cloning Lasso tool. Drag completely around the flawed area like you would when selecting with the Lasso tool. If you need to, you can apply a slight feather of 0.5 to 2 pixels, depending on the

Figure 3-7: Drag around the flawed area.

**Book VIII
Chapter 3**

Fixing Flaws and
Removing What's
Not Wanted

resolution, to soften the edge of the selection. I selected my area without a feather.

You can actually select your flawed area with any selection tool you like. If you use another selection tool, after you have your selection, select the Patch tool and proceed to Step 4.

4. **Drag your selection to the area on your image that you want to clone (or sample) from, as shown in Figure 3-8.**

5. **When you release the mouse button, Photoshop patches your flawed selection with the cloned pixels.**

Figure 3-8: Drag the selection to the area you want to sample.

6. **Repeat the process, as needed.**

After several patches, the wall looks almost as good as the girl, as shown in Figure 3-9.

Zeroing In with the Spot Healing Brush

Whereas the Healing Brush tool is designed to fix larger flawed areas, the Spot Healing Brush tool is designed for smaller blemishes and little imperfections. The biggest difference between the Healing Brush and the Spot Healing Brush is that the Spot Healing Brush doesn't require you to specify a sampling source. It automatically takes a sample from around the area to be retouched. The good news is it's quick and easy. The downside is that it doesn't give you as much control over the sampling source. Consequently, reserve this tool for small and simple flaws. Follow these steps to quickly fix little, nitpicky imperfections with the Spot Healing Brush tool:

Figure 3-9: The Patch tool repaired the wall.

1. **Open your image and grab the Spot Healing Brush tool.**

   The small moles in Figure 3-10 are examples of small areas you can fix with the Spot Healing Brush.

2. **On the Options bar, click the Brush Preset Picker and select your desired diameter, hardness, and other options for your brush tip.**

   Try to select a brush that's a little larger than the flawed area.

PhotoSpin

Figure 3-10: Watch these moles disappear.

3. **Select a blending mode from the Options bar.**

   Like the Healing Brush, you can select the Replace mode. Most likely, the Normal mode will work the best.

4. **Select a type from the Options bar.**

   You have a choice among Proximity Match, Create Texture, and the new Content Aware:

   - *Proximity Match:* Samples the pixels around the edge of the selection to use to fix the flawed area.

   - *Create Texture:* Uses all the pixels in the selection to create a texture to fix the flaw.

   - *Content-Aware:* Compares and uses actual content from the image close to the flaw. Try using the Content-Aware option when removing large items like cars, litter, scratches on your image, and other annoying elements.

5. **Choose Sample All Layers to heal an image by using all visible layers.**

   If you leave this option unselected, you heal only from the active layer.

   Click the Tablet icon (at the end of the Options bar) to control the size of the brush. The pressure you apply will then override any settings in the Brush panel.

6. **Click, or click and drag, the area you want to fix.**

   In Figure 3-11, I used the Spot Healing Brush for the moles and spots on the upper lip and cheeks. But for the mole over the eyebrow, I broke out the Healing Brush. I

Figure 3-11: I used the Spot Healing Brush and the Healing Brush to remove a few moles.

found I needed more control of the sampling source because the mole is so close to the hair of the eyebrow.

For retouching skin, try Proximity Match first and, if it doesn't work, undo and try Create Texture or Content-Aware. You may get better results filling the flawed area by using the Edit⇨Fill command. See how in Book IV, Chapter 2.

Colorizing with the Color Replacement Tool

The Color Replacement tool allows you to replace the original color of an image with the foreground color. You can use this tool in a variety of ways. Create the look of a hand-painted photo by colorizing a grayscale image. Or maybe you just want to change the color of an object or two, such as a couple flowers in a bouquet. And although Photoshop has a bona-fide Red Eye tool, you can use the Color Replacement tool to easily paint away red-eye.

The great thing about the Color Replacement tool is that, like the other healing tools, it completely preserves the tonality of the image. The color that you apply doesn't obliterate the midtones, shadows, and highlights like it would if you were using the regular Brush tool. The Color Replacement tool works by first sampling the original colors in the image and then replacing those colors with the foreground color. By specifying different sampling methods, limits, and tolerance settings, you can control the range of colors that Photoshop replaces.

This weapon in the arsenal of retouching tools is a cinch to use. Follow these steps to replace color:

1. **Open your image and select the Color Replacement tool.**

   Remember, it shares a flyout menu with the regular Brush and Pencil tools.

   It looks like a brush with a square and two arrows next to it. You can press B (or Shift+B) to select it.

2. **On the Options bar, click the Brush Preset Picker.**

   In the drop-down panel that appears, select your desired diameter, hardness, and other options for your brush tip.

3. **On the Options bar, select your desired blend mode:**

   • *Color:* The default mode that works well for most colorizing jobs. Use this mode if you're trying to get rid of red-eye.

   • *Hue:* Similar to color, but less intense, providing a lighter effect.

   • *Saturation:* Set your foreground color to Black in the Tools panel and set the mode to Saturation to convert a color image to grayscale.

- *Luminosity:* The exact opposite of the Color mode. Although it can create a beautiful effect between two image layers, it doesn't provide that great an effect with this tool.

  For a full "scientific" definition of each blending mode, check out Book V, Chapter 3.

4. **Select your sampling method from the icons on the Options bar.**

   The default of Continuous allows you to sample and replace color continuously while you drag your mouse. Select Once to replace colors only in areas containing the color that you first sample. Finally, select Background Swatch to replace colors only in areas containing your current Background color.

5. **Select your sampling limits mode.**

   The default of Contiguous lets you replace the color of pixels containing the sampled color that are adjacent to each other directly under the brush. Discontiguous lets you replace the color of the pixels containing the sampled color wherever it occurs under your brush. Find Edges allows you to replace the color of pixels containing the sampled color while preserving the sharpness of the edges of the objects.

6. **Specify your tolerance percentage.**

   Tolerance refers to a range of color. A high tolerance lets you replace a broad range of color. A low tolerance limits the replacement of color to only areas that are similar to the sampled color.

7. **Choose whether you want anti-aliasing.**

   Remember, anti-aliasing slightly softens and smoothes the edge of the selected or sampled areas.

   Click the Tablet icon (at the end of the Options bar) to control the size of the brush. The pressure you apply overrides any settings in the Brush panel.

8. **After you establish your settings, click or drag in your image.**

   The foreground color, which in my example is black, replaces the original colors of the sampled areas. (See Figure 3-12.) Of course, the exact effect you get depends on your settings.

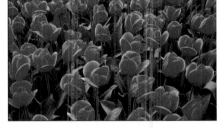

Figure 3-12: Use the Color Replacement tool to replace the original color in your image with your current foreground color.

Getting Rid of Dreaded Red-Eye

Red-eye occurs when the subject of a picture looks directly into the flash, and the unfortunate result is that eerie reddish luminescence in the eyes that says, "I may very well be a demon child."

Many cameras have a red-eye prevention mode, but that's little solace when you have a great picture that features bright red pupils as its most dominant feature. If you've been hanging around in Photoshop for a while, you're probably aware that you can get the same result many different ways. This holds true for getting rid of red-eye, as well. You can use the regular Brush tool with a Color blend mode and paint away the red. Or you can use the Color Replacement tool with a black foreground to color away the crimson. Additionally, you can use the Red Eye tool.

 TIP

If you need to fix the green, blue, or yellow eye that occurs in animals, the Red Eye tool isn't effective. You will want to use the other two techniques mentioned above.

Follow these steps for a quick way to get the red out and restore your image to a less zombielike look:

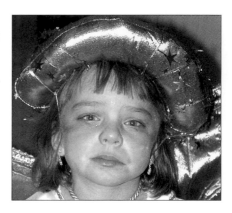

Figure 3-13: This photo needs an exorcist.

1. **Open the original photo with red-eye showing.**

   I'm using a photo of an unhappy angel, shown in Figure 3-13.

2. **Select the Red Eye tool.**

   Using the default settings, click the red portion of the eye in your image, as shown in Figure 3-14. This one-click tool darkens the pupil and retains the tonality and texture of the eye.

3. **If you're not happy with the results, tweak one or both of the following options:**

   • *Pupil Size:* Use the slider to increase or decrease the size of the pupil.

   • *Darken Pupil:* Use the slider to darken or lighten the color of the pupil.

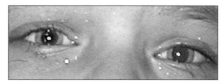

Figure 3-14: Click the red-eye with the Red Eye tool to make it vanish.

4. **If all goes well, your image is now cured of the dreaded red-eye, as shown in Figure 3-15.**

The Red Eye tool works only with RGB or Lab color images. For details on these color modes, see Book II.

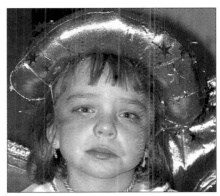

Figure 3-15: The ultimate cure for red-eye, but not tears.

Working with Vanishing Point

The Vanishing Point command enables you to make realistic edits in images that have perspective planes. With Vanishing Point, you specify the planes in your images and then, by using a variety of techniques, such as painting or cloning, add or eliminate objects on those planes.

For example, say you have a building that has only one window on the side. You have a remodeling project in mind in which you want to add more light in the room, so you want to add three more windows on that side. Using Vanishing Point, you can easily add those windows, all of which will be scaled and angled by staying true to the perspective of the side of that building.

Besides editing flaws from or features into your digital photos, other great uses for Vanishing Point include mocking up covers for books or DVDs, and putting graphics on various packaging containers.

Follow these steps to use this incredible feature:

1. **Open an image that needs editing.**

Creating a new layer is a good idea so that you can isolate your Vanishing Point result from your original image layer. You get further editing advantages by adding a layer if you want to change opacity settings, blend modes, and so on.

If you want the Vanishing Point results to only be applied to a specific part of your image, be sure to make the selection (or add a mask) before selecting the Vanishing Point command.

If you need to paste an element into the Vanishing Point dialog box, be sure to copy the item before selecting the Vanishing Point command. This copied element can be from the same image or a different image. It can also be a text layer.

2. **Choose Filter⇨Vanishing Point.**

   The Vanishing Point dialog box appears, as shown in Figure 3-16.

Create Plane tool

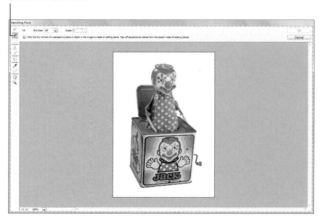

PhotoSpin

Figure 3-16: Boxes are good candidates for working with the Vanishing Point command.

3. **Grab the Create Plane tool (second tool from the top), and then click at each of the four corners of your plane to establish your editing surface.**

   Be as accurate as you can when specifying the plane on your image.

   A bounding box with *nodes* at each corner and a grid appears over the plane surface, as shown in Figure 3-17. Feel free to tweak the plane to perfection — just move or resize the plane by using the Create Plane or Edit Plane tools. Photoshop informs you if your plane has a problem by displaying a bounding box and grid as red or yellow. If you have a problem grid, adjust the bounding box until it becomes blue (indicating the plane is valid) by moving a corner node. ***Note:*** You may have to move multiple nodes.

4. **Use the Grid Size slider, accessed by clicking the double-headed arrow, to adjust the size of the grid units to better line up the plane and grid with the elements that may be in your image, such as tiles, texture, windows, or doors.**

5. **(Optional) If desired, you can use the Create Plane tool and Ctrl-drag (⌘-drag on the Mac) an edge node of the plane to "tear off" an additional plane.**

For example, you can extend the plane around to another side, as I did in Figure 3-17, and create another plane. This process keeps the planes related to each other and ensures that your edit is in the correct scale and angle. Make sure you get your first plane exact because after you create an additional plane, you can no longer edit the first plane, except to expand it by dragging the edge nodes.

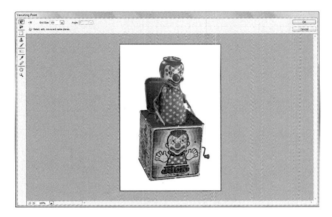

Figure 3-17: Define your editing plane with the Create Plane too .

Your second planes have to be perpendicular! You can tear off another plane and position it out at an angle. After creating your additional plane, grab either the Create Plane or Edit Plane tool, hold down Alt (Option on the Mac), grab the center node on the side opposite from your axis, and swing it out at your desired angle. You can also enter a value, or slide the slider, in the Angle option at the top of the Vanishing Point dialog box.

At this point, you can simply create perspective planes, click OK, and bail out. The planes you established appear when you call up the Vanishing Point command again.

6. **After you establish your perspective planes, select an editing task:**

   • *Make a selection.* Select the Marquee tool and drag a selection in the plane, as I did in Figure 3-18. Specify your selection options, either before or after the selection. You can feather the selection to get soft edges. Or you can adjust the opacity of the selection. You can also choose a Heal option. Move Mode allows you to specify the selection as Destination or Source. Select Destination to select the area you move the marquee to. Source fills an area with the contents of the marquee when you move the marquee and release. If you want to select your entire plane, just double-click with the Marquee tool.

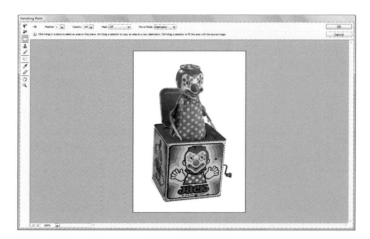

Figure 3-18: Make a selection with the Marquee tool on your plane.

- *Clone.* Select the Marquee or Transform tool and Alt-drag (Option-drag on the Mac) the selection to create a copy of the selection. Transform (scale, rotate, or move) the selection to your liking. Clone as many times as you want. When you move the selection, it adjusts to fit the perspective of the plane, as shown in Figure 3-19.

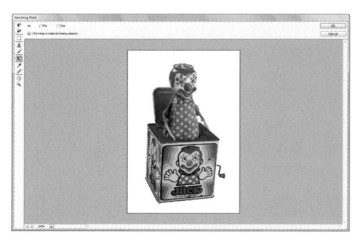

Figure 3-19: Your cloned selection conforms to fit the perspective of the destination plane.

Note: You have access to multiple undos within the Vanishing Point dialog box. But they're limited to your single editing session. Press Ctrl+Z (⌘+Z on the Mac) to undo.

- *Move a selection.* Grab the Marquee or Transform tool and drag the selection. Hold down the Shift key to constrain the move.

- *Transform a selection.* To scale the selection, select the Transform tool, move the cursor on top of a node, and drag. To rotate, move the cursor next to a node until you see a curved double arrow. Then, drag in the direction of your desired rotation. Select the Flip or Flop options to flip the selection horizontally or vertically.

- *Fill a selection with a piece of the image.* With the Marquee tool, Ctrl-drag (⌘-drag on the Mac) and make the selection you want as the source image. You can also choose Source from the Move Mode pop-up menu and drag the selection to the source image. You can then move or clone the selection. If the selection needs to be scaled or rotated, grab the Transform tool.

- *Clone by stamping with part of the image.* This technique works exactly like the regular Photoshop Clone Stamp tool. With the Stamp tool, Alt-click (Option-click on the Mac) the area you want to define as the source for your cloning. Then, drag your mouse on the portion of the image where you want the clone to appear. If you drag in a perspective plane, the Stamp tool paints the cloned area in perspective. You can specify options for your brush diameter, hardness, and opacity.

- *Select a Heal option.* The Off option allows you to clone without blending color, lighting, and shading of the surrounding pixels. The Luminance option allows you to clone by using the lighting and shading of the surrounding pixels, but keeping the color of the source (or sampled area). The On option enables you to clone by blending the color, lighting, and shading of the surrounding pixels. Select Aligned to sample pixels while maintaining the current sampling point, even when you release the mouse. Deselect this option to sample pixels from the sampling point of each mouse click.

- *Paint with color.* Select the Brush tool and specify your options, which are similar to the clone options. Click the Brush Color swatch. Select your desired color from the Color Picker and paint by dragging within your image. Like stamping, the brush size and shape adjust to stay true to the perspective.

- *Paste a copied element from the Clipboard before selecting the Vanishing Point command.* Press Ctrl+V (⌘+V on the Mac) to paste your element. With your Marquee tool, position the element on your plane, where it adjusts to fit the perspective.

- *Move around, measure, and magnify, as needed.* The Hand, Zoom, and Measure tools make measuring and navigation easy. You can also access the Magnification pop-up menu and the plus (+) and minus (–) buttons at the bottom of the window.

7. Click OK.

No one will be the wiser that your composite image, shown in Figure 3-20, doesn't really exist in the world as we know it. Save your edited image as a native Photoshop (.psd), TIFF, or JPEG file to ensure that your perspective planes are saved.

Figure 3-20: Your Vanishing Point-edited image looks unedited and unchanged.

Book IX

Photoshop and Print

So you've toiled away and gotten your images picture perfect? Not a flaw, colorcast, or stray pixel to be found? Congratulations! It's time to flaunt your editing prowess and share those images with the world. This book gives you the vitals on how to get those images print-ready. You can find information on how to set up images for offset printing. I also explain how to create panoramas from multiple images and how to work with High Dynamic Range (HDR) images.

Chapter 1: Prepping Graphics for Print

In This Chapter

✓ **Picking the right resolution, mode, and format**

✓ **Prepress and working with a service bureau**

✓ **Printing vector images**

✓ **Managing color when printing**

✓ **Creating color separations**

*P*reparing images for the screen is a snap compared to what you have to go through to get images ripe for the printing process. If all you ever want to do is print your images to a desktop laser or inkjet printer, the task is a little easier, but you still must consider some guidelines. And prepping your images for offset printing? Well, throw in an additional set of guidelines. It's not rocket science, mind you. If you stick to the basic rules and, more importantly, spend some time developing a good working relationship with your service bureau and offset printer, you're good to go.

Getting the Right Resolution, Mode, and Format

If you're not familiar with the concept of resolution, I suggest taking a look at Book II, Chapter 1. That's where I cover all the basics on resolution, pixel dimension, resampling, and other related topics. For full descriptions on color modes and file formats, see Book II, Chapter 2. That said, the following sections give you the lowdown on the proper settings for an image that will ultimately go to print.

Resolution and modes

Table 1-1 provides some guidelines about what resolution settings to use for the most common types of output. Remember, these are just *guidelines*. They aren't chiseled in stone to withstand the sands of time or anything lofty like that. You need to communicate with your service bureau, offset printer, or client and get specifications and/or recommendations. (See the section "Working with a Service Bureau," later in this chapter.)

Table 1-1	Recommended Resolutions and Image Modes		
Device	*Notes*	*Recommended Resolution*	*Mode*
Fuji Frontier photo printer	Wallets to 10 x 15 inches. Great for printing digital photos.	300 dpi	RGB
Online photo printers, such as Shutterfly	Check recommended size and resolution settings on the vendor's Web site.	1024 x 768 for 4-x-6 print; minimum of 1600 x 1200 for 8-x-10 print	RGB
Digital presses	Brands include Xeikon, Xerox, IBM, Indigo*, Scitex, Heidelberg, and so on.	255 to 300 dpi	CMYK
Epson color inkjets	Resolutions depend on the print setting. Epson recommends ⅓ of the horizontal resolution, but do test prints; settings may be higher than you need.	720 dpi × ⅓ = 240 dpi; 1440 dpi × ⅓ = 480 dpi; 2880 dpi × ⅓ = 960 dpi	RGB
Color separations	Film separations or direct to plate for offset printing.	2 × lines per inch (lpi); 2 × 133 lpi = 266 dpi; 2 × 150 lpi = 300 dpi; 2 × 175 lpi = 350 dpi**	CMYK and spot colors
Laser printers	Color or B&W printouts.	2 x lpi = 170 dpi	Grayscale or RGB

*Indigo presses can handle a fifth spot color, if necessary.
**See the section "Screen frequencies," in this chapter.

Screen frequencies

For the recommended resolution for color separations in Table 1-1, I list 2 multiplied by the number of lines per inch. The lines per inch, or *lpi,* pertains to the screen frequency of the output device. Screen frequencies are measured in lines per inch in a halftone screen. You may also hear the terms *screen ruling* or *line screen.* When images are printed, they're converted into a series of dots called *halftones.* When you print your halftone, you print it by using a halftone screen of a certain value. The average screen frequency for printing four-color images is 133 to 175 lpi. Therefore, when you multiply that number by 2, you need to create your images by using a resolution setting of 266 to 350 dots per inch (dpi).

File formats

As far as file formats go, what you choose depends on a couple issues:

- ✔ What you intend to do with the image — print it to a laser printer, order prints from an online photo printer?

- ✔ What does your service bureau, offset printer, client, director, or another interested party prefer?

Most publications (newspaper, magazines) will accept PDFs only because of their capability to embed fonts and links within the document, thereby eliminating a lot of headaches. For more on PDFs, see Book II, Chapter 2.

Table 1-2 lists some of the more popular recommended formats for specific jobs, but again, communicate with the parties involved to see what's ultimately the best format to use.

Table 1-2	Recommended File Formats
Job	**Formats**
Color inkjet printouts	EPS, TIFF, PDF, PSD
Color separations	PSD, PDF, EPS, TIFF, DCS 2.0
Spot color separations	PSD, PDF, DCS 2.0 if importing into another application
Magazines/brochures	EPS, TIFF, PDF
Newspapers	TIFF, PDF
Importing to page layout programs	TIFF, EPS, PSD, PDF
Importing to illustration programs	EPS, TIFF, DCS, PSD, PDF
Slides	TIFF, PowerPoint, PICT, PCX, EPS (some bureaus can't do EPS)
Photo prints	JPEG, TIFF
Word documents	TIFF, EPS, PNG
E-mailing for workflow review	PDF

Working with a Service Bureau

Service bureaus handle photo processing and various photographic output options, such as prints (of varying sizes) and slides. Mounting and lamination services may also be provided. Many service bureaus provide scanning services, including high-end drum scanning. A common service is taking scans or digital photos and burning them onto CDs or DVDs. Many service bureaus provide output to color separations to film and RC paper. Larger bureaus may even have a digital press to handle a short-run (500 or less), on-demand printing need.

Getting the ball rolling

Developing a good working relationship with your service bureau and/or offset printer can save you a lot of time, money, and frustration. These folks are the experts and know their equipment and processes. And believe me, they're only too willing to help. The fewer problems they have with your files, the better they like it. You can do some things to keep the relationship on solid footing:

- **Get a dialogue going about the specs.** If your file is going directly to a newspaper, magazine, or other publication, talk with the art director, graphics production coordinator, or other knowledgeable person about the graphic specifications required.

- **Build a lasting relationship.** Consistency is also key. When you find a good bureau or offset printer, stick with it for all your jobs. Jumping from one company to another because a quote came in a little cheaper doesn't always pay off in the long run. If you're a faithful customer, often your service bureau or offset printer will match that lower quote if it can.

- **Get on the Web.** Many service bureaus have Web sites where you can find a listing of services they offer, price lists, file specs, and even downloadable order forms. Larger offset printers also have general information, online requests for quote applications, and more. Larger offset printers may provide services such as scanning and film-separation output, so be sure to check the Web site for details.

Using a prepress checklist

To prepare your file for print, use the following list to ensure your file is ready and rarin' for problem-free output. Note that this list isn't all-inclusive when it comes to prepress; I include tips that pertain to Photoshop only.

- **Always transform your images in their native application.** Size, crop, rotate, shear, and reflect art in Photoshop. Transforming images in an illustration or page layout program is complex and time-consuming.

- **Ensure that images can first print from Photoshop.** Do this before importing the images into an illustration or page layout program.

- **If you're placing Photoshop EPS images into a page layout or illustration program, set the halftone screen frequency in the destination program instead of embedding it in each image in Photoshop.** Or better yet, don't set any halftone screen frequencies in your images and let your service bureau or offset printer handle setting them in the other program.

- **When saving Photoshop images for print purposes, stick to TIFF, EPS, native PSD, or PDF file formats.** If you're unsure of the proper format to use for a specific job, ask your offset printer or service bureau.

- **Make sure that you use the proper color mode.** For example use CMYK for color separations and RGB for slide output.

- **Create vector shapes and paths efficiently.** Use the fewest number of anchor points possible to create the path and delete any unnecessary or stray points. Leave your flatness setting blank. Photoshop uses the default setting for the output device, which is usually a safe bet.

- **Limit the number of typefaces.** Downloading takes time. Limiting the number of typefaces also makes your document look more sophisticated and polished.

- **Make sure that all scanning is at the appropriate dpi.** For more on resolution, see Book II, Chapter 1.

- **If your image is to bleed (extend to the edge of the printed page), take that into account when creating your image.** Note that you need to allow for ⅛ to ¼ of an inch on any side that will bleed to allow for slippages when the paper is cut.

- **Always specify colors from a Pantone color swatch chart and then select the color, whether process or spot, in Photoshop.** *Never* trust the way colors look onscreen because of calibration deficiencies and differences between RGB and CMYK color models.

- **Make spot color names consistent.** Make sure that the Photoshop spot color names exactly match those of any programs to which you are importing your image, such as an illustration or page layout program. Otherwise, you may get an additional color separation.

- **Print and provide laser or inkjet prints of your file, both separations (if warranted), and a composite print.** Print all prints with printer marks — crop marks, registration marks, labels, and so on.

- **Provide all fonts used in your file.** Provide both screen and PostScript printer fonts, if applicable.

- **Choose File⇨Save As for your final save to squeeze down to the smallest file size.**

- **Organize your files into folders.** For example, put the image files together in one folder, all the fonts in another, and so on.

- **Communicate any trapping needs to your service bureau or offset printer.** *Trapping* is also known as spreading and choking, where you create slight overlaps where your colors meet to avoid registration problems on the printing press. For color separations, indicate whether you created the trapping yourself or if you want the service bureau/offset printer to do it.

Some file format warnings

If you save your file as an EPS or DCS and re-open the file in Photoshop, Photoshop rasterizes the vector data to pixels. Save the original in the native PSD format.

If you save your layered file as an EPS, Photoshop converts your vector type to clipping paths. Extensive and small type creates complex clipping paths, which can be time-consuming and sometimes difficult to print. You can either flatten your file or deselect the Include Vector Data option in the Save as EPS Options dialog box. Either choice rasterizes the type into pixels at the resolution of your image. You may want to consider eliminating the type in your image file and applying it either in a drawing or page layout program that can retain vector type.

Saving and Printing Vector Data in a Raster File

Photoshop allows you to create vector shapes and vector type with the Pen tools, shape tools, and type tools. (I explain how in Book III.) Technically, the vector shapes are clipping paths applied to a bitmap, or *raster,* layer. But the clipping path is *still* a vector path, thereby retaining vector qualities. This vector data is resolution-independent, which means that it prints at the resolution of the PostScript output device. Photoshop sends the printer separate images for each type and shape layer, which are printed on top of the raster image and clipped by using their vector paths. The edges of the vector path print at the full resolution of the PostScript printer, but the contents, such as the colored pixels or the image pixels within the vector path, print at the resolution of the Photoshop file. (All portions of the type are resolution-independent.) Therefore, type and shapes always have crisp, hard edges, with curves appearing smooth and never jagged.

Remember that the only file formats that allow you to retain vector data are PSD, PDF, DCS, and EPS. When saving to DCS or EPS, be sure to select the Include Vector Data option in their respective Options dialog boxes. All other file formats rasterize the vector data.

Choosing Color Management Print Options

I highly recommend checking out the color management section in Book II, Chapter 3. In that chapter, I go into great detail about the concept of color spaces, ICC profiles, and so on. In this section, I cover the color management options you can find in the Print dialog box.

Different output devices operate in different color spaces. Monitors, desktop printers, large-format printers, film recorders, offset printers, and so on all have their own unique color space. The color management options enable you to convert the color space of your image while printing. So, for example, if the ICC (color) profile of your image is sRGB, you can choose to have your image's color space converted to the color space of your Epson printer when you print.

Unfortunately, I can't tell you what specific settings to choose. This choice is a widely debated topic, and different printers have their strengths, shortcomings, and quirks. My advice is to take an hour and a pack of paper, run test prints to see which settings give you the most accurate result, and stick with those. You may even get different results from different types of paper.

When you have some free time, follow these steps to experiment with the Color Management settings and discover what print settings work best:

1. **Choose File⊃Print to open the Print dialog box, shown in Figure 1-1.**

2. **Select Color Management from the pop-up menu in the top-right portion of the Print dialog box.**

3. **Select either Document or Proof.**

   Remember, you're experimenting. So select one, and then try the other:

   • *Document:* Uses the color profile of your image.

   • *Proof:* By default, Proof uses the color profile of your Working CMYK color space, which you defined in your Color Settings dialog box. You can change this profile, however, by choosing View⊃Proof Setup⊃ Current Custom Setup. For details on proofs, see Book II, Chapter 3.

Figure 1-1: Specify the settings in the Color Management portion of the Print dialog box.

4. **Select a method from the Color Handling pop-up menu.**

The options differ, depending on whether you chose Document or Proof in Step 3.

If you chose Document in the Print area, here are your options:

- *Printer Manages Colors:* Sends the document unchanged to the printer, tagged with its color profile. The printer driver then picks an appropriate color profile and converts your document's colors to the final printout. Just make sure you enable color management in your printer dialog box.

- *Photoshop Manages Colors:* Tells Photoshop to handle the color conversion, using the settings you select from the Printer Profile and Rendering Intent pop-up menus. Photoshop also checks whether you selected the Black Point Compensation option with this setting. If you did, make sure you disable any color management in your printer dialog box.

- *Separations:* Select this option if you want to print color separations. (See the following section.) Note that your image must be in CMYK mode.

If you chose Proof in the Print area, you see the same options, but a couple of them produce different results:

- *Printer Manages Colors:* Works only with a PostScript (PS level 2 or higher) printer, which manages the color conversion of the proof to the print based on your selection of Simulate Paper Color or Simulate Black Ink.

- *Photoshop Manages Colors:* Tells Photoshop to handle the color conversion of the proof to the print, using the printer profile specified in the pop-up menu and your choice of simulation. Unless you have a lot of dark colors, I recommend leaving it on Simulate Paper Color.

5. **If you chose Photoshop Manages Colors in Step 4, select your printer and paper type from the Printer Profile pop-up menu.**

Profiles associated with the current printer you select in the Printer submenu are sorted and placed at the top of the profile list.

Although you may be able to change the Rendering Intent setting, I recommend leaving this at the default setting of Relative Colorimetric, especially when printing photos or multicolored artwork. If, by chance, your image has a lot of areas of solid saturated color, you can try Saturation. Also, leave the Black Point Compensation check box at the default setting of selected or deselected (depending on your Color Handling choice) — unless, of course, you're a color guru and have a better reason not to. Setting this option enables your printer to more accurately print the blacks in your image.

When you select Photoshop Manages Color, you have three additional options located directly below the image preview. These options are strictly preview options and affect only how you see your image on the computer screen. The Match Print Colors option displays a soft proof of your print based on the profiles, color management options, and printer you select. See Book II, Chapter 3, for more on soft proofs. The Gamut Warning option displays colors that will be *out of gamut,* or out the range of printable colors. These colors appear as gray pixels by default. And, finally, the Show Paper White option simulates the white point of the paper you select in the Printer Profile submenu. My paper of choice is Premium Matte, as shown in Figure 1-1.

6. **Mac users, click the Print Settings button to choose paper size, quality/media settings, and other options, depending on your exact printer. Click OK.**

7. **When you finish making your selections, click Print.**

Windows users, your final dialog box appears. Depending on your printer, options will vary. In Windows 7, click the Preferences button and search for paper/media and quality options. Depending on whether your printer is an Epson, Canon, HP, or other, the names of these settings vary.

If you selected the Photoshop Manages Colors option, you should turn off color management in your particular printer's dialog box.

That's all there is to it. If you want more information on printing, check out Book I, Chapter 3. For more explanation on color management, see Book II, Chapter 3.

If all you want to do is print color prints on your desktop printer I recommend starting by selecting Document in the Print area and selecting Photoshop Manages Colors for Color Handling, which gives you the most control over printing. If you have a little time and paper to burn, then print another copy by using the Printer Manages Colors option. Do a side-by-side comparison to see which one looks superior. You can also crack the seal on the documentation that came with your printer for any recommendations.

Getting Four-Color Separations

It's necessary to *color-separate* your image whenever you plan to print your image to an offset press. Your image must first be in CMYK color mode. (Choose Image➪Mode➪CMYK Color.) Then, the composite color image gets digitally separated into the four-color channels — cyan, magenta, yellow, and black — and is output. (These colors are also known as *process colors.*) Sometimes, the separation output is onto film, and sometimes, it's output directly to aluminum printing plates. The plates are put on an offset press, paper runs through each of the four inked rollers (cyan first, then magenta, yellow, and finally black), and out comes your composite image.

Before you take your image to a service bureau or offset printer to get color separations, it's wise to get what are called *laser separations.* Basically, you're color-separating your image, not to film or plates, but to paper.

If your image doesn't separate to paper, most likely it won't to film or plates, either. You can go back and correct the problem, rather than pay upward of $80 to $150 an hour to have the service bureau or offset printer correct it for you. Consider laser separations a cheap insurance policy.

Follow these steps to get laser separations from your desktop printer:

1. **Be sure your image mode is CMYK. If it isn't, choose Image⇨Mode⇨ CMYK Color.**

   I'm assuming your image is a four-color image. But it may also be a grayscale, duotone, tritone, or quadtone image, in which case, no conversion to CMYK is necessary. (See Book II, Chapter 2, for more on modes.)

   After the conversion, you have an image with four channels — Cyan, Magenta, Yellow, and Black, like the one shown in Figure 1-2.

2. **Choose File⇨Print, and then select Color Management from the pop-up menu in the top-right portion of the Print dialog box that appears.**

3. **In the Print area, select Document.**

   The setting should say U.S. Web Coated (SWOP) v2.

4. **Select Separations from the Color Handling pop-up menu.**

   This option prints each channel from the image to a separate plate, or in the case of laser separations, paper.

5. **Select Output from the pop-up menu in the top-right portion of the dialog box, and then select additional options as you desire.**

   For general print options, see Book I, Chapter 3. For additional options, see Table 1-3.

   Note that if you're printing to a non-PostScript printer, some of these options may not be available. You see a preview of most of these options when you apply them to your file.

6. **Click the Print button.**

   If all goes well, four pieces of paper, one for each of the four CMYK channels, print. If you're printing a grayscale, duotone, tritone, or quadtone image, you get one to four pieces of paper, one for each color used. If that doesn't happen, something's amiss, and it's time for troubleshooting. Be sure to take these laser separations with you when you hand over your file to the service bureau or offset printer.

Corbis Digital Stock

Figure 1-2: Color images are separated into four process colors.

Table 1-3	Output Options	
Option	*What It Does*	*Recommendation*
Calibration Bars	Prints an 11-step grayscale bar outside the image area to gauge how accurately the shades are being printed. When you're printing separations, this option prints a gradient tint bar and color bar.	Select this option.
Registration Marks	Prints crosshair and target marks outside the image area, allowing you to line up the four plates or pages.	Select this option.

continued

Table 1-3 *(continued)*

Option	What It Does	Recommendation
Corner Crop Marks	Adds crop marks at the corners of the image to indicate where to trim the image.	Select this option.
Center Crop Marks	Adds crop marks at the center of each side of the image to indicate where to trim the image.	Select this option.
Description	Prints the description as entered in the File➪File Info area.	Select if you have entered a description.
Labels	Prints the filename and channel name on each plate or page.	Select this option.
Emulsion Down	*Emulsion* is the side of the film that's light sensitive. Allows the film to be printed with the emulsion side down.	Leave this option deselected for laser separations. When the service bureau or offset printer prints the separations to film or plates, it may select this option.
Negative	Prints black as white and white as black, and every other color inverts accordingly.	Leave this option deselected for laser separations. When the service bureau or offset printer prints the separations to film or plates, it may select this option.
Interpolation	Anti-aliases low-resolution images by resampling.	Available only for PostScript Level 2 or laser printers. Leave it deselected.
Include Vector Data	See the "Saving and Printing Vector Data in a Raster File" section, in this chapter.	Leave this option selected if you have type or vector paths.

Creating Spot Color Separations

Photoshop allows you to add separate channels for spot colors (see Book VI, Chapter 1, for more on channels), which can then be color-separated. Spot, or *custom,* colors are premixed inks manufactured by various ink companies, the most popular in the U.S. being Pantone. A spot color is often used for a logo, type, or small illustration. Spot colors are also used when you need to apply metallic inks or varnishes to your print job. Spot colors can be used rather than, or in addition to, the four process CMYK colors.

If you're delving into the world of spot colors, I highly recommend that you choose your color from a printed Pantone swatch book, available from www.pantone.com. Because your screen is an RGB device and you're setting up your file for a CMYK output device, the colors you see on screen don't match the colors that are ultimately on paper — at best, they're a ballpark match. For accuracy, you must select the colors from the printed swatch book. For more on working with color, see Book II, Chapter 3.

Creating a spot channel

Follow these steps to create a spot channel:

1. **On a separate layer, create the graphic or type to which you want to apply the spot color.**

2. **Ctrl-click (⌘-click on the Mac) the thumbnail of the layer to select the graphic and then choose Edit⇨Fill to fill it with any solid color at an opacity of 100 percent.**

3. **With your selection active, choose Window⇨Channels and then select New Spot Channel from the Channels panel pop-up menu.**

   You can apply a spot color only to an active selection. It can't be applied to just a layer.

   The New Spot Channel dialog box appears, as shown in Figure 1-3.

   Figure 1-3: Adding an additional color separation in Photoshop requires creating a spot color channel first.

4. **In the Name text box, enter a name for your spot color. In the Ink Characteristics area, click the color swatch.**

   I recommend naming your spot color according to the spot color you want to use, such as Pantone 7417C.

   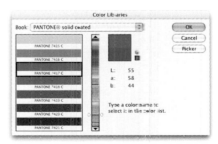

   When you click the color swatch, the Color Picker appears.

5. **Click the Color Libraries button in the Color Picker and select your Pantone color from the Color Libraries dialog box that appears (see Figure 1-4), and then click OK.**

   Figure 1-4: Select an appropriate color from the Color Libraries dialog box.

6. **In the New Spot Channel dialog box, select a Solidity value between 0 percent and 100 percent.**

A value of 100 percent represents an ink that's completely opaque, such as a metallic ink, which completely covers the inks beneath it. A value of 0 percent represents a transparent ink, such as a clear varnish. But the solidity value affects only the screen view and composite prints; it doesn't affect the separations. It can help you see where a "clear" varnish will print.

Figure 1-5: The Channels panel displays the spot channel.

7. **Click OK to close the dialog box.**

Your spot channel appears in the Channels panel and is filled in the image, as well. I created a spot channel for my crest graphic and for the type (Pantone 7417C), as shown in Figure 1-5.

In the printing process, spot colors are overprinted on top of the four-color image, as shown in Figure 1-6. That means that the spot color is applied at the end of the printing process and is printed over the other inks. This can sometimes cause lighter spot colors to darken somewhat.

If you need your spot color graphic to knock out the underlying image, create it in an illustration or page layout program. A *knockout* is a hole left in the four-color image, which is filled with the spot ink. The spot ink doesn't print over the other inks.

Corbis Digital Stock

Figure 1-6: Spot colors are often used for color-critical logos that print on top of your image.

8. **Save the image in the native Photoshop, Photoshop PDF, or Photoshop DCS 2.0 (Desktop Color Separations) format.**

TIFFs also support spot channels, but your page layout program may not recognize them.

If the image is being separated directly out of Photoshop, leave it as a PSD or PDF file. If you want to import it into a different program, such as InDesign, or QuarkXPress, you must save it as a DCS file. If your image is a duotone, tritone, or quadtone image, you also have to go through a few more hoops. You must first convert it to multichannel mode by choosing Image⇨Mode.

In the DCS 2.0 Format dialog box, make sure that the Include Halftone Screen and Include Transfer options aren't selected.

Import the image into your destination application and set your screen angles.

Editing a spot channel

After you create a spot channel, you can edit it. Select the channel in the Channels panel and use a painting or editing tool to paint with black, white, or any shade of gray, just as you would with an alpha channel. To change any of the options of the spot channel, double-click the spot channel thumbnail, or select it and then select Channel Options from the panel pop-up menu. Select a different color or solidity.

TIP

Converting an alpha channel to a spot channel

If you want to convert an alpha channel to a spot channel, select the alpha channel in the Channels panel and select Channel Options from the panel's pop-up menu. Rename the channel and select Spot Color. Click the color swatch and select a color from the Color Libraries section of the Color Picker. Click OK, then click OK again. Note that Photoshop converts all areas containing nonwhite pixels (unselected to partially selected areas) to the spot color. With the channel still selected in the Channels panel, choose Image⇨Adjustments⇨Invert to apply the spot color to the white pixels or selected areas of the alpha channel. For details on alpha channels, see Book VI, Chapters 1 and 3.

Chapter 2: Using Photomerge and Merge to HDR Pro

In This Chapter

✐ **Creating a panorama from multiple shots**

✐ **Merging photos for superior quality**

Sometimes, working with just a single shot isn't quite enough. You couldn't quite squeeze that beautiful mountain vista into one photo; it took three shots. Not to worry, that's what Photoshop's Photomerge command is for. This great command seamlessly stitches multiple shots of your panorama into a single image. Similarly, trying to capture the entire tonal range of an image can be tough. The Merge to HDR Pro command enables you to take multiple exposures of an image and later merge those exposures into a single High Dynamic Range image, allowing for superior image quality. And as if that alone isn't enough, these two commands are found on Photoshop's Automate menu, meaning they're quite easy to use.

Using the Photomerge Command

The Photomerge command allows you to combine multiple images into one continuous panoramic image. For example, you can take several overlapping photos of a mountain range and put them together into one panoramic shot using the Photomerge dialog box, as shown in Figure 2-1.

If you know you ultimately want to create a Photomerge composition, you can make things easier by making sure that when you shoot your photos, you overlap your individual images by 15 to 40 percent, but no more than 70 percent. Adobe also recommends that you avoid using distortion lenses (such as fish-eye) and your camera's zoom setting. Finally, try to stay in the same position and keep your camera at the same level for each shot. Using a tripod and rotating the head can help you achieve this consistency. If you are lucky enough to have a nice, long parallel surface handy (like a sidewalk), try taking spaced photos using your tripod along this surface.

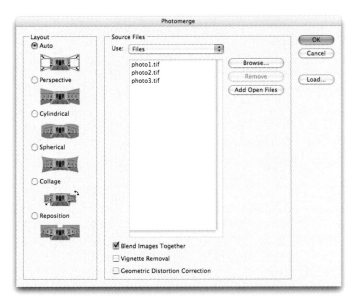

Photodisc

Figure 2-1: Select several overlapping shots to create one panoramic image.

Follow these steps to assemble your own Photomerge composition:

1. **Choose File⇨Automate⇨Photomerge.**

   You can also select your desired source images and choose Tools⇨ Photoshop⇨Photomerge in Adobe Bridge. Using Bridge is a timesaver because you can quickly and visually select your images.

2. **In the Photomerge dialog box, shown in Figure 2-1, select your source files.**

   From the Use pop-up menu, you can select from Files (which uses individual files you select) or from Folder (which uses all images in a folder. Click the Add Open Files button to use all currently open files. Or click the Browse button to navigate to your desired files or folder.

   If you want to delete a file from the list, select it and click Remove.

3. **Select Blend Images Together to correct the color differences that can occur from blending images with different exposures.**

   Photoshop then blends the colors and tones.

   If the Blend Images Together option doesn't help, you can always create a blending group. First, in your Layers panel, create a new group containing the layer you want to change. Next, change the group Blend mode to Normal. Finally, add an adjustment layer, such as Levels or Exposure, in the group above the layer you want to change. For more on adjustment layers, see Book V, Chapter 1. For more on blend modes, see Book V, Chapter 3.

4. **Select Vignette Removal to correct exposure problems caused by *lens vignetting* (when light at the edges of images is reduced and therefore edges are darkened).**

5. **Select Geometric Distortion Correction to correct for lens distortions, such as radial distortion, barrel distortion (bulging out), and pincushion distortion (pinching in).**

   You can use this option to align shots taken with a fish-eye lens.

6. **In the Layout area, select your desired project mode, as shown in Figure 2-1.**

   The thumbnail illustration visually demonstrates each mode but I'll give you a little more description of each:

   - *Auto:* Select the Auto mode to make Photoshop analyze your images on its own.

   - *Perspective:* Select this mode if your images have been shot with perspective, or at acute angles. This mode is also recommended for High Dynamic Range (HDR) images.

   - *Cylindrical:* Select this option if you shot your images with a wide-angle lens or when your images have that nasty "bow-tie" distortion. This mode is also good for those 360-degree, full panoramic shots.

   - *Spherical:* This mode is handy when stitching together a 360-degree panorama, in which you have a wide field of view, both horizontally and vertically. Use this option for shots taken with a wide-angle lens.

   - *Collage:* This projection method aligns images by rotating, positioning, and uniformly scaling each image. It may be the best choice for pure panoramas, but you can also find it useful for stitching together images based on common features.

   - *Reposition:* When you select this mode, Photoshop doesn't take into account any distortion, but merely scans the images and positions them in what it considers the best position.

7. **Click OK.**

   Photoshop marches off and attempts to automatically align and "stitch" your source images into a new Photoshop image, shown in Figure 2-2. Hopefully, all goes well; however, if Photoshop can't align and merge, it presents an alert that says "some images could not be aligned."

No matter which projection mode you select, Photoshop leaves your merged image in layers. In addition to those layers, Photoshop may also add a layer mask to each layer to better blend and composite your merged image. These layer masks act like any other layer masks, meaning you can edit them to your liking. For more on layer masks, see Book VI, Chapter 3.

Photodisc

Figure 2-2: The Photomerge command enables you to combine multiple images into one continuous panoramic shot.

Using the Merge to HDR Pro Command

Have you ever caught an early matinee and emerged molelike from the pitch-black theater into the bright light of high noon, only to have to squint for a while because your eyes burned? Or on the flip side, have you blindly tumbled into your seat, popcorn scattering all over the aisle in that same darkened theater because you just came in from the bright daylight? In both cases, your eyes needed some time to adjust to the abrupt change from extreme dark to extreme light or vice versa. Cameras suffer from the same problem. But although our eyes can eventually adapt to varying brightness levels, cameras and devices, such as computer monitors and scanners, can capture only a fixed dynamic, or tonal, range. In digital imaging tech talk, *dynamic range* is the ratio of the darkest and brightest values a device can capture simultaneously.

In the past, digital photography aficionados were hindered when performing higher-end, image-editing tasks in Photoshop because they were forced to work within a limited dynamic range. Recent versions of Photoshop have provided users with plenty of support for High Dynamic Range (HDR) images. HDR images, which contain 32 bits of data per channel, are superior to non-HDR images because they can capture a much larger dynamic range — in fact, they're able to represent the entire dynamic range of the real world.

Photographers can take multiple exposures of an image and then later merge those multiple exposures into a single photo in Photoshop, thereby capturing the entire dynamic range into a single HDR image. Although you can use the Merge to HDR Pro command on 8- or 16-bit images, be aware that only 32-bit images can store all the HDR data.

Adobe offers a few tips to maximize your success with the Merge to HDR Pro command:

- ✓ Use a tripod when shooting multiple exposures of the same scene to ensure you're capturing the exact same shot each time.

- ✓ Make sure you take enough shots to cover the entire dynamic range of your subject. Shoot for a minimum of three, but try for five to seven, if not more.

- ✓ Vary the shutter speed to create different exposures, instead of varying your aperture or ISO, which can cause noise, vignetting, and altering of depth of field.

- ✓ Make sure the exposure difference between the shots is one or two Exposure Value (EV) steps apart. Use one or two f-stops apart as a guide.

- ✓ Don't vary the lighting in the shots.

- ✓ Don't shoot anything that's moving. The scene needs to be static.

Follow these steps to use this improved feature:

1. **Choose File➪Automate➪Merge to HDR Pro.**

   The Merge to HDR Pro dialog box appears, as shown in Figure 2-3.

   Note that you can also access this command in Bridge by choosing Tools➪Photoshop➪Merge to HDR Pro.

   You can even create 32-bit images via the File New dialog box. Simply select 32-bit from the Bit Depth pop-up menu to the right of the Color Mode pop-up menu.

Figure 2-3: Select two or more files to merge in the Merge to HDR Pro dialog box.

2. **Select either Files or Folder from the Use pop-up menu.**

   You can also select Add Open Files if you want to use files that are currently open in Photoshop. Just make sure that they've been saved first.

3. **If you selected Files or Folder in Step 2, click the Browse button, select the images, and click Open. If you're using files that you already have open, move on to Step 4.**

   If you choose an image by accident, simply select it and click Remove.

4. **(Optional) Select Attempt to Automatically Align Source Images if you want Photoshop to try to line up your various exposures.**

This is a good idea if you shot your photos without the use of a tripod. Also note that your images need to be the same dimension and resolution for this command to work.

5. **Click OK.**

You may get a mini dialog box that asks you to manually set your exposure value, as shown in Figure 2-4. You need to specify your exposure time (shutter speed), f-stop (aperture), and ISO (film speed) for all your images.

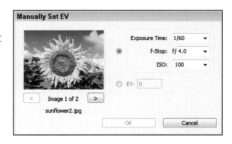

A second dialog box appears with thumbnails of your chosen images on the bottom and a large preview of the merged image in the center.

Figure 2-4: Manually specify your exposure value.

6. **Based on how you like the merged image, you can select or deselect any of the thumbnails in the source area, at the bottom of the dialog box, by selecting or deselecting the check boxes.**

Photoshop may bark that you don't have enough dynamic range to get a "useful" HDR image, in which case, you have to bail out.

If you want to zoom in and out of your images, click the – and + buttons, or use the View pop-up menu at the bottom of the Preview window.

7. **In the Mode menu, shown in Figure 2-5, select your desired bit depth for the merged image.**

Be sure to leave your 32-bit image set to 32 Bit if you want to capture and store the entire dynamic range.

8. **On the histogram, use the White Point slider to set the white point for the merged image if you want to see a better preview.**

The dynamic range of HDR images surpasses what your monitor can show. So, when you view these images on your computer, they can look pretty nasty — too dark and undersaturated. If you adjust the preview with the White Point slider, Photoshop provides a better display of the image without altering the image data at all. Remember that if your image is 32-bit, adjusting the white point affects only the preview, not the actual image data. That preview adjustment should then be saved in the HDR file and applied whenever the file is opened in Photoshop. But, if your image is 16- or 8-bit, adjusting the white point applies the adjustment to the actual image data itself.

You can save your settings for use later by choosing Preset⇨Save Preset.

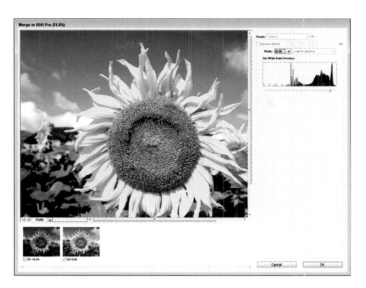

Figure 2-5: Specify your desired bit depth and adjust your white point.

By default, the Merge to HDR Pro command automatically calculates a response curve based on an analysis of the tonal range of your images.

9. **(Optional) If you want to save a curve for later use, click the response curve menu in the upper-right corner of the dialog box and choose Save Response Curve.**

Camera response curves have to do with how your camera sensor analyzes light.

10. **(Optional) Select Remove Ghosts if you have images with objects you wish to remove.**

For example, if you have a shot where a car or person moved into the shot and you want it removed, selecting this option will do so. Photoshop will display a green box around the image thumbnail with the best tones, which will then be used as the base image for the merged photo.

11. **Click OK.**

Your merged HDR image appears in all its full dynamic glory in its own image window.

Even if you want to ultimately convert your 32-bit image to 16-bit or even 8-bit, always make your exposure and contrast corrections first and then convert it. You'll get your dynamic range the way you want it. To adjust exposure and contrast, select your desired bit depth from the Mode pop-up menu, and select your desired conversion method from the pop-up menu. Here is a brief explanation of each conversion method:

✒ **Exposure and Gamma:** Adjusts the brightness (Exposure) and contrast (Gamma) of the image.

✒ **Highlight and Compression:** Compresses the highlight values so they fall within the tonal range of an 8- or 16-bit image.

✒ **Equalize Histogram:** This is an automatic method that compresses the dynamic range but tries to retain contrast.

✒ **Local Adaptation:** Enables you to adjust the tones by adjusting local brightness regions in your image. Set the following options:

- Click the *Curve* tab and make adjustments to the curve. The histogram of that curve shows the Luminance (amount of light) value. Each red tick mark represents one exposure value (or f-stop).

- For *Edge Glow,* adjust the Radius slider to specify the size of the local brightness regions. Strength indicates how far apart the values of two pixels must be before they are not part of the same brightness region.

- For *Tone and Detail,* adjust the Gamma setting accordingly. Lower settings emphasize midtone values, while higher settings emphasize shadows/highlights. A Gamma setting of 1 indicates that dynamic range is maximized. Adjust Exposure to adjust f-stops. Specify the Details, Shadow, and Highlight settings to adjust sharpness and contrast of dark and light areas, respectively.

Finally, click the Color tab and adjust the Vibrance (saturation while minimizing clipping) and Saturation (color intensity).

For more on the dynamics of curves, see Book VIII, Chapter 1. Note that you can also choose Image⇨Mode⇨16-Bits or 8-Bits/Channel and make your exposure and contrast adjustments in the same HDR Conversion dialog box that you can get through the Merge to HDR Pro dialog box.

Keep in mind that you also have the option of creating layers within a 32-bit image. This, of course, opens up a whole world of creative possibilities, giving you the ability to composite multiple images. You can also apply another half dozen or so blend modes on those layers, including Hue, Saturation, and Color. As an added bonus, you can even paint on those 32-bit layers, as well as add type. You can have your way with the following tools: Brush, Pencil, Shape, Clone and Pattern Stamp, History Brush, Eraser, Gradient, Blur, Sharpen, Smudge, and Type.

Finally, don't be surprised to encounter a different dialog box when you select a color for an HDR image. HDR images have their very own Color Picker (in the Extended Version of Photoshop only).

If you copy a layer, selection, or entire image from an 8-bit or 16-bit file, you encounter a profile mismatch because of the differences in the color profiles' gamma values. Convert your profile to match your HDR image. For more on color profiles, see Book II, Chapter 3.

Index

M

www.librex.co.uk

Photoshop® CS5 All-in-One For Dummies®

Published by
Wiley Publishing, Inc.
111 River Street
Hoboken, NJ 07030-5774

www.wiley.com

Copyright © 2010 by Wiley Publishing, Inc., Indianapolis, Indiana

Published by Wiley Publishing, Inc., Indianapolis, Indiana

Published simultaneously in Canada

For general information on our other products and services, please contact our Customer Care Department within the U.S. at 877-762-2974, outside the U.S. at 317-572-3993, or fax 317-572-4002.

For technical support, please visit www.wiley.com/techsupport.

Wiley also publishes its books in a variety of electronic formats. Some content that appears in print may not be available in electronic books.

Library of Congress Control Number: 2010925703

ISBN: 978-0-470-60821-0

Manufactured in the United States of America

10 9 8 7 6 5 4 3 2

WILEY

About the Author

Barbara Obermeier is principal of Obermeier Design, a graphic design studio in Ventura, California. She's the author or co-author of over 19 publications, including *Photoshop Elements 8 For Dummies, How-to-Wow with Illustrator,* and *Digital Photography Just the Steps For Dummies,* 2nd Edition. Barb also teaches graphic design at Brooks Institute.

Dedication

I would like to dedicate this book to Gary, Kylie, and Lucky, who constantly remind me of what's really important in life.

Author's Acknowledgments

I would like to thank my excellent project editor, Nicole Sholly, who kept me and this book on track; Bob Woerner, the world's best Executive Editor; Andy Cummings, who gives Dummies a good name; David Busch, for his great contribution to the first edition; Dennis Cohen, for his technical editing; and all the hard-working, dedicated production folks at Wiley. A special thanks to Ted Padova, colleague, fellow author, and friend, who always reminds me there is eventually an end to all those chapters.

Publisher's Acknowledgments

We're proud of this book; please send us your comments at http://dummies.custhelp.com. For other comments, please contact our Customer Care Department within the U.S. at 877-762-2974, outside the U.S. at 317-572-3993, or fax 317-572-4002.

Some of the people who helped bring this book to market include the following:

Acquisitions, Editorial, and Media Development

Project Editor: Nicole Sholly

Executive Editor: Bob Woerner

Copy Editors: Heidi Unger, Brian Walls

Technical Editor: Dennis R. Cohen

Editorial Manager: Kevin Kirschner

Media Development Project Manager: Laura Moss-Hollister

Media Development Assistant Project Manager: Jenny Swisher

Media Development Associate Producers: Josh Frank, Marilyn Hummel, Douglas Kuhn, Shawn Patrick

Editorial Assistant: Amanda Graham

Sr. Editorial Assistant: Cherie Case

Cartoons: Rich Tennant (www.the5thwave.com)

Composition Services

Project Coordinator: Katherine Crocker

Layout and Graphics: Claudia Bell, Samantha Cherolis, Joyce Haughey, Erin Zeltner

Proofreader: Melissa D. Buddendeck

Indexer: Sherry Massey

Publishing and Editorial for Technology Dummies

> **Richard Swadley,** Vice President and Executive Group Publisher

> **Andy Cummings,** Vice President and Publisher

> **Mary Bednarek,** Executive Acquisitions Director

> **Mary C. Corder,** Editorial Director

Publishing for Consumer Dummies

> **Diane Graves Steele,** Vice President and Publisher

Composition Services

> **Debbie Stailey,** Director of Composition Services

Contents at a Glance

Table of Contents

Introduction

There's a reason why Photoshop is the world's industry standard in image-editing software. The depth and breadth of the program is unparalleled. Photoshop immediately sucks you in with its easy-to-use interface and powerful tools and commands. It's so feature rich that you soon begin to lose track of time and start blowing off your commitments just to try one more thing. And just when you think you've finally explored every nook and cranny and mastered the program, you suddenly read a tip in a book or magazine that enlightens you about something you didn't know. Or even more likely, you stumble upon some great effect while working on a late-night project. That's the beauty of Photoshop. It's the program that just keeps giving.

The depth and breadth of Photoshop has downsides, too, of course. You must make a major time commitment and invest much effort to master it — hence the large number of books written on the program. Walk into your neighborhood bookstore or type Photoshop in the Search field at any online bookseller's site, and you see a barrage of choices. Some books are general reference books, some are targeted toward the novice user, and others focus on a specific mission, such as color management or restoration and retouching.

About This Book

This book is written for the person who has a good grasp of using a computer and navigating the operating system and at least a cursory knowledge of Photoshop. It is intended to be a comprehensive reference book that you can read cover to cover or reach for when you're looking for specific information about a particular task.

Wherever I can, I sneak in a useful tip or an interesting technique to help you put Photoshop to work for your project needs.

Sometimes, knowing *how* to use a tool doesn't necessarily mean that you know *what* to do with it. That's why this book contains several Putting It Together exercises that help you make a connection between the multiple Photoshop tools at your disposal and the very specific task you need to accomplish. Want to get the red out of a subject's eyes or create a collage?

Just check out the Putting It Together sections in Books III through IX. These sections present info in easy-to-follow numbered steps, in a hands-on style, building on what's presented in the chapter so that you can go to the next level, put concepts to work, and move on to the next task.

You can find images that appear within the Putting It Together sections on this book's companion Web site (www.dummies.com/go/photoshopcs5 aiofd), so you can follow along precisely with the steps.

What's in This Book

This book is broken into minibooks, each covering a general topic. Each minibook contains several chapters, each covering a more specific topic under the general one. Each chapter is then divided into sections, and some of those sections have subsections. I'm sure you get the picture.

You can read the book from front to back, or you can dive right into the minibook or chapter of your choice. Either way works just fine. Anytime a concept is mentioned that isn't covered in depth in that chapter, you find a cross-reference to another book and chapter where you find all the details. If you're looking for something specific, check out either the Table of Contents or the Index.

The Cheat Sheet at Dummies.com (find more information inside the front cover) helps you remember all the shortcuts you'll use most often. Print it, tape it to your monitor, and glance over it when you need to.

And finally, I have pictures. Lots of them. In full, living color. Many of these pictures have callouts that point to specific steps or identify important concepts, buttons, tools, or options. With a program like Photoshop, an image often speaks louder than words.

This book contains nine minibooks. The following sections offer a quick synopsis of what each book contains.

Book 1: Photoshop Fundamentals

Ready to get your feet wet with the basics of Photoshop? Head to Book I. Here's where you get familiar with the Photoshop environment — the desktop, menus, and panels. I also briefly introduce the key tools and explain what each one does.

Photoshop has such an abundance of tools — and so many ways to use those tools — I can't possibly cover them all in this book. But if you're looking for details on the less commonly used features or perhaps more information about using tools you're already familiar with, you'll find them on this book's companion Web site (www.dummies.com/go/photoshopcs5aiofd).

In this book, I cover how to get started on Photoshop and how to view and navigate your image window. Here's also where I give you all the important details about the o'mighty Adobe Bridge, and the new Mini Bridge, and how to customize your workspace and preference settings.

Finally, I go into the bare basics of printing, and then how to save files and close Photoshop.

Book II: Image Essentials

This book covers all those nitpicky — but critical — details about images, such as size, resolution, pixel dimension, image mode, and file format. Turn to this book to find out how to safely resize your image without causing undue damage.

You can also find out how to crop images and increase their canvas size. In addition, I breeze through basic color theory and get you started using and managing color.

But wait — there's more. I give you the lowdown on the History panel and brushing and erasing to history. And, if that's not enough, I throw in a chapter on using and creating actions for enhanced productivity.

Book III: Selections

This important book gives you all the juicy details and techniques on creating and modifying selections and paths. You find out about each of the selection tools and also the powerful — albeit sometimes unruly — Pen tool and its accompanying Paths panel.

Book IV: Painting, Drawing, and Typing

If you want to know about the drawing and painting tools, this book is for you. Here I cover the Brush and Pencil tools, including the new Mixer Brush tool, along with the multifaceted Brush panel and new Brush Preset Picker panel. I also show you how to create vector shapes by using the shape tools, and how to fill and stroke selections.

Head to this book to find out how to create both gradients and patterns and, last but not least, become familiar with the type tools and how to use them to create and edit standard type, type on and in a path, and type with special effects.

Book V: Working with Layers

Layers are an integral component in a Photoshop image, and Book V is where I explain them. In this book, you discover how to create and edit layers and how to use multiple images to create a multilayered composite image. You find out various ways to manage layers for maximum efficiency, including using the Layer Comps panel. I also show you how to enhance layers by applying different blend modes, opacity settings, layer styles, and styles. I round out the minibook by covering Smart Objects. And finally, I introduce you to working with the Auto Align and Auto Blend features.

Book VI: Channels and Masks

This book gives you all the how-tos you need to work with channels and masks. I show you how to save and edit selections as alpha channels so that you can reload them later. And I show you how to work with the various kinds of masks — quick masks, clipping masks, layer masks, and channel masks — and how you can use each to select difficult elements. I also cover other masking techniques, such as erasing and using the Color Range command. Finally, I introduce you to the Masks panel, a powerful ally to the masking arsenal.

Book VII: Filters and Distortions

I filled this book with tons of handy tips and techniques on using filters to correct your images to make them sharper, blurrier, cleaner, and smoother — whatever fits your fancy. I give you the scoop on the Smart Filters feature, which enables you to apply filters nondestructively. You also find out how to use filters to give your image a certain special effect, such as a deckled edge or water droplets. Finally, I introduce the Liquify command so that you can see the wonder of its distortion tools — and how they can turn your image into digital taffy.

Book VIII: Retouching and Restoration

You find everything you need to know about color correction or color enhancement in Book VIII — getting rid of colorcasts, improving contrast and saturation, remapping, and replacing colors.

In addition, I include a chapter on using the focus and toning tools to manually lighten, darken, smooth, soften, and sharpen areas of your image. You get to see how you can use the Clone Stamp tool, the Healing tools, and the Red Eye tool to fix flaws and imperfections in your images, making them good as new. I also show you the Color Replacement tool and how to replace your image's original color with the foreground color. Finally, you get some tidbits on how to work with the fascinating Vanishing Point feature, which can make editing and compositing images a whole lot easier.

Book IX: Photoshop and Print

This book gives you the lowdown on preparing your images for print. You find details on how to get the right resolution, image mode, and file format. You also discover how to set up both process and spot color separations for those offset print jobs.

About the Web Site

For those Web graphics enthusiasts, you find lots of great bonus chapter material on this book's companion Web site (www.dummies.com/go/photoshopcs5aiofd). Find out how to optimize your images for maximum quality and quick download times. You also find information on slicing and animating your images and creating a photo gallery that you can easily post on the Web.

Conventions Used in This Book

You'll find that this book is cross-platform. Windows commands are given first, followed by Mac commands in parentheses, like this:

Press Enter (or Return on the Mac) to begin a new line.

And occasionally, text is specific to one platform or another. You'll find that figures are divided into both platforms as well.

Often, the commands given involve using the keyboard along with the mouse. For example, "Press Shift while dragging with the Rectangular Marquee tool to create a square," or "Alt-click (Option-click) on the eyeball to redisplay all layers."

When you see a command arrow (⇨) in the text, it indicates that you should select a command from the menu bar. For example, "choose Edit⇨Define Custom Shape" means to click the Edit menu and then choose the Define Custom Shape command.

This book has been written using Photoshop CS5 and, more specifically, the Standard version. Despite that fact, you can still glean valuable info if you're using version CS4 or CS3. It may take a little more time to understand how a panel or options have changed, and of course, the topics covering new features won't be applicable.

Speaking of new features, when writing this book, it wasn't exactly crystal clear what new CS5 features Adobe would be including in the Standard versus Extended versions of Photoshop. So if I've included (or not) a particular tool or command that you don't have, my apologies in advance.

Icons Used in This Book

While perusing this book, you'll notice some icons beckoning you for your attention. Don't ignore them; embrace them! These icons point out fun, useful, and memorable tidbits about Photoshop, plus facts you'd be unwise to ignore.

Seasoned users will appreciate this icon, which kindly points out new features introduced in Photoshop CS5.

This icon indicates information that makes your Photoshop experience easier. It also gives you an icebreaker at your next cocktail party. Whipping out, "Did you know that pressing the bracket keys enlarges or shrinks your brush tip?" is bound to make you the center of conversation.

This icon is a reminder of things that I already mentioned and want to gently re-emphasize. Or I might be pointing out things that I want you to take note of in your future Photoshop excursions.

The little bomb icon is a red flag. Heed these warnings, or else Photoshop may show its ugly side.

This icon marks eggheady graphics or Photoshop info that goes beyond the basics.

This icon points to related content you'll find on this book's companion Web site, which you can find at www.dummies.com/go/photoshopcs5aiofd.

Book I

Photoshop Fundamentals

The 5th Wave   By Rich Tennant

"I've got the red-eye reduction, I'm just seeing if there's a button that'll fix your hair."

Don't know where to start? Well, unless you have a burning question on something very specific, this is a great place to dive in. And I promise you won't flounder. There's nothing like a general overview to get you feeling confident enough to tackle more sophisticated features.

In this book, I introduce you to the Photoshop environment with all its components, from the desktop to the many panels. I show you each of the 71 tools and briefly explain what each tool does. From there, I show you how to open existing files or create new ones and then how to save and print those files, as well as how to view and navigate around your image window. In that same chapter, I give you details on using Adobe Bridge, a powerful browser and file-management tool, as well as the new mini Bridge. Finally, I explain how to customize your workspace and preferences so you can tailor Photoshop to better suit your personal image-editing needs and interests. I guarantee you won't find a more accommodating image editor around.

Wright Beach, Ca

Chapter 1: Examining the Photoshop Environment

In This Chapter

✔ **Starting Photoshop**

✔ **Examining the Photoshop desktop**

✔ **Working with panels**

✔ **Discovering the Application bar**

✔ **Investigating the Menu bar and the Options bar**

*A*s environments go, the Photoshop working environment is pretty cool: as inviting as a landscaped backyard and not nearly as likely to work you into a sweat. Each of Photoshop's many tools — with more options than a Swiss Army knife — is custom-designed for a specific chore. When you're familiar with your surroundings, you'll be eager to make like Monet in his garden, surrounded by panels, brushes, buckets of paint, and swatches of color, ready to tackle the canvas in front of you.

Launching Photoshop and Customizing the Desktop

You start Photoshop the same way you launch any other program with Windows or the Mac OS. As with other programs, you can choose the method you find the easiest and most convenient. In Windows, you can launch programs from the Start menu or an icon on the taskbar. In Mac OS X, you may have a Photoshop icon on the Dock. In either Windows or Mac OS X, you can double-click a Photoshop shortcut or alias icon if you have one on your desktop. Finally, you can double-click an image associated with Photoshop, which then launches Photoshop along with the file.

When you launch Photoshop, the workspace, shown in Figure 1-1, appears. Like the real-world desktop where your keyboard and monitor reside, the Photoshop desktop is a place for you to put all the images you're working with.

Within the Photoshop application window, you see a variety of other windows and boxes, such as the image window that enables you to view and edit images. The application window contains the stuff you're probably used to seeing in other programs — a title bar at the top of the window, a status bar at the bottom (unless you have it turned off) if you're a Windows user, and menus to help you execute commands and get important information about your image files. However, the arrangement of controls may be a little unfamiliar to you. Photoshop arranges controls into groups, or *panels*.

Your virtual desktop can become as cluttered as the real thing, but Adobe has built in some special features (located on the Options bar, which I discuss later in this chapter) that let you keep stuff close at hand but tuck things away so they're not constantly underfoot (or under-mouse, so to speak).

Options bar   Document window   Dock

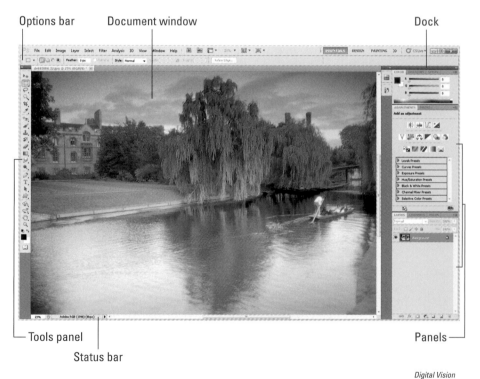

Tools panel   Panels

Status bar

Digital Vision

Figure 1-1: The Photoshop desktop consists of many components, including an image window, panels, and bars.

After you arrange your Photoshop desktop the way you like it for a specific project, you can even save the desktop and reuse it whenever you work on that project (see Book I, Chapter 5 for details).

Every image you work on appears within the confines of the image window. However, you can move some components, such as the various panels and the Options bar, both inside and outside the Photoshop application window.

The following sections show you how to customize the workspace so you can get to work.

Setting display settings with the Window menu

The Window menu, shown in Figure 1-2, controls the display of panels and some other elements of the Photoshop workspace. (Find out more about maneuvering panels in the section "Playing with Panels," later in this chapter.)

The top two entries on the Window menu enable you to control the display arrangement of your open documents and manage your workspaces.

On the Window⇨Arrange submenu, you can tell Photoshop to *cascade* (stack) or *tile* (butt edge to edge) all open documents. Your images must be floating in their windows to enable this option (Window⇨Arrange⇨Float All in Windows).

Photoshop also sports what's referred to as an application frame. Open documents are tabbed together neatly, one stacked behind the other. If you yearn for the old days and want your images to float within the application, choose Float in Window (for the currently selected image only) and Float All in Windows (for all your images) commands in the Arrange submenu.

Table 1-1 gives you the lowdown about the other options on the Window⇨Arrange submenu.

The remaining bulk of the Window menu contains a list of panels (in alphabetical order) and currently open documents.

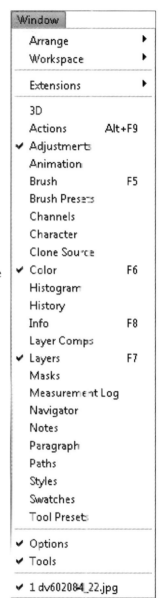

Figure 1-2: Access all panels via the Window menu.

Table 1-1	The Window⇨Arrange Submenu
Menu Command	*What It Does*
Consolidate All to Tabs	Takes your open floating documents and tabs them together under the Options bar.
Match Zoom	Takes your open documents and matches the magnification percentage of your active document.
Match Location	Takes your open documents and matches the location of your active document. For example, if you're viewing the lower-left corner of your active document and choose Match Location, all your open documents display from the lower-left corner.
Match Rotation	Takes your open documents and matches the canvas rotation of your active document.
Match All	Employs all Match commands simultaneously.
New Window	Opens another view of the same image, allowing you to work on a close-up part of the image while viewing results on the entire image.
Minimize (Mac only)	Hides the image while placing the image's thumbnail on the Dock. Click the thumbnail to restore the image in Photoshop.
Bring All to Front (Mac only)	If you have multiple applications launched, thus multiple document windows open, this command brings all Photoshop documents to the front, ahead of any document windows from other open applications.

Setting up the status bar

Each Photoshop image window comes equipped with a status bar. Many people tend to associate status with wealth, so I think there's a good reason to accept the free wealth of information that the status bar offers:

✔ On the far left of the bar is a box that displays an active image's current zoom level (such as 33.33%). Incidentally, the title bar of the document itself also shows the zoom level.

If you installed Photoshop to a networked computer and you activate the workgroup features, which enable file sharing and other perks, you see the icon for the Workgroup Services pop-up menu just to the right of the zoom-info box.

✔ To the right of the zoom level is the display area for file and image information — which, by default, shows the document profile.

To display other types of information, click the right arrow in the status bar, choose Show, and select one of the following options from the menu that appears (as shown in Figure 1-3):

✔ **Adobe Drive:** If you're a Version Cue user, you can select this option, which enables you to connect to Version Cue servers. When you connect via Adobe Drive, you can open and save Version Cue files. Adobe has decided to discontinue Version Cue, so the future of the Adobe Drive feature is unknown.

PhotoDisc

Figure 1-3: The status bar provides a wealth of vital information about your image.

✔ **Document Sizes:** When you select this option, Photoshop displays two numbers to approximate the size of the image. The first number shows you the size of the file if you were to flatten (combine) all the layers into one and save it to your hard drive in the native Photoshop file format. The number on the right shows the size of the file, including layers, channels, and other components, and how much data Photoshop has to juggle while you're working on the file. You want this option active when you need to keep track of how large your image is.

✔ **Document Profile:** When you select this option, the status bar displays the name of the color profile that the image uses, as well as the number of bits per channel. You probably won't use this option unless you need to know the profiles of all the open documents while making complex color corrections. (You can find more information about profiles in Book II, Chapter 3.)

✔ **Document Dimensions:** When you select this option, the status bar shows you the size of the image by using the default measurement increment you've set in Photoshop's Preferences (pixels, inches, picas, and so on). You might need this information to reference the physical dimensions of your open files. For information on setting preferences in Photoshop, see Book I, Chapter 5.

✔ **Measurement Scale:** Displays the scale of the document. For example, 1 pixel=1.0000 pixels.

✔ **Scratch Sizes:** Scratch space is the virtual memory set aside on your hard drive to simulate RAM and make editing large files easier. Enabling this option shows two measurements for an active image. On the left, you see the amount of real memory and virtual memory that all open images are using. On the right, you see the total amount of RAM available for working with images. Photoshop needs a lot more memory and disk space to work on an image while that image is open, shown by the Scratch Sizes display, as opposed to the Document Size display that shows only the file size of the document.

✔ **Efficiency:** This indicator helps you gauge whether you really have enough RAM to perform a task. It shows the percentage of time Photoshop spends actually working on an operation, compared to the time it must spend reading or writing image information to or from your hard disk. If the value dips below 100 percent most of the time, you need to allocate more memory to Photoshop (if you're using a Windows PC). For more information on parceling out RAM, see Book I, Chapter 5.

✔ **Timing:** This number shows you how long it took you to complete your most recent incredible feat.

✔ **Current Tool:** This option shows you the name of the tool currently in use.

✔ **32-Bit Exposure:** This option is for adjusting the preview image for viewing 32-bit High Dynamic Range (HDR) images. The slider control is available only if you have an HDR image open. Book IX, Chapter 2 covers HDR.

Playing with Panels

Many image-oriented programs use panels of a sort, and Photoshop has had panels (formerly called palettes) since version 1.0 (released in January 1990). However, since Photoshop 3.0, the program has used a novel way of working with panels. Rather than standalone windows, Photoshop uses grouped, tabbed panels, which overlap each other in groups of two or three (or more, if you rearrange them yourself). To access a panel that falls behind the one displayed on top, click the panel's tab. By default, some panels, such as Tool Presets, appear alone.

Book I
Chapter 1

Examining the
Photoshop
Environment

Panels may contain sliders, buttons, drop-down lists, pop-up menus (as shown in Figure 1-4), and other controls. You also find icons at the bottom of many panels. For example, at the base of the Layers panel are command icons that let you create a new layer, add a layer style, or trash a layer that you no longer want. Many panels — such as the Brush, Styles, Actions, and Color panels — include options for defining sets of parameters (called *presets*) that you can store for reuse at any time.

Whatever name you call them, palettes or panels, they still hold the same information. They're streamlined and easily tucked away and expanded, as needed. By default, the panels are anchored in the top-right by a multitiered dock.

Here's how to open, close, and otherwise manipulate a panel group, which can be accessed easily from the Window menu:

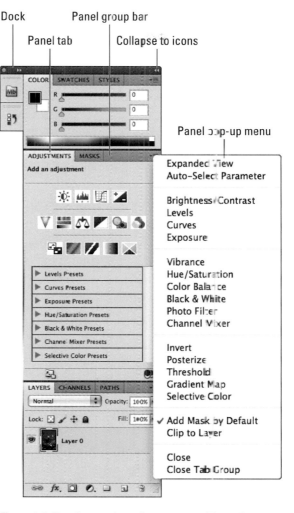

Figure 1-4: Panels contain various command icons for editing and managing your image.

✔ **To expand a panel:** Panels are represented by icons when collapsed. To expand a panel, simply click its icon. You can also select a panel by choosing it in the Window menu.

✔ **To bring a panel to the front of its group:** When the panel group is expanded, the visible panel is the panel that has a check mark next to it on the Window menu. In this mode, you can select only one panel in any group because only one tab in a group can be on top at one time. When you select a panel from the Window menu, you have no way of knowing which panels are grouped together because Adobe lists panels alphabetically, rather than by groups. To bring a specific panel to the front, click its tab (when expanded) or icon (when collapsed).

✔ **To move a panel out of its group:** Grab the panel's tab with your mouse and drag it to its new location, such as another group, the panel dock, or the Photoshop desktop. If you move the panels out of their groups or drag them onto the desktop so they stand alone, any of them can be selected in the Window menu.

✔ **To collapse a panel:** Click the gray area next to the tab.

✔ **To close a panel:** Select a check-marked panel in the Window menu. The whole panel group closes. You can also select Close or Close Tab Group from the panel's pop-up menu.

Here are some more panel-manipulation tips:

✔ **Expand or collapse the dock.** To do so, click on the double triangles at the top of the dock.

✔ **Reduce a panel to its icon.** Drag the panel by its tab and position it below the existing column of icons. Release your mouse button to make the panel collapse to its corresponding icon.

✔ **Save space by keeping panels in groups.** You can move all the panels in a group by dragging the gray area to the right of the group's tab. Access an individual panel by clicking its tab to bring it to the front. As a result, several panels occupy the screen space required by only one.

✔ **Use the Window menu if you can't find a panel.** On the Window menu, select the panel's name to make it visible or to bring it to the top of its group.

✔ **Customize, customize, customize.** After you use Photoshop for a while, creating your own custom panel groups based on the panels you most often use can be a real timesaver. For example, if you don't use the Paths panel very often but can't live without the Actions panel, you can drag the Paths panel to another group or to the panel dock area, and put the Actions panel in the same group as the mission-critical Layers and Channels panels.

✔ **Restore default panel locations, when desired.** If you decide you don't like the way you've arranged your panels, you can choose Window➪Workspace➪Essentials (Default) to return them to the default configuration (the way they were when Photoshop was installed).

Many panels (for example, the Swatches and Character panels) allow you to reset the settings back to their defaults. To do so, select Reset from the panel's pop-up menu located in the top-right corner.

Working with Your First Photoshop File

So many menus, so little time! The second you begin working with Photoshop, you may be convinced that Adobe's flagship image editor has approximately 8,192 different menu selections for you to choose from. In truth, Photoshop has only about 500-plus separate menu items, including some duplicates. That figure doesn't count the 100 or so entries for filter plug-ins (which can expand alarmingly when you add third-party goodies). However, even 500-plus menu items are considerably more than you find in the most ambitious restaurants. Basically, if you want to do something in Photoshop, you need to use the Menu bar (or its equivalent command snuggled within a panel menu). If you're using the Mac OS, the Photoshop Menu bar may share space with Finder components (such as the Apple menu).

The following sections offer a summary of what you can find and where you can find it.

Photoshop also helps you by providing efficient context menus, which change their listings depending on what you're doing. You don't see options you don't need; you see options appropriate to what you're working on. Right-click (Right-click or Control-click on the Mac) to bring up the menu.

Opening, printing, and saving files

The File menu offers a cornucopia of file options, from opening new images and opening saved files to browsing existing files, closing files, and saving files. You'll find automate, scripts, and print commands, too. To open a file, choose File⇨Open and navigate to the folder containing the file you want to open. Select the file and click Open. For detailed instructions on the many ways you can open files, see Book I, Chapter 3.

Making selections

Selections let you work with only part of an image. You can select an entire layer or only portions of a layer with one of the selection tools, such as the Marquee or Magic Wand tool. The Select menu offers several commands to modify your selection — from capturing more pixels to softening the edges of the selection. The Select menu (shown in Figure 1-5) is short and sweet, but the capability and control that the menu unleashes is nothing short of an image-editing miracle.

Understanding selections is such an important cornerstone to your Photoshop knowledge that I devote an entire minibook (Book III) to showing you how to use them.

Making simple image edits

The Edit menu contains tools that enable you to cut, copy, or paste image selections in several ways. You can fill selections or *stroke* their outlines (create a line along their edges), which I explain in more detail in Book IV, Chapter 2. You can use the Edit menu to rotate, resize, distort, or perform other transformations (changes in size or shape) on your selections (see Book III, Chapter 3). Additionally, you can undo the last change you made in Photoshop, fade a filter, check your spelling, or find and replace text.

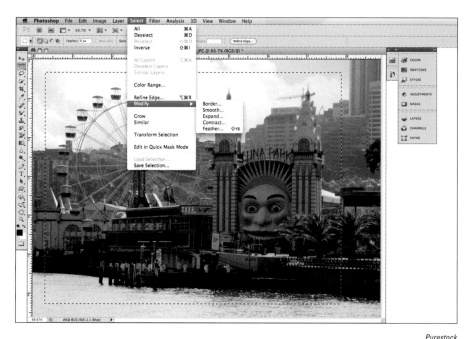

Purestock

Figure 1-5: The Select menu offers commands for making, modifying, saving, and loading your selections.

Adjusting size, color, and contrast

You'd think the Image menu (shown in Figure 1-6) might have something to do with making changes to an entire image document, wouldn't you? In practice, some of the entries you find here do apply to the whole document, but others can apply to only particular layers or selections.

For example, the Mode menu item allows you to change an entire image from color to grayscale. The Image Size, Canvas Size, Image Rotation, Crop, and Trim selections all change the whole document in some way. On the other hand, you can only apply the changes wrought from the Adjustments submenu to an entire image if the document consists of only a background and has no layers. If the document has more than one layer, then adjustments such as Color Balance, Hue/Saturation, or Levels work only with a single layer or a selection on that layer.

The Variables and Apply Data Set commands work with data-driven graphics. Briefly, data-driven graphics make it possible to quickly produce multiple versions of an image for print and Web projects. Multiple versions allow for target audience customization for projects such as direct mail pieces. For example, you can base hundreds of versions of a brochure or Web banner on a single template. The Variables define which elements change within a template. A Data Set is a collection of variables and associated data.

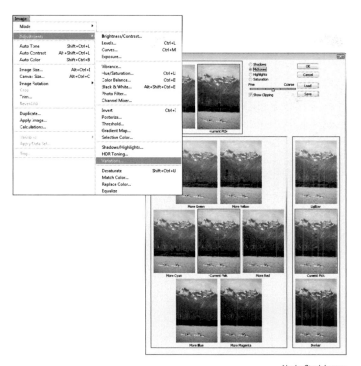

Alaska Stock Images

Figure 1-6: The Image menu is where you find commands for adjusting the size, color, and contrast of your image.

You'll find yourself turning to the Image menu more often than many of the other menus, partially because it's so useful and partially because, for some reason, many of the options don't have keyboard shortcuts that let you bypass the menu.

Creating layers

Layers give you a way of stacking portions of an image — like sheets of acetate — on top of one another so that you can work on individual pieces separately. Then, when you're satisfied with your changes, you can either combine the changes into a final image or leave them in layers for maximum editing flexibility.

The Layers feature, which gets an entire book of its own (Book V), lets you create new and duplicate layers, delete one or several layers, change layer properties (such as a layer's name), or add special features, such as drop shadows or beveled edges, to objects in a layer. You can also create special kinds of layers to make adjustments or mask portions of an image. The menu has selections for changing the order of the layers (moving a specific layer to the front or top of the stack, and so on) and grouping layers. Figure 1-7 shows an image that has three layers: The first layer is the symphony image, the second layer is the instrument, and the third layer contains the type.

You also can merge layers down, combine them with all other visible layers, or flatten them into one single-layer image (or background). Although consolidating your layers makes the file smaller, flattening is irreversible after you close the file. Storing an unflattened version of a file is always a good idea in case you want to make more changes later on.

Applying filters

A filter is an effect that changes an entire layer, channel, or selection. Some common filters include the Blur and Sharpen filters, as well as the Distort filters, such as Spherize. The Filter menu, shown in Figure 1-8, consists almost entirely of cascading categories of image-transmogrifying plug-ins. You can wade through this menu to find the perfect effect to apply to an image or selection. Book VII has everything you need to know about filters.

PhotoSpin

Figure 1-7: Layers enable you to edit elements individually in your document.

After you apply a filter, Photoshop copies the filter command to the top of the Filter menu for easy accessibility, in case you want to reapply the filter with the exact same settings.

The Filter Gallery command allows you to apply several filters simultaneously in one neat editing window.

Liquify and Vanishing Point are more like mini-programs than filters. The rest of the Filter menu consists of 14 filter categories, each containing from two to more than a dozen options:

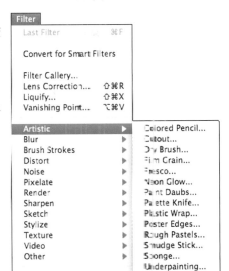

Figure 1-8: The Filter menu is bursting at the seams with plug-ins to improve, enhance, or completely transform your image.

- ✓ Single-step filters, such as Blur, Facet, and Clouds, are simple to use but make a huge impact on an image. Just select each filter to apply it; it has no options to specify.

- ✓ Dialog box-based filters let you select options galore. These filters utilize preview windows, buttons, slider controls, and menus to distort, pixelate, sharpen, stylize, apply textures, and perform other functions.

- ✓ The Filter menu also provides an opportunity to convert for Smart Filters. If you convert your layer to a Smart Object, you can then apply a Smart Filter. A Smart Filter is smart because it doesn't alter your image pixels, but merely hovers above them, thereby allowing you to re-edit, or even remove, the filter if necessary. For the scoop on this cool (and very useful) feature, see Book VII, Chapter 1.

If you install additional filters from third parties, Photoshop lists them at the very bottom of the Filter menu. You can find third-party filters at such Web sites as www.alienskin.com, www.andromeda.com, and www.autofx.com.

Unifying with the Application bar

The Application bar, shown in Figure 1-9, located at the far end of the main menu in Windows and directly below the main menu on the Mac consolidates commands and features previously found, or also found, elsewhere in the application. For more details on most of these commands, check out Book I, Chapter 4. Here's what you can find on this bar:

- ✓ **Application icon:** The Photoshop icon is displayed to simply identify the application. In Windows, clicking the icon displays the standard system menu.

✏ **Launch Bridge:** This button allows you to access the image-management application, Bridge, with a mere click.

✏ **View Extras:** Click this icon to select whether to show guides, the grid, or rulers from the drop-down list. For more on these items, see Book I, Chapter 4.

✏ **Magnification Percentage:** Displays the current magnification percentage. Click the down arrow to select from preset percentages of 25%, 50%, 100%, and 200%. Or enter your desired magnification percentage in the text field.

✏ **Hand and Zoom tools:** Select these tools from the Application bar or Tools panel — your choice. Use the Hand tool to move around your image window and the Zoom tool to zoom in and out. For more on these two tools, see Book I, Chapter 4.

✏ **Rotate View tool:** Select this tool from either the Application bar or Tools panel. This tool actually rotates your entire image window, not just the image within the boundaries of the window.

✏ **Arrange Documents tool:** Click the down arrow to select various viewing configurations. Depending on the number of open images you have, various configurations will be available. You can also choose to float, rather than tab, your open images; create a new window; and display actual pixels or fit your entire image onscreen. See explanations of the Match commands in the earlier "Setting display settings with the Window menu" section in this chapter.

✏ **Screen Mode Switcher:** Click the down arrow to select from standard, full screen with Menu bar, and full screen modes.

✏ **Workspace Switcher:** Click the down arrow to select a different workspace. Selecting the Essentials workspace resets all your panels and menus to the default settings.

If you're a Mac user and don't care for this bar, hide it by choosing Window⇨Application Bar to deselect it. Also, if you use other CS5 applications, you may find a similar Application bar.

Simplifying your edits with the Options bar

The Options bar, shown in Figure 1-10, is a great feature because it eliminates the need to access a separate options panel for each tool. The bar remains available at all times, docked below the Menu and Application bars (unless you decide to hide it for some bizarre reason), and the options change when you switch tools. If the default location doesn't work for you, feel free to move it anywhere you please.

Application bar

Figure 1-9: The Application bar unifies commonly used features in one centralized location.

Options bar

Alaska Stock Images

Figure 1-10: The ubiquitous Options bar is dynamic and reflects various options for the tool in use and operation being performed.

Because the Options bar changes its appearance with each active tool, I can't explain all the components you might find there, but all Options bars do have some common characteristics:

- **Gripper bar:** Grab this little bar, on the far left, with the mouse and drag to undock or dock the Options bar. You can let the Options bar float anywhere in the workspace.

- **Tool Presets/Options pop-up menu:** This box displays the icon of the currently active tool. Click the down arrow to access a drop-down list that includes a selection of brush tips (for painting and erasing tools); a flyout menu that lets you select presets (saved settings) for various tools; and additional options to set, such as the size of the icons used to represent brush tips. You may also reset a particular tool — or all tools — to the Photoshop default values.

- **Bar options:** Additional options, such as mode, opacity, feather, type styles, and fonts are arrayed on the rest of the Options bar.

Viewing and navigating the image

A hodgepodge of functions is sprinkled throughout the View menu. Some of them, such as Proof Setup, Proof Colors, and Gamut Warning, won't trouble you until you've become a fairly advanced Photoshop user. For new Photoshop users, the commands to zoom into and out of the image are likely the most familiar. You can also choose your screen mode, which lets you view your image full-screen with the Menu bar and panels, or full-screen with just panels.

You're better off accessing some functions, especially the zoom features, through keyboard shortcuts. See Book I, Chapter 5 for details.

From the View menu, you can select which extras Photoshop displays. You can choose to show (or hide) the following, as shown in Figure 1-11:

- **Layer Edges:** Displays a blue-stroked box that surrounds the boundaries of the content of the selected layer.

- **Selection Edges:** Moving lines that define the boundary of a selection, which are very useful for obvious reasons.

Figure 1-11: Viewing and navigating your image are the main tasks on the View menu.

- **Target Path:** Lines and curves that define a shape or select part of an image. You definitely want to see them if the paths need editing.

- **Grid and Guides:** Lines that display onscreen, which are great when you're aligning selections, objects, or other components, and potentially distracting when you're not.

- **Count:** Bulleted numbers indicating your counted elements will appear. The Count feature is only in the Extended version of Photoshop.

- **Smart Guides:** Smart Guides enable you to precisely position and align layer content, and only appear when needed.

- **Slices:** Rectangular pieces of an image to which you can optimize or apply Web features. If you slice the image, you probably want to view the results.

- **Notes:** Onscreen notes that you can create and view. Notes can sometimes be confusing, unless you're already confused; then notes can help you sort out what's what.

- **Pixel Grid:** Displays a pixel grid when you are zoomed into your image at a magnification greater than 500%.

- **3D Axis:** Show the X, Y, and Z Axis orientation of a 3-D object. This option is only in the Extended version of Photoshop.

The View menu holds the controls for turning on and off the snap feature in Photoshop. (The *snap feature* makes objects magnetically attracted to grids, guides, or other objects.) You can also create new guides, lock and clear slices (see Bonus Chapter 2 for slice-and-dice information), and turn rulers on or off. (The Introduction has details about finding bonus chapters on this book's companion Web site.)

Introducing Adobe ConnectNow

Adobe provides a useful and, more importantly, free Web conferencing application that enables users to share ideas and collaborate on projects online. Using any computer platform and any browser, users can participate in online meetings and work sessions. ConnectNow enables users to share their files, audio, and video. You can participate via chats, whiteboard, Webcam, and notes.

With CS5, Adobe moved the ConnectNow feature to Acrobat.com (https://acrobat.com) and added even more functionality. The only requirements are

- **An Adobe.com user ID:** Get one at www.adobe.com.

- **An Adobe ConnectNow account:** Sign up at www.adobe.com/acom/connectnow.

- **Adobe Flash Player:** Download it at www.adobe.com/shockwave/download/download.cgi?P1_Prod_Version=ShockwaveFlash.

Follow these steps to access Adobe ConnectNow (shown in Figure 1-12) from within Photoshop:

1. **Choose File⇨Share My Screen to launch Adobe ConnectNow.**

   You can also access Adobe ConnectNow from this Web address: `www.adobe.com/acom/connectnow`.

   You can go directly to `https://acrobat.com`.

2. **From the Menu bar, choose Files to create a new document, presentation, table, or PDF. Choose Meetings to start a meeting, invite participants, or share your screen or Webcam.**

This great application deserves far more space than I can cram into this section. In fact, it probably deserves its own mini user manual. Be sure to visit `www.adobe.com/acom/connectnow` if you're interested in trying Adobe ConnectNow. You can find a ton of detailed information on using this great tool.

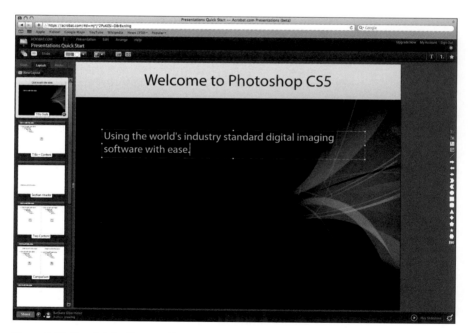

Figure 1-12: Use Adobe ConnectNow to participate in an online Web conference.

Chapter 2: Getting to Know the Tools Panel

In This Chapter

✔ Using the Tools panel

✔ Looking at what each tool does

✔ Creating tool presets

After you have a good grasp of the overall Photoshop environment (described in Book I, Chapter 1), you're ready to dive into the cache of gadgets that — along with the menus, panels, and dialog boxes — make it all happen. Just like you can use a saw, hammer, and nails to transform a pile of 2x4s into a garden gazebo, you can use the Lasso, Healing Brush, and Smudge tools to convert a mediocre photo into a masterpiece that's fit for framing. But remember, behind every garden gazebo is a carpenter who knew how to use the tools required to build it.

Turning On the Tools Panel

You can access the Tools panel by choosing Window⇨ Tools. Here are a few tips for using the Tools panel:

✔ To quickly hide and show the Tools panel (along with the other panels), press Tab.

✔ To move the Tools panel anywhere within the Photoshop window, drag the title bar. Re-dock the Tools panel by dragging it back to its original location.

By default, the Tools panel is a single column. Click the double triangle at the top of the panel to display a two-column configuration.

Selecting tools

To select a tool, simply click it in the Tools panel. A small black triangle in the bottom-right corner of a tool slot indicates that more tools are hidden behind that tool on a *flyout menu,* shown in Figure 2-1 (note that the Tools panel in Figure 2-1 is from the Extended Version of Photoshop). Click and hold down your desired tool to access the flyout menu. You can also access tools by using keyboard shortcuts (which are listed in the Cheat Sheet at Dummies.com; find more information inside the front cover).

Note: 3D tools are in the Photoshop CS5 Extended version only.

Figure 2-1: The Photoshop Tools panel offers a multitude of tools for your editing pleasure.

For the most part, you can access a hidden tool by pressing the Shift key along with the keyboard letter of the visible tool. For example, to select the Pencil tool, which shares the flyout menu with the Brush tool, press Shift+B.

If you don't like having to press the Shift key to access a hidden tool, choose Edit⇨Preferences⇨General (Photoshop⇨Preferences⇨General on the Mac) and deselect the Use Shift Key for Tool Switch option. You can then rotate through the tools by pressing the same letter repeatedly.

When you hover your mouse pointer over a tool, color control, or icon, you see a tooltip. The *tooltip* tells you the name of the tool or icon and its keyboard shortcut, if any. Although helpful at first, it can get annoying after a while. Turn it off by deselecting the Show Tool Tips option in the Interface section of the Preferences dialog box.

Getting to know your tools

The Tools panel is divided into three sections: tools, color swatches, and icons for Quick Mask or Standard mode. The following sections introduce you to the tools. The following list details the other residents of the Tools panel shown in Figure 2-2:

- ✔ **Foreground Color and Background Color:** *Color swatches* represent the current foreground and background colors. When using some of the tools and applying some commands, you may apply one of these colors. The small black-and-white swatches represent the default colors.

  - Click the Default Colors icon to reset the colors to the default.
  - Click the curved arrow icon to switch the foreground and background colors.

  For everything you need to know about color, see Book II, Chapter 3.

- ✔ **Edit in Quick Mask Mode:** The default editing mode is Standard mode. To edit in Quick Mask mode, click the icon. I cover Quick Masks, which offer a way to view, make, and edit a selection, in Book VI, Chapter 2.

Color swatches

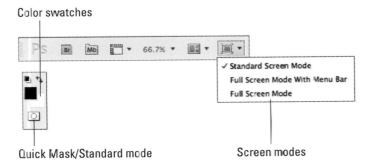

Quick Mask/Standard mode   Screen modes

Figure 2-2: The Tools panel's color, masking, and viewing options.

The Screen modes can be found in the Application bar (Window⇨Application Bar on the Mac only). This bar is located at the top of the application window, to the right of the Menu bar on the PC and directly below the Menu bar on the Mac. Click the icon located on the far right of the Application bar to access various view modes. The default Standard Screen Mode enables you to see your entire Photoshop desktop. You can also select Full Screen Mode with Menu Bar, which hides your desktop background and other open images. Or click Full Screen Mode, which hides everything but your current image. When you select Full Screen Mode, a warning tells you that you must press F to return to Standard Screen mode. In addition to viewing modes, you can also find other handy items in the Application bar; see Book I, Chapter 1 for details.

Introducing the Photoshop Tools

I'm giving you just a very brief description of what each tool does. You're thoroughly initiated on each of the tools while you go through the book. Don't want to go page by page through the book? Okay, you're in luck; I also give you the exact spot where you can find more on each of the tools. For what it's worth, I've organized the tools into logical groupings — although some can cross over into other groups, and some are so unique that they don't fit well in any group.

Using selection tools

The selection tools are the workhorses of Photoshop. They allow you to capture and isolate pixels so that you can edit or manipulate just a portion of an image. Marquee tools capture rectangular or elliptical selections, or single rows or columns of pixels. Figure 2-3 shows an example of an elliptical selection. Whereas the lasso tools make freeform selections, the Magic Wand tool creates selections by picking up pixels of similar colors. The Quick Selection tool enables you to "paint" your desired selection. And the Move and Crop tools do just what their names describe — move and crop images. See Book III, Chapter 1 for details on all the selection tools except the Move and Crop tools. You can find Move-tool details in Book III, Chapter 3, and Book V, Chapters 1 and 5. Crop-tool details reside in Book II, Chapter 1.

Creating and modifying paths

The path tools create and modify *paths,* which are elements comprised of straight and curved segments and anchor points. You can then use these paths as a basis for a selection or to define a shape.

Because of their precision, you may find that using path tools to create a difficult selection usually yields better results than you can achieve with the selection tools.

Figure 2-3: The Elliptical Marquee tool (left) lets you make an elliptical selection; the Move tool (right) enables you to move a selection within your image.

The Path Selection and Direct Selection tools select your paths and path components after you draw the path. Figure 2-4 shows examples of using the Pen tool and Direct Selection tool, respectively. (For more on the Pen tools, see Book III, Chapter 2.)

Corbis Digital Stock

Figure 2-4: The Pen tool creates a path of anchor points and segments; use the Direct Selection tool to select and manipulate those points and segments.

Using painting tools

Generally, the painting tools allow you to apply color or erase pixels. In the case of the Gradient tool, you can apply multiple colors simultaneously. And with the Art History Brush tool, you paint on a stylized effect rather than color. The Color Replacement tool lets you replace the color within your image with the foreground color. Figure 2-5 shows an example of a heart drawn with the Custom Shape tool, painted with the Brush tool (using the Scattered Rose brush tip), Special

Figure 2-5: The painting tools can add texture and color to a basic shape; the Eraser tool erases pixels to reveal your background color.

Effects brush (left), and later (right) partially erased with the Eraser tool.

The new Mixer Brush tool simulates traditional, natural media painting methods, such as blending and mixing color together and varying the wetness within a brushstroke. See Book IV, Chapter 1 for more on the Mixer Brush tool.

All the painting tools rely on the Brushes panel for the size, shape, texture, and angle for the tip of the tool. See Book IV, Chapters 1 and 2, for details on most of the painting tools. You can find an explanation of the Eraser's Erase to History option in Book II, Chapter 4.

Using tools for cloning and healing

The cloning and retouching tools are the powerhouse tools to break out when you need to do some image repairs. These tools allow you to duplicate portions of your image, paint with a pattern, or seamlessly fix scratches, wrinkles, and other blemishes. The unique History Brush tool lets you actually paint a previous version of your image back into your current image — perfect for undoing mistakes.

The Spot Healing Brush quickly removes small blemishes and hickeys of all kinds. The Red Eye tool removes the nasty red reflections in the eyes of your loved ones, as shown in Figure 2-6. Be sure to check out Book VIII, Chapter 3 for info on cloning, pattern stamping, and healing. You can find History Brush details in Book II, Chapter 4.

Figure 2-6: The Red Eye tool is a quick and easy way to correct demon eyes.

Creating effects with typographical tools

Type tools pretty much do what their moniker suggests — create type of varying sorts. The Horizontal Type tool and Vertical Type tool create regular old type, and type on a path; the Mask Type tools create selections in the shape of letters — which you can then fill with images, patterns, colors, and so on. Figure 2-7 shows text created using both the Horizontal Type and Horizontal Type Mask tools. (For type tool details, see Book IV, Chapter 3.)

life's a beach

Corbis Digital Stock

Figure 2-7: You can easily create vector type (left) or a type mask (right) in Photoshop.

Using focus and toning tools

The focus and toning tools allow you to enhance your image by altering the pixels in various ways. You can lighten, darken, blur, smudge, sharpen, saturate, or desaturate color in selected portions of your image.

These tools work best for touching up smaller areas, rather than the entire image. For example, in Figure 2-8, I used the Smudge tool to spike the groom's hair. (I hope he doesn't take it personally.) To saturate the orange on the right, I used the Sponge tool. See Book VIII, Chapter 2 for all you want to know about focus and toning tools.

Creating shapes

The shape tools allow you to create vector-based elements in your image. You can fill these elements with the foreground color or leave them as an empty path.

Although vector-based elements are the heart and soul of the shape tools, you can also create shapes filled with pixels of the foreground color. For shape details, see Book IV, Chapter 1. For more on resolution, see Book II, Chapter 1. Figure 2-9 shows the Custom Shape (left) and Rectangle and Ellipse tools (right) in action.

Corbis Digital Stock

Figure 2-8: You can make your images stand out from the crowd with the Smudge (left) or Sponge (right) tool.

Figure 2-9: Create shapes from large preset libraries (or from your own imagination) with the shape tools.

Viewing, navigating, sampling, and annotating tools

Photoshop has an abundance of tools to help you view and navigate your image window. These tools allow you to zoom in (as shown in Figure 2-10) and out, move your image within the window, and measure distances and angles. The Eyedropper and Color Sampler tools let you pick up and sample color respectively — handy for grabbing or evaluating color in an image. The Notes tool creates written notes that you can leave within an image window — useful for collaboration purposes or simply for reminders to yourself. (See Book II, Chapter 3 for more on the Eyedropper and Color Sampler tools. For the lowdown on the Measure, Zoom, and Hand tools, see Book I, Chapter 4.)

Figure 2-10: The Zoom tool enables you to zoom in and out of your image.

Bonus Chapter 3 covers the Notes tool. See the Introduction for details about this book's companion Web site.

Using tools for the Web

Photoshop doesn't have a whole lot of tools dedicated to the preparation of Web images. That's mainly because Adobe's other programs (Fireworks, Dreamweaver, and Flash) take up the slack in that department. In the Tools panel, you find the Slice tool and Slice Select tool, which allow you to create and select slices. *Slices* are rectangular sections from an image that you can optimize and turn into Web features. For example, you might slice an image and, in Dreamweaver, apply rollovers and image maps to those slices separately for the best viewing experience on your Web page.

See Bonus Chapter 2 for all you need to know about slicing. The Introduction has all the details about this book's Web site.

Photoshop also provides a whole array of 3-D tools, which you can use to create graphics for Web animation, but only in the Extended version.

Saving Time with Tool Presets

Tool presets enable you to create tool settings that you can save and use again. Creating tool presets is a real timesaver if you use specific tool settings on a frequent basis. For example, I make numerous 2-x-2-inch and 2-x-3-inch rectangular selections on images I use in a newsletter. Because I saved the settings as presets, I don't have to redefine them each time I want to select an image for my project.

Creating custom tool presets

Follow these short and simple steps to create your own custom tool preset:

1. **Select the tool you want to create a preset for.**

2. **Select the option you want for the tool on the Options bar.**

   For example, if you selected the Rectangular Marquee tool in Step 1, you may want to select Fixed Size from the Style pop-up menu and then enter your desired Width and Height values.

3. **Click the Tool Preset Picker button on the Options bar, as shown in Figure 2-11 (it's on the far-left side of the Options bar).**

   Or you can choose Window⇔Tool Presets to work through the Tool Presets panel.

Tool Preset Picker button   Create a new tool preset

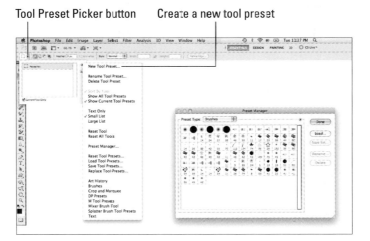

Figure 2-11: Create a custom tool preset for tool settings that you
use often.

4. **Click the Create New Tool Preset button (the dog-eared-page icon).**

   Or, if you're using the Tool Presets panel, choose New Tool Preset
   from the panel menu. If the tool doesn't allow for presets, such as
   the Measure tool, for example, the Create New Tool Preset button
   is gray.

5. **Name the preset and click OK.**

   Your new preset is saved and ready for reuse.

6. **To select the tool preset, you can do one of three things:**

   • Click the Tool Preset Picker button and select a preset from the
     picker's pop-up menu.

   • Select a preset in the Tool Presets panel.

   • Select a preset in the Preset Manager (Edit⇨Preset Manager). Then,
     choose Tools from the pop-up menu and select your preset.

The Tool Presets panel contains a trash can icon that enables you to delete a
preset quickly. Select the preset and drag it to the trash.

Managing your presets

You can manage your presets by selecting options from the Tool Preset
Picker pop-up menu. Table 2-1 describes these options.

Table 2-1	The Tool Preset Picker Pop-Up Menu
Option	*What It Does*
New Tool Preset	Creates a new preset.
Rename Tool Preset	Renames the preset. (Select the preset in the list and then select this option.)
Delete Tool Preset	Deletes a preset. (Select the preset in the list and then select this option.)
Sort by Tool	Groups your presets by tool.
Show All Tool Presets	Shows the presets for all your tools.
Show Current Tool Presets	Shows the presets for the active tool only.
Text Only	Gives you the name of the preset without the icon.
Small List	Shows a small icon, along with the preset name.
Large List	Shows a larger icon with the preset name.
Reset Tool	Closes the active preset and returns to the default tool setting.
Reset All Tools	Returns all tools to their defaults.
Preset Manager	Opens the Preset Manager, which manages all the various libraries of preset brushes, swatches, gradients, styles, patterns, contours, custom shapes, and tools. You can also load other libraries and the custom preset libraries you've created. Additionally, you can rename or delete a preset.
Reset Tool Presets	Replaces your current tool presets with the default presets. If you want to restore the defaults but keep your custom tool presets, select Append.
Load Tool Presets	Loads tool presets that you've previously saved or acquired elsewhere.
Save Tool Presets	Saves a custom set of tool presets for later retrieval. The saved file has a `.tpl` extension.
Replace Tool Presets	Replaces your current tool presets. Allows you to load a `.tpl` file that replaces your current tool presets.
Art History, Brushes, Crop and Marquee, DP Presets, M Tool Presets, Mixer Brush Tool, Splatter Brush Tool Presets and Text options	Allows you to either append or replace your current tool presets with the tool presets from each of those individual libraries.

Chapter 3: Starting, Finishing, and Getting It on Paper

In This Chapter

✔ **Opening images**

✔ **Saving images**

✔ **Closing down Photoshop**

✔ **Printing from Windows and the Mac**

*A*lthough you can create some interesting images from scratch in Photoshop, most of the time you work with digital pictures that already exist. These pictures may be images captured by your scanner or photos you've snapped with your digital camera.

Photoshop offers you a lot of different options for opening existing images, creating new images, and saving original files or copies to your hard drive. After you open, edit, and save your files, you may want to transfer those images from screen to paper. This chapter takes you through the steps you need to know to get your photos in and out of Photoshop.

Browsing for Files

If you don't know the exact filename or location of an image, you can use Adobe Bridge to search for and open files. (Check out Book I, Chapter 4 for a complete description of Bridge.) Finding a file is about as easy as you might expect: Choose File⇨Browse in Bridge or press Alt+Ctrl+O (Option+⌘+O on the Mac). The Bridge window opens, as shown in Figure 3-1.

You can also just click the Launch Bridge button, which is a Br icon on the Application bar.

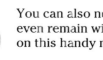

You can also now browse in the new Mini Bridge, which can even remain within your application window as a panel. For more on this handy new addition, see Book I, Chapter 4.

iStockphoto

Figure 3-1: Adobe Bridge allows you to efficiently search for your images.

In the default workspace, to navigate to a folder you want to search, click the Folders tab and locate your desired folder from the list. Click an image in the lightbox area to see it in the Preview window (which shows up on the right side of the Bridge). Bridge graciously provides information about the file in the Metadata panel located below the Preview.

When you find a file you're sure you want to open, either double-click it, choose File⇨Open, or choose File⇨Open With (and then choose your desired application) on the Bridge menu.

Opening an Image

If you know where an image file is stored, you can open the file in a similar way to opening a word-processing, spreadsheet, or other file. Follow these steps to open a file:

1. In Photoshop, choose File⇨Open.

Or press Ctrl+O (⌘+O on the Mac).

The standard Open dialog box for Windows or the Mac OS (operating system) appears. The layout of the dialog box differs slightly between the two. Figure 3-2 shows the Windows version and Figure 3-3 the Mac version.

Figure 3-2: Opening a file in Photoshop on a PC in Windows.

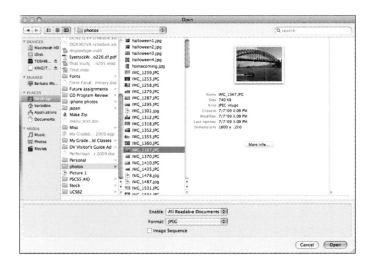

Figure 3-3: Mac OS X Open dialog box.

2. **Navigate to the folder that contains your file.**

   From the Files of type list (Windows) or Enable list (Mac OS), you can select which types of files you want to display.

   To view all files, select All Formats (Windows) or All Readable Documents (Mac OS).

3. **Click the name of the image file you want to open.**

   To select multiple files, click the first file and then Ctrl-click (⌘-click on the Mac) each additional file.

   You may see a preview of the image in the Open dialog box's Preview window.

4. **After you select the file you want, click the Open button.**

   The file opens in Photoshop.

   If you choose File⇨Open Recent, a submenu lists the last files you worked on. Click a filename to open it or simply type the number next to the filename. You can specify the number of files that appear on this menu in the File Handling section of the Preferences dialog box. (For the lowdown on how to specify this value, jump ahead to Book I, Chapter 5.)

Opening special files

Photoshop needs to know the image format of a file (whether it's a TIFF, PCX, PSD, or JPEG file, for example) before it can open the file. Photoshop uses different methods in Windows and Mac OS to determine the format of an image file:

✔ In Windows, Photoshop looks at the file extension (.tif, .pcx, .psd, and so forth), and if it finds a standard image format extension, it assumes that the file was saved using that format.

   File extensions are hidden by default in Windows. You, like many other users, may have changed the default to display file extensions.

✔ Mac OS X uses a similar system based on filename extensions. File extensions may or may not be hidden in the Mac OS. Showing or hiding file extensions can be accomplished via any file's Info dialog box. Select the file in the Mac OS X Finder and press ⌘+I to make the Info dialog box pop up. In this dialog box, you can show or hide the extension for that file and change what application is associated with that file (or all files with the same extension).

For compatibility reasons, Macintosh applications such as Photoshop usually use the Windows file extension. However, when you move files from one platform to the other, they can easily be misidentified. With Photoshop's

Open As feature, you can specify the format that you think (or know) a given file uses. This facility works slightly differently in Windows than in the Mac OS.

Opening specific files using the Windows OS

In Windows, follow these steps to open a specific file:

1. **Choose File⇨Open As and navigate to the file you want to open.**

2. **From the Open As drop-down list, select the file format you want to use.**

3. **Double-click the file's icon.**

   If you selected the right format in Step 2, the file opens in Photoshop. If the file doesn't open, you may have selected the wrong format. Select another and try again.

Opening specific files using the Mac OS

The standard Open dialog box includes an Enable option at the bottom. Select All Documents from the Enable pop-up menu. Then, you can select the file format you want to try directly from the Format list.

Opening as a Smart Object

Photoshop enables you to open a file as a Smart Object. Choose File⇨Open as Smart Object to create a special layer that can contain both raster and vector data. Smart Objects are beneficial because they allow you to transform and manipulate your image data non-destructively. (For details on Smart Objects, see Book V, Chapter 5.)

Placing Files

In Photoshop, use File⇨Place to put PDF (Portable Document Format), Adobe Illustrator (AI), EPS (Encapsulated PostScript), PSD, JPEG, TIFF, BMP, GIF, PNG, and several other lesser-used file formats into separate layers of their own. These files are often created by programs other than Photoshop (such as Adobe Acrobat or Adobe Illustrator) or acquired from your digital camera. Although Photoshop can open these files independently, you can use the Place feature if you want to combine them with an existing image.

Follow these steps to place a PDF, Adobe Illustrator, or EPS file:

1. **Open an existing document into which you want to place a file.**

2. **Choose File⇨Place.**

   The Place dialog box opens.

3. **Navigate to the file you want to insert and then double-click the file.**

   If you're placing an Illustrator file, make sure it was saved with PDF Compatibility selected in the Illustrator Options dialog box. Otherwise, it may not be placed.

   For some types of files, such as multipage PDF files, you may see a dialog box like the one shown in Figure 3-4, which lets you specify which page you want to place. You can also select either the entire Page or just a particular Image on the page. Finally, select how much of your image you want to place from the Crop To pop-up menu. The default bounding box crops to the smallest area that includes text and graphics.

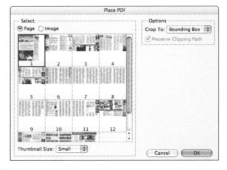

Figure 3-4: Use the Place command when importing a page from a multipage PDF into an existing file.

   Photoshop automatically places PDFs, JPEGs, TIFFs, or PNGs (among other image types) as Smart Objects. For more on Smart Objects, see Book V, Chapter 5.

   Your image appears in a bounding box in the center of your Photoshop image.

4. **If you want, reposition the artwork by positioning your cursor inside the bounding box and dragging.**

   You can also transform (scale, rotate, and so on) your placed artwork, if you want — by dragging or rotating the handles on the bounding box or by entering values on the Options bar. Hold down the Shift key to constrain the proportions when scaling.

   You don't have to be concerned if your placed image is a Smart Object, but be careful about sizing non–Smart Object images. If you enlarge them too much, you may degrade the quality of your image. For more information on transforming images, see Book III, Chapter 3. Avoid degradation of quality by creating a Smart Object, which I explain in Book V, Chapter 5.

   Note that when you place a file, you can't edit the text or vector artwork in it within Photoshop. Why? Because Photoshop rasterizes the file, using the resolution of the file into which you placed it. You can, however, edit a Smart Object in the program it was created in, such as Illustrator. See Book V, Chapter 5 for details. Note that when art is larger than the Photoshop image, Photoshop downsizes the art so that it fits the image. See Book II, Chapter 1 for more on rasterizing and resolution.

5. **If you're placing vector artwork, select Anti-Alias on the Options bar if you want to soften the edges of the artwork during the transformation.**

   Not selecting the option produces a hard edge.

6. **Double-click inside the bounding box to commit the placed image to a new layer.**

   You can also press Enter (Return on the Mac) or click the Commit button (the check icon) on the Options bar.

Creating a New Image

At some point, you'll want to create a new image from scratch. You may want an empty canvas to paint on or need a blank image as scratch space. Or you may want to paste a copied selection into a new document.

Follow these steps to use the New feature to create a new image:

1. **Choose File⇨New.**

   Or press Ctrl+N (⌘+N on the Mac).

   The New dialog box appears, as shown in Figure 3-5.

2. **Type a name for the new file.**

   If you don't specify a name, Photoshop creates one for you, such as Untitled-1, Untitled-2, and so forth.

Figure 3-5: Specify all your desired options in the New dialog box.

3. **If you want to create content for mobile devices (such a cellphone, PDA, or mini portable PC), click the Device Central button.**

   What follows is a fairly quick, easy process:

   a. *Specify your desired preferences by choosing Edit⇨Preferences (Device Central⇨Preferences on the Mac) and selecting your default Phone ID, language, and fonts in the Preferences dialog box. Click OK.*

      You may also specify your levels of Undo.

   b. *In the dialog box's main window, click the Browse tab to select a category from the Library Filter in the bottom left and then choose one or more devices from the list in the Device Library, as shown in Figure 3-6.*

c. *Click the Create tab and then under the New Document tab, select the type of content you want to create, such as a full-screen graphic or wallpaper, from the Content Type drop-down menu.*

To create a custom size, check the Custom Size option at the bottom and enter your desired dimensions.

d. *Click Create.*

Your new, blank document, sized and ready for art, opens in Photoshop. Note that the default is 72 ppi, RGB color mode, using an sRGB color profile. For more on resolution and modes, see Book II, Chapter 2.

If you want to preview how your content will look, choose File⇨Save for Web & Devices. See Bonus Chapter 1 on this book's Web site for details.

Note that you can also access the Device Library dialog box by choosing File⇨Device Central. And you find the same command in both Adobe Illustrator and Flash.

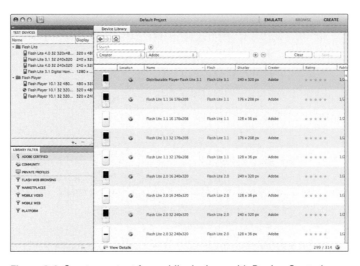

Figure 3-6: Create content for mobile devices with Device Central.

4. **In the New dialog box, select a preset image category from the Preset pop-up menu.**

Choose from common categories such as U.S. Paper, Photo, Web, Mobile and Devices, and Film and Video.

The Clipboard provides the size that corresponds with an image that you copied. Here are a couple of other preset tips:

- You can also choose to match the size of any open file. Open files are listed at the bottom of the Preset list.

- If you select Custom, Photoshop also allows you to create a user-defined custom preset based on your defined settings: After you define your values, click the Save Preset button in the New Document Preset dialog box. Name your preset. Choose any or all the options you want to include in your preset. When you choose not to include an option, Photoshop displays the last used value for that option. Click OK. Your custom preset now appears near the top of the Preset list.

5. **If you selected an image category from the Preset menu in Step 4, select your desired preset Size for that category.**

6. **Or, if you chose Custom in Step 4, enter the width and height of your image manually by typing the width and height of your choice in the text boxes.**

   Note that any Preset sizes automatically revert to Custom when any of the preset's values are changed, and that when you change the units for either the width or height, the other dimension also changes. You can hold down the Shift key to change both width and height independently.

   Like with other Photoshop dialog boxes, you may change from the default unit of measurement of pixels to another, such as inches.

7. **Enter the resolution for the new document.**

   When you select a Preset image category and size, the recommended resolution is entered for you. You can change this resolution if desired, but remember that selecting the right resolution at this point in the creation process is important because if you need to change the resolution later, you degrade image quality. (For more information on selecting an appropriate resolution, see Book II, Chapter 1.)

   Note that Photoshop gives you the size of your image file, based on your settings, in the lower-right portion of the dialog box. This information is good to know if you're targeting a specific file size for your image.

8. **From the Color Mode drop-down list, select a color mode.**

   Your choices include Bitmap, Grayscale, RGB Color, CMYK Color, and Lab Color.

9. **Select your desired color depth for your document.**

   Only 1-bit color depth is available for bitmap images. (Each pixel is either black or white.) The 8-bit and 16-bit color depths are available for the other color modes. And you may also create a new 32-bit image in RGB or Grayscale modes. For details on modes and color depths, see Book II, Chapter 2.

10. **In the Background Contents drop-down list, select an option for how you want the background layer to be filled.**

   Your choices are white, the current background color, or transparent.

11. **Click the Advanced button to display a couple of additional options:**

   • *Color Profile:* Assigns a *color profile* (a definition of the way color looks in a document) to your new document. The default, Adobe RGB (1998), is fine when creating a new document unless you have good reason not to. This setting provides a nice, large *gamut* (range) of RGB colors.

   • *Pixel Aspect Ratio:* Selects an *aspect ratio* (the relationship of width to height of a pixel). The default setting of Square Pixels is fine for print or Web images. Images for digital video content may require a non-square aspect ratio, such as D1/DV NTSC.

12. **Click OK when you finish entering your options.**

   Photoshop creates the new image.

Saving a File

Before you exit Photoshop, you want to save your file on your hard drive or other media. Don't worry if you forget to do this; Photoshop won't let you exit without first asking you if you want to save any files that you've changed or newly created.

Saving files from time to time while you work on them is a good idea so that you always have a recent copy safely stored on your drive.

Follow these steps to save a file:

1. **Choose File➪Save to store the current file with its present name.**

   Choose File➪Save As to store a file already saved with a different name, or even a file with the same name but in a different location.

   The dialog box appears, as shown in Figure 3-7.

2. **Navigate to the folder where you want to store the file.**

3. **Type a name in the File Name (Save As on the Mac) text box.**

4. **Select a format from the Format drop-down list.**

   Some file formats have special capabilities and requirements. For details on file formats, see Book II, Chapter 2.

Figure 3-7: Saving a file frequently is one of the smartest things you can do in Photoshop.

5. **In the Save and Color options areas, select or deselect (if available) the following check boxes, as desired:**

- *As a Copy:* Save the file as a copy.

- *Notes:* Include or delete notes you have created with the Note tool in the saved copy. (See Bonus Chapter 3 for more on notes. The Introduction has details about this book's bonus material on the Web.)

- *Alpha Channels:* Include or ignore *alpha channels* (stored selections). (See Book VI, Chapter 1 for a discussion of channels.)

- *Spot Colors:* Enable spot colors in the saved file. (For more information on spot colors, see Book IX, Chapter 1.)

- *Layers:* Include layers or simply flatten the image to one layer. (See Book V, Chapter 1 for the lowdown on layers.)

- *Use Proof Setup:* Enable proof setup, which includes an onscreen preview of how the image will look when printed or viewed on a specific device. (See Book II, Chapter 3 for more information.)

- *ICC Profile (Windows)/Embed Color Profile (Mac):* Embed a color profile in the file based on the settings established in your Color Settings dialog box. Leave this value at the default setting, but check out Book II, Chapter 3 for information on the specialized situations when you might want to change it.

- *Thumbnail (Windows only):* Embed a thumbnail image in the file if you've defined thumbnails as optional in Photoshop's Preferences. (You can find more on preferences in Book I, Chapter 5.)

- *Use Lower Case Extension (Windows only):* Use lowercase extensions (that is, .tif rather than .TIF), regardless of how you type the filename.

6. **Depending on which file format you select, you may get an additional dialog box of options.**

   For specifics on these file format options, see Book II, Chapter 2.

7. **Click Save to store the image.**

Closing and Quitting

When your session is finished, you want to close up shop and quit Photoshop. PC users, in addition to using the traditional File⇨Exit option, can close Photoshop in any of the following ways:

- ✔ Choose Close from the Windows Control menu in the upper-left corner of the Photoshop title bar.

- ✔ Click the Close (X) button in the upper-right corner of the Photoshop title bar below Windows.

- ✔ Press Ctrl+Q.

Mac users can choose Photoshop⇨Quit Photoshop or press ⌘+Q.

When you use any of these methods, Photoshop asks you whether you want to save any open file that hasn't been saved (or hasn't been saved since it was modified in this session). Click the Yes button to save and close the files.

You can also close any open files without exiting Photoshop by pressing Ctrl+Alt+W (⌘+Option+W on the Mac).

You want to have a backup copy of an image safe on your hard drive prior to an editing session. If you change your mind about the modifications you make to an image, you can always return to the backup copy. Choose File⇨ Save As and enter a new name for the file. You can also select the As a Copy check box and append the word "copy" to the current filename.

Getting It on Paper

Hard-copy prints have become a hugely popular output option, thanks largely to the swarm of inexpensive photo-quality inkjet printers that are vying for your discretionary dollars. Today, anyone can afford a printer capable of producing sparkling prints from digital images. The chief problem is restraining the urge to print everything in sight before your ink tank (and wallet) runs dry.

Actually, making the prints is only a minor puzzle, and one addressed in the following sections. You can print most images with just a few clicks. Most of the advanced options I discuss in this chapter are needed only for special situations or specialized applications, and they're not discussed in detail; the following sections cover only the basics. If you need more detailed information on printing, see Book IX, Chapter 1.

Many photofinishers, service bureaus, or even retail outlets can make prints from your Photoshop-edited images if you burn them to a CD, save them to a USB flash drive, or upload them to an FTP site over the Internet. Vendors such as Shutterfly (www.shutterfly.com), Kodak Gallery (www.kodakgallery.com), and Snapfish (www.snapfish.com) offer prints of all sizes, calendars, and professionally printed and bound photo books. One of my favorite places to get great quality photos, photo books, and even photos printed on canvas is Costco.

Taking a look at printers

You can print Photoshop images on any kind of printer — but aside from the occasional 200-copy print run of black-and-white "Have You Seen This Kitty?" posters, monochrome laser printers are not high on the list of favored Photoshop output hardware.

More often, you're choosing a full-color printer — probably an inkjet model, but possibly other models (such as dye-sublimation, thermal-wax, solid-ink, or even color laser) — as your printer. Although all these printers produce roughly similar results, they do have some differences, as detailed in the following list:

- **Inkjet printers:** These printers paint the page by spraying a jet of ink one dot at a time, under precision computer control. They produce better results when used with photo paper designed especially for inkjets. Inkjet printers generally provide excellent full-color output, but the cost of consumables (ink and paper) can add up fast.

- **Dye-sublimation printers:** These printers potentially offer better-looking prints, but the printers and materials are more expensive than inkjet printers. They use a continuous ribbon of color panels in a roll that's the same width as the print, with each panel used only once. The print head's tiny heating elements can melt dots of dye over a range of 256 values to generate up to 16.8 million colors.

✔ **Thermal-wax printers and solid-ink printers:** These printers use blocks of wax or resin that are melted and sprayed directly onto a page. These devices are commonly used in printing barcodes and labels for clothing, autos, and aircraft.

✔ **Color Laser:** Color laser printers use colored toner and apply ink in four passes. They tend to be a little more expensive, and the quality isn't as good as a nice inkjet print. They do usually print much faster than inkjet printers.

Printing an image

The process of printing an image in Photoshop is slightly different in the Windows and Mac operating systems. The chief differences are in the Print Settings (previously the Page Setup) dialog box, in which you can select a printer and specify orientation, paper size, and other parameters. The following sections take a closer look at the Print Settings dialog box in the two operating systems. Note that unlike the old Page Setup command, the Print Settings command cannot be accessed via the File menu, but instead it's tucked away as a button in the Print dialog box.

Print settings in Microsoft Windows

With Windows applications such as Photoshop, you open the Print Settings dialog box by choosing File➪Print and clicking the Print Settings button. The Properties dialog box then appears. On the Main and Page Setup tabs, you can select the paper size, orientation (portrait or landscape), and other things — such as which paper tray to use, as shown in Figure 3-8. Click Save, or Preview, to return to the main Print dialog box.

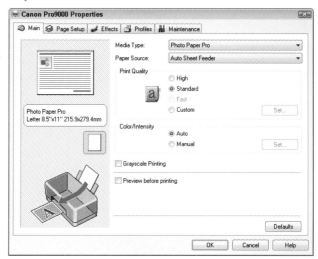

Figure 3-8: Set your desired paper size in the Windows Properties dialog box.

Print settings in the Mac OS

Choose File⇨Print and click the Print
Settings button. You can set the
desired printer, page size, and additional parameters, depending on your
printer, as shown in Figure 3-9. Click
Save, or Preview, to return to the main
Print dialog box.

 In Mac OS X, you can also select a
printer directly from the Print dialog
box, just like you can in Windows. Also
in Mac OS X, if you're connected
directly to a printer via the USB port,

Figure 3-9: The Mac Print dialog box
offers options for a printer and paper size.

the system automatically detects the printer. If you're on a network, select a
printer from the Printer pop-up menu in the Print dialog box.

Setting printing options

Photoshop has a couple printing modes to choose from, depending on how
much control you need and how much of a hurry you're in. Here are your
options:

- **Print One Copy:** A quick way to print a hard copy using the default settings.

- **Print (Ctrl+P on a PC, ⌘+P on the Mac):** Opens a generous Print dialog
  box that includes a Preview pane and many options. This dialog box is
  almost identical in Windows and Mac operating systems. Figure 3-10
  shows the Windows version.

Digital Vision

Figure 3-10: The Print dialog box gives you a multitude of options.

To set your print options, follow these steps:

1. **Choose File⇨Print.**

   The Print dialog box opens.

2. **Select your desired printer from the Printer drop-down list.**

3. **Specify the number of copies you want.**

4. **(Mac only) Select Send 16-Bit Data if your image is 16-bit.**

5. **Click the Print Settings button if you need to revisit that dialog box.**

   In Windows, this dialog box may look different than the one you see when choosing File⇨Page Setup, depending on which printer you selected in the Print dialog box. You may see specific settings customized for your printer, such as print quality, special effects, and so on. These settings vary from printer to printer, so be sure to consult your printer's instruction manual.

6. **Change your page orientation in the Print dialog box by clicking the Portrait or Landscape button next to the Print Settings button.**

7. **Use the Top and Left boxes in the Position area to indicate where you want the image to appear on the page.**

   To center the image, select the Center Image check box. You can also click and drag the image in the preview window to position it if the Bounding Box option is selected.

8. **If you aren't centering your image, select your desired unit of measurement from the Units drop-down list at the bottom of the dialog box.**

9. **If you want to scale the image up or down, select the scale percentage and/or enter height and width values in the Scaled Print Size area.**

   You can also scale the image by clicking and dragging the corner handles of the image in the preview window. However, make sure the Bounding Box option is selected. Scaling in the Print dialog box doesn't change the physical dimensions of the image, just the print size. But keep in mind that scaling up may give you a less-than-optimum printout. Additional options include

   - *Scale to Fit Media:* Sizes your image to fit on a particular paper size.

   - *Match Print Colors:* Gives you a soft proof in your preview. For more on soft proofs, see Book II, Chapter 3.

   - *Gamut Warning:* This option displays colors that will be *out of gamut,* or out of the range of printable colors. These colors appear as gray pixels by default.

   - *Show Paper White:* This option simulates the white point of the paper you choose in the Printer Profile submenu. (Choose Color Management from the menu at the top-right to access the Printer Profile submenu.)

The Match Print Colors, Gamut Warning, and Show Paper White options are available only when your Color Handling is set to Photoshop Manages Colors. For details on color management when printing, see Book IX, Chapter 1.

- *Bounding Box:* Places the handles around the image area and allows for visual sizing.

- *Print Selected Area:* Allows you to print only part of a large image. You need to make the selection before choosing the Print command.

- *Units:* Select your desired unit of measurement.

Your document's resolution is now displayed, as well.

10. **Choose Output from the drop-down list located in the top-right.**

The other option on the drop-down list, Color Management controls advanced proofing and color-profile tasks. (Check out Book IX, Chapter 1 for information on printing using color management and Book II, Chapter 3 for more detail on general color-management topics.)

11. **Select the Output printing options you want to apply:**

- *Background:* The area surrounding the printed image is called the *background,* not to be confused with the *background color* on the Colors panel or the *background layer* of an image. You can change this color from the default (white) to any other color.

- *Border:* The dialog box that pops up lets you add a black border around an image in any width from 0 to 10 points, 0 to 3.5 millimeters, or 0 to 0.15 inches.

- *Bleed:* A *bleed* is an image that extends right up to the edge of the paper size on one or more edges. In effect, you're cropping inside the image area. In practice, most printers don't actually print right to the edge, so to bleed, say, a 5-x-7-inch image, you need to print it on a larger sheet of paper, such as 6 x 8 inches. Clicking the Bleed button opens a dialog box in which you enter a width in inches, millimeters, or points inside the edge of the image.

- *Interpolation:* This option is available with only some printers, particularly PostScript Level 2 (or higher models), to even out the jagged appearance of diagonal lines. Just be aware that interpolation can help only so much, and in some cases, it can be damaging. For more on interpolation, see Book II, Chapter 1.

- *Include Vector Data:* If you have vector artwork in your image, be sure to include this option. For more info on printing vector data, see Book IX, Chapter 1.

12. **Select options for marking the area outside the print area.**

These options include several items that appear only when the print area is smaller than the paper size:

- *Calibration Bars:* This option adds an 11-step grayscale bar outside the image area when printing to a paper size that's larger than the image area. You can use calibration bars to gauge how accurately the gray tones of an image are being reproduced.

- *Registration Marks:* Registration marks are handy when you're printing with multiple plates for color separations, such as those used in four-color or duotone processes. These marks help keep the plates aligned so the image is printed properly.

- *Corner Crop Marks:* Selecting this box prints crop marks at the corners of the image, which indicate where trimming should take place. You can see these and other marks in Figure 3-11.

- *Center Crop Marks:* These crop marks show where the page will be trimmed at the top, bottom, and each side.

- *Description:* To include a description on a printout, choose File➪File Info and enter the text you want to appear. Then, select the Description box in the Print dialog box.

Corner crop marks   Center crop mark

Registration mark   Label

Corbis Digital Stock

Figure 3-11: Crop marks are handy to print.

- *Labels:* Selecting this check box prints the document name and channel name on the image. (See Book VI, Chapter 1 for more on channels.)

13. **Set the options that apply when you're printing to film for color separations, if that's the case.**

    Be sure to talk to your service bureau or offset printer representative for their recommendations. (For more tips, see Book IX, Chapter 1.)

    Here are your choices:

    - *Emulsion Down:* The side of a film or photographic print paper that's light-sensitive is called the emulsion side. You must specify whether you want the emulsion side up or side down for film output. Emulsion Down is the most common film output choice, although some publications may request Emulsion Up. The default is Emulsion Up. (The check box isn't selected.) This option isn't available with all printers.

    - *Negative:* When you print an image on paper, you usually want a positive image; in which case, you shouldn't select the Negative check box. If you're printing the image on film (as is the case if you're printing color separations), your printer will probably request a negative.

14. **Click Print.**

Chapter 4: Viewing and Navigating Images

In This Chapter

↳ **Exploring the image window**

↳ **Zooming within an image**

↳ **Moving with the Hand tool**

↳ **Traveling around with the Navigator**

↳ **Selecting screen modes**

↳ **Positioning and measuring precisely**

↳ **Finding images with Adobe Bridge**

↳ **Sharing images in a PDF or Web gallery**

↳ **Introducing Mini Bridge**

*P*hotoshop offers a variety of ways to view your image documents while you work with them. You can pull back to look at the big picture or zoom in to work on a tiny portion of the image in minute detail. A useful Navigator panel is also at hand to show you exactly where you are in an image and help you move to a specific spot with a click of the mouse button. Should you want to align objects precisely on the screen, Photoshop offers grids and guides with some "magnetic" properties. If you're having trouble finding the image you want, using an uber-browser, called Adobe Bridge, helps you search visually. And the new Mini Bridge is a compact browsing tool that docks itself as a panel in your Photoshop window.

This chapter introduces you to all these viewing and navigating aids, each designed to help you spend less time cruising around the images and more time working with them.

Looking at the Image Window

Each Photoshop image document resides in its own window. A great feature of this window is that you can open multiple image windows for the same image. This feature comes in handy because sometimes you want to look at an image from two perspectives. For example, you may want to get up close and personal with an image to edit pixels, but you still want to view the full image in a fairly large size, as shown in Figure 4-1. In either case, all you need to do is create a new image window for the same image. You can size each window separately, and you can center the window on any portion of the image you want.

Corbis Digital Stock

Figure 4-1: Creating a new image window enables you to view the overall image while editing an area in close-up view.

Here's a quick list of what you can do with multiple windows:

- **Keep different parts of an image straight by creating multiple windows.** Select the document window you want and then choose Window⇨ Arrange⇨New Window for (*filename*) from the Menu bar. You can size and position the new window, and zoom in or out, without affecting the view of the original window.

- **Keep windows organized by cascading them.** If you find that you've created so many windows that you can't view them all easily, Photoshop can automatically arrange them for you in its working space. Choose Window⇨Arrange⇨Cascade to create an overlapping stack of windows arranged from the upper-left to the lower-right side of your display. Be sure, however, that your images are all floating in windows. (Choose Window⇨Arrange⇨Float All in Windows.)

✔ **Keep from losing important windows by tiling them.** Choose Window⇨Arrange⇨Tile to arrange the windows side by side without overlapping. Photoshop shrinks the document windows so they all fit onscreen, but it doesn't change the zoom amount.

You can also click the Arrange Documents icon (next to the last icon) in the Application bar. Select from among a variety of layouts for your image windows. For example, you can choose to Tile All Vertically.

✔ **Tidy up by closing windows you don't need anymore.** To close a specific window when your images are tabbed, click its Close button in the upper-right (upper-left on the Mac) corner of its title bar. If your images are in floating windows, click in the top-right (top-left on the Mac) corner.

✔ **Close all windows in one fell swoop.** To close all windows, choose File⇨Close All. You can also press Alt+Ctrl+W (Option+⌘+W on the Mac).

✔ **Minimize/maximize a document.** Note that your images must be in floating windows to view the Minimize and Maximize icons.

✔ **Bring all Photoshop documents to the front (in Mac OS).** The Mac OS allows you to work in multiple applications and multiple files simultaneously. Choose Window⇨Arrange⇨Bring All to Front to bring all your Photoshop documents to the forefront.

One image, two monitors

For many image-editing enthusiasts and professionals, one monitor simply isn't enough. If you have Windows Vista or 7 installed, or any recent Mac OS, you can set up your computer so that you can use two monitors to edit an image. The extra space offers advantages for viewing and navigating your images.

In Windows, you can drag the image window anywhere in the Photoshop working space. If you want to drag it to a second display screen (and your video card supports spanning two displays), you have to stretch the Photoshop working space (or application window) across both displays. This works great if both monitors are the same size. But if the monitors are significantly different sizes, it doesn't work so well. Either way, make sure your monitors are set to the same resolution. Remember that you can also move panels and dialog boxes onto a second monitor.

Although explaining how to set up multiple monitors on various operating systems is beyond the scope of this book, you can likely find details on how to set up an additional monitor in your operating system's Help feature.

Zooming In and Out of Image Windows

Photoshop offers several ways to zoom in or out of an image, but you'll probably find yourself using one method, such as the keyboard shortcuts, almost instinctively. Each method has advantages of its own. The following sections offer a quick discussion of the main zoom features, as well as some of the lesser-known zooming tricks.

Zooming with keyboard shortcuts

The keyboard shortcuts are the quickest and easiest way to zoom, after you use them enough to remember what they are. Table 4-1 offers a rundown of the handiest zoom keyboard shortcuts, which work no matter what tool you're using. When you press a keyboard shortcut, Photoshop zooms in or out by one of its preset increments (such as 200%, 100%, 50%, 33%, 25%, and so forth). The maximum magnification Photoshop now allows is 3,200%; the minimum magnification is less than 1%, way more than you'd ever need.

Table 4-1	Zooming with Keyboard Shortcuts	
To Do This	*Windows Shortcut*	*Mac Shortcut*
Zoom in.	Ctrl+the plus key (Press Ctrl and the + key.)	⌘+the plus key
Zoom out.	Ctrl+the minus key (Press Ctrl and then the – key.)	⌘+the minus key
Zoom in to a point centered on where you click the mouse button.	Spacebar+Ctrl-click	Spacebar+⌘-click
Zoom out from a point centered on where you click.	Spacebar+Alt-click	Spacebar+Option-click

Using the Zoom tool

Click the Zoom tool in the Tools panel or press Z to activate it. Click anywhere in the image to magnify it by one of the preset magnifications mentioned in the preceding section. Hold down the Alt key (or the Option key on the Mac) and click with the Zoom tool to zoom out. In either case, the zoom centers on the point you click.

Double-click the Zoom tool in the Tools panel to display your image at 100% magnification.

The Zoom tool's big advantage is its zoom selection facility. With the Zoom tool, drag in your image to create a temporary selection. When you release the button, Photoshop zooms in to fill the image window at the highest magnification that includes the selected area.

When the Zoom tool is active, you also have additional zoom tools on the Options bar, as shown in Figure 4-2. Selecting plus (+) or minus (–) sets the default magnification of the Zoom tool to either enlarge or reduce the image.

When you zoom in and out, Photoshop doesn't alter the size of the document window, so your image may become too large for its window (in which case, scroll bars appear so you can view the rest of the image) or too small (in which case, a gray border appears around the image).

Figure 4-2: Zoom options include handy buttons for fitting your image onscreen and displaying the image's print size.

Select the Resize Windows to Fit option on the Options bar to make Photoshop automatically change the size of the document window to show the full document in view, up to the size of the Photoshop working area.

Select the Zoom All Windows option to have Photoshop size all open documents simultaneously. For the other options on the Options bar, see the following section.

Select the new Scrubby Zoom option for quick on-image zooming. With the Zoom tool, drag on your image to the left to zoom out and drag to the right to zoom in.

Photoshop offers animated zooms. This feature enables you to zoom in smoothly when you hold down your mouse button with the Zoom tool active. Be sure to select the Animated Zoom option in the Preferences settings. For details on setting this, and other zoom preferences, see Book I, Chapter 5.

Other ways to zoom

Although you'll likely use the zoom methods mentioned in the preceding section most often, Photoshop offers some other ways to zoom that come in handy from time to time as well:

- **Zooming from the View menu:** Choose View➪Zoom In or View➪Zoom Out to enlarge or reduce the image from the Menu bar. You can also choose from these options on the View menu:

  - *Fit on Screen:* Enlarges the image to the maximum size that fits within the application window.

  - *Actual Pixels:* Shows your image onscreen at a 1:1 pixel ratio.

  - *Print Size:* Shows the image at the size that it will print.

  The above options also appear on the Options bar — with the additional option of Fill Screen, which does just that with your image.

  To resize windows to fit onscreen when you're not using the Zoom tool, choose Edit➪Preferences➪General (or Photoshop➪Preferences➪General on the Mac) and select the Zoom Resizes Windows option.

- **Typing ratios in the Magnification box:** The Magnification box at the bottom of each document shows the current magnification ratio. Type an exact magnification ratio in this box and press Enter (Return on the Mac) to produce a custom zoom level. This box is handy if you need a specific amount of enlargement or reduction.

  Another Magnification box appears in the Navigator panel, along with some other options for zooming. I describe them in the section "Cruising with the Navigator Panel," later in this chapter.

- **Zooming with the Application bar:** Select a preset zoom level from or enter any desired percentage in the Zoom Level drop-down list on the Application bar.

↙ **The following commands live on the Window⇨Arrange submenu:**

- *Match Zoom:* Choose Match Zoom to have all your open documents match the magnification percentage of your active document.

- *Match Location:* Choose this command to match the locations of all your open documents with the location of your active document. For example, if you're viewing the center portion of an image, choosing this command then adjusts the views of all your open documents to the center, as well.

- *Match Rotation:* This command enables you to match the canvas rotation of your active document, created by using the Rotate View tool.

- *Match All:* And finally, Match All does all three commands simultaneously.

 ↙ **Magnifying by dragging:** With the Zoom tool, drag around the portion of the image you want to zoom into. A selection marquee appears, and when you release the mouse button, that portion of the image fills your document window. To freeze and then move the selection marquee around the image, begin your drag and then hold down the spacebar while dragging the marquee to a new location.

 Note that when you now zoom in greater than 500%, a pixel grid appears. Instead of having pixels butt up against one another flush, like in previous versions of Photoshop, a thin, gray line separates each pixel.

If you don't like the display of the pixel grid, disable it by deselecting Pixel Grid under the View⇨Show submenu.

Handling the Hand tool

The Hand tool helps you to quickly move around in an image document and works similarly to a scroll bar.

 The Hand tool is more of a function than an actual tool because you rarely need to click the Hand tool to use it. Simply hold down the spacebar while using any other tool, and the cursor changes into the Hand icon, enabling you to move the image around in its window by dragging.

Here are some tips for using this tool:

↙ **Press H to activate the tool.** To activate the Hand tool without clicking its icon in the Tools panel, just press the H key. You can also select this tool from the Application bar.

↙ **Use the Options bar to change the size of a window.** When the Hand tool is active, the Actual Pixels, Fit on Screen, Fill Screen, and Print Size buttons appear on the Options bar. Click these buttons to display your image in a 1:1 pixel ratio (100% magnification); make the entire image fit within your screen; make the image fill your application working space; or make the document appear in the size it'll be when printed.

✔ **Use the Hand tool while zooming.** When the Hand tool is active, you can hold down the Alt key (Option key on the Mac) and click the image to zoom out, or hold down the Ctrl key (⌘ key on the Mac) and click to zoom in — without needing to press the spacebar like you would with the normal keyboard shortcut.

✔ **Scroll All Windows.** When the Hand tool is active, this option, in the Options bar, enables you to move around all open documents simultaneously.

✔ **Double-click the Hand tool.** Resizes the document image to a Fit on Screen magnification.

✔ **Press the Page Up or Page Down buttons to change the view.** These buttons move the view up or down by a window.

Now that you've become friendly with the Zoom and Hand tools, here's one last tip. If you hold down the Shift key while scrolling with the Hand tool or zooming with the Zoom tool, all open image windows scroll or zoom together. This trick can come in especially handy, for example, when you create another view of the same document. (Choose Window⇨Arrange⇨New Window.)

Rotating with the Rotate View tool

Sharing the flyout menu with the Hand tool is the Rotate View tool. This tool actually rotates your entire image window, as shown in Figure 4-3.

Follow these steps to use the Rotate View Tool:

1. **Select the Rotate View tool from the Tools panel or Application bar.**

2. **Place your tool cursor in the image window and hold down the mouse button.**

   A compass rose appears.

Figure 4-3: Rotate your entire image window.

3. **Drag the cursor clockwise (or counterclockwise) to rotate the image window.**

   Note that you can see the numeric rotation angle in the Options bar. Check the Rotate All Windows option to simultaneously rotate all open documents.

4. **When you reach your desired rotation angle, release the mouse button.**

5. **If you want to undo your rotation, click the Reset View button in the Options bar.**

   Choosing Edit⇨Undo or using the History panel to undo doesn't revert your image to the original 0-degree rotation.

 If you're a MacBook user, or if you are using a Windows 7 computer with a multi-touch trackpad, you may be aware that you can use your trackpad to flick, rotate, or zoom. You may also have been annoyed when you did these things inadvertently, in which case you can disable Gestures in your General Preferences settings.

Cruising with the Navigator Panel

Some Photoshop users don't use the *Navigator panel* (which is a roadmap to your image document) nearly as often as they could, and there's a simple reason for that: In its default size, the Navigator panel is just too darned small to be of use.

Most new Photoshop users see the tiny Navigator window and decide that working with such a small thumbnail image isn't worth the bother. There's a quick fix, and after you've seen exactly what the Navigator panel can do for you, it may become one of your favorite tools. Here are the keys to using the Navigator panel, which you open by choosing Window⇨Navigator:

✔ **Resize the Navigator panel.** Before you begin working with the Navigator panel, shown in Figure 4-4, grab the size box at the lower-right corner of the Navigator panel and drag it down and to the right to create a jumbo version with a much larger, more viewable thumbnail. It's easiest to resize when you pull the panel out of the dock and let it float.

 Resizing works really well if you're using a second monitor. Placing the jumbo-sized Navigator panel on the second monitor works great. For more on working with two monitors, see the sidebar "One image, two monitors," in this chapter.

 The Navigator panel is one panel that you probably want readily accessible. It's most useful when it's visible at all times. Undock the Navigator panel by pulling the tab of the panel to the left. Position the Navigator panel to one side of your image so it's ready for instant use.

✔ **View the thumbnail.** The entire Navigator window shows the full document image, with an outline called a *View box* showing the amount of image visible in the document window at the current zoom level.

✔ **Change the view.** Click anywhere in the thumbnail *outside* the View box to center the box at that position. The comparable view in your main document window changes to match.

✔ **Move the view.** Click anywhere in the thumbnail inside the View box and then drag to move the box to a new position. The main document window changes to match the new view.

Corbis Digital Stock

Figure 4-4: The Navigator panel is more productive and user-friendly when enlarged.

✔ **Zoom in or out.** Click the Zoom In button (which has an icon of two large pyramids) or Zoom Out button (which has an icon of two smaller pyramids) to zoom in or out. Or drag the Zoom slider that resides between the two icons. The View box changes size when you zoom in or out, and Photoshop magnifies or reduces the view in the original document window to match, as well.

✔ **Specify an exact magnification.** The lower-left corner of the Navigator panel has a Magnification box. It shows the current magnification, and you can type a new value to zoom to the exact magnification level you need.

If the View box color is too similar to a dominant color in your image, you can select a new color for its outline by selecting Panel Options from the Navigator panel pop-up menu.

Choosing a Screen Mode

Photoshop's working area can become horribly cluttered. And here's a secret: The more adept you become, the more cluttered the desktop becomes. Just when you begin to appreciate a neatly docked Options bar and the convenience of displaying panels, you realize that you've gobbled up all your free working space.

Photoshop now has three different screen modes (or maybe five, depending on what you consider to be a screen mode). Each mode shows or hides some of the elements on the screen at the press of a key or click of the mouse button. Select a mode by clicking the Screen Mode icon at the right end of the Application bar, or by choosing View⇨Screen Mode. The final two modes are accessible via keyboard commands. Table 4-2 shows you how to unclutter your screen quickly.

Table 4-2	Cleaning Up Working Space Clutter	
Do This . . .	*. . . To Change to This Screen Mode*	*What's Happening*
Press Shift+Tab.	Hide all panels.	All the panels in your working space — except for the Tools panel — vanish. When you need to access them again, press Shift+Tab again.
Press the Tab key.	Hide all panels and the Options bar.	All the panels (including the Tools panel) and the Options bar vanish, leaving you with a clean workspace showing only the Menu bar, Application bar, and any open documents (or the Mac, the Application bar may not display).
Click the Screen Mode button in the Application bar.	Full Screen mode with Menu bar.	Only the active document window is visible, along with the panels, Menu bar, Application bar, and Options bar. The document window is maximized, and the other documents are hidden.
Click the Screen Mode button in the Application bar.	Full Screen mode.	View the image alone with all other components hidden, as shown in Figure 4-5.
Click the Screen Mode button in the Application bar.	Standard Screen mode.	The default Photoshop screen appears, displaying all menus and panels.

Press the F key to cycle between the last three screen modes in Table 4-2.

If you hide the Tools panel in any Screen Mode, simply hover your mouse over the left side of the screen to make your Tools panel reappear.

Getting Precise Layout Results

Photoshop includes numerous useful features that help you lay out your images precisely. There are dozens of reasons to make a selection in a particular place, position an object at an exact location, or align several objects along the same imaginary line. Here are a few examples:

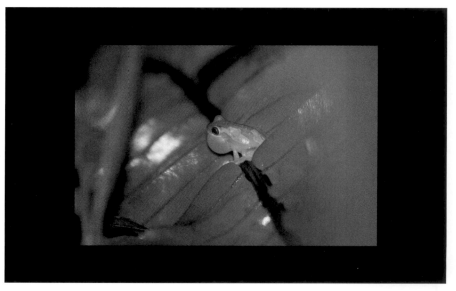

Dynamic Graphics, Inc.

Figure 4-5: View your image in Full Screen mode.

✔ You want to draw parallel lines exactly 50 pixels apart to create a "window blind" effect.

✔ You're creating a set of thumbnails that need to be aligned in neat rows and columns.

✔ You want to create an object that's the exact same size (in one or more dimensions) as another object already in your image.

You have several tools to help you do this and more.

Creating guides

Guides are nonprintable horizontal and vertical lines that you can position anywhere you like within a document window. Normally, they're displayed as solid blue lines, but you can change guides to another color and/or to dashed lines.

To use guides, choose Edit➪Preferences➪Guides, Grid & Slices (or Photoshop➪Preferences➪Guides, Grid & Slices on the Mac), as I discuss in Book I, Chapter 5. Guides would be useful even if they were only, well, guides. However, they have another cool feature: Objects and tools dragged to within 8 screen pixels of a guide are magnetically attracted to the guide and snap to it. That makes it ridiculously easy to align objects precisely. Because the objects snap to the guides, you can be confident that you've placed the objects exactly on the guide and not just near it. You can turn off the Snap to Guides feature if you want a little more control in your arrangements.

To place guides, follow these steps:

1. **Make sure that rulers are visible in your image.**

   Choose View➪Rulers to display them, if necessary.

2. **Click in the horizontal ruler and drag down to create a new horizontal guide. Release the mouse button when the guide is in the location you want.**

   Anytime you create a guide by dragging from the ruler, the Show Guides option automatically switches on. At other times, you can show or hide guides by choosing View➪Show➪Guides or by pressing Ctrl+semicolon (⌘+semicolon on the Mac).

3. **Click in the vertical ruler and drag to the right to create a new vertical guide.**

   When you release the mouse button, your new guide stops.

   You can also create a horizontal guide by Alt-clicking in the vertical ruler (Option-clicking on the Mac), or create a vertical guide by Alt-clicking in the horizontal ruler (Option-clicking on the Mac). Use whichever method is faster for you.

   Finally, you can choose View➪ New Guide and enter your desired orientation and position.

4. **Use the Move tool (press V to activate it) to reposition your guides.**

   Look for the guides in Figure 4-6.

Corbis Digital Stock

Figure 4-6: Nonprinting guides allow you to precisely position your elements.

Using guides

After the guides are in place, here are a few of the things you can do with them:

- **Turn the Snap to Guides feature on or off.** Choose View➪Snap To➪Guides.

- **Lock all guides so you don't accidentally move them.** Choose View➪Lock Guides. You can also press Alt-Ctrl+semicolon (Option+⌘+semicolon on the Mac).

- **Remove all guides and start from scratch.** Choose View➪Clear Guides.

- **Change a horizontal guide to a vertical guide (or vice versa).** Hold down the Alt key (Option key on the Mac) while you drag the guide with the Move tool.

- **Align a guide at a precise location on the ruler.** Hold down the Shift key while you drag a guide to force it to snap to the ruler ticks.

- **Create a new guide in a precise location.** Choose View⇨New Guide, click the Horizontal or Vertical option, and type a distance from the ruler where you want the new guide to reside.

- **Hide and show guides.** Click the View Extras icon in the Application bar and select Show Guides from the drop-down list to toggle the view off and on.

Using grids

The Photoshop grid feature offers a convenient canned set of guidelines already nicely arranged for you at preset intervals. You can use a grid for any application where you want to align objects in a pleasing, geometrically precise arrangement.

Grids share some features in common with guides but boast a few differences, too:

- Like guides, grids don't print with your image. They're used only as reference lines in your onscreen image, as shown in Figure 4-7.

- Objects and tools can optionally snap to the lines on a grid, depending on whether you have View⇨ Snap To⇨Grid turned on or off.

- You can show or hide grids by choosing View⇨Show⇨Grid. Or click the View Extras icon in the Application bar and select Show Grids from the drop-down list to toggle the view off and on.

Corbis Digital Stock

Figure 4-7: Grids enable you to arrange elements along evenly spaced lines.

- You can change the color of the grid and select solid lines, dashed lines, or dots for the grid by choosing Edit⇨Preferences⇨Guides, Grid, Slices (Photoshop⇨Preferences on the Mac).

- You can specify the distance between grid lines and the number of subdivisions between grid lines in the Preferences dialog box. For more information on setting grid and guide preferences, see Book I, Chapter 5.

Measuring Onscreen

You can measure distances and objects within Photoshop many different ways. The rulers, used in combination with guides, are a good way to mark distances precisely so that you can create objects of a particular size. You can change the increments used for these measurements in Photoshop's Preferences, as I detail in Book I, Chapter 5.

However, Photoshop also has a handy Ruler tool that you can use to lay measurement outlines in any direction. These lines tell you a great deal more than just the size of the object you're measuring. You can also measure angles and determine the exact coordinates of an object.

When you use the Ruler tool, the Options bar offers a readout of information that includes the following values:

- ✔ **X, Y — the X and Y coordinates of the start of the line:** For example, if you start at the 1-inch position on the horizontal ruler and the 3-inch position on the vertical ruler, the X and Y values on the Options bar are 1.0 and 3.0, respectively. (You select the increments for the X and Y values on the ruler in Photoshop's Preferences.)

- ✔ **W, H — the horizontal (W) and vertical (H) distances traveled from the X and Y points:** A 1-inch long, perfectly horizontal line drawn from the X,1 and Y,3 positions shows a W value of 1.0 and an H value of 0.0.

- ✔ **A:** The angle of the first line or the angle between two lines.

- ✔ **L1:** The total length of the line.

- ✔ **L2:** The total length of the second line.

- ✔ **Clear:** Press the Clear button to delete your current measurement.

You can now straighten your image using the Ruler tool. Simply drag along the horizontal axis you wish to align to with the Ruler. Then click the Straighten button in the Options bar.

Measuring an object

To measure an object, follow these steps:

1. **Select the Ruler tool.**

   It's tucked away in the Tools panel with the Eyedropper. Press I, or Shift+I, to cycle between the Eyedropper, Color Sampler, Note, and Ruler tools until the Ruler tool appears.

2. **Click at a starting location for the measuring line and then drag to the end location.**

Hold down the Shift key while dragging to constrain the line to multiples of 45 degrees.

3. **Release the mouse button to create the measurement line, as shown in Figure 4-8.**

Measuring an angle

You can measure an angle by drawing two lines and reading the angle between them from the Options bar. Just follow these steps:

1. **Select the Ruler tool in the Tools panel.**

   It's tucked away with the Eyedropper. Press I, or Shift+I, to cycle through the tools until the Ruler tool appears.

Figure 4-8: The Ruler tool is your onscreen measuring device.

2. **Click at a starting location for the first line and drag to the end location.**

   You can hold down the Shift key while you drag to constrain the line to multiples of 45 degrees.

3. **Release the mouse button to create the first line.**

4. **Hold down the Alt key (the Option key on the Mac) and click the end-point of the first line that you want to use to measure the angle.**

5. **Drag the second line and release the mouse button when you reach your desired length.**

6. **On the Options bar, read the angle between the two lines (labeled A).**

   You can also see the length of each line, as shown in Figure 4-9.

Using the Info Panel

The Info panel, accessible under the Window menu, shown in Figure 4-10, displays a variety of information, depending on what tool you're using. To specify which status info options you want displayed, or whether you want Tool Hints shown, select Panel Options from the Info panel pop-up menu. For example, if you're using the Ruler tool, the information in the Info panel duplicates the measurements shown on the Options bar. Selecting other tools modifies the Info panel's appearance to reflect the functions of that tool. Here's some of the information you can find out by keeping the Info panel visible on your desktop:

✔ When using most tools, the Info panel displays the X and Y coordinates of the cursor, as well as the color values of the pixel directly beneath the cursor.

Figure 4-9: The Ruler tool also serves as a digital protractor.

⤺ When making a selection with the marquee tools, the Info panel shows both the X and Y coordinates of the cursor, as well as the width (W) and height (H) of the selection.

⤺ When dragging with the Crop or Zoom tools, the Info panel shows the width and height of the marquee used to define the cropping or zoom borders. The Crop tool's current angle of rotation (A) is also displayed.

⤺ With the Line, Pen, and Gradient tools, the Info panel shows the X and Y coordinates of the starting position for the line, path, or gradient you're defining, as well as the distance (L) of the line you've dragged, the change in X and Y directions (Delta X and Delta Y), and the angle (A).

☑ When you use a transformation command, the Info panel displays the percentage change in the Width, Height, Angle, Angle of Horizontal Skew (H), and Angle of Vertical Skew (V). For more on transformations, see Book III, Chapter 3.

☑ When you use a color adjustment, such as Levels, and that adjustment dialog box or adjustment layer is active, the Info panel displays before-and-after color values beneath the mouse cursor. See Book VIII, Chapter 1 for more on color adjustments.

☑ After you make a selection with the Lasso or Magic Wand tools, the Info panel shows the Width and Height of the selection's bounding rectangle.

☑ Select Panel Options from the Info panel's pop-up menu. In the Info Panel Options dialog box that appears, you can define a second color readout, in addition to the default readout, using a different color model if you want, as shown in Figure 4-11. In addition to the regular color modes, the default Actual Color option displays values in the current mode of the document. Proof Color displays values based on the setting chosen in View➪Proof Setup. The Total Ink option displays the percentage CMYK ink under the cursor based on the settings in the CMYK Setup dialog box in the Color Settings (Advanced). You can also define a measurement increment for the mouse cursor (in inches, pixels, millimeters, and so forth)

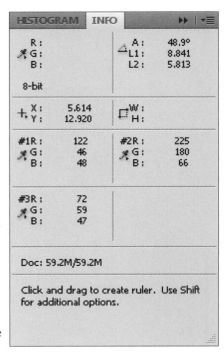

Figure 4-10: The Info panel displays useful file information, such as measurements and color readouts.

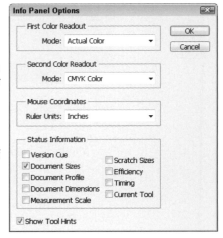

Figure 4-11: Set a different color mode in the Info Panel Options dialog box.

independently of the increment you've selected in Preferences. You can also choose to display other types of information about your file. For more info on these options, see Book I, Chapter 1.

Working with Extras

Extras are the optional items displayed on your screen, such as grids, pixel grids, guides and Smart Guides, selection and layer edges, notes, slices, and the *target path* (a line drawn with the Pen tool). Although you can turn on and off the display of each option independently, the Extras function helps you to create a set of extras that you want to see or hide. You can then turn them all on or off at the same time.

The following list explains how to show or hide these extras:

- ✒ To turn one extra on or off, choose View➪Show and then select the extra you want to show.

- ✒ You can also hide and show your guides, grid, and ruler by clicking the View Extras icon in the Application bar.

- ✒ To show or hide extras in a group, choose View➪Show➪Show Extras Options. Select each extra that you want to show in the dialog box that appears, as shown in Figure 4-12.

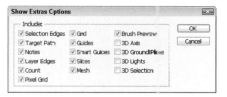

Figure 4-12: Pick and choose the extras you want to show in your image window.

- ✒ To show or hide all the extras you've selected in the Extras Options dialog box, choose View➪Extras or press Ctrl+H (⌘+H on the Mac).

Managing Images with Adobe Bridge

Adobe Bridge, shown in Figure 4-13, is command and control central for not just Photoshop, but the entire Adobe Creative Suite. So, if you haven't embraced Bridge yet, it won't be long before you appreciate the omnipresent power of this application.

Adobe Bridge enables you to visually browse your network, hard drives, and external media to find the exact image you need, and it has a multitude of viewing, sorting, cataloging, and organizing features to manage all your assets — photographic, illustrative, video, written, and so on. Bridge is so multifaceted that, although you can access it from any Adobe application, it's also a standalone program.

Favorites panel

Menu bar

Folders panel

Application bar

Metadata panel

Preview panel

Keywords panel

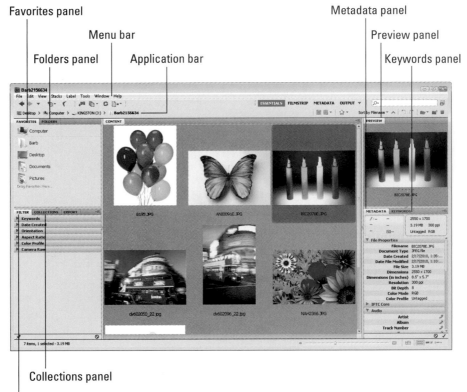

Collections panel

Filter panel

Figure 4-13: Adobe Bridge enables you to visually explore and locate your digital media assets.

Here's a brief description of what Bridge offers:

- **File browsing and asset management:** View, search, organize, and process your files. You can open, move, delete, rotate, label, and rate your images. You can also import and edit your photos from your digital camera.

- **Camera Raw:** You can open and edit Camera Raw files directly from Bridge and save them in a format that's compatible with Photoshop. You can edit JPEG and TIFF files, as well.

- **Color management:** You can use Bridge to synchronize the color settings across all your Creative Suite applications to ensure color accuracy and consistency. This capability requires you have the applications installed on your computer.

✏ **Perform automated tasks:** You can perform automatic tasks like batch processing directly from Bridge.

✏ **Create projects:** Finally, you can create projects, such as slide shows, PDF presentations, and Web galleries.

You can access Bridge in several ways:

✏ In Photoshop, choose File➪Browse in Bridge.

✏ Click the Bridge icon in the Application bar.

✏ To launch Bridge directly, choose Start➪Adobe Bridge in Windows. (Click the Bridge icon in the Dock or double-click the Bridge icon in the `Applications/Adobe Bridge CS5` folder on the Mac.)

Brief anatomy of Bridge

Before I dive headlong into the applicable operations of Bridge, let me give you a brief anatomical breakdown of each of its main components. (Refer to Figure 4-13.)

✏ **Menu bar:** Commands found on the Menu bar allow you to open or delete images, get photos from your camera, create stacks, add file info, and search for images. You can also label files and append their *metadata* (information about your file). The Menu bar also offers options for sorting and viewing files. Finally, on the Tools➪Photoshop menu, you have access to basically the same Automate menu that you find in Photoshop itself, plus a couple unique commands, which I cover in the section "Using the Menu bar and buttons," later in this chapter.

✏ **Application bar:** You find some often-used commands on the Application bar at the top of the application window. Click the right- and left-arrow buttons to go forward and back among your files and folders. Click the down-pointing arrow button to go to a parent or favorites location. Click the Boomerang icon to go back to Photoshop. Click the arrow-and-clock icon to access a recent file or folder. Click the camera icon to get photos from a camera. The Refine icon offers several options:

   • *Review Mode:* This mode leaves the Bridge interface and displays your images full screen. You can find more details about this mode in the section "View menu," later in this chapter.

   • *Batch Rename:* In this dialog box, you can rename, move, or copy a folder of images in one fell swoop. Bridge runs a script and processes the images simultaneously.

   • *File Info:* This command brings up a comprehensive metadata panel in which you can edit info about your file. For more details, see Bonus Chapter 3 on the Web.

Click the shutter icon to open an image in Camera Raw. Click the page icon to Output to the Web or PDF (more on this feature coming up in this chapter).

✔ **Folder hierarchy:** A bar that appears below the Menu and Application bars lists the current location (such as a folder on your hard drive) on display. Click the right-pointing arrow to view the particular folder's hierarchy, as well as Favorites and Recent Folders.

✔ **Shortcut buttons:** Open a recent file, create a new folder, and rotate or delete files with a click of the button. You can also switch to Compact mode (which I explain how to do in the following section). Enter a description of what you're looking for in the Search field and choose where you search via the drop-down menu.

✔ **Favorites panel:** Located in the upper-left of the Bridge window, this panel provides easy access to folders, files, and, if you're a Creative Suite user, the Bridge Home. Drag whatever hard drives, folders, or files you want to include in your Favorites panel.

✔ **Folders panel:** Also located in the upper-left portion of the Bridge window, this panel shows the folder hierarchy on your computer. If an image file is available to your computer, Bridge lets you use this panel to find it.

✔ **Filter panel:** Enables you to see your assets sorted by various criteria. For example, you can view your images by date created, keywords, file type, and even the ISO setting of your camera. Select your criteria in the Filter panel, as shown in Figure 4-14, and view the results in the Content window. Click the No icon (a circle with a diagonal line) at the bottom of the Filter panel to clear all filters. Click the pushpin icon to keep the filter intact when browsing for files in Bridge.

✔ **Collections panel:** If you've already gone through the trouble of meticulously naming your files, or you're like me and are too darned lazy to do so, then the Collections panel is for you. It's a lot less time-consuming than using keywords — simply select, or find, your desired images

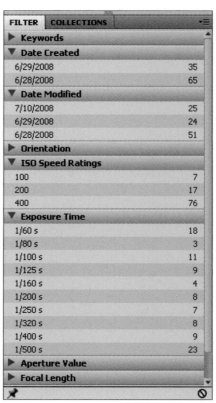

Figure 4-14: The Filter panel sorts and displays your assets.

in the Content area (technically referred to as the *light table*) and click the New Collection icon at the bottom of the panel. If you want to include selected files into a new collection, click Yes when prompted. Name your collection. To add a file to an existing collection, simply select the image(s) and drag it (or them) into the folder icon in the Collections panel. To delete a collection, select the collection and click the trash icon. Click the time-saving New Smart Collection icon to have Bridge go out and collect your files based on established criteria. Choose where to look and by what criteria. To add another criterion, click the plus sign. Specify match settings — any or all — and specify whether you want to include subfolders and non-indexed files. Click Save. If all goes well, you have a collection, or digital photo album, in short order.

✔ **Export panel:** Drag files from your light table area onto the Export panel. Click the up-pointing arrow to export the files to your hard drive. In the Export dialog box, under the Destination tab, choose what folder you would like to export your files to. Choose your image specifications under the Image Options tab. Click Export. This is a quick and easy way to copy files you need for a project onto your desktop.

✔ **Workspace controls:** Select from a variety of presets — Essentials (the default workspace), Filmstrip, or Metadata located at the top of the Bridge window. You can find additional workspaces in the pop-up menu to the right of the Metadata button. You can also find commands to create a new workspace, and delete and reset workspaces. Find details on creating a new workspace in the following section.

✔ **Preview panel:** In the top-right portion of the Bridge window is a preview of the currently selected file. You can reduce or enlarge the preview by dragging the separator bars on the left and bottom of the Preview panel. To more closely examine a portion of your image in the Preview panel, simply click the image. That portion then appears in a loupe window over your image. Hold down and drag the loupe to view other portions of the image. To close the loupe, simply click in the loupe window.

✔ **Content light table:** The largest area of the Bridge window is reserved for displaying the content. This window shows thumbnail images of all the files in the currently selected folder, along with information about each file. In addition, any subfolders are shown with a folder icon.

✔ **Keywords panel:** This feature lets you tag your images with keywords, such as the names of people or places, to enable easier locating and sorting of images.

✔ **Metadata panel:** The Metadata panel shows information about your images. The File Properties section shows items such as filename, date of creation, date last modified, image format, size, and so on. Any file information for images added via File⇨File Info appears in the IPTC section of the Metadata panel. Likewise, you can also enter or edit file information directly in the IPTC section in Bridge. Finally, the Camera Data section displays information associated with your digital photos, such as the make and model of your camera, exposure, and ISO speed. You can also display other types of metadata, such as Camera Raw information, by selecting them in the Preferences dialog box, accessed via the Metadata panel pop-up menu.

In Bonus Chapter 3 on this book's companion Web site, you can find out about the Notes feature and advanced features of the Metadata panel. See the Introduction for details about this book's Web site.

✓ **Viewing controls:** At the bottom of the Bridge window is a slider that reduces or enlarges the content thumbnails. Note that you can enlarge thumbnails up to 640 pixels. There are also icons to view your content as thumbnails, details, or a list.

Configuring the Bridge window

Bridge, being as enormous and full-featured as it is, is surprisingly flexible when it comes to how you configure its various panels. Here's a rundown of how to customize your Bridge window:

✓ To size the entire Bridge window, diagonally drag any corner or edge of the window. (On the Mac, drag the lower-right corner.)

✓ To resize panels, drag the bar that divides them. Position your cursor over the bar (the cursor changes to a double-headed arrow), and then click and drag the bar to size the panel.

✓ Switch to Compact mode by clicking the icon in the upper far-right corner of the Application window. This command condenses your Bridge window to just a portion of your light table and the Application bar. Click the Ultra Compact Mode icon to reduce the window to just the Application bar. Click the Switch to Full Mode icon to revert. Other viewing options are available in the drop-down menu in the top-right corner when you're in one of the compact modes.

✓ You can drag and regroup the tabbed panels in Bridge, just like you can with Photoshop panels. To collapse a panel, double-click its tab.

✓ After you configure your Bridge, you can save it as a workspace preset that you can then call up at anytime. For example, you may want one workspace for working with photos and yet another when working with layout or word-processing files. Simply choose Window➪Workspace➪ New Workspace. Provide a name, choose to save your window location and sort order of images as part of the workspace, and click Save. Note that you can also select New Workspace from the Workspace drop-down menu in the Application bar. To access the workspace, choose Window➪ Workspace and then select the name of your saved preset. It also appears as its own icon in the Workspace area at the top of the Bridge window. You may also select from several preset workspaces designed for specific tasks. For example, if viewing files is your most important task, then select the Light Table preset, shown in Figure 4-15. Not happy with a workspace?

Choose Window➪Workspace➪Delete Workspace and select your work-space from the Workspace drop-down list in the Delete Workspace dialog box. Or simply reset your workspace back to the Essentials workspace, the default.

Figure 4-15: The Light Table workspace focuses on the best viewing configuration in the Bridge.

Using the Menu bar and buttons

The Menu bar is a visual testimony to the numerous capabilities of Bridge. The following sections provide a brief rundown of what you find on each menu.

File menu

Here's what you find on the Bridge's File menu:

- **New Window:** If you want one window to remain displayed as is, choose this command to create another Bridge window.

- **New Folder:** This command creates a new folder in the location listed in the folder hierarchy. You can also click the Create a New Folder button in the row of shortcut buttons.

- **Open:** After you select a thumbnail in the Content window, you can choose the Open command to open the image in Photoshop or another CS5 application. Of course, you can also simply double-click the selected file(s). To open multiple files, just hold down Ctrl (⌘ on the Mac) while selecting.

- **Open With:** Select a file and choose the Open With command. Select your program of choice from the submenu that appears.

✔ **Open Recent:** Choose from your most recent ten files.

✔ **Open in Camera Raw:** Select a Camera Raw file and choose this command to edit the Raw settings. You can also open JPEG or TIFF files.

✔ **Test in Device Central:** Select a file and then this command, which launches the Adobe Device Central mini-application. In this mini-application, you can see how your image will look on a variety of mobile devices. See Book I, Chapter 3 for details on Device Central.

✔ **Close Window:** When you have enough of Bridge, choose this command.

✔ **Delete (Move to Trash on the Mac):** If you want to eliminate a file, select it and choose this command. Kiss that file goodbye by emptying the trash. You can also click the trash can icon in the top-right portion of the Bridge window. Remember that when you trash things via the Bridge, you're actually deleting them from the desktop, as well.

✔ **Eject (Mac only):** Select your media and then this command to eject that media from your computer.

✔ **Return to (*program*):** Choose this command to leave the Bridge and return to your program of choice.

✔ **Reveal in Explorer (Finder on the Mac):** This command brings up your operating system's window and reveals the location of the selected file.

✔ **Reveal in Bridge:** This command visually escorts you to where your selected file resides.

✔ **Get Photos from Camera:** Select your desired device (camera or card reader) and import your images into your chosen folder and subfolder. Click Get Photos to start the download. Click Advanced Dialog if you want to apply metadata to the imported images.

✔ **Move to:** Select a file and move it to another location on your computer or network.

✔ **Copy to:** Select a file and copy it to another location on your computer or network.

✔ **Export to Hard Drive:** This command can be used in lieu of the Export panel, which is described earlier in this chapter.

✔ **Place:** Select a file, choose Place, and then choose one of the CS5 applications, such as InDesign, from the submenu. That program then imports your selected file.

✔ **Add to Favorites:** You can choose to add or remove a folder from your Favorites. If you're not familiar with Favorites, it's a special folder that lists your favorite files, folders, programs, and drives for quick and handy access. You can easily find the Favorites panel and the Folders panel in the top-left portion of the Bridge window. And, depending on your operating system, you'll come across numerous ways to access your Favorites.

✔ **File Info:** This feature lets you add some of your own metadata, such as title, author, copyrights, dates, credits, and so on. This information can come in handy for photographers and reporters. You can also edit (replace, append, save, and delete) some other data, such as IPTC data. But feel free to leave this data as it is.

Many commands, such as Open, Copy, Delete, and Label, are available via a context menu. Simply select an image or folder, and right-click (Control-click on the Mac) to access the menu.

Edit menu

On the Bridge's Edit menu, here are your options:

✔ **Preferences:** Mac users can access the Preferences window from the Adobe Bridge CS5 menu, rather than Edit. Briefly, **General** preferences control the way the Bridge looks and feels. For example, you can control how light or dark to make the Content window for your files. **Metadata** preferences control which type of data is displayed in the Metadata panel. Check out Bonus Chapter 3 to find out more about metadata. You can assign names and keyboard shortcuts to your colored **Labels.** Specify which application to use to open files of certain types. The **File Type Associations** are specific to the Bridge only **Thumbnails** settings have to do with items such as showing additional lines of data along with the thumbnail image. I suggest leaving those settings at their default unless you're certain you want to change them.

✔ **Undo/Cut/Copy/Paste/Duplicate:** I lumped these commands together because they're all self-explanatory. Undo undoes your last executed command. Select a file(s) and cut, copy, duplicate, or paste it from or into your folder.

✔ **Select All/Deselect All:** These two commands quickly select or deselect all the files in your selected folder.

✔ **Invert Selection:** Selects everything that's currently not selected and deselects everything that is.

✔ **Find:** This command enables you to find files in selected folders, including subfolders, based on a variety of criteria such as filename, dates, labels, or keywords. Click Find, and the files matching your criteria appear in the Bridge Content window.

✔ **Develop Settings:** If you have Camera Raw images, you can open them directly in the Bridge and apply the default Camera Raw settings or settings from a previous conversion. You can also copy, paste, and clear settings via this submenu.

✔ **Rotate:** The rotate commands rotate your images in varying degrees and directions. When you open the image, Photoshop applies the rotation. You can also click the rotate buttons.

✔ **Creative Suite Color Settings:** See whether the color settings of all your Creative Suite applications are synchronized. (The Creative Suite applications must be installed on your computer.) If they aren't, and you want them to be, select your desired setting from the list and click Apply.

✔ **Camera Raw Preferences:** Choose this command to establish your Camera Raw image, cache, and DNG (Digital Negative) File Handling settings. Mac users can find the Camera Raw Preferences window on the Adobe Bridge CS5 menu, rather than Edit. For more on Camera Raw, see Book II, Chapter 2. For more on Camera Raw Preferences, see Book I, Chapter 5.

View menu

Here's what the View menu has to offer:

✔ **Full Screen Preview:** Select this option to fill your screen with your selected image only. Press Esc to return to the Bridge application window.

✔ **Slideshow:** This neat option leaves the Bridge interface and displays just the images, full screen, from your selected folder.

✔ **Slideshow Options:** Choose settings for your slide show, including the duration of your slide display, type and duration of your transitions, and whether to display a caption, among others.

✔ **Review Mode:** This mode leaves the Bridge interface and displays your image(s) full screen. Click the forward- and back-arrow buttons to cycle through the images. Click the down-pointing arrow button to eliminate an image from the Review mode display. Click the magnifying glass icon to open a window in which you can enlarge portions of your image for a more detailed view. Click the Next icon to create a new collection from the images displayed in Review mode and then return to the Bridge interface. Click the X icon to just return to the Bridge interface.

✔ **Compact Mode:** Select this option to get a pared-down Bridge with just a Content window and Application bar — no panels.

✔ **As Thumbnails/Details/List:** Display your content in the default view of thumbnails. View it with Details, where you get a large thumbnail along with metadata, ratings, and labels, as shown in Figure 4-16. Or view it as a list, with smaller thumbnails, filenames, and some metadata.

✔ **Show Thumbnail Only:** This option shows just the thumbnail of the image without the accompanying data, such as filename, date, and so on.

✔ **Grid Lock:** This option provides a grid of horizontal and vertical lines around your thumbnails in the Content light table.

✔ **Show Reject Files:** Display files that you've labeled with the harsh moniker of Reject.

✔ **Show Hidden Files:** Select this option to see files that Photoshop doesn't recognize.

✔ **Show Folders:** This option enables you to view folder icon thumbnails, in addition to image thumbnails.

✔ **Show Items from Subfolders:** Select this option to have all the files within your subfolders displayed.

✔ **Show Linked Files:** Select this option to display content files linked to a specific file that uses links, or reference files, or OLE (Object Linking and Embedding).

✔ **Sort:** From this menu, select the criteria by which you want to sort your files. The default is by the name of your file, but a ton of other options, such as label, rating, or date, are up for grabs. After you select the criteria, Bridge displays your files accordingly.

Figure 4-16: View your content as Details.

✔ **Refresh:** If you've renamed a file, the order of your files isn't updated in the Bridge's window. Choose Refresh to get your files in order.

Stacks menu

You can select a group of images and create a stack, which makes the images easier to manage and cuts down on clutter in your Content window. The top image thumbnail in the stack is visible in the Content window, and the number of images in the stack is visible on the top-left corner of that thumbnail, as shown in Figure 4-17. It's not mandatory, but normally, you want to create stacks from similar images, such as multiple exposures of the same subject, multiple poses of a portrait, and so on. Here are the options found in the Stacks menu:

✔ **Group as Stack:** Select your desired photos and choose this command to create a stack.

✔ **Ungroup from Stack:** Select a photo and choose this command to remove it from the stack.

✔ **Open/Close Stack:** Select Open to display each image in the stack (surrounded by an outline). Choose Close to collapse the stack.

Closed stack   Open stack

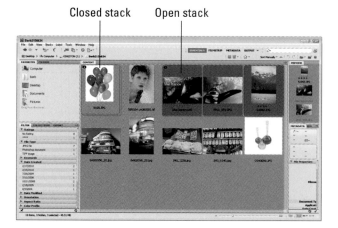

Figure 4-17: Create stacks from groups of images.

✔ **Promote to Top of Stack:** First, open the stack and select your desired image. Choose this command to have that image appear on top of the stack.

✔ **Expand/Collapse All Stacks:** Opens and displays, or closes, all images in all stacks.

✔ **Auto Stack Panorama/HDR:** This script looks at the metadata (EXIF) of your images, and if it finds two or more files that have a timestamp within 18 seconds of each other, it first inspects the images by using the Auto Align algorithm. If everything is good to go, it creates a group, or stack, of panorama shots. It also creates a stack for HDR (High Dynamic Range) shots if it also finds different exposure value (EV) settings in the metadata. You can then process these stacks in Photoshop by choosing Tools➪Process Collections in Photoshop.

Label menu

The Label menu offers commands for rating and labeling your files:

✔ **Rating:** Rank your files using the one- to five-star system. You can now also apply a Reject rating, for those images that aren't up to par. Use the View➪Sort menu or the Rating shortcut button to choose your desired ranking. Files with that ranking then appear in the Content window.

✔ **Labels:** Label your files for quick identification and organization. Again, use the View➪Sort menu, or the Sort shortcut or Rating shortcut buttons to choose and view the labeled files.

Note that you can also assign labels and ratings to folders.

Tools menu

Here are the offerings on the Tools menu:

- **Batch Rename:** Choose this command to rename multiple image files within a folder in one execution. You can rename the files and keep them in the same folder or move them to a new folder. Click the Browse button to select that folder. Then, designate how your files are named by selecting an option from the pop-up menu or typing your own name. Choose the starting number for renamed images and specify whether you want to enable the naming convention to be compatible with another platform.

- **Device Central:** This command launches Adobe's Device Central, a mini-application that lets you create graphics for mobile devices, such as cell phones. See Book I, Chapter 3 for more details.

- **Create Metadata Template and Edit Metadata Template:** Choose which metadata you want to include in the template. Name the template and save it. Choose Edit Metadata Template if you need to later modify the template.

- **Append Metadata and Replace Metadata:** Allow you to add or substitute existing metadata based on a template. To create a template, choose Tools⇨Create Metadata Template.

- **Cache:** *Cache* is memory that stores frequently used data, such as thumbnails and file info, to allow for quicker loading when you display a previously viewed image or folder. Building a cache for a subfolder enables you to store the information for a selected folder. If you purge the cache, you delete ranking and thumbnail information, thereby creating more disk space. Exporting a cache lets you export to the folder selected in the Folders panel. Cache allows you to burn a CD without generating thumbnails. Purging the cache can also fix problems with thumbnails and previews that aren't displaying properly.

- **Photoshop:** Some of the features are the same as those on the Photoshop File⇨Automate submenu. See Book IX, Chapter 2 for more on Photomerge and Merge to HDR Pro. For more info on batch processing, see Book II, Chapter 5. For details on the Lens Correction feature, see Book VII, Chapter 2. The Load Files into Photoshop Layers command takes your selected images in Bridge and creates a new layered file in Photoshop, using those selected images. The Process Collections in Photoshop command searches for stacked Panorama and HDR images (see the "Stacks menu" section, earlier in this chapter), and imports them into Photoshop for processing into composite images.

Window menu

If you've configured the Bridge just to your liking and want to save it as a workspace for future retrieval, choose Workspace⇨New Workspace. You can also select from preset workspaces that are configured for specific tasks, such as optimum viewing of thumbnails or pinpointing metadata. Finally, under the Workspace submenu, you find commands to reset and delete your various Bridge workspaces. See details on workspaces in the section "Managing Images with Adobe Bridge," earlier in this chapter.

You can also choose to display or hide your various panels in the Window menu. Finally, you can open a new synchronized Bridge window, enabling you to perform your Bridge activities within two windows.

You should be aware that Photoshop has bestowed the Content window with light table powers. You can drag images around to reorder, group, or rank them. What the heck? You can just drag them around to give them a little exercise, if you want. Sitting in the Bridge window all day can make a file a little stiff.

Using keywords

Keywords are descriptive labels that you attach to files. They help to categorize your images, enabling you to more efficiently and quickly locate your desired files. Here's the lowdown on creating and using keywords:

- ✔ **To create a new keyword (a categorical folder which contains keywords):** Click the plus sign (+) icon at the bottom of the Keywords panel, as shown in Figure 4-18, or select New Keyword from the Keywords panel pop-up menu. Specify your keyword and press Enter (Return on the Mac).

- ✔ **To create a new sub keyword:** Select your desired keyword, click the arrow-and-plus-sign (+) icon at the bottom of the Keywords panel, or select New Sub Keyword from the Keywords panel pop-up menu. Type the keyword you want to add and press Enter (Return on the Mac).

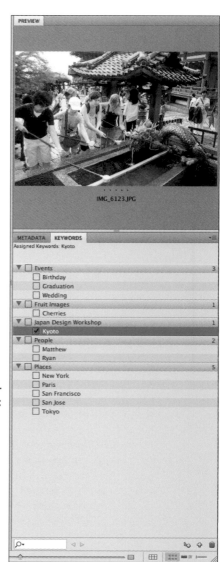

Figure 4-18: Create keywords to organize, and later sort, your images.

✔ **To rename an existing keyword or sub keyword:** Select the keyword and then select Rename from the Keywords panel pop-up menu. Provide a new name and press Enter (Return on the Mac).

Renaming a keyword in the panel doesn't also rename it if you've applied it to a file.

✔ **To delete a keyword or sub keyword from the panel:** Select the keyword; then click the Trash icon or select Delete from the Keywords panel pop-up menu. Again, deleting the keyword doesn't delete it from any files that you've previously applied it to.

✔ **To apply a keyword or sub keyword:** Select the file or files, and then check the box to the left of the keyword in the panel.

✔ **To remove a keyword or sub keyword from a file:** Select the file(s) and deselect the check box to the left of the keyword in the panel.

✔ **To search for images labeled with certain keywords:** Select Find from the Keywords panel pop-up menu. Choose your desired folder or disk from the Look In menu or choose Browse to navigate to your desired location. Select your criteria from the pop-up menus and select your matching specifications — any or all. To add additional criteria fields, click the plus sign (+). Specify whether to include all subfolders and non-indexed files. When you finish, click the Find button. All images containing your entered keyword appear in the Content window of the Bridge. Select your desired images and then click the New Collection button in the Collections panel to store and arrange your images in a digital photo album, referred to as a *collection.*

✔ **To search for keywords:** Use the Quick Find field (the magnifying glass icon) by entering a keyword and selecting Contains, Equals, or Starts With from the pop-up menu.

Creating PDF Presentations

In Bridge, you can use the ultra-efficient PDF generation feature to create a single, multipage document from multiple images. This feature is great for several reasons. First, your recipient doesn't need to have any specific hardware, software, utilities, or fonts to open and view the presentation. Your recipient needs only the Acrobat Reader program, a free download from www.adobe.com. In addition, sending a single file that contains multiple images is a great way to share your photos with family and friends. You avoid the hassle of having to e-mail your images as separate attachments. Finally, the PDF format offers excellent compression, thereby squeezing your file size down significantly without sacrificing image quality. Just be sure to check your final file size so that you don't choke your recipients' e-mail inboxes!

Follow these steps to create a PDF presentation:

1. **Select your desired images and choose Window⇨Workspace⇨Output.**

   You can also select Output from the Workspace shortcut menu in the top-right portion of the Application window. Finally, you can also click the Output to Web or PDF button in the Application bar.

   The Output panel appears, as shown in Figure 4-19.

Click PDF

Figure 4-19: Create a PDF presentation by using Bridge's Output panel.

2. **Click the PDF icon, as shown in Figure 4-19.**

3. **Select a Template from the pop-up menu.**

   Presets, such as 2-UP Greeting Card and 4*5 Contact Sheet, are available. The Maximize Size preset places one image per page at the maximum size. I chose the Fine Art Mat template, which surrounds each image with significant white space, similar to a framing mat.

4. **In the Document area, select a page preset and size.**

   Note that you can enter a custom size in the Width and Height fields. Select either Portrait or Landscape orientation. Select your desired background color. Specify whether you want High or Low Quality. Select High if you want to be able to print the PDF with optimum results. Select Low if your PDF is meant to be viewed only onscreen. Finally, if you want to secure your PDF via a password or disable printing, select those options. Both options can be good when sending a PDF for approval purposes only.

5. **In the Layout section, specify how you want your images to be arranged on the page.**

   Because I want one image per page, I'm leaving it as 1 Column and 1 Row. Specify your margin measurements and other options for spacing and rotation.

6. **In the Overlays section, if you want the filename and/or file extension below each image, select your desired font size and color.**

   In addition, you have the option of adding a header or footer to each of the pages in your PDF.

7. **If you want your file to be viewed as a slide show, specify your viewing options in the Playback area:**

   - *Open in Full Screen Mode:* Opens the PDF in Full Screen mode, where the page fills the screen.

   - *Automatic advance to the next page:* Specify how long each image appears onscreen in the Duration field.

   - *Loop After Last Page:* Enables the presentation to continually run. If not selected, the presentation stops after the last image.

   - *Transition:* From the pop-up menu, select how you want one image to transition to the next. For certain transitions, you can also specify the Direction and Speed of the transition.

8. **Finally, if you want watermarked text (which will be overlaid on the images), such as a copyright notice, enter the text and specify the font attributes and colors.**

   You can also specify the Opacity (transparency) percentage.

9. **Select View PDF After Save to have your PDF file open in Acrobat or Acrobat Reader.**

   Preview may open for Mac users, depending on your settings.

10. **Click Save. Name your file and click Save again.**

    Bridge then creates your PDF, as shown in Figure 4-20.

Figure 4-20: A PDF created by Bridge.

Creating a Web Gallery

If you're proud of your Photoshop artistry and you want to show it off to the world on a Web page, doing it in Bridge is the way to go. It's a breeze to use, so even if you don't know anything about HTML — except that it's an acronym you hear a lot — you can create a Web-based display page for your images with very little trouble.

All you need to do is select the images you want to include on your Web page, select a style, enter a little information, and sit back and watch while Bridge does the rest. Of course, tell all your friends and colleagues where to find it.

If you want to know more about creating Web pages and posting them for anyone and everyone who has Internet access to see, check out *Web Sites Do-It-Yourself For Dummies,* by Janine Warner (Wiley).

A Web gallery is a Web page that includes small thumbnails and links that enable visitors to view those images in a larger size. But using thumbnails isn't your only option. The gallery can also showcase one image at a time in large form and change the view at intervals, just like a slide show.

The advantage of displaying your images in a Web gallery (compared to simply constructing one humongous page that shows all the images at their full file sizes) is that viewers who have slow Internet connections don't have to wait for all the images to download. Even visitors who have fast Internet connections will appreciate not being inundated with a flood of images.

To create your Web gallery, follow these steps:

1. **Select your desired images and choose Window⇨Workspace⇨ Output.**

   You can also select Output from the Workspace shortcut menu in the top-right portion of the Application window. Finally, you can also click the Output to Web or PDF in the Application bar. The Output panel appears.

2. **Click the Web Gallery icon.**

3. **Select a template from the pop-up menu.**

   Presets, such as Filmstrip and Slideshow, are available. I chose the Lightroom Flash Gallery template, as shown in Figure 4-21. Photoshop will automatically select the Style, based on your chosen template.

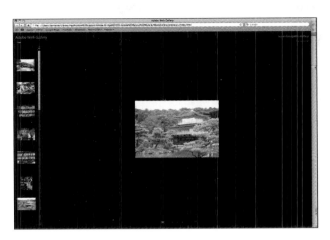

Figure 4-21: A finished Web Gallery in Adobe Bridge.

4. **(Optional) To get an idea of what the template will look like, click the Refresh Preview button.**

   You can also click Preview in Browser to see how your Web gallery looks in your default Web browser.

5. **In the Site Info area, specify your desired site, gallery titles, and description. Also, enter your contact info and e-mail or Web address, if desired. If you want everyone to know that your Web gallery is copyrighted, tell them so.**

   Be aware that putting an e-mail link on a Web page invites spam. So, be sure to have your e-mail client's spam filter on full bore if you plan to include your e-mail address.

6. **Specify the colors you want for your text, headers, menu, background, border, and controls in the Color Palette section.**

   I left mine at the default colors.

7. **In the Appearance area, specify whether you want your Web page to be laid out as scrolling, left-aligned, paginated, or a slide show.**

   I chose paginated so that visitors can navigate through the site by page.

8. **Select the size of your preview and thumbnails.**

9. **In the Create Gallery section, click either Save to Disk or Upload.**

   If you select Save to Disk, click Browse to navigate to the location where you want to save your Web gallery files. Then, click Save.

If you select Upload, enter the FTP server address, your username, your password, and the folder name. Then, click a second Upload button. If you're unsure about this information, check with your ISP (Internet service provider).

Introducing Mini Bridge

Mini Bridge is a new extension in Photoshop CS5 that enables you to easily and quickly browse for files without leaving the application, like you must with full-blown Bridge. Once you open Mini Bridge, it remains on your screen as a panel until you choose to close it. The Mini Bridge panel is divided into what is referred to as *pods,* or mini panels.

To open Mini Bridge, do one of the following:

- Choose File➪Browse in Mini Bridge.
- Click the Mini Button icon in the Application bar.
- Choose Window➪Extensions➪Mini Bridge.

Click the Settings button to specify these Mini Bridge preferences:

- **Bridge Launching:** Choose how Mini Bridge launches and how it communicates with the big cheese Bridge.
- **Appearance:** Adjust the brightness of the user interface (UI) by lightening the panel background. You can also adjust the lightness of the Content and Preview pod backgrounds. Select Color Manage Panel to apply your monitor's ICC profile to thumbnails and image previews. See Book II, Chapter 3 for more on ICC profiles.
- **Manage Modules:** Select which applications you want enabled when you launch Mini Bridge. You can check for updates by clicking the gear icon.

Here are few things you can do with Mini Bridge, shown in Figure 4-22:

- Browse for files by clicking the Browse Files button on the Home page.
- Open or place a file using Mini Bridge by selecting it in the Content pod and dragging it into Photoshop. You can also double-click to open it in its associated application.
- Click the Tools button above the Content pod to access Photoshop-automated commands such as Batch processing and Photomerge.

✓ Click the Panel view button to bring up the various pods, such as Navigation, Preview, and Path.

✓ Search for files using the Search button (magnifying glass icon).

✓ Adjust the view of your panel and how it displays thumbnails and content using the controls at the bottom.

✓ Sort your files in the Content pod by using the Sort, Filter, and Select buttons above the pod.

✓ Click the Preview button in the bottom-right corner and preview files by opening a panel-sized preview, full-screen preview, or slide show preview, or you can compare images in Review mode.

✓ Add an item to Favorites or a Collection by dragging it from the Content pod to the list in the Navigation pod.

✓ Go to Bridge by clicking the Br icon in the top-right corner.

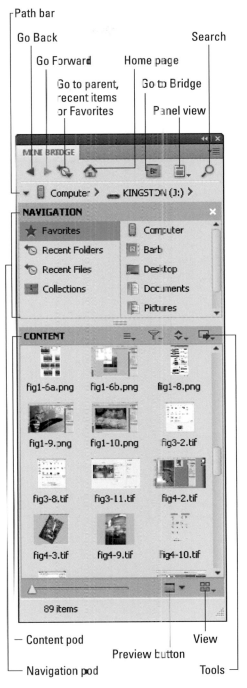

Figure 4-22: Browse the Mini Bridge and keep it docked as a panel

Chapter 5: Customizing Your Workspace and Preferences

*N*ow, more than ever, Photoshop lets you have it your way without having to make a trip down to the local burger shack. You can easily customize the look of your workspace, specifying everything from the location of panels to the arrangement of dialog boxes when you begin a session. You can even store these physical layouts and recall them anytime you like. And, in addition to customizing your keyboard shortcuts, you can also customize your menus to highlight certain workflow commands.

Photoshop also makes it easy to choose how certain tools and features operate. You can choose how the cursors for tools such as brushes look, tell Photoshop your preferred way of storing files, and specify just how much memory you want to set aside for image editing. You can set all these preferences once and then forget them, or you can change them from time to time when your needs change. This chapter shows you how to customize your workspace and preferences so that Photoshop works your way.

Creating Workspace Presets

Photoshop is a complicated program; the more you learn, the more complicated (and routine) your activities become. For one project, you may find yourself using the Styles panel repeatedly to add special effects to layers. For your next project, you may never use the Styles panel but require frequent access to the Paths panel to create curves that you use to make selections. And so it goes.

Use custom workspaces to save time and effort, or to instantly clean up a messy desktop.

Custom workspaces come in handy if you share a computer with students, family members, or coworkers. Those who prepare images for various mediums and purposes have different needs that may call for special workspaces, too.

You can start with one of the many preset workspaces. Select a workspace from the Workspace Switcher in the Application bar, or by choosing Window⇨Workspace. Photoshop CS5 offers preset workspaces for various workflows, such as design, motion, and photography. These presets can modify menu and/or keyboard shortcuts. They can also modify which panels are visible. You can select a preset, then establish your panel preferences, and save the modified workspace as your own custom workspace. Read on to find out how.

You can tailor your workspace in these ways:

- **Combine panels to group together the ones you use most often.** Drag a panel's tab into another panel group to add it to that group. If the Layers, Channels, and History panels are the ones you use most often, you might want to group them together. You can collapse panels that you rarely use down to space-saving icons, minimize them to just their title bars, or close them altogether.

  Before saving your workspace preset, show or minimize, collapse, or close the panels (however you prefer them) and move them to the locations you want on your screen.

- **Position dialog boxes.** Although they don't save with the workspace, per se, Photoshop's Menu bar dialog boxes pop up in the same location they appeared the last time you used them. You may want to drag them to a specific place on your screen so that they appear there every time. When I'm working with a large image, I sometimes position dialog boxes on the screen of my second monitor to maximize the area for the image on my main display.

- **Customize the Options bar.** You can grab the gripper bar at the left edge of the Options bar and drag it to another location. For example, you can dock the bar on the right, along with your other panels, or have it float in a specific place on your Photoshop desktop. Photoshop stores these settings with your workspace preset.

- **Set Photoshop's font size.** You can change the size of the font for text that's displayed on the Options bar and panels. Choose Edit⇨Preferences⇨Interface (Photoshop⇨Preferences⇨Interface on the Mac). Select Small, Medium, or Large from the UI Font Size pop-up menu in the Interface dialog box. The change takes place the next time you start Photoshop.

Other settings concerning the appearance of screen modes, menu colors, and the actions of panels are located in the Preferences settings, described in the section "Setting Your Preferences," later in this chapter.

Creating and Deleting Workspace Presets

After you set up your custom workspace, you can save it by choosing Window⇨Workspace⇨New Workspace. In the New Workspace dialog box that appears, type a name for your saved workspace.

Panel locations are saved by default. You have the additional options of selecting which components — keyboard shortcuts and menus — you want to capture in your custom workspace, as shown in Figure 5-1. After you adjust your desired settings, click the Save button.

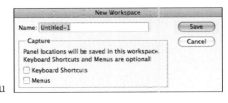

Figure 5-1: Select which components to save in your custom workspace.

Your saved workspace now appears as an item on the Workspace submenu.

Want to return to the way Adobe sees the world of Photoshop? Choose Window⇨Workspace⇨Essentials (Default).

To delete a saved workspace, choose Window⇨Workspace⇨Delete Workspace. In the Delete Workspace dialog box that appears, select the name of the workspace you want to remove from the drop-down list. Click the Delete button, and your preset is gone, gone, gone.

You can create a workspace, as well as delete it or select a preset, by using the handy Workspace Switcher on the right side of the Application bar. The Workspace Switcher highlights the name of the current workspace. Simply click the other workspaces displayed in the bar or click the down-pointing arrow and make your selection from the submenu.

Customizing Keyboard Shortcuts

For those of you who are like me — I avoid using a mouse, and prefer the ease and speed of keyboard shortcuts — Photoshop offers customizable keyboard shortcuts. You can assign shortcuts to menu commands, panel commands, and tools. You can edit, delete, or add to the Photoshop default set or create your own custom set. Follow these steps to customize keyboard shortcuts:

1. **Choose Edit⇨Keyboard Shortcuts. In the Keyboard Shortcuts and Menus dialog box that appears (see Figure 5-2), make sure the Keyboard Shortcuts tab is selected.**

    You can also choose Window⇨Workspace⇨Keyboard Shortcuts & Menus.

Figure 5-2: Customize keyboard shortcuts for enhanced productivity.

2. **Select your desired set of keyboard shortcuts from the pop-up menu.**

   You can also create a new set by clicking the New Set button (the disk with a down-pointing arrow icon).

   Clicking New Set makes a copy of the selected set for you to then edit and customize. If you create a new set, name the set (leaving it with a .kys extension) and keep it stored in the Keyboard Shortcuts folder.

3. **Select Application Menus, Panel Menus, or Tools from the Shortcuts For drop-down list.**

   Click the triangle next to the menu heading to expand the particular menu headings.

4. **Select your desired command from the list. Type the shortcut keys you want to assign to that command in the shortcut field.**

   If a shortcut has already been assigned to that command, you can simply type over it.

   If the keyboard shortcut you type is already being used, Photoshop warns you that if you accept the shortcut, it'll be removed from the original command.

5. **Click Accept to assign the shortcut to the command or tool.**

   If you later change your mind and want to use the original keyboard shortcut (if there was one), click Use Default. If you decide you don't want the shortcut at all, click Delete Shortcut. And if you make a mistake, just click Undo.

Application and Panel menu commands must include a Ctrl (⌘ on the Mac) and/or a Function (F) key in the keyboard shortcut.

6. **When you finish, click the Save Set button (the disk icon).**

   If you want to delete the set, click the Delete Set button (the trash icon).

7. **Click the Summarize button to save the keyboard shortcut set as an .htm file, which loads in your Internet browser.**

   You can then print the file and keep it as a handy reference of your shortcuts.

8. **Click OK to exit the dialog box.**

Customizing Menus

Adobe takes the customization club to yet another level by adding the ability to customize menus, as shown in Figure 5-3. You have the choice of colorizing chosen menu items or hiding the menu items altogether.

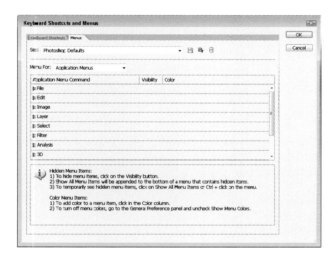

Figure 5-3: Customize menu items to show only those you use.

Follow these steps to make the Photoshop menus your own:

1 **Choose Edit➪Menus.**

   You can also choose Window➪Workspace➪Keyboard Shortcuts & Menus.

   The Keyboard Shortcuts and Menus dialog box appears. (Refer to Figure 5-3.)

2. **Click the Menus tab, and in the Set drop-down list at the top, select the Photoshop Defaults set or another preset.**

   Or to create a new menu, click the New Set button (the disk with a down-pointing arrow icon).

   Clicking New Set makes a copy of the selected set for you to then edit and customize. If you select a new set, name the set (leaving it with a .mnu extension), and keep it stored in the Menu Customization folder.

3. **Select Application Menus or Panel Menus from the Menu For drop-down list. Click the triangle to expand the individual menu headings.**

4. **Select one of the following options for your desired command:**

   • *Visibility:* To hide or show a menu item, click the Visibility button.

     Be careful not to hide the really critical commands, such as Open or Save.

   • *Color:* To add color to a menu item, click the Color swatch (or the word None) and select a color from the drop-down list.

5. **When you finish making changes, click the Save All Changes to the Current Set of Menus button (the disk icon).**

   To delete a menu set, click the Delete Set button (trash can icon).

   Or, to create a new set based on the current menu, click the Create a New Set Based on the Current Set of Menus button.

6. **In the Save dialog box, enter a name for the set and click Save.**

7. **Click OK to exit the dialog box.**

If you've hidden some menu items and decide you want to temporarily show them while working in Photoshop, choose Show All Menu Items from the menu that has the hidden items.

To turn off menu colors (they're on by default), choose Edit⇨Preferences⇨Interface (Photoshop⇨Preferences⇨Interface on the Mac) and deselect Show Menu Colors.

Setting Your Preferences

Photoshop stores settings for many different options in various Preferences files on your hard drive. The first time you run Photoshop after a new installation, you probably want to customize preferences to suit your own needs.

You can access the Preferences dialog box by choosing Edit⇨Preferences (Photoshop⇨Preferences on the Mac). The first category of settings that appears in the submenu are the General Preferences (shown in Figure 5-4). You can choose any of the other Preferences categories from the submenu.

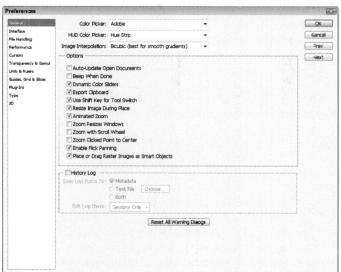

Figure 5-4: The General Preferences pane specifies a lot of the "look and feel" of your Photoshop interface.

After you're in any Preferences dialog box, you can move between the pane by clicking the Prev or Next buttons that appear in each of the Preferences panes. If you like keyboard shortcuts, you can switch to the other Preferences pane by pressing Ctrl+1, Ctrl+2 (⌘+1, ⌘+2 on the Mac), and so forth. The following sections give you a rundown of what you can do with the settings in the different Preferences panes.

Setting general preferences

The General Preferences pane is where you select some options that are, well, general in nature. You can select some choices from drop-down lists, and others are check boxes you can select or deselect to activate or disable that option. Here's a rundown of options in the upper part of the pane:

- **Color Picker:** Use the familiar Adobe Color Picker to select precise colors or work with the Windows or Macintosh system color pickers, as desired. You might want to use the Windows or Apple color picker, for example, if you've previously defined some custom colors outside Photoshop and now want to make them available for a Photoshop project.

- **HUD Color Picker:** The HUD (heads-up display) Color Picker lets you quickly select colors within the image window without having to access the Color Picker. Choose whether you want a strip or wheel of color. For more on using the HUD Color Picker, see Book II, Chapter 3.

- ✔ **Image Interpolation:** When Photoshop resizes an image, it must either create new pixels (when making the image larger) or combine existing pixels (to make the image smaller). To do this, the program examines neighboring pixels and uses the information to derive the new or replacement pixels. You can select the type of mathematical algorithm Photoshop uses to do this, though you likely want to stick with the default option, Bicubic (Best for Smooth Gradients). You can find out more about interpolation and the other algorithms in Book II, Chapter 1.

In the Options section of the General Preferences dialog box, you find nearly a dozen check boxes that you can select or deselect, as described in the following list:

- ✔ **Auto-Update Open Documents:** When you're working on an image and move to another application to work on the same image, you'll probably want the changes made in the other application to reflect in the document still open in Photoshop. Select this check box so that Photoshop monitors the document and updates its version whenever the document is changed in the other application.

- ✔ **Beep When Done:** I remember the bad old days when computers were slow and Photoshop would take a minute or two to apply the Gaussian Blur filter or perform calculations when merging even moderate-sized image layers. The Beep When Done signal was my cue to stop watching television and resume working with Photoshop. Although most operations are a lot faster today, if you're working with very large images or simply like to be notified when a step is finished, the beep option can be useful (or incredibly annoying to your coworkers).

- ✔ **Dynamic Color Sliders:** The sliders in the Color panel change colors to match the settings you make. If your computer is on the slow side, you can turn off this feature to improve performance.

- ✔ **Export Clipboard:** When this feature is active, Photoshop transfers its private clipboard (used only within Photoshop) to the general Windows or Macintosh Clipboard so that you can paste information into other applications. If you activate this option, switching from Photoshop to other applications takes a little longer, and Photoshop's clipboard contents replace whatever was in your system Clipboard when you switched.

The clipboard is generally a poor vehicle for moving image data between applications because the transferred information may not be of the best quality. Instead, save your file and open it in the other application. If you do this, you can turn off the Export Clipboard option, saving you some time when switching between applications. Additionally, many applications support the dragging and dropping of files between programs.

✔ **Use Shift Key for Tool Switch:** When this feature is active, you can change from one tool in the Tools panel to another in the same flyout menu (say, to change from the Gradient tool to the Paint Bucket tool) by pressing the Shift key and the keyboard shortcut for that tool

✔ **Resize Image During Paste/Place:** By default, when you place or paste files that are larger than the document they're being pasted or placed into, the files are resized to fit. Deselect this option to have the file import with its exact dimensions, as shown in Figure 5-5.

✔ **Animated Zoom:** This option enables you to zoom in smoothly, rather than in increments, when holding down the mouse button or pressing Ctrl+plus/equal sign (+/=) (⌘+plus/equal sign [+/=] on the Mac).

✔ **Zoom Resizes Windows:** Select this check box if you want your document windows to grow and shrink to fit your document while you zoom in and out. Deselect this check box if you want the document's window to always remain the same size; you might want to deselect the check box if you frequently work with several documents side by side and don't want them to change relative size while you zoom in and out.

Not resized

Resized

Photo Disc

Figure 5-5: Select the Resize Image During Paste/Place check box to have your image automatically resized upon import.

✔ **Zoom with Scroll Wheel:** This handy option enables your mouse scroll wheel to become a zooming tool, regardless of which tool you're using.

✔ **Zoom Clicked Point to Center:** If selected, when you click the Zoom tool at a specific location, that location then becomes the center of your image window.

✔ **Enable Flick Panning:** If selected, when you quickly drag and release with the Hand tool, the image continues to move, slowly decelerating to a stop.

✔ **Place or Drag Raster Images as Smart Objects:** Select this option to create Smart Object layers when using the File➪Place command or when dragging and dropping raster images from other applications from the browser or from your desktop.

In the History Log section, you can have Photoshop record all your editing commands. The History Log feature is handy if you want to present a finished, fully edited image to a client or manager, but need to be able to show the steps of how you got there. Or maybe you want a record of the steps so that you can repeat them on other images and don't want to rely on your memory.

You have a few formats in which you can save your history log:

✔ **Metadata:** Saving the log to *metadata* (information embedded in your image file) allows you to view the log in the Bridge window and in the History tab of the File➪File Info dialog box. For more on Bridge, see Book I, Chapter 4.

✔ **Text File:** You can save the log to a text file. Click the Choose button to provide a name and location for the file.

✔ **Both:** This option saves the log as both metadata and a text file.

✔ **Edit Log Items:** You select Sessions Only, Concise, or Detailed. The Sessions Only option records your editing until you close the file or quit Photoshop. The Concise option keeps a comprehensive log (multiple sessions), but in short and sweet steps. The Detailed option provides a comprehensive, detailed log. For example, a concise log entry may be just Crop, whereas a detailed log entry may be Crop to rectangle, also providing the original and cropped dimensions, the angle, and the resolution values.

The last option in the General Preferences dialog box is the Reset All Warning Dialogs button. If you've turned off the display of certain warnings by selecting the Don't Show Me This Dialog Box Again check box, you can reactivate all the warnings by clicking this button.

Customizing the interface

The Interface preferences, shown in Figure 5-6, deal with the "look" of Photoshop. Here's the scoop:

- ✔ **Screen Modes:** When using the Application Frame, you can select the color of the background around your image. You can also select whether your image edge is surrounded by a line, drop shadow, or nothing at all.

- ✔ **Show Channels in Color:** When selected, this option tells Photoshop to show each of the color channels (for example, Red, Green, and Blue; or Cyan, Magenta, Yellow, and Black) in their respective colors in the Channels panel. In most cases, you don't want to use this feature. You need to be able to see the channels in their grayscale form to perform image-editing tasks such as converting from color to grayscale or channel masking, or for selective sharpening on certain channels. Book VI, Chapter 1 introduces channels.

- ✔ **Show Menu Colors:** Check this option to have the ability to view customized menus in color.

- ✔ **Show Tool Tips:** Photoshop can display little pop-up reminders about tools and other objects on your screen. If you find these reminders distracting, deselect this check box to turn off tool tips.

- ✔ **Enable Gestures (Mac only):** Enables you to use your Macintosh trackpad for controls such as rotation of the document canvas. If you are annoyed by the inadvertent rotation of your canvas, deselect this option.

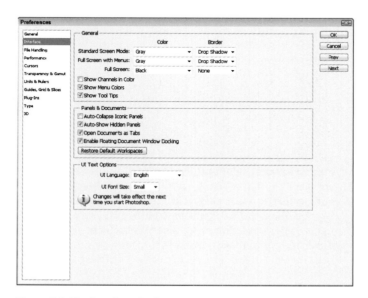

Figure 5-6: The Interface Preferences category specifies the "look" of Photoshop.

✔ **Auto-Collapse Iconic Panels:** If selected, panels automatically collapse down to just their icons when you click somewhere else within the Photoshop application.

✔ **Auto-Show Hidden Panels:** If selected, this option automatically shows any hidden panels.

✔ **Open Documents as Tabs:** Selecting this new option opens documents tabbed to the Application Frame. If you deselect this option, images "float," like in previous versions of Photoshop.

✔ **Enable Floating Document Window Docking:** Lets you dock floating document windows as tabs when dragging one document window to another document window. Holding down Ctrl (Control on the Mac) while dragging a floating window also temporarily turns on the preference while you're working in Photoshop.

✔ **Restore Default Workspaces:** Click this button to reset all of your workspaces back to their default settings.

✔ **UI Text Options:** Specify the size of the text displayed in dialog boxes, panels, and so on. Select from Small, Medium, or Large.

Deciding how you want files handled

The options in the File Handling Preferences pane, shown in Figure 5-7, control how Photoshop handles files when they're opened and closed. Here's the lowdown on these options:

✔ **Image Previews:** Storing a preview thumbnail with an image can speed up browsing for the image you want. You can tell Photoshop to save a preview by default or to ask you first (in case you want to create images that are a little smaller in size, especially for the Web). Or you can also choose not to ever save a preview. Mac users need to select the kinds of image previews they need. Select the Icon option to enable an image icon to appear on the desktop. Select the Macintosh Thumbnail option to see a preview in the Open dialog box. Select the Windows Thumbnail option to see a preview in a Windows OS dialog box. Finally, select the Full Size option to save a low-resolution version of the file to use in applications that can open only low-resolution (72 ppi) Photoshop images.

✔ **File Extension (Append File Extension on the Mac):** You can select whether the file extensions appended to filenames (such as `.psd`, `.tif`, and so forth) are consistently uppercase or lowercase, as you prefer. On the Mac, you can choose whether to add extensions by selecting from the Always, Never, or Ask When Saving options. If you want cross-platform compatibility with PCs or you're creating Web graphics, select the Always option. Mac users, select the Use Lower Case option to save extensions as lowercase characters.

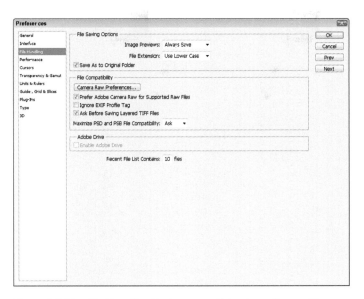

Figure 5-7: The File Handling Preferences dialog box offers settings for opening and saving files.

✔ **Save As to Original Folder:** When you choose File⇨Save As, your file will save to the folder you last saved that image.

✔ **Camera Raw Preferences:** Here are the details on these preferences, as shown in Figure 5-8:

- When a Camera Raw (CR) file is processed, the image settings can be saved in two different places — a sidecar .xmp file or a Camera Raw database file. Create a separate sidecar .xmp file if you want to archive your images or exchange them with other people because it's a collaborative workflow. If you archive the files to a CD or DVD, copy them to a hard drive before opening them because CR can't write an XMP file to read-only media. If you store your setting to a CR database file, the settings are saved in the folder Document and Settings/[*username*]/Application Data/Adobe/CameraRaw (Users/[*user name*]/Library/Preferences on the Mac).

- When you reopen a CR image, the image settings you used when the file was last opened are reapplied. Select which Default Image Settings you want applied. The only settings that aren't stored are color profile, bit depth, pixel dimensions, and resolution.

- The cache in Camera Raw stores data for file thumbnails, metadata, and file info. You can choose to increase the cache, if desired. Note that 1GB holds data for around 200 images. If your cache gets bloated or corrupted, clicking the Purge Cache button deletes the data.

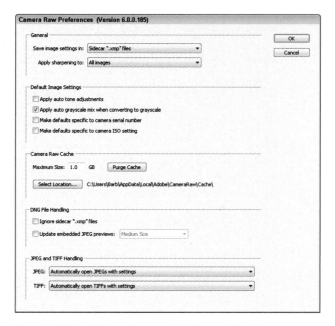

Figure 5-8: Establish preferences for Camera Raw images.

- DNG stands for Digital Negative, a popular format for storing CR images. DNG image settings are usually embedded in the file itself. If you want to stick with the norm, select the Ignore Sidecar ".xmp" Files option. If you want a JPEG preview of your image, select the option and choose from a Medium or Full Size preview.

- Another important setting is the JPEG and TIFF Handling option. Camera Raw (CR) enables you to open and edit both JPEGs and TIFFs. If you select Automatically Open All Supported JPEGs (or TIFFs), any JPEG or TIFF automatically opens in CR, rather than Photoshop. If you select Automatically Open JPEGs (or TIFFs) with Settings, CR opens any JPEG or TIFF with Camera Raw (crs) tags. So, any files that you have previously opened and edited, and then closed by clicking Done in CR, will open in CR. Because working with Camera Raw images can be a little complex, Adobe offers a lot of documentation and videos on working with these types of images. Check out www.adobe.com.

✔ **Prefer Adobe Camera Raw for Supported Raw Files:** Select this setting to have ACR open any and all Raw file formats supported by Photoshop.

✔ **Ignore EXIF Profile Tag:** When this option is selected, Photoshop ignores the sRGB tag that many digital cameras add to their EXIF (camera) data. The sRGB tag is widely used by digital cameras, but it's not well respected among many high-end digital photography professionals.

✔ **Ask Before Saving Layered TIFF Files:** Photoshop can save an advanced type of TIFF file that includes layers, exactly like with its own native PSD files. However, many applications can't read these files. If you always open TIFF files in Photoshop, or you're using recent versions of other Creative Suite applications that can accept layered TIFFs and you don't mind creating larger TIFF files in the process, you can disable this option. Otherwise, Photoshop asks you for confirmation each time you want to save a TIFF file that contains layers.

✔ **Maximize PSD File and PSB File Compatibility:** Photoshop lets you choose an option for file compatibility.

Not all applications can handle the more sophisticated features that may be stored in a PSD file (such as fancy layer effects). If you frequently open PSD files in applications other than later versions of Photoshop, you may want to set this option to Always. Keep in mind that you may lose some features when you choose this option. Select Ask to have Photoshop prompt you when you save a file about whether you want to apply the option. Or select Never to ignore the option completely.

When you maximize compatibility, Photoshop saves a *composite* (flattened) version along with the layered file to ensure that older applications (such as Photoshop version 2) can read the files. However, this option can make your file size balloon significantly.

The PSB (large file) format is like the PSD format in that it supports most Photoshop features. Currently, only Photoshop CS (along with Photoshop Elements 7 and 8) and higher can open PSB files. Again, keeping this option selected ensures maximum compatibility with any future programs that may accept this format.

If you plan to use your PSD files in InDesign or Illustrator, you should have the Maximize Compatibility feature selected because the performance of these programs is faster when you have a composite along with the layers, especially with large files that have a lot of layers.

✔ **Adobe Drive:** Select this option if your computer is located on a network and you need to share your files with others in your collaborative workgroup by using a server.

✔ **Recent File List Contains:** Type a value from 0 to 30 to specify the number of recently used files you want displayed in the Open Recent list on the File menu.

Handling performance options

Everything you need to specify Photoshop's performance can be found in the Preferences pane. Here are the options, as shown in Figure 5-9:

✔ **Memory Usage:** The perennial question: How much memory does Photoshop require? The perennial answer: As much as you can cram into your computer! Memory is so inexpensive right now that you have no excuse for not having at least a gigabyte of RAM, and more is even better if you're using an operating system that can handle extra memory efficiently, such as Windows Vista or 7, or Mac OS X. Version CS5 runs at its best with at least 2 gigabytes of RAM, even better with 4 gigabytes.

When you cram your RAM, you want to make sure Photoshop can use as much as you can spare. You can use the Memory Usage slider, shown in Figure 5-9, to allocate your memory. Use a value of 50 to 80 percent, depending on how much memory you have to spare. Allocating more to Photoshop reduces the RAM for other applications, so if you have other programs that need a lot of memory, select a prudent value.

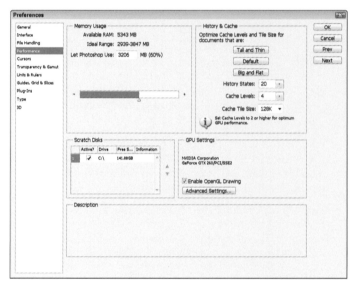

Figure 5-9: Adjust the Memory Usage setting to allocate the maximum amount of RAM Photoshop gobbles up.

✔ **History States:** Photoshop remembers how your document looks at various stages of editing, storing all the image information on your hard drive and listing the individual states in the History panel. (For more information on using the History panel, see Book II, Chapter 4.) Keeping track of every change you make requires a lot of memory and hard drive space, so you can specify how many resources to use by typing a value into this box. The default is 20. (The max is 1000.) If you have resources to burn and frequently find yourself stepping way back in time to modify or delete a step, you can type a larger number. If your resources are skimpy and you don't anticipate making many changes to earlier steps (or are willing to take frequent snapshots or save interim images), you can enter a smaller number.

✔ **Cache Levels:** You can set aside the amount of memory for storing screen images in the Cache Levels setting, to speed up redraws of a reduced-view image on your screen while you make changes. You can specify the number of copies of your image stored in memory, from the default value of 4 up to 8 levels. CS5 has added Cache Optimize buttons to make it easier to decide the number of cache levels. You can use Tall and Thin (2 cache levels) if you have a smaller file with lots of layers. You can choose Big and Flat (5 cache levels) if your file is bigger with fewer layers. The Default setting gives a cache level of 4. In addition, you are able to specify the Cache Tile Size, which determines the amount of data Photoshop processes at one time. Bigger tiles can result in faster processing of larger files. Smaller tiles may be better for smaller files with more layers.

✔ **Scratch Disks:** Scratch disks are areas on your hard drive that Photoshop uses to substitute for physical RAM when you don't have enough RAM to work with the images you open. Scratch disks are no replacement for physical memory, but Photoshop needs scratch disks many times, even if you have huge amounts of memory.

Photoshop uses your startup drive (the drive used to boot your operating system) as its first scratch disk by default. That may not be the best choice because your startup drive is usually pretty busy handling requests of your operating system. Ideally, your scratch disk(s) should be a different hard drive and, preferably, the fastest one you have available.

If you have more than one hard drive, select one other than your startup drive as your first scratch disk.

If you don't have a second hard drive, you can improve scratch disk performance by creating a *partition* on an existing drive for use as a scratch disk. Remember to keep the scratch disk *defragmented* (that is, with the files all organized together on your hard drive) by using your favorite defragmentation utility.

✔ **GPU Settings:** Photoshop attempts to auto-detect your video card and lists the make and model. Select Enable OpenGL Drawing to enhance the performance of your graphics display and speed up your screen redraw. If some of your tool cursors don't appear while you edit an image, try deselecting this option to see whether it fixes the problem. You must select this option to enable viewing options such as flick panning, animated zooms, and the Rotate View tool.

Adjusting your cursors

The Cursors Preferences pane, shown in Figure 5-10, enables you to set several options that control how cursors display onscreen.

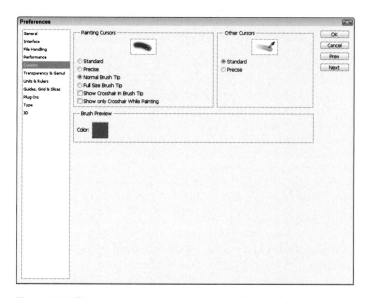

Figure 5-10: Choose the way your cursors are displayed — from crosshairs to brush tips.

The following list describes the Cursor options:

✔ **Painting and Other Cursors (shown in Figure 5-11):** Select the Standard option to show a tool's cursor as an icon representing the tool itself (although I don't know why you'd want to do this). Here's the lowdown on the other settings:

- *Precise:* Switches to a cursor that has crosshairs, which is useful for positioning the center of a tool's operational area in a particular place.

- *Normal Brush Tip:* Displays a 50% point for the brush tip, which means that the diameter of the brush tip reflects feathering of 50% or more. The wispier feathered areas of 50% or less are outside the diameter area shown.

- *Full Size Brush Tip:* Displays the full size of the diameter of the brush tip.

- *Show Crosshair in Brush Tip:* A great hybrid. It shows a crosshair in the center of either of the brush tips — great for precision retouching.

- *Show Only Crosshair While Painting:* Cursor switches to just a crosshair when painting. This can be helpful when using large brushes. Showing the diameters of very large brushes can be cumbersome and slow.

Most users prefer to set the painting cursors to Normal or Full Size Brush Tip and the other cursors to Precise. Some folks complain that precise cursors are hard to see against some backgrounds, but you can always press the Caps Lock key to toggle precise cursors on or off.

✓ **Brush Preview:** To change the color of your brush editing preview, click the color swatch, which takes you to the Color Picker, where you can select your desired color.

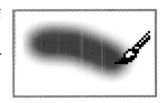

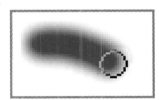
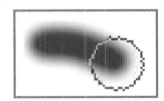
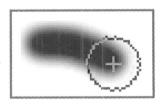
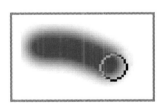

Adjusting transparency and gamut

Photoshop uses colors and patterns to represent information about an image that's normally invisible, such as areas that are transparent or parts of an image that contain colors that can't be represented by your current display or printing system. The Transparency & Gamut Preferences pane, shown in Figure 5-12, enables you to tailor these displays to your own preferences.

For example, transparency is typically shown onscreen by using a gray-and-white checkerboard pattern. You can change the pattern and colors if you prefer another type of display.

Here's a rundown of the options you find in this pane:

Figure 5-11: Photoshop offers six brush tips.

✔ **Grid Size:** You can choose small, medium, large, or no grid at all. You may want to switch from the default medium-sized grid to a large grid if you're using a very high-resolution setting (such as the 1920 x 1200 pixel setting I use on my monitor) so that the grid is a little easier to see. (I don't bother with this, myself.) Or you can switch to a smaller grid if you're working at a lower resolution.

✔ **Grid Colors:** The default light grid is the least obtrusive, but you can switch to a medium or dark grid, if you want. Also, you're not limited to gray-and-white checkerboard squares. To select custom colors, click the white and gray squares below the Grid Colors list.

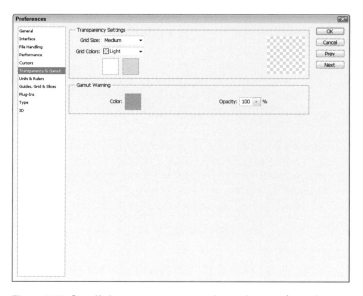

Figure 5-12: Specify how transparency and out-of-gamut (meaning out-of-range) colors are displayed in the Transparency & Gamut Preferences pane.

✔ **Gamut Warning:** You can adjust the color used to represent out-of-gamut colors and to specify the transparency for the warning color. Double-click the Color box to set the hue and select the transparency with the Opacity slider. The gamut warning is generally used before converting RGB images to CMYK to see which colors will be lost. For more information on color gamuts, see Book II, Chapter 2.

A *gamut* is the range of colors that can be displayed or printed. In Photoshop talk, out-of-gamut colors generally are those that can't be represented by cyan, magenta, yellow, and black and, therefore, can't be printed. To turn gamut warnings on or off, choose View➪Gamut Warning. I recommend leaving the gamut warning on. That way, you know what's happening with your image's colors.

Setting measurement preferences

In the Units & Rulers Preferences pane, shown in Figure 5-13, you can set the units used to measure things onscreen (inches, pixels, millimeters, and so forth) and to define a default column size when typing text in multiple columns. In addition, you can define the resolution of the image when you choose File⇔New and select a preset from the Preset Sizes list. (See Book I, Chapter 3 for more on preset sizes.)

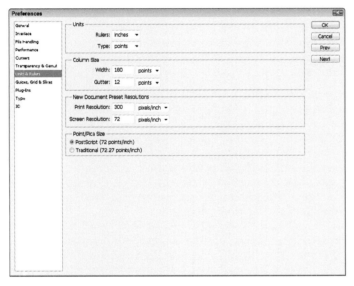

Figure 5-13: Specify your units of measurement and default Photoshop resolution settings in the Units & Rulers Preferences dialog box.

In the Units area of the pane, you find these options:

- ✔ **Rulers:** Select the measurement units that Photoshop uses for rulers. Your choices are pixels, inches, centimeters, millimeters, points, picas, or percent. The most popular units are inches and millimeters, but if you're working with publications and specifying in picas, you might prefer that increment instead. If you're prepping Web graphics, you may prefer to have your rulers incremented in pixels.

- ✔ **Type:** Select the measurement used to represent the dimensions of type. Point size is almost universally used, but pixels and millimeters are also available. You may want to use pixels if you're trying to fit type into a specific-sized area of an image.

In the Column Size area, you can specify the following:

- ✔ **Width:** The width of the column in inches, centimeters, millimeters, points, or picas.
- ✔ **Gutter:** The width of the area separating columns, also in inches, centimeters, millimeters, points, or picas.

In the New Document Preset Resolutions area, you can set the following:

- ✔ **Print Resolution:** The default is 300 pixels per inch, a good overall print setting to keep. You can change to another value and use pixels per centimeter as a measurement, if you want. This resolution setting affects the Photo, International Paper, and U.S. Paper presets found in the New dialog box.
- ✔ **Screen Resolution:** Generally, 72 pixels per inch works with most images that are prepped for screen viewing. You can select another resolution and use pixels per centimeter, if you like. This resolution setting affects the Web and Film and Video presets found in the New dialog box.

Changing the resolution of an image after you created it can impact the sharpness of your image and degrade quality. Choosing the final resolution you want when you create a document is best, whether you specify the resolution manually or use these presets.

In the Point/Pica Size area, you can select whether you want to use a measurement of 72 points per inch (which first became relevant in the Macintosh realm and spread as desktop publishing became widespread) or the traditional 72.27 points per inch definition used in the precomputer era. Unless you have a special reason to choose otherwise, use the PostScript (72 points per inch) option.

Setting up guides, grids, and slices

Guides are nonprinting lines you can create on your screen to make it easier to align objects. *Grids* are vertical and horizontal lines in the background that make lining up objects even easier. *Slices* are sections of an image you can create for Web page graphics so that each slice can be loaded and treated separately (usually in a table or similar arrangement). For more information on using grids and guides, see Book I, Chapter 4. Figure 5-14 shows the Guides, Grid & Slices Preferences pane.

In the Guides and Smart Guides areas, you can set these options:

- ✔ **Color:** Either select a color from the drop-down list or click the color sample swatch to select your own color. You may want to change the default color if that color is too similar to a dominant color in your image.
- ✔ **Style (for guides only):** Select from lines or dashed lines. If you work with images that contain many horizontal and vertical lines that extend across most of an image, dashed lines may be more visible.

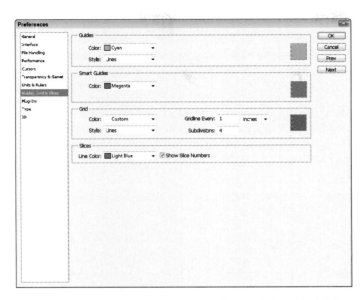

Figure 5-14: Change the colors and styles of your guides and grids for maximum contrast against your image in the Guides, Grid & Slices Preferences pane.

In the Grid area, these are your options:

- ✔ **Color:** Select a color from the drop-down list or click the color sample patch to define a specific hue.
- ✔ **Style:** You can select lines, dashed lines, or dots.
- ✔ **Gridline Every:** Select the distance between gridlines.
- ✔ **Subdivisions:** Select the number of subdivisions for each gridline.

In the Slices area, these are your choices:

- ✔ **Line Color:** From the drop-down list, select a color for the lines that surround each slice.
- ✔ **Show Slice Numbers:** If you select this check box, Photoshop adds a slice number to the display of slices, which makes it easier to keep track of individual slices.

For a full explanation of slices, check out Bonus Chapter 2. See the Introduction for details about this book's companion Web site.

Adding plug-ins

Plug-ins are mini software programs that add features to Photoshop. The Plug-Ins folder is where Photoshop stores all your filters and other plug-in add-ons. A default folder is created when you install Photoshop.

Photoshop allows you to specify an additional folder to search other than its own Plug-Ins folder. This additional folder may come in handy if you want to keep your third-party add-ons separate from Photoshop's native plug-ins. An auxiliary plug-ins directory (not nested within Photoshop's own Plug-Ins folder) can simplify managing those extra filters, and you can turn off their use (potentially speeding up Photoshop's load time) by deselecting the Additional Plug-Ins Folder check box in this dialog box, as shown in Figure 5-15. You can also use this option when you have some plug-ins installed for another application and want to share them with Photoshop without having to make extra copies in your Photoshop Plug-Ins directory.

Figure 5-15: Plug-ins, like filters, add features to Photoshop.

Here are a couple tips on using plug-ins:

✔ **To activate a new plug-ins folder:** Select the Additional Plug-Ins Folder check box. In the dialog box that appears, navigate to the folder you want to use and select it. Click Choose. You then need to exit Photoshop and restart the program to activate the new directory.

✔ **If you have a plug-in or folder you want to deactivate:** Use a tilde (~) as the first character of the plug-in or folder name. Photoshop ignores the plug-in(s) or folder(s) specified. Just remove the tilde from the name to activate the plug-in or folder. This can come in handy if you're having a program glitch and want to deactivate your plug-ins to troubleshoot whether they're causing the problem.

✓ **Extension Panels:** Choose whether to allow Extension panels like Kuler and CS Live to connect to the Internet for updates and new goodies. Also choose whether to have your Extension panels load when you start Photoshop.

Specifying type options

The Type Preferences enable you to establish your font options, shown in Figure 5-16, as follows:

✓ **Use Smart Quotes:** Smart quotes are the curly quotes that typographers use for quotation marks and apostrophes. Straight quotes should be used for abbreviations for feet and inches. I recommend leaving this option selected by default.

✓ **Show Asian Text Options:** If deselected (the default), Photoshop hides Asian text options in the Character and Paragraph panels.

✓ **Enable Missing Glyph Protection:** If certain *glyphs* (characters) are missing, Photoshop makes a substitution if this option is selected.

✓ **Show Font Names in English:** Photoshop displays Asian font names in English if this option is selected (and you select the Show Asian Text Option).

✓ **Font Preview Size:** Specify whether you want a small, medium, or large font for the font menu display of your Type tool.

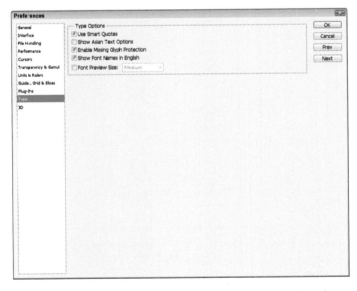

Figure 5-16: The Type preferences establish your typographic options.

Using the Preset Manager

Many of the panels and tools Photoshop works with can use settings that you store on your hard drive as presets. For example, you can create custom colors and brush tips, build your own gradients, create a library of shapes, or compile a set of styles to apply to layers.

You want to become familiar with the Preset Manager, which provides a central management tool for all the options that are individually available from the panels and tools themselves. Just like with the tools, you can select, edit, and delete presets. The only thing you can't do with the Preset Manager is actually create a preset. You must do this with the Tool Preset Picker, Tool Presets panel, Gradient Editor, Brushes panel, and other locations. For more details, see Book I, Chapter 2. Here are some tips on using the Preset Manager, shown in Figure 5-17:

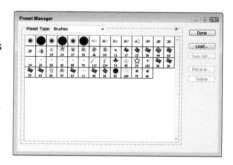

Figure 5-17: The Preset Manager is the central management tool for all Photoshop presets for all panels.

- ✔ To show the Preset Manager, choose Edit⇨Preset Manager. To hide it, click Done.

- ✔ To select a specific type of preset to work with, select it from the Preset Type drop-down list.

- ✔ To load an existing set of presets from your hard drive, click the Load button and navigate to the presets you want to access. You can also select a preset library listed on the pop-up menu of each preset type.

- ✔ To store a new or modified group of settings, click the Save Set button and type a name.

- ✔ To give a particular preset a new name, select the preset in the dialog box, click the Rename button, type the new name, and click OK.

You can rename multiple presets consecutively by clicking and Ctrl-clicking (⌘-clicking) the items that you want to rename, and then clicking the Rename button. Photoshop asks you to supply a new name for each, in turn.

- ✔ To quickly load the default preset library for any tool or panel, select Reset *[Preset]* from the Preset Manager pop-up menu. You can also replace your current preset library with another.

- ✔ Different preset display options are available on the Preset Manager pop-up menu.

Book II
Image Essentials

To me, when people say that a bit of information is *essential,* they mean, "Hey, you really gotta know this stuff or else!" Well, technically, you could skip this book, and Photoshop wouldn't be any wiser — but I don't recommend it. In this book, I cover the nitty-gritty of topics like resolution, image modes, and file formats. Fun? Nope. Dry? Most likely, unless you're the type who gets excited about pixel dimensions. But having a good handle on the information in this book is critical to ensuring good-looking images.

I show you how to safely size your images without causing them to turn to mush. You can also find information on cropping images and increasing canvas sizes, as well as an important chapter on both applying color and color managing your files. If you want to know more about how to undo your mistakes, you'll want to check out the chapter on the History panel. And finally, if all this information makes your head spin and you need a breather, look at the chapter on Actions. Actions can automate a lot of your frequently executed Photoshop techniques, giving you more time to stop and smell those roses you just photographed.

Chapter 1: Specifying Size and Resolution

In This Chapter

⮕ Comparing raster (pixel) and vector images

⮕ Understanding how pixels appear on different monitors

⮕ Working with the Image Size command

⮕ Resampling images (if you must)

⮕ Adjusting the canvas size

⮕ Cropping an image

Size and resolution are slippery subjects. A digital image's size may refer to its file size, how big you want it to be on a printed page (such as 3 x 5 or 8 x 10 inches), the size you want it be onscreen (full screen or just part of the screen), or how densely packed the pixels are (its resolution). To use Photoshop's tools so that an image looks good in print *or* onscreen, you need to know not only what type of size you're working with, but also what the image's resolution is — and how both of these factors might affect the image's appearance.

Given all the factors in size and resolution, it's not surprising that Photoshop has evolved into a Swiss Army knife. It offers multiple tools for specifying, viewing, or changing an image's size. In this chapter, I give you a bit of background in both size and resolution so that you know what tools to use and how to use them. In Book IX, you can find out how to use the basics I cover here in order to tailor size and resolution specifically for print.

I also explain how to change image size without harming your image. Yes, you can harm your image. Not intentionally, of course. But it can happen quicker than you can close a dialog box. However, with a firm understanding of how pixels live and breathe, you can ensure that your images are safe from damage.

Putting Images under the Microscope

Digital images fall into two camps — *vector* images, which are created by mathematical formulas, and *raster* images, which are made up of pixels arranged in a grid. Photoshop allows you to produce both types of images and even to combine both types within a single file. Table 1-1 gives you the skinny on vector and raster images.

Table 1-1	Characteristics of Vector and Raster Graphics			
Graphic Type	How It Works	File Size	Image Degradation Possible?	Resolution-Dependent?
Vector	Mathematical formulas precisely locate and connect geometric objects and segments.	Usually small	No	No
Raster	Breaks pieces of an image into a grid made up of pixels.	Usually large	Yes	Yes

Even though Photoshop can produce vector graphics, its primary mission is to create awe-inspiring raster images. And because the issue of resolution is so critical to raster images, this chapter primarily discusses methods for sizing and resizing raster images. I cover producing vector art in more detail in Book IV, Chapter 1.

Vector images

One cool thing about vector images — also called *object-oriented images* — is that when you zoom in on them, they don't look blocky. That's because vector images are made of *segments* (whether curved or straight) and *anchor points,* which are elements that indicate the endpoints of the segments. Both segments and anchors are defined by mathematical objects called *vectors.* Vectors use a unique mathematical formula to define the specific location of an object, as well as its geometric shape. Vector images, one of which is shown in Figure 1-1, are usually the product of drawing programs, such as Adobe Illustrator, but Photoshop is also capable of producing a vector or two.

Figure 1-1: Graphics that need clean lines work great in vector format.

Here are a few more handy things to know about vector graphics

- ✔ **A curve is still a curve, even at 20,000 feet.** Because they're mathematically defined, vector graphics can be sized and otherwise transformed without an inkling of quality loss. Take that little 2-inch spot illustration and size it up to mural size, and it appears identical.

- ✔ **You can get pretty pictures in small packages.** Vector-image files can be small because file size depends on the complexity of the vector objects, not on the size of the illustration.

- ✔ **Vector images are independent — resolution-independent, that is.** Not only can they be transformed and printed without degrading their quality, but they also have no built-in resolution — they take on the resolution of the output device. For example, if you print my logo in Figure 1-1 to an *imagesetter* (a high-end printing device used for color separations) at 3600 dots per inch (dpi), the image comes out at 3600 dpi. Print it to a 300-dpi laser printer, and what do you get? A 300-dpi image.

Because your monitor can display images only on a grid, vector images display onscreen as pixels. This accounts for the jagged appearance you sometimes see when you zoom into a curved vector object. But don't worry; it prints just fine.

Raster images

Raster images are usually the result of the digitizing of *continuous-tone* images, such as photographs or original painted or drawn artwork. Raster images are made up of a grid of squares called pixels. (*Pixel* is short for picture element; it's the smallest component of a digital image.) If you've ever looked at a bathroom wall made up of those small square tiles reminiscent of the '40s, you're familiar with what a grid of pixels looks like up close: Each pixel lives in a specific location on that grid, and each contains a single color. When you edit a raster image, you're editing one or more pixels, rather than an object-oriented shape.

But how do you fit a round peg into a square hole? By faking it. Unlike the true mathematical curve that's possible when you're drawing vector shapes, raster images must try to approximate a curve by mimicking the overall shape with square pixels. So, the elliptical shapes of my beanie (shown in Figure 1-2) have to fit within this system of squares. Fortunately, the pixels'

Figure 1-2: Raster images are composed of a grid of square pixels.

mimicry is unnoticeable in high-resolution images viewed at a reasonable distance. But when you zoom in, you can see that a curve in an image (such as the curve of my beanie) is indeed made up of square pixels.

Raster graphics work great for photorealistic or painterly images in which subtle gradations of color are necessary. On the downside, because they contain a fixed number of pixels, raster graphics can suffer a degradation of quality when they're enlarged or otherwise transformed. They're also large in file size.

Bitmap (another name for raster) images are resolution-dependent. Because they contain a fixed number of pixels, the resolution of the device they're being printed to is only one of two factors that influence the quality of the image. The quality of the output also depends heavily on the resolution of the image. For example, an image with 72 dots per inch (dpi) doesn't look any better printed on a 600-dpi printer than it does on a 1200-dpi printer. Likewise, a 300-dpi image doesn't look as good printed on an old 72-dpi dot-matrix printer as it does on a 1200-dpi printer.

Viewing Raster Images Onscreen

When you view images onscreen, pixel dimensions come into play — especially if you're putting images on the Web — because the display of images is based on 1 image pixel per 1 screen pixel. The most important issue, then, is making sure that your image fits inside your (or your audience's) monitor when viewed at 100 percent.

When you view an image onscreen, the display size is determined by the pixel dimension, plus the size and setting of the monitor. You therefore need to determine what monitor resolution your audience is likely using and size your graphics accordingly. Table 1-2 illustrates how an 800-x-600-pixel image might display differently, depending on monitor resolution.

Table 1-2	Displaying an Image on Different Monitors	
Size of Monitor	*Resolution (in Pixels)*	*How Does an 800-x-600-Pixel Image Display?*
24-inch monitor	1920 x 1080	The image fills a small portion of the screen.
22-inch monitor	1680 x 1050	The image fills a small portion of the screen.
17-inch monitor	1024 x 768	The image fills part of the screen.
	800 x 600	The image fills the screen, with each pixel appearing larger.
15-inch monitor	800 x 600	The image fills the screen.
		Larger images can't be viewed in their entirety.

You may also hear people referring to monitor resolution in graphic display standards, such as XGA (1024 x 768 pixels), UXGA (1600 x 1200 pixels), WQXGA (2560 x 1600 pixels), and so on.

Resolution is measured in pixels per inch, or *ppi*. You may also run across the term *samples per inch (spi)*, often used when talking about scanners. Another term you see often is *dots per inch (dpi)*, always used in reference to printers, imagesetters, and other paper-outputting devices. You may hear people refer to dpi as *printer resolution*.

When displaying images onscreen, the recommended resolution setting is somewhere between 72 ppi and 96 ppi, even though resolution isn't really a factor in preparing screen images. That's just because monitors display somewhere in the 72- to 96-ppi range.

So, if you change the physical dimensions of an image, it's always at a one-to-one ratio with the monitor. If you view an image whose resolution is higher than that of the monitor, the image appears larger onscreen than in print. For example, try opening (or dragging and dropping) a 300-ppi JPEG file into a browser window. It explodes on your screen. Because the monitor can display only 72 to 96 ppi, it needs a ton of space to show all the pixels.

Using the Image Size Command

A time will come when you need to mess with the resolution or dimensions of an image. You may want to

- ✔ Change the file size.
- ✔ Make sure the resolution is appropriate for print.
- ✔ Adjust the dimensions so that they're just right for viewing onscreen.
- ✔ Change the width, height, and/or resolution of your image for printing or some other kind of output.

Photoshop — powerhouse that it is — allows you to size an image in all these ways with the Image Size command on the Image menu. Follow these steps to resize your image:

1. **Open the image and then choose Image⇨Image Size.**

   The Image Size dialog box opens, as shown in Figure 1-3. This is where the magic happens.

2. **Note the current state of your image and decide whether any of the following values need to change in order to get a nice-looking image for the desired output (print or the Web):**

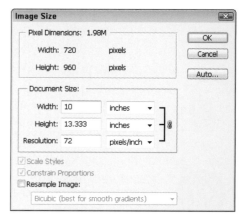

Figure 1-3: The Image Size dialog box is one of the most important in Photoshop.

- *The current pixel dimensions and the resulting file size:* My example shows 720 pixels in width and 960 pixels in height for a file size of 1.98MB (megabytes).

- *The current document size:* The size of your image when it prints on media, such as paper.

- *The resolution:* My example is 72 ppi, which is good for displaying onscreen or on the Web, but inadequate for printing. I'll see some *pixelation* (visible little squares) on my printout. Therefore, to print, I need to reduce the size of the image so that my total pixels are packed into a smaller area, to give the image cleaner lines.

3. **Make sure the Constrain Proportions check box is selected.**

The chain-and-bracket icon in the Document Size area indicates that the Constrain Proportions check box is selected. Nine times out of ten, you want your image to stay proportional. With the option selected, changing one value in the Document Size area makes the other values change automatically so that the proportions stay intact.

You can also select the Scale Styles check box, which allows you to scale or not scale any effects or styles that you've applied to your layer(s). This option is available only if you select Constrain Proportions. (For more on styles, see Book V, Chapter 4.)

4. **Make sure that the Resample Image check box is deselected.**

When you *resample,* you add or delete pixels in the image. Although you sometimes need to resample, doing so isn't good for your image. (I explain why in the following section.)

5. **Enter any new values in the dialog box.**

For example, because I want to print my image, I enter a new value of 300 pixels per inch for my resolution in the Document Size area. The other values automatically change.

6. Click OK.

You won't notice any difference in the way your image appears onscreen because you haven't added or deleted any pixels; you've merely compacted them into a smaller space.

Congratulations! You've just safely resized your image. You can proudly say, "No pixels were harmed in the making of this image."

Resampling Images

Resampling means you're changing the pixel dimensions of an image. When you *downsample* (or resample down), you're eliminating pixels and therefore deleting information and detail from your image. When you *upsample* (or resample up), you're adding pixels. Photoshop adds these pixels by using interpolation. *Interpolation* means Photoshop analyzes the colors of the original pixels and "manufactures" new ones, which are then added to the existing ones.

You can specify the interpolation method in the Image Size dialog box. The default that appears in the dialog box is based on the interpolation method you specified in your General Preferences dialog box. Here are your five choices:

- **Nearest Neighbor:** This method is fast and provides for the smallest file size, but it's less precise than the other options and therefore the lowest quality.

- **Bilinear:** Considered a medium-quality method, it works by averaging the color of the pixel above, below, and to the right and left of each pixel.

- **Bicubic:** This method is the slowest but most precise.

- **Bicubic Smoother:** A good method to use when you must upsample images, but it can slightly affect the sharpness of the image.

- **Bicubic Sharper:** This is a good method when downsampling an image.

If you really must resample, especially when upsampling, I recommend leaving the method set to Bicubic Smoother. Notice I said *if you really must.* Here are some reasons why you might choose to add or delete pixels:

- You no longer have access to the original artwork, which you could otherwise rescan at the proper resolution and size.

- You no longer have access to the original high-resolution version of the file.

- You want to print a photo at a specific dimension, but the image's current resolution won't allow for decent-quality output.

- You absolutely can't replace the low-resolution image with another of higher resolution.

Resampling isn't a recommended activity, especially when it pertains to upsampling. As smart as Photoshop is, having to manufacture pixels isn't an exact science. Your image tends to lose detail and sharpness and get blurry and mushy. Overall blurriness and goopy edges tend to be an unfortunate side effect of interpolation, as shown in Figure 1-4. The bottom line is that your resampled image never looks as good as the original. Downsampling isn't as scary. You're deleting pixels, and therefore detail, but the degradation is virtually undetectable to the eye.

Original   Resampled

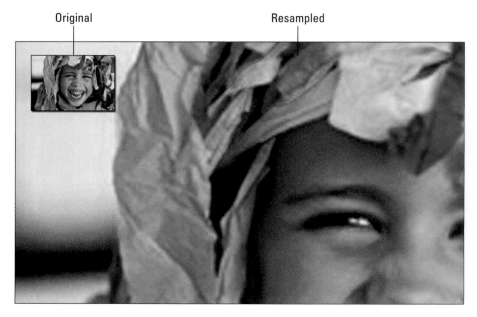

Figure 1-4: Fuzzy, blurry images are a result of resampling.

Adding pixels to an image

To add pixels to an image, follow these steps:

1. **With your desired image open, first choose Image⇨Duplicate to make a copy of your original. With the duplicate active, choose Image⇨Image Size.**

   The Image Size dialog box appears.

   This is where the havoc happens. Be careful!

2. **Make sure that the Resample Image option is selected.**

   The Width and Height in the Pixel Dimensions area are now text boxes into which you can enter values. They're no longer fixed values as they are when Resample Image is deselected.

3. **Enter a higher value for the resolution and, if desired, enter a higher value for the width or height.**

   In my example, I entered a resolution of 300 ppi.

   The pixel dimensions increased dramatically, and so did the file size (from a mere 299.5K to 5.08MB), as shown in Figure 1-5.

   If you get all discombobulated when working in the dialog box, press Alt (Option on the Mac). The Cancel button changes to a Reset button. Click it, and you're back to where you started. This is a good shortcut to remember because it holds true for many of Photoshop's dialog boxes.

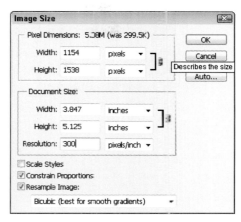

Figure 1-5: Increasing the pixel dimensions in an image causes your image to degrade in quality.

4. **Leave your Interpolation method set to Bicubic (Best for Smooth Gradients), which is a good option when upsampling.**

5. **Click OK.**

   Photoshop now goes through its interpolation ritual and churns out a newly resampled image. Do a side-by-side comparison to the original, looking at both at 100% view. Your original should look a whole lot better than the resampled image. And, for a real shocker, try printing out the two images and seeing what kind of degradation takes place.

Taking pixels out of an image

When you *downsample,* you eliminate pixels and therefore delete information and detail from your image. Although I've emphasized the pitfalls of resampling up, you can sometimes damage your image by downsampling, as well.

Granted, downsampling is sometimes necessary when you're converting high-resolution print graphics into Web graphics. For example, you may be forced to take images used for a corporate brochure and repurpose them into content for the company's Web site. You probably won't notice much degradation in image quality because the images are just being viewed onscreen. In addition, downsampling can occasionally camouflage the moiré patterns caused by scanning halftones. (For more on halftones, check out Book VII, Chapter 1.) Keep in mind, however, that 72 ppi isn't sufficient for printing an image, as shown in Figure 1-6.

You should never need to make an image smaller than 72 ppi.

2.25 x 3.375 inches
300 ppi

2.25 x 3.375 inches
72 ppi

Purestock

Figure 1-6: Downsample your images to 72 ppi for display on the Web, but not for print.

TIP

A potpourri of image-size do's and don'ts

Here are some tips and tricks to keep in mind when you're messing around with image size and resolution settings:

- **Use the Smart Sharpen or Unsharp Mask filter after you resample.** Choose Filter⇨ Sharpen⇨Smart Sharpen or Unsharp Mask. These filters heighten the contrast between pixels to give the illusion of sharpening or forcing the image more into focus.

- **Don't change your settings — just print.** If you want to leave the size and resolution settings untouched, but you need to print your image at a different size, use the Scaled Print Size option in the Print dialog box. (For details, see Book I, Chapter 3.)

- **Start out with the proper dimensions.** It goes without saying, but I'll say it anyway: Try to enter the proper dimensions and resolution when creating a new document. You don't want to find yourself in the unfortunate situation of creating your file at 72 ppi, spending hours getting it just perfect, and then remembering you were supposed to prep it for print and really needed it to be 300 ppi. Be sure you scan images at a high-enough resolution, too.

- **Don't use a higher resolution than you need.** All you do is create an unnecessarily huge file with a slower print time. In some cases, it may actually make your printout look darker and muddier.

- **Look no further than this book.** Use the handy, dandy table of recommended resolution settings in Book IX, Chapter 1 for a variety of output devices.

To remove pixels from an image, follow the steps in the preceding section and change the image settings accordingly.

If you have to downsample your image significantly — for example, to 25 percent of its original size — you may get better results if you do several successive 50-percent downsamples, applying an Unsharp Mask or Smart Sharpen filter on the image in between each image sizing. (For more on the Unsharp Mask filter, see Book VII, Chapter 1.)

Changing the Canvas Size

I've probably harped on you to the point that you're slightly paranoid, or at least ultra-conscious, of using the Image Size command. Well, you can relax because the Canvas Size command is as safe as can be. Unlike the Image Size command, which enlarges or reduces the dimensions or resolution of your image, the Canvas Size command merely changes the size of the *canvas,* or page, on which the image sits.

When you increase the size of the canvas, Photoshop fills the expanded area outside the image with your chosen color. Increasing your canvas size can come in handy if you're trying to add a frame or border around your image. If you make the canvas smaller, Photoshop *crops* (cuts away) the image. Follow these quick-and-easy steps to change your canvas size:

1. **Choose Image⇨Canvas Size.**

   The Canvas Size dialog box, shown in Figure 1-7 appears. The current size of your canvas appears at the top of the dialog box.

2. **Enter new values in the Width and Height text boxes.**

   You can also change the unit of measurement by using the pop-up menus.

   Select the Relative check box to be able to specify an amount of space for Photoshop to add or remove around your image. This feature is handy when you're adding or removing equal amounts of canvas around images with fractional measurements.

3. **Specify your desired anchor placement.**

   The anchor shows how the image sits inside the canvas. By default, Photoshop centers the image and adds or removes the canvas around it. Click any of the other eight squares to have Photoshop add or remove the canvas asymmetrically around the image.

   If you reduce either the Width or Height value and then click OK, an alert box appears asking if you really want to proceed because you'll be clipping the image. This is actually another way of cropping an image, albeit not one you'll use every day. See the following section for more on cropping.

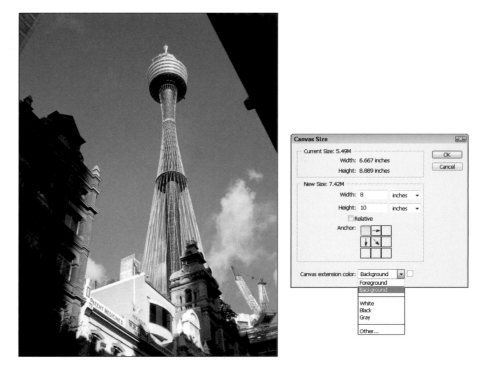

Figure 1-7: Increasing your canvas size adds to the area around your image.

4. **Select your canvas color from the Canvas Extension Color pop-up menu and click OK.**

   Choose from Foreground, Background, White, Black, Gray, or Other. If you select Other, Photoshop transports you to the Color Picker, where you can select any color you desire. The small swatch to the right of the pop-up menu displays the current background color. You can also click this swatch to access the Color Picker (which I explain how to use in Book II, Chapter 3).

Cropping an Image

Even a novice photographer knows that cropping an image can make a composition stronger. *Cropping* entails cutting away background clutter or endless expanses of empty space in order to focus in on your desired subject.

This simple process can transform a ho-hum photograph into a visually exciting one. Take a look at my example in Figure 1-8. I mean, it doesn't take Ansel Adams to figure out which image is stronger. (It would be even better if the fence weren't in the background, but hey, that's nothing that a little Photoshop retouching can't take care of. Check out Book VIII; it's all about retouching and restoration techniques.)

Figure 1-8: Cropping is one of the easiest ways to improve the composition of your image.

Sure-fire cropping tips

Even though cropping is about as simple an image-editing maneuver as you can get, you need to know about a few other options:

✓ **Perspective:** If you need a nonrectangular cropping marquee, select this check box on the Options bar. (Your crop marquee must be active.) This feature allows the corner handles to move independently. Note that when you apply the actual crop, the photo is transformed into a rectangular shape, thereby distorting the image based on your applied perspective.

✓ **Front Image:** Also in the Options bar, this setting enables you to crop one image so that it's the exact same size as another image. Open two images and crop the first one. Click Front Image. Photoshop enters the width, height, and resolution values from the first image on the Options bar. Drag the Crop tool on your second image and adjust the marquee, as desired. Double-click inside the marquee. Photoshop automatically crops your second image to match your first.

✓ **Delete and Hide:** If your image doesn't contain any layers — that is, it consists only of a background — any cropped areas are permanently deleted from your file. However, if your image consists of one or more layers (see Book V for the lowdown on layers), you have the choice of deleting or hiding your cropped area. Delete eliminates the cropped area, whereas Hide just hides the cropped area. You can see the hidden areas if you move the layer by using the Move tool. Another way to see the hidden area is to choose Image⇒Reveal All. Photoshop expands the canvas to show all areas in all layers, except for the Background layer.

✓ **Width, Height, and Resolution:** If you want to crop an image to an exact measurement, enter a value in these text boxes on the Options bar. These options are available only when the Crop tool is active and you haven't yet dragged a cropping marquee. But be careful about the value you use for the Resolution setting. Remember, resampling isn't a good thing. To remove the entered settings, click the Clear button on the Options bar.

Using the Crop tool

The most popular way to crop an image is by using the Crop tool. This simple tool is as easy and effective to use as a T-square and an X-ACTO knife, just without the possibility of bodily injury. Select the Crop tool in the Tools panel or press C on the keyboard. Then, follow these steps:

1. **With the Crop tool, drag around the part of the image you want to keep and then release your mouse button.**

   While you drag, a *marquee* (a dotted outline) appears and displays the cropping boundaries. Don't worry if your cropping marquee isn't exactly correct. You can adjust it in Step 2.

   The area outside the cropping marquee appears darker than the area inside in order to better frame your image. Adobe calls this a *shield*. You control the color and *opacity* (the amount of transparency) of the shield by adjusting the settings on the Options bar. If, for some strange reason, you don't want the shield, deselect the Shield check box.

   Version CS5 gives you an added aid in framing your image. Choose None, Grid, or Rule of Thirds from the new Crop Guide Overlay setting in the Options bar. The Rule of Thirds is a photographic principle that advocates placing elements most appealing to the eye at one of the four intersecting points of the rule of thirds grid.

   Figure 1-9 shows a great example of way too much useless background. I dragged around the only thing I want to retain — the pirate girl.

2. **Adjust the cropping marquee by dragging the handles.**

   The small squares on the sides and corners of the cropping marquee are called *handles*. When you hover your mouse over any handle or the marquee itself, your cursor changes to a double-headed arrow, indicating that you can drag.

Handle   Cropping marquee   Shield

Rule of Thirds grid

Figure 1-9: The area around your cropping marquee appears darker so that you can better frame your image.

To move the entire marquee, position your mouse inside the marquee until you see a black arrowhead cursor and then drag. Adjust the marquee until you're satisfied.

You can also drag the *origin point* (the circle icon in the center) to change the axis of rotation.

If you move your mouse outside the marquee, the cursor changes to a curved, double-headed arrow. Dragging with this cursor rotates the marquee. This feature can be extremely useful when you need to rotate and crop a crooked image. By using the Crop tool, you can perform both commands in one step and often more quickly and accurately. Just be aware that rotation, unless it's in 90-degree increments, resamples your image — which, if done repeatedly, can damage your image. (See the earlier section, "Resampling Images," for more on resampling.) Getting the rotation right the first time around is for the best.

3. **Double-click inside the cropping marquee.**

   You can also just press Enter (Return on the Mac) or click the Commit (check mark icon) button on the Options bar. Photoshop discards the area outside the marquee, as shown in Figure 1-10. If you want to cancel the crop, just press Esc or click Cancel (the slashed circle icon) on the Options bar.

Figure 1-10: Eliminating background clutter allows you to hone in on your subject.

Cropping with the Marquee tool

If you get bored with using the Crop tool, you can also crop a selected area by choosing Image➪Crop. Simply make a selection with any of the tools and then choose this command. Although using the Rectangular Marquee tool for your selection makes the most sense, you don't have to.

You can use Image➪Crop with any selection — circular, polygonal, kidney bean, even feathered. Photoshop can't crop to those odd shapes but it gets as close to the outline as it can. (For all you need to know on selections, see Book III, Chapter 1.)

Using the Trim command

The fabulous Trim command trims away transparent or solid-colored areas around your image. Choose Image➪Trim, and a dialog box appears. Select Transparent Pixels (for layered images), Top Left Pixel Color, or Bottom Right Pixel Color as a basis for the trim. Then, choose to trim away the Top, Bottom, Left, or Right side(s) from the image, and click OK.

This command works great for quickly eliminating black-and-white borders around images.

Using the Crop and Straighten Photo command

Choose File➪Automate➪Crop and Straighten Photos. Photoshop then looks for rectangular areas in your document, extracts each one into its own document, and straightens those individual images, as shown in Figure 1-11.

The Crop and Straighten Photos command is fabulous if you want to save time by scanning multiple images initially into one document. (And the command works on single images, as well.) This command is a real manual-labor timesaver, and I wholeheartedly endorse it.

You can now also straighten images using the Ruler tool. Here's how:

1. **Select the Ruler tool from the Tools panel.**

   It shares a flyout menu with the Eyedropper tool. You can also press I or Shift I to cycle through the tools.

2. **Click at the starting point of the axis you wish to straighten. Drag the tool at the ending point of that axis. Release the mouse.**

3. **Click the Straighten button in the Options bar.**

Figure 1-11: The Crop and Straighten command extracts and straightens your images into separate files.

Chapter 2: Choosing Color Modes and File Formats

In This Chapter

✔ **Choosing the right color mode**

✔ **Switching a file's color mode**

✔ **Focusing on file formats**

*I*n addition to choosing a size and resolution (discussed in Book II, Chapter 1), you need to decide on a color mode and file format for your image. Usually, you base this decision on the final use for the image. Are you importing it into a page-layout program for offset printing? Posting it on a Web page? Using it for a newspaper article?

When you know an image's final destination, you can make intelligent choices about which color mode and file format are best. This chapter gives you some background information to help you make those choices so that you don't end up having to do extra work, spend extra time, or waste extra money.

Selecting a Color Mode

Every file has a *color mode*, also called an *image mode* or just plain *mode*. To determine the color mode of an image, look in the title bar of the image window or choose Image⇨Mode. Color modes define the color values used to display the image. Photoshop offers eight modes and enables you to convert images from one mode to another. The color mode you choose for a particular image depends on a couple of factors:

✔ **The file format you plan to save it in:** Some modes call for specific file formats. You may find that a certain format is unavailable because your file isn't in the appropriate color mode.

✔ **The end use for the image:** Do you plan to post the image on the Web? Or are you putting it in a brochure that will be offset printed? For more on prepping images for print, see Book IX, Chapter 1. For details on getting images ready for the Web, see Bonus Chapter 1.

Basic RGB and CMYK color theory

When you view an RGB image, you're looking at an image made of three colors — red, green, and blue. These colors are

- The primary colors of light (additive color)

- The colors that correspond to the three types of cones inside your eyes

- The colors that comprise white light from the sun

- The colors your monitor uses when displaying images

The CMYK color scheme (subtractive color) is based on the light-absorbing quality of ink on paper. In theory, a white light hits these inks. Some visible wavelengths are absorbed, or subtracted, and others are reflected back to your eyes. CMYK images comprise various percentages of only four colors of ink — cyan, magenta, yellow, and black. These colors correspond to the inks used in the offset printing process.

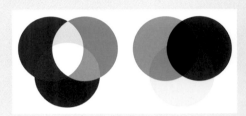

The following sections provide a brief description and example of each mode and any file-format or usage connections.

 Color modes affect the number of colors that display, as well as the size of the file and the number of channels. One or more channels — in which the color data is stored — represents each mode. Grayscale images have one color channel — Black. CMYK images have four color channels — Cyan, Magenta, Yellow, and Black. (For the lowdown on channels, see Book VI, Chapter 1.)

RGB Color

Uses: RGB is the gold standard for most scanners, all monitors, all digital cameras, and some desktop inkjet printers. And it's the primary color mode (with Indexed Color being secondary) to use with any images to be viewed onscreen (whether on the Web or in any kind of multimedia presentation).

File formats: Just about every file format, except GIF, can handle an image in RGB mode.

RGB is a very good overall work mode. Images in RGB mode have full access to all Photoshop commands, including filters and image adjustments. RGB images contain values of 0 to 255 for each of three colors — red, green, and blue. With

8 bits of color information for each of the three colors, these 24-bit images can reproduce up to 16.7 million colors onscreen. 48-bit images (16 bits per color) can display even more. Most scanners also scan images in RGB, all monitors display in RGB, and most desktop inkjet printers prefer to print RGB (rather than CMYK) images. But always do a test print with both modes to be sure.

The RGB mode in Photoshop varies according to the RGB Working Space setting you select in the Color Settings dialog box. For details on color settings, see Book II, Chapter 3.

RGB also supports High Dynamic Range or HDR, (32-bit per color) images.

CMYK Color

Uses: CMYK is the standard for images that are color-separated for offset printing. Some other composite printing devices also require images to be in CMYK mode.

File formats: CMYK can handle just about every major format except GIF.

CMYK images, such as the one shown in Figure 2-1, contain a percentage of one or more four-process color inks — cyan, magenta, yellow, and black. Darker colors have higher percentages, whereas lighter colors have lower percentages. Pure white is created when all four colors have a value of 0 percent. Like RGB mode, the CMYK mode in Photoshop can vary according to the CMYK Working Space setting you select in the Color Settings dialog box.

Make sure that you do your image editing in RGB mode, where you have access to the full range of filters and adjustments. When you complete your editing, convert the image from RGB to CMYK. (For details, see the section "Converting from RGB to CMYK," later in this chapter.)

Corbis Digital Stock

Figure 2-1: CMYK is the mode needed for offset-printed images.

Grayscale

Uses: Grayscale mode, shown in Figure 2-2, is for black-and-white (and all shades of gray in between) images.

File formats: All the most commonly used file formats accept Grayscale mode.

Grayscale images contain up to 256 levels of gray. Each pixel has a brightness value ranging from 0 (black) to 255 (white). You can scan an image in Grayscale mode, or you can convert color images to grayscale. If you convert a color image to grayscale, Photoshop discards all the color information, and the remaining gray levels represent the luminosity of the pixels. (Check out the "Converting to grayscale" section, later in this chapter.) You can also convert a grayscale image to a color image; although this process doesn't actually convert your grayscale image to color, it enables you to apply color on top of the grayscale image.

Corbis Digital Stock

Figure 2-2: Images in grayscale mode contain 256 levels of gray.

High Dynamic Range (HDR) images can also support Grayscale mode. For more on HDR images, see Book IX, Chapter 2.

Monotone, Duotone, Tritone, and Quadtone

Uses: Because printing presses can print only about 50 gray levels per ink color, duotones and multitones — which use two to four inks — are used to increase the range of tones of grayscale images. Duotones and multitones are often created by using black and spot colors (premixed inks), although you can also use process colors. (For more on spot colors, see Book IX, Chapter 1.)

File formats: The only file formats that can save duotones, tritones, and quadtones are native Photoshop, Photoshop 2.0, EPS, PDF, Large Document Format, or Photoshop Raw.

These modes create one-color, (monotone), two-color (duotone), three-color (tritone; shown in Figure 2-3), and four-color (quadtone) images. Photoshop lumps all the various tone modes under duotone. You can find a pop-up menu in the Duotone options dialog box, from which you can select the various options. Unlike RGB and CMYK images, in which the components of the image display with different colors, the monotones, duotones, tritones, and quadtones have the colors mixed throughout the image. The colored inks are often used to reproduce tinted grays, not the different colors you find in RGB and CMYK images.

To access the Duotone mode, you must first convert the color image to grayscale (see how later in this chapter). Then, choose Image➪ Mode➪Duotone. In the dialog box that appears, select Monotone, Duotone, Tritone, or Quadtone from the pop-up menu. Then, select ink colors — either spot or process — by clicking the appropriate swatches. Finally, you can adjust the

Corbis Digital Stock

Figure 2-3: Tritone images mix three inks throughout the image.

Curves settings by dragging the graph line. This tells Photoshop how to distribute the ink(s) among the various tones. You don't have access to the individual color channels in Duotone mode. The only manipulation you can do in that mode is to specify the Curves settings.

If you're new to these modes, you need to know that Photoshop offers numerous preset duotones, tritones, and quadtones. To access these presets, select one from the Preset pop-up menu. Sometimes, printing these types of images can be challenging, so starting with these presets is a good idea if you're inexperienced.

Indexed Color

Uses: Indexed Color mode is primarily for Web graphics and multimedia displays.

File formats: Indexed Color mode supports a variety of formats, with GIF being the most popular. Other formats supported include Photoshop, Photoshop 2.0, Photoshop Raw, BMP, EPS, IFF Format, ElectricImage, Large Document Format, PCX, PDF, PICT, PICT Resource, PNG, Targa, and TIFF.

Indexed Color mode, shown in Figure 2-4, uses 256 colors or less; what graphics aficionados call 8-bit color. When you convert an image to indexed color, Photoshop builds a Color Lookup Table (CLUT), which stores and indexes the color. (The Color Table option appears in the Mode menu.) If a color in the original image isn't in the table, Photoshop chooses the closest match or makes a new one from the available colors. Using fewer colors reduces the file size, which is why the GIF file format — a very popular Web-graphics format — uses this mode. (See the "GIF" section, later in this chapter.)

Corbis Digital Stock

Figure 2-4: Indexed Color mode uses 256 colors or less.

The Indexed Color mode doesn't support layers, and editing capabilities are limited. For more on indexed color, see Bonus Chapter 1 on this book's Web site. (The Introduction has details about the companion Web site.)

Lab Color

Uses: Lab Color mode provides a consistent color display, which is ideal for high-end image retouching.

File formats: You can save an image in Lab Color mode in native Photoshop, Photoshop Raw, EPS, TIFF, PDF, JPEG 2000, Large Document Format, or Photoshop DCS 1.0 and 2.0 formats. You can save images containing 48 bits (16 bits per channel) in Photoshop, Photoshop Raw, PDF, Large Document Format, and TIFF formats.

Lab Color mode is usually thought of as the internal color mode that Photoshop uses when converting from one color mode to another — for example, when going from RGB to CMYK. It's also the mode preferred by color-retouching experts because it's considered to be *device-independent* (it appears consistent on various devices).

Lab Color mode consists of a lightness channel and two additional channels (*a* and *b*), shown in Figure 2-5, which contain the range of colors from green to red (*a*) and blue to yellow (*b*).

HDR images containing 32 bits per color can be saved in Photoshop, FXG, Large Document Format, OpenEXR, Radiance, Portable Bit Map, and TIFF file formats. OpenEXR and Radiance are two types of HDR file formats. OpenEXR images are used in film visual effects. Radiance images are often used in 3-D modeling programs. See more on HDR images in Book IX, Chapter 2.

Bitmap

Uses: This mode is best for scanned *line art* (that is, art composed entirely of lines, such as a line drawing of a camera you might see in a manual) and signatures (your John Hancock).

> **TIP**
>
> When scanning line art, be sure to crank up your scanning resolution to 1200 ppi or so to ensure a good-quality bitmap image.

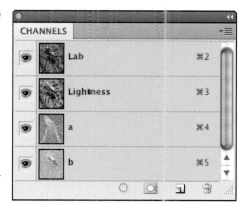

Figure 2-5: Lab Color mode is the preferred editing mode for color experts because it's device-independent.

File formats: Photoshop, Photoshop 2.0, EPS, TIFF, PDF, BMP, PNG, GIF, Large Document Format, PCX, PICT, PICT Resource, Portable Bit Map, and Wireless Bitmap.

Bitmap images contain pixels that are either black or white, exclusively. You must convert color images to grayscale before you can access Bitmap mode. When you choose Image⇨Mode⇨Bitmap, a dialog box appears, offering options for resolution and method. The various methods give several appearances, one of which is shown in Figure 2-6, so try each one to see which you prefer. When you select Custom Pattern, you can then select a pattern from the drop-down menu.

If you save a file in Bitmap mode as an EPS (see the section "EPS," later in this chapter), you can convert the white areas in the image to transparent areas. Transparency enables you to overlay the file on a background containing color or an image, and only the dark pixels show.

Corbis Digital Stock

Figure 2-6: Bitmap mode enables you to choose a method, such as Pattern Dither.

Multichannel

Uses: Multichannel mode is for special printing needs or as an intermediate mode when converting between color modes.

File formats: The only file formats available for multichannel images are native Photoshop, Photoshop 2.0, Photoshop DCS 2.0, Large Document Format, or Photoshop Raw formats.

The Multichannel mode, shown in Figure 2-7, comprises multiple gray-scale channels, each containing 256 levels of gray. Whenever you delete or mix channels, you end up with a multichannel image. You can also convert any image with more than one channel to this mode. In a multichannel image, each channel becomes a spot channel, with 256 levels of gray.

Corbis Digital Stock

Figure 2-7: Deleting or mixing channels creates a multichannel image.

For more on channels, see Book VI, Chapter 1.

You'll also find various bit depths under the Mode menu. For info on bit depth, see the Book VI, Chapter 1 sidebar, "A little bit about bit depth."

Converting to a Different Color Mode

Sometimes, your image starts out in one color mode and then you find you need to convert the image to another mode. Maybe you have to strip the color out of an image you're submitting to the local newspaper. Or maybe you have to convert your RGB image to CMYK to get it ready for an offset print job.

When you convert modes, you're permanently changing the color values in your image, so save a backup image, just in case.

The following sections offer pointers for the most common conversions you'll make. If you want to convert an image into an indexed color for the Web, your best bet is to use the Save for Web option, which I cover in Bonus Chapter 1 on this book's companion Web site (you can find out about the Web site in the Introduction).

Converting from RGB to CMYK

As I mention several times in this book, CMYK is the image mode necessary for high-end composite printing and offset printing. You first want to perform all your necessary image-editing tasks in RGB mode for the following reasons:

- The image size is smaller because RGB mode has only three channels.
- The RGB color space provides more device independence because it isn't reliant on inks.
- You have full accessibility to filters and image adjustments.
- RGB mode provides a large color gamut, so Photoshop preserves more colors after it makes image adjustments.

When you finish editing the image in RGB mode, you can convert the image from RGB to CMYK (you can perform any fine-tuning in CMYK mode, if necessary). If you're new to this procedure, you may be surprised at what can result. You may see a color shift (from slight to major) because the *color gamut* (range of colors) of the RGB model (16.7 million) is much larger than that of CMYK (approximately 55,000).

The extent of the shift depends on the colors in the RGB image and how many of them are out of gamut. Photoshop replaces RGB colors that are out of gamut with the closest match available within the CMYK gamut, often replacing the electric blues, fiery reds, and sunny yellows with duller, muddier CMYK equivalents. Unfortunately, you can't do anything to prevent this replacement. It's just the way of the world of color. However, if you can select colors (instead of acquiring them from a scan), be sure that you don't select any colors that are out of gamut to begin with. You can also *soft proof* colors (preview the effects of your CMYK conversion without actually converting) by choosing View➪Proof Setup➪Working CMYK. Check out Book II, Chapter 3 for details about selecting colors and soft proofing.

Converting to grayscale

You can convert a color image to grayscale in a multitude of ways, as shown in Figure 2-8. The following sections cover a few that you may want to try.

Quick-and-dirty method

Choose Image➪Mode➪Grayscale. Photoshop then asks you whether you want to discard color information. Click Discard. If your image contains multiple layers, Photoshop first asks whether you want to merge your layers. If you want to keep your layers, click the Don't Merge button.

Although this method does the job in stripping color from your image, you may be left with an image that's flat and lacking contrast. You can apply a Levels adjustment (choose Image➪Adjustments➪Levels) to boost the contrast, or you can try one of the other conversion methods.

Image⇨Mode⇨Grayscale Lab mode Best channel

Corbis Digital Stock

Figure 2-8: Photoshop gives you many ways to convert a color image to grayscale.

Be aware that you can no longer apply color to your image after you convert it. If you choose a color in the Color panel, the color appears gray in the foreground and background color icons. If you *want* to apply color to your grayscale image, convert it back to RGB or CMYK mode.

Lab Color mode method

This method most likely provides a better grayscale image than the quick-and-dirty method I describe in the preceding section. Make sure that you finish all your edits that require layers before you follow these steps:

1. **Choose Image⇨Mode⇨Lab Color.**

   As I mention in the earlier "Lab Color" section, converting to Lab Color mode converts the channels into a lightness channel and *a* and *b* channels containing ranges of color. If you have layers, you're prompted for whether you want to merge your layers. You can choose either option because, in Step 2, you have to flatten the image if you want to proceed with the operation. For details on working with layers, see Book V.

2. **Choose Window⇨Channels. Delete the *a* channel by dragging it to the trash can icon at the bottom of the panel.**

   Again, if you have layers, click OK to flatten your layers. If you select Cancel, you abort the operation.

   If you delete the *a* channel, the *b* channel then changes its name to Alpha 2.

3. **Delete the Alpha 2 channel.**

   That leaves you with the lightness channel, which is now named Alpha 1.

4. **Choose Image⇨Mode⇨Grayscale.**

   Your color image is now a grayscale one.

Best channel method

If you look at the individual channels in the image, one often stands out as being a very good grayscale image by itself. (If channels are a mystery to you, check out Book VI, Chapter 1 for details.) You may find that the Red channel provides a good grayscale image when the subject is people because humans have a lot of red in their skin. Or you may find that the Green channel looks good in a scenic shot. The Blue channel rarely yields a nice image, though. Most of the crud picked up in a digital image finds its way into the Blue channel.

In the Channels panel, select each channel and view its contents. Find the channel that looks the best, select it, and then choose Image⇨Mode⇨Grayscale. If you have layers, Photoshop asks whether you want to flatten your layers. Click OK. Photoshop then asks whether you want to discard all the other channels. Click OK.

You can also use the Channel Mixer to create custom grayscale images. For more on the Channel Mixer, see Book VI, Chapter 1.

Finally, you have yet one more way to convert to grayscale, via the Black & White feature in the Image⇨Adjustments submenu. For details, see Book VIII, Chapter 1.

Using the Conditional Mode Change command

Photoshop enables you to specify instances in which one mode changes into another so that you can utilize the conversion command in an action. Briefly, an *action* is a collection of recorded and saved commands that you can replay repeatedly. (For details on actions, see Book II, Chapter 5.) Sometimes, when you incorporate a mode conversion as part of an action, you get an error message because the file you're opening may not have the same mode you specified as the source mode in the action. For example, you may have specified CMYK as your source mode in the action, but the action opens a file in Grayscale mode. You get an error message because the Grayscale mode of the file doesn't match the CMYK source mode. The Conditional Mode Change command takes care of this problem. Follow these steps to add this command to your action:

1. **Start creating and recording your action.**

2. **Choose File⇨Automate⇨Conditional Mode Change.**

   The Conditional Mode Change dialog box, shown in Figure 2-9, appears.

3. **Select the mode(s) you want as valid for the source mode.**

   Other options include the All or None buttons to select (respectively) all modes or no modes.

4. **Select your desired target mode from the Mode pop-up menu.**

5. **Click OK.**

   If all goes well, Photoshop incorporates the Conditional Mode Change command as a step in your action.

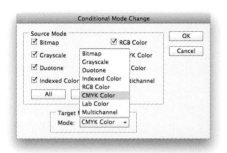

Figure 2-9: Include the Conditional Mode Change command in your action to ensure all images are processed, regardless of the image's mode.

Choosing the Right File Format

A critical component in saving a file is choosing the file format. The file format is the way the file's data is represented and saved. Photoshop generously offers numerous file formats to choose from. Some you'll use frequently, and others you'll probably never set eyes on. I provide quite a bit of detail on the formats you'll use most frequently in the following sections.

If a file format doesn't appear in the Open, the Save, or another dialog box, you may need to install the optional plug-in for that particular format.

TIFF

TIFF, *Tagged Image File Format,* is by far one of the best and most useful formats. One of the great qualities of TIFFs is that they are and have always been totally cross-platform. Additionally, almost every program on the planet can import TIFFs. Okay, so that's a slight exaggeration. Almost every word processing, presentation, page-layout, drawing, painting, and image-editing program can import TIFFs. This file format works especially well for printed or color-separated images.

Photoshop enables you to save layers and transparency (explained in detail in Book V) and use various methods of compression. You have the option of having Photoshop warn you that including layers increases your file size. To enable this option, select the Ask Before Saving Layered TIFF Files check box in the File Handling section of the Preferences dialog box (Edit➪Preferences➪File Handling on a Windows computer or Photoshop➪Preferences➪File Handling on the Mac). Photoshop saves the layers, along with a flattened version of the image. Be aware that some applications, such as PowerPoint, may display only the flattened version (in which case, transparency isn't preserved).

It should come as no surprise that the most commonly used format offers a variety of options — all of which are available in the TIFF Options dialog box (shown in Figure 2-10). The following sections give you everything you need to know about your options so that you can make an informed decision, based on your intended uses for the image.

Image Compression

Compression makes your file sizes smaller, but at a cost. If your files are unusually large, compression makes them save and open more slowly. TIFF files can be up to 4GB in size. Be careful, however, because older versions of Photoshop and other applications don't support file sizes larger than 2GB.

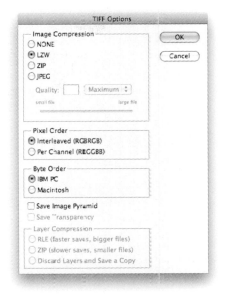

Figure 2-10: The TIFF Options dialog box offers a multitude of options for saving TIFFs.

Book II
Chapter 2

Choosing Color
Modes and File
Formats

Photoshop offers three methods of compression, besides the option of None, which (of course) leaves your image uncompressed:

✔ **LZW:** This method has been around for eons and is a *lossless* compression scheme, which means that data isn't deleted to make your file smaller. LZW is especially good for compressing images with large areas of a single color. Most programs that support TIFF also support LZW compression, so you can use this method without much hesitation.

✔ **Zip:** Zip compression is also a lossless method and is popular in the Windows arena. Like LZW, it works well with images that have large areas of a single color.

✔ **JPEG:** This method, although popular and very effective, is a lossy compression process. When compressing, JPEG deletes data to reduce the file size. (That's where the *loss* in *lossy* comes from.) JPEG compression is a cumulative compression scheme, which means that it recompresses every time it saves. Over time, this can degrade image quality.

I recommend that you stick with LZW compression, if possible. If you need to create a JPEG, however, minimize the degradation of lossy compression by leaving your image in either TIFF or native Photoshop file formats while editing. When you finish editing and need to compress the image save the file as a JPEG at a high-to-maximum-quality setting.

Pixel Order

Specify how Photoshop arranges the data in the color channels of the TIFF file. Interleaved stores the samples from individual channels interleaved with each other (for example, RGBRGBRGB). Per Channel stores them consecutively (for example, RRRGGGBBB). Previously, Photoshop wrote all TIFFs as Interleaved. However, Per Channel offers better compression and speed, and Adobe swears that all applications support the format.

Byte Order

Byte order is the way bits of data are arranged and stored. Specify whether you want to save the TIFF for a Mac or a PC. If you want to be able to use the image on both platforms, select IBM PC. Macs are much more forgiving when exchanging files.

Save Image Pyramid

This option enables you to save multiple resolutions of an image. The top of the pyramid is the lowest resolution, and the bottom of the pyramid is the highest resolution. If the program supports them, you can choose to open any of the resolutions. Photoshop can open the image only at the highest resolution within the file. I recommend leaving this option deselected.

Save Transparency

Select this option to preserve transparent areas when the TIFF is opened in other applications. Of course, those applications must also support transparency. If you open a TIFF with transparency in Photoshop, the transparent areas are *always* preserved, whether or not you select the option. This option is disabled if your image has no transparent areas.

Layer Compression

If your file has layers and you choose to save them, you have the choice of RLE (Run Length Encoding) or Zip compression. Because RLE compression is also lossless, you have the choice of faster saves (RLE) or smaller files (Zip). When you select the Zip option, Photoshop discards the layers, thereby flattening the image, and then saves a copy. Your original layered file remains intact. This option is disabled if your image has no layers.

JPEG

JPEG, the acronym for Joint Photographic Experts Group, is a file format that uses lossy compression (explained in the "Image Compression" section, earlier in this chapter). The JPEG file format offers 13 compression settings — the higher the quality, the less the compression.

JPEG compression is very effective and can squeeze your file size to practically nothing. Because the compression is lossy, I don't recommend this format for high-end printing. JPEG supports RGB, CMYK, and Grayscale image modes.

If you want to post your image on the Web, you have to save it as a JPEG, GIF, or PNG. JPEG works great with photographic images that have a wide range of colors. You're better off using the Save for Web feature when saving as a JPEG. You think 13 levels of compression is a lot? With Save for Web, you get around 100 levels of compression, along with some other options. Check out Bonus Chapter 1, on this book's companion Web site, for the low-down on all the JPEG options and settings. (The Introduction contains details about the book's companion Web site.)

JPEG 2000

JPEG 2000 is a cousin to standard JPEG; it provides a few more bells and whistles, including better compression rates and more quality settings. In addition to the standard lossy compression algorithms, JPEG 2000 (shown in Figure 2-11) also offers lossless compression and can support 16-bit images, alpha and spot channels, and transparency (8-bit images only). You can save in this format when using the following image modes: RGB, CMYK, Grayscale, and Lab Color.

One of the coolest features of this format is its support of a *Region of Interest (ROI)*. This feature enables you to choose a region of an image that you can then optimize to ensure the best quality. You save an alpha channel (explained in Book VI) to define that vital portion of the image where detail retention is critical. You can then compress the rest of the image more heavily and with lesser quality, resulting in a smaller file size. For more details on JPEG 2000, see Bonus Chapter 1 on this book's companion Web site (which I talk about in the Introduction).

Purestock

Figure 2-11: The JPEG 2000 format is a souped-up version of an old favorite.

Although praising the qualities of JPEG 2000 is fine, be warned that you currently need a plug-in to view these files on the Web, and support is still spotty. In the future, this format may become a standard for the Web and for digital cameras.

GIF

GIF is another file format used for Web graphics. GIFs support transparency — but on the down side, you must save GIFs in the Indexed Color mode, which offers only 256 colors (or even fewer). Although this format is great for making tiny files, it's not so great for continuous-tone images in which the number of colors displayed is critical. Therefore, the GIF format is usually reserved for illustrations (spot illustrations, buttons, logos, and so on) and type with large areas of flat colors and sharp details. For the whole story on GIFs, head to this book's companion Web site (discussed in the Introduction) and check out Bonus Chapter 1.

PNG is the last major file format used for Web images. PNGs support transparency and 24-bit color. For more info, see Bonus Chapter 1 (located at this book's companion Web site).

EPS

EPS is short for *Encapsulated PostScript.* PostScript is a page-description language developed by Adobe and used by many printers. The EPS format can contain both vector and raster graphics. (For details on vector and raster graphics, see Book II, Chapter 1.) The EPS format tends to create larger file sizes and doesn't have a built-in compression scheme as do JPEGs or TIFFs. EPS is a recommended file format for creating color separations for high-end, four-color print jobs. This is also the file format to use for images with clipping paths (explained in Book III) and one of the few formats that supports Duotone mode. In addition to duotones, EPS supports Lab Color, CMYK, RGB, Indexed Color, Grayscale, and Bitmap modes. Additionally, you use this format when creating a DCS (Desktop Color Separations) file. It doesn't support alpha channels. Finally, EPS is the format of choice for importing to and from drawing programs, such as Illustrator and CorelDRAW.

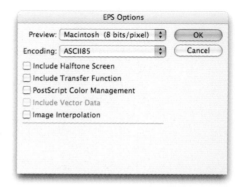

Figure 2-12: When saving an EPS, specify your options.

Here are the options when saving in the EPS format, as shown in Figure 2-12:

- ✓ **Preview:** If you import your EPS into another application, this option provides a low-resolution image for you to view. I recommend choosing 8-bit TIFF, which works on both PC and Mac.

- ✓ **Encoding:** This option specifies the way an image is sent to the PostScript printer. Choose Binary if you can; it produces smaller files and keeps all original data. If you're having printing problems, choose ASCII. JPEG compresses the file, but discards data and may cause color-separation problems. Avoid it, if possible.

- ✓ **Include Halftone Screen** and **Include Transfer Function:** Use these options for offset print jobs. Let your friendly service bureau or commercial printing expert specify these options.

- ✓ **Transparent Whites:** If your image is in Bitmap color mode, this option enables white areas to appear transparent.

- ✓ **PostScript Color Management:** This option converts the file's color data to the printer's color space. I don't recommend selecting this option if you're importing your image into a document that's color managed. (For more on color management, see Book II, Chapter 3.)

- ✓ **Include Vector Data:** When selected, this option preserves any vector graphics, such as type and shapes. However, that data is preserved only when you import the file into another program. If you reopen the EPS in Photoshop, your vector data is rasterized.

- ✓ **Image Interpolation:** This option *anti-aliases* low-resolution images — softens their edges when they're printed.

PDF: The universal donor

PDF is the acronym for *Portable Document Format,* which is the native format of Adobe Acrobat. This format, developed by Adobe, can contain editable text, vector, and raster data. PDF files are often used for electronic documentation that will be downloaded from the Web.

PDFs are extremely useful in the imaging world. Anyone with a computer running Windows, Mac OS, or Unix can read a PDF. All you need to view a PDF file is Adobe Acrobat Reader, which is available as a free download from the Adobe Web site. If you save your image as a PDF and e-mail it to (or post it on the Web as a downloadable file for) a colleague, manager, client, or friend, that person can see your image — colors, fonts, and all — exactly the way you see it. The other nice thing about PDFs is that they have an automatic compression process that makes the files small and manageable for mail transfer or loading on the Web.

When you save a file as a Photoshop PDF, you have all the same save options of the native Photoshop format. PDF supports layers, alpha channels, spot colors, and annotations, so select these options if you have any. It also supports the same image modes as the native Photoshop format. Additionally, you can also save 16-bit images as PDFs. After choosing your initial options, you get an alert dialog box that informs you that the settings you just chose may be overridden by the settings you choose next.

The Save Adobe PDF dialog box offers a multitude of options. At the top of the dialog box are settings for presets, standards, and compatibility, as shown in Figure 2-13:

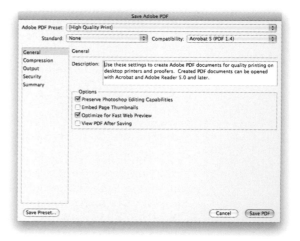

Figure 2-13: The Save Adobe PDF dialog box offers a smorgasbord of options.

✔ **Adobe PDF Preset:** Select a preset setting from the pop-up menu. Photoshop then kindly gives you a description of that setting, including what versions of Acrobat can open that PDF. The default setting of High Quality Print creates PDF files suitable for good-quality printing on desktop printers. Stick with the default as an overall setting — unless you want to create a PDF specifically to view onscreen or e-mail for approval purposes, in which case, select Smallest File Size.

PDF/X is an ISO (International Organization for Standardization) standard for graphic content exchange designed for the prepress purpose workflow. Ask your service provider or offset print house if it prefers one of the PDF/X formats, rather than the generic PDF, for final file output. For specifics on the criteria of each PDF/X format, check the Acrobat Help file.

✔ **Standard:** Accept the default associated with your chosen preset or choose a flavor of PDF/X from the pop-up menu.

✔ **Compatibility:** Specify the version of Acrobat you want your file to be compatible with. Note, however, that Acrobat 4 and 5 don't support layers. When you change either the Standard or Compatibility options, (Modified) is added to your preset name.

In addition to the options along the top, described in the preceding list, this massive, multi-tiered dialog box offers the following categories in which you can refine your choices, if you want:

- ✔ **General:** The General category of settings contains the PDF presets, editing options, Acrobat version compatibility choices, and viewing options.

- ✔ **Compression:** The PDF format, by nature, includes excellent compression, but you can compress and downsample your image even further to reduce (or maybe to simply adjust) the size of the PDF file. You can find details about downsampling in Book II, Chapter 1.

  If optimum print quality is a concern, you're better off not downsampling your image at all.

- ✔ **Output:** The Output area covers how to handle the color data in your file when you export to PDF. I recommend keeping the default settings of your presets, unless you're sure of what you're doing. An understanding of color management, explained in Book II, Chapter 3, helps you interpret the options in this area.

- ✔ **Security:** If you want to apply some restrictions on who can open your PDF, including what they can then do with it, you've come to the right spot. You can assign a password for opening the file in either Acrobat or Photoshop (or Preview on a Mac), but if you forget the password, there's no way to extract it from your file. Make sure you write it down somewhere! You can also choose whether you want your user to be able to print or change the document.

- ✔ **Summary:** This option gives you a rundown of all your specified options and alerts you to anything it finds not so kosher.

Acrobat 4 users can't open PDFs that have 128-bit RC4 encryption.

You can also combine multiple images into a single, multi-paged PDF document or slide show. This is a great way to e-mail images to coworkers, family, and friends. The best way to accomplish this is to do it within Adobe Bridge, where you have a multitude of options to customize your PDF. Click the PDF button on the Output tab in the top-right corner in Bridge and specify your options.

Photoshop

Of course, I can't forget the native Photoshop format (.psd). This format offers several benefits. First, along with TIFF and PDF, Photoshop enables you to save layers in your image. The other formats flatten the layers into a single background. This format works well if you're going to spend a considerable length of time working on your image. The Photoshop format also supports all image modes, is the fastest format for opening and saving, and offers all the various save options.

Like TIFF, the Photoshop format uses a lossless compression process, although it's invisible to you. If you need to open a file in an older version of Photoshop, be sure to save it as a native Photoshop file. Finally, almost all drawing and layout programs now support the importing of Photoshop files.

QuickTime users should be aware that it provides a PSD translator that allows you to open PSD files in any application, such as Microsoft Word, that has the QuickTime translators enabled.

Photoshop Raw

This format is designed to transfer images among applications and platforms. The Photoshop Raw format can be useful if you want to transfer an image to or from a mainframe computer or other device that doesn't support the standard graphic formats. Don't confuse it with the Camera Raw format I describe in the following section. The Photoshop Raw format supports CMYK, RGB, Lab Color, Grayscale, and Multichannel images. The format allows for any pixel or file size, but it doesn't support layers.

You may never have to save a file in the Photoshop Raw format. If you do, you can likely accept the defaults for File Type, Creator, and Header. Save Channels In and Byte Order are similar to Pixel Order and Byte Order, discussed earlier in this chapter.

Camera Raw

The Camera Raw file format is the format used by many digital cameras to capture and save image data and the image's metadata, as shown in Figure 2-14. This format captures everything about an image and is the closest possible thing to a digital negative. Each camera has its own proprietary raw image format. Fortunately, Photoshop can support most camera models, especially higher-end cameras. If, by chance, your new camera isn't supported, check www.adobe.com periodically for updates.

Camera Raw files utilize a lossless scheme to capture and save image data, similar to TIFFs (explained in the "TIFF" section, earlier in this chapter). This approach is advantageous because no data is lost through compression as it is with the JPEG format. Camera Raw files also have the advantage of being smaller than uncompressed TIFFs. Of all the digital camera file formats, only Camera Raw images contain the actual, unadulterated data captured by the digital camera's sensor without any camera adjustments, filters, and other processing. Many die-hard photographers consider this file format to be the pure digital "negative," so to speak. They prefer to analyze, manipulate, and adjust the image data themselves, instead of leaving those decisions to the mercy of the camera. This file format also prevents the loss of any image data that can sometimes occur when a file is converted from its native format to a more commonly used format, such as TIFF or PSD. But Camera Raw can save your files as DNG (Digital Negative), TIFF, PSD, or JPEG formats, if you desire.

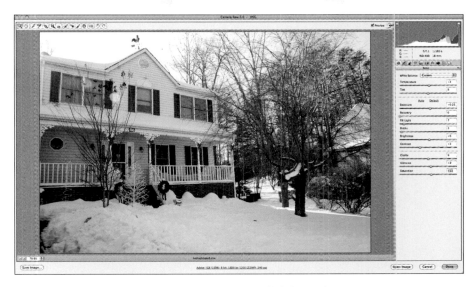

Figure 2-14: The Camera Raw format is as close to a digital negative as you can get.

Version CS5 introduces Camera Raw 6.0 and incorporates newer processing (version 2.0) that employs better sharpening and noise reduction. Here's just a brief sampling of some of the capabilities of Camera Raw:

- Select multiple Camera Raw files, as well as JPEGs and TIFFs, in Adobe Bridge and then edit the settings in one fell swoop.

- Make adjustments in white balance, exposure, shadows, contrast, saturation, sharpness, and so on. Your settings are applied to all selected files.

- Save your files in Adobe Bridge or import them into Photoshop for further enhancements.

- Rate your files inside Camera Raw.

- Crop, rotate, straighten, and sharpen your images.

- Correct lens distortion, reduce noise, color fringe, spots, red-eye, and other flaws.

- The Fill Light feature is similar to the Shadow function in Photoshop's Shadow/Highlight feature. Move the slider (0 to 100) to lighten dark areas while leaving light areas undisturbed.

- Camera Raw files are processed in their own thread, which means you can do double duty — editing some files while saving others simultaneously.

✔ Camera Raw also offers what's referred to as *localized corrections* — using an Adjustment Brush, you can "paint" areas by using varying brush sizes to correct very specific portions of your image. Similarly, you can use the Graduated Filter to apply more or less adjustment to your image in a gradual, gradient-like manner. This is Camera Raw's digital answer to using a Neutral Density analog filter when capturing a shot. The Graduated Filter can come in handy, especially when adjusting landscape shots.

Adobe has added additional camera support in version CS5 — but if, by chance, the Camera Raw feature still doesn't support your particular camera model, contact Adobe to see whether it will be supporting your model in the near future. If your camera doesn't capture images in the Camera Raw format at all, don't worry. You're fine with TIFF or JPEG, especially because you can edit these two formats in the Camera Raw dialog box. However, if your camera is capable of saving images in Camera Raw format, check out its capabilities. Visit `www.adobe.com/products/photoshop/cameraraw.html` for detailed information showing all you need to know about working with Camera Raw.

BMP

BMP (Bitmap) is a standard Windows file format commonly used for saving images that you want to make part of your computer's resources, such as the wallpaper that you see on your Windows desktop. BMP is also a format used by computer programmers. BMP supports RGB, Indexed Color, Grayscale, and Bitmap image modes.

Here are your options when saving a BMP file:

✔ **File Format:** Choose between Windows and OS/2.

✔ **Depth:** Although you can select a bit depth, I recommend leaving the default setting Photoshop selects for you.

✔ **Compress (RLE):** The compression scheme used is lossless, which is great, but don't select this option if you're creating wallpaper. Windows won't recognize it.

✔ **Flip Row Order:** This option enables Windows to recognize the file by reading the first row of pixels first and the last row last. It's for programmers who are coding for Windows applications. Leave it deselected unless you're one of them.

Don't worry about the Advanced Modes option. It's even more eggheady than the other options and strictly programming territory.

Large Document Format (PSB)

Work with humongous files? Then you'll be pleased to know that the Large Document Format supports files of any size. Besides the Photoshop Raw and TIFF file formats, the Large Document Format is the only other format that can save files larger than 2GB. Even better, the coveted features, such as layers, layer effects, and filters, are all supported by this format. If you want to work with large files, just make sure you have the Maximize PSD and PSB File Compatibility option set to Always in the File Handling pane of your Preferences.

Large Document Format files can be opened in Photoshop CS or later, *only* (and Photoshop Elements 7 and 8 if you happen to also own those programs). So, make sure any recipients of your files have the latest and greatest version of Photoshop. This limitation isn't confined to older versions of Photoshop, either. Be forewarned that many other applications, and even some operating systems, fall to their knees when presented with a file size larger than 2GB.

Other file formats

Although you may never need to use any of these formats, just to satisfy any curiosities, here's a quick description of each.

- ✓ **Cineon:** A Kodak film format containing 10-bits per channel.

- ✓ **Dicom (Digital Imaging and Communications in Medicine):** Used for transfer and storage of medical images (PS Extended only)

- ✓ **Digital Negative (DNG):** Archival format for Camera Raw images containing raw image data as well as metadata.

- ✓ **FXG:** A vector graphics XML file format used to describe graphic files and intended for new Flash-authoring applications.

- ✓ **IFF:** Includes Maya IFF and Amiga IFF, supporting image, sound and video files.

- ✓ **PCX:** An old PC vector drawing format.

- ✓ **PICT:** Stands for Macintosh Picture and is Apple's original format for Mac graphics. Not used much since 2001, except for occasional old slides and screen presentations.

- ✓ **Photoshop DCS 1.0 and 2.0:** Version of the EPS format that enables you to save desktop color separations (DCS).

- ✓ **Pixar:** High-end format used for 3-D images and animation.

- ✓ **Portable Bit Map:** Supports monochrome (1-bit) images used for exchanging files between various platforms.

- ✓ **Scitex:** Used for high-end imaging on a Scitex system.

- ✓ **Targa:** An old PC video format.

- ✓ **WBMP:** Supports 1-bit images used for mobile devices.

Chapter 3: Using and Managing Color

In This Chapter

✔ **Choosing foreground and background colors**

✔ **Defining color**

✔ **Establishing color management settings**

✔ **Getting consistent color among multiple applications**

✔ **Soft proofing colors**

Color in Photoshop takes on two personalities. On one hand, choosing colors and applying them is easy, fun, and stress-free. On the other hand, managing color — that is, making what you see onscreen match what comes out on paper (or in your browser) — can be difficult and frustrating.

Unfortunately, you have to be well-versed in both picking great colors and managing colors for print. What's the use of creating the next *Mona Lisa* in Photoshop only to find that it looks like a fifth-generation color Xerox copy? In this chapter, I start by showing you how to define and apply color; then, I ease you into the world of color management.

If you haven't already read the section on color theory in Book II, Chapter 2, you might want to give it a gander before you dive into this chapter. Knowing a little color theory may make this chapter a little more understandable.

Dealing with Foreground and Background Colors

Photoshop has two categories of color — a foreground color and a background color. You apply the *foreground color* when you use the type tools, the painting tools, or the shape tools. The foreground color is also the beginning color of a default gradient applied by the Gradient tool. The *background color* is the color you apply with the Eraser tool (assuming you don't have layers) and is the ending color of the default gradient. When you increase the size of your canvas, you fill the additional canvas with the background color (also assuming you don't have layers). You can find the swatches that represent the two color categories in the lower part of the Tools panel, as shown in Figure 3-1.

The default color for the foreground is black; the background is white. Click the small icon labeled in Figure 3-1 or simply press the D key to return the colors to the defaults. To switch the foreground and background colors, click the curved arrow in the Tools panel or press the X key.

Here are a few tips to help you get a handle on using tools with foreground and background colors:

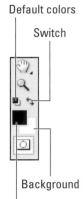

Default colors

Switch

Background

Foreground

Figure 3-1: Photoshop color swatches are at the bottom of the Tools panel.

✒ **Blend the foreground and background by using the Gradient tool.** When you drag with the Gradient tool across the canvas and the gradient is set to the default, you get a blending of the foreground and background colors.

✒ **Fill selected areas with the foreground color.** Just click your canvas with the Paint Bucket tool to select areas based on a Tolerance setting and fill those areas with the foreground color.

✒ **Apply the background color by erasing.** If you're working on a background, rather than a layer, you can use the Eraser tool to apply the background color. Some people prefer to say you're erasing to the background or canvas color.

If you use the Eraser tool on a layer, you erase to transparency. See Book V for the scoop on layers.

✒ **Add more background to your canvas and fill it with the background color.** When you enlarge your canvas size, Photoshop, by default, automatically fills the added canvas with the background color.

If you enlarge a layer, the extra canvas is transparent. See Book II, Chapter 1 if the word *canvas* seems foreign to you.

Defining Color

Like with nearly everything else in Photoshop, you can select color in several ways. In the following sections, I explain each of these color-definition options:

✒ Click a color in the Color Picker.

✒ Move the sliders in the Color panel.

✒ Sample color from your image (or elsewhere) with the Eyedropper tool.

✒ Grab a color from the Swatches panel.

Poking around Color Picker

When you click either the Foreground or Background color swatch in the Tools panel, you're transported magically to the Color Picker. This huge dialog box, shown in Figure 3-2, allows you to select a color from the color spectrum (called a *color slider*) or define your color numerically.

Color field   Color slider Color values

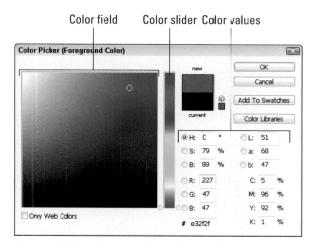

Figure 3-2: Using the Color Picker is one of the many ways to specify color in Photoshop.

Choosing a color visually is fine for Web or multimedia work, but not recommended for print work. Among other reasons, your monitor uses an RGB (red, green, and blue) color model, whereas printers use a CMYK (cyan, magenta, yellow, and black) model. For more on this and other color-management issues, see "Color Management Essentials," later in this chapter. For the basics of color theory, see Book II, Chapter 2.

To select a color visually, follow these steps:

1. **Click either the Foreground or Background color swatch in the Tools panel.**

   The Color Picker dialog box appears. (Refer to Figure 3-2.)

2. **Drag the color slider to get in the ballpark of the color you want.**

3. **To fine-tune your choice, click in the large square on the left.**

   This square area is called a *color field*. The circular icon targets your selected shade. The dialog box displays your new chosen color, as well as the current, or original, foreground or background color.

   The numeric values also change accordingly to represent the exact shade you've chosen.

Alternatively, if you know the numeric values of the color you want to use, you can plug in the values in the text boxes on the right side of the Color Picker. For example, RGB values are based on brightness levels, from 0 to 255, with 0 being black and 255 being the pure color or white. CMYK values are based on percentages (0 to 100) of the four process colors — cyan, magenta, yellow, and black. You can enter the hexadecimal formula (six digit alpha numeric color code) for Web colors.

4. **When you're satisfied with the color, click OK. Note that you can add your new color to your Swatches panel, if desired. Click the Add to Swatches button. Name your new swatch and click OK.**

5. **Click OK to exit the Color Picker.**

The new HUD (Heads Up Display) Color Picker is a nifty onscreen tool that lets you quickly select colors. This can come in handy when you want to choose colors based on your image and want to have your Color Picker adjacent to those colors. To choose a color from the HUD Color Picker, select any painting tool. Then press Shift+Alt+right-click (Control+Option+⌘ on the Mac) and click in your image window to display the HUD Color Picker. Drag to select your desired hue and shade (you can release the keys while you drag). You'll see the appearance of a circle target to help pinpoint your desired color, as shown in Figure 3-3.

Figure 3-3: Using the new HUD Color Picker enables you to quickly choose colors in your image window.

You can do pretty much the same thing in the Color panel that you can do with the Color Picker. I prefer the Color panel, so I go into more detail about that approach in the following section.

Mixing with the Color panel

To open the Color panel, shown in Figure 3-4, choose Window➪Color. A couple of swatches in this panel may look vaguely familiar. That's because they represent the foreground and back- ground colors — just like the swatches in the Tools panel. And (also like the Tools panel swatches) the infamous Color Picker appears if you click the swatches in the Color panel. But forget the Color Picker; you don't need to go there. Everything you need is right here in this tiny panel.

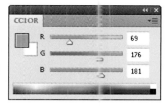

Figure 3-4: The Color panel is a compact but efficient way to select colors.

Before you use the Color panel to define your colors, you should know which color model you want to use. Here's a short description of each:

- ✔ **Grayscale:** For working strictly in black, white, and shades of gray. You get one slider, K, which represents black. Move the slider to get shades of gray, including complete white and complete black.

- ✔ **RGB (Red-Green-Blue):** For anything that's viewed onscreen — from multimedia and slide presentations to content for the Web. You can use it for printing on most desktop inkjet printers.

- ✔ **CMYK (Cyan-Magenta-Yellow-Black):** Used in printing.

- ✔ **Web Color:** Used strictly for the Web. If you select this model, make sure that you also select Make Ramp Web Safe from the Color panel options menu. The Ramp is the color spectrum bar at the bottom of the Color panel.

- ✔ **HSB (Hue-Saturation-Brightness):** Based on percentages of saturation and brightness, and an angle (0 to 360 degrees), which corresponds to a loca- tion on the color wheel. (I don't cover this model in Book II, Chapter 2.)

- ✔ **Lab (Lightness, a, b):** Contains three channels: one for lightness, one (a) that contains colors from green to red, and one (b) that contains colors from blue to yellow. Lab is more complex to understand and work with than the other models — and it's the color model of choice for high-end color experts. (By the way, Lab is also Photoshop's native color mode.)

When you want to define a color according to a color model, I think the Color panel is the way to go. Follow these quick-and-easy steps to define a color by using the Color panel:

1. **Open the Color panel by choosing Window⇨Color.**

2. **Make sure the color swatch you want to define, Foreground or Background, is selected on the left side of the Color panel.**

   An outline appears around the selected swatch.

3. **Select your desired color model from the Color panel pop-up menu by clicking the down-pointing arrow in the upper-right corner.**

   You'll probably be using RGB, CMYK, or Web Color the majority of the time.

   If you want to use the RGB color model but also want to ensure that any color you choose is printable, select CMYK Spectrum from the Color panel options menu. By default, all the colors in the ramp are printable. Just be sure to choose your colors by clicking in the ramp.

4. **In the Color panel, move the sliders for each component of the color model or enter numeric values.**

   You can also select a color by clicking inside the color ramp at the bottom of the Color panel. Click the small swatches at the far-right end of the color ramp to change your color to black or white.

5. **To make sure your desired color works with the color mode you've selected, keep an eye open for an alert icon.**

   Here are a few more tips to keep in mind when working with the Color panel:

   • If you're working in RGB or CMYK, this alert icon is known as the *gamut alarm* and looks like the triangular warning. Its appearance is Photoshop's way of saying, "Hey, you! That color you mixed won't print the way you think it will because it's out of gamut." Remember, *gamut* is the range of colors a device can either display or print.

   • Because the RGB color model has a much wider gamut than the CMYK color model, some of the colors can be viewed only onscreen and not reproduced on paper.

   • If a color is out of gamut, Photoshop offers you a substitution. Inside a little square to the right of the gamut alarm icon, the closest printable color to the one you chose appears.

   • If you're working in Web Colors, be on the lookout for a small cube icon. Click either the icon or the square to use the closest Web-safe color. The cube indicates that the color you mixed isn't a Web-safe color. Clicking the cube tells Photoshop that you want to use its Web-safe alternative, instead. A Web-safe color ensures that the color won't *dither* (mix available colors to simulate a missing color) when displayed in the browser.

6. **Click either the icon or the square if you want to use the closest printable color, rather than your original choice.**

Grabbing color from the Swatches panel

Another way to define a foreground or background color is by clicking a color in the Swatches panel, shown in Figure 3-5. Choose Window➪Swatches to bring up the panel.

You can have any tool active when you use the Swatches panel to define a color because as soon as you move the tool over the Swatches panel, it temporarily changes to an Eyedropper icon that samples the color.

Figure 3-5: The Swatches panel allows you to grab and store colors.

Besides being a way to select your foreground and background colors, the Swatches panel acts like a traditional artist's paint palette in digital form by letting you store as many colors as you want in the panel for later use.

To change the background color, either select the background swatch icon in the Color panel or simply Ctrl-click (⌘-click on the Mac) a swatch in the Swatches panel.

Here are some of the things you can do with the Swatches panel:

- ✓ **Customize the Swatches panel's display.** You can choose how to display the Swatches panel by selecting Small or Large Thumbnail (swatch thumbnails) or Small or Large List (swatch thumbnails along with a name) from the Swatches panel pop-up menu. (Click the down-pointing triangle in the upper-right portion of the panel to open the menu.)

- ✓ **Use preset colors.** To load a particular preset swatch library, select it from the list on the Swatches panel pop-up menu. Click Append to add the library to the existing swatches or OK to replace the existing swatches. You can find libraries specific for Web graphics and for implementing spot colors, such as those created by Pantone, Toyo, and Focoltone.

    You can also select Load Swatches from the Swatches panel pop-up menu. In the Load dialog box, navigate to the Color Swatches folder by following this path: Adobe\Adobe Photoshop CS5\Presets\Color Swatches; then, select your desired library.

    You can also work with swatches by using the Preset Manager. (For more on the Preset Manager, see Book I, Chapter 5.)

- ✓ **Customize your own Swatches panel.** To add a color to the Swatches panel, do one of the following:

    - Click the New Swatch icon at the bottom of the Swatches panel.

    - Select New Swatch from the Swatches panel pop-up menu. Name your swatch and click OK.

Book II
Chapter 3

Using and Managing Color

- Click an empty spot in the Swatches panel. (Your cursor changes to a paint bucket icon.) Name your swatch and click OK. Or Alt-click (Option-click on the Mac) on an empty spot to add the color and bypass the Name dialog box. Note that the color that's added depends on whether your foreground or background swatch is selected.

✔ **Delete swatches that you don't want anymore.** To delete a swatch, drag it to the trash can icon at the bottom of the Swatches panel.

✔ **Create your own library of swatches.** To save a set of swatches as a library, select Save Swatches from the Swatches panel pop-up menu. Name your swatch library (leave the file extension as `.aco`) in the Save dialog box. Click Save.

✔ **Save swatches to share with other Adobe Creative Suite applications.** Select Save Swatches for Exchange from the Swatches panel pop-up menu, and your color panel is saved in a format (with an `.ase` extension) that you can then load into sister applications, such as Illustrator and InDesign.

I recommend saving libraries in a subfolder of the Presets folder. Follow this path: `Adobe\Adobe Photoshop\Presets\Color Swatches`; then, create your own folder, name the file, and click Save.

✔ **Restore your default swatch libraries.** To return to the default library of swatches, select Reset Swatches from the Swatches panel pop-up menu. You can choose to either replace or append to the current library.

Lifting and sampling color

Photoshop lets you change foreground or background colors by lifting them from the image with the Eyedropper tool. Using the Eyedropper tool comes in handy when you want to sample an existing color in an image for use in another element. For example, if I want my text to be the same color as the flower in my image, I click a petal with my Eyedropper tool, which then lifts (samples) the color and makes it my new foreground color. I then create my type, which uses that foreground color. *Voilà* — color coordination at its finest.

Here are some handy tips for using the Eyedropper tool to suck up color from one place and use it elsewhere in your image:

✔ **Select any color you want from any image that's open.** If you have multiple images open, you can click inside an image that you're not working on. In fact, if that doesn't knock your socks off, you can lift any color you see onscreen, even from a file in another application, such as Illustrator, or from your desktop. Just click and drag your Eyedropper from the image window onto the color you want to sample. Be sure that you can see both application windows simultaneously.

✔ **Select your sampling area.** You have only two options (found on the Options bar) to worry about when using the Eyedropper tool. You can select the color of just the single pixel you click (Point Sample). Or Photoshop averages the colors of the pixels in a 3-x-3-, 5-x-5-, 11-x-11-,

31-x-31-, 51-x-51-, or 101-x-101-pixel radius. You can also choose to sample from just your currently active layer or all your layers.

✓ **Make colors Web ready with a right-click of your mouse button.** For you Webbies out there, if you right-click (Control-click on the Mac) your image to bring up the context menu, you have one more option — Copy Color as HTML. This option converts the sampled color to a hexadecimal color code and copies the code to the Clipboard so that you can paste the code into an HTML file.

✓ **Toggle between the Eyedropper and other tools.** For your productive painting pleasure, when you're using the Brush, Pencil, Color Replacement, Gradient, Paint Bucket, or Shape tool, holding down Alt (Option on the Mac) allows you to temporarily access the Eyedropper tool. Release the key to return to your original tool.

✓ **Toggle between the background and the foreground.** If the foreground color swatch is active, Alt-click (Option-click on the Mac) with the Eyedropper tool to lift a new background color. If the background color swatch is active, Alt-clicking (Option-clicking on the Mac) lifts a new foreground color.

To use the Eyedropper tool, you first need to decide whether you want to change the foreground or background color. Then, follow these steps:

1. **Select the foreground (or the background) in the Tools panel or the Color panel.**

2. **Select the Eyedropper tool in the Tools panel (or press the I key).**

   Fortunately, the Eyedropper looks exactly like a real eyedropper.

3. **Click the color in your image that you want to use.**

   That color becomes your new foreground (or background) color.

Using the Color Sampler tool to measure color

The Eyedropper's cousin, the Color Sampler tool, looks like an eyedropper with a small target next to the icon. It also shares the Eyedropper's flyout menu.

The "Sampler" moniker is kind of misleading because this tool only *measures* the colors you click. In addition to merely obtaining the numeric value of a color, the Color Sampler tool can monitor changes to your image after you apply color-correction techniques and filters.

Follow these steps to use the Color Sampler tool:

1. **Select the Color Sampler tool in the Tools panel and then click the color you want to measure.**

   A target icon, labeled #1, appears on your image.

Photoshop opens the Info panel automatically and shows you the numeric values for that color (as shown in Figure 3-6).

2. **Repeat Step 1 up to three more times for a total of four targeted colors.**

   Target icons appear for your second, third, and fourth samples.

3. **With the Color Sampler tool, drag the targets to sample new areas of your image, if you want. Delete a target by Alt-clicking (Option-clicking on the Mac) it.**

   You can actually measure a fifth color by just moving the Color Sampler cursor around the image. The numeric value appears in the upper portion of the Info panel.

Color target icons

Figure 3-6: The Color Sampler tool measures up to five colors in your image.

Finding and Sharing Color Themes with Kuler

Kuler is an online community that provides color themes for you to browse, download, create, edit, and upload for sharing with others. Use these themes when creating graphic print projects or Web sites. All you need to participate is an Internet connection and an Adobe ID. (See www.adobe.com to sign up if you don't have one already.)

Here are basics of how to use Kuler:

1. **Choose Window⇨Extensions⇨Kuler.**

2. **Click the Browse button. In the Browse panel, enter your desired tag word in the Search field (magnifying glass icon) and press Enter (Return on the Mac).**

   For example, I entered the word *organic,* as shown in Figure 3-7. All the themes tagged with the word *organic* then appear in the list of themes. You can also search by criteria such as Highest Rated or Most Popular from the Search Results drop-down list. Click the up- and down-pointing arrow buttons at the bottom of the panel to view previous and next sets of themes. Click the double curved arrow to refresh the themes from the Kuler community.

3. **Choose a theme from the list, click the right-pointing arrow, and choose one of the following submenu items:**

   - *Edit the Theme:* Choosing this option takes you to the Create panel, as shown in Figure 3-8. In the color wheel, select your desired color by clicking on the color's associated circle icon. To edit the color, move the circle icon within the wheel or drag your color sliders (or enter a hexadecimal formula) at the bottom of the panel. You also have icons above the color sliders to add your foreground or background color as the base color (the color around which your theme is based) and to add and delete colors from the theme. Finally, to change your base color, select a color in your theme and click the button labeled Affect the Other Colors in the Theme Based on a Harmony. Hover your mouse over the buttons, and a tooltip indicates which button is which.

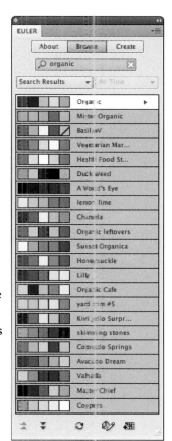

**Book II
Chapter 3**

**Using and
Managing Color**

Figure 3-7: Search for color themes in Kuler.

You can also click the Color Wheel/Pencil icon at the bottom of the panel to edit the theme.

- *Add to Swatches Panel:* This option adds the colors in the theme to your Swatches panel. (Choose Window⇨Swatches.)

  You can also click the Swatches icon at the bottom of the panel to add to the Swatches panel.

- *View Online in Kuler:* Selecting this option launches your browser and opens your theme in the Kuler community Web site.

4. **Click the Save Theme button at the bottom of the panel.**

   You can also click the Swatches icon at the bottom of the panel to add the theme to your Swatches panel. Finally, click the up arrow icon in the bottom right of the Create panel to upload the theme to the Kuler community Web site.

To create a new theme, click the Create panel and basically follow the same steps as editing the theme, described in Step 3.

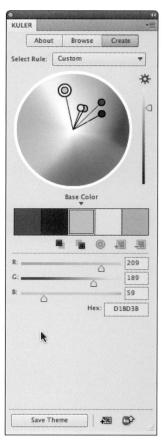

Figure 3-8: Edit your color theme using the color wheel.

Color Management Essentials

Grab some Tylenol. You're about to delve into the rather confusing and sometimes cantankerous world (or as some users would call it — underworld) of color management. It's by far the biggest headache of every graphics professional's day-to-day experience. And I'm sure quite a few home users also scratch their heads wondering why their digital photos looked so great onscreen and turned into a muddy mess on paper.

Reproducing color isn't an exact science. In fact, sometimes you'd think it takes an act of voodoo magic to get the output you want. Don't throw up your hands and live with whatever output comes out the other end; if you can't change the color, you can at least change your attitude toward color. Getting a handle on color management requires four things — some knowledge, some patience, a significant amount of time to experiment and test, and (most importantly) acceptance. Acceptance of the unfortunate fact that you don't live in a WYSIWYG world: What you get in one medium is sometimes merely an approximation of what you see in another.

Why? Well, I start with the basic gripe of many users while they look disapprovingly at their printout — "But it didn't look like that on the screen!" As detailed in Book II, Chapter 2, you can work with two major color models — RGB (Red-Green-Blue) and CMYK (Cyan-Magenta-Yellow-Black). The RGB color model (16.7 million colors), which all monitors use, has a significantly wider range of color (called a *gamut* in computer lingo) than the CMYK color model (approximately 55,000 colors) that printers use. So, many of the colors you see onscreen fall outside the CMYK gamut — and therefore can't be reproduced on paper. And, in some cases, some CMYK colors fall outside the RGB gamut. Programs such as Photoshop do their best by providing colors that are the closest match. But those out-of-gamut bright and vibrant colors are matched with duller, darker versions, at best.

And, if that difference alone isn't enough to complicate matters, hardware devices that share the same color model can possess different gamuts within that color model. For example, the RGB color space of a monitor can differ from the RGB color space of a scanner. Not only that, but you can also have different color spaces within the same type of device. A 15-inch generic monitor doesn't display color equal to a 24-inch Samsung or Apple monitor. Likewise, an Epson printer may not share the same color space as a Hewlett-Packard or Canon printer. So, when you take into account the differences that can occur among platforms, monitors, printers, browsers, scanners, applications, paper and other substrates, or any of the almost infinite number of possible permutations, it makes you want to return to the days of quill and parchment. Techies often call this mind-numbingly large number of possible inconsistencies *device-dependent color.* In other words, the color is dependent upon the hardware device. And device-dependent color varies. That's just the cold, harsh reality, and nothing's changing that.

But Adobe, being the kind and benevolent software mega-giant that it is, has developed a color-management system designed to be *device-independent.* The 5-cent explanation of this system is that you first identify your working color spaces. Photoshop then *tags* your files with that color space by embedding a color profile (also known as an ICC profile) with your files. The program analyzes any color space in which you either view or output a file and makes adjustments on the fly so that the color is viewed and printed reasonably accurately and consistently, in theory, independent of the device. Photoshop also reads the embedded color profile (or lack thereof) of any file you open and addresses how you want to deal with that profile if it doesn't match your working color space.

In the following sections, I give you the 25-cent explanation — which I hope is enough to get you started in managing color. If color management is an extremely critical workflow issue for you, I recommend buying a book or two strictly devoted to nothing but managing color. It's well worth the money. One of my personal favorites is *Color Management for Digital Photographers For Dummies,* by Ted Padova and Don Mason (Wiley).

Setting up your work environment

One aspect of color management that people often overlook is setting up a good working environment for digital image editing. You may wave your hand impatiently and say, "Yeah, yeah, I just want to get to the important stuff." This *is* the important stuff. Don't worry. Setting up a good work environment won't cost you much. Just do these things:

- **Keep your computer desktop a neutral gray.** Colors and patterns behind your images influence the way that you perceive those images. Creating a neutral, gray desktop is the closest you can get to mounting your work on gray, black, or white matte board (and not neon green or paisley), the way professional graphic designers and photographers do.

- **Keep your lighting as consistent as possible.** For example, avoid working on images in full, bright afternoon sun and then again under a single desk lamp late at night. Likewise, view onscreen images and your printed output under the same lighting.

- **Keep the walls of your work environment as neutral as your monitor desktop.** You don't have to paint your office gray, but try to avoid a lot of colorful posters and artwork around and behind your monitor.

- **Speaking of monitors, if you're using an LCD (flat screen) monitor, be sure you're sitting directly in front of it.** Color shifts quite a bit on LCDs if you're viewing it at even a slight angle. So, no slumping in your chair!

- **Keep a swatch book (or two) handy, such as those from Pantone or Trumatch, to select your colors.** Don't make a decision based on what you see onscreen. These books give you a true representation of how onscreen color looks when printed on paper. Just be sure to keep them out of the light and update them periodically when the colors start to fade.

  Be prepared for a healthy monetary investment when you buy a swatch book. These little buggers can cost anywhere from $75 to $200. You can purchase swatch books from some larger art supply stores or order them online. You can purchase Pantone books from www.pantone.com. Do a Web search for others, such as Trumatch, Focoltone, and Toyo.

- **Take some time to test your *workflow* (production methods) and your computer system.** Scan images using multiple settings, print images using multiple settings, and view your images using different browsers on different monitors and different platforms.

Get to know the strengths, limitations, and quirks of every piece of your equipment. Experiment with Photoshop. I know; I know. You have a life. But trust me — it's an investment with great returns.

Calibrating your monitor

Calibrating your monitor and creating an ICC profile of your monitor ensures that your monitor doesn't display any red, green, or blue *colorcasts* (traces of color) and that it provides as neutral a gray screen as possible. Calibration is incredibly important if you want to standardize your image display — knowing that how you view your image today will be how you view your image tomorrow or next week.

If you really want to do a good calibration job, consider investing in a combination hardware/software calibration package. These products used to be really pricey, but you can get a starter package for as little as $79. You can choose from several manufacturers, including Datacolor (http://spyder.datacolor.com) and X-Rite (www.xrite.com).

If you're a Windows 7 user, you can check out Display Color Calibration. Choose Start⇨Control Panel and type calibrate display in the Search field. Click Calibrate Display Color. Click Next and follow the instructions. If you're a Mac OS X user and on a super-tight budget, you can use the Display Calibrator Assistant. Choose Apple⇨System Preferences and click Displays in the System Preferences dialog box. Then click the Color tab and click the Calibrate button. Answer the questions in the Display Calibrator Assistant. (See Figure 3-9.)

Figure 3-9: Mac users can use the Display Calibrator Assistant to calibrate their monitors.

The Display Calibrator Assistant attempts to remove any colorcasts and get as neutral a gray background as it can. It also creates a profile of your monitor for Photoshop, Illustrator, and other programs so that those applications know how your monitor displays color.

When you calibrate your monitor, display an image for which you already know the color values. For example, use an image that you've worked with and for which you have a good print, and then use that image each and every time you calibrate. Your goal is to match the digital image on your screen to the printed image. You should calibrate every so often because monitors can drift and degrade. Some experts say weekly is best; others are more liberal and say monthly is fine.

Not only is letting your monitor warm up a prerequisite before you calibrate, it's also a good idea before you sit down to tackle any image-adjustment work.

Establishing Your Settings

After you calibrate your monitor (see the preceding section) and adequately arrange your work environment (described earlier in this chapter), you need to nail down the color settings and make sure they're the right match for your intended output.

You establish these settings in the Color Settings dialog box, the rather intimidating dialog box shown in Figure 3-10. To open it, choose Edit➪Color Settings. In the Color Settings dialog box, you can choose from predefined settings established for specific types of output, or you can customize your own settings to fit your individual needs. The following sections offer more details about the settings you can choose in the Color Settings dialog box.

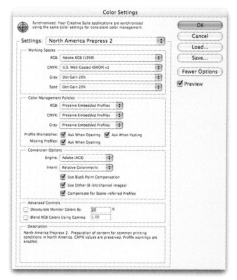

Figure 3-10: The Color Settings dialog box is command central for establishing your color-management system.

While you're perusing the dialog box, hover your cursor over any item to make a great description of that item appear at the bottom of the dialog box.

Handling Photoshop's predefined settings

In the Color Settings dialog box, Photoshop allows you to take the easy route and select from a long list of predefined color settings based on your desired output. After you set up the predefined settings, Photoshop provides all the appropriate working color spaces and color-management policies you need to get good color results.

Being the smart program that it is, Photoshop won't steer you down the wrong path with its predefined settings. The only way you can mess up the predefined settings is if your output doesn't match the setting. For example, the Web Graphics Defaults setting isn't appropriate for your high-end, four-color print job because these two mediums use color in completely different ways. (See Book II, Chapter 2 for details if you're curious why this is so.)

Be sure to click the More Options button in the Color Settings dialog box to access the full set of predefined color settings. Here's a brief description of the main settings in the Settings drop-down list at the top:

- **Custom:** Allows you to manually assign your own settings. When you define a custom configuration, save your settings so that you can reload them later, if necessary.

- **Monitor Color:** Emulates the color of most video applications. Reserve it for screen images only. Avoid it for producing print images.

- **North America General Purpose 2:** Provides all-purpose general color settings for screen and print images in North America. It uses the same CMYK, Grayscale, and Spot working spaces as North America Prepress 2, but uses the Web standard of sRGB for the RGB working space.

Book II
Chapter 3

Using and
Managing Color

- **North America Newspaper:** For prepping content for North American newspaper presses. CMYK values are preserved, and all profile warnings are enabled.

- **North America Prepress 2:** Provides color settings for print images in North America. Preserves the CMYK working space and brings any profile warnings to your attention.

- **North America Web/Internet:** Gives color settings for Web images in North America. Uses sRGB for the RGB working space.

- **ColorSync Workflow (Mac only):** Uses ColorSync 3.0 Color Management System and ColorSync profiles. It's not recognized by the Windows platform.

- **Europe General Purpose 2:** Provides general color settings for screen and print images in Europe. Profile warnings are disabled.

- **Europe General Purpose 3:** Same as 2, but it offers updated CMYK ICC profiles for offset printing on coated paper.

- **Europe Prepress 2:** Provides color settings for print images in Europe. Preserves the CMYK working space and brings any profile warnings to your attention.

- **Europe Prepress 3:** Same as 2, but it offers updated CMYK ICC profiles for offset printing on coated paper.

- **Europe Web/Internet:** Gives color settings for Web images in Europe. Uses sRGB for the RGB working space.

- **Europe Web/Internet 2:** Same as Web/Internet, but it offers updated CMYK ICC profiles for offset printing on coated paper.

- **Japan Color for Newspaper:** Provides settings to be used for newspaper presses in Japan. Preserves the CMYK working space and alerts you to any profile warnings.

- **Japan General Purpose 2:** Provides general color settings for screen and print images in Japan.

- **Japan Magazine Advertisement Color:** Gives color settings for preparing images by using the color standards of the Japanese Magazine Publisher Association.

- **Japan Prepress 2:** Provides color settings for print images in Japan. Preserves the CMYK working space and brings any profile warnings to your attention.

- **Japan Web/Internet:** Gives color settings for Web images in Japan. Uses sRGB for the RGB working space.

- **Photoshop 5 Default Spaces:** Uses the default color settings found in Photoshop 5, the first version to use color management.

You can always use a predefined setting as a starting point and adjust whatever individual settings you need to. If you do, your predefined setting name automatically changes to Custom.

Indicating your working spaces

If you select one of the predefined color settings from the Settings drop-down list, Photoshop plugs in all the necessary remaining options in the dialog box. (If you select the Custom option, Photoshop leaves whatever settings were there previously because it knows you're going to choose your own settings, anyway.)

When you select one of the predefined color settings, the first group of settings that Photoshop plugs in contains your working spaces. *Working spaces* are the color profiles associated with the RGB, CMYK, Grayscale, and Spot color modes. If you select the Custom color setting, you need to choose your own working spaces.

Each of the four working spaces is equally important, so I advise you to read all the following sections — and read them in order — if you're serious about color management.

RGB working spaces

Table 3-1 gives you a quick view of your RGB working space options.

Table 3-1	RGB Working Space Options	
Working Space	*What It Does*	*Recommendation*
Monitor RGB	Sets the working space to your current monitor space (which it gets from the monitor profile you established during calibration). Forces Photoshop to turn off color management.	I don't recommend this setting unless you have a specific need to use it.

Working Space	What It Does	Recommendation
ColorSync RGB	Sets the working space to the profile specified in the Apple ColorSync control panel. This is the default setting for the ColorSync Workflow pre-defined setting.	For Macintosh only.
Adobe RGB (1998)	The default setting for all the Prepress predefined settings. It's the best color profile to use for viewing 24-bit (8-bit mode) images and converting RGB files to CMYK. Provides a large gamut of RGB colors.	I recommend this option as a general setting for all print work and as an overall setting if you're unsure what to choose.
Apple RGB	Can be used for older Mac OS scanners and monitors.	Unless you're the proud owner of a 13-inch Apple monitor, I'd avoid it.
ColorMatch RGB	Use this working space only with Radius PressView monitors.	I don't think I need to give you a recommendation on this one! You Radius PressView users know who you are.
ProPhoto RGB (also called ROMM RGB)	Provides a large color gamut. Good for viewing 48-bit (16-bit mode) images. You may see banding in 24-bit (8-bit mode) images.	Good for output to dye sublimation and inkjet photo printers.
sRGB	The default setting for Web Graphics Defaults. This color profile represents a standard, Trinitron PC monitor — the monitor of choice for many of the world's Web surfers. This option can also be used with Windows scanners. Avoid it for print work because of its limited RGB color gamut.	If your goal is to ensure your Web graphics look relatively the same in Los Angeles as they do in Bangladesh, sRGB is a good profile to use.

If you click the More Options button in the Color Settings dialog box, you get even more RGB, as well as CMYK, Grayscale, and Spot settings. These settings include profiles for monitors, printers, and various video formats. For the most part, you can stick with the main working spaces and be covered.

You can save and load any custom settings, including the individual RGB, CMYK, Grayscale, and Spot working spaces, as well as your entire group of color settings.

After you set RGB working spaces, don't forget that you also have to configure the other three working spaces, as described in the following sections.

CMYK working spaces

CMYK working spaces are a little more involved than RGB options (listed in the preceding section). CMYK working spaces serve a threefold purpose:

- Photoshop converts your RGB file to the CMYK color space when you choose Image➪Mode➪CMYK.

- You view your RGB image in the CMYK color space when you choose View➪Proof Setup➪Working CMYK. See the section "Proofing Colors in the Final Output (Soft Proofing)," later in this chapter, for more on soft proofing colors.

- The CMYK color space determines how a CMYK file is displayed on an RGB monitor.

Europe (FOGRA), Japan, and the United States have specific color profiles for printing. Those CMYK options are divided between those for coated and uncoated paper, and sheet-fed or Web printing presses. The latter two have different percentages of ink coverage and paper stock. Macs also have a ColorSync Generic CMYK profile. I'd leave the setting at U.S. Web Coated (SWOP) v2 unless your commercial printer tells you otherwise.

Grayscale working spaces

Grayscale working spaces have to do with two parameters — viewing and dot gain of grayscale images (Image➪Mode➪Grayscale). You can select Gray Gamma 1.8 for a Macintosh monitor or Gray Gamma 2.2 for a PC monitor. You can also view an image according to how it will print, based on typical dot gain.

For those Mac users using Mac OS 10.6, Snow Leopard, you can set your Gray Gamma to 2.2.

Dot gain is how much ink the paper absorbs, thereby increasing the size of every halftone dot. When continuous-tone images are digitized, they're converted into a series of dots known as a *halftone*.

If you're preparing graphics for the Web, you may want to set your working space to Gray Gamma 2.2 — whether or not you're using a Mac — because most of the Web surfers worldwide are PC users.

For print work, leave the setting at Dot Gain 20% unless your commercial printer tells you otherwise. You can enter any desired percentage in the Custom Dot Gain option.

Don't forget — you still have to adjust another working space, which I cover in the following section.

Spot working spaces

Spot working spaces have to do with spot colors. *Spot colors* are premixed inks that are printed in addition to, or in lieu of, the four process colors — cyan, magenta, yellow, and black. Unless your commercial printer tells you otherwise, stick with a setting of Dot Gain 20%.

Working with your newly defined settings

After you define your color profiles in the Color Settings dialog box, you may want to get a handle on how these newly established settings affect how Photoshop works. Although the settings typically affect only how Photoshop works in the background, you nevertheless might want to be aware of the following key changes:

- **By default, any new images you create use the color profile you selected in the Color Settings dialog box.** Every file you create on your computer now uses the colors within the gamut of your color profiles (either RGB or CMYK, depending on your document color mode). Overall, this default setting should make managing color in Photoshop easier. For example, if you mostly work with multimedia or Web images and have specified your color settings accordingly, you don't need to worry about whether each color will display accurately because you've set the defaults to reflect that color mode. But, if you want to prep an image for print, those defaults won't work, and you need to change your individual working spaces to those that are print oriented or to a preset, such as North American Prepress.

- **The color settings you select are used to display any *untagged images* (images that don't have an embedded color).** An example of an untagged image is a Photoshop file created before version 5 — that is, before Photoshop supported embedded color profiles.

- **Your settings define how Photoshop converts your images from one working space to another.** For example, say you choose North America Prepress 2 from the Settings drop-down list in the Color Settings dialog box. In this case, the default for CMYK is U.S. Web Coated (SWOP) v2, which is a specific CMYK setting for a Web printing press and coated paper, among other things. (This setting appears in the Working Spaces area of the Color Settings dialog box.) When you convert an RGB image to CMYK (Image➪Mode➪CMYK) prior to sending it off to the printer, Photoshop automatically tags the image with the U.S. Web Coated (SWOP) v2 color profile.

✔ **When you save a file, make sure that you select the ICC Profile (Embed Color Profile on the Mac) option in the Save or Save As dialog box, if it's available.** See Figure 3-11. (Some file formats don't support color profiles.) This selection ensures that Photoshop tags the file with the specified color profile and that its origins are always known.

Figure 3-11: Select the ICC (or Color) Profile check box when you save an image.

Setting color-management policies

After you establish working color spaces, the next step is to establish the default color-management policy for each color mode. In other words, you need to tell Photoshop how to interpret and manage the color profiles of files it opens.

Photoshop looks at the color profile of a file, compares it to your working spaces, and then employs the default policies you've established. If the file has the same color profile as yours, there isn't an issue. You're good to go.

But sometimes, this isn't the case — like in these situations:

✔ **The file you open has no profile.** These can be older files, files that were created with color management turned off, or files created in other applications that don't employ color management.

✔ **The file you open has a color profile that doesn't match your working space.** Say that you have a Web designer friend, and his settings are based on the North America Web/Internet option. He gives you a file, and you open it in Photoshop on your computer. You do mostly print work, so your settings are based on the North America Prepress 2 option. Photoshop then displays an alert that says the file has an embedded color profile that doesn't match your current RGB working space — his working space is sRGB and yours is Adobe RGB (1998). The alert then goes on to describe the default policy that's invoked on the file, as shown in Figure 3-12.

If you've selected a predefined setting, the policies have already been established for you, and those should work fine. I do recommend, however, that if you change the policies of any of the predefined settings, don't choose Off as your option, unless you have a good reason. (***Remember:*** Color management is a *good* thing.)

To set your color-management policies, follow these steps:

1. **Open the Color Settings dialog box by choosing Edit⇨Color Settings.**

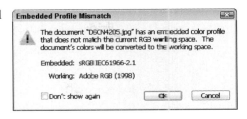

Figure 3-12: Photoshop alerts you when you open a file whose color profile doesn't match yours.

2. **In the Color Management Policies area, select from the following three options for each color mode:**

   • *Off:* This option turns color management off for any new files you create, import, or open. However, if the opened or imported file's color profile matches your current working space, the profile is preserved.

   • *Preserve Embedded Profiles:* This option displays the files in their original embedded color space. No color conversion occurs. Untagged files remain untagged but use the current working space for display.

   • *Convert to Working RGB (or CMYK or Grayscale, depending on your image mode):* This option converts any files with missing or mismatched embedded profiles to your working RGB space. Untagged files remain untagged but use the current working space for display.

3. **Decide whether you want to select the Ask When Opening check box for Profile Mismatches.**

   If you don't select the Ask When Opening option for Profile Mismatches, Photoshop displays the Embedded Profile Mismatch alert message (see Figure 3-12), describing which default policy will occur. You can then select the Don't Show Again check box, and from that point forward,

   Photoshop executes the policy without displaying an alert. For files with missing profiles, Photoshop simply invokes the default policy without an alert.

   If you select the Ask When Opening check box for Profile Mismatches, Photoshop not only displays an Embedded Profile Mismatch alert, but also provides you with options for handling the color of that file, thereby overriding the default policy, as shown in Figure 3-13.

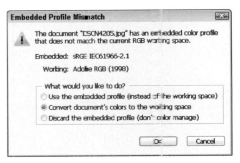

Figure 3-13: Selecting the Ask When Opening option allows you to override your default color-management policy setting.

The options in the alert are similar to the default policies of the Color Settings dialog box. Here's a brief explanation of each option in the alert:

- *Use the Embedded Profile (Instead of the Working Space):* Photoshop displays the file in its original embedded color space and doesn't perform any color conversions.

- *Convert Document's Colors to the Working Space:* Photoshop converts the file from its embedded color space to your working color space.

- *Discard the Embedded Profile (Don't Color Manage):* Photoshop doesn't utilize any color management when opening files but displays the file in your working space.

Be cautious about making any CMYK conversions. If you encounter a Profile Mismatch with a CMYK image, you probably want to preserve the image's embedded profile unless you're absolutely sure it should be converted to another CMYK working space. But, if the image doesn't have a profile, then, by all means, convert it to your CMYK working space.

4. **Decide whether you want to select the Ask When Pasting check box for Profile Mismatches.**

   If you select the Ask When Pasting option for Profile Mismatches, Photoshop prompts you when you drag and drop layers or selections that have the same color mode (see Book II, Chapter 2 for more on modes) but different color profiles. In the Paste Profile Mismatch alert dialog box, you have two options:

   - *Convert (Preserve Color Appearance):* Photoshop converts and matches the appearance of the color, rather than the RGB numerical values. For example, the RGB color of R 152, G 122, B 250 may be a different shade of purple in one RGB working space versus another. If you preserve the numerical values, the shades won't match. If you preserve the appearance, Photoshop attempts to maintain the two shades.

   - *Don't Convert (Preserve Color Number):* Photoshop doesn't convert the appearance of the color, but instead matches the RGB numerical values.

   If you don't select the Ask When Pasting check box, Photoshop pastes the color appearance between RGB images and pastes the numerical values between CMYK images.

5. **Decide whether you want to select the Ask When Opening check box for Missing Profiles.**

   If you do select the check box, Photoshop displays a Missing Profile alert and also provides you with the following options, as shown in Figure 3-14:

Figure 3-14: Photoshop alerts you when opening an image without a color profile and asks you how you want to proceed.

- *Leave As Is (Don't Color Manage):* This option leaves the image untagged and without a color profile, but displays the image in your working space.

- *Assign Working RGB (or CMYK or Grayscale, depending on your image mode):* your working space. Photoshop tags the image with your working space and displays it in that working space. If you change your working space, the image retains the old working space.

- *Assign Profile:* This option allows you to assign any color profile contained within the pop-up menu. You can use this option if you know where the untagged image originated. For example, if you scanned your image and your scanner doesn't embed profiles, you can assign the scanner profile.

Unless you have a specific reason not to, I recommend that you assign your working RGB space to those orphan files.

6. **If you're done working in the Color Settings dialog box, click OK to exit.**

I recommend selecting the Ask When Opening and Ask When Pasting check boxes. With these boxes selected, you know when a profile mismatch occurs — and you have the choice of picking your course of action, which includes overriding the defaults you set in the policy settings. So you can evaluate whether you want to preserve or convert on a file-by-file basis. For example, if you're a print designer and a Web designer gives you a file, you get a profile mismatch alerting you that the file has the sRGB color space and that it doesn't match your working space of Adobe RGB (1993). If you're going to use the image as-is for Web content, you tell Photoshop to preserve the embedded profile and not to make any conversion. But if you want to repurpose the image (for, say, a logo), you have to instruct Photoshop to convert the file to your working RGB space. (Of course, ultimately you have to also convert the image mode to CMYK for printing purposes.)

To find out the color profile of an image, select Document Profile from the pop-up menu at the bottom of the image window (which I describe in detail in Book I, Chapter 1). Also, if an image has a color profile that differs from your working space, an asterisk appears outside the parentheses in the title bar. An untagged image displays a pound sign. By the way, when you select More Options in the Color Settings dialog box, you have a few additional options regarding color conversion engines and rendering intents, which are methods of color translation. I recommend putting your trust in Photoshop and leaving these options at their defaults unless you're a bona fide color expert.

Getting Consistent Color among Adobe Applications

If you have a complete Adobe workflow (like I do), you may want to use the same color settings for all your Adobe applications. Illustrator, InDesign, and

Acrobat share a similar Color Settings dialog box. They have a few minor differences, but nothing major. If an element doesn't exist in one application's Color Settings dialog box, Adobe merely plugs in the default setting. You can choose the same predefined color setting from the Settings pop-up menu in each application, or you can use a shortcut.

With the advent of Adobe Bridge (explained in Book I, Chapter 4), getting consistent color across all your Creative Suite applications is merely a button click away. Just follow these steps:

1. **Simply launch Bridge and choose Edit⇨Creative Suite Color Settings.**

   In the Suite Color Settings dialog box, shown in Figure 3-15, you can immediately tell whether the color settings across all your Creative Suite applications are synchronized. (*Synchronized* is Adobe's cool name for *the same.*)

2. **If they're not and you want the settings to be the same, first click the Show Expanded List of Color Settings Files to ensure you have the full list of possibilities.**

3. **Then, just select your desired predefined color setting from the list and click the Apply button.**

Figure 3-15: Get consistent color among your Adobe Creative Suite apps.

   Bridge then ensures that each Creative Suite application uses that color setting. You can also select a previously saved custom setting. If you want to see where your saved color settings files reside, just click the Show Saved Color Settings Files button.

You don't have to synchronize your color settings. You may want to have different settings in InDesign, a page-layout program, than you have in Dreamweaver, a Web-page-creation application. In the Color Settings dialog box in each Creative Suite application, a message appears at the top to let you know whether your suite color settings are synchronized.

You can save your custom Color Settings in Photoshop by clicking the Save button in the Color Settings dialog box. To ensure that all your Adobe applications can access the settings file, save it to a default location:

✔ For Microsoft Windows, the default location is the `AppData/Roaming/Adobe/Color/Settings` folder.

✔ For Mac OS X users, the default folder is `Users/CurrentUser/Library/ApplicationSupport/Adobe/Color/Settings`.

You can also place saved custom color settings files that you've received from other people (for example, reps from your offset print house) in this location.

Proofing Colors in the Final Output (Soft Proofing)

Photoshop allows you to preview onscreen how your image will look on a variety of output devices. First, choose View➪Proof Setup and select your desired setup. The Working options are based on the working spaces you specified in the Color Settings dialog box (described earlier in this chapter):

✔ **Legacy Macintosh RGB:** Display your image as it'll appear on a standard Macintosh monitor running Mac OS 10.5 or earlier.

✔ **Internet Standard RGB (sRGB):** Display your image as it'll appear on a standard Windows monitor or a Macintosh monitor running Mac OS 10.6 or earlier.

✔ **Monitor RGB:** Allows you to view the image by using your current monitor's color space. This setting essentially turns off your RGB working space and lets you see the image without any color management.

✔ **Custom:** Allows you to choose a specific device. For example, choosing U.S. Web Coated (SWOP) v2, from the Device to Simulate drop-down menu, lets you to see how your RGB images will look when they're converted to CMYK for printing. Or you can choose your desktop inkjet printer profile from the Device to Simulate drop-down menu to see how your images will look when printed to that device.

After you select your setup, choose View➪Proof Colors to view the image in your chosen working space. For the most reliable results, use a good-quality monitor and set up a good viewing environment (described earlier in this chapter). Also, keep in mind that although soft proofing is a good thing, it's no substitute for a good-quality hard-copy proof. Some things — such as the type and quality of paper, certain inks, and so on — can't be accurately simulated onscreen.

Photoshop also offers two proof setup settings to view how images will appear to those who are colorblind. Color Blindness Protanopia mimics red-green colorblindness with less sensitivity to red light. Color Blindness Deuteranopia mimics red-green color blindness with less sensitivity to green light.

Chapter 4: Time Travel — Undoing in Photoshop

In This Chapter

✔ Undoing and redoing

✔ Reverting to the state you last saved

✔ Exploring the History panel

✔ Viewing an image's states

✔ Looking at the History options

✔ Taking snapshots

✔ Erasing with the Erase to History option

✔ Brushing back in time with the History Brush tool

*W*hen Thomas Wolfe said, "You can't go home again," he wasn't talking about Photoshop. If you change your mind about something you do and want to return to your starting place (or any point in between), Photoshop is very forgiving. My favorite image editor offers many different ways to reverse actions, undo what you did, reapply effects you've cancelled, and change your mind as often as a new apartment owner deciding where to put the couch.

This chapter helps you master Photoshop's powerful time-traveling features, including the Undo command, the History panel, and such tools as the Art History Brush and the Eraser.

Undoing What's Done with the Undo Command

Your first stop in your journey through time is the Undo/Redo command. This command simply reverses the last action you took or reapplies that action if you just undid it. For example, if you apply a brush stroke that you don't like, use Undo to remove that stroke. Then, if you immediately change your mind, you can redo it by using the command again.

To undo your last action, choose Edit⇨Undo or simply press Ctrl+Z (⌘+Z on the Mac).

Press the Undo/Redo shortcut keys rapidly to toggle an effect on and off if you want to compare the before and after effects quickly. When you decide which way to go, stop toggling. This procedure works best if you press Ctrl+Z (⌘+Z on the Mac) to apply both Undo and Redo.

The Undo/Redo command works for only a single command. If you do anything else after you apply a command and then change your mind about that command, you have to resort to one of the other time-travel techniques described later in this chapter.

If you can't undo or redo an action, Undo/Redo is gray in the menu, showing that it's unavailable. However, you can often use the History panel to remove the action. See the section "Working with the Almighty History Panel," later in this chapter, for details on how to use the History panel.

If you want to free the memory that the Undo command uses, choose Edit⇨Purge⇨Undo. If the item is gray, the buffer is already empty. You can't undo this action, so do it only if Photoshop is acting sluggish.

Reverting to What's Saved

Revert replaces your current file with the last saved file, effectively wiping out everything you've done since you last saved the file. You can revert to the last version of the file by choosing File⇨Revert. Although you lose all the changes in your current file when the last saved version replaces it onscreen, the Revert command is stored on the History panel. You can find out how to remove a command from the History panel in the section "Introducing History panel options and tools," later in this chapter.

Working with the Almighty History Panel

Undoing and redoing commands, explained in the preceding sections, are kid's stuff compared to the power of the almighty History panel. (Choose Window⇨History.) Think of this tool as a recipe that lists the steps (how many appear depends on what you specify in your preferences, which I talk about in the following section) that you took to cook up your image in its present state. By using the History panel, you can browse through the recipe and return to any step in the list to begin work anew from that point.

Understanding states and snapshots

You can't go too far in your use of the History panel without understanding two important concepts, as well as how the concepts are different

✔ **States:** *States* is just another way of saying steps. At any given point in your image-editing activities, Photoshop saves your edits into states.

By default, Photoshop remembers 20 states for an image. You can increase the number to as many as 1,000 in the Performance Preferences dialog box. Choose Edit➪Preferences➪Performance (or Photoshop➪ Preferences➪Performance in Mac OS X) and enter a new value (or move the slider) in the History States box.

Boosting this number can eat up your available memory quite quickly. You may want to leave the states set to 20 and save snapshots of your image, as I describe in the section "Taking Snapshots," later in this chapter. When you reach the limit of 20 steps, the oldest step (at the top of the list) is deleted to make room for the latest one at the bottom.

✔ **Snapshots:** You can save temporary copies of an image at any state. This enables you to revert to a previous state any time during your work session by selecting a particular snapshot to work from. See "Taking Snapshots," later in this chapter, to find out how to use snapshots.

When you have these concepts down, you can get to the business of understanding how the tools in the History panel use states and snapshots to help you go back in time (and back to the future again) to undo, redo, and modify each miniscule edit you make to your images.

Introducing History panel options and tools

The History panel has several useful components you should know about, as shown in Figure 4-1:

✔ **Snapshot thumbnail:** This miniature image of the saved snapshot image gives you a copy of your document that has all the current states included. (For more on snapshots, see the section "Taking Snapshots," later in this chapter.)

✔ **Source state column:** Click in this column to the left of a particular snapshot or state, and when you begin painting with the History Brush tool or erasing with the Erase to History option, Photoshop uses the snapshot or state that you select in this column as the source.

✔ **History state:** A particular step or edit in your document's list of steps. An icon appears in this column showing what kind of action occurred in that state.

REMEMBER

Source state column

Source state

Snapshot thumbnail

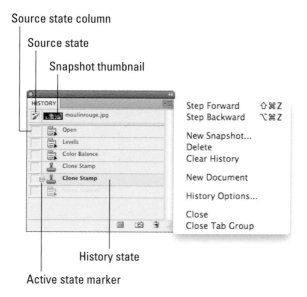

Figure 4-1: The indispensable History panel lets you undo up to 1,000 steps.

History state

Active state marker

- ✔ **Active state marker:** This slider points to the currently active state. You can drag it up or down to change the current state.

- ✔ **Create new document from current state:** Click this icon to create a duplicate copy of your image at the currently selected state. Your new document starts out with a nearly empty history list. The only state that's present is Duplicate State.

- ✔ **Create new snapshot:** Click this icon to store an image of your document, preserving all the states listed.

- ✔ **Delete current state:** Click this icon to remove a selected state.

- ✔ **Undone states:** These gray states are undone when you select an earlier state in the list.

- ✔ **Open state:** The original document that you first opened.

- ✔ **Current history state:** The active state that you've selected in the history list.

Viewing an Image's Various States

You can move back to any state listed in the History panel, remove a state to cancel a step, or perform other time-travel stunts by using the History panel. The following sections outline some basic time-shifting techniques that you can use.

Going back to a particular state

To go back in time and resume editing at a particular point, just click the state to which you want to return. All subsequent states appear gray, or *undone*. Then, begin editing your image as usual. As soon as you perform a new step, all the states that follow your reentry point vanish. It's like applying the Undo command (Ctrl+Z on a PC, ⌘+Z on the Mac) to a group of steps with one click.

If you intentionally (or accidentally) begin editing while a previous state is high-lighted, and then you change your mind, immediately undo your action — press Ctrl+Z (⌘+Z on the Mac). The subsequent steps that were removed reappear.

Reviewing your image at different states

To review how your image looked at previous states, just click the state that you want to see. (You can also drag the active state marker up and down the list.) The document image immediately changes to reflect that earlier state. You can move back and forth between any two points in the history list, if you like. As long as you don't make any editing changes during your time-traveling jaunt, your current history list is preserved.

Purging and clearing all states

To remove a state and all the steps that follow it, select the state and then press the Delete key or click the trash can icon.

You can clear all the states except the most recent one from the panel by selecting Clear History from the panel pop-up menu. (Click the down arrow in the upper-right corner of the panel to make this menu appear.) All your snapshots will be preserved. You can undo your clearing only if you choose Edit➪Undo immediately after you execute the command. You can also delete all the states except the last one in the history list and keep the snapshots you've saved by choosing Edit➪Purge➪Histories. You can clear or purge your history list when you no longer need the states it includes — if you either want to save memory or return to the original state of your document. When purging, just be sure that you really, seriously are not interested in going back later to make changes because you can't undo this command.

Navigating the history list

You can move up and down the history list, even if the list isn't visible on your screen. Choose Edit➪Step Forward to move forward in the history list and Edit➪Step Backward to move back. The best way to access these commands is to use the keyboard shortcuts:

- Press Alt+Ctrl+Z (Option+⌘+Z on the Mac) to move backward (up the history list).
- Press Shift+Ctrl+Z (Shift+⌘+Z on the Mac) to move forward (down the history list).

Looking at the History Options Dialog Box

The History panel has five options that change its behavior. To access these options, select History Options from the History panel pop-up menu, which opens the History Options dialog box, shown in Figure 4-2. For a rundown of the various settings, see Table 4-1.

Figure 4-2: Change the History panel's behavior in this dialog box.

Table 4-1	Setting History Panel Options	
Option	*What It Does*	*Recommended Setting*
Automatically Create First Snapshot	This option, selected by default, tells Photoshop to create a snapshot of the image when you first open it, before you make any changes. You can return to this snapshot at any time by clicking its name in the History panel.	Checked. Consider it free insurance — you can always return to your original image, if necessary.
Automatically Create New Snapshot When Saving	This option tells Photoshop to create a new snapshot each time you save the image.	Depends. If you're like me and save every couple of minutes, you probably don't want to select this option; otherwise, you end up with a panel filled with unwanted snapshots.
Allow Non-Linear History	Selecting this option lets you edit or delete a state without removing all the states that follow it. When the Non-Linear History capability is active, you can edit an intermediate state in the history list, leaving the other steps below it unchanged.	Unchecked. Use this option with caution because steps are interdependent. A change that you remove may form the basis for another edit later on, so deleting it can cause weird results.

Option	What It Does	Recommended Setting
Show New Snapshot Dialog by Default	This option ensures that Photoshop asks you to name any new snapshot that you create.	Checked. Applying names to snapshots makes remembering the state of the image when you saved the snapshot easy. Even if this option is unchecked, however, you can still access the dialog box by pressing the Alt (Option on the Mac) key when you click the camera icon.
Make Layer Visibility Changes Undoable	This option records the toggling on and off of the visibility of your layers.	Unchecked. Showing and hiding layers doesn't affect image pixels.

Taking Snapshots

Snapshots are duplicates of your image at a particular point in time, similar to saving a document with an alternate name to create a copy of that document. (Photoshop automatically names the snapshots Snapshot 1, Snapshot 2, and so on.) However, snapshots are temporary copies, available only during your current work session.

You can use snapshots to alternate between versions of an image when you're making major changes. For example, if you plan to apply several filters and adjustments that will drastically modify your image, you may want to save a snapshot before you apply the filters and adjustments and then save another snapshot after you apply them. You can then click either snapshot to switch from one version to the other quickly, as shown in Figure 4-3.

The second you close a file, the snapshots you've taken disappear forever. If you want a more permanent way to save versions of your file, see the Layer Comps panel discussion in Book V, Chapter 2.

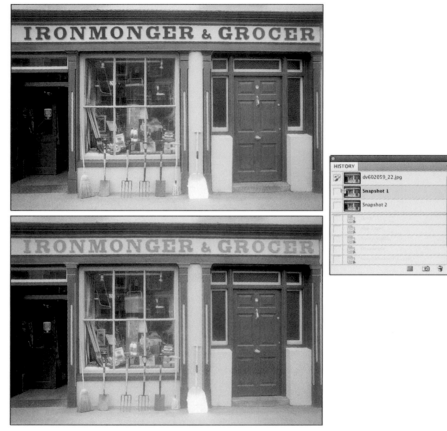

Digital Vision

Figure 4-3: Use snapshots to compare before and after images when you apply a filter or adjustment.

To take a snapshot, follow these steps:

1. **Select the state at which you want to take a snapshot.**

   You can select the most recent state that has all your latest editing changes, or you can select an earlier state. Just make sure that you take the snapshot before your desired state is eliminated.

2. **Select New Snapshot from the panel pop-up menu.**

   You can also click the New Snapshot icon at the bottom of the History panel. Either way, the New Snapshot dialog box opens. Photoshop names your first snapshot Snapshot 1.

3. **In the Name box, enter a name for the snapshot.**

   Use a name that helps you remember the contents of that particular snapshot.

You can add or change the name of the snapshot later by double-clicking the snapshot name in the history list and typing the new name.

4. If you like, select a snapshot subtype in the From menu.

Full Document, which is the default, creates a snapshot of all the layers in the image at the currently selected state. This keeps all of your separate layers. You can also take a snapshot of merged layers. This merges all of your layers into a single layer. Finally, you can just snap the Current Layer. Book V explains working with layers.

5. Click OK to create the snapshot.

If you no longer need a snapshot, you can select the snapshot and click the trash can icon, drag the snapshot to the trash can icon, or select Delete from the History panel's options menu.

Restoring Part of an Image

Although the concept may seem like quantum physics, you can erase and brush on an image by using previously saved states or snapshots.

What? Okay, let me try this again. You can erase portions of an image to a history state, as well as paint on an image from a history state. So, traveling through time doesn't have to be an all-or-nothing experience; you can erase or paint portions of a different state onto your currently active state.

For example, suppose you apply a blur filter to a face and decide later that you want to make the eyes sharp again. You can use the Eraser tool with the Erase to History option selected, or use the History Brush tool, to paint over the eyes with information from an earlier state before you blurred them, as shown in Figure 4-4.

Using the Eraser with the Erase to History option

Use the Eraser with the Erase to History option when a portion of an earlier state or snapshot contains information that you want to include in an image that you've extensively edited. To erase and restore to a portion of an earlier state or snapshot, just follow these steps:

1. In the History panel, click in the far-left column of the state or snapshot that you want to use as the source for the Eraser tool with the Erase to History option.

A brush icon appears to the left of the state's listing in the History panel, indicating that Photoshop will use this state as the source for the Eraser tool with the Erase to History option.

Purestock

Figure 4-4: You can easily restore portions of your edited image to an earlier state.

2. **Select the Eraser tool.**

   You can also press the E key to access the tool.

3. **Select the Erase to History option on the Options bar.**

4. **Select any other Eraser tool options that you want to use, such as Brush size and type, Mode, Opacity and Flow percentages, or Airbrush.**

   The Mode options include a Brush, Pencil, or Block tip for your brush. For details on the other options, see "Selective Erasing with the Eraser Tools" in Book VI, Chapter 2.

5. **Select your desired layer in the Layers panel and, in the History panel, select the state that you want to erase to.**

6. **Drag your eraser on the portion of the image you want to erase.**

   Photoshop removes the image in the layer and replaces it with the image in the state that you specified as the source in Step 1.

You can convert the Eraser tool so that it temporarily uses the Erase to History option by holding down the Alt key (Option key on the Mac) while you erase or paint.

Using the History Brush tool

You can use the History Brush tool to apply an image area from a different state or snapshot to your current state. Use this tool to restore a portion of an image to an earlier state, while leaving the rest of the heavily modified image alone. The History Brush has an advantage over the Eraser tool because the History Brush gives you access to many blend modes. Just follow these steps to use the History Brush:

1. **In the History panel, click in the far-left column of the state or snapshot that you want to use as the source for the History Brush tool. (Refer to Figure 4-1.)**

   A brush icon appears in the column, indicating that Photoshop will use this state as the source for the History Brush tool.

   In my example, I chose my original image just after I cropped it.

2. **Select the History Brush tool in the Tools panel.**

   You can also press Y to select the tool.

3. **On the Options bar, select any other brush options that you want to use — such as Brush size and type, Mode, Opacity and Flow percentages, and Airbrush.**

   For details on the brush options, see Book IV, Chapter 1.

4. **Select your desired layer in the Layers panel and, in the History panel, select the state that you want to paint back to.**

5. **Drag with the History Brush tool to paint over the portion of the image you want to restore.**

   Photoshop paints over the image in the layer with the image from the state you specified as the source in Step 1.

   In Figure 4-5, I painted my original faces by using a 10–15% Opacity setting over my Water Paper-filtered image.

Figure 4-5: Painting with the History Brush tool

Using the Fill with History feature

If you can easily select the area that you want to replace with a specific state, you can use the Fill with History feature. Suppose you don't like the sky in a particular image. You select the sky area and then add clouds by using the Clouds filter. After you make those changes, you want to put the original sky back, but you don't want to reverse any of the other edits you performed. Just follow these steps to replace an area by using the Fill with History feature:

1. **Click in the far-left column of the state you want to use as the source for the Fill with History function in the History panel.**

   For example, select the state that has the original sky.

2. **With your current state active, use your favorite selection tools to select the area that you want to replace.**

   For example, if you remembered to save your original sky selection before you added clouds, you can choose Select➪Load Selection and retrieve that selection. Book III covers selection tools in detail.

3. **Choose Edit➪Fill and then select History from the Use pop-up menu.**

4. **Click OK to fill the selection with the image area from the selected state.**

Using the Art History Brush tool

The Art History Brush tool is an interesting variation on the plain old History Brush tool. Both tools paint over an image by using information from a previous state. The Art History Brush tool, however, includes several choices on the Options bar that let you apply brush-stroke effects to your image when you paint:

- **Style:** The Style menu contains various-shaped brush stroke styles, such as Tight Short, Loose Medium, Dab, or Loose Curl.

- **Area:** This option controls the area that the paint stroke covers, independent of the brush size you select. The larger the brush size, the more area it covers.

- **Tolerance:** This option adjusts the amount of the change applied to your image. A low tolerance value lets you apply strokes anywhere in the image, regardless of color values. A high tolerance value limits Art History strokes to areas that are very different from the source state or snapshot, making your image less dramatically different from the original.

You can use these options to create an interesting hand-painted effect, which you can control quite easily after you have some practice.

When Photoshop won't let you go back

Sometimes, you may see a No symbol (a slashed circle) when you try to use the Eraser with the Erase to History option, the History Brush tool, or the Fill with History command. Your current image must be the same file size (have the same number of pixels) as the state you're trying to go back to. Such actions as cropping, trimming, using the Image Size or Canvas Size commands, or rotating any amount other than 180 degrees can prevent you from going back to a previous state. However, if you happen to have a square image, you can still use the Eraser with the Erase to History option if you rotate that image in 90-degree increments.

The Art History Brush tool often works best when you use a state that's quite different from the state you're painting over. For example, you can apply a heavy filter that makes the image almost unrecognizable and then use that filtered image to paint with the Art History Brush tool. You can even completely fill an image with color or texture and then work with that.

To paint with the Art History Brush tool, follow these steps:

1. **Apply any effects and filters that you want to use to a chosen state.**

   See Book V, Chapter 4 for the details on effects. See Book VII, Chapters 1 and 2 for filter info.

   I started by applying a Rough Pastels filter to my beach scene.

2. **Click in the far-left column in the History panel to select the state that you want to use as the source for the Art History Brush tool.**

3. **Select the Art History Brush tool from the Tools panel.**

   You can also press Y to select it.

4. **Select from the choices on the Options bar.**

   Several of the options, such as Brush, Mode, and Opacity, are similar to the options available with the ordinary Brush tool. The new options are Style, Area, and Tolerance, explained earlier.

5. **Paint with the brush to get the effect you want, as shown in Figure 4-6.**

Don't forget that you can use the History panel to reverse Art History strokes if you change your mind about them!

Purestock

Figure 4-6: The Art History Brush tool lets you paint back to history with artistic flair.

Chapter 5: Creating Actions for Productivity and Fun

In This Chapter

✓ Working with actions in the Actions panel

✓ Playing preset actions

✓ Recording a new action

✓ Editing and organizing actions

✓ Using actions sets

✓ Processing batches of files

✓ Creating droplet applets

*P*ractice makes perfect — but when repeating the same steps in Photoshop over and over, the result is often tedium and impatience. You don't want to have to reinvent the wheel each time you go for a spin around the block, so why repeat the actions that carry out specific tasks in Photoshop if you don't have to? Photoshop lets you record steps by using a fast and fun feature called Actions. Photoshop also has presets for popular actions, such as creating a wood frame, simulating water reflections, or providing a molten-lead look. This chapter shows you how to take advantage of Photoshop's presets, as well as its macro recording and editing capabilities.

Using the Actions Panel

Not surprisingly, Photoshop has a panel dedicated to the automation of various chores. To view the Actions panel, choose Window⇨Actions (or press F9 on a PC, Opt+F9 on the Mac) or click the Actions icon in the panel dock. You can view the Actions panel in two modes, Button and List. Each mode is useful in its own way. You can access the mode you're not currently using via the Actions panel pop-up menu:

✓ **Button mode:** A convenient, compact mode that hides all the inner workings of the actions, presenting only a list of buttons that you can click to trigger a particular macro. Button mode is fast and easy; just click and go.

✔ **List mode:** Shown in Figure 5-1 is the default display in which each action appears as a folder-like heading. You can open a heading to reveal all the steps within that action or collapse the heading to hide those steps. You need to be in List mode when you record an action and when you edit individual steps. List mode also lets you perform only a select number of the steps in an action.

When you're working in List mode, the Actions panel has these three columns:

✔ **The left column:** Contains check boxes that you can select or deselect to include or exclude actions (or steps within an action).

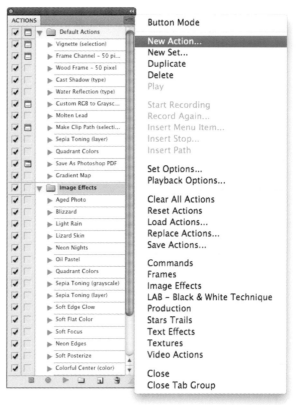

Figure 5-1: The Actions panel lets you create and store actions — a set of recorded steps that automate repetitive tasks.

✔ **The middle column:** Toggles on or off whether actions display dialog boxes. Some actions include options that you can select while running the macro. For example, the Vignette (Selection) action, which creates a faded frame around a selection, includes a dialog box that lets you specify the width of the fading. This dialog box appears only after you select this middle column; if you deselect the column, the action uses a default value. Adobe refers to this setting as Modal control.

✔ **The right column:** This widest column shows the name of the set of actions (folder icon) or the individual action. Click the right-pointing arrow to the left of the action's name to reveal the individual steps of the action. If you've assigned any keyboard shortcuts to your action, they also appear in this column.

Introducing Preset Actions

Preset actions are the actions created by the kind folks at Adobe that come with Photoshop. You can also get other preset actions from Adobe's Web site, as well as from third-party vendors. You may need to load an action into the panel so that it's ready to use. After an action is loaded, you can apply all the steps in that action in one fell swoop by playing the action. The following sections explain how to work with preset actions in more detail.

Loading preset actions

Photoshop's preset actions are located in a series of files in the Actions folder. The default actions load by, um, default when you first open Photoshop. However, you can open and use other preset actions. They include Frames (for putting frames around your images), Text Effects (for enhancing your text), and Image Effects (which let you give your image the appearance of being aged or neon, for example), among others.

Photoshop CS5 adds a couple new preset actions. Using LAB-Black and White Technique is a nice way to convert a color image into grayscale. Star Trails Rotation creates circular, glowing motion trails, as shown in Figure 5-2.

Follow these steps to load preset actions:

1. **In the Actions panel, click the panel pop-up menu arrow and select Load Actions.**

   In the Load dialog box, Photoshop opens the Actions folder in the Presets folder. This folder contains several sets of actions presets. If the folder is empty, navigate to `C:\Program Files\Adobe\Adobe Photoshop CS5\Presets\Actions`. (On the Mac, go to `Macintosh HD\Applications\Adobe Photoshop CS5\Presets\Actions`.)

Original

Star Trails Rotation applied

NASA

Figure 5-2: Photoshop comes with a wide array of interesting preset actions that can quickly transform your image.

2. **Select one of the actions sets.**

3. **Click the Load button.**

Easier, Photoshop's additional actions presets also appear at the bottom of the Actions panel pop-up menu. You can add any of them to your current list of actions by selecting the set's name.

The new actions presets appear in the Actions panel below the default actions. You can show or hide the actions in Default Actions or any of the other sets by clicking the expand/collapse arrow in the third column.

You can also make actions available — or unavailable — for an entire set by clicking the first column in the Actions panel to the left of the actions set's folder icon.

Here are some other tidbits about loading and working with preset actions:

✔ Any actions sets that you create (as I describe in the section "Creating and Saving Actions Sets," later in this chapter) appear in the pop-up menu if you save them in the Photoshop Actions folder. If you save them somewhere other than the Actions folder, you can navigate to that folder by using the usual file navigation commands.

✔ To remove the existing actions and replace them with the set you're loading, select Replace Actions from the panel pop-up menu.

✔ To reset the Actions panel to the Default Actions set (removing all other sets that you may have loaded), select Reset Actions from the panel pop-up menu.

✔ To clear all actions from the Actions panel, select Clear All Actions from the panel pop-up menu. (You might want to do this if you're creating your own set of actions from scratch.)

✔ To rename an actions set, select it and then select Set Options from the panel pop-up menu.

If you do a Google search for *Photoshop Actions*, you get a barrage of user-created actions, ranging from functional to funky. You can save these actions to your computer so that you can then load them into Photoshop. ***Remember:*** Check any file that you download from the Internet for viruses and other malware, using an antivirus program or a similar utility.

Playing a preset action

You perform an action on an image by playing that action. To play a preset action, just open the file that you want to apply the action to, and then do one of the following:

✔ In Button mode, click the action that you want to play. You don't have any other options.

✔ In List mode, select the action that you want to play, and then click the Play Selection button at the bottom of the Actions panel or select Play from the panel pop-up menu.

If you want to play back just one step of an action (say, for testing purposes), select the step that you want to play in List mode, and then Ctrl-click (⌘-click on the Mac) the Play button in the Actions panel. You can also simply double-click the step in the list while holding down the Ctrl key (the ⌘ key on the Mac).

Creating a New Action

When you create an action, you automate a series of steps. The hardest part about creating a new action is figuring out what functions you want to automate. Think about steps that you carry out over and over, and whether you could be more productive if you had an action that could do them for you. For example, you might want to create your own action to reduce images to a constant width of 500 pixels for display in an eBay auction. However, performing color-correction tasks for your eBay images is more difficult to automate because your images may vary in their original color and contrast.

Note that you can now even record your custom print settings as part of your action. This can save loads of time, if you have taken a bit of time to set up custom print settings that you want to use time and time again.

After you decide what you want to automate, examine the actual steps so that you can record them. After you record the steps, creating a new action involves little more than starting Photoshop's macro recorder and carrying out the steps that you want to include in the action.

While you're working out the kinks in your action, I highly recommend that you do so on a *copy* of your original file. That way, if things go awry, your original file is safe from harm.

Here are the steps to follow to create a new action:

1. **Open an image.**

2. **Display the Actions panel in List mode by unchecking Button Mode in the panel pop-up menu.**

3. **Click the Create New Action button at the bottom of the Actions panel.**

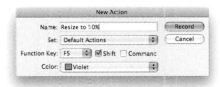

Figure 5-3: Name your new action and specify your other options.

   You can also select New Action from the panel pop-up menu.

   The New Action dialog box opens, as shown in Figure 5-3.

4. **In the Name text box, enter a name for the action.**

5. **In the Set pop-up menu, select the actions set in which you want to save the new action.**

   An *actions set* is merely a folder that contains individual actions for organizational purposes. Feel free to use an existing set or create your own.

6. **(Optional) To associate the action with a function-key shortcut, select the name of the function key from the Function Key drop-down list.**

   This step associates the action with a button on the keyboard. Associating an action with a function key, such as F2, F3, and so on, can cut down the time it takes you to perform common actions. Try to use keyboard shortcuts that aren't already associated with other Photoshop tasks.

   Select the Shift or Ctrl (Shift or ⌘ on the Mac) check box to use either one of these keys with the function key.

   Any keyboard shortcut that you assign to an action overrides the default function already assigned to the keyboard shortcut. A few exceptions exist in which the operating system wins in the case of a conflict. You can revert to the original shortcut by choosing Edit⇨Keyboard Shortcuts. See Book I, Chapter 5 for details.

   To avoid conflicts, Mac users can check for system keyboard shortcuts. To do so, look under the Keyboard Shortcuts tab in the Keyboard & Mouse section of the Systems Preferences under the Apple menu.

7. **In the Color drop-down list, select a color to mark your action in Button mode.**

   This option enables you to group related actions by color.

8. **Click the Record button in the New Action dialog box to begin recording.**

9. **Carry out all the steps that you want to record.**

10. **Click the Stop Playing/Recording button at the bottom of the Actions panel to finish the action.**

    Your new action appears in the Actions panel, in both List and Button modes.

Editing and Managing Actions

After you create a new action, you can try it out by opening an image and clicking the Play button in the Actions panel. If the action doesn't perform the way you expect, you may need to edit your action to fine-tune it. You also may need to edit an action to add features or change the action's behavior in some way. (For example, you might decide that you want your resizing action to change the size to 45 percent, rather than 50 percent.) Photoshop enables you to edit your actions fairly easily. However, certain actions won't run on certain files. For example, if your action involves adjusting the opacity of a layer and you run it on an image without layers, it won't work. You have to include a step that creates a layer first.

You have a lot of editing options; you can change the action's name, keyboard shortcut, or color coding. Just double-click the action name in the Actions panel and then enter a new name; or select the action, select Action Options from the panel pop-up menu, and change the information in the dialog box, as desired. You can also hold down the Alt key (Option key on the Mac) and double-click the action's name in the Actions panel to open the Actions Options dialog box.

Rerecording an action

As easy as editing an action is, your best option is often to simply rerecord the action from scratch. If the action isn't long or complex, you can often rerecord it in less time than editing the existing action. You can rerecord an action two ways:

- ✔ **Create a new action from scratch.** Perform all the steps again to replace the old action with a new one, saving the action with the same (or a different) filename.

- ✔ **Use the clever Record Again feature.** Photoshop runs through the steps that you already recorded, opening the dialog boxes that you used the first time so that you can enter new values.

This Record Again method is very handy if you want to change only some of the parameters, keeping the steps the same and in the same order. You don't even have to remember what steps you used. Photoshop runs through them for you while you record the steps, or macro, again.

To rerecord a macro with the Record Again option, select the name of the macro that you want to rerecord and select Record Again from the panel pop-up menu. When the different dialog boxes appear, enter the new values that you want and click OK until the macro is finished.

Editing an action

You can edit individual steps of an action. Here are some of the editing changes that you can make:

- ✔ **Move a step.** To move a step from one place in the action to another, click the step that you want to relocate and drag it to its new place in the action list.

- ✔ **Add a step in the middle.** To add a new step in the middle of an existing action, select the step that you want to precede the new step. Click the Record button and perform the steps that you want to add. Click the Stop Recording button when you finish.

✔ **Add a step to the end.** To add a new step at the end of an existing action, select the name of the action, click the Record button, and perform the steps that you want to add. Click the Stop Recording button when you finish.

✔ **Remove a step.** Click the step that you want to delete and then drag the step to the trash icon, or click the trash icon and then click OK in the dialog box that appears. (Alt-click the trash icon [Option-click on the Mac] to bypass the dialog box and delete the step without confirmation.) You can also select a step and select Delete from the panel pop-up menu.

✔ **Duplicate a step.** Hold down the Alt key (Option key on the Mac) and drag the step that you want to duplicate to another location in the Actions panel. Photoshop then creates a copy of the step, leaving the original step where it was, as shown in Figure 5-4.

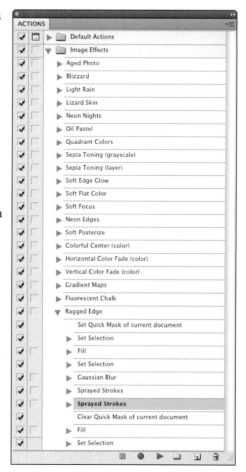

Figure 5-4: Duplicate a step in an action.

Slowing down action playback

When you play back an action to test it, the action may run too quickly for you to see exactly what's going on. To slow things down, select Playback Options from the panel pop-up menu and select a playback speed in the Playback Options dialog box.

Select Accelerated to zip through an action at normal speed, Step by Step to command Photoshop to briefly stop between actions so that you can examine what's happened, or Pause For to create a short pause before moving on. (Make sure that you specify for how many seconds you want to pause.) If you want to get really fancy, you can select the Pause for Audio Annotation check box and use your microphone to describe what each step does.

You can remove or duplicate an entire action by using the procedures described in the preceding list for removing a step or duplicating a step.

Creating and Saving Actions Sets

If you create your own sets of actions, you may want to include them in custom sets that you can load or remove, as needed. Just follow these steps:

1. **Display the Actions panel in List mode.**

2. **Click the Create New Set button in the Actions panel or select New Set from the panel pop-up menu.**

   The New Set dialog box appears.

3. **Enter a name for your actions set in the New Set dialog box and click OK.**

4. **Drag any existing actions that you want to include from their locations in the Actions panel to a new location within your new set folder.**

5. **Create any new actions that you want to include within the new set.**

   See the section "Creating a New Action," earlier in this chapter.

6. **Select the name of the set and choose Save Actions from the panel pop-up menu.**

7. **Save the set in the Actions folder (which you can find in the Presets folder within the Adobe Photoshop CS5 folder).**

Batch Processing Actions

Photoshop's Batch feature lets you apply an action to a group of files. Suppose you want to make changes to a series of files. You can open each file in Photoshop, play the desired macro, and then save the file. However, that might take a few minutes (or much longer if you have several files to process). If you want to keep your original file, too, you have to remember to save each file in a new folder. Batch processing can automate tedious chores for you.

To try this useful tool, copy some files (at least five or six) to a new folder and follow these steps:

1. **Make sure that all the files are in a single folder of their own.**

   Any subfolders will be included in that folder.

   Photoshop, by default, works on all the files in a folder. You have to use Adobe Bridge if you want to choose only some of those files by using the Batch feature. You can find out more about Adobe Bridge in Book I, Chapter 4.

2. **Choose File⇨Automate⇨Batch.**

   The Batch dialog box opens, as shown in Figure 5-5.

3. **In the Set pop-up menu, select the set that contains the action you want to apply.**

   If you have only one set of actions loaded, that set appears by default.

4. **In the Action pop-up menu, select the action that you want to apply.**

5. **In the Source pop-up menu, select Folder.**

Figure 5-5: By batch-processing an action on a group of files, you can take a coffee break and still get work done.

You can also select Opened Files to process files that you already opened in Photoshop, Import to process a series of files captured with your scanner or transferred from your digital camera, or Bridge to process files that you selected in Adobe Bridge.

6. **Click the Choose button, navigate to the folder that you want to use, and click OK (in Windows) or Choose (in Mac OS).**

7. **Select other options in the Source area, as desired.**

   Here's a description of your choices:

   - *Override Action "Open" Commands:* Normally, Photoshop opens each of the files in the selected folder automatically and processes them — so your action doesn't have to contain an Open command. However, if the macro *does* contain an Open command, select this option. With this option active, Photoshop overrides Open commands in the actions that use specific files (rather than batched files).

   - *Include All Subfolders:* Select this option to process files in subfolders within the folder that you specify.

   - *Suppress File Open Options Dialogs:* Select this option to have Photoshop disregard any options that possibly could be selected upon opening a file.

   - *Suppress Color Profile Warnings:* When Photoshop opens a file that contains its own color profile, it asks whether you want to use that profile or Photoshop's default profile. Selecting this check box suppresses that choice; Photoshop always uses its own default color profile. I explain color profiles in Book II, Chapter 2.

8. **In the Destination area, tell Photoshop what to do with each file after the action has been applied to it.**

   Choose one of the following options from the drop-down list:

   * *None:* Leaves the file open on your Photoshop desktop without saving it (unless the action itself contains a Save command).

   * *Save and Close:* Closes the files in the same folder in which Photoshop found them. Your original file is overwritten, so use this option only when you don't want to save the original or you have another copy.

   * *Folder:* Saves the document in a folder.

9. **If you chose Folder in Step 8, click the Choose button and navigate to a destination folder for your files.**

10. **Select the Override Action "Save As" Commands check box to ignore any Save As parameters in the action and use the filenames of the files (as specified in the File Naming section described in Step 11).**

11. **In the File Naming section, specify how you want Photoshop to create the filenames for the new, processed files by selecting options from the drop-down lists.**

    You can select options from six pop-up menus, depending on how long and complicated you want the filenames to be.

    When you process large numbers of files, these naming tools can help you keep track of when and how the files were created.

12. **Select the Windows, Mac OS, or Unix check box to specify what operating system you want the saved filenames to be most compatible with.**

13. **In the Errors pop-up menu, select whether you want Photoshop to stop processing a batch when it encounters an error or whether you want it to simply continue and list the errors in a file. If you select the latter option, click the Save As button and, in the Save dialog box, specify a name and location for the log.**

    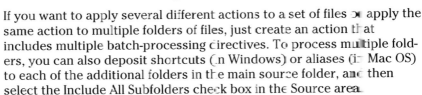

    If you want to apply several different actions to a set of files or apply the same action to multiple folders of files, just create an action that includes multiple batch-processing directives. To process multiple folders, you can also deposit shortcuts (in Windows) or aliases (in Mac OS) to each of the additional folders in the main source folder, and then select the Include All Subfolders check box in the Source area.

14. **When you finish selecting options in the Batch dialog box, click OK to start the batch processing.**

Creating Droplets

Droplets are drag-and-drop mini-applications — essentially applets — in macro form that can exist outside Photoshop on your desktop, on your task-bar, or within a folder. They're always available, so you can apply them to any image files you want. Think of them as batches waiting to happen.

You just need to drag the file or files that you want to process onto the drop-let. Photoshop doesn't even have to be open at the time. When you drop the file or files, the droplet opens Photoshop and carries out the steps in the action embedded in the droplet's instructions. You must use an existing action as the core of the droplet.

To create a droplet, follow these steps:

1. **Choose File⇨Automate⇨Create Droplet.**

   The Create Droplet dialog box opens, as shown in Figure 5-6.

2. **In the Save Droplet In area, click the Choose button and enter a name and location on your hard drive for the droplet application.**

   The location isn't of overriding importance because after you create the droplet, you can drag it to your desktop, a toolbar, or wherever you like.

Figure 5-6: Create and manage your droplets in this dialog box.

   The rest of the Create Droplet dialog box is the same as the Batch dialog box (described in the preceding section), except that you don't have to specify a source. Droplets use the files dropped on them as their source files.

3. **In the Play area, select the actions set, action, and options.**

4. **Select a destination from the Destination pop-up menu.**

5. **Specify any file-naming options you want.**

6. **Specify how Photoshop should process errors.**

7. **When you finish, click OK to create the droplet.**

   To use the droplet, just select the file, files, or folders that you want to process and drag them to the droplet applet.

Book III
Selections

The 5th Wave   By Rich Tennant

"How's it going? You get a handle on that Lasso function yet?"

*1*f there's one technique that separates the really good Photoshop users from the wannabes, it's the ability to make a top-notch selection. Pick up any tabloid and you'll agree with me that a lot of those wannabes seem to be gainfully employed! This book, along with Book VI, gives you a complete arsenal of selection commands, methods, and techniques. In this book, I give you information on how to create and modify selections and paths by using various Photoshop tools, such as the Marquee, Lasso, Magic Wand, Quick Selection, and Pen tools. After you go through this book, you can put those wannabes to shame.

Chapter 1: Making Selections

In This Chapter

✔ **Capturing selections with the Marquee tools**

✔ **Roping selections with the Lasso tools**

✔ **Picking up pixels with the Magic Wand tool**

✔ **Selecting quickly to save time**

*N*o matter how much you know about Photoshop, if you can't make a good selection, your work will look like it belongs with the creatively (but poorly) composed images in those weekly tabloid rags. You know what I'm talking about — those pictures that go alongside headlines like "Bat Boy Wins Bake-Off" and "Woman with 16 Fingers Wins Typing Contest."

Making accurate selections is the key to creating and editing images effectively so that the result looks flawless. Fortunately, Photoshop offers a bevy of tools and techniques for creating selections, from the simple to the complex. Photoshop offers three basic methods of creating a selection: using a selection tool or method, using the Pen tool, or creating a mask

In this chapter, I give you the foundation you need to use the selection and Pen tools. In fact, the rest of Book III covers these tools in detail. I cover the more complex method of masking in Book VI.

Defining Selections

The tools I discuss in this chapter require you to take a little piece of a larger image so that you can dig in and make some serious edits. Defining a selection means that you specify which part of the image you want to work with. Everything within a selection is fair game for manipulation and is considered *selected*. Everything outside the selection is protected, or *unselected*. Simple enough, right? Well, you can also have partially selected pixels. Confused yet? A *partially selected* pixel has usually been anti-aliased, feathered, or masked. (I cover anti-aliasing and feathering in the section "Using the Marquee options," later in this chapter. You can find out about masking in Book VI.)

When you use a selection tool to define a selection, a moving dotted outline called a *selection marquee* appears.

Marqueeing When You Can

Photoshop geeks call the selection marquee by a variety of names. Sometimes it's referred to as a marquee, other times as a selection, and you might even hear people call it a selection outline, an outline, selection edges, or just plain old edges. A favorite name for these dotted lines is marching ants. Throughout the book, I usually call them *selection marquees.* Boring? Maybe. Accurate? Yup. Whatever you want to call the selection marquee, how you create one depends on the particular Marquee tool or command you use.

The Marquee tools are the easiest selection tools to use — so I suggest that you use them when you can.

In the Photoshop repertoire of tools, you find four types of Marquee tools: Rectangular Marquee, Elliptical Marquee, Single Row Marquee, and Single Column Marquee.

Using the Rectangular Marquee tool

The Rectangular Marquee tool creates rectangular, including square, selections. Use this tool when you want to zero in on an image, plucking it out of a larger background to provide a better focal point.

Follow these steps to make a selection with the Rectangular Marquee tool:

1. **Select the Rectangular Marquee tool from the Tools panel.**

   You can also use the keyboard shortcut — press the M key.

2. **Click and drag from one corner of the area that you want to select to the opposite corner.**

   While you drag, the selection marquee appears. The marquee follows the movement of your mouse cursor (a crosshair or plus sign icon). For example, in Figure 1-1, I dragged from the lower-left corner to the upper-right corner.

Selection marquee

Purestock

Figure 1-1: The Rectangular Marquee selects part of your image.

3. **Release your mouse button.**

   You now have a full-fledged rectangular selection.

If you want to create a perfect square, hold down the Shift key after you begin dragging. When you have your desired selection, release the mouse button and then the Shift key.

If you want to drag your selection from the center outward, rather than from corner to corner, hold down the Alt (Option on the Mac) key after you begin dragging. When you have your desired selection, release your mouse button and then release the Alt (Option on the Mac) key.

Using the Elliptical Marquee tool

The Elliptical Marquee tool is designed for elliptical, including circular, selections. You can easily select objects such as clocks, balls, and full moons by using this tool.

When you select with the Elliptical Marquee tool, you don't drag from corner to corner per se; you drag from one corner of the ellipsis's bounding box to the other, which makes the process a little tougher. Here are the steps:

1. **Select the Elliptical Marquee tool from the Marquee flyout menu in the Tools panel.**

   You can also use the keyboard shortcut. If the Elliptical Marquee tool is visible, press the M key. If the Rectangular Marquee is visible, you must press Shift+M.

2. **Position the crosshair near the area that you want to select and then drag around your desired element.**

   While you drag, the selection marquee appears.

   You may find it easier to create an elliptical selection by holding down the Alt (Option on the Mac) key and dragging from the center outward. First, click the mouse button, and then before you move the mouse, hold down Alt (Option on the Mac) and drag. Release your mouse and then the key when you have your desired selection. If you want to draw from the center out and want a perfect circle, hold down the Shift key, as well. When you have your desired selection, release your mouse button and then the Shift+Alt (Shift+Option on the Mac) keys. This technique works for creating squares, also.

3. **When you're satisfied with your selection, release your mouse button.**

   Your elliptical selection is alive and well, as shown in Figure 1-2.

   • If you need to move the selection marquee to better center your selection, click and drag inside the marquee.

Book III
Chapter 1

Making Selections

- You can move a selection with any of the Marquee tools by pressing the spacebar while you're drawing.

- If the selection isn't quite the right shape and size, jump to Book III, Chapter 2 to find out how to make perfect selections.

Using the Single Column and Single Row Marquee tools

The Single Row and Single Column Marquee tools select a single row or single column of pixels. If you don't go blind using them, these tools can occasionally come in handy for selecting and repairing a thin scratch or fold line on an image, or for getting rid of an artifact, such as a colored line, that has somehow appeared on a scanned image. (You can find out more about making repairs in Book VIII.)

Photodisc

Figure 1-2: The Elliptical Marquee is the tool of choice for selecting round objects.

To use either of these tools, click either the row or column of pixels that you want to work on. You don't have to do any dragging, but it does help to zoom into your image so that you can better position the tool on the offending row or column.

For more on zooming, see Book I, Chapter 4. Check out Figure 1-3 to get familiar with a single-row selection.

The Single Row and Single Column Marquee tools don't have keyboard shortcuts, so you're stuck with having to click the tools to select them.

Using the Marquee options

If drawing from the center outward or creating a perfect circle or square doesn't give you enough control, you may want to look at the marquee settings provided by the Options bar. These options allow you to make selections that are even more precise by specifying exact measurements.

You must select the options on the Options bar *before* you make your selection with the Marquee tools.

Figure 1-3: The Single Row Marquee tool selects just one row of pixels.

For now, you can ignore the first five icons on the left side of the Options bar, as shown in Figure 1-4. The first icon has to do with tool presets, which I cover in Book I, Chapter 2. The next four icons are the selection-option icons (which I discuss in Book III, Chapter 3).

Figure 1-4: Specify all your marquee settings or the Options bar.

Here's the lowdown on each of the remaining options:

✔ **Feather:** *Feathering* softens, or feathers, the edges of a selection. The amount of softening depends on the radius — the higher the radius, the softer the edge, as shown in Figure 1-5. The radius measures how far in all directions the feather effect extends.

You can use feathering to create a subtle and natural transition between selections or to create a special effect in which an image slowly fades out to the background or to transparency. To feather while you're selecting, select the Feather option on the Options bar before you use the Marquee tools. You can feather a selection after the fact by using the Select⇨Modify submenu. Check out Book III, Chapter 2 for more feathering details.

Feather radius 4 pixels

Feather radius 20 pixels

Figure 1-5: Applying a feather to your selection blurs the edges.

✔ **Anti-Alias:** Whereas feathering completely blurs edges, anti-aliasing just slightly softens the edge of an elliptical selection so that very hard, jagged edges aren't quite so prominent, as shown in Figure 1-6. You don't have an option in which you can enter a pixel value for anti-aliasing. An anti-aliased edge is always 1 pixel wide.

For the most part, I recommend keeping the Anti-Alias option selected, especially if you plan to create composite images. Anti-aliasing helps create natural-looking blends between multiple selections. However, if want a crisp, linear edge, deselect this option.

✔ **Style:** The Style drop-down list contains these three settings:

  • *Normal:* This setting enables you to freely drag a selection to any desired dimension.

- *Fixed Aspect Ratio:* This option allows you to specify a ratio of width to height in a selection. For example, if you enter 2 for width and 1 for height, you *always* get a marquee selection that's twice as wide as it is high, no matter what the size. If you enter 1 for both dimensions, you get perfect circles or squares.

- *Fixed Size:* Select this option to specify exact values for the Width and Height. This option comes in handy when several images need to be the same exact size, such as in a row of headshots in a corporate brochure.

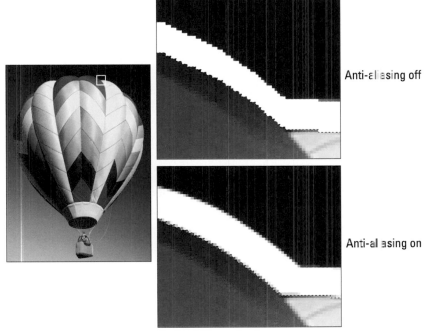

Anti-aliasing off

Anti-aliasing on

Figure 1-6: Anti-aliasing slightly softens your selection edges.

✔ **Width and Height:** When you select a Fixed Size from the Style drop-down list, you can enter values in the Width and Height text boxes. To swap the Width and Height values, click the double-headed arrow button.

Even though the default unit of measurement in the Width and Height text boxes is pixels (px for short), you can enter any unit of measurement that Photoshop recognizes — pixels, inches, centimeters, millimeters, points, picas, or percents. After the number, simply type the word or abbreviation of your desired unit of measurement. Photoshop even lets you enter mixed units of measurements, so if you want a selection 100 pixels by 1.25 inches, you can specify that.

✔ **Refine Edge:** Although you probably won't need to fine-tune a simple marquee selection, that's what this option does. You can apply Refine Edges to any selection, and it appears on the Options bar of the Marquee, Lasso, Magic Wand, and Quick Selection (where it'll come in handy) tools. You can even use it to refine a layer mask. (See Book V, Chapter 3 for more on layer masks.) You can also apply this command to any existing selection by choosing Select⇨Refine Edge.

Here's the lowdown on this option's settings (shown in Figure 1-7), which are greatly improved in CS5:

- *View Mode:* Choose a mode from the pop-up menu to preview your selection. For example, Marching Ants shows the moving marquee, Overlay displays the red overlay you get when working in Quick Mask mode, and On Black and On White show the selection against a black or white background. Hover your cursor over each mode to get a tooltip. Press F to cycle through the various modes. Show Original shows the image without a selection preview. Show Radius displays the image with the selection border.

- *Smart Radius:* Select this option to have Photoshop automatically adjust the radius for hard and soft edges near your selection border.

- *Radius:* Specify the size of the selection border you will refine. Increase the radius to improve the edge of areas with soft transitions or a lot of detail. Move the slider while looking at your selection to find a good setting.

- *Smooth:* Smoothes out jigs and jags along the selection edge.

- *Feather:* Move the slider to create an increasingly softer, more blurred edge.

- *Contrast:* Removes artifacts while tightening soft edges by increasing the contrast. Try using the Smart Radius option first before playing with Contrast.

- *Shift Edge:* Decreases or increases your selection border. Slightly decreasing your selection border can help to *defringe* (eliminate undesirable background pixels) your selection edges.

- *Decontaminate Colors:* Replaces background fringe with the colors of your selected element. Note that because decontamination changes the colors of some of the pixels, you will have to output to, or create, another layer or document to preserve your current layer. To see the decontamination in action, choose Reveal Layer for your View mode.

- *Amount:* Changes the level of decontamination.

- *Output To:* Choose whether you want to output your refined, decontaminated selection to a selection on your current layer, layer mask, layer, layer with layer mask, new document, or new document with layer mask.

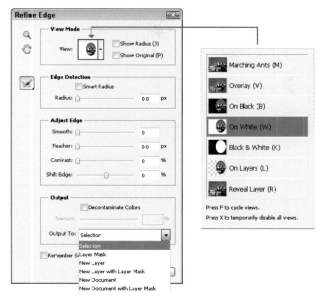

Figure 1-7: Fine-tune your selections with Refine Edges.

- *Refine Radius tool:* Brush around your border to adjust the area you are refining. To understand exactly what area is being included or excluded, change your View mode to Marching Ants. Use the right and left brackets to decrease and increase the brush size.

- *Zoom tool:* Enables you to zoom into your image to see the effects of your settings.

- *Hand tool:* Lets you pan around your document window to see the effects of your settings in various portions of your image.

Lassoing (When You Can't Marquee)

Unfortunately, not much in life is perfectly rectangular or elliptical. Most of the time, you have to deal with irregular shapes that have *extrusions* and *protrusions* (otherwise known as bumps or bulges) of some sort. That's where the Lasso tools come in handy. This group of tools allows you to make freeform selections.

Photoshop offers three Lasso tools: the Lasso tool itself (which I call the regular Lasso to distinguish it from the others), the Polygonal Lasso tool, and the Magnetic Lasso tool. Each of the Lasso tools has its own special purpose in the realm of freeform selections. But, in the category of simplicity, the Lasso tools are almost as easy to use as the Marquee tools. You just have to drag around the part of the image that you want to select. Just don't indulge in too much caffeine. A steady lasso hand is a good lasso hand.

The selection you make is only as good as how accurately you can trace around your desired element. If you don't make an exact selection the first time around, you can always go back and make corrections (which I cover in Book III, Chapter 3).

If, when making a selection, you find yourself fighting with your mouse (and losing), you may want to invest in a digital drawing tablet, such as a Wacom tablet. Using the stylus and the tablet can make mastering tools such as the Lasso a whole lot easier.

The Lasso and Polygonal Lasso tools both have only three choices on the Options bar to worry about — Feather, Anti-Aliased, and Refine Edges. These options work exactly the way they do with the Marquee tools. To find out more, check out the earlier section "Using the Marquee options."

To make a selection by using the Lasso tool, follow these steps:

1. **Select the Lasso tool from the Tools panel.**

   The tool looks like (well, yeah) a rope. You can also use the keyboard shortcut; press the L key.

2. **Position the cursor somewhere on the edge of the element that you want to select.**

   The *hot spot* (the lead point) of the Lasso cursor is the end of the rope. If you need a little visual assistance, press your Caps Lock key, which switches your cursor to a crosshair.

   Zoom in on the image if the element and the background don't have a lot of contrast.

   In my example, I started at the top of the butte, as shown in Figure 1-8.

3. **Trace around the element and try to capture only what you want to retain in your selection.**

   While you trace, a line forms that follows the movement of your mouse.

   Don't release your mouse button until you complete the selection by returning to the starting point to close the loop. When you release your mouse button, Photoshop thinks you're done and closes the selection, as shown in Figure 1-9.

4. **Continue tracing until you return to your starting point; release the mouse button.**

   Recognizing that you're now done, Photoshop presents you with a selection marquee that matches your Lasso line. (See Figure 1-10.)

Lasso cursor

Corbis Digital Stock

Figure 1-8: The Lasso tool is for freeform selections.

Closed selection marquee

Corbis Digital Stock

Figure 1-9: Don't release your mouse button too soon.

Selected area

Corbis Digital Stock

Figure 1-10: After tracing around your object, release your mouse, and Photoshop presents you with an accurate selection marquee.

Selecting straight sides with the Polygonal Lasso tool

Whereas the regular Lasso tool is great for selecting undulating, curvy elements, the Polygonal Lasso tool shines when it comes to the more regimented, straight-sided subjects, such as city skylines, buildings, and stairways.

Unlike the regular Lasso tool, the Polygonal Lasso tool has rubber band-like qualities, and instead of dragging, you click and release the mouse button at the corners of the object that you're selecting. It's like digital connect-the-dots. (Bonus: Less manual dexterity required.)

The following steps show you how to select with the Polygonal Lasso tool:

1. **Select the Polygonal Lasso tool in the Tools panel.**

   You can also use the keyboard shortcut. Press the L key and then press Shift+L until you get the Polygonal Lasso tool. It looks like the regular Lasso tool, but it has straight sides.

2. **With the Polygonal Lasso tool selected, click to establish the beginning of the first line of your selection.**

   A corner is always a good place to start.

3. **Move the mouse and click at the next corner of the object. Then, continue clicking at the various corners of your object.**

   The line stretches out from each corner that you click, like a rubber band.

4. **To close your selection, return to the first point that you clicked and click one last time.**

When you place your cursor over the starting point, a small circle appears next to your cursor, a sure sign that you're at the right place for closing the selection. A selection marquee that matches your Polygonal Lasso line appears, as shown in Figure 1-11.

Corbis Digital Stock

Figure 1-11: The Polygonal Lasso tool is perfect for selecting straight-sided objects.

Book III
Chapter 1

Making Selections

Which tool do you use if you have an object with both curves and straight sides? You can have two, two, *two* tools in one! Hold down the Alt (Option on the Mac) key to have the Polygonal Lasso tool temporarily transform into the regular Lasso tool. Then, click and drag to select the curves. Release the Alt (Option) key to return to the Polygonal Lasso tool. This trick works with the other Lasso tools, as well.

Attracting with the Magnetic Lasso tool

The last member of the lasso tool trio is the Magnetic Lasso, which I admit can be somewhat tricky to use and sometimes even downright obstinate. The Magnetic Lasso tool works by analyzing the colors of the pixels between the elements in the foreground and the elements in the background. Then, it snaps to the edge between the elements, as if the edge had a magnetic pull.

The Magnetic Lasso tool performs best when your image has a lot of contrast between the foreground and background elements — for example, a dark mountain range against a light sky or a shadow against a stucco wall.

The Magnetic Lasso tool also has some unique settings — which you can adjust on the Options bar — to tame its behavior. I cover those settings in the following section. For now, follow these steps to use the tool:

1. **Select the Magnetic Lasso tool in the Tools panel.**

   You can also use the keyboard shortcut: Press the L key and then press Shift+L until you get the Magnetic Lasso tool. The tool looks like a straight-sided lasso with a little magnet on it.

2. **Click the edge of the object you want to select.**

   You can start anywhere; just be sure to click the edge between the element you want and the background you don't want.

3. **Move your cursor around the object without clicking.**

   The Magnetic Lasso tool creates a selection line similar to the other lasso tools. It also adds little squares, called *points,* along that selection line, as shown in Figure 1-12. These points pin down the selection line the way you might section off an area of your yard with ropes and stakes.

Magnetic Lasso point

iStockphoto

Figure 1-12: The Magnetic Lasso tool detects the edge of your object.

Here are a couple more tips to keep in mind when working with the Magnetic Lasso tool:

- If the Magnetic Lasso tool starts veering off the edge of your object, back up your mouse and click to force a point down on the line.

- If the Magnetic Lasso tool adds a point where you don't want one, simply press your Backspace (Delete on a Mac) key to delete it.

4. **Continue moving your mouse around the object; return to your starting point and click the mouse button to close the selection.**

Like with the Polygonal Lasso tool, a small circle appears next to your cursor, indicating that you're at the correct place to close the selection. The selection marquee appears when the selection is closed.

Adjusting the Magnetic Lasso options

The Magnetic Lasso tool comes equipped with a few settings on the Options bar that control the sensitivity of the tool.

I recommend starting out by messing around with the Magnetic Lasso tool using its default settings. If the tool isn't cooperating, then play with the options.

The first icon, on the far left, has to do with tool presets, and the next four icons are the selection option icons. (Check out Book III, Chapter 3.) The Feather, Anti-Alias, and Refine Edge options work the way they do with the Marquee tools. (See the earlier section "Using the Marquee options.") The following list explains the remaining options:

- **Width:** This option, measured in pixels from 1 to 256, determines how close to the edge you have to move your mouse before the Magnetic Lasso tool recognizes the object you're selecting. Decrease the value if the object's edge has a lot of indentations and protrusions or if the image has low contrast. Increase the value if the image has high contrast or smooth edges.

  When using the Magnetic Lasso tool, you can change the Width value from the keyboard by pressing the left bracket ([ ) key to lower the value and the right bracket ( ]) key to increase the value.

- **Edge Contrast:** Measured in percentages from 1 to 100, this option specifies the required contrast between the object you're selecting and its background before the Magnetic Lasso tool hugs the edge between them. If your image has good contrast between the foreground and background, use a high percentage.

✓ **Frequency:** This setting, measured in percentages from 0 to 100, specifies how many points to place on the selection line. The higher the percentage, the greater number of points. If the object you want to select has a fairly smooth edge, keep the percentage low. If the edge is jagged or has a lot of detail, a high percentage may be more effective in getting an accurate selection line.

✓ **Tablet Pressure (Pen icon):** If you own a pressure-sensitive drawing tablet, select this option to make an increase in stylus pressure causing the edge width to decrease.

Performing Wand Wizardry

The Magic Wand. The name is intriguing, isn't it? Any tool that has the audacity to call itself the Magic Wand must be so powerful that it can grant your every selection wish with a mere swoosh. Unfortunately, it's not quite so awe-inspiring. A better name for this tool would be the Click-'n-Select tool. You click your image, and the Magic Wand tool makes a selection that contains areas of similar color based on the color of the pixel you clicked.

Simple enough. What's not quite so simple is how to determine *how* similar the color has to be to get the Magic Wand tool to select it. That's where the important Tolerance setting comes in. Before you tackle tolerance (and find out how it affects the Magic Wand tool's performance), you first need to get the hang of using the Magic Wand tool. In case you haven't used the Magic Wand before, I ordered the following sections with this in mind, so read them in order.

Selecting with the Magic Wand tool

Like with the Magnetic Lasso tool (covered in the section "Attracting with the Magnetic Lasso tool," earlier in this chapter), the Magic Wand tool works best when you have high-contrast images or images that have a limited number of colors. As shown in Figure 1-13, a black-and-white checkered flag is a perfect example of something that the Magic Wand tool effectively selects. I click the top of a black square, and the Magic Wand tool picks up all the other surrounding black pixels. I can now easily change the color of my black squares to red or yellow in one fell swoop.

Figure 1-13: The Magic Wand tool works best on images with limited colors.

As you can see, Figure 1-14 is a poor candidate for the Magic Wand tool. This image contains a ton of colors — and no definitive contrast between the glass, the wine, and the background. Although it takes only one click to select the black squares on the flag, other high-contrast candidates may take a few clicks. And some images may need you to make a tweak or two to the Tolerance setting, described in the following section.

Setting your tolerance

Sometimes, an image may contain a few shades of a similar color. Consider a cloudless sky, for example. A few shades of blue make up the bright blue yonder. By using the Magic Wand tool, if you click a darker shade of blue in the sky, Photoshop selects all similar shades of blue, but the lighter shades remain unselected. This is usually a sure sign that you need to increase your Tolerance level. The *Tolerance* setting determines the range of color that the Magic Wand tool selects. Tolerance is based on brightness levels that range from 0 to 255:

Corbis Digital Stock

Figure 1-14: Trying to select an image with a lot of color variation can be an exercise in futility.

 ✔ Setting the Tolerance to 0 selects one color only.

 ✔ Setting the Tolerance to 255 selects all colors — the entire image.

To use the Magic Wand tool and adjust Tolerance settings, follow these steps:

1. **Select the Magic Wand tool in the Tools panel.**

   Press the W key and then press Shift+W until you get a tool that looks like the weapon of choice for many Disney characters.

2. **Click the portion of the image that you want to select; use the default Tolerance setting of 32.**

   The pixel that you click determines the base color. The default value of 32 means that the Magic Wand tool selects all colors that are 16 levels lighter and 16 levels darker than the base color.

   If you selected everything you wanted the first time you used the Magic Wand tool, stretch your arm and give yourself a pat on the back. If you didn't (which is probably the case), go to Step 3.

3. **Enter a new Tolerance setting on the Options bar.**

   If the Magic Wand tool selected more than you wanted it to, lower the Tolerance setting. If it didn't select enough, raise the setting.

4. Click the portion of the image that you want to select.

Changing the Tolerance level doesn't adjust your current selection.

The Magic Wand tool deselects the current selection and makes a new selection — based on your new Tolerance setting, as shown in Figure 1-15. If it still isn't right, you can adjust the Tolerance setting again. I regret that I can't give you a magic formula that you can use to determine the right value. It's all about trial and error.

Tolerance of 16   Tolerance of 64

iStockphoto

Figure 1-15: Finding the right Tolerance is the key to selecting with the Magic Wand.

Using the Magic Wand Options bar

If you get a selection close to what you want, stop there and then use the selection-refining techniques I discuss in Book III, Chapter 2. But before you do that, you need to know about the other Magic Wand settings on the Options bar. Besides Anti-Alias and Refine Edge, which I discuss in the earlier section "Using the Marquee options," the three remaining options are as follows:

✓ **Contiguous:** When you turn on this option, the Magic Wand tool selects *only* pixels that are adjacent to each other. If you turn off the option, the Magic Wand tool selects all pixels within the range of tolerance, whether or not they're adjacent to each other.

✓ **Sample All Layers:** This option is valid only when you have multiple layers in your image. (For more on layers, see Book V.) If you have multiple layers and this option is on, the Magic Wand tool selects color from all visible layers. If you turn off this option, the Magic Wand selects colors from the active layer only.

✔ **Sample Size:** Although this option affects the Magic Wand tool, it appears on the Options bar *only* when you select the Eyedropper tool. (For more on the Eyedropper, see Book II, Chapter 3.) Select the Eyedropper tool and, in the Sample Size pop-up menu that appears, select from the following options:

- *Point Sample:* Samples just the color of the pixel you clicked.

- *3 by 3 Average:* Averages the color of the pixel you clicked and the surrounding eight pixels.

- *5 by 5 Average:* Averages the color of the pixel you clicked and the surrounding 24 pixels.

- *11 by 11 Average:* Averages the color of the pixel you clicked and the surrounding 120 pixels.

- *31 by 31 Average:* Averages the color of the pixel you clicked and the surrounding 960 pixels.

- *51 by 51 Average:* Averages the color of the pixel you clicked and the surrounding 2,600 pixels.

- *101 by 101 Average:* Averages the color of the pixel you clicked and the surrounding 10,200 pixels.

Saving Time with the Quick Selection Tool

We all never have enough time. Luckily, Adobe heard our cries and gave us a great tool. Think of it as a combo Brush, Magic Wand, Lasso tool. Easy to use — with surprisingly good results — it's sure to become part of your selection arsenal. To make short work of selecting by using this tool, follow these steps:

1. **Select the Quick Selection tool from the Tools panel.**

   The tool looks like a wand with a marquee around the end. It shares the Magic Wand tool's flyout menu. You can also press the W key, and then press Shift+W until you get the tool.

2. **If you're making a new selection, be sure that the selection option is set to New Selection or Add to Selection on the Options bar.**

3. **Select your desired brush settings from the Brush picker on the Options bar.**

4. **If your image has layers and you want to make a selection from all the layers, select the Sample All Layers option.**

   If you leave this option unselected, you select only from the current layer.

Book III Chapter 1

Making Selections

5. **Select the Auto-Enhance option to have Photoshop assist you by automatically refining your selection by implementing an algorithm.**

6. **Click and drag over the desired areas of your image.**

   Your selection grows while you drag, as shown in Figure 1-16.

   If you stop dragging and click in another portion of your image, your selection includes that clicked area.

7. **Change your selection as needed.**

   You have three options to change your selection:

   - To add to your selection, hold down the Shift key while dragging across your desired image areas. (If the Add to Selection option is selected on the Options bar, you don't have to hold down the Shift key.)

   - To delete from your selection, press the Alt (Option on the Mac) key while dragging across your unwanted image areas.

   - You can also select the Add to Selection and Subtract from Selection options on the Options bar.

Purestock

Figure 1-16: Paint a selection with the Quick Selection tool.

8. **If you need to further fine-tune your selection, click the Refine Edges option on the Options bar.**

   I explain settings in detail in the "Using the Marquee options" section, earlier in this chapter.

Chapter 2: Creating and Working with Paths

In This Chapter

🖊 **Working with the Pen tools**

🖊 **Using the Paths panel**

🖊 **Loading paths as selections (and vice versa)**

🖊 **Editing, saving, and selecting paths**

Although the Marquee, Lasso, and Magic Wand tools are fun, friendly, and easy to wield (see Book III, Chapter 1), sometimes they don't quite have the horsepower to make a precise selection. Therefore, either you spend a lot of time cleaning up what you've selected (see Book III, Chapter 3 for more on that topic), or you live with a ho-hum selection. That's where the Pen tool and its related cronies come to the rescue. The Pen tool creates paths that you can then convert into selections.

Because the Pen tool (along with the related path-editing tools) offers control and precision, it can nail that accurate selection. The only problem is that the Pen tool is far from fun, friendly, and easy. Many new users try the Pen a few times but end up muttering in disgust and returning gratefully to the Lasso tool. However, I guarantee that if you dedicate a good chunk of time to mastering the Pen tool, you can turn up your elite little nose at the simple Lasso tool.

Introducing Paths

Unlike the other selection tools, the Pen tool doesn't initially produce a selection marquee. When you select the Pen tool and start clicking and dragging around your image, you create a path. Paths have three types of components — anchor points, straight segments, and curved segments.

Curved paths are *Bézier paths* (after Pierre Bézier — who, in the 1970s, invented the equation used for CAD CAM programs). They're based on a mathematical cubic equation in which the path is controlled by direction lines that end in direction points (often referred to as *handles*), as shown in Figure 2-1. The length and angle of direction lines control the pitch and angle of the Bézier curve.

The following list introduces the different kinds of anchor points (refer to Figure 2-1) that Photoshop puts at your disposal. You can use some or all of these anchor points in a single path:

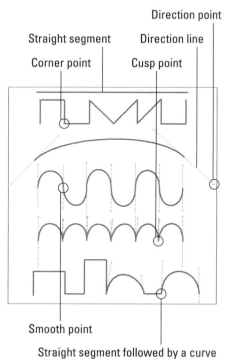

Figure 2-1: The Pen tool creates Bézier curves, which are comprised of many different components.

- **A true corner point:** Has no direction lines. Use corner points when you're selecting objects that have straight sides, such as stairs or barns.

- **A smooth point:** Has two direction lines pointing in opposite directions that are dependent on one another. Use smooth points when selecting objects that have alternating curves, such as a sea of rolling waves.

- **A cusp point:** Has two direction lines that are independent of one another. Use cusp points when you're selecting an object that has curves going the same direction, such as the petals on a daisy.

- **A point between a straight segment and a curve:** A corner point that has only one direction line.

After you create a Bézier path, you can then edit the path by moving, adding, deleting, or converting anchor points and by manipulating the direction lines. You can also transform paths by choosing Edit⇨Transform Paths. When you transform a path, you can scale, rotate, skew, distort, change the perspective of, or warp the path. (See Book III, Chapter 3 for details.)

The path hovers over the image in its own space. You control the path via the Paths panel, where you can save it, duplicate it, stroke it with color (apply color to the edge only), fill it with color or a pattern, and (most importantly) load it as a selection. I say "most importantly" because nine times out of ten, you painstakingly create a path as a means to an accurate selection marquee. You may use the path as a clipping path one other time: to hide a part of a layer or part of an image.

Creating a Path with the Pen Tool

The best way to get the hang of the Pen tool is to dive right in and work with it. Start with straight lines, which are very easy, and then move on to the more difficult curves. The more you practice with the Pen, the more comfortable and proficient you can become. It definitely is an example of the old adage, "You get out what you put into it."

Knowing your Pen tool options

Although every path consists of three basic components — segments, points, and direction lines — the Pen tool enables you to use these components to create a few different types of paths. See Book IV, Chapter 1 for more information on the following options, accessible from the Pen tool's Options bar. You must choose one of the following:

- ✔ **Shape Layers:** This option creates a shape on a new layer that's called, not surprisingly, a shape layer. After you create the path that defines the shape, Photoshop fills the shape with the foreground color and stores the path as a vector mask (see Book VI, Chapter 3) in the Paths panel. A shape layer is a unique entity.

- ✔ **Paths:** This option enables you to create a traditional path that hovers over the image. The path you create is a *work path* — which is temporary, appears in the Paths panel, and is unsaved. If you're creating a path that you eventually want to load as a selection, this is your option.

- ✔ **Fill Pixels:** This option is available only when you're using the shape tools. It allows you to create a shape and fill it with the foreground color, but it doesn't create a shape layer, nor does it retain the path.

For a detailed explanation of vector images (shape layers and paths) and raster images (such as those created with fill pixels), see Book II, Chapter 1.

Creating your first work path

Making a work path is the easiest of the three options, and you'll use it frequently after you get the hang of using the Pen tool. The following steps show you how to create a simple, straight path:

1. **Open an image you want to practice on.**

   I suggest choosing an image that has an element with straight edges and curves, if you also want to practice creating curved paths in the next few sections.

2. **Select the Pen tool from the Tools panel.**

   You can just press the P key, too.

3. **On the Options bar, click the Paths button.**

   You can see this button in Figure 2-2.

4. **To create a straight line, click and release your mouse button at the points where you want the line to begin and to end, leaving anchor points at those positions.**

   You don't need to do any dragging to create straight segments. When you click and add your anchor points, Photoshop creates straight segments that connect the anchor points, as shown in Figure 2-3.

5. **To draw a constrained line — horizontal, vertical, or 45-degree angle — hold down the Shift key while you click.**

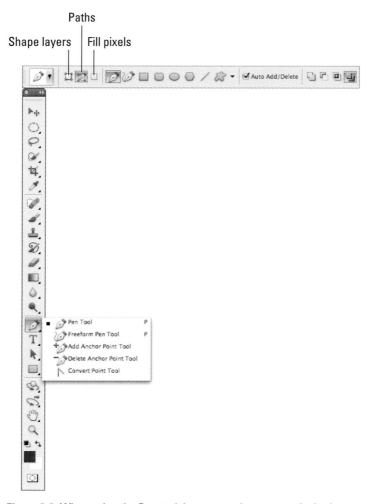

Figure 2-2: When using the Pen tool, be sure to choose your desired path type from the Options bar.

Straight segment Anchor points

Corbis Digital Stock

Figure 2-3: Drawing straight lines with the Pen tool requires nothing more than clicks.

6. **To end the path, click the Pen tool in the Tools panel to deselect it.**

   Or use this very handy shortcut:

   a. *Hold down the Ctrl key (⌘ on the Mac).*

      The Direct Selection tool (the white arrow) appears.

   b. *Click away from the line and release the Ctrl key (⌘ on the Mac).*

      The Pen tool reappears.

      With your path now deselected, you're free to start another, uncon-
      nected path, if you need to.

Check out the following sections if you want to add other kinds of segments to the path. Otherwise, skip to the section "Closing a path," later in this chapter.

Drawing curves

You're probably never going to create a simple work path that doesn't have curves as well as straight lines. I mean, not much in life is perfectly linear. Most things have undulations here and there. Picking up from the preceding section, follow these steps to create curved paths:

1. **If you're adding on to a previously created open path, be sure to position your cursor on the last anchor point you created on that open path before you continue.**

   A slash mark or a small square appears next to your cursor. If you're starting a new path, position the cursor where the curve begins.

2. **Whichever appears — the slash mark or the square — click and drag toward the direction you want the bump of the curve to go. Release the mouse button when you're done.**

   Here are some quick pointers for this stage of the procedure:

   • If you're creating a new path, an anchor point and two direction lines (which have direction points at their ends) appear. If you're adding a curve to your straight segment, an anchor point and one direction line with one direction point appear. The direction lines and direction points control the angle and pitch of the curve.

   • How do you know how far you should drag? Use the Rule of Thirds. Imagine that your curve is a piece of string that you've laid out in a straight line. Divide that line into thirds. Generally, the distance you drag your mouse cursor is approximately one-third the length of that line.

   • How do you establish the angle? Drag straight from the anchor point for a steeper curve and at an angle from the anchor point for a flatter curve. The element in my example is a flatter curve; therefore, I dragged up and to the right at an angle of just a few degrees, as shown in Figure 2-4.

Anchor point   Direction line

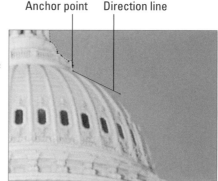

Corbis Digital Stock

Figure 2-4: Dragging at an angle of about 45 degrees or less begins the path of the flat curve.

3. **Move the cursor to the end of the curve and click and drag in the opposite direction, away from the bump.**

   Another anchor point and a set of two direction lines and points appear. Photoshop creates the curve segment between the anchor points, as shown in Figure 2-5. Here are a couple other handy pointers:

   - If you drag both direction lines in the same direction, you create a curve shaped like an *S*.

   - On the Options bar, click the down arrow at the end of the row of tools and choose the Rubber Band option. With this option selected, Photoshop draws a segment between the last anchor point you created and wherever your cursor is located, which gives you a kind of animated preview of how the path will appear. I find the option distracting, but some users love it.

Second anchor point

Curve segment   Direction line

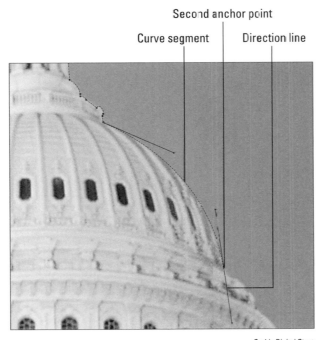

Corbis Digital Stock

Figure 2-5: Finish the curve by dragging in the opposite direction.

4. **To draw more alternating curves, repeat these steps, dragging in an opposite direction each time.**

Book III
Chapter 2

Creating
and Working
with Paths

Connecting a straight segment to a curve segment

If you need to create a straight segment after creating a curve (or vice versa), you need to convert the point where the path changes from curved to straight. To convert a point, follow these steps:

1. **Position your cursor over the second anchor point in the existing curve and hold down the Alt key (Option on the Mac).**

   A caret (which looks like an upside down V) appears next to the Pen cursor.

2. **Click and release your mouse button over the anchor point. Also release the Alt key (Option on the Mac).**

   The bottom direction line disappears. You've converted a smooth point into a corner point with one direction line. This action now allows you to create a straight segment.

It's no coincidence that the icon for the Convert Point tool is also a caret. Whenever you see a caret symbol in Photoshop, it's an indication that you're converting an anchor point, from smooth to corner or vice versa.

3. **Move your mouse to the end of the straight edge that you want to select, and then click and release your mouse button.**

   You can press the Shift key while you click if you want the line to be constrained horizontally, vertically, or at an angle that's a multiple of 45 degrees.

   Photoshop connects the two anchor points with a straight segment, as shown in Figure 2-6.

Corner point with one direction line   Straight segment

Corbis Digital Stock

Figure 2-6: To connect a straight segment to a curve segment, you must first convert the point.

Connecting curve segments with cusp points

If you want to create a curve that goes in the same direction as a curve that's adjacent to it, you have to take a couple additional steps, in addition to following the steps in the earlier "Drawing curves" section:

1. **Convert the point — this time from smooth to cusp — by positioning your cursor over the second anchor point in the existing curve and holding down the Alt (Option on the Mac) key.**

2. **Click and drag toward the bump of the curve. Release the mouse button and then release the Alt (Option on the Mac) key.**

   Essentially, your actions are pulling the direction line out from the anchor point. Both direction lines move to the same side of the anchor point, yet they're independent of each other, creating the cusp point, as shown in Figure 2-7.

3. **Move your cursor to where you want the curve to end and drag away from the bump to create your second curve.**

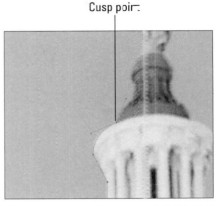

Cusp point

Corbis Digital Stock

Figure 2-7: You can connect two curves that go in the same direction with a cusp point.

 Try to keep anchor points on either side of the curve, not along the top. Also, try to use the fewest number of anchor points possible to create your path. That way, the path results in a much smoother curve. It also can reduce the possibility of printing problems.

Closing a path

To close the path, return to your first anchor point and click. A small circle appears next to your Pen cursor, indicating that you're closing the path.

Congratulations! You're now the proud owner of a work path. (See Figure 2-8.) Don't worry if the path isn't perfect; you can find out how to edit paths in the section "Editing Paths," later in this chapter. If your path is perfect and you want to save it, skip ahead to the section "Working with the Paths Panel," later in this chapter.

 If your path is incomplete and you want to continue drawing it, either click or click and drag the endpoint with the Pen tool. A slash mark or small square appears next to the Pen cursor.

Creating subpaths

You can create a series of lines or curves. For example, you may want to create a border consisting of some decorative curve shapes, which you could later stroke with color. (See Book IV, Chapter 2.) You can then save these *subpaths* under a single path name. To create a series of subpaths, simply end one path before starting another. Make sure that the paths aren't hidden when you do so; otherwise, Photoshop eliminates the previous path when you start another.

**Book III
Chapter 2**

Creating
and Working
with Paths

Corbis Digital Stock

Figure 2-8: To close your work path, return to your first anchor point and click.

Working with the Paths Panel

Working hand in hand with the Pen tool is the Paths panel. Think of the Paths panel as a kind of Command and Control Center for your paths. Although it isn't mandatory, opening your Paths panel (shown in Figure 2-9) is a good idea before you create a path so that you can stay apprised of what's happening with your image. To open the panel, choose Window⇨Paths.

Figure 2-9: The Paths panel allows you to save, delete, stroke, fill, and make selections from your paths.

The icons at the bottom of the Paths panel, from left to right (as shown in Figure 2-9), are

- Fill Path with Foreground Color
- Stroke Path with Brush
- Load Path as Selection

✔ Make Work Path from Selection

✔ Create New Path

✔ Delete Current Path

The following sections highlight some of the stuff you can do with the Paths panel.

Creating a path

When you create a path, it appears in the Paths panel as a work path.

A work path is temporary and unsaved, and you can have only one work path in the Paths panel at a time.

If the work path is selected when you begin another path, your actions are added to the current work path. If the existing work path is hidden and you begin drawing another path, that new work path replaces the existing one.

Creating a new path

You can save yourself a lot of grief if you make sure that your path is saved before you start creating it. If you select New Path from the Paths panel pop-up menu *before* you create the path, Photoshop saves the work path, and it becomes a saved path (also called a *named* path). You can also click the Create New Path icon at the bottom of the Paths panel.

Saving a work path

To save a work path, double-click the path in the Paths panel. Or choose Save Path from the Paths panel pop-up menu. (Click the down arrow in the upper-right of the panel to open the menu.) Then, provide a name in the Save Path dialog box that appears and click OK.

After you save your path, you can reload it at any time. Unlike layers, paths take up very little storage space, so don't hesitate to save them. You don't want to go through all that work again if you don't have to. Unlike work paths, you can have as many saved paths as your heart desires.

Deleting, duplicating, and renaming a path

To delete a path, drag the path to the trash can icon at the bottom of the panel. Or choose Delete Path from the Paths panel pop-up menu

You can duplicate a saved path by selecting the path in the Paths panel and selecting Duplicate Path from the Paths panel pop-up menu. You can also drag the saved path on top of the Create New Path icon at the bottom of the panel.

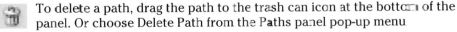

To rename a path, double-click the path name in the Paths panel. Then, enter the new name directly within the panel.

Stroking a path

You can use the Stroke Path command to paint a stroke along the path. You can select which painting or editing tool to use to stroke the path. Follow these steps:

1. **Select the path in the Paths panel. Then, select Stroke Path from the Paths panel pop-up menu.**

   Or hold down the Alt (Option on the Mac) key and click the Stroke path that has the brush icon (an outlined circle) at the bottom of the panel.

    You can also click the Stroke Path icon without holding down the Alt (Option on the Mac) key. This option bypasses the dialog box in Step 2 and just strokes your path with whatever setting you used previously.

2. **In the dialog box that opens, select one of the many painting or editing tools that you want to use to apply color to the stroke. Click OK.**

   Make sure that you verify your chosen tool's settings on the Options bar because Photoshop uses those settings to stroke your path. Photoshop also applies your current foreground color to the stroke.

   If you're using a pressure-sensitive drawing tablet, you can select the Simulate Pressure check box to create strokes that have varying widths. If everything has gone well, you end up with a stroked path like the one shown in Figure 2-10.

   If you select one or more paths by using the Direct Selection tool (the white arrow in the Tools panel), the Stroke Path command changes to Stroke Subpath(s), enabling you to stroke only the selected paths.

Corbis Digital Stock

Figure 2-10: Photoshop allows you to apply a stroke of color to your paths.

 Although paths live in their own space, independent of layers, and don't print, after you stroke or fill them, they do become part of your image layer and will print. Make sure the currently active layer is the one you want your stroked or filled path to appear on before you perform the operation.

Filling a path

You can fill the interior of a path with color by choosing the Fill Path command. Follow these steps:

1. **Select the path in the Paths panel and select Fill Path from the Paths panel pop-up menu.**

   A dialog box gives options for Contents, Opacity, Blending, and Rendering. Briefly, for your Contents options, choose among various colors, Pattern, or History. (For more on the Contents and Opacity options, see Book IV, Chapter 2.)

   You can also hold down the Alt (Option on the Mac) key and click the Fill Path with Foreground Color icon (a solid circle) at the bottom of the panel. Clicking the Fill icon without holding down the Alt (Option on the Mac) key fills the path with the foreground color and the other settings at their defaults.

2. **In the dialog box, leave the Blending Mode option set to Normal.**

   Using the Layers panel to apply your blending modes is better because you have more flexibility (see Book V for more on layers). Here's the scoop on the remaining options:

   - The Feather option gradually blurs the edges of the fill into the background. Enter the feather radius in pixels. The more pixels, the greater the blur or feather.
   - The Anti-Alias option just slightly softens the very edge of the fill by one pixel so the edges don't appear as ragged.

   If you select one or more paths by using the Direct Selection tool, the Fill Path command changes to Fill Subpath(s), enabling you to fill only the selected paths.

3. **After you set your options, click OK.**

   Your path is filled — similar to mine, which is shown in Figure 2-11.

**Book III
Chapter 2**

Creating and Working with Paths

Corbis Digital Stock

Figure 2-11: If stroking your path with color isn't enough, you can fill it instead.

Loading Paths as Selections

Creating a path is usually the means to an end — an accurate selection. Therefore, you frequently use the Paths panel to load your path as a selection.

Follow these steps to get the lowdown on how to do just that. Open an image, make a selection by using the Pen tool, and get started:

1. **Select Make Selection from the Paths panel pop-up menu.**

   Alternatively, you can also hold down Alt (Option on the Mac) and click the Load Path as Selection icon in the Paths panel.

    To bypass the Make Selection dialog box, simply click the Load Path as Selection icon at the bottom of the Paths panel without holding down the Alt (Option on the Mac) key.

2. **Feather or anti-alias your selection in the Make Selection dialog box.**

   You have these options:

   • Feather your selection by entering a pixel value in the Feather Radius box. (For more on feathering, see Book III, Chapter 3.)

   • Leave the feather radius at 0 for a hard-edged selection.

   • My personal recommendation: Select the Anti-Alias option. This option slightly softens the edge of the selection by one pixel so that it doesn't appear so jagged.

   • If you have no other selections active, the Operation option will default to New Selection. If you happen to have another selection active when you load your current path as a selection, you can choose to add to, subtract from, or intersect with that other selection.

   After the path is made into a selection (as shown in Figure 2-12), it acts like any other selection.

If you need a selection refresher, see Book III, Chapter 1. If you want to save your selection (saving a selection creates an alpha channel), jump ahead to Book VI, Chapter 1, where I explain details on working with channels.

 Here's one of my favorite shortcuts: To quickly load the path as a selection, select the path and then press Ctrl+Enter (⌘+Return on the Mac). You can also Ctrl-click (⌘-click on the Mac) your path name in the Paths panel to do the same. Just be aware that you bypass the Make Selection dialog box and its options when you use the shortcuts.

Corbis Digital Stock

Figure 2-12: The main reason to create a path is to achieve an accurate selection.

Turning a Selection into a Path

Although you probably won't use this option nearly as often as you use the option to turn a path into a selection, the option is, indeed, available: You can create paths from existing selections.

Creating a path from a selection can come in handy if you need to save a path as a clipping path (where areas of the image outside the path are hidden, but not deleted). To create a path from a selection, follow these steps:

1. **If you've been reading from the beginning of this chapter, you probably have a selection onscreen ready to go. If you're just now jumping in, select the desired element in your image.**

2. **With the selection marquee active, select Make Work Path from the Paths panel pop-up menu.**

   You can also create a path from a selection by holding down Alt (Option on the Mac) and clicking the Make Work Path from Selection icon in the Paths panel. If you just click the icon without holding down Alt (Option on the Mac), you also make a path, but you bypass the dialog box.

3. **In the dialog box that appears, enter a Tolerance value.**

   The Tolerance value controls how sensitive Photoshop is to the nooks and crannies in the selection when it creates the path:

   - The lower the value, the more sensitive it is, and the more closely the selection follows your path.

   - Too low a value, such as 0.5, may create too many anchor points.

   - Too high a value, such as 10 (the max), rounds out your path too much. Start with the default setting of 2.0.

   You can always tweak the path later (check out the section "Editing Paths," later in this chapter).

4. **If the path is still showing, simply click in the gray area below the path names in the Paths panel.**

   This action deselects the path.

5. **Select the work path in the Paths panel and select Save Path from the Paths panel pop-up menu. Name the path and click OK.**

Using the Kinder Freeform Pen

Confession: There's a more amicable incarnation of the Pen tool — the Freeform Pen tool. This tool is kind of a hybrid Lasso/Pen tool. Just click and drag around the element you want to select, and the tool creates an outline that follows your cursor, exactly like the Lasso.

After you release your mouse button, Photoshop provides the anchor points, lines, and curves for that path. In this way, the Freeform Pen works exactly like the Pen.

In my humble opinion, the Freeform Pen rates just an okay. The downside is that you're back to needing a steady hand in order to get an accurate selection. The Freeform Pen tool's probably one notch better than the Lasso tool because you get a path that you can refine before you load it as a selection. I'd rather pay my dues and get skilled with the regular Pen.

Here are some Freeform Pen tips:

- To create straight segments by using the Freeform Pen, hold down Alt (Option on the Mac) while pressing the mouse button and then click to create the anchor point.

✔ Holding down Alt (Option on the Mac) temporarily turns the Freeform Pen into the regular Pen. When you want to return to using the Freeform Pen, release Alt (Option on the Mac), keeping the mouse button clicked.

If you release Alt (Option on the Mac) after releasing the mouse button, Photoshop ends your path, and you can do nothing about it.

The following sections give you the scoop on the options (which you can find by clicking the down arrow on the Options bar) that go hand in hand with the Freeform Pen tool. (See Figure 2-13.)

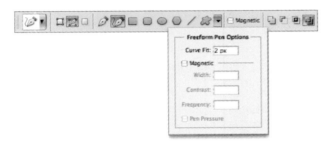

Figure 2-13: The Freeform Pen is a cross between the Lasso and the Pen tools, and it requires a steady hand to create paths.

Curve Fit

The Curve Fit option lets you adjust the amount of error Photoshop allows when trying to fit your cursor movement to a path. You can enter a value from 0.5 to 10 pixels; the default setting is 2 pixels.

At the default setting, Photoshop doesn't register any movement of your cursor that's 2 pixels or less. Setting the value to 0.5 pixels makes the Freeform Pen very sensitive to your movement and forces the tool to follow the edge closely.

The disadvantage of this option is that using it also causes unnecessary anchor points. Although a value of 10 pixels corrects this problem by making the option less sensitive, your path may not be as accurate if you back off on the sensitivity.

I recommend trying the Freeform Pen at each of these settings and then getting a feel for the kind of path it makes.

Magnetic

When selected, the Magnetic option makes the Freeform Pen act much like the Magnetic Lasso tool. (See Book III, Chapter 1.) Click anywhere on the edge of the element you want to select. Release your mouse button and then move the cursor around the edge. The tool snaps to the edge of your element, creating anchor points and segments. You can

- **Manually control the magnetism.** If the Freeform Pen tool starts to veer off course, you can force an anchor point down manually by clicking. To delete the most recent anchor point, press Backspace (delete on the Mac).

- **Create straight segments.** To create straight segments, Alt-click (Option-click on the Mac) to temporarily get the regular Pen. Alt-drag (Option-drag on the Mac) to temporarily access the regular Freeform Pen. To return to the Magnetic Freeform Pen tool, release Alt (Option on the Mac), click again, and continue moving the cursor.

To close a path by using the magnetic Freeform Pen, double-click or return to your starting anchor point.

Width, Contrast, Frequency, and Pen Pressure

The Width, Contrast, and Frequency settings are specifically for the Magnetic option and work just like the Magnetic Lasso options. Width specifies how close to the edge (1–256) the tool must be before it detects an edge. Contrast (1–100) specifies how much contrast must be between pixels for the tool to see the edge. Frequency (0–100) specifies the rate at which the tool lays down anchor points. For more details, see Book III, Chapter 1.

The Pen Pressure option is available only if you're using a pressure-sensitive drawing tablet. It allows you to adjust how sensitive the tool is based on how hard you press down with the stylus.

Creating Paths without the Pen

I want to let you in on a fun way to create paths. Yes, I said fun. (You have to assume that by *fun,* I mean no Pen tool is involved in the method.)

You can grab any of the shape tools and create a work path. However, before you do, be sure to click the Paths icon on the Options bar. The icon looks like a Pen cursor with a square path around it. Click and drag the shape tool of choice onto your canvas and presto, an instant path. These shapes can come in handy for creating small spot illustrations, logos, and Web buttons.

Follow these steps:

1. **Open an existing image and select a shape tool.**

   In the example shown in Figure 2-14 I used the Custom Shape tool. For details on the shape tools and their options, see Book IV Chapter 1.

2. **Choose a shape from the Custom Shape Picker drop-down panel on the Options bar.**

   I chose a fish shape for my example.

3. **Choose the Paths option on the Options bar. Using the Shape tool, click and drag a path in your image window. Press the Shift key while dragging to constrain the shape's proportions.**

   You can then use the Paths panel to load the path as a selection. (See the section "Loading Paths as Selections," earlier in this chapter.)

Book III
Chapter 2

Creating and Working with Paths

Photodisc

Figure 2-14: Using the Custom Shape tool is a fun and painless way to create paths.

4. **Choose Layer⇨New⇨Layer via Copy.**

   You just put the selection on its own layer. You can hide your original background image by clicking the eyeball icon in the Layers panel. For more on layers, see Book V.

5. **If you want, add some type with the Type tool.**

   Then, you can jazz it up — like this, for example:

   - If you want to give your type some motion, click the Create Warped Text button on the Options bar. You can also apply drop shadows, bevels, and other effects by choosing Layer⇨Layer Style.

   - For my example, I chose the Arc style warp in the Warp Text dialog box.

   - I also applied a Bevel and Emboss and Drop Shadow Layer Style to both the selection and the type. (For more on type, see Book IV, Chapter 3.)

6. **Delete the original image layer.**

   Figure 2-15 shows the image I ended up with — fun and very easy.

Photodisc

Figure 2-15: After adding some type and a few effects, you have a fun composite image.

Editing Paths

Often, using the Pen tool to get a reasonably decent, but not perfect, path is easier and less time consuming. After you have that path, go back and edit it for more accuracy. Although following the Eyeball-It-Then-Fix-It strategy is valuable at any time in your Photoshop career, it's especially true when you're figuring out how to use the Pen tool.

Photoshop offers you a bevy of editing tools that can make your path repair a snap. These tools even share the Pen tool's flyout menu. Additionally, the arrow tools, which Adobe calls the Path Selection and Direct Selection tools, are extremely helpful when it comes to fine-tuning your path. You

may find (as I do) that the Direct
Selection tool is one of your favorite
tools — so simple to use, yet so functional. Figure 2-16 shows both sets
of tools.

To edit a path, follow these steps:

1. **If you can't see the path you want
   to edit, select the path in the
   Paths panel.**

   This selection activates the
   path.

2. **To see the individual anchor
   points so that you can edit them,
   select the Direct Selection tool
   (the white arrow) and then click
   anywhere along the path.**

   You now see the individual
   anchor points and segments
   that comprise the path. Most
   of the anchor points, if not all,
   are hollow because they're
   unselected, as shown in
   Figure 2-17.

3. **If you need to move an anchor
   point, click it with the Direct
   Selection tool.**

   When selected, the point
   becomes solid, also shown
   in Figure 2-17.

4. **Drag to move the anchor
   point.**

   If you need to, you can move a
   curved or straight segment in the
   same fashion.

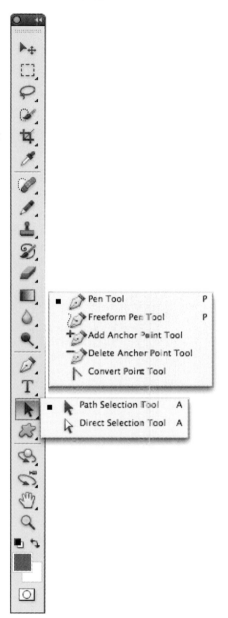

Figure 2-16: The compadres of the Pen tool
help to refine your paths to perfection.

Book III
Chapter 2

Creating
and Working
with Paths

5. **If you need to move an entire path, use the Path Selection tool (the black arrow).**

   You can also select multiple paths by holding down the Shift key while clicking the paths.

   If you move any part of the path beyond the boundary of the image canvas, it's still available — just not visible. Use the Zoom tool to zoom out until you see the hidden portion of the path.

6. **Using the Direct Selection tool, manipulate the direction lines to change the shape of the curve. First, click the anchor point of the curve to select it. Then, click and drag the direction point going the same direction as the bump.**

   By lengthening or shortening the direction line, you can control how steep or flat the curve is. By rotating the direction line, you change the slope of the curve, as shown in Figure 2-18. Here are a few more editing pointers:

Unselected anchor point

Selected anchor point

Corbis Digital Stock

Figure 2-17: Hollow anchor points are unselected; solid points are selected.

Corbis Digital Stock

Figure 2-18: By manipulating the direction lines, you can change the shape of a curve.

- **To add an anchor point in your path:** Use the Add Anchor Point tool. Click in the path where you need an anchor point. This tool always adds a smooth point, no matter where you click.

- **To delete an anchor point:** Select the Delete Anchor Point tool, position the cursor over the anchor point, and click it. The anchor point disappears while you keep your path intact.

- **To convert an anchor point from smooth to corner or vice versa:** Select the Convert Point tool. Position your cursor over your desired anchor point. If the anchor point is a corner point, drag away from the anchor point to create the direction lines that create a smooth point. If the point is a smooth point, simply click and release the anchor point to convert it into a corner point.

  To convert a smooth point to a cusp point, make sure the direction lines are showing and then drag a direction line to break it into independent direction lines. Finally, to convert a cusp point back to a smooth point, just drag out from the anchor point.

- **To copy a path:** Select the path by using the Path Selection tool. Then, hold down Alt (Option on the Mac) and drag away from the path. While you drag, you carry a copied path with you.

- **To delete a path:** Select the path by using the Path Selection tool and press the Backspace key (Delete key on the Mac). You can also select a point on the path by using the Direct Selection tool and pressing Backspace (Delete on the Mac) twice.

Using the Options Bar

Quite a few options appear on the Options bar when the Pen tool or Path Selection/Direct Selection tools are active. Here's the scoop on those options:

- **Auto Add/Delete:** Enables you to add or delete an anchor point by using the regular Pen tool.

- **Show Bounding Box:** Places a box around the path, allowing you to transform the path. The bounding box isn't a path or part of your image. It's merely a visual guide to assist you in transformations. For more on transformations, see Book III, Chapter 3.

- **Path state buttons (Add, Subtract, Intersect, and Exclude):** Combine all visible paths by adding, subtracting, intersecting, or excluding paths. Click your desired button to direct Photoshop on how to control the overlapping portions of the path(s) when you convert it to a selection. For example, clicking the Add button selects all areas, whether or not they overlap. Clicking Intersect selects only the overlapping areas.

Book III
Chapter 2

**Creating
and Working
with Paths**

- ✒ **Combine button:** Allows you to group paths as a single unit. Select your desired paths and click the Combine button. When you select any one of the paths, all the paths within the group are selected.

- ✒ **Align and Distribute buttons:** Align two or more paths, and distribute three or more paths. The icons give you a good visual clue as to how the alignment or distribution will appear.

Chapter 3: Modifying and Transforming Selections and Paths

In This Chapter

↙ **Adding and subtracting from a selection**

↙ **Using the Select commands**

↙ **Feathering selections**

↙ **Moving and cloning a selection**

↙ **Transforming pixels, selections, and paths**

1 f you're like me, you may find it tough to get the perfect selection the first time around. I mean, all you need is one too many cups of coffee, and that Lasso tool seems to take on a mind of its own. That's okay. Photoshop is too benevolent to leave you hanging with a mediocre selection. Multitudes of techniques are available to modify and transform your selections. You can add or remove pixels from your selection, scale your selection outline, smooth jagged edges, or switch what's selected for what isn't. Knowing how to clean up and modify your selections helps you to nail your desired element with precision.

If you haven't already thumbed through the first two chapters of Book III and gotten a good grasp of how to create selections by using the mighty Photoshop Tools panel, go ahead and browse those chapters now.

Achieving Selection Perfection

Although the selection tools, such as the Lasso, Quick Selection, and Magic Wand tools, usually do a decent job of capturing the bulk of your selection, making an accurate selection often requires another sort of tool — concentration. Give your selections a little extra attention, and you'll be amazed by the results. By adding and subtracting from the outline here and there, you can refine a selection and ensure that you capture only what you really want — and nothing that you don't.

The following sections show you how to use keyboard shortcuts, along with your mouse, to make perfect selections. If you're not one for keyboard shortcuts, you can use the selection option buttons on the Options bar to create a new selection, add to a selection, subtract from a selection, or intersect one selection with another. You just need to grab the selection tool of your choice, click the selection option button you want, and drag (or click if you're using the Magic Wand or the Polygonal Lasso tool).

When adding to a selection, a small plus sign (+) appears next to your cursor. When subtracting from a selection, a small minus sign (–) appears. When intersecting two selections, a small multiplication sign (×) appears.

Adding to a selection

If your selection doesn't quite contain all the elements you want to capture, you need to add those portions to your current selection.

For you keyboarders, to add to a current selection, simply hold down the Shift key and drag around the pixels you want to include when using the regular Lasso tool or the Rectangular or Elliptical Marquee tools. You can also hold down the Shift key and click the area you want when using the Magic Wand tool, or drag the area you want when using the Quick Selection tool.

To include an area that has straight sides in your selection, you can hold down the Shift key and click around the area when using the Polygonal Lasso tool. And although you may not have much need to do it, you can hold down the Shift key and click when using the Single Column or the Single Row Marquee tool. I wouldn't use the Magnetic Lasso tool to add to a selection; it's excessively cumbersome.

To add to your selection, you don't have to use the same tool that you used to create the original selection. Feel free to use whatever selection tool you think can get the job done. (See Book III, Chapters 1 and 2 for details on selection tools and methods.)

Follow these steps to add to the circular selection, such as the one shown in Figure 3-1:

1. **Make your first elliptical selection by selecting the larger circle with the Elliptical Marquee tool.**

   Be sure you hold down the Alt key (Option on the Mac) to draw from the center out. See the left image in Figure 3-1.

2. **To add the smaller circular area you will need to hold down two keys. Hold down the Shift key to add to the selection and then hold down the Alt key (Option on the Mac) to draw from the center out. You must press and hold down the keys in this order.**

3. **Drag around the smaller selection by using the Elliptical Marquee tool.**

   The resulting selection is shown in the example on the right in Figure 3-1.

 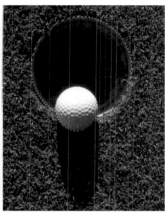

Figure 3-1: The original selection appears on the left; the selection after adding is on the right.

Subtracting from a selection

Just like you can add to a selection marquee, you can also subtract from, or take a chunk out of, a selection. Here's how to subtract from a current selection using the following tools:

- ✔ **The regular Lasso tool or the Rectangular and Elliptical Marquee tools:** Hold down the Alt (Option on the Mac) key and drag around the pixels you want to subtract.

- ✔ **The Magic Wand and the Quick Selection tools:** Hold down the Alt (Option on the Mac) key and click the area you want to remove.

- ✔ **The Polygonal Lasso tool:** To subtract a straight-sided area, hold down the Alt (Option on the Mac) key and click around the area.

- ✔ **The Single Column and the Single Row Marquee tools:** You can hold down the Alt (Option on the Mac) key and click. The Single Column and the Single Row Marquee tools come in handy when you want to get rid of just the edge of a selection.

In Figure 3-2, I selected the outside of the frame by using the Polygonal Lasso tool. I didn't use the obvious tool of choice — the Rectangular Marquee tool — because the frame wasn't completely straight. To deselect the inside of the frame from the selection, I held down the Alt (Option on the Mac) key and clicked each corner of the inside of the frame when using the Polygonal Lasso tool, resulting in the selection shown in Figure 3-2.

Figure 3-2: Press Alt (Option on the Mac) to delete from your existing selection.

Intersecting two selections

What happens when you hold down the Shift and Alt (Option on the Mac) keys together? Not a collision, but an intersection. Holding down both keys while dragging with the Lasso or the Marquee tool, or clicking with the Magic Wand tool, creates the intersection of the original selection with the second selection.

To retain only the part of an image where two selections overlap, hold down Shift+Alt (Shift+Option on the Mac) and then drag.

You can select a portion of an image by using the Polygonal Lasso tool. Then, hold down Shift+Alt (Shift+Option on the Mac) and drag with the Rectangular Marquee tool. The resulting intersection of the two selections appears.

Getting the Keys to Behave

Photoshop has a little glitch in its way of doing things. Well, not so much a glitch as a conflict. With so many ways of doing things, somewhere along the line you may have to jigger with Photoshop to get it to do what you want. For example, how does Photoshop know whether you want to create a perfect square or add to a selection when you press the Shift key?

Let me lay this out for you:

- ✔ When you make an initial selection with the Rectangular or the Elliptical Marquee tool, holding down the Shift key constrains the proportions of the selection, thereby allowing you to create a perfect square or a perfect circle.

- ✔ If you hold down Alt (Option on the Mac) when using either of these tools, you can draw from the center out.

- ✔ If you hold down Alt (Option on the Mac) when using the Lasso tool, the Lasso tool temporarily becomes the Polygonal Lasso tool.

Unfortunately, despite numerous requests, the capability to read users' minds wasn't a Photoshop CS5 upgrade feature. The following steps show you what you have to do to get Photoshop to recognize your wishes.

To add a perfectly square or round selection to an existing selection, follow these steps:

1. **Hold down Shift and drag when using the Rectangular or the Elliptical Marquee tool.**

   Your selection is unconstrained.

2. **While you drag, keeping your mouse button pressed, release the Shift key for just a moment and then press and hold it again.**

   Your unconstrained selection suddenly snaps into a constrained square or circle.

3. **Release the mouse button before you release the Shift key.**

   If you don't release the mouse button before you release the Shift key, the selection shape reverts to its unconstrained form.

To delete part of a selection while drawing from the center out, follow these steps:

1. **Hold down Alt (Option on the Mac) and drag when using the Rectangular or the Elliptical Marquee tool.**

2. **While you drag, keeping your mouse button pressed, release the Alt (Option on the Mac) key for just a moment and then press and hold it again.**

   You're now drawing from the center outward.

3. **Release the mouse button before you release the Alt (Option on the Mac) key.**

   See Figure 3-3.

Digital Vision

Figure 3-3: You can delete from an existing selection and draw from the center out simultaneously.

Use the preceding steps when you're selecting a doughnut, tire, inflatable swim ring, and other circular items that have holes in the middle.

Using the Select Menu

Although you can add, subtract, and intersect selections by using the Shift and Alt (Option on the Mac) keys and the selection option buttons on the Options bar, you can do much more with the commands on the Select menu. In this menu, you can find ways to expand, contract, smooth, and fuzz your selection, and even turn your selection inside out. You can also use this menu to automatically select similar colors and create selection borders. I show you how to do all this in the following sections. With this kind of knowledge, imperfect selections will soon be a thing of the past.

Selecting all or nothing

The All and the Deselect commands are pretty self-explanatory. To select everything in your image, choose Select⇨All. To deselect everything, choose Select⇨Deselect. The key commands Ctrl+A (⌘+A on the Mac) and Ctrl+D (⌘+D on the Mac), respectively, come in very handy and are easy to remember.

In most cases, you don't have to select everything in your image. If you don't have an active selection marquee, Photoshop naturally assumes that you want to apply whatever command you execute to the entire image.

Reselecting a selection

If you've taken 20 minutes to carefully lasso a spiny sea anemone from its ocean home, the last thing you want is to lose your coveted selection marquee. But that's exactly what happens if you accidentally click the canvas when you have an active selection tool in hand. The selection marquee disappears.

Sure, you can choose Edit⇨Undo if you catch your mistake right away. Technically, you can also access the History panel to recover your selection. (See Book II, Chapter 4 for more on history.) However, a much easier solution is to choose Select⇨Reselect. This command retrieves your last selection.

Besides immediately bringing back a selection you accidentally deselected, the Reselect command can come in handy if you decide to select an element for a second time. For example, if you do such a great job retouching your spiny anemone that you decide to add, by copying, another anemone to your image, go ahead; it's all up to you. By using the Reselect command, you can easily load the selection again, rather than start the selection from scratch.

The Reselect command works for only the last selection you made, so don't plan to reselect a selection you made last week — or even ten minutes ago — if you've selected something else in the meantime.

Swapping a selection

Sometimes, selecting what you don't want is easier than selecting what you do want. For example, if you're trying to select your pet dog, photographed against a neutral background, why spend valuable time meticulously selecting him with the Pen or the Lasso tool, when you can just click the background with the Magic Wand tool? (Don't forget to use the Shift key to select bits of background you might have missed the first time.)

After you select the background, just choose Select⇨Inverse. Presto, you now have Fido the Retriever selected and obediently awaiting your next command, as shown in Figure 3-4.

Feathering a selection

In Book III, Chapter 1, I describe how to *feather* (blur the edges of) a selection when using the Lasso and the Marquee tools by entering a value in the Feather box on the Options bar. This method of feathering requires that you set your feather radius *before* you create your selection.

Unfortunately, using this method, a problem arises if you want to modify the initial selection. When you select with a feather, the marquee outline of the selection adjusts to take into account the amount of the feather. Therefore, the resulting marquee outline doesn't resemble your precise mouse movement. As a result, modifying, adding, or subtracting from your original selection is pretty tough.

A much better way to feather a selection is to make your initial selection without a feather, as shown in the top image of Figure 3-5. Clean up your selection as you need to, and then apply your feather by choosing Select⇨Modify⇨Feather. In the dialog box, enter a Feather Radius value and click OK. The resulting selection appears in the bottom image of Figure 3-5.

The *radius* is how far out in all directions the feather extends. A radius of 8 means the feather extends 8 pixels from the selection outline. A large feather radius makes the image appear to fade out.

Figure 3-4: Sometimes, you want to select what you don't want and then invert your selection.

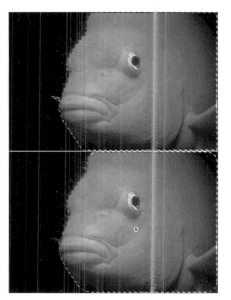

Corbis Digital Stock

Figure 3-5: You can more easily clean up your selection prior to applying a feather.

TIP

Deleting a straight-sided selection

If you have an existing selection, holding down Alt (Option on the Mac) when using the Lasso tool subtracts from the selection. If you want to subtract a straight-sided selection from an existing selection, you can hold down Alt (Option on the Mac) and begin to drag. Then, release Alt (Option on the Mac) and select the Polygonal Lasso tool. But this process can be tricky and is really unnecessary. I recommend just grabbing the Polygonal Lasso tool itself to delete your straight-sided selection. Ditto for adding and getting intersections with straight-sided selections.

Using the other Modify commands

In addition to the Feather command, the Select⇨Modify menu contains a group of other modification commands that are lumped categorically. With the exception of the Contract command, you probably won't use these options every day. When you do use them, however, you'll find they prove pretty handy. Here's the lowdown on each command:

- **Border:** This command selects the area around the edge of the selection marquee. You specify the width of the area, from 1 to 200 pixels, and you get a border marquee. Select a foreground color, choose Edit⇨Fill, pick Foreground Color from the Use drop-down list, and then click OK to fill your border with color. (By the way, you can also achieve a similar look by choosing Edit⇨Stroke. See Book IV, Chapter 2 for details.)

- **Smooth:** If your selection marquee seems a bit ragged around the edges, try selecting the Smooth command to round the nooks and crannies. Enter a sample radius value from 1 to 100 pixels. Photoshop examines each selected pixel and then includes or deselects pixels in your selection based on the range specified by the radius amount. If most of the pixels are selected, Photoshop includes the strays; if most of the pixels are unselected, Photoshop removes the pixels. Start with 2 pixels — and if that doesn't seem like enough, increase it by a few more pixels or so.

WARNING!

   Use this command with great caution. It's just too easy to get mushy, ill-defined selections.

- **Expand:** This command allows you to increase the size of your selection by a specified number of pixels, from 1 to 100. This command can come in handy if you just missed the edge of a circular selection and want to enlarge it, as shown in Figure 3-6.

- **Contract:** To shrink your selection by 1 to 100 pixels, choose Contract. I use this command a lot, in conjunction with the Feather command, when compositing multiple images.

Photodisc

Figure 3-6: The Expand command increases your selection, enabling you to pick up missed pixels around the edges.

Applying the Grow and Similar commands

The Grow and the Similar commands are close cousins to the Magic Wand tool, and to a lesser extent, the Quick Selection tool. (For more on the Magic Wand tool and the Tolerance setting, check out Book III, Chapter 1.) If you're familiar with the modus operandi of the Magic Wand tool, you know that you rarely get the perfect selection on the first click. That's because you're making an intelligent guess about what Tolerance setting can pick up the pixels you want.

The Grow command compensates a little for the Magic Wand tool's inaccuracy. For example, if you need to include more in your selection, you can increase the Tolerance setting and try again — hold down Shift and click the area you need to include. Or you can choose Select⇨Grow. The Grow command increases the size of the selection by including adjacent pixels that fall within the range of Tolerance.

The Similar command is like Grow, only the pixels don't have to be adjacent to be selected. The command searches throughout the image and picks up pixels within the Tolerance range, wherever they may fall.

Both commands use the Tolerance value that's displayed on the Options bar when you have the Magic Wand tool selected. Adjust the Tolerance setting to include more or fewer colors by increasing or decreasing the setting, respectively.

The Refine Edge command, which has been upgraded in version CS5, helps to fine tune your selection. Find out the details in Book III, Chapter 1.

Book III Chapter 3

Modifying and Transforming Selections and Paths

Moving and Cloning Selections

When you have your selection refined to ultimate perfection, you may then want to move it or clone it. To move a selection, simply grab the Move tool (the four-headed arrow) at the top right of the Tools panel, and then drag the selection.

Photodisc

Figure 3-7: When you move a selection by using the Move tool, you leave a hole that reveals the background color.

Sounds easy enough, right? When you move the selection, however, be warned that the area where the selection used to reside fills with the background color, as shown in Figure 3-7. The background appears, of course, only if you're moving both the selection outline and the image pixels. You can move just the selection outline (without the pixels), as I explain in the section "Moving the selection outline, but not the pixels," later in this chapter. Additionally, if you're moving a selection on a layer, you're left with transparent pixels. When you use the Move tool, your cursor icon changes to a pair of scissors, letting you know that you're cutting out the selection.

The Move tool has some notable options on the Options bar:

- **Auto-Select Layer:** Select the topmost layer directly under the Move tool cursor, not necessarily the selected area.

- **Auto-Select Group:** Select the entire layer group that the selected layer belongs to.

- **Show Transform Controls:** Show handles on the bounding box of your selected area.

Cloning

If the idea of leaving a big hole in your image doesn't appeal to you, you can copy and move the selection, leaving the original image intact, as shown in

Figure 3-8. Just hold down Alt (Option on the Mac) and drag when using the Move tool. This action is often referred to as *cloning* because you're essentially making a duplicate of a selected area and then moving that duplicate elsewhere.

When cloning, your cursor icon changes to a double-headed arrow, notifying you that you're duplicating the selection.

Corbis Digital Stock

Figure 3-8: Hold down Alt (Option on the Mac) while dragging to clone your selection and not leave a nasty hole.

Moving the selection outline, but not the pixels

If all you want to do is move the selection marquee without moving the pixels underneath, avoid using the Move tool. Instead, grab any selection tool — a Marquee tool, a Lasso tool, or the Magic Wand tool — and then click inside the marquee and just drag. That way, you move only the outline of the element, not the element itself. You can also use the arrow keys to nudge a selection marquee.

Transforming Pixels

After you perfectly select your element, you may find you need to resize or reorient that element. *Transforming* involves scaling, rotating, skewing, distorting, warping, flipping, or adjusting the perspective of your pixels.

Follow these steps to transform a selection:

1. **Create your selection.**

   I'll leave this task up to you; just use your well-honed selection expertise (or refer to earlier sections in this chapter for help).

   You can also apply transformations to a layer or to multiple layers. (For more on this topic, see Book V.)

2. **Choose Edit➪Transform.**

   If all you want is a single transformation, this command is adequate. However, if you want multiple transformations, you're wise to stick with the Free Transform command.

3. **Choose a transformation type from the submenu:**

   • *Scale:* Increases or decreases the size of your selection.

   • *Rotate:* Freely rotates your selection in either direction.

- *Skew:* Distorts your selection on a given axis.

- *Distort:* Distorts your selection with no restrictions on an axis.

- *Perspective:* Applies a one-point perspective to your selection.

- *Warp:* This option is like a mini-Liquify command, which you can use to distort your selection by manipulating a mesh grid that overlays your image. (Book VII, Chapter 3 covers Liquify.)

- *Rotate 180°, 90° CW (Clockwise), or 90° CCW (Counterclockwise):* Rotates the selection by specified amounts.

- *Flip Horizontal or Vertical:* Flips your selection along the vertical and horizontal axes, respectively.

As soon as you select your desired distortion and release the mouse button, the *bounding box* or *transform box* surrounds your selection, complete with handles on the sides and corners. You don't get a bounding box when you select the Flip or Rotate (by degrees) transformations (which just get applied to your image).

4. **Depending on which transformation type you choose in Step 3, drag the appropriate handle:**

- *Scale:* Corner handles work best for this transformation. Hold down Shift to scale proportionately. You can also click the Maintain Aspect Ratio (lock icon) on the Options bar to do the same. Hold down Alt (Option on the Mac) to scale from the center.

- *Rotate:* Move your cursor outside the bounding box. When the cursor becomes a curved arrow, drag clockwise or counterclockwise. Hold down Shift to rotate in 15-degree increments.

- *Skew:* Drag a side handle.

- *Distort:* Drag a corner handle.

- *Perspective:* Drag a corner handle.

- *Warp:* Drag any control point or line on the default custom mesh grid to distort your selection. You can pretty much drag anywhere on the image, even in between mesh lines, to apply the warp. You can't, however, add or delete control points.

With the Warp transformation, you have some additional options. The Options bar has a drop-down list with various warping styles, such as arch, wave, and twist. In fact, these styles are the same ones you find on the Warp Text menu. (See Book IV, Chapter 3.) When you choose one of the styles, Photoshop then applies the mesh grid for that style. Here's the lowdown on the remaining options:

- *Change the warp orientation:* Change the direction of some styles, such as wave, flag, and fish.

- *Bend:* Increase or decrease the value, or drag the handle on the warp style, to increase the distortion.

- *H% and V%:* Increase the percentages to increase the horizontal (H) and vertical (V) distortions.

- *Switch between Free Transform and Warp mode:* Switch between the Free Transform box and the Warp mesh grid.

To warp an image in an even more flexible way, check out the new Puppet Warp feature in Book VII, Chapter 3.

Choosing Rotate 180°, 90° CW, or 90° CCW, or Flip Horizontal or Vertical executes the command. Handle-dragging isn't necessary.

Photoshop executes all the transformations, except Warp, around a point called the *reference point* (dotted square icon). The reference point appears in the center of the transform box by default.

You can move the center point anywhere you want, even outside the bounding box. Additionally, you can set your own reference point for the transformation by clicking a square on the reference point locator on the Options bar. Each square corresponds with a point on the bounding box.

5. **(Optional) Choose a second transformation type from the Edit⇨ Transform submenu, if desired.**

If you're an ultra-precise type of person, you can also numerically transform the selection by entering values on the Options bar.

In Figure 3-9, I executed all the transformations at the same time.

Execute all your transformations in one fell swoop, if possible. In other words, don't scale a selection and five minutes later rotate it and five minutes after that distort it. Every time you apply a transformation to an image, you're putting it through an interpolation process. You want to limit how many times you interpolate an image because it has a degrading effect — your image starts to appear soft and mushy. Only flipping or rotating in 90-degree increments is interpolation-free. For more on interpolation, see Book II, Chapter 1.

For best results when transforming, make sure to set your interpolation method to Bicubic. This setting can be found in your Preferences settings under General.

Handle

Bounding box

Selection marquee

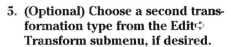

Alaska Stock Images

Figure 3-9: Apply all transformations at the same time to minimize interpolation.

If you want to be able to transform your image nondestructively, and indefinitely, use Smart Objects. See Book V, Chapter 5 for details.

6. **After you transform your selection to your liking, click the Commit button on the Options bar, or press Enter (Return on the Mac).**

   To cancel the transformation, press Esc or click the Cancel button on the Options bar.

   Your image is now magically transformed. If your image isn't on a layer, you can leave a hole filled with the background color after your image is transformed. Check out Book V to avoid this calamity.

To repeat a transformation, choose Edit➪Transform➪Again.

To duplicate an item while transforming, hold down the Alt (Option on the Mac) key when selecting the Transform command.

Transforming Selection Marquees

To transform just the selection marquee — without affecting the underlying pixels — make your desired selection and then choose Select➪Transform Selection. Photoshop doesn't have a submenu with individual transformations to choose from. Instead, you must apply the transformations as you do with the Free Transform command: by using the keyboard shortcuts. You can also enter values on the Options bar to transform numerically, or you can access the context menu. To move the selection marquee and the bounding box, simply drag inside the marquee or nudge it by pressing the keyboard arrow keys. Transforming selections is particularly handy when you're trying to select elliptical objects. Getting a precise selection the first time around is often hard, so you may need to apply a transformation. For example, in Figure 3-10, I scaled, rotated, and distorted the marquee around my clockface to get a more accurate selection.

Corbis Digital Stock

Figure 3-10: Transform a selection marquee without affecting underlying pixels.

Using Content-Aware Scaling

Content-aware scaling is a cool image-sizing feature also known as *seam carving*. This method of scaling enables you to resize and reshape your images without overdistorting the content and composition of those images. It also preserves image quality much better than traditional transformations. Although the exact way the algorithm works is technically complex, don't worry. It's pretty darn simple to use. Here's how to apply content-aware scaling:

1. **Choose your desired layer in the Layers panel. If you want to isolate the scaling to a selection on the layer, make that selection now.**

   Content-aware scaling doesn't work on adjustment layers, layer masks, individual channels or Smart Objects. For more on layers and Smart Objects, see Book V. For more on channels, see Book VI. If you're scaling a Background layer, choose Select⇨All.

2. **Choose Edit⇨Content-Aware Scale.**

3. **Specify your options on the Options bar as follows:**

   - *Reference Point:* Click a square in the reference point box to specify the axis point. The default location is the center.

   - *Use Relative Positioning for Reference Point (triangle icon):* Select this option to specify the new axis point in relation to its current position.

   - *Amount:* This option specifies the ratio of content-aware scaling to normal scaling. To minimize distortion, specify your Threshold amount. Start with a higher percentage and then adjust accordingly, if necessary.

   - *Protect:* You can designate areas that you want to protect from scaling by selecting them and saving them as alpha channels. (See Book VI, Chapter 1.) If you have an alpha channel, choose it from this submenu.

   - *Protect Skin Tone (man icon):* Select this option to preserve skin tones from distorting when scaling.

4. **Click and drag one of the handles of the scale box that surrounds your layer or selection to resize your image.**

   You can upscale (make your image bigger) or downscale (make your image smaller). You can also use the Horizontal and Vertical Scale numerical fields on the Options bar. Select Maintain Aspect Ratio to keep the scaling proportional (chain icon).

5. **When you have completed your scale, double-click inside the scale box, or press Enter (Return on the Mac) on your keyboard.**

   Check out Figure 3-11 to see the difference between a layer resized with Content-Aware Scale and a layer resized with Free Transform. Note how there is less distortion with the first method.

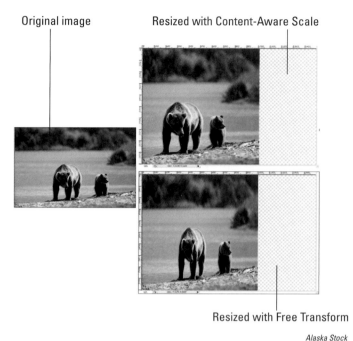

Original image

Resized with Content-Aware Scale

Resized with Free Transform

Alaska Stock

Figure 3-11: Resize your image using content-aware scaling.

Transforming Paths

After you create a bounding box around the path (see Book III, Chapter 2 for more on paths), the transformation technique for paths is the same as it is for selections and selection marquees, except that you can apply the Distort, Perspective, and Warp commands only to whole paths. The major difference between transforming paths and transforming selections is in how you select the path.

To select all paths, follow these steps:

1. **Choose Window➪Paths.**

2. **Click the pathname in the Paths panel.**

3. **Choose Edit➪Transform Path and choose your desired transformation from the submenu.**

   You can also choose Edit➪Free Transform Path.

To select a single path, follow these steps:

1. **Choose Window➪Paths.**

2. **Click the pathname in the Paths panel.**

3. **Select the Path Selection tool.**

4. **Click the path with the Path Selection tool.**

5. **Choose Edit⇨Transform Path and choose your desired transformation from the submenu.**

   You can also choose Edit⇨Free Transform Path. In Figure 3-12, I transformed the path by rotating it.

To select part of a path, follow these steps:

1. **Choose Window⇨Paths.**

2. **Click the pathname in the Paths panel.**

3. **Select the Direct Selection tool.**

4. **Select the points you want with the Direct Selection tool.**

5. **Choose Edit⇨Transform Points and choose your desired transformation from the submenu.**

Figure 3-12: Apply transformations to paths.

You can also choose Edit⇨Free Transform Points.

Putting It Together

Removing a Person (Without Getting in Trouble with the Law)

Follow these steps to seamlessly remove an unwanted element (in this case, a person) from an image:

 TIP

When you first attempt this technique, start with an image that has an element that isn't attached to something you want to keep in the image.

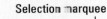

Selection marquee

1. **Open an image that contains something you want to remove.**

2. **Use the selection tool of your choice to select the element that you want to remove.**

   You don't have to be super-precise, so feel free to grab the Lasso tool. If you need a Lasso refresher, see Book III, Chapter 1. When you make your selection, be careful not to cut off any portion of your element. Otherwise, you leave some stray pixels — a dead giveaway that something was once there. Using the Lasso tool, I made a rough outline around the woman on the right, as shown in the figure.

Purestock

continued

continued

3. **Position your cursor inside the selection marquee, press and hold the mouse button and hold down the Shift key, and then drag your selection to move it horizontally (or vertically, if the image warrants it) to an area of the photo that you want to clone.**

   The selection marquee, shown in the figure, is the only thing that I moved.

4. **With the Move tool selected, position your cursor inside the selection marquee, hold down Alt+Shift (Option+Shift on the Mac), and then drag to move the cloned area on top of the element that you're removing. Carefully match up the edges, release your mouse button, and then release the Alt and Shift keys (Option and Shift on the Mac).**

5. **Choose Select⇨Deselect.**

   The cloned area now covers the element that you want to remove, as shown in the figure. In the example, the beach/ocean selection now covers the woman.

   Depending on your image, you may want to choose Select⇨Modify⇨Feather and enter a pixel or two before you move the cloned area. Feathering softens the edges and smoothes out the transition between the cloned area and the background. (See the section "Feathering a selection," in this chapter, for more on feathering.) I didn't feather my selection because it didn't really need it. Try it both ways to see which looks better. Use the History panel to undo your steps, if necessary. (See Book II, Chapter 4 for more on the History panel.)

   The final step is to clean up any telltale signs that the element was there.

Area to be cloned

Purestock

Cloned area covers woman

Purestock

6. **Select the Clone Stamp tool and select a medium-size feathered brush from the Brush Preset picker on the Options bar or from the Brushes panel, hold down Alt (Option on the Mac), and click a good area next to a flaw; release Alt (Option on the Mac) and then click the flaw.**

   If the Clone Stamp is a mystery to you, be sure to check out Book VIII, Chapter 3.

   Repeat this step until you fix all the flaws and the clone blends in seamlessly with the background. Don't get carried away with the Clone Stamp tool, or you end up with a smudgy mess. Being light-handed is a good thing, as I was in the now-retouched image. Nobody can tell that only two people stand where three people once stood.

Purestock

   The technique demonstrated here is actually now "old school." Another way to quickly eliminate objects is to use the new Content-Aware Fill feature. See Book IV, Chapter 2 for details on this awesome tool.

Book IV

Painting, Drawing, and Typing

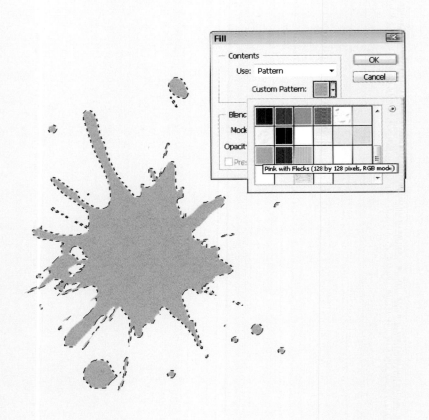

*L*ike a Swiss Army knife, Photoshop does it all. This book describes all you need to know about Photoshop's drawing and painting tools. I first give you the lowdown on the ubiquitous brush. The brush — which is found not only in the Brush tool itself but within several other painting and editing tools — has more variations than you can shake a stick at. I also cover how to create vector shapes with the Shape tools and how to fill and stroke your selections with color. If one color is not enough, keep reading until you get to the section on gradients and patterns. I give you the steps for using the many Photoshop presets and also for creating your own gradients and patterns. Rounding out this section will be an introduction to the 3-D tools. And finally, because man doesn't communicate by images alone, you can find lots of useful information about creating type. Not just regular old run-of-the-mill type, mind you (which is covered, of course), but type on a path, type with shadows and bevels, type filled with images, type warped into shapes — you get the . . . um . . . picture.

Chapter 1: Painting and Drawing with Photoshop

In This Chapter

↙ **Making pencil sketches and brush strokes**

↙ **Managing brushes with the Brush panel**

↙ **Using Brush presets**

↙ **Understanding vectors**

↙ **Creating basic and custom shapes**

↙ **Setting Geometry options**

*Y*ou're definitely going to want to brush up on your painting and drawing techniques now that you don't have to worry about messing up your clothes. Painting is one of the basic skills you need to work in Photoshop. After you master the art of painting strokes and working with brushes, you're well on your way to mastering more-advanced techniques, such as masking and retouching, which benefit from strong painting skills. (I introduce the full range of Brush tools in Book I, Chapter 2.)

Hand in hand with painting, of course, is drawing. Photoshop's shape tools add an important dimension to your drawing capabilities. This chapter introduces you to a plethora of tools and techniques. I start with painting and then move on to drawing. Embrace both, and they can serve you well.

Introducing the Pencil and Brush Tools

The Pencil and Brush tools are like peanut butter and chocolate. Not only do they work well together, but they also share many important traits. Just as important, however, are their differences. You can access these tools in the Tools panel. Press B to make the Brush tool appear by default. To access the Pencil, press Shift+B. You can toggle between these tools, along with the Color Replacement tool and Mixer Brush tool, by pressing Shift+B again. Find out more about using these tools in the following sections.

Finding out what the Pencil tool does

The Pencil and Brush tools are very much alike, except that the Pencil tool has hard edges by default (as shown in Figure 1-1) and the Brush tool can have soft, feathered edges. The Pencil tool can also erase what it creates!

Figure 1-1: The Pencil tool draws hard-edged strokes and is perfect for digital sketches.

You can do all the following with the Pencil tool:

- Drag the mouse to draw freehand lines.

- Click at one point, release the mouse button, and then Shift-click at a second point to draw a straight line between the points. As long as you hold down the Shift key, you can keep clicking to draw straight lines between each of the points.

- Press the Alt key (the Option key on the Mac) and click any area of your drawing to switch the foreground color to that hue.

- When using the Pencil, as well as the Brush, Color Replacement, and Mixer Brush tools, press and hold down the V key to access the Move tool temporarily. Release the V key to return to the original tool. This handy shortcut enables you while drawing or painting to move a layer or selection without having to go back and forth to the Tools panel.

The Pencil tool also offers the Auto Erase option, which you activate from the Options bar at the top. Auto Erase is a handy feature that lets you remove portions of your pencil strokes without switching to the Eraser tool. When you have Auto Erase turned on, the operation of the Pencil tool is slightly different from the default. The effect of either of the following actions is that Photoshop erases lines you've drawn:

✔ When you click an area of the drawing other than an area that's foreground colored (for example, the pencil lines you've already drawn), the Pencil tool begins drawing a line in the foreground color (this is the default mode).

✔ When you click an area of the drawing that's foreground colored (such as the pencil lines you've drawn), the Pencil tool draws by using the background color.

Because the Pencil tool doesn't use soft-edged lines to draw, anything other than straight vertical or horizontal lines has rough, jagged edges (often called *jaggies*), as shown in the close-up image in Figure 1-2. Jaggies aren't objectionable in some cases, especially in higher-resolution images, but if you zoom in on an area containing pencil lines, the jaggies are readily apparent. I show you how to modify the characteristics of the lines drawn with the Pencil tool in the section "Working with the Brush panel," later in this chapter.

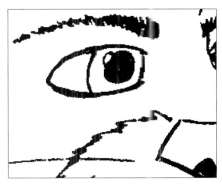

Figure 1-2: Zooming in on hard-edged strokes displays jagged edges.

Using the Pencil tool

If you're ready to start using the Pencil tool, keep in mind that lines that aren't vertical or horizontal look jagged up close. However, this doesn't necessarily pose a problem in all cases, especially when working with Web graphics. Those same hard edges can lend themselves to producing crisp-edged images for display in a browser window. To try out the Pencil tool, follow these steps:

1. **Activate the Pencil tool by selecting it from the Tools panel.**

   The Pencil tool shares a flyout menu with the various Brush tools. You can press Shift+B to make it appear if it's hidden underneath the Brush tool.

   The Pencil tool's current brush tip (usually the 1-pixel brush unless you select something else) appears in the Brush Preset Picker on the Options bar.

   Click the thumbnail or arrow in the Brush box to summon the Brush Preset Picker panel if you want to select a different-size pencil tip.

2. **If you want to draw using anything other than Normal mode, select a mode from the Mode options menu.**

   Blend modes other than Normal cause colors to interact and blend in different ways. (You can find more about modes in Book V, Chapter 3.)

3. **Select opacity for your pencil strokes.**

   If you want whatever is in the background to show partially through your strokes, select opacity of less than 100 percent by using the slider or by typing an opacity percentage directly into the text box.

4. **Click and drag with the mouse to create your pencil lines.**

Painting with the Brush tool

The Brush tool is a basic tool used throughout Photoshop in various incarnations, so master its use as quickly as possible.

The most important difference between the Brush and the Pencil tools is that, by default, the Brush tool produces soft-edged lines that Photoshop renders smoother by a process known as *anti-aliasing*. This technique substitutes partially filled pixels along the edges of lines to produce the illusion of gradual fading. Our eyes merge the transparent pixels together, so the line looks smooth rather than hard-edged.

Although jagged edges are most apparent in diagonal lines, Photoshop applies anti-aliasing to brush stroke edges, even in horizontal and vertical lines. The fuzzier the brush, the more semi-filled pixels used to produce the effect, as shown in Figure 1-3.

Pencil line   Hard-edge brush line

Soft-edge brush line

Figure 1-3: Strokes from the Pencil and Brush tools vary in the softness of their edges.

The Brush tool shares most of the basic features found in the Pencil tool, except the Auto Erase feature isn't available:

- Select the Brush tool from the Tools panel or press B or Shift+B until you get the Brush.
- Select a brush tip from the Brush Preset Picker on the Options bar.
- Select a mode and opacity from the options on the Options bar.

✔ Drag to paint, click and Shift-click to paint straight lines, and hold down the Shift key while dragging to constrain the Brush tool to horizontal or vertical lines.

✔ Press the Alt key (the Option key on the Mac) and click an area of color to switch the foreground color to that color.

The Brush tool has several other options to select from:

✔ **Flow:** *Flow* determines how quickly the Brush tool applies the paint. You can set a flow rate from 1 to 100 percent by using the Flow slider or by typing a percentage directly into the text box. You might think of it as controlling how liquid the paint is. At low flow rates, Photoshop applies the paint slowly so the color is less intense; at higher flow rates, the paint quickly reaches its full strength while you drag.

✔ **Airbrush:** Click the Airbrush button on the Options bar to switch the Brush tool (as well as many of the other tools that use brush tips) to Airbrush mode. This mode produces the spray effect you get with a traditional airbrush. The longer you hold down the mouse button, the more paint pumps out of the tool, and the wider the airbrush effect spreads, as shown in Figure 1-4.

Figure 1-4: Using the Airbrush option with the Brush tool enables you to create smoky strokes.

✔ **Toggle the Brush Panel:** On the left side of the Options bar is a button (a panel icon) that shows or hides the Brush panel. This button is a quick way to access this valuable panel, and it's available with the Pencil tool and other tools that use brush tips, too. I show you how to use the Brush panel in the upcoming "Working with the Brush panel" section.

Blending with the Mixer Brush tool

The new Mixer Brush tool takes painting one notch higher toward achieving a more realistic, natural media look to the brush strokes. This tool allows you to blend colors (see Figure 1-5) and vary your wetness within a single brush stroke. The Mixer Brush tool uses two paint wells — a "reservoir" that deposits color (Adobe calls it paint) on the canvas and a "pickup" that receives, or picks up, color from the canvas (which can be an image or color you've applied). This is a great tool to try if you want to paint over a photo to make it look more painterly but don't want to apply a filter.

Here's how to use the Mixer Brush tool:

1. **Select the Mixer Brush tool from the Tools panel.**

   This tool shares the same flyout menu as the Brush, Pencil, and Color Replacement tools.

2. **To load color into your reservoir, Alt+click (Option+click) where you wish to sample that color. You can also choose your desired Foreground color from the Tools panel.**

   When you load color from your canvas, your brush tip reflects any color variation in the sampled area. If you want the brush tip to use a single color based on your sampled area, select the Load Solid Colors Only from the Current Brush Load (swatch icon) drop-down menu on the Options bar.

3. **Choose a brush from the Brush Presets panel.**

4. **Set your desired options in the Options bar.** For a description on the various options, see "Painting with the Brush tool" earlier in this chapter and "Choosing a brush-tip shape" later in this chapter.

   Here is a brief rundown on options specific to the Mixer Brush tool:

   - *Current Brush Load Swatch:* Load Brush fills your brush with reservoir color. Clean Brush removes color from your brush. Load Solid Colors Only, as mentioned above, enables you to pick up a uniform versus varied color from your sampled area.

   - *Load Brush after Each Stroke/Clean Brush after Each Stroke:* Automatically loads your brush with reservoir color and then cleans your brush after each stroke. These two options are good options if you want to paint over a photo, for example, to make it look like a painting.

   - *Blending Brush Combinations:* Choose presets, from Dry, Moist, Wet, Very Wet, with variations of mixing levels. Experiment with these combos to see the look they provide.

   - *Specify percentages of Wet, Load, Mix, and Flow:* Wet percentages specify how much color the brush picks up from the canvas. Higher numbers give more paint. Load specifies how much color is loaded in the reservoir. Lower percentages enable the stroke to "dry" out more quickly. Mix controls the ratio of canvas color to reservoir color. A mix percentage of 100% grabs all color from the canvas, whereas 0% gets all color from the reservoir. Flow specifies how much color is pumped out when the Airbrush option is enabled.

   - *Sample All Layers:* Enables you to pick up or blend color from all layers, not just your active layer.

5. **Drag on your image to paint. If you have selected the Airbrush option, you can also hold down your mouse to "build" your color.**

Mixer Brush applied

Original

Figure 1-5: The Mixer Brush tool enables you to blend two colors or more.

Working with the Brush panel

You'll find the Brush panel extremely useful for changing the characteristics of preset brush tips and for creating your own. You can also access and select brush presets, as I discuss in the section "Using the preset brushes," later in this chapter.

You can view the Brush panel in several ways:

- ✓ Choose Window⇨Brush from the menu bar.
- ✓ Click the Brush panel's icon in the Photoshop panel dock.
- ✓ Toggle the Brush panel's button on the left side of the Options bar.
- ✓ Press F5 to toggle the Brush panel open or closed.
- ✓ Grab the Brush panel's icon and drag it out of the dock and onto your Photoshop desktop. This mode keeps the Brush panel easily accessible until you put it away by dragging it to the dock, clicking its Close box, or rendering it hidden by choosing Window⇨Brush.

The Brush panel displays a list of brush properties on the left and includes a brush-stroke preview at the bottom of the panel.

The largest pane in the panel, on the right, shows various types of information, such as the size and type of brush tip, or the different controls offered for any of the 11 properties you can set.

No longer does the Brush panel have to share a space with the Brush presets. Click the new Brush Presets button located in the upper-left of the Brush panel; a separate Brush Presets panel appears. Additionally, preset previews appear on the right side of the Brush panel, as well as a Size (diameter) slider.

Choosing a brush-tip shape

When you select Brush Tip Shape on the left side of the Brush panel, a scrolling box shows the available brush tips, as shown in Figure 1-6.

The 11 brush parameters you can choose to apply and edit display in the left column. You can select any of these options to apply them to the currently selected brush. Click the option name to edit its characteristics. You must select the parameter name to access the options. Toggling the parameter on by checking the check box doesn't work. Here are the Brush Tip Shape characteristics:

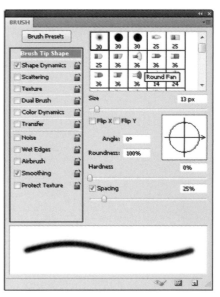

Figure 1-6: The Brush panel offers a multitude of different brush tips.

✏ **Shape Dynamics:** Controls the amount of jitter (randomness or variation) produced when you draw a stroke, the minimum diameter, tilt, angle and roundness jitter, minimum roundness, and other options. The higher the value, the greater the variance for each option.

Some of these options apply only when you're using a pressure-sensitive digital tablet. Check your digital tablet's instruction manual for more information on how to customize brushes for your tablet.

The Flip X and Flip Y jitter option flips the brush shape across the horizontal axis (X) or the vertical axis (Y). For example, if your brush is an L shape and you select Flip X, your brush shape becomes a backward L. Check Flip Y to make your brush shape an upside-down L shape. Check both to make your brush shape an upside-down, backward L shape.

✏ **Scattering:** Controls the number and position of brush marks in a stroke. The higher the value, the higher the number of brush marks and the farther apart they are. When you select Both Axes, Photoshop distributes the brush marks radially, as if on a curve. Count controls the number of brush marks at each spacing point. The higher the value, the greater the number of marks.

✔ **Texture:** Allows you to impart a texture pattern (using the foreground color) to a brush stroke; a Photoshop preset texture or one of your designs. Select Invert to reverse the light and dark pixels in the pattern. Scale sizes the pattern in each stroke. Texture Each Tip renders each tip when it's stroked, giving a more saturated effect. Depth controls how prominent the pattern appears against the brush stroke. Minimum Depth specifies the minimum depth that the paint of each stroke shows through the pattern. Mode lets you choose one of Photoshop's blending modes, as I describe in Book V, Chapter 3. You can find more about creating and working with patterns in Book IV, Chapter 3.

✔ **Dual Brush:** You can use two tips to draw with a single brush. This option lets you select the characteristics of the second tip by using the same type of attributes — such as diameter, spacing, and scatter — that you applied to the first tip. You can also specify a blending mode between the two tips.

✔ **Color Dynamics:** Uses your foreground and background colors to adjust how the color varies during a stroke, allowing you to create a multicolored brush. Slight variations give the stroke a more natural, organic look. You can introduce slight (or major) jitter to the hue, saturation, brightness, and purity of the colors, as well as some randomness between the foreground and background colors when you draw a stroke. Without color dynamics, the stroke color remains constant.

✔ **Transfer:** Controls the buildup of color; that is, how much color transfers onto the brush tip. Options include introducing randomness into the opacity and flow factors of a brush, again making the brush stroke look more natural and less machine-generated. The new Wet and Mix options are available when you select the Mixer Brush tool. Experiment with all the dynamics to see exactly how they can affect your image. The Flow and Opacity settings in the Brush panel don't override those settings on the Options bar.

Here's a list of brush-tip characteristics, which you can find on the left side of the Brush panel:

✔ **Noise:** Adds random pixels to brush tips, giving them texture and an organic quality. This option is more apparent in feathered brushes.

✔ **Wet Edges:** The brush tip leaves a stroke that looks more like watercolor, with paint building up along the edges.

✔ **Airbrush:** Gives the brush tip a soft, airbrushed look.

✔ **Smoothing:** Smoothes curves when you draw arcs with the brush. This option is more noticeable when you use a pressure-sensitive drawing tablet.

✔ **Protect Texture:** Ensures that all brush tips that use a texture use the same texture. Therefore, you can switch back and forth between brush tips while painting and still achieve a consistent texture.

Figure 1-7 shows the range of possibilities these options offer.

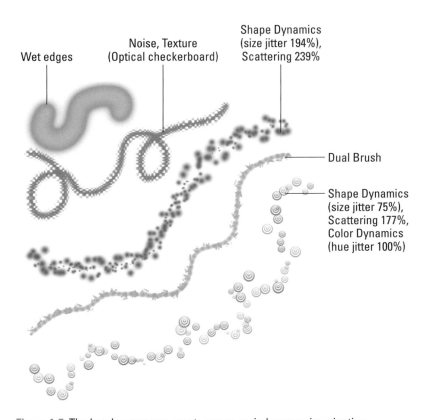

Figure 1-7: The brushes you can create are as varied as your imagination.

 You can lock any of the brush characteristics by clicking the small lock icon to the right of the characteristic. Locking a characteristic ensures that the settings don't change after you have your brush just so. This works especially well if you want the size of your brush to correlate with the amount of pressure you apply to a stylus when using a drawing tablet. By locking settings, you override any specifications set by preset brushes. You can select the Reset All Locked Settings option from the Brush panel pop-up menu to bring back the default settings of the brush. To clear all brush options, select Clear Brush Controls from the Brush panel pop-up menu.

 If you really like a brush you've created, feel free to save it as a preset that you can access again and again. Simply select New Brush Preset from the pop-up menu on the Brush panel or from the Brush drop-down panel on the Options bar.

Using the preset brushes

Photoshop has two brush panels, in a sense. In addition to the Brush panel, the Brush Preset Picker (shown in Figure 1-7) on the Options bar appears when you click the down arrow next to the box displaying the active brush tip.

With CS5, Photoshop offers a separate, dedicated Brush Presets panel, as shown in Figure 1-8.

Photoshop has a large number of pre-designed brush presets that you can use. The default set includes round, hard-edged brushes (which still have softer edges than the Pencil tool) and round soft-edged brushes. There are also airbrush, spatter, and natural media brush-tip presets, as well as a group of brush-tip shapes, such as stars, leaves, and other shapes. In CS5, you also get a set of new "bristle" tip brushes. You can also download brushes galore from the Web, so go crazy. Just Google "photoshop brushes" and watch in amazement as you get page after page of available downloads.

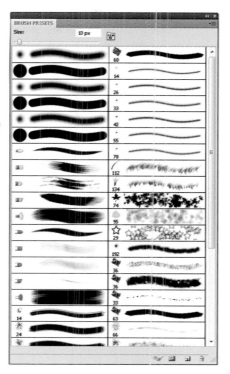

Figure 1-8: The Brush Presets panel offers a deluge of premade brushes.

A preset brush's pixel diameters appear as text next to a thumbnail image of the brush shape when the panel's display is in default mode. To use one of these brushes, just click the Brush Preset Picker arrow or thumbnail on the Options bar, or click the brush in the Brush Presets panel and then select the brush you want from the scrolling preset list. You can augment your choices with any of the following options:

✔ **Move the Size slider to change the diameter of the selected brush.** This is a quick way of getting a slightly larger or smaller brush when none of the presets meets your needs exactly. For example, the hard-round brush preset is 13 pixels in diameter. You can click this brush tip and move the slider to the right to get a hard-edged brush in any size up to 2,500 pixels.

To change the brush size by using the keyboard when a tool is active, press the] key (the right bracket) to increase the size and the [key (the left bracket) to decrease the size. The amount of change varies according to the initial size of the brush. To adjust the size more dramatically, continue to press the bracket key.

✔ **Click the curved arrow icon to restore the brush to its original size.**

✔ **Select any of the libraries of additional brush-tip presets provided with Photoshop.** Click the Brush Preset Picker or the Brush Presets panel's pop-up menu and select one of the brush libraries shown at the bottom. They have names like Special Effect Brushes and Faux Finish Brushes. Select whether to append the brushes to your current set or to replace the current set with the library you select from the dialog box that appears.

✔ **CS5 has provided a new set of preset brush tips referred to as "bristle" brushes.** These brushes create realistic brush stokes that appear to have been made using natural, not digital, media. You can specify options for the brush tips to change the shape, bristles (density), length, thickness, stiffness (flexibility), angle, and spacing.

You can also manage brush-tip libraries by using the Preset Manager. (See Book I, Chapter 5 for information on using the Preset Manager.) Click the Preset Manager icon at the bottom of the Brush Presets panel to access it directly.

✔ **Select a custom library of brush tips that you've created.** Click Load Brushes to append new brushes to your current collection or to replace them with the new library.

✔ **In the Brush Preset Picker, if the Hardness option is available, adjust the slider to make the brush more (higher) or less (lower) fuzzy.**

In addition to the presets Photoshop offers, you can create your own presets to use when you need them. Book I, Chapter 2 explains how to create your own presets.

Viewing preset brushes

You can change the way brushes are shown in the Brush Preset Picker, the Brush panel, and the Brush Presets panel by selecting a viewing mode from the Picker's or panels' pop-up menus:

✔ **Text Only:** Displays the names of the brush tips in several columns (depending on how wide you've made the panel).

✔ **Small Thumbnail:** The default view, with a thumbnail image of the brush tip and its diameter in pixels.

✔ **Large Thumbnail:** Provides a closer look at the brush tip.

✔ **Small List:** Shows a column list of the brush tips with their text names and small thumbnails.

✔ **Large List:** Shows a column list of the brush tips with their text names and larger thumbnails.

✓ **Stroke Thumbnail:** Shows a typical stroke from the selected brush so you can see how it looks when applied.

✓ **Bristle Brush Preview** (in the Brush Preset panel): Click the first icon on the bottom left to toggle a preview window of the Bristle Brush tip, which appears on the image window. Click the preview window to view the brush from different angles.

Putting It Together

Colorizing Black-and-White Images

Just as there are valid artistic reasons for shooting a photo in black and white, there are equally reasonable rationales for changing a grayscale image into a color one. Perhaps the picture is an old one, taken before color film was widely used, and you want to colorize it. Or you may come across a monochrome image that would look even better in color. Photoshop lets you restore black-and-white pictures to their original colors or create entirely new color schemes. If you can imagine an image in color, use Photoshop to add the hues you want to see.

IT Stock Free

**Book IV
Chapter 1**

**Painting
and Drawing
with Photoshop**

In my example, which you can find on this book's Web site (see the Introduction for details), I chose a black-and-white photo of an adorable boy. Rather than a full-color treatment that attempts to duplicate a color photograph, I want to apply a technique that mimics the hand-colored look of the venerable Marshall's Photo Coloring System of

continued

continued

pigments, photo oils, spot colors, retouch pencils, and other products so popular in the '50s and '60s (and enjoying a rebirth today). Although I've worked with a Marshall's kit myself, Photoshop is a lot faster and easier, and less messy.

1. **Open a grayscale image in Photoshop.**

2. **Choose Image⇨Mode⇨RGB Color to convert the grayscale image to a full-color image (even though it presently still lacks any color).**

3. **Choose Layer⇨New⇨Layer.**

   This creates a new transparent layer to paint on, as shown in the figure. Although you can paint directly on an image layer (or a copy of an image layer), using an empty layer is safer and gives you more flexibility in backtracking when you make a mistake. (For more information on working with layers, consult Book V.)

4. **In the New Layer dialog box that appears, name the layer and then click OK.**

   You can paint all your colors on a single layer, but you may find that using a separate layer for each part of the face lets you fade that color in and out as required to blend smoothly with your other hues.

5. **Select the Color mode from the Blend Mode drop-down list in the Layers panel.**

   Photoshop uses this mode to combine the painting layer with the image layer, enabling you to apply color while retaining the details of the underlying image.

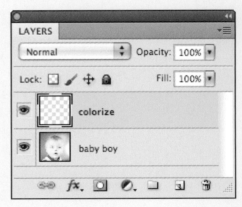

6. **Select a color you want to apply from the Swatches panel or use the Color panel to mix your own.**

   You can find information on color in Book II, Chapter 3.

7. **Select the Brush tool in the Tools panel.**

8. **Click the down arrow next to the Brush Preset Picker on the Options bar and select a brush from the list.**

   Hard-edged brushes appear first, and the soft-edged brushes follow. I would start with a soft-edged brush.

   The Airbrush option on the Options bar creates a very subtle and soft effect. Just be sure you pick the kind of brush that works best for the area of the picture you're colorizing. (Use a small, fuzzy brush for smaller areas, and use a bigger, sharper brush for more defined lines and wider areas.)

9. **Paint all the parts of the image where you want to apply color.**

If you make a mistake, you can erase the bad strokes without affecting the underlying grayscale image because you're painting on a separate layer.

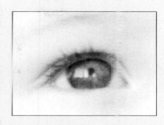

In my example, I chose a nice, light blue color to change the color of the boy's eyes, as shown in the figure. A small fuzzy brush is perfect for a small area such as the eyes.

Change brushes as necessary by clicking the Brush Preset Picker on the Options bar and selecting a larger or smaller brush.

10. **When you finish with that area of the image, create a new layer for each of the main components of the photograph and repeat Steps 4 through 9 with an additional color.**

I painted the eyes, lips, cheeks, hair, and hair highlights separately because creating natural, subtle effects with people's skin, hair, and eyes takes a special touch:

- *Eyes:* When painting the eyes, paint only the irises and leave the pupils their original black color. Don't paint over the catchlights in the eyes, either. (*Catchlights* are reflections of light sources, such as windows or the flash.)

- *Lips:* Color the inner surface of the lips a darker, rosier pink than the outer surface. Lips look best when portrayed in at least two shades. Don't forget to color the gums with an even lighter pink.

- *Hair:* Hair looks best when the highlights and darker portions are slightly different colors.

- *Cheeks:* To put a little blush in the cheeks, choose the Airbrush option on the Options bar and work with a relatively large brush size. Apply a good dash of color to each cheek and a lighter bit of color to the forehead and chin. I used a 300-pixel brush for this high-resolution image.)

  I left the clothes and background uncolored to emphasize that the focal point is the boy's face.

11. **For the overall skin tone, I chose a different technique, using the Hue/Saturation command. This technique works especially well with those who have naturally dark complexions. You can choose to paint the skin with a brush or use this technique:**

- Duplicate the grayscale image layer and then choose Image➪Adjustments➪ Hue/Saturation.

- Choose the Colorize option and move the Hue slider to the left to produce a sepia tone. I set my Hue to 36. Set Saturation to 25 percent and click OK to colorize this layer.

continued

Book IV
Chapter 1

Painting and Drawing with Photoshop

continued

✔ Use the Eraser tool to remove everything in the colorized layer that isn't skin. In my example, I removed the hair, background, eyes, lips, teeth, and clothing. The result is a nice sepia tone to the face.

Be sure to pick a color that's as close to real life as possible. If the subject has darker skin, you may need to move away from rosier blush tones.

12. **When you finish coloring your layers, you can experiment with different opacity levels for each colorized layer to see whether more-transparent hues might look better.**

Drawing with Vector Shapes

Although I'm a big fan of photos and all the pixels that make up those photos, sometimes you have to call on a vector or two. Maybe you need to create a simple line art graphic for a Web page. Or perhaps you want to add a logo to a poster. In these instances, drawing a vector shape with the Pen or Shape tool is the way to go.

Before you begin creating vector shapes in Photoshop, having a firm grasp on the basics of pixels versus vectors is a big help. Vectors describe a shape mathematically; pixel images, on the other hand, describe the same shape in terms of a map of pixels. The key difference is that, while you increase the size of a pixel-based image, it begins to look blocky. Because vector images are based on mathematical formulas, they look good at any size. Figure 1-9 shows both types of image. I explain the difference between vector and pixel-based images in more detail in Book II, Chapter 1.

When you create vector objects in a program like Photoshop, they're comprised of paths, which are made of anchor points, and straight and curved segments, or *lines*. You can create these points and lines by working with the preset shapes or by creating your own shape. The presets are easier to work with, but the custom shapes enable you to be more creative. In the following sections, I walk you through the steps for creating vector shapes, as well as the various options.

Vector image   Pixel image

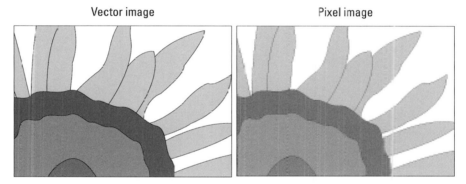

Figure 1-9: Photoshop images fall into one of two camps — vector or pixel.

Drawing a preset shape

Follow these steps to draw a preset shape in your document:

1. **Select a Shape tool from the Tools panel.**

   You can also press U and select the shape tool from the Options bar. You can select from the following shape tools (shown in Figure 1-10):

   - *Rectangle/Ellipse:* The rectangle and ellipse have no special parameters on the Options bar; however, they both behave much like their counterparts among the selection tools. For example, you can hold down the Shift key while dragging a shape to produce a perfect square or circle; hold down Shift+Alt (Shift+Option on the Mac) to draw the shape outward from the center. You have other Geometry options that let you determine how you draw the shapes (unconstrained, fixed size, from center, and so forth).

   - *Rounded Rectangle:* This shape has the same options as the rectangle shape, with the addition of a box in which you can type the radius of the circle used to round the corners of the rectangle.

   - *Polygon:* This shape includes a box in which you can enter the number of sides (from 3 to 100) you want for the polygon, as well as Geometry options.

Shape mode   Shape tools   Custom shape panel

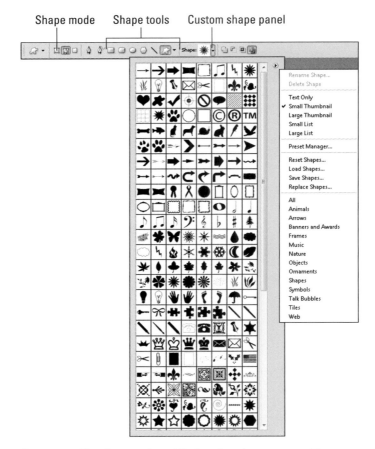

Figure 1-10: The shape tools and Options bar give you everything you need to make shapes, from simple squares to ornate *fleur-de-lys.*

- *Line:* You can give the line shape a width from 1 to 1,000 pixels and assign a layer style and/or fill color. You can also enter parameters for an arrowhead at either or both ends.

- *Custom:* You can find numerous preset custom shapes to choose from. As with any shape, you hold down Shift to constrain proportions or Alt (Option on the Mac) to draw from the center out.

2. **Select the mode for the shape you want to draw from the three icons on the Options bar.**

   Here's a list of ways in which you can create a shape (all options are on the Options bar):

   - *Shape Layers:* Click this icon to create the shape in a new layer of its own. When you select this mode, icons appear on the Options bar that let you select a layer style and/or fill color.

Shape Layers is a good choice if you want to keep your shapes in separate layers so you can manipulate them further. (Some options include making the shapes appear to have been added together, subtracted from each other, and so on.) Photoshop links shapes in a shape layer to a vector mask, which can show or hide portions of an image. You can find out more about shape layers and vector masks in the sections "Creating your own custom shape" and "Using vector masks," later in this chapter. The shapes remain scalable until you change them into pixels by choosing Layer⇨Rasterize⇨Shape.

- *Paths:* Click this icon to create the shape with a path, which "hovers" over your image. The shape appears as a path that you can edit by using the Pen tools and the Paths panel. (For everything you need to know about paths, check out Book III, Chapter 2.)

- *Fill Pixels:* Click this icon to create a shaped area filled with the foreground color. This option doesn't produce a vector shape, but instead fills the shape with pixels. The process is similar to filling a selection created with the Rectangular or Elliptical Marquee tools or painting on your canvas with a painting tool. When you select this mode, the Options bar includes choices that let you specify a blending mode, the transparency of the filled area, and whether you want the area anti-aliased. You can't edit a shape created with this option, except to modify the pixels.

3. **Select your options — on the Options bar (if any) and in the Geometry options drop-down panel, which also resides on the Options bar.**

   The Options bar changes to reflect each type of shape; each type has its own options, which are listed in Step 1. For detailed explanations on the various Geometry options, see the section "Setting Geometry options," later in this chapter.

   If you chose the Custom Shape tool in Step 1, click the drop-down arrow to access the Shapes panel. Select the shape that works for you. You can access more preset shape libraries via the pop-up menu at the top of the panel (refer to Figure 1-10).

4. **Drag in the document to draw the shape you've defined.**

   The shape appears in the image window. If you chose the Shape Layer mode in Step 2, the shape also appears in the Layers panel in its own layer. A rectangle filled with the foreground color appears in the image column, and the shape itself is shown in the mask column as a vector mask, as you can see in Figure 1-11. The black layer peeks through my vector mask, which is in the shape of pinwheels.

Drawing multiple shapes in a shape layer

After you create a shape layer, you can draw additional shapes in the layer, adding to the vector mask associated with that layer. You can add, subtract, overlap, and intersect shapes in exactly the same way you do with selections, as described in Book III, Chapter 3. Follow these steps:

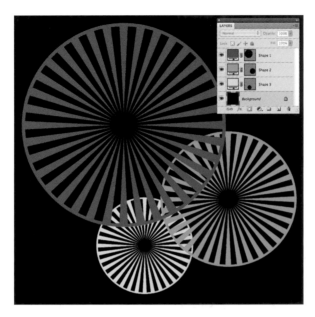

Figure 1-11: When you create a shape layer, you're creating a layer of color that shows through a vector mask (path) in the form of your shape.

1. **After you create the first shape, as I explain in the preceding section, select your desired state button on the Options bar:**

   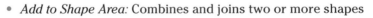

   • *Add to Shape Area:* Combines and joins two or more shapes

   • *Subtract from Shape Area:* Subtracts one shape from another shape

   • *Intersect Shape Areas:* Creates a shape only from the areas that overlap

   • *Exclude Overlapping Shape Areas:* Creates a shape only from the areas that don't overlap

2. **Grab your desired shape tool and draw the next shape.**

Hold down the Shift key to temporarily switch to Add to Shape Area while drawing a new shape. Hold down the Alt (Option on the Mac) key to temporarily switch to Subtract from Shape Area. This works just like adding or subtracting selections.

Setting Geometry options

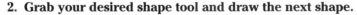

Geometry options for your shapes (rectangle/rounded rectangle, ellipse, polygon, line, and custom) help define how the shapes look. Click the down arrow on the Options bar to access the Geometry options. The following sections show you what you can do with these options.

Rectangular-shape Geometry options

Here are the Geometry options for the rectangle and rounded rectangle shapes, as shown in Figure 1-12:

- **Unconstrained:** When you select this option (the default), Photoshop defines the size and proportions of the rectangle while you drag.

- **Square:** Select this button to constrain the shape to a perfect square. (You can also hold down the Shift key to do the same thing on the fly.)

- **Fixed Size:** This option lets you draw rectangles only in fixed sizes. Specify the exact size by entering a width and height.

Figure 1-12: Geometry options define how your particular shape appears.

- **Proportional:** This option lets you define an aspect ratio, or proportion, for the rectangle. Type 3 into the W box and 4 into the H box to constrain yourself to drawing any size rectangle with fixed proportions in a 3:4 ratio.

- **From Center:** Select this option to expand the shape from the center point you click.

- **Snap to Pixels:** This option snaps the edges of a rectangle or rounded rectangle to the pixels on your screen.

Elliptical-shape Geometry options

The ellipse shape has the same options that are available for rectangles (also shown in Figure 1-11). Of course, instead of being able to create a perfect square, you can restrain the shape to be a perfect circle. Also, the Snap to Pixels option (available for rectangles) doesn't exist for ellipses.

Polygonal-shape Geometry options

The Geometry options for the polygon shape, as shown in Figure 1-13, include:

- **Radius:** Controls the distance from the center of a polygon to its outer points.

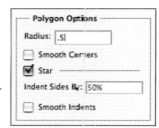

Figure 1-13: Choose between a polygon and a star.

✔ **Smooth Corners:** Select this option to round off the corners.

✔ **Star:** Select this option to create a star shape — that is, a polygon in which the sides indent inward, rather than extend outward from the corner points.

✔ **Indent Sides By:** The value entered here determines the amount the sides indent inward.

✔ **Smooth Indents:** Rounds off the inner corners created by indenting the sides.

✔ **Sides:** Directly in the Options bar, indicate the number of sides for your polygon or the number of points for your star.

Line Geometry options

The line's Geometry settings include whether to put arrowheads at the start or end of the line, as shown in Figure 1-14, or both. Figure 1-14 also shows how changing the width, length, and concavity settings affect the arrowhead shapes.

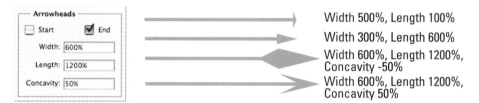

Figure 1-14: By specifying the width, length, and concavity, you can change the appearance of your arrowheads.

Custom-shape Geometry options

The custom shape options are similar to those you find for the other Geometry shapes — with a couple additions, shown in Figure 1-15:

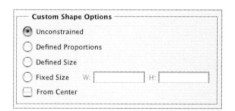

Figure 1-15: You can size your shape without losing its original proportions by checking the Defined Proportions option.

✔ **Defined Proportions:** When you use this option, Photoshop limits any shapes created by using this new custom shape to the *proportions* you use when you create it now. That is, you can change the size of a new shape, but only in proportion with the original custom shape that you created.

✔ **Defined Size:** When you use this option, Photoshop limits any shapes generated based on this new custom shape to the size you set now.

Creating your own custom shape

You can create your own custom shape by defining the shape with a vector mask, work path, or saved path. You can find out more about creating work paths and saved paths in Book III, Chapter 2. To create a shape and add it to your shape library, follow these steps:

1. **Select the Pen tool from the Tools panel or press Shift+P until the Pen tool is selected.**

2. **Select the Shape Layers icon on the Options bar and use the pen to draw the shape you want to create.**

   Book III, Chapter 2 describes the techniques for adding, removing, and adjusting the shapes of curves with the Pen tool.

   Photoshop automatically places the shape you create in its own shape layer as a vector mask. Find out more about what you can do with a vector mask in the following section.

3. **In the Paths panel, select the path or vector mask you want to convert into a custom shape.**

4. **Choose Edit⇨Define Custom Shape from the menu bar.**

   The Shape Name dialog box appears, as shown in Figure 1-16.

Figure 1-16: Create your own shapes when you tire of the presets.

5. **Enter a descriptive name for your new shape in the dialog box and then click OK.**

   The new shape appears in the custom shapes pop-up panel on the Options bar.

6. **Select Save Shapes from the Shapes panel's pop-up menu to store your new library on your hard drive.**

Although you can't create a shape with the Preset Manager, you can use the Preset Manager to manage the shapes in your shape library.

Using vector masks

When you create a shape in Shape Layer mode, Photoshop automatically saves the shape as a vector mask. Essentially, a shape layer has two components. First, Photoshop entirely fills the layer with color. Then, Photoshop places the shape, which (again) is comprised of a path, on top. The thumbnails in the Layers panel visually display this concept. The color peeks through the outline of the shape, and Photoshop hides (or masks) the rest of the layer. In other words, vector masks clip away the color of a shape layer. If you delete a vector mask, you're left with just a layer of solid color.

Like all vector objects, vector paths print at the full resolution of the printer and are resolution-independent.

You can edit a shape that Photoshop has saved as a vector mask at any time. Simply click the vector mask thumbnail to select it. Then, use the Shape and Pen tools to edit the shape.

Here are some additional things you can do with a vector mask:

✔ To remove a vector mask, drag its thumbnail in the Layers panel to the Trash icon at the bottom of the panel. You can also select the layer and choose Layer➪Vector Mask➪Delete.

✔ To enable or disable a vector mask, Shift-click its thumbnail in the Layers panel, or select the layer and choose Layer➪Vector Mask➪Disable (or Enable). Photoshop marks the thumbnails of disabled vector masks with an X.

✔ You can convert a vector mask to a layer mask by selecting the layer and choosing Layer➪Rasterize➪Vector Mask.

There is an additional tool to refine masks — both vector and pixel. Choose Window➪Masks to bring up this useful panel. Move the Feather slider to soften the edges of your hard-edged vector mask. Drag the Density slider to control the opacity of the areas outside the vector mask. For more details on this great panel, see Book VI, Chapter 3.

Manipulating shapes

You can manipulate shapes you create by using a variety of tools. Here's a quick list of the things you can do:

✔ **Move:** Select the Move tool (press V) to move shapes in their layer.

✔ **Delete:** Select a shape and press Delete to remove it.

✔ **Adjust anchor points:** Use the Direct Selection tool to manipulate anchor points, direction handles, lines, and curves.

✔ **Transform shapes:** Choose Edit➪Transform Path or with the Move tool selected, select the Show Transform Controls option on the Options bar to transform shapes. For more information, see Book III, Chapter 3.

✔ **Align and distribute shapes:** Use active buttons on the Options bar when you have the Move tool selected to change alignment and distribution along an imaginary line (shown on the button).

✔ **Clone a shape:** Hold down Alt (Option on the Mac) and move the shape with the Path Selection tool.

You can find more information on manipulating shapes in Book III, Chapter 2.

Remember that if you select the Fill Pixels option on the Options bar, you're stuck with limited editing capabilities.

Chapter 2: Filling and Stroking

In This Chapter

✔ **Filling and stroking selections or paths**

✔ **Building and applying gradients**

✔ **Creating and applying patterns**

*P*hotoshop offers several ways to create elements such as geometric shapes, out of pixels. Filling and stroking these elements are two of the most venerable commands at your disposal. You can also paint geometric elements on your canvas by hand or convert vector shapes to pixels (see Book IV, Chapter 1 for more on that topic). Therefore, if you need pixels arranged into regular circles, ellipses, and polygons, the Fill and Stroke facilities of Photoshop are worthy of your consideration.

Here's how they work:

✔ The Fill command adds color, a pattern, or content to a selection of any shape (or form) you've created.

✔ The Stroke command applies color around the selection outline only.

This chapter shows you how to create these objects by filling and stroking selections and paths, how to add smooth gradient blends, and the best ways to apply patterns. After reading this chapter, you'll have your fill of different strokes.

Another way of filling is by using a fill layer, which you can use to fill a shape. Because fill layers work a little differently from the types of fills discussed in this chapter, I cover them in Book V, Chapter 1.

Filling a Selection with a Solid Color

When you just want to add a solid color, you use either the foreground or the background color. (These colors appear at the bottom of the Tools panel, as I explain in Book I, Chapter 2.) The following steps show you the basics of filling a selection with either the foreground or the background color (you have plenty of other Fill options, which I discuss in the following sections):

1. **Create your selection on a layer.**

   See Book III for all you need to know about selections and Book V for the scoop on layers.

2. **Select a fill color as the foreground or background color.**

   Choose Window⇨Color. In the Color panel, use the color sliders to mix your desired color. For more on choosing color, see Book II, Chapter 3.

3. **Choose Edit⇨Fill.**

   The Fill dialog box, shown in Figure 2-1, appears. In this dialog box, under Contents, you can select whether to fill with the foreground or the background color. You also can select Color (which launches the Color Picker), Black, 50% Gray, White, History, Pattern, or the new Content-Aware option.

4. **Click OK.**

   The color that you choose fills the selection.

Figure 2-1: You can fill your selection with color, history, a pattern, or content.

You can select a blending mode, the fill opacity, and choose whether to fill the entire selection or only the portions of the selection that contain pixels (the nontransparent areas). I recommend not adjusting your Blending Mode or Opacity settings in the Fill dialog box; instead create a new layer for your fill and adjust those settings in the Layers panel, where you have more flexibility. For all you need to know about layers, check out Book V.

Fill Options and Tips

After you make a selection, you're ready to use one of the Fill options. You can use the Fill dialog box (as described in the preceding section) to fill the selection with the foreground or the background color; you can also choose to fill the selection with color, black, white, gray, a pattern, history, or content. Photoshop is full of shortcuts and options. Here are just a few:

- ✔ With the selection active, press Alt+Backspace (Option+Delete on the Mac) to fill the selection with the foreground color. All areas within the selection, including transparent areas, fill with the color.

- ✔ Fill only the pixels in a selection with the foreground color, leaving any transparent pixels transparent, by pressing Alt+Shift+Backspace (or Option+Shift+Delete on the Mac). For more on transparency, see Book V, Chapter 1.

   Lock the transparent pixels in a layer (and its selections) by clicking the Transparency icon in the Lock area of the Layers panel.

✔ If you're working on the Background layer, you can also fill the selection with the background color by pressing the Backspace (Delete on the Mac) key. This opens the Fill dialog box. Choose your desired Fill option from the Use drop-down menu. (Pressing Backspace/Delete on other layers creates a transparent area that shows the image in the layer underneath the selection.)

✔ By selecting the Color option in the Fill dialog box, you access the Color Picker where you can select any color of the rainbow to fill your selection. For more on using the Color Picker, see Book II, Chapter 3.

✔ Select the Content-Aware option in the Fill dialog box to fill the selection with similar content that's close to your selection, as shown in Figure 2-2. If you are trying to create a realistic composite, be sure to look at the results closely. Sometimes this option can create soft or choppy edges.

Selection marquee

Selection filled with content

iStockphoto

Figure 2-2: Fill your selection with content from your image.

✔ Select the Pattern option in the Fill dialog box to fill the selection with a pattern. Click the arrow next to the pattern swatch and select a pattern from the pop-up panel. Click the Pattern panel pop-up menu to select more pattern libraries.

✔ Select the History option in the Fill dialog box to restore the selection to a state or snapshot of the image. For more on working with the History panel, see Book II, Chapter 4.

✔ Paint part or all the interior of the selection by using any of the Brush tools, as shown in Figure 2-3. This option lets you partially fill a selection by using a bit of flexibility and creativity. When you paint a selection by using Brush tools, Photoshop confines the paint inside the boundaries of your selection. For more on painting, see Book IV, Chapter 1.

✔ Pour color from the Paint Bucket tool into the selection.

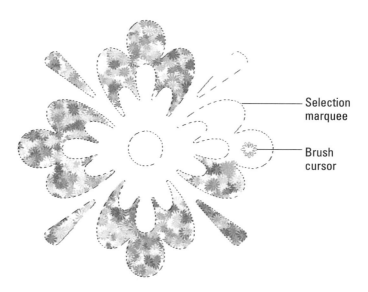

Selection marquee

Brush cursor

Figure 2-3: The marquee confines your brushstrokes to your selected area.

Pouring with the Paint Bucket Tool

The Paint Bucket tool, available in the Tools panel (where it shares a flyout menu with the Gradient tool), operates much like a combination of the Brush tool and the Magic Wand tool, as you can see by looking over its options.

To use it, select the tool (press Shift+G until it's active) and click inside the selection you want to fill. Here are your options, all of which are on the Options bar:

✔ **Fill:** You can select whether to fill with the foreground color or a pattern.

✔ **Pattern:** When you select Pattern on the Options bar, you can select a preset pattern, load patterns from your pattern libraries, or create a pattern of your own. You can find more information on patterns in the section "Working with Patterns," later in this chapter.

✔ **Mode:** You can select a fill blend mode, too, although you'll be better served to set your blend mode via your Layers panel due to better editing flexibility. You can find more information on these modes in Book V, Chapter 3.

✔ **Opacity:** Adjust this value to make your fill semitransparent.

✔ **Tolerance:** Like the Magic Wand tool, you can choose a Tolerance level (0 to 255) that specifies how similar in color a pixel must be before it's selected for painting. You can find more information on Tolerance levels in Book III, Chapter 1.

✔ **Anti-Alias:** Choose this option to blend in the paint smoothly with the areas not filled.

✔ **Contiguous:** When selected, the paint fills only pixels that are touching within your selection. When deselected, paint fills all pixels within the Tolerance level that you specify within your selection.

✔ **All Layers:** This option applies paint based on the colors in all layers that are within the selection and Tolerance level you specify.

As with other tools that fill, you can prevent the Paint Bucket tool from filling the transparent pixels. Just select the Transparency icon in the Lock area of the Layers panel.

Stroking a Selection

Stroking enables you to create outlines of selections, layers, or paths. Stroking a selection creates a border around the selection. It's up to you to decide whether to put the border inside, outside, or centered on the selection. (Photoshop doesn't care.)

To stroke a selection, follow these steps:

1. **In the Tools or Colors panel, choose a foreground color and make a selection of your choice.**

2. **Choose Edit➪Stroke.**

3. **In the Stroke dialog box, adjust the settings and the options, as shown in Figure 2-4:**

- *Width:* You can select 1 to 250 pixels. You can also type a value by using another measurement, such as inches, but Photoshop converts it to pixel values before applying.

- *Color:* Click in the Color box to select the hue you want from the Color Picker.

- *Location:* Select where Photoshop should apply the stroke in relation to your selection border. The Inside option always gives you sharp corners on a rectangle. The Center and Outside options can result in blunt, mitered corners.

- *Mode:* This determines how the stroke color merges with other colors on the same layer.

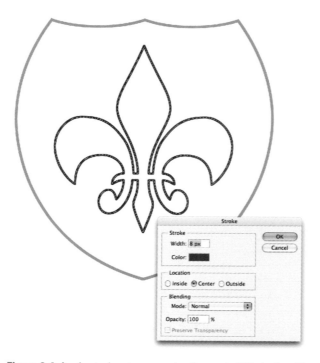

Figure 2-4: Apply strokes to your selection up to 250 pixels wide.

- *Opacity:* The default value is 100%. If you want the stroke to be semi-transparent, type another value.

- *Preserve Transparency:* Select this option to apply the stroke only to nontransparent pixels.

4. Click OK to apply the stroke.

I recommend leaving the Blending Mode and Opacity setting options in the Stroke dialog box alone. Instead of adjusting these settings, create a new layer for your stroke and then choose different Blending Mode and Opacity settings in the Layers panel. This approach maximizes your ability to make edits.

Working with Gradients

A *gradient* is a wonderful blend of colors that you can apply to a layer or selection, gradually fading from one hue to another. Gradients can involve more than two colors, producing a veritable rainbow of variations. You can apply gradients by using preset selections of colors, or you can create your own gradient.

You can create the following gradient effects:

- **Foreground to background:** A transition from the current foreground color to the background color.

- **Foreground to transparent:** A transition from the current foreground color to transparent, allowing whatever's under the transparent portion to show.

- **Black to white:** A transition from black to white.

- **An array of colorful selections:** Including rainbows, coppery sheens, and other effects.

You can load other libraries of gradients from the Gradient panel menu's libraries. They have names such as Color Harmonies, Metals, and Special Effects. For more information on managing preset libraries, see Book I, Chapter 5.

In addition to being able to control the appearance and application of a gradient, you also have the opportunity to adjust the Gradient tool's options, all of which are on the Options bar:

- **Mode:** Select any of Photoshop's blending modes.

- **Opacity:** Select how transparent the gradient is.

- **Reverse:** Reverse the order in which the colors are applied.

✔ **Dither:** Add *noise,* or random information, to produce a smoother gradient that prints with less *banding* (color stripes caused by the limitations of the printing process to reproduce a full range of colors).

✔ **Transparency:** This option determines whether Photoshop ignores the gradient's transparency settings when you apply a gradient. If you deselect this option, all portions of the gradient are fully opaque. I show you how to work with a gradient's transparency in the section "Adding transparency to a gradient," later in this chapter.

Applying a preset gradient to a selection

Here's how to apply a preset gradient:

1. **Select the layer from the Layers panel and/or make the selection that you want to apply the gradient to.**

2. **Select the Gradient tool from the Tools panel (or press G or Shift+G) until the Gradient tool becomes active.**

3. **Select one of the preset gradients from the Gradient Picker drop-down menu on the Options bar.**

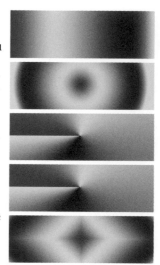

CS5 now provides a new preset called Neutral Density. Based on an analog-graduated, neutral-density lens filter, this preset is great when you want to correct an image that may have an overly bright (or overexposed) sky in comparison to the rest of the image. Create a new layer over your image layer and drag the Gradient tool (set to Linear) from the top to the bottom, using this preset. Then play with various blend modes for that layer. Overlay and Soft Light usually work well. You can also try using this new preset when layer masking. (See Book VI, Chapter 3.)

4. **Select the gradient type by clicking one of the icons on the Options bar.**

Figure 2-5 illustrates each gradient type:

Figure 2-5: You can choose from five gradients.

- *Linear:* Blends the colors of the gradient from start color to end color in a straight line

- *Radial:* Blends the colors outward in a circular pattern

- *Angle:* Creates a counterclockwise sweep around the starting point, resembling a radar screen

- *Reflected:* Blends the colors by using symmetrical linear gradients on either side of the starting point

- *Diamond:* Blends the colors outward in a diamond pattern

5. Choose any other options you want from the Options bar.

I explain these options in the section "Working with Gradients," earlier in this chapter.

6. Place the cursor at the position in the layer or selection where you want to place the starting color of the gradient.

7. Drag in any direction to the point you want to place the end color.

Longer drags result in a subtle transition between colors, whereas shorter drags result in a more abrupt transition. Press the Shift key while dragging to restrain the direction of the gradient to an even 45-degree angle, as well as perfectly horizontal or vertical.

8. Release the mouse button to apply the gradient.

The gradient I created is shown in Figure 2-6.

Figure 2-6: Indulge your love of color with Photoshop gradients.

Customizing and editing gradients

Although Photoshop includes dozens of gradient presets, you may want to create your own. Perhaps you want to create a gradient with your company colors or build one to match the predominant colors in an image. Or, you might want to create a gradient that includes more than two colors. The Gradient Editor lets you create your own gradient preset, using as many colors as you want, which you can save and reuse at any time.

The Gradient Editor has many options, but it's easy to use when you know what all the controls and options do. Follow these steps to create a simple smooth gradient:

1. **Select the Gradient tool from the Tools panel.**

2. **Click in the gradient sample window (not the arrow) on the Options bar.**

   The Gradient Editor dialog box opens, as shown in Figure 2-7.

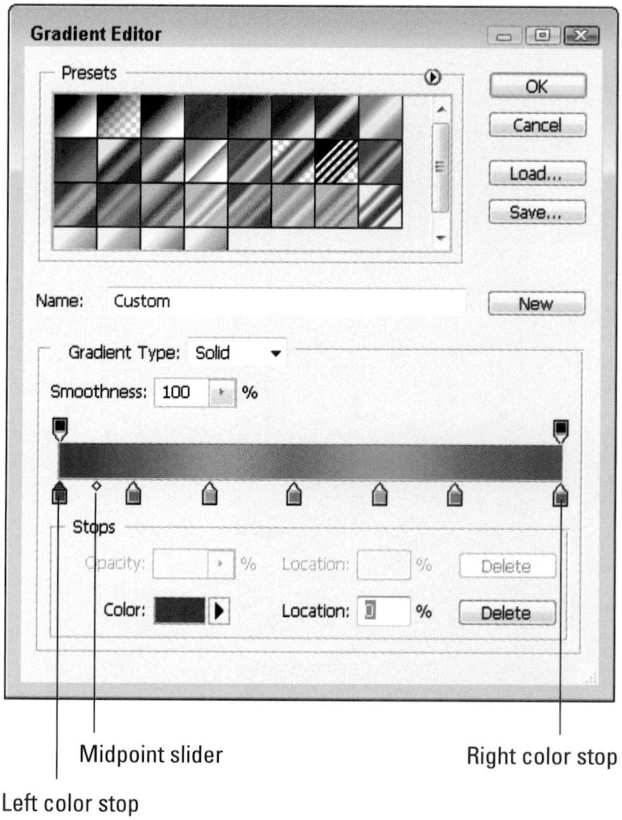

Figure 2-7: The Gradient Editor enables you to create custom gradients.

3. **Pick an existing gradient preset from the Presets area to use as the basis for your new gradient.**

4. **Select Solid or Noise from the Gradient Type pop-up menu.**

   As soon as you start to edit the existing gradient, the name of the gradient changes to Custom. A Noise gradient is one containing random colors. Because the colors are random, each time you create a noise gradient, the result is different. If you choose Noise, you can select which color mode to use and the roughness of the gradient and then select a range of acceptable colors.

5. **Adjust the Smoothness slider.**

   Click and drag the slider (click the right arrow) or enter a value to determine how smoothly to blend your colors into one another.

   If you choose Noise in Step 4, the slider changes to Roughness. This option affects how smoothly or abruptly a color transitions into another.

6. **You can set the following options only if you choose Noise in Step 4:**

   - *Color Model:* Select your desired color model or limit the range of colors by adjusting the sliders. See Book II, Chapter 2 for more on color models.

   - *Restrict Colors:* Limits the colors to printable CMYK colors only. See Book II, Chapter 2 for details.

   - *Add Transparency:* Lets you include transparency in your gradient, if desired.

   - *Randomize:* Changes the colors in your gradient. Each time you click Randomize, you get a new set of colors.

7. **To define the color of the starting point for your gradient, click the left color stop button under the gradient bar.**

   The triangle above the stop turns black to indicate you're working with the starting point of the gradient. Because Noise gradients are random, you can't define the colors.

8. **Select the starting color by using one of these methods:**

   - Double-click the left color stop and select a color from the Color dialog box that appears.

   - Click the Color box in the Stops area of the dialog box and choose a color from the Select Stop Color dialog box that opens.

   - Select Foreground, Background, or User Color from the Color pop-up menu in the Stops area of the Gradient Editor dialog box.

If you select color with the Foreground or Background option, the color in the gradient changes automatically when you change the foreground or the background color. The change doesn't affect any gradients you've already created, but it does affect any future gradients. However, when you open the Gradient Editor again, you can revert to the original foreground or background color you used when you created the gradient by selecting the User Color option from the Color pop-up menu in the Stops area.

- Position the cursor (it appears as an Eyedropper icon) anywhere in the gradient bar to select a start color from the bar, or position the cursor anywhere within an image on your screen and then click to select the color under the cursor.

9. **Click the end point color stop at the right side of the gradient bar and use any of the methods described in Step 8 to choose the end color of the gradient.**

10. **Change the location of the start and end points of the colors by moving the color stops to the left or right. Click and drag the midpoint slider (a diamond icon that appears when you click an adjacent color stop) to adjust where the color mixes equally, 50-50.**

You can also change the position of the midpoint by typing a value into the Location box. The position of the color stops can also be changed this way.

Because the center point of the gradient is halfway between the start and end points, the gradient proceeds smoothly from one color to the other, meeting to blend evenly in the middle. Moving the color stops and the midpoint changes the proportions.

11. **(Optional) Want to add another color? Just click below the gradient bar at the position you want to add the next color, and then define a color for the new color stop.**

12. **(Optional) Repeat Step 11 for additional colors.**

Heck, you can keep going like this for hours.

13. **For the additional color stops, move the stops to the left or right to adjust the location of the start and end points for each color. Then, adjust the midpoint sliders between the colors.**

14. **If you change your mind, you can redefine the color or click the Delete button.**

You can also remove a color stop by dragging it down or up from its position on the gradient bar.

15. **After your edits are complete, give your gradient a name, if you want, and click the New button.**

    Your gradient is added to the Presets menu. Figure 2-8 shows an example of a unique gradient that I created in the Gradient Editor.

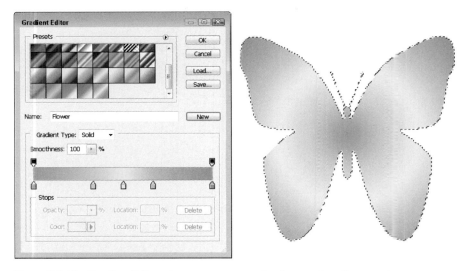

Figure 2-8: The Gradient Editor gives you more creative license than the presets.

Adding transparency to a gradient

By default, a gradient has 100-percent opacity in the start color and progresses to 100-percent opacity in the end color. If you like, you can have the gradient fade out to transparency so that the portion of the image under the gradient shows through. To add transparency to a gradient, follow these steps:

1. **Create a gradient, as described in the preceding sections.**

2. **Select the left opacity stop.**

    This stop is located just above the gradient bar, as shown in Figure 2-9.

3. **Use the Opacity slider to specify the amount of transparency for the gradient at its start point.**

    You can also type a value into the Opacity box.

4. **Select the right opacity stop, and then slide the Opacity slider or enter a percentage in the text box to specify transparency for the gradient at its end point.**

    The lower the percentage, the less opaque the color.

Opacity stop   Opacity slider

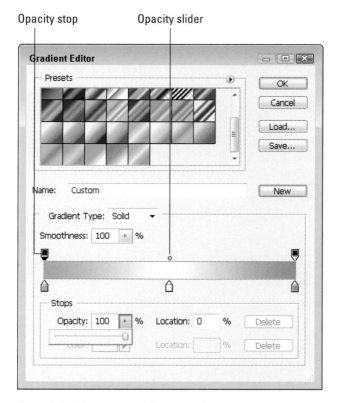

Figure 2-9: Lighten your gradients by adjusting the opacity of your colors.

5. **Move the opacity stops to the right or left to adjust the location where Photoshop applies each stop's opacity setting.**

6. **Move the midpoint slider (a diamond icon) to adjust how the color and the transparency mix.**

7. **Click above the gradient bar to add more opacity stops if you want to vary the transparency of the gradient at different points.**

   For example, you could fade transparency from 100 percent to 50 percent and back to 100 percent to produce a particular effect. Figure 2-10 shows a gradient with varying levels of transparency.

Gradients ordinarily proceed smoothly from one color to another. If you want a less homogeneous appearance, adjust the Smoothness slider to a value of less than 100 percent (click the right arrow to access the slider).

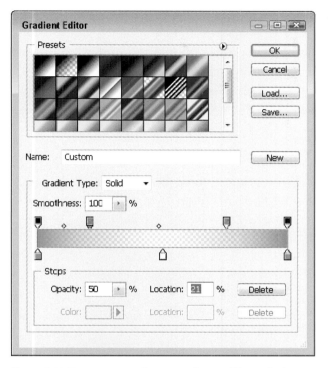

Figure 2-10: Transparency gives a gradient a different look.

Managing and Saving Gradients

If you're smart, you'll store the gradients you create so that you can use or edit them again later. Before you can save them, however, be sure to add them to the gradient Presets (see "Customizing and editing gradients" earlier in this chapter). Here are some tips for managing your gradients:

- ✔ To save a gradient, click the Save button in the Gradient Editor dialog box. You save the current presets, including your new gradient, under the current library's name or another name that you choose.

- ✔ To load gradient presets into the Gradient Editor, click the Load button and select the name of the gradient library that you want to add to the Presets list.

- ✔ To add an additional set of presets to the current presets, select the name of the presets from the Gradient Editor's pop-up menu

For more information about managing gradient presets with the Preset Manager, see Book I, Chapter 5.

Working with Patterns

Patterns are textures or repeating configurations of pixels that you use to fill selections or layers. You can apply patterns with painting tools, smear them around your image with the Pattern Stamp tool, or use them as a basis for the Healing Brush and Patch tools. Photoshop offers a large selection of patterns; you can download an even larger selection, and you can even create your own.

You select patterns from panels that appear on the Options bar for many of the tools just mentioned, much like brush tips and gradients, and you manage them in much the same way, using the Preset Manager (see Book I, Chapter 5). The following sections show you how to apply a preset pattern and create your own pattern.

Applying a preset pattern

Although you can apply patterns with many tools, this chapter sticks with applying patterns as fills. To fill a layer or selection with a preset pattern, follow these steps:

1. **Choose the layer from the Layers panel and/or make the selection you want to fill with a pattern.**

2. **Choose Edit⇨Fill and then select Pattern from the Use pop-up menu.**

3. **In the Custom Pattern panel, select the pattern you want to fill with.**

   Here are some tips in choosing a pattern:

   • Choose a pattern from the drop-down panel, as shown in Figure 2-11.

   • Replace the current patterns with new patterns by selecting Replace Patterns from the panel pop-up menu (click the arrow on the right side of the dialog box). Then, select the new pattern library from the dialog box that appears.

   • Append new patterns to the current set by selecting Load Patterns from the panel pop-up menu.

   • Append one of the preset libraries that come with Photoshop by selecting the pattern from the list at the bottom of the panel pop-up menu.

4. **Choose any other Fill options you want to apply, such as Mode, Opacity, or Preserve Transparency.**

   The Preserve Transparency option prevents Photoshop from filling the transparent areas on your layer with a pattern.

   I recommend adjusting the Mode and Opacity settings in the Layers panel rather than the Fill dialog box. This approach allows you maximum flexibility if you want to make edits later.

5. **Click OK to fill the layer or selection with the chosen pattern.**

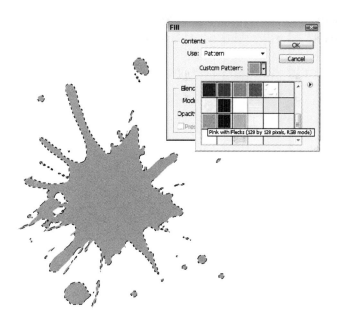

Figure 2-11: Fill your selection with pink flecks or one of the many other Photoshop preset patterns.

Creating a new pattern

You can create your own pattern, basing it on an existing image or one you create yourself. Select a small portion of an image to build an abstract pattern or use a recognizable object to define that object as a pattern stamp. You can use anything, from a logo to your signature, as a pattern.

To create your own pattern, follow these steps:

1. **Open the image that contains the area you want to use as a pattern or create an image from scratch.**

2. **Make any modifications to the image to produce the exact pattern that you want.**

3. **Use the Rectangular Marquee tool to select the area you want to convert into a pattern.**

   If you don't make a selection, Photoshop uses your entire image as a basis for the pattern.

   If you're using a selection to define your pattern, you must use a rectangular selection. You can't use a feathered selection of any kind.

4. **Choose Edit⇨Define Pattern.**

5. **Enter a name for your pattern in the Define Pattern dialog box.**

   Your new pattern appears in the Pattern panel for use.

Chapter 3: Creating and Editing Type

In This Chapter

✔ **Discovering different kinds of type**

✔ **Getting to know the type tools**

✔ **Entering text**

✔ **Making type follow a path**

✔ **Using the Character and Paragraph panels**

✔ **Editing text**

✔ **Creating character and paragraph styles**

✔ **Exploring masking, shaping, and warping effects**

*F*or an image-editing program, Photoshop has surprisingly good tools for creating type. Over time, features have been added that let you create paragraphs of text or simple lines of text used as headlines or labels. You can change the spacing between characters, warp your type, check your spelling, or create selections in the shape of text. Drop shadows, beveled type, and other special effects are yours quickly and easily. And you can even place text on or inside a path.

You may still want to use Adobe Illustrator or InDesign to create professional layouts in which you can keep text and image files separate, or where you have to place buckets full of text at small point sizes. But if what you're looking for is a great-looking image that includes great-looking snippets of text, Photoshop can do the job. This chapter introduces you to Photoshop's basic type tools, as well as its more advanced type capabilities.

Selecting a Type Mode

The text you create in Photoshop can be categorized in several different ways, but ultimately, you're either adding just a little text (such as a word or single line of text) or a lot (maybe a paragraph or so). Accordingly, Photoshop separates type into two modes:

✔ **Point type:** Use this mode to create a headline or label. You can create point type by clicking in your image and typing; the line appears while you type and grows to whatever length you need (even if that length is wider or taller than your image). Point type never wraps around to a new line. To wrap to the next line, you must insert a hard return by pressing Enter (Return on the Mac).

✔ **Paragraph type:** Use this mode to enter longer blocks of text on an image. It's (unsurprisingly) similar to the kind of type you're accustomed to working with in word processing programs. In Paragraph mode, all the text goes into a resizable bounding box, and if a line is too long, Photoshop automatically wraps it around to the next line.

There is a third way to enter type — on a path. This unique way to create type is described in the later section, "Creating Type on or in a Path."

The Point type and Paragraph type modes each operate a bit differently, although they share many features and options. I explain each of them separately in the sections "Entering Text in Point Type Mode" and "Entering Text in Paragraph Type Mode," later in this chapter.

Understanding Different Kinds of Type

Whether you're using Point type mode or Paragraph type mode, you can select several type options, each designed to help you work with, display, print, and edit text. These options determine how Photoshop enables you to work with text in a file:

✔ **Vector type:** All text in Photoshop is initially created as vector-based type. Vector type provides scalable outlines that you can resize without producing jaggy edges in the diagonal strokes. You can also edit type in this mode, adding or subtracting characters or adjusting attributes, such as kerning and tracking. Vector type is always of optimum quality and appears crisp and clean. (See Book II, Chapter 1 for more details on vector and rasterized images.)

✔ **Rasterized type:** When Photoshop converts vector type into pixels, that text is *rasterized.* When text is rasterized, it's no longer editable; instead, it's a frozen graphic of what the text looks like. When you finish editing vector type and want to merge the text with the other pixels in an image (or to perform some manipulations that can be done only with rasterized text, such as applying filters), you can transform the vector type into pixels by rasterizing it. You can't resize rasterized type without losing some quality or risking a bad case of the jaggies.

✔ **Pixel fonts:** *Pixel fonts* are tiny fonts designed for display at small sizes on computer screens, especially Web sites. Pixel fonts are designed so that every pixel corresponds to a pixel on your screen. These fonts, with names such as MINI 7, MiniSerif, and Tenacity, are created in fixed sizes (say, 7 pixels high for MINI 7 or 10 pixels high for Tenacity and PixelDust). Diagonal lines are avoided as much as possible, with the font designs favoring horizontal and vertical strokes. As a result, pixel fonts look crisp and clear at small sizes without anti-aliasing (smoothing around the edges). Indeed, you shouldn't use anti-aliasing with pixel fonts, nor should you attempt to resize or rescale them. You can buy or download pixel fonts, install them on your computer, and use them just like you use other fonts. You can see some examples of pixel fonts in Figure 3-1.

FFF NADADOR BOLD

FFF MANAGER BOLD

FFF HARMONY

FFF FORWARD

Figure 3-1: Unlike traditional fonts, pixel fonts are designed to fit into the pixel grid of your screen.

Exploring the Type Tools

Strictly speaking, Photoshop has four type tools (found in the Tools panel), but two of them are simply vertically oriented versions of the main two text implements. You can use either Paragraph or Point type mode with any of the type tools:

- **Horizontal Type:** Use this tool to enter point or paragraph type oriented horizontally on your screen. If you want text that's oriented at an angle other than vertical, you can rotate it by choosing Edit⇨Transform⇨ Rotate after you enter the text. This tool creates the type on its own type layer, except when used in Bitmap, Multichannel, or Indexed Color modes, which don't support layers. (Book II, Chapter 2 covers these modes.)

- **Vertical Type:** The Vertical Type and Vertical Type Mask tools (described in the following bullet) are handy for entering Asian characters. However, you can also use this tool to enter Roman character point type oriented in a vertical column. You can also use the Vertical Type tool to create columns of paragraph text, but the results look a little strange. Note that the columns also go from right to left. After you enter your text columns, you can rotate the text to an orientation other than vertical by choosing Edit⇨ Transform⇨Rotate. Like the Horizontal Type tool, this tool creates type in its own type layer, except with file formats that don't support layers.

- **Horizontal Type Mask/Vertical Type Mask:** These tools operate identically to their siblings described in the two preceding bullets, with two exceptions. Instead of adding filled type, both the Horizontal and Vertical Type Mask tools create a selection border in the shape of the type you enter. Both tools add a selection marquee to the current active layer. You can do anything with a type selection that you can do with any other selection, including saving it (Select⇨Save Selection) for reuse later. You can find a longer discussion of the type mask tools in the section "Creating type outlines," later in this chapter.

The Horizontal and Vertical Type tools have some interesting options, which I explain in the following section. You can also set controls in the Paragraph and Character panels, which I discuss in the sections "Working with the Character Panel" and "Working with the Paragraph Panel," later in this chapter.

Entering Text in Point Type Mode

If you're image oriented (and why wouldn't you be if you're using Photoshop?), you're probably not planning to include a novella with your graphics.

Point type is great for headlines, labels, and similar small amounts of text. You can also use it to create logos and headings for Web pages. The Web is one place where text that isn't tack-sharp can still do the job.

Although a Photoshop image is generally not the place you want to insert a whole lot of text, you can add larger blocks of text that are professional and effective — read the section "Entering Text in Paragraph Type Mode," later in this chapter. You can modify how point type and paragraph type are displayed by using the Paragraph and Character panels.

To enter point type, just follow these steps:

1. **Open a saved image or create a new Photoshop document.**

2. **Select either the Horizontal or Vertical Type tool from the Tools panel, or press T to select the type tool if the one you want is visible.**

   Press Shift+T to cycle through the four available type tools until the one that you want is active.

   Your cursor looks like an I-beam, similar to the one you see in a word processing program.

3. **Click the area of the image where you want to insert the text.**

   Where you click is called the *insertion point.*

   A small horizontal line about one-third of the way up the I-beam shows where the baseline (on which the line of text rests) is for horizontal type. If you select the Vertical Type tool, the cursor is rotated 90 degrees. The baseline is centered in the I-beam and represents the center axis of the vertical column of text you type.

4. **Select any of the type options from the Options bar, Character panel, or Paragraph panel.**

   To access the panels, click the Character and Paragraph toggle button on the Options bar or select either panel on the Window menu.

   I describe these options in the sections, "Working with the Character Panel" and "Working with the Paragraph Panel," later in this chapter.

5. **Type your text. Press Enter (or Return on the Mac) to begin a new line.**

   Lines of point type don't wrap around. When you press Enter or Return, you're inserting a hard carriage return that doesn't move. You have to remove hard returns if you want to change the length of the lines you type.

6. **When you finish entering the text, click the Commit (the check mark icon) button on the Options bar. You can also press Ctrl+Enter (⌘+return on the Mac).**

   A new type layer with your text is created. The layer appears in your Layers panel, as indicated by the T icon.

Entering Text in Paragraph Type Mode

Paragraphs are best allocated to captions, text descriptions, or slightly longer chunks of text that accompany an image.

Paragraph type is similar to the text you enter in a word processing program, except that it's contained inside a border, called a text box or a *bounding box*. While you type into a text box, the lines of text wrap around to fit the dimensions of the box. If you resize the box, Photoshop adjusts the wrapped ends to account for the new size.

You can type multiple paragraphs, use typographical controls, and rotate or scale the type. You can easily resize paragraph type (and point type, too) by entering a new point size value in the Character dialog box without having to reselect all the text. Just make sure the text layer is selected in the Layers panel and the Text tool is active. This approach works for all the other text characteristics, as well.

To enter paragraph type, follow these steps:

1. **Open a saved image or create a new Photoshop document.**

2. **Select either the Horizontal or Vertical Type tool from the Tools panel, or press T to select the type tool if the one you want is active.**

   Press Shift+T to cycle through the four available type tools until the one you want is active.

   Your cursor looks like an I-beam, similar to the one you see in a word processing program.

3. **Insert and size the text box by using one of the following methods:**

   • Drag to create a text box of an arbitrary size. After you release the mouse button, you can drag any of the handles at the corners and sides of the box to customize the size.

- Hold down the Alt (Option on the Mac) key and drag a box of any size. The Paragraph Text Size dialog box appears. You can enter the exact dimensions of the box you want to create. When you click OK, a bounding box of the size you specified appears, complete with handles for resizing the box later, if you want.

4. **Select the type options you want from the Options bar, or Character or Paragraph panel.**

5. **Enter your text. To start a new paragraph, press Enter (Return on the Mac).**

   Each line wraps around to fit inside the bounding box, as you can see in Figure 3-2.

   If you type more text than fits in the text box, an overflow icon (plus sign) appears in the bottom-right handle. You can resize the text box by gripping any of the eight handles and dragging.

6. **Click the Commit button on the Options bar. (The button looks like a check mark.) You can also press Ctrl+Enter (⌘+return on the Mac).**

   Photoshop creates a new type layer.

Wisconsin's Finest

Paragraph text appears inside a resizable bounding box. The text wraps around from line to line and reflows as the box is made larger or smaller.

Paragraph text is ideal for entering larger amounts of text in Photoshop.

Figure 3-2: Paragraph text automatically wraps to conform to your bounding box.

To convert point type to paragraph type or vice versa, select the type layer in the Layers panel. Then choose Layer⇨Type⇨Convert to Point Text or Convert to Paragraph Text.

Creating Type on or in a Path

Photoshop also offers the ability to place type in and on a path. The way you create path type in Photoshop is very similar to the way you create path type in InDesign and Illustrator. Follow these steps:

1. **Grab the Pen or Shape tool. Select the Paths option on the Options bar and create your path. For more on paths, see Book III, Chapter 2.**

   You can also copy and paste an existing path, or import a path from Illustrator or another compatible drawing program.

2. **Using the regular Type tool (either Horizontal or Vertical), click on or inside the path.**

When clicking on the path, your type cursor changes to indicate type on a path. If you clicked inside the path and are filling it with type, a bounding box appears.

3. **Type your desired text and marvel at how the type glides along or inside the path, as shown in Figure 3-3.**

   Commit the type by clicking the Commit button (the check mark) on the Options bar. You can also press Ctrl+Enter (⌘+return on the Mac). After you commit the type, the path itself doesn't appear unless you stroke or fill it with color, as I did with my smaller heart.

4. **To adjust the starting (x icon) or ending point (circle icon) for the type on a path, click either point with the Path Selection tool and drag the type to a new position.**

5. **Edit the text (changing characters, colors, alignment, and so on) just as you would with regular type.**

6. **Adjust the path by using any of the path tools — the Direct Selection tool, the Convert Point tool, and so on.**

   The type magically reflows along the newly adjusted path.

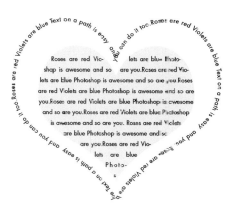

Figure 3-3: Make a visual statement with your type by putting it on or in the path of your choice.

To create regular point or paragraph type when you click near a path, hold down the Shift key when clicking, telling Photoshop you don't want path type.

Using the Options Bar

The Options bar contains a group of options, shown in Figure 3-4. Some (but not all) of these options are duplicated in the Character panel. Those options that appear in both places are the most frequently used options. Talk about convenience.

Figure 3-4: The text options on the Options bar.

Your options, from left to right, include

✔ **Change Text Orientation:** Use this handy button to toggle between vertical and horizontal text orientations. Just select the type layer you want to transform and with the type tool selected, click the Text Orientation button on the Options bar. This option works with point type and paragraph type, although the results you get from switching the paragraph type to vertical orientation may look odd.

✔ **Font Family:** Select the font/typeface you want from the drop-down list.

You will find one of these abbreviations before the font name: a (Adobe Type 1 [PostScript]) fonts; TT (TrueType); O (OpenType). Those fonts with no abbreviations are bitmapped fonts.

✔ **Font Style:** Some fonts can have additional styles, such as light or demibold, and other styles are assigned as separate typefaces. Only the styles available for a particular font appear in the list.

If a font you want to use doesn't offer bold or italic style, you can simulate either or both by selecting a faux style in the Character panel.

✔ **Font Size:** Select the size of the text from this list or type a size in the text box. Generally, text sizes are shown in points, with 72 points equaling approximately 1 inch. (A 36-point font is ½ inch in size at 72 pixels per inch [ppi].)

If you don't like points, you can switch to millimeters or pixels in the Units & Rulers Preferences dialog box. (You can find instructions for doing this in Book I, Chapter 5.)

✔ **Anti-Aliasing:** This list includes four different types of smoothing to use on your text, plus *none* (which leaves your text unsmoothed). For small type, try Sharp to avoid your type from being too fuzzy around the edges. But the exact results depend on the typeface, so be sure to take a gander at your type. Bonus Chapter 1 (on this book's Web site) explains anti-aliasing in detail. See the Introduction for details about the Web site.

✔ **Text Alignment:** Three buttons specify whether Photoshop aligns your Horizontal Type tool text left, center, or right. When you use the Vertical Type tool, the buttons transform into Top, Center (vertically), and Bottom choices.

✔ **Text Color:** Click in this box to select a color from the Color Picker.

✔ **Create Warped Text:** This option lets you warp and bend text by using 15 different types of distortion.

✔ **Toggle Character and Paragraph Panels:** Click this button anytime a type tool is active to show or hide the Character and Paragraph panels.

✔ **Cancel:** Click this button (or press the Esc key) to cancel the text entry you're making.

✔ **Commit:** Click this button to apply the text to a type layer.

Working with the Character Panel

The Character panel (shown in Figure 3-5), which is usually paired with the Paragraph panel, lets you format the appearance of individual type characters. Choose Window⇨ Character or click the Character panel icon (capital letter A) in the dock. Five of the options in the Character panel are exactly the same as those on the Options bar. The duplicated features include Font Family, Font Style, Font Size, Anti-Aliasing, and Text Color. The other menus, buttons, and text boxes provide

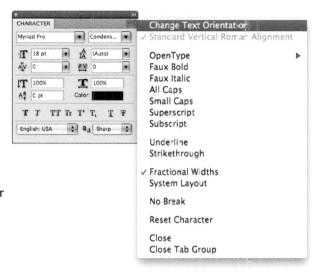

Figure 3-5: The Character panel offers type specification options galore.

additional functions. I discuss these options in the following sections.

Leading

Leading is the amount of space between the baselines of consecutive lines of type, usually measured in points. (The *baseline* is the imaginary line on which a line of type rests.) You can select a specific amount of leading or allow Photoshop to determine the amount automatically by choosing Auto from the Leading menu.

Wider line spacing can make text easier to read (as long as you don't go overboard!) or can be used for artistic effect. Tighter line spacing makes for more compact text but can decrease readability if your tightening goes too far.

When you select Auto Leading, Photoshop multiplies the type size by a value of 120 percent to calculate the leading size. So, Photoshop spaces the baselines of 10-point type 12 points apart. You can change this automatic value by clicking the Paragraph panel and selecting Justification from the panel's menu. A dialog box appears, containing several values. Type the amount you want in the Auto Leading box. If all this seems confusing, I recommend experimenting with leading to get a true idea of how various values affect the space between lines of text.

Tracking

Tracking is the amount of space between letters in a word, line, or paragraph. You can specify negative tracking to squeeze all the letters together more closely or positive tracking to let them spread out a bit.

Don't confuse tracking with *kerning,* which deals with the space between two individual letters. Tracking sets a value to evenly space all the letters you select, and kerning helps you close or widen the gap between two individual letters, officially called a *letter pair.*

One use for tracking is to help lines of text fit a specified horizontal space, and you can make this technique work if you use it judiciously. Beginners typically overdo tracking, squeezing letters together so tightly they touch, or spreading them apart so that wide gaps appear. You can see examples of tracking in Figure 3-6.

This is normal tracking.
This is loose tracking.
This is tight tracking.

Figure 3-6: Tracking adjusts the spaces between your selected letters.

To track a set of characters or a line, select the text you want to squeeze or expand, and select a value either from 0 to –100 or 0 to 200 from the Tracking menu, or type a specific value (from –1000 to 10000) in the Tracking text box. Each unit is equal to $\frac{1}{1,000}$ of an *em* (the width of an em dash in a particular typeface), so a setting of –100 reduces the space between characters by $\frac{1}{10}$ the width of an em dash (quite a lot!).

Kerning

Kerning is a technique for adding or removing space between pairs of letters to make them fit together more closely and aesthetically. For example, the letters A and V are a natural fit and often look better when kerned slightly closer. If you select Metrics in your Kerning option, Photoshop automatically tries to kern the characters to provide an attractive look, like that shown in the kerned pair in Figure 3-7. The Optical option kerns a pair of letters based on their particular shape. The kerning tables are built into the individual font. Be warned that cheap fonts sometimes have poorly created kerning tables or no tables at all — another good reason to stick with quality fonts.

To manually kern letters, click the point between the two characters and select a percentage either from 0 to –100 or 0 to 200 from the Kerning menu, or type a specific value (from –1000 to 10000) in the Kerning text box. Like with the Tracking menu, the values represent $\frac{1}{1,000}$ of an em.

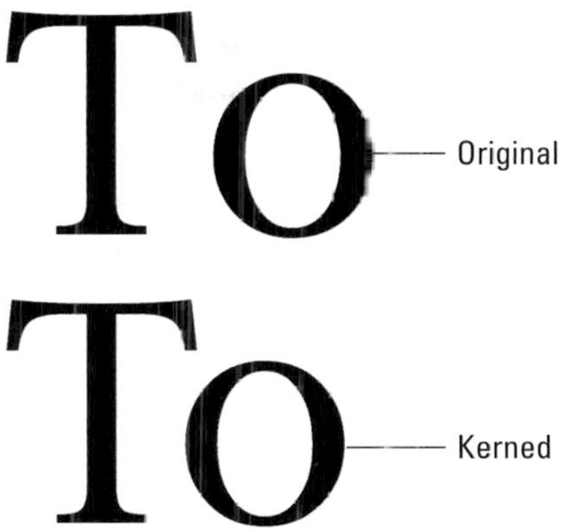

Vertical and Horizontal Scale

The Vertical and Horizontal Scale options represent the relationship between the height and width of the text. By default, this relationship is 100%. To make the width of the type proportionately 50% more than the height, enter 150% into the Horizontal Scale box. You can see examples of scaling in Figure 3-8.

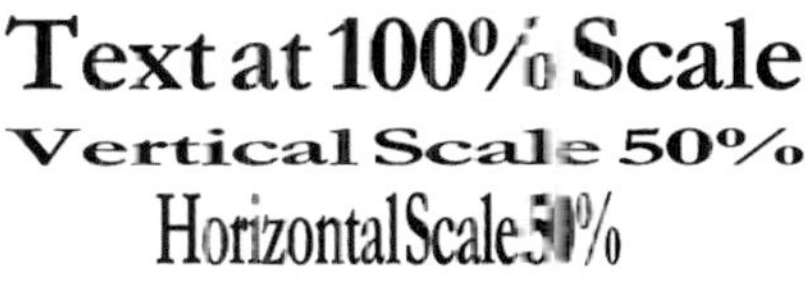

Be careful about using the Scale options. Type designers create fonts with very specific proportions. When you deviate from those proportions, you can destroy what was once a beautifully designed typeface.

Figure 3-7: Kerning a pair of letters can enhance their appearance.

Text at 100% Scale
Vertical Scale 50%
HorizontalScale 50%

Figure 3-8: Be wary of using Vertical or Horizontal Scale.

Baseline shift and text attributes

The Baseline option adjusts the height above or below a typeface's normal baseline. You can employ this option to adjust the height of bullets and symbols, such as trademark and registration marks. A bar with several buttons in the Character panel lets you turn on or off several type attributes with a single click. Table 3-1 covers the many text attributes.

Table 3-1		Character Panel Text Attributes
Icon	*Name*	*What It Does*
T	Faux Bold	Creates a fake bold. ***Warning:*** Applying faux styles can distort the proportions of a font. It's really best to use fonts as they were originally designed — and if there's no bold font style, *c'est la vie.*
T	Faux Italic	Creates a fake italic. Like with faux bold, take caution when using this attribute to prevent distortion.

continued

Table 3-1 *(continued)*

Icon	Name	What It Does
TT	All Caps	Changes the case of the characters in selected text to all capitals or back to their original case when you turn it off.
Tᴛ	Small Caps	Creates uppercase letters about the size of lower-case letters in a font. Less obtrusive than full-size caps in text passages. Photoshop either uses the small caps characters built into many fonts or creates faux small caps for you.
T¹	Superscript	Raises and reduces a character automatically to create a superscript, as in E=MC^2.
T₁	Subscript	Lowers and reduces the character below the baseline, creating a subscript.
T	Underline	Underlines the selected characters.
⫪	Strikethrough	Provides a ~~strikethrough~~ effect to the selected characters. In legal applications, strikethrough is widely used to show sections that have been removed, but in their original context.
English: USA	Character Set	Selects the language you want to use for Photoshop's spell checker and for hyphenation. The option includes variations, such as English: USA or English: UK, and French or Canadian French.

You can also find the attributes in Table 3-1 on the Character panel pop-up menu. And the menu lists a few other attributes that aren't displayed directly in the panel:

- **Change Text Orientation:** Rotates your text horizontally or vertically.

- **Standard Vertical Roman Alignment:** Displays the text in the standard alignment you're used to seeing — across the page.

- **OpenType:** When you work with OpenType fonts, you may find that they include tables of various font attributes. These tables allow you to apply various styles, such as true diagonal fractions; alternate Old Style numerals; fancy cursive type uppercase letters (Swash and Titling); ligatures (designed to fix the kerning of certain awkward letter combinations, such as fi and tt); and ornamental fonts (think dingbats or wingdings), such as leaves and flowers.

- **Fractional Widths:** This setting is the default display. When type gets small, the spacing between characters may vary by fractions of a pixel.

Photoshop has to favor one pixel or the other, and sometimes the appearance is strange. Overall, however, it provides the best spacing for the legibility and appearance of the type. But, for small type to be displayed on the Web, the readability may be impaired due to some characters running together and words having gaps.

✓ **System Layout:** Displays the text by using the operating system's default text handling, similar to what you see in WordPad or TextEdit. This option doesn't allow fractions of pixels and removes any antialiasing. This is a good option for text to be displayed on the Web.

✓ **No Break:** Prevents words from breaking at the end of lines. You may want to select this option to prevent words such as proper names, dates, initials, and so forth from breaking. Select your text and then select the option.

✓ **Reset Character:** Select this option to reset your character attributes (font family, size, style, and so on) back to Photoshop's default.

Working with the Paragraph Panel

You can use the Paragraph panel, shown in Figure 3-9, to format any or all paragraphs in a type layer. Choose Window⇨Paragraph or click the Paragraph panel icon (backward P icon called a pilcrow) in the dock. Simply select the paragraph or paragraphs that you want to format by clicking an individual paragraph with the Type tool. You can drag a selection to select multiple paragraphs, or in the Layers panel, click a type layer that contains the paragraphs to format all of them at the same time.

The Paragraph panel's pop-up menu gives you access to Justification and Hyphenation dialog boxes. You can use these to customize the default settings that Photoshop uses for these functions. As a side note, if you're not familiar with the word *glyph* used in the Justification dialog box, it's another word for a font character.

Figure 3-9: Use the Paragraph panel to align and indent your text.

**Book IV
Chapter 3**

**Creating and
Editing Type**

Changing paragraph alignment

At the top of the Paragraph panel, you see a set of seven alignment buttons. Three of these buttons align nonjustified text. They include the following:

- ✔ **Left Align Text:** All text is even with the left margin and allowed to be ragged on the right side of the column.

- ✔ **Center Text:** Text is evenly centered in its column and ragged on both right and left edges.

- ✔ **Right Align Text:** All text is even with the right margin and allowed to be ragged on the left side.

With vertical type, these choices align the text to the top, a center axis, and the bottom of a column.

Changing paragraph justification

Four options in the Paragraph panel produce justified text, in which Photoshop inserts spaces between characters as necessary so that each line is flush on both left and right sides. In addition, you choose to make the last line flush left, flush right, centered, or force justified on both sides with spaces inserted by Photoshop. This last option sometimes calls for some manual tweaking to avoid a final line that's squeezed or expanded too much. You can apply justification options to paragraph type only, not point type.

The "rules," or criteria, that Photoshop uses for creating justified text can be found in the Justification dialog box, accessible via the Paragraph panel pop-up menu.

For vertical type, the justification choices are Top align, Center, Bottom align, or Justify (four options).

Changing paragraph indentation

Three options in the Paragraph panel let you enter an amount of indentation between the sides of the text bounding box and the actual text. You can specify the amount of indentation from the left or right, and for the first line of the paragraph (creating a first line that's indented more than the others in the paragraph). For vertical type, the indentations are rotated 90 degrees.

Changing spacing between paragraphs

Two options in the Paragraph panel let you specify the amount of space between paragraphs. You can specify the amount of space before every paragraph, the amount after every paragraph, or both.

Breaking long words across two lines

The final option in the Paragraph panel is the Hyphenate check box, which specifies whether Photoshop hyphenates words that are too long to fit on a line or leaves them intact. Turning on hyphenation can prevent awkward spacing, particularly with justified text that would otherwise contain a lot more spaces between characters to make a line fit.

The criteria that Photoshop uses for creating hyphenated text can be found in the Hyphenation dialog box, accessible via the Paragraph panel pop-up menu.

The Paragraph panel's pop-up menu has a few additional options:

- **Roman Hanging Punctuation:** Controls whether punctuation marks (quotations, dashes, colons, and so on) appear inside or outside the margins. Select this option to have the punctuation marks appear outside.

- **Adobe Single-Line Composer:** Composition includes using a host of parameters (such as word and letter spacing, and hyphenation) to determine where a line should break. This option composes type one line at a time and offers more manual control over where lines break. The option favors compressing or expanding word spacing over hyphenation, but prefers hyphenation over compressing or expanding letter spacing. This option is selected by default.

- **Adobe Every-Line Composer:** Looks at multiple, possible breaking points for a range of lines. The option can optimize earlier lines in the paragraph to avoid weird breaks later on in the paragraph. Emphasis is given to even spacing of letters and words over hyphenation. This option can provide more even spacing and fewer hyphens.

- **Reset Paragraph:** Resets all the paragraph attributes back to the Photoshop defaults.

Editing Text

You can apply all the options described in this chapter while you enter text, or later, when you're rearranging words or fixing typos and other errors. To make changes to the text itself, just follow these steps:

1. **Open a saved image or create a new Photoshop document.**

2. **Select the appropriate Type tool.**

3. **In the Layers panel, select the existing type layer you want to modify or, for a new type layer, click the Type tool in the document.**

4. **To modify existing text, drag the mouse from the insertion point to select characters to copy, delete, or format. For new type, begin typing at the place you clicked. Press the Backspace or Delete key as you type to eliminate characters.**

5. **When you're done entering your changes, click the Commit button.**

Finding and replacing text

You can make global changes in a text layer, switching all occurrences of a set of characters to another string. For example, you might have typed

Book IV
Chapter 3

Creating and
Editing Type

Ghandi a few dozen times before remembering that Mahatma's name is spelled *Gandhi.* To replace text, follow these steps:

1. **Open a saved image or create a new Photoshop document.**

2. **In the Layers panel, select the type layer you want to modify.**

3. **Choose Edit➪Find and Replace Text.**

   The Find and Replace Text dialog box appears, as shown in Figure 3-10.

Figure 3-10: Make global changes to your text with the Find and Replace command.

4. **Type or paste the text you want to replace in the Find What box.**

5. **Enter the replacement text in the Change To box.**

6. **(Optional) If you want the search to locate only text that exactly matches the case of the Find string (for example, *FREEdom* but not *Freedom*), select the Case Sensitive option.**

7. **(Optional) To ignore the search word embedded in another word (say, to find *the* but not *there* or *they*), select Whole Word Only.**

8. **Click Find Next.**

9. **When each string is found, select whether you want to**

   - *Change:* This option changes only the string of text just located. Click this button if you're looking for one particular occurrence.

   - *Change All:* This option changes all occurrences of the search text with the replacement string in your text.

   - *Change/Find:* This option changes the found text and then looks for the next occurrence.

Checking your spelling

Photoshop can check your spelling by using an internal dictionary that you can update with words of your own. Even though you're not likely to enter huge amounts of text in Photoshop, that's no excuse for misspelling the words that you do include. Indeed, because it's so difficult to change text after you've rasterized a text layer, the spell checker can save you a great deal of work. Follow these steps to use it:

1. **Open a saved image containing type layers.**

2. **Make sure that you've specified the correct language in the Character panel's Character Set menu.**

3. **Select the text that you want to check or select a type layer, in the Layers panel, to check all the text on that layer.**

4. **Choose Edit⇨Check Spelling.**

5. **When Photoshop identifies a possible error in the Not in Dictionary box, click Change to substitute the recommended correction for the word that's spelled incorrectly.**

   Or you can choose from one of these options:

   - *Ignore:* Leaves the word alone and continues to check the rest of the text.

   - *Ignore All:* Ignores all instances of the word for the rest of the spell-check session.

   - *Suggestions:* Select a different word from the Suggestions text box or type in the correct spelling yourself.

   - *Change All:* Corrects all occurrences of the misspelled word.

   - *Add:* Adds the unfamiliar word to Photoshop's dictionary.

   Deselect the Check All Layers option to check only the currently selected layer.

6. **Click Done when you finish.**

   The Check Spelling dialog box closes.

Masking, Shaping, and Warping Type

You can do a lot more with type than create labels, captions, or paragraphs of text. Type can become an integral part of your decorative design, especially when you stylize, warp, or otherwise transform it in interesting ways.

Your Photoshop text can have character, too, communicating messages with more than just words. The text of a beach scene can appear to be wavy, or watery and translucent. Halloween type can take on a ghostly or spooky appearance. Type can be romantic, otherworldly, cheerful, or comical. It all depends on how you create and apply it.

The following sections show you some of the tricks you can perform by masking, warping, and shaping your type so that your words come to life and add something special to your images.

Playing with type layer opacity

Layers are like stacks of digital overlays on which each of the elements of your image reside. (Check out Book V, Chapter 1 for the lowdown on layers.) You can change the transparency of a type layer, like you can with any other layer in Photoshop, reducing the *opacity* (transparency) of the type so that it allows the underlying layer to show through. Take a look at Figure 3-11, which shows type at varying levels of opacity over an image.

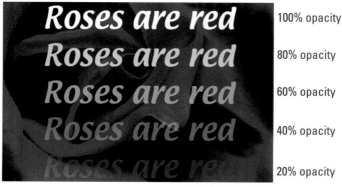

Corbis Digital Stock

Figure 3-11: Varying the opacity of your type is as easy as dragging a slider.

Changing the opacity of a type layer can convey an idea of gradual visibility of words onto an image. When working with opacity in multiple layers of type, you can create a sort of nonanimated fade-in, each with a greater opacity. Figure 3-12 shows an example of this effect.

Another way to alter the transparency of type is to use a layer mask. (Check out Book VI, Chapter 3 for more information on layer masks.) By using a layer mask, you can customize your transparency with maximum flexibility and still edit the text to change the wording, font size, font, or anything else. Simply apply a gradient, or grab a brush and paint on the layer mask. I used the fun Drippy Water Color Brush and painted on my layer mask, as shown in Figure 3-13.

The first Putting It Together project in this chapter, "Ghosting Your Type," shows you another way to use type opacity to create a ghostly effect.

Figure 3-12: Gradually fade your type to get the message across.

PhotoSpin

Figure 3-13: Creating a layer mask on your type layer gives you more flexibility with your transparency effects.

Creating fade effects

To create text that appears to fade out, just follow these steps:

1. **Enter the words** fading out slowly **(or other text of your choice) into a new type layer.**

   You can find out how to enter text in the section "Entering Text in Point Type Mode," earlier in this chapter.

2. **Choose Layer⇨Layer Mask⇨Reveal All.**

   This step creates a mask that can show or hide some of the layer. With Reveal All selected, the layer defaults to showing everything on the layer without hiding any of it. For details on layer masks, see Book VI, Chapter 3.

3. **Press D to make sure that Photoshop's colors are the default black and white.**

4. **Select the Gradient tool from the Tools panel.**

   Or press Shift+G until the Gradient tool is active. For more on working with gradients, see Book IV, Chapter 2.

5. **Select the Linear Gradient fill from the Options bar.**

6. **In the Options bar, click the Gradient picker (down-pointing arrow) and select the Foreground to Background gradient.**

   This is, by default, the first one in the panel, unless you've changed the defaults.

7. **Click the layer mask's icon in the Layers panel to make sure it's active. You will see brackets around the layer mask thumbnail icon.**

8. **Click on the left side of the type layer and drag to the right side.**

   Photoshop creates a gradient in the layer mask that's black on the right and fades to white on the left, as shown in Figure 3-14. So, the mask is most transparent on the left side (where the mask is white) and least transparent on the right side (where the mask is black). It reveals more of the original type on the left and fades it out on the right, as you can see in the figure.

FADING OUT SLOW

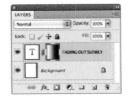

Figure 3-14: Fade your text gradually by applying a gradient on a layer mask.

Putting It Together

Ghosting Your Type

Need some ghostly, semitransparent type? You can twist, transmogrify, and transform your text by using Photoshop's arsenal of features. Create your type from scratch in an empty document or add the type to an existing picture or background. (You can find my example image on this book's Web site.) For the heck of it, these steps show you how to add ghostly writing to an existing image. Just follow these steps:

1. **Open the background image you want to overlay with the ghost type.**

Any image, ectoplasmic or not, will do.

2. **Select the color you want to use for your text from the Swatches panel.**

Black and orange are good Halloween colors, but you can use any contrasting color.

You can also sample a color from your image by using the Eyedropper tool. Simply click your desired color, and it then becomes your new foreground color.

3. **Select the Horizontal Type tool from the Tools panel and then click the area where you want to add the text.**

The vertical cursor that appears is the size that the text will be.

4. **Select a font, style, and size from the drop-down lists on the Options bar.**

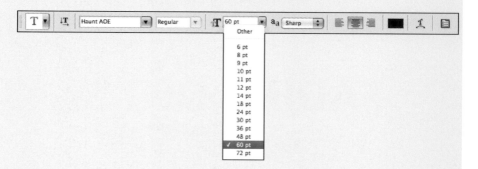

5. **Select an anti-aliasing method to help smooth the edges of your type.**

Anti-aliasing, which I cover in the section "Using the Options Bar," in this chapter, softens a hard edge by adding partially transparent pixels.

6. **Type your text.**

   The text appears on top of the background.

7. **Click the Commit button (the check mark icon) on the Options bar to insert the text you've typed into a layer of its own. You can also press Ctrl+Enter (⌘+return on the Mac).**

8. **To change the opacity of the type, adjust the Opacity setting in the Layers panel.**

   To make additional changes to the text, use a filter. For example, if you want to make the text wavy, select the Wave filter from the Filter➪Distort menu. Or you can use other filters from the array discussed in Book VII. Just remember, when you use a filter, a warning pops up, informing you that the type layer must be *rasterized* (converted from editable text to pixels) first. Click OK, and you're on your way.

9. **When you're satisfied with the look, save your image for additional editing later or choose Layer➪Flatten Image to combine the text and background.**

Creating type outlines

In addition to its Vertical and Horizontal Type tools (discussed in the section "Exploring the Type Tools," earlier in this chapter), Photoshop includes Vertical and Horizontal Type Mask tools. These tools function almost identically to their conventional counterparts, with one important exception: Type mask tools don't create a new layer. Instead, they create a selection that hovers over the currently active layer, like the one shown in Figure 3-15.

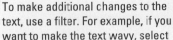

Figure 3-15: Type mask tools create selection marquees from your letter shapes.

You can treat the selections created with the type mask tools just as you can any other selection. Try the following:

✔ Move type mask selections around your document when any of the selection tools are active.

✔ Store type selections as alpha channels by choosing Select➪Save Selection. I introduce selections in Book III, Chapter 3. You can find out how to save selections and make alpha channels in Book VI, Chapter 1.

✔ Skew type selections (or change them in some other way) by using Select➪Transform Selections. You can find more information on transforming selections in Book III, Chapter 3.

✔ Convert a selection into an editable path, as described in the section "Transforming type into vector shapes and paths," later in this chapter. Book III, Chapter 2 also introduces the joy of working with paths.

✔ Use the selection to cut or copy portions of an image in text-shaped chunks, as shown in Figure 3-16. You can find out how this last suggestion works by following the steps in the Putting It Together project, "Carving Your Type in Stone," at the end of this chapter, in which you find out how to create an image that looks like words carved in stone.

Rasterizing your type layer

The Type tool creates editable type layers. You can change the wording, spacing, font, font size, and other factors as much as you want, as long as the type remains in a type layer.

However, after you make all the changes you want, you may need to convert your type layer to pixels in the form of rasterized type. After they're rasterized, you can apply filters, paint on the type, and apply gradients and patterns. Rasterizing type layers allows you to merge the type with other pixels in your image and, eventually, flatten the image to create a finished document suitable for use with other programs.

Digital Vision

Figure 3-16: Use a type mask to create type from an image.

Rasterizing type the other way

In addition to rasterizing a type layer in the usual way, you can also rasterize it by merging it with a nontype layer. For example, in your Layers panel, if your type layer is directly on top of a text layer that has already been rasterized, you can merge the layers by choosing Layer➪Merge down or pressing Ctrl+E (⌘+E on the Mac).

You may also come across the opportunity to rasterize a type layer because Photoshop reminds you to. Some commands, particularly filters, operate only on pixels. When you try to use them, you may see a warning dialog box. Often, the dialog box includes an option for immediately converting the type layer to rasterized form.

After you convert your type to pixels, you can no longer edit the type. Nor can you resize the text without risking jaggies. Rasterize your type only when you're certain you won't need to edit or resize it anymore. Make a copy of the type layer before you rasterize it and toggle off the visibility of the copy, and make sure you save an unflattened copy of the document with all layers intact. By making these copies, if you need to edit the type, you can use the layered file that has the unrasterized text. For more on layers, see Book V.

To rasterize your type, select the type layer that you want to convert to pixels. Then, choose Layer➪Rasterize➪Type. The type is shown in the Layers panel on a transparent background.

Transforming type into vector shapes and paths

By default, regular type created with the Type tool is vector-based type, not bitmapped, rasterized type. But you can also convert regular type (each character) to individual vector shapes. The individual characters then become shapes defined by vector masks. You can edit the shapes like any shapes created with the shape tools, by manipulating anchor points, and straight and curved segments. See Book IV, Chapter 1 for the lowdown on shapes. And you can also convert regular type to work paths, where each character becomes a path, editable by using the selection arrows and Pen tools, like any other path. Type is usually converted into a path in order to create a vector mask based on the type. (An image is contained within the editable paths created by the letterforms.) For more on paths, see Book III, Chapter 2. For more on vector masks, see Book VI, Chapter 3.

So, you can convert regular type to shapes in the form of a vector mask or work path. You convert type to vector shapes and paths in order to edit it with the Pen tools. Here are the ways to do that:

- ✔ To convert type to an editable work path, choose Layer➪Type➪Create Work Path.

- ✔ To convert type to shapes, choose Layer➪Type➪Convert to Shape.

**Book IV
Chapter 3**

**Creating and
Editing Type**

Here are the chief things to know about type converted into a shape or path:

✔ Like a type layer, you can resize it without producing jagged diagonal lines.

✔ You can edit the shape of the characters, but you can't edit the text itself, as shown in Figure 3-17.

✔ You must rasterize the converted type before you can merge it with pixel-based layers or apply special effects with filters. You can apply layer styles to any kind of type, however. Be sure to check out Book V, Chapter 4 for all you need to know about layer styles.

✔ If you've converted your type into a shape, it becomes a vector mask exactly like other vector masks in Photoshop, and you can edit the shape of the characters by using the Pen tools. You can find detailed information on editing vector masks in Book VI, Chapter 3.

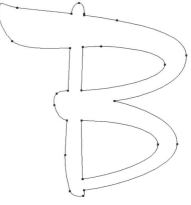

Figure 3-17: Converting your type to a path allows you to alter the shape of the letters.

Wreaking havoc on your type

Photoshop's great automated Warp feature can twist your type in predictable ways that are not only repeatable but, thanks to the controls in their dialog boxes, also customizable. The cool part is that even though type has been warped, it remains fully editable until you rasterize it. All you need to do to warp your text is click the Warp icon on the Options bar, which opens the multifaceted Warp Text dialog box (shown in Figure 3-18), and then choose your warp style and distortion options in that dialog box.

Web designers take note: You can't warp text that has a faux bold style applied (found in the Character panel).

You can find a whole list of special effects in the Warp Text dialog box, such as Arc, Arch, Bulge, Flag, Wave, Fish, Fisheye, and Twist. Each of these effects provides a special look to your type, as shown in Figure 3-19.

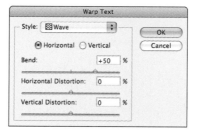

Figure 3-18: Choose from a number of warp styles.

Each effect has a dialog box of its own that allows you to set the parameters for the amount, direction, degree of distortion, amount of bend, and so forth. You can watch your type warp right onscreen and tailor the distortion however you like. You can apply most asymmetrical warp effects to type in either horizontal or vertical directions. Fisheye, Inflate, and Twist are among those effects that can't be rotated because they're already oriented in horizontal and vertical directions that you can control with sliders.

Figure 3-19: Even after you warp your text, it remains fully editable.

 Putting It Together

Carving Your Type in Stone

You can use a type tool to create selections shaped like text and then use images themselves as textures for the type. A type selection can cut out any part of a picture for use any way you want.

Follow these steps to carve letters into a stone texture image:

1. **Open the stone texture image you want to use.**

 I'm using a sandstone wall, but you can use other kinds of stone, wood, or any texture that interests you. Best of all, the embossed look that results is only one of many different looks you can achieve simply by making small changes in the layer style that you apply to the text.

2. **Select the Horizontal Type Mask tool from the Tools panel and then click the area where you want to enter your text.**

3. **Select the font, font style, font size, and other text parameters from the drop-down lists on the Options bar.**

4. **Enter the text you want to use onto the texture you've chosen. Then, click the Commit button (the check mark icon), or press Ctrl+Enter (⌘+return on the Mac) on the Options bar to set your text.**

The selection in the shape of the text appears where you typed the text.

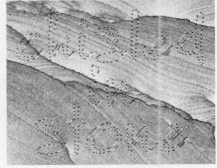

Corbis Digital Stock

continued

**Book IV
Chapter 3**

**Creating and
Editing Type**

continued

5. **Press Ctrl+C (⌘+C on the Mac) to copy the selected area of your chosen texture (the brick in the shape of the text, in my example), and then press Ctrl+V (⌘+V on the Mac) to paste a text-shaped section of that texture in a layer of its own.**

   The text blends in with what's in the background layer (in my example, the sandstone) and is invisible (for now).

6. **Choose Layer⇨Layer Style⇨Bevel and Emboss to open the Layer Style dialog box.**

   In the Layer Style dialog box, you can find dozens of different effects that you can create.

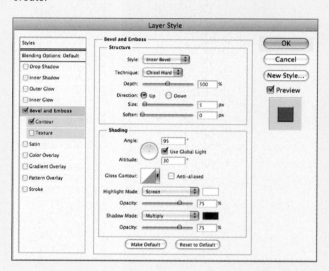

7. **Experiment with the settings in the Layer Style dialog box to try out different looks and achieve various effects:**

   ✔ Select the kind of beveling or embossing you want from the Style and Technique drop-down lists in the Structure area.

   I selected Inner Bevel and Chisel Hard to produce a dramatic, hard-edged embossing effect.

   ✔ Move the Depth slider to the right to increase the depth of the bevel.

   I set the value at 500% for a raised effect. A lower value produces a less 3-D effect, and a higher value produces a more drastic 3-D effect.

   ✔ Select the Contour check box in the layer styles column on the left side of the dialog box for an even more pronounced 3-D look.

   ✔ In the Shading area, you can adjust controls that allow you to change the apparent angle of the illumination that produces the bevel's shadow.

   I moved the angle to 95 degrees (roughly straight overhead), but I left the other controls alone.

You can find details about how to use the other options in the Layer Style dialog box in Book V, Chapter 4.

8. **Click OK to apply the effects that you've chosen.**

9. **(Optional) As a last touch, choose Image⇨Adjustments⇨Levels to darken the text layer so that it stands out even more distinctly from the background. Drag the midtones (gray triangle) and shadows (black triangle) adjustments to the right, while keeping an eye on your image.**

   For more info on how to use the Levels adjustment, see Book VIII, Chapter 1.

Book V

Working with Layers

*L*ayers are like modern appliances. Sure, you could live without a microwave, a dishwasher, and a vacuum cleaner, but cooking and cleaning would take a lot longer — and it wouldn't be nearly as convenient. Layers give Photoshop users the ultimate in editing flexibility. This in turn saves production time, giving you more time to let your creative juices flow.

In this book, I give you information about how to create and edit layers. You see how to take multiple images and create single composite images. I also cover how to manage your layers by using layer sets and layer comps. And you find out how to enhance your layers by using adjustment layers, layer styles, blend modes, and various opacity settings. Finally, you'll want to check out the chapter on Smart Objects. These intelligent objects allow you to transform elements indefinitely without loss of quality.

Chapter 1: Creating Layers

In This Chapter

✓ Backgrounds versus layers

✓ Taking a look at the types of layers

✓ Working with the Layers panel

✓ Creating layers

✓ Compositing with multiple layers

✓ Transforming layers

✓ Automatically aligning and blending layers

People are often surprised and even downright shocked when I tell them that pretty much everything they can do with layers they can also do without them. Not using layers would be more technically challenging and a heck of a lot more tedious, but you could still get the job done. The benefit to using layers is that you have tremendous flexibility. The changes you make to the pixels on the individual layers are permanent, but the interaction between the pixels on different layers is dynamic. You can make endless edits as long as those layers exist. Layers make working in Photoshop a lot more forgiving, allowing you to make changes quickly and productively.

But hey, it's not just the technical and practical aspects that make layers so wonderful. Layers also allow you to express your creative side, compositing several images into one with just a drag of the mouse. The only downside to layers is that each one makes your file size grow and, therefore, can slow your system performance. Additionally, you can save layers in only a few file formats. Nevertheless, the downsides are a small price to pay for something that makes your image-editing life so much easier.

Getting to Know the Layers Panel

In terms of a real-world analogy, think of layers as sheets of acetate, similar to those clear plastic sheets used with overhead projectors. You draw different elements on the various sheets. What you draw on one sheet doesn't affect the other sheets. You can show just one sheet, or you can stack several on top of one another to create a combination image. You can reshuffle the order of the sheets, add new sheets, or delete old sheets. Any space on the sheet that doesn't have a mark on it is clear, or transparent.

That's how layers work in Photoshop. You can place elements on separate layers, yet show them together to create a combination image, or *composite*. You can also add, delete, or rearrange layers. Unlike sheets of acetate, however, you can adjust how opaque or transparent the element on the layer is, as well as change the way the colors between layers interact (blending modes).

As with every other important aspect of Photoshop, the program houses layers in a single location, called a panel. It's time to formally meet the powerful panel that controls the operations of layers. To display the Layers panel, shown in Figure 1-1, choose Window⇨Layers or, easier yet, press F7.

Active layer

Type layer

Figure 1-1: Layers give you tremendous editing flexibility.

The order of the layers in the Layers panel represents the order in the image. The top layer in the panel is the top layer in your image, and so on.

For some tasks, you can work on only one layer at a time. For other tasks, you can work on multiple layers simultaneously.

Here's the lowdown on how to work with the Layers panel:

- ✔ **Select a layer.** Simply click its name or thumbnail. Photoshop then highlights the *active layer.*

- ✔ **Select multiple contiguous layers.** Click your first layer and then Shift-click your last layer.

- ✔ **Select multiple noncontiguous layers.** Ctrl-click (⌘-click on the Mac) your desired layers.

✔ **Select all layers except the background.** Choose Select⇨All Layers.

✔ **Select layers of similar type.** If you want to select all the type layers, for example, select a layer and then choose Select⇨Similar Layers.

✔ **Deselect all layers.** Choose Select⇨Deselect Layers or click in the area below the bottom layer or background.

✔ **Select the actual element (the nontransparent pixels) on the layer.** Ctrl-click (⌘-click on the Mac) the layer's thumbnail in the panel. If you forget this handy shortcut, you can also select your layer in the Layers panel and then choose Select⇨Load Selection. Make sure that the layer name that appears in the Channel pop-up menu is *[layer name]* Transparency and click OK.

✔ **Create an adjustment or fill layer.** Click the Create a New Fill or Adjustment Layer icon at the bottom of the panel. You can also click an adjustment icon in the new Adjustments panel. See "Introducing Different Types of Layers," later in this chapter, for more on these layers.

✔ **Duplicate an existing layer.** Drag the layer to the Create a New Layer icon at the bottom of the panel. See the following section for more on creating layers.

✔ **Rename a layer.** When you create a new layer, Photoshop provides default layer names (Layer 1, Layer 2, and so on). If you want to rename a layer, simply double-click the layer name (the name, not the thumbnail) in the Layers panel, enter the name directly in the Layers panel, and press Enter (Return on the Mac).

Although it may seem tedious to give your layers meaningful names, it can help your productivity, especially when the number of layers in your file starts to increase.

This renaming shortcut works throughout Photoshop (the Channels panel, the Paths panel, and so on). You can also select the layer and select Layer Properties from the Layers panel options menu or choose Layer⇨Layer Properties.

✔ **Determine what layer holds the element you want to edit.** Select the Move tool and Ctrl-click (⌘-click on the Mac) the element. Photoshop automatically activates the appropriate layer. Or you can right-click (Control-click on the Mac) the element. A context menu appears, telling you what layer the element resides on and enabling you to select that layer.

You can use the keyboard shortcut Alt+] (right bracket) (Option+] on the Mac) to move up one layer; Alt+[(left bracket) (Option+[on the Mac) to activate the next layer down.

✔ **Adjust the interaction between colors on layers and adjust the transparency of layers.** You can use the blending modes and the Opacity and Fill options at the top of the panel to mix the colors between layers and adjust the transparency of the layers. For details, see Book V, Chapter 3.

✔ **Delete a layer.** Drag it to the trash icon at the bottom of the Layers panel. You can also choose Layer➪Delete➪Layer or choose Delete Layer from the panel options menu.

If you've gone a little layer crazy and created a bunch of empty layers, you can get rid of them quickly. Just choose File➪Scripts➪Delete All Empty Layers to delete layers that don't contain any content.

✔ **Change the size of the layer thumbnails.** Choose Panel Options from the panel menu and select a thumbnail size. You can also choose whether to display just the boundary of the layer contents or the whole document in the thumbnail. Finally, you can choose to have a layer mask on your fill layer by default and have your layer effects appear in expanded view. Fill layers are described in the section "Taking advantage of fill layers," later in this chapter, and layer effects are covered in Book V, Chapter 3.

The remaining icons at the bottom of the Layers panel allow you to link layers, and create layer styles, layer masks, and layers groups, all of which warrant sections of their own. See Book V, Chapter 4 for more on layer styles and Book V, Chapter 2 for more on layer groups. Check out Book VI, Chapter 3 for more on layer masks.

The preceding list represents just the tip of the iceberg. You can also view and hide layers, and link, lock, color-code, rearrange, merge, flatten, and animate layers. Book V, Chapter 2 covers most topics in detail.

Looking at the Background and Layers

When you create a new image with white or background colored contents, scan an image into Photoshop, or open a file from a stock photography CD or your own digital camera, basically, you have a file with just a *background*.

An image contains at most only one background, and you can't do much to it besides paint on it and make basic adjustments. You can't rearrange the background in the stack of layers — it's always on the very bottom of the Layers panel. You also can't change the opacity or blend mode of a background. What you can do is convert a background to a layer, and then the world's at your feet.

To convert a background into a layer, follow these steps:

1. **Double-click Background in the Layers panel.**

   Alternatively, you can choose Layer➪New➪Layer from Background. Note that Background is italic in the Layers panel, as shown in Figure 1-2.

2. **Name the layer or leave it at the default name of Layer 0.**

Figure 1-2: A newly opened image in Photoshop contains only a background.

You can also color-code your layer in this dialog box or by selecting Layer Properties from the panel pop-up menu. Color-coding your layer just makes it stand out more noticeably in the Layers panel.

3. Click OK.

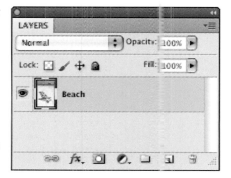

Photoshop converts your background into a layer, as indicated in the Layers panel. Note that the layer name is no longer italic, as shown in Figure 1-3.

Figure 1-3: Double-click the background to convert it into a layer.

When you create a new image with transparent contents, the image doesn't contain a background; instead, the image is created with a single layer. You can also convert a layer into a background by selecting it and then choosing Layer⇨New⇨Background from Layer. However, this option is available only when no background exists.

Introducing Different Types of Layers

Although turning the background into a layer (discussed in the preceding section) is a popular activity, Photoshop refers to *layers* in the plural for a reason. Image editing would be no fun if you didn't have a variety of different layers to mess around with.

Photoshop Standard offers five types of layers (Extended gives you two more — Video and 3D). Four of the five have very specific purposes in the life of your image. Some you may never use, and some you'll use only occasionally. But the vanilla-flavored type, which you'll use the most, is simply called a layer.

Using plain vanilla layers

The regular layer is the one that most closely matches the acetate analogy (discussed in the section "Getting to Know the Layers Panel," earlier in this chapter). You put various elements on separate layers to create a composite image. You can create blank layers and add images to them, or you can create layers from images themselves. You can create as many layers as your computer's RAM lets you. Sometimes, layers are created automatically by a specific action.

Because each layer in an image is a separate entity, you can edit, paint, transform, mask, or apply a filter on a layer without affecting the other layers. After an element is on a layer, you no longer have to make a selection (get the selection outline) to select it — you simply drag the element with the Move tool. The element freely floats in a sea of transparency. Because showing "clear" areas or transparency is impossible on a computer monitor, Photoshop uses a gray-and-white checkerboard, by default, to represent the transparent areas of a layer.

Because you'll work with regular layers on a daily basis, I spend the majority of Book V discussing them.

Playing around with layer masks

A *layer mask* is like a second sheet of acetate that hovers over a layer. You can use layer masks with regular layers, adjustment layers, fill layers, and Smart Filters. For example, you may paint on a layer mask (typically with black, white, and various shades of gray) to selectively hide or display an adjustment (or an image on a regular layer). Any black areas on the mask hide the adjustment, any white areas show the adjustment, and anything in between (gray) partially shows the adjustment. The Masks panel gives you even more flexibility because it includes options for controlling the density and feather of the mask. I cover layer masks in detail in Book VI, Chapter 3.

Using adjustment layers

An *adjustment layer* is a special kind of layer used mostly for color correction. What's great about adjustment layers is that you can apply that color correction without permanently affecting any of your layers. Adjustment layers apply the correction to all the layers below them, without affecting any of the layers above them.

Because the color correction actually resides on a layer, you can edit, delete, duplicate, merge, or rearrange the adjustment layer at any time. You have more flexibility in your image-editing chores and more freedom for experimentation. Additionally, none of this experimentation harms your image because it takes place above the image on an adjustment layer.

Photoshop has 15 kinds of adjustment layers, and you can use as many as your heart desires. The adjustments offered are the same adjustments you find on the Image➪Adjustments menu. For specifics on each adjustment, including what it corrects, see Book VIII, Chapter 1. Here's how to create an adjustment layer:

1. **Open an image of your choice.**

   Because you're applying an adjustment layer, you may want to use an image that's in need of some color correction. In the case of adjustment layers, you don't need to convert your background into a layer. I chose an image that was oversaturated.

2. **Choose Layer➪New Adjustment Layer. From the submenu, choose your desired adjustment. In the New Layer dialog box, name the layer (if you want), leave the other options at their defaults, and click OK.**

   For my example, I chose Hue/Saturation.

   You can also just click the Create a New Fill or Adjustment Layer icon (the black and white circle icon) at the bottom of the Layers panel and choose an adjustment from the pop-up menu that appears.

   The dialog box pertaining to your adjustment appears in the Adjustments panel. The adjustment layer also appears in the Layers panel, shown in Figure 1-4. The adjustment layer icon and a thumbnail appear on the adjustment layer. The thumbnail represents a layer mask. For more on layer masks, check out the "Playing around with layer masks" sidebar, in this chapter.

3. **Make the necessary corrections and then click OK.**

The adjustment layers have their own panel. Choose Window➪Adjustments to bring up the panel, shown in Figure 1-4. Click an icon to apply one of the 15 adjustments. The dialog box pertaining to your adjustment appears within the panel. You can also select a preset for an adjustment. Presets appear in the list window of the Adjustments panel (click the right-pointing arrow next to the adjustment name) or, after you select the adjustment, in the pop-up menu directly to the right of the adjustment name in that particular adjustment's dialog box. Here are a few tips to keep in mind when working with this panel:

✔ Click the arrow at the bottom of the panel to switch between the adjustment list and adjustment controls windows.

✔ Click the manila envelope icon to switch between compact and expanded views of the panel.

✔ Click the triple circle icon to have the new adjustment affect all the underlying layers. Click again (to return to the default setting) to have the new adjustment clip to, or just affect, only the layer directly under the adjustment layer.

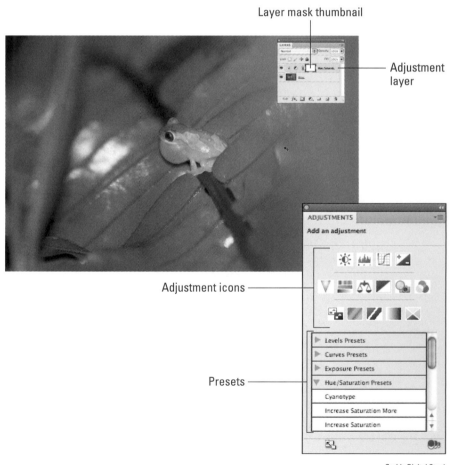

Corbis Digital Stock

Figure 1-4: Applying your corrections with an adjustment layer, rather than directly on the image, allows for more editing flexibility.

In the adjustment controls window, you can

 ✔ Click the double circle to toggle between having the adjustment layer affect all layers or just the layer directly below the adjustment.

 ✔ Click the eye icon to toggle visibility of the adjustment layer.

 ✔ Click the eye and curved arrow icon to view a previous state.

 ✔ Click the curved arrow to reset the default settings for the adjustment layer.

 ✔ Click the Trash icon to delete the adjustment layer.

✔ Access the panel pop-up menu to make adjustments, reset an adjustment, change the view of the panel, save and load presets, or close the panel.

In my example, the layer mask is white, so my adjustment shows up full strength over my image. You can also apply an adjustment layer to a selected portion of your image by painting on your layer mask. Like with regular layers, you can also adjust the opacity, fill, and blending modes of an adjustment layer. For more on these options, see Book V, Chapter 3.

 If you want to view your image without the adjustment, click the eye icon in the left column of the Layers panel to hide the adjustment layer. You can find more about viewing layers in Book V, Chapter 2. If you want to delete the adjustment layer, simply drag it to the trash icon in the Layers panel, or choose Delete➪Layer from the Layer menu or the Layers panel options menu. You can also perform these commands via the new Adjustments panel.

Editing adjustment layers

After you create an adjustment layer, you can easily edit it. Simply click the adjustment layer icon in the Layers panel. In the adjustment's dialog box, make any edits and then click OK. The only adjustment layer that you can't edit is the Invert adjustment. It's either on or off.

Isolating your adjustments

If you don't use an adjustment layer when you make color corrections, the correction you apply affects only the *active layer* (the layer highlighted in the Layers panel). However, you can also isolate your adjustment layer to a single layer or a portion of a single layer.

Here are some tips for using and isolating adjustment layers:

✔ **Correct part (but not all) of a layer.** To enable the adjustment layer to correct only a portion of a layer, make a selection before you create the adjustment layer. The adjustment affects only the pixels within the selection outline.

The adjustment affects the pixels within the selection outline *on each layer that resides below the adjustment layer.* In addition to selecting a part of a layer, you can also create and select a closed path (see Book III, Chapter 2 for more on paths).

Another way to correct part of a layer is to paint on the adjustment layer mask. Painting with black hides the adjustment, painting with various levels of gray partially hides the adjustment. For more on layer masks, see Book VI, Chapter 3.

✔ **Clip to the layer.** By default, when you apply a new adjustment layer, that adjustment clips to the layer directly below the adjustment layer. This means that the adjustment layer will affect only that underlying layer. However, you can click the circles icon at the bottom of the Adjustment Layers panel to have the adjustment affect all underlying layers.

✔ **Create a layer group.** You can create a *layer group* (described in Book V, Chapter 2) and place the layers you want adjusted in that group. Then, make sure that the blending mode is set to any mode except Pass Through. For more on modes, see Book V, Chapter 3.

Taking advantage of fill layers

A *fill layer* lets you add a layer of solid color, a gradient, or a pattern. Like adjustment layers, fill layers also have layer masks, as indicated by the mask icon thumbnail in the Layers panel.

You can create as many fill layers as you want, just as you can with regular layers and adjustment layers. You can also edit, rearrange, duplicate, delete, and merge fill layers. Additionally, you can blend fill layers with other layers by using the opacity, fill, and blending mode options in the Layers panel.

Like with an adjustment layer, to confine the effects of a fill layer to a portion of the image, make a selection, or create and select a closed path, before you create the fill layer (see Book III, Chapter 2 for more on paths). Editing or changing the contents of a fill layer is similar to editing or changing the contents of an adjustment layer (see the preceding section for details), except that fill layers don't have their own panel. To edit a fill layer, double-click the fill layer thumbnail in the Layers panel.

Here's how to create a fill layer:

1. **Open an image of your choice.**

   In this case, open an image that would look good with a border or text. For my example, I created the word *fujiyama* by using the Horizontal Type Mask tool (for details, see Book IV, Chapter 3). If you don't have an active selection, the fill layer encompasses your entire canvas.

2. **Choose Layer➪New Fill Layer. From the submenu, choose your desired adjustment. Name the layer, leave the other options at their defaults, and click OK.**

   For my example, I chose Pattern from the submenu.

   You can also just click the Create a New Fill or Adjustment Layer icon at the bottom of the Layers panel and select a fill from the pop-up menu.

3. **Follow the steps that correspond with the option you chose in Step 2:**

   - *Solid Color:* Select your desired color from the Photoshop Color Picker. (For more on color, see Book II, Chapter 3.)

   - *Gradient:* Select a preset gradient from the pop-up panel or click the gradient preview to display the Gradient Editor, where you can create your own gradient. Set additional gradient options, as desired. (For gradient details, see Book IV, Chapter 2.)

   - *Pattern:* Select a pattern from the pop-up panel. Drag the scale slider to adjust the size of the pattern. I scaled my Crayon on Vellum pattern 120%, as shown in Figure 1-5. Click Snap to Origin to position the origin of the pattern with the document window. Finally, select the Link with Layer option to specify that the pattern moves with the fill layer if you move it.

   Figure 1-5: Choose from a variety of preset patterns for your fill layer.

4. **Click OK.**

   After you close the dialog box, the fill layer appears in the Layers panel. Similar to adjustment layers, a layer mask is created on the fill layer. In my example, shown in Figure 1-6, *fujiyama* appears white on the layer mask, thereby allowing my pattern to show through. The remaining areas are black, hiding my pattern. I added a couple layer styles (Drop Shadow and Inner Bevel) to my type to jazz it up a bit. If you want to do the same, jump ahead to Book V, Chapter 4.

   If you want to delete the fill layer, do one of four things: Drag it to the trash icon in the Layers panel; choose Delete➪Layer from the Layer menu; choose Delete Layer from the Layers panel options menu; or the easiest, press the Backspace key (Delete on the Mac) on your keyboard.

You can rasterize a fill layer to convert it to a regular raster image. Choose Layer➪Rasterize➪Fill Content. A raster image enables you to use painting tools or filters on the layer. I introduce raster images in Book II, Chapter 1.

Figure 1-6: Your chosen fill shows through your selected areas.

Making use of shape layers

Believe it or not, Photoshop isn't just about photos and painting. Photoshop also has a whole slew of shape drawing tools — six, to be exact. You can fill those shapes with solid color, gradients, or patterns. When you create a shape, it resides on its own unique shape layer. A shape layer contains a *vector mask,* similar in concept to the adjustment layer mask described in the section "Using adjustment layers," earlier in this chapter.

If you look at the Layers panel, you can see that the Shape layer has two thumbnails: One is filled with color, and the other contains the path of the shape, as shown in Figure 1-7. To state it simply, the color is peeking through the path of the shape, and the rest of the layer is hidden or masked. The paths that constitute a shape are *vector paths;* when printed, they retain their smooth curves without the jagged edges you often see from bitmap editing programs. Although you can edit, move, and transform shapes, your ability to edit shape layers is limited. To apply filters and most other special effects, you must first *rasterize* the shape layers — that is, convert the vector paths to pixels. For more details on shapes, see Book IV, Chapter 2.

Using type layers

To create type, such as the type shown in Figure 1-8, click your canvas with the Type tool (horizontal or vertical) and type your desired text. After you commit your text by pressing Enter on the numeric keypad or clicking the Commit button on the Options bar (it looks like a check mark), you've created a type layer. In the Layers panel, you see a layer with a T icon, indicating that it's a type layer. Initially, the name of the type layer corresponds to the text you typed (you can change the layer name, if you want). Like shapes, the text in Photoshop is true vector type and, if left in that format, always prints smooth and without jaggies.

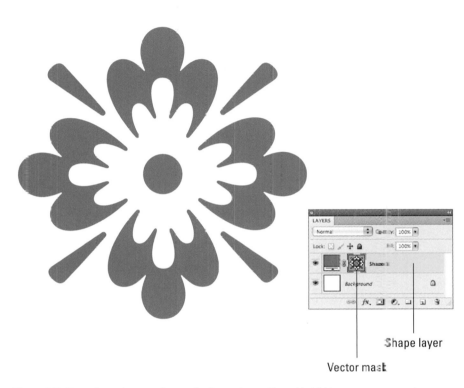

Shape layer

Vector mask

Figure 1-7: On a shape layer, color peeks through a path and is hidden everywhere else.

Another great thing about type in Photoshop is that it's live; you can edit the text at any time. You can also change the orientation, apply anti-aliasing (softening of the edges), create paths from the type, and even warp it into various distortions. You can also convert the type to a shape. Like with regular layers, you can move, re-arrange, copy, and change the layer options (opacity, fill, and mode) of a type layer. If, however, you want to apply certain special effects, such as filters, you must first *rasterize* (convert into pixels) the text. For everything you need to know about type, see Book IV, Chapter 3.

Figure 1-8: Type layers automatically appear when you create and commit type.

Making Layers

As I mention in the section "Using plain vanilla layers," earlier in the chapter, good, old-fashioned, regular layers are the backbone of the layers world. The following sections look at the various ways to create these layers.

Creating a new layer

You can create a new layer in a couple ways:

✏ **To create a new blank layer in an image that's open:** Click the Create a New Layer icon at the bottom of the Layers panel. You can also create a new layer by selecting New Layer from the panel pop-up menu or by choosing Layer⇨New⇨Layer. Both methods open a dialog box in which you name your layer and specify other options for grouping, color-coding, blending, and opacity (all of which I explain in other chapters in Book V). Provide a name for your layer and click OK. If you chose the first method, a layer with the default name of Layer 1 appears in the Layers panel.

When you click the Create a New Layer icon, the layer is added above your active layer. By holding down the Ctrl key (⌘ on the Mac) when you click, Photoshop adds the new layer below the active layer.

✏ **To create an entirely new document with a layer:** Choose File⇨New. In the New dialog box that appears, select the Transparent for the Background Contents option. Your new file then appears with Layer 1, rather than a background.

When your new transparent layer is ready and waiting, you can put content on the new layer in several ways:

✏ Use one of the painting tools and paint directly on the layer.

✏ Make a selection on another layer or the background (for the difference between the two, see the preceding sections in this chapter) within the same document or from another image entirely. Then, choose Edit⇨Copy. Select your new blank layer in the Layers panel and choose Edit⇨Paste.

✏ Make a selection on another layer (or the background) within the same document or from another image and then choose Edit⇨Cut. Select your new blank layer and choose Edit⇨Paste. Remember that Photoshop deletes the selection from the source and adds it to your new layer, as shown in Figure 1-9.

✏ Transfer an entire image to your new layer by choosing Select⇨All and then either Edit⇨Copy or Edit⇨Cut. Select your new blank layer and choose Edit⇨Paste.

Figure 1-9: Cutting and pasting a selection from one layer to another leaves a transparent hole on the original layer.

Using Layer via Copy and Layer via Cut

Another way to create a layer is to use the Layer via Copy command on the Layer menu. Make a selection on a layer or background and choose Layer⇨New⇨Layer via Copy. The copied selection is placed on a new layer with the default name of Layer 1. You can do the same with the Layer via Cut command, but in this case, Photoshop deletes the selected area from the source layer or background, and places it on the new layer. The source layer is left with a gaping transparent hole (refer to Figure 1-9). If you used the background for the source, your background color fills the space. Remember that you can use these two commands only within the same image. You can't use them between multiple images.

Duplicating layers

If you want to duplicate an existing layer, select it in the Layers panel. Then, drag the layer to the Create a New Layer icon at the bottom of the panel. You can also duplicate a layer by selecting Duplicate Layer from the panel pop-up menu or by choosing Layer⇨Duplicate Layer. As with creating a new layer, both methods prompt you with a dialog box to name your layer and include other options. Provide a name for your layer and click OK. If you chose the first method, Photoshop provides the default name of the original layer with the word *Copy* appended to the name.

Duplicating layers can be especially handy when you want to experiment with a special effect but don't want to harm your original image.

Compositing with Multiple Images

Often, when working with layers, you're not confined to using a single image. I mean, you can do only so much to that family portrait taken at the local photo studio. But take your family and put them in front of the ruins at Machu Picchu or the summit at Mount Everest (you can even add faux snow with a technique I show you in Book VII), and you have endless hours of fun. When you get the hang of working with several images, you'll find myriad new creative possibilities. And you're not limited to just plain old snapshots. You can incorporate type, vector illustrations, and scans of just about anything you can place on a scanning bed. Apply some layer styles, maybe a filter or two (see Book VII), and you have an image worthy of some major wall space.

Copying and pasting images

In the "Creating a new layer" section, earlier in this chapter, I explain how to use the Copy, Cut, and Paste commands within the same image or between two images when you want to fill a new blank layer with content. You can also use the Copy and Paste commands without having a blank layer ready. When you copy and paste a selection without a blank layer, Photoshop automatically creates a new layer from the pasted selection. You can go about your merry way and perform all your layer creations by using only those commands. However, I rarely use them when working with multiple images. I prefer the drag-and-drop method, which I describe in the following section.

The Copy Merged command on the Edit menu creates a merged copy of *all* the visible layers within the selection.

Dragging and dropping layers

To copy an entire layer from one document to another, simply select your desired layer in the Layers panel, grab the Move tool, and in your image window, drag and drop that layer onto your destination document. Or simply drag the thumbnail of your layer in the Layers panel onto your destination document. Photoshop automatically introduces the dropped layer as a *new* layer above the active layer in the image. You don't need to have a selection outline to copy the entire layer. However, if you want to copy just a portion of the layer, make your desired selection, as shown in Figure 1-10, before you drag and drop with the Move tool. If you want the selected element centered on the destination image, hold down the Shift key while you drag and drop. See the "Bypassing the clipboard" sidebar for more on dragging and dropping.

In CS5, you can also drag and drop a file, not just within Photoshop, but from most anywhere — your desktop, your Web browser, and other applications. Simply open a Photoshop document and drag and drop from your source onto that document. By doing so, you create a new layer in that document.

To drag and drop your images, be sure to specify that your images float rather than specifying they're tabbed. To do so, choose Window⇨Arrange⇨ Float All in Windows.

Bypassing the clipboard

Yes, you can always cut and paste, or copy and paste, a layer from one image to another, but I prefer to drag and drop, rather than copy and paste, between two images. By dragging and dropping, you bypass the temporary storage area for copied and stored data, the *clipboard*. (Whenever you copy or cut a selection, Photoshop stores the selection on the clipboard until you're ready to paste it to its new home.) So, what's wrong with that? Well, nothing, unless you're working with high-resolution images. Storing images on the clipboard, even on a temporary basis, can slow down your system.

Keeping your clipboard clear of data ensures that Photoshop is running lean and mean so that you can drag and drop more images, selections, and layers more quickly and more efficiently. If you want to perform a little spring cleaning on your clipboard, you can always choose Edit⇨Purge⇨Clipboard, which empties your clipboard of any stored data. Take my advice and try the drag-and-drop method. I guarantee that, like me, you'll be flexing your trigger finger — all the better to drag and drop even faster.

Cortis Digital Stock

Figure 1-10: Dragging and dropping a selection keeps your clipboard lean and mean.

What if you have multiple elements on one layer and want to select only one of the elements to drag and drop? Simply grab the Lasso tool and draw around the object. You don't have to be super-precise, but don't include any portion of the other elements on the layer. Then, hold down the Ctrl key (⌘ key on the Mac) and press the up-arrow key once. The element then is neatly selected. Not only can you drag and drop the element, but you can also move or edit it without affecting the other pixels on the layer. Flip to Book III, Chapter 1 for help with making selections.

Using the Paste Special commands

Photoshop has added a couple new paste commands. In addition to Paste Into, you will find Paste in Place and Paste Outside. All three commands are lumped under the new Edit⇨Paste Special submenu.

Paste Into

Let's start with my favorite — Paste Into. You may occasionally want to place an image on a separate layer, yet have it fill a selection. That's where this command comes into play. Paste Into enables you to insert a copied or cut selected image into a selection outline.

For example, if you want to make it appear as if a snake is poking its head out of the opening of a cave, or a bottle is poking out of a can, as shown in Figure 1-11, Paste Into is your command. Be sure to check out the Putting It Together project, in this chapter, to get more practice at this practical technique.

Layer mask

PhotoSpin

Figure 1-11: Use the Paste Into command to make one layer appear as though it is emerging from another.

Follow these steps to insert a copied or cut selected image into a selection outline:

1. **Make the selection on the layer that you want the image to fill.**

    I call this the destination layer.

2. **Select the image that will fill that selection.**

    I call this the source image.

3. **Choose Edit⇨Copy.**

4. **Return to the destination layer and choose Edit⇨Paste Special⇨ Paste Into.**

   Photoshop converts the selection outline on the destination layer into a layer mask. The pasted selection is visible only inside the selection outline. In my example, my bottle is showing only inside my selection. The bottom of the bottle is hidden, making it look like my bottle is sitting inside the can.

Paste Outside and Paste in Place

The opposite of Paste Into is Paste Outside. The Paste Outside command pastes a copied selection outside another selection, rather than inside. If you are copying between two images and you want to paste the selection of your source image into the same relative location in your target image, choose the Paste in Place command.

Transforming Layers

When compositing multiple images, you'll no doubt have to scale some of your image to fit it into your layout. Fortunately, Photoshop makes scaling an easy chore by providing you with the Transform and Free Transform commands on the Edit menu. Transforming layers is almost identical to transforming selections, except that you don't need to make a selection first. After an element is on a layer, you can just choose the appropriate transformation command and off you go. Additionally, you can apply a transformation to multiple layers simultaneously if you select the multiple layers first. I explain each transformation in detail in Book III, Chapter 3.

Try to perform all your transformations in one execution. Don't go back numerous times and apply various transformations. Each time you transform pixels, you're putting your image through the *interpolation* process (increasing, decreasing, or remapping pixels). Done repeatedly, your image may start to turn into mush. If not mush, it won't be as pristine and crisp as it was before.

If your image looks jagged after you transform it, you may have your preferences set incorrectly for your interpolation method. Choose Edit⇨ Preferences⇨General (Photoshop⇨Preferences⇨General on the Mac) and select the Bicubic option from the Image Interpolation pop-up menu. Bicubic enables a smoother appearance to your interpolated pixels. You can also try Bicubic Smoother when resampling up (upsampling) and Bicubic Sharper when resampling down (downsampling). For more on resolution and re-sampling, see Book II, Chapter 1.

When the Move tool is active, you can transform a layer without choosing a command. Simply select the Show Transform Controls option on the Options bar. This option surrounds the contents (or an active selection) of the layer with a bounding box with handles. Drag these handles to transform the contents.

Using Puppet Warp

Being a puppet master is an easy task with CS5's new transform command — Puppet Warp. Think of Puppet Warp as a lighter-weight Liquify filter (see Book VII, Chapter 3). This command enables you to distort specific areas of an image via a mesh overlay and the placement of pins.

You can apply a Puppet Warp on regular layers, shape layers, type layers, Smart Objects, and even vector masks. Here's how:

1. **Select your desired layer in the Layers panel.**

2. **Choose Edit⇨Puppet Warp.**

3. **On the Options bar, shown in Figure 1-12, specify your desired settings:**

Figure 1-12: Specify your Puppet Warp distort settings.

- *Mode:* Determines the elasticity of the mesh. Distort will give you an ultra-stretchy mesh, while Rigid will do the opposite.

- *Density:* Specifies the spacing of the mesh, where small changes in moving the pins result in larger warps. Also a good mode for larger images. Rigid is the opposite and recommended when your object is more stiff, as with human appendages.

- *Expansion:* Expand or contract the outer edges of the mesh.

- *Show Mesh:* Deselect to display only the pins, and not the mesh.

4. **On your image, click to add a pin to an area you want to distort or anchor.**

5. **Drag a selected pin to warp the mesh, as shown in Figure 1-13.**

6. **To rotate around a pin automatically, select Auto on the Options bar, and drag. To rotate a fixed number of degrees, select Fixed on the Options bar, press the Alt (Option on the Mac) key and position your cursor near, but not over, the pin. Drag to rotate.**

   Your degree of rotation appears on the Options bar.

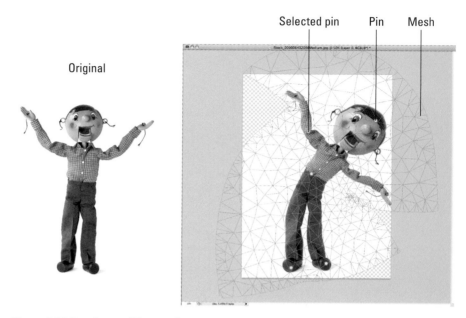

Figure 1-13: Use Puppet Warp to give marionettes newfound flexibility.

7. **You can also do the following:**

   - To show a mesh area that you've overlapped over another, click the Pin Depth buttons on the Options bar.

   - To select multiple pins, Shift+click on your desired pins. Release the Shift key to drag all pins simultaneously.

   - To delete a pin, select it and press Backspace (Delete on the Mac). Or Alt (Option on the Mac) and click over a pin.

   - Click Remove All Pins (the curved arrow icon) on the Options bar to do just that.

   - To select all pins, press Ctrl (⌘ on the Mac). To deselect all pins, press Ctrl+D (⌘+D on the Mac). To hide the mesh, press Ctrl+H (⌘+H on the Mac).

   - To exit Puppet Warp, click the slashed circle icon, or press Esc.

8. **After you warp to your desired result, press Enter (Return on the Mac) or click the check icon on the Options bar.**

Auto-Align Layers

One of the coolest features in Photoshop is the Auto-Align Layers command. How many times have you taken photos at a reunion, wedding, or other family event where not one of the shots is perfect? In one shot, Aunt Marlene has her eyes closed. In another, Momma Sue is looking to the side for Junior who should be in the photo. The Auto-Align Layers feature enables you to take these multiple images and composite them into that perfect shot by aligning your image and then letting you mask out the parts of the image that you don't want.

You can also use the Auto-Align Layers feature to stitch together images, such as panoramic shots or scans of oversized images — that is any series of images that have even a slight overlap.

Follow these steps to Auto-Align your layers:

1. **Create a new document with the same dimensions as your source images.**

2. **Open all your source images. With the Move tool, drag and drop each image into the new document.**

   Each image should be on a separate layer.

3. **If you desire, you can choose a layer to use as a reference. Lock the reference layer.**

   If you don't set a reference layer, Photoshop analyzes the layers and then selects the layer in the center of the final composite as the reference.

4. **In the Layers panel, select all the layers you want to align and choose Edit⇨Auto-Align Layers.**

5. **Choose one of the projection methods:**

   - *Auto:* Photoshop analyzes the layers, decides which method would create the best composite, and then applies the alignment.

   - *Perspective:* Photoshop designates one of the layers as the reference layer. The remaining layers are transformed so that content is aligned.

   - *Collage:* This option enables you to move, rotate, and scale your layers to get your desired layout.

   - *Cylindrical:* This is a good option for panoramic shots. It places the reference layer in the center and then places remaining layers on an unfolded cylinder to minimize distortion.

   - *Spherical:* This option also places the reference layer in the center and places the remaining layers on a sphere to correct distortion. This option comes in handy when you want to align shots taken with a wide-angle lens.

   - *Reposition:* A good option when you need to stitch together oversized scanned images. And the option to select if you're trying to create the perfect shot I describe in the introduction of this section

6. **Check options to correct for lens problems, such as Vignette Removal and Geometric Distortion.**

Vignetting is an exposure problem caused when light at the edges of the images is reduced and the edges become darkened. *Geometric Distortion* refers to such problems as barrel (bulging out) and pincushion (pinching in) distortions.

7. **Click OK.**

Photoshop finds and aligns the common areas of the layers, as shown in Figure 1-14. If you're stitching together images, you're done. If the composite has visible seams or inconsistencies, you can apply the Auto-Blend Layers command described in the following section.

Figure 1-14: Use Auto-Align Layers to stitch or composite multiple images.

If you're creating the perfect shot, add a layer mask to your top layer, set your foreground color to black, and use the Brush tool (with the appropriate tip size) to paint over the portions you want to hide or delete. In a mask, black hides pixels, so the layer underneath shows through. Repeat this process of layer masking your content until you have the shot you want. For more on layer masks, see Book VI.

Auto-Blend Layers

You may have images that need to be stitched together. For example, you may need to stitch together a series of panoramic shots you took or an oversize image you had to scan in several sections because it couldn't fit on your scanner. As you can see in Figure 1-15, the Auto-Blend command helps to smooth out the telltale seams or weird color inconsistencies that occur when stitching together shots with different exposures or contrast settings. You can also use the File⊅Automate⊅Photomerge command to stitch together images. For more on Photomerge, see Book IX, Chapter 2.

Figure 1-15: Seamlessly blend your images with the Auto-Blend command.

You can also use this command to blend a stack of several images together. For example, say you took several shots, at varying depths of field, of a group of flowers, which caused some flowers to be in focus and others to be blurry. You can blend them together to get a composite shot with all the flowers in focus.

Follow these steps to blend layers:

1. **Create a new document and then open all your source images. With the Move tool, drag and drop each image into the new document.**

   Each image should be on a separate layer.

2. **Select all the layers and choose Edit⇨Auto-Align Layers.**

   Note that you can try to align the layers yourself manually.

3. **Choose a projection method (see details in the preceding section), then click OK.**

4. **Select all the layers (avoiding the Background layer, if you have one) and choose Edit⇨Auto-Blend Layers.**

5. **Select your Blend Method — either Panorama or Stack Images.**

   Select Panorama for, well, panoramic shots. Select Stack Images for non-panoramic images, such as shots of flowers with varying depths of field. Select the Seamless Tones and Colors option to optimize the blending of the multiple images.

6. **Click OK.**

   This command automatically applies layer masks to each layer, as necessary. These layer masks attempt to hide under- and overexposed areas.

You can apply this command only on RGB or Grayscale images. You can't apply it to background layers and Smart Objects (and video or 3-D layers in the Extended version of Photoshop).

Putting It Together

Creating Layers and Using the Paste Into Command to Make a Collage

If you remember your elementary-school days, you probably remember cutting out a bunch of pictures from magazines and pasting them on a piece of construction paper. Well, with Photoshop, the idea of a collage isn't much different, but the activity is a little more refined. Maybe you want to let loose your artistic side. Or maybe you need to combine several images as part of a job. Whatever your reason, you can use the steps here to get started on your first collage. And, if *collage* is too froufrou a word for you, you can substitute it with *composite* — which has the definition "derived from many components." I usually do.

Creating a collage takes many steps. Throughout Book V, you can find several ongoing Putting It Together projects, all of which lead you to a finished collage. Be sure to save your collage file so that you can work on it while you make your way through this minibook.

If you're short on photos, you can go to www.gettyimages.com. Be sure to register so that you can have access to a huge gallery of free comping images. *Comping images* are small, low-resolution images used for internal corporate or personal non-commercial use only. You can also purchase high-resolution images for a song ($1 to $5) at www.istockphoto.com or www.stockxpert.com.

To create the first layer of your collage, follow these steps:

1. **Decide on two images you want to use in your collage and open them by choosing File⇨Open.**

   I recommend picking an image to use as your main canvas and then opening up a supporting image that you can select and then drag onto that main image. However, if you want, you can also start with just a blank document. For my example, I chose a travel theme and opened an image of the Grand Canyon and another image of a passport, as shown in the figure.

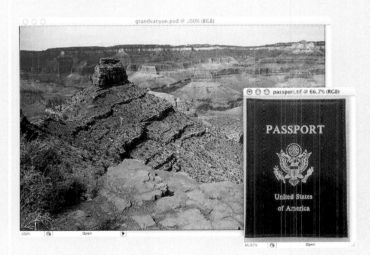

2. **Choose Window⇨Layers to open the Layers panel.**

   Always be sure that the Layers panel is visible whenever you're creating a composite from multiple images. You need to see what's happening while you drag and drop, and be aware of what layer you're working on at all times.

continued

continued

3. **Select the desired element in the supporting image.**

Feel free to use whatever selection method suits your fancy, but remember, the finished collage will look only as good as its individual selections. For more on making selections, see Book III.

Because the contrast between my passport and the background behind it was very good, I grabbed the Magic Wand tool, set the Tolerance to 50, and clicked the passport. I then held down the Shift key and, with the Lasso tool, circled the remaining pixels in the gold type that the Magic Wand tool didn't pick up.

4. **Choose Select⇨Modify⇨Contract and, in the Contract Selection dialog box, enter a value. Then, choose Select⇨Modify⇨Feather and enter a value in the Feather Selection dialog box.**

Contract the selections lightly (I chose a value of 1 pixel) before you apply a feather (I chose a 0.5 pixel value) to avoid picking up some of the background during the feathering process. Note that the values you choose depend on the resolution of your images — the lower the resolution, the smaller the value needed.

Using a small feather helps to avoid the harsh, I-cut-it-out-with-a-pair-of-pinking-shears look.

5. **With the Move tool, drag and drop the selection onto the background image.**

The Layers panel shows that you've produced a layer. You'll notice that your main image remains as the background below the layer, as shown in the figure.

Don't worry if your element isn't the right size. You can find a Putting It Together project in Book V, Chapter 2 that shows you how to scale the layer.

6. **Choose File⇨Save As. In the Save As dialog box, name the file *collage* and make sure the format is Photoshop.**

   Keep the file in a handy spot on your hard drive so that you can find it when you're ready to do more with your collage.

In the preceding steps, I showed you how to create a layer by dragging and dropping a passport onto a background image of the Grand Canyon. The process I demonstrate in the following steps is a little different. It entails pasting one selection into another.

Sticking with my travel theme, I opted to take the image of a compass and paste it into the background so that the compass looks like it's peeking out from the side of the canyon. To paste one selection into another on your collage, follow these steps:

1. **Choose File⇨Open. Select the file you saved from the preceding exercise. Also, open a new supporting image.**

2. **Choose Window⇨Layers to open the Layers panel.**

   Always keep the Layers panel visible whenever you're creating a composite from multiple images.

3. **Select the part of the supporting image that you want to use.**

   Feel free to use whatever selection method you desire, but try to get as accurate a selection as you can.

   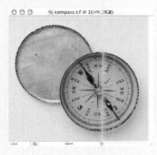

   For my compass image, I used the Elliptical Marquee tool, while holding down the Alt key (Option on the Mac), to draw from the center out to select the bottom portion of the compass. With the same tool, I held down the Shift key, then the mouse button, and then the Alt key (Option) to add the top portion of the compass, as shown in the figure.

4. **Contract and feather the selection (as described in Step 4 in the preceding set of steps).**

   Unless you're going for some special effect, be consistent with the treatment of the edges of each of your elements in your composite.

5. **Choose Edit⇨Copy.**

6. **In your saved collage file, move the first supporting image (the image you added in the preceding set of steps) to the side with the Move tool. Then, use the Lasso tool (or any other selection tool) to create a selection in which to paste your new supporting image.**

   I want the compass image to look like it's peeking up from behind the side of the canyon, so I made a selection in the cliffs of the Grand Canyon.

continued

continued

7. **Choose Edit⇨Paste Special⇨Paste Into.**

   If you use the Move tool to move the pasted image around the canvas, you see that the pasted image is invisible outside the boundaries of the selection outline, as shown in my collage.

   Don't be concerned if your element isn't the right size. I show you how to scale your layer in Book V, Chapter 2.

   The Layers panel shows a second thumbnail next to the compass thumbnail. This thumbnail represents the layer mask created automatically when you pasted into a selection. A layer mask allows portions of the layer to show and be hidden. In my example, the white areas on the layer mask are where my compass shows through. Those white areas correspond to the selection I made in Step 6. The black areas represent where my compass would be hidden if I were to move it into those areas. For more on layer masks, see Book VI, Chapter 3.

8. **Choose File⇨Save.**

Chapter 2: Managing Layers

In This Chapter

✓ Viewing, shuffling, and moving layers

✓ Aligning and distributing layers

✓ Linking and locking layers

✓ Creating layer sets

✓ Flattening and merging layers

✓ Using the Layer Comps panel

*H*opefully, you had the time and inclination to check out the first chapter of Book V. That's where you get all the basic information on creating layers. In this chapter, you get the scoop on how to manage the layers you've created. And unlike some coworkers, clients, or family members, layers are downright agreeable to being managed — even micromanaged, for that matter. The beauty of layers is that they're so darn easy to get along with. You can hide them, shuffle them, link and lock them, herd them into groups, and even smush them together into one loving, collective layer. Yes, Photoshop has a whole slew of ways to get your layers in the orderly and organized fashion you deserve.

Often, hiding all the layers in your image except for the one you want to edit is useful. You can focus on the element at hand without the distraction of all the other components of the image. You can hide a layer with a single quick click of the mouse button, as I describe in the following list:

✓ **Hide all the layers but one.** Select the layer you want to display. Alt-click (Option-click on the Mac) the eye icon for that layer in the left column of the Layers panel. To redisplay all the layers, Alt-click (Option-click on the Mac) the eye icon again.

✓ **Hide an individual layer.** Click the eye icon for that layer, as shown in Figure 2-1. To redisplay the layer, click the blank space in the eye column.

You can also hide layer styles or entire layer groups by using the same method as with layers. You can find out more about layer groups in the section "Creating Layer Groups," later in this chapter. For the lowdown on layer styles, see Book V, Chapter 4.

Figure 2-1: You can hide and show individual layers to better focus your tasks.

Only layers that are visible will print. Hiding layers for printing can be useful if you want to have several versions (each on a separate layer) of an image for a project within the same document. You can view selective layers, print them, get approval from the powers-that-be, and then delete the layers with the scrapped versions. Only one file to manage — even I can handle that.

If clicking is just too strenuous for you, try this neat trick: Drag through the eye column to hide or display multiple layers in one fell swoop. Now that's technology.

Rearranging Layers

You can shuffle the order of layers like clear sheets of acetate used with over-head projectors. The *stacking order* of the layers in the Layers panel corresponds to the order of the layers in the document. If you want to move a layer to another position in the stacking order, drag the layer (or layer group) up or down in the Layers panel. While you drag, you see a fist icon. Release your mouse button when a highlighted line appears where you want to insert the layer.

Alternatively, you can change the order by selecting the layer (or layer group) and then choosing Layer⇨Arrange. Then, select one of the following commands from the submenu:

- ✒ **Bring to Front and Send to Back:** Send the layer to the very top or very bottom of the stacking order.

- ✒ **Bring Forward and Send Backward:** Move the layer one level up or down.

- ✒ **Reverse:** Switches the order of your layer stack if you have two or more layers selected.

If your image has a background, it always remains the bottommost layer. If you need to move the background, first convert it to a layer by double-clicking the name in the Layers panel. Enter a name for the layer and click OK.

Moving Layer Elements

Rearranging layers is different from moving the content on the layer. Because the elements on a layer are free floating on a bed of transparency, it's a piece of cake to move the element whenever necessary. Moving the element has no effect on any of the other layers, and it doesn't harm the image one iota.

To move an image on a layer, first select that layer in the Layers panel and then just drag it with the Move tool (the arrow pointer with a tiny four-headed arrow), located in the Tools panel; it doesn't get any simpler than that. Here are a few more handy tips when moving an image and using the Move tool:

- ✒ **Move the layer in 1-pixel increments.** Press an arrow key (located between the keyboard and keypad) when you have the Move tool selected. To move the layer in 10-pixel increments, press Shift when you press the arrow key.

- ✒ **Find out what layer holds the element you want to move (or edit in some other way).** If you have the Auto-Select and Layer options selected in the Options bar, select the Move tool and click the element. Photoshop automatically activates the layer that the element resides on. If you don't have this option selected, then Ctrl-click (⌘-click on the Mac) the element. Or you can right-click (Control-click on the Mac) the element. A context menu appears, telling you what layer the element resides on, and then enables you to select that layer from the context menu. It also lists the background layer.

- ✒ **Switch to a layer when you click with the Move tool on any part of a layer.** Select the Auto-Select and Layer options on the Options bar. But be careful if you use this option, especially if you have a lot of overlapping elements; you may inadvertently select a layer when you don't want to.

- ✒ **Select the Auto-Select and Group options on the Options bar to select the layer group that the selected layer is in.** For more on groups, see the section "Creating Layer Groups," later in this chapter.

✔ **Display a bounding box that has handles around the elements on your layer.** Select the Show Transform Controls check box on the Options bar. This box can be useful if all your elements are melting into one another in an indistinguishable conglomeration.

I recommend keeping this option selected so that you essentially have the same controls (scale, rotate, and so on) you have if you chose Edit⇨ Free Transform. For more on transformations, see Book III, Chapter 3.

Putting It Together

Transforming and Moving Layers in a Collage

When you have a couple images in your collage (see the Putting It Together project in Book V, Chapter 1), you can start transforming them to your liking. Moving and scaling are the manipulations you'll probably do the most. Photoshop enables you to transform layers without affecting any other layer within the image. (For more on transformations, see Book V, Chapter 1 and Book III, Chapter 3.) To transform and move images in a collage, follow these steps:

1. **Choose File⇨Open. Select your saved collage file in the dialog box that opens.**

2. **Choose Window⇨Layers to open the Layers panel.**

3. **In the Layers panel, select the layer you want to transform.**

   In my example, I chose the layer that has the passport on it.

4. **Choose Edit⇨Free Transform.**

   By choosing Free Transform rather than Transform, you interpolate the image only once, rather than twice. For more on interpolation, see Book II, Chapter 1.

5. **Shift-drag a corner transformation handle to scale the image down to the desired size but maintain the proportions, which reduces the amount of distortion.**

   I reduced the passport in my example to about half its original size.

6. **Position the cursor just outside the handle until a curved arrow appears. Rotate the image the desired amount.**

   The figure shows my example; I rotated the passport about 35 degrees.

7. **When you transform the selection to your liking, double-click inside the transform box or press Enter (Return on the Mac).**

8. **Transform the element that has a layer mask. In the Layers panel, choose the layer and follow Steps 4 through 7.**

   In my example, that's the compass layer.

   Be sure to click the layer's thumbnail and not the layer mask thumbnail. Otherwise, you transform the layer mask thumbnail, rather than the element.

9. **When you transform the selection to your liking, double-click in the transform box.**

   I scaled the compass slightly so that the top of the compass became visible. Then, I rotated the compass to show more of the compass face, rather than the cover.

10. **Choose File➪Save.**

You probably already have a pretty good sense of the possibilities (which are infinite) available to you when you create and change collages. Of course, you can always add more stuff to a collage and rearrange the layers, as needed. Just follow these steps:

1. **Choose File➪Open and select your collage file. Also open another image.**

   I chose a boarding pass image.

2. **Choose Window➪Layers to open the Layers panel if it isn't already visible.**

3. **Select the desired element in the supporting image.**

   It goes without saying that making the selection accurate can only enhance your composite. I selected the boarding pass with the Polygonal Lasso tool.

4. **Contract and feather the image's edges and use the Move tool to drag the selection into the collage file.**

   For the most professional appearance possible, use consistent values for modifying and feathering all the selections in this composite.

5. **Position and transform the selection, as needed.**

   Follow the directions provided in the preceding steps list. In my example, I scaled the boarding pass to the same size as the passport, rotated it clockwise, and positioned it a little lower than the passport.

continued

continued

6. **In the Layers panel, rearrange your layers, if needed, by selecting a layer and dragging it above another layer.**

In my image, I dragged my passport layer above my boarding pass layer, as shown in the figure.

Because the layers are independent entities, you can shuffle them indefinitely like a deck of cards.

7. **Choose File↔Save.**

Aligning and Distributing Layers

If you're a precision junkie like me, you'll appreciate Photoshop's capability to align and distribute your layers. These commands can be especially useful when you need to align items such as navigation buttons on a Web page mock-up or a row of headshots for a corporate publication. Follow these steps to align and distribute your layers:

1. **In the Layers panel, select the layers you want to align, as shown in Figure 2-2.**

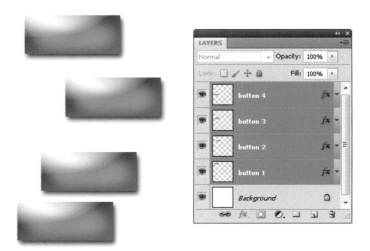

Figure 2-2: Select the layers you want to align in the Layers panel.

2. **Choose Layer➪Align and select one of the alignment commands.**

Photoshop provides you with handy little icons that illustrate the various alignment types. You also find these icons as buttons on the Options bar when you have the Move tool selected, as shown in Figure 2-3. Feel free to use either method.

Figure 2-3: The Options bar offers different alignment buttons.

Depending on which alignment type you choose, Photoshop aligns to the layer element that's the farthest to the top, bottom, left, or right. If you align to the center, Photoshop splits the difference among the various layer elements.

3. **In the Layers panel, select three or more layers that you want to distribute evenly.**

4. **Choose Layer➪Distribute and select one of the distribute commands.**

The distribute commands evenly space the layers between the first and last elements in either the row or column.

For the word-challenged, you can find an icon illustrating the distribution types. And like alignment, the distribute icons appear as buttons on the Options bar when you have the Move tool selected. You can see the buttons from Figure 2-2 precisely aligned and evenly distributed in Figure 2-4.

You can also align a layer to a selection outline by following these steps:

1. **Make your desired selection in the image.**

2. **Select a layer or layers in the Layers panel.**

3. **Choose Layer➪Align Layers to Selection and choose an alignment type from the submenu.**

Note that the Align Layers to Selection command doesn't appear in the Layer menu until you have both layers and an active selection outline.

For the Auto-Align Layers option, the last icon on the Options bar, check out Book V, Chapter 1.

Figure 2-4: The aligned and evenly distributed buttons.

Linking Layers

You'll probably find that you don't need to link layers in most cases. Simply select multiple layers and apply your command — moving, scaling, rotating, and so on. Occasionally, however, you may want to link layers so that they stay grouped as a unit until you decide otherwise. To link layers, follow these short steps:

1. **Select the layers or layer groups in the Layers panel.**

2. **Click the Link Layers icon at the bottom of the Layers panel, as shown in Figure 2-5.**

   A link icon appears to the right of the layer name in the Layers panel.

   To remove a link, click the Link Layers icon again.

Link layers

Figure 2-5: Use the Link command if you need a longer-term grouping of your layers.

If you find the need to quickly select all the linked layers in your Layers panel, select just one of the layers and then choose Select Linked Layers from either the Layer menu or the Layers panel pop-up menu. This technique can come in handy, for example, when working on Web pages with a lot of linked layers containing buttons or labels in a navigation bar.

Putting It Together

Selecting Layers in a Collage and Adjusting Their Size

When you're working on composites, you may find the need to adjust the size or angle of more than one layer. You can select the layers you want to scale or rotate and transform all the layers at the same time. This strategy enables you to adjust all the layers the same amount at the same time — thus ensuring that they stay proportional in size. If you want to be certain that all the layers stay selected during the transformation process, you can link them for extra insurance. Follow these steps:

1. **Open your saved collage file.**

   Make sure that the Layers panel is visible.

2. **Select the layers you want to transform. If you want to link them, simply click the Link Layers icon at the bottom of the Layers panel.**

   In my example, I selected Layers 1 and 3 — my passport and boarding pass.

3. **Choose Edit⇨Free Transform and Shift-drag the corner transformation handle to scale the layers. When you're satisfied, double-click inside the transform box or press Enter (Return on the Mac).**

   Because both layers are selected, any transformation you apply, including moving and scaling, affects both layers, as shown in the figure.

4. **Save the file when you're done.**

Locking Layers

After you get your layers the way you want them, you may want to lock them to prevent them from being changed, as shown in Figure 2-6. To lock a layer, select it in the Layers panel and select one or more of the lock options at the top of the Layers panel. See Table 2-1 for details about each option.

You can also choose Layer⇨Lock Layers or select Lock Layers from the Layers panel pop-up menu.

When you select the Lock All option, a solid, dark gray lock icon appears on the layer, indicating the layer is fully locked. When you select any of the other lock options, the lock appears light gray and hollow, indicating the layer is partially locked.

Lock options   Fully locked

Partially locked

Figure 2-6: Locking prevents unwanted edits.

By default, the background is locked and can't be unlocked until you convert the background into a layer by choosing Layer⇨New⇨Layer from Background. In addition, by default, type layers have the Lock Transparent Pixels and Lock Image Pixels options selected. These options are grayed out and can't be deselected. However, if you need to paint on the type layer, you can always rasterize it, thereby removing all locking options. For more on type, see Book IV, Chapter 3.

If you have layer groups, you can choose Layer⇨Lock All Layers in Group or select Lock All Layers in Group from the Layers panel pop-up menu.

Table 2-1		Lock Options in the Layers Panel
Button	*Name*	*What It Does*
	Lock Transparent Pixels	Prevents you from painting or editing any transparent areas on your layer. To quickly select or deselect the Lock Transparent Pixels check box, press the forward slash key (/).
	Lock Image Pixels	Prevents you from painting or editing your layer. You can still select, move, or transform items on the layer.
	Lock Position	Prevents you from moving and transforming the layer but gives you free rein on everything else.
	Lock All	Prevents you from painting, editing, moving, or transforming your layer. (But you can still make selections.)

Color-Coding Layers

To visually distinguish your layers in the Layers panel, Photoshop lets you color-code your layers or layer groups, as shown in Figure 2-7. Choose Layer⇨Layer Properties or select Group Properties from the Layers panel pop-up menu. Choose a color from the drop-down list and click OK.

For a great timesaver, right-click (Control-click on the Mac) the layer's eyeball icon to make a context menu listing the colors appear.

I find that color-coding works especially well with layer groups. First, organize your layers into groups, such as navigation buttons, type, images, border, background, and so on. Then, assign a color to each group. By using the same color-coding system from one project to the next, you can get a little productivity boost by instinctively knowing where to find your elements.

Creating Layer Groups

I don't know about you, but having a file cabinet full of neatly labeled manila folders containing all my vital paperwork is very satisfying. It's compact. It's organized. It's "at the ready," as they say in the military. Fellow geeks can revel in Photoshop's digital answer to the manila folder, which enables you to organize layers into *layer groups.* You can expand or collapse layer groups to see or hide their contents. In their collapsed state, layer groups are a great antidote for the annoying scrolling that you must do in an abundantly layered file. And groups enable you to apply opacity settings, blend modes, and layer styles to multiple layers at a time.

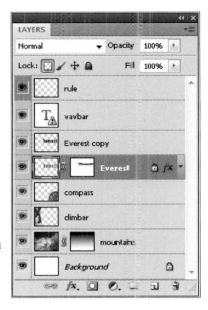

Figure 2-7: Color-coding layers helps to visually identify and organize your layers.

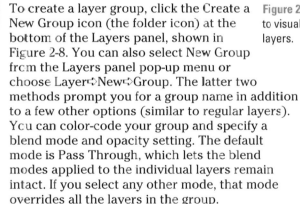 To create a layer group, click the Create a New Group icon (the folder icon) at the bottom of the Layers panel, shown in Figure 2-8. You can also select New Group from the Layers panel pop-up menu or choose Layer⇨New⇨Group. The latter two methods prompt you for a group name in addition to a few other options (similar to regular layers). You can color-code your group and specify a blend mode and opacity setting. The default mode is Pass Through, which lets the blend modes applied to the individual layers remain intact. If you select any other mode, that mode overrides all the layers in the group.

After you create your group, drag your layers into the group folder in the Layers panel. If the group is collapsed when you drag or if you drag a layer on top of the group icon itself, Photoshop places the layer at the bottom of the layer group. If the group is expanded, you can drag the layer to a specific location within the group. To collapse or expand the group, click the triangle icon to the left of the folder icon.

Although layer groups are pretty straightforward, keep these few points in mind:

Expanded group

Create a New Group

Collapsed group

Figure 2-8: Grouping layers provides better layer manageability

✔ Like with regular layers, you can select, duplicate, show, hide, lock, and rearrange layer groups. See other sections in this chapter for more on these commands.

✔ You can nest layer groups. Create (or drag) one layer group into another layer group. In CS4, you were limited to five or fewer levels of nested groups. Now, however, in CS5, you can nest more than five.

✔ You can create a layer group from selected layers. Select the layers that you want to be in a group, and then select New Group from Layers from the Layers panel pop-up menu or choose Layer⇨New⇨Group from Layers. Name the group in the dialog box that appears and click OK.

✔ If you select a layer within a group and then choose Layer⇨Arrange, the command applies to the stacking order only within the layer group.

✔ You can merge layer groups. Select the group and select Merge Group from the Layers panel pop-up menu or choose Layer⇨Merge Group. For more on merging, see the following section.

✔ You can rename your group by double-clicking the group name in the Layers panel. You can also choose Layer⇨Group Properties or select Group Properties from the Layers panel pop-up menu.

✔ In addition, you can lock layers within a group. Select Lock All Layers in Group from the Layers panel pop-up menu or choose Layer⇨Lock All Layers in Group.

Flattening and Merging Layers

Being the true layers evangelist that I am, I tout the glories of layers in the first two chapters of this minibook. And layers are wonderful. But they do have a dark side. They can make your file go from slim and trim to bulky and bloated. You not only get a larger file size that slows your computer system performance, but you're also limited to the file formats that allow you to save layers: Photoshop's native format (.psd), TIFF (.tif), Large Document Format (.psb), and PDF (.pdf). If you save your file in any other format, Photoshop smashes your layers down into a background. This file limitation often forces users to save two versions of every layered file — one as a native Photoshop file and one as something else, such as EPS or JPEG, to import into another program. For more on file formats, see Book II, Chapter 2. To curb large file sizes or use layered images in a wider range of formats, you have a couple options:

✔ **Merging layers:** Combines visible, linked, or adjacent layers into a single layer (not a background). The intersection of all transparent areas is retained. You can merge layers or layer groups. You can also merge adjustment or fill layers (see Book V, Chapter 1 for details), but they can't act as the target layer for the merge. Merging layers can help decrease your file size and make your document more manageable. You're still restricted to the layer-friendly file formats, however.

✔ **Flattening an image:** Combines all visible layers into a background. Photoshop deletes hidden layers and fills any transparent areas with white. Flattening is usually reserved for when you're completely finished editing your image.

When you convert an image from one color mode to another, that conversion may cause the file to flatten. Look out for the warning dialog box that prompts you of this result, and go back and save a copy of your file as a native Photoshop file, thereby preserving your layers. See Book II, Chapter 2 for details about color modes.

Merging layers

You can merge your layers several ways. To use the first option, follow these steps:

1. **Ensure that all the layers (and layer sets) that you want to merge are visible, as shown in Figure 2-9.**

Figure 2-9: Merging layers can make your file size a lot smaller.

2. **Choose Merge Visible from the Layers panel pop-up menu or the Layer menu.**

   All visible layers are smushed into a single layer, as shown in Figure 2-9.

Hold down Alt (Option on the Mac) when choosing Layer⇨Merge Visible. Photoshop merges those layers onto a new layer.

You can also merge layers by following these steps:

1. **Position the layer or layer groups that you want to merge adjacent to each other in the Layers panel.**

2. **Select the top layer of those you want merged.**

3. **Choose Merge Down from the Layers panel pop-up menu or the Layer menu.**

   If the top layer is a layer group, the command is called Merge Group.

   Merge Down merges your selected layer with the layer directly below it.

Flattening layers

To flatten an image, follow these steps:

1. **Ensure that all the layers you want to retain are visible.**

   Photoshop discards all hidden layers.

2. **Choose Layer⇨Flatten Image or select Flatten Image from the Layers panel pop-up menu.**

   The transparent areas of your flattened image are filled with the background color and appear as a background layer in the Layers panel, as shown in Figure 2-10.

Figure 2-10: Flatten your layers only if you're reasonably sure you won't need individual layers any longer.

   Photoshop doesn't prompt you with a warning like, "Are you sure you really want to do this?" But if you mistakenly flatten your image, you can undo the command immediately by choosing Edit⇨Undo. If you go ahead and perform another action, then undo your mistake by using the History panel. However, if the flattening step is no longer in the History panel, there's no way to undo the flattening. See Book II, Chapter 4 for the scoop on the History panel.

Putting It Together

Checking Your Collage for Flaws and Consolidating Layers

When you begin a project, you may think you know what you want the final result to look like. But when your creative juices start flowing, you may decide that something doesn't look right. For example, while I was working on my collage, I discovered that the sky behind and above the canyon was a little on the ordinary side.

1. **Open the saved collage file and open a new image that you want to incorporate into the collage.**

   In my example, I thought the sky needed some kick, so I opened an image that contained a sky I liked.

2. **Select the part of the image that you want to add to your collage, as shown in the figure.**

   Most of the time, consistency is key. In my example, however, I didn't need to feather the image. Because I'm going to paste it into the old sky, the edges of the element won't be seen.

Photodisc

3. **Choose Edit⇨Copy.**

4. **In the collage image, select the portion of the image into which you want to paste your copied element.**

   Because I'm pasting the image into the background image, I first needed to make the selection I wanted to paste into. I used the Magic Wand tool. After a couple of additional Shift-clicks, I selected the entire sky behind the canyon.

5. **Choose Edit⇨Paste Into.**

   The element you copied (in my case, the new sky) appears inside the selected area of your collage, as shown in the figure.

When you're close to finalizing your collage, you might want to consolidate layers. Minimizing the number of layers makes projects easier to manage and your file size smaller, which is great when you get ready to add the finishing touches to your collage.

Be sure that before you merge your layers, you'll never have to manipulate them separately, especially if the elements on the layer overlap each other, as mine do.

To consolidate two layers, follow these steps:

1. **Select the layers in the Layers panel.**

continued

continued

2. **Select Merge Layers from the Layers panel pop-up menu.**

   The two layers merge and become one.

3. **Choose File⇨Save.**

Working with the Layer Comps Panel

The Layer Comps feature doesn't really add more layer functionality, but because it shares a similar moniker, I explain it in this minibook.

What Layer Comps does is enable you to create and save multiple versions of your project within a single master file. Through the Layer Comps panel, Photoshop records all the vital statistics of your layers, including their visibility, position, and blending options. These statistics come in handy when you want to show a client or art director various design versions within a single document. That's right: No longer do you have to save the various renditions of a design or project in multiple files. Just be aware that layer comps do add to your file size.

The following steps walk you through the day-to-day operation of the Layer Comps panel:

1. **Choose Window⇨Layer Comps to display the panel, shown in Figure 2-11.**

Corbis Digital Stock

Figure 2-11: The Layer Comps panel enables you to create and save multiple versions of a project within a single document.

2. **Create all your desired layer content.**

If you perform all your editing on just a background layer, you can't save the document as a layer comp.

3. **When you have a version of the document that you want to save as a comp, click the New Layer Comp button at the bottom of the panel or select New Layer Comp from the panel pop-up menu.**

The New Layer Comp dialog box appears.

To create a comp and bypass the options dialog box, hold down the Alt (Option on the Mac) key when you click the New Layer Comp button.

4. **Name your layer comp and select the attributes you want recorded — Visibility, Position, and Appearance (Layer Style) of the layers. Click OK.**

You can also add an optional comment about the configuration you're capturing, as shown in Figure 2-12.

Figure 2-12: Add project details in the Comment field.

If you add a comment, you see a triangle just to the left of the layer comp name. (Refer to the sunflower solo comp shown in Figure 2-11.) Click the triangle to see your comment in the panel.

5. **Continue creating your various configurations of the document, capturing a layer comp after each.**

6. **To display a particular layer comp, click in the left column in the Layer Comps panel.**

A document icon appears, which indicates that particular layer comp is selected.

7. **To efficiently cycle through all your layer comps, click the Apply Next Selected Layer Comp or Apply Previous Selected Layer Comp icon (the arrows) at the bottom of the Layer Comps panel.**

You can also, less efficiently, apply layer comps by selecting the particular layer comp and selecting Apply Layer Comp from the panel pop-up menu. The document icon moves to that layer, and Photoshop displays that layer comp.

Here are a few more Layer Comp tidbits:

✓ **To rename a layer comp:** Simply double-click its name in the panel.

✓ **To delete a layer comp:** Select it and click the trash can icon in the Layer Comps panel. You can also drag the layer comp to the trash can icon or select Delete Layer Comp from the panel pop-up menu.

✔ **To duplicate a layer comp:** Select it and drag it onto the New Layer Comp icon in the panel or select Duplicate Layer Comp from the panel pop-up menu.

✔ **To update a particular layer comp with the currently active configuration of the document:** Select the layer comp, and then select Update Layer Comp from the panel pop-up menu or click the Update Layer Comp button at the bottom of the panel.

✔ **To display your document at its latest configuration (but not necessarily the latest saved layer comp):** Select Restore Last Document State from the panel pop-up or simply click in the column to the left of the Last Document State item in the Layer Comps panel.

✔ **To rearrange the order of the layer comps:** Simply drag it to a new location in the panel.

To output your layer comps, choose File⇨Scripts⇨Layer Comps to Files. Select this command to make Photoshop export your layer comps to individual files. In the dialog box that appears, shown in Figure 2-13, provide a destination and prefix name for your file. Indicate whether you want to include Selected Layer Comps Only. (You must select them before you choose the command.) Leave that option deselected to have Photoshop export all layer comps. Then, choose your desired file type and specify whether you want to Include ICC Profile (see Book II, Chapter 2) and Maximize Compatibility. (See Book I, Chapter 5.) Click Run and then sit back and watch the magic happen.

Figure 2-13: Have Photoshop automatically export your layer comps into individual files.

The Layer Comps to WPG (Web Photo Gallery) command is an optional plug-in that you'll find on your installation disc in the Goodies folder. And you won't find the Layer Comps to PDF command in the Scripts submenu at all. You can find it in the Adobe Output Module in Adobe Bridge. For more on creating PDFs and Web galleries, see Book I, Chapter 4.

Chapter 3: Playing with Opacity and Blend Modes

In This Chapter

✔ Adjusting opacity and fills

✔ Applying blend modes for effects

✔ Setting the blend options

In this chapter, I show you how to let down your hair and get those creative juices flowing. Yes, I'm about to say the "F" word: Fun.

This chapter, along with Book V, Chapter 4, focuses on how to tweak the layers you've made. Maybe you want to make one of your layers semitransparent so that you can see the layer beneath it; or say you want to try blending the colors between a couple layers in a way that's slightly offbeat. Look no further.

Although some techniques in this chapter may reek of complexity, keep in mind that you don't need to totally understand them. Take these techniques as far as you want. And remember, there's no substitute for good, old experimentation. Before you jump into these techniques, it helps to have a handle on the methods of layer creation and management that I explain in Book V, Chapters 1 and 2.

Adjusting Layer Opacity

By far one of the easiest ways to make your image look oh-so-sophisticated is to have one image ghosted over another, as shown in Figure 3-1. Creating this effect is a snap with the Opacity option in the Layers panel. You adjust the opacity in two ways:

✔ Select your desired layer in the Layers panel. Then, either access the slider by clicking the right-pointing arrow, entering a percentage value in the Opacity text box, or simply scrubbing over the word Opacity (it converts to a two-way arrow).

You can now select more than one layer at a time and change the Opacity (or Fill Opacity) values in one fell swoop.

Figure 3-1: Adjusting the opacity enables one image to ghost over another.

✔ You can also double-click a layer thumbnail, choose Layer➪Layer Style➪ Blending Options, or select Blending Options from the Layers panel pop-up menu. (Click the triangle in the upper-right corner to open the menu.)

Any of these methods brings up the Layer Style dialog box, where you can enter a value or drag the slider for opacity.

The Opacity setting allows you to mix the active layer with the layers below it in varying percentages from 100% (completely opaque) to 0% (completely transparent). Remember that you can adjust the opacity only on a layer, not a background.

You can also change the Opacity percentage by using keyboard shortcuts. With any tool active, except a painting or editing tool, press a number key. Press 5 for 50 percent, 25 for 25 percent. If you're entering a two-digit value, just be sure you type the numbers quickly, or else Photoshop interprets the numbers as two different values. You get the picture. Note that for the default of 100 percent, you must press 0.

Adjusting the Fill Opacity

In addition to adjusting the regular opacity for a layer, you can also adjust the fill opacity. Fill opacity works a little differently from regular opacity. The regular Opacity setting affects layer styles (see Book V, Chapter 4) and blend modes (see the following section) that have been applied to the layer. Fill opacity, however, affects only the pixels or shapes that reside on the layer. It doesn't affect the styles or blends. As you can see in Figure 3-2, the drop shadow and emboss styles in the bottom example show through full strength.

Figure 3-2: Fill opacity (bottom) affects only layer pixels, not styles or blend modes that have been applied to the layer.

To adjust the Fill Opacity setting, select your desired layer, or layers, in the Layers panel, and then enter a value in the Fill Opacity text box or drag the pop-up slider. The other methods for adjusting fill opacity are similar to the regular opacity option.

Creating Effects with Blend Modes

Photoshop's 25 blend modes (27 when you work with the painting and editing tools) determine how the colors in different layers interact with each other. Blend modes can produce a multitude of interesting, sometimes even bizarre, effects. And what's more, you can easily apply, change, or discard blend modes with no permanent damage to your layers.

Most options in the Blend Mode pop-up menu (located under the Layers tab) in the Layers panel are the same as those on the Mode pop-up menu on the Options bar. The exceptions are the Behind and Clear modes, which you can find only on the Options bar because they're available for use only with painting and editing tools.

I urge you to pick an image with a few layers and apply each blend mode to get a good handle on what the various blend modes do. In fact, try a few different images because the effects may be subtle or intense, depending on the colors in the image. Throw in some different opacity percentages, and you're on your way to endless hours of creative fun.

You'll find these modes called *blend modes, painting modes, brush modes, layer modes, calculations,* or just plain *modes.* They're usually referred to as *blend modes* or *layer modes* when used with layers and painting modes, and *brush modes* when used in conjunction with a painting or editing tool.

General blend modes

In the General category, you find the following modes, which are shown in Figure 3-3 and explained in Table 3-1.

Table 3-1	General Blend Modes
Blend Mode	*Description*
Normal	You're probably very familiar with the Normal blend mode by now. It's the default that lets each pixel appear in its very own unadulterated state. The other three modes are used only in certain circumstances.
Dissolve	The effects of Dissolve can be seen only with a layer that has an opacity setting of less than 100% — the lower the opacity, the more intense the effect. The effect is created by allowing some pixels from lower layers, which are randomized, to show through the target layer.
Behind	Available only when you have a painting or editing tool active. Type must be rasterized, and Lock Transparency must be deselected. It allows you to edit or paint only on the transparent areas of the layer, giving the illusion that the strokes are behind the layer.
Clear	Available only when you have a painting or editing tool active. Type must be rasterized, and Lock Transparency must be deselected. It allows you to edit or paint with transparency, giving the appearance that holes are being punched into your image.

Blend modes that darken

Overall, the blend modes in this category all produce effects that darken your image, as shown in Figure 3-4. However, one of my favorite uses for the Darken blend mode is a little different. Scan a handwritten letter or sheet of music and layer it over an image. Apply the Darken blend mode to the letter or sheet-music layer. The white areas of the paper become transparent, and only the letters or musical notes display, creating a nice composite image. Table 3-2 describes these modes.

Normal   Dissolve

Behind   Clear

Figure 3-3: The Behind and Clear blend modes are available only with a painting or editing tool.

Darken   Multiply

Color Burn   Linear Burn

Darker Color

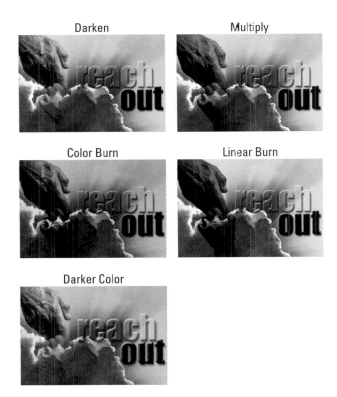

Figure 3-4: These blend modes darken, or burn, your layers.

Table 3-2	Blend Modes That Darken
Blend Mode	*Description*
Darken	If the pixels on the layer are lighter than those below, the lighter pixels turn transparent. If the pixels on the layer are darker, they appear unchanged. It's a great mode, as is Darker Color, for superimposing scanned text or line art because it allows the white color of the paper to essentially drop out, leaving only the dark letters or lines.
Multiply	Burns the layer into the layers underneath. The Multiply mode darkens all colors where they mix. With layers, it's comparable to sticking two slides in the same slot in a slide projector. If you're painting, each successive stroke creates a darker color, as if drawing with markers.
Color Burn	Darkens the layers underneath and burns them with color. Increases contrast. Blending with white pixels has no effect. It's like applying a dark dye to your image.
Linear Burn	Darkens the layers underneath by decreasing the brightness. This is similar to Multiply but tends to make portions of your image pure black. Blending with white pixels has no effect.
Darker Color	When blending two layers, the darker of the two colors will be visible.

Blend modes that lighten

If you have blend modes that darken, having modes that lighten just makes good sense. So, if you have the need to throw some digital bleach on your brightly colored pixels, try a couple of these blend modes, which I describe in Table 3-3. Figure 3-5 shows examples of these effects.

Table 3-3	Blend Modes That Lighten
Blend Mode	*Description*
Lighten	If the pixels on the layer are darker than those below, the darker pixels turn transparent. If the pixels on the layer are lighter, they appear unchanged. This is the opposite of Darken.
Screen	Lightens the layer where it mixes with the layer underneath. Blending with black pixels has no effect. It's like putting two slides in two different projectors and pointing them at the same screen. Screen is the opposite of Multiply.

Blend Mode	Description
Color Dodge	Lightens the pixels in the layers underneath and infuses them with colors from the top layer. This is like bleaching your layer. Blending with black pixels has no effect.
Linear Dodge (Add)	Lightens the layers underneath by increasing the brightness. It's similar to Screen but tends to make parts of your image pure white. Blending with black pixels has no effect.
Lighter Color	When blending two layers, the lighter of the two colors will be visible.

Figure 3-5: These blend modes lighten, or dodge, your layers.

Lighting blend modes

This group of blend modes plays with the lighting in your layers. Some of these blend modes, such as Pin Light, are reserved for the occasional wacky special effect. The following list and images explain and show each mode:

✔ **Overlay:** Multiplies the dark pixels in the top layer and screens the light pixels in the underlying layers. Enhances the contrast and saturation of colors.

Overlay

✔ **Soft Light:** Darkens the dark pixels and lightens the light pixels. If the pixels on the top layer are lighter than 50% gray, the lighter pixels are lightened further. If the pixels on the top layer are darker than 50% gray, the mode darkens pixels. Blending with black or white results in darker or lighter pixels, but it doesn't make parts of your image pure black or pure white. It's similar to Overlay, but softer and subtler, like shining a soft spotlight on the image.

Soft Light

✔ **Hard Light:** Multiplies the dark pixels and screens the light pixels. It's like shining a bright, hard spotlight on the image. If the pixels on the top layer are lighter than 50% gray, they're screened. If the pixels on the top layer are darker than 50% gray, the mode multiplies the pixels. You can use this mode to add highlights and shadows to an image. Blending with black or white gives you black and white.

Hard Light

✔ **Vivid Light:** If the pixels on the top layer are darker than 50% gray, this mode burns (or darkens) the colors by increasing the contrast. If the pixels on the top layer are lighter than 50% gray, the mode dodges (or lightens) the colors by decreasing the contrast. Vivid Light is a combination of Color Burn and Color Dodge.

Vivid Light

✔ **Linear Light:** If the pixels on the top layer are darker than 50% gray, the mode burns (or darkens) the colors by decreasing the brightness. If the pixels on the top layer are lighter than 50% gray, the mode dodges (or lightens) the colors by increasing the brightness. It's a combination of Linear Burn and Linear Dodge.

Linear Light

✔ **Pin Light:** Replaces the colors of pixels, depending on the colors in the top layer. If the pixels on the top layer are darker than 50% gray, the mode replaces pixels darker than those on the top layer and doesn't change lighter pixels. If the pixels on the top layer are

Pin Light

lighter than 50% gray, the mode replaces the pixels that are lighter than those pixels on the top layer and doesn't change pixels that are darker. Pin Light is a combination of Darken and Lighten and it's useful for special effects.

Hard Mix

✔ **Hard Mix:** Similar to Vivid Light, but it reduces the colors to a total of eight — cyan, magenta, yellow, black, red, green, blue, and white. Although the results depend on the mix of existing colors on the top and bottom layers, this mode usually creates a highly posterized effect.

Blend modes that invert

If the blend modes discussed in the preceding sections are a tad too tame for you, you may want to check out the inverters — Difference and Exclusion (described in Table 3-4). These blend modes invert your colors and can produce some interesting special effects, as shown in Figure 3-6.

Difference · Exclusion

Figure 3-6: The Difference and Exclusion blend modes invert colors.

Table 3-4	**Blend Modes That Invert**
Blend Mode	*Description*
Difference	Produces a negative, or inverted, effect according to the brightness values on the top layers. If the pixels on the top layer are black, the mode doesn't change the colors of the underlying layers. If the pixels on the top layer are white, the mode inverts the colors of the underlying layers. This can produce bizarre results.
Exclusion	Similar to Difference, but with less contrast and saturation. If the pixels on the top layer are black, the mode doesn't change the colors of the underlying layers. If the pixels on the top layer are white, the mode inverts the colors of the underlying layers. Medium colors blend to create gray.

HSL color model blend modes

These blend modes use the HSL (Hue, Saturation, and Lightness) color model to mix colors. My favorite blend mode in this group is Color, which allows you to apply color to images without obscuring the tonality. The Color mode is great for "hand painting" grayscale images. See details on this technique in Book IV, Chapter 1. Table 3-5 lists these modes, and Figure 3-7 shows their effects.

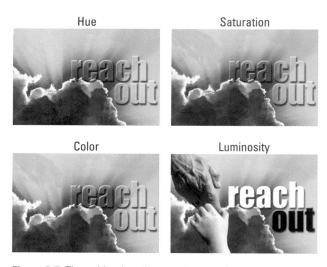

Hue

Saturation

Color

Luminosity

Figure 3-7: These blend modes use the Hue, Saturation, and Lightness color model to mix colors.

Table 3-5	HSL Color Model Blend Modes
Blend Mode	**Description**
Hue	Blends the luminance (brightness) and saturation (intensity of the color) of the underlying layers with the hue (color) of the top layer.
Saturation	Blends the luminance and hue of the underlying layers with the saturation of the top layer.
Color	Blends the luminance of the underlying layers with the saturation and hue of the top layer. This mode is great for colorizing gray-scale (with a color mode set to RGB) images because it preserves the shadows, highlights, and details of the underlying layers.
Luminosity	Blends the hue and saturation of the underlying layers with the luminance of the top layer. Preserves the shadows, highlights, and details from the top layer and mixes them with the colors of the underlying layers. Luminosity is the opposite of Color.

The following blend modes work with 8-, 16-, and 32-bit images: Normal, Dissolve, Darken, Multiply, Lighten, Linear Dodge, Difference, Hue, Saturation, Color, Luminosity, Lighter Color, and Darker Color.

Working with the Advanced Blending Options

If you want to get serious about layers, then you need to know about the Advanced Blending Options, which you can find in the Layer Style dialog box. These options allow you to tailor the way your layer styles and blend modes interact with your layers. Getting to the advanced options is just like accessing opacity and blend modes: You can double-click a layer thumbnail, choose Layer⟹Layer Style⟹Blending Options, or select Blending Options from the Layers panel pop-up menu. The massive Layer Style dialog box rears its multi-paneled head, as shown in Figure 3-8.

(By the way, if you're ready to know more about these blending features, skip to Book V, Chapter 4, where I cover layer styles.)

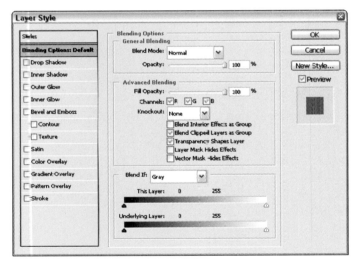

Figure 3-8: The Layer Style dialog box is home to Advanced Blending Options.

Advanced options to blend with

The advanced options aren't for the faint of heart. To be frank, the options are, well, advanced, so you might find them a tad too eggheady for your taste. But if not, here you go:

✐ **Fill Opacity:** I cover this in the section "Adjusting the Fill Opacity," earlier in this chapter.

✔ **Channels:** This option allows you to restrict your blending options to specific channels only. For all you need to know about working with channels, check out Book VI.

✔ **Knockout:** This option allows you to specify which layers have holes in them so that you can view the layers underneath. You first have to use the Fill Opacity option to set the opacity of the knockout. The lower the opacity, the more the hole shows; therefore, set it to 0% (like in my example in Figure 3-9) to see all the way through. Set the Knockout to Shallow to create a hole through one layer group (see Book V, Chapter 2) or a clipping group. (See Book V, Chapter 4.) Set the Knockout to Deep to create a hole all the way through to the background. If you're working with just layers, and not layer groups or clipping groups, the knockout cuts through to the background. If there's no background, it cuts through to transparency.

Figure 3-9: A knockout cuts holes in your layers to enable you to view the layers underneath.

✔ **Blend Interior Effects as Group:** This option applies the blend mode of the layer to interior layer effects, such as inner glows, satin and color overlay, and so on. Deselect this option to prevent the blend mode from affecting the layer effects. You can see the difference in Figure 3-10.

✔ **Blend Clipped Layers as Group:** The blend mode of the bottom layer in the clipping group affects all the other layers in the group. Deselect this option to make each layer retain its own blend mode and appearance.

✔ **Transparency Shapes Layer:** Confines layer effects and knockouts to opaque areas of a layer. Deselect this option to apply the mode's layer effects and knockouts to the entire layer. (See Figure 3-11.)

Blend Interior Effects as Group selected

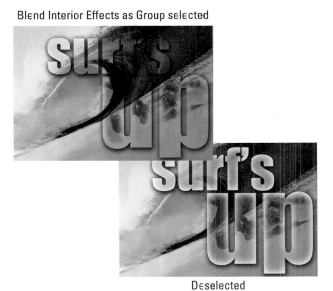

Deselected

Figure 3-10: The Blend Interior Effects as Group option applies the blend mode of the type layers to the layer's inner glow, bevel and emboss, and color overlay.

- ✔ **Layer Mask Hides Effects:** Confines layer effects to the area designated by the layer mask. (For more on layer masks, see Book VI, Chapter 3.)
- ✔ **Vector Mask Hides Effects:** Confines layer effects to the visible area designated by a vector mask, as shown in Figure 3-12. (For more on vector masks, see Book VI, Chapter 3.)

Transparency Shape Layer selected   Deselected

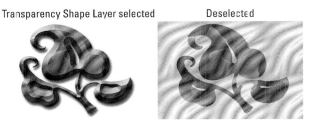

Figure 3-11: The Transparency Shapes Layer restricts layer styles to the opaque areas of a layer.

Figure 3-12: Choose to confine your effects to the vector mask, or not.

Blend If options

By using the slider bars, you can specify which colors are visible in the active layer and which colors show through from the underlying layers. You can select a specific channel from the Blend If pop-up menu to apply the option to a single channel. The default channel, Gray, affects all channels in the image. The two sliders at the bottom of the Layer Style dialog box do the following:

✓ **This Layer:** Allows you to set a blending range. In other words, you can hide certain colors according to the brightness values in the active layer. By dragging the black triangle to the right, you exclude darker colors. By dragging the white triangle to the left, you exclude lighter colors.

✓ **Underlying Layer:** Forces the colors from the underlying layers to show through the active layer. Again, dragging the black and white triangles excludes ranges of colors.

Excluding and forcing colors can result in some harsh color transitions. You can provide for a smoother transition between blended and unblended areas by splitting the slider into two parts, allowing the pixels to gradually fade to transparency. Alt-drag (Option-drag on the Mac) on either the black or white triangle in either slider bar to split the triangle into two halves. The left and right triangles mark the beginning and end of the blending range, where pixels fade into or out of view.

Putting It Together

Fine-Tuning and Adjusting Opacity Settings in Your Collage

If you've followed along with the Putting It Together projects I discuss in Book V, Chapters 1 and 2, you may have a collage that you're pretty satisfied with. You just need to make the final tweaks and then go to sleep (or go home to your spouse and children).

One of the most important tweaks you can make is to opacity. Follow these steps to adjust the opacity settings on some of the layers:

1. **Open your saved collage file.**

   If the Layers panel isn't already visible, open it.

2. **Select a layer in your collage and move the opacity slider to the left or right.**

   If you want the layer to be more opaque, move the slider to the right. If you're interested in making the layer more transparent, move the slider to the left.

   I chose Layer 4 and adjusted the opacity to 75%. I like the blue sky in my collage, but it's a tad too vibrant in comparison to the rest of the image. Adjusting the opacity tones it down and allows the blue to blend in more naturally.

3. **Save the file and move on to the next layer you want to adjust.**

   If you have more complicated opacity settings to adjust, keep reading.

4. **Select the background layer and then select Duplicate Layer from the Layers panel pop-up menu. Click OK to close the Duplicate Layer dialog box.**

continued

continued

Making a copy of the background is great because it allows you to add a blend mode, like you do in Step 5, and then adjust it to get just the right amount of the effect.

For example, if you want to define an element in your collage, but applying it directly on the layer makes the effect too intense, make a copy of the layer. I wanted to pump up the definition of the canyon in my collage, but when I used the blend mode directly on the background, the result looked too harsh.

By the way, I couldn't resist the urge to include a pair of hiking boots in my collage.

5. **Select the background copy layer and select a mode (such as Vivid Light) from the Mode pop-up menu in the Layers panel.**

The definition likely looks great, but the contrast is over the top.

6. **Adjust the opacity to tone it down.**

I changed the opacity in mine to 35%.

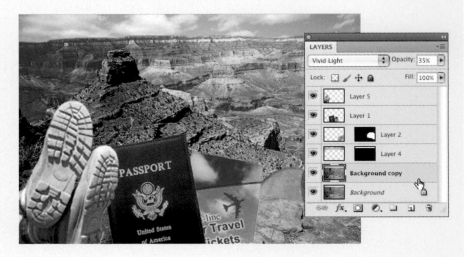

7. **When you're satisfied with the opacity and contrast, save the collage file.**

Chapter 4: Getting Jazzy with Layer Styles and Clipping Groups

In This Chapter

✔ **Getting the facts on layer styles**

✔ **Using the Styles panel**

✔ **Creating a custom style**

✔ **Clipping layers**

After you have all the basic elements in your layered composite image, you may want to give it a little pizzazz and finesse. Maybe a headline would pop out a little more if you beveled the edge, or maybe that silhouetted image would take on a little more dimension if you placed a drop shadow behind it. This chapter is where you find out how to do that and more. (If you're wondering how to create a composite image with layers, see Book V, Chapters 1, 2, and 3, which introduce the basics of creating composites with layers.)

Layer Styles Basics

Back in the day, creating a drop shadow in Photoshop took a concerted effort. And beveled or embossed type? Well, I'll just say that you really had to have the inside scoop on some Photoshop tricks. Now, however, Photoshop makes creating these kinds of effects as easy as selecting an option.

In this chapter, you may see the terms *effect* and *style* used interchangeably. Technically, however, Adobe says that after layer effects are applied to a layer, they become part of a layer's *style*. You can save and load styles, but not effects. So, if you apply a bunch of effects and want to be able to easily re-create the look, save it as a style.

When you get started with layer effects and styles, keep the following tips in mind:

✔ You can apply layer effects to regular layers, shape layers, fill layers, and type layers, but not to backgrounds, completely locked layers, or layer groups. For more on backgrounds, see Book V, Chapter 1. For details on locking layers and creating layer groups, see Book V, Chapter 2.

- Layer effects are *dynamically linked* to the contents of a layer. If you move or edit the contents of the layers, the effects are updated.

- When you apply effects, they become part of the layer's style. A styled layer has an fx symbol next to the layer's name in the Layers panel. You can expand (to view the individual effects) or collapse the layer style by clicking the triangle icon next to the florin.

- Drag the fx symbol from one layer to another to move it. Or Alt+drag (Option+drag on the Mac) the fx symbol from one layer to another to copy the style easily.

- If you create a style so fantastic that you want to save it for later use, you can save a custom style as a preset and store it in the Styles panel. (See the section "Saving your own style," later in this chapter.)

- Feel free to cut loose and have some fun. Layer styles are completely nondestructive. They don't muck around with your actual pixel data. If you don't like them, edit them. If you really don't like them, delete them to go back to your original unstylized image.

Introducing the Many Layer Styles

Layer effects fall into a few categories. You can add shadows, glow effects, beveled and embossed edges, and overlay colors and patterns, and you can, of course, tweak to your heart's content. This list introduces the various effects that you can apply. (In the following sections, I explain how you apply each layer style and tweak its settings.)

- **Shadows:** Add a soft drop or inner shadow to the contents of a layer. You can adjust the blend mode, color, opacity, angle, size, and contour to suit your needs. Figure 4-1 shows examples of both types of shadows.

Drop Shadow   Inner Shadow

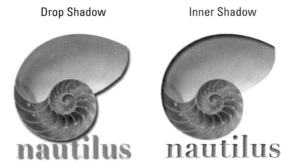

Figure 4-1: Add dimension by applying an inner or drop shadow to your object or type.

✔ **Glows:** Add a soft highlight that appears on the outside or inside edges of the contents of a layer, as shown in Figure 4-2. Like shadows, you can fine-tune the appearance by adjusting numerous options.

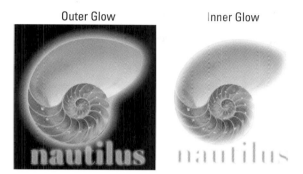

Figure 4-2: Inner and outer glows add a soft highlight to edges.

✔ **Bevels:** Create a 3-D edge on either the outside or inside edges of the contents of a layer, giving the element some dimension. Similarly, emboss effects make elements appear raised off of or punched into the page. Satin creates a satiny or draped fabric effect over your element. All these effects (shown in Figure 4-3) offer numerous options to adjust their appearances.

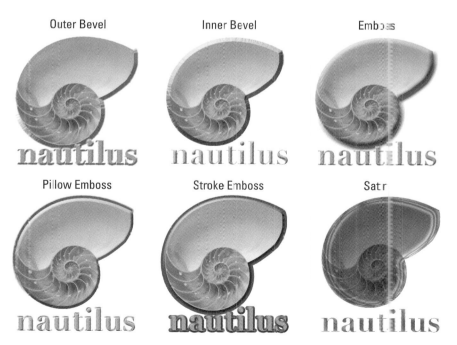

Figure 4-3: Bevel and Emboss make your element look raised or punched.

✔ **Overlays:** Apply a fill of color, a gradient, or a pattern over the contents of your layer, as shown in Figure 4-4. You can adjust the opacity of the overlay, among other options, so that your original element shows through more clearly. You can also surround your layer with a stroke consisting of a color, gradient, or pattern.

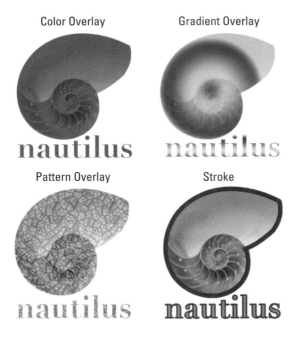

Color Overlay   Gradient Overlay

Pattern Overlay   Stroke

Figure 4-4: Overlays cover your object or type.

Applying a Layer Effect

Follow these steps to apply a layer effect:

1. **Select your desired layer in the Layers panel.**

2. **Choose Layer➪Layer Style and choose an effect from the submenu.**

   You can also click the Add a Layer Style icon in the Layers panel and select an effect from the pop-up menu.

   An intimidating Layer Style dialog box with a ton of options rears its head, as shown in Figure 4-5.

3. **Select the Preview check box in the top-right portion of the dialog box so you can see your effects while you apply them.**

4. **To accept the default settings, just click OK.**

   Or you can experiment with the settings.

   You can use sliders or check boxes, enter values in the text boxes, and so on. The following sections in this chapter describe the options and settings in detail.

5. **If you refine your effect settings, click OK when you finish.**

   Photoshop applies your effect to your layer, as indicated by the fx icon.

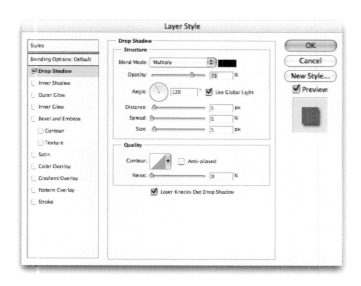

Figure 4-5: The Layer Style dialog box allows you to easily turn effects off and on with a mere check of a box.

Managing and Editing Layer Styles

You can always just apply the layer effect with Photoshop's default settings, but what fun is that? To edit a style, double-click the Effect name or the Effects label, double-click the layer thumbnail or double-click the Layer Style icon in the Layers panel, and make your desired adjustments in the Layer Style dialog box. If you double-clicked the layer thumbnail or the icon, be sure to select your desired effect from the left side of the dialog box to get access to your effect's settings.

The following sections give you the details on each of the options. But a picture is worth a thousand words. Experiment to see these effects come alive.

Managing layer styles

Here are a few pointers to keep in mind when working with and editing layer styles:

- ✔ **Choose several effects at one time.** Simply select the check box for the effect on the left side of the Layer Style dialog box. To access the options for each effect, you must click the effect name so that it's highlighted.

- ✔ **Remove an effect.** Deselect the check box associated with it.

- ✔ **Move a style onto a separate layer.** By default, layer styles are attached to a layer. To put a style on a separate layer, select the styled layer and choose Layer⇨Layer Style⇨Create Layer. You see a new layer in the Layers panel with a name, such as `Layer 0's Drop Shadow`.

  Although separating a style onto its own layer may give you more manual editing capability and allow you to apply filters, you lose all editing ability with the Layer Style dialog box. Also, the style won't dynamically update when you change the layer itself. Your style basically becomes just a generic mass of colored pixels.

- ✔ **Copy and paste effects onto other layers.** Select the layer containing the effect and choose Layer⇨Layer Style⇨Copy Layer Style. Select the layer or layers on which you want to apply the effect and choose Layer⇨Layer Style⇨Paste Layer Style. Even easier, you can also just hold down the Alt (Option on the Mac) key and then drag and drop an effect from one layer to another.

- ✔ **Hide effects.** Choose Layer⇨Layer Style⇨Hide All Effects to hide all effects on the image, not just the selected layer.

- ✔ **Display hidden effects.** Choose Layer⇨Layer Style⇨Show All Effects.

- ✔ **Remove all the effects on a layer.** Choose Layer⇨Layer Style⇨Clear Layer Style. You can also drag the *Effects bar* (what Adobe calls the name Effects) or fx icon to the trash can icon in the Layers panel.

- ✔ **Remove a single effect.** Simply drag and drop the single effect to the trash can icon in the Layers panel.

- ✔ **Resize a layer effect.** Select your desired layer in the Layers panel. Choose Layer⇨Layer Style⇨Scale Effects. Select Preview and enter a value between 1 and 1,000 percent. This command allows you to scale the effect without scaling the element.

Editing drop shadow or inner shadow effects

If you used the default settings to apply your drop shadow or inner shadow and want to do some tweaking, edit by following these steps:

1. **In the Layers panel, double-click the Effect name.**

   Or you can double-click the layer thumbnail or the Layer Style icon (fx icon).

   The Layer Style dialog box opens. If you double-clicked the layer thumbnail or the Layer Style icon, you need to click the Drop Shadow or Inner Shadow name on the left side of the dialog box.

2. **Change the Blend Mode setting to adjust how the colors of the shadow mix with the colors of your elements.**

   Usually, the default mode, Multiply, works best.

3. **Adjust the Opacity setting to change how transparent the shadow appears.**

4. **To select a shadow color, open the Color Picker by clicking the swatch to the right of the Blend Mode setting.**

5. **Establish the angle of your light source.**

6. **Select the Use Global Light option to ensure that all the shadows and highlights of all your elements are consistent.**

   You don't want one layer to look like it's 6 a.m. and another to look like it's 2 p.m. The neat thing is that if you change the angle on one layer style, all the styles (with the Use Global Light option selected) you've applied to your layers adjust to that new angle dynamically.

7. **Specify how far the shadow is offset from your element with the Distance setting.**

8. **Adjust the Spread, Choke, and Size settings to specify the boundary, intensity, and size of the shadow.**

9. **Select the Layer Knocks Out Drop Shadow option if you have a transparent object on top of the shadow.**

   This option prevents the shadow from showing through the object.

10. **After you refine your effect settings, click OK.**

    Your effect is edited and ready to go, as shown in Figure 4-6.

    You can also choose to apply various contours and noise to your shadow. See the section "Playing with Contours," later in this chapter, for details.

Figure 4-6: Effects such as shadows are live, enabling you to edit them at any time.

Changing default inner and outer glow effects

The inner and outer glow effects possess many of the same settings as the shadows. But unlike shadows, glows offer the option of using a gradient, which can produce an interesting halo effect, as shown in Figure 4-7.

PhotoSpin

Figure 4-7: Colorize a glow with a gradient.

Follow these steps to edit your own glow:

1. **Double-click the layer thumbnail or the Layer Style icon (the fx icon).**

   The Layer Style dialog box opens.

2. **Click the name of the Effect and specify Blend Mode, Opacity, Color, Spread, and Size settings.**

   If you're editing an inner glow effect, you see the options of Source (Center or Edge) and Choke, rather than Spread. The Center option applies the glow over the entire image except the edge, whereas the Edge option applies only to the element's edge. The Choke option behaves similarly to the way the Spread option behaves.

3. **If you want to use a gradient rather than a solid color, select a preset gradient from the Gradient drop-down panel or click the Gradient Editor button to edit or create your own gradient.**

   Book IV, Chapter 2 explains the Gradient Editor in detail.

4. **In the Technique option, select either the Softer or Precise setting.**

   Choose Softer to apply a blurred glow. This option doesn't preserve detailed edges of the element.

   Choose Precise to create a glow that's good for hard-edged elements, such as type. This option does preserve the details.

5. **Use the Range and Jitter options for the Contour setting.**

   For more on contours, see the "Playing with Contours" section, later in this chapter.

6. **After you refine your effect settings, click OK.**

   Your effect is edited and ready to rock.

Editing Bevel and Emboss Effects

Because Photoshop offers five bevel and emboss styles, you have a ton of options. Some are similar to those found with the shadow and glow effects, whereas others are unique. The Layer Style dialog box is divided into four panels.

Structure

This panel contains the most relevant options:

- **Technique:** These settings of Smooth, Chisel Hard, or Chisel Soft determine how soft or hard the edge of the bevel is. Chisel Hard works well with type and harder-edged elements. You can see an example of each in Figure 4-8. I used a depth of 700% and a size of 8.

Smooth   Chisel Hard   Chisel Soft

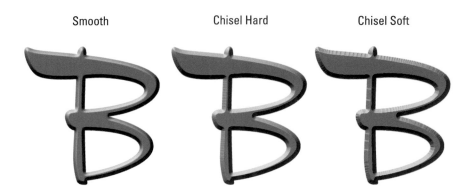

Figure 4-8: Choose from three types of bevels.

- ✒ **Depth:** Affects how raised or sunken the edge of the bevel or pattern appears.

- ✒ **Direction:** For these settings, Up positions the highlight along the edge closest to the light source and the shadow on the opposite edge. Down does the opposite, positioning the shadow near the light source.

- ✒ **Size:** Controls the size of the bevel or emboss effect.

- ✒ **Soften:** Blurs the shading of the effect.

Shading

Because of the 3-D nature of bevel and emboss effects, Photoshop has settings for Highlight and Shadow (each with separate Blend Modes and Opacity options) and Angle. Because bevels and embosses are more dimensional, an additional setting of Altitude affects the light source.

Texture

In the Texture panel (click Texture on the left side of the Layer Style dialog box), you can apply a pattern onto your layer that creates a texture, as shown in Figure 4-9. Adjust the scale and depth of the pattern, and link the pattern to the layer, if desired. If you link the pattern and layer, the pattern moves when you move the layer. The Snap to Origin command aligns the pattern origin with the document if you select the Link with Layer option. If you don't select the option, the Snap to Origin command aligns the pattern to the upper-left corner of the layer.

Figure 4-9: Textures add patterns onto your elements.

Contour

Contours change the distribution of the colors in the effect, as shown in Figure 4-10. You can use the various presets offered to create interesting, and sometimes bizarre, shadows, glows, bevels, and other effects. For details on contour and its various iterations, see the section "Playing with Contours," later in this chapter.

Figure 4-10: A Falling Slope Descending contour.

Editing Satin Effects

You can adjust the color, blend modes, opacity, angle, distance, and size — all of which I explain in the preceding sections. You can also adjust the contour, which is discussed in the section "Playing with Contours," later in this chapter.

Changing Overlay Effects

Shadows, being based in reality, are the kinds of effects you'll find yourself using frequently. On the other hand, you'll probably use overlay effects only occasionally, if at all. In most cases, overlays are reserved for the realm of the special effect. But, in case you need to apply an overlay, here are the options:

- **Color Overlay:** Adjust the Blend Mode, Opacity, and Color settings of the overlay. This effect, along with the Gradient Overlay and Pattern Overlay, is best used with an opacity setting of less than 100% or a blend mode other than Normal. That way, the elements underneath aren't totally obliterated.

- **Gradient Overlay:** Choose a preset gradient from the drop-down Gradient picker or click the Gradient swatch to access the Gradient Editor to create your own. The Align with Layer option uses the bounding box of the layer to calculate the gradient. Specify the angle, style (Linear, Radial, Angle, Reflected, or Diamond), and scale of the gradient. Reverse flips the gradient. Adjust the Blend Modes and Opacity settings.

- **Pattern Overlay:** Select a preset pattern from the Pattern picker drop-down panel. Snap to Origin and Link with Layer work the same as with Bevel and Emboss. Select Blend Modes and Opacity settings. Use the Scale slider to size the pattern. Figure 4-11 shows a fabric pattern overlay on a rose.

Figure 4-11: I created this fabric rose with the Denim pattern and an Overlay blend mode.

Changing Stroke Effects

Specify the size of your stroke in pixels and whether you want it to ride the outside, center, or inside of the edge of the element. Determine the Blend Mode and Opacity settings. Specify whether to fill your stroke with a color, gradient, or pattern. Select your desired color, gradient, or pattern from the corresponding options. These options are similar to those of overlay effects, described in the preceding section.

Playing with Contours

Several of the layer effects have various options for contours. *Contours* change the distribution of the colors in the effect. The default setting for all the effects except satin is *linear contour*. In an effect with a linear contour, the opacity drops off in a straight line.

But you're not limited to the linear contour option. Click the arrow of the Contour option to make a variety of preset contours appear in a drop-down menu, as shown in Figure 4-12. Click the panel arrow to load the complete contour preset library by choosing Contours at the bottom of the pop-up menu. You can also click the Load Contours command to load other libraries you may have saved previously or acquired from friends, colleagues, or third-party vendors.

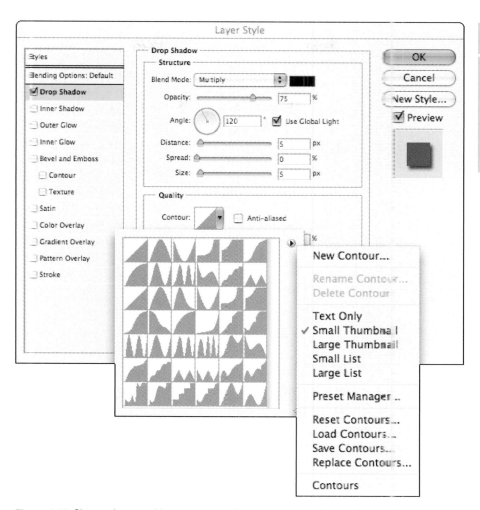

Fig**ure** 4-12: Choose from a wide assortment of preset co**n**tours for your layer s**t**yles.

The presets offer contours such as Ring, Rolling, Sawtooth, and Steps, all of which create rings of transparency within the shadows and glows. If you use contours with bevel and emboss effects, you can create nooks, crannies, bumps, and lumps that are highlighted and shaded.

In the Contour panel pop-up menu, you can also find options for naming and deleting contours, as well as saving, loading, resetting, and replacing contour libraries. Using different contours can create fun and funky shadows and glow, as shown in Figure 4-13.

Figure 4-13: A Ring-Triple contour on the drop shadow of my beveled text and oval adds a metallic touch.

Adjusting contour settings

You're using Photoshop, the Swiss Army Knife of the graphics-editing world, so you can do a whole lot more than select a preset contour and apply it to a layer. Depending on the effect you're working with, you can change the appearance of the contour in a variety of ways:

- **Noise:** Randomizes the colors of selected pixels in the drop or inner shadows to give a gritty effect.

- **Anti-Aliasing:** Slightly softens the edge pixels of a contour.

- **Range:** Controls how much of the glow is targeted for the contour. Reduce the Range setting to get a less feathered, tighter, and larger glow.

- **Jitter:** Doesn't affect the appearance of the default glow, but with other gradients, the Jitter setting varies the color and opacity of selected pixels to give a roughened effect.

- **Invert:** Turns the colors of the satin effect inside out.

- **Gloss Contour:** Changes the distribution of color in the effect over the layer. It creates a metallic effect when used with the Bevel and Emboss styles. The Contour option that appears indented below the Bevel and Emboss style in the Styles list does the same for the edges of the layer. It creates shaded and highlighted nooks and crannies when used with the Bevel and Emboss styles.

Modifying contours with the Contour Editor

If the preset contours just don't do it for you, feel free to create your own by following these steps:

1. **Open the Contour Editor dialog box, shown in Figure 4-14, by clicking the Contour thumbnail in the Layer Style dialog box.**

2. **Click the line on the Mapping grid to add points and drag the line to adjust the slope.**

   You can also select a point on the Mapping line and enter values in the Input and Output boxes.

3. **To create a sharp corner, rather than a curve, select a point and click the Corner option.**

4. **When you have the contour to your liking, click the New button, give it a name in the Contour Name dialog box that appears, as shown in Figure 4-15, and click OK.**

   Photoshop saves your custom contour as a preset and makes it available in the Contour panel.

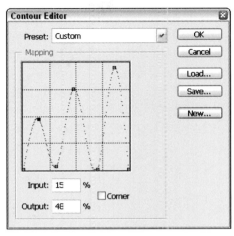

Figure 4-14: Create a custom contour if the presets don't meet your needs.

Figure 4-15: Name your custom contour.

You can save custom contours for reloading later or for trading with friends and neighbors. (Try giving them away on Halloween.) Photoshop saves a contour as a .shc file in the Contours folder in the Presets folder in the Photoshop application folder.

Applying and Modifying Preset Styles

In addition to layer effects, Photoshop also offers you a multitude of preset layer styles that you can access via the Styles panel, in the Window menu, shown in Figure 4-16.

You can also access these styles by using the Style picker drop-down panel on the Options bar, when the Pen or shape tools are active and you have the Shape Layer option selected. And you can find the Styles panel nestled at the top of the Layer Style dialog box, as well.

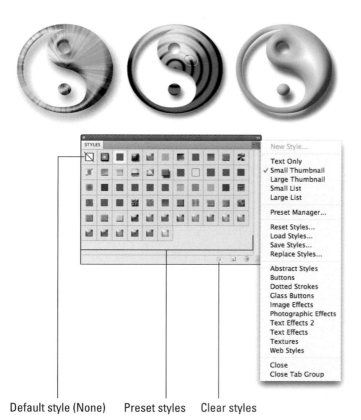

Default style (None)   Preset styles   Clear styles

Figure 4-16: Use the Styles panel to apply effects such as Angled Spectrum (left), Striped Cone (center), and Star Glow (right).

Here are the many splendid ways to apply a preset style:

- Select the layer and click a style in the Styles panel.

- Drag and drop a style from the Styles panel onto a layer in the Layers panel.

- Drag and drop a style directly onto the image window. When your cursor is over the element to which you want to apply the style, release your mouse button.

- Double-click the layer thumbnail in the Layers panel. Select Styles in the upper-left side of the Layer Style dialog box. Choose a style from the panel. Click OK to close the Layer Style dialog box.

✏ If you're using a Pen or shape tool, select the Shape Layer option. Then, select a style from the Style picker drop-down panel on the Options bar before drawing the shape.

By default, applying a style over another style replaces it. To add a style along with another, hold down the Shift key while clicking or dragging the style.

Managing preset styles

Here are some additional points to remember when using the Styles panel. You can do any of the following:

✏ **Load another Style preset library.** In the Styles panel, the Style picker drop-down panel in the Options bar, or the Styles panel in the Layer Style dialog box, you can select Load Styles from the panel pop-up menu to add a library to your current preset list. (Refer to Figure 4-16.) Select the library and click Load. You can also select Replace Styles. Even easier, just select a preset library from the bottom of the menu and click OK to replace or append your current list.

✏ **Use the Preset Manager to load Style preset libraries.** You can also rename, delete, and save whole libraries of presets. See Book I, Chapter 5.

✏ **Return to the default library of presets.** Select Reset Styles from the Styles panel pop-up menu.

✏ **From the Styles panel pop-up menu, select a viewing option for your panel.** You can select Small or Large Thumbnail or Small or Large List. And, of course, there's also Text Only, but what fun is it if you can't see the presets?

✏ **Rename a preset style.** Although there are a lot of ways to rename a preset style, it's easiest to double-click the style in the Styles panel. If you're in Thumbnail view, type a new name in the dialog box and click OK. If the view is set to Small List or Large List, simply type a new name directly in the Styles panel and press Enter (Return on the Mac).

✏ **Save a set of preset styles as a library.** Select Save Styles from the Styles panel pop-up menu, from the Styles panel of the Layer Style dialog box pop-up menu, or from the Style picker drop-down panel pop-up menu on the Options bar. Name the library, navigate to the Styles folder in the Presets folder in the Photoshop folder, and click Save.

✏ **Delete a preset style.** Drag the style to the trash can icon in the Styles panel or Alt-click (Option-click on the Mac) the style. You can also select Delete Style from the Styles panel of the Layer Style dialog box or the Style picker drop-down panel on the Options bar.

↙ **Clear a style (that is, remove it from the layer).** Select your desired layer in the Layers panel and click the Clear Style button in the Styles panel. You can also click the Default Style (None) swatch in the stand-alone Styles panel or the ones located in the Layer Style dialog box or on the Options bar.

↙ **Change the style or color of the currently active shape layer.** Click the link icon on the Options bar and select a different style or color. This option allows you to experiment with different styles for that shape.

Conversely, if you deselect the link icon, Photoshop doesn't change the style of the active shape layer when you select a different style. This option allows you to select a different style or color for a new shape layer without affecting the previous shape layer.

Saving your own style

If you get bored using the preset style libraries, or if you really went to town and created a custom style that you think is so fabulous that you'll want to use it again and again, you can easily save it to the Styles panel. Just follow these steps to save a custom style:

1. **Create your own custom style by applying layer effects and/or styles to your layer.**

   Starting with an existing preset style and modifying the settings to suit your needs is also easy.

2. **After you complete your style, click the Create New Style button in the Styles panel or select New Style from the Styles panel pop-up menu.**

   You can also simply click in an empty space in the Styles panel. Or you can double-click the fx icon or effect name to open the Layer Style dialog box, in which you can click the New Style button.

3. **In the New Style dialog box, shown in Figure 4-17, name your style and select your desired options.**

   The Include Layer Effects check box includes any effects you applied via the Effects section of the Layer Style dialog box — drop shadows, bevels, and so on.

   The Include Layer Blending Options check box includes any blending you did by using the Blending Options section of the Layer Styles panel. Photoshop adds your new style to the end of the Styles panel. If you want to edit your custom style, you must select each individual effect in the Layers panel and adjust the settings in the Layer Styles dialog box.

In the Styles panel, Alt-click (Option-click on the Mac) to create a new style and bypass the dialog box. Your style gets the default name of Style 1.

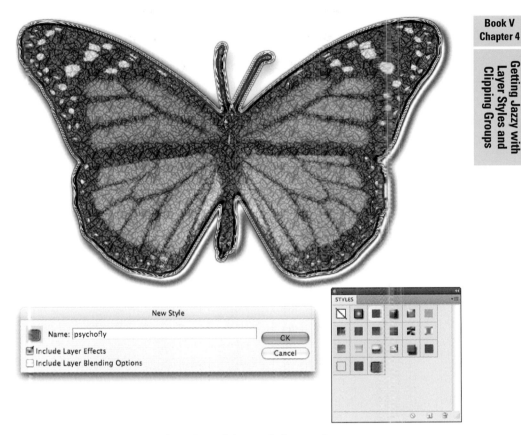

Figure 4-17: Create a custom style and save it in your Styles panel.

Clipping Layers into Masks

In a *clipping mask,* the bottommost layer (also known as the *base layer*) acts as a mask for the layers above it. The layers in the group clip to the opaque areas of the base layer and don't show over the transparent areas of the base layer.

At this point, you might be saying, "Huh?" Instead of trying to decipher the definition, a better way to understand a clipping mask is to just create one. Follow the steps in this section, and I know that rather than "Huh," you'll be saying "Yeah, baby," just like Austin Powers.

Creating a clipping mask works well if you want to fill type with different images on multiple layers.

Managing clipping masks

Here's some clipping mask trivia:

- To remove a single layer from the clipping mask, you can simply Alt-click (Option-click on the Mac) the line between the two layers in the Layers panel. Or you can select the layer and choose Layer⇨Release Clipping Mask. Both commands remove the selected layer and any layers above it from the clipping mask.

- To ungroup all the layers in the clipping mask, select the clipped layer and choose Layer⇨Release Clipping Mask.

- You can also apply clipping masks to adjustment and fill layers. If you clip between a regular layer and an adjustment layer, or a regular layer and a fill layer, the adjustment or fill layer affects only the pixels of the adjacent underlying layer, rather than all the underlying layers. For more on adjustment and fill layers, see Book V, Chapter 1.

Using the steps that follow, I created a new document with a white background. I took the Custom Shape tool, selected the Fill Region option (see Book IV, Chapter 1 for more on shapes), and drew a heart on my second layer. I added a drop shadow and inner bevel to my heart for added dimension, but this step isn't mandatory.

I then opened an image of an island and dragged and dropped that image onto my composite. I opened an image of some dolphins, selected a couple dolphins, and dragged and dropped them onto my composite.

And, finally, I created some type and applied a drop shadow and inner bevel to the type, as shown in Figure 4-18.

Follow these steps to create your own clipping mask:

1. **Open or create an image that has several layers.**

2. **Hold down Alt (Option on the Mac) and position your mouse cursor over the line dividing two layers in the Layers panel.**

   Your cursor changes to two overlapping circles with a small arrow icon. You can also choose Layer⇨Create Clipping Mask.

Figure 4-18: In a clipping mask, layers clip to the opaque areas of a base layer.

3. **Click your mouse button.**

   I did this three times: in between my type and the dolphin layer, in between the dolphin and the island layer, and in between the island layer and my heart shape. Notice how all my images and my type clip to the base layer (the heart shape) in the Layers panel. (Refer to Figure 4-18.)

   Nothing outside the boundaries of the heart shape is visible on any of the layers in the clipping mask, as shown in Figure 4-18. The down-pointing arrow icons beside each layer on the Layers panel indicate that the layers are clipped. The clipping mask takes on the opacity and blend mode of the base layer.

Putting It Together

Adding Text and Layer Styles to a Collage

If you've been reading Book V from the beginning, then you may have a nearly complete collage on your hands. If you're at all interested in using words with your images, then now (at the end of the project, not the beginning) is the time to add them. Adding type can turn a good composite into a dynamite and cohesive image that conveys exactly what you want. I'm no Shakespeare and can't help you create the perfect tag line, but I can show you how to add text to your collage. Adding layer styles gives you versatility in the kinds of effects you can apply to layers, so I show you how to apply those to a collage. To add and adjust type, follow these steps:

1. **Open the saved collage file.**

Make sure that the Layers panel is open.

2. **Select the Eyedropper tool from the Tools panel. Click a color in the collage that you like.**

The color you sampled is now the foreground color.

3. **Select the Type tool. On the Options bar, select a font, style, point size, and other formatting options.**

I recommend choosing an easy-to-read serif font and applying a bold style to it. I'm using Times Bold, and I set the point size to 100.

I set the Anti-Aliasing option to Crisp and the Alignment option to Left, but you can explore your options until you're dizzy (or your deadline passes).

4. **Click inside your image and type some text.**

I typed `Go outside` for my travel collage.

5. **Select the Move tool from the Tools panel and position the type in the collage.**

I put my text in the upper-left corner.

6. **Adjust your settings as you desire.**

If you want to add a second, smaller line of text, grab the Type tool again, click the image, and reduce the point size from the Options bar. You can change other settings, as well.

7. **When you're satisfied with your changes, click under the first line of text and type your next line.**

Under `Go outside`, I typed `and play`, as shown in the figure.

With the Move tool, fine-tune the position of the type.

When you're satisfied with the size, style, color, and appearance of the type in your collage, you can make some more large-scale changes by creating layer styles. Follow these steps:

1. **Add a drop shadow.**

Make sure that you select Use Global Light so that all the layers use the same angle.

In the Layers panel, select the layer that includes the first line of text. Then, choose Layer⇨Layer Style⇨Drop Shadow. Make sure the Drop Shadow box is selected in the left column.

You can change the angle so that the light source is coming from one direction or another. (Mine's set at 120% so that the light's coming from the upper-left.)

2. **Add bevels and embossing.**

Click the Bevel and Emboss style in the left column.

Make sure that you actually select the style and not just the box; otherwise, the right panel with all the options doesn't appear.

In my example, I selected Inner Bevel from the Style pop-up menu in the right panel. Then, I selected Chisel Soft from the Technique pop-up menu. My idea was to give the type a carved-in-stone look.

3. **Click OK when you're satisfied with the styles you've created in the layer so far.**

continued

continued

4. **Apply the same styles to the layer that includes the second line of text, as shown in the figure.**

To get the exact same settings without having to make every adjustment again, right-click (Control-click on the Mac) the fx icon on the first layer you worked on and select Copy Layer Style from the context menu that appears. Select the second type layer and right-click (Control-click on the Mac) on the layer name, and then select Paste Layer Style from the context menu that appears.

5. **Make any last adjustments and choose File⇨Save.**

You're all done. If you feel like it, keep adding to or refining the collage when you figure out new tricks.

Chapter 5: Working with Smart Objects

In This Chapter

✔ **Creating Smart Objects**

✔ **Converting Smart Objects**

✔ **Editing Smart Objects**

*W*ith the advent of Smart Objects, Photoshop has significantly cut your editing time while letting you transform your objects indefinitely without fear of quality loss. That's right. Vector files, raster files — it doesn't matter to these intelligent fellows. And with Smart Objects, you create the art once, and then if you want to show the art again, you use what are called *instances*. These instances can be linked to your original art, which makes editing a breeze. This chapter tells you all about this feature — the ultimate in digital recycling.

Introducing Smart Objects

A Smart Object is actually what Adobe refers to as a *container,* in which a bitmap (raster) or vector image's source data is embedded. So, in essence, a Smart Object is composed of two files, one inside the other. Adobe uses the analogy of a new file, the *child,* which is embedded into the original file, the *parent.* This source data of the child is contained in the Smart Object parent but keeps all its native characteristics and is fully editable.

Here are a few advantages of Smart Objects:

✔ **Transform with minimum degradation.** In Book III, Chapter 3, I warn you about the negative side of transformations. When transforming traditional layers, your image goes through the process of resampling, which then causes degradation of quality. With Smart Objects, you can perform multiple transformations on your artwork without losing any additional image quality. Photoshop does this by actually using your *original* source data to render the additional transformations.

✔ **Preserve nonnative file data.** Photoshop transforms any nonnative image information, such as Illustrator vector artwork, into a format it can recognize without altering the native data.

✔ **Edit the Smart Object, and all instances are dynamically updated.** If you make changes to the original Smart Object, all instances (duplicates of the original) are automatically changed, as well. No need to change them individually. This can be a real timesaver, especially if you've gone crazy with the number of instances you've used, such as on a map or Web home page.

✔ **Apply a Smart Filter.** Layers must first be converted to Smart Objects before you can apply a Smart Filter. Smart Filters are a totally non-destructive way to apply filters that can then be edited indefinitely. For details on this great feature, see Book VII, Chapter 1.

Creating Smart Objects

You can create a Smart Object in a few ways. You can import the artwork via the Place command. You can also copy and paste the artwork from Illustrator into Photoshop. Or you can convert a Photoshop layer into a Smart Object. Finally, you can create one Smart Object from another. I discuss the specific steps for each way in the following sections.

Placing artwork

You may not have much experience in using the Place command in Photoshop because most activities involve opening images and creating new ones. But with the advent of Smart Objects, you may call on this command more frequently. Follow these steps to place artwork:

1. **Choose File⇨New and create a new blank Photoshop document, using your desired size and settings.**

   If you're unsure about creating a new file, see Book I, Chapter 3. You can also use an existing Photoshop file.

2. **Choose File⇨Place. In the Place dialog box, locate and select your desired artwork. Click the Place button.**

   If your file is in any format besides Illustrator or PDF, it pops right onto your canvas, as shown in Figure 5-1. Note the bounding box and X around and across the image, which is an indication that the image has been placed.

Figure 5-1: Create a Smart Object by placing your artwork into a Photoshop file.

If your file is a native Illustrator or PDF file, the Open as Smart Object dialog box appears, asking you for additional information, as shown in Figure 5-2. If it's a multipaged PDF, you can select the page or image you want placed. Select your cropping options. Not sure what they mean? Just select one and view the thumbnail to see how the image appears in relationship to the page. By the way, you can also select between a Small, Large, and Fit Page thumbnail view.

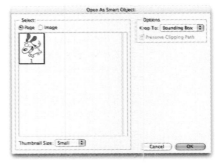

Figure 5-2: When placing an Illustrator or PDF file, specify your options in the Open as Smart Object dialog box.

If you happen to deselect the Create PDF Compatible File option when saving your native Illustrator file, you see a nasty warning in the Place PDF dialog box telling you to go back and resave your file with the option checked and then place the file again. Don't take it personally. Illustrator was programmed based on PDF core code and sometimes doesn't like it when you strip it of the connection.

You can also select the image in Adobe Bridge and choose File➪Place➪ In Photoshop. See Book I, Chapter 4 for details on working with Bridge.

3. **Using the bounding box, transform (scale, rotate, and so on) your image to your desired dimensions and then position it on your canvas, as shown in Figure 5-3.**

   Remember, you can rest assured that your transformations are applied without degrading the quality of your image.

   If your image is larger than the Photoshop canvas, it's automatically sized to fit within the canvas dimensions. If you need a refresher on transforming and moving, see Book III, Chapter 3.

Figure 5-3: Transform and position your image before committing it into your file.

   If you're placing a PDF, EPS (most of them), or native Illustrator file, specify the Anti-Alias option on the Options bar. Select it to create a softer, blended edge. Deselect it to produce a hard edge.

4. **After you have your image the way you want it, you can double-click inside the bounding box, press Enter (Return on the Mac), or click the Commit (check mark icon) button on the Options bar.**

   When the artwork is committed, the native file data is embedded into the Photoshop file, and the artwork is rasterized on its own layer. The Smart Object icon appears on those layers, as shown in Figure 5-4.

   If you change your mind and don't want to commit the image, press Esc or click the Cancel button on the Options bar.

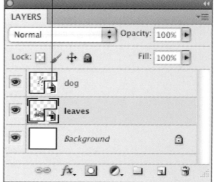

Figure 5-4: The Smart Object icon.

Copying and pasting

Before you copy and paste artwork from Illustrator into Photoshop as a Smart Object, be sure to check the PDF and AICB (no transparency support) options in the File Handling and Clipboard preferences in Illustrator.

Leave the default of Preserve Appearances and Overprints selected. By doing so, you can control how your artwork is rasterized in Photoshop. If left deselected, Photoshop rasterizes the art without your vital input. Follow these steps to copy and paste artwork as a Smart Object from Illustrator into Photoshop:

1. **Open your desired Adobe Illustrator file in Illustrator.**

2. **Select your artwork and choose Edit⇨Copy.**

3. **Switch to Photoshop. Open your desired Photoshop document or create a new document.**

4. **Choose Edit⇨Paste.**

5. **In the Paste dialog box, shown in Figure 5-5, select the Smart Object option and click OK.**

   Your image is imported and appears in a bounding box, and the Layers panel shows that you pasted the image as a Smart Object, as shown in Figure 5-5.

6. **Using the bounding box, transform (scale, rotate, and so on) your image to your desired dimensions and position it on your canvas.**

   Perspective, Distort, and Warp transformations are unavailable to Smart Objects.

Figure 5-5: Specify how you want the artwork pasted.

Because you chose Smart Object in the Paste dialog box in Step 4, remember that you can transform your artwork without degrading it before you place it into Photoshop. Like with the Place command, the native file data is embedded into the Photoshop file, and the art is rasterized on its own layer after the artwork is committed.

7. **Commit the artwork by double-clicking inside the bounding box, pressing Enter (Return on the Mac), or clicking the Commit (check mark icon) button on the Options bar.**

Converting a layer into a Smart Object and vice versa

If you want to convert a layer into a Smart Object, follow these steps:

1. **Select your desired layer in the Layers panel.**

2. **Choose Layer⇨Smart Objects⇨Convert to Smart Object.**

   You can also select the command from the Layers panel pop-up menu. After you convert a layer into a Smart Object, you see the Smart Object icon in the lower-right corner of the layer thumbnail.

You can also convert a Smart Object into a layer. You may want to do this if you need to paint on your artwork.

Follow these steps to make the conversion:

1. **Select your desired layer in the Layers panel.**
2. **Choose Layer⇨Rasterize⇨Smart Object.**

   Your Smart Object is rasterized at its current size, so be sure it's the size you want before you execute the command. Your Smart Object icon disappears, and you're left with a normal, run-of-the mill layer.

Creating one Smart Object from another

Sometimes, you may want to use one Smart Object as the basis for another. Depending on your needs, you can keep the new Smart Object linked to or unlinked from the original. If it remains linked, modifying the original automatically modifies the duplicate. If unlinked, you can modify the original without changing the duplicate. In addition, you're free to change the duplicate without worrying about affecting the original.

Follow these steps to create a Smart Object from another:

1. **Select the Smart Object layer in the Layers panel.**
2. **Create a duplicate Smart Object that's linked to or unlinked from the original:**

   - *An unlinked object:* Choose Layer⇨Smart Objects⇨New Smart Object via Copy.

   - *A linked object:* Choose Layer⇨New⇨Layer via Copy.

   A new Smart Object layer appears in the Layers panel, as shown in Figure 5-6.

You can also drag and release the Smart Object layer over the Create a New Layer icon at the bottom of the Layers panel. This action creates a duplicate Smart Object that's linked.

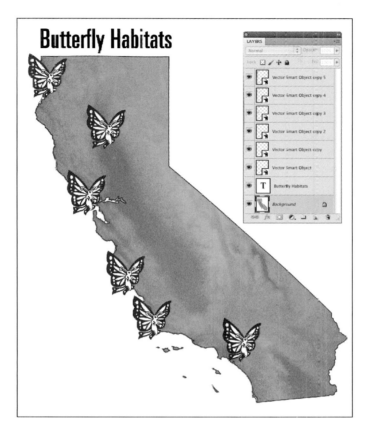

Figure 5-6: You can duplicate a Smart Object and either have it linked to or unlinked from its original.

Editing Smart Objects

One of the great things about Smart Objects is that you can edit the contents, or source data. If the source content is a vector-based PDF, AI, or EPS file and was prepared in Illustrator, it opens in that program. If the source content is raster-based, a Camera Raw file or a vector file (like a shape layer) and created in Photoshop, the file opens in Photoshop. (For details on vector versus raster images, see Book II, Chapter 1.)

Follow these steps to edit the contents of a Smart Object:

1. **In your document, select the Smart Object layer in the Layers panel.**

2. **Choose Layer⇨Smart Objects⇨Edit Contents.**

   Or you can simply double-click the Smart Objects layer thumbnail in the Layers panel.

   A dialog box appears, telling you to save your changes and save the file in the same location.

3. **Click OK to close the dialog box.**

   The Smart Object opens in the program in which it was created, either Illustrator or Photoshop.

4. **Edit your file *ad nauseam*.**

5. **Choose File⇨Save to incorporate the edits.**

6. **Close your source file.**

7. **Return to your Photoshop document, which contains your Smart Object.**

   If all goes as expected, all instances of the Smart Object are updated. For example, my butterflies went from purple in Figure 5-6 to blue in Figure 5-7.

Replacing contents

When replacing the contents of a Smart Object with new contents, you automatically update all instances of that Smart Object in your document, which can be a real productivity enhancer. Just follow these short steps:

Butterfly Habitats

Figure 5-7: The Photoshop document automatically reflects any editing you do to your Smart Object.

1. **Select the Smart Object layer in the Layers panel.**

2. **Choose Layer⇨Smart Objects⇨Replace Contents.**

3. **In the Place dialog box, locate your new file and click the Place button.**

4. **Click OK if you're presented with a dialog box, and the new contents pop into place, replacing the old contents, as shown in Figure 5-8.**

   All instances of that Smart Object are also updated in your document.

To replace the contents of a single instance of a Smart Object, you have to make sure that the Smart Object isn't linked to other Smart Objects. To create an unlinked Smart Object, select the Smart Object instance you want to change, choose Layer➪Smart Objects➪New Smart Object via Copy. Make your desired replacement and then delete the original Smart Object.

Butterfly Habitats

Figure 5-8: I replaced the contents of my blue butterflies with that of a rarer species.

Exporting contents

You can export your Smart Object and save it to a hard drive or external media. Photoshop exports the contents of your Smart Object in its original placed format, such as JPEG, native Illustrator (.ai), TIFF, PDF, and so on. Follow these steps:

1. **Select the Smart Object in the Layers panel.**

2. **Choose Layer➪Smart Objects➪Export Contents.**

3. **In the Save dialog box, navigate to your destination and click Save.**

   If your Smart Object was created from layers, it exports in the PSB format. Remember, you can open the .psb file only in Photoshop. It won't open in another program.

The last command in the Layer➪Smart Objects submenu is Stack Mode. Unfortunately, this command is available only in the Extended version. People in the science, forensics, medical, and pro video fields are probably thrilled over its capabilities. How about the rest of us? Well, using image stacks can help to decrease the noise in your images across multiple exposures. In this case, *noise* can be defined not just as the grainy or wavy little artifacts throughout your image, but also anything that you don't want in the picture — cars, birds, annoying people walking in front of your scenic shot. If this sounds like something worthwhile for your workflow, it may be worth checking out an upgrade.

Book VI
Channels and Masks

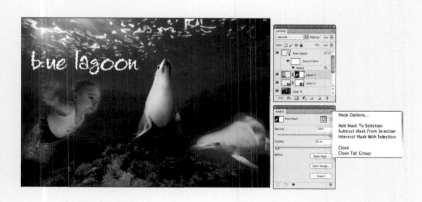

*1*f you have the basics down and are ready for something a little more challenging, this is your book. Here, I help you start working with channels and creating masks. Creating masks is one of the most accurate ways to make a selection and is especially useful in tackling more difficult selections.

In this book, I show you different ways of creating a mask, from quick masks to layer masks to channel masks. If you've ever flung your mouse or stylus pen in frustration because you couldn't select the hair on your loved one's photo, you'll be well-served by reading this book and getting up to speed on masking techniques.

Chapter 1: Using Channels

*I*f you're reading this, it probably means that you didn't quickly thumb through this chapter, say "Yuck, boorrrrringgg!" and move on to sexier topics such as blending, filtering, and retouching. You knew that would be a huge mistake.

The wonderful thing about channels is that they offer you greater control and selectivity when doing those very things — blending, filtering, and retouching. Channels give you one more level of control when editing your images. You can use individual channels for layer-blending options and filters, as well as starting points for masks.

Channels also come into play when saving selections for later use or for adding spot (custom) colors to your image. You can also use channels to turn color images into nicely contrasted grayscale images. And finally, you can play around with the colors in an image by mixing up the channels. So bear with me. The topic of channels may be a bit dry and technical, but in the end, channels enable you to hold the envious title of Master Editor.

To understand how channels work, you'll find it helpful to know a few things about colors — specifically, the various color modes, which I cover in Book II, Chapter 2.

Understanding Channels

When you look at a color image, you see one big, 24-bit, composite collection of colored pixels. Technically speaking, however, Photoshop doesn't see that at all. Photoshop perceives a color image as individual bands of 8-bit, grayscale images. RGB images have three bands; CMYK images have four bands.

I know it's strange to think of a color image as being composed of several grayscale images, but it's true. Each one of these bands, or grayscale images, is a *channel*. Specifically, they're color channels. If you just can't get past the fact that a color image is the sum of several grayscale channels, as shown in Figure 1-1, then just think of channels as holding tanks for color data.

Purestock

Figure 1-1: A color image is composed of 8-bit grayscale images referred to as channels.

Another way of relating channels to the real world is in terms of hardware. Here's how the most common hardware handles color:

- When you offset-print a CMYK image, the process separates the colors (see Book IX, Chapter 1) into four colors — cyan, magenta, yellow, and black. Paper passes through four individual rollers on the printing press, and each roller contains one of those four colored inks.

- Scanners scan in RGB via a pass of red, green, and blue sensors over your image.

- Digital cameras capture images in RGB.

- CRT screens display images via red, green, and blue tubes.

In addition to color channels, there are channels called *alpha channels* (covered in the section "Introducing Alpha Channels," later in this chapter) and others called *spot channels* (discussed in Book IX, Chapter 1). Photoshop now supports up to 56 channels per file. So knock yourself out! Just remember that each channel you add increases your file size.

A little bit about bit depth

When you're standing around the water cooler or the color printer and hear people talking about a 1-bit or an 8-bit image, they're referring to something called bit depth. *Bit depth* measures how much color information is available to display and print each pixel. A higher bit depth means the image can display more information — specifically, more colors. For example, a 1-bit image can display two color values — black and white. That's why a purely black-and-white image is called a bitmap image. Likewise

✓ An 8-bit image can contain up to 256 grayscale levels (2^8). Grayscale images are 8 bit (1 channel, 8 bits).

✓ A 24-bit image can contain about 16 million colors (2^{24}). RGB images are 24 bit (3 channels × 8 bits).

✓ CMYK images are 32 bit (4 channels × 8 bits). CMYK images, however, are limited to the number of colors that are physically reproducible on paper, which is around 55,000.

✓ High Dynamic Range (HDR) images are 96 bit (3 channels [RGB] × 32 bits) Theoretically, they're capable of having about 65 million colors, but in reality, the maximum range is determined by what colors were captured by the camera.

Bit depths typically range from 1 to 64 bits.

Briefly, you can use alpha channels to create, store, and edit selections, defining them not by a selection outline, but by black, white, and varying shades of gray pixels — in other words, a grayscale image. Black pixels represent unselected areas of the image, white pixels represent selected areas, and gray pixels represent partially selected pixels.

You can create spot channels when you want to add a spot (or custom) color to your image. Spot colors are premixed inks often used in addition to or in lieu of CMYK colors.

All images, no matter what their color mode, have at least one channel. Grayscale, Bitmap, Duotone, and Indexed Color (for GIF Web images) modes have only one channel. RGB and CMYK images have three and four channels, respectively. They also contain a composite channel, which reflects the combination of the individual color channels and gives you the full color display.

Working with Channels

Like with layers (which I discuss in Book V), channels have their own panel that acts as command central for viewing, creating, and managing tasks. The first step is accessing channels by choosing Window⇨Channels. The Channels panel appears, as shown in Figure 1-2.

Viewing channels without a remote

Selecting a channel in the Channels panel automatically makes it appear in the image window. To select a channel, click the channel thumbnail or name in the panel. To select more than one channel, Shift-click. To show or hide a channel, click in the eye column in the far left of the panel. You can also drag through the column to hide or show the channels quickly.

CMYK, RGB, and Lab images have a *composite* channel, in addition to their individual channels. This composite channel is the combination of all the channels in the image and is named after the color mode. For example, the composite channel in Figure 1-2 is the first one, called CMYK.

Corbis Digital Stock

Figure 1-2: The Channels panel stores all the image's channels, from spot to alpha channels.

Changing the default channel view

The default setting is to view your channels in grayscale. You can, however, view them in color. To do so, choose Edit➪Preferences➪Interface (Photoshop➪Preferences➪Interface on the Mac) and select Show Channels in Color.

Although this option *graphically* exemplifies the way an image comprises separate color channels, it really does you no good if you want to work with your channels for editing. That's because the color view obscures details and makes measuring the impact of adjustments and filters more difficult. You need to see the channels in their true grayscale form for that.

If you select or show more than one channel, even in the default grayscale view, the channels always appear in color.

To change the size of the thumbnail that appears, select Panel Options from the Channels panel pop-up menu. Select your desired thumbnail size. If you're working with several channels and you have a dinosaur of a computer, you can also choose None to turn off the thumbnails — which improves performance.

Duplicating and deleting channels

Duplicating channels is something you may do quite often. I know I do. And deleting channels isn't just for neat freaks: Channels take up a lot of memory, so getting rid of the ones you no longer need is always good.

Here are some instances when duplicating channels is a good idea:

- **When you want to create a channel mask:** First, you find a suitable channel and then make a duplicate. (For more on this technique, see Book VI, Chapter 3.) You can use channel masks to select difficult elements involving fine details, such as hair, fur, smoke, and so on.

- **When you want to make a backup copy of the channel before doing some editing:** Having a backup, just to be on the safe side, is always a good idea. For example, you may want to apply an Unsharp Mask filter to one or two channels to improve the focus of the image. For more on the Unsharp Mask filter, see Book VII, Chapter 1.

- **To insert a copy of an alpha channel into another image:** For example, maybe you spent an hour creating elaborate alpha channels for shadows and highlights on a product photographed in flat lighting.

  You may have 12 products, all the same shape but different colors, that you need to apply those highlights and shadows to. Instead of re-creating the wheel each time, you could simply duplicate the alpha channels into each file.

Duplicating channels

To duplicate a channel, follow these short steps:

1. **Select your desired channel in the Channels panel.**

2. **Select Duplicate Channel from the panel pop-up menu.**

   The Duplicate Channel dialog box appears, as shown in Figure 1-3.

3. **In the Duplicate section, in the As field, name the channel.**

   You can also drag the channel to the New Channel icon at the bottom of the panel. If you do this, Photoshop provides a default name and bypasses Steps 3 through 6.

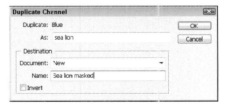

Figure 1-3: Name and provide a destination for your duplicate channel.

   You can also duplicate a channel to another image by dragging the channel. Open your destination image and drag the desired channel from your current image into the destination image window. The duplicated channel appears in the Channels panel.

4. **In the Destination section, select a file from the Document drop-down list.**

Or choose New to create a new image.

You can choose your current image or any open image with the same pixel dimensions as your current image. (For more on pixel dimensions, see Book II, Chapter 1.)

If you choose New, Photoshop creates a new image that has a single channel. Provide a name for the file.

5. **Select Invert if you want to reverse the selected and unselected areas of the duplicate channel.**

You use the Invert option primarily when you duplicate an existing alpha channel. For more on alpha channels, see the section "Introducing Alpha Channels," later in this chapter.

6. **Click OK.**

The dialog box closes. Your duplicate channel appears in the Channels panel, as shown in Figure 1-4.

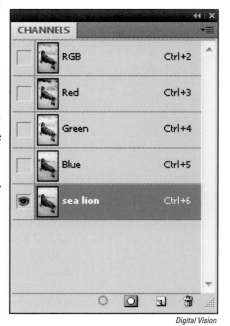

Digital Vision

Figure 1-4: You can duplicate channels for masking, as well as for backup purposes.

Replacing one channel over another

To replace the contents of one channel with another, you can use the copy-and-paste method. In your current image, select your desired channel in the Channels panel. Choose Select➪All and then Edit➪Copy. Select the channel in the destination image that you want to replace and choose Edit➪Paste. The pasted content of the channel replaces the original content.

Deleting unwanted channels

To delete an unwanted channel — something you definitely want to do because channels can eat up a lot of space — select the channel in the Channels panel and do one of the following:

✔ Drag the channel to the trash at the bottom of the panel.

✔ Select Delete Channel from the panel pop-up menu.

✔ Click the trash and then click Yes in the dialog box.

✔ Alt-click (Option-click on the Mac) the trash.

Rearranging and renaming channels

Although you can't shuffle or rename color channels, you can do so with spot and alpha channels. To move a spot or alpha channel, simply drag it up or down in the Channels panel. When you see a dark line appear where you want the channel to go, release your mouse button. You can move a spot or alpha channel above a color channel only in a multichannel image. In short, in a multichannel image, each channel becomes an independent spot channel, and the channels no longer have a relationship with each other. Multichannel images don't support layers. For more details, see Book II, Chapter 2.

To rename a spot or alpha channel, double-click the name in the Channel panel and type a new name. You can also select Channel Options from the panel pop-up menu.

Splitting channels

You can split the channels of your image into separate images in separate files. For example, in Figure 1-5, you see the Red, Green, Blue, Alpha, and Spot channels split into individual channels. Choose Split Channels from the panel pop-up menu. When you do so, your original image closes. The channel files have the name of your original image plus the channel name. You can split channels only on a flattened image — in other words, an image that has no individual layers.

Corbis Digital Stock

Figure 1-5: Be sure to save all changes in your original image before you split it because Photoshop closes your file.

You might want to split channels if you need to save your original file in a format that doesn't preserve channels — such as EPS, which doesn't support alpha channels. Or you may want to split channels to merge them later on.

Merging channels

You can merge channels into a single image. The channels must be opened as separate images, in grayscale mode, and have the same pixel dimensions. You can merge channels only when they're flattened images and have no layers.

Merging color channels can create some unique special effects. For example, by mismatching your channels when you merge them, you can create bizarre, and sometimes beautiful, color shifts.

To merge channels, follow these steps:

1. **Open your split channel files and activate any one of them.**

2. **Choose Merge Channels from the Channels panel pop-up menu.**

3. **In the Merge Channels dialog box, choose your desired color mode, as shown in Figure 1-6.**

   Any modes that are unavailable are grayed out. You may not have enough channels for the grayed-out modes.

Figure 1-6: Choose the color mode and number of channels in this dialog box.

4. **Enter the number of channels you want.**

   When you choose your mode in Step 3, Photoshop automatically fills in the number of channels for the mode. If you deviate and enter something different, the file becomes a multichannel file.

5. **Click OK.**

6. **Select your channels in the dialog box that appears.**

   In my example, the Merge CMYK Channels dialog box appears. If you want to merge the channels normally, make sure that each channel matches (Red for Red, and so on). If you want to rearrange the channels, you can mix them, as I did in Figure 1-7, so that the Cyan channel is mixed with the Magenta channel, and so on.

7. **If you're merging into a multi-channel image, click Next.**

   Repeat this step for each channel.

8. **Click OK.**

   You've now merged your files into a single image, which appears in your Photoshop window.

Figure 1-7: You can mismatch your channels when merging them to create a unique effect.

Photoshop closes individual channel files and merges any spot channels as alpha channels.

Check out Figure 1-8 to see how my sunflower went from yellow to magenta just by merging the layers a little differently.

If you have an image that includes alpha or spot channels, select Multichannel from the Mode drop-down list in Step 3; otherwise, Photoshop doesn't include those channels in the merged image. After you merge the image, Photoshop gives all the channels the names Alpha 1, Alpha 2, Alpha 3, and so on. To get back to a color composite, choose Image➪Mode➪RGB Color or CMYK Color.

Original

Split and merged

Photodisc/Getty Images

Figure 1-8: When you split and merge channels, you can create botanical specimens from another world.

Using Painting and Editing Tools with Channels

Sometimes, it's better to edit individual channels rather than the composite image. Mediocre flatbed scanners often reproduce, and digital cameras sometimes capture, an image that's slightly soft or out of focus. You may want to counteract that effect by applying an Unsharp Mask or Smart Sharpen filter. Before you do, you should examine each channel separately. You may find that the Blue channel contains a lot of garbage — artifacts, dithering, and other nasty crud.

Blue channels are notorious for acquiring this junk, so try to avoid sharpening this channel unless you *really* want to accentuate what's already ugly.

Instead of applying the Unsharp Mask or Smart Sharpen filter on Blue channels, select the Red and Green channels in the Channels panel and then choose Filter➪Sharpen➪Unsharp Mask or Smart Sharpen. Similarly, you can apply a Gaussian Blur filter to a channel to soften the unsightly pattern (called a *moiré* pattern) caused by scanning a halftone. (See Book VII, Chapter 1 for more on moiré patterns, and filters are covered throughout Book VI.)

Although Unsharp Mask, Smart Sharpen, and Gaussian Blur are a few corrective filters that you'll use frequently, I also find it useful to apply a special-effect filter to individual channels. Sometimes, applying a filter to the composite image produces an effect that's, well, overdone. Applying the filter to one or two channels can produce an effect that's subtler and less in-your-face. For example, in Figure 1-9, I applied a filter to just the Blue channel for the flower on the top. Using individual channels can also be useful for applying filters that produce monochromatic images, such as the Graphic Pen or Photocopy filters. (Be sure your foreground and background colors are black and white.) If you apply the filter to the entire image, you get a black-and-white image. If you apply it to an individual channel, you retain some color.

You can select a color channel and then edit that channel by using a painting or editing tool in the image. Keep these facts in mind:

- Painting with white adds the color channel's color at full intensity in the composite image.

- Painting with black removes the color in the composite image.

- Painting with a value of gray adds color at varying levels of intensity in the composite image.

Photodisc/Getty Images

Figure 1-9: By editing individual color channels, you can selectively and subtly apply filters (top) or adjust color (bottom).

For example, if you paint with white on the Blue channel in an existing image, Photoshop adds more blue to the color composite image. But if you paint with black, Photoshop adds yellow to the image because when you remove blue, you're left with the opposite (or complementary) color — yellow. To perform this channel magic, select the Brush tool and then select your desired brush size from the Options bar. Select your desired color in the Color panel. Select the channel you want to edit in the Channels panel and paint on the image. You can see the results by selecting the composite channel in the Channels panel. Refer to Figure 1-9 to see how I gave a flower a channel-color makeover.

The results are a little different if you try this technique on a blank CMYK canvas. For example, when you paint with black on the Cyan channel, your composite color image displays cyan. When you paint with white, you get no change.

Introducing Alpha Channels

You use alpha channels for selections that are incredibly detailed or that you want to save and reuse. To make that selection, an alpha channel uses black, white, and shades of gray to create a mask. The selected pixels are white, and unselected pixels are black. For example, in the alpha channel of the image shown in Figure 1-10, the selection includes the lanterns and trees;

they appear white in the alpha channel. If an alpha channel includes gray areas, those areas are partially selected (or partially unselected, depending on whether you think the glass is half full or half empty).

Original image

Alpha channel mask

Corbis Digital Stock

Figure 1-10: The alpha channel makes selecting this shape much easier than using the Lasso or Magic Wand tool.

Book VI
Chapter 1

Using Channels

You can create a mask by first duplicating a color channel and then editing that channel with painting and editing tools and filters. (See Book VI, Chapter 3 for the details.) You can also create an alpha channel by saving a selection you've created. After you create a channel mask or save a selection as an alpha channel, you can load that channel to use it as a selection in any image. The following sections explain how to save a selection as an alpha channel and load a selection.

Saving a selection as an alpha channel

One of the great things about alpha channels is that you can save them and then retrieve them time and time again, which can be especially handy if you've taken a lot of time and effort to create the selection. Why reinvent the wheel if you want to select the element again in the future? Sure, you can create a mask by using Quick Mask mode and Color Range (see Book VI, Chapter 2), but those masks are only temporary.

After you make the initial selection, saving it is a piece of cake. Follow these steps:

1. **Make a selection in your image. (See Book III for help.)**

2. **Choose Select⇨Save Selection.**

   You can also click the Save Selection as Channel button (a circle on a square icon) at the bottom of the Channels panel. A new channel appears with the default name of Alpha 1, bypassing Steps 3 and 4.

3. **Select a destination image in the Document pop-up menu.**

   You can select your current image, any other open image that has the same pixel dimensions, or a new image.

4. **Select a destination channel from the Channel pop-up menu.**

   You can select a new channel, an existing alpha channel, or a layer mask. (See Book VI, Chapter 3 for more on layer masks.)

   • If you select New, name the channel.

   • If you select an existing alpha channel or layer mask, select your desired operation: Replace, Add To, Subtract From, or Intersect. These commands add to, subtract from, or intersect your current selection with the existing alpha channel.

5. **Click OK.**

   Your alpha channel is complete and appears in the Channels panel, as shown in Figure 1-11.

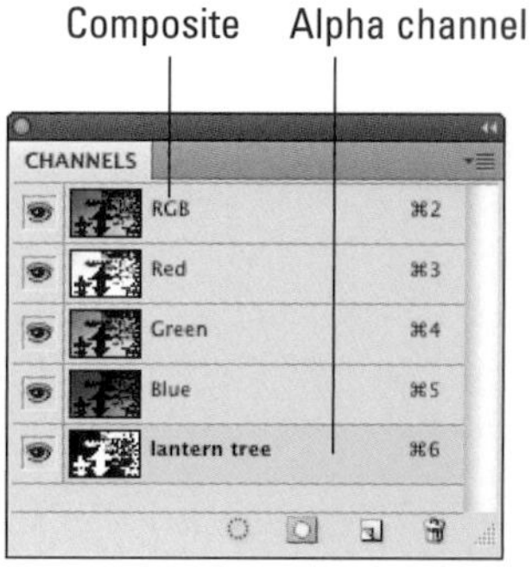

Composite   Alpha channel

Figure 1-11: Saving your selection as an alpha channel allows you to efficiently reuse the selection.

Loading an alpha channel

If you've gone through the trouble of creating an alpha channel, it's no doubt because you want to easily load (or access) the selection again and again. To load an alpha channel, use any one of these many methods:

🖰 Choose Select⇨Load Selection. In the Load Selection dialog box, select your document and channel. Click Invert to swap selected and unselected areas. If your image has an active selection, choose how you want to combine the selections.

🖰 Select the alpha channel in the Channels panel, click the Load Channel as Selection icon at the bottom of the panel, and then click the composite channel.

🖰 Drag the channel to the Load Channel as Selection icon.

🖰 Ctrl-click (⌘-click on the Mac) the alpha channel in the Channels panel.

🖰 Ctrl+Shift-click (⌘+Shift-click on the Mac) to add the alpha channel to an active selection.

🖰 Ctrl+Alt-click (⌘+Option-click on the Mac) to subtract the alpha channel from an active selection.

🖰 Ctrl+Alt+Shift-click (⌘+Option+Shift-click on the Mac) to intersect the alpha channel with an active selection.

Adding channels can start to bloat your file size, so use them judiciously. The Photoshop native format and TIFF format compress channel information and therefore are good file formats to use when working with a lot of channels. The only formats that preserve alpha channels are Photoshop, TIFF, PDF, PICT, Pixar, Photoshop Raw. BMP, TGA (Targa), and PSB (Photoshop large format).

Using the Channel Mixer

The Channel Mixer actually does what its name implies — it mixes color channels. This feature lets you repair bad channels and produce grayscale images from color images. It also allows you to create tinted images and more intense special effects. Finally, it allows you to do the more mundane tasks of swapping or duplicating channels.

Although some Photoshop elitists worldwide tout the Channel Mixer as an advanced feature not to be mucked with by amateurs, I say, "Give it a whirl." Intimidation is a nasty roadblock to creative fun. Just make a backup copy of an image before diving into the mix by following these steps:

1. **Select the composite channel in the Channels panel.**

   If you have an RGB image, the composite channel is the RGB channel; for CMYK images, it's the CMYK channel.

2. **Choose Image⇨Adjustments⇨ Channel Mixer.**

   The Channel Mixer dialog box appears, as shown in Figure 1-12.

3. **If desired, select a Preset from the pop-up menu.**

   CS5 provides an assortment of Black and White presets you can use to convert your color images to grayscale. This is a great conversion method because it preserves detail and provides very good contrast control.

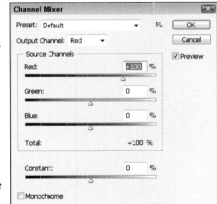

Figure 1-12: Among its many capabilities, the Channel Mixer enables you to repair bad channels.

4. **For Output Channel, select the channel in which to blend one or more source (existing) channels.**

For example, if your Blue channel is lousy, select it from the Output Channel drop-down list. Note that if you're using one of the black and white presets, you have only the Gray channel available.

5. **Drag any source channel's slider to the left to decrease the channel's effect on the Output channel or drag to the right to increase the effect.**

Because my Blue channel contains artifacts and dithering picked up by the scanner, I'm raising the Red and Green values from 0% to 25% and lowering the Blue value from 100% to 50%. To retain good contrast, try to use a combo of Red, Green, and Blue values that add up to close to 100%.

You can also enter a value from –200% to +200%. Using a negative value inverts the color data of the source channel.

6. **Tinker with the Constant option to add a Black or White channel of varying opacity.**

This option adjusts the grayscale value of the selected Output channel. Drag the slider to a negative value to get a Black channel. Positive values give a White channel.

This option brightens or darkens the overall image, but it may cause strange color shifts if adjusted to the extreme. I recommend leaving it at 0 most of the time. But try it. It may help.

7. **Select Monochrome to apply the same settings to all output channels, producing a color image that has only values of gray.**

This is another great way to produce a grayscale image from a color image. Adjust the individual sliders to mix the values until you're satisfied with the contrast.

You can save (and load) any of your custom settings by clicking the Preset Option button just to the left of the OK button.

8. **Click OK to exit the Channel Mixer.**

After you exit the Channel Mixer, choose Image⇨Mode⇨Grayscale to complete the conversion.

If you select and then deselect the Monochrome option, you can modify the blend of each channel separately. By doing so, you can create color images that appear to be hand-tinted with color inks. Go for the subtle treatment or a more intensely colored look.

Swapping color channels can produce some bizarre color effects. For example, try selecting the Red channel from the Output Channel drop-down list. Set the Red source channel to 0 and then set the Green source channel to 100. Try other combinations, Green for Blue, Blue for Red, and so on. Sometimes, they can be downright freakish, but occasionally you may stumble on one that's worthy.

Putting It Together

Giving Flat Art Highlights and Shadows

Sometimes, you need to give your art — whether it's a photo or another type of image — a little shine and shadow to bring it to life. You can do this by creating and saving your selections as alpha channels and filling them with translucent color. The great thing about alpha channels is that because you save them with your document, you can use them time and time again. Just follow these steps:

Book VI
Chapter 1

Using Channels

1. **Create a simple piece of artwork to use as a basis for your shadows and highlights.**

I created a pool ball by creating two layers. On each layer, I used the Elliptical Marquee tool to create different-sized circles. I filled each circle with a separate color, as shown in the figure. To follow along with these steps, you can download this image from this book's Web site. (See the Introduction for details.)

2. **Choose Window⇨Channels.**

The Channels panel appears.

Be sure to keep this panel visible because you'll be creating new channels for the highlights.

3. **Select the Pen tool from the Tools panel and create a path for the highlight.**

I created a path for the highlight on the top-left portion of the ball in my example, assuming that the light source is coming from the upper-left corner. If the Pen tool seems like a foreign object to you, check out Book III, Chapter 2.

4. **Choose Window⇨Paths.**

The Paths panel appears.

5. **Click the Load Path as Selection icon (a dotted circle) at the bottom of the Paths panel.**

Your work path disappears and a selection marquee appears.

6. **Choose Select⇨Save Selection.**

The Save Selection dialog box appears.

continued

continued

7. **Name the channel. Make sure to select New Channel under Operation and click OK.**

An additional channel appears in the Channels panel, as shown in the preceding figure. This new channel is the alpha channel — your saved selection.

8. **Click the Create a New Layer icon (the dog-eared page) in the Layers panel. Double-click the layer name and rename it.**

I named mine *large highlight.*

Putting your highlights and shadows on separate layers is important so that you can apply different opacity settings and also retain the ability to tweak them later, if needed.

9. **Choose Edit⇨Fill, select the White option for Contents, and leave all the other options at their default settings. Click OK to close the Fill dialog box.**

Your highlight is now filled with white. Don't worry; it won't stay this opaque.

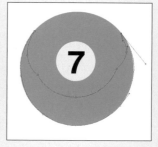

10. **In the Layers panel, adjust the Opacity setting to 50%.**

The highlight now appears translucent. (Refer to the preceding figure.)

11. **Select the Pen tool and create a path for the highlight on the bottom of the object, as shown in the figure.**

Make sure the path matches up to the edge of the object. Use the Direct Selection tool if you need to adjust the anchor points or curve segments of the path.

12. **In the Paths panel, click the third icon from the left at the bottom of the panel.**

The work path disappears, and a selection marquee appears.

13. **Choose Select⇨Save Selection. In the Save Selection dialog box that appears, name the channel. Make sure to select New Channel under Operation and click OK.**

Mine is called *bottom highlight*. Another alpha channel appears in the Channels panel.

14. **Repeat Steps 8 through 10, but adjust the opacity to only 30% as shown in the figure.**

15. **Use the Pen tool to create a path for the smaller shadow.**

For example, I created a path on the bottom-right portion of the ball.

16. **Load the path as a selection in the Paths panel and choose Select⇨Modify⇨Feather. In the Feather Selection dialog box, enter 3 pixels and click OK.**

The idea is to give the shadow a softer edge.

17. **Repeat Steps 6 through 10, but fill the selection with black, rather than white, and adjust the opacity to 20%.**

The shadow is shown in the figure.

18. **Use a selection tool to add a cast shadow.**

In my example, I used the Elliptical Marquee tool to create an ellipse at the base of the ball by holding down Alt (Option on the Mac) and dragging the mouse. The resulting selection is shown in the figure.

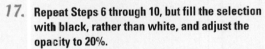

Then, I feathered the selection 25 pixels before I saved the selection.

The cast shadow needs to have really fuzzy edges, thus the large number of pixels for the feather.

19. **Repeat Steps 8 and 9, filling the selection with black.**

My highlighted and shadowed pool ball is ready to roll, shown in the figure.

If your cast shadow layer is above your object, you have to change the stacking order and move your shadow layer so that it's below your object.

Now that you've spent all this time on the front end creating your alpha channels, you can save time on the back end by using those alpha channels to apply highlights and shadows to similar artwork.

continued

continued

20. **To load alpha channels, choose Select⇨Load Selection and select an alpha channel from the Channel pop-up menu. Then, repeat the applicable steps for creating new layers, filling them with color, and adjusting their opacity.**

In my example, I took the highlights and shadows I created with lucky pool ball number 7 and loaded them as alpha channels in pool ball number 5.

Chapter 2: Quick-and-Dirty Masking

In This Chapter

↙ **Using Quick Masks**

↙ **Working with Color Range**

↙ **Selecting by erasing**

Masking is essentially just another way of making a selection. Instead of defining your selection with a selection outline, masks define your selection with up to 256 levels of gray, which allows you to have varying levels of selection. Photoshop *masks* (or protects) unselected pixels from any commands you execute. Photoshop doesn't mask selected pixels, making them fair game to any executed commands.

Different types of masks have different purposes — channel masks, layer masks, and vector masks. You can use them to temporarily make a selection, save and load selections, define vector shapes, selectively apply an adjustment layer or filter, blend one layer into another, and so on. Although selecting with the Marquee, Lasso, Magic Wand, and Pen tools can be fine, you'll soon find that these tools have a limited repertoire: You can't use them with much accuracy on more complex images. That's when you turn to masking.

Most things that pack a powerful punch are either expensive or hard to master, or both. Well, you already forked out a pretty penny for Photoshop. And yes, masking isn't for those who get their selections via a drive-thru window. To help you with the learning curve, in this chapter I ease you into masking by using Photoshop's automated masking tools. Although they aren't quite as accurate as the hardcore masking I cover in Book VI, Chapter 3, they're easier on you, and with certain images (or a serious time crunch), the quick-and-dirty masking tools get the job done.

Working with Quick Masks

As you can probably guess from the name, Quick Masks allow you to create and edit selections quickly without having to bother with the Channels panel. Although you don't really create an end-product mask per se, the way you go about getting your selection is "masklike." They're also user-friendly in that they allow you to see your image while you're working. You can begin your Quick Mask by using a selection tool or a painting tool. After you have your Quick Mask, you can edit the mask by using any painting or editing tool.

Quick Masks are temporary, so if you create one you really like, be sure to choose Select➪Save Selection at the end of the following steps. (Note that you have to be out of Quick Mask mode to do this.) That way, you can save the selection as an alpha channel. For more on saving selections as alpha channels, see Book VI, Chapter 1.

Follow these steps to create your very own Quick Mask:

1. **Open a new document and, using any selection tool, select the element you want in your image.**

   Don't worry about getting the selection perfect. You can fine-tune your selection after you have the Quick Mask in place. Note that you can also just paint your mask from scratch. But I think that starting with a selection is easier.

2. **Click the Edit in Quick Mask Mode button in the Tools panel (or press the Q key).**

   If your Quick Mask settings are at the default, a color overlay covers and protects the area outside the selection, as shown in Figure 2-1. The selected pixels are unprotected.

3. **Refine the mask by using a painting or editing tool.**

   Paint with black to add to the mask, thereby making the selection smaller. Even though you're painting with black, your strokes show up as a red overlay, as shown in Figure 2-2. This red overlay is a visual carryover from back in the day when artists used Rubylith (red transparent material) to mask portions of their art during airbrushing. Paint with white to delete from the mask, making the selection larger. Paint with a shade of gray to partially select the pixels. Partially selected pixels take on a semitransparent look, perfect for feathered edges.

Digital Vision

Figure 2-1: When using a Quick Mask, a color overlay represents the unselected (or protected) areas.

4. **After you finish editing your mask, shown in Figure 2-3, click the Edit in Standard Mode button in the Tools panel to exit the Quick Mask.**

   You can also press the Q key.

   The overlay disappears, and a selection outline appears. Your selection is ready and waiting for your next command. The selection outline correlates with the unmasked or selected areas of the Quick Mask. Don't be surprised if the wispy or soft edges you so diligently selected aren't readily apparent when you switch back to normal editing mode. When you composite your selected image with another, your hard quick-masking work will be evident.

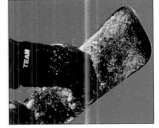

Digital Vision

Figure 2-2: Clean up your Quick Mask.

TIP

You can change Quick Mask options by double-clicking the Quick Mask Mode button in the Tools panel. When you add a Quick Mask to a selection, by default a red overlay covers the masked area. The overlay has an opacity setting of 50%. In addition to changing the color (to provide better contrast with your image, perhaps) and opacity of the overlay, you can also choose whether you want the overlay to represent the masked (unselected, protected) areas or the selected (unprotected) areas.

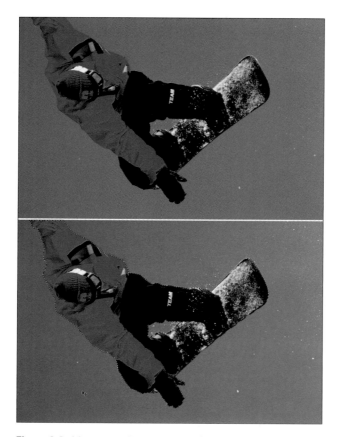

Figure 2-3: After you refine your mask (top), click the Edit in Standard Mode button (Q) to convert your mask into a selection outline (bottom).

Using the Color Range Command

The Color Range command allows you to select similarly colored pixels in a selection or within an entire image. You can think of it as a smarter Magic Wand tool (which I talk about in Book III, Chapter 1). Unlike the Magic Wand tool, however, Color Range lets you adjust your selection before you ultimately get the selection outline. It does this by using Fuzziness (a cousin of Tolerance, also discussed in Book III, Chapter 1), which allows you to select colors relative to how closely they resemble the sampled colors. Photoshop selects all the identical colors, partially selects similar colors, and doesn't select dissimilar colors. You adjust the fuzziness, and Photoshop adjusts the selection.

Starting with Color Range basics

Here are some Color Range command tips before you get started:

↗ You can save and load Color Range settings by clicking the appropriate buttons in the dialog box. But heck, after you have a selection, you can also choose Select⇨Save Selection to save it as an alpha channel.

↗ You can select a color range based on preset colors or tones that you choose from the Select drop-down list. For example, choosing red automatically selects all the red in the image. Choosing midtones selects all the medium-range tones in the image. And Out-of-Gamut (only available for RGB and Lab modes) selects all colors that can't be printed by using CMYK colors. For more on modes, see Book II, Chapter 2.

If you choose the Color Range command when you have an active selection, Photoshop selects only colors within the selection outline and ignores the rest of your image.

Executing the Color Range command

Follow these steps to work with the Color Range command:

1. **Choose Select⇨Color Range.**

   The Color Range dialog box appears in full glory.

2. **Choose Sampled Colors from the Select drop-down list and then select the Eyedropper tool in the dialog box.**

3. **Select a display option — Selection or Image.**

   I recommend leaving the setting at the default of Selection so that you can see the mask while you build it. You can toggle between the two views by pressing Ctrl (⌘ on the Mac).

4. **Either in the image itself or in the image preview in the Color Range dialog box, click to sample your desired colors.**

   The image preview changes to a mask. Black areas show unselected pixels, white areas show selected pixels, and gray areas show partially selected pixels.

   Your goal is to try to make what you want to select all white and what you don't want to select all black, as shown in Figure 2-4. And if you want some things partially selected, they can remain gray.

Figure 2-4: When using the Color Range command, your desired selection area appears white in the preview box.

5. **Adjust the selection by adding or deleting colors.**

   You can select or delete as many colors in your image as you want.

   Use the Add to Sample tool (the plus eyedropper icon) to add, and use the Subtract from Sample tool (the minus eyedropper icon) to delete.

   You can be lazy like me and just stick with the regular eyedropper icon. Simply hold down Shift+Alt (Shift+Option on the Mac) to add and delete.

6. **Fine-tune the range of colors by dragging the Fuzziness slider.**

   The Fuzziness ranges extend from 0 to 200. A higher value selects more colors, and a lower value selects fewer colors. While you adjust the fuzziness, the mask dynamically updates.

   If you can't quite get the control you want with the Fuzziness slider, try selecting the Localized Color Clusters option. Instead of just maintaining a single color cluster from the colors you select, this option enables you to select multiple color clusters. This option can help with obtaining cleaner, more precise selections, especially when you're trying to select more than just one color. Adjust the Range slider to fine-tune the range, or area, of your selection.

   The Invert option selects what's currently unselected and deselects what's currently selected. And if you totally muck things up, you can reset the dialog box by holding down Alt (Option on the Mac) and clicking Reset.

7. **Select a Selection Preview from the drop-down list to preview the selection in the image window.**

   - *None:* Displays the image normally.
   - *Grayscale:* Displays just the grayscale mask.
   - *Black Matte and White Matte:* Displays the selection against a black or white background.
   - *Quick Mask:* Shows the mask over your image, using your Quick Mask settings.

8. **Click OK.**

   Your image appears with a selection outline based on the Color Range mask.

   Now, do what you will with your nice, clean selection.

   I decided my Thai dancer needed to be in a more exotic locale, so I transported her (by dragging and dropping with the Move tool onto another image) to a mystical Shangri-La, shown in Figure 2-5.

Corbis DigiFal Stock, Digital Vision

Figure 2-5: With a clean selection made with the Color Range command, you can send people to locales never before visited.

Selective Erasing with the Eraser Tools

The eraser tools let you erase portions of an image to the background color, to transparency, or even to the way your image looked earlier in your editing session. There are three eraser tools — the regular Eraser, the Magic Eraser, and the Background Eraser. All three share a tool flyout menu.

The eraser tools look like real erasers, so you can't miss them. But just in case you do, press E and then Shift+E to toggle through the three tools.

When you erase pixels, those pixels are gone. Gone. For good. Before using the eraser tools, it might be wise to make a backup of your image. You can save the image either as a separate file or as another layer. That way, if things run amok, you have some insurance.

Erasing to the background or transparency

The Eraser tool allows you to erase areas on your image to either the background color or to transparency. Select the Eraser tool, drag through the desired area on your image, and you're done.

If the image contains just a background, you erase to the background color, as shown in Figure 2-6. If the image is on a layer, you erase to transparency.

Corbis Digital Stock

Figure 2-6: The Eraser tool erases either to the background color (left) or, if on a layer, to transparency (right).

I rate this tool in the same category as the Lasso tool. It's quick; it's easy, but it has limited applications. Use it only for minor touchups. The Eraser tool definitely isn't a tool to use on its own for making accurate selections.

The most useful function I find for the Eraser tool is to clean up my channel masks. Set the mode to Block, zoom into your mask, and clean up those black and white pixels. See Book VI, Chapter 3 for more on channel masks.

These options on the Options bar control the Eraser tool:

✓ **Mode:** Select from Brush, Pencil, and Block. When you select Brush or Pencil, you have access to the Brush Preset picker panel on the far left of the Options bar.

Use the Brush Preset drop-down picker panel to select from a variety of brush sizes and styles. Block has only one size, a square of 16 x 16 pixels. But because the block size remains constant, if you zoom way in, you can perform some detailed erasing.

✓ **Opacity:** Specify a percentage of transparency for the erasure. Opacity settings less than 100 percent only partially erase the pixels. The lower the Opacity setting, the less it erases. This option isn't available for the Block mode.

✓ **Flow:** Set a flow rate percentage when using Brush mode. Flow specifies how fast Photoshop applies the erasure and is especially handy when using the Airbrush option.

- **Airbrush:** Click the button when using Brush mode to turn your brush into an airbrush. With this option, the longer you hold your mouse button down, the more it erases.

- **Erase to History:** This option allows you to erase back to a selected source state or snapshot in the History panel. You can also hold down Alt (Option on the Mac) to temporarily access the Erase to History option. See Book II, Chapter 4 for more information.

- **Brush Panel:** Click the toggle button to bring up the full Brushes panel.

Selecting and erasing by color

The Magic Eraser tool works like a combination Eraser and Magic Wand tool. It both selects and erases similarly colored pixels:

- **When you click a layer:** The Magic Eraser tool erases pixels of a similar color based on a specified range and leaves the area transparent, as shown in Figure 2-7.

- **When you click the background:** The Magic Eraser tool automatically converts the background to a layer and then does the same thing.

- **When you click a layer with locked transparency:** The Magic Eraser tool erases the pixels and replaces the area with the background color.

The Tolerance value defines the range of colors that Photoshop erases, just like it does with the Magic Wand tool. The value determines how similar a neighboring color has to be to the color that you click. A higher value picks up more colors, whereas a lower value picks up fewer colors. In my example in Figure 2-7, I set my Tolerance value to 8 and clicked in the upper-left of my image. Photoshop selected and erased only a limited shade of black due to my lower Tolerance setting.

Here are the other options:

- **Anti-Alias:** Creates a slightly soft edge around the transparent area.

- **Contiguous:** Selects only similar colors that are adjacent to each other. Deselect this option to delete similar-colored pixels wherever they appear in your image.

Corbis Digital Stock

Figure 2-7: Clicking with the Magic Eraser simultaneously selects and erases similarly colored pixels.

✔ **Sample All Layers:** Samples colors using data from all visible layers, but erases pixels on the *active* layer only.

✔ **Opacity:** Works like it does for the regular Eraser tool.

Removing an image's background

 The Background Eraser tool is probably the most sophisticated of the eraser-tool lot. It erases away the background (in the composition of the image, not the Layers panel) from an image and leaves the foreground untouched — in theory, anyway.

Like the Magic Eraser tool, the Background Eraser tool erases to transparency on a layer. If you drag on the background, Photoshop converts the background into a layer.

To use the Background Eraser tool, you need to carefully keep the crosshair that appears in the center of the cursor, also known as the *hot spot,* on the background pixels while you drag. Then Photoshop deletes all background pixels under the brush circumference. But, if you get close to a foreground pixel with the hot spot, that pixel is gobbled up, as well. As you can see from my example in Figure 2-8, I got a little too close to the man's face in some spots, and it left him a little chewed up.

Here's the rundown on the options, found on the Options bar, for the Background Eraser:

Background Eraser chews up man's face.

Corbis Digital Stock

Figure 2-8: Be careful when using the Background Eraser, or else you can inadvertently eat up pixels.

✔ **Brush Preset picker:** Provides various settings to customize the size and appearance of your eraser tip. The size and tolerance settings at the bottom are for if you use a pressure-sensitive drawing tablet. You can base the size and tolerance on the pen pressure or position of the thumbwheel.

✔ **Sampling:** The three settings (represented by icons) determine what areas should and shouldn't be erased. The default Continuous setting allows you to sample colors continuously while you drag through the image. The Once setting erases only areas that contain the color you first clicked. If the background is pretty much one color, you can try this option. The Background Swatch setting erases only the areas containing the background color.

✔ **Limits:** The Contiguous setting erases similar colors that are adjacent to one another. The Discontiguous setting erases similar colors to whatever's under the brush tip, regardless of whether they're adjacent. The Find Edges setting erases contiguous pixels while retaining the sharpness of the edges.

✔ **Tolerance:** Works just like the Magic Eraser Tolerance setting.

✔ **Protect Foreground Color:** Prevents you from erasing areas that match the foreground color.

Putting It Together

Framing a Photo with Quick Mask

Sometimes, you may want to add a decorative border or edge to your image. Maybe you're creating a postcard or greeting card, and the standard rectangular shape image just doesn't provide enough pizzazz. Although adding a border or edge might look difficult, it is a snap with the Quick Mask command. Just follow these steps:

1. **Using any selection tool, create a selection on your image.**

I started with a rectangle in my image and then chose Select➪Inverse to turn the selection inside out.

2. **Click the Edit in Quick Mask Mode button in the Tools panel.**

A color overlay covers and protects the area outside the selection, as shown in the figure.

Your selected area is open for you to edit as you so desire.

3. **Grab the Brush tool, choose the Heavy Stipple brush, and set the brush diameter to 168 pixels.**

You can find the Heavy Stipple brush in the Wet Media Brushes library of the Brushes panel. See Book IV, Chapter 1 for more on the Brushes panel.

4. **Paint around the edges of the mask with black to add to the masked area.**

5. **Adjust the Flow setting to 35% to get a semitransparent area and then click a few more times.**

You can also paint with gray to get the same effect.

continued

continued

6. **Again, adjust your brush diameter (this time to 80 pixels) and add a few random clicks here and there.**

7. **Switch your color to white and repeat the steps, clicking around the image and also in the interior of the mask.**

   Because white adds to the selected area, your image starts to show through.

   I ended up with a mottled mess, shown in the figure.

   You can also apply a filter or adjustment (Image⇨Adjustment) to the Quick Mask. See this technique in action in Book VII, Chapter 2.

8. **Click the Edit in Standard Mode button to exit the Quick Mask mode.**

   The overlay disappears, leaving you with a selection outline, shown in the figure.

   The selection outline correlates with the unmasked or selected areas of the Quick Mask. If you had a feathered mask, such as mine, the selection outline runs halfway between the selected and unselected areas of the mask, creating a soft transition.

9. **Your selection is ready and waiting for your next command.**

   In my example, I deleted my selection, thereby filling the hole with my background color of white and leaving me with a stippled image. Note that because my brush was feathered and also varied in the Flow settings, some of my image is also feathered and semitransparent.

Chapter 3: Getting Exact with Advanced Masking Techniques

In This Chapter

✓ **Creating and editing layer masks**

✓ **Using vector masks**

✓ **Working with channel masks**

If you haven't already checked out Book VI, Chapter 2, which covers Photoshop's quick-and-easy masking tools, you might want to breeze through that chapter first, especially if the word *mask* brings to mind an image from Halloween rather than a selection technique. In this chapter, I dive into some manual masking techniques.

Layer masks are tremendously useful, and if you're like me, you'll find yourself addicted to them. They can be fantastic for blending layers and making multiple images dissolve into one another. Vector masks create shapes defined by vector paths and produce clean, smooth-edged graphic elements.

Channel masks are probably the most time-consuming of the masking lot, but they're powerful and accurate. Like anything in life, the more you practice using them, the faster and better you get.

But Photoshop CS5 includes a feature to help in your masking tasks — the Masks panel. This handy panel enables users to add, control, and refine masks of all sorts.

After you get through this final chapter of Book VI, you'll be familiar with every masking technique Photoshop has to offer. By then, you'll be prepared to use masks to select a very hairy orangutan, dyed green, perched in a tree in a lush rainforest. And how many people can say that?

Working with the Masks Panel

The Masks panel, shown in Figure 3-1, enables you to add, control, and refine your layer, vector, and filter masks. I explain layer and vector masks in the sections "Working with Layer Masks" and "Creating and Editing

Vector Masks," later in this chapter. Details on filter masks can be found in Book VII, Chapter 1. For now, I cover just the features in this panel because they may assist you in getting your mask exactly the way you want it:

- **Thumbnail:** Shows what layer or mask is currently selected in your file.

- **Add Pixel Mask/Select Pixel Mask:** Click this icon to add a layer mask. If you added a layer mask by another means, such as via the Layers panel or Layer menu, the icon is automatically selected. Remember that when working with masks, black hides areas of your image, white shows areas of your image, and any gray areas are partially hidden at varying percentages, depending how dark or light the gray is.

- **Add Vector Mask/Select Vector Mask:** Click this icon to add a vector mask. If you added a vector mask by another means, the icon is automatically selected.

- **Select Filter Mask:** This icon appears only when a Smart Filter has been applied. For more on Smart Filters, see Book VII, Chapter 1.

- **Density:** Think of this option as a kind of opacity control for your mask. To lessen the transparency of the masked (or hidden) area, select the mask and drag the slider to the left.

- **Feather:** The Feather option softens the edges of the mask, creating more of a dissolve between your layers when creating a composited image. To see the effect on the actual mask itself, hold down Alt (Option on the Mac) and click the mask thumbnail in the Layers panel, which temporarily hides the layer and shows only the mask. Hold down Alt (Option on the Mac) and click to display the layer again.

- **Mask Edge:** Click this button to bring up the Refine dialog box. In this dialog box, you can fine-tune the edges of your masks to your liking. For an explanation of the Refine Edge dialog box, see Book III, Chapter 1.

- **Color Range:** Click this button to open the Color Range dialog box. Color range is yet another way to create a selection or mask. For details on this feature, see Book VI, Chapter 2.

- **Invert:** This option reverses the colors of the mask. Therefore, black areas become white, white becomes black, dark gray converts to light gray, and so on.

- **Load Selection from Mask:** Click this option to load your mask as a selection. Note that the black areas of your mask are unselected, the white areas are selected, and the gray areas are partially selected. For more on selections, see Book III.

- **Apply Mask:** Click this icon to have your mask permanently applied to the layer. The mask is then deleted. Be careful when applying this option because you can no longer edit the mask and refine your visible areas.

- **Disable/Enable Mask:** Click this icon to show or hide your mask.

- **Delete Mask:** Click the trash can icon to delete the mask.

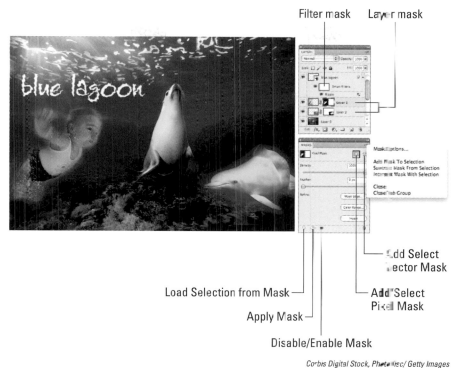

Filter mask   Layer mask

Add Select
Vector Mask

Add Select
Pixel Mask

Load Selection from Mask

Apply Mask

Disable/Enable Mask

Figure 3-1: The Masks panel aids in adding and refining various types of masks.

- ✓ **Mask Options:** This first command in the panel pop-up menu enables you to change the color and opacity of your mask overlay.

- ✓ **Add Mask to Selection, Subtract Mask from Selection, Intersect Mask with Selection:** These commands, also in the panel pop-up menu, allow you to add to, delete from, or intersect with existing selections made from your masks.

- ✓ **Close/Close Tab Group:** The final commands in the panel pop-up menu close the Masks panel and the group that the Mask panel belongs to, respectively.

Working with Layer Masks

Like any other mask, a *layer mask* is a grayscale image that you can edit to your heart's content. Layer masks are excellent for blending layers of images together and creating soft transitions between elements.

For versatility, layer masks are unparalleled. They allow you to gradually brush in transparency and opacity on a selective pixel basis. Paint with black to hide portions of the layer; paint with white to display portions; and paint in varying shades of gray to partially show elements. You can even apply gradients, image adjustments, and filters to your layer masks to create interesting special effects.

After you get the concept of layer masks, you'll never use the eraser tools (covered in Book VI, Chapter 2) again. You won't have to because one of the great things about layer masks is that you can forever edit, or even delete them, with no permanent harm whatsoever to the image.

Creating layer masks

To create a layer mask, select your desired layer and choose Layer⇨Layer Mask⇨Reveal All or Hide All.

- **Reveal All:** Creates a mask filled with white, which shows the layer.

- **Hide All:** Creates a mask filled with black, which hides, or *masks,* the layer and shows nothing but transparency.

You can also click the Add Layer Mask icon at the bottom of the Layers panel (which, by default, selects Reveal All). Or you can click the Add a Pixel Mask icon in the Masks panel.

You can't add a layer mask to a background layer. You must convert the background layer to a regular layer if you want to use a layer mask on the background of an image.

You can also use an existing selection to create a layer mask. Select your desired layer and make a selection by using one of the selection tools. Choose Layer⇨Layer Mask⇨Reveal Selection or Hide Selection. You can also click the Add Layer Mask button in the Layers panel to create a mask that reveals the selection.

After you create the layer mask, you can grab the painting tool of your choice and apply your grayscale color. ***Remember:*** Add white to the mask to display the image. Add black to hide the image. Add gray to make the layer semitransparent.

Using the Gradient and Brush tools on a layer mask

I must confess: I use two of the layer masking tools more than the others:

- **The Gradient tool:** Setting this tool to a linear gradient of black to white or white to black is truly awesome. Select the layer mask in the Layers panel and drag with the Gradient tool on the layer mask to create the gradient. The darker areas of the gradient gradually hide the image, whereas the lighter areas gradually show the image.

✓ **The Brush tool:** With a large, feathered tip, using the Airbrush option and the Flow set to around 10%, this tool is amazing. With these settings in place, you can create feathered edges that blend one layer into another without any harsh lines. Again, select the layer mask in the Layers panel and drag with Brush tool on the layer mask.

In Figure 3-2, which is an image with two layers (the flag on the bottom and the girl on top), I used a combination of both these tools. I started with the black-to-white linear gradient, which I dragged from the left edge of my image through to the right edge. I then took the Brush tool with a large feathered tip (265 pixels), selected the Airbrush option, set the Flow to 10%, set my foreground color to black, and worked my way around the profile of the girl's face to get rid of some more of the background behind her.

TIP

To edit a layer mask, click the Layer Mask thumbnail in the Layers panel. Select your desired painting or editing tool, and paint or edit the mask to perfection. Just be sure that you're working on the layer mask, rather than editing the image itself. Otherwise, you apply paint directly to your image. You can tell because you see brackets around the layer mask thumbnail in the Layers panel. You also see the Pixel Mask icon highlighted and the mask thumbnail displayed in the Masks panel.

No layer mask

With layer mask

Figure 3-2: Layer masks enable you to seamlessly blend two layers.

Managing layer masks

Here are some tips to help you work with your layer masks. You can do the
following:

- ✐ **Load a layer mask.** *Loading* a layer mask means getting a selection outline based on the layer mask. Simply Ctrl-click (⌘-click on the Mac) the
  Layer Mask thumbnail. You can also click the Load Selection from Mask
  icon in the Masks panel.

- ✐ **View the mask without viewing the image.** Sometimes when you're
  editing a layer mask, you may find it helpful to see the mask itself without having to view the image, too. For example, in Figure 3-3, I hid the
  image of the little girl and the flag to see the layer masks. Simply Alt-click
  (Option-click on the Mac) the Layer Mask thumbnail to view the mask
  and hide the image on the layer.

  To redisplay the image, Alt-click (Option-click on the Mac) again or click
  the eye icon in the far left column.

- ✐ **View the layer mask as a red over-**
  lay. If you prefer to see your layer
  mask as a red overlay, Alt+Shift-
  click (Option+Shift-click on the
  Mac) the Layer Mask thumbnail.
  You can also click the eyeball icon
  on the layer mask in the Channels
  panel.

Figure 3-3: Check out just your layer mask
without the image.

- ✐ **Click again with the same keys to**
  remove the overlay. You can
  change the opacity and color of the
  overlay in the Layer Mask Display
  Options dialog box, which you
  access by double-clicking the layer mask channel in the Channels panel.
  You can also change it by selecting Mask Options from the Masks panel
  pop-up menu.

- ✐ **Paste a copied selection into a layer mask.** Simply Alt-click (Option-
  click on the Mac) the Layer Mask thumbnail. Choose Edit⇨Paste and
  then choose Select⇨Deselect. Click the image thumbnail in the Layers
  panel to return to the image.

  The copied selection can consist of anything, but this technique comes
  in particularly handy when you're copying one layer mask into another.

- ✐ **Create a mask from the transparent areas of a layer.** Select the layer in
  the Layers panel and choose Layer⇨Layer Mask⇨From Transparency.

- ✐ **Disable (temporarily hide) or enable a layer mask.** Just Shift-click the
  Layer Mask thumbnail or choose Layer⇨Layer Mask⇨Disable or Enable.
  Or click the Disable/Enable Mask icon in the Masks panel.

✔ **Unlink a layer from its layer mask.** By default, Photoshop links a layer mask to the contents of the layer. This link allows them to move together. To unlink a layer from its layer mask, click the link icon in the Layers panel. Click the icon again to re-establish the link. You can also choose Layer➪Layer Mask➪Unlink or Link.

✔ **Delete a layer mask.** Just drag the Layer Mask thumbnail to the trash can icon in the Layers panel. Click Delete in the dialog box. Or you can choose Layer➪Layer Mask➪Delete. Finally, click the Delete (trash can) icon in the Masks panel.

✔ **Apply a layer mask.** When you apply a layer mask, you essentially fuse the mask to the layer, so your mask is permanently applied to the layer. Photoshop replaces all black areas in the mask with transparent pixels and all gray areas with partially transparent pixels; all white areas are unaffected. Drag the thumbnail to the trash can icon in the Layers panel. Click Apply in the dialog box. You can choose Layer➪Layer Mask➪Apply or click the Apply Mask icon in the Masks panel.

Putting It Together

Making a Photo Gradually Fade from Color to Grayscale

Layer masks are extremely powerful when it comes to blending multiple images so that one seems to dissolve into the others. In this project, I don't show you how to use a layer mask to blend different images, but rather the same image — one in color and one in grayscale. Follow these steps:

1. **Open a copy of your favorite color image, like the one shown in the figure.**

The subject matter isn't critical here, so feel free to whip out that old prom picture.

2. **Choose Image➪Duplicate.**

Accept the default name and click OK in the dialog box that appears.

3. **With the duplicate image active, choose Window➪Channels.**

View each of the channels to find the one that gives you the best grayscale image.

4. **Select your desired channel in the Channels panel.**

If you need a refresher on channels, see Book VI, Chapter 1. The Red channel gives the best contrast for the portrait in my example. Because skin tones tend to have a lot of red in them, the Red channel usually provides the best grayscale image of a person.

continued

continued

5. **Choose Image⇨Mode⇨Grayscale and click OK in the Discard Other Channels alert box.**

   Photoshop has now stripped the color from the image, shown in the figure.

   This is only one way to convert a color image to grayscale. There are a lot of others. Check them out in Book II, Chapter 2.

6. **Choose Window⇨Layers.**

   The Layers panel appears.

7. **Holding down the Shift key with the Move tool selected, drag and drop your grayscale image onto your color image.**

   This action automatically creates a new layer from the grayscale image. (See Book V for more information about layers.)

   By holding down the Shift key, you keep the grayscale image centered over the color image.

8. **Close your duplicate image.**

9. **Press D to access the default colors.**

   This step gives you a black foreground swatch and a white background swatch in your Tools panel.

   Now, I show you how to use one of my favorite techniques, a black-to-white gradient, on the layer mask.

10. **Make sure that the grayscale layer is the active layer in the Layers panel and click the Add Layer Mask icon at the bottom of the panel.**

    It's the icon that looks like a dark square with a white circle on top. Photoshop adds a second thumbnail on your layer, indicating that a layer mask has been applied.

    A layer mask acts like a piece of clear acetate over your layer.

11. **Select the Gradient tool and then select the default gradient of Foreground to Background.**

    To get the default gradient, click the Gradient Picker on the Options bar and select the first gradient.

    It should be a gradient of white to black because it's based on the current foreground and background colors, which reverse when you select the Layer Mask thumbnail. For a gradient refresher, see Book IV, Chapter 2.

12. **Drag the gradient from the top of your image to the bottom.**

    Or from left to right. Or at a diagonal. It's your call.

13. **Experiment with long drags and short drags. The angle and length of your mouse movement determine how the layer mask reveals the underlying image.**

In my example, I dragged from the bottom of the image to the top and stopped about two-thirds of the way up.

Where black appears on the layer mask, the grayscale image is hidden. Where white appears on the mask, the grayscale image shows through and everything in between allows the grayscale image to partially show.

Although I used a linear gradient in my example, you can experiment with the other types, as well. Radial gradients can provide some interesting effects.

14. **When you complete your mask, save and close the file.**

Creating and Editing Vector Masks

Whereas layer masks let you create soft-edged masks, vector masks create hard-edged masks defined by shapes created by a vector path on a layer. Vector-based shapes produce clean, smooth, and well-defined edges that are never jagged. And you can size and transform vector shapes without ever degrading the appearance of the element. (For an introduction to vector images, see Book IV, Chapter 1.)

You create a vector mask when you create a shape with any one of the shape tools. You can also create a vector mask when you convert type to a shape. (Choose Layer➪Type➪Convert to Shape.) See Book IV, Chapter 3.

Adding a vector mask to a layer

To add a vector mask to layer, follow these steps:

1. **Select the layer in the Layers panel and choose Layer➪Vector Mask➪Reveal All or Hide All.**

   I describe Reveal All and Hide All in the "Creating layer masks" section, earlier in this chapter. Remember that you can't add a vector mask to a background layer. You can also click the Add a Vector Mask icon in the Masks panel.

2. **Select the Paths icon in the Options bar. On the vector mask, create a path with the Pen tool or grab any shape tool and create a shape.**

   See Book III, Chapter 2 for more on paths and Book IV, Chapter 1 for more on shapes.

   I selected the Custom Shape tool and dragged a sunburst shape on my vector mask. Notice how everything inside the path (represented by the white area on the vector mask thumbnail) is visible and everything outside the path (represented by the gray areas on the vector mask thumbnail) is hidden, or masked, as shown in Figure 3-4.

   Like layer masks, you can add vector masks only to layers, not backgrounds. If necessary, simply convert your background to a layer by double-clicking the background in the Layers panel.

3. **If your vector mask is satisfactory, save your file and then close it.**

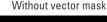
Without vector mask   With vector mask

Figure 3-4: Everything outside of a vector mask is hidden, or masked, from display.

Another way to add a vector mask is to select your desired layer, draw a work path with the Pen tool or one of the shape tools, and then select Layer➪ Vector Mask➪Current Path.

Managing vector masks

Here are a few vector mask tips. You can perform the following tasks:

- ✔ **Edit a vector mask path.** Use the pen tools and the Direct Selection tool, as described in Book III, Chapter 2.

- ✔ **Add multiple shapes or paths to the existing vector mask.** All you need to do is drag another shape with any of the shape tools. Or add another path with the Pen tool. You can also add, delete, and intersect shapes and paths using the Add, Subtract, Intersect, and Exclude icons in the Options bar.

- ✔ **Remove a vector mask from a layer.** Drag the thumbnail to the trash can icon in the Layers panel or choose Layer➪Vector Mask➪Delete. You can also click the Delete (trash can) icon in the Masks panel.

- ✔ **Disable (temporarily hide) or enable a vector mask.** Shift-click the vector mask thumbnail or choose Layer➪Vector Mask➪Disable (or Enable). You can also click the Disable/Enable Mask icon in the Masks panel.

- ✔ **Rasterize a vector mask.** *Rasterizing* (or turning the mask into a pixel-based image) converts the vector mask into a layer mask. Choose Layer➪Rasterize➪Vector Mask.

- ✔ **Apply layer styles to vector shapes.** This is a quick-and-easy way to create buttons for a Web page or a custom logo, as shown in Figure 3-5. Just select the layer, not the vector mask, and choose Layer➪Layer Style. Select your style of choice. For details on layer styles, see Book V, Chapter 4.

Figure 3-5: Adding layer styles to your shapes can make them really shine.

Creating Channel Masks

Photoshop's channel masks are probably the most time-consuming masks to use because they require a lot of manual labor. Not heavy lifting, mind you, but work with the tools and commands in Photoshop.

But, don't get me wrong; it's time well spent. Channel masks can usually accurately select what the other Photoshop tools can only dream about — wisps of hair, tufts of fur, a ficus benjamina tree with 9,574 leaves.

You can create a channel mask in a lot of ways, but I'm here to offer you one that works most of the time. To create a channel mask, follow these steps:

1. **Analyze your existing channels to find a suitable candidate to use to create a duplicate channel.**

   This is usually the channel with the most contrast between what you want and don't want. For instance, in my example, the Blue channel provided the most contrast between the windmills and the sky, which I wanted to mask, and the background, which I didn't.

   To duplicate the channel, drag your desired channel thumbnail to the New Channel icon at the bottom of the Channels panel. After you duplicate the channel, it then becomes an alpha channel and is named (channel) copy.

2. **Make sure the alpha channel is selected in the Channels panel and choose Image⇨Adjustments⇨Levels.**

   Using the histogram and the sliders in the Levels dialog box, increase the contrast between the element(s) you want and don't want selected. Click OK when you're done to close the dialog box.

3. **Select a tool, such as the Brush or Eraser tool, and paint and edit the alpha channel to refine the mask.**

   See Figure 3-6. I used the combo of the Brush and Eraser set to Block mode to clean up my mask.

4. **When you complete the mask, click the Load Channel as Selection icon (the dotted circle icon on the far left) at the bottom of the Channels panel. Then, click your composite channel at the top of the list of channels.**

   This step loads your mask as a selection, giving you that familiar selection outline. You can also use one of my favorite keyboard shortcuts: Ctrl-click (⌘-click on the Mac) directly on the alpha channel to load the mask as a selection.

   Your selection is now ready to go.

5. **You can leave it within the original image, or drag and drop it onto another image with the Move tool, as I did in Figure 3-7.**

   Because my new sky was darker than my original, I also darkened my windmills so the lighting would be more consistent. If you've done a good job, nobody will be the wiser that the two images never met in real life.

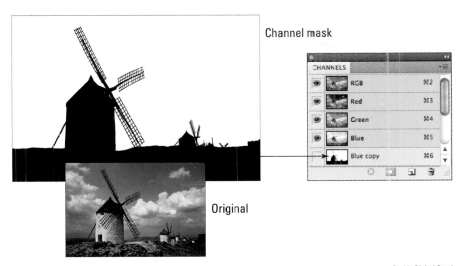

Channel mask

Original

Figure 3-6: Use the Levels and Photoshop painting and editing tools to refine your channel mask.

Figure 3-7: When combining multiple images, masking is usually the most accurate method.

Putting It Together

Masking Hair, Fur, and Other Wispy Things

Hair, fur, fuzz, and other objects with complex or loosely defined edges can prove difficult to select with the run-of-the-mill selection techniques. But that's where masking can save the day. Because a mask allows for a 256-level selection, it does a great job of picking up those elusive strands of hair and such that would otherwise probably be cut off in the selecting process.

Perhaps you've seen those photos where everyone in a composite image appears to have helmet hair? Here are the steps to avoid the Aqua Net look and select even the smallest wisp of hair:

1. **Choose File➪Open.**

   Select an image that contains something hairy, furry, or fuzzy. A portrait is an ideal choice (unless the subject is hair challenged).

   For your first attempt at this technique, starting with an image that has a pretty simple and uncluttered background is best.

   In my example, I used an image of a pensive, young urban professional shown in the figure.

2. **Choose Window➪Channels.**

   View each channel by clicking the channel name in the Channels panel.

   Each channel is an independent gray-scale image and a potential starting point for a mask.

   It's best to start with the channel that contains the most contrast between what you want to select and what you don't. If it's a toss-up, go with the channel that makes selecting the difficult part of the image easiest. (In my example, that's the hair, so I chose the Blue channel.)

3. **Choose Duplicate Channel from the Channels panel pop-up menu. In the Duplicate Channel dialog box, name the channel *mask* and click OK.**

   You've created an alpha channel for the mask, shown in the figure. Now, you can edit the mask without harming the original channel.

4. **Make sure the alpha channel is selected in the Channels panel and choose Image➪Adjustments➪Levels. Boost the contrast in the image by dragging the Input sliders for shadows, midtones, and highlights.**

Make the element(s) you want to select to be all white or all black with a little gray in the wispy areas. In other words, you want to change most of the pixels in the image to either black or white.

If you need help using the Levels adjustment, see Book VIII, Chapter 1.

Remember, the goal is to select the person and his or her hair. You can do that in one of two ways:

- By selecting the person
- By selecting the background first and then inverting the selection

In a mask, traditionally, white represents a selected area, black represents an unselected area, and gray represents a partially selected area.

In my example, because my guy is darker than the background, I adjusted the contrast to make the subject as black as I could while making the background lighter. You can see the result in the figure.

5. **When you're done, click OK to close the Levels dialog box.**

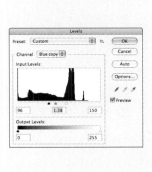

6. **Refine the mask by selecting the Eraser tool and selecting Block Mode from the Options bar.**

TIP

The Block Eraser is a great tool for cleaning up masks. It allows you to paint inside the mask without creating any feathered edges.

7. **Press D to access the default colors.**

Remember, the Eraser tool paints with the background color, so be sure you have the color you want before you drag. Press X to switch the foreground and background colors.

continued

8. **Clean up your mask by painting with black and white, as shown in the figure.**

Make sure to use short strokes so you can undo any mistakes you make.

9. **Use the Zoom tool if you need to touch up the details.**

The Block Eraser tool has only one size, so you have to zoom in to paint thinner strokes and zoom out to erase a larger area.

Remember to leave some gray around the wispy areas, as seen in the figure; otherwise they may look chopped off.

Take your time and be as accurate as you can. Patience makes a big difference.

TIP

If you're not sure what you need to paint on the mask and you want to refer to the color image, simply click the composite channel (either RGB or CMYK, depending on your image) at the top of the Channels panel. Then click the mask channel again to return to your mask. Or you can view both the mask and the composite simultaneously. Your mask appears as a red overlay.

Your mask is refined and ready to go.

10. **Click the first icon on the left at the bottom of the Channels panel to load the mask as a selection.**

Or Ctrl-click (⌘-click on the Mac) the channel mask.

A selection marquee appears around your mask.

TIP

If you want to soften the edge a little, you can choose Select⇨Modify⇨Feather and enter a value somewhere between 0.5 pixel (for a low-resolution image) to 2 pixels (for a high-resolution image). Feathering allows for a soft, natural-looking transition between your masked element and the background. I used a 1-pixel feather for my image.

11. **Return to the composite image by clicking the RGB channel (or CMYK, if warranted).**

The selection outline appears in your composite image, shown in the figure.

12. **If you need to invert your selection, choose Select⇨Inverse.**

In my example, I just filled my background with a solid color, so I left the background selected.

13. **Choose Window⇨Color and mix a color of your choice. Choose Edit⇨ Fill, and in the Fill dialog box, choose Foreground Color for your Contents. Click OK.**

Photoshop now replaces the background with a solid color. Check the edges to see how clean your mask is.

14. **Make any final edits you need to make.**

My guy looked like he spent too much time at the local tanning booth, so I toned down the redness in his skin by using the Variation commands (see Book VIII, Chapter 1), as shown in the figure.

15. **When you're happy with your channel mask, save and close the file.**

It takes practice to get masking down to a science, but, believe me, it's worth your time. Nine times out of ten, a channel mask lends a much better selection than any of the easier, quicker selection tools and techniques.

Book VI
Chapter 3

**Getting Exact with
Advanced Masking
Techniques**

TIP

Instead of filling the background with a color, you can also open a second image and, with the Move tool, drag and drop your masked element into the second image. A couple of things to keep in mind when compositing with two images: First, try to use two images whose lighting isn't so dissimilar that it looks artificial. Take into account the time of day, the angle of the light, and so on. Second, try to select two images whose levels of focus make sense. If you need to soften one of the images, apply the Gaussian Blur filter. If your mask is good, your person should look right at home in his or her new digs.

Book VII
Filters and Distortions

The 5th Wave   By Rich Tennant

"Hey — let's put scanned photos of ourselves through a ripple filter and see if we can make ourselves look weird."

*G*ot an image that needs to be sharper or maybe less dusty? How about an image that needs to look like it was wrapped in plastic and then Xeroxed on a circa-1970 photocopier? Either way, this is the book that describes the fine-tuning and the folly of filters.

Filters can do wonders in correcting your images, making them look better than the original. And if it's special effects you're interested in, look no further. Filters can make your image look ripped, sprayed, wet, hot — and just about any other adjective you're interested in. The best news is that Photoshop offers Smart Filters: filters that work their magic without damaging your pixels. If distortions are more your thing, you won't be disappointed with the Liquify command, for which image warping, pushing, bloating, and puckering are daily activities.

Chapter 1: Making Corrections with Daily Filters

In This Chapter

✓ Understanding how filters work

✓ Introducing Smart Filters

✓ Sharpening soft areas

✓ Improving an image with blurring

✓ Smoothing defects with Median and Facet filters

✓ Fading a filter's effects

✓ Applying filters repeatedly or selectively

*F*ilters have a long and glorious history, ranging from performing essential tasks (such as removing abrasive particles from the oil in your car's crankcase) to even more important chores involving the pixels in your Photoshop images. In both cases, filters (also called *plug-ins* because they can be installed or removed from Photoshop independently) seize tiny, almost invisible bits of stuff and rearrange them in useful ways. The results are something you'd never want to do without.

This chapter introduces you to the basics of Photoshop's filter facilities and starts you on the road to plug-in proficiency.

You Say You Want a Convolution?

All filters do one simple thing in a seemingly complicated way: They make Photoshop do your bidding. Deep within a filter's innards is a set of instructions that tells Photoshop what to do with a particular pixel in an image or selection. Photoshop applies these instructions to each pixel in the relevant area by using a process the techies call *convolution* (creating a form or shape that's folded or curved in tortuous windings), but which we normal folk simply refer to as *applying a filter*.

Corrective and destructive filters

Filters fall into two basic categories:

⬩ **Corrective filters:** Fix problems in an image. They fine-tune color, add blur, improve sharpness, or remove such nastiness as dust and scratches. Although corrective plug-ins can be fairly destructive to certain pixels, they don't change the basic look of an image in general. You might not even notice that a corrective filter has been applied unless you compare the new version of the image with the original.

⬩ **Destructive filters:** Tend to obliterate at least some of an image's original detail (some to a greater extent than others) while they add special effects. They may overlay an image with an interesting texture, move pixels around to create brush strokes, or distort an image with twists, waves, or zigzags. You can often tell at a glance that a destructive filter has been applied to an image: The special effect often looks like nothing that exists in real life.

An unaltered image (such as the image on the left in Figure 1-1) can be improved by using a corrective filter such as Unsharp Mask (center) or changed dramatically with a destructive filter such as Find Edges (right).

Corbis Digital Stock

Figure 1-1: Filters range in variety from the corrective (center) to the destructive (right).

Filter basics

Whether a filter is corrective or destructive, it falls into one of two camps. Here's the scoop:

⬩ **Single-step filters:** The easiest filters to use, single-step filters have no options and use no dialog boxes. Just select the filter from the menu and watch it do its stuff on your image or selection. The basic Blur and Sharpen filters are single-step filters.

✔ **Mini-application filters:** Most filters come complete with at least one dialog box, along with (perhaps) a few lists, buttons, and check boxes. And almost every mini-app filter has sliders you can use to adjust the intensity of an effect or parameter. (See Figure 1-2.) These filters are marked in the menus with an *ellipsis* (a series of dots) following their names; like with other menu commands that show those dots, it's an indication that you're about to be presented with a dialog box where more options are lurking.

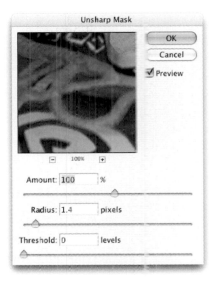

Figure 1-2: Mini-application filters require you to specify various settings before applying your filter.

The controls themselves are easy to master. The tricky part is figuring out what the various parameters you're using actually do. How does changing brush size affect your image when you're using a brush-stroke filter? What happens when you select a particular pattern with a texturizing filter? You can read descriptions of how various filter controls affect your image, but your best bet is to simply experiment until you discover the effects and parameters that work best for you. Just be sure that you save a copy of the original image; filters do permanent damage to files — modifying, adding, and deleting pixels.

Adobe also provides a command under the Filter menu — Browse Filters Online. Selecting this command launches your browser and takes you to the Photoshop Marketplace, where you'll find lots of downloadable Photoshop goodies — filters, brushes, shapes, patterns, actions, user groups work-shops, and so on.

Introducing Smart Filters

In my humble opinion, Smart Filters is one of the best recent features of Photoshop. Smart Filters are the same filters we all know and love, but they are applied to your image nondestructively. Technically, the filters are applied to your pixel data, but Photoshop always retains the original pixel data inside the Smart Object. Then, each time a filter is edited, Photoshop installs the original pixel data and reapplies the filter. Never mind how it's done behind the curtain; just know that Smart Filters act like layer effects, appending themselves to your layer, where they can be edited, rearranged, and deleted at any time. For more on Smart Objects, see Book V, Chapter 5.

Here are the steps to apply a Smart Filter:

1. **Create a Smart Object by doing one of the following:**

   - Choose File⇨Open as Smart Object. Select your file and click Open.

   - In an existing file, choose File⇨Place. Select your file size and position the image to your liking, and press the Commit button in the Options bar in Photoshop.

   - Select a layer in the Layers panel and choose Layer⇨Smart Objects⇨ Convert to Smart Object.

   - Select a layer in the Layers panel and choose Filter⇨Convert for Smart Filters.

   - Copy and paste Illustrator content as a Smart Object into Photoshop.

2. **Select your desired filter from the Filter menu.**

   Any filter applied to a Smart Object becomes a Smart Filter.

   Your Smart Filter is appended beneath your Smart Object layer, as shown in Figure 1-3.

Figure 1-3: Apply Smart Filters for nondestructive effects.

You can also apply the Shadows/Highlights and Variations adjustments as Smart Filters. These are found under the Image⟹Adjustments submenu.

When you add a Smart Filter to a layer, Photoshop automatically adds a layer mask. Technically, when a layer mask is applied to a Smart Filter, it's called a *filter mask*. Correspondingly, an alpha channel appears in the Channels panel, as shown in Figure 1-4.

By default, the entire filter is displayed, as evidenced by an all-white filter mask. But the application of a filter mask enables you to selectively hide and show the effects of the filter, shown in Figure 1-4, where I applied the filter to the background (as indicated by the white in the filter mask) but not to the sea lion (as indicated by the black in the filter mask). If you made a selection on the layer before applying a Smart Filter, the mask will reflect that selection. For more Smart Filter masking details, see the following bulleted list. For information on masking in general, check out Book VI.

Note that the Masks panel enables you to control and fine-tune masks of all types, including layer masks, vector masks, and filter masks. Check out Book VI, Chapter 3 to find out details on using this great panel.

Filter Mask

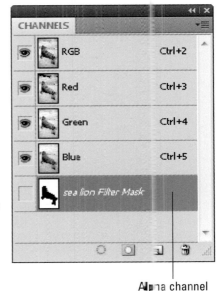

Alpha channel

Figure 1-4: Smart Filters come equipped with their own mask.

3. **Edit the filter as often as you like by simply double-clicking the filter name in the Layers panel.**

   You can also right-click (Control-click on the Mac) the filter name to access a context menu from which you can select Edit Smart Filter. (Refer to Figure 1-3.)

Your filter's dialog box appears, enabling you to adjust the parameters, as desired. You can't edit *single-step filters* (those that don't display a dialog box but are automatically applied). You can, however, double-click to reapply certain filters, such as Clouds and Difference Clouds, that reside in the Render filter submenu.

4. **(Optional) If desired, adjust the blend modes and opacity settings of the Smart Filter by right-clicking (Control-clicking on the Mac) on the filter line in the Layers panel to access a context menu. From that menu, select Edit Smart Filter Blending Options.**

   In the dialog box that appears, select your desired blend mode from the Mode pop-up menu. Adjust your opacity by entering a percentage or moving the slider. This is a great way to tone down the effect of the filter and achieve a more subtle appearance. Doing so is similar to fading a filter (described in the section "Fading a Filter," later in this chapter), only better because you can infinitely edit the settings.

5. **Add as many filters as you need to the Smart Object.**

   Filters reside in a grouped stack.

6. **(Optional) If you no longer want the filter, delete it by selecting it in the Layers panel and dragging it into the trash at the bottom of the panel.**

   To delete an entire Smart Filter group (multiple filters), grab the Smart Filters line in the Layers panel and drag it into the trash. You can also delete the filters by right-clicking (Control-clicking on the Mac) the filter name and selecting Delete Smart Filter from the context menu that appears. You can also delete all filters by right-clicking (Control-clicking on the Mac) the Smart Filters line in the Layers panel and choosing Clear Smart Filters from the context menu.

Here's everything else you need to know about the ins and outs of working with Smart Filters:

✏ Any file format that supports layers, such as PSD, TIFF, and PDF, supports Smart Filters.

✏ You can't apply Liquify or Vanishing Point as Smart Filters.

✏ Click the eye icon next to the filter name in the Layers panel to display or hide the individual Smart Filter. Click the eye of the Smart Filters group to toggle on or off all the filters.

✏ When executing commands, such as a transformation (scale, rotate, and so on), on a layer that has a Smart Filter, Photoshop alerts you that it'll turn off the Smart Filter in the preview during the transformation and reapply it after the transformation is complete. You may select the Do Not Show Again option to bypass the alert box from then on.

✔ You can rearrange the order of multiple filters by dragging them up or down the list in the Layers panel.

✔ To move a smart filter, drag the filter from one Smart Object layer to another. To copy Smart Filters, hold down Alt (Option on the Mac) while dragging.

✔ In the cases of multiple filters, only a single filter mask is applied to all filters within the group.

✔ You can use most of the same tools used to edit regular layer masks, such as the Brush and Gradient tools, to edit filter masks.

✔ You can adjust the Density and Feather options of the filter mask by using the Masks panel. See Book VI, Chapter 3 for details.

✔ Filter masks aren't linked to the Smart Objects, so if you move either one with the Move tool, the other doesn't move along with it.

✔ To hide the filter mask, hold down Shift and click the filter mask thumbnail in the Layers panel. You can right-click (Control-click on the Mac) the filter mask thumbnail and select Disable Filter mask from the context menu that appears.

✔ To delete the filter mask, drag the thumbnail to the trash at the bottom of the Layers panel. You can also right-click (Control-click on the Mac) on the filter mask thumbnail and select Delete Filter Mask from the context menu that appears. In addition, you can also add, subtract, or intersect the mask as a selection in this same context menu.

✔ To display just the filter mask, hold down Alt (Option on the Mac) and click the filter mask thumbnail in the Layers panel.

✔ To add a filter mask, right-click (Control-click on the Mac) the Smart Filter line in the Layers panel and select Add Filter Mask from the context menu that appears.

Sometimes, when converting from one color mode to another, such as when going from RGB to CMYK, certain filters can't be supported. Photoshop prompts you with an alert box saying so and asks you whether you want to rasterize the layer. Rasterizing essentially converts your Smart Object into a regular layer and fuses your Smart Filters onto that layer. Bye-bye Smart Filter. If you choose not to rasterize, any Smart Filters that can't be displayed are annotated with an alert icon (a triangle with an exclamation mark) in the Layers panel.

Sharpening What's Soft

Sometimes, your images aren't as sharp as you want. Sometimes, your images have a tiny bit of softening caused by scanning an image or perhaps by capturing a photo on your digital camera. Or perhaps you want only a particular part to be sharper so that it stands out from its surroundings.

All sharpening tools operate by increasing the contrast between adjacent pixels. If you look at a sharpened image side by side with the original version (as shown in Figure 1-5), you see that no new information has been provided. Instead, the contrast is boosted so edges are more distinct. The dark parts of the edges are darker; the light parts at their boundaries are lighter.

Photoshop has six main sharpening features, only five of which are actually filters, on the Filter⇨Sharpen menu. The sixth (the Sharpen tool) isn't a filter, strictly speaking. It is a tool in the Tools panel and is more like a paintbrush that lets you sharpen areas selectively by using strokes.

Figure 1-5: Sharpening an image boosts the contrast of neighboring pixels and gives the illusion of improved focus.

Sharpen

The Sharpen filter is best used for minimal touchups in small areas. This single-step filter increases the contrast between all the pixels in the image or selection. Although this filter makes the image look sharper, it can add a grainy look to solid areas that aren't part of the edges.

Sharpen More

The Sharpen More filter, a single-step filter, increases the contrast between pixels even more than the regular Sharpen filter. Like the Sharpen filter, Sharpen More is best relegated to noncritical sharpening because it doesn't do a very good job of sharpening large areas. Also, it doesn't provide the control you need for more intense projects.

Sharpen Edges

The Sharpen Edges filter is a single-step filter that's superior to the Sharpen and Sharpen More filters because it concentrates its efforts on the edges of images, adding sharpness without making the image grainy or noisy. It's best used for quickie fixes.

Smart Sharpen

The newest member of the Sharpen team is definitely a keeper: Smart Sharpen does a great job of detecting edges and sharpening them less destructively. Like the veteran Unsharp Mask filter, discussed in the next section, this filter gives you a lot of control over the sharpening settings, as shown in Figure 1-6. Here's the scoop on those settings:

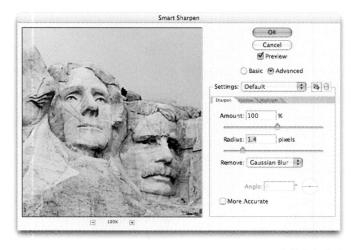

Corbis Digital Stock

Figure 1-6: The Smart Sharpen filter gives the most control over your sharpening specifications.

✔ **Preview:** Obviously, keep this option selected so that you can take a gander at what's happening as you sharpen. You'll appreciate the large preview.

✔ **Basic and Advanced:** The only difference between the two views is that with the Advanced view, you can control the amount of sharpening in the Shadow and Highlight areas of your image. Use the following controls to fine-tune the amount of sharpening in your light and dark areas:

  • *Fade Amount:* Determine the amount of sharpening.

  • *Tonal Width:* Specify the range of tones you want to sharpen. Move your slider to the right to sharpen only the darker of the shadow areas and the lighter of the highlight areas.

- *Radius:* Specify the amount of space around a pixel that's used to determine whether a pixel is in the shadow or the highlight area. Move your slider to the right to specify a greater area.

✓ **Settings:** You can save your sharpening settings so that you can load them for later use without having to re-create them. Click the disk/down-pointing arrow icon to do so.

✓ **Amount:** Use this control to vary the amount of edge sharpening. A higher value increases the contrast between pixels around the edges. Your choices range from 1 percent to 500 percent. For subtle amounts of sharpening, anything around 100 percent or less provides the effect you're looking for without making the image appear overly contrasty (yes, that's a technical term) or unrealistic.

✓ **Radius:** This slider controls the width (in pixels) of the edges that the filter will modify. The higher the value, the wider the edge that's affected. Your range varies from 0.1 pixel (for fine control) to 64 pixels (for broader sharpening effects). How you use this control varies chiefly on the resolution of your original image. Low-resolution images (100 pixels per inch and lower) look best when you use only a small radius value, from a fraction of a pixel up to 3 or 4 pixels.

A good rule to consider when you select a radius is to divide your image's ppi resolution by 150 and then adjust from there. For example, if you have a 150 ppi image, set the radius at 1 and then tweak from there.

✓ **Remove:** Specify the algorithm to be used to remove the blurriness in the image. Gaussian Blur is the method used by Unsharp Mask and is good for removing that hazy type of blurriness. Lens Blur detects and sharpens the edges and detail in the image, and it does a good job of reducing those nasty halos that can occur from sharpening. Motion Blur reduces the blurriness that can occur when you move your camera (or your subject moves).

✓ **Angle:** Specify the direction of motion if you choose Motion Blur as your algorithm.

✓ **More Accurate:** Check this option to make Photoshop provide a more accurate removal of blurriness. It takes longer, but it's worth the wait, as shown in Figure 1-7.

Corbis Digital Stock

Figure 1-7: Smart Sharpen can take your soft, mushy photo and make it come to life.

Unsharp Mask

Don't feel bad: Everyone is confused by the name *Unsharp Mask* the first time they encounter it. This filter provides a sophisticated attempt to duplicate a sophisticated photographic effect called (you guessed it) *unsharp masking,* in which two sheets of film are sandwiched together to create a final image. One sheet is the original film negative (or a duplicate), and the second is a positive image (the "normal" photograph) that's blurred slightly. When the two are put together, the light and dark areas cancel each other out, except at the edges — because of the blurring of the positive mask, which causes the edges to spread at those points.

Unsharp masking is a tricky procedure in the darkroom. It's much more precise in the digital realm because Photoshop can easily control the width of the areas to be masked, as well as a relative brightness level to use before beginning to apply the masking effect.

In the Unsharp Mask dialog box, you can find two of the same controls that you have with Smart Sharpen (see the preceding section) — Amount and Radius. You also have another option, called Threshold. Threshold controls the difference in brightness that must be present between adjacent pixels before the edge is sharpened. That is, you need to have a distinct contrast between adjacent pixels along an edge in order to sharpen the edge. Your choices range from brightness values of 0 to 255. Selecting a low value emphasizes edges with very little contrast difference (which is usually what you want). You're generally better off leaving this control at 0 unless your image has a lot of noise. Higher values force Photoshop to provide edge sharpening only when adjacent pixels are dramatically different in brightness. Increasing the threshold too much can cause some harsh transitions between sharpened and unsharpened pixels.

In most cases, the Amount and Radius sliders are the only controls you need to use. Threshold is most useful when the first two controls create excessive noise in the image. You can sometimes reduce this noise by increasing the Threshold level a little.

Sharpening always increases contrast, so keep this in mind if you plan on adjusting the contrast of your image with other commands and tools. Sharpening is usually one of the last commands you apply when correcting and enhancing your images.

Blurring What's Sharp

What, me blurry? The answer is yes, if you have an image that contains unwanted *grain* (the roughness or noise added by the photographic film) or perhaps an ugly pattern of halftone dots used in a printed image.

Applying the Lens Blur filter

If you've ever played with the aperture settings on a camera, you're probably well aware that you can determine how shallow or deep your depth of field is. Depth of field relates to the *plane of focus* (the areas in a photo that are in front of or behind the focal point, and that remain in focus) or how in-focus the foreground elements are when you compare them to the background elements. If you use a Lens Blur filter on an alpha channel (see Book VI, Chapter 1 for more on alpha channels), the alpha channel acts as a depth map. This approach is great for taking a fully focused image and creating a shallow depth of field in which the foremost object is in focus and the background elements get blurrier the farther they are from the focal point. You can achieve this effect by creating an alpha channel filled with a white-to-black gradient — black where you want the most focus, white where you want the least focus or most blur.

Here's a brief description of setting the Lens Blur filter options:

- **Source:** If you have an alpha channel, select it from this pop-up menu. The Lens Blur option interprets the various grayscale values of the alpha channel and applies the blur according to the value set in the Blur Focal Distance option. Choose Transparency to make an image get blurrier while it gets more transparent. Choose Layer Mask to apply the blur according to the grayscale values on the layer mask. (See Book VI, Chapter 3 for more on layer masks.) If your image contains none of these options, choose None. Photoshop applies the blur on the image.

- **Blur Focal Distance:** Specifies how blurry or in focus an area of the image is. Drag the slider to specify the value or click the crosshair cursor on the part of the image that you want to be in full focus.

- **Iris:** The Iris settings are meant to simulate a camera lens. Specify the shape of the lens, as well as the radius (size of the iris), curvature, and rotation of that shape.

- **Specular Highlights:** The Lens Blur filter averages the highlights of an image, which, if left uncorrected, cause some highlights to appear grayish. These controls help to retain *specular highlights,* or those highlights that should appear very white. Set the Threshold value to specify which highlights should be *specular* (remain white). Set a Brightness value to specify how much to relighten any blurred areas.

- **Noise:** Blurring, of course, obliterates any noise (or *film grain*) that an image may have. This absence of noise can cause the image to appear inconsistent or unrealistic, in many cases. Drag the slider to add noise back into your image.

You might need to blur a background to make the foreground seem sharper or blur a portion of an image to create an angelic glow. Here are your blurring options (all in the Filter➪Blur menu):

- **Average:** This single-step filter calculates the average value (or color) of the image or selection and fills the area with that average value. This option can help you smooth the values of areas that contain a lot of noise.

✓ **Blur:** Also a single-step filter, Blur provides overall blurring of an image.

✓ **Blur More:** This filter provides a significantly increased amount of blurring compared to the regular, old-fashioned Blur filter.

✓ **Box Blur:** The Box Blur filter blurs your image in the shape of, well, a box or square.

✓ **Gaussian Blur:** This filter offers a radius control to let you adjust the amount of blurring more precisely. It also has a really cool name.

The Gaussian Blur filter is an excellent tool because it gives you a great deal of control over the amount and type of blurring you get, especially when compared to the single-step Blur and Blur More filters, which apply a fixed amount of blur. Use these latter two filters when you simply want to desharpen an image a tad, and turn to Gaussian Blur when you're looking for a specific effect.

✓ **Lens Blur:** This filter simulates the blurring that can occur when you capture an image with a camera. For details, see the sidebar "Applying the Lens Blur filter," in this chapter.

✓ **Motion Blur:** This filter simulates the blur you see in objects that are moving.

✓ **Radial Blur:** This filter produces the kind of blur you might get when photographing a revolving automobile tire. You can also get a zoom effect with this filter.

✓ **Shape Blur:** The Shape blur basically blurs your image according to the shape you choose from the panel. The shape choices you have are the same as those with the Custom Shape tool. Move the Radius slider to the right for a larger blur. You can see an example of different shape blurs in Figure 1-8.

✓ **Smart Blur:** This filter lets you control how Photoshop applies the blur to edges and other details of the image.

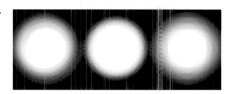

Figure 1-8: The Shape Blur blurs your image in a variety of shapes.

✓ **Surface Blur:** This filter blurs the surface or interior of the image, rather than the edges. If you want to preserve your edge details but blur everything else, this is your filter.

Smoothing with the Facet and Median Filters

One reason you might want to blur an image is to reduce dust and scratches, or to smooth away sharp edges. In the following sections, I show you how to use the versatile Facet and Median filters to soften an image.

Although the Facet and Median filters smooth images by eliminating some detail, you can compensate for the blurring effect by applying the Smart Sharpen filter or Unsharp Mask (covered earlier in this chapter) with a low radius setting to sharpen things up a little.

The Facet filter

The Facet filter breaks up an image by using a posterizing effect. It gathers blocks of pixels that are similar in brightness and converts them to a single value, using geometric shapes. (When you posterize an image, you reduce it to a very small number of tones.)

The geometric shapes make the image look more randomly produced, while eliminating much of the banding effect you get with conventional posterizing filters.

The effects of the Facet filter are subtle and best viewed at close range. The original image in Figure 1-9 contains some dust, scratches, and a few other defects. Instead of retouching them one by one, I used Facet.

Facet is a single-step filter, so you don't need to adjust any controls. Just choose Filter⇨Pixelate⇨Facet and evaluate your results. You can apply the filter multiple times. However, even one application smoothes out the picture and eliminates the worst of the artifacts.

Original	Single Facet filter	Multiple Facet filter

iStockphoto

Figure 1-9: The Facet filter can simply eliminate annoying artifacts or convert your image into a "painted" piece.

If you apply the Facet filter multiple times, your image takes on a kind of pointillist, stroked look that becomes obvious. Using the filter over and over on the same image can yield quite interesting special effects.

The Median filter

The Median filter (look for it on the Filter➪Noise menu) operates similarly to the Facet filter in that it reduces the difference between adjacent pixels by changing the values of some of them. In this case, it assigns the median values of a group of pixels to the center pixel in the group. Unlike the Facet filter, the Median filter gives you a bit of control. You can choose the radius of the group that Photoshop uses to calculate the median value. Median tends to make an image look a bit blurrier because it reduces the contrast of adjacent pixels. However, it does a good job of smoothing the image and removing artifacts.

Putting It Together

Creating an Angelic Glow

Sometimes, a little blur can add a soft, romantic mood or angelic glow that can improve glamour photos, pictures of kids, or even something as mundane as a flower. The secret is to apply only enough blurring to provide the soft effect you want without completely obliterating your original subject. Assuming, of course, that your subject doesn't *deserve* obliteration; that the kids are your own (or those of a close friend or relative); and that they are, in fact, of that rare angelic variety.

You don't want to use this effect on other subjects, such as men, who generally like a rugged, masculine appearance. Many senior citizens regard the age lines on their faces as badges of distinction earned over a long, rewarding life. Don't try softening them up with glowing effects, either.

To add an angelic glow to your little angel, just follow these steps:

1. **Open the image in Photoshop.**

   I used one of a cute little girl.

2. **Choose Layer➪Duplicate Layer to create a copy of the image layer.**

3. **Select Filter➪Blur➪Gaussian Blur.**

   Gaussian Blur softens the upper layer, producing an airy glow.

continued

**Book VII
Chapter 1**

**Making Corrections
with Daily Filters**

continued

4. **Move the Radius slider to the right to produce a moderate amount of blur and then click OK to apply the blur-ring effect, as shown in the figure.**

   I used a value of 7.

5. **In the Layers panel, select Lighten from the Blending Modes pop-up menu.**

6. **Use the Opacity slider (click the right-pointing arrow to access the slider) to reduce the amount of glow (if it's too much for your tastes).**

   I reduced my Opacity to 65 percent.

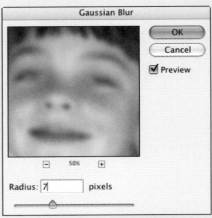

7. **Choose Layer⇨Flatten Image to combine all the layers.**

   Experiment with different amounts of Gaussian Blur until you find the perfect glowing effect, as I did in my figure.

Applying a Filter Again

You can reapply the last filter you worked with — using the same settings — by pressing Ctrl+F (⌘+F on the Mac). (It's also the first command on the Filter menu.) You might want to do this to strengthen the effect of a filter on a particular image, layer, or selection. Or you simply may want to apply the same filter to a succession of images or selections.

To bring up the dialog box for the last filter you applied, press Ctrl+Alt+F (Windows) or ⌘+Option+F (Mac). This shortcut can be very useful when you apply a filter and then decide you want to go back and use different settings. After applying the filter, press Ctrl+Z (⌘+Z on the Mac) to undo, and then press Ctrl+Alt+F (⌘+Option+F on the Mac) to bring up the filter's dialog box. The dialog box opens with the settings you used last time, allowing you to make adjustments and then reapply the filter.

Fading a Filter

Sometimes, you may not want the full effects of a filter applied to your image or selection. Often, applying a filter full strength tends to give it that artificial "Photoshopped" look. Photoshop has a handy Fade Filter facility that lets you control the intensity of the filter's effects. You can access this feature by choosing Edit⇨Fade or by pressing Shift+Ctrl+F (Shift+⌘+F on the Mac). The Fade Filter facility also has a Preview option, so you can preview the changes you're making to the original image.

You must fade your filter *immediately after* you use the filter. If you use a painting or editing tool after applying the filter, for example, Fade Filter doesn't appear on the Edit menu anymore. Photoshop replaces it with Fade Brush Tool or whatever your last execution was.

You can fade the effect in the Fade dialog box in the following ways:

- **Adjust opacity settings.** Just about every filter allows you to adjust opacity, so most of the time, the Opacity slider is all you need to adjust the strength of the filter applied to your image.

- **Use a blending mode.** Use one of the blend modes in Photoshop to merge the filter effect with the original image. For more on blend modes, see Book V, Chapter 3.

  You can also fade a filter's effect by applying a filter to a duplicate layer or to a selection on that layer. Then adjust the opacity or blend mode of the filtered layer so that it merges with the unfiltered layer underneath it.

You can also apply a Smart Filter to your layer or selection. By doing so, you get the utmost flexibility in editing the filter's opacity and blend modes — not just once, but infinitely. For more about Smart Filters, see the section "Introducing Smart Filters," earlier in this chapter.

Book VII Chapter 1

Making Corrections with Daily Filters

Selectively Applying a Filter

You don't need to apply filters to an entire image or an entire layer. You can achieve some of the best effects when you apply a filter to only a portion of an image — say, to an object in the foreground but not on the background. Your choices include the following:

- **Selections:** Make a selection and apply the filter only to that selection. You can use Quick Mask mode (see Book VI, Chapter 2) to paint a selection. This technique can give you a high degree of control; it even lets you feather the edges of the selection so the filter effect fades out.

✔ **Channels:** You can store selections as alpha channels (visible in the Channels panel, of course). But you can also choose to apply a filter to only one of the other channels, such as the Red, Green, or Blue channels in an RGB image. By using this technique, you can create a filter effect that's applied to only one color in an image. (Check out Book VI, Chapter 1 for information about channels.)

✔ **Layer Masks:** You can use a layer mask to create a selection where you apply the filter to that selection only. Or you can actually apply the filter to the layer mask itself for a special effect, as shown in Figure 1-10.

✔ **History Brush:** Use the History Brush tool to paint a filter onto a portion of the image. Apply the filter to the entire image. Then in the History panel, select the state just before you applied your filter. Set your source state to the filter state and then paint the part of your image you want filtered. For details on working with the History panel, see Book II, Chapter 4.

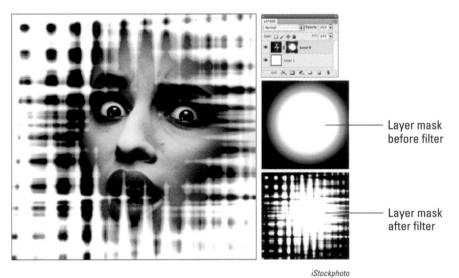

Layer mask before filter

Layer mask after filter

iStockphoto

Figure 1-10: Apply a filter to your layer mask to create a special effect.

Because a Smart Filter comes equipped with its own layer mask, you can selectively apply the filter to your layer in varying percentages. For details, see the section "Introducing Smart Filters," earlier in this chapter.

Putting It Together

Sprucing Up a Scanned Halftone

Publications use only a limited number of ink colors to reproduce a photograph. Every tone you see in a black-and-white image must be reproduced by using pure black ink and the white (okay, dirty beige) of the paper. Full-color images are represented by combining CMYK (cyan, magenta, yellow, and black). Printers can't use various shades of gray ink to create grayscale photos. They also can't use different strengths of color inks to generate the rainbow of hues you see in an image onscreen. To get at least some of that subtlety, photographs have to be converted to a pattern of dots before they can be printed.

Our eyes blend the dots together to produce the illusion of a grayscale or color image with smooth gradations of tone. However, a problem arises if you want to reuse a photograph and don't have access to the original. Scanners can capture the halftone dots, but the resulting image usually has an unpleasant pattern called *moiré*.

You have several ways of reducing the moiré effect, usually by blurring the image so that the dots merge and the underlying pattern vanishes. Many scanners have a *descreen* setting that partially eliminates the effect, but that setting sometimes actually blurs your image more than you want. Fortunately, you can usually do a pretty good job in Photoshop. But remember that, if there's any way possible, scanning from continuous-tone images always yields the best quality.

In the following steps, I demonstrate an easier way to eliminate a moiré pattern. (Over the years, I managed to lose the original negative and print.) You can see the dreadful moiré pattern that resulted when I scanned the clip.

To rid your scanned halftone print of bothersome moiré, follow these steps:

1. **Open the image in Photoshop.**

2. **Zoom in so that you can see the halftone pattern clearly while you work, as shown in the figure.**

3. **Choose Filter⇨Blur⇨Gaussian Blur.**

   The Gaussian Blur dialog box appears.

   You can also first convert your image to a Smart Object and then apply your Gaussian Blur and Smart Sharpen filters as Smart Filters. See the section "Introducing Smart Filters," in this chapter.

**Book VII
Chapter 1**

**Making Corrections
with Daily Filters**

continued

continued

4. **Move the Radius slider to the right until the halftone pattern is blurred, and then click OK to apply the blur.**

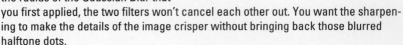

I used a value of 1.7 pixels in my figure.

5. **Choose Filter⇨Sharpen⇨Smart Sharpen to restore some of the image's sharpness now that you've eliminated the pattern. Choose Gaussian Blur for the Remove algorithm.**

As long as the Radius value for the Smart Sharpen filter doesn't exceed the radius of the Gaussian Blur that you first applied, the two filters won't cancel each other out. You want the sharpening to make the details of the image crisper without bringing back those blurred halftone dots.

6. **Move the Amount slider to the right to sharpen the image.**

Try to find a setting that does the job without making the image appear unnaturally sharp or show too much contrast. I used 150 percent in my figure.

Calculate a starting Radius value by dividing the ppi (pixels per inch) of the scanned image by 150. If a moiré pattern reappears, reduce the Radius value.

7. **Click OK to apply the sharpness.**

The result of my blur-and-sharpen exercise is shown in the final figure.

Chapter 2: Applying Filters for Special Occasions

In This Chapter

✔ Using the Filter Gallery

✔ Applying artsy effects and brush strokes

✔ Adding distortion and noise — on purpose

✔ Breaking up an image

✔ Rendering different effects

✔ Sketching and texturizing images the easy way

✔ Putting other filters to work

*P*hotoshop has dozens of filters that let you enhance your image in unusual ways. You can create Old Masters portraits from common snapshots, shatter your image into a thousand sparkling pieces, create clouds in a cloudless sky, create stained glass, or perform hundreds of other tricks.

The big challenge in using these filters is figuring out what each filter can do and how to apply it to the best effect. This chapter builds on Book VII, Chapter 1 by introducing you to more of those fabulous Photoshop plug-ins — and shows you some typical applications for them. Several Putting It Together projects have step-by-step instructions. For the first few examples, I provide you with the settings I used to achieve particular looks. However, filter effects vary greatly when applied to different images, so you have to play with the filter controls yourself when you use these techniques with your own images.

You can apply a filter to a layer, selection, or channel. And you can also fade a filter, change opacity settings, and use layer masks to soften the effects of filters. In fact, in some cases, you may *have* to decrease the effect of a filter because full strength can look overdone. On the other hand, when applied selectively, the same filter may look subtle and sophisticated. Although filters can be a blast to play with, you want to exercise some restraint when applying them for a real project. Getting carried away with the effects is easy, but the simplest effect is often the most beautiful.

Working in the Filter Gallery

The Filter Gallery (a dialog box-like gizmo that Adobe refers to as an *editing window*) gives you an alternative route to access and apply filters. To put it onscreen, choose Filter⇨Filter Gallery. In this window, you can apply multiple filters, as well as edit or delete them later. This feature has made filters more flexible, more user-friendly, and easier to apply.

Follow these steps to get up and running in the Filter Gallery:

1. **Choose Filter⇨Filter Gallery.**

   The Filter Gallery dialog box appears, as shown in Figure 2-1.

2. **Click your desired filter category folder.**

   The folder expands and displays the filters in that category. A thumbnail illustrating the filter's effect accompanies each filter. To collapse the filter category folder, simply click it again.

3. **Select the filter you want to apply.**

4. **Specify any settings associated with the filter.**

   You get a large preview of your image in the left side of the dialog box. Use the magnification controls to zoom in and out of the preview. When you change your settings, the preview dynamically updates itself. To preview a different filter, simply select that filter.

   If you want your custom settings to be the new default for the filter, simply hold down the Ctrl key (⌘ key on the Mac) while you are specifying your settings. The Cancel button changes to Default. After you have established your settings, release the Ctrl (or ⌘) key. Your new settings then become the new default.

5. **When you're happy with the filter, click OK to apply the filter and exit the dialog box. But if you want to apply another filter, leave the dialog box open and proceed to Steps 6, 7, and 8.**

6. **If you want to apply another filter, click the New Effect Layer button at the bottom of the dialog box.**

   Clicking this button duplicates the existing filter.

7. **Select your new filter, which then replaces the duplicate.**

   Photoshop lists each of the filters you apply to the image in the bottom-right of the dialog box.

8. **When you're done, click OK to apply the second filter and exit the dialog box.**

   You can apply as many filters as you want to your image. But, often, less is more.

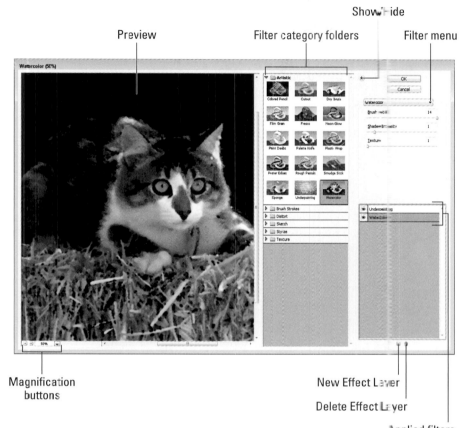

Show/Hide

Preview   Filter category folders   Filter menu

Magnification buttons

New Effect Layer

Delete Effect Layer

Applied filters

Corbis Digital Stock

Figure 2-1: The Filter Gallery enables you to apply and edit multiple filters with in a single dialog box.

Book VII
Chapter 2

Applying Filters for
Special Occasions

Here are some other helpful tips to keep in mind when you're using the Filter Gallery:

- To delete an applied filter, select it in the list in the lower-right portion of the dialog box and click the Delete Effect Layer button (the trash can icon) at the bottom of the dialog box.

- To edit an applied filter's settings, select it in the list and make any necessary changes. Click OK to reapply. Although you can edit a particular filter's settings, that edit affects any subsequent filters you've made after applying that particular filter.

✔ You can rearrange the order of the applied filters. Simply select and drag the filter up or down within the list.

Rearranging the order of the applied filters changes the resulting effect of the filters.

✔ To resize the Filter Gallery dialog box, drag the lower-right corner.

✔ To hide the Filter menu and provide the maximum real estate for the preview box, click the arrow to the left of the OK button.

✔ You can choose any of the filters found in the Filter Gallery from the Filter menu itself. Choosing a Filter menu filter launches the Filter Gallery automatically — but not all filters are available in the Filter Gallery. You have to access some of them individually from the Filter menu.

Don't be misled into thinking that the Filter Gallery is like layer styles, where the styles can be removed and the underlying pixel data is returned to its pristine, original state. Regular filters change the pixels of an image permanently, and after you apply one, you can't remove it. So, be sure that you really like what you've done and that you have a backup copy of that precious family photo or critical project image.

That being said, if you do want your filters to act like layer styles, they can. You can apply a Smart Filter to any layer that you first convert into a Smart Object. Smart Filters enable you to apply a filter nondestructively, without altering any underlying pixels. For more on Smart Filters, see Book VII, Chapter 1.

Getting Artsy

Quite a few Photoshop filters produce artistic effects. You can find a large collection of them in the Sketch and Stylize submenus. However, the Artistic menu contains 15 versatile filters that you can use to add brush strokes to your images, wrap them in plastic, create posterlike effects, and manufacture other interesting looks.

Many Photoshop users employ these filters to create images that look as if they were painted. What those users might not tell you, unless pressed, is that artsy filters can make terrible photos look better — or, in some cases, pretty darn good. These filters can disguise a multitude of photographic sins, turning shoebox rejects into pretty decent digital transformations. The photo of a clock in Figure 2-2 is, arguably, not very interesting — and (worse) it's blurry. I moved the camera while I was taking the photo.

Figure 2-2: This photo isn't that interesting and is slightly out of focus.

To improve this image, I employed filters on the Filter⇨Artistic menu. Try one of the following filters:

- **Poster Edges:** A quick application of this filter improves the photo 100 percent. (See the left photo in Figure 2-3.) The filter not only gives the picture an artsy, posterlike look, but it also enhances the edges to make the clock's outline appear sharper.

  I set the Poster Edges filter's Edge Thickness to 4, bumped the Edge Intensity up to a value of 6 to create dramatic-looking edges, and set the Posterization level to 6 to allow more tones for a bit more realism.

- **Rough Pastels:** This filter, shown in the right photo in Figure 2-3, gives the look of a fine art piece created with oil pastels. I used the settings of 8 for the Stroke Length and Stroke Detail, 100% Scale, and 20 for Relief. I left my light source at Bottom.

- **The Dry Brush:** This filter can add an even more stylistic effect, reducing details to a series of broad strokes.

- **Colored Pencil:** This filter crosshatches the edges of your image to create a pencil-like effect.

- **Cutout:** This effect assembles an image from what looks like cut-out paper shapes, which resemble a kid's art project.

- **Film Grain:** This photographic effect diffuses an image with thousands of tiny dots that simulate clumps of film grain. (Think of old home movies.)

- **Fresco:** This effect looks (supposedly) like pigments applied to fresh, wet plaster. Okay, I guess . . . if you squint.

- **Paint Daubs:** This effect uses smears of color from your choice of a half-dozen different brush types. Very Jackson Pollock.

Figure 2-3: The Poster Edges filter (left) and the Rough Pastels filter (right) help

✐ **Plastic Wrap:** This filter can produce a wet look, particularly when you apply it to a selection and then fade the filter so it doesn't overpower the detail in your image.

✐ **Watercolor:** This nice pastel effect diffuses an image while adding an interesting, watery texture.

Stroking Your Image with Filters

You can find more stroking filters on the Brush Strokes submenu, along with some interesting texturizing filters that can spruce up less-than-perfect photos and add a new look to even your best shots.

Choose Filter⇨Brush Strokes to find the stroking filters that can provide hours of fun, including

✐ **Ink Outlines:** Adobe describes this filter as producing the look of a corroded ink drawing.

✐ **Spatter:** This filter generates the look you might get from a sputtering airbrush, as shown in Figure 2-4. I set my Spray Radius to 25 and my Smoothness to 10.

✐ **Accented Edges:** Use this filter to make a subject jump out from its background by emphasizing the edges of all the objects in the picture.

Corbis Digital Stock

Figure 2-4: The Spatter filter gives this portrait a nice painted texture.

Putting It Together

Creating Exotic Edges for Your Images

An attractive border can give your image an edge. If you want an edgy look or want to take your work right to the edge, you can apply this technique faster than you can say, "Overworked metaphor!" Photoshop lets you apply deckled looks and other effects to the borders of your image by using any of several plug-ins built right into your trusty Filters menu.

Follow these easy steps to the edge of image immortality:

1. **Choose a photo that you think could use a decorative border and open it in Photoshop.**

2. **With the Rectangular Marquee tool, select the portion of the image you're framing, as shown in the figure.**

3. **Double-click the Quick Mask Mode icon in the Tools panel. In the Quick Mask dialog box that appears, choose Selected Areas in the Color Indicates area.**

4. **Click OK to enter Quick Mask mode.**

Photoshop highlights the rectangle you selected in color, as shown in the figure.

5. **Choose Filter➪Blur➪Gaussian Blur, set the Radius, and click OK.**

To give the image a softer edge when the selection is deckled, I've set the Radius to 30.

6. **Choose Filter➪Brush Strokes➪ Sprayed Strokes.**

7. **Adjust the Stroke Length and Spray Radius sliders to acquire the desired effect.**

The higher the resolution, the higher the value you may need. In this case, I moved the Stroke Length and Spray Radius sliders to the max of 20 and 25 (respectively).

Imagestate

Book VII
Chapter 2

Applying Filters for Special Occasions

continued

continued

8. **Select your desired Stroke Direction from the drop-down list.**

I selected Right Diagonal for my image.

9. **Click OK to apply the effect to the Quick Mask selection.**

After application, the edges of the quick mask overlay (highlighted area) appear frayed, as shown in the figure.

10. **Press Q to exit Quick Mask mode.**

A selection border with ragged edges appears around the selection.

11. **Press Ctrl+C (⌘+C on the Mac) to copy the selected area, and then press Ctrl+V (⌘+V on the Mac) to paste it into a new layer.**

12. **Create a new layer and fill it with the color you want for the background.**

I filled my background with white.

13. **In the Layers panel, move the colored background layer underneath your deckled image.**

14. **Choose Layer⇨Flatten Image. When prompted, if you want to discard hidden layers, click OK.**

The finished image appears, as shown in the final figure.

Distorting for Fun

With a couple exceptions, Photoshop's Distortion filters twist, turn, and bend your images in surprising ways, turning ordinary objects into wavy images, pinched shapes, and bloated spheres.

The first exception? The Diffuse Glow filter distorts images only to the extent that it imbues them with a soft, romantic, fuzzy look that can make the sharpest image look positively ethereal.

I've never figured out why Adobe dumped this useful filter into the Distort submenu, but there it is. (And here it is applied to a girl in Figure 2-5.)

Corbis Digital Stock

Figure 2-5: Give your photo a heavenly aura with the Diffuse Glow filter (left).

The second exception was the Lens Correction filter when it resided under the Distort submenu. It got moved out and supersized in CS5. This awesome filter fixes distortions caused by the camera lens. Choose Filter⇨Lens Correction. In the dialog box, you will find Auto Correction and Custom tabs. Make it easy and try the Auto Corrections or move right to the Custom settings and manually make corrective adjustments.

Here's the lowdown on the new Automatic Correction settings:

- **Correction:** Select the problem you want to correct. Find explanations of each in the Custom tab information. Note that if the corrections extend or contract your image beyond its original dimensions, choose Auto Scale Image. Choose how you want your edges filled from the Edge pop-up menu — with black, white, transparency, or extended with pixels from the image.

- **Search Criteria:** Choose your camera make and model, as well as your lens model. Choosing the correct equipment will assist Photoshop in making more accurate corrections.

✔ **Lens Profiles:** Select a matching profile. For zoom lenses, right-click (Control-click on the Mac) and choose the most similar focal length. If you don't find your lens profile, click the Search Online button to find profiles uploaded by other photographers. If you want to save a profile for later use, click the Lens Profiles pop-up menu and choose Save Online Profile Locally.

Here are the settings under the Custom tab:

✔ **Geometric Distortion:** Correct abnormalities such as *barrel* and *pin-cushion* distortions, in which straight lines appear (respectively) bowed out or in. Select the Remove Distortion tool and drag on the image — or you can also drag the Remove Distortion slider.

✔ **Chromatic Aberration:** Got colored fringe around your subjects? Photographers call this nastiness *chromatic aberration.* Fringe, aberration, whatever it's called — get rid of it by using the Red/Cyan or Blue/Yellow Fringe sliders. The Move Grid, Hand, and Zoom tools can help make your adjustments more user-friendly.

✔ **Vignette:** If your images suffer from vignetting, in which the edges are darker than the center, slide the Amount slider to specify the amount of lightening or darkening. Slide the Midpoint slider to specify the width affected by the Amount.

✔ **Transform:** Correct perspective issues, often caused by tilting your camera when shooting, by using the Transform sliders of Vertical and Horizontal Perspective. Adjust the Angle to rotate the image to compensate for camera tilt or tweak your perspective adjustments. You may also use the Straighten tool to rotate a tilted image, as shown in Figure 2-6. Drag along the line in your image that you wish to straighten. Finally, to eliminate blank areas in your image created by correcting geometric distortions, use the Scale setting, which will crop off those areas.

✔ **Preview/Show Grid:** Choose whether to see your image with or without a grid overlay (of which you can specify the size). Many problems, such as perspective issues, are easier to fix using a grid as a guide.

✔ **The Move grid, Hand, and Zoom tools:** Can help make your adjustments more user friendly. You can also control your magnification using the zoom controls in the lower-left corner of the dialog box.

The Lens Correction filter works with 8-bit and 16-bit images only.

You can fix several photos simultaneously by batch-processing them with the Lens Correction automated command. Choose File➪Automate➪Lens Correction.

Other filters of this ilk can produce wavy images, add pond ripples, pinch images, or transform them into spheres. Check out Figure 2-7 to see distortions of a wall clock.

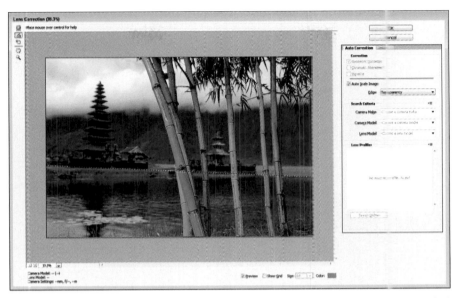

Figure 2-6: Use the Straighten tool to fix the horizon line in the Lens Correction dialog box.

Zigzag in
Pond Ripples mode   Normal   Wave   Glass in
Frosted mode   Spherize

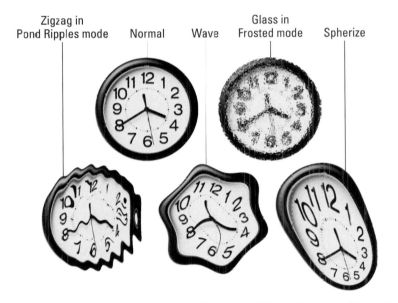

Figure 2-7: A normal clock takes on Dali-esque qualities with various Distort filters.

The Glass filter can do the following to your images:

- Add a glass-block texture
- Add a canvas texture
- Create frosted-glass fuzziness
- Break up your image with tiny lenses

 Don't like any of Photoshop's textures? No biggie; you can also load your own texture. Click the Texture pop-up menu (the right-pointing arrow) and select Load Texture.

Pumping Up the Noise

Noise in images consists of any graininess or texture that occurs, either because of the inherent quality of the image or through the editing process. Noise filters, such as the Photoshop Add Noise plug-in, produce random texture and grain in an image. If you're new to image editing, you might wonder why you'd want to add noise to an image in the first place. Wouldn't it be smarter to remove it? Well, sometimes. In practice, you can find a lot of applications, including the following, that call for a little noise here and there:

- **Adding texture:** Objects that become too smooth, either because of blurring or other image editing you may have done, often look better when you add some noise to give them a texture. This technique is particularly useful if one object in an image has been edited, smoothed, or blurred more than the other objects in the image.

- **Blending foreign objects into a scene:** When you drop a new object into the middle of an existing scene, the amount of grain or noise in the new object is often quite different from the objects it's joining.

  For example, say you've decided to take a photo of your house and want to insert a certain luxury car in your driveway. Unfortunately, your digital photo of your brother-in-law's luxo-mobile is a lot sharper than the picture of your house. Adding a little noise can help the two objects blend more realistically. You may even forget that the car isn't yours.

- **Improving image quality:** Images that contain smooth gradients often don't print well because some printers can't reproduce the subtle blend of colors from one hue to another. The result is *objectionable banding* in your printed image: You can see distinct stripes where the colors progress from one to another. Adding a little noise can break up the gradient enough that your printer can reproduce the blend of colors, and the noise/grain itself is virtually invisible on the printed sheet.

Pumping Down the Noise

Although the Add Noise filter adds grain, the other filters in the Noise submenu don't add noise at all; instead, they make noise and *artifacts* (flaws, such as the dust and scratches on old film) less noticeable. Choose Filter➪ Noise to find your tools, which include

- ✔ **Despeckle:** This filter makes dust spots in your image less noticeable by decreasing the contrast of your entire image — except at the edges. That translates into a slightly blurry image (which masks the spots) that still retains sharpness along the edges of image components. You end up with a little blur to soften the image but enough detail in the edges that the picture still looks good.

- ✔ **Dust & Scratches:** This filter concentrates its blurring effect on only those areas of your image that contain scratches and other artifacts. Photoshop performs this magic by looking at each pixel in an image and moving out in a radial direction until it encounters an abrupt transition in tone. (That's a signal that a spot or scratch has been found.) You can specify the radius in which Photoshop searches for the little culprits, from 1 to 100 pixels. Be careful not to overdo it. Too much of this filter can obliterate the detail in the image. Leave the Threshold at 0. If you journey into the world of mush, try using Edit➪Fade right after you apply the filter.

   When working with any of the Noise filters, be very conservative at first. All the Noise filters involve destruction of image data. Remember, that's just the nature of filters, in general — changing pixel data. A little bit can help — and be just the effect you're looking for. Just a little bit more, however, may completely wreck things.

- ✔ **Median:** This filter reduces contrast around dust motes, thus hiding them, in a slightly different way. This filter looks at the pixels surrounding each pixel in the image and replaces the center one with a new pixel that has the median brightness level of that group. The process is a little hard to describe succinctly, but basically, the bright spots darken while the rest of the image isn't affected. For more on the Median filter, see Book VII, Chapter 1.

- ✔ **Reduce Noise:** This filter, shown in Figure 2-8, is designed to remove luminance noise and JPEG artifacts that can appear on digital photos. *Luminance noise* is grayscale noise that makes images look overly grainy. Here's some info on the options:

  - • *Strength:* Specify the amount of noise reduction. You can reduce noise in the overall image or (if you click the Advanced button) channel by channel.

    Be sure to check out the Blue channel, in particular. It's often the channel that captures all the crud.

  - • *Preserve Details:* A higher number preserves edges and details but reduces the amount of noise removal. Find a happy medium.

- *Reduce Color Noise:* Removes random colored pixel artifacts.

- *Sharpen Details:* Counteracts the fact that removing noise reduces sharpness, as well.

- *Remove JPEG Artifact:* Check this option to remove the annoying blocks and halos that can occur because of low-quality JPEG compression.

You can also save and reload your settings. Click the disk/arrow icon. In the New Filter Settings dialog box, enter a name for your settings and click OK. To load your settings, choose your desired settings from the Settings drop-down list.

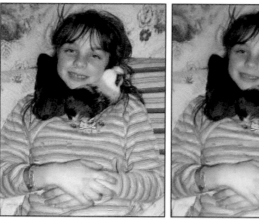

Figure 2-8: The Reduce Noise filter attempts to remove noise while retaining some sharpness in edges and details.

Breaking Your Image into Pieces

The Pixelate filters in Photoshop break your images into bits and pieces, providing more of those painterly effects you can get with brush strokes and artistic filters.

The Pixelate submenu includes the Crystallize filter (applied to the little girl shown in Figure 2-9), as well as plug-ins that produce color halftone effects, fragmented images, and the pointillize effect (used in the "Creating Snow and Rain" Putting It Together project, in this chapter).

Corbis Digital Stock

Figure 2-9: The Crystallize filter breaks your image into polygonal shapes.

Rendering

In computerese, *rendering* means creating something from nothing, in a way. That's why all rendering filters in Photoshop produce special effects by creating a look, object, or lighting effect that's melded with your original image.

Using the Clouds filter

The Clouds filter can muster a sky full of clouds from scratch with a few clicks of the mouse, as in the now-cloudy picture shown in Figure 2-10. This filter creates clouds using random values from the foreground and background colors. Indeed, most Photoshop veterans use this filter so much that they have a surprising number of clouds in their images. Find it at Filter➪Render➪Clouds. To create a more contrasty cloud effect, hold down Alt (Option on the Mac) quickly when choosing the command. If you don't like the first set of clouds you get, apply the filter again and again until you do. If you want a more "realistic" sky, try using a dark sky blue for your foreground color and a very light blue, or white, color for your background color. Be sure to apply the filter on its own layer, if you don't want to obliterate the original contents of your image.

Brand X Pictures

Figure 2-10: Got clouds? Make your own with the Clouds filter.

Need a quick Web background image? Create a 128-x-128-pixel (or some multiple of that size) image and apply the Clouds filter. It tiles seamlessly on your Web page.

Creating fibers

This filter can create a textilelike effect out of thin air. Choose Filter⇨ Render⇨Fibers. In the dialog box that appears, move the Variance slider to increase the contrast between light and dark areas. Move the Strength slider to increase the tightness of the weave of the fibers. Click the Randomize button to get another variation of the effect of the filter.

Using other rendering filters

Other useful filters on the Render submenu (at Filter⇨Render) include

✔ **Difference Clouds:** Use this filter to create puffy objects in the sky (or foggy clouds at lower levels). Instead of performing this magical feat the way the Clouds filter does, the Difference Clouds filter uses image information to figure the difference in pixel values between the new clouds and the image they're joining. The result is a unique cloud effect. Try applying the filter repeatedly to create a marbleized effect.

✔ **Lens Flare:** This filter creates the reflection effect that plagues photographers when they point their cameras toward a strong light source, such as the sun. Photoshop mimics several different kinds of photographic lenses, giving you useful flares that can spice up concert photos, add a sunset where none existed, and create other kinds of lighting bursts. In the Lens Flare dialog box, specify a location for the center of the flare by clicking the image thumbnail or dragging the crosshair.

✔ **Lighting Effects:** As a sort of photo-studio lighting setup, this filter uses pixels to do its work. You can set up 16 different lights and manipulate how they illuminate your photo.

Putting It Together

Creating Snow and Rain

Sometimes, you may come across a photo that needs a little bit of atmosphere thrown in to give it extra punch. And I mean *atmosphere* literally. By using a couple of filters and a blend mode, you can add some rain or snow to any image. Just follow these steps to create either rain or snow:

1. **Open a color image. If it isn't currently in RGB mode, choose Image⇨Mode⇨ RGB Color.**

Make sure you're in RGB mode; the blend mode used in these steps doesn't work correctly with CMYK images.

2. **Drag the background layer to the Create a new layer icon at the bottom of the Layers panel.**

You now see a layer named Background Copy in the Layers panel.

3. **Double-click the name Background Copy and type** Snow.

This isn't a mandatory step. I'm just being ultra-organized.

Book VII
Chapter 2

Applying Filters for Special Occasions

continued

continued

4. First, set your background color to white. With the Snow layer active, choose Filter⇨Pixelate⇨Pointillize. In the dialog box, set your cell size to whatever value you prefer. Click OK.

The bigger the cell size, the bigger the snowflakes or raindrops.

For rain, you might try a cell size of 3 (which is the minimum) or 4. For snow, try a larger cell size, between 6 and 9. I used a value of 7 in my image.

5. On the Snow layer, choose Image⇨Adjustments⇨Threshold. Move the slider all the way to the right, to a max value of 255.

This adjustment takes the colored cells and turns them to either black or white.

By using a value of 255, all brightness values less than 255 turn black, and the remaining value turns white.

6. On the Snow layer, select Screen from the Mode pop-up menu in the Layers panel.

The Screen blend mode lightens the Snow layer, where it mixes with the background. Blending with black pixels has no effect; therefore, they drop out, as shown in the figure.

7. Choose Filter⇨Blur⇨Motion Blur. In the dialog box that opens, specify the Angle and Distance values.

If you want the wind to appear to be blowing hard, set the angle more diagonally, around 45 degrees. If you want the precipitation to appear to be coming straight down, set the angle to 90 degrees. Setting the distance elongates the pointillized cells that you created in Step 4, making them look a little more realistic. For snow, start with a range of about 8 to 12 pixels. For rain, start a little higher, around 15 to 25 pixels. I used a value of 12 pixels in my figure.

If you're creating rain, proceed to Step 8. If you're a snow person, you're done, as shown in the figure.

8. **Choose Filter⇨Sharpen⇨Unsharp Mask.**

   The Unsharp Mask dialog box appears.

9. **Specify the Amount, Radius, and Threshold values and click OK.**

   The Unsharp Mask filter gives the illusion of sharpening the focus of the image by increasing the contrast between the pixels.

   I used an amount of 500%, a Radius of 1, and kept the Threshold at 0. This gives the raindrops a little more definition.

10. **Choose Filter⇨Blur⇨Motion Blur. In the dialog box that appears, specify the Angle and Distance values.**

    Again, the angle is up to you, but make it consistent with the value that you used in Step 7. Set the distance according to how you want your rain to appear — a moderate spring rain or a torrential, close-to-hurricane type of downpour. In the image shown here, I used 45 degrees and 25 pixels.

Getting Organic with the Sketch Filters

The Sketch filter submenu contains a few filters that don't really belong there. That's because many current Photoshop filters were acquired from Aldus Corporation (now defunct), and Adobe had to shoehorn them into the organizational structure of Photoshop. But no matter — they work nonetheless.

If you were to encounter a picture of Michelangelo's *David,* shown in Figure 2-11, you might be tempted to sketch the famous sculpture by using one of the filters you can find when you choose Filter⇨Sketch.

Perhaps a Conté Crayon effect or a Graphic Pen and Ink look would be nice. But the Sketch submenu also includes other artistic effects, such as the Note Paper look, a halftone screen, chalk and charcoal, and even a bas-relief effect that turns flat images into a Michelangelo-esque sculpture.

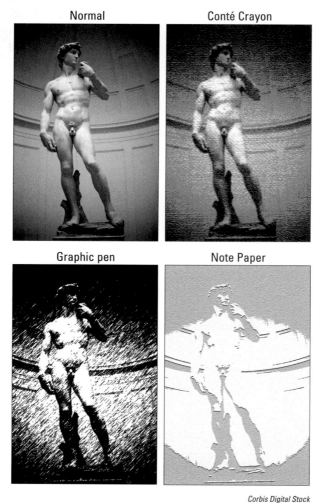

Corbis Digital Stock

Figure 2-11: Give your digital photos a more organic feel with the Sketch filters.

You can also experiment with these other Sketch filters:

- **Chrome:** Creates a polished chrome effect. Use the Levels adjustment to add more contrast, if necessary.

- **Photocopy:** Gives that infamous, anachronistic look (dating back to the days when photocopiers didn't do a very good job of reproducing half-tone images). Creates areas of black and white with little gray value when the default foreground and background colors of black and white are selected.

✔ **Plaster:** Creates a look that resembles molten plastic more than it looks like plaster. The filter uses the foreground and background values to color the image.

✔ **Stamp:** Mimics a rubber or wooden-block stamp (not very sketchlike, indeed!).

✔ **Reticulation:** Adds texture by reproducing a veritable photographic disaster — the wrinkling of film emulsion that occurs when you move film from one developing chemical to another that has an extremely different temperature. (Think hot developer followed by a bath in cold water.) The highlights look grainy; the shadow areas look thick and goopy.

✔ **Torn Edges:** Creates the look of ragged paper and colorizes the image, using the foreground and background colors.

✔ **Water Paper:** Creates the look of paintlike daubs on fibrous wet paper.

Even if the Sketch filters don't all produce sketchy effects, they do have one thing in common: They give your images an organic look that's decidedly uncomputerlike.

Putting It Together

Adding Water Droplets and Other Wet Effects

You can find a lot of techniques for creating nice, neat, round drops of water by using Photoshop. Unless you've just waxed your car and expect a rain shower within moments, however, perfectly beaded water droplets can be fairly rare. In real life, you're likely to encounter some sloppy drops and driblets. This technique simulates that look; you could use it to add sparkling water drops to a flower, create a wet-look texture for artistic effect, or add a three-dimensional *trompe l'oeil* ("fools the eye" optical illusion. Find the flower image I use on this book's companion Web site if you want to follow along. Follow these steps to add wet effects:

1. **Open a plain old bone-dry photograph in Photoshop.**

   I'm using a flower photograph, which will look great wet.

2. **Press D to make sure you have the foreground and background colors in Photoshop set to the default values of black and white.**

3. **Choose Window⇨Channels to bring up the Channels panel. From the Channels panel menu, choose New Channel.**

   This choice creates a new alpha channel for the water droplets. (For more on channels, see Book VI.)

continued

continued

4. **In the Color Indicates area of the New Channel dialog box, select the Selected Areas radio button and set Opacity to 100%. Click OK.**

5. **Select Filter⇨Render⇨Clouds to create a motley cloud effect to use as the basis for your random water droplets.**

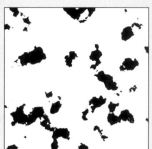

To view your alpha channel, select it in the Channels panel.

6. **Choose Image⇨Adjustments⇨Threshold, and then move the slider to create black blotches that will become water droplets, as shown in the figure. Click OK.**

I used a value of 83, but because the Clouds filter produces random results, you may find that a different value works better for you.

7. **Choose Filter⇨Blur⇨Gaussian Blur and move the Radius slider enough to blur the jagged edges of the droplets. Click OK.**

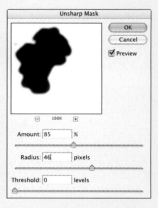

I used a value of 3.8 pixels.

8. **Choose Filter⇨Sharpen⇨Unsharp Mask and adjust the Amount and Radius sliders to firm up the edges of the droplets. Click OK.**

I found that an Amount of 85% and a Radius of about 46 creates soft-edged-but-distinct water droplets, as shown in the figure.

9. **Ctrl-click (⌘-click on the Mac) the new channel in the Channels panel to load the selection you've created, as shown in the figure.**

10. **Click the RGB Channel in the Channels panel to return to your full-color picture.**

The droplets appear as selections.

11. **Choose Layer⇨New⇨Layer via Copy to create a new layer for the droplets to reside in.**

12. **Choose Layer⇨Layer Style and select Bevel and Emboss. Specify your options and click OK.**

The bevel/embossing effect adds a third dimension to the drops. You can experiment with the depth and size controls to get the exact effect you want. I used the Inner Bevel style, set to the Smooth Technique in the Structure area of the dialog box. I used the sliders to increase the Size of the bevel to 27 pixels and Softened the edges by 11 pixels.

13. **If you like, you can choose Image⇨Adjustments⇨Levels to darken the droplets against their background. Click OK.**

The final image looks like a print that has been drenched with liquid.

Adding Texture

Photoshop lets you add a lot of interesting textures (which are in the Filter⇨ Texture menu) to your image, such as the cracked canvas effect generated by the Craquelure filter (see Figure 2-12) or the pixel effect produced by the Patchwork filter.

Corbis Digital Stock

Figure 2-12: The Craquelure filter gives an Old-World painting feel to your image.

You can find other filters on this menu to help you create mosaic effects, add yet another kind of film grain, and create stained-glass effects in your images. But the most versatile filter in this set is the Texturizer, shown in Figure 2-13. The Texturizer filter enables you to apply various kinds of textures to your images or selections, including Canvas, Sandstone, Burlap, or Brick.

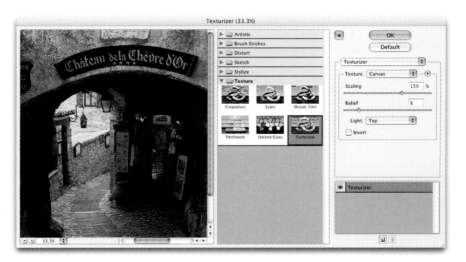

Corbis Digital Stock

Figure 2-13: You can apply either preset or custom-made textures to your images with the Texturizer filter.

You can select the relative size of the texture compared to the rest of your image by using the Scaling slider and adjust the amount of 3-D relief effect. You can even select the direction of the light source that produces the 3-D look, selecting from top, bottom, either side, or any of the four corners of the image. If those variations aren't enough for you, then create your own texture, save it as a Photoshop PSD file, and use that file to texturize your image.

You can find a handful of other filters that allow you to load your own textures, including Rough Pastels, Underpainting, and Conté Crayon.

Looking at the Other Filters

The Video and Other categories are the homes of the oddest of the odd. For example, the Other submenu is home to the Custom filter, which is no filter at all — it's a dialog box that has a matrix in which you can type numbers that Photoshop uses to process the pixels in your image in unexpected ways. The center box in the matrix represents a pixel in your image; the surrounding boxes represent the pixels that surround that pixel. The numbers you type tell Photoshop whether to darken or lighten pixels. You can experiment to see what will happen, and, if you like the effect, tell all your friends that you *meant* to do that.

The High Pass filter, also in the Other category, applies an effect opposite to the Gaussian Blur filter. It finds and keeps the details in the edges where it finds distinct color or tonal differences and turns the rest of the image gray. When converting a continuous-tone image into a bitmap (black and white only) image, applying this filter is useful before applying the Threshold adjustment. See Book VIII, Chapter 1 for more on the Threshold command. The High Pass filter is also handy for creating a channel mask. (See Book VI, Chapter 3 for details about working with channel masks.)

Two other filters that help with masking are the Minimum and Maximum filters. The Minimum filter expands the black areas while decreasing white areas (a process known as *choking* in traditional photography). The Maximum filter expands the white portions while decreasing black areas (known as *spreading*). The radius value you enter tells the filter how many pixels to expand or decrease from the edges of your selection.

The Video menu contains its own share of strange filters, including the NTSC Colors filter, which performs the rather obscure function of converting all the colors in your image to match the colors used for television reproduction. (NTSC stands for *National Television Systems Committee*.) You can use this filter to process digital presentations or slides that you want to show on television, if you're really, really particular about how the colors are portrayed.

Book VII
Chapter 2

Applying Filters for Special Occasions

Chapter 3: Distorting with the Liquify Command

In This Chapter

✔ Checking out the Liquify window

✔ Liquifying an image

✔ Protecting/unprotecting with freezing and thawing

✔ Canceling your transformations with Reconstruction

✔ Extending transformations to other areas

*L*iquify is the only Photoshop filter that gets a chapter of its own. But, then again, Liquify is no ordinary filter; it's the ultimate in image distortion tools and is therefore a good deal more complex than most of its kin on the Filter menu. What other filter has its own hefty tools panel, loads of buttons, several different modes, and more than a dozen option categories that amount to dozens more variations?

The Liquify command lets you push and pull on parts of your image; twist, turn, and pinch other parts; bloat sections; freeze portions in place so that they remain immune to the transformations going on around them; and perform selective reconstructions if you don't like everything you've done. You can perform this magic with a remarkable degree of control, too. You can almost be assured that every celebrity photo that appears on a magazine cover has been run through the Liquify gauntlet a time or two.

This chapter explores all the features of the Liquify command and shows you how to use these features to create sensational images.

Exploring the Liquify Window

At first glance, the Liquify window is a little daunting. It's a little daunting on second, third, and fourth glances, too. But when you quit glancing and dive into this versatile filter, you'll find that the tools and options make a lot of sense.

You open the Liquify window by choosing Filter⇨Liquify, and there, the Liquify Tools panel appears on the left, as shown in Figure 3-1. The other options available with Liquify (which I describe in the section appropriately named "The Options Areas," later in this chapter) appear on the right side of the window. The Tools panel includes a dozen tools that you can use to paint and distort your image.

Like with Photoshop's main Tools panel, you can activate each tool by pressing a letter associated with its name.

Purestock

Figure 3-1: The intimidating Liquify window is really quite user-friendly after you get familiar with its tools and settings.

The painting tools

The first group of tools is used to paint distortions on your image. Shown in this list with their keyboard shortcuts in parentheses, the painting tools (refer to Figure 3-1) are the following:

✔ **Forward Warp (W):** This tool is faintly reminiscent of the Smudge tool, but it doesn't blur the pixels quite as much as it pushes them forward while you drag, creating a stretched effect. Use the Warp tool to push pixels where you want them to go, using short strokes or long pushes.

When compared to a tool like the Smudge tool, which tends to destroy detail, the Warp tool can preserve detail within distortions.

Imagestate

 ✔ **Twirl Clockwise (C):** Place the cursor in one spot, press the mouse button, and watch the pixels under your brush rotate like a satellite photo of a tropical storm. Or drag the cursor to create a moving twirl effect. Pixels move faster in the center than along the edges of the brush. To twirl the other way, hold down the Alt (Option on the Mac) key while you drag or hold down the mouse button.

Try this technique with the other tools I describe in this list. (With some tools, the effect is more obvious than with others.) Simply hold down the mouse button. The longer you hold down the mouse button, the more prominent the effect becomes.

 ✔ **Pucker (S):** This tool is the equivalent of the Pinch filter, squishing pixels toward the center of the area covered by the brush while you hold down the mouse button or drag. To reverse the pucker direction, which essentially applies a bloat, hold down the Alt (Option on the Mac) key while you hold down the mouse button or drag.

**Book VII
Chapter 3**

**Distorting with the
Liquify Command**

✔ **Bloat (B):** Here is an analog to the Spherize filter, pushing pixels toward the edge of the brush area while you hold down the mouse button or drag the mouse. To reverse the bloat direction — doing so applies a pucker — hold down the Alt (Option on the Mac) key while you hold down the mouse button or drag.

 ✔ **Push Left (O):** Formerly known as the Shift Pixels tool, this odd tool moves pixels to the left when you drag the tool straight up. Drag down to move pixels to the right. Drag clockwise to increase the size of the object being distorted. Drag counterclockwise to decrease the size. To reverse any of the directions, hold down the Alt (Option on the Mac) key while you hold down the mouse button or drag.

✔ **Mirror (M):** Formerly known as the Reflect tool, the Mirror tool drags a reversed image of your pixels at a 90-degree angle to the motion of the brush. Hold down the Alt key (Option key on the Mac) to force the reflection in the direction opposite the motion of the brush (for example, to the left of a brush moving right, or above a brush moving down). This tool is a good choice for producing shimmery reflections.

✔ **Turbulence (T):** This tool adds a random jumbling effect to your pixels when you click and hold down your mouse. It acts similarly to the Forward Warp tool when you click and drag. You can use the Turbulence tool to re-create maelstroms of air, fire, and water with (well, yeah) clouds, flames, and waves.

The other tools

The remaining tools in the Liquify Tools panel (refer to Figure 3-1) are

✔ **Reconstruct (R):** This tool lets you reverse or alter — completely or partially — the distortions you've made. You can retrace your steps if you went overboard in your warping activities.

✔ **Freeze Mask (F):** Use this tool to protect areas from changes. It paints the frozen area with a red overlay, just like Quick Mask mode.

✔ **Thaw Mask (D):** This tool unprotects areas by erasing the red protective "freeze" tone. This is a lot like erasing areas you've painted in Quick Mask mode.

✔ **Hand (H):** The Hand tool works exactly like the standard Photoshop Hand tool. Click and drag the image to move it around within the Preview window. You can find more about the Hand tool in Book I, Chapter 4.

✔ **Zoom (Z):** The Zoom tool works exactly like the standard Photoshop Zoom tool. Indeed, you can also zoom in and out by using Ctrl and the plus sign (⌘ and the plus sign on the Mac) and Ctrl and the minus sign (⌘ and the minus sign on the Mac) shortcuts. See Book I, Chapter 4, for more on using the regulation Zoom tool.

Separate from the Liquify Tools panel and in the lower-left corner of the Liquify window is a magnification box with a pop-up menu that you can use to select magnifications from 6 percent to 1600 percent. Or, if you like buttons, click your way to magnification by using the +/– zoom control buttons.

The Options Areas

On the right side of the Liquify window (refer to Figure 3-1), you can find some menus and buttons that let you specify options for the tools, for reconstructing and freezing, and for viewing. I point them all out to you here and cover exactly how to use them in the rest of this chapter:

- **Load Mesh and Save Mesh:** Liquify lets you show or hide a crisscross area called a *mesh,* shown in Figure 3-2. The mesh provides a visual map of the distortions you've applied. The mesh starts out as a square grid and changes while you apply distortions. The mesh lets you clearly see exactly what you've done to the image and, even better, provides a way to save those distortions on your hard drive so that you can load and reapply them to the same (or a different) image later.

- **Tool Options:** You can use the Tool Options area to apply parameters to the painting tools. You can specify the following options:

  - *Brush Size:* Specifies the width of the brush from 1 to 1500 pixels.

**Book VII
Chapter 3**

**Distorting with the
Liquify Command**

Purestock

Figure 3-2: The mesh provides a visual map of your applied distortions.

- *Brush Density:* Specifies how fast the brush effect levels off at its edges. For example, with a feathered brush, the effect is stronger in the center and lighter at the edges.

- *Brush Pressure:* Specifies the speed at which you distort while you drag. Lower is slower.

- *Brush Rate:* Specifies the speed at which you distort while you keep a tool, such as the Twirl tool, stationary. Again, lower is slower.

- *Turbulent Jitter:* Determines how tightly the brush jumbles pixels. When using the Turbulence tool, this option gives the stroke a more natural, organic look.

When you select the Reconstruct tool, you can also select a Reconstruct mode from the pop-up menu. (I explain each of these modes in the section "Extending and Cloning Distortions," later in this chapter.)

If you have a pressure-sensitive stylus tablet, you can also choose to use the amount of pressure you apply to control the width of your brush stroke.

✓ **Reconstruct Options:** Here, you can select one of several Reconstruct modes. Reconstruct and Restore All buttons let you reverse all changes made on unfrozen areas (a little at a time) or revert to your last set of distortions. I show you how to use these options in the section "Reconstructing an Image," later in this chapter.

✓ **Mask Options:** Consider freezing and masking one and the same when you're immersed in the Liquify dialog box. The mask options let you freeze areas from existing selections, layer masks, transparent areas, or alpha channels in your image. You can also invert the frozen area (thawing frozen portions of the image and freezing the previously thawed areas), and thaw all the areas that were frozen with one click. Here's the lowdown on the options, each of which is indicated by a double-circle icon:

- *Replace Selection:* Allows you to freeze or mask areas of your image based on an existing selection, transparent area, alpha channel, or layer mask. (For more on alpha channels and layer masks, see Book VI, Chapters 1 and 3, respectively.)

- *Add to Selection:* Displays the mask in the image and then enables you to add to the frozen areas by using the Freeze tool. Adds pixels to the currently frozen areas.

- *Subtract from Selection:* Subtracts pixels from the currently frozen areas.

- *Intersect with Selection:* Masks only those pixels that are selected and currently frozen.

- *Invert Selection:* Inverts selected pixels and currently frozen areas.

  Click None to remove frozen areas. Click Mask All to freeze the entire image. Click Invert All to exchange frozen and thawed areas.

✔ **View Options:** You can show or hide frozen (masked) areas, the mesh, or the image. Also, if you select the Show Mesh option, you can select the mesh size and color. If you select the Show Mask option, you can select the color that indicates frozen areas. For example, if your image contains a lot of red, you may want to change the freeze color to blue to create more contrast.

Finally, you can also apply a backdrop that shows how the image being liquified will appear when merged with other layers. To view your distorted image along with other layers, select the Show Backdrop option and then select the particular layer you want to view, or select All Layers from the Use pop-up menu. You can now choose whether you want the backdrop in front, behind, or blended with the distorted image. Specify an opacity percentage for the displayed layers so they won't obliterate the image being distorted. The default (50%) allows you to see both your image and layers well so that you can keep track of your distortions.

Transforming an Image

Liquify seems impossibly complex on the surface, but it's as easy to apply as finger paint after you play with it a little. Here's a step-by-step scenario of the things you might do to apply some distortion to your own image:

1. **Select and open an image you want to transmogrify with Liquify; select a layer.**

2. **If you don't want to distort the whole layer, you can make your desired selection.**

   You can also use a layer mask, alpha channel, selection, or transparent area to define what portions you want to distort.

3. **Choose Filter➪Liquify.**

   The Liquify dialog box appears.

4. **If applicable, load your selection, layer mask, transparent area, or alpha channel into the Mask Options area.**

   Make sure you select the Show Mask option in the View Options area. If you have a saved selection (also known as an alpha channel), you have an alpha channel option to choose from. Otherwise, you don't see that option.

5. **You can also select the Freeze Mask tool and paint over the areas that you want to mask or protect.**

   After you freeze an area, you may want to get rid of the freeze highlighting for a while. Deselect the Show Mask option in View Options to turn off the display.

6. **In the View Options area, make sure that the Show Mesh and Show Image options are both selected.**

TIP

You can hide any or all of these at any time to get a different view of your image. For example, you might want to hide the frozen areas and mesh to view only your image with the distortions you've applied so far. Or you might want to look only at the mesh, as shown in Figure 3-3, to get a look at the distortions by themselves. Being able to examine the liquification process in several different ways is one reason that Liquify is so controllable.

7. **If you're having trouble seeing the mesh (or think the mask color will blend in with a dominant color in your image), use the View options to change the size and color of the mesh and the hue of the mask.**

If you want to see your image distortions against a backdrop, you can select that option, as well.

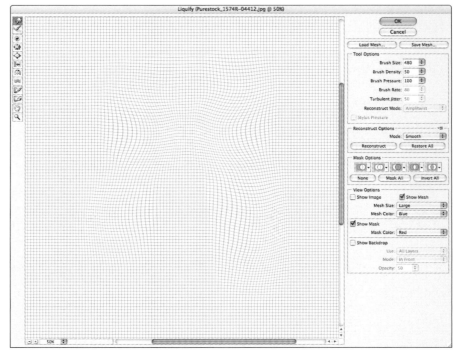

Purestock

Figure 3-3: You can choose to view just the mesh if you want a good look at how the actual distortions are mapped.

8. **Use the painting tools to apply various effects to your image, as shown in Figure 3-4.**

   Remember to adjust the brush size and pressure to get the exact coverage you want.

   At various points while you work, you may decide you want to freeze parts of the image from further changes (either temporarily or permanently).

9. **If you decide you want to work on an area again, select the Show Mask option to display the frozen areas (if necessary). Then select the Thaw Mask tool and erase all or part of the freeze.**

10. **Use the Reconstruct tool or options to partially or fully reverse or modify your distortions.**

    If you want to start over, click Restore All to get back to your original image. All option settings stay as is. Hold down the Alt (Option on the Mac) key and click Reset to revert back to your original image and reset all options to their default settings.

Book VII
Chapter 3

Distorting with the
Liquify Command

Figure 3-4: Use the various Painting tools to apply your desired distortions.

11. **When you finish, save the mesh you created by clicking Save Mesh. Give the mesh a name and store it on your hard drive.**

    This step is totally optional, but saving your work is a good idea if you really like what you've done.

12. **Apply the distortion to your image by clicking OK and exiting the Liquify dialog box.**

Mastering Freezing and Thawing

Liquify's capability to protect areas by freezing, and unprotect areas by thawing, deserves a closer look. Consider freezing the equivalent to masking. Here's a summary of the things you need to know:

Purestock

Figure 3-5: Protect areas from distortion by freezing them.

✔ **The easiest way to freeze/ unfreeze is to use the Freeze Mask and Thaw Mask tools to paint the areas you want to protect or unprotect, as shown in Figure 3-5.** Use the brush controls to modify how either tool paints or erases. When you set brush pressure to less than 100 percent, the opacity of the mask you're painting determines how frozen that area is. For example, if an area is only 25-percent frozen, using a distortion tool on that area produces only three-quarters the distortion you get in an area that's completely thawed.

✔ **You can use active or saved selections to define a frozen or masked area.** This is a great capability; you can use all the selection tools in Photoshop to define frozen/unfrozen areas before you invoke Liquify. You can, for example, select a portion of your image by using the Magic Wand or Quick Selection tool, another portion by using Quick Mask mode, and then save them all (choose Selection⇨Save Selection) as alpha channels. Then, when you use Liquify, choose any of those saved selections, or alpha channels, to freeze an area.

> ✔ **Select the basis that you want to use for your mask from the pop-up menu of the Replace Selection command (the far-left icon under Mask Options).**

You can also select a layer mask to define your mask. This is a great way to apply your distortions at varying degrees of intensity. Where the mask reveals more, the distortion is more prominent. Where the mask hides more, the distortion is subtler. For details on layer masks, see Book VI, Chapter 3.

> ✔ **To thaw all frozen areas, click the None button in the Mask Options area.**

> ✔ **To freeze all thawed areas, click the Mask All button in the Mask Options area.**

> ✔ **To reverse your frozen/unfrozen areas, click the Invert All button.** That which was frozen is thawed, and that which was unfrozen is frozen. Amen!

Reconstructing an Image

One of the most powerful capabilities of Liquify is that it can reconstruct your image fully or partially — restoring some or all of the image to its pre-Liquify state. This capability gives you a great deal of control over exactly how Photoshop transforms your image; you can backtrack any part of the transformation exactly the way you want. Here are some of your options:

> ✔ **To cancel all the changes made on your image (say, you really, really messed up), click the Restore All button in the Reconstruct Options area.** The image returns to its original state (as it was when you first opened the Liquify window) and removes distortions in both frozen and unfrozen areas.

> ✔ **To change only unfrozen areas of your image to their original states, select the Revert mode in the Reconstruct Options area of the dialog box, and then click the Reconstruct button multiple times until you get to your desired image.** The frozen areas remain distorted, but everything else returns to normal.

Use this option when you're displeased with some sections but like the distortions in others. Freeze the stuff you like and let Liquify cancel the changes elsewhere.

> ✔ **To paint portions of your image back to normalcy, select Revert mode in the Tool Options area, and then select the Reconstruct tool from the Liquify Tools panel.** You can use the Reconstruct tool to restore the areas that you paint. The image reverts more quickly at the center of the brush, so you have an extremely fine degree of control in how you revert your image. The mesh may help you see exactly what portions are being restored, too.

✔ **You can also click the Reconstruct button to have Photoshop apply an overall reconstruction.** Click the button to make Photoshop reconstruct once. Click it again to remove even more distortion.

If you don't necessarily want to reconstruct your image back to its original condition, but rather want to alter, extend, or clone your distortions, you can select Reconstruct modes other than Revert. See the following section, which talks about the other Reconstruct modes.

Extending and Cloning Distortions

Liquify allows you to extend distortions you've made in frozen areas into parts of the image that are unfrozen. If you have an image that has the requisite frozen and unfrozen portions, first select a mode — which determines specific ways in which Photoshop extends the image from the frozen areas into the unfrozen area.

Reconstruct modes

The Reconstruct modes include the following four:

✔ **Rigid:** This mode keeps rigid right angles in the mesh's grid, which can generate some mismatches (Adobe calls these *discontinuities*) at the edges where the frozen and unfrozen portions meet. This mode restores unfrozen areas to close approximations of their original states.

✔ **Stiff:** Adobe describes this as a *weak magnetic field,* attracting the edges between the frozen and unfrozen areas strongly where they meet and producing less distortion in unfrozen areas farther away from the edges.

✔ **Smooth:** This mode smoothly spreads the frozen areas' distortions through the unfrozen areas. It produces a smooth blending effect, as shown in Figure 3-6.

✔ **Loose:** This mode generates an even smoother blending effect between frozen and unfrozen areas than the Smooth mode.

Corbis Digital Stock

Figure 3-6: The Smooth mode smoothly blends frozen distortions into unfrozen areas.

Use the Reconstruct tool to expand the frozen-area distortions into the unfrozen area, using the mode you've selected to blend the pixels while you paint. You can drag to paint, or click and Shift-click to paint in straight lines (much like you do with Photoshop's regular Brush tools).

More Reconstruct modes

There are three Reconstruct modes that work slightly differently than the four discussed in the preceding section. These modes more or less clone particular distortions you've already applied elsewhere in the image. Like the Clone Stamp tool, these modes allow you to select part of the distortion and apply (or clone) copies of the selection to other parts of your image:

 ✔ **Displace:** Displace copies the amount of displacement at the starting point of the distortion to unfrozen parts of your image. You can use this mode to displace parts of your image to a different position in the image.

 ✔ **Amplitwist:** Amplitwist displaces, scales, and rotates unfrozen areas to match the distortion that exists at the starting point.

 ✔ **Affine:** Affine does much the same thing as Amplitwist, using displacement, scaling, rotation, and skew in the distortion to modify unfrozen areas to match those distortions that exist at the starting point.

Each time you click the mouse button, you create a new starting point, so if you're trying to extend a distortion effect from a single starting point, don't release your mouse button until you're done using the Reconstruct tool.

Using Displace, Amplitwist, and Affine

The Displace, Amplitwist, and Affine Reconstruct modes use different combinations of distortion factors — such as displacement, scaling, rotation, or skew. Unlike the other modes, the Reconstruct button isn't available for these three. You can use these modes only with the Reconstruct tool. To use Displace, Amplitwist, or Affine, follow these steps:

1. **Open an image to work on and choose Filter⇨Liquify.**

2. **Select the Reconstruct tool.**

3. **Select one of the three modes — Displace, Amplitwist, or Affine — from the Reconstruct Mode pop-up menu in the Tool Options area.**

4. **Click a place in the image where you want to clone the applied distortion.**

5. **Drag with the mouse in the unfrozen areas to apply that distortion.**

6. **To change the origin of the distortions being copied, click again anywhere in a distorted area to select a new sampling point. Then resume dragging in unfrozen areas.**

   Your image takes on a distorted appearance, like the one shown in Figure 3-7.

7. **When you finish, click OK to apply the distortion.**

Book VII
Chapter 3

Distorting with the
Liquify Command

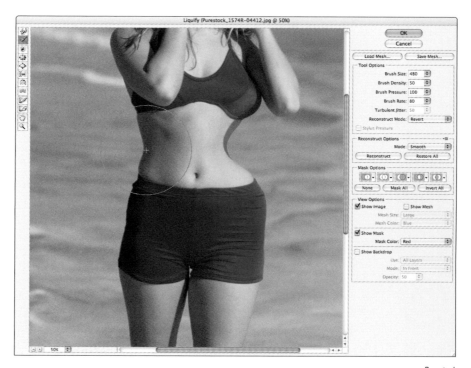

Purestock

Figure 3-7: Undo your distortions by using one of the various flavors of the Reconstruct tool.

Book VIII

Retouching and Restoration

Although taking the perfect photo is a great goal, it's one that is often just beyond our reach. Not to worry though, if you're a Photoshop owner. In this book, you find out what you need to know about correcting color in all its permutations — contrast, saturation, replacing, remapping, and so on. You find details on using the focus and toning tools to manually adjust the tones, textures, and colors in your images. I also give you details on how you can give your images a digital spa day with the two Healing Brushes and the Patch and Red Eye tools. You learn how to remove blemishes, wrinkles, and every other one of nature's imperfections. After you master these techniques, you'll be on your way to doing your own digital extreme makeovers. But whatever you do, don't leave this book without checking out the Vanishing Point feature. This single command alone may be well worth the money you plunked down for Photoshop.

Chapter 1: Enhancing Images with Adjustments

In This Chapter

✔ Selecting automatic color correction

✔ Using simple manual color correction tools

✔ Introducing professional correction tools

✔ Switching colors with mappers and other tools

*P*hotoshop can provide magical transformations to images, making them unrecognizable from the original. But sometimes what you really want is simply to make an image look the same as the original — only better. Perhaps the colors are a little too warm, or the shadows a bit inky, but you don't want an image that looks more processed than a freeze-dried floral arrangement. You'd be happy to have everyone admire your image without a clue that you've made major corrections in Photoshop.

Welcome to the world of image enhancements. This chapter concentrates on the things you can do to correct color, contrast, hue, and color saturation. After you master the basic tools, you can explore some even more sophisticated things that you can do by using features such as Photoshop's Adjustment Layers (in Book V, Chapter 1), which let you dynamically apply your changes in remarkably flexible ways. But before you dive into image adjustments, make sure you remove any flaws, such as dust, scratches, blemishes, and other nasty items, from your image. Check out Book VIII, Chapter 3 to find out about fixing imperfections.

Introducing the Histogram Panel

One of the first things you want to do before you make any color or tonal adjustments to your image is to take a good look at the quality and distribution of the tones throughout your image. I don't mean just eyeballing the composite image on your screen. I'm talking about getting inside your image and looking at its guts with the Histogram panel — and keeping it onscreen so you can see its constant feedback on your image adjustments.

A histogram displays the *tonal range* (also referred to as the *key type*) of an image, as shown in Figure 1-1. It shows how the pixels are distributed by graphing the number of pixels at each of the 256 brightness levels in an image. On this graph, pixels with the same brightness level are stacked in bars along a vertical axis. The higher the line from this axis, the greater the number of pixels at that brightness level. You can view the distribution for each color channel separately or for the composite image as a whole.

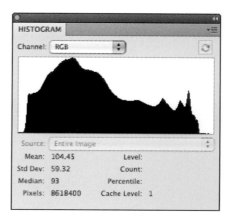

Figure 1-1: The Histogram panel displays how pixels are distributed at each of the 256 brightness levels.

From this graph, you can then determine whether the image contains enough detail in the shadow, midtone, and highlight areas. This information helps you determine what image adjustments you may need to make. The following steps walk you through the basics of using the panel and interpreting the information you find there:

1. **Choose Window➪Histogram to bring up this graphical wonder.**

   By default, the histogram displays the tonal range of the whole image, in the composite image's color mode, such as RGB, CMYK, Grayscale, and so on. For details on color modes, see Book II, Chapter 2.

2. **Select Compact View, Expanded View, or All Channels View from the Histogram panel pop-up menu:**

   • *Compact View:* The default. Displays only a histogram of the whole image (or your chosen selection or channel) with no controls or statistics.

   • *Expanded View:* Shows a histogram with statistics and controls for selecting and viewing the histogram of individual channels. This view also has controls for refreshing the histogram to show uncached data and choosing a selected layer (on the Source pop-up menu). Refer to Figure 1-1 to see this view.

   • *All Channels View:* Shown in Figure 1-2, this view displays all the options of the Expanded View, plus the individual histograms for each color channel. You may also choose to view your channels in color.

3. **Choose a different source in the Channel and/or Source pop-up menu, if needed.**

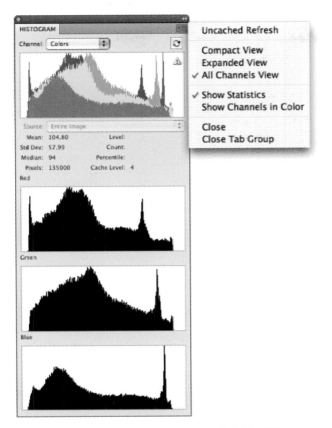

Figure 1-2: The All Channels View displays individual histograms for each color channel, as well as the composite channel.

For example, instead of seeing a histogram for an entire image, you can display the histogram of an individual channel, alpha channel, or spot channel from the Channel pop-up menu. You can also focus on the selected layer or an adjustment layer. Just select the layer in the Layers panel and choose Selected Layer or Adjustment Composite from the Source pop-up menu.

For more on adjustment layers, see Book V, Chapter 1.

4. **If the Cached Data Warning icon (a triangle with an exclamation mark) appears in the upper-right corner of the histogram, click the Uncached Refresh button just above the icon to see a histogram that reflects the image's current state.**

The warning lets you know that Photoshop is reading the histogram from cache rather than showing your image's current state. *Cache* is a reserved, high-speed section of your computer's memory. The image cache allows the histogram to display faster because it's calculating the histogram based on a representative sampling of the pixels in your image.

Unless it's really bogging down your workflow, I recommend viewing your image's histograms by using uncached data.

5. **With the Histogram panel displaying the controls and data you want to check, examine the tonal range in the histogram.**

An image with good tonal range displays pixels in all areas. An image with poor tonal range has gaps in the histogram, as shown in Figure 1-3.

The rest of this chapter explains ways you can correct color problems that you find.

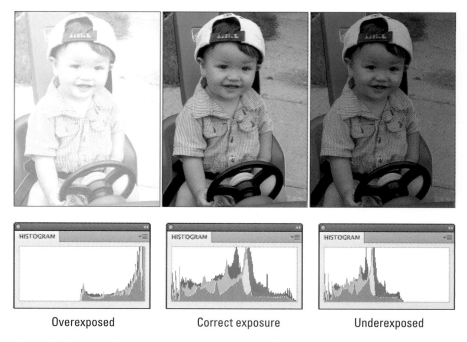

| Overexposed | Correct exposure | Underexposed |

Figure 1-3: Images with poor tonal range have noticeable gaps in the histogram.

6. **If you're into numbers, check the statistics to evaluate your image, as well.**

See the sidebar "Understanding the histogram statistics," in this chapter, for how to interpret these details.

Position your cursor within the histogram to see statistics about a specific value. Drag your cursor within the histogram to see statistics about a range of values. (Photoshop highlights the range.)

Understanding the histogram statistics

The Histogram panel gives you all kinds of statistics about the pixels in your image. Some of these statistics, such as Standard Deviation, may be for those who live in the land of Probability and Statistics. But you may be able to glean some useful information from the other statistics that can help you in your image-adjusting tasks. Here's a brief explanation of each statistic:

✔ **Mean:** Average intensity value

✔ **Standard Deviation:** How much the intensity values vary

✔ **Median:** Middle value of the intensity values.

✔ **Pixels:** Total number of pixels used to represent the histogram

✔ **Cache Level:** The current level of image cache used to calculate the histogram

These statistics display a value only when you position or drag your cursor in the histogram. (Each value corresponds only to the portion of the histogram under your cursor.)

✔ **Level:** Intensity level

✔ **Count:** The total number of pixels corresponding to that intensity leve

✔ **Percentile:** The number of cumulative pixels (in percentages) at or below that level, from 0% (left) to 100% (right)

When you make adjustments based on problems you see in the histogram, be sure to select any Preview options in the dialog boxes of your image adjustments, such as Levels. That way, the Histogram panel displays both the original and adjusted histograms, as shown in Figure 1-4.

Choosing Automatic Color Correctors

Photoshop has three automatic correction tools that can, in many cases, improve appearance with a simple click of a menu command: Auto Tone, Auto Color, and Auto Contrast. Before you use them, first note their pros and cons:

✔ **The upside:** These controls are easy to use. You don't need to know much about toning, color balance, or contrast to use the automatic correctors. (That's why they're automatic.) But you can find out more

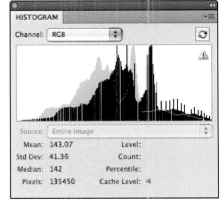

Figure 1-4: View both the original and adjusted histograms.

about correcting tone, color balance, and contrast in sections later in this chapter, when I explain how to make adjustments manually.

✔ **The downside:** An automatic control's ease of use almost always comes with a downside. In the case of the color correctors, none likely can do as good a job as you can do manually, and sometimes automatic controls even do more harm than good.

If you have an average image (one that doesn't require a great deal of correction), you can try the automatic color correctors to see whether they help. I explain how in the following sections. If you don't want to try the automatic controls, apply the manual tools explained in sections later in this chapter to produce the exact look you want.

You have the choice of applying the automatic color correctors, as well as any of the other image adjustments, to all or just a portion of your image. To isolate any adjustment to just a portion of your image, either make a selection (see Book III) or apply the adjustment to a layer. (See Book V.)

Auto Tone

The Auto Tone command, formerly known as Auto Levels, uses a bit of built-in Photoshop intelligence to automatically apply the Levels command (discussed in the section "Leveling for better contrast," later in the chapter) to your image.

Auto Tone works best with average images that could use a bit of tweaking but have a lot of detail in the *highlights* (the brightest portions of an image that contain detail), *shadows* (the darkest portions of an image that contain detail), and midtones.

Auto Tone defines the very lightest and darkest pixels of each of the three colors as white and black, respectively, and then arranges the midtone pixels in between. While it balances the tones in your image, the command may reduce colorcasts or even introduce some. You can fine-tune the color manually after Auto Tone has done its work.

To try out the Auto Tone command, just choose Image➪Auto Tone or press Shift+Ctrl+L (Shift+⌘+L on the Mac).

Although Auto Tone can improve your contrast, it may also produce an unwanted *colorcast* (a slight trace of color). If this happens, cancel the command and try the Auto Contrast command. If that still doesn't improve the contrast, try the Levels command instead. Even better, try your Levels adjustment on an adjustment layer. If it doesn't work, you can always delete it. No harm, no muss. For more on adjustment layers, see Book V, Chapter 1.

Auto Color

The Auto Color command adjusts both the color and contrast of an image, based on the shadows, midtones, and highlights that it finds in the image. You usually use this command to remove a colorcast (or bias) or balance the color in your image. Sometimes, using Auto Color can be helpful in correcting oversaturated or undersaturated colors, as well. You can access the command by choosing Image➪Auto Color or by pressing Shift+Ctrl+B (Shift+⌘+B on the Mac).

Although Auto Color can do a good job on its own, you can customize the parameters it uses to make its color corrections in the Auto Color Correction Options dialog box, which I discuss in the section "Setting Auto Color Correction Options," later in this chapter. Figure 1-5 shows an image corrected by using Auto Tone and Auto Color.

Figure 1-5: Using Auto Tone and Auto Color quickly improved the contrast and colors of this snapshot.

Auto Contrast

Like its manually operated cousin, the Brightness/Contrast command, the Auto Contrast command fiddles with the overall contrast and colors (if you're working with a color image) in an image, instead of making adjustments to each color individually. Auto Contrast converts the lightest and darkest pixels to white and black, respectively, making all highlights in the image lighter and all shadows darker without changing the color values. This command may not do as good a job at improving contrast as Auto Tone does, but it retains the color balance of an image and doesn't cause any nasty colorcasts.

TIP

Try using this command on hazy images. If you find it overdoes the adjustment, try choosing Edit⇨Fade and bringing down the Opacity level to blend the adjusted image with your original image. For more on using the Fade command, see Book VII, Chapter 1.

To use Auto Contrast, choose Image⇨Auto Contrast or press Alt+Shift+Ctrl+L (Option+Shift+⌘+L on the Mac).

Setting Auto Color Correction Options

You can use the Auto Color Correction Options dialog box to tweak exactly how Photoshop applies its Auto Tone, Auto Color, and Auto Contrast controls, as well as for the manually operated Levels and Curves commands. You can apply the settings only to a particular image-editing session or save the settings as defaults for all your Photoshop work.

Setting color correction options is a more advanced task, and you can make best use of the tools if you already understand manual color and contrast corrections. You can brush up on your color theory, too, in Book II, Chapter 3.

To customize the automatic options, follow these steps:

1. **Open an image and choose Image⇨Adjustments⇨Levels or press Ctrl+L (⌘+L on the Mac).**

   You can also use the Curves command by pressing Ctrl+M (⌘+M on the Mac).

2. **Click the Options button in the dialog box to access the Auto Color Correction Options dialog box, shown in Figure 1-6.**

3. **In the Algorithms area, click the method you want Photoshop to use to adjust the tones.**

   Your choices include

   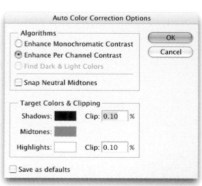

   Figure 1-6: After you know the basics, customize the auto correction options.

   • *Enhance Monochromatic Contrast:* This option applies the same changes to the Red, Green, and Blue channels, making brighter areas appear lighter and shadow areas appear darker, with no changes made to the colors. (This is the method used by the Auto Contrast command.)

   • *Enhance Per Channel Contrast:* This option individually adjusts the red, green, and blue colors so that each has its own best balance of light and dark tones, even if the color balance changes a bit. (This is the algorithm used by the Auto Tone command.)

- *Find Dark & Light Colors:* This option locates the average lightest and darkest pixels, and uses their values to maximize the contrast of the image. (This is the algorithm used by the Auto Color command.)

4. **Select the Snap Neutral Midtones check box if you want Photoshop to base its gamma, or midtone, correction values around a neutral color located in the image.**

   The Auto Color command uses this option.

5. **In the Target Colors & Clipping area, enter a value in each of the Clip text boxes.**

   Setting clipping values between 0.5% and 1% eliminates the too-dark and too-light pixels.

   These values adjust the percentage of black and white pixels that Photoshop removes from the darkest and lightest areas of the image. This option is useful because every image includes some very dark pixels that contain no real image information, as well as some very light pixels that are completely washed out. Factoring in these two kinds of pixels when you adjust tonal values is a waste. By setting the clipping values between 0.5% and 1%, you leave these no-good pixels out of the picture, so to speak.

6. **Click the Shadows, Midtones, or Highlights swatch.**

   The Color Picker appears, allowing you to set a preferred value for the darkest, medium, and lightest areas.

7. **Select the Eyedropper tool from the Tools panel.**

8. **Move your mouse over the image and locate the dark, middle, or light tone you want to use. Click it when you find it.**

9. **Click OK to exit the Color Picker. Repeat Steps 6 through 8 for each of the three colors you want to change.**

   When you move the mouse over the image, the values in the Info panel change, helping you pick the shadow, midtone, or highlight area you want.

10. **Back in the Auto Color Corrections Options dialog box, select the Save as Defaults check box to store the settings you just made for subsequent use in any Photoshop session.**

    If you don't select the check box, Photoshop applies the changes you made to only the current session.

11. **Click OK to exit the Auto Color Correction Options dialog box.**

    Your options are now customized. Note that these changes also affect the Auto buttons in the Levels and Curve dialog boxes.

Using Simple Color Correctors

Photoshop has several simple manual tools you can use to fix color in ways that are different from the Auto Tone, Auto Contrast, and Auto Color commands. They're the Brightness/Contrast control, Color Balance, Shadows/Highlights, Exposure, HDR Toning, the ever-popular Variations tool, and the Desaturate command (all found in the Image⇨Adjustments menu). In the following sections, you can find out when to use (and when not to use) each of them.

Applying Brightness/Contrast

Beginners gravitate to the Brightness/Contrast control because it seems so intuitive to use. If your image is too dark, move a slider to make it lighter; if it's too light, move the same slider to make it darker. Right? You can fix an image that's overly contrasty or overly flat-looking the same way. Right?

Maybe.

I say *Maybe* and not flat out *No* because, in recent versions, Adobe has improved the command, as demonstrated in Figure 1-7. Instead of applying all its adjustments equally to all areas of your image (whether they need it or not), it now applies adjustments proportionately to your image, like the Levels and Curves adjustments do. Just avoid the Use Legacy option, which reverts the Brightness/Contrast command back to its pre-CS3 algorithm, thereby turning your image into a mess.

Even though Adobe has improved the Brightness/Contrast command, you're better off using Levels and Curves, which can tailor your image enhancements to the exact portions of the image you want to work with.

Tweaking with the Color Balance controls

Figure 1-7: The Brightness/Contrast command attempts to improve tonal values in your image.

With an understanding of color theory (which I explain in Book II, Chapter 3), you can probably use the Color Balance controls to make some simple changes to the color in your image. The difficult part is recognizing exactly which color you need to add or subtract from your image in the first place.

Resisting the urge to go nuts with sliders

If you're like me, you like clicking options, adjusting values, and sliding sliders back and forth. Thankfully, Photoshop is happy to oblige you with options to make you feel so powerful that you can take on any project.

Was that a sinister laugh I heard? Easy there, partner. I'm about to tell you something that will break your heart at first — but you'll thank me later: Always pick a single slider and stick with it when you're trying to compensate for any colorcast. Moving two sliders is a waste because you can accomplish anything you want with just one.

For example, if you move both the Cyan/Red and Magenta/Green sliders an equal amount to the left (adding cyan and magenta), you're actually just adding blue. Moving three sliders is even worse because, depending on the amount and direction of movement, the three sliders are likely to at least partially cancel each other out or multiply the effects. However, if a cast is in just one area, such as the shadows, and a different colorcast is in another area, it may be useful to do more than one adjustment.

Colors are subtler than you might think. For example, a slight colorcast toward cyan can look a lot like a slightly green or blue colorcast. Is your image too red, or does it have too much magenta?

Use the Variations command that I describe in the section "Correcting colorcast with Variations," later in this chapter, to figure out how to tell the various colorcasts apart. The Variations command displays each of the different types of colorcasts in an array so you can compare them.

To use the Color Balance controls, follow these steps:

1. **Choose Image⇨Adjustments⇨Color Balance or press Ctrl+B (⌘+B on the Mac) to access the Color Balance dialog box.**

2. **Choose the Shadows, Midtones, or Highlights option to select the tones of an image you want to work on.**

   Usually, Midtones is the best choice, unless your image has a colorcast in the shadows or highlights that doesn't affect the overall image. That can sometimes happen when a subject is close to a colored wall or other object that reflects light onto, say, the shadowed side of a subject.

3. **Select the Preserve Luminosity option.**

   When this option is selected, Photoshop modifies the colors of the image, but the brightness and contrast of the tones stay the same. If you're not happy with the results, deselect the option.

4. **Move the Cyan/Red, Magenta/Green, or Yellow/Blue slider to add or subtract color, watching the effects of your adjustments on the original image.**

The Color Levels boxes show the amount of each color that Photoshop adds and subtracts while you move the sliders. Figure 1-8 shows an example of subtracting green to improve the color in an image.

Purestock

Figure 1-8: Use the Color Balance adjustment to remove colorcasts from an image.

The colors are arranged by their opposites on the color wheel. Dragging the slider toward Cyan adds cyan to the image and subtracts its complement, red. Dragging toward Green adds green to the image and subtracts magenta.

Fixing lighting with Shadows/Highlights

The Shadows/Highlights adjustment is a great feature that offers a quick and easy method for correcting over- and underexposed areas in your image. This command works well on a subject photographed with the light source coming from behind (backlit), giving that subject a dark foreground. The adjustment can also bring out the detail in harsh shadow areas in subjects shot in bright, overhead light, as shown in Figure 1-9.

Original   Adjusted with Shadows/Highlights

Figure 1-9: The Shadows/Highlights adjustment is a quick way to correct the lighting in your images.

To familiarize yourself with this tool, follow these steps:

1. **Open an image in dire need of repair and choose Image⇨Adjustments⇨ Shadows/Highlights.**

   Note that you can also adjust CMYK images, as well as RGB.

   When the dialog box appears, the correction is automatically applied in your preview. If you don't see any change, make sure you've selected the Preview check box. The default settings in the dialog box are meant to correct backlit images, so they may or may not do the right correction job for you with the default settings.

2. **Move the Amount slider to adjust the amount of correction for your Shadows and/or your Highlights.**

   The higher the percentage, the lighter the shadows and the darker the highlights. You can also enter a value in the percentage text box.

3. **If you're happy with the results, you can click OK and be done with the adjustment. However, if you crave more control, click the Show More Options check box at the bottom of the dialog box.**

   A whole array of sliders magically appears, as shown in Figure 1-10.

4. **Drag the Tonal Width slider to increase or decrease the range of tones adjusted in the shadows or highlights.**

**Book VIII
Chapter 1**

**Enhancing Images
with Adjustments**

The lower the percentage, the narrower the range of tones that are affected. For example, by using a very low percentage, only the darkest parts of the shadow or the lightest parts of the highlight are corrected. A higher percentage includes a wide range of tones, including midtone areas. The appropriate percentage to use varies among images, so start with the default setting of 50% and work in small increments from there.

If, when lightening the shadow areas, you find the midtones and highlights getting too light, reduce the Tonal Width percentage of the Shadows. But, if you start seeing artifacts, you've set the percentage too high.

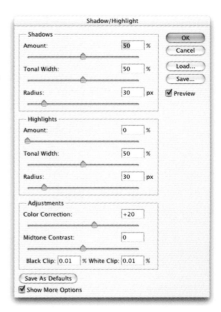

Figure 1-10: The Shadows/Highlights dialog box offers controls for adjusting the amount of correction in your shadow, midtone, and highlight areas.

5. **Drag the Radius slider to increase or decrease the number of pixels used in the local neighborhood.**

   To fix lighting, this command lightens or darkens pixels according to the luminance (brightness) of the surrounding pixels, technically called a *local neighborhood.* The best local neighborhood size depends on the particular image, so play with this slider and view the results. If the Radius is too small, your main subject may lack contrast. Conversely, if it's too large, your background may be overly bright or dark. Adobe recommends setting the radius to approximately half the size of the main subject in your image. So, if your subject takes up roughly 600 pixels, then set your radius to 300 pixels.

6. **Make additional changes in the Adjustments area, as needed:**

   • *Color Correction:* Available for color images only, this control enables you to correct the colors in *only* the adjusted portions of your image. Often, when you increase or decrease the Amount of Shadows or Highlights, you bring out the "hidden" colors. Generally, higher Color Correction values make colors more saturated, whereas lower values make colors more desaturated.

   • *Brightness:* Available for grayscale images only. Move the slider left to darken and right to lighten.

- *Midtone Contrast:* Move the slider left to reduce contrast and right to increase contrast. Just be aware that when you increase the Midtone Contrast, you may also undesirably darken shadow areas and lighten highlight areas.

- *Black Clip/White Clip:* As I explain in the section "Setting Auto Color Correction Options," earlier in this chapter, setting clipping values between 0.5% and 1% eliminates the too-dark and too-light pixels.

7. **Click the Save as Defaults button to save and make your settings the defaults.**

   If you want to reset the settings back to the original defaults, hold down Shift and click the Save as Defaults button. You can save as many settings as you want. Click the Load button to reload a particular setting. To save the settings as new settings, but not as the defaults, click the Save button.

8. **Click OK to apply the adjustment and exit the dialog box.**

Adjusting exposure

This Exposure adjustment is primarily meant to correct tonal values of High Dynamic Range (HDR) images, which are 32 bits. (In layman's terms, the bits indicate how much information is stored about the color. The more bits, the better the color.) But you can apply Exposure adjustments to 16-bit or even 8-bit images, as well. This command works by using a linear color space, also known as gamma 1.0, rather than your image's color space, to make tonal adjustments. Figure 1-11 shows an example of an image helped by this adjustment.

If you use the Exposure adjustment with 16-bit or 8-bit images, the slider's adjustments may be too drastic. Hold down the Ctrl (⌘ on the Mac) key when your mouse is over the number field and drag to access the scrubby sliders, which offer a less-dramatic adjustment when you slide the control. Also, keep an eye on your image. The Exposure adjustment sometimes *clips,* or loses, data on lower-bit images.

1. **Choose Image⇨Adjustments⇨Exposure.**

2. **Adjust any of the following:**

   - *Exposure:* This option adjusts mainly the highlights and pretty much ignores the darkest shadows.

   - *Offset:* This option darkens the shadow and midtone values, and leaves the highlights alone.

   - *Gamma Correction:* This option adjusts the image's gamma, or *midtone,* values.

Figure 1-11: Fix tonal values with the Exposure adjustment.

To apply the Exposure adjustment, follow these steps:

3. **Use the Eyedroppers to adjust the luminance, or *brightness*, values in the image.**

   Note that this is different from Levels, where the eyedroppers adjust all the color channels:

   - *Set Black Point Eyedropper:* Sets the Offset. The pixel you click becomes the black point.

   - *Set White Point Eyedropper:* Sets the Exposure. The pixel you click becomes the white point.

   - *Midtone Eyedropper:* Sets the Exposure. The pixel you click becomes the middle gray value.

4. **Click OK to apply the adjustment.**

   To save the settings, click the Save Preset button (to the right of OK). Name the preset and click Save in the Save dialog box. Apply the preset later by clicking the Load button.

Using HDR Toning

This new adjustment enables you to apply HDR contrast and exposure settings to your images. While mostly aimed toward 32-bit images, it can also be applied to 16-bit and 8-bit images.

To apply the HDR Toning adjustment, follow these steps:

1. **Open a 32-, 16-, or 8-bit image.**

   Make sure the image is in RGB or Grayscale mode. Also, your image cannot contain any layers and must consist of a Background only.

2. **Choose Image⇨Adjustments⇨HDR Toning.**

3. **Choose your desired method from the pop-up menu and any subsequent settings.**

   For an explanation of these settings, see Book IX, Chapter 2.

You can use HDR Toning to create a stylized appearance — oversaturated, overly sharp, and illustrative, as shown in Figure 1-12. Play with the Glow and Detail sliders under the Local Adaptation method and experiment.

Original   Adjusted with HDR Toning

Figure 1-12: Create a stylized look with HDR Toning.

**Book VIII
Chapter 1**

**Enhancing Images
with Adjustments**

Correcting colorcast with Variations

Photoshop's Variations feature is a variation (so to speak) on the profes-sional photographer's *ring around* (a set of color prints, each made with slightly different color balance) or *test strip* (a single print of an image made so that each section is shown using a different color balance). Both tools let you view several renditions of an image and choose the best one visually by comparing them. You might want to use Variations when you're unsure exactly how the color is biased and you want to compare several versions of an image to see exactly what the colorcast is.

Although not as sophisticated as some color correction techniques, the Variations feature has the advantage of being quick and simple, and it doesn't require a lot of training to use.

The Putting It Together project "Correcting Tinted, Faded Photos," in this chapter, walks you through the steps for using the Variations dialog box.

Washing out color with Desaturate

Sometimes, you don't want any color at all. Photoshop's Desaturate com-mand can wash all the color out of a layer or selection.

Just because you can do something doesn't mean you should. Use this command with caution because neither the Desaturate command nor Photoshop's Image➪Mode➪Grayscale command is the best technique for converting a color image to monochrome. Simply removing the color can produce an image that appears to be too low in contrast, which is another kettle of fish altogether. See Book II, Chapter 2, along with the section "Converting to Black & White," later in this chapter, for a better way to cre-ate grayscale images.

However, if you simply want to eliminate the color from a layer or image selection quickly, the Desaturate command does the job. To apply it, select your desired layer in the Layers panel, select the area you want to operate on, and then choose Image➪Adjustments➪Desaturate or press Shift+Ctrl+U (Shift+⌘+U on the Mac).

Using the Saturation control in the Hue/Saturation command gives you bet-ter control over the degree of desaturation you desire, while leaving the image looking richer. I show you how to play with saturation by using the Hue/Saturation controls in the section "Getting colorful with Hue/Saturation," later in this chapter.

Putting It Together

Correcting Tinted, Faded Photos

In this Putting It Together project, I employ the Variations feature to restore the color in a scan of a color print originally made in 1965. Unfortunately, the years have not been kind to this photo; it has a slight, but annoying, greenish tinge because the magenta dye layer of the print has faded. As a result, the other two color layers, cyan and yellow, appear proportionately stronger when compared to the magenta that remains, and cyan and yellow make a shade of green.

I plan to use the Variations feature of Photoshop to restore the magenta layer in this photo that's green with age.

To correct colorcast in an old photograph by using the Photoshop Variations feature, follow these steps:

1. **In Photoshop, open an old, fading photo that needs color correction.**

In this case, I'm using an old, faded, greenish-looking picture, shown in the figure, but any colorcast works.

continued

continued

2. **Choose Image⇨Adjustments⇨Variations from the menu bar.**

   The Variations dialog box appears.

3. **Select the Show Clipping option to tell Photoshop to show any areas of the image that will be "overwhelmed" by the correction you're contemplating.**

   That is, no new information is added.

4. **If you want to use corrections you saved, load those settings by clicking the Load button. Otherwise, skip to Step 5.**

5. **Make adjustments with the Fine/Coarse slider.**

   In my example, the greenish picture needs some magenta, so I dragged the Fine/Coarse slider to the left. I wanted to have a smaller increment of change when I adjusted the color.

   You can also click one of the tick marks to move the slider to that position. Photoshop doesn't allow setting the control to any of the intermediate positions between the marks.

6. **Make sure that you've selected the Midtones radio button, and then click the Preview window containing the amount of color you want to add.**

   Watch the Current Pick thumbnail, which reflects the correction.

   In my case, I need to click the More Magenta image.

   Click several times if your initial application isn't enough or click other Preview windows to add additional colors.

   Photoshop applies your corrections only to the middle tones of the image. In many cases, that's sufficient. However, sometimes shadows take on a particular hue, or the highlights may gain colorcasts of their own.

7. **Click the Highlights and/or Shadows radio buttons to add colors only to those parts of the photo.**

   Variations isn't the best tool to make complex color corrections, so be careful.

   You might be able to see a highlight color in the shadows under the pillow, most noticeable in the More Magenta preview. The highlight is the Clipping indicator showing that the change made by that Preview window is too much for that particular area of the picture. That is, Photoshop can't add any more magenta to the highlighted area without losing detail in the image.

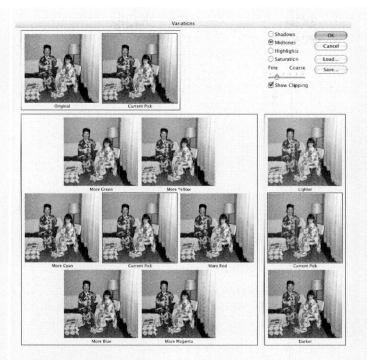

8. **Click the Darker preview (in the lower-right corner of the dialog box) to make the photo a little darker.**

   Adjust the Fine/Coarse slider to adjust the amount of change, or gradually darken and lighten the image by clicking multiple times.

   In my case, only one click is necessary.

9. **Click the Saturation radio button to brighten the colors and use the Fine/Coarse slider to control how much saturation you add or remove.**

   The Variations feature also lets you adjust the purity of color, or *saturation*, of the colors in an image. Now, only three previews appear: a less-saturated version, the current choice, and a more-saturated version. My photo was washed out, or under-saturated, so I clicked the More Saturation button.

10. **To save your settings, click the Save button, apply a name to the settings, and store them in the folder of your choice.**

continued

continued

I recommend saving your settings, especially if you're working on a copy of the original image and want to apply the same corrections later, or if you plan to correct several photos that have the same color defects.

Working with Professional Color Correctors

The simple color correctors I discuss in the section "Using Simple Color Correctors," earlier in this chapter, usually aren't enough to provide thorough color correction if you have a really problematic image on your hands. Fortunately, Photoshop has the kind of professional tools needed to make sophisticated color corrections for higher-end color printing. You don't have to be a pro to use the Levels or Curves commands, nor to work with the Hue/Saturation controls. But you'll feel like one after you master these powerful tools.

Leveling for better contrast

If you want to adjust tonal values of images (the brightness or darkness of tones) or correct colors (the relationship between the colors), the Levels command is the tool for you. It offers more control than the Auto Tone command, which I discuss in the section "Auto Tone," earlier in this chapter. The

Levels command is also a much more sophisticated tool than the Brightness/ Contrast control because you can work with individual tones, brightening or darkening individual tones as you want, and you have a great deal more information to help you make your choices.

Open the Levels dialog box, shown in Figure 1-13, by pressing Ctrl+L (⌘+L on the Mac) or choosing Image⇨ Adjustments⇨Levels. The graph shown in the center of the dialog box is a histogram, which I describe in detail in the section "Introducing the Histogram Panel," earlier in this chapter. You can use this dialog box, histogram and all, for evaluating and adjusting levels in the following ways:

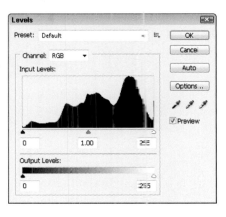

Figure 1-13: The Levels dialog box offers controls for adjusting the contrast in your image.

- ✔ **Visually check the distribution of dark, midtone, and light values.**

- ✔ **View separate histograms for each channel.** The default histogram displays information for the entire image. To see the histogram of an individual channel, select it from the Channel pop-up menu. For an RGB image, you can view the Red, Green, and Blue channels. For a CMYK image, you can view the Cyan, Magenta, Yellow, and Black channels. You can view the histograms of each channel simultaneously by using the Histogram panel.

- ✔ **Adjust the black and white points based on the histogram.** The three triangles at the bottom of the histogram, in black, gray, and white, represent the shadow on the left, midtone in the middle, and highlight on the right. Even though they're located where they are, many images have no black tones at the far-left side of the scale nor white tones at the far-right side.

  One of the simplest corrections you can do is to move the black and white sliders so that they actually correspond to the pixels containing dark and light tones. Simply slide the black triangle so that it corresponds to the first true black pixels in the image (the beginning of the histogram), and then move the white triangle to align it with the lightest pixels (the end of the histogram). That ensures that Photoshop doesn't waste tones by allocating them to areas of the image that actually have no image detail. Figure 1-14 shows an example of an image that was rescued by the use of the Levels adjustment.

Figure 1-14: Applying the Levels command to a dark photo dramatically improves the contrast.

✔ **See exactly what happens when you use the Auto Tone command.** When you click the Auto button, which applies the same adjustments as the Auto Tone command, Photoshop applies its own suggested changes, resetting the white point and the black point, and redistributing the gray values of the pixels in between. Afterward, the histogram shows that the pixels fill the complete range from white to black.

Setting black and white points manually

For more control, you can use the Eyedropper tools in the Levels dialog box to set the black and white points. Just follow these steps:

1. **Open an image and choose Image⇨Adjustments⇨Levels.**

   Make sure you have the Info panel open (Window⇨Info), and display the HSB and RGB color modes. (To do this, select Panel Options from the Info panel pop-up menu and select HSB and RGB from the Color Readout pop-up menus.) See Book II, Chapters 2 and 3 for more on color modes.

   Remember that you can also apply certain adjustments, such as Levels, via an adjustment layer rather than directly to the image itself. Adjustment layers provide more editing flexibility if you later decide you need to tweak the adjustment. For more on adjustment layers, see Book V, Chapter 1.

2. **Select the White Eyedropper tool and move it around the image while watching the Info panel.**

3. **Look for the lightest white in the image, which may be anywhere from 90% to 100% in brightness (the B under HSB). Select that point by clicking.**

4. **Using the Black Eyedropper tool, repeat the process outlined in Steps 2 and 3 to select the darkest black in the image, which may be anywhere from 0% to 10% in brightness (B).**

   The combination of these two choices redistributes the pixels from pure white to pure black.

You can also set the white and black points by moving the position of the white and black triangles on the input sliders (just under the histogram). Or you can enter numbers in the Input Levels boxes. The three boxes represent the black, gray, and white triangles, respectively. Use the numbers 0 to 255 in the white and black boxes.

5. **Use the Gray Eyedropper tool to remove any colorcasts. Select an area of your image that should be neutral gray, one in which the Info panel shows equal values of red, green, and blue.**

   Note that the Gray Eyedropper tool isn't available when you're working on grayscale images.

   Although you generally make changes to the entire document by using the RGB channel, you can apply changes to any one of an image's component color channels by selecting the specific channel in the Channel pop-up menu at the top of the Levels dialog box. (Refer to Figure 1-13.) You can also make adjustments to selected areas only. This can be helpful when one area of your image needs adjusting but others don't. See Book III, Chapter 1 for details on making selections.

6. **Adjust the output sliders at the very bottom of the Levels dialog box.**

   Moving the black triangle to the right reduces the contrast in the shadows and lightens the image. Moving the white triangle to the left reduces the contrast in the highlights and darkens the image.

7. **Adjust the midtones with the gray triangle slider. (It appears between the black and white input sliders, just under the histogram.)**

   The values you're adjusting are called the *gamma values*.

   Dragging this triangle to the left lightens the midtones. Dragging it to the right darkens the midtones while leaving the highlights and shadows alone. You can also move the gray triangle by entering numbers from 9.99 to 0.1 in the center option box. The default value (1.0) lies exactly in the middle of the range.

   If you're working with a series of similar images (such as a bunch of video captures), you can save the settings to reuse them later.

   You can also select a preset Levels setting, such as Increase Contrast or Lighten Shadows, from the Preset pop-up menu in the Levels dialog box. Use a preset as your starting point and then fine-tune the adjustment manually by adjusting the input sliders, as described in the preceding steps.

8. **Click the Save button to store your settings.**

   This step saves the settings, but it doesn't apply them. Just click the Load button to retrieve them.

9. **Click OK to apply your settings and exit the dialog box.**

**Book VIII
Chapter 1**

**Enhancing Images
with Adjustments**

Adjusting curves for hard-to-correct photos

The Curves command is one of the most advanced Photoshop correction tools available, offering sophisticated control over the brightness, contrast, and midtone *(gamma)* levels in an image; I'm talking about control that's far beyond what the Levels and Brightness/Contrast dialog boxes offer. This section introduces you to the functions of the Curves command, but you'll want to practice using it a great deal to gain the kind of experience you need to work with it effectively.

Whereas the Brightness/Contrast dialog box lets you change an image globally, and the Levels command allows you to change the shadows, highlights, and midtones separately, Curves goes far beyond either of those settings. It lets you change pixel values at 16 different points (which include start and end points) along an image's tonal range. You can work with the combined Red, Green, and Blue color channels (or CMYK channels) or apply your changes to the individual colors. Often, images that just can't be fixed to your satisfaction with Levels can be helped with the Curves adjustment, as shown in Figure 1-15.

PhotoDisc/Getty Images

Figure 1-15: The Curves adjustment offers more control and sophistication than many other color correction tools.

Working with the Curves dialog box

You access the Curves dialog box, shown in Figure 1-16, by choosing Image⇨Adjustments⇨Curves or by pressing Ctrl+M (⌘+M on the Mac).

The following tips help you to begin understanding how to interpret the information and use the tools in this dialog box:

- **The horizontal axis maps the brightness values as they are before image correction (input).**

- **The vertical axis maps the brightness values after correction (output).** Each axis represents a continuum of 256 levels, divided into four parts by finely dotted lines. In the default mode, the lower-left corner represents 0,0 (pure black) and the upper-right corner is 255,255 (pure white). By default, the dialog box shows a 4-x-4 (quarter tone) grid; Alt-click (Option-click on the Mac) inside the grid to toggle it to a 10-x-10 (10% increment) grid. If you have the Curve Display Options visible, you can use the Quarter Tone or 10% Increment display buttons.

- **Whenever you open the Curves dialog box, the graph begins as a straight line.** Unless you make changes, the input is exactly the same as the output, a direct 1-to-1 correlation.

- **You can expand the Curve Display Options and specify the following:**

  - *Show Amount Of:* Choose between Light and Pigment to display the brightness levels or percentages. To keep things simple, I'd leave them at the default of Light (levels), where darker values are at the bottom-left and lighter values are at the top-right. Choose between a simple or detailed grid (icons).

  - *Show:* If you're adjusting curves for individual channels, choose Channel Overlays to superimpose those individual curves.

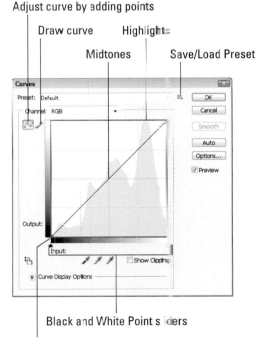

Figure 1-16: The Curves dialog box offers maximum control for adjustment of your image's color and tones.

Select Baseline to show your original straight line curve. Choose to display a histogram overlay. For more on histograms, see the section "Introducing the Histogram Panel," earlier in this chapter. Select Intersection Line to display horizontal and vertical lines to help you align your points while you drag them on the curve.

↙ **The Eyedropper can show you pixel values.** When you use the Eyedropper tool to click in the image, a circle appears on the graph to show you the value of the pixel being sampled. At the bottom of the Curves grid box, you can read the pixel's input and output values.

↙ **Auto sets black and white values.** When you click the Auto button, the darkest pixels in the image (the deep shadows) are reset to black, and the lightest areas are set to white. Like with the Levels dialog box, this option is the easiest way to make a correction but may not be the best.

↙ **Eyedropper tools can also set black, white, and gray values.** The Curves dialog box has black, white, and gray Eyedropper tools you can use to set the black, white, and midtone points, just like you can with Levels.

↙ **Select the Show Clipping options to have Photoshop display where clipping occurs in the image during your corrections.** Remember, clipping occurs when a pixel's values are lighter or darker than the highest or lowest value that can be displayed in the image, resulting in loss of detail in those areas.

Adjusting curves

If you click at any point on the curve other than the end points, Photoshop adds a control point that shows your position. You can remove a control point by dragging it downward until it's completely off the graph or by dragging it on top of the next point up or down from it on the graph. You can add up to 14 points to the curve.

Curve presets are located at the very top of the Curves dialog box. If you're a Curves novice, trying one of these presets is a good way to get your feet wet in how curves work. Note that when you select a preset, a curve is loaded into your dialog box. You can also use a preset as a starting point and then tweak it further with your own adjustments. Experiment with the curves to see how they affect the image. For example:

↙ Click the Auto button to have Photoshop analyze your image's color and tonal values and make an automatic adjustment. Again, you can use this preset as a starting point and tweak from there.

↙ Flattening a curve lowers contrast.

↙ Making a curve steeper heightens contrast.

↙ Moving a curve downward (if the display is set to Light) darkens the image. Moving it upward lightens.

- ✔ If your display is set to Light, adjust your highlights by moving points in the top-right of the curve, shadows by adjusting points in the bottom-left of the curve, and midtones by moving points in the center of the curve.

- ✔ A gently sloped S-shaped curve increases contrast, especially in the highlight and shadow areas. Using a curve like this also helps to define the midtones.

- ✔ For ultimate control, Photoshop lets you draw a curve with the precise shape you want, creating an arbitrary curve or map. Click the Pencil tool and then draw peaks and valleys in the Curves dialog box. Watch the changes in your original image.

- ✔ You can also add points to the curve by holding down Ctrl (⌘ on the Mac) and clicking your image. Adding points is beneficial if you want to preserve an area in your image.

- ✔ If you want to adjust the color in your image, select your desired channel from the Channel pop-up menu and then adjust the curve. For more on channels, see Book VI.

Arbitrary maps, such as the one shown in Figure 1-17, create distinctive solarization color effects when Photoshop warps the colors of your image. They're fun to play with, maybe useful now and then, but not nearly as practical as S curves.

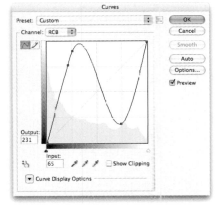

Figure 1-17: Going crazy with the Curves maps can result in a solarization-like effect.

Book VIII
Chapter 1

Enhancing Images
with Adjustments

After you create a custom curve, you may want to save it (a good idea) to load and apply it to other photos with similar contrast issues. Click the Preset Options button (just to the left of the OK button) and select Save Preset from the pop-up menu that appears.

Converting to Black & White

Photoshop provides a great way to convert a color image to grayscale with the Black & White feature. For other ways to make your image grayscale, see Book II, Chapter 2 and the section "Washing Out Color with Desaturate," earlier in this chapter.

The great thing about the Black & White feature is that, like the Channel Mixer (which you can read about in Book VI, Chapter 1), you have a lot of control over how your colors are converted.

Here's how to go to grayscale by using Black & White:

1. **Choose Image➪Adjustments➪Black & White.**

   Your Black and White dialog box appears, as shown in Figure 1-18. In addition, Photoshop automatically applies a default conversion to your image.

Dreamstime

Figure 1-18: Convert color images to grayscale with the Black & White adjustment.

2. **Adjust the conversion to your liking by doing one of the following:**

   - *Choose a Preset:* Select a preset conversion (or a custom one you saved previously) from the pop-up menu. Note that you can also use one of the presets as a starting point and then adjust from there.

   - *Click Auto:* This option analyzes your image's color values and then converts to grayscale, while trying to maximize your gray tonal values. Again, this conversion can be used as a starting point.

- *Adjust the sliders:* Do your own thing. Drag the sliders left to darken and right to lighten the tones. That's what I did in my example in Figure 1-18. Note that your mouse turns into an eyedropper when you move or click over your image. Click areas of your image to highlight that dominant color in your dialog box. Click and drag on the image itself with the eyedropper to move the color slider for that color, making it darker or lighter.

3. **If desired, select the Tint button to apply a tone of color to the black-and-white image.**

   Adjust the Hue and Saturation sliders to choose a tint color and intensity of that color. Click the color swatch to access the Color Picker, where you can select another color.

If you totally goof up your image, hold down Alt (Option on the Mac) and click the color chip to reset that adjustment. To reset all adjustments, hold down Alt (Option on the Mac) to convert the Cancel button into Reset, and then click that button.

After you establish a custom conversion setting, save it to apply to other similar images by selecting Save Preset from the Preset Options pop-up menu, just to the left of the OK button.

Getting colorful with Hue/Saturation

Photoshop's Hue/Saturation controls let you adjust colors based on their hue, saturation, and lightness. The Hue/Saturation dialog box doesn't work with the Red, Green, and Blue (or Cyan, Magenta, Yellow, and Black) channels of an image. Instead, it operates on the different colors, or hues. You can select all the colors (Master) or one color to modify from the Edit pop-up menu.

Three sliders are in the Hue/Saturation dialog box. (See Figure 1-19.)

- ✓ **Hue:** Shifts all the colors clockwise or counterclockwise around the color wheel, depending on the direction you move the slider. I moved my Hue slider to the left to turn the image green and purple.

- ✓ **Saturation:** Increases or decreases the richness of the colors in an image. I moved my Saturation slider to the right to increase the saturation and make the image almost glow.

- ✓ **Lightness:** Modifies the brightness values.

You can adjust any of these values by moving the sliders and watching the results in the image window. The top color bar at the bottom of the dialog box represents the colors in their order on the color wheel before you made any adjustment. The lower color bar shows how the modifications you make affect the colors.

**Book VIII
Chapter 1**

Enhancing Images
with Adjustments

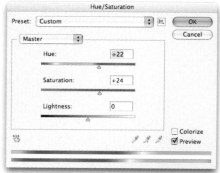

ImageState

Figure 1-19: The Hue/Saturation command enables you to adjust colors based on their hue (color), saturation (intensity), or lightness (brightness).

Select the slider (the pointing finger icon) to adjust your Hue and Saturation values. With the icon selected, drag directly on your image to adjust the Saturation. Hold down the Ctrl (⌘ on the Mac) key and drag on your image to adjust the Hue.

When you select an individual color to adjust, sliders appear between the color bars so that you can define the range of color to be adjusted. You can select, add, or subtract colors from the range by selecting one of the Eyedropper tools and clicking in the image.

You can also select a Hue/Saturation preset, such as Old Style or Sepia, from the Preset pop-up menu in the Hue/Saturation dialog box.

The Hue/Saturation dialog box also lets you colorize images, a useful option for creating sepia-colored images, like in the Putting It Together project "Making a New Photo Look Old," in this chapter.

Using the Colorize option

Use the Colorize option in the Hue/Saturation dialog box to change the color of any selected area to a new, solid color. This option is unlike the Hue slider, which changes only individual pixels based on their present color values. Just follow these steps:

1. **Open an image and access the Hue/Saturation dialog box by choosing Image⇨Adjustments⇨Hue/Saturation or pressing Ctrl+U (⌘+U on the Mac).**

2. **Select the Colorize option.**

3. **Drag the Hue slider in either direction to change a color.**

   Photoshop doesn't colorize pure white pixels and pure black pixels because colorization affects only gray pixels (from a brightness value of 1 to 254).

   You can also adjust the Saturation and Lightness, if desired

Pumping up the Vibrance

Think of the Vibrance adjustment as a souped-up, more intelligent Hue/ Saturation command. This adjustment increases the saturation in an image but does it in a nonlinear fashion. Therefore, pixels with a lower saturation get more adjustment, and pixels with a higher saturation get less. As a bonus. the adjustment includes a built-in skin-tone protector to prevent faces from becoming overly red. Choose Image⇨Adjustments⇨Vibrance. In the Vibrance dialog box, move the Vibrance and Saturation sliders to the right to increase each. But use a light touch with this adjustment. A little goes a long way, as shown in Figure 1-20.

Figure 1-20: The Vibrance command increases saturation in a nonlinear way.

Putting It Together

Making a New Photo Look Old

Black-and-white photography is a newer phenomenon than you might think. Daguerreotypes and other early photographs frequently had a brownish or bluish tone to them. You can create sepia-toned masterpieces of your own. (Or, if you want, you can create a tint in green, blue, or another shade.) Toned pictures can create a mood or otherwise transform a mundane photo into something interesting.

In this Putting It Together project, I chose a recent photo of a boy and his donkey in Java, Indonesia. Without any nasty anachronisms, such as automobiles or satellite dishes, aging this image is easy.

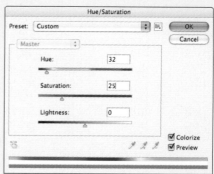

Corbis Digital Stock

The Photoshop Hue/Saturation feature is all you need to perform this time-traveling magic. Just follow these easy steps:

1. **Open the image in Photoshop and convert it to black and white by choosing Image⇨Adjustments⇨ Black & White. Click OK.**

   You choose this command rather than the Image⇨Mode⇨Grayscale command to convert the photo to black and white because you're going to continue to work with it as a color image — the image just won't have colors until you add them. For more info on the Black & White adjustment, see the earlier section, "Converting to Black & White."

Corbis Digital Stock

2. **Choose Image⇨Adjustments⇨ Hue/Saturation.**

   The Hue/Saturation dialog box appears.

3. **Select the Colorize check box so that you can add color to the image.**

4. **Adjust the Hue slider to produce the tone you're looking for.**

   To produce a rich sepia tone, move the Hue slider to the far left. If you prefer green, blue, or some other shade, you can experiment with this slider to get the exact color you want.

5. **Adjust the Saturation slider to modify the richness of the color.**

   I used a setting of 25, as shown in the figure. When you move the slider to the right, the color becomes more pure. You end up with a striking red at the far-right position.

6. **Adjust the Lightness slider to lighten or darken the photo, depending on your mood.**

Generally, you want to leave the Lightness slider at the default middle position. To create a darker, moodier picture, move it to the left; to produce a more faded look, move it to the right.

7. **When you're satisfied with your changes, click OK.**

Now, my photo looks like a vintage postcard.

You can create similar effects by using the Photoshop Duotones, Tritones, and Quadtones features. See Book II, Chapter 2 for more information on these tools. You can also try the Tint options in the Black & White adjustment. (See the section "Converting to Black & White," in this chapter.)

Corbis Digital Stock

Matching Color between Documents

The Match Color command enables you to match colors in a single image or between images — a source image and a target image. But it doesn't stop there. You can also match colors between layers or even selections. You can further refine your correction by adjusting the luminance and color intensity (saturation).

This command is great for getting rid of colorcasts in a single image. It also works wonders for matching the color of the lighting between two images or layers — for example, use it if you want to realistically composite an image shot under fluorescent lighting and one shot in natural light.

The Match Color command works only with RGB images, but be sure to apply this command before you perform any color conversions.

Follow these steps to use the Match Color command to match one image with another:

1. **Open the two images you want to match.**

If you want, you can make selections in one or both of those images — for example, if you're creating a composite image from two separate images and want to match the lighting color or skin tones. Without selections, the overall target image is matched to the source image. In my example in Figure 1-21, I selected an image taken outdoors in natural light and one taken inside under fluorescent lights (which give that image a nasty green colorcast). I want to use the girl in each image in a composite and therefore want to try to match the skin tones.

Figure 1-21: The Match Color command lets you match colors within a single image or between two images.

2. **Make sure your target image (the one that needs to be corrected) is the active file, and choose Image⇨Adjustments⇨Match Color.**

   If you're using a specific layer in your target image, select that layer prior to choosing the command. Make sure you select the Preview option so that you can view your adjustments on the fly.

3. **In the Match Color dialog box, shown in Figure 1-22, select your source image from the Source pop-up menu in the Image Statistics area.**

   Select None if you're working with only one image (if the source image and target image are the same).

   Remember, the source image contains the colors you want to match in the target image.

4. **If you're using a particular layer in your source image, select it from the Layer pop-up menu.**

   Or choose the Merged option to match the colors from all the layers.

Figure 1-22: Match color between two images with different lighting.

5. **If you have selections in your images, you can select one of the following options:**

   - If you have a selection in your target image but want to match the colors from the whole image, select the Ignore Selection when Applying Adjustment option.

   - Select the Use Selection in Source to Calculate Colors option if you want to use the colors in the selection in the source image to calculate the adjustment. Deselect this option to ignore the selection in the source image and match the colors from the entire source image.

   - Select the Use Selection in Target to Calculate Adjustment option if you have a selection in the target image and want to use the colors in the selection to calculate the adjustment. If it's deselected, the adjustment is calculated using the colors of the whole image.

6. **Select the Neutralize option to remove any colorcasts in the target image.**

When using the Match Color command, your cursor becomes the Eyedropper tool. This allows you to sample colors on your images and look at the color values in the Info panel while making your adjustments.

7. **Adjust the luminance by moving the slider or entering a value.**

   A higher value increases the brightness in the target image. A lower value decreases brightness.

8. **Adjust the color intensity of your target image.**

   A higher value increases the color saturation, and a lower value decreases the saturation. Moving the slider to 1 desaturates the image to grayscale.

9. **Use the Fade option to control the amount of adjustment that is applied to the target image, moving the slider to the right to reduce the amount.**

   If you move the slider all the way to the right, the image returns to its original colors.

10. **If you want to save your settings to use on other images, click the Save Statistics button. Then, in the Save dialog box that appears, name the file, specify the location, and click Save.**

    To reload the settings later, click the Load Statistics button and navigate to the file.

11. **Click OK to apply the adjustment and exit the dialog box.**

My image, shown in Figure 1-23, has less of that nasty green cast from the fluorescent lighting.

Figure 1-23: These tones are a better match with the target image.

Switching Colors with Replace Color

The Replace Color command creates interesting creative effects by allowing you to substitute one set of colors for another. It builds a mask, using colors you select, and then replaces the selected colors with others that you specify. You can adjust hue, saturation, and lightness of the masked colors.

Just follow these steps:

1. **Choose Image⇨Adjustments⇨Replace Color.**

   The Replace Color dialog box appears, as shown in Figure 1-24.

2. **Choose either Selection or Image:**

   • *Selection:* Shows the mask in the Preview window. The masked area is black, semitransparent areas are shades of gray, and unmasked areas are white.

For details on masks, see Book VI, Chapter 2.

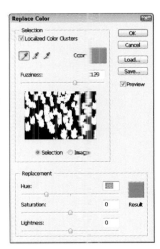

- *Image:* Shows the full image itself in the Preview window. Use this option if you zoomed in on the original image to select colors more easily, but you still want to be able to see the full image in the preview.

3. **Click the colors you want to select.**

   You can click the colors in either the image itself or the Preview window.

4. **Shift-click or use the plus (+) Eyedropper tool to add more colors.**

5. **Press the Alt key (Option key on the Mac) and click, or use the minus (–) Eyedropper tool and click, to remove colors.**

6. **To add colors similar to the ones you select, use the Fuzziness slider to refine your selection, adding or subtracting from the selection based on the tolerance value.**

Corbis Digital Stock

Figure 1-24: The Replace Color adjustment enables you to substitute one color for another.

If your selection isn't quite cooperating, try selecting the Localized Color Clusters option to assist you in obtaining a cleaner, more precise selection. The Localized Color Clusters option is especially handy if the color you're trying to select is somewhat varied.

7. **Move the Hue, Saturation, and Lightness sliders to change them to new values.**

8. **When you like the result, click OK to apply the settings.**

Figure 1-25 shows my images before and after replacing color.

Corbis Digital Stock

Figure 1-25: Don't like the color of your flowers? Use the Replace Color command to change it.

Increasing and Decreasing Color

Increasing and decreasing color is a popular Photoshop activity, so the fact that Photoshop offers more than one way to do so is no surprise. In addition to the Selective Color command, which I describe in the following section, several other commands are a lot easier to understand — and a lot easier to use.

This is the place to start reading if you want to know all about the Gradient Maps command and the various color mapper tools, all of which are designed to change the arrangement of the colors in your photos in ways that *don't* produce realistic-looking images. Images that have been color-mapped are certainly interesting to look at.

Using the Selective Color command

You use the Selective Color command (in the Image⇨Adjustments menu) chiefly to manipulate the amount of process colors (that is, cyan, magenta, yellow, and black) used in printing an image. In the Selective Color dialog box, select the color you want to edit from the Colors pop-up menu. Adjust the CMYK sliders to modify the selected color.

With the Relative method selected, you can add or subtract color. For example, if a pixel is 30 percent cyan and you add 20 percent cyan, Photoshop adds 6 percent cyan to the pixel (20 percent of 30 percent is 6 percent).

With the Absolute method selected, Photoshop bases the amount of change on the exact value you enter. For example, if a pixel is 30 percent cyan and you add 20 percent cyan, the pixel changes to a total of 50 percent cyan.

Using gradient maps

Gradient maps convert your image to grayscale and then replace the range of black, gray, and white tones with a gradient of your choice, in effect colorizing your image — often, in startling ways.

Photoshop maps the lightest tones of your image to one color in the gradient and changes the darkest tones to the other color of the gradient (assuming you're using just two colors for the gradient). Photoshop changes all the formerly gray tones to an intermediate color between the two. When you use multiple colors or fancy gradients, the image really gets interesting. Just follow these steps to try out this feature:

1. **Open an image and access the gradient map, shown in Figure 1-26, by choosing Image⇨Adjustments⇨Gradient Map.**

2. **Choose the gradient you want from the gradient list.**

   This list is exactly like the one offered with the Gradient tool. You can edit the gradient used for your map exactly like you do for the

Gradient tool. For more information on choosing gradients, see Book IV, Chapter 2.

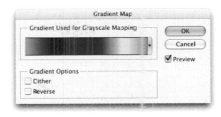

3. **Choose either or both of these options:**

   - *Dither:* Adds random noise to smooth out the gradient and reduces banding.

   - *Reverse:* Changes the direction of the gradient. Use the Reverse option to create a negative quickly.

Figure 1-26: A gradient map replaces the tones in your images with a gradient.

4. **Click OK to apply the gradient map.**

   If the effect is a little too intense for your taste, try fading the gradient map (Edit⇔Fade Gradient Mask) and then adjusting the opacity percentage and/or applying a different blend mode.

Adding color with photo filters

Photographers will appreciate the Photo Filter command, which is reminiscent of the analog method of placing a colored filter in front of a camera lens to tweak the color balance and color temperature of the light coming through the lens. This is a great way to make an image appear cooler or warmer. Have a portrait where your subject appears a little too bluish? Apply a Warming filter and bring some rosiness back into his or her cheeks. You can also apply a colored filter to add a tint of color to your image. Figure 1-27 shows how I warmed up an overly cool image.

To apply the Photo Filter adjustment, follow these steps:

1. **Open your image and choose Image⇔Adjustments⇔Photo Filter to apply the filter to the entire image.**

   If you want to apply the filter to one or more layers, choose Layer⇔New Adjustment Layer⇔ Photo Filter.

Corbis Digital Stock

Figure 1-27: Photo Filters adjust the color balance and color temperature of an image.

2. **Make sure you have the Preview option selected so you can view the results.**

3. **In the Photo Filter dialog box, select the Filter radio button to choose a preset filter from the Filter pop-up menu or select the Color radio button to select a custom color for your filter.**

   See Table 1-1 for a brief description of the filters in the Filter pop-up menu.

   If you opt for the custom color, click the swatch to select a color from the Color Picker.

4. **Select the Preserve Luminosity check box if you don't want the filter to darken your image.**

   Note that some photo pros advocate not selecting this option, but it's up to you.

5. **Adjust the Density slider to control the amount of color applied to your image.**

   A higher value provides a stronger adjustment. Use the Density control with restraint. Anything above 50 percent produces a severe effect.

6. **Click OK to apply the adjustment and exit the dialog box.**

Table 1-1	Photo Filters
Name	*Effect of Filters*
Warming Filter (85, LBA) and Cooling Filter (80, LBB)	Adjusts the white balance in an image. A photo shot in a high color temperature of light makes an image blue. Warming Filter (85, LBA) makes the colors warmer, more yellow. Similarly, an image shot in light of a low color temperature benefits from the Cooling Filter (80, LBB), which makes the colors more blue.
Warming Filter (81) and Cooling Filter (82)	Similar to the preceding filters but for minor adjustments.
Colors	These filters adjust the hue of an image. You can select a color to get rid of a colorcast. For example, if your image is too green, select magenta. If it's too blue, select yellow. You can also select a color to apply a special effect.

Playing with the color mappers

Photoshop also includes some fun-filled color mapping commands (in the Image⇨Adjustments menu), so-called because they change the colors of your image in specific ways. Two of them, Invert and Equalize, can't even have any options. They're akin to single-step filters that you apply and forget. (I cover filters in Book VII.) I show all the color mappers in Figure 1-28.

| Invert | Equalize | Threshold | Posterize |

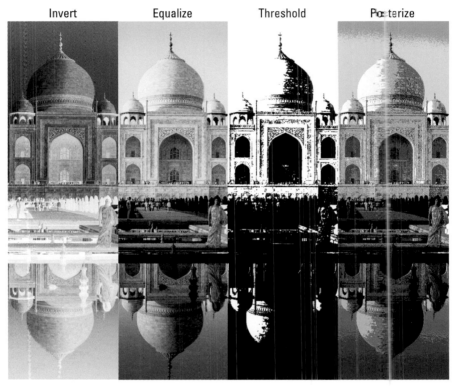

Corbis Digital Stock

Figure 1-28: The Color Mappers change the colors in your image in specific ways, such as reversing colors or converting your image to black and white.

Invert

Invert simply reverses all the colors and tones in your image, creating a negative image. Photoshop changes black tones to white, white tones to black, dark grays to light grays, and colors to their complements. For example, a light yellow color becomes a dark blue, and so forth.

Some folks mistakenly think they can use this command to create a positive (or color-correct) version of a scanned color negative. It isn't so simple because color negatives have an orange mask overlaying the color information. Converting a color negative correctly requires a lot of color correcting and tweaking. If you have sophisticated scanning software, you may have a command that does the conversion. A couple third-party Photoshop filters also do the duty. But to do it manually requires a lot of color correcting and tweaking. Something you may not want to try at home!

Equalize

This command locates the lightest and darkest pixels in an image, defines them as white and black, respectively, and then changes all the other pixels in between to divide the grayscale values evenly. Depending on your image, this process may increase contrast or otherwise alter the color and tones when the values are evenly distributed.

Threshold

Threshold converts your image to black and white, with all pixels that are brighter than a value you specify represented as white, and all pixels that are darker than that value as black. You can change the threshold level to achieve different high-contrast effects.

Posterize

This color mapper creates an interesting graphic effect by reducing the number of colors in your image to a value you specify, from 2 to 255. Low values provide distinct posterlike effects. While you increase the number of color levels, the image begins to look either more normal or a bit like a bad conversion to Indexed Color.

Putting It Together

Cleaning Up a Line Art Scan

Line art consists of (you guessed it!) lines, rather than the continuous tones of a photograph or painting. Line art can consist of outlines, shapes (like you find in a bar chart), patterns (like the fills in the bar chart), or freehand drawings (like those produced in pen or pencil).

What you don't want to see when you scan line art is an extra color: the background color of the paper. Often, the paper appears as a dull gray, and you may see other artifacts you don't want, such as wrinkles or spots in the paper.

Luckily, Photoshop has a handy Threshold command that you can use to determine which tones appear as black and which are dropped altogether. You end up with a nice black-and-white line art image with all the intermediate tones removed.

Follow these instructions to clean up a piece of line art (to test-drive these steps, download my example image from this book's Web site, which I talk about in the Introduction):

1. **Open a line drawing in Photoshop, as shown in the figure.**

2. **Choose Image⇨Adjustments⇨ Threshold from the menu bar.**

   The Threshold dialog box includes a chart called a *histogram*. The histogram includes a series of vertical lines showing how many of an image's tones are represented by a certain brightness level. You can see that a relatively small number of tones are represented by a brightness value of 93, marked by the gray triangle at the bottom of the histogram. Many more tones are used at the other levels, forming a sloping mountain in the chart.

3. **Move the slider to the right until the tones you want to appear in the image are shown.**

   The more you move the slider to the right, the darker the image gets. A threshold of about 170 seems about right for this image.

4. **Click OK to apply the modification.**

   Some small artifacts may remain in your image, as shown in the figure. These are spots and parts of wrinkles that are darker than the page background, approaching the darkness of the line art itself.

5. **To clean up these slight defects, use the Eraser tool.**

Chris Blair

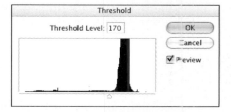

**Book VIII
Chapter 1**

**Enhancing Images
with Adjustments**

Chapter 2: Repairing with Focus and Toning Tools

In This Chapter

✓ **Dodging and burning**

✓ **Manipulating color with the Sponge tool**

✓ **Smudging rough spots smooth**

✓ **Blurring for effect**

✓ **Focusing on sharpness**

*O*ne of the coolest things about Photoshop is the way it offers several tools to accomplish similar results, but with distinctly individualized looks. The focus and toning tools in Photoshop are examples of this. The focus tools blur, sharpen, and smudge your image in much the same way as the Blur, Sharpen, and Liquify filters (which I cover in Book VII). The toning tools lighten, darken, and change the richness of color in your image a bit like commands, such as Levels, Curves, and Hue/Saturation (covered in Book VIII, Chapter 1).

But where their counterparts operate only on layers or selections, the focus and toning tools let you *paint* the effects you want directly onto your image. Using these tools, you can often create subtler, natural looks tailored to meet your exact needs, as I explain in this chapter.

 While you work through this chapter, keep in mind all the tips I give you in Book IV, Chapter 1 about using brushes. Most of that information applies to the brushlike focus and toning tools, as well.

Lightening and Darkening with Dodge and Burn Tools

Dodging and burning originated in the darkroom, where photographers salvage negatives containing areas that are too dark or too light by adding or subtracting a bit of exposure when an enlarger makes prints.

An enlarger makes a print by projecting an image of a negative onto a piece of photosensitive paper. During the exposure, the darkroom technician can reduce the amount of light falling onto the paper by placing some object (often a disc-shaped piece of cardboard or metal impaled on a piece of wire) in the light path to *dodge* part of the image. The worker can *burn* other parts of an image by exposing only a small portion through an opening, such as the fingers in a cupped pair of hands. The Dodge and Burn tools in Photoshop adopt their icons from those popular real-world tools used to achieve these darkroom effects.

However, the Photoshop counterparts are a great deal more flexible. For example, the worker in a darkroom varies the size of the dodging or burning tool by moving it up or down in the light path. Unfortunately, the closer the real-world tool gets to the paper, the sharper it appears, forcing the darkroom worker to move the tool more rapidly and frequently to blur the edges of the effects. With the Photoshop Dodge and Burn tools, you can set the size of the tool and its softness independently by selecting a brush of the size and the hardness or softness you require.

You can also set the Photoshop tools to operate primarily on shadows, midtones, and highlights. You can adjust the degree of lightening and darkening applied by specifying an exposure, too.

The Dodge (used to lighten) and Burn (used to darken) tools can be very effective, but you can't add detail that isn't there. Keep the following in mind:

- ✔ When you lighten very dark shadows that contain little detail, you end up with grayish shadows.

- ✔ Darkening very light areas that are completely washed out doesn't look very good, either.

In either case, you want to use the Dodge and Burn tools in moderation and work only with small areas. To dodge or burn a portion of an image, just follow these steps:

1. **Open an image with under- or overexposed areas and select the Dodge or Burn tool from the Tools panel.**

   Press the O key to choose the active toning tool or press Shift+O to cycle through the available toning tools until the one you want is active.

2. **In the Options bar, make these adjustments:**

   a. *Select a brush from the Brush Preset Picker or toggle open the larger Brush panel.*

   Larger, softer brushes spread the dodging and burning effect over a larger area, making blending with the surrounding area easier.

   You can choose the same brushes available with any of the painting tools, including preset brushes from your library.

   b. *Under the Range options, select Shadows, Midtones, or Highlights.*

Use Shadows to lighten or darken detail in the darker areas of your image, Midtones to adjust the tones of average darkness, and Highlights to make the brightest areas even lighter or (more frequently) darker.

In Figure 2-1, the original image (top) had mostly dark areas, so I dodged the shadows. Note the increased detail in the eyes, teeth, and hair. I also gave a couple swipes to the highlight areas with the Burn tool.

c. *Select the amount of the effect to apply with each stroke by using the Exposure slider or text box.*

d. *Enable the airbrush option for a softer, more gradual effect.*

e. *Check the Protect Tones option.*

This setting provides more natural and subtle dodging and burning results by preserving the hues and tones of the image pixels.

f. *If you are using a pressure-sensitive tablet, click the last icon. Doing so overrides any settings you made in the Brush panel.*

Figure 2-1: The Dodge and Burn tools are effective when touching up smaller dark and light areas.

3. **Paint over the areas you want to lighten or darken with the toning brush, gradually building up the desired effect.**

Using a soft-edged brush is often best when dodging and burning. You want to create a realistic, not retouched, appearance.

The Exposure control is similar to the Opacity control offered by other painting tools, but it's especially important with dodging and burning.

Using a low value is best (I often work with 10-percent exposure or less) so that you can carefully paint in the lightening or darkening you want.

High exposure values work too quickly and produce unnatural-looking, obviously dodged or burned areas in your images.

4. **If you go too far, press Ctrl+Z (⌘+Z on the Mac) to reverse your most recent stroke.**

5. **When you finish, choose File⇨Save to store the image.**

Turning Down the Color with the Sponge Tool

The Sponge tool, which soaks up color like, well, a sponge, reduces the richness or intensity (or saturation) of a color in the areas you paint. It can also perform the reverse, imbuing a specific area with richer, more vibrant colors.

Surprisingly, the Sponge tool also works in grayscale mode, pushing light and dark pixels toward a middle gray, providing a darkening or lightening effect to those pixels. Unlike the Hue/Saturation or Desaturate commands (Image➪Adjustments), which work only on layers or selections, you can use the Sponge tool on any area that you can paint with a brush.

You can use the Sponge tool on an image in subtle ways to reduce the saturation in selected areas for an interesting effect. For example, you may have an object that's the center of attention in your picture simply because the colors are so bright (or even garish). The Sponge tool lets you reduce the color saturation of that area (and only that area) to allow the other sections of your image to come to the forefront. You can also use the Sponge tool to make an artistic statement: You could reduce or increase the saturation of a single person in a group shot to make that person stand out (perhaps as being more colorful than the rest). To use the Sponge tool, just follow these steps:

1. **Open an image and select the Sponge tool from the Tools panel.**

   Press the O key to choose the Sponge if it's the active toning tool or press Shift+O to cycle through the Sponge, Dodge, and Burn tools until the Sponge tool is active.

2. **In the Options bar, make the following changes:**

   a. *Select a brush from the Brush Preset Picker or the larger Brush panel.*

      Use large, soft brushes to saturate/desaturate a larger area.

      Smaller brushes are useful mostly when you need to change the saturation of a specific small object in an image.

   b. *Select either Desaturate (reduce color richness) or Saturate (increase color richness) from the Mode pop-up menu.*

   c. *Select a flow rate (the speed with which the saturation/desaturation effect builds up while you apply the brush) with the Flow slider or text box.*

   d. *If you want an even softer effect, select the Airbrush icon.*

   e. *Select the Vibrance option.*

      This setting allows saturation for each color to reach its fullest level, but the setting stops saturation after that point to avoid *clipping* (when colors fall outside the printable range). At the same time, it allows saturation to continue for any colors that haven't reached the clipping point.

   f. *If you are using a pressure-sensitive tablet, click the last icon. Doing so overrides any settings you made in the Brush panel.*

3. **Paint carefully over the areas you want to saturate or desaturate with color.**

   In Figure 2-2, I saturated the little girl to make her a focal point and desaturated the parents and surroundings.

Purestock

Figure 2-2: The Sponge tool saturates (increases richness) and desaturates (decreases richness) color.

Smoothing with the Smudge Tool

Although grouped among the focus tools, the Smudge tool performs more of a warping effect, something like the Warp tool in the Liquify dialog box (see Book VII, Chapter 3 for information on this command).

Smudge pushes your pixels around on the screen as if they consisted of wet paint, using the color that's under the cursor when you start to stroke. However, don't view the Smudge tool as a simple distortion tool that produces only comical effects. I use it on tiny areas of an image to soften the edges of objects in a way that often looks more natural than blurring tools. The Smudge tool can come in handy when retouching images to create a soft, almost painted look, as shown in Figure 2-3. Just don't go gung-ho, or you may obliterate detail that you want to preserve.

TIP Smudged areas may be obvious because of their smooth appearance. Adding a little texture by using the Noise filter after you smudge is often a good idea if you want to blend in a smudged section with its surroundings. You can find tips on applying the Noise filter in Book VII, Chapter 2.

**Book VIII
Chapter 2**

**Repairing
with Focus and
Toning Tools**

To apply the Smudge tool, just follow these steps:

1. **Open the image and select the Smudge tool from the Tools panel.**

2. **Select the settings you want from the Options bar:**

   a. *Select a brush from the Brushes panel.*

   Use a small brush for smudging tiny areas, such as edges. Larger brushes produce drastic effects, so use them with care.

   b. *Select a blending mode from the Mode pop-up menu.*

   c. *Select the strength of the smudging effect with the Strength slider or text box.*

   Low values produce a lighter smudging effect; high values really push your pixels around.

   d. *If your image has multiple layers and you want Photoshop to use the color information from all the visible layers to produce the smudge effect, select the Sample All Layers option.*

Photodisc

Figure 2-3: The Smudge tool can give your fruit, or other elements, a soft, painted look.

   The smudge still appears only on the active layer, but the look is a bit different, depending on the contents of the underlying layers.

3. **Use the Finger Painting option to begin the smudge by using the foreground color.**

   You can get some interesting effects with this option. You can switch the Smudge tool into Finger Painting mode temporarily by holding down the Alt key (the Option key on the Mac) while you drag. If you are using a pressure-sensitive tablet, click the last icon. Doing so overrides any settings you made in the Brush panel.

4. **Paint over the areas you want to smudge.**

5. **Watch the screen carefully while you smudge so that you can redirect your daubs to achieve the look you want.**

   This tool can be a little on the destructive side. If you're looking to preserve reality, use it with restraint. If you want to get wild, go crazy.

6. **When you finish, choose File⇨Save to store your image.**

Softening with the Blur Tool

Adding a little blur here and there can save an image with a few defects. Blurring can also be used for artistic effect — say, to add a little motion to a soccer ball frozen in time by a too-fast shutter speed. You can also blur portions of your image to emphasize and focus on a particular element, as shown in Figure 2-4, where I blurred the empty slide cases a bit to draw attention to the image. The Photoshop Blur tool makes painting your blur effects exactly where you want them easy.

Figure 2-4: Use the Blur tool to soften a rough edge or make your element a focal point by blurring its surroundings.

The Blur tool doesn't push pixels around the way the Smudge tool does. Instead, the Blur tool decreases the contrast among adjacent pixels in the area painted.

The mechanics of using the Blur tool and several of its options are similar to those of the Smudge tool (which I talk about in the preceding section). Just follow these steps:

1. **Open an image and select the Blur tool from the Tools panel.**

2. **In the Options bar, specify these settings:**

   a. *Select a brush from the Brush Preset Picker or the larger Brush panel.*

      Use a small brush for applying small areas of blur. Use larger brushes with caution to, for example, blur the entire background to make a foreground object appear sharper in comparison.

   b. *Select a blending mode from the Mode pop-up menu.*

   c. *Select the strength of the blurring effect with the Strength slider or text box.*

   d. *If your image has multiple layers and you want to blur based on the pixel information in all the visible layers in your image, select the Use All Layers option.*

      Selecting this option can produce a smoother blur when you merge the layers later.

   e. *If you are using a pressure-sensitive tablet, click the last icon. Doing so overrides any settings you made in the Brush panel.*

3. **Paint over the areas you want to blur.**

4. **When you finish, choose File⊅Save to store your image.**

Cranking Up the Focus with the Sharpen Tool

In theory, the Sharpen tool is nothing more than the Blur tool (discussed in the preceding section) in reverse — instead of decreasing contrast among pixels, the Sharpen tool increases the contrast. In practice, however, you need to use this tool with a bit more care than the Blur tool. Where blurred areas tend to fade from a viewer's notice (at least, in terms of how his or her eyes perceive them), sharpened areas of an image jump out at people.

If you blur an area a little too much, you may not even notice. But even a small area that has been oversharpened can change the entire appearance of an image — and not flatteringly.

You can often successfully sharpen small areas with the Sharpen tool. Sometimes, the eyes in a portrait can benefit from a little sharpening, as shown in Figure 2-5. Or you might want to sharpen an area to make it stand out more distinctly against a slightly blurred background.

Stockphoto

Figure 2-5: Use the Sharpen tool sparingly and in small areas, such as in the eyes of this portrait.

Follow these simple steps to use the Sharpen tool:

1. **Select the Sharpen tool from the Tools panel.**

2. **Make the following changes in the Options bar:**

   a. *Select the brush of your choice from the Brushes panel.*

   b. *Select a blending mode from the Mode pop-up menu.*

   c. *Select the strength of the sharpening effect with the Strength slider or text box.*

   Using a fairly low value (say, 25 percent or less) is a good idea because you can build up sharpness slowly, being careful not to overdo it. You know you've gone too far with the sharpness when the pixels start to look noisy and grainy.

   d. *Use the information on all your layers for Photoshop's contrast-increasing algorithms by selecting the Use All Layers option.*

   e. *Choose Protect Detail to enhance the details in the image and minimize artifacts. If you leave this option unselected, your sharpening is more pronounced.*

   f. *If you are using a pressure-sensitive tablet, click the last icon. This overrides any settings you made in the Brush panel.*

3. **Paint over the areas you want to sharpen.**

4. **When you finish, choose File⇨Save to store your image.**

Sharpening increases contrast so be careful when using the Sharpen tool if you plan to adjust the Levels or Curves controls, too. Any change that increases contrast in the whole image also boosts the contrast of an area you've sharpened.

The Unsharp Mask and Smart Sharpen filters offer more options and better overall control, so unless you really need to paint the sharpening effect, you're usually better off using a filter. If you really want to apply the effect with brushstrokes, you can always apply the Unsharp Mask filter to a whole layer, take a snapshot, undo the filter operation, and then use the snapshot as a source to paint from, using the History panel. See Book II, Chapter 4 for information on how to paint from the History panel. Finally, for maximum flexibility, try using Smart Filters, which enable you to endlessly edit your filter. For more on Smart Filters, see Book VII, Chapter 1.

Putting It Together

Fixing an Underexposed Foreground

Sometimes, editing tools just don't cut the mustard when it comes to fixing large areas of an underexposed image. Instead, you have to use three tools together to repair the damage: a filter, a fill, and a blend mode.

If you're like me, you've taken at least a couple photos where your subject was lit from behind, thereby underexposing the foreground and burying the subject in the shadows. You can try the Shadows/Highlights adjustment, on the Image⇨Adjustments menu, which usually does a good job of fixing the problem. But if you're not satisfied with that adjustment, you can follow this old-school method. Or you can even go for a combo plate and use them both. Follow these steps to bring your subject back into the light:

1. **Open the image in need of repair.**

2. **Choose Image⇨Duplicate.**

3. **In the dialog box that appears, name the duplicate file (I named mine Nick after my friend) and click OK.**

4. **On the duplicate image, choose Image⇨Mode⇨Grayscale. Click Discard in the dialog box that appears to discard the color information.**

Photoshop has now stripped the color from the image. Don't worry; this is just an intermediary step.

continued

continued

5. On the duplicate image, choose Filter⇨Blur⇨Gaussian Blur. In the Gaussian Blur dialog box, enter a radius value and click OK.

For a low-resolution image (72 ppi), a value of 5 pixels is enough. For higher-resolution images (300 ppi), use 20 pixels. Your goal is to get rid of the detail in the image.

6. Return to the original image and choose Select⇨Load Selection.

In the Load Selection dialog box, make sure the Document drop-down list shows your file from Step 2.

7. Select Gray for the Channel. Select the Invert box. In the Operation area, leave the setting as New Selection, as shown in the figure. Click OK to load the selection.

You're loading the only available channel in the duplicate grayscale image as a selection. A selection outline appears, which corresponds to the blurry gray areas in your duplicate image.

8. Choose Edit⇨Fill.

9. In the Fill dialog box that appears, shown in the figure, select 50% Gray from the Use pop-up menu. Select Color Dodge from the Mode pop-up menu. Leave the Opacity at 100%. Click OK.

Although Photoshop fills the selection with 50-percent gray, the Color Dodge mode *lightens* the pixels in the image, creating a kind of bleaching effect.

10. You can now see the subject of your image in a better light, like in my image.

Chapter 3: Fixing Flaws and Removing What's Not Wanted

In This Chapter

✔ **Making copies with the Clone Stamp tool**

✔ **Healing digitally with the Healing Brush tool**

✔ **Applying patches with the Patch tool**

✔ **Zapping with the Spot Healing Brush tool**

✔ **Applying color with the Color Replacement tool**

✔ **Eliminating red-eye**

✔ **Using Vanishing Point**

Say that you want to duplicate an element in your image. That's easy enough, right? Make a selection and copy and paste it into the new location. Presto. That works fine most of the time. But what if the element has a shadow behind it, next to it, above it, or below it? What a pain. The better method is to clone the element by using the Clone Stamp tool. It's quick, easy, and no one will know that only one element was there originally.

Here's another hypothetical situation: What if some unsightly flaw mars your otherwise perfect image? Or maybe the corporate executive, whose head shot you took last week, has requested a little digital Botox around the eyes and mouth.

In this chapter, I reveal secrets of cloning that won't make medical ethicists scream. I show you how to heal scars, scratches, and other imperfections without calling a plastic surgeon. And you can use Vanishing Point to add or remove windows or doors without forking out a dime to a contractor.

Cloning with the Clone Stamp Tool

The Clone Stamp tool, one of Photoshop's more popular tools, always arouses a "Wow," "Cool," or similar remark of approval when demonstrated.

Believe it or not, you can also reach for this tool when retouching imperfections, such as scratches, scars, bruises, and other minor flaws. In fact, that used to be one of its major functions. In some retouching instances, it does a great job, although the advent of the Healing Brush and Patch tools has relegated the Clone Stamp tool more to the pure cloning functions and less to the hard-core retouching jobs.

Using the Clone Stamp tool

The Clone Stamp tool works its magic by taking sampled pixels from one area and *cloning* (or copying) them onto another area. Cloning often works better than making a selection and then copying and pasting it because cloning allows you to retain soft edges on details such as shadows, giving you a more realistic duplicate image. To assist you with your cloning tasks, the Clone Source panel enables you to see a preview (in an overlay style) of the source pixels you're cloning.

Follow these steps to clone an element without any genetic engineering:

1. **Open an image and select the Clone Stamp tool from the Tools panel.**

   Press the S key (or Shift+S if the Pattern Stamp is currently active) on the keyboard.

   You have several options to choose from on the Options bar.

2. **Select a brush and change its size or hardness in the Brush Preset Picker to better control the area that you're cloning.**

   For more information on brushes, see Book IV, Chapter 1.

   I recommend having your Clone Stamp tool cursor display your Full Size Brush Tip so you can judge the amount of the area you're cloning. To do so, choose Edit➪Preferences➪Cursors (Photoshop➪Preferences➪ Cursors on the Mac). Select the Full Size Brush Tip radio button in the Painting Cursors area of the dialog box.

   I used a 65-pixel, feathered brush.

   Click the Tablet icon (at the end of the Options bar) to control the size of the brush. The pressure you apply will then override any settings in the Brush panel.

3. **Select the blend mode of your choice on the Options bar.**

   Selecting a mode such as Difference, Multiply, or Color can produce some interesting special effects. For more on modes, see Book V, Chapter 3. I left my setting at Normal.

4. **To make the clone more or less opaque, use the Opacity slider or text box on the Options bar.**

   I left the opacity at 100%. If you are using a pressure-sensitive tablet, and you want the pressure you apply to set the opacity, click the Tablet Opacity icon.

5. **Specify how fast the Clone Stamp tool applies the clone by adjusting the Flow Rate percentage.**

   Again, I left my option at 100%.

6. **Select the Airbrush option for airbrushing capabilities, if desired.**

7. **Select or deselect the Aligned option, depending on your preference.**

   With Aligned selected, the clone source moves when you move your cursor to a different location. If you want to clone multiple times from the same location, deselect the Aligned option. I left mine selected.

8. **Select the All Layers option from the Sample drop-down list to clone part of an image with multiple layers.**

   Selecting this option enables you to sample pixels in all the visible layers for the clone. If you select the Current Layer option, the Clone Stamp tool clones only from the active layer. If you select the Current and Below option, you sample pixels from the current layer and all layers below it.

9. **If you select All Layers in Step 8, you can choose whether to ignore any adjustment layers when cloning. To do so, click the Adjustment Layer icon on the Options bar.**

   By ignoring adjustment layers, you may prevent the bizarre results that can sometimes occur by double-applying your adjustment layers during the cloning process.

10. **Choose Window⇨Clone Source to open the Clone Source panel, as shown in Figure 3-1. Specify the following options:**

    * *Sampling Sources:* In Step 11, you define a sampling source by Alt-clicking (Option-clicking on the Mac) the area of the image that you want to clone. However, if you want to create multiple sampling sources, you can do so in the Clone Source panel by selecting a different Clone Source button and repeating this Alt-clicking (Option-clicking on the Mac) process on other areas of your image. You probably don't need to use more than one source. Multiple sampling sources are useful for video editors who have to work with tight registration between frames that need cloning.

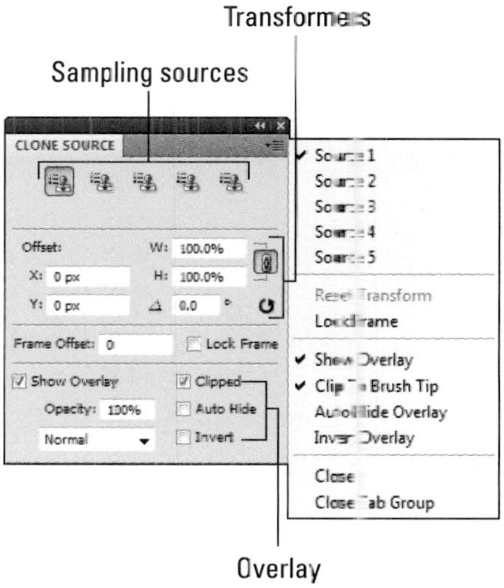

Figure 3-1: The Clone Source panel assists in the cloning process.

- *Transformations:* Adjust the rotation, position, or scale of your clone. Select the link icon to maintain your Width (W) and Height (H) aspect ratio. Click the small curved arrow below the link icon to reset your transformation settings (W, H, and Rotation). I wanted my cloned tiger to be a twin of the one that's already in the image, so I left the settings at their default.

You can use scrubby sliders by hovering over the transformation label (H, W, and so on) of a field and dragging left or right. Hold down Alt (Option on the Mac) while dragging to make your changes slower. Hold down Shift while dragging to make your changes faster.

- *Overlay:* If desired, select the Show Overlay option. Applying an overlay is especially useful when cloning subjects that need to be in alignment with the underlying image. Adjust the Opacity to your desired percentage. I used 30% in my example. If you want, select the Auto-Hide option. If you select this option, when you release your mouse, you see a ghosted preview of how your cloned pixels will appear on the image. While you're painting, however, the overlay is hidden. Select a blending mode for your overlay from the Blending Mode drop-down list. Depending on your source pixels, a blend mode other than Normal may work better in aligning your cloned image with the underlying image. Check Invert to reverse the colors and tones in your overlay. This setting may also assist you in aligning areas.

To display the overlay temporarily, hold down Alt+Shift-click (Option+Shift-click on the Mac) after setting your source. You can drag your overlay around and then, after you have your desired location, release the mouse to set it down.

You can find most of the same options in the Clone Source panel pop-up menu.

If you select the Clipped option, the overlay is clipped, or contained, only within the boundaries of your brush. In my opinion, this makes it a lot easier to clone exactly what you want.

11. Alt-click (Option-click on the Mac) the area of your image that you want to clone.

By clicking the area you want to clone, you're defining the *source*.

12. Click or drag along the area where you want the clone to appear, as shown in Figure 3-2.

While you drag, Photoshop displays a crosshair icon along with your Clone Stamp cursor. The crosshair represents the source you're cloning from, and the Clone Stamp cursor shows where the clone is being painted. While you move the mouse, the crosshair moves, as well. This provides a continuous reference to the area of your image that you're cloning. Keep an eye on the crosshair, or you may clone something you don't want. Try to clone your entire object in one fell swoop so it doesn't get fragmented.

Photo Disc/Getty Images

Figure 3-2: When using the Clone Stamp tool, drag along the area where you want your clone to appear.

When you successfully complete the cloning process, you have two identical objects. Figure 3-3 shows my identical twin Siberian tigers.

Figure 3-3: My twin Siberian tigers are the products of cloning.

13. Save the image and close it.

Tips for excellent cloning results

Here are a few useful tidbits regarding the Clone Stamp tool:

- ✔ **Use the Clone Stamp tool to fix simple flaws.** To clean up a flaw that's pretty straight, such as a stray hair or scratch, Alt-click (Option-click on the Mac) with the tool to define the source. Then, click at one end of the straight flaw and Shift-click at the other end. The cloned source pixels then cover up the flaw.

- ✔ **Pay attention to the origin point for sampling.** Depending on what you're cloning (for example, when covering up a flaw), if you keep sampling from the same point without ever varying it, the area you're cloning starts to look like ugly shag carpeting. Or, at best, starts to appear blotchy and overretouched.

- ✔ **Zoom out occasionally to check how your image looks overall.** Doing so helps you avoid those funky telltale clone stamp repetitive patterns and blotches.

 ✔ **When cloning patterns, use the Pattern Stamp tool,** which shares the flyout menu with the Clone Stamp tool. Select a custom pattern from the Pattern Picker on the Options bar. Drag with the Pattern Stamp tool, and you see the pattern appear.

Digital Bandaging with the Healing Brush Tool

The Healing Brush and Patch tools are similar to the Clone Stamp tool. They let you clone pixels from one area and apply them to another area. But that's where the similarities end; the healing tools leave the Clone Stamp tool eating their dust.

The problem with the Clone Stamp tool is that it doesn't take the tonality of the flawed area — the shadows, midtones, and highlights — into consideration. Therefore, if the pixels you're sampling from aren't shaded and lit exactly like the ones you're covering, you have a mismatch in color, which makes seamless and indecipherable repairs hard to achieve.

That's where the Healing Brush tool comes in. This very intelligent tool clones by using the *texture* from the sampled area (the source) and then the *colors* around the brush stroke when you paint over the flawed area (the destination). The highlights, midtones, and shadows remain intact, and the result of the repair is more realistic and natural — not retouched and phony. Follow these steps to heal your favorite, but imperfect, photo:

 1. **Open your image and select the Healing Brush tool.**

   My guy, shown in Figure 3-4, looks like he could stand to get some "work done," as they say in Hollywood. You can also heal between two images. Just make sure that they have the same color mode.

2. **On the Options bar, click the Brush Preset Picker.**

   In the drop-down panel, select your desired diameter and hardness, as well as spacing, angle, and roundness if you want, for your brush tip. You will most likely specify your brush settings several times while retouching your image. Using the appropriate brush size for the flaw you're repairing is important.

   Click the Tablet icon (at the end of the Options bar) to control the size of the brush. The pressure you apply will then override any settings in the Brush panel.

3. **On the Options bar, leave the blending mode set to Normal.**

   You can change your blending mode, if necessary. The Replace mode preserves textures, such as Noise or Film Grain, around the edges of your strokes when using a

Figure 3-4: The Healing Brush can make these wrinkles practically disappear.

soft brush. For most simple retouching jobs, such as this one, you can leave it at Normal.

4. **Select a Source option.**

   You have a choice between Sampled and Pattern:

   - *Sampled:* You'll probably use this option, which uses the pixels from the image, 99 percent of the time.

   - *Pattern:* You can probably infer that it uses pixels from a pattern you select from the Pattern Picker.

   For my example, I'm sticking with Sampled because I don't think my guy would look that good with a Tie-Dye or Nebula pattern across his face. He's just way too corporate for that.

5. **Select how you want to align the sampled pixels.**

   When you click or drag with the Healing Brush tool, Photoshop displays a crosshair along with the Healing Brush cursor. The crosshair represents the sampling point, also known as the *source*. While you move the Healing Brush tool, the crosshair also moves, providing a constant reference to the area that you're sampling. However, if you deselect the Aligned option on the Options bar, Photoshop applies the source pixels from your original sampling point, despite how many times you stop and start dragging. I left the Aligned option selected in my example.

6. **Select the All Layers option from the Sample drop-down panel to heal an image by using all visible layers. Select Current Layer if you want to heal only from the active layer. Choose Current Layer and Below to heal from your active layer and all layers beneath it.**

You can use the Clone Source panel with the Healing Brush tool and the Clone Stamp tool. For details, see the section "Cloning with the Clone Stamp Tool," earlier in this chapter.

For maximum flexibility, select the Sample All Layers option and, in the Layers panel, add a new, blank layer above the image you want to heal. Select this blank layer and when you heal the image, the pixels appear on the new layer and not on the image itself. You can then adjust opacity and blending modes, and make other tweaks to the "healed" pixels.

7. **If you selected All Layers in Step 6, you can choose whether to ignore any adjustment layers when healing.**

By ignoring adjustment layers, you may prevent the bizarre results that can sometimes occur when your adjustment layers get double-applied during the healing process. To do so, click the Adjustment Layer icon on the Options bar.

8. **Establish the sampling point by Alt-clicking (Option-clicking on the Mac).**

Make sure to click the area of your image you want to clone *from*.

In my example, I clicked the smooth area on the chin and portions of the forehead.

9. **Release the Alt (Option on the Mac) key and click or drag over the area of your image that contains the flaw.**

Pay attention to where the crosshair is located because that's the area you're sampling from.

In my example, I brushed over the wrinkles under and around the eyes and on the forehead, as shown in Figure 3-5. I also zapped some dark spots here and there.

10. **Save the file, close it, and send in your invoice for your digital dermabrasion.**

Figure 3-5: In just 5 or 10 minutes, this gentleman lost about 10 years.

Patching without Seams

Although the Patch tool is similar to the Healing Brush tool in theory, its application method is slightly different. Instead of painting over the flaws with a brush, you select your flawed area and apply a patch to that selection.

The Patch tool does a good job in fixing larger flawed areas or isolated imperfections, rather than a few wrinkles or scars here and there. What's more, it's a breeze to use.

Follow these steps to patch an area in need of repair:

1. **Open your image and select the Patch tool.**

   It looks like a patch of material. The girl in my image, shown in Figure 3-6, is virtually flawless, although I can't say the same for the wall she's leaning against.

Figure 3-6: The Patch tool can fix the flaws on the wall.

2. **Select Source or Destination on the Options bar.**

   Select Source if you want to select the flawed area. Select Destination if you want to select the good area you want to clone from.

   Select the Transparent option to patch from your source pixels with less opaqueness.

You can use the Clone Source panel with the Patch tool. For details, see the section "Cloning with the Clone Stamp Tool," earlier in this chapter.

3. **Drag around the flawed area of your image, as shown in Figure 3-7.**

   Think of the Patch tool as a kind of super-cloning Lasso tool. Drag completely around the flawed area like you would when selecting with the Lasso tool. If you need to, you can apply a slight feather of 0.5 to 2 pixels, depending on the

Figure 3-7: Drag around the flawed area.

Book VIII
Chapter 3

Fixing Flaws and Removing What's Not Wanted

resolution, to soften the edge of the selection. I selected my area without a feather.

You can actually select your flawed area with any selection tool you like. If you use another selection tool, after you have your selection, select the Patch tool and proceed to Step 4.

4. **Drag your selection to the area on your image that you want to clone (or sample) from, as shown in Figure 3-8.**

5. **When you release the mouse button, Photoshop patches your flawed selection with the cloned pixels.**

6. **Repeat the process, as needed.**

After several patches, the wall looks almost as good as the girl, as shown in Figure 3-9.

Figure 3-8: Drag the selection to the area you want to sample.

Zeroing In with the Spot Healing Brush

Whereas the Healing Brush tool is designed to fix larger flawed areas, the Spot Healing Brush tool is designed for smaller blemishes and little imperfections. The biggest difference between the Healing Brush and the Spot Healing Brush is that the Spot Healing Brush doesn't require you to specify a sampling source. It automatically takes a sample from around the area to be retouched. The good news is it's quick and easy. The downside is that it doesn't give you as much control over the sampling source. Consequently, reserve this tool for small and simple flaws. Follow these steps to quickly fix little, nitpicky imperfections with the Spot Healing Brush tool:

Figure 3-9: The Patch tool repaired the wall.

1. **Open your image and grab the Spot Healing Brush tool.**

   The small moles in Figure 3-10 are examples of small areas you can fix with the Spot Healing Brush.

2. **On the Options bar, click the Brush Preset Picker and select your desired diameter, hardness, and other options for your brush tip.**

   Try to select a brush that's a little larger than the flawed area.

PhotoSpin

Figure 3-10: Watch these moles disappear.

3. **Select a blending mode from the Options bar.**

   Like the Healing Brush, you can select the Replace mode. Most likely, the Normal mode will work the best.

4. **Select a type from the Options bar.**

   You have a choice among Proximity Match, Create Texture, and the new Content Aware:

   - *Proximity Match:* Samples the pixels around the edge of the selection to use to fix the flawed area.

   - *Create Texture:* Uses all the pixels in the selection to create a texture to fix the flaw.

   - *Content-Aware:* Compares and uses actual content from the image close to the flaw. Try using the Content-Aware option when removing large items like cars, litter, scratches on your image, and other annoying elements.

5. **Choose Sample All Layers to heal an image by using all visible layers.**

   If you leave this option unselected, you heal only from the active layer.

   Click the Tablet icon (at the end of the Options bar) to control the size of the brush. The pressure you apply will then override any settings in the Brush panel.

6. **Click, or click and drag, the area you want to fix.**

   In Figure 3-11, I used the Spot Healing Brush for the moles and spots on the upper lip and cheeks. But for the mole over the eyebrow, I broke out the Healing Brush. I

Figure 3-11: I used the Spot Healing Brush and the Healing Brush to remove a few moles.

**Book VIII
Chapter 3**

Fixing Flaws and Removing What's Not Wanted

found I needed more control of the sampling source because the mole is so close to the hair of the eyebrow.

For retouching skin, try Proximity Match first and, if it doesn't work, undo and try Create Texture or Content-Aware. You may get better results filling the flawed area by using the Edit⇨Fill command. See how in Book IV, Chapter 2.

Colorizing with the Color Replacement Tool

The Color Replacement tool allows you to replace the original color of an image with the foreground color. You can use this tool in a variety of ways. Create the look of a hand-painted photo by colorizing a grayscale image. Or maybe you just want to change the color of an object or two, such as a couple flowers in a bouquet. And although Photoshop has a bona-fide Red Eye tool, you can use the Color Replacement tool to easily paint away red-eye.

The great thing about the Color Replacement tool is that, like the other healing tools, it completely preserves the tonality of the image. The color that you apply doesn't obliterate the midtones, shadows, and highlights like it would if you were using the regular Brush tool. The Color Replacement tool works by first sampling the original colors in the image and then replacing those colors with the foreground color. By specifying different sampling methods, limits, and tolerance settings, you can control the range of colors that Photoshop replaces.

This weapon in the arsenal of retouching tools is a cinch to use. Follow these steps to replace color:

1. **Open your image and select the Color Replacement tool.**

   Remember, it shares a flyout menu with the regular Brush and Pencil tools.

   It looks like a brush with a square and two arrows next to it. You can press B (or Shift+B) to select it.

2. **On the Options bar, click the Brush Preset Picker.**

   In the drop-down panel that appears, select your desired diameter, hardness, and other options for your brush tip.

3. **On the Options bar, select your desired blend mode:**

   • *Color:* The default mode that works well for most colorizing jobs. Use this mode if you're trying to get rid of red-eye.

   • *Hue:* Similar to color, but less intense, providing a lighter effect.

   • *Saturation:* Set your foreground color to Black in the Tools panel and set the mode to Saturation to convert a color image to grayscale.

- *Luminosity:* The exact opposite of the Color mode. Although it can create a beautiful effect between two image layers, it doesn't provide that great an effect with this tool.

  For a full "scientific" definition of each blending mode, check out Book V, Chapter 3.

4. **Select your sampling method from the icons on the Options bar.**

   The default of Continuous allows you to sample and replace color continuously while you drag your mouse. Select Once to replace colors only in areas containing the color that you first sample. Finally, select Background Swatch to replace colors only in areas containing your current Background color.

5. **Select your sampling limits mode.**

   The default of Contiguous lets you replace the color of pixels containing the sampled color that are adjacent to each other directly under the brush. Discontiguous lets you replace the color of the pixels containing the sampled color wherever it occurs under your brush. Find Edges allows you to replace the color of pixels containing the sampled color while preserving the sharpness of the edges of the objects.

6. **Specify your tolerance percentage.**

   Tolerance refers to a range of color. A high tolerance lets you replace a broad range of color. A low tolerance limits the replacement of color to only areas that are similar to the sampled color.

7. **Choose whether you want anti-aliasing.**

   Remember, anti-aliasing slightly softens and smoothes the edge of the selected or sampled areas.

   Click the Tablet icon (at the end of the Options bar) to control the size of the brush. The pressure you apply overrides any settings in the Brush panel.

8. **After you establish your settings, click or drag in your image.**

   The foreground color, which in my example is black, replaces the original colors of the sampled areas. (See Figure 3-12.) Of course, the exact effect you get depends on your settings.

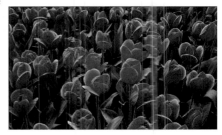

Figure 3-12: Use the Color Replacement tool to replace the original color in your image with your current foreground color.

Getting Rid of Dreaded Red-Eye

Red-eye occurs when the subject of a picture looks directly into the flash, and the unfortunate result is that eerie reddish luminescence in the eyes that says, "I may very well be a demon child."

Many cameras have a red-eye prevention mode, but that's little solace when you have a great picture that features bright red pupils as its most dominant feature. If you've been hanging around in Photoshop for a while, you're probably aware that you can get the same result many different ways. This holds true for getting rid of red-eye, as well. You can use the regular Brush tool with a Color blend mode and paint away the red. Or you can use the Color Replacement tool with a black foreground to color away the crimson. Additionally, you can use the Red Eye tool.

TIP

If you need to fix the green, blue, or yellow eye that occurs in animals, the Red Eye tool isn't effective. You will want to use the other two techniques mentioned above.

Follow these steps for a quick way to get the red out and restore your image to a less zombielike look:

1. **Open the original photo with red-eye showing.**

   I'm using a photo of an unhappy angel, shown in Figure 3-13.

2. **Select the Red Eye tool.**

   Using the default settings, click the red portion of the eye in your image, as shown in Figure 3-14. This one-click tool darkens the pupil and retains the tonality and texture of the eye.

3. **If you're not happy with the results, tweak one or both of the following options:**

   • *Pupil Size:* Use the slider to increase or decrease the size of the pupil.

   • *Darken Pupil:* Use the slider to darken or lighten the color of the pupil.

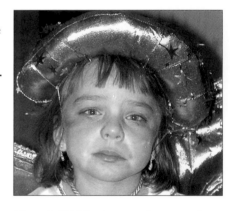

Figure 3-13: This photo needs an exorcist.

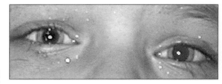

Figure 3-14: Click the red-eye with the Red Eye tool to make it vanish.

4. **If all goes well, your image is now cured of the dreaded red-eye, as shown in Figure 3-15.**

The Red Eye tool works only with RGB or Lab color images. For details on these color modes, see Book II.

Working with Vanishing Point

The Vanishing Point command enables you to make realistic edits in images that have perspective planes. With Vanishing Point, you specify the planes in your images and then, by using a variety of techniques, such as painting or cloning, add or eliminate objects on those planes

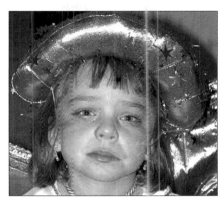

Figure 3-15: The ultimate cure for red-eye, but not tears.

For example, say you have a building that has only one window on the side. You have a remodeling project in mind in which you want to add more light in the room, so you want to add three more windows on that side. Using Vanishing Point, you can easily add those windows, all of which will be scaled and angled by staying true to the perspective of the side of that building.

Besides editing flaws from or features into your digital photos, other great uses for Vanishing Point include mocking up covers for books or DVDs, and putting graphics on various packaging containers.

Follow these steps to use this incredible feature:

1. **Open an image that needs editing.**

   Creating a new layer is a good idea so that you can isolate your Vanishing Point result from your original image layer. You get further editing advantages by adding a layer if you want to change opacity settings, blend modes, and so on.

   If you want the Vanishing Point results to only be applied to a specific part of your image, be sure to make the selection (or add a mask) before selecting the Vanishing Point command.

   If you need to paste an element into the Vanishing Point dialog box, be sure to copy the item before selecting the Vanishing Point command. This copied element can be from the same image or a different image. It can also be a text layer.

2. Choose Filter↪Vanishing Point.

The Vanishing Point dialog box appears, as shown in Figure 3-16.

Create Plane tool

PhotoSpin

Figure 3-16: Boxes are good candidates for working with the Vanishing Point command.

3. Grab the Create Plane tool (second tool from the top), and then click at each of the four corners of your plane to establish your editing surface.

Be as accurate as you can when specifying the plane on your image.

A bounding box with *nodes* at each corner and a grid appears over the plane surface, as shown in Figure 3-17. Feel free to tweak the plane to perfection — just move or resize the plane by using the Create Plane or Edit Plane tools. Photoshop informs you if your plane has a problem by displaying a bounding box and grid as red or yellow. If you have a problem grid, adjust the bounding box until it becomes blue (indicating the plane is valid) by moving a corner node. ***Note:*** You may have to move multiple nodes.

4. Use the Grid Size slider, accessed by clicking the double-headed arrow, to adjust the size of the grid units to better line up the plane and grid with the elements that may be in your image, such as tiles, texture, windows, or doors.

5. (Optional) If desired, you can use the Create Plane tool and Ctrl-drag (⌘-drag on the Mac) an edge node of the plane to "tear off" an additional plane.

For example, you can extend the plane around to another side, as I did in Figure 3-17, and create another plane. This process keeps the planes related to each other and ensures that your edit is in the correct scale and angle. Make sure you get your first plane exact because after you create an additional plane, you can no longer edit the first plane, except to expand it by dragging the edge nodes.

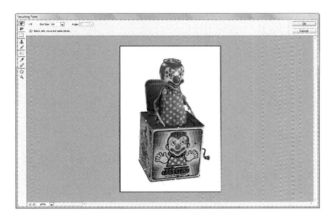

Figure 3-17: Define your editing plane with the Create Plane tool.

Your second planes have to be perpendicular! You can tear off another plane and position it out at an angle. After creating your additional plane, grab either the Create Plane or Edit Plane tool, hold down Alt (Option on the Mac), grab the center node on the side opposite from your axis, and swing it out at your desired angle. You can also enter a value, or slide the slider, in the Angle option at the top of the Vanishing Point dialog box.

TIP

At this point, you can simply create perspective planes, click OK, and bail out. The planes you established appear when you call up the Vanishing Point command again.

6. **After you establish your perspective planes, select an editing task:**

   - *Make a selection.* Select the Marquee tool and drag a selection in the plane, as I did in Figure 3-18. Specify your selection options, either before or after the selection. You can feather the selection to get soft edges. Or you can adjust the opacity of the selection. You can also choose a Heal option. Move Mode allows you to specify the selection as Destination or Source. Select Destination to select the area you move the marquee to. Source fills an area with the contents of the marquee when you move the marquee and release. If you want to select your entire plane, just double-click with the Marquee tool.

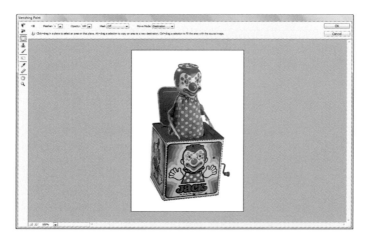

Figure 3-18: Make a selection with the Marquee tool on your plane.

- *Clone.* Select the Marquee or Transform tool and Alt-drag (Option-drag on the Mac) the selection to create a copy of the selection. Transform (scale, rotate, or move) the selection to your liking. Clone as many times as you want. When you move the selection, it adjusts to fit the perspective of the plane, as shown in Figure 3-19.

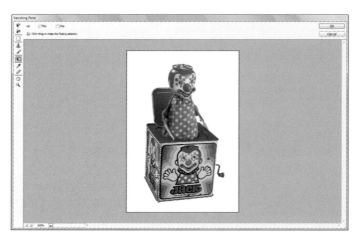

Figure 3-19: Your cloned selection conforms to fit the perspective of the destination plane.

Note: You have access to multiple undos within the Vanishing Point dialog box. But they're limited to your single editing session. Press Ctrl+Z (⌘+Z on the Mac) to undo.

- *Move a selection.* Grab the Marquee or Transform tool and drag the selection. Hold down the Shift key to constrain the move.

- *Transform a selection.* To scale the selection, select the Transform tool, move the cursor on top of a node, and drag. To rotate, move the cursor next to a node until you see a curved double arrow. Then, drag in the direction of your desired rotation. Select the Flip or Flop options to flip the selection horizontally or vertically.

- *Fill a selection with a piece of the image.* With the Marquee tool, Ctrl-drag (⌘-drag on the Mac) and make the selection you want as the source image. You can also choose Source from the Move Mode pop-up menu and drag the selection to the source image. You can then move or clone the selection. If the selection needs to be scaled or rotated, grab the Transform tool.

- *Clone by stamping with part of the image.* This technique works exactly like the regular Photoshop Clone Stamp tool. With the Stamp tool, Alt-click (Option-click on the Mac) the area you want to define as the source for your cloning. Then, drag your mouse on the portion of the image where you want the clone to appear. If you drag in a perspective plane, the Stamp tool paints the cloned area in perspective. You can specify options for your brush diameter, hardness, and opacity.

- *Select a Heal option.* The Off option allows you to clone without blending color, lighting, and shading of the surrounding pixels. The Luminance option allows you to clone by using the lighting and shading of the surrounding pixels, but keeping the color of the source (or sampled area). The On option enables you to clone by blending the color, lighting, and shading of the surrounding pixels. Select Aligned to sample pixels while maintaining the current sampling point, even when you release the mouse. Deselect this option to sample pixels from the sampling point of each mouse click.

- *Paint with color.* Select the Brush tool and specify your options, which are similar to the clone options. Click the Brush Color swatch. Select your desired color from the Color Picker and paint by dragging within your image. Like stamping, the brush size and shape adjust to stay true to the perspective.

- *Paste a copied element from the Clipboard before selecting the Vanishing Point command.* Press Ctrl+V (⌘+V on the Mac) to paste your element. With your Marquee tool, position the element on your plane, where it adjusts to fit the perspective.

- *Move around, measure, and magnify, as needed.* The Hand, Zoom, and Measure tools make measuring and navigation easy. You can also access the Magnification pop-up menu and the plus (+) and minus (–) buttons at the bottom of the window.

7. **Click OK.**

No one will be the wiser that your composite image, shown in Figure 3-20, doesn't really exist in the world as we know it. Save your edited image as a native Photoshop (.psd), TIFF, or JPEG file to ensure that your perspective planes are saved.

Figure 3-20: Your Vanishing Point-edited image looks unedited and unchanged.

Book IX

Photoshop and Print

So you've toiled away and gotten your images picture perfect? Not a flaw, colorcast, or stray pixel to be found? Congratulations! It's time to flaunt your editing prowess and share those images with the world. This book gives you the vitals on how to get those images print-ready. You can find information on how to set up images for offset printing. I also explain how to create panoramas from multiple images and how to work with High Dynamic Range (HDR) images.

Chapter 1: Prepping Graphics for Print

*P*reparing images for the screen is a snap compared to what you have to go through to get images ripe for the printing process. If all you ever want to do is print your images to a desktop laser or inkjet printer, the task is a little easier, but you still must consider some guidelines. And prepping your images for offset printing? Well, throw in an additional set of guidelines. It's not rocket science, mind you. If you stick to the basic rules and, more importantly, spend some time developing a good working relationship with your service bureau and offset printer, you're good to go.

Getting the Right Resolution, Mode, and Format

If you're not familiar with the concept of resolution, I suggest taking a look at Book II, Chapter 1. That's where I cover all the basics on resolution, pixel dimension, resampling, and other related topics. For full descriptions on color modes and file formats, see Book II, Chapter 2. That said, the following sections give you the lowdown on the proper settings for an image that will ultimately go to print.

Resolution and modes

Table 1-1 provides some guidelines about what resolution settings to use for the most common types of output. Remember, these are just *guidelines*. They aren't chiseled in stone to withstand the sands of time or anything lofty like that. You need to communicate with your service bureau, offset printer, or client and get specifications and/or recommendations. (See the section "Working with a Service Bureau," later in this chapter.)

Table 1-1	Recommended Resolutions and Image Modes		
Device	*Notes*	*Recommended Resolution*	*Mode*
Fuji Frontier photo printer	Wallets to 10 x 15 inches. Great for printing digital photos.	300 dpi	RGB
Online photo printers, such as Shutterfly	Check recommended size and resolution settings on the vendor's Web site.	1024 x 768 for 4-x-6 print; minimum of 1600 x 1200 for 8-x-10 print	RGB
Digital presses	Brands include Xeikon, Xerox, IBM, Indigo*, Scitex, Heidelberg, and so on.	255 to 300 dpi	CMYK
Epson color inkjets	Resolutions depend on the print setting. Epson recommends ⅓ of the horizontal resolution, but do test prints; settings may be higher than you need.	720 dpi × ⅓ = 240 dpi; 1440 dpi × ⅓ = 480 dpi; 2880 dpi × ⅓ = 960 dpi	RGB
Color separations	Film separations or direct to plate for offset printing.	2 × lines per inch (lpi); 2 × 133 lpi = 266 dpi; 2 × 150 lpi = 300 dpi; 2 × 175 lpi = 350 dpi**	CMYK and spot colors
Laser printers	Color or B&W printouts.	2 x lpi = 170 dpi	Grayscale or RGB

*Indigo presses can handle a fifth spot color, if necessary.
**See the section "Screen frequencies," in this chapter.

Screen frequencies

For the recommended resolution for color separations in Table 1-1, I list 2 multiplied by the number of lines per inch. The lines per inch, or *lpi*, pertains to the screen frequency of the output device. Screen frequencies are measured in lines per inch in a halftone screen. You may also hear the terms *screen ruling* or *line screen*. When images are printed, they're converted into a series of dots called *halftones*. When you print your halftone, you print it by using a halftone screen of a certain value. The average screen frequency for printing four-color images is 133 to 175 lpi. Therefore, when you multiply that number by 2, you need to create your images by using a resolution setting of 266 to 350 dots per inch (dpi).

File formats

As far as file formats go, what you choose depends on a couple issues:

- What you intend to do with the image — print it to a laser printer, order prints from an online photo printer?

- What does your service bureau, offset printer, client, director, or another interested party prefer?

Most publications (newspaper, magazines) will accept PDFs only because of their capability to embed fonts and links within the document, thereby eliminating a lot of headaches. For more on PDFs, see Book II, Chapter 2.

Table 1-2 lists some of the more popular recommended formats for specific jobs, but again, communicate with the parties involved to see what's ultimately the best format to use.

Table 1-2	Recommended File Formats
Job	**Formats**
Color inkjet printouts	EPS, TIFF, PDF, PSD
Color separations	PSD, PDF, EPS, TIFF, DCS 2.0
Spot color separations	PSD, PDF, DCS 2.0 if importing into another application
Magazines/brochures	EPS, TIFF, PDF
Newspapers	TIFF, PDF
Importing to page layout programs	TIFF, EPS, PSD, PDF
Importing to illustration programs	EPS, TIFF, DCS, PSD, PDF
Slides	TIFF, PowerPoint, PICT, PCX, EPS (some bureaus can't do EPS)
Photo prints	JPEG, TIFF
Word documents	TIFF, EPS, PNG
E-mailing for workflow review	PDF

Working with a Service Bureau

Service bureaus handle photo processing and various photographic output options, such as prints (of varying sizes) and slides. Mounting and lamination services may also be provided. Many service bureaus provide scanning services, including high-end drum scanning. A common service is taking scans or digital photos and burning them onto CDs or DVDs. Many service bureaus provide output to color separations to film and RC paper. Larger bureaus may even have a digital press to handle a short-run (500 or less), on-demand printing need.

Getting the ball rolling

Developing a good working relationship with your service bureau and/or offset printer can save you a lot of time, money, and frustration. These folks are the experts and know their equipment and processes. And believe me, they're only too willing to help. The fewer problems they have with your files, the better they like it. You can do some things to keep the relationship on solid footing:

- **Get a dialogue going about the specs.** If your file is going directly to a newspaper, magazine, or other publication, talk with the art director, graphics production coordinator, or other knowledgeable person about the graphic specifications required.

- **Build a lasting relationship.** Consistency is also key. When you find a good bureau or offset printer, stick with it for all your jobs. Jumping from one company to another because a quote came in a little cheaper doesn't always pay off in the long run. If you're a faithful customer, often your service bureau or offset printer will match that lower quote if it can.

- **Get on the Web.** Many service bureaus have Web sites where you can find a listing of services they offer, price lists, file specs, and even downloadable order forms. Larger offset printers also have general information, online requests for quote applications, and more. Larger offset printers may provide services such as scanning and film-separation output, so be sure to check the Web site for details.

Using a prepress checklist

To prepare your file for print, use the following list to ensure your file is ready and rarin' for problem-free output. Note that this list isn't all-inclusive when it comes to prepress; I include tips that pertain to Photoshop only.

- **Always transform your images in their native application.** Size, crop, rotate, shear, and reflect art in Photoshop. Transforming images in an illustration or page layout program is complex and time-consuming.

- **Ensure that images can first print from Photoshop.** Do this before importing the images into an illustration or page layout program.

- **If you're placing Photoshop EPS images into a page layout or illustration program, set the halftone screen frequency in the destination program instead of embedding it in each image in Photoshop.** Or better yet, don't set any halftone screen frequencies in your images and let your service bureau or offset printer handle setting them in the other program.

✔ **When saving Photoshop images for print purposes, stick to TIFF, EPS, native PSD, or PDF file formats.** If you're unsure of the proper format to use for a specific job, ask your offset printer or service bureau.

✔ **Make sure that you use the proper color mode.** For example, use CMYK for color separations and RGB for slide output.

✔ **Create vector shapes and paths efficiently.** Use the fewest number of anchor points possible to create the path and delete any unnecessary or stray points. Leave your flatness setting blank. Photoshop uses the default setting for the output device, which is usually a safe bet.

✔ **Limit the number of typefaces.** Downloading takes time. Limiting the number of typefaces also makes your document look more sophisticated and polished.

✔ **Make sure that all scanning is at the appropriate dpi.** For more on resolution, see Book II, Chapter 1.

✔ **If your image is to bleed (extend to the edge of the printed page), take that into account when creating your image.** Note that you need to allow for ⅛ to ¼ of an inch on any side that will bleed to allow for slippages when the paper is cut.

✔ **Always specify colors from a Pantone color swatch chart and then select the color, whether process or spot, in Photoshop.** *Never* trust the way colors look onscreen because of calibration deficiencies and differences between RGB and CMYK color models.

✔ **Make spot color names consistent.** Make sure that the Photoshop spot color names exactly match those of any programs to which you are importing your image, such as an illustration or page layout program. Otherwise, you may get an additional color separation.

✔ **Print and provide laser or inkjet prints of your file, both separations (if warranted), and a composite print.** Print all prints with printer marks — crop marks, registration marks, labels, and so on.

✔ **Provide all fonts used in your file.** Provide both screen and PostScript printer fonts, if applicable.

✔ **Choose File⇨Save As for your final save to squeeze down to the smallest file size.**

✔ **Organize your files into folders.** For example, put the image files together in one folder, all the fonts in another, and so on.

✔ **Communicate any trapping needs to your service bureau or offset printer.** *Trapping* is also known as spreading and choking, where you create slight overlaps where your colors meet to avoid registration problems on the printing press. For color separations, indicate whether you created the trapping yourself or if you want the service bureau/offset printer to do it.

Some file format warnings

If you save your file as an EPS or DCS and re-open the file in Photoshop, Photoshop rasterizes the vector data to pixels. Save the original in the native PSD format.

If you save your layered file as an EPS, Photoshop converts your vector type to clipping paths. Extensive and small type creates complex clipping paths, which can be time-consuming and sometimes difficult to print. You can either flatten your file or deselect the Include Vector Data option in the Save as EPS Options dialog box. Either choice rasterizes the type into pixels at the resolution of your image. You may want to consider eliminating the type in your image file and applying it either in a drawing or page layout program that can retain vector type.

Saving and Printing Vector Data in a Raster File

Photoshop allows you to create vector shapes and vector type with the Pen tools, shape tools, and type tools. (I explain how in Book III.) Technically, the vector shapes are clipping paths applied to a bitmap, or *raster*, layer. But the clipping path is *still* a vector path, thereby retaining vector qualities. This vector data is resolution-independent, which means that it prints at the resolution of the PostScript output device. Photoshop sends the printer separate images for each type and shape layer, which are printed on top of the raster image and clipped by using their vector paths. The edges of the vector path print at the full resolution of the PostScript printer, but the contents, such as the colored pixels or the image pixels within the vector path, print at the resolution of the Photoshop file. (All portions of the type are resolution-independent.) Therefore, type and shapes always have crisp, hard edges, with curves appearing smooth and never jagged.

Remember that the only file formats that allow you to retain vector data are PSD, PDF, DCS, and EPS. When saving to DCS or EPS, be sure to select the Include Vector Data option in their respective Options dialog boxes. All other file formats rasterize the vector data.

Choosing Color Management Print Options

I highly recommend checking out the color management section in Book II, Chapter 3. In that chapter, I go into great detail about the concept of color spaces, ICC profiles, and so on. In this section, I cover the color management options you can find in the Print dialog box.

Different output devices operate in different color spaces. Monitors, desktop printers, large-format printers, film recorders, offset printers, and so on all have their own unique color space. The color management options enable you to convert the color space of your image while printing. So, for example, if the ICC (color) profile of your image is sRGB, you can choose to have your image's color space converted to the color space of your Epson printer when you print.

Unfortunately, I can't tell you what specific settings to choose. This choice is a widely debated topic, and different printers have their strengths, shortcomings, and quirks. My advice is to take an hour and a pack of paper, run test prints to see which settings give you the most accurate result, and stick with those. You may even get different results from different types of paper.

When you have some free time, follow these steps to experiment with the Color Management settings and discover what print settings work best:

1. **Choose File⇨Print to open the Print dialog box, shown in Figure 1-1.**

2. **Select Color Management from the pop-up menu in the top-right portion of the Print dialog box.**

3. **Select either Document or Proof.**

   Remember, you're experimenting. So select one, and then try the other:

   • *Document:* Uses the color profile of your image.

   • *Proof:* By default, Proof uses the color profile of your Working CMYK color space, which you defined in your Color Settings dialog box. You can change this profile, however, by choosing View⇨Proof Setup⇨ Current Custom Setup. For details on proofs, see Book II, Chapter 3.

Figure 1-1: Specify the settings in the Color Management portion of the Print dialog box.

4. **Select a method from the Color Handling pop-up menu.**

   The options differ, depending on whether you chose Document or Proof in Step 3.

   If you chose Document in the Print area, here are your options:

   - *Printer Manages Colors:* Sends the document unchanged to the printer, tagged with its color profile. The printer driver then picks an appropriate color profile and converts your document's colors to the final printout. Just make sure you enable color management in your printer dialog box.

   - *Photoshop Manages Colors:* Tells Photoshop to handle the color conversion, using the settings you select from the Printer Profile and Rendering Intent pop-up menus. Photoshop also checks whether you selected the Black Point Compensation option with this setting. If you did, make sure you disable any color management in your printer dialog box.

   - *Separations:* Select this option if you want to print color separations. (See the following section.) Note that your image must be in CMYK mode.

   If you chose Proof in the Print area, you see the same options, but a couple of them produce different results:

   - *Printer Manages Colors:* Works only with a PostScript (PS level 2 or higher) printer, which manages the color conversion of the proof to the print based on your selection of Simulate Paper Color or Simulate Black Ink.

   - *Photoshop Manages Colors:* Tells Photoshop to handle the color conversion of the proof to the print, using the printer profile specified in the pop-up menu and your choice of simulation. Unless you have a lot of dark colors, I recommend leaving it on Simulate Paper Color.

5. **If you chose Photoshop Manages Colors in Step 4, select your printer and paper type from the Printer Profile pop-up menu.**

   Profiles associated with the current printer you select in the Printer submenu are sorted and placed at the top of the profile list.

    Although you may be able to change the Rendering Intent setting, I recommend leaving this at the default setting of Relative Colorimetric, especially when printing photos or multicolored artwork. If, by chance, your image has a lot of areas of solid saturated color, you can try Saturation. Also, leave the Black Point Compensation check box at the default setting of selected or deselected (depending on your Color Handling choice) — unless, of course, you're a color guru and have a better reason not to. Setting this option enables your printer to more accurately print the blacks in your image.

When you select Photoshop Manages Color, you have three additional options located directly below the image preview. These options are strictly preview options and affect only how you see your image on the computer screen. The Match Print Colors option displays a soft proof of your print based on the profiles, color management options and printer you select. See Book II, Chapter 3, for more on soft proofs. The Gamut Warning option displays colors that will be *out of gamut,* or out the range of printable colors. These colors appear as gray pixels by default. And, finally, the Show Paper White option simulates the white point of the paper you select in the Printer Profile submenu. My paper of choice is Premium Matte, as shown in Figure 1-1.

6. **Mac users, click the Print Settings button to choose paper size, quality/media settings, and other options, depending on your exact printer. Click OK.**

7. **When you finish making your selections, click Print.**

   Windows users, your final dialog box appears. Depending on your printer, options will vary. In Windows 7, click the Preferences button and search for paper/media and quality options. Depending on whether your printer is an Epson, Canon, HP, or other, the names of these settings vary.

   If you selected the Photoshop Manages Colors option, you should turn off color management in your particular printer's dialog box.

   That's all there is to it. If you want more information on printing, check out Book I, Chapter 3. For more explanation on color management, see Book II, Chapter 3.

If all you want to do is print color prints on your desktop printer, I recommend starting by selecting Document in the Print area and selecting Photoshop Manages Colors for Color Handling, which gives you the most control over printing. If you have a little time and paper to burn, then print another copy by using the Printer Manages Colors option. Do a side-by-side comparison to see which one looks superior. You can also crack the seal on the documentation that came with your printer for any recommendations.

Getting Four-Color Separations

It's necessary to *color-separate* your image whenever you plan to print your image to an offset press. Your image must first be in CMYK color mode. (Choose Image➪Mode➪CMYK Color.) Then, the composite color image gets digitally separated into the four-color channels — cyan, magenta, yellow, and black — and is output. (These colors are also known as *process colors.*) Sometimes, the separation output is onto film, and sometimes, it's output directly to aluminum printing plates. The plates are put on an offset press, paper runs through each of the four inked rollers (cyan first, then magenta, yellow, and finally black), and out comes your composite image.

Before you take your image to a service bureau or offset printer to get color separations, it's wise to get what are called *laser separations*. Basically, you're color-separating your image, not to film or plates, but to paper.

If your image doesn't separate to paper, most likely it won't to film or plates, either. You can go back and correct the problem, rather than pay upward of $80 to $150 an hour to have the service bureau or offset printer correct it for you. Consider laser separations a cheap insurance policy.

Follow these steps to get laser separations from your desktop printer:

1. **Be sure your image mode is CMYK. If it isn't, choose Image⇨Mode⇨ CMYK Color.**

   I'm assuming your image is a four-color image. But it may also be a gray-scale, duotone, tritone, or quadtone image, in which case, no conversion to CMYK is necessary. (See Book II, Chapter 2, for more on modes.)

   After the conversion, you have an image with four channels — Cyan, Magenta, Yellow, and Black, like the one shown in Figure 1-2.

2. **Choose File⇨Print, and then select Color Management from the pop-up menu in the top-right portion of the Print dialog box that appears.**

3. **In the Print area, select Document.**

   The setting should say U.S. Web Coated (SWOP) v2.

4. **Select Separations from the Color Handling pop-up menu.**

   This option prints each channel from the image to a separate plate, or in the case of laser separations, paper.

5. **Select Output from the pop-up menu in the top-right portion of the dialog box, and then select additional options as you desire.**

   For general print options, see Book I, Chapter 3. For additional options, see Table 1-3.

   Note that if you're printing to a non-PostScript printer, some of these options may not be available. You see a preview of most of these options when you apply them to your file.

6. **Click the Print button.**

   If all goes well, four pieces of paper, one for each of the four CMYK channels, print. If you're printing a grayscale, duotone, tritone, or quadtone image, you get one to four pieces of paper, one for each color used. If that doesn't happen, something's amiss, and it's time for troubleshooting. Be sure to take these laser separations with you when you hand over your file to the service bureau or offset printer.

Corbis Digital Stock

Figure 1-2: Color images are separated into four process colors.

Table 1-3	**Output Options**	
Option	*What It Does*	*Recommendation*
Calibration Bars	Prints an 11-step grayscale bar outside the image area to gauge how accurately the shades are being printed. When you're printing separations, this option prints a gradient tint bar and color bar.	Select this option.
Registration Marks	Prints crosshair and target marks outside the image area, allowing you to line up the four plates or pages.	Select this option.

continued

Table 1-3 *(continued)*

Option	What It Does	Recommendation
Corner Crop Marks	Adds crop marks at the corners of the image to indicate where to trim the image.	Select this option.
Center Crop Marks	Adds crop marks at the center of each side of the image to indicate where to trim the image.	Select this option.
Description	Prints the description as entered in the File➪File Info area.	Select if you have entered a description.
Labels	Prints the filename and channel name on each plate or page.	Select this option.
Emulsion Down	*Emulsion* is the side of the film that's light sensitive. Allows the film to be printed with the emulsion side down.	Leave this option deselected for laser separations. When the service bureau or offset printer prints the separations to film or plates, it may select this option.
Negative	Prints black as white and white as black, and every other color inverts accordingly.	Leave this option deselected for laser separations. When the service bureau or offset printer prints the separations to film or plates, it may select this option.
Interpolation	Anti-aliases low-resolution images by resampling.	Available only for PostScript Level 2 or laser printers. Leave it deselected.
Include Vector Data	See the "Saving and Printing Vector Data in a Raster File" section, in this chapter.	Leave this option selected if you have type or vector paths.

Creating Spot Color Separations

Photoshop allows you to add separate channels for spot colors (see Book VI, Chapter 1, for more on channels), which can then be color-separated. Spot, or *custom,* colors are premixed inks manufactured by various ink companies, the most popular in the U.S. being Pantone. A spot color is often used for a logo, type, or small illustration. Spot colors are also used when you need to apply metallic inks or varnishes to your print job. Spot colors can be used rather than, or in addition to, the four process CMYK colors.

If you're delving into the world of spot colors, I highly recommend that you choose your color from a printed Pantone swatch book, available from www.pantone.com. Because your screen is an RGB device and you're setting up your file for a CMYK output device, the colors you see onscreen don't match the colors that are ultimately on paper — at best, they're a ballpark match. For accuracy, you must select the colors from the printed swatch book. For more on working with color, see Book II, Chapter 3.

Creating a spot channel

Follow these steps to create a spot channel:

1. **On a separate layer, create the graphic or type to which you want to apply the spot color.**

2. **Ctrl-click (⌘-click on the Mac) the thumbnail of the layer to select the graphic and then choose Edit➪Fill to fill it with any solid color at an opacity of 100 percent.**

3. **With your selection active, choose Window➪Channels and then select New Spot Channel from the Channels panel pop-up menu.**

   You can apply a spot color only to an active selection. It can't be applied to just a layer.

   The New Spot Channel dialog box appears, as shown in Figure 1-3.

   Figure 1-3: Adding an additional color separation in Photoshop requires creating a spot color channel first.

4. **In the Name text box, enter a name for your spot color. In the Ink Characteristics area, click the color swatch.**

   I recommend naming your spot color according to the spot color you want to use, such as Pantone 7417C.

   When you click the color swatch, the Color Picker appears.

   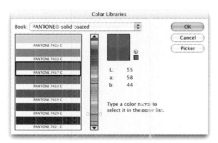

5. **Click the Color Libraries button in the Color Picker and select your Pantone color from the Color Libraries dialog box that appears (see Figure 1-4), and then click OK.**

   Figure 1-4: Select an appropriate color from the Color Libraries dialog box.

6. **In the New Spot Channel dialog box, select a Solidity value between 0 percent and 100 percent.**

   A value of 100 percent represents an ink that's completely opaque, such as a metallic ink, which completely covers the inks beneath it. A value of 0 percent represents a transparent ink, such as a clear varnish. But the solidity value affects only the screen view and composite prints; it doesn't affect the separations. It can help you see where a "clear" varnish will print.

Figure 1-5: The Channels panel displays the spot channel.

7. **Click OK to close the dialog box.**

   Your spot channel appears in the Channels panel and is filled in the image, as well. I created a spot channel for my crest graphic and for the type (Pantone 7417C), as shown in Figure 1-5.

   In the printing process, spot colors are overprinted on top of the four-color image, as shown in Figure 1-6. That means that the spot color is applied at the end of the printing process and is printed over the other inks. This can sometimes cause lighter spot colors to darken somewhat.

   If you need your spot color graphic to knock out the underlying image, create it in an illustration or page layout program. A *knockout* is a hole left in the four-color image, which is filled with the spot ink. The spot ink doesn't print over the other inks.

Corbis Digital Stock

Figure 1-6: Spot colors are often used for color-critical logos that print on top of your image.

8. **Save the image in the native Photoshop, Photoshop PDF, or Photoshop DCS 2.0 (Desktop Color Separations) format.**

   TIFFs also support spot channels, but your page layout program may not recognize them.

If the image is being separated directly out of Photoshop, leave it as a PSD or PDF file. If you want to import it into a different program, such as InDesign, or QuarkXPress, you must save it as a DCS file. If your image is a duotone, tritone, or quadtone image, you also have to go through a few more hoops. You must first convert it to multichannel mode by choosing Image⇨Mode.

In the DCS 2.0 Format dialog box, make sure that the Include Halftone Screen and Include Transfer options aren't selected.

Import the image into your destination application and set your screen angles.

Editing a spot channel

After you create a spot channel, you can edit it. Select the channel in the Channels panel and use a painting or editing tool to paint with black, white, or any shade of gray, just as you would with an alpha channel. To change any of the options of the spot channel, double-click the spot channel thumbnail, or select it and then select Channel Options from the panel pop-up menu. Select a different color or solidity.

Converting an alpha channel to a spot channel

If you want to convert an alpha channel to a spot channel, select the alpha channel in the Channels panel and select Channel Options from the panel's pop-up menu. Rename the channel and select Spot Color. Click the color swatch and select a color from the Color Libraries section of the Color Picker. Click OK, then click OK again. Note that Photoshop converts all areas containing nonwhite pixels (unselected to partially selected areas) to the spot color. With the channel still selected in the Channels panel, choose Image⇨Adjustments⇨Invert to apply the spot color to the white pixels or selected areas of the alpha channel. For details on alpha channels, see Book VI, Chapters 1 and 3.

Chapter 2: Using Photomerge and Merge to HDR Pro

In This Chapter

✏ **Creating a panorama from multiple shots**

✏ **Merging photos for superior quality**

Sometimes, working with just a single shot isn't quite enough. You couldn't quite squeeze that beautiful mountain vista into one photo; it took three shots. Not to worry, that's what Photoshop's Photomerge command is for. This great command seamlessly stitches multiple shots of your panorama into a single image. Similarly, trying to capture the entire tonal range of an image can be tough. The Merge to HDR Pro command enables you to take multiple exposures of an image and later merge those exposures into a single High Dynamic Range image, allowing for superior image quality. And as if that alone isn't enough, these two commands are found on Photoshop's Automate menu, meaning they're quite easy to use.

Using the Photomerge Command

The Photomerge command allows you to combine multiple images into one continuous panoramic image. For example, you can take several overlapping photos of a mountain range and put them together into one panoramic shot using the Photomerge dialog box, as shown in Figure 2-1.

If you know you ultimately want to create a Photomerge composition, you can make things easier by making sure that when you shoot your photos, you overlap your individual images by 15 to 40 percent, but no more than 70 percent. Adobe also recommends that you avoid using distortion lenses (such as fish-eye) and your camera's zoom setting. Finally, try to stay in the same position and keep your camera at the same level for each shot. Using a tripod and rotating the head can help you achieve this consistency. If you are lucky enough to have a nice, long parallel surface handy (like a sidewalk), try taking spaced photos using your tripod along this surface.

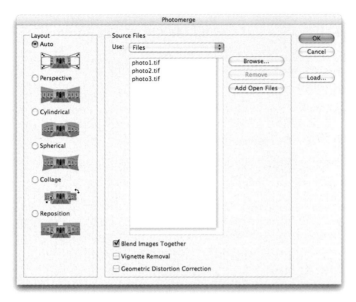

Photodisc

Figure 2-1: Select several overlapping shots to create one panoramic image.

Follow these steps to assemble your own Photomerge composition:

1. **Choose File⇨Automate⇨Photomerge.**

   You can also select your desired source images and choose Tools⇨ Photoshop⇨Photomerge in Adobe Bridge. Using Bridge is a timesaver because you can quickly and visually select your images.

2. **In the Photomerge dialog box, shown in Figure 2-1, select your source files.**

   From the Use pop-up menu, you can select from Files (which uses individual files you select) or from Folder (which uses all images in a folder. Click the Add Open Files button to use all currently open files. Or click the Browse button to navigate to your desired files or folder.

   If you want to delete a file from the list, select it and click Remove.

3. **Select Blend Images Together to correct the color differences that can occur from blending images with different exposures.**

   Photoshop then blends the colors and tones.

   If the Blend Images Together option doesn't help, you can always create a blending group. First, in your Layers panel, create a new group containing the layer you want to change. Next, change the group Blend mode to Normal. Finally, add an adjustment layer, such as Levels or Exposure, in the group above the layer you want to change. For more on adjustment layers, see Book V, Chapter 1. For more on blend modes, see Book V, Chapter 3.

4. **Select Vignette Removal to correct exposure problems caused by** *lens vignetting* **(when light at the edges of images is reduced and therefore edges are darkened).**

5. **Select Geometric Distortion Correction to correct for lens distortions, such as radial distortion, barrel distortion (bulging out), and pincushion distortion (pinching in).**

   You can use this option to align shots taken with a fish-eye lens.

6. **In the Layout area, select your desired project mode, as shown in Figure 2-1.**

   The thumbnail illustration visually demonstrates each mode but I'll give you a little more description of each:

   * *Auto:* Select the Auto mode to make Photoshop analyze your images on its own.

   * *Perspective:* Select this mode if your images have been shot with perspective, or at acute angles. This mode is also recommended for High Dynamic Range (HDR) images.

   * *Cylindrical:* Select this option if you shot your images with a wide-angle lens or when your images have that nasty "bow-tie" distortion. This mode is also good for those 360-degree, full panoramic shots.

   * *Spherical:* This mode is handy when stitching together a 360-degree panorama, in which you have a wide field of view, both horizontally and vertically. Use this option for shots taken with a wide-angle lens.

   * *Collage:* This projection method aligns images by rotating, positioning, and uniformly scaling each image. It may be the best choice for pure panoramas, but you can also find it useful for stitching together images based on common features.

   * *Reposition:* When you select this mode, Photoshop doesn't take into account any distortion, but merely scans the images and positions them in what it considers the best position.

7. **Click OK.**

   Photoshop marches off and attempts to automatically align and "stitch" your source images into a new Photoshop image, shown in Figure 2-2. Hopefully, all goes well; however, if Photoshop can't align and merge, it presents an alert that says "some images could not be aligned."

No matter which projection mode you select, Photoshop leaves your merged image in layers. In addition to those layers, Photoshop may also add a layer mask to each layer to better blend and composite your merged image. These layer masks act like any other layer masks, meaning you can edit them to your liking. For more on layer masks, see Book VI, Chapter 3.

Figure 2-2: The Photomerge command enables you to combine multiple images into one continuous panoramic shot.

Using the Merge to HDR Pro Command

Have you ever caught an early matinee and emerged molelike from the pitch-black theater into the bright light of high noon, only to have to squint for a while because your eyes burned? Or on the flip side, have you blindly tumbled into your seat, popcorn scattering all over the aisle in that same darkened theater because you just came in from the bright daylight? In both cases, your eyes needed some time to adjust to the abrupt change from extreme dark to extreme light or vice versa. Cameras suffer from the same problem. But although our eyes can eventually adapt to varying brightness levels, cameras and devices, such as computer monitors and scanners, can capture only a fixed dynamic, or tonal, range. In digital imaging tech talk, *dynamic range* is the ratio of the darkest and brightest values a device can capture simultaneously.

In the past, digital photography aficionados were hindered when performing higher-end, image-editing tasks in Photoshop because they were forced to work within a limited dynamic range. Recent versions of Photoshop have provided users with plenty of support for High Dynamic Range (HDR) images. HDR images, which contain 32 bits of data per channel, are superior to non-HDR images because they can capture a much larger dynamic range — in fact, they're able to represent the entire dynamic range of the real world.

Photographers can take multiple exposures of an image and then later merge those multiple exposures into a single photo in Photoshop, thereby capturing the entire dynamic range into a single HDR image. Although you can use the Merge to HDR Pro command on 8- or 16-bit images, be aware that only 32-bit images can store all the HDR data.

Adobe offers a few tips to maximize your success with the Merge to HDR Pro command:

✔ Use a tripod when shooting multiple exposures of the same scene to ensure you're capturing the exact same shot each time.

✔ Make sure you take enough shots to cover the entire dynamic range of your subject. Shoot for a minimum of three, but try for five to seven, if not more.

✔ Vary the shutter speed to create different exposures, instead of varying your aperture or ISO, which can cause noise, vignetting, and altering of depth of field.

✔ Make sure the exposure difference between the shots is one or two Exposure Value (EV) steps apart. Use one or two f-stops apart as a guide.

✔ Don't vary the lighting in the shots.

✔ Don't shoot anything that's moving. The scene needs to be static.

Follow these steps to use this improved feature:

1. Choose File➪Automate➪Merge to HDR Pro.

The Merge to HDR Pro dialog box appears, as shown in Figure 2-3.

Note that you can also access this command in Bridge by choosing Tools➪Photoshop➪Merge to HDR Pro.

You can even create 32-bit images via the File New dialog box. Simply select 32-bit from the Bit Depth pop-up menu to the right of the Color Mode pop-up menu.

Figure 2-3: Select two or more files to merge in the Merge to HDR Pro dialog box.

2. Select either Files or Folder from the Use pop-up menu.

You can also select Add Open Files if you want to use files that are currently open in Photoshop. Just make sure that they've been saved first.

3. If you selected Files or Folder in Step 2, click the Browse button, select the images, and click Open. If you're using files that you already have open, move on to Step 4.

If you choose an image by accident, simply select it and click Remove.

4. **(Optional) Select Attempt to Automatically Align Source Images if you want Photoshop to try to line up your various exposures.**

This is a good idea if you shot your photos without the use of a tripod. Also note that your images need to be the same dimension and resolution for this command to work.

5. **Click OK.**

You may get a mini dialog box that asks you to manually set your exposure value, as shown in Figure 2-4. You need to specify your exposure time (shutter speed), f-stop (aperture), and ISO (film speed) for all your images.

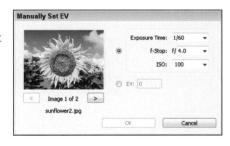

Figure 2-4: Manually specify your exposure value.

A second dialog box appears with thumbnails of your chosen images on the bottom and a large preview of the merged image in the center.

6. **Based on how you like the merged image, you can select or deselect any of the thumbnails in the source area, at the bottom of the dialog box, by selecting or deselecting the check boxes.**

Photoshop may bark that you don't have enough dynamic range to get a "useful" HDR image, in which case, you have to bail out.

If you want to zoom in and out of your images, click the – and + buttons, or use the View pop-up menu at the bottom of the Preview window.

7. **In the Mode menu, shown in Figure 2-5, select your desired bit depth for the merged image.**

Be sure to leave your 32-bit image set to 32 Bit if you want to capture and store the entire dynamic range.

8. **On the histogram, use the White Point slider to set the white point for the merged image if you want to see a better preview.**

The dynamic range of HDR images surpasses what your monitor can show. So, when you view these images on your computer, they can look pretty nasty — too dark and undersaturated. If you adjust the preview with the White Point slider, Photoshop provides a better display of the image without altering the image data at all. Remember that if your image is 32-bit, adjusting the white point affects only the preview, not the actual image data. That preview adjustment should then be saved in the HDR file and applied whenever the file is opened in Photoshop. But, if your image is 16- or 8-bit, adjusting the white point applies the adjustment to the actual image data itself.

You can save your settings for use later by choosing Preset⇨Save Preset.

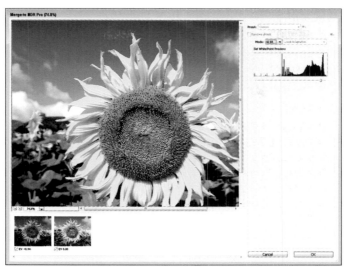

Figure 2-5: Specify your desired bit depth and adjust your white point.

By default, the Merge to HDR Pro command automatically calculates a response curve based on an analysis of the tonal range of your images.

9. **(Optional) If you want to save a curve for later use, click the response curve menu in the upper-right corner of the dialog box and choose Save Response Curve.**

    Camera response curves have to do with how your camera sensor analyzes light.

10. **(Optional) Select Remove Ghosts if you have images with objects you wish to remove.**

    For example, if you have a shot where a car or person moved into the shot and you want it removed, selecting this option will do so. Photoshop will display a green box around the image thumbnail with the best tones, which will then be used as the base image for the merged photo.

11. **Click OK.**

    Your merged HDR image appears in all its full dynamic glory in its own image window.

Even if you want to ultimately convert your 32-bit image to 16-bit or even 8-bit, always make your exposure and contrast corrections first and then convert it. You'll get your dynamic range the way you want it. To adjust exposure and contrast, select your desired bit depth from the Mode pop-up menu, and select your desired conversion method from the pop-up menu. Here is a brief explanation of each conversion method:

✔ **Exposure and Gamma:** Adjusts the brightness (Exposure) and contrast (Gamma) of the image.

✔ **Highlight and Compression:** Compresses the highlight values so they fall within the tonal range of an 8- or 16-bit image.

✔ **Equalize Histogram:** This is an automatic method that compresses the dynamic range but tries to retain contrast.

✔ **Local Adaptation:** Enables you to adjust the tones by adjusting local brightness regions in your image. Set the following options:

- Click the *Curve* tab and make adjustments to the curve. The histogram of that curve shows the Luminance (amount of light) value. Each red tick mark represents one exposure value (or f-stop).

- For *Edge Glow,* adjust the Radius slider to specify the size of the local brightness regions. Strength indicates how far apart the values of two pixels must be before they are not part of the same brightness region.

- For *Tone and Detail,* adjust the Gamma setting accordingly. Lower settings emphasize midtone values, while higher settings emphasize shadows/highlights. A Gamma setting of 1 indicates that dynamic range is maximized. Adjust Exposure to adjust f-stops. Specify the Details, Shadow, and Highlight settings to adjust sharpness and contrast of dark and light areas, respectively.

Finally, click the Color tab and adjust the Vibrance (saturation while minimizing clipping) and Saturation (color intensity).

For more on the dynamics of curves, see Book VIII, Chapter 1. Note that you can also choose Image➪Mode➪16-Bits or 8-Bits/Channel and make your exposure and contrast adjustments in the same HDR Conversion dialog box that you can get through the Merge to HDR Pro dialog box.

Keep in mind that you also have the option of creating layers within a 32-bit image. This, of course, opens up a whole world of creative possibilities, giving you the ability to composite multiple images. You can also apply another half dozen or so blend modes on those layers, including Hue, Saturation, and Color. As an added bonus, you can even paint on those 32-bit layers, as well as add type. You can have your way with the following tools: Brush, Pencil, Shape, Clone and Pattern Stamp, History Brush, Eraser, Gradient, Blur, Sharpen, Smudge, and Type.

Finally, don't be surprised to encounter a different dialog box when you select a color for an HDR image. HDR images have their very own Color Picker (in the Extended Version of Photoshop only).

If you copy a layer, selection, or entire image from an 8-bit or 16-bit file, you encounter a profile mismatch because of the differences in the color profiles' gamma values. Convert your profile to match your HDR image. For more on color profiles, see Book II, Chapter 3.

Index

U